COASTAL AND OCEAN LAW

CASES AND MATERIALS

Second Edition

By

Joseph J. Kalo
Graham Kenan Professor of Law
University of North Carolina School of Law

Richard G. Hildreth
Professor of Law
Co-Director, Ocean and Coastal Law Center
University of Oregon School of Law

Alison Rieser
Professor of Law
University of Maine School of Law

Donna R. Christie
Elizabeth C. and Clyde W. Atkinson Professor of Law
Florida State University School of Law

Jon L. Jacobson
Professor Emeritus of Law
University of Oregon College of Law

AMERICAN CASEBOOK SERIES®

WEST GROUP

A THOMSON COMPANY

Mat #18378434

ISBN 0–314–25876–0

TEXT IS PRINTED ON 10% POST
CONSUMER RECYCLED PAPER

To Dad and Mom, Monica, Joe, Angela, Ted, Kristy, and Lauren.

JJK

To Mary Lou, Cliff, Caroline, Emily, Ian, and Judy without whose support my participation in this book would not be possible.

RGH

To Jenna, who loves all sea creatures, and to Les, who gives the smallest ones names.

AR

To the memory of Alice C. Repetske.

DRC

To Mary.

JLJ

Preface to the Second WestGroup Edition

The Coastal Zone Management Act of 1972 is now thirty years old. Thirty-three of the 35 eligible states and territories have developed programs approved by the federal government, bringing 95,331 miles of coast under the management of the Act. The development of Indiana's program will incorporate 45 of the remaining 108 miles of national coastline into the program. Only Illinois is not participating. This sustained program effort has brought 99.9% of the nation's shoreline into the program. Why has development of planning and management programs for the coasts continued to be a matter of state and national focus and importance?

The short answer is that the coast has become a vanishing resource. Coastal beaches are critically eroding; the vast majority of coastal wetlands have been drained, filled and lost; only about 700 miles of sandy shoreline has been characterized as remaining "undeveloped" by the Department of Interior.[1] Offshore, fisheries and coral reefs are suffering from overexploitation and the effects of land-based pollution. The need to address these critical problems has not diminished since 1972. Use of the coastal zone has also bred conflicts that only continue to intensify. The concentration of population on the coast - more than 750 people per square mile - and intense industrial and recreational use have spawned numerous user conflicts and tested the limits of the carrying capacity of the coastal ecosystems. The legal battle between the public interest and private property rights that has reached the U.S. Supreme Court several times since the 1980s has often focused on the rare shoreline property that is still available for development.

Common law recognized the restlessness of the boundary between the sea and shore, but the legal regimes that developed in domestic and international law were generally directed either toward the land mass or the high seas, ignoring the intimate interrelationship of the land and sea. These legal systems largely overlooked the importance and special needs of the coastal zone, that is, the coast and nearshore ocean. Today, however, the coastal zone itself has become the subject

---

[1] The Coastal Barrier Resources Act has required the federal government to identify the areas of undeveloped barrier islands and spits around the country and deny federal funding and subsidies for development of those areas. *See* 16 U.S.C. § 3501-3510.

v

of an increasingly comprehensive legal regime. The quantity and uniqueness of this body of law reflects the importance of the coastal zone for human habitation, transportation, industrial and energy siting, living and nonliving resource exploitation, and recreation, as well as a heightened awareness of the ecological significance and dynamic nature of the coasts.

The modern era of coastal zone management can be traced to the Commission on Marine Science, Engineering, and Resources, also known as the Stratton Commission, which was created by Congress in 1966 to investigate and make recommendations on United States' marine law and policy. This Commission is credited with coining the term "coastal zone" and with focusing national attention on the coastal zone's importance and peril. The Commission's final report, *The Nation and the Sea* (1969), found that:

> The coast of the United States is, in many respects, the Nation's most valuable geographic feature. It is at this juncture of the land and sea that the great part of this Nation's trade and industry takes place. The waters off the shore are among the most biologically productive regions of the Nation.

The Stratton Commission also found, however, that the value of the coast as a vital natural system and as a focal point for industry and recreation was threatened by rapidly increasing population and intense commercial, residential, and recreational development. The conclusion that our coasts were in jeopardy was bolstered by the Department of Interior's 1970 National Estuary Study which documented the accelerating rate at which coastal wetlands and estuaries were being altered or destroyed.

The report of the Stratton Commission's three-year study identified the coast as a *national* resource and concluded that the federal government had a direct responsibility for navigation and commerce in coastal waters and a shared interest in conservation and economic development in coastal areas. The report also recognized that "[r]apidly intensifying use of coastal areas already has outrun the capabilities of local governments to plan their orderly development and to resolve conflicts."

The Stratton Commission's report and the National Estuary Study spurred Congress to introduce a series of bills and proposals which culminated in the Coastal Zone Management Act of 1972 (CZMA). The

Act declared a national policy "to preserve, protect, develop, and where possible, to restore or enhance, the resources of the Nation's coastal zone for this and succeeding generations." This policy was not implemented, however, by imposing a federal land and water management scheme on the coastal zone. The congressional findings stated:

> The key to effective protection and use of the land and water resources of the coastal zone is to encourage the states to exercise their full authority over the lands and waters in the coastal zone by assisting the states, in cooperation with Federal and local governments and other vitally affected interests, in developing land and water use programs for the coastal zone, including unified criteria, standards, methods, and processes for dealing with land and water use decisions of more than local significance.

State developed and implemented programs now create the framework to address the problems of the coast in the context of modern uses and conflicts.

The "wet side" of the coastal zone, the marginal sea, is also receiving more attention from a legal and management perspective. Historically, the sea appeared to be infinite, bearing inexhaustible resources and incapable of being seriously disturbed by human activities. The advancement of technology has resulted in the means to pollute even the vast oceans and to overexploit resources to the point of extinction. Evolving international and domestic perspectives about control over ocean resources, as well as conflicting, duplicative, or inadequate jurisdictional regimes and authorities, have created major challenges for effective management of the ocean and its resources. Often international law developments - such as the United Nations Convention on the Law of the Sea, the most ambitious international treaty ever negotiated - have outpaced domestic legal responses in the United States.

Since 1998, the federal government has, however, focused significant attention on the oceans. A Coral Reef Task Force produced a National Action Plan; federal agencies were directed to establish an integrated national system of Marine Protected Areas; and an Ocean Exploration initiative was announced to develop a national ocean exploration strategy. Finally, with enactment of the Oceans Act of 2000, the federal government has begun its first comprehensive review of national oceans policy since the Stratton Commission.

The Oceans Act establishes a sixteen-member Commission on Ocean Policy that is charged to hold public hearings nationally and produce a report:

▸ assessing existing ocean-related facilities and technologies, and reviewing opportunities for development of ocean products and technologies;

▸ assessing the current and future supply of and demand for ocean resources;

▸ reviewing existing and planned Federal ocean and coastal activities;

▸ reviewing federal laws and regulations governing ocean and coastal activities to identify and resolve inconsistencies and contradictions;

▸ reviewing relationships of federal, state, and local governments in planning ocean activities; and

▸ reviewing the effectiveness of state and federal efforts to integrate ocean and coastal management, and the adequacy of existing federal interagency ocean policy coordination.

The report is to include conclusions and recommendations to change U.S. law to achieve a coordinated, comprehensive policy for the responsible use and stewardship of ocean and coastal resources.

This book is a response to the need of lawyers and policy makers to understand the unique and inherently astatic natural and legal landscape of the coastal zone. Law courses generally focus on a field of law, like torts, or the regulation of some activity, like corporate law. Rarely does a course or textbook focus on a place. But the ocean and its shores are unique places. Many of the legal assumptions and rules traditionally applied to more stable inland areas are simply not consistent with the coastal environment, and the law has evolved to reflect that.

This book is not intended nor designed to be a comprehensive treatise on coastal and ocean law. No attempt is made to examine every statute or every issue; the book attempts to avoid significant overlap with materials more appropriately covered in environmental, international, or administrative law. The aim of the book is to provide the tools to examine, in some depth, the significant features of state, federal, and international coastal and ocean law. Each chapter is organized around significant issues affecting the coasts and oceans. In addition to cases, statutory materials and regulations, problems and questions are included to provide the reader with a specific context and to raise the issues that the reader should think about in reading and analyzing the materials.

Most citations and footnotes have been deleted from the edited opinions and other primary and secondary source material included in this book. Such deletions are not indicated by any editorial notations, such as "citations omitted." However, deletions of text are indicated by asterisks or ellipses. We hope that anyone interested in case or other authority cited in an opinion will pursue that line of investigation by examining the original opinion.

This book is the fourth edition of *Coastal and Ocean Law*, and although it has now evolved significantly, recognition should be given to earlier works that contributed to the development of this text: Richard Hildreth's and Ralph Johnson's *Ocean and Coastal Law* (1983), Joseph J. Kalo's *Coastal and Ocean Law* (1989), the first edition of this text, and Donna Christie's *Florida Ocean and Coastal Law and Policy* (1985, 1992), as well as class materials developed by Alison Rieser and Jon Jacobson. This text represents the accumulated experience gained by teaching, evaluating, and revising these materials for more than two decades.

Joseph J. Kalo wishes to thank the University of North Carolina Law School for making the time available to complete this work, Marilyn Steele and Marion White, whose patience and word processing skills were essential to the completion of this book, his research assistant, Nancy Tennie Hunter, class of 2003, and all the students who have taken the course over the years and pushed me to a greater understanding of coastal and ocean law.

Richard Hildreth wishes to thank the Oregon Sea Grant Program and the University of Oregon School of Law for their long standing support of his work in ocean and coastal law. That work would not have been possible without the aid and comfort provided over the years by his colleagues at the University of Oregon Ocean and Coastal Law Center, Andrea Coffman, Dianne Bass, and co-author, Jon Jacobson.

Alison Rieser wishes to thank the Pew Fellows Program in Marine Conservation for a fellowship in 1999-2002 to explore the role of science in marine conservation law, the Jessie B. Cox Charitable Trust and the University of Maine Sea Grant College Program for supporting her development of teaching materials in ocean and coastal law, the faculty and dean of the University of Maine School of Law for providing an opportunity to teach courses in this area, the administrative staff of the Law School, and the dozens of students whose enthusiasm for this field of law made its teaching a pleasure.

Donna Christie wishes to thank the Florida State University College of Law, and particularly Dean Donald Weidner, for continuing to support her research and work on this text. She is grateful to have enthusiastic students who find continual excitement in this area of the law. Finally, she thanks Jim Christie for making her remember to the enjoy the coasts she seeks to protect.

We all sincerely thank our retiring co-author Jon Jacobson for his contributions and his inspiration. We have cherished his friendship and wish him a fulfilling and totally satisfying retirement.

- February 2002

Editor's Note

Most footnotes are omitted from edited materials without indication. The footnotes throughout each chapter are numbered consecutively. Therefore, the footnote numbers that appear in the edited materials do not necessarily correspond with the numbering that appears in the original. Back to back deletions from different paragraphs are shown with only one set of asterisks, and deletions of dissenting or concurring opinions are not always indicated.

Acknowledgments

We are indebted to the following authors and publishers for their generosity in giving us permission to reprint excerpts from copyrighted materials:

Thomas Addison and Timothy Burns, The Army Corps of Engineers and Nationwide Permit 26: Wetlands Protection or Swamp Reclamation, 18 Ecology Law Quarterly 619 (1991). Reprinted with permission.

Lee G. Anderson, "Marine Fisheries" in Current Issues in Natural Resources Policy (P. Portney, ed. 1982). Reprinted with the permission of Resources for the Future, Inc.

Dennis W. Arrow, The Proposed Regime for the Unilateral Exploitation of Deep Seabed Mineral Resources, 21 Harvard International Law Journal 337 (1980). Permission granted by the Harvard International Law Review © (1980) and President and Fellows of Harvard College.

Ernest R. Bartley, The Tidelands Oil Controversy (1953). Copyright © 1953, renewed 1981, University of Texas Press. Reprinted with permission.

Neal D. Black, Note, Balancing the Advantages of Individual Transferable Quotas Against Their Redistributive Effects: The Case of *Alliance Against IFQs v. Brown*, 9 Georgia International Environmental Law Review 727 (1998). Reprinted with permission of the publisher, Georgetown University and Georgetown International Environmental Law Review. Copyright © 1997.

Donna R. Christie and Richard Hildreth, Coastal and Ocean Management in a Nutshell (2d ed. 1999). Copyright © 1999 West Publishing Company. Reprinted with the permission of West Group.

Environmental Law Reporter, Vol. 11, No. 36, p. 1347 (Jan. 2, 1981). Copyright © 1981 by The Bureau of National Affairs, Inc. (800-372-1033) Reprinted with permission.

Daniel P. Finn, Interagency Relationships in Marine Resource Conflicts, 4 Harvard Environmental Law Review, 359 (1980). Permission granted by the Harvard Environmental Law Review © 1980 and the President and Fellows of Harvard College.

Richard Hildreth, C. Terenzi and L. Thomas, Evaluation of the New Carissa Incident for Improvement to State, Federal, and International Law, 16 Journal of Environmental Law and Litigation 101, 135-136 (2001). Reprinted with permission.

G. Kevin Jones, The Development of Outer Continental Shelf Energy Resources, 11 Pepperdine Law Review 9 (1983). Reprinted with permission of the Pepperdine Law Review.

John Warren Kindt, Ocean Dumping, 13 Denver Journal of International Law and Policy 335 (1984). Reprinted with the permission of the Denver Journal of International Law and Policy.

Robert B. Krueger, The Background of the Continental Shelf and the Outer Continental Shelf Lands Act, 10 Natural Resources Journal 442 (1970). Reprinted with the permission of the Natural Resources Law Journal.

Marian Macpherson, Integrating Ecosystem Management Approaches into Federal Fishery Management Through the Magnuson-Stevens Fishery Conservation and Management Act, 6 Ocean and Coastal Law Journal 1 (2001). Reprinted with permission by the Marine Law Institute, University of Maine Law School. Copyright © 2001.

Frank E. Maloney and Richard C. Ausness, The Use and Legal Significance of the Mean High Tide Line in Coastal Boundary Mappings, 53 North Carolina Law Review 185 (1974). Copyright © 1974 by the North Carolina Law Review Association. Reprinted with permission.

Eva Morreale, Federal Power in the Western States: The Navigation Power and the Rule of No Compensation, 3 Natural Resources Journal 1 (1963). Reprinted with the permission of the Natural Resources Law Journal.

James L. Nicoll, Jr. Marine Pollution and Natural Resources Damages: The Multi-million Dollar Damage Award and Beyond, 5 University of San Francisco Maritime Law Journal 323 (1993). Reprinted with the permission of the the University of San Francisco Maritime Law Journal.

Note, Right, Title and Interest in the Territorial Sea: Federal and State Claims in the United States, 4 Georgia Journal of International and Comparative Law 463, 469 (1974). Reprinted with permission.

Restatement (Second) of Torts, sec. 929(1)(a) and comment (b) (1979). Reprinted with the permission of the American Law Institute.

Alison Rieser, Prescriptions for the Commons: Environmental Scholarship and the Fishing Quotas Debate, Harvard Environmental Law Review, Volume 23, Number 2, 393-421 (1999). Reprinted with permission by the President and Fellows of Harvard College and the Harvard Environmental Law Review. Copyright © 1999.

William H. Rodgers, Jr., Environmental Law (Second Edition 1994). Copyright © 1994 West Publishing Company. Reprinted with Permission of West Group.

Aaron L. Shalowitz, Boundary Problems Raised by the Submerged Lands Act, 54 Columbia Law Review 1021 (1954). Reprinted with the permission of the Columbia Law Review

William B. Stoebuck, Nontrespassory Takings In Eminent Domain (1977). Copyright © 1997 by Michie, a division of Reed Elsevier Inc. and Reed Elsevier Properties Inc and reproduced with permission of Michie. Further reproduction is not authorized.

Summary of Contents

Table of Contents

Table of Cases and Administrative Decisions

The principal cases and decisions are in Roman type. Cases or decisions cited or discussed in the text are bold type. References are to pages.

Table of Constitutional Provisions, Statutes, and Regulations, and International Treaties and Conventions

Only materials quoted in whole or significant part in the text
are included in this table.

COASTAL AND OCEAN LAW

CASES AND MATERIALS

Second Edition

Chapter One

PUBLIC AND PRIVATE INTERESTS IN COASTAL LANDS AND WATERS

SECTION 1. INTRODUCTION

Within the coastal zone exists a complex mix of common law private and public rights and interests. Generally, legal title to land located above the mean high-tide line to the line of vegetation (the dry sand area) and beyond (the uplands) will be in private hands. However, legal title to the lands below the mean high-tide line (the wet sand area and submerged lands) will be in the state.

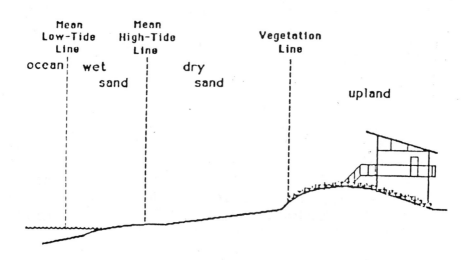

Typical divisions of the beach. Note that, in Delaware, Maine, Massachusetts, Pennsylvania, and Virginia, private rights may extend to the mean low-tide line. [Adapted from D. Brower, Access to the Nation's Beaches: Legal and Planning Perspectives 19-20, 60-61 (1978)].

1

Coastal waters themselves, of course, are not subject to private ownership and are under the control of the state. Title to the lands located below the mean high-tide line, sometimes referred to as *sovereignty lands or public trust lands*, is generally in the state and such lands are said to be held by the state in public trust. The beneficiary of this trust is the public, who has the right, subject to reasonable limitations, to use public trust lands and associated navigable (or public trust) waters for a wide variety of commercial and recreational purposes. In this chapter, the origins and scope of this public trust doctrine are examined first.

Although coastal waters and submerged lands are public trust resources, that does not preclude the existence of private property interests in those same resources. For example, owners of land abutting navigable waters, by reason of their adjacency, may have certain distinctive common law rights or privileges to use adjacent navigable waters and submerged lands. These rights are known as *littoral rights* in saltwater bodies and freshwater lakes, and *riparian rights* in rivers and other freshwater bodies. Frequently, however, judges, lawyers, and others will use the terms interchangeably. Although the nature and extent of these rights or privileges may vary considerably from state to state, to some degree, a common core exists.

The extent of, and relationship between, public rights and private property interests in coastal waters and submerged lands implicates fundamental notions of private property that find expression in the "takings" clause of the Fifth Amendment to the United States Constitution. Not infrequently, when the government acts to protect public rights and interests in coastal lands and waters, those adversely affected by the government's actions will claim that there is a "taking" of some private property interest for which compensation is required. But, part of the legal process is the judicial adjustment and redefining of common law property interests. A private property interest thought to exist may be defined out of existence. If the asserted private property interest does not exist, then it would seem the takings claim predicated on it disappears. A significant question is: are there circumstances in which this common law process of shaping and defining the nature and extent of public and private rights can itself be a "taking"?

Whatever restraints the "takings" clause might otherwise place on government conduct, a rather unique exception to the "takings" clause exists when the federal government acts to protect or improve navigation in coastal waters. This exception falls under the heading of the *navigation servitude.* In essence, all state-created property rights and interests in coastal waters and submerged lands are subordinate to this navigation servitude.

As public use of coastal areas has increased, courts have increasingly found that the public's rights are not necessarily limited to those rights reflected in the traditional public trust doctrine. In some cases, the public's public trust rights have been expanded to include the right of access to, and the use of, privately owned, dry sand beach and other areas. Such a process of extension of public rights, as you can imagine, is very controversial. Courts also use traditional common law property principles, such as those relating to the acquisition of public prescriptive easements, customary rights and implied dedications, to expand public rights of access and use. Expanded public trust rights and those derived from other traditional common law doctrines are the subject of the last part of this chapter.

As with many rights developed through the common law process, the exact parameters of common law littoral rights and public trust rights may be uncertain. The views of private waterfront landowners, public officials, and the general public about access to, and use of, our limited coastal resources frequently diverge. Clashes are inevitable. How the courts resolve these conflicting views, interests, and rights is the heart of this chapter.

SECTION 2. TITLE TO LANDS UNDER COASTAL WATERS

The traditional American common law rule is that the beds of nonnavigable coastal waters belong to the adjacent landowners. If one person owns the land on both sides of a coastal creek or stream, then that person owns the bed too. If the banks are owned by different people, then each owns to the thread of the creek or stream. The owner of the bed of nonnavigable waters may be able to exercise exclusive control over the overlying waters. However, if the waterbody is navigable then title to the submerged lands is normally in the state, with the overlying waters available for use by the public. Such submerged lands are frequently said to be held by the state in a special, distinct capacity and are referred to as either "sovereignty" or "public trust" lands. As such, the state's authority to dispose of such lands may be more limited than its power over other state-owned property.

This concept of "sovereignty" or "public trust" lands is traceable back to Roman law and English common law. The Romans developed the "natural law" principle that the sea belonged to no one, that use rights in it, and on its shores, were common to all. This was necessary to protect the empire's dependence upon navigation for trade and communication, as well as fishing.

However, during the early Middle Ages, commerce and navigation declined in importance throughout Europe, and in England much of the coast passed into private ownership. Early grants of coastal lands lacked precision, and the English sovereigns seem to have acquiesced as feudal lords assumed that their titles extended out into the sea.

Beginning with the signing of the Magna Carta, and particularly after Sir Matthew Hale's treatise, De Jure Maris (1670), there emerged a new interest in reestablishing public rights (the *jus publicum*) in coastal waters and navigable rivers. Hale's treatise laid the groundwork for the English common law rule that title to lands over which the tide ebbed and flowed was *prima facie* in the Crown and held by it in a sort of trust for the public (the public rights of use being navigation and fishing). This trust did not preclude a Crown grant of tidelands to private individuals, but the burden was on private landowners to prove that such a grant indeed had occurred.

In the next case -- Phillips Petroleum Company v. Mississippi -- the specific issue is whether ownership of submerged lands under nonnavigable-in-fact tidal waters is in state or private hands. But the broader question in *Phillips Petroleum* is whether the submerged lands are "lands under navigable waters," title to which passed to Mississippi on statehood.

As you read *Phillips Petroleum*, you will see that the phrase "navigable waters" has different meanings depending on the question being asked. *Phillips Petroleum* is a title determination case, but it is a case involving title to submerged lands in a state other than one of the original thirteen. The definition of navigable waters for purposes of determining title to submerged lands in one of the original thirteen states is not necessarily the same as the one used in *Phillips Petroleum*. To add to the complexity, the definition in *Phillips Petroleum* is not necessarily the definition that would be used to determine whether, as a matter of state law, submerged lands remained in state hands after statehood or passed, in one fashion or another, into private hands.

Even when title to submerged lands is in private hands, that does not necessarily mean that the owner of the submerged lands controls the overlying waters. Generally, the public is entitled to use navigable waters for navigation, fishing, and water recreation. But, the definition of "navigable waters" for purposes of public use may be different and broader than "navigable waters" for title determination purposes.

This does not exhaust the different meanings of "navigable waters." Navigable waters may mean one thing if the question is whether a particular federal statute applies; it may mean another if the question is whether the waterway is subject to the federal navigation servitude; and still another if the question is whether federal admiralty jurisdiction exists. With such variations in possible meaning, it is important when reading cases to keep in mind that a definition of navigable waters (or navigability) reached in one context may not be applicable in another context.

PHILLIPS PETROLEUM COMPANY v. MISSISSIPPI
Supreme Court of the United States, 1988
484 U.S. 469

JUSTICE WHITE delivered the opinion of the Court.

The issue here is whether the State of Mississippi, when it entered the Union in 1817, took title to lands lying under waters that were influenced by the tide running in the Gulf of Mexico, but were not navigable in fact.

I

As the Mississippi Supreme Court eloquently put it: "Though great public interests and neither insignificant nor illegitimate private interests are present and in conflict, this in the end is a title suit." Cinque Bambini Partnership v. State, 491 So. 2d 508, 510 (1986). More specifically, in question here is ownership of 42 acres of land underlying the north branch of Bayou LaCroix and 11 small drainage streams in southwestern Mississippi; the disputed tracts range from under one-half acre to almost ten acres in size. Although the waters over these lands lie several miles north of the Mississippi Gulf Coast and are not navigable, they are nonetheless influenced by the tide, because they are adjacent and tributary to the Jourdan River, a navigable stream flowing into the Gulf. The Jourdan, in the area involved here, is affected by the ebb and flow of the tide. Record title to these tracts of land is held by petitioners, who trace their claims back to prestatehood Spanish land grants.

The State of Mississippi, however, claiming that by virtue of the "equal footing doctrine" it acquired at the time of statehood and held in public trust all land lying under any waters influenced by the tide, whether navigable or not, issued oil and gas leases that included the property at issue. This quiet title suit, brought by petitioners, ensued.

The Mississippi Supreme Court, affirming the Chancery Court with respect to the lands at issue here, held that by virtue of becoming a State, Mississippi acquired "fee simple title to all lands naturally subject to tidal influence, inland to today's mean high water mark. * * *" Id. Petitioners' submission that the State acquired title to only lands under navigable [in fact] waters was rejected.[1]

---

[1] The Chancery Court had held that 140 acres of the lands claimed by petitioners were public trust lands. The Mississippi Supreme Court reversed with respect to 98 of these 140 acres, finding that these tracts were artificially created tidelands (caused by road construction), and therefore were not part of the public trust created in 1817. Since

We granted certiorari to review the Mississippi Supreme Court's decision, 479 U.S. 1084 (1987), and now affirm the judgment below.

II

As petitioners recognize, the "seminal case in American public trust jurisprudence is Shively v. Bowlby, 152 U.S. 1 (1894)." Reply Brief for Petitioners 11. The issue in Shively v. Bowlby was whether the state of Oregon or a prestatehood grantee from the United States of riparian lands near the mouth of the Columbia River at Astoria, Oregon, owned the soil below the high-water mark. Following an extensive survey of this Court's prior cases, the English common law, and various cases from the state courts, the Court concluded:

"At common law, the title and dominion in lands flowed by the tide water were in the King for the benefit of the nation. * * * Upon the American Revolution, these rights, charged with a like trust, were vested in the original States within their respective borders, subject to the rights surrendered by the Constitution of the United States. * * *

The new States admitted into the Union since the adoption of the Constitution have the same rights as the original States in the tide waters, and in the lands under them, within their respective jurisdictions." Id., at 57.

Shively rested on prior decisions of this Court, which had included similar, sweeping statements of States' dominion over lands beneath tidal waters. Knight v. United States Land Association, 142 U.S. 161, 183, (1891), for example, had stated that, "It is the settled rule of law in this court that absolute property in, and dominion and sovereignty over, the soils under the tide waters in the original States were reserved to the States, and that the new States since admitted have the same rights, sovereignty and jurisdiction in that behalf as the original States possess within their respective borders." On many occasions, before and since, this Court has stated or restated these words from *Knight* and *Shively*.

Against this array of cases, it is not surprising that Mississippi claims ownership of all of the tidelands in the State. Other States have done as much. The 13 original States, joined by the Coastal States Organization (representing all coastal States), have filed a brief in support of Mississippi, insisting that ownership of thousands of acres of tidelands

---

these lands were neither tidelands in 1817, nor were they added to the tidelands by virtue of natural forces of accretion, they belonged to their record title holders. 491 So.2d at 520.

Because the State did not cross-petition, this portion of the Mississippi Supreme Court's decision is not before us. The only issue presented here is title to the 42 acres which the Mississippi Supreme Court found to be public trust lands.

under nonnavigable waters would not be disturbed if the judgment below were affirmed, as it would be if petitioners' navigability-in-fact test were adopted. * * *

Petitioners rely on early state cases to indicate that the original States did not claim title to nonnavigable tidal waters. * * * But it has been long established that the individual States have the authority to define the limits of the lands held in public trust and to recognize private rights in such lands as they see fit. Shively v. Bowlby, 152 U.S. at 26. Some of the original States, for example, did recognize more private interests in tidelands than did others of the 13 -- more private interests than were recognized at common law, or in the dictates of our public trusts cases. * * * Because some of the cases which petitioners cite come from such States (i.e., from States which abandoned the common law with respect to tidelands), they are of only limited value in understanding the public trust doctrine and its scope in those States which have not relinquished their claims to all lands beneath tidal waters.

Finally, we note that several of our prior decisions have recognized that the States have interests in lands beneath tidal waters which have nothing to do with navigation. For example, this Court has previously observed that public trust lands may be used for fishing -- for both "shell-fish [and] floating fish." See, e.g., Smith v. Maryland, 18 How. 71, 75 (1855). On several occasions the Court has recognized that lands beneath tidal waters may be reclaimed to create land for urban expansion. E.g., Hardin v. Jordan, 140 U.S. 371, 381-382 (1891); Den v. Jersey Co., 15 U.S. (How.) 426, 432 (1854). Because of the State's ownership of tidelands, restrictions on the planting and harvesting of oysters there have been upheld. McCready v. Virginia, 94 U.S. (4 Otto) 391, 395-397 (1877). It would be odd to acknowledge such diverse uses of public trust tidelands, and then suggest that the sole measure of the expanse of such lands is the navigability of the waters over them.

Consequently, we reaffirm our long standing precedents which hold that the States, upon entry into the Union, received ownership of all lands under waters subject to the ebb and flow of the tide. Under the well-established principles of our cases, the decision of the Mississippi Supreme Court is clearly correct: the lands at issue here are "under tide waters," and therefore passed to the State of Mississippi upon its entrance into the Union.

III

Petitioners do not deny that broad statements of public trust dominion over tidelands have been included in this Court's opinions since the early 19th century. Rather, they advance two reasons why these previous statements of the public trust doctrine should not be given their apparent application in this case.

A

First, petitioners contend that these sweeping statements of state dominion over tidelands arise from an oddity of the common law, or more specifically, of English geography. Petitioners submit that in England practically all navigable rivers are influenced by the tide. Brief for Petitioners 19. See The Propeller Genesee Chief v. Fitzhugh, 12 How. 443, 454 (1852). Thus, "tidewater" and "navigability" were synonyms at common law. See Illinois Central R. Co. v. Illinois, 146 U.S. 387, 436 (1892). Consequently, in petitioners' view, the Crown's ownership of lands beneath tidewaters actually rested on the navigability of those waters rather than the ebb and flow of the tide. * * *

The cases relied on by petitioners, however, did not deal with tidal, nonnavigable waters. And we will not now enter the debate on what the English law was with respect to the land under such waters, for it is perfectly clear how this Court understood the common law of royal ownership, and what the Court considered the rights of the original and the later entering States to be. As we discuss above, this Court has consistently interpreted the common law as providing that the lands beneath waters under tidal influence were given the States upon their admission into the Union. See Shively v. Bowlby, 152 U.S. at 57.* * * It is true that none of these cases actually dealt with lands such as those involved in this case, but it has never been suggested in any of this Court's prior decisions that the many statements included therein -- to the effect that the States owned all the soil beneath waters affected by the tide -- were anything less than an accurate description of the governing law.

B

Petitioners, in a related argument, contend that even if the common law does not support their position, subsequent cases from this Court developing the American public trust doctrine make it clear that navigability -- and not tidal influence -- has become the sine qua non of the public trust interest in tidelands in this country.

It is true that *The Genesee Chief*, 12 How. at 456-457, overruled prior cases of this Court which had limited admiralty jurisdiction to waters subject to tidal influence. Cf. *The Thomas Jefferson*, 10 Wheat. 428, 429 (1825). The Court did sharply criticize the "ebb and flow" measure of admiralty inherited from England in *The Genesee Chief*, and instead insisted quite emphatically that the different topography of America -- in particular, our "thousands of miles of public navigable water[s] * * * in which there is no tide" -- required that "jurisdiction [be] made to depend upon the navigable character of the water, and not upon the ebb and flow of the tide." 12 How. at 457. Later, it came to be recognized as the "settled law of this country" that the lands under navigable freshwater lakes and rivers were within the public trust given the new States upon their entry into the Union, subject to the federal navigation easement and the power of Congress to control navigation on those streams under the Commerce Clause. Barney v. Keokuk, 94 U.S. (4 Otto) 324, 338 (1877). See also Illinois Central R. Co. v. Illinois, 146 U.S. at 435-436.

That States own freshwater river bottoms as far as the rivers are navigable, however, does not indicate that navigability is or was the prevailing test for state dominion over tidelands. Rather, this rule represents the American decision to depart from what it understood to be the English rule limiting Crown ownership to the soil under tidal waters. In Oregon ex rel. State Land Board v. Corvallis Sand & Gravel Co., 429 U.S. 363, 374 (1977), after recognizing the accepted doctrine that States coming into the Union had title to all lands under the tidewaters, the Court stated that Barney v. Keokuk, had "extended the doctrine to waters which were nontidal but nevertheless navigable, consistent with [the Court's] earlier extension of admiralty jurisdiction."

This Court's decisions in *The Genesee Chief* and Barney v. Keokuk extended admiralty jurisdiction and public trust doctrine to navigable freshwaters and the lands beneath them. But we do not read those cases as simultaneously withdrawing from public trust coverage those lands which had been consistently recognized in this Court's cases as being within that doctrine's scope: all lands beneath waters influenced by the ebb and flow of the tide.* * *

C

Finally, we observe that not the least of the difficulties with petitioners' position is their concession that the States own the tidelands bordering the oceans, bays, and estuaries -- even where these areas by no means could be considered navigable, as is always the case near the shore. Tr. of Oral Arg. 6. It is obvious that these waters are part of the sea, and the lands beneath them are State property; ultimately, though, the only proof of this fact can be that the waters are influenced by the ebb and flow of the tide. This is undoubtedly why the ebb-and-flow test has been the measure of public ownership of tidelands for so long.

Admittedly, there is a difference in degree between the waters in this case, and nonnavigable waters on the seashore that are affected by the tide. But there is no difference in kind. For in the end, all tidewaters are connected to the sea: the waters in this case, for example, by a navigable, tidal river. Perhaps the lands at issue here differ in some ways from tidelands directly adjacent to the sea; nonetheless, they still share those "geographical, chemical and environmental" qualities that make lands beneath tidal waters unique. Cf. Kaiser Aetna v. United States, 444 U.S. 164, 183 (1979) (Blackmun, J., dissenting).

Indeed, we find the various alternatives for delineating the boundaries of public trust tidelands offered by petitioners and their supporting amici to be unpersuasive and unsatisfactory. As the State suggested at argument, see Tr. of Oral Arg. 22-23, and as recognized on several previous occasions, the ebb and flow rule has the benefit of "uniformity and certainty, and * * * eas[e] of application." See, e.g., Cobb v. Davenport, 32 N.J.L. 369, 379 (1867). We are unwilling, after its lengthy history at common law, in this Court, and in many state courts, to abandon the ebb and flow rule now, and seek to fashion a new test to govern the limits of public trust tidelands. Consequently, we hold that the lands at issue in this case were within those given to Mississippi when the State was admitted to the Union.

IV

Petitioners in passing, and amici in somewhat greater detail, complain that the Mississippi Supreme Court's decision is "inequitable" and would upset "various * * * kinds of property expectations and interests [which] have matured since Mississippi joined the Union in1817." They claim that they have developed reasonable expectations based on their record title for these lands, and that they (and their predecessors-in-interest) have paid taxes on these lands for more than a century.

We have recognized the importance of honoring reasonable expectations in property interests. Cf. Kaiser Aetna v. United States, supra, 444 U.S. at 175. But such expectations can only be of consequence where they are "reasonable" ones. Here, Mississippi law appears to have consistently held that the public trust in lands under water includes "title to all the land under tidewater." Rouse v. Saucier's Heirs, 166 Miss. 704, 713, 146 So. 291, 291-292 (1933). Although the Mississippi Supreme Court acknowledged that this case may be the first where it faced the question of the public trust interest in non navigable tidelands, 491 So. 2d at 516, the clear and unequivocal statements in its earlier opinions should have been ample indication of the State's claim to tidelands. Moreover, cases which have discussed the State's public trust interest in these lands have described uses of them not related to navigability, such as bathing, swimming, recreation, fishing, and mineral development. See, e.g., Treuting v. Bridge and Park Comm'n of City of Biloxi, 199 So.2d 627, 632-633 (Miss.1967). These statements, too, should have made clear that the State's claims were not limited to lands under navigable waterways. Any contrary expectations cannot be considered reasonable.

We are skeptical of the suggestions by the dissent * * * that a decision affirming the judgment below will have sweeping implications, either within Mississippi or outside that State. The State points out that only one other case is pending in its courts which raises this same issue.

Tr. of Oral Arg. 19. And as for the effect of our decision today in other States, we are doubtful that this ruling will do more than confirm the prevailing understanding -- which in some States is the same as Mississippi's, and in others, is quite different. As this Court wrote in Shively v. Bowlby, 152 U.S., at 26 "there is no universal and uniform law upon the subject; but * * * each State has dealt with the lands under the tide waters within its borders according to its own views of justice and policy."

Consequently, our ruling today will not upset titles in all coastal states, as petitioners intimated at argument. Tr. of Oral Arg. 32. As we have discussed * * * many coastal States, as a matter of state law, granted all or a portion of their tidelands to adjacent upland property owners long ago. Our decision today does nothing to change ownership rights in States which previously relinquished a public trust claim to tidelands such as those in issue here.

Indeed, we believe that it would be far more upsetting to settled expectations to reverse the Mississippi Supreme Court decision. As amici note, see, e.g., Brief for State of California et al. as Amici Curiae 19, many land titles have been adjudicated based on the ebb-and-flow rule for tidelands -- we cannot know how many titles would have to be adjusted if the scope of the public trust was now found to be limited to lands beneath navigable tidal waters only. If States do not own lands under non navigable tidal waters, many State land grants based on our earlier decisions might now be invalid. Cf. Hardin v. Jordan, 140 U.S. at 381-382. Finally, even where States have given dominion over tidelands to private property owners, some States have retained for the general public the right to fish, hunt, or bathe on these lands. These long-established rights may be lost with respect to nonnavigable tidal waters if we adopt the rule urged by petitioners.

The fact that petitioners have long been the record title holders, or long paid taxes on these lands does not change the outcome here. How such facts would transfer ownership of these lands from the State to petitioners is a question of state law. Here, the Mississippi Supreme Court held that under Mississippi law, the State's ownership of these lands could not be lost via adverse possession, laches, or any other equitable doctrine.* * * We see no reason to disturb the "general proposition [that] the law of real property is, under our Constitution, left to the individual States to develop and administer." Hughes v. Washington, 389 U.S. 290, 295 (1967) (Stewart, J., concurring). * * * Consequently, we do not believe that the equitable considerations petitioners advance divest the State of its ownership in the disputed tidelands.

V

Because we believe that our cases firmly establish that the States, upon entering the Union, were given ownership over all lands beneath waters subject to the tide's influence, we affirm the Mississippi Supreme Court's determination that the lands at issue here became property of the State upon its admission to the Union in 1817. Furthermore, because we find no reason to set aside that court's state-law determination that subsequent developments did not divest the State of its ownership of these public trust lands, the judgment below is Affirmed.

JUSTICE KENNEDY took no part in the consideration or decision of this case.

JUSTICE O'CONNOR, with whom JUSTICE STEVENS and JUSTICE SCALIA join, dissenting.

Breaking a chain of title that reaches back more than 150 years, the Court today announces a rule that will disrupt the settled expectations of landowners not only in Mississippi but in every coastal State. Neither our precedents nor equitable principles require this result, and I respectfully dissent from this undoing of settled history.

* * *

In my view, the public trust properly extends only to land underlying navigable bodies of water and their borders, bays, and inlets. This Court has defined the public trust repeatedly in terms of navigability. It is true that these cases did not involve waters subject to the ebb and flow of the tide. But there is no reason to think that different tests of the scope of the public trust apply to saltwater and to freshwater. Navigability, not tidal influence, ought to be acknowledged as the universal hallmark of the public trust.

* * *

American cases have developed the public trust doctrine in a way that is consistent with its common law heritage. Our precedents explain that the public trust extends to navigable waterways because its fundamental purpose is to preserve them for common use for transportation. * * *

Although the States may commit public trust waterways to uses other than transportation, such as fishing or land reclamation, this exercise of sovereign discretion does not enlarge the scope of the public trust. Even the majority does not claim that the public trust extends to every waterway that can be used for fishing or for land reclamation. Nor does the majority explain why its tidal test is superior to a navigability test for the purpose of identifying waterways that are suited to these other uses.

Because the fundamental purpose of the public trust is to protect commerce, the scope of the public trust should parallel the scope of federal admiralty jurisdiction. This Court long ago abandoned the tidal test in favor of the navigability test for defining federal admiralty jurisdiction, describing the ebb and flow test as "purely artificial and arbitrary as well as unjust." The Propeller Genesee Chief v. Fitzhugh, 12 How. 443, 457 (1852). * * *

For public trust purposes, navigable bodies of water include the nonnavigable areas at their boundaries. The question whether a body of water is navigable is answered waterway by waterway, not inch by inch. The borders of the ocean, which certainly is navigable, extend to the mean high-tide line as a matter of federal common law. Hence the States' public trusts include the ocean shore over which the tide ebbs and flows. This explains why there is language in our cases describing the public trust in terms of tidewaters: each of those cases concerned the shores of a navigable body of water. This does not imply, however, that all tidally influenced waters are part of the sea any more than it implies that the Missouri River is part of the Gulf of Mexico.

The Court holds today that the public trust includes not only tidewaters along the ocean shore, but also discrete bodies of water that are influenced by the tide but far removed from the ocean or any navigable tidal water, such as the separate little streams and bayous at issue here. * * *

II

The controversy in this case concerns more than cold legal doctrine. The particular facts of this case, to which the Court's opinion gives short shrift, illustrate how unfortunate it is for the Court to recognize a claim that appears belated and opportunistic.

Mississippi showed no interest in the disputed land from the time it became a State until the 1970s. Petitioners, or prior titleholders, recorded deeds on the land and paid property taxes throughout this period. App. to Pet. for Cert. 41a. In 1973, Mississippi passed the Coastal Wetlands Protection Law. Miss.Code Ann. §§ 49-27-1 to 49-27-69 (Supp.1987). This statute directed the Mississippi Marine Resources Council to prepare maps identifying state-owned wetlands. The maps, drawn from aerial photographs, were intended to show the probable scope of state-owned wetlands in order to aid state agencies in planning to protect them. § 49-27-65. But the Mineral Lease Commission decided to use the maps as a basis for issuing oil and gas leases on what appeared to be state-owned lands. The Commission leased 600 acres to respondent Saga Petroleum U.S., Inc.

Petitioners, holders of record title, filed a complaint in Chancery Court to quiet title to the * * * contested acres. * * * The land now claimed by Mississippi consists of slightly more than 42 acres underlying the north branch of Bayou LaCroix and 11 small drainage streams.

These waterways are not used for commercial navigation. None of the drainage streams is more than a mile long; all are nameless. Mississippi is not pressing its claim for the sake of facilitating commerce, or even to protect the public's interest in fishing or other traditional uses of the public trust. Instead, it is leasing the land to a private party for exploitation of underlying minerals. Mississippi's novel undertaking has caused it to press for a radical expansion of the historical limits of the public trust.

* * *

The Court's decision departs from our precedents, and I fear that it may permit grave injustice to be done to innocent property holders in coastal States. I dissent.

Notes and Questions

1.   **Navigable in law.** For many purposes, nonnavigable-in-fact tidal waters are considered to be "navigable-in-law" and therefore "navigable waters." See, e.g., 33 CFR §§ 329.4, 329.11, and 329.12 (in Chapter 2, infra).

2.   **The equal footing doctrine.** The subject of the controversy in *Phillips Petroleum* was the ownership of tidelands located in waters that are not navigable-in-fact. What is the basis of the claim of Mississippi, a state carved out of the Southwest Territory? The answer lies in the *equal footing doctrine*. The original thirteen colonies, when they first became independent states, which was prior to the formation of the United States, succeeded to the sovereign rights of the English crown. One of these rights was the ownership of lands under navigable waters and the right to convey such lands subject to any recognized public trust rights. When the United States acquired a new territory, it held any submerged land in trust for future states to be carved out of the territory. When a new state was formed, sovereignty over submerged lands under navigable waters then passed to the new state which continued to hold the lands subject to the public trust. See, e.g., Pollard's Lessee v. Hagan, 44 U.S. 212, 224 (1845).

The fact that the federal government held territorial submerged lands in trust for future states did not necessarily mean that the federal government could never validly convey those lands to private parties prior to statehood. The Supreme Court, in Shively v. Bowlby, 152 U.S. 1 (1894), declared that the Property Clause permitted Congress to convey territorial public trust lands [and so defeat the title of a new State] "in order to perform international obligations, or to effect the improvement of such lands for the promotion and convenience of commerce with foreign nations and among the several States, or to carry out other public purposes appropriate to the objects for which the United States holds the Territory." Id. at 48. See also Summa Corp. v. California ex rel. State Lands Commission, 466 U.S. 198, 204-09 (carrying out treaty provisions represents an "international duty") reh'g denied, 467 U.S. 1231 (1984) (dicta); United States v. City of Anchorage, 437 F.2d 1081 (1971) (grant of public trust lands to federally owned and operated railroad deemed a "public purpose"); United States v. Alaska, 423 F.2d. 764 ("public purpose" served by grant to game refuge) cert. denied, 400 U.S. 967 (1970).

According to the United States Supreme Court, there is a "strong presumption against conveyance by the United States" of title to the bed of a navigable water. Montana v. United States, 450 U.S. 544, 552, reh'g denied, 452 U.S. 911 (1981). It is unclear whether this "strong presumption against conveyance" is constitutionally mandated or represents merely a congressional policy. See Utah Division of State Lands v. United States, 482 U.S. 193, 207 (1987) (Court inferred a congressional policy, not a constitutional obligation, to retain public trust property for future States); but see State of North Dakota ex. rel. Board of University and School Lands v. Andrus, 506 F.Supp. 619, 623 (1981), aff'd, 671 F.2d 271 (1982) (presumption arises from the constitutional doctrine of equal footing). No matter what the source of this presumption, a court will not infer a conveyance of public trust lands unless in the grant itself an "intention was definitely declared or otherwise made very plain, or was rendered in clear and especial words, or unless the claim confirmed in terms embraces the land under the waters of the stream." *Utah Division of State Lands*, supra, at 198. The Supreme Court, however, has never determined that the United States did in fact grant to private parties sovereign lands prior to statehood. But see Choctaw Nation v. Oklahoma, 397 U.S. 620 (United States grant to Indian Nations upheld due to the unusual history behind the particular Indian treaties involved in this case. Arguably the Indian tribes represented a sovereign nation, not individuals), reh'g denied, 398 U.S. 945 (1970).

3. **Federal definitions of navigability.** As the majority opinion in *Phillips Petroleum* points out, no comprehensive federal definition of navigability exists. The earliest federal definitions of navigability appear in admiralty jurisdiction cases. Because, in the absence of a statute, only torts occurring on navigable waters fall within federal admiralty jurisdiction, the classification of the waters upon which the tort

occurred is of some significance.

The history of admiralty jurisdiction in the 1800s is one of expansion beyond that which existed in England. In The Steamboat Thomas Jefferson, 23 U.S. 428 (1825), the Court held that admiralty "navigable waters" meant the sea or waters subject to the ebb and flow of the tide, the so-called English rule of navigability. However, as the country grew westward to include the Great Lakes and vast inland river systems, the Court discarded the limitations of the English rule. The reach of admiralty jurisdiction was broadened to include all fresh waters that were used for commercial navigation between the states and between the United States and foreign countries. The Propeller Genesee Chief v. Fitzhugh, 53 U.S. (12 How.) 443 (1851); Jackson v. The Steamboat Magnolia, 61 U.S. (20 How.) 296 (1857); The Eagle, 75 U.S. (8 Wall.) 15 (1868); Ex parte Boyer, 109 U.S. 629 (1884). Although unanswered questions still exist as to the exact definition of navigable waters for purposes of federal admiralty jurisdiction, there has been no significant United States Supreme Court opinion on the topic since the 1880s.

In 1870, the Court's attention shifted to the relationship of navigability to the federal government's power under the Commerce Clause. In The Daniel Ball, 77 U.S. (10 Wall) 557 (1870), the issue was whether a federal safety regulation applied to a ship that operated solely on a river in Michigan, upon which goods moved in interstate commerce. If the river was a "navigable water of the United States" within the meaning of the federal statute, and if Congress had the power under the Commerce Clause to pass such a statute, then The Daniel Ball was subject to the regulation. The Court answered both questions affirmatively. In addressing the first issue, Justice Field, the author of *Illinois Central*, infra, attempted to provide a comprehensive definition of navigability.

> The doctrine of the common law as to the navigability of waters has no application in this country. Here the ebb and flow of the tide do not constitute the usual test, as in England, or any test at all of the navigability of waters. There no waters are navigable in fact, or at least to any considerable extent, which are not subject to the tide, and from this circumstance tide water and navigable water there signify substantially the same thing. But in this country the case is widely different. Some of our rivers are as navigable for many hundreds of miles above as they are below the limits of tide water, and some of them are navigable for great distances by large vessels, which are not even affected by the tide at any point during their entire length. A different test must, therefore, be applied to determine the navigability of our rivers, and that is found in their navigable capacity. Those rivers must be regarded as public navigable rivers in law which are navigable in fact. And they are navigable in fact when they are used, or are susceptible of being

used, in their ordinary condition, as highways for commerce, over which trade and travel are or may be conducted in the customary modes of trade and travel on water. And they constitute navigable waters of the United States within the meaning of the acts of Congress, in contradistinction from the navigable waters of the States, when they form in their ordinary condition by themselves, or by uniting with other waters, a continued highway over which commerce is or may be carried on with other States or foreign countries in the customary modes in which such commerce is conducted by water.

Id. at 563. The "navigability" test of *The Daniel Ball* was subsequently expanded in other Commerce Clause cases, of which United States v. Appalachian Electric Power Co., 311 U.S. 377 (1940), is perhaps the most significant. In that case, the Court said:

To appraise the evidence of navigability on the natural condition only of the waterway is erroneous. Its availability for navigation must also be considered. "Natural and ordinary condition" refers to volume of water, the gradients and the regularity of the flow. A waterway, otherwise suitable for navigation, is not barred from that classification merely because artificial aids must make the highway suitable for use before commercial navigation may be undertaken.

* * * Although navigability to fix ownership of the river bed or riparian rights is determined * * * as of the formation of the Union in the original states or the admission to statehood of those formed later, navigability, for the purpose of the regulation of commerce, may later arise. An analogy is found in admiralty jurisdiction, which may be extended over places formerly nonnavigable. There has never been doubt that the navigability referred to in the cases was navigability despite the obstruction of falls, rapids, sand bars, carries or shifting currents. The plenary federal power over commerce must be able to develop with the needs of that commerce which is the reason for its existence. * * *

Id. at 407-09.

Despite the broad language of these cases, they do not provide a comprehensive federal navigability test. Each case must be read in its context. When this is done, it is clear that the following questions are not resolved by these decisions or *Phillips Petroleum*. First, is the expanded definition of *Appalachian Electric Power Co.* applicable to title determination cases? Second, if a test of navigability is "navigable in fact," what is meant by "navigable in fact?" Navigable in fact by what types of vessels and for what purposes? Finally, in *The Daniel Ball*, in dicta, the court provides a definition of "navigable waters of the States." If that is a federal common law definition of state navigable waters, in what situations is it to be applied?

Phillips Petroleum addresses the "ebb and flow" branch of the test for navigable waters. What is the test for determining whether nontidal waters, impressed with the public trust, passed to the state pursuant to the equal footing doctrine? Are only waters that are part of "a continued highway over which commerce is or may be carried on with other States or foreign countries" public trust waters that passed to the newly created states upon statehood? If so, what would be the status of a body of water that prior to statehood lay entirely within the territory, with no connections with any waters that lay outside the territory, and was placed entirely within the geographic boundaries of a newly carved out state? Are public trust waters simply the fortuitous consequence of the drawing of lines on a map? See Utah v. United States, 403 U.S. 9 (1971) (at time of statehood, Utah acquired title to Great Salt Lake, an entirely intrastate body of water).

4. Once "navigable waters" and associated submerged lands pass to the state, may a state adopt a broader definition of navigable waters? If it does, wouldn't the state be engaged in a taking of private property in violation of the Fifth Amendment or does Oregon ex rel State Land Board v. Corvallis Sand and Gravel Company, 429 U.S. 363 (1977) (discussed in Section 3, on page 55), mean that a state is entitled to develop its own rules of property for all land within its borders? Does the Fifth Amendment permit a state to modify, over time, its definition of navigability? Could a state adopt one definition of navigable waters for title purposes and a broader definition for the purpose of determining what waters are open to public trust uses? Would this avoid any "takings" problem?

The fact of the matter is that state definitions of navigability do evolve over time. For example, the Arkansas Supreme Court expanded its definition of navigable-in-fact to include streams that can be used for recreational purposes. Earlier cases had suggested that a waterway had to be used for commercial navigation to be "navigable." These cases were distinguished on the ground that the issue of whether streams useful for only recreational boating could be "navigable waters" had not been before the court. State v. McIlroy, 268 Ark. 227, 595 S.W.2d 659, cert. denied, 449 U.S. 843 (1980). See also Kelly ex. rel. MacMullan v. Hallden, 51 Mich. App. 176, 214 N.W.2d 856 (1974). It is important to note that in these cases, the courts were not deciding whether title to the submerged land lying under the body of water was in the state or in private hands. The issue was only the right of the public to use the water for navigation or other public trust uses. This right of public use is sometimes referred to as a navigation easement. In a few states the public has the right to use the bottom for purposes incidental to the use of the water. But public ownership of submerged lands does not necessarily follow the public right to use the overlying water body. For a further discussion of these issues, see 1 and 4 Water and Water Rights §§ 6.02(f), 6.03(a), 30.03, 32.01-.03(a) (1991).

SECTION 3. A STATE'S AUTHORITY OVER SUBMERGED LANDS UNDER NAVIGABLE WATERS

A. ILLINOIS CENTRAL RAILROAD

[Illinois Central Railroad Co. v. Illinois, 146 U.S 387 (1892), is the cornerstone of the public trust doctrine as it exists today in the United States. The roots of the *Illinois Central* controversy lie in an 1869 Illinois legislative act that purported to grant the railroad title to submerged lands lying in the Chicago harbor. The Act provided, in part, that:

> * * * the fee to said lands shall be held by said company in perpetuity, and * * * said company shall not have power to grant, sell, or convey the fee to the same * * * and provided also, that nothing herein contained shall authorize obstructions to the Chicago harbor, or impair the public right of navigation; nor shall this act be construed to exempt the * * * railroad * * * from any act of the general assembly which may be hereafter passed regulating rates of wharfage and dockage to be charged in said harbor.

Id. at 406, n.3.

If the railroad accepted the grant, it was to pay certain specified sums to the City of Chicago and a percentage of the revenues derived from the use of facilities placed upon the submerged lands to the State of Illinois. The first payment to Chicago was tendered but never accepted by the city. No payment was ever made to the State because the litigation was instituted before any facilities were constructed upon the disputed lands.

The 1869 Act generated substantial adverse publicity and a call for its repeal. A new legislature was elected, and in response to public feeling, it acted quickly in 1873 to repeal the 1869 Act. The State then filed an action to determine title. The action was initially filed in state court, but the railroad subsequently removed the case to the federal circuit court.

Although the 1869 Act could be read as conveying only a limited interest in the submerged lands to the railroad, the railroad's position was that the Act conveyed absolute title to the company with the complete power to use and dispose of any of the submerged lands. The limiting language was viewed as only preventing the transfer of the technical fee title.

When the case reached the United States Supreme Court, two Justices disqualified themselves. One, Chief Justice Fuller, had represented the railroad in the lower courts; the other, Justice Blatchford, was a stockholder in the railroad.

The Supreme Court (4-3) affirmed the decision of the circuit court, which had declared the 1869 grant invalid. The majority opinion was written by Justice Field, a Justice known for his railroad sympathies. In his opinion, Justice Field stated:]

* * *

The act, if valid and operative to the extent claimed, placed under the control of the railroad company nearly the whole of the submerged lands of the harbor, subject only to the limitations that it should not authorize obstructions to the harbor or impair the public right of navigation, or exclude the legislature from regulating the rates of wharfage or dockage to be charged. With these limitations the act put it in the power of the company to delay indefinitely the improvement of the harbor, or to construct as many docks, piers and wharves and other works as it might choose, and at such positions in the harbor as might suit its purposes, and permit any kind of business to be conducted thereon, and to lease them out on its own terms, for indefinite periods. * * *

The question, therefore, to be considered is whether the legislature was competent to thus deprive the state of its ownership of the submerged lands in the harbor of Chicago, and of the consequent control of its waters; or, in other words, whether the railroad corporation can hold the lands and control the waters by the grant, against any future exercise of power over them by the State.

That the State holds the title to the lands under the navigable waters of Lake Michigan, within its limits, in the same manner that the State holds title to soils under tide water, by the common law, we have already shown; and that title necessarily carries with it control over the waters above them whenever the lands are subjected to use. But it is a title different in character from that which the State holds in lands intended for sale. It is different from the title which the United States hold in the public lands which are open to pre-emption and sale. It is a title held in trust for the people of the State that they may enjoy the navigation of the waters, carry on commerce over them, and have liberty of fishing therein freed from the obstruction or interference of private parties. The interest of the people in the navigation of the waters and in commerce over them may be improved in many instances by the erection of wharves, docks and piers therein, for which purpose the State may grant parcels of the submerged lands; and, so long as their disposition is made for such purpose, no valid objections can be made to the grants. It is grants of parcels of lands under navigable waters, that may afford foundation for wharves, piers, docks, and other structures in aid of commerce, and grants of parcels which, being occupied, do not substantially impair the public interest in the lands and waters remaining, that are chiefly considered and sustained in the adjudged cases as a valid exercise of legislative power consistently with the trust to the public upon which such lands are held by the State. But that is a very different doctrine from the one which would sanction the abdication of the general control of the State over lands under the navigable waters of an entire harbor or bay, or of a sea or lake. Such abdication is not consistent with the exercise of that trust which requires the government of the State to preserve such waters for the use of the public. The trust devolving upon the State for the public, and which can only be discharged by the management and control of property in which the public has an interest, cannot be relinquished by a transfer of the property. *The control of the State for the purposes of the trust can never be lost, except as to such parcels as are used in promoting the interests of the public therein, or can be disposed of without any substantial impairment of the public interest in the lands and waters remaining.* It is only by observing the distinction between a grant of such parcels for the improvement of the public interest, or which when occupied do not substantially impair the public interest in the lands and waters remaining, and a grant of the whole property in which the public is interested, that the language of the adjudged cases can be reconciled. General language sometimes found in opinions of the courts, expressive of absolute ownership and control by the State of lands under navigable waters, irrespective of any trust as to their use and disposition, must be read and construed with reference to the special facts of the particular cases. A grant of all the lands under the navigable waters of a State has never been adjudged to be within the legislative power; and any attempted grant of the kind would be held, if not absolutely void on its face, as subject to revocation. *The State can no more abdicate its trust over property in which the whole people are interested, like navigable waters and soils under them, so as to leave them entirely under the use and control of private parties, except in the instance of parcels mentioned for the improvement of the navigation and use of the waters, or when parcels can be disposed of without impairment of the public interest in what remains, than it can abdicate* its police powers in the administration of government and the preservation of the peace. In the administration of government the use of such powers may for a limited period be delegated to a municipality or other body, but there always remains with the State the right to revoke those powers and exercise them in a more direct manner, and one more conformable to its wishes. So with trusts connected with public property, or property of a special character, like lands under navigable waters, they cannot be placed entirely beyond the direction and control of the State.

The harbor of Chicago is of immense value to the people of the State of Illinois in the facilities it affords to its vast and constantly increasing commerce; and the idea that its legislature can deprive the State of control over its bed and waters and place the same in the hands of a private corporation created for a different purpose, one limited to transportation of passengers and freight between distant points and the city, is a proposition that cannot be defended.

The area of the submerged lands proposed to be ceded by the act in question to the railroad company embraces something more than 1,000 acres, being, as stated by counsel, more than three times the area of the outer harbor, and not only including all of that harbor but embracing adjoining submerged lands which will, in all probability, be hereafter included in the harbor. It is as large as that embraced by all the merchandise docks along the Thames at London; is much larger than that included in the famous docks and basins at Liverpool; is twice that of the port of Marseilles, and nearly if not quite equal to the pier area along the water front of the city of New York. And the arrivals and clearings of vessels at the port exceed in number those of New York, and are equal to those of New York and Boston combined. Chicago has nearly twenty-five per cent of the lake carrying trade, as compared with the arrivals and clearings of all the leading ports of our great inland seas. * * * It is hardly conceivable that the legislature can divest the State of the control and management of this harbor and vest it absolutely in a private corporation. Surely an act of the legislature transferring the title to its submerged lands and the power claimed by the railroad company to a foreign State or nation would be repudiated, without hesitation, as a gross perversion of the trust over the property under which it is held. * * * It would not be listened to that the control and management of the harbor of that great city -- a subject of concern to the whole people of the State -- should thus be placed elsewhere than in the State itself. All the objections which can be urged to such attempted transfer may be urged to a transfer to a private corporation like the railroad company in this case.

Any grant of the kind is necessarily revocable, and the exercise of the trust by which the property was held by the State can be resumed at any time. Undoubtedly there may be expenses incurred in improvements made under such a grant, which the State ought to pay; but, be that as it may, the power to resume the trust whenever the State judges best is, we think, incontrovertible. The position advanced by the railroad company in support of its claim to the ownership of the submerged lands and the right to the erection of wharves, piers, and docks at its pleasure, or for its business in the harbor of Chicago, would place every harbor in the country at the mercy of a majority of the legislature of the State in which the harbor is situated.

We cannot, it is true, cite any authority where a grant of this kind has been held invalid, for we believe that no instance exists where the harbor of a great city and its commerce have been allowed to pass into the control of any private corporation. But the decisions are numerous which declare that such property is held by the state, by virtue of its sovereignty, in trust for the public. The ownership of the navigable waters of the harbor and of the lands under them is a subject of public concern to the whole people of the State. The trust with which they are held, therefore, is governmental and cannot be alienated, except in those instances mentioned of parcels used in the improvement of the interest thus held, or when parcels can be disposed of without detriment to the public interest in the lands and waters remaining.

This follows necessarily from the public character of the property, being held by the whole people for purposes in which the whole people are interested. * * *

The soil under navigable waters being held by the people of the State in trust for the common use and as a portion of their inherent sovereignty, any act of legislation concerning their use affects the public welfare. It is therefore appropriately within the exercise of the police power of the State.

* * * The legislature could not give away nor sell the discretion of its successors in respect to matters, the government of which, from the very nature of things, must vary with varying circumstances. The legislation which may be needed one day for the harbor may be different from the legislation that may be required at another day. Every legislature must, at the time of its existence, exercise the power of the State in the execution of the trust devolved upon it. We hold, therefore, that any attempted cession of the ownership and control of the State in and over the submerged lands in Lake Michigan, by the act of April 16, 1869, was inoperative to affect, modify or in any respect to control the sovereignty and dominion of the State over the lands, or its ownership thereof, and that any such attempted operation of the act was annulled by the repealing act of April 15, 1873, which to that extent was valid and effective. There can be no irrepealable contract in a conveyance of property by a grantor in disregard of a public trust, under which he was bound to hold and manage it.

* * *

Affirmed.

Id. at 450-51, 452-56, 459-60 (emphasis added).

Notes and Questions

1.   Does the public trust doctrine apply to federally-owned submerged lands? See District of Columbia v. Air Florida, Inc., 750 F.2d 1077, 1083-86 (D.C. Cir. 1984) (dicta); United States v. 1.58 Acres of Land, 523 F. Supp. 120 (D. Mass. 1981) (dicta) (federal government is as restricted as the states in the disposition of sovereignty lands); but see Utah Division of State Lands v. United States, 482 U.S. 193 (1987).

2.   State police powers and the Contract Clause. The position of the railroad in *Illinois Central* was that the legislation was in effect a contract which could not be repealed by a later legislature without violating the Contract Clause of the United States Constitution. Why wasn't the action of the state of Illinois a violation of the Contract Clause? Consider the following case, Stone v. Mississippi, 101 U.S. 814 (1879):

In 1867, the Mississippi legislature passed legislation incorporating a private corporation and granting that corporation the right to conduct a lottery within the state. Shortly thereafter, in 1869, a new state constitution was adopted. The new constitution declared that "The legislature shall never authorize any lottery; nor shall the sale of lottery-tickets be allowed; nor shall any lottery heretofore authorized be permitted to be drawn, or tickets therein sold." Acting pursuant to this constitutional mandate, the 1870 legislature passed legislation prohibiting all lotteries within the state. The State then sued the corporation on the ground that it was conducting a prohibited lottery. The corporation defended on the basis that the rights granted by the 1867 statute could not be abrogated by a later state constitution or legislation.

The unanimous opinion of the Supreme Court began with the somewhat reluctant acknowledgment that a charter to a private corporation was within the protection of the Contract Clause. However, the Court then noted that, unless a valid contract was entered into, there was nothing to be protected by the Contract Clause. Thus, "[w]hether the alleged contract exists * * * or not, depends on the authority of the legislature to bind the State and the people of the State in that way." Id. at 817. Although nothing in the pre-1869 state constitution prohibited the legislature from granting the right to conduct lotteries, the Court noted "[a]ll agree that the legislature cannot bargain away the police power of a State." Id. Without attempting to define the limits of this police power the Court stated that it certainly included all matters affecting the public health and public morals and thus a lottery was a proper subject of regulation under state police powers. Consequently, a contract in which the legislature or state purported to give up the right to regulate or prohibit a lottery was invalid and unenforceable.

In explaining its decision the Court stated:

* * * the power of governing is a trust committed by the people to the government, no part of which can be granted away. The people, in their sovereign capacity, have established their agencies for the preservation of the public health and the public morals, and the protection of public and private rights. These several agencies can govern according to their discretion, if within the scope of their general authority, while in power; but they cannot give away nor sell the discretion of those that are to come after them, in respect to matters the government of which, from the very nature of things, must "vary with varying circumstances." They may create corporations, and give them, so to speak, a limited citizenship; but as citizens, limited in their privileges, or otherwise, these creatures of the government creation are subject to such rules and regulations as may from time to time be ordained and established for the preservation of health and morality.

The contracts which the Constitution protects are those that relate to property rights, not governmental. It is not always easy to tell on which side of the line which separates governmental from property rights a particular case is to be put; but in respect to lotteries there can be no difficulty. * * * Any one, therefore, who accepts a lottery charter does so with the implied understanding that the people, in their sovereign capacity, and through their properly constituted agencies, may resume it at any time when the public good shall require, whether it be paid for or not. All that one can get by such a charter is a suspension of certain governmental rights in his favor, subject to withdrawal at will. He has in legal effect nothing more than a license to enjoy the privilege on the terms named for the specified time, unless it be sooner abrogated by the sovereign power of the State. It is a permit, good as against existing laws, but subject to future legislative and constitutional control or withdrawal.

Id. at 820-21. See also A. Weisburd, Territorial Authority and Personal Jurisdiction, 63 Wash. U. L.Q. 377, 384 (1985).

   3.   *Illinois Central*: A matter of federal constitutional law or the law of the individual states?

   A central issue is the legal foundation of the public trust doctrine. There is no question that the public trust doctrine is widely accepted by the states. And there is no question that state decisions affirming the existence of the public trust doctrine almost always cite *Illinois Central* as authority. See, e.g., CWC Fisheries, Inc. v. Bunker, 755 P.2d 1115, 1117-18 (Alaska 1988); Caminiti v. Boyle, 107 Wash.2d. 662, 670, 732 P.2d 989, 997 (1987); Shepard's Point Land Co. v. Atlantic Hotel, 132 N.C. 517, 525-28, 44 S.E. 39, 41-42 (1903); State v. Black River Phosphate Co., 32 Fla. 82, 13 So. 640, 645-47 (1893). However, when faced with determining the validity of an alleged conveyance of submerged lands under navigable waters, the courts frequently avoid the difficult issue of the constitutional basis of the public trust doctrine.

In most cases, conveyances of public trust lands are treated as valid but as subject to the pubic's continuing public trust use rights. In many of these cases, the courts use a variety of approaches to find that there was no valid conveyance of the submerged land free of the public trust. In some cases, courts strictly construe against the grantee the language of the authorizing legislation or the deed of conveyance. For example, in Boston Waterfront Dev. Corp. v. Commonwealth, 378 Mass. 629, 637-38, 393 N.E.2d 356, 361 (1979), a statute granting certain submerged land to a corporation in fee simple also contained language that "nothing herein shall be understood as authorizing * * * interfere(nce) with the legal rights of * * * [others]." This language was construed to mean that the submerged lands were conveyed subject to the public trust. See also, e.g., Coastal States Gas Producing Co. v. State Mineral Board, 199 So.2d 554, 557-58 (La. App 1967); CWC Fisheries, Inc. v. Bunker, 755 P.2d 1115 (Alaska 1988) (unless legislative intent to give up the public interest in any tideland statute is clearly expressed or necessarily implied, the court will interpret the grant as preserving the public interest). In other cases, courts conclude that the particular state entity or agency that made the alleged conveyances of submerged lands under navigable water lacked the necessary legislative authorization. See, e.g., Martin v. Busch, 93 Fla. 535, 573, 112 So. 274, 286-87 (1927).

But when nonconstitutional grounds for invalidating a conveyance of submerged lands do not exist, the issue of what exactly is the constitutional basis of the public trust doctrine cannot be ignored. If the United States Constitution is the source of the doctrine, what federal constitutional provision permits the United States Supreme Court to impose a public trust upon state owned land? Is there both a federal public trust doctrine and the public trust doctrine of individual states? If so, how do the doctrines differ? Finally, if no express provision of the federal or state constitution prohibits legislative disposals of submerged lands, why should a state or federal court be permitted to invalidate state legislation conveying submerged lands to private parties by means of an extra-constitutional doctrine, such as the public trust doctrine? When the people adopt constitutions defining the powers of the various branches of the federal and state governments, and the constitutions do not in any express manner limit the power of the Congress or state legislatures to dispose of federal or state owned submerged land, then haven't the people spoken? Compare C. Wilkinson, The Headwaters of the Public Trust: Some Thoughts on the Source and Scope of the Traditional Doctrine, 19 Envtl. L. 425 (1988), with J. Huffman, A Fish Out Of Water: The Public Trust Doctrine in a Constitutional Democracy, 19 Envtl. L. 527 (1988).

In Gwathmey v. State of North Carolina, 342 N.C. 287, 464 S.E.2d 674

(1995), the North Carolina Supreme Court directly addressed the question of whether a constitutional public trust doctrine limits the authority of a state legislature to dispose of public trust submerged lands. The case involved a state agency's conveyances between 1926 and 1945 of salt marsh located in one of North Carolina's estuarine sounds. The State argued that the marshlands could not be conveyed free of the public trust and the legislature did not have the power to do anything which would impair public trust interests in such lands. The Court responded that

> It is true that lands submerged by waters which are determined to be navigable in law are subject to the public trust doctrine. However, the assumption that such lands may not be conveyed by the General Assembly without reservation of public trust rights is incorrect.

> * * *

> No constitutional provision throughout the history of our State has expressly or impliedly precluded the General Assembly from conveying lands beneath navigable waters by special grant in fee simple and free of any rights arising from the public trust doctrine. See [J. Kalo and M. Kalo, The] Battle to Preserve North Carolina's Estuarine Marshes: The 1985 Legislation, Private Claims to Estuarine Marshes, Denial of Permits to Fill, and the Public Trust, 64 N.C. L. Rev. at 576-77. *The public trust doctrine is a common law doctrine.* In the absence of a constitutional basis for the public trust doctrine, it cannot be used to invalidate acts of the legislature which are not proscribed by our Constitution. Thus, in North Carolina, the public trust doctrine operates as a rule of construction creating a presumption that the General Assembly did not intend to convey lands in a manner that would impair public trust rights. * * * However, this presumption is overcome by a special grant from the General Assembly *expressly* conveying lands underlying navigable waters in fee simple and without reservation of any public trust rights. [citations omitted].

Id. at 301-04; S.E.2d at 682-84. See also Providence Chamber of Commerce v. State, 657 A.2d 1038, 1041-43 (R.I. 1995) (public trust is a common law doctrine). But see New York v. DeLyster, 759 F. Supp. 982, 990 (W.D.N.Y. 1991) (*Illinois Central* "involved a fundamental issue of federal law concerning the nature of a state's sovereignty, and the powers assumed by the state upon its admission to the Union.").

The North Carolina Supreme Court's view of the essential nature of the public trust doctrine is supported by language in United States Supreme Court cases decided subsequently to *Illinois Central*. Two years after *Illinois Central* was decided, the Court handed down Shively

v. Bowlby, 152 U.S. 1 (1894). *Shively* concerned the title to submerged land located below the high water mark in the Columbia River, a navigable river in Oregon. The Court held that the issue was a matter to be determined by state law, stating that:

> * * * The title and rights of riparian or littoral proprietors in the soil below the high water mark * * * are governed by the laws of the several States, subject to the rights granted to the United States by the Constitution.

> The United States, while they hold the country as a Territory, * * * may grant * * * titles or rights in the soil below the high water mark of tide waters. But they have never done so by general laws; and * * * have acted upon the policy * * * of *leaving the administration and disposition of the sovereign rights in navigable waters, and in the soil under them, to the control of the States * * * when organized and admitted to the Union.*

Id. at 57-58 (emphasis added). Later, in Appleby v. City of New York, 271 U.S. 364 (1926), the Court seemed to retreat from its holding in *Illinois Central*. In *Appleby*, the Court held that a state could convey fee title to submerged lands if the legislature decided it was in the public interest. In its view, the *Illinois Central*

> * * * case arose in the Circuit Court of the United States, and the conclusion reached was necessarily a statement of Illinois law, but the general principle and the exception have been recognized the country over. * * *

Id. at 395. And more recently, in Idaho v. Coeur d'Alene Tribe of Idaho, 521 U.S. 261, 285 (1997), the Court observed that "[w]hile *Illinois Central* was 'necessary a statement of Illinois law,' Appleby v. City of New York * * *, it invoked the principle in American law recognizing the weighty public interests in submerged lands." See also E. Pearson, Illinois Central and the Public Trust Doctrine in State Law, 15 Va. Envir.L.J. 713 (1996).

B. ALIENATION OF PUBLIC TRUST LANDS: CRITERIA FOR VALIDITY

What criteria should determine the validity of state created private rights in public trust lands and waters? Consider the next case.

PEOPLE v. CHICAGO PARK DISTRICT
Supreme Court of Illinois, 1976
66 Ill. 2d 654, 360 N.E.2d 773

WARD, CHIEF JUSTICE.

The General Assembly passed Senate Bill 782 (Laws of 1963, at 1229-31) on June 17, 1963, and it was signed by the Governor on June 26, 1963. The bill, in essence, provided for the conveyance by the State of Illinois of 194.6 acres of land submerged in waters of Lake Michigan to the United States Steel Corporation, hereafter referred to as defendant, upon its paying to the State Treasurer $19,460 and upon the Chicago Park District reconveying to the State an interest in the land it had received by certain legislation. * * *

The defendant, which proposes to construct a steel plant on the land to be reclaimed, tendered its draft on August 13, 1973, in the amount of $19,460 to the State Treasurer, but it was returned three days later. The Attorney General commenced this action by filing a complaint in the circuit court of Cook County. The complaint sought a declaratory judgment that "An Act for the sale to United States Steel Corporation of the interest of the State of Illinois in certain lands" (Senate Bill 782) was void. * * * The trial court allowed the plaintiffs' motion for summary judgment, holding that Senate Bill 782 was void on the grounds that it violated the public trust doctrine, the fourteenth amendment of the United States Constitution, and the following provisions of the Illinois Constitution of 1970: article I, section 2; article IV, section 13; and article VIII, section 1(a). The defendant appealed. * * *

The defendant argues that * * * Senate Bill 782 does not violate the public trust doctrine or any of the constitutional provisions as the Attorney General alleges and that the trial court's judgment was erroneous.

Any discussion of the public trust doctrine in Illinois must begin with Illinois Central Railroad Co. v. Illinois, 146 U.S. 387 [Discussion of *Illinois Central* omitted.]

A short time [after the *Illinois Central* decision] * * * another question involving submerged lands was presented to this court. In Illinois Central R.R. Co. v. City of Chicago, 173 Ill. 471, 50 N.E. 1104 (*Illinois Central II*), the plaintiff railroad sought to prevent the city of

Chicago from interfering with its plan to fill in 4.48 acres of land submerged in Lake Michigan between 25th and 27th Streets in Chicago. The plaintiff proposed to construct an engine house on the reclaimed land, and it alleged in its complaint the necessity of constructing the engine house on this site. The plaintiff contended that it had the power under the charter granted to it by the State to reclaim this land. This court, citing People ex rel. Moloney v. Kirk, 162 Ill. 138, 45 N.E. 830, declared that the State held title to the submerged lands in trust for the benefit of the people and that it could not sell these lands. 173 Ill. 471, 485, 50 N.E. 1104. It went on to say that in *Illinois Central I* the Supreme Court had held that 'grants of parcels of lands for wharves, piers, docks, and other structures in aid of commerce, and grants of parcels which do not impair the public interests in the lands and waters remaining' could be allowed. 173 Ill. 471, 485, 50 N.E. 1104, 1108. But the court concluded:

> It is not proposed here to take or appropriate the land in question for the erection of wharves, docks or piers, the construction of which may facilitate or aid the navigation of the waters of the lake, but the sole purpose seems to be to appropriate the submerged land for the private use of the railroad company. It is unreasonable to believe that the legislature, in the enactment of section 3 of the charter of the railroad company, ever intended to place in the hands of the company unlimited power to go on, from time to time, and appropriate to its own use parcel after parcel of the lands covered by the waters of Lake Michigan; and, if such unlimited power was contemplated it transcended its authority. It, in effect, undertook to part with governmental powers, which it could not do.

173 Ill. 471, 487, 50 N.E. 1104, 1109.

It can be seen that the State holds title to submerged land, as is involved here, in trust for the people, and that in general the governmental powers over these lands will not be relinquished. (See generally R. Clark, [Waters and Water Rights] § 36.4(A) (1967); R. Powell, The Law of Real Property, par. 160.) It is within this general framework that we are called upon to decide whether the legislative grant here was valid. In two of the discussed decisions (*Illinois Central I* and *II*) direct grants of submerged lands to private interests were held void. In the one case (People ex rel. Moloney v. Kirk) in which a grant of private interests was upheld, it was observed that the main purpose of the statute was to allow public officials to construct a needed extension of Lake Shore Drive for direct public benefit. 162 Ill. 138, 155-56, 45 N.E. 830. In none of these cases, nor in later cases decided by this court (Fairbank v. Stratton, 14 Ill. 2d 307, 152 N.E.2d 569; Bowes v. City of Chicago, 3 Ill. 2d 175, 120 N.E.2d 15), was a grant upheld where its primary purpose was to benefit a private interest.

[I]t may be pointed out that, in considering what is the public interest, courts are not bound by inflexible standards.

We have no difficulty in finding that, in this latter half of the twentieth century, the public rights in tidal lands are not limited to the ancient prerogatives of navigation and fishing, but extend as well to recreational uses, including bathing, swimming and other shore activities. The public trust doctrine, like all common law principles, should not be considered fixed or static, but should be molded and extended to meet changing conditions and needs of the public it was created to benefit.

Borough of Neptune City v. Borough of Avon-By-The-Sea (1972), 61 N.J. 296, 309, 294 A.2d 47, 54-55, and cases and authorities cited therein; see also Marks v. Whitney (1971), 6 Cal. 3d 251, 98 Cal. Rptr. 790, 491 P.2d 374.

On this question of changing conditions and public needs, it is appropriate to observe that there has developed a strong, though belated, interest in conserving natural resources and in protecting and improving our physical environment. The public has become increasingly concerned with dangers to health and life from environmental sources and more sensitive to the value and, frequently, the irreplaceability of natural resources. This is reflected in the enactment of the Illinois Environmental Protection Act (Ill.Rev.Stat. 1975, ch. 111 ½, par. 1001 Et seq.) in 1971 and in the ratification by the people of this State of sections 1 and 2 of article XI of the 1970 Constitution, which declare:

The public policy of the State and the duty of each person is to provide and maintain a healthful environment for the benefit of this and future generations. The General Assembly shall provide by law for the implementation and enforcement of this public policy.

Each person has the right to a healthful environment. Each person may enforce this right against any party, governmental or private, through appropriate legal proceedings subject to reasonable limitation and regulation as the General Assembly may provide by law.

It is obvious that Lake Michigan is a valuable natural resource belonging to the people of this State in perpetuity and any attempted ceding of a portion of it in favor of a private interest has to withstand a most critical examination.

The defendant steel company plans to construct an additional facility which will extend its South Work's Plant some 194 acres into Lake Michigan. The general area in question is bordered on the north by a public beach, Rainbow Park, at 79th Street; on the south by the United States Government breakwater protecting Calumet Harbor, and on the east by the Illinois-Indiana state line in Lake Michigan. These waters, which are adjacent to waters presently in important public use, would be irretrievably removed from the use of the people of Illinois. It cannot be said there will not be an adverse effect on the public use of these adjacent waters. We would also observe that in *Illinois Central II* it was said of the grant there: "(T)he sole purpose seems to be to appropriate the submerged land for the private use of the railroad company." 173 Ill. 471, 487, 50 N.E. 1104, 1109. Here, too, we can perceive only a private purpose for the grant.

The defendant contends that the General Assembly has determined that the land in question will be used for a public purpose and that this court should not overturn this determination. The defendant points to section 1 of Senate Bill 782, which states:

It is hereby declared that the grant of submerged land contained in this Act is made in aid of commerce and will create no impairment of the public interest in the lands and waters remaining, but will instead result in the conversion of otherwise useless and unproductive submerged land into an important commercial development to the benefit of the people of the State of Illinois.

The defendant argues, too, that a public purpose will be served in that the plant facilities which will be erected on the reclaimed land will provide a large number of jobs and will boost the economy of the city of Chicago and of the State. We judge these arguments to be unpersuasive.

While the courts certainly should consider the General Assembly's declaration that given legislation is to serve a described purpose, this court recognized in People ex rel. City of Salem v. McMackin, 53 Ill. 2d 347, 354, 291 N.E.2d 807, 812, that the "self-serving recitation of a public purpose within a legislative enactment is not conclusive of the existence of such purpose."

In order to preserve meaning and vitality in the public trust doctrine, when a grant of submerged land beneath waters of Lake Michigan is proposed under the circumstances here, the public purpose to be served cannot be only incidental and remote. The claimed benefit here to the public through additional employment and economic improvement is too indirect, intangible and elusive to satisfy the requirement of a public purpose. In almost every instance where submerged land would be reclaimed there would be employment provided and some economic benefit to the State. This court has upheld grants where the land was to be used for a water filtration plant (Bowes v. City of Chicago, 3 Ill. 2d 175, 120 N.E.2d 15) and for an exposition hall (Fairbank v. Stratton, 14 Ill. 2d 307, 152 N.E.2d 569), but it has upheld a grant to private individuals in only one instance, People ex rel. Moloney v. Kirk, 162 Ill. 138, 45 N.E. 830. There, however, as has been pointed out, the main purpose of the legislation was to benefit the public by the construction of an extension of Lake Shore Drive. The benefit to private interest was to further a public purpose and was incidental to the public purpose. (See also, City of Milwaukee v. State (1927), 193 Wis. 423, 214 N.W. 820.) Any benefit here to the public would be incidental. We judge that the direct and dominating purpose here would be a private one.

For the reasons given, the judgment of the circuit court is affirmed.

Notes and Questions

1.   When a state alienates, in fee simple, submerged lands under navigable waters, must the conveyance be for a "public purpose"? See, e.g., International Paper Company of Moss Point v. Mississippi State Highway Department, 271 So.2d 395 (Miss. 1972). If so, what is an acceptable public purpose? Must the contemplated private use provide a public benefit? Would a conveyance of submerged land, which would be filled, be valid if it was to a group of doctors who were going to construct a hospital? Must the contemplated purpose be a water dependent use? See City of Madison v. State, 1 Wis. 2d 252, 258-59, 83 N.W.2d 674, 678 (1957). Must the purpose be a use related to accepted public trust uses? If so, what is the source of the requirement that any conveyance of submerged lands under navigable waters be for a specific purpose? See generally 4 Water and Water Rights §§ 30.02(d)-(d)(3) (1996).

2.   If any conveyance of submerged lands must be for a "public purpose," does that only require a deliberate and reasoned decision by the legislature that the transaction, of which the conveyance is a part, affirmatively promotes the public interest in submerged lands? See West Indian Co., Ltd. v. Government of Virgin Islands, 844 F.2d 1007, 1019 (3rd. Cir. 1988), cert. denied, 488 U.S. 802 (1988); J. Sax, The Public Trust Doctrine in Natural Resources Law: Effective Judicial Intervention, 68 Mich. L. Rev. 471 (1970). If so, what constitutes a "deliberate and reasoned decision"?

3.   May the state be indirectly divested, free of the public trust, of submerged lands under navigable waters? If the state has a Marketable Title Act or Torrens Act, does either act apply to claims to public trust lands?

Most states have statutes that abrogate the ancient legal maxim "*nullius tempus occurrit regi*," or "time does not run against the king." Nowadays, in most situations, one can acquire title to state owned land by adverse possession. The courts, however, have been reluctant to apply the doctrine of adverse possession to public trust lands. See, e.g., O'Neill v. State Highway Dep't Bd., 50 N.J. 307, 320, 235 A.2d 1, 8 (1967); Coastal States Gas Producing Co. v. State Mineral Bd., 199 So.2d 554, 557 (La. App. 1967); State ex rel Rohrer v. Credle, 322 N.C. 522, 369 S.E. 2d 825 (1988) (exclusive right to take oysters from lands under navigable waters cannot be acquired by prescriptive use). Absent a statute, such as N.C. Gen. Stat. § 1-45.1 (1985), that expressly prohibits the adverse possession of public trust lands, on what grounds can you distinguish allowing adverse possession of some state owned lands but not public trust lands? Assuming that a state's adverse possession statute applied to public trust lands, what difficulties would a claimant encounter in proving the requisite elements of adverse possession?

In order to increase alienability of land and to simplify title transactions, a number of states have passed Marketable Title Acts. See, e.g., West's Fla. Stat. Ann. §§ 712.01-.10 (1979); N.C. Gen. Stat. §§ 47B-1 to 47B-9 (1984); Conn. Gen. Stat. Ann. § 47-33(b-h) (Supp. 1985). Under the provisions of these acts, the owner of title to land that has been of record for the requisite number of years has a title that is marketable subject only to claims that are exempted from the operation of the acts, encumbrances inherent in or arising after the instrument constituting the root of title, and claims that have been preserved by re-recording. All other conflicting claims are extinguished by the acts. If the particular state act does not expressly exempt the title or interests owned by the state or its political subdivisions, then two questions arise: (1) can the act be invoked to divest the state of title to submerged land under navigable waters, and (2) can the act be invoked to terminate the public's right to engage in public trust activities in such lands and waters?

4. One of our nation's most valuable resources is the millions of acres of saltwater marshlands that serve as vital links in the production of fish and shellfish. Yet, despite the apparent limitations *Illinois Central* placed upon the disposal of submerged lands, many states did sell and purport to convey fee simple title to large portions of these wetlands. Much was sold for pennies an acre. This, of course, was done primarily at a time when such wetlands were viewed as swamps, serving no purpose other than to breed mosquitos and other noxious insects. Today, many of these transactions are being challenged as violations of the public trust doctrine. See M. Kalo and J. Kalo, The Battle to Preserve North Carolina's Estuarine Marshes: The 1985 Legislation, Private Claims to Estuarine Marshes, Denial of Permits To Fill, And The Public Trust, 64 N.C. L. Rev. 565 (1986) Do they violate the public trust? Before you view the challengers as the good guys, charging forth to save the environment from pillagers, think about what the private parties are doing or might do with the land in dispute. If the state or other challengers win the lawsuits and the conveyances are declared invalid, does that prevent

the state from entering into a more profitable arrangement that permits other private companies to engage in the same acts as those engaged in or planned by the present private claimant to the land? See, e.g., Phillips Petroleum Co. v. Mississippi, supra. In other words, is it just a battle over who gets the money?

5. If a state agency sells submerged lands under navigable waters to private investors and the investors make some improvements, and they invest significant sums in development plans for a project involving the submerged land, subsequently the state may still challenge the validity of the original sale? If the state is successful, must the state reimburse the investors for the original purchase price (with interest?), the real property taxes that were paid, the development planning costs, and other sums invested in the proposed project? Would the answer change if the state was revoking a conveyance that a state agency had the authority to make as opposed to challenging the authority of the agency to make the conveyance in the first instance?

C. STATE PUBLIC TRUST MANAGEMENT OBLIGATIONS

In the management of public trust waters and submerged lands, does the state have any affirmative obligations? Many people and companies use public trust waters and submerged lands for either private recreational purposes or for profit. The uses range from individual recreational piers and duck blinds to fish pound nets, fish farms, large scale marinas, and restaurants built over the water. Each of these uses, and many others, involve some appropriation of public trust lands and waters and, to some extent, the exclusion of the general public from the appropriated area. As the manager of the public trust, can the state charge these users "rent" or "equitable compensation" for their use of public trust waters and submerged lands? Is this good public policy? Is the state under a legal obligation to collect "rent"?

CAMINITI v. BOYLE
Supreme Court of Washington, 1987
107 Wash. 2d 662, 732 P.2d 989

ANDERSEN, JUSTICE.

This action was commenced by a petition filed in this court seeking a writ of mandamus directed to the Commissioner of Public Lands and the State Treasurer. Petitioners ask us to declare unconstitutional the state statute (RCW 79.90.105) which allows owners of residential property abutting state-owned tidelands and shorelands to install and maintain private recreational docks on such lands without payment to the state. * * * Having now considered the parties' briefs and oral argument on the merits, we decline to hold the statute unconstitutional. Issuance of the writ will be denied.

The case was submitted on agreed facts. Those pertinent to our disposition of the case are as follows:

By the Laws of the State of Washington of 1983 * * * (RCW 79.90.105), the following legislation became effective on June 13, 1983:

The abutting residential owner to state-owned shorelands, tidelands, or related beds of navigable waters, other than harbor areas, may install and maintain without charge a dock on such areas if used exclusively for private recreational purposes and the area is not subject to prior rights. This permission is subject to applicable local regulation governing construction, size, and length of the dock. This permission may be revoked by the department upon finding of public necessity which is limited to the protection of waterward access or ingress rights of other landowners or public health and safety. The revocation may be appealed as a contested case under chapter 34.04 RCW. Nothing in this section prevents the abutting owner from obtaining a lease if otherwise provided by law.

Prior to the effective date of RCW 79.90.105, approximately 370 residential owners of private land abutting public aquatic lands were paying the State approximately $35,000 in annual rental for private recreational docks on public aquatic lands, outside of harbor areas, pursuant to the then statutorily authorized leasing program. * * *

There is one principal issue.

ISSUE

Does RCW 79.90.105, which allows owners of residential property abutting state-owned tidelands and shorelands[2] to install and maintain private recreational docks on such lands free of charge, violate article 17, section 1 of the Washington State Constitution or the "public trust doctrine"?

---

[2] In addition to referring to state-owned shorelands and tidelands, RCW 79.90.105 also deals with "*related beds* of navigable waters, other than harbor areas. * * * " (Italics ours.) Bedlands are those lands lying beyond the line of navigability of rivers and lakes and those lands beyond the low-tide mark of tidal waters. RCW 79.90.050. Bedlands in tidal waters may present unique problems, particularly with respect to federal regulation of navigable waters. However, the parties have chosen to argue this case primarily with respect to tidelands and shorelands which, as a practical matter, are those principally involved. As a consequence, bedlands will not be separately dealt with herein other than to point out by this note that what we hold concerning tidelands and shorelands generally applies to bedlands as well.

DECISION

The short answer to the question posed by this issue is "no." Upon admission into the Union, the state of Washington was vested with title in, and dominion over, its tidelands and shorelands. Since statehood, the Legislature has had the power to sell and convey title to state tidelands and shorelands. Prior to 1971, when the Legislature by statute changed its policy, the state had sold approximately 60 percent of its tidelands and 30 percent of its shorelands. The Legislature has never had the authority, however, to sell or otherwise abdicate state sovereignty or dominion over such tidelands and shorelands. By enacting the statute at issue in this case (RCW 79.90.105), the Legislature has seen fit to grant only a revocable license allowing owners of land abutting state-owned tidelands and shorelands to build recreational docks thereon subject to state regulation and control. The Legislature did not thereby surrender state sovereignty or dominion over these tidelands and shorelands, but through the Department of Natural Resources and local subdivisions of state government continues to exercise control over them.

By our state constitution, "[t]he state of Washington asserts its ownership to the beds and shores of all navigable waters in the state up to and including the line of ordinary high-tide, in waters where the tide ebbs and flows, and up to and including the line of ordinary high water within the banks of all navigable rivers and lakes. * * * " Const. art. 17, § 1 (part). This was but a formal declaration by the people of rights which our new state possessed by virtue of its sovereignty, and which declaration had the effect of vesting title to such lands in the state.

As this court has repeatedly held, under the foregoing constitutional provision the state of Washington has the power to dispose of, and invest persons with, ownership of tidelands and shorelands subject only to the paramount public right of navigation and the fishery. * * *

The state's ownership of tidelands and shorelands is not limited to the ordinary incidents of legal title, but is comprised of two distinct aspects.

The first aspect of such state ownership is historically referred to as the *jus privatum* or private property interest. As owner, the state holds full proprietary rights in tidelands and shorelands and has fee simple title to such lands. Thus, the state may convey title to tidelands and shorelands in any manner and for any purpose not forbidden by the state or federal constitutions and its grantees take title as absolutely as if the transaction were between private individuals. In the case before us, the state has not by this statute conveyed title to the land, but as will be discussed shortly, has given a revocable license only.

The second aspect of the state's ownership of tidelands and

shorelands is historically referred to as the *jus publicum* or public authority interest. The principle that the public has an overriding interest in navigable waterways and lands under them is at least as old as the Code of Justinian, promulgated in Rome in the 5th Century A.D. This *jus publicum* interest as expressed in the English common law and in the common law of this state from earliest statehood, is composed of the right of navigation and the fishery. More recently, this interest was more particularly expressed by this court in Wilbour v. Gallagher, 77 Wash. 2d 306, 316, 462 P.2d 232 (1969), as the right

> of navigation, together with its incidental rights of fishing, boating, swimming, water skiing, and other related recreational purposes generally regarded as corollary to the right of navigation and the use of public waters.

The state can no more convey or give away this *jus publicum* interest than it can "abdicate its police powers in the administration of government and the preservation of the peace." Thus it is that the sovereignty and dominion over this state's tidelands and shorelands, as distinguished from *title*, always remains in the state, and the state holds such dominion in trust for the public. It is this principle which is referred to as the "public trust doctrine." Although not always clearly labeled or articulated as such, our review of Washington law establishes that the doctrine has always existed in the State of Washington.

The test of whether or not an exercise of legislative power with respect to tidelands and shorelands violates the "public trust doctrine" is found in the following language of the United States Supreme Court:

> The control of the State for the purposes of the trust can never be lost, except as to such parcels as are used in promoting the interests of the public therein, or can be disposed of without any substantial impairment of the public interest in the lands and waters remaining.

Accordingly, we must inquire as to: (1) whether the state, by the questioned legislation, has given up its right of control over the *jus publicum* and (2) if so, whether by so doing the state (a) has promoted the interests of the public in the *jus publicum*, or (b) has not substantially impaired it.

* * *

Turning * * * to the above stated test for violations of the "public trust doctrine," and applying that test to the questioned statute (RCW 79.90.105), we observe as follows.

Right of control. Petitioners argue that "[a] common thread in judicially-pronounced public trust doctrine tests is deciding whether the state has retained adequate control over trust resources." We agree.

By enacting RCW 79.90.105, the Legislature has given up relatively little right of control over the *jus publicum*, and has not conveyed title to any state-owned tidelands or shorelands. The statute in question relates only to residential owners whose property abuts public tidelands or shorelands.[3] * * * In Washington, abutting landowners have no riparian rights in state-owned tidelands and shorelands; accordingly, the ultimate state control is that the Legislature having by this statute given abutting landowners the license to use its tidelands and shorelands, can likewise revoke that license by repealing the statute in the event it sees fit to do so. * * *

Promotion of the interests of the public. The statute also promotes the interests of the public in the *jus publicum*, albeit to a limited degree. The Shoreline Management Act of 1971, discussed above, stresses that "coordinated planning is necessary in order to protect the public interest associated with the shorelines of the state while, at the same time, recognizing and protecting private property rights consistent with the public interest." The statute under review expresses a part of that policy; it is a practical recognition that one of the many beneficial uses of public tidelands and shorelands abutting private homes is the placement of private docks on such lands so homeowners and their guests may obtain recreational access to navigable waters. No expression of public policy has been directed to our attention which would encourage water uses originating on public docks, as they do, while at the same time discouraging any private investment in docks to help promote the use of public waters.

Impairment of the jus publicum. In any event, nothing in the statute substantially impairs the *jus publicum*. Private docks cannot, of course, block public access to public tidelands and shorelands, and the public must be able to get around, under or over them. Recreational docks existed on public tidelands and shorelands before enactment of the statute, and still do; the principal difference being that under current statutory policy there is no obligation to pay rental or lease fees.

* * *

The writ petitioned for is denied.

PEARSON, C.J., and DOLLIVER, UTTER, BRACHENBACH, CALLOW and DURHAM, JJ., and SCHUMACHER, J. Pro Tem., concur.

DORE, JUSTICE (dissenting). * * * (omitted)

Notes and Questions

1.   In many states, littoral and riparian owners have the right to wharf out and other similar rights. In such states, may the state charge littoral and riparian owners a fee or annual rent when the owners exercise their rights and build docks, piers, or similar structures on the public trust lands adjacent to their waterfront property? Does it matter whether the riparian owner's use is commercial or non-commercial?

2.   To what extent may the state issue licenses or leases to non-riparian or non-littoral owners that authorize such licensees or lessees to engage in activities on public trust lands? Does it matter whether the public will be totally excluded from the area subject to the license or lease? For example, under what circumstances, if any, may the state grant the right to close off public trust lands and associated waters to a fish farm? May the state, by lease, allow a private club to have exclusive use of the wet sand beach and waters that lie adjacent to the club's uplands? Do the terms of the lease matter? Does the length of the lease matter? Must the terms of the lease be the least restrictive of the public's right to use public trust lands and waters that is consistent with the legitimate needs of the licensee or lessee? See, e.g., Cartens   v. California Coastal Commission, 182 Cal.App.3d 377, 227 Cal.Rptr. 135 (1986).

In Ryals v. Pigott, 580 So.2d 1140, 1151 (Miss. 1990), the court said: "Waters which are public by virtue of the (Mississippi) Constitution and the Equal Footing Doctrine may not-by legislative enactment or judicial decree-be withdrawn from public use." Is this a more expansive public trust doctrine applicable to all "public waters," irrespective of who holds legal title to the submerged lands?

3.   If the state collects a fee or rent for use of public trust lands or waters, must the funds collected be used for a public trust purpose or may the legislature use them for any other public purpose?

4.   If the placement of rip-rap or a seawall will inevitably cause the loss of the wet sand beach, may public interest groups challenge the issuance of a permit to construct such beach hardening devices on the grounds that the public trust doctrine requires the preservation of the wet sand beach for public access and use? If such an objection to the issuance of the permit is not made before the coastal permit agency, is it waived? If the coastal permit agency nonetheless issues the permit, would a public interest group have standing to appeal the agency's decision? See, e.g., Save Our Dunes v. Alabama Department of Environmental Management, 834 F.2d 984 (11th Cir. 1987) (Under Alabama law, concern, knowledge, and general use of beaches are not sufficient, in and of themselves, to make plaintiffs an "aggrieved" person with standing to appeal adverse agency determination.)

5.   Assuming that a county otherwise has the authority to ban the use of motorized personal watercraft, i.e., jet skiis, does such a ban violate the public trust doctrine by completely excluding one segment of the recreational public from navigable waters? See Weden v. San Juan County, 135 Wash.2d 678, 958 P.2d 273 (1998)(holding it does not).

SECTION 4. THE TRADITIONAL TRIAD AND JUDICIAL EXPANSION OF PUBLIC TRUST USES

English common law and the common law of most states recognize the right of any person to use navigable waters for navigation, commerce and fishing -- the so-called traditional triad of public trust rights. Many American courts have expanded these public trust rights beyond the traditional triad to include other uses such as hunting, bathing, swimming, general recreation, using the bottom for anchoring, standing or other purposes, and conservation. See, e.g., Matthews v. Bay Head Improvement Ass'n, 95 N.J. 306, 321, 471 A.2d 355, 363, cert. denied, 469 U.S. 821 (1984); Marks v. Whitney, 6 Cal. 3d 251, 259, 491 P.2d 374, 380, 98 Cal.Rptr. 790, 796 (1971); Swan Island Club v. White, 114 F. Supp. 95, 103-05 (1953); White v. Hughes, 139 Fla. 54, 59, 190 So. 446, 449 (1939); Arnold v. Mundy, 6 N.J.L. 1 (1821) (one of the first cases recognizing the existence of the public trust doctrine in the United States); N.C. Gen. Stat. § 1-45.1 (purporting to codify common law public trust rights); see also J. Stevens, The Public Trust: A Sovereign's Ancient Prerogative Becomes The People's Environmental Right, 14 U.C. Davis L. Rev. 195, 221-23 (1980); Comment, The Public Trust Doctrine In Maine's Submerged Lands: Public Rights, State Obligation And The Role of The Courts, 37 Me. L. Rev. 105, 107-13 (1985); Comment, The Public Trust in Tidal Areas: A Sometime Submerged Traditional Doctrine, 79 Yale L.J. 762, 781-86 (1970). In some jurisdictions, public trust rights are apparently open-ended. See, e.g., Marks v. Whitney, supra. Does this raise a potential issue of a taking by judicial modification of the common law?

The "takings" clause of the Fifth Amendment to the United States Constitution provides that:

nor shall private property be taken for public use, without just compensation. * * *

Most "takings" occur through legislative or executive action. For example, the executive branch, through its agents, seizes private property for public use. Or the legislature passes a statute that so restricts the uses to which private property may be put that the court finds that in effect the law is the equivalent of an appropriation of the property for public use. But the "takings" issue may also arise in a different context -- the promulgation and modification of property rules through the common law process. If a court expands the definition of "navigable," and thereby gives the public access to waters that everyone formerly thought were closed to the public, or adds to the public uses encompassed by the public trust doctrine, or manipulates common law doctrines to assure the public has access to the dry sand beach, the question presented is whether there is a "taking" of private property rights for public use in violation of the Fifth Amendment? What are relevant factors in determining whether a "taking" has occurred in this context? See B. Thompson, Judicial Takings, 76 Va. L. Rev. 1449 (1990).

SECTION 5. PRIVATE PROPERTY INTERESTS IN COASTAL WATERS AND LANDS: LITTORAL AND RIPARIAN RIGHTS

A. INTRODUCTION

Although the state has the power to regulate coastal water uses and generally holds title to coastal submerged lands, property owners whose lands abut coastal waters may also have common law rights in adjacent coastal waters and submerged lands. Although these common law *littoral* and *riparian* rights may vary widely among the individual states, according to an early twentieth century authority, Henry Farnham, the traditional common law rights included:

(1) The right to have the water remain in place and to retain, as nearly as possible, its natural character.[3]

(2) The right of access, which included:
   (a)   The right to maintain contact with the body of water;

   (b)   The right to accretions;

   (c)   The first right to purchase adjacent submerged land if it is sold by the state;

   (d)   If filling of submerged land is permitted by the state, the preferential right to fill adjacent submerged land.

(3) Subject to reasonable restrictions, the right to wharf out to the navigable portion of a body of water.

---

[3] The 19th century common law riparian rules were based on the natural flow theory, which required that the riparian owner's use of the waterbody leave it substantially unchanged except for minor effects of the use. As a result of industrialization and increased economically and socially useful needs of water, most American jurisdictions have adopted the reasonable use theory. This theory allows the riparian owner to make reasonable use of the water for any purpose. See generally, e.g., Restatement of Torts, Second, Chapter 41, Introductory Note (1979).

(4) The right of free use of the water immediately adjoining the property for the transaction of such business associated with his wharves or other such structures.

I. Farnham, Water and Water Rights § 62 (1904); see also, e.g., Smith Tug & Barge Co. v. Columbia-Pacific Towing Corp. 250 Or. 612, 616, 443 P.2d 205, 208 (1968); 3 American Law of Property § 12.32 (1952); 1 Water and Water Rights § 6.01(a) (1991). For a detailed discussion of the specifics of the general rights listed above, see Game & Fresh Water Fish Commission v. Lakes Islands, Ltd., 407 So.2d 189, 191-92 (Fl. 1982).

One common feature of this list of rights is allowing the waterfront owner to maintain his or her adjacency to the water body. But what is meant by adjacency, and where exactly is the boundary when the level of the body of water may fluctuate with rising and falling tides?

Since the 17th Century and the publication of Lord Hale's De Jure Maris, the boundary between privately owned uplands and the publicly owned foreshore or tidelands has generally been the "ordinary high-tide line." In the United States, the federal common law rule is that the "ordinary high-tide line" is the "mean high-tide line," which is the average of all high-tides over an 18.6 year cycle, as determined by the Department of Commerce, National Oceanic Survey. See Borax Consolidated Ltd. v. Los Angeles, 296 U.S. 10, 26-27 (1935). The "ordinary high-tide line" is not the highest line reached by the tides during any month or period of years, and thus, areas of the foreshore which are flooded on occasion by tidal waters are the subject of private ownership. As the sea level rises, the mean high-tide line will move shoreward. Since, in many areas, the shore has a very gradual slope, a small vertical change in water level may cause a large horizontal movement of a boundary on the ground. See G. Cole, Water Boundaries 1-55 (1997) (a detailed discussion of the techniques used to locate the mean high-tide line); see also F. Maloney and R. Ausness, The Use and Legal Significance of the Mean High Water Line in Coastal Boundary Mapping, 53 N.C. L. Rev. 185 (1974).

In thinking about this division between the public and the private, consider for a moment coastal beaches with which you are familiar and how these beaches are used. In light of these considerations, is using the mean high-tide line a realistic way of separating the public from the private?

In addition to separating publicly owned foreshore from privately owned upland, the *mean high-tide line* marks the outer limits of a body of navigable waters. That which is waterward is part of the navigable body of water; that which is landward is considered part of the uplands.[4] Thus, a navigable body of water is more than its navigable channels. It includes the full breadth of the water body from mean high-tide line to mean high-tide line.[5]

One further observation is necessary to complete this discussion. The *Borax* rule is a federal common law rule applied to determine the seaward boundary of a federal patent or grant of oceanfront property. This rule may not be applicable in other settings. As a matter of state law the dividing line between public and private interests may be something other than the mean high-tide line as defined by federal law. In fact, at least five states (Maine, Massachusetts, Virginia, Delaware, and Pennsylvania) recognize the existence of some private interests extending to the low-tide line.

B. THE RIGHT OF ACCESS

(1.) Accretion, Erosion, Avulsion, And Reliction

In most coastal states, tidal boundaries are considered to be ambulatory; that is, the physical location of the mean high (or low) water line may shift because of natural or artificial changes in the location of the shoreline. Accordingly, littoral owners may gain or lose land by virtue of accretion, reliction, erosion, or avulsion.

* * * Accretions or accreted lands consist of additions to the land resulting from the gradual deposit by water of sand, sediment or other material. The term applies to such lands produced along both navigable and non-navigable water. Alluvion is that increase of earth

---

[4] In some situations, it is physically impossible to use the mean high-water mark as a means of separating uplands from submerged lands. For example, dense mangrove swamps cover parts of Florida's coast. Under those conditions, locating the mean high water mark is not possible. Rather than apply a purely fictional tidal rule, Florida's courts sometimes use *meander lines* to define the boundary between public and private lands. See Florida Bd. of Trustees of the Internal Improvement Trust Fund v. Wakulla Silver Springs Co., 362 So.2d 706 (Fla. Dist. Ct. App. 1978); cf. Utah v. United States, 425 U.S. 948 (1976) (involving title to lands exposed by the evaporation of Utah's Great Salt Lake). But see St. Joseph Land and Dev. Co. v. Florida St. Bd., 365 So.2d 1084 (Fla. Dist. Ct. App. 1979).

The meander line is a straight line or series of straight lines connecting points on the shore. The meander line is primarily for determining the quantity of public land in the subdivision being surveyed and is not intended as an exact measurement. For a discussion of the problems of using meander lines as boundaries, see D. Maloney, The Ordinary High Water Mark: Attempts at Settling an Unsettled Boundary Line, 13 Land & Water L. Rev. 465, 489-92 (1965).

[5] When dealing with non-tidal waters, the outer limits of navigability are determined by the location of the ordinary high water mark.

on a shore or bank of a stream or sea, by the force of the water, as by a current or by waves, which is so gradual that no one can judge how much is added at each moment of time. The term "alluvion" is applied to the deposit itself, while accretion denotes the act, but the terms are frequently used synonymously.

Reliction refers to land which formerly was covered by water, but which has become dry land by the imperceptible recession of the water. Although there is a distinction between accretion and reliction, one being the gradual building of the land, and the other the gradual recession of water, the terms are often used interchangeably. The term "accretion" in particular is often used to cover both processes, and generally the law relating to both is the same.

Erosion is the gradual and imperceptible wearing away of land bordering on a body of water by the natural action of the elements. Avulsion is either the sudden and perceptible alteration of the shoreline by action of the water, or a sudden change of the bed or course of a stream forming a boundary whereby it abandons its old bed for a new one.

As a general rule, where the shoreline is gradually and imperceptibly changed or shifted by accretion, reliction or erosion, the boundary line is extended or restricted in the same manner. The owner of the littoral property thus acquires title to all additions arising by accretion or reliction, and loses soil that is worn or washed away by erosion. However, any change in the shoreline that takes place suddenly and perceptibly does not result in a change of boundary or ownership. Normally a landowner may not intentionally increase his estate through accretion or reliction by artificial means. However, the littoral owner is usually entitled to additions that result from artificial conditions created by third persons without his consent.

* * *

F. Maloney and R. Ausness, The Use and Legal Significance of the Mean High Water Line in Coastal Boundary Mapping, 53 N.C. L. Rev. 185, 224-26 (1974). See also Lechuza v. California Coastal Commission, 70 Cal. Rptr.2d 399,411-16 (Cal. App. 1997) (judgment in quiet title action between state and private oceanfront landowner does not quiet title to a fixed boundary line and seaward private boundary remains ambulatory).

(2.) The Right To Accretions

(a.) The General Rule

The general common law rule is that all accretions belong to the waterfront owner to whose land they attach. Such a rule has a number of justifications. First, a person is a littoral or riparian owner if a water body constitutes one or more of the described boundaries of his or her property. In such a case, in order for the boundary to remain the same, the accretions must become the property of the waterfront owner. Second, the reason waterfront property commands a premium price is because of its access to the water. Unless the accretions became the property of the waterfront owner, she could gradually be cut off from access to the water and lose one of the most important and valuable features of the property. Third, accretions, in many cases, involve relatively small additions to the upland. To the extent that such additional uplands can be put to productive use, as a practical matter, the waterfront owner is the only one situated to put the accreted land to use. Fourth, if the waterfront owner is to lose land to erosion, then it seems only fair to allow her to benefit from the reverse process of accretion.

(b.) The General Rule And Equity

FORD v. TURNER
District Court of Appeal of Florida, 1962
142 So. 2d 335

WHITE, *JUDGE*.

Appellants H. H. Ford and Robert Ford and wives were principal defendants in a quiet title suit which resulted in favor of the plaintiff-appellee Walter S. Turner, Jr. The litigation involves an apparent increment or increase of land in the form of an elongated strip physically attached to the southerly end of Captiva Island near Blind Pass in Lee County on the lower Gulf Coast of Florida. * * *

The record reveals, however, that the general topography of the involved area has altered considerably since the turn of the century. The great geodetic changes between 1900 and 1958 are reflected in the following sketches derived from exhibits in evidence. The approximate relative location of the disputed tract, which purportedly 'accreted' to the plaintiff's land, is indicated on Sketch 2 [which appears following the text of the case].* * *

According to the defendants' exhibits, the Ford property did originally front on the open Gulf of Mexico. A series of aerial photographs dated 1937, 1939, 1944, 1953 and 1958 show that Captiva

Island has built up in a southerly direction until that island has almost completely paralleled Ford's original Gulf frontage, leaving only a navigable channel separating Ford's property and the 'accreted' portion of Captiva Island with the Island fronting on the Gulf.* * *

Generally the margin or bed of a stream, or other body of water constituting a boundary, continues to be the boundary notwithstanding any accretion or erosion which changes the location of the body of water. The boundary lines of land so located thus extends or restricts as that margin gradually changes or shifts by reason of accretion or erosion. Feig v. Graves, Fla. App.1958, 100 So.2d 192, 196. The newly formed land belongs to the owner of the land to which it is an accretion, and not to the one originally owning the land in that place. See 8 A.L.R. 640, 41 A.L.R. 395 and numerous cases cited.

One witness testified that the accretion to plaintiff's land extended southeastward approximately 9,000 feet. One of the defendants' contentions, as stated, is that accretion can not thus extend laterally but only frontward.* * *

We have studied the authorities cited by defendants in support of their contention that accretion must be immediately in front of the land to which it has attached and that the owner cannot follow it laterally. See III Farnham, Waters and Water Rights, § 845(a), pgs. 2489-2490. Most of the cited cases, however, applied to rivers and streams or non-tidal waters where the owners' boundaries extended to the center of the stream bed in contradistinction to the instant case where the lands border tidal waters in which the title to the submerged land is held by the State of Florida in trust for the use and benefit of its citizens.* * *

Florida is bordered by water on the east, south and west. The numerous islands or keys are constantly changing by various methods of accretion, alluvion, erosion, reliction and avulsion, giving rise to myriad problems. Public policy demands a definite standard of quieting title to these areas despite the fact that occasionally some hardship may occur. * * *

Affirmed.

SKETCH 2

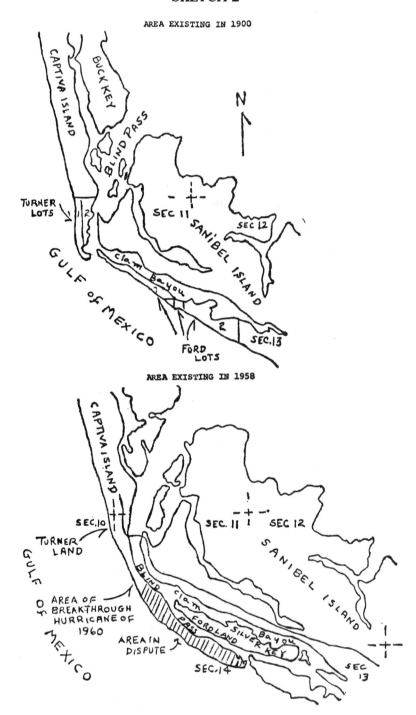

Notes and Questions

1.   On facts quite similar to *Ford*, the Supreme Court of Washington held that lateral accretions that cut off a littoral owner's direct access to the ocean belonged to that person and not to the littoral owner to whose uplands the accretions actually adhered.   Hudson House, Inc. v. Rozman, 82 Wash.2d 178, 509 P.2d 992 (1973).   See also Strom v. Sheldon, 12 Wash.App. 66, 527 P.2d 1382 (1974).   See generally 3 American Law of Property § 15.27 (1952).   For a criticism of *Ford*, see Note, Accretion: A New Slant, 17 U. Miami L. Rev. 417 (1963).

2.   Who owns accretions that result from the construction of a groin, jetty, or similar structure? Is the waterfront owner entitled only to accretions created by natural processes? The general common law rule is that the waterfront owner is entitled to all accretions created by natural or artificial sources, unless the accretions are artificially induced by the waterfront owner.   See also, e.g., Bd. of Trustees of Internal Improvement Trust Fund v. Sand Key Associates, Ltd., 512 So.2d 934 (Fla. 1987) (common law rule). But see, e.g., People v. Hector, 241 Cal. App.2d 484, 50 Cal.Rptr. 654 (1966) (If artificially induced accretions would result in the transfer of state owned tidelands to private ownership, the California rule is that waterfront owners are not entitled to such accretions). Frequently, such questions are resolved by statute. See, e.g., N.C. Gen. Stat. §§ 146-6(a) and (b).

3.   In Norfolk, Virginia, a couple purchased an unbuildable one acre, waterfront lot on Chesapeake Bay in 1981.   Then a "miracle" occurred! In 1984 sand rapidly began to accrete. In fact, it accreted as fast as the City of Norfolk could dump it on a withered city beach two miles upshore. Longshore currents carried the City's sand directly to the lot. Today, the lot is fronted by a five acre beach. The City claims the beach is "public land" and plans to scoop up the sand and return it to the beach where it was originally dumped. Can the city do that? See C. Zaneski, "Drifting Sand Shapes into a Property Dispute," The Virginian-Pilot and The Ledger-Star, November 5, 1988, at A1.

4.   What happens when erosion causes the mean high-tide line to move shoreward,   eventually crossing the fixed boundary line of formerly non-littoral or non-riparian land? Does the land become littoral or riparian and subject to the rules of erosion and accretion?   See generally American Law of Property § 15.27 (1952); C. Dunscombe, Riparian and Littoral Rights 37 (1970). Consider the following situation. In 1965, the plaintiff purchased two inland lots in a development located near the north end of a barrier island. The recorded plat showed the location of the lots and of a planned adjacent public road. Over a period of several years, but before any significant construction occurred in the development, the northern inlet separating this barrier island from the next one migrated southward, completely washing away

the northern end of the island, including plaintiff's lots. Neither the plaintiff nor any of the other affected lot owners made any attempt to reclaim submerged lots. However, in 1978, the original developer obtained permits from both the state and the U.S. Army Corps of Engineers allowing him to reconstruct the northern end of the island.

Over the next few years, sand and other fill material was deposited in the inlet until the inlet was completely closed. A new inlet was then opened near the original 1965 location. The filled area was roughly the size of the original washed out area, but not in exactly the same location. Plaintiff's original lots would now be oceanfront lots, but located seaward of the beach setback line and therefore unbuildable.

After the filling was completed, the enterprising developer prepared a new plat, with new lots and a new road, the locations of which did not correspond to the original 1965 plat, and filed the plat with the state. All of these new lots have been sold and summer homes valued at one-half million dollars or more constructed upon them.

The plaintiff has now filed suit seeking a declaration that she is the owner of two lots, located in the positions in which they appear in the 1965 plat, and that she has an easement of ingress and egress over the area identified as a public road on the 1965 plat. At this time, that road would run right through the center of a number of houses constructed upon 76 of the "new" lots. Is the plaintiff still the owner of the two lots? Does she have a right of ingress and egress over the area shown in the original plat? See Ward v. Sunset Beach and Twin Lakes Inc., 53 N.C. App. 59, 279 S.E.2d 889 (1981); United States v. 2,134.46 Acres of Land, 257 F.Supp. 723 (D.N.D. 1966); N.C. Gen. Stat. § 146-6.

(c.) *Whose General Rule: State Or Federal Common Law?*

Generally state law determines the nature and the extent of a property right. Thus, one would think that the question of whether a waterfront owner was entitled to accretions, or suffered losses as the result of erosion, would be a matter of state common law or statutes. But this is not always true.

In Hughes v. Washington, 389 U.S. 290 (1967), the state of Washington claimed title to accretions to oceanfront property owned by Mrs. Hughes. Mrs. Hughes title was traceable back to a pre-statehood federal patent. The state supreme court held that under state law Mrs. Hughes had no right to any accretions that formed between her upland property and the ocean. The United States Supreme Court reversed, holding that the question of Mrs. Hughes' right to accretions was a matter of federal common law. And, the federal common law rule was the traditional common law rule which vested title to accretions in the adjacent upland owner. According to the Court, the question was one that:

> deals with waters that lap both the lands of the State and the boundaries of the international sea. This relationship, at this particular point of the marginal sea, is too close to the vital interest of the Nation in its own boundaries to be governed by any law but the "supreme Law of the Land".

Id. at 293. A few years later, the Court seemed to back away from its conclusion in *Hughes*.

In Oregon ex rel. State Land Board v. Corvallis Sand and Gravel Company, 429 U.S. 363 (1977), the United States Supreme Court held that the *Hughes* rule -- that the common law rights of littoral owners whose title is traceable to a federal patent are determined by federal common law -- did not apply to riparian owners whose title is also traceable to a federal patent. According to the Court, federal law only determined the initial boundary between submerged lands that passed to the state upon statehood, and the uplands, which were the subject of a federal patent. "[T]hereafter * * * the land is subject the laws of the State." Id. at 376. Thus, the rights of the riparian owner, whose title was traceable to a federal patent, were to be determined by state property law rules and not federal law.

The issue of whether federal common law or state law determines the present-day property rights of persons who trace their title back to a federal patent goes to a fundamental notion inherent in our federal system, that each newly admitted state enters the Union on an "equal footing" regarding political standing and sovereignty. The rights of riparian owners in the original thirteen states, political entities that existed prior to the founding of the Union, were a matter of the states' existing, differing, evolving common law. To hold that "[a]n original State * * * [was] free to choose its own legal principles to resolve property disputes relating to lands under its riverbeds; [but], a subsequently admitted State * * * [must] apply the federal common-law rule, which may result in property law determinations antithetical to the desires of that State * * * " would be a perverse application of the *equal footing doctrine*. Id. at 378. "Under our federal system, property ownership is not governed by a general federal law, but rather by the laws of the several States." Id.

Surprisingly, *Hughes* was not overruled by the *Corvallis* majority. Instead, the majority attempted to distinguish *Hughes* on the dubious basis that the property in *Hughes* was oceanfront property, the boundaries of which are "`too close to the vital interest of the Nation in its own boundaries to allow to be governed by any law but the supreme Law of the Land.'" Id. at 377 n.6 (citing Hughes v. Washington, 389 U.S. 290, 293 (1967)).

Later, in California v. United States, 457 U.S. 273, reh'g denied, 458 U.S. 1131 (1982), the Supreme Court reaffirmed the *Hughes* rule. The issue was whether the United States or the State of California had title to oceanfront land created through accretion to land owned by the United States. The accretion followed the construction of two jetties extending seaward from the land owned by the United States. Under California law, a distinction is drawn between accretion resulting from natural forces and that which the effect of artificial conditions. The former belongs to the littoral owner; the latter belongs to the State. The Court, however, held "that a dispute over accretion to oceanfront property where title rests with or *was derived* from the Federal Government is to be determined by federal law." Id. at 273 (emphasis added). According to the Court, the federal rule is that accretions of whatever cause belong to the littoral owner. Id. at 288. See also Wilson v. Omaha Indian Tribe, 442 U.S. 653 (1979).

The *Hughes* decision and its progeny leaves a number of questions unanswered. Does the *Hughes* rule apply to property on all tidal waters if title is traceable to a federal patent? Would it apply to property in Puget Sound? If oceanfront property is located in one of the original thirteen states, and therefore title could not be traced to a federal patent, does federal or state law determine the rights of oceanfront property owners? Does United States v. California, 381 U.S. 139 (1965) or the Submerged Lands Act of 1954 (see Chapter Four, infra) have any bearing on this question?

(3.) Interfering With The Natural Processes Of Erosion And Accretion

When jetties, groins, or other structures that interfere with the natural movement of sand are constructed and as a consequence erosion occurs down-current from the structure, is a littoral owner, whose property is sand starved and thus eroded entitled to sue anyone for damages? Does the injured littoral owner have a public or private nuisance action against anyone? Does either the riparian reasonable use rule or common enemy rule apply to shoreline erosion control activities?

LUMMIS v. LILLY
Supreme Judicial Court of Massachusetts, 1982
385 Mass. 41, 429 N.E.2d 1146

NOLAN, JUSTICE.

The defendants filed a motion to dismiss or for summary judgment in answer to a complaint in three counts alleging nuisance, unreasonable use, and unjust enrichment, resulting from the defendants' installation and maintenance of a stone groin on their Cape

Cod waterfront property, which almost adjoins the plaintiff's littoral property.* * *

From the record we learn that the defendants have owned their property since at least 1965. * * * The plaintiff purchased his property (Lummis property) in 1975. An engineer's plan of the area reveals that both properties are on that part of the shore of Buzzards Bay in Cape Cod known as Sippewisset Beach and that they are almost contiguous. In 1966, Josiah Lilly applied to the Massachusetts Department of Public Works for a license "to build and maintain a stone groin." The license was granted under the following terms and conditions: "* * * Nothing in this license shall be construed as authorizing encroachment on property not owned or controlled by the licensee except with the consent of the owner or owners thereof. This license is granted subject to all applicable Federal, State, County and Municipal laws, ordinances and regulations." Lilly also received a permit from the United States Army Engineer Division "to construct and maintain a stone groin and place riprap" on his property, under conditions which do not require recital because they are not material to this case. A groin was then built.

A groin was defined in one expert's affidavit as "a solid structure which lies generally perpendicular to the shoreline and extends from the backshore out across the foreshore of the beach. The function of a groin is to interrupt the littoral drifting of sand along the shore, thereby producing deposition of sand on the updrift side of the structure and widening the beach." According to the same expert the "[l]ittoral drifting continues on the downdrift side of the structure and since the sand which is transported away is not replaced by sand from the updrift side, the beach narrows on the downdrift side of the groin." The Lummis property is on the downdrift side and these conditions, as they affect the Lummis property, are precisely the damage alleged by the plaintiff.

The narrow but important issue is whether we should apply the rule of "reasonable use" as most recently enunciated by this court in Tucker v. Badoian, 376 Mass. 907, 384 N.E.2d 1195 (1978), to the rights of owners of oceanfront property.

In *Tucker*, the court rejected, as to the problems of surface water, the standard which came to be known as the "common enemy" rule. It had been formulated (though not so named) in the early case of Gannon v. Hargadon. * * * The common enemy rule was expressed in *Gannon* * * * as follows: "The right of an owner of land to occupy and improve it in such manner and for such purposes as he may see fit, either by changing the surface or the erection of buildings or other structures thereon, is not restricted or modified by the fact that his own land is so situated with reference to that of adjoining owners that an alteration in the mode of its improvement or occupation in any portion of it will cause water, which may accumulate thereon by rains and snows falling on its surface or flowing on to it over the surface of adjacent lots, either to stand in unusual quantities on other adjacent lands, or pass into and over the same in greater quantities or in other directions than they were accustomed to flow." The rights of private landowners with respect to surface waters were governed by the common enemy rule from the time of *Gannon* to *Tucker*. The pristine harshness of the common enemy rule was soon relaxed to impose liability on a landowner who used artificial contrivances to cause surface waters to accumulate or to flow onto neighboring land in unreasonable quantities.

The common enemy rule has never been successfully invoked in decisions adjudicating the rights of riparian landowners. From earliest times, these rights have been enforced under the standard of reasonable use. In Stratton v. Mount Hermon Boys' School, 216 Mass. 83, 85, 103 N.E. 87 (1913), the "reasonable use" rule was articulated as follows: "[E]ach riparian owner must conduct his operations reasonably in view of like rights and obligations in the owners above and below him. The right of no one is absolute but is qualified by the existence of the same right in all others similarly situated. The use of the water flowing in a stream is common to all riparian owners and each must exercise this common right so as not essentially to interfere with an equally beneficial enjoyment of the common right by his fellow riparian owners. Such use may result in some diminution, obstruction or change in the natural flow of the stream, but the interference cannot exceed that which arises from reasonable conduct in the light of all circumstances, having due regard to the exercise of the common right by other riparian owners." Support for this rule * * * can be found in Restatement (Second) of Torts § 850 (1979).

Our jurisprudence on the rule governing littoral rights is not abundant. * * * A more recent case to address the problem directly is Jubilee Yacht Club v. Gulf Ref. Co., 245 Mass. 60, 140 N.E. 280 (1923), in which the plaintiff sought damages and injunctive relief because of the defendant's construction of a breakwater. The defendant in the present action relies heavily on *Jubilee*, in which the court denied the plaintiff relief because the defendant "merely exercised the ordinary rights of an owner in fee." Id. at 64, 140 N.E. 280. There, the court analogized the defendant's construction of the concrete breakwater to "acts * * * committed by the owner of adjoining property away from the seashore. * * * The building of fences, walls or other structures, or making excavations on his own land ordinarily is within the absolute right of the owner of a fee without reference to the incidental injury which may thereby be caused to his neighbor." Id. at 62, 140 N.E. 280.

To the extent that the *Jubilee* decision approved of a rule applicable to littoral owners other than that of reasonable use we choose not to follow it. There is no sound reason for imposing the obligation of reasonable use on riparian owners, while permitting littoral owners to use their property without any limitations. See Mears v. Dole, 135 Mass. 508, 510 (1883).

1. Reasonable use. On remand, the trial judge will be faced with weighing the evidence to resolve whether the defendants have made a reasonable use of their property as that use affects the plaintiff's property. There are several factors which the judge may consider in determining whether the maintenance of the stone groin in its present form constitutes a reasonable use. Factors considered relevant to reasonable use by riparian owners can be considered in evaluating the same question when applied to littoral owners.

Among those factors are the license which the defendant secured and whether the conditions of the license have been met. Neither the license from the Department of Public Works nor the permit from the United States Army Engineer Division is conclusive on the issue of reasonable use. It is settled that a license does not immunize the licensee from liability for negligence or nuisance which flows from the licensed activity.

Other factors bearing on the reasonableness of the use are the purpose of the use, the suitability of the use to the water course, the economic value of the use, the social value of the use, the extent and amount of harm it causes, the practicality of avoiding the harm by adjusting the use or method of use of one owner or the other, the practicality of adjusting the quantity of water used by each owner, the protection of existing values of water uses, land, investments, and enterprise, and the justice of requiring the user who is causing harm to bear the loss. Restatement (Second) of Torts § 850A (1979). See Stratton v. Mount Hermon Boys' School, 216 Mass. 83, 85, 103 N.E. 87 (1913).

2. Nature of relief. This case was decided by entry of summary judgment for the defendants. As a result, the judge did not consider the issue of the relief, if any, to which the plaintiff would be entitled. We need not reach this issue. At a minimum, the plaintiff might be entitled to equitable relief from prospective injury, if an unreasonable use of the groin is found. In such case, equitable relief in the form of an injunction or an order to reduce the size of the groin or to modify its shape may be in order.

As to relief for damages sustained prior to the entry of judgment, it appears that the plaintiff's claim is founded more nearly on longstanding principles enunciated in connection with the rights of riparian owners than on principles similar to the rights of landowners concerned with surface water, recently announced prospectively in Tucker v. Badoian, supra. [citations omitted.] On this record, we cannot determine what, if any, damages may be recoverable by the plaintiff.

The judgment dismissing the plaintiff's complaint is reversed and the case is remanded to the Superior Court for action consistent with this opinion.

So ordered.

Notes and Questions

1.   In 1998, after obtaining all necessary state and federal permits, the City of New Inlet constructed two jetties to protect the navigation channel leading from the ocean through the inlet to the Port of New Inlet. The permits required that the city construct and operate a sand transfer plant on the north side of the inlet. The sand bypassed by the sand transfer plant was to be placed on the shoreline south of the inlet in such a way as to insure the proper distribution by longshore currents to the beaches to the south of the inlet. A town to the south of City of New Inlet claims that the city is not operating the plant in a proper manner, that the beaches to the south are sand starved, that the town and other littoral owners have a vested right in the sand accretions that would naturally accrue but for the existence of the jetties, and that the city is liable for damages to all the littoral owners to the south whose beaches are being deprived of sand. Is the town correct?

2.   If a littoral owner's property is experiencing severe erosion, may the state nonetheless deny the property owner permission to construct a seawall or other beach hardening structure on the grounds that any such structure will inhibit the natural movement of the mean high-tide line, and if the natural processes are inhibited, the wet sand area will eventually be eroded away and there will be no wet sand area (public beach) left? See Shell Island Homeowners Association v. Tomlinson, 134 N.C. App. 217, 228 517 S.E. 2d 406, 414 (1999) (littoral and riparian owners have no statutory or common law right to erect hardened structures in areas of environmental concern to protect their property from erosion). May the state go so far as to order the removal of seawalls and similar structures that were erected in the past with the permission of the state?

3.   Rising sea levels, ocean storms and the natural wave processes annually cause significant losses of valuable beachfront property. Often these property owners will seek to reclaim the lost land. Due to the expense and the likelihood that any reclamation may be only temporary, property owners will attempt to have the state or federal government subsidize all or part of the project. When such reclamations occur to whom should the reclaimed beach belong? In the absence of a statute, where should the line between public and private ownership be drawn?

See, e.g., Carolina Beach Fishing Pier v. Town of Carolina Beach, 277 N.C. 297, 177 S.E.2d 513 (1970).

4.   If the federal or state government plans to replenish a beach and the statute below is in effect, will the federal or state government need the permission of each littoral owner to place fill below the mean high-tide line? Above the mean high-tide line? Who owns the nourished beach?

The title to land in or immediately along the Atlantic Ocean or Gulf of Mexico raised above the mean high water mark by publicly financed projects that involve hydraulic dredging or other deposition of spoil materials or sand vests in the State. Title to such lands raised through projects that receive no public funding vests in the adjacent littoral proprietor. All such raised lands shall remain open to the free use and enjoyment of the people of the State, consistent with the public trust rights in ocean beaches, which rights are part of the common heritage of the people of this State.

C. THE SCOPE OF THE RIGHT OF ACCESS

(1.) The Water Area Over Which The Littoral Right Exists

DORRAH V. MCCARTHY
Supreme Court of Georgia, 1995
265 Ga. 750, 462 S.E.2d 708

FLETCHER, PRESIDING JUDGE

Property owners William and Margaret Dorrah sued to stop their neighbor Brian McCarthy from constructing a dock in the navigable tidal waters in coastal Chatham County. The trial court ruled that McCarthy was a riparian owner because his property adjoins the high water mark of the river and that the Department of Natural Resources did not abuse its discretion in allowing equitable access to navigable water in the tidal basin among adjoining waterfront property owners. We agree that the state exercised its discretion reasonably when it adopted an equitable approach in apportioning use of its tidelands among riparian owners on the curving shoreline and affirm.

McCarthy and Dorrahs own adjoining lots that abut the high water mark or marsh line on a curving inlet in a tidal basin of the Wilmington River. In 1987, McCarthy applied for a permit to build a dock in the basin's navigable waters, but DNR rejected the proposal. In 1993, the DNR commissioner requested a legal opinion concerning the proper method for allocating use of state-owned bottoms on the navigable the waters between adjoining waterfront property owners. The attorney general concluded that the straight-line extension method, which extends the side boundary lines of property, was generally acceptable, but rigid adherence to it could cause inequitable results by denying access to deep water to a riparian or littoral owner. Based on this official opinion, DNR changed its policy and granted McCarthy a revocable license to construct a dock in the tidal waters. The Dorrahs sued McCarthy and the DNR commissioner, seeking an injunction to stop construction and a declaratory judgment that the license was illegal. The trial court denied both, and the Dorrahs appealed.

* * *

Although the courts in this state have not previously considered how to divide the riparian owner's right of access on a curving shoreline, other states provide persuasive authority for the principle of equitable apportionment. Many jurisdictions have adopted the general rule that allocates access to tidal waters according to the riparian owner's frontage on the high water line. The "fundamental rule" in dividing the tidelands is "to give each parcel a width at its outer or seaward end proportional to that which it has at the high water mark." Other states have eschewed a general rule in favor of case-by-case adjudication based on equitable principles.

We hold that the Georgia Department of Natural Resources exercised its discretion reasonably in adopting a policy granting equitable access to the tidelands and tidal waters among the waterfront property owners. When a shoreline is relatively straight, extending the property lines straight out to the navigable waters is a fair method for allocating access among riparian owners. When the shoreline curves, however, the straight-line method is inadequate. It can result in overlapping claims for use of state-owned water bottoms and in denying access to water altogether to some riparian owners. * * *

Judgment affirmed.

All the Justices concur.

Note

A number of methods are used by courts and regulatory agencies to allocate, among waterfront property owners, the water area lying between their uplands and the deep water (or line of navigation). In addition to those described in *Dorrah*, there is the method used in the next case–*In Re Protest of Mason*. In *Mason* the area through and over which the littoral owner is entitled to exercise his or her right of access, including the right to wharf out, is delineated by the following method. First, in front of the littoral property, draw an imaginary line that locates the beginning of navigable or deep water. Next, beginning at the line of deep water, draw two imaginary lines that are (1) perpendicular to the imaginary line of deep water and (2) if extended, will intersect with the shore at the point where the littoral property owner's property lines meet the water's edge.

Another method is to draw the lines perpendicular to the shore and then out to the imaginary line of deep water. See, e.g., C. Dunscombe, Riparian and Littoral Rights 37 (1970). For a description of other methods see generally A. Daniel Tarlock, Law of Water Rights § 3.17[1][b] (1998). As the *Dorrah* court points out, to achieve equitable results a number of jurisdictions will use different methods in different cases depending on the configuration of the shoreline and the location of deep water. See, e.g., Pine Knoll Shores Association v. Cardon, 126 N.C. App 155, 484 S.E.2d 446 (1997); Water Street Associates Limited Partnership v. Innopak Plastics Corporation, 230 Conn. 764, 646 A.2d 790 (1994).

(2.) The Nature Of The Right Of Access

IN RE PROTEST OF MASON
North Carolina Court of Appeals, 1985
78 N.C. App. 16, 337 S.E.2d 99

BECTON, JUDGE.

This case began with the application of Joseph A. Huber to the Marine Fisheries Commission (Commission) to lease public bottom land in Core Sound for clam culture. Clyde Mason, Jr., protested the proposed lease. On 14 April 1984, after an administrative hearing and a final agency hearing, the Commission ordered that the lease be issued to Huber with certain conditions. Following is a more detailed recitation of the facts and procedural history of this case.

On 9 July 1982, Huber submitted an application for a lease for shellfish cultivation in a 1.8 acre area of the public bottom of Core Sound, Carteret County, North Carolina.

* * *

Huber's lease application included a map of the proposed area to be used for clam culture. The map showed that the area would begin at the highwater mark of Core Sound and extend outward in such a way as to overlap Mason's area of riparian access across the Sound. The water depth in this area varies from zero at the shore side of the lease area to a depth of one and one-half to four and one-half feet at the waterward side. It is not disputed that Mason owned the riparian rights involved herein, that Core Sound is navigable, or that Mason's riparian area is overlapped by the proposed lease area.

* * *

On 22 September 1983, the Commission approved Huber's proposed lease (which had been amended on 15 September 1983). On 7 October 1983, Mason requested an administrative hearing. An administrative hearing was held, and the hearing officer issued a proposed order on 14 March 1984. The Commission then held a final hearing. It reviewed the entire record, including the findings and conclusions of the administrative hearing officer, and it issued a final order on 14 April 1984 granting to Huber a lease subject to several specific conditions.

Mason petitioned the superior court to review the Commission's decision. * * * In the petition, Mason included a recitation of the facts in the case, some of which varied from the findings of the Commission. The trial court issued its own findings of fact and conclusions of law and held that (1) the Commission violated the United States and North Carolina Constitutions by issuing the lease to Huber because it constituted a taking of the vested riparian rights of Mason for a private purpose without compensation. * * * The trial court reversed the Commission's order and denied the issuance of the lease.

The Commission appeals, asserting that the trial court erred by * * * (3) improperly and erroneously concluding that riparian access areas must extend to the nearest federally maintained channel; and (4) erroneously concluding that Mason's riparian rights were taken and that he was entitled to compensation. We disagree with the Commission on its first two assignments of error, and we hold that the trial court properly reversed the Commission's order. But we agree with the Commission on its last two assignments of error, and we modify the reasoning of the trial court to the extent it relies on the conclusion that Mason's riparian rights were taken.

* * *

Riparian rights are vested property rights that cannot be taken for private purposes or taken for public purposes without compensating the owner, and they arise out of ownership of land bounded or traversed by navigable water. * * * The State may regulate, protect and promote the shellfish industry and protect the public rights in navigable waters. The legislature vested the authority to promote the shellfish industry in the Marine Fisheries Commission, but it also mandated that the Commission may not lease a bottom area if the lease would impinge upon riparian rights. G.S. § 113-202(a)(4).

The trial court in the case at bar concluded that Mason's riparian rights were seriously encumbered in that the lease would interfere with Mason's rights to "navigation, recreation, access to the navigable portions of Core Sound, potential future accretions and all other rights of usage to which petitioner is entitled * * * by virtue of his riparian ownership." We believe the Commission properly and conscientiously considered the potential conflicts between the proposed lease and Mason's riparian rights, and the trial court erroneously concluded that the lease, as issued, would impinge upon Mason's riparian rights. * * *

The * * * area to consider is the area covered by the lease as issued, with the conditions imposed by the Commission. These conditions are explicitly authorized by the legislature:

In the event the Secretary finds the application inconsistent with the applicable standards, the Secretary shall recommend that the application be denied or *that a conditional lease be issued* which is consistent with the applicable standards. G.S. § 113-202(d) (emphasis added). And, if a protest is filed, "[t]he Marine Fisheries Commission may impose special conditions on leases so that leases may be issued which would otherwise be denied." Id. § 113- 202(h) (quoted language eliminated by 1985 amendments). The Commission used this authority to impose the following conditions: 1. All stakes must be a minimum of nineteen feet apart; 2. All stakes should be at a height clearly visible to boaters; 3. The matting must be maintained so as not to pose a threat to navigation; 4. The lease area must be set back at least 100 feet from the Protestant's shoreline as shown in Protestant's Exhibit 21; and 5. That portion of the lease area within the limits of the Protestant's areas of riparian rights shall be made subject to the lawful exercise of those rights including the right to build a pier for access to navigable waters within the lease. Upon six months notice that the Protestant, or his successor in interest, has obtained the necessary permits for and intends to build a pier within the lease area, the leaseholder shall remove all equipment which interferes with the pier and reasonable access to the pier.

The first three conditions were designed to guard the public's right of navigation and recreation (including Mason's) as required by G.S. § 113-202(a)(3). The Commission recognized the problem:

On the proposed lease site, the number of stakes, if unregulated as to proximity and height, could pose an impermissible obstruction to navigation in an area commonly plied by boats eighteen to twenty-three feet long, Finding of Fact 4(e). While the Commission requires lease boundary stakes no further than fifty yards apart, 15 NCAC 3C.0305(a)(3), it sets no minimum distance for stakes generally. And it concluded that the conditions, combined with the protection already afforded the public under G.S. § 76-40(a) (prohibiting deposit of various wastes in navigable water) and (c) (1981) (prohibiting abandonment of structures on floor of navigable waters), would render "such matting and stakes * * * compatible with other public uses of the area." The fourth condition, requiring a one hundred foot set-off, also protects the public's right and Mason's right to navigation and recreation in the riparian area. The set-off, based upon 15 NCAC 3c.0302(a)(3), recognizes Mason's right to make reasonable use of the water as it flows past the shore.

The final condition imposed by the Commission protected Mason's right to access to "deep" or "navigable" water. The Commission concluded that the lease as proposed "could interfere with [Mason's] riparian right to build a pier or other structure out to deep water." The Commission noted, however, that Mason's Exhibit 22 (the map) did not, as a matter of law, show Mason's area of riparian access because it extended the area of access to the federal channel. The Commission nevertheless found that the proposed lease area generally extends substantially waterward of Mason's property. The trial court specifically found: 7. The riparian area of petitioner's land is that area included within parallel lines drawn from the perpendicular to the water course as established by the NOAA Chart aforesaid to the termini of petitioner's land lines at the highwater mark as shown by protestant's Exhibit 22. Exhibit 22 shows the riparian area extending all the way to the federally maintained channel.

As the Commission correctly noted, the riparian access zone does not necessarily extend this far. It only extends as far as necessary to provide access to the "navigable parts" of the waterway. See Shepard's Point Land Co., 132 N.C. at 538, 44 S.E. at 46. Thus, the question becomes: What is navigable? In this State, "all water courses are regarded as navigable in law that are navigable in fact." State v. Baum, 128 N.C. 600, 604, 38 S.E. 900, 901 (1901). "The navigability of a watercourse is therefore largely a question of fact for the jury, and its best test is the extent to which it has been so used by the public when unrestrained." Id. Thus, the Commission was correct in concluding that the right of access to "navigable" water in the case at bar depended upon "the context of the actual shoreline, the sound, and local usage." We further point out that the lateral boundaries of the zone of riparian access should be determined in accordance with the Coastal Area Management Act (CAMA) regulation 15 NCAC 7h.0208(b)(6)(F) (1983) (concerning the proper placement of piers that may interfere with adjacent property owner's riparian access area):

The line of division of areas of riparian access shall be established by drawing a line along the channel or deep water in front of the properties, then draw a line perpendicular to the line of the channel so that it intersects with the shore at the point the upland property line meets the water's edge. Here we note that these imaginary lines drawn from the channel or deep water represent the lateral boundaries between access zones and do not represent the distance each zone extends away from the shore. Each access zone extends only as far as necessary to ensure access to navigable waters, as described above.

Even though the findings of the Commission indicate that the small craft customarily used in the proposed lease area are able to navigate up to the shore, there was no error in the Commission's conclusion that Mason is entitled to some access to deeper water through the area of the proposed lease. Otherwise, Mason would be boxed in. The Commission was well within its authority to condition the lease on the provision of this zone of access. See G.S. §§ 113-202(d), (h). * * *

For the reasons set forth above, we affirm the result and modify the reasoning of the trial court.

Modified and affirmed.

WEBB and *MARTIN, JJ.,* concur.

Problem

A non-profit sailing club requested a permit to build an extension and addition to its pier. The neighboring littoral property owners objected on the ground that there would be too much noise and activity in the waters adjacent to their property and the sailing club's property. The permit was nonetheless granted, and the pier was built. The neighbors subsequently hired a surveyor who determined that part of the extension and addition is located within one of the adjacent littoral owners' area of access. Does that adjacent littoral owner have a claim of trespass? See, e.g., Langley v. Meredith, 237 Va. 55, 376 S.E.2d 519 (1989) (encroaching pier to be removed). Can she get an injunction ordering the removal of the offending portion of the pier? See Flowers v. Blackbeard Sailing Club, Ltd., 115 N.C. App. 349, 444 S.E.2d 636 (1994) (objecting riparian landowner must pursue administrative remedies before coastal commission).

Notes and Questions

1. At common law in England, the placement of a wharf or other structure in navigable waters was unlawful and, if it interfered with public navigation, a public nuisance. But in the United States, to promote the development of navigation and commerce, riparian owners were encouraged to erect wharves and piers. Gradually, by custom and usage or by statute, most eastern and Gulf of Mexico states permitted riparian owners to wharf out. However, in some jurisdictions, the law distinguished between riparian owners and owners of property adjacent to the ocean or gulf. As to the latter, their only rights are those associated with accretion, erosion, reliction, and other shore processes. Such oceanfront or gulf-front owners have no common law right to construct piers or wharfs in ocean waters. See generally C. Dunscombe, Riparian and Littoral Rights 7-15, 21-23 (1970); but see Capune v. Robbins, 273 N.C. 581, 160 S.E.2d 881 (1968).

In Pacific Coast states, the recognition of riparian rights was limited. In Washington, the right to wharf out is a revocable, statutory right. Oregon originally granted upland owners no riparian rights of access or wharfage over tidelands as against the state or its grantees. Bowlby v. Shively, 22 Or. 410, 30 P. 154 (1892), aff'd, Shively v. Bowlby, 152 U.S. 1 (1894). Later, the Oregon Supreme Court modified its position in *Bowlby*. The riparian owner on navigable water had, in the absence of any statute regulating or prohibiting such activity, the "right" to construct a log boom or other structure adjacent to his property. Coquille M & M Co. v. Johnson, 52 Or. 547, 98 P. 132 (1908).

In a number of jurisdictions, there is uncertainty as to whether a common law right to wharf out exists. Within a single jurisdiction, precedents may be in conflict. See, e.g., Peoples Counsel of Baltimore County v. Maryland Marine Manufacturing Co., Inc., 316 Md. 491, 560 A.2d 32 (1989) (concluding that the right to build a wharf or other structure can only come from the state, but citing a number of conflicting Maryland decisions of all vintages). See generally 1 Water and Water Rights § 6.01(a)(2) (1991 Edition).

In those jurisdictions in which the right to wharf out is a recognized common law incident of ownership of waterfront property, it may be regarded as a vested property right, such as in North Carolina, or only as a priority that such owners have. Port Clinton Associates v. Bd. of Selectmen of the Town of Clinton, 217 Conn. 588, 597-98, 587 A.2d 126, 142 (1991) (riparian rights are so limited by superior public rights that they are a mere "franchise."); Watts v. Lawrence, 703 So.2d 236 (Miss. 1997) ("littoral rights * * * are not property rights per se; they are merely licenses or privileges"). Whatever the essential nature of the right, the exercise of it in all jurisdictions is subject to significant regulation and typically requires the obtaining of both federal and state permits.

2. The traditional right of access includes the right to fill in adjacent shallows and dredge channels through adjacent shallows to reach the navigable part of the waters. This right is subject to reasonable regulation. However, if the riparian or littoral owner has reasonable access, the owner has no right to dredge submerged lands to either improve or maintain a particular level of access without the permission of the owner of the submerged lands. See Town of Oyster Bay v. Commander Oil Corporation, 700 N.Y. S. 2d 47 (App. Div. 1999).

3. Conversely, if the submerged lands underlying navigable waters are held by the state as public trust property and navigable waters are open to all the public, should a coastal state develop criteria for what portion of these public trust lands and waters may be physically occupied by the piers and docks of private littoral owners? What should the criteria be?

4.   Along many parts of the coast, the construction and sale of dockominiums is a growing phenomenon. See, e.g., M. Cheng, Dockominiums: An Expansion Of Riparian Rights That Violates The Public Trust Doctrine, 16 B.C. Envtl. Aff. L. Rev. 821 (1989); C. Hall, Dockominiums: In Conflict With The Public Trust Doctrine, 24 Suffolk U. L. Rev. 331, 332-35 (1990). In order to accomplish their goals, the developers of such projects must address the question of the severability of the riparian right of access from the ownership of adjacent uplands. In some jurisdictions, as a matter of common law, the riparian right of access is in effect an easement appurtenant and, as most such easements, is not severable from the dominant estate. However, in other jurisdictions, riparian rights may be severed. See, e.g., Simons v. French, 25 Conn. 346, 352 (1856); William v. Skyline Dev. Corp., 265 Md. 130, 155-56, 288 A.2d 333, 348 (1972). In such jurisdictions, the right to wharf may be subdivided by plat and rectangular portions conveyed and sold to individuals, without regard to whether they own any adjacent uplands. And even in some of those jurisdictions that, as a matter of common law, would not allow severance of riparian right, if the riparian rights are part of a condominium development and the jurisdiction has enacted a version of the Uniform Condominium Act, the riparian right of access may be subdivided and sold as separate units.

5.   Does a riparian owner's right to wharf out mean that she can occupy the whole area of access if she wishes, for example by building a large marina? If the marina will also extend beyond the beginning of deep water, does the riparian owner have a common law right of use measured by the reasonable use doctrine? See, e.g., Walker v. N.C. Department of Environment, Health, and Natural Resources, 111 N.C. App. 851, 433 S.E.2d 767 (N.C. App. 1993) (no independent littoral or riparian right to construct large scale marina without first obtaining easement from the state).

6.   Is the right to wharf out limited to water dependent uses? For example, may a riparian owner build a restaurant that extends out over the water? See generally 1 Water and Water Rights § 6.01(a)(2) (1991)(must have navigational function).

7.   To what extent may the government limit oceanfront property owners' right of direct access to the water? Suppose, without obtaining easements or releases of littoral rights, the government nourishes a beach by placing a pipe below the mean high tide line, pump sand below the mean high tide line, creating a new beach berm and dry sand beach seaward of the original mean high tide line. The area between the where the sand is discharged and the existing beach above the mean high tide line is filled in by wind and water action moving the discharged sand into the gap. Once the project is completed, all access to the beach is limited to designated walkways a quarter of a mile apart.

Between the walkways, is placed a continuous sand fence. Relying on the statute in note 4, page 65, could the government claim both title to the nourished dry sand beach and the right to limit the access of oceanfront property owners to the newly created beach to use of the walkways only?

LEE COUNTY, FLORIDA v. KIESEL
United States District Court of Appeals, First District, 1998
705 So.2d 1013

NORTHCUTT, JUDGE

We affirm a partial final judgment in this inverse condemnation action.* * * The trial court found that the Kiesels were entitled to compensation because a bridge the county built over the Caloosahatchee River obstructed the Kiesels' riparian right of view. * * *

Evidence at the bench trial reflected that the Kiesels purchased their riverfront property in 1987 for $160,000 and constructed a house at the cost of $265,000. After the home was built, the county proceeded with the alignment and construction of the bridge. The bridge makes landfall on property adjacent to the Kiesel home; none of the Kiesels' property was condemned for the construction. The bridge is not aligned perpendicularly to the shoreline, but extends over the river at an angle, reaching across the view from the Kiesels' property. * * *

The trial court found that "[a]s a result of the angle at which the bridge is constructed across the front (river side) of the Kiesel property, it substantially and materially interferes with and disturbs the view across the waters of the Caloosahatchee River from the said property." The court concluded that "as a direct and proximate result of such substantial and material interference, the market value of the Kiesel property has substantially decreased, having been estimated by Plaintiffs' expert real estate appraisal witness as being in the range of $185,250 to $227,000."

* * *

Owners of uplands along navigable waters enjoy common law riparian rights, one of which is the right to an unobstructed view over the water to the channel. These rights constitute property, which the government may not take or destroy without paying just compensation to the owners. * * *

Shorelines do not often neatly parallel channels, and property lines are not always perpendicular to shorelines or channels. Consequently, it is impossible to devise a rule for every case that would define the physical parameters of the riparian right of view or establish what degree of intrusion would constitute an obstruction. * * * [In Hayes v. Bowman, 91 So.2d 795 (1957), the Florida Supreme Court stated:]

> We * * * hold that the common law riparian right to an unobstructed view and access to the Channel over the foreshore across the waters toward the Channel must be recognized over an area as near 'as practicable' in the direction of the Channel so as to distribute equitably the submerged lands between the upland and the Channel. * * * An upland owner must in all cases be permitted a direct, unobstructed view of the Channel and as well a direct, unobstructed means of ingress and egress over the foreshore and tidal waters to the Channel. * * *

> In making such 'equitable distribution' the Court necessarily must give due consideration to the lay of the upland shore line, the direction of the Channel and the co-relative rights of adjoining upland owners.

91 So.2d at 801-02.

* * * to constitute a compensable obstruction of the riparian right of view, the interference must be more than a mere annoyance. It must substantially and materially obstruct the land owner's view to the channel. * * *

Finding no merit in the county's other issues, we affirm the order under review.

CAMPBELL, A.C.J., and **FRANK, J.**, Concur.

Notes and Questions

1.   Is the recognition of the right of view simply a way in which the court can find a justification for awarding damages for the decline in the value of plaintiffs' waterfront property that was caused by the placement of an unsightly bridge offshore? Does the placement of visible stakes within the *Mason* plaintiff's area of access also give rise to a claim of interference with his right of view of the waters of the sound? Cf. Harding v. Commissioner of Marine Resources, 510 A.2d 533, 536-37 (Me. 1985) (Aquaculture leasing statute does not require consideration of effect on upland property values). Florida is one of the few states that recognize a riparian right of view.

2.   If, after obtaining all necessary state and federal permits, a soundfront property owner builds a marina within its area of access, may neighboring soundfront property owners successfully attack the location and use of the marina's docks and piers on the ground that the

marina is a "nuisance" and interferes with their correlative riparian rights?   See Heston v. Ousler, 119 N.H. 58, 398 A.2d 536 (1979) (upholding a master's finding that the location and use of defendant's docks constituted a nuisance).   If so, what specific circumstances would be sufficient to support such a conclusion?   What should the remedy be? Is the question of whether the marina would be a nuisance one that must be raised before the permit granting agencies?

BECKER v. LITTY
Maryland Court of Appeals, 1989
318 Md. 76, 566 A.2d 1101

ADKINS, JUDGE.

Boone Creek is a tidal estuary located near Oxford, Talbot County, Maryland.   A somewhat tortuous channel at its mouth leads to the Choptank River.   The Creek is divided into what are known as the North and Southeast Branches.   At the confluence of these branches is Sol's Island, containing perhaps as much as five acres of land.   A bridge spanning the roughly 240 feet from Sol's Island to the mainland is the focus of controversy in this case, which raises, among other issues, important questions of riparian rights, the preemptive effect of a United States Coast Guard bridge permit, and standing.   We shall resolve these issues, but, because the record before us clearly does not reflect a number of matters that bear on the ultimate disposition of the case, we shall remand under Maryland Rule 8-604(d), for further proceedings.

I. Facts

In May 1986, appellee Suzanne Hanks Litty acquired title to Sol's Island, then an essentially uninhabited tract of land accessible only by air or via the waters of Boone Creek.   She and her husband, appellee Ernest Litty (the Littys), decided to build a residence on the island. They also decided, it seems, that an aerial or aquatic commute would have its drawbacks.   In October 1986, the Littys obtained a United States Coast Guard permit to build a private, one-lane, fixed bridge across the aforesaid 240 feet between Sol's Island and the mainland.   The permit specified that the bridge should have three feet of vertical clearance over Boone Creek at mean high water.

Although the Coast Guard had given public notice of the application for the bridge permit, and also had notified certain federal and State agencies, some of the Littys' Boone Creek neighbors did not become aware of the situation until after the permit had issued.   When they learned of the permit, those neighbors lost no time in protesting to the Littys, the Coast Guard, and others.   Despite these objections, the Littys actively prepared for erection of the bridge.

On 11 January 1988, appellants William B. Becker and his wife Jean, along with 12 others who owned property, or in most cases both owned property and resided on the shores of Boone Creek, filed a complaint against the Littys seeking to enjoin construction of the bridge. Because the individual appellants assert essentially identical interests, we shall refer to them, collectively, as "the Beckers." On 2 February 1988, the Circuit Court for Talbot County (Wise, J.) issued an interlocutory injunction barring construction of the bridge. On 25 August it dissolved that injunction and granted summary judgment in favor of the Littys and against the Beckers. We frame the issues in this appeal by explaining the Beckers' theories below, and the trial court's reasons for rejecting them.

II. Issues and Rulings in the Circuit Court

The Beckers' and their co-parties' properties are located at various spots on the North and Southeast Branches of Boone Creek. In the circuit court they asserted that they owned various vessels by which they navigated between the branches of the Creek and from the Creek to the Choptank River. They alleged that Boone Creek to the south and southeast of Sol's Island was too shallow to permit navigation as a practical matter. Thus, the only way they could move between the branches, and for those whose properties lay on the Southeast Branch, into the Choptank, was through the narrow channel between Sol's Island and the mainland. A bridge with only three feet of vertical clearance would effectively block this navigation. This, averred the Beckers, would deprive them of their riparian rights and cause substantial depreciation in the values of their properties.

Judge Wise did not accept any of these arguments. He held that the Beckers were complaining about interference with a right of navigation, which is a public right, as opposed to one of the bundle of rights possessed by riparian owners. * * *

III. Riparian Rights

Before us the Beckers restate their riparian rights argument. In essence, they assert that there can be no interference with what they claim is their right, as the owners of riparian property, to navigate on the waters of Boone Creek and the Choptank River. We assume, arguendo, that the bridge, if constructed pursuant to the Coast Guard permit, will have that effect. But we hold that Judge Wise did not err in rejecting this argument.

* * *

The riparian owner has * * * a right of access to water. That is, a right of access "to the water in front of his fast land." The owner has the right, under proper circumstances, to reach that water for purposes such as fishing, bathing, and making certain improvements into the water. That is why, for example, the riparian owner is entitled to reliction and accretion. But once the right of access is gratified, this particular right of a riparian owner goes no further. It does not encompass a right of free navigation.

The right to navigate on navigable waters is a public right, not one that attaches only to the owner of riparian property. "The public [has] a right, at common law, to navigate over every part of a common navigable river.* * * " Garitee v. M. & C.C. of Balto., 53 Md. 422, 436 (1880). * * *

Other courts have reached similar results.* * * Webb v. Giddens, 82 So.2d 743, 745 (Fla. 1955), did reach a contrary conclusion. There, a riparian owner who rented boats was totally cut off from the main body of the lake where people used the boats. The Florida court allowed the owner access to the lake. In a later case, the Supreme Court of Florida did state that "a riparian owner's interest in waterway navigation is the same as a member of the public except where there is some special injury to the riparian owner," but the injury was very different from the present case. Game & Fresh Water Fish Comm'n v. Lake Islands, 407 So. 2d 189 (Fla. 1982). In *Lake Islands*, the property owners lost all access to their islands, whereas in the present case, the Beckers can still get to their property by land and still have access to Boone Creek.

In short, other jurisdictions, like Maryland, hold that a general right to navigation is not a riparian owner's right, but a right of the general public. The Littys' bridge will not deprive the Beckers of their riparian rights of access to the water in front of their properties. They still have that access. * * *

For the reasons stated, we reject the Beckers' riparian rights claim.

Notes and Questions

1. The right of access to waters fronting littoral and riparian lands is not absolute. As *Lilly* illustrates, it is possible to effectively cut off certain types or levels of access to navigable waters without infringing on the protected common law right of access.

2. Is the right of access to navigable water illusory if once a littoral owner reaches the navigable portion of the water body the littoral owner is unable to actually use the water body for navigation?

3. Does a littoral owner have any recourse if another littoral owner, within her area of access, constructs a wharf or pier that interferes with the ability of vessels to reach the first littoral owner's wharves or piers?

See, e.g., Bond v. Wool, 107 N.C. 126 (1890) (construction and placement of a pier that effectively cut off the ability of fishing vessels to navigate to neighbor's wharves did not constitute an interference with the neighbor's common law right of access to navigable waters); see also Bloom v. Water Resources Commission, 157 Conn. 528, 254 A.2d 884 (1969) (positioning of new marina in such a way as to jeopardize an adjacent oyster operation did not invalidate permits issued for marina construction and operation).

SECTION 6. THE NAVIGATION SERVITUDE

A. FEDERAL NAVIGATION SERVITUDE

Under the Commerce Clause, the federal government has extensive powers over arteries of interstate and foreign commerce. But usually when the federal government acts to aid the movement of goods in interstate commerce by improving the arteries of commerce, such as the interstate highway system and it removes private structures that are impediments to the project, the government is required by the Fifth Amendment of the United States Constitution to pay fair compensation to the owners of such structures. When, however, the federal government acts to aid navigation in the nation's waterways and removes obstructions or private structures or otherwise destroys or diminishes private riparian rights, it is not required to pay compensation to the owners of such structures and property interests! The justification for no-compensation is the *federal navigation servitude*. Although compensation is not required, Congress may elect nonetheless to compensate the property owner for some or all of the loss sustained. See, e.g., 33 U.S.C. § 595a (1982) (compensation for real property above the high water mark taken by the United States shall include the fair market value based upon all uses to which the property may reasonably be put). As you read the following materials, think about these questions:

(1) What kinds of interests are burdened by the navigation servitude?

(2) What is the geographic extent of the navigation servitude?

(3) How does the navigation servitude differ from the public trust doctrine?

(4) What does "in aid of navigation" encompass?

(5) What is the justification for this "taking without paying" power?

LEWIS BLUE POINT OYSTER CO. v. BRIGGS
Supreme Court of the United States, 1913
229 U.S. 82

MR. JUSTICE LURTON delivered the opinion of the court.

This was an action to restrain the defendant in error from dredging upon certain lands under the waters of Great South Bay in the State of New York. The defense was that the lands upon which he was engaged in dredging were under the navigable waters of the bay, which was a navigable area of the sea, over which enrolled and registered vessels passed in interstate commerce; that Congress had provided for the dredging of a channel some 2,000 feet long and 200 feet wide across said Bay, and that defendant was engaged as a contractor with the United States in dredging the channel so authorized. The plaintiff in error, plaintiff below, averred that this channel would pass diagonally across submerged land in said bay which it held as lessee under the owner of the fee in the bed of the bay. The land so held under lease had been planted with oysters and had been long used for the cultivation of that variety of oyster known as the "Blue Point." The claim was that the dredging of such a channel would destroy the oysters of the plaintiff, not only along the line of excavation, but for some distance on either side, and greatly impair the value of his leasehold for oyster cultivation.

The New York Court of Appeals held that the title of every owner of lands beneath navigable waters was a qualified one, and subject to the right of Congress to deepen the channel in the interest of navigation, and such a "taking" was not a "taking" of private property for which compensation could be required. The judgment of the courts below discharging the injunction and dismissing the action was therefore affirmed.

The case comes here upon the claim that the dredging of such a channel, although in the interest of navigation, is a taking of private property without just compensation, forbidden by the Fifth Amendment to the Constitution of the United States.

* * * If the public right of navigation is the dominant right and if, as must be the case, the title of the owner of the bed of navigable waters holds subject absolutely to the public right of navigation, this dominant right must include the right to use the bed of the water for every purpose which is in aid of navigation. This right to control, improve and regulate the navigation of such waters is one of the greatest of the powers delegated to the United States by the power to regulate commerce. Whatever power the several States had before the Union was formed, over the navigable waters within their several jurisdictions, has been delegated to the Congress, in which, therefore, is centered all of the

governmental power over the subject, restricted only by such limitations as are found in other clauses of the Constitution.

By necessary implication from the dominant right of navigation, title to such submerged lands is acquired and held subject to the power of Congress to deepen the water over such lands or to use them for any structure which the interest of navigation, in its judgment, may require. The plaintiff in error has, therefore, no such private property right which, when taken, or incidentally destroyed by the dredging of a deep water channel across it, entitles him to demand compensation as a condition.

* * *

The conclusion we reach, is that the court below did not err in dismissing the action of the plaintiff in error, and the judgment is accordingly

Affirmed.

Notes and Questions

1.   Before reacting to *Blue Point Oyster*, some more background on the navigation servitude is helpful. Professor Eva Morreale, in Federal Power in Western Waters: The Navigation Power and The Rule of No Compensation, 3 Nat. Resources. J. 1, 2 n.6 (1963), wrote:

It is important to note * * * that the terms "*navigation power*" and "*navigation servitude*" describe two related but nevertheless distinct phenomena. Navigation power designates the regulatory power which Congress, under the commerce clause and since Gibbons v. Ogden, exercises over navigable waters. Navigation servitude designates the rule that certain private property may be taken in the exercise of the navigation power without the payment of compensation.

What is the justification for this no-compensation rule?

2.   The federal navigation servitude, in its traditional form, could be used to avoid payment of compensation to adversely affected private property owners when the only purpose of the particular federal activity was in aid of navigation. Gradually, the navigation servitude was transformed. In 1931, Justice Brandeis, wrote: "That purposes other than navigation will also be served could not invalidate the exercise of the authority conferred, even if those other purposes would not alone have justified an exercise of Congressional power." Arizona v. California, 283 U.S. 423, 456 (1931). Mr. Justice Brandeis implied, however, that aid of navigation had to be the primary purpose. Ten years later, in Oklahoma v. Atkinson, 313 U.S. 508, 534 (1941), the Court

noted: "That ends other than flood control will also be served, or that flood control may be relatively of lesser importance, does not invalidate the exercise of the authority conferred on Congress." The requirement that navigation be the primary purpose had vanished. Aid of navigation need only be a purpose.

3.   In United States v. Certain Parcels of Land situated in the City of Valdez, 666 F.2d 1236 (1982), the City of Valdez, Alaska, sought compensation for a ferry terminal facility condemned by the federal government and incorporated into a Coast Guard vessel traffic control and safety facility.   In part, the City of Valdez asserted that the government could not rely on the navigation servitude to avoid compensation because construction of the facility did not aid "navigation in fact."   According to the city, the government only improves navigation when it removes obstructions in navigable waters. Since the ferry terminal was not removed, but instead incorporated into a new dock, the city contended that it did not aid navigation, that the government took the facility for its own use, and that the government had to compensate the city for the value of the terminal. (Interestingly, the ferry terminal facility was constructed entirely with federal funds, by the U.S. Army Corps of Engineers, for the city after a 1964 earthquake destroyed the original facility owned by the State of Alaska).

The Ninth Circuit rejected the petitioners claim.   The court dismissed the city's assertion that the exercise of the navigation servitude requires that the government act to aid navigation in fact. According to the court, only a purpose to improve and protect navigation is essential.   Under such circumstances, "private improvements connected to fastlands but located in navigable waters may be altered or removed by the government without compensating the owner." Id. at 1240.

4.   The U.S. Army Corps of Engineers ordered some wharf owners to remove pilings from their wharves and suspended the wharf owners' federal permit right to maintain such structures.   When the wharf owners sued, alleging a taking, the district court held that (1) the wharf owners' state-created right to maintain a wharf on state owned submerged lands was subordinate to the federal navigation servitude and (2), under the applicable regulations, the Corps retained the power to modify, revoke, or suspend plaintiffs' rights under their federal permit if such was necessary in the public interest. Donnell v. United States, 834 F.Supp. 19 (D. Me. 1993).

5.   What waters are subject to the navigation servitude? Read the discussion in note 3, which follows *Phillips Petroleum*, supra.   For additional reading on the navigation servitude, See, e.g., W. Stoebuck, Nontrespassory Taking in Eminent Domain 100-20 (1977).

APPLEGATE v. UNITED STATES
United States Court of Federal Claims, 1996
35 Fed Cl. 406

MILLER, JUDGE.

This case is before the court on plaintiffs' motion for summary judgment as to liability; plaintiffs' motion for partial summary judgment based on the Assignment of Claims Act, 31 U.S.C. § 3727 (1994); and defendant's motion for summary judgment. Plaintiffs seek compensation for an alleged taking in violation of the Fifth Amendment through erosion due to construction of a federal harbor project. By their motions plaintiffs contend: 1) that erosion of their properties above the mean high-water mark, beyond the limits of the Federal Government's navigational servitude, amounts to a physical taking; 2) that the Government caused the erosion of their properties through construction of the Canaveral Harbor project * * *. Defendant asserts entitlement to summary judgment on the bases: 1) that plaintiffs have no compensable expectancy in accreting beaches or in the uninterrupted flow of sand. * * *

Facts

The following facts are undisputed, unless otherwise indicated. This constitutional takings case involves over 300 plaintiffs and more than 350 parcels of land. * * *

Plaintiffs are owners of beachfront property south of Port Canaveral in Brevard County, Florida. This coastline fronts on the Atlantic Ocean to the south of the projection of Cape Canaveral. Prior to the events giving rise to this action, the area consisted of a 41-mile long arc of white sandy beaches. All of the plaintiffs, save one, acquired interests in the properties that are the subject of this action at various times after construction began on the federal project in question.

During the 1950s the Corps undertook construction of the Canaveral Harbor Project (the "Project") * * *. The Project was designed to provide a deep-water harbor on the east coast of Florida in Brevard County, immediately south of Cape Canaveral. The Project included the dredging of a channel from the deep water of the Atlantic Ocean through a barrier island into the Banana River Lagoon, as well as turning basins, dikes, locks, and other harbor mechanisms. Construction of the Project began in 1950.

As part of the Project, the Corps constructed two jetties projecting from the shoreline eastward into the Atlantic Ocean. * * * Plaintiffs and defendant contest the purpose of the jetties and their effect on the harbor and adjacent lands.

* * *

DISCUSSION

* * *

2. Permanent Physical Occupation: Taking Through Erosion

* * *

Plaintiffs claim a physical invasion of their properties through flooding and erosion caused by the Corps' construction of the Project. They contend that the construction interfered with the natural southerly littoral flow of sand that, before construction of the Project, provided regular, natural replenishment and maintenance of their beachfront properties. Defendant maintains that plaintiffs have no compensable expectancy in the littoral flow of sand because the Government has exceptional power to regulate waters in the public interest, including the flow of sand beneath the MHWM. * * *

It is well settled that flooding and attendant erosion of private property by the Government amount to a taking. United States v. Dickinson, 331 U.S. 745, 750 (1947). * * *

Takings cases involving navigable waters present unique considerations. The United States holds broad powers to regulate along bodies of water and maintains an exclusive navigation servitude, United States v. Rands, 389 U.S. 121, 123 (1967), which reflects the superior interests of the United States in navigation and the nation's navigable waters. United States v. Twin City Power Co., 350 U.S. 222, 224 (1956). * * *

The holdings of the Supreme Court and the Federal Circuit establish that the Government owes no compensation for injury or destruction of a claimant's rights when they lie within the scope of the navigational servitude, which encompasses, at least, properties below the MHWM. * * * However, the Supreme Court "has never held that the navigational servitude creates a blanket exception to the Takings Clause. * * * " Kaiser-Aetna [v. United States,] 444 U.S. [164,] at 172.

The Federal Circuit recognizes that compensation may be required "where improvements to navigation made by the government result in erosion to land located above or outside * * * the high-water mark at the time of construction." * * * Whether the Government's action went so far as to amount to a taking then is a separate inquiry from the existence of the navigational servitude itself. Kaiser-Aetna, 444 U.S. at 174; Owen [v. United States,] 851 F.2d [1404,] 1416.

* * *

Binding precedent supports a ruling, as a matter of law, that flooding and erosion on plaintiffs' properties caused by governmental action above the MHWM is a compensable taking. Owen, 851 F.2d at 1416. The same line of cases denies compensation to a landowner for damage to property within the broad navigational servitude held by the United States, specifically the littoral flow of sand below the MHWM.

A judgment as a matter of fact and law in a takings case requires proof of causation. Proof of actual and proximate causation of plaintiffs' damages due to construction of the Project by the Corps is a difficult undertaking on summary judgment. * * *

1) Proof of Loss

Fundamental to proving causation in a takings case is marshaling evidence of the actual taking of property. Public Water, 133 Ct. Cl. at 352, 135 F. Supp. at 890. Plaintiffs filed their complaint in 1992. * * * Plaintiffs Don and Gayle Applegate and Noro and Company, d/b/a Pelican Landing Resort, were permitted to represent the claims of similarly situated plaintiffs. Plaintiffs' counsel certified to the court that the test plaintiffs represent the similar claims of all plaintiffs. During the following months, the court ordered plaintiffs to provide defendant with information on the actual and specific physical losses due to dune and bluff erosion caused by construction of the Project. To date plaintiffs have not provided any information on actual loss of property for any plaintiff, including the test plaintiffs. As a result, plaintiffs currently face a June 28, 1996 deadline to provide such information, after which the sanction of dismissal will be imposed. Applegate v. United States, 35 Fed. Cl. 47, 58-59 (1996) (order denying motion to dismiss and compelling discovery); Applegate v. United States, No. 92-832L (Fed. Cl. Mar. 27, 1996) (order denying reconsideration and extending deadline).

* * * Without an appropriate showing of the amount of beachfront allegedly lost, the court cannot rule as a matter of fact and law that any loss occurred and that any plaintiff in this case therefore is entitled to compensation for a taking of property.

2) Proof of Causation

To entitle a claimant to compensation, the Fifth Amendment requires that the Government actually take the property interest at issue. In cases involving indirect action, a necessary and difficult element of proof is causation. Collectively, plaintiffs and defendant have presented hundreds of pages of documents. Review of the evidence submitted on summary judgment leads to the ineluctable conclusion that the burdens attendant to resolution on summary judgment as to causation, in light of the conflicting evidence, are insurmountable. The evidence presents conflicting scenarios regarding the causes, history, and current state of erosion on beaches south of Canaveral Harbor.

Among the disputes that directly relate to causation is the nature of beach creation and renourishment. Plaintiffs assert that Brevard County beaches are the product of the natural southerly littoral flow of sand, which also causes sustaining accretion, relying on letters from Corps engineers, Corps reports, and the holding in Pitman. 457 F.2d at 978. Disputing plaintiffs' theory that the littoral flow of sand created the beaches, defendant rejoins with an alternative explanation of the process by which the beaches of Peninsular Florida were formed, relying on the Affidavit of David V. Schmidt, Chief, Coastal Section, Plan Formulation Branch, Planning Division, Jacksonville District, U.S. Army Corps of Engineers.

* * *

3. Assignment of Claims

Plaintiffs argue that a landowner may recover damages for a taking of property that precedes his ownership of the affected property. Plaintiffs assert that they are entitled to compensation dating back to the initial construction of the Project, regardless of the date of purchase.

* * *

"[I]t is undisputed that '[since] compensation is due at the time of taking, the owner at that time, not the owner at an earlier or later date, receives the payment'." [United States v.] Dow[357 U.S.] at 20-21.* * * Furthermore "[i]t is well established * * * that the Assignment of Claims Act prohibits the voluntary assignment of a compensation claim against the Government for the taking of property." * * *

Since plaintiffs are barred by law from claiming damages prior to ownership, and no valid assignment occurred, plaintiffs are precluded from recovering damages for any property taken before the date for each purchase of property.

* * *

CONCLUSION

Accordingly, based on the foregoing,

IT IS ORDERED, as follows:

1. Plaintiffs' motions for summary judgment are denied.

* * *

4. Assuming that plaintiffs comply with the court's order of February 29, 1996, requiring them to respond to outstanding discovery requests by June 29, 1996, a status conference shall be held * * *.

Notes and Questions

1. Did the court hold that the plaintiffs had a property right in the natural littoral flow of sand in the ocean waters lying in front of their beach property? Other than the fact that the federal government is the defendant, isn't this case the same as Lummis v. Lilly?

2. Was the plaintiffs' legal problem simply the difficulty of proving that the Corps' jetties and other activities were the source of the erosion threatening their property and if these were a cause, the erosion was attributable to that and not to natural forces? Does proof of cause and loss present almost insoluble and extremely expensive problems of proof for plaintiffs attempting to recover in such cases?

3. Are the critical facts here the construction of the jetty and the cutting of an artificial channel through a barrier island? Should the navigation servitude insulate the federal government from liability if the Corps was dredging a natural coastal river to protect the river channel from siltation and the consequence was increased erosion of down current beaches?

4. In developed areas it would not be unusual for coastal properties to change hands frequently. If a property owner may only recover for erosion that has taken place during that person's period of ownership, doesn't this, as a practical matter, preclude the successful prosecution of takings claims predicated upon alleged erosion of beach property resulting from governmental activities?

5. The federal government settled the *Applegate* litigation by agreeing to pay for an $8 million dollar beach restoration project and an additional $5 million dollars in damages and attorneys' fees to oceanfront property owners. T. O' Mieilia, Palm Beach Considers Suing U.S. Over Beaches, Palm Beach Post, Wednesday, December 15, 1999.

B. STATE NAVIGATION SERVITUDES

The Commerce Clause grants the federal government power over interstate commerce, including the use of and activities involving navigable waters of the United States. Under the Supremacy Clause, this power of the federal government is superior to any such power of the individual states. But if Congress has not seen fit to exercise its power over a particular navigable waterway, a state may regulate navigation there. In addition to this state navigation power, a state navigation servitude may also exist in a particular state. The existence of such a servitude can be traced back to an early New York case, Lansing v. Smith, 4 Wend. 9 (N.Y. 1829), in which the court held that a riparian owner on navigable water was not entitled to compensation when access to his wharf was impeded by a state-licensed pier. The grant of the riparian property to the owner was viewed as being subject to an implied reservation of power to regulate commerce. By 1897, several other states had recognized such a servitude. E.g., Holyoke Water Power Co. v. Connecticut River Co., 52 Conn. 570 (Conn. 1884); Green Bay & M Canal Co. v. Kaukauna Water Power Co., 90 Wis. 370, 61 N.W. 1121, 63 N.W. 1019 (1895). Most often the existence of a state navigation servitude has been asserted in dicta, recognizing the doctrine, but finding it

> inapplicable because the state's activity has been held not to be carried out under the navigation power. The net result being that the scope of the state navigation power has been most narrowly constricted. * * *

> So reluctant have state courts been to invoke the navigation servitude that one might question the vitality of the state branch of the navigation servitude. * * *

W. Stoebuck, Nontrespassory Taking in Eminent Domain 114-15 (1977).

In Wernberg v. State, 516 P.2d 1191 (1973), reh'g denied, 519 P.2d 801 (Alaska 1974), the Alaskan Supreme Court addressed the issue of the existence and extent of the Alaskan state navigation servitude. The case involved highway construction that had the effect of blocking Wernberg's access to the deep waters of Cook Inlet. After the construction of the highway, Wernberg, a commercial fisherman and littoral owner, could no longer navigate his fishing vessels into Cook Inlet. The state opposed the payment of any compensation to the appellant on the ground that any right of access of a littoral owner was subordinate to the state navigation servitude. The court rejected the state's argument. In its opinion, the court observed that, where recognized, state navigation servitudes are governed by one of three rules:

> (1) the general rule; (2) the public purpose rule; *** [or] (3) the Louisiana exception. The general rule requires the state to compensate the riparian owner for infringement of his property rights unless the project causing the harm is in aid of navigation. The public purpose rule, on the other hand, requires no compensation if the offending project is for any public purpose. Under the Louisiana exception, the scope of the servitude extends to projects "in aid of navigation" that are miles from the actual

boundaries of the watercourse, allowing the state to burden all property in between without payment of compensation.

Id. at 1196. The court then said that the state could take riparian or littoral property rights for a purpose other than to aid navigation, but then the Alaskan constitution requires that compensation be paid.

If compensation must be paid, what does the state navigation servitude add to the police powers of the state to take private property rights for a public purpose so long as compensation is paid? Is the state navigation servitude meaningful in Alaska?

In its opinion the court also stated that state navigation servitudes are subordinate to the federal one,

but where the federal government has not acted, it allows the state, in aid of navigation, to take private riparian rights without paying the compensation that would otherwise be required by the fourteenth amendment.

Id. Does this mean that if the state had been acting "in aid of navigation," Wernberg would not have been entitled to compensation for loss of his access to the deep waters of Cook Inlet?

The "public purpose" rule discussed in *Wernberg*, is best exemplified by the California Supreme Court's decision in Colberg, Inc. v. State ex rel. Department of Public Works, 62 Cal.Rptr. 401, 432 P.2d 3 (1967), cert. denied, 390 U.S. 949 (1968), a decision that sharply contrasts to what most other state courts have been doing. In *Colberg*, the plaintiffs owned a shipyard, located on riparian land, at the end of a tidal waterway. The State planned to construct a fixed low level bridge between plaintiff's shipyard and the mouth of the waterway. As a result, the ship access from the mouth of the waterway to the shipyards would be substantially diminished. Relying on the state navigation servitude, the California Supreme Court denied compensation. The court said that "whatever the scope and character of * * * [plaintiffs'] right to have access to those navigable waters,* * * such right is burdened with a servitude in favor of the state which comes into operation when the state properly exercises its power to control, regulate, and utilize such waters." Id. at 12-13. Perhaps more significantly, the court stated:

The limitation of the servitude to cases involving a strict navigational purpose stems from the time when the sole use of navigable waters for purposes of commerce was that of surface water transport. * * * That time is no longer with us. The demands of modern commerce, the concentration of population in urban centers fronting on navigable waterways, the achievements of science in devising new methods of commercial intercourse -- all of these factors require that the state, in determining the means by which the general welfare is best to be served through the utilization of navigable waters held in trust for the public, should not be burdened with an outmoded classification favoring one mode of utilization over another.

Id. at 12. Consequently, in California the navigable servitude applies whenever the state exercises its power over navigable waters to improve commercial intercourse, whether navigational or otherwise. See Note, Colberg, Inc. v. State: Riparian Landowner's Right to Eminent Domain Relief for State Impairment of Access to a Navigable Waterway, 72 Dick. L. Rev. 375, 380 (1968).

Would the federal government be required to compensate in a situation in which it engaged in activities with similar consequences to those in *Colberg*? Is the expansion of the state navigation servitude in California in effect a taking by judicial decision in violation of the Fifth Amendment? Does *Colberg* in effect proclaim a state navigational servitude for every form of governmental activity that affects navigable waters?

SECTION 7. PUBLIC ACCESS TO AND USE OF COASTAL LANDS AND WATERS

A. BEACH ACCESS PROBLEM

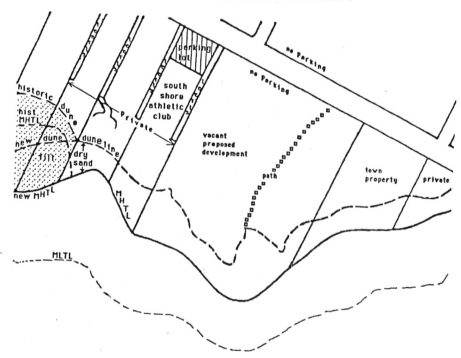

The map above shows a beach area. In addition to the information provided in the map, assume that membership in the South Shore Athletic Club, a nonprofit association, is open to any resident of the town, but in fact only nonbeachfront property owners join the club. The club employs a number of private security guards to patrol the parking lot, recreational facilities and the beach shoreward of the mean high-tide line. Finally, the town taxes any property owned by any nonprofit organization at a lower rate than that which is generally applied.

The town property to the north is open to residents and nonresidents at a fee of $10.00 per person per day. The whole beach is patrolled by town public safety officers and trash and garbage receptacles are provided all along the beach by the town, with regular daily pickups. Two years ago the beach area to the south was extended and a new dune line created. Seventy-five percent of the cost was paid for by the adjacent littoral owners and twenty-five percent by the town. Except for the downtown area, there is very little on-street parking. Near the beach, most streets are "no parking" and no public parking lots are provided. Where parking is permitted, it is for residents only.

Using the map, cases and other materials, identify the beach access issues that exist in this setting. If additional information is needed, specify the needed information and explain the significance of the needed facts. Be careful to separate the vertical access issues -- how the public gets from a public road to the public portion of the beach -- from the horizontal access issues -- what portions of the dry and wet sand are open to public use -- and the incidental access issues, such as the provision of adequate public parking. Among the specific issues you should consider are:

a. Can South Shore Athletic Club be forced to open its beach to all members of the public?

b. Can the town require individuals to pay $10.00 a day for use of the town beach? Must the town provide public parking lots? On street public parking? Must the town provide changing and restroom facilities?

c. Can the town require any developer of the vacant property to dedicate an easement to allow the public a pathway to the beach? Is the path that exists already a public way? May the town trade the path for a sideline easement to the beach? What other devices are available to the town to provide public beach access?

d. Does the public have any right to cross private property to reach the wet sand area? Is the public entitled to use the dry sand for recreational purposes? Can the town prohibit the placement of any fences or other barriers or structures on the dry sand area?

e.   If the town is not permitted to limit the use of the beach area, isn't there a significant danger that the resource may be overburdened and the quality of the beach environment destroyed? If so, how should the government manage, allocate, and protect the important resource?

B. EXPANSION OF THE PUBLIC TRUST DOCTRINE ABOVE THE MEAN HIGH-TIDE LINE

MATTHEWS v. BAY HEAD IMPROVEMENT ASS'N
Supreme Court of New Jersey, 1984
95 N.J. 306, 471 A.2d 355, cert. denied, 469 U.S. 821

SCHREIBER, J.

The public trust doctrine acknowledges that the ownership, dominion and sovereignty over land flowed by tidal waters, which extend to the mean high water mark, is vested in the State in trust for the people.   The public's right to use the tidal lands and water encompasses navigation, fishing and recreational uses, including bathing, swimming and other shore activities. Borough of Neptune City v. Borough of Avon-by-the-Sea, 61 N.J. 296, 309, 294 A.2d 47 (1972). In *Avon* we held that the public trust applied to the municipally-owned dry sand beach immediately landward of the high water mark.[6]

The major issue in this case is whether, ancillary to the public's right to enjoy the tidal lands, the public has a right to gain access through and to use the dry sand area not owned by a municipality but by a quasi-public body.

* * *

I

Facts

The Borough of Bay Head (Bay Head) borders the Atlantic Ocean. * * * A beach runs along its entire length adjacent to the Atlantic Ocean. There are 76 separate parcels of land that border the beach. All except six are owned by private individuals. Title to those six is vested in the Association.

---

[6]   The dry sand area is generally defined as the land west (landward) of the high water mark to the vegetation line or where there is no vegetation to a seawall, road, parking lot, or boardwalk. New Jersey Beach Access Study Commission, Public Access to the Oceanfront Beaches: A Report to the Governor and Legislature of New Jersey 1 (1977).

The Association was founded in 1910 and incorporated as a nonprofit corporation in 1932. * * *

Nine streets in the Borough, which are perpendicular to the beach, end at the dry sand. The Association owns the land commencing at the end of seven of these streets for the width of each street and extending through the upper dry sand to the mean high water line, the beginning of the wet sand area or foreshore. In addition, the Association owns the fee in six shore front properties, three of which are contiguous and have a frontage aggregating 310 feet. Many owners of beachfront property executed and delivered to the Association leases of the upper dry sand area. These leases are revocable by either party to the lease on thirty days' notice. Some owners have not executed such leases and have not permitted the Association to use their beaches. Some also have acquired riparian grants from the State extending approximately 1000 feet east of the high water line.

* * *

Membership is generally limited to residents of Bay Head. Class A members are property owners. Class B are non-owners. Large families (six or more) pay $90 per year and small families pay $60 per year. Upon application residents are routinely accepted. Membership is evidenced by badges that signify permission to use the beaches. Members, which include local hotels, motels and inns, can also acquire badges for guests. The charge for each guest badge is $12. Members of the Bay Head Fire Company, Bay Head Borough employees, and teachers in the municipality's school system have been issued beach badges irrespective of residency.

Except for fishermen, who are permitted to walk through the upper dry sand area to the foreshore, only the membership may use the beach between 10:00 a.m. and 5:30 p.m. during the summer season. The public is permitted to use the Association's beach from 5:30 p.m. to 10:00 a.m. during the summer and, with no hourly restrictions, between Labor Day and mid-June.

No attempt has ever been made to stop anyone from occupying the terrain east of the high water mark. During certain parts of the day, when the tide is low, the foreshore could consist of about 50 feet of sand not being flowed by the water. The public could gain access to the foreshore by coming from the Borough of Point Pleasant Beach on the north or from the Borough of Mantoloking on the south.

* * * The Association's avowed purpose was to provide the beach for the residents of Bay Head.

* * *

The trial court held that the Association was not an arm of the Borough of Bay Head, that the Association was not a municipal agency, and that nothing in the record justified a finding that public privileges could attach to the private properties owned or leased by the Association. A divided Appellate Division affirmed. The majority agreed with the trial court that the Association was not a public agency or a public entity and that the action of the private owners through the Association established no general right in the public to the use of the beaches.

* * *

II

The Public Trust

* * *

In order to exercise * * * rights guaranteed by the public trust doctrine, the public must have access to municipally-owned dry sand areas as well as the foreshore. The extension of the public trust doctrine to include municipally-owned dry sand areas was necessitated by our conclusion that enjoyment of rights in the foreshore is inseparable from use of dry sand beaches. * * *

III

Public Rights in Privately-Owned Dry Sand Beaches

In * * * [earlier cases] our finding of public rights in dry sand areas was specifically and appropriately limited to those beaches owned by a municipality. We now address the extent of the public's interest in privately-owned dry sand beaches. This interest may take one of two forms. First, the public may have a right to cross privately owned dry sand beaches in order to gain access to the foreshore. Second, this interest may be of the sort enjoyed by the public in municipal beaches * * * namely, the right to sunbathe and generally enjoy recreational activities. * * *

Exercise of the public's right to swim and bathe below the mean high water mark may depend upon a right to pass across the upland beach. Without some means of access the public right to use the foreshore would be meaningless. To say that the public trust doctrine entitles the public to swim in the ocean and to use the foreshore in connection therewith without assuring the public of a feasible access route would seriously impinge on, if not effectively eliminate, the rights of the public trust doctrine. This does not mean the public has an unrestricted right to cross at will over any and all property bordering on the common property. The public interest is satisfied so long as there is reasonable access to the sea.

[T]he particular circumstances must be considered and examined before arriving at a solution that will accommodate the public's right and the private interests involved. Thus an undeveloped segment of the shore may have been available and used for access so as to establish a public right of way to the wet sand. Or there may be publicly-owned property, such as in *Avon*, which is suitable. Or, as in this case, the public streets and adjacent upland sand area might serve as a proper means of entry. The test is whether those means are reasonably satisfactory so that the public's right to use the beachfront can be satisfied.

The bather's right in the upland sands is not limited to passage. Reasonable enjoyment of the foreshore and the sea cannot be realized unless some enjoyment of the dry sand area is also allowed. The complete pleasure of swimming must be accompanied by intermittent periods of rest and relaxation beyond the water's edge. The unavailability of the physical situs for such rest and relaxation would seriously curtail and in many situations eliminate the right to the recreational use of the ocean. * * * We see no reason why rights under the public trust doctrine to use of the upland dry sand area should be limited to municipally-owned property. It is true that the private owner's interest in the upland dry sand area is not identical to that of a municipality. Nonetheless, where use of dry sand is essential or reasonably necessary for enjoyment of the ocean, the doctrine warrants the public's use of the upland dry sand area subject to an accommodation of the interests of the owner.

We perceive no need to attempt to apply notions of prescription, dedication, or custom, as an alternative to application of the public trust doctrine. Archaic judicial responses are not an answer to a modern social problem. Rather, we perceive the public trust doctrine not to be "fixed or static," but one to "be molded and extended to meet changing conditions and needs of the public it was created to benefit." Avon, 61 N.J. at 309, 294 A.2d 47 [sic].

Precisely what privately-owned upland sand area will be available and required to satisfy the public's rights under the public trust doctrine will depend on the circumstances. Location of the dry sand area in relation to the foreshore, extent and availability of the publicly-owned upland sand area, nature and extent of the public demand, and usage of the upland sand land by the owner are all factors to be weighed and considered in fixing the contours of the usage of the upper sand.

Today, recognizing the increasing demand for our State's beaches and the dynamic nature of the public trust doctrine, we find that the public must be given both access to and use of privately-owned dry sand areas as reasonably necessary. While the public's rights in private beaches are not co-extensive with the rights enjoyed in municipal beaches, private landowners may not in all instances prevent the public from exercising its rights under the public trust doctrine. The public must be afforded reasonable access to the foreshore as well as a suitable area for recreation on the dry sand.

V

The Beaches of Bay Head

[The court held that the Bay Head Improvement Association was a quasi-public entity and that its membership must be opened up to the public at large.]

* * *

The Public Advocate has urged that all the privately-owned beachfront property likewise must be opened to the public. Nothing has been developed on this record to justify that conclusion. We have decided that the Association's membership and thereby its beach must be open to the public. That area might reasonably satisfy the public need at this time. We are aware that the Association possessed, as of the initiation of this litigation, about 42 upland sand lots under leases revocable on 30 days' notice. If any of these leases have been or are to be terminated, or if the Association were to sell all or part of its property, it may necessitate further adjudication of the public's claims in favor of the public trust on part or all of these or other privately-owned upland dry sand lands depending upon the circumstances. However, we see no necessity to have those issues resolved judicially at this time since the beach under the Association's control will be open to the public and may be adequate to satisfy the public trust interests. We believe that the Association and property owners will act in good faith and to the satisfaction of the Public Advocate. Indeed, we are of the opinion that all parties will benefit by our terminating this prolonged litigation at this time.

The record in this case makes it clear that a right of access to the beach is available over the quasi-public lands owned by the Association, as well as the right to use the Association's upland dry sand. It is not necessary for us to determine under what circumstances and to what extent there will be a need to use the dry sand of private owners who either now or in the future may have no leases with the Association. Resolution of the competing interests, private ownership and the public trust, may in some cases be simple, but in many it may be most complex. In any event, resolution would depend upon the specific facts in controversy.

None of the foregoing matters were fully argued or briefed, the disputes concerning rights in and to private beaches having been most general. All we decide here is that private land is not immune from a possible right of access to the foreshore for swimming or bathing purposes, nor is it immune from the possibility that some of the dry sand may be used by the public incidental to the right of bathing and swimming.

We realize that considerable uncertainty will continue to surround the question of the public's right to cross private land and to use a portion of the dry sand as discussed above. Where the parties are unable to agree as to the application of the principles enunciated herein, the claim of the private owner shall be honored until the contrary is established.

* * *

The judgment of the Appellate Division is reversed in part and affirmed in part. Judgment is entered for the plaintiff against the Association. Judgment of dismissal against the individual property owners is affirmed without prejudice. No costs.

For reversal in part; affirmance in part -- Chief Justice WILENTZ and Justices CLIFFORD, SCHREIBER, HANDLER, POLLOCK and O'HERN -- 6.

Opposed -- None.

Notes and Questions

1.   The beach access cases are somewhat similar to the cases on the rights of private owners of uplands to wharf out, fill, and dredge in navigable waters. Once again, public use rights are in conflict with traditional concepts of exclusive private ownership. As in the wharf-out cases, an understanding of the various zones involved is critical. Review the diagram adapted from *Brower*, supra, at the beginning of this chapter.

2.   Is the *Matthews* application of the public trust doctrine limited to property owned or controlled by public or quasi-public entities? Doesn't the logic of *Matthews* extend to privately owned dry sand areas? If it does, is there a "takings" issue when the public trust is expanded beyond traditional waters or uses?

3.   The battle over the public's right to use dry sand beaches continues. In North Carolina, in a recently filed lawsuit a number of oceanfront property owners assert that, since their title extends to the

mean high tide line, the public has no right to use the dry sand beach landward of that line. For a discussion of the case and related issues, see J. Kalo, The Changing Face of the Shoreline: Public and Private Rights to the Natural and Nourished Dry Sand Beaches of North Carolina, 78 N.C. L. Rev. 1869 (2000). New Hampshire legislation attempting to assert public trust rights to "the furthest landward limit reached by the highest tidal flow" over the nineteen-year tidal cycle ("the highest syzygy line"), was found to be an unconstitutional taking of private property. Purdie v. Attorney General, 143 N.H. 661, 732 A. 2d 442 (1999). Public rights in New Hampshire extend to only the mean high tide line, which is the common law boundary between public and private shorelands. The history of the beach access movement in Connecticut and New Jersey is discussed in M. Poirer, Environmental Justice and the Beach Access Movements of the 1970s in Connecticut and New Jersey: Stories of Property and Civil Rights, 28 Conn. L. Rev. 719 (1996).In the most recent chapter of that story, the Appellate Court of Connecticut held that portions of a town ordinance limiting the use of a town park, including a beach area, to town residents and their guest, was void as a violation of the public trust doctrine and public policy. Leydon v. Town of Greenwich, 57 Conn. App. 712, 750 A. 2d 1122 (Conn. App. 2000).

4.   Massachusetts is what is referred to as a "low-tide" state; that is, a littoral owner's boundary extends to the low water, not high water, line.   Between the mean high water and extreme low water line, however, the public has limited rights. Historically, these rights did not include the right of the general public to walk on the beach! When the legislature proposed the bill recognizing such a right, the Massachusetts court, in an advisory opinion, held that the proposed law would constitute a taking of private property rights in the foreshore (the right to exclude the general public) and the proposed law failed to provide fair compensation to those whose property rights would be adversely affected. Thus, the proposed law would violate both the Massachusetts and United States Constitutions. In re Opinion of the Justices, 365 Mass. 681, 313 N.E.2d 561 (1974). See also Bell v. Town of Wells, 557 A.2d 168 (Me. 1989)(statute defining public rights to use intertidal land to include general recreational purposes held to be an unconstitutional taking of private property).

C. OBTAINING PUBLIC ACCESS THROUGH OTHER LEGAL THEORIES

The public trust doctrine is not the only theory that has been advanced in the efforts to assert the public right of access to the beach or the public right to use the dry sand area of the beach. Prescription, dedication, and custom are among the other approaches used to address this issue. What advantages and disadvantages do you see as to the use of each of these theories as a means of determining whether the public can use the dry sand or may cross uplands to reach the beach area?

(1.) Public Prescriptive Easements And Beach Access

A public prescriptive easement across privately owned, beachfront property may arise when the public crosses the private land to reach the wet sand beach. If the public use meets the traditional common law requirements of being (1) open and notorious, (2) continuous and uninterrupted, and (3) adverse for the prescribed period of time, then the public would acquire a permanent easement. See generally J. Bruce and J. Ely, The Law of Easements and Licenses in Land §§ 5.09[1] and [3] (1995). Establishing such public use, however, may present insurmountable problems of proof. See, e.g., City of Daytona Beach v. Toma-Rama, Inc., 294 So.2d 73, 77 (Fla. 1974)(use not adverse to owner and treated as permissive); Town of Manchester v. Augusta County Club, 477 A.2d 1124, 1130 (Me. 1984) (presumption that public use of undeveloped land was permissive). See also Comment, Sunbathers Versus Property Owners: Public Access to North Carolina Beaches," 64 N.C.L.Rev. 159, 164-66 (1985). On the other hand, unsuccessful efforts by a landowner to prevent an aggressive public from crossing her land may establish that the use was nonpermissive. Concerned Citizens v. Holden Beach Enterprises, 329 N.C. 37, 404 S.E.2d 677 (1991), describes a on-going battle, extending over 20 years, between sunbathers and fishermen who were using a beach path crossing undeveloped land to reach an inlet and the owner of the land. Despite the presence of "No Trespassing" signs, which people used for firewood, the placement of fences and gates, which people pulled down and destroyed, and a private security guard and guardhouse, who people ignored and drove past, the public continued to use the path. According to the court, the repeated, futile attempts by the owner to prevent the public from crossing his land established that the public use was indeed adverse and not permissive. And although some people were deterred, that did not interrupt the public use because most were not. At trial, the frustrated agent of the owner asked: "'[W]hat does it take to keep somebody out of a place[?] * * * [H]ave you got to set a tank up, a machine gun, or what [?]'" Id. at 51, S.E.2d at 686.

Another issue in the *Concerned Citizens* case was whether the evidence established that the public had in fact used a specific, identifiable path for the full statutory period. During the time people were walking or driving across the property to reach the inlet, storms, hurricanes, winds, high water, and erosion altered the configuration of the island and the dune field and other terrain through which people traveled. As a result, the precise course of the pathway they traveled also changed, an the defendant's argument was that no easement existed. The court, however, held that, so long as there was a "substantial identity" to the area traversed, the fact that the dynamic quality of the environment necessitated changes in the precise route would not require a finding that there was no easement.   Whether "substantial identity" existed was a question of fact for the jury.

Problem

Assume that, in 1999, a developer purchases a vacant tract of oceanfront land. On examining the tract, the developer sees a large number of trails winding through the dunes to the beach and suspects a significant number of people have been crossing the property to reach the ocean. The developer comes to you and asks you for advice as to what she can do to either foreclose or terminate any public prescriptive easements. You also know that town ordinances do not allow any fences on the road-upland side of the boundary. Sideline fences, however are permissible. What advice would you give to the developer?

(2.) Implied Dedication And Beach Access

Another common law theory that may be used to establish the existence of a public way for access to the beach is that of implied dedication. The common law theory of prescriptive easements requires use by the public for a specified period of years, generally, in the absence of a specific statute, the same time period as is applied to claims of adverse possession without color of title. However the theory of implied dedication is not usually dependant upon establishing public use for a set period of time. In an implied dedication case, the essential requirements are established by acts or circumstances that show the landowner intended to donate an easement to the public and that such an offer was impliedly accepted. The difficulty, of course, is precisely what acts or circumstances constitute such an intent and acceptance. In a line of beach access cases, the California Supreme Court held that an implied dedication could be inferred solely from the public's use of a pathway or road to reach a beach. See, e.g., Gion v. City of Santa Cruz, 2 Cal.3d 29, 89 Cal. Rpt. 162, 465 P.2d 50 (1970). To protect landowners from a clearly unintended dedication of land to public use and encourage landowners to allow the public to use privately-owned land for recreational purposes, some state legislatures have passed statutes that prevent the finding of an implied dedication when the only evidence of an intent to dedicate is the fact that the public used it without objection by the landowner, West's Ann. Cal. Civ. Code § 1009, Oregon Rev. Stat. § 105.655. However, the statute may not apply to privately-owned property that is used by the public to access the beach. See, e.g., West's Ann. Cal Civ. Code § 1009(d)(key provision is not applicable to coastal property lying within 1000 yards of MHTL of Pacific Ocean). In some jurisdictions, an essential component of an implied dedication are acts of maintenance of the area by public authorities. See, e.g., Seaway Co. v. Attorney General, 375 S.W.2d 923 (Tex.Civ.App. 1964). The latter requirement evidences judicial sensitivity to imposing continued maintenance responsibilities, and fiscal obligations, upon local or state governments in the absence of some solid evidence that such obligations would not be unwelcome. See, e.g., Emanuelson v. Gibbs, 49 N.C.App. 417, 420, 271 S.E.2d 557, 559 (1980); Bradford v. Nature Conservancy, 224 Va. 181, 198; 294 S.E.2d 866, 875 (1982); Marx v. Department of Commerce, 220 Mich.App. 66, 73, 558 N.W.2d 460, 464-65 (1997).

(3.) Customary Access Rights

In State ex rel. Thornton v. Hays, 254 Or. 584, 462 P.2d 671 (1969), the Oregon Supreme Court applied the common law doctrine of customary rights to establish the public's right to use the dry sand beaches of the state. The essential requirements of such a claim of a right of customary use are (1) A long and general usage, which in the case of beach usage the court traced back to use by Indians prior to the arrival of settlers, (2) without interruption by private landowners, (3) peaceful and free from dispute, (4) reasonable, (5) certain as to its scope and character, (6) without objection by landowners, and (7) is not contrary to other customs or laws. According to the court, all of these conditions existed with respect to the dry sand area of the beaches of the state and therefore such beaches are open to public use. A few other jurisdictions also recognize the doctrine of custom. See, e.g., County of Hawaii v. Sotomura, 55 Haw. 176, 182, 517 P.2d 57, 61 (1973); Public Access Shoreline Hawaii v. Hawaii County Planning Commission, 79 Hawaii 425, 903 P.2d 1246 (Haw. 1995), cert. denied, 517 U.S. 1163 (1996) (coastal zone management act requires protection of customary rights); United States v. St. Thomas Beach Resorts, Inc., 336 F.Supp. 769, 772-73 (D.V.I. 1974).

Was the decision in *Thornton* an unconstitutional taking of Oregon beachfront owners' private property? In Hay v. Bruno, 344 F.Supp. 286 (D. Or. 1972), a three-judge panel held that the Oregon statutes confirming public customary rights along the ocean shore (held and administered as state recreation areas) are constitutional and do not violate the rights of the owners of "dry sand areas." See also Stevens v. City of Cannon Beach, 317 Or. 131, 854 P.2d 449 (1993), cert. denied with two dissents, 62 U.S.L.W. 3619, 3621 (1994) (common law doctrine of custom does not constitute a taking); D. Bederman, The Curious Resurrection of Custom: Beach Access and Judicial Takings, 96 Col. L. Rev. 1375 (1996).

There are indications that the United States Supreme Court may find unconstitutional the use of the doctrine of custom as a basis for public rights to privately owned dry sand beaches. Dissenting from the denial of certiorari in City of Cannon Beach, Justice Scalia said:

> To say that this case raises a serious Fifth Amendment takings issue is an understatement. The issue is serious in the sense that

involves a holding of questionable constitutionality; and it is serious in the sense that the land-grab (if there is one) may run the entire length of the Oregon coast.

Stevens v. City of Cannon Beach, 510 U.S. 1207, 1212 (1994). Justice Scalia's concern could more than just professional. The doctrine of custom is asserted as a basis for the public's right to use the dry sand beaches of North Carolina. The plaintiffs in that litigation (see note 3, following the Bay Head Improvement case, supra) are oceanfront property owners in the same coastal development in which Justice Scalia is a non-oceanfront property owner

(4.) Creating Beach Access By Regulation

Another approach available for providing public access is the subdividing of shoreline areas in such a manner as to provide for all streets, other than those running parallel to the beach, to extend to the beginning of the MHTL or dry sand. Of course, public access really isn't complete unless there is adequate public parking available within a reasonable walking distance from the beach. What legal issues are raised when conditions requiring dedication of public access are included in zoning permits for coastal development? This allows development without obstructing the public way of passage to the beach. In addition, where large areas of shoreline are developed, the zoning ordinance may provide that a public way be provided from a public roadway to the recreation area at designated intervals along the shoreline.

Coastal zone management authorities may also attempt to require dedication of public access as a condition for obtaining a coastal zone development permit. However, in Nollan v. California Coastal Commission, 483 U.S. 825 (1987), the U.S. Supreme Court held, on the facts of the case, that requiring the dedication of a lateral public easement across the oceanfront lot as a condition for permitting the rebuilding of a house was an unconstitutional taking. *Nollan* and the taking issue is discussed in Chapter Three.

SECTION 8. REGULATORY RESTRICTIONS ON PUBLIC ACCESS

Public trust uses are subject to reasonable regulation. But what criteria should be used to determine if the regulation is reasonable? If title to submerged lands underlying public waters is in private hands, such as a private hunt club, could the legislature prohibit public hunting without permission of the submerged land owner in such areas? If you represented an association of duck hunters attempting to persuade a court to find such legislation invalid, what objections and arguments would you make?

Under what circumstances may a state restrict public access to public trust lands? See, e.g., People v. Deacon, 87 C.A.3d Supp. 29, 151 Cal. Rptr. 277 (1978) (county ordinance prohibiting motorcycle use for tidelands access upheld). How effective is the public trust doctrine in resolving potential conflicts between competing public trust uses, e.g. offshore oil and gas development and fishing? See R. Hildreth, The Public Trust Doctrine and Conflict Resolution in Coastal Waters, 3 Coastal Zone '89: Proceedings of the Sixth Symposium on Coastal and Ocean Management 2604 (1989). See also Atlantic Richfield Co. v. State Lands Comm'n, 21 ELR 21320 (Cal Super. Ct. Los Angeles County Jan. 24 1990) (California State Lands Commission denial under public trust doctrine of an oil company's proposal to build new platforms on an existing offshore oil lease is valid if the proposal presents an unacceptable environmental risk). If public access to public trust lands is restricted, must the restrictions be the least required to achieve legitimate public interests or needs? See, e.g., Carstens v. California Coastal Comm'n, 182 Cal.App. 3d 277, 277 Cal. Rptr. 135 (1986).

In Riveria v. United States, 910 F. Supp. 239 (D.VI. 1996), the plaintiffs challenged the closure of a beach in a federal park that was ordered as part of the partial shutdown of the federal government during the 1995 budget dispute between the President and Congress. The plaintiffs alleged that the closure violated the Virgin Islands Open Shoreline Act which protects the public's right to use and enjoy the beaches of the islands. The district court issued a preliminary injunction ordering the reopening of the beaches.

Chapter Two

PROTECTING WATER QUALITY
AND WATER HABITATS

SECTION 1. INTRODUCTION

Intense development pressure on the fragile coast and recognition of the importance of maintaining the integrity of the coastal environment has led to increased, frequently controversial, governmental regulation of activities affecting coastal waters. The primary focus of this chapter is the role of the federal government in this process.

The examination of the federal role opens with a brief look at the National Environmental Policy Act of 1969 (NEPA). The heart of NEPA is the requirement that in certain circumstances an Environmental Impact Statement (EIS) must be prepared either before the government itself may engage in activities that have the potential of significantly affecting the environment or before the government may issue a permit or other necessary approval for non-federal activities having a similar potential. The EIS is supposed to identify the potential adverse consequences of the proposed activities and to identify less environmentally harmful alternatives that are available to achieve the desirable objectives of the activities. The high volume of both federal activities and private activities within the highly sensitive coastal environment that require federal permission means that many projects raise issues of whether the requirements of NEPA have been adequately satisfied.

Frequently, development activities will touch upon coastal waters. Two statutory programs administered by the United States Army Corps of Engineers limit the nature and extent of such activities. The older is the permit program established pursuant to the Rivers and Harbors Act of 1899. The prime objective of this act and its associated permit program is to insure that development activities in coastal waters do not impede or interfere with the navigability of these waters. The other program, the Section 404 permit program, has a somewhat different

97

goal. The Section 404 program is a product of the Clean Water Act [CWA] and is directed at maintaining or enhancing the quality of the nation's waters. Although each of these two programs is discussed in this chapter, the Section 404 program is the more significant and more controversial of the two and, accordingly, it is examined in more detail.

Another section of the Clean Water Act, Section 401, is an extremely important tool in the effort to maintain and improve the quality of the nation's waters. Section 401 requires applicants for federal licenses and permits (including Section 404 permits) for discharges into navigable waters to provide a certification from the state that the discharge will not violate state water quality standards. Section 401 as it relates to coastal water quality and the protection of water habitats is discussed at the end of this chapter.

SECTION 2. CONTROLLING FEDERAL ACTIVITIES THAT MAY AFFECT COASTAL WATERS

A. THE CIVIL WORKS ACTIVITY OF THE U.S. ARMY CORPS OF ENGINEERS

With an annual budget in excess of $3.8 billion, the Army Corps of Engineers is the largest civil engineering firm in the world. Originally created by Congress by the Act of March 16, 1802, ch. 9, § 26, 2 Stat. 132 et. seq., its initial role was to erect and maintain frontier fronts and other defense facilities. However, soon its purpose was expanded to include construction and maintenance of coastal installations. Then, over the course of the nineteenth century its purpose was extended to include the maintenance and improvement of the nation's rivers, harbors, and other navigable waterways. Today, its national, multipurpose civil works program also includes flood control, hydroelectric power production, irrigation, and improvement of water supplies and water quality.

One major activity of the Corps in coastal areas is maintenance of commercial harbors and navigation channels. The maintenance of these areas requires the Corps to dredge, and dispose of, more than 300 million cubic yards of material each year. If all that material were placed within its city limits, Washington, D.C. would be covered with five feet of dredge material. An additional 80 million cubic yards of material is dredged each year in connection with new Corps projects.

Another significant Corps coastal activity is its coastal engineering projects. The future of the country's open ocean beaches, coastal property, and coastal recreational dependent communities is being shaped by the Corps' attempts to control shoreline erosion through the construction of jetties, groins, seawalls, and other beach stabilization structures and its beach replenishment programs. For a comprehensive examination of the Corps' beach erosion control and stabilization projects, see generally, O. Pilkey and K. Dixon, The Corps and the Shore (1996). See also, C. Dean, Against the Tide: The Battle For America's Beaches (1999).

The Corps' Civil Works Program, under the civilian supervision of the Assistant Secretary of the Army for Civil Works, is the responsibility of the Chief of Engineers of the U.S. Army. To implement its civil works programs, the Corps is organized into geographic divisions headed by a division commander, usually with the rank of brigadier general. The divisions are further subdivided into districts, headed by the district engineer, usually with the rank of colonel. The 11 divisions and 36 local districts boundaries generally correspond with the watershed boundaries of major river basins. Actual planning and construction are done by district offices. Although the Corps is part of the U.S. Army, civilian employees perform most of the planning, construction, operational, and regulatory functions of the Corps. For a short official history of the Corps, see The History of the US Army Corps of Engineers, EP 870-1-45, U.S. Army Corps of Engineers (1998). For more critical examinations of the Corps, see, e.g., R. Smythe, The U.S. Army Corps of Engineers, Audubon Wildlife Report 1989/1990 3-59; O. Pilkey and K. Dixon, The Corps and the Shore (1996). The website for the Corps is <www.usace.army.mil/>.

B. DISCLOSURE OF THE ENVIRONMENTAL COSTS OF FEDERAL COASTAL ACTIVITIES: THE NATIONAL ENVIRONMENTAL POLICY ACT OF 1969

The coastal area is the target of numerous public and private "development" projects that, if carried out, may have both short and long term adverse effects upon the people, topography, water resources, fish, and wildlife in the area. Yet these projects may also provide resources or facilities needed for national defense, the improvement of the public welfare, or the maintenance of a healthy economy.

When the federal government, through entities such as the Corps, plays any significant role in the encouragement, promotion, or implementation of coastal development projects, the governmental entity must abide by the mandate of the National Environmental Policy Act of 1969 (NEPA). NEPA is one of a number of environmental statutes, passed in the late 1960s and early 1970s, intended to reshape our nation's relationship to its environment. Read the following NEPA provisions carefully. What exactly is the mandate of NEPA? What are the critical words and phrases?

NATIONAL ENVIRONMENTAL POLICY ACT

42 U.S.C. § 4321. Congressional declaration of purpose

The purposes of this chapter are: To declare a national policy which will encourage productive and enjoyable harmony between man and his environment; to promote efforts which will prevent or eliminate damage to the environment and biosphere and stimulate the health and welfare of man; to enrich the understanding of the ecological systems and natural resources important to the Nation; and to establish a Council on Environmental Quality.

42 U.S.C. § 4331. Congressional declaration of national environmental policy

(A) The Congress, recognizing the profound impact of man's activity on the interrelations of all components of the natural environment, particularly the profound influences of population growth, high-density urbanization, industrial expansion, resource exploitation, and new and expanding technological advances and recognizing further the critical importance of restoring and maintaining environmental quality to the overall welfare and development of man, declares that it is the continuing policy of the Federal Government, in cooperation with State and local governments, and other concerned public and private organizations, to use all practicable means and measures, including financial and technical assistance, in a manner calculated to foster and promote the general welfare, to create and maintain conditions under which man and nature can exist in productive harmony, and fulfill the social, economic, and other requirements of present and future generations of Americans.

(B) In order to carry out the policy set forth in this chapter, it is the continuing responsibility of the Federal Government to use all practicable means, consistent with other essential considerations of national policy, to improve and coordinate Federal plans, functions, programs, and resources to the end that the Nation may --

(1) fulfill the responsibilities of each generation as trustee of the environment for succeeding generations;
(2) assure for all Americans safe, healthful, productive, and esthetically and culturally pleasing surroundings;
(3) attain the widest range of beneficial uses of the environment without degradation, risk to health or safety, or other undesirable and unintended consequences;
(4) preserve important historic, cultural, and natural aspects of our national heritage, and maintain, wherever possible, an environment which supports diversity and variety of individual choice;

(5) achieve a balance between population and resource use which will permit high standards of living and a wide sharing of life's amenities; and
(6) enhance the quality of renewable resources and approach the maximum attainable recycling of depletable resources.

(C)   The Congress recognizes that each person should enjoy a healthful environment and that each person has a responsibility to contribute to the preservation and enhancement of the environment.

42 U.S.C. § 4332. Cooperation of agencies; reports; availability of information; recommendations; international and national coordination of efforts

The Congress authorizes and directs that, to the fullest extent possible: (1) the policies, regulations, and public laws of the United States shall be interpreted and administered in accordance with the policies set forth in this chapter, and (2) all agencies of the Federal Government shall --

(A)   utilize a systematic, interdisciplinary approach which will insure the integrated use of the natural and social sciences and the environmental design arts in planning and in decision making which may have an impact on man's environment;

(B)   identify and develop methods and procedures, in consultation with the Council on Environmental Quality * * *, which will insure that presently unquantified environmental amenities and values may be given appropriate consideration in decision making along with economic and technical considerations;

(C)   include in every recommendation or report on proposals for legislation and other major Federal actions significantly affecting the quality of the human environment, a detailed statement by the responsible official on --

(1) the environmental impact of the proposed action,
(2) any adverse environmental effects which cannot be avoided should the proposal be implemented,
(3) alternatives to the proposed action,
(4) the relationship between local short-term uses of man's environment and the maintenance and enhancement of long-term productivity, and
(5) any irreversible and irretrievable commitments of resources which would be involved in the proposed action should it be implemented.

Prior to making any detailed statement, the responsible Federal official shall consult with and obtain the comments of any Federal agency which has jurisdiction by law or special expertise with respect to any environmental impact involved * * *

(E) study, develop, and describe appropriate alternatives to recommended courses of action in any proposal which involves unresolved conflicts concerning alternative uses of available resources;

(F) recognize the worldwide and long-range character of environmental problems and, where consistent with the foreign policy of the United States, lend appropriate support to initiatives, resolutions, and programs designed to maximize international cooperation in anticipating and preventing a decline in the quality of mankind's world environment;

(G) make available to States, counties, municipalities, institutions, and individuals, advice and information useful in restoring, maintaining, and enhancing the quality of the environment;

(H) initiate and utilize ecological information in the planning and development of resource-oriented projects; and

(I) assist the Council on Environmental Quality * * *

Note On NEPA, The EIS, And Judicial Review

NEPA is a significant piece of federal environmental legislation. It expresses an across-the-board national policy of preserving and protecting the environment. It does not prohibit agency action that may result in environmental degradation, but it requires the environmental costs of any major agency action to be disclosed to the public and to be a significant consideration in the decision-making process. Disclosure of the potential environmental impact of contemplated agency action is effectuated through the statutorily mandated environmental impact statement (EIS) described in 42 U.S.C. § 4332(2)(C). One significant aspect of an EIS is the description of alternatives to the contemplated agency action.

Of course, frequently the critical question is whether an EIS is even required for the proposed action. Although some types of agency actions always require the preparation of an EIS, many may not. Since an EIS is only required for actions that "significantly affect the human environment," NEPA has no application to them. As to others, the agency will prepare a brief preliminary assessment, called an environmental assessment (EA), examining the impacts of, and alternatives to, the proposed action to determine whether a NEPA EIS is required. If, based on the EA, the agency finds no significant impact, a FONSI (finding of no significant impact) is prepared, no EIS is prepared. On the other hand, if in the EA the agency determines there will or may be such an impact, then an EIS is prepared.

NEPA has generated a great deal of environmental litigation as opponents of a particular contemplated agency action seek to prevent agency from going forward with its plans. When a court reviews an administrative agency's compliance with NEPA requirements, the standard of review may pose an insurmountable barrier to the opponents.

NEPA's mandate is procedural, not substantive in nature. Therefore, the Administrative Procedure Act, 5 U.S.C. § 706(2)(A), applies when a court reviews an agency's compliance with NEPA Under that act, in order to set aside an agency decision the court must find that the decision was *arbitrary and capricious.* Since NEPA does not elevate environmental considerations to a special position or mandate that they be given greater weight than other relevant consideration when an agency evaluates alternatives to a given proposal, it is difficult for a court to find an agency's decision arbitrary or capricious. As long as the agency articulates in its EA or EIS a rational connection between the facts found and the choice made, a court is virtually unable to tamper with the ultimate decision reached. See Strycker's Bay Neighborhood Council v. Karlen, 444 U.S. 223, 227-28 (1980) (agency does not have to elevate environmental concerns over other appropriate considerations); Baltimore Gas and Elec. Co. v. Natural Resources Defense Council, Inc., 462 U.S. 87, 97-98 (1983) (role of reviewing court is to insure the agency adequately considered and disclosed environmental impact of its actions and that its decision was not arbitrary or capricious); Robertson v. Methow Valley Citizen's Council, 490 U.S. 332, 351 (1989) ("[N]EPA merely prohibits uninformed -- rather than unwise -- agency action."); Marsh v. Oregon Natural Resources Council, 490 U.S. 360, 371 (1989) ("NEPA does not work by mandating that agencies achieve particular substantive environmental results").For a more detailed discussion of NEPA, see, S. Novick, 2 Law of Environmental Protection, Chapter 9 (Environmental Law Institute 2001).

SECTION 3. THE FEDERAL GOVERNMENT AS A REGULATOR OF STATE AND PRIVATE COASTAL ACTIVITIES

A. COASTAL DEVELOPMENT PROBLEM

Coastal Development Company has plans to develop a large tract of coastal property. Its plan envisions a large, integrated residential-commercial community consisting of marinas, single-family dwellings, condominiums, restaurants and other commercial businesses. Coastal purchased the tract of land in the late 1960s.

The property fronts on the Gulf of Mexico, and is bordered on one side by a coastal river that empties into the Gulf at one corner of Coastal's land. Mangroves are situated on the Gulf side and most of the coastal river side of the property. Numerous small ponds and wetlands dot the tract. Near the center of the property is a three-quarter of a mile long and one-half mile wide freshwater lake. At the north end of the lake there is a small, non-navigable stream which feeds the lake. At the southern end of the lake there is a canal connecting the lake with the coastal river. Fifteen feet wide, four to five feet deep and one mile in length, the canal was created in 1971 when Coastal, with state permission, dredged the natural creek that ran between the lake and the river. In its earlier, undredged, natural state, the creek was frequently used by canoeists and rafters to travel to and from the lake and coastal river, but the canoeists and rafters would have to portage at two or three locations where the water was both shallow and extremely rocky. Due to these shallow, rocky spots, other types of watercraft could not move between the river and the lake.

Among Coastal's plans are:

(1) the dredging of a tidal lagoon for a marina and the clearing of adjacent red and black mangroves to construct shoreside marina facilities and a seafood restaurant. The red mangroves generally grow below MHTL; the black mangroves generally grow above MHTL but below HTL.

(2) the construction of a finger canal development in the uplands adjacent to the freshwater lake. The main finger canal will join the lake. The upland area in which the development is to be sited contains several acres of freshwater, forested wetlands and several small freshwater ponds.

(3) the construction of a suspension bridge from the shore of the freshwater lake to a small island located 300 feet offshore. The island will be used as a recreational facility for those owning lots on the lake or in the finger canal development.

(4) the filling of a ten acre swamp consisting of some open water, cypress trees, and water vegetation.

(5) the filling of a small, one acre pond containing some open water. This pond is not hydrologically connected with any of the other bodies of water or streams on the property. It was artificially created as the result of the removal ten years ago of upland soil for use as fill in a road that was being constructed across the property. The removal of soil left a pit of an average depth of three feet that gradually filled with water running off slightly higher surrounding land.

(6) the trapping of beavers and destruction of a beaver dam blocking a small, non-navigable stream that flows into the freshwater lake. As a result of the dam, the waters of the stream have spread out in the low lying area above the dam. Within fifty feet of the original bed of the stream, there are now many obligate hydrophytes. On the other side of this vegetation, extending an additional one hundred feet are facultative hydrophytes. Presently there is little open water. Once the beavers are removed and the dams destroyed, the stream will flow in its original bed. The developer then plans to remove much of the obligate and facultative hydrophytes.

Which, if any, of the developer's proposed activities are covered by the Rivers and Harbors Act of 1899, and which, if any, are covered by the Clean Water Act Section 404?

B. RIVERS AND HARBORS ACT OF 1899

In addition to its own civil works activities, the Corps also regulates the activities of other parties in coastal areas. The Corps' power is derived from Congress, which has the power to "regulate commerce with foreign nations, and among the several states." U.S. Const. art. I, § 8, cl. 3. Although control over navigable waters is not specifically granted to the federal government by the Constitution, the United States Supreme Court held in Gibbons v. Ogden, 22 U.S. (9 Wheat.) 1 (1824), that the power to regulate commerce includes the power to regulate navigation and thus navigable waters. Through various congressional acts, Congress has granted to the Secretary of the Army the power to maintain the navigability of the waters of the United States. The Secretary of the Army in turn has delegated that responsibility to the Corps.

> Congress granted the Corps its first regulatory authority in order to preserve federal control over maintaining navigability of the Nation's waters. In 1888, the Supreme Court held that, in the absence of a federal regulatory scheme, states could authorize or prohibit dams, bridges, or other obstructions to navigation. Congress responded by enacting the Rivers and Harbors Act of 1890, requiring prior approval of the Secretary of War for all construction activities and other obstructions to navigation. * * * These provisions were continued largely unaltered * * * in the Rivers and Harbors Act of 1899, and have remained essentially unchanged since then.

T. Addison and T. Burns, The Army Corps of Engineers and Nationwide Permit 26: Wetlands Protection or Swamp Reclamation, 18 Ecology L.Q. 619, 624 (1991).

Read the following provisions of the Rivers and Harbors Act of 1899 carefully. A major issue is the extent of the Corps' jurisdiction, or, to put it differently, what constitutes "navigable waters of the United States."

(1.) Selected Provisions of the Rivers and Harbors Act of 1899

Section 9

33 U.S.C. § 401. Construction of bridges, causeways, dams or dikes generally; exemptions

It shall not be lawful to construct or commence the construction of any bridge, causeway, dam, or dike over or in any port, roadstead, haven, harbor, canal, navigable river, or other navigable water of the United States until the consent of Congress to the building of such structures shall have been obtained. * * *

Section 10

33 U.S.C. § 403. Obstruction of navigable waters generally; wharves; piers, etc.; excavations and filling in

The creation of any obstruction not affirmatively authorized by Congress, to the navigable capacity of any of the waters of the United States is prohibited; and it shall not be lawful to build or commence the building of any wharf, pier, dolphin, boom, weir, breakwater, bulkhead, jetty, or other structures in any port, roadstead, haven, harbor, canal, navigable river, or other water of the United States, outside established harbor lines, or where no harbor lines have been established, except on plans recommended by the Chief of Engineers and authorized by the Secretary of the Army; and it shall not be lawful to excavate or fill, or in any manner to alter or modify the course, location, condition, or capacity of, any port, roadstead, haven, harbor, canal, lake, harbor of refuge, or inclosure within the limits of any breakwater, or of the channel of any navigable water of the United States, unless the work has been recommended by the Chief of Engineers and authorized by the Secretary of the Army prior to beginning the same.

* * *

(2.) Geographic Scope

LESLIE SALT CO. v. FROEHLKE
United States Court of Appeals, Ninth Circuit, 1978
578 F.2D 742

SNEED, Circuit Judge:

These appeals deal with the scope of the regulatory jurisdiction of the U.S. Army Corps of Engineers ("Corps") over "navigable waters of the

United States" as that term is used, first, in the Rivers and Harbors Act of 1899, 33 U.S.C. § 401 et seq., and, second, in the Federal Water Pollution Control Act of 1972. 33 U.S.C. § 1251, et seq.

Suit was initiated on March 29, 1972, by the Sierra Club against Leslie Salt Co. ("Leslie"), seeking a declaratory judgment that Leslie's diked evaporation ponds in and around Bair Island in San Francisco Bay were built in violation of the Rivers and Harbors Act of 1899 because Leslie had failed to seek or obtain permits from the Corps. The action also sought a permanent injunction ordering removal of the dikes or, in the alternative, prohibiting further construction or maintenance of dikes at Bair Island. Leslie then sued the Corps on December 20, 1973, seeking a declaration that the regulatory jurisdiction of the Corps over tidal marshlands in San Francisco Bay under both the Rivers and Harbors Act of 1899 and the Federal Water Pollution Control Act of 1972 ("FWPCA") is delimited by the line of mean high water ("MHW"). The Sierra Club was permitted to intervene in this action.

* * *

I. Facts

Leslie owns some 35,000 acres of property along the shores of south San Francisco Bay. Appellant Mobil Oil Estates Ltd. (Bair Island Investments) is the owner of a 3,000-acre parcel in San Mateo County known as "Bair Island." * * * In its natural condition, the property was marshland subject to the ebb and flow of the tide. Commencing in 1860, the land was diked and reclaimed and has since that time been used primarily for salt production by means of solar evaporation of Bay waters introduced into Leslie's salt ponds. These dikes were completed, for the most part, in 1927, although some work continued through 1969. Because of these dikes, the land in question has not been subject to tidal action on a regular basis, although most of it is periodically inundated by Bay waters for salt production. The Bair Island property was removed from salt production in 1965; because of the continued maintenance of dikes on the island, it has become dry land.

In 1971 and 1972, the San Francisco District of the Corps published two Public Notices (No. 71-22 on June 11, 1971, and No. 71-22(a) on January 18, 1972), stating that the Corps had changed its policy and would henceforth require permits for all "new work" on unfilled marshland property within the line of "former mean higher high water," whether or not the property was presently diked off from the ebb and flow of the tides.

In these Public Notices the Corps purported simply to redefine the scope of its regulatory authority within the ambit of the Rivers and

Harbors Act of 1899, sections 9 and 10 of which prohibit filling or the construction of any "dam," "dike," "obstruction," or "other structures" within the "navigable water of the United States," without the prior authorization of the Corps of Engineers. 33 U.S.C. §§ 401, 403.

An understanding of the technical tide line terminology is critical to this case. Every 24.8 hours, both the Pacific and Atlantic coasts of the United States experience two complete tidal cycles, each including a high and a low-tide. The Gulf coast tides, known as diurnal, have but one high and one low-tide each lunar day. On the Atlantic coast, the difference between the two daily tidal cycles, known as semi-diurnal tides, is relatively slight. Accordingly, there is in most instances little difference between the two high-tides or between the two low-tides in a given day on the east coast. The two daily Pacific coast tidal cycles (known as "mixed type" tides), however, in most locations are substantially unequal in size, with one high-tide significantly higher than the other. The mean high water line is the average of both of the daily high-tides over a period of 18.6 years; the mean higher high water line is the average of only the higher of the two tides for the same period of time. Thus, on the Atlantic coast the difference between the MHW and the MHHW is relatively small, while on the Pacific coast generally it is relatively large. Sierra Club v. Leslie Salt Co., supra, 412 F. Supp. at 1098-99.

We shall first discuss Leslie's suit and then turn to that of the Sierra Club.

II. Leslie's Suit

* * *

B. Scope of Corps' Jurisdiction Under Rivers and Harbors Act.

Analysis of the Rivers and Harbors Act must begin by acknowledging that it does not define the terms "navigable water of the United States" or "waters of the United States." Pertinent regulations defining these terms have recently been adopted by the Corps. On July 25, 1975, after the San Francisco District of the Corps issued the two Public Notices dealing with the use of the MHHW line as the limit of its jurisdiction, the Corps promulgated the following definition of "navigable waters of the United States":

> The term, "navigable waters of the United States," is administratively defined to mean waters that have been used in the past, are now used, or are susceptible to use as a means to transport interstate commerce landward to their ordinary high water mark and up to the head of navigation as determined by the Chief of Engineers, and also waters that are subject to the ebb and flow of the tides

shoreward to their mean high water mark (*mean higher high water mark on the Pacific coast*). See 33 C.F.R. 209.260 (ER 1165-2-302) for a more definitive explanation of this term.

33 C.F.R. § 209.120(d)(1) (emphasis added).   Regulation 209.260, adopted September 9, 1972, provides in most pertinent part, as follows:

Shoreward limit of jurisdiction. Regulatory jurisdiction in coastal areas extends to the line on the shore reached by the plane of the mean (average) high water. *However, on the Pacific coast, the line reached by the mean of the higher high waters is used.*

33 C.F.R. § 209.260(k)(1)(ii) (emphasis added).

Prior to these amendments the Regulation did not address itself to the shoreward limit of its jurisdiction and deferentially set forth its views regarding what constitutes navigable water as merely "the views of the Department since the jurisdiction of the United States can be conclusively determined only through judicial proceedings." 33 C.F.R. § 209.260(a) (1971).

Leslie contends that the district court's ruling upholding the Corps' regulations is contrary to every reported decision defining the boundaries of tidal water bodies. Conceding that Congress may in theory have the power under the Commerce Clause to legislate with respect to land between the MHW and the MHHW line, Leslie argues that the "navigable waters of the United States" within the meaning of the Rivers and Harbors Act have consistently been judicially extended only to the MHW line. In response, the Corps and the Sierra Club argue that the extent of Rivers and Harbors Act jurisdiction on the Pacific coast is an issue of first impression for any appellate court, and has arisen in only two previous court cases.[1] They urge that the Corps' use of the MHHW line on the Pacific coast is a logical and reasonable attempt to "harmonize" its regulatory program throughout the country. Inasmuch as Leslie accurately describes the state of the authorities, the Corps and Sierra Club in effect invite us to read the Act differently than in the past to accommodate the desire of the Corps to extend its jurisdiction on the Pacific coast. We decline the invitation because we believe it is misdirected. It should be addressed to Congress rather than the Judiciary.

Turning to the authorities, the Supreme Court in 1915 held that federal regulatory jurisdiction over navigable tidal waters extends to the

---

[1] One of these is unreported, United States v. Freethy, No. 73-1470 (N.D.Cal. Feb. 24, 1975); the other makes only passing mention of the use of the MHHW line as the Corps' limit of jurisdiction, United States v. Kaiser Aetna, 408 F, Supp. 42, 50 n. 18 (D. Hawaii 1976), appeal docketed, No. 76-1968 (9th Cir. May 3, 1976).

MHW line. Willink v. United States, 240 U.S. 572, 580 (1916). While *Willink* was concerned with the boundaries of the tidal waters on the Atlantic coast, the case is significant because it deals directly with the relationship between the federal navigational servitude and the Corps' regulation of "navigable waters of the United States." The servitude, which reaches to the limits of "navigable water," permits the removal of an obstruction to navigable capacity without compensation. See 33 U.S.C. § 403. Accordingly, an expansion of "navigable water" shoreward diminishes the protection of the Fifth Amendment. We think an interpretation of the Act which accomplishes this, first advanced seventy-two years after its enactment, should be viewed with skepticism to say the least.

* * *

Consistent with *Willink* * * * is the leading case defining the extent of tidal water bodies on the Pacific coast. Borax Consolidated, Ltd. v. City of Los Angeles, 296 U.S. 10 (1935) originated in a property dispute brought by Los Angeles to quiet title to land on an island in Los Angeles harbor. At issue was the proper boundary between tidelands as to which the State possessed original title upon admittance to the Union, and uplands, which became public lands of the United States at the time of their acquisition from Mexico. * * *

The Supreme Court, affirming a decision of this court, held that the tideland extends to the MHW mark as technically defined by the United States Coast and Geodetic Survey: that is, "the average height of all the high waters" at a given place over a period of 18.6 years. Id. at 26-27 (emphasis added).

* * *

The district court below distinguishes *Borax* on the grounds that the Supreme Court was dealing with an issue of *title* and "made no reference to the federal navigational servitude under the Rivers and Harbors Act or to the distinction of MHHW and MHW." Sierra Club v. Leslie Salt Co., supra, 412 F. Supp. at 1101. However, *Borax* cannot be brushed aside so easily. The considerations involved in the regulation of navigable waters under the commerce power are intimately connected to the question of title to tidelands. The term "navigable waters" has been judicially defined to cover: (1) nontidal waters which were navigable in the past or which could be made navigable in fact by "reasonable improvements." United States v. Appalachian Electric Power Co., 311 U.S. 377 (1940); * * * and (2) waters within the ebb and flow of the tide. The Propeller Genesee Chief v. Fitzhugh, 53 U.S. (12 How.) 443 (1851); * * * Tideland, by definition, is the soil underlying tidal waters. To fix the shoreward boundary of tideland there must be fixed the shoreward limit of tidal water which, in turn, should fix the shoreward limit of "navigable waters" in the absence of a contrary intent on the part of Congress. To fix the limit of "navigable water," for the purposes of the Rivers and Harbors Act, further shoreward than *Borax* fixed the limit of "tidal water" assumes the existence of an intent of Congress at the time of the Act's enactment of which we have no evidence.

* * *

This long-standing recognition that, for the purpose of fixing a shoreward limit, the terms tide water and navigable water are interchangeable strongly suggests that in *Borax* the Supreme Court, in the course of settling a title dispute, also fixed the shoreward boundary of navigable water on the Pacific coast. This is buttressed by the fact that since *Borax* and *Willink*, the MHW line has been routinely cited as the boundary of federal regulatory jurisdiction over tidal waters by every court to consider the question, with the two recent exceptions upon which the Corps and Sierra Club rely. United States v. Stoeco Homes, Inc., supra, 498 F.2d 597 (3d Cir. 1974), cert. denied, 420 U.S. 927 (1975); United States v. Holland, 373 F. Supp. 665 (M.D. Fla. 1974); United States v. Cannon, 363 F. Supp. 1045 (D. Del. 1973); United States v. Pot-Nets, 363 F. Supp. 812 (D. Del. 1973); United States v. Lewis, 355 F. Supp. 1132 (S.D. Ga. 1973). * * * Although these cases all arose on the Atlantic or Gulf coasts, each implicitly accepts *Borax*, a Pacific coast case, as enunciating a rule applicable to all coasts of the United States. Taken together, they indicate the extent to which the MHW line has been consistently accepted as the boundary of "navigable waters of the United States." * * *

Moreover, we have already indicated that more is involved than simply an expansion of the Corps' regulatory authority. As stated by the Supreme Court in United States v. Virginia Electric Co., 365 U.S. 624 (1961):

> This navigational servitude sometimes referred to as a "dominant servitude," * * * or a "superior navigation easement," * * * -- is the privilege to appropriate without compensation *which attaches to the exercise of the "power of the government to control and regulate navigable waters in the interest of commerce."* United States v. Commodore Park, 324 U.S. 386, 390.

United States v. Virginia Electric, 365 U.S. at 627-28 (emphasis added). The navigational servitude reaches to the shoreward limit of navigable waters. To extend the servitude on the basis of a recently formulated administrative policy is to impose an additional burden of unknown magnitude on all private property that abuts on the Pacific coast.

We wish to point out, however, that our interpretation of the Rivers and Harbors Act is not governed by a belief that the Act represents the full exertion by Congress of its authority under the Commerce Clause. * * *

We hold that in tidal areas, "navigable waters of the United States," as used in the Rivers and Harbors Act, extend to all places covered by the ebb and flow of the tide to the mean high water (MHW) mark in its unobstructed, natural state. Accordingly, we reverse the district court's decision insofar as it found that the Corps' jurisdiction under the Rivers and Harbors Act includes all areas within the former line of MHHW in its unobstructed, natural state.

Our holding that the MHW line is to be fixed in accordance with its natural, unobstructed state is dictated by the principle recognized in *Willink*, supra, that one who develops areas below the MHW line does so at his peril. * * *

[The court's discussion of the scope of the Corps' regulatory authority under the CWA, Section 404, appears in the next section of materials.]

Notes and Questions

1. In *Leslie Salt*, the area in question was no longer subject to inundation by tidal waters; nonetheless, the court upheld the Corps' jurisdiction over areas below the MHW line "fixed in accordance with its natural, unobstructed state." Leslie Salt Co. v. Froehlke, 578 F.2d 742, 753 (9th Cir. 1978). The San Francisco District of the Army Corps of Engineers determines the location of the MHW line in its natural state by using U.S. Geological Survey maps from the 1850s to 1890s. W. Want, Law of Wetlands Regulation § 4.07[3].

2. How workable is the MHW (or mean high-tide) line as the upland limit of the Corps' jurisdiction under the Rivers and Harbor Act? Recall the boundary determination discussion in Chapter One, supra. Does that limit mean the Corps lacks the authority to enjoin activities taking place above the mean high-tide line? See Problem One in the next subsection.

3. The phrase "navigable waters of the United States" as used in the Rivers and Harbors Act of 1899 means what it meant at the time the Act was passed by Congress. The Corps' attempts to give it a more expansive reading to include any body of water that is a segment of a commercial highway consisting of water, rail, and road connections, were rebuffed by the courts. See, e.g., Minnehaha Creek Watershed Dist. v. Hoffman, 597 F.2d 617 (8th Cir. 1979); Hardy Salt Co. v. Southern Pac. Transp., 501 F.2d 1156 (10th Cir. 1974).

Since the Rivers and Harbors Act of 1899 was an exercise by

Congress of its power under the Commerce Clause, * * * the extent of federal regulatory jurisdiction under the Act is to be determined in accordance with the basic test set forth in *The Daniel Ball*. The Rivers and Harbors Act of 1899 was a recompilation of two earlier acts, the Rivers and Harbors Act of 1890 and the Rivers and Harbors Act of 1894. Legislative history of the Rivers and Harbors Act of 1899 indicates that it was understood by its drafters to be merely a restatement of existing law. See United States v. Pennsylvania Chem. Corp., 411 U.S. 655, 666 (1973). The extent of federal regulatory power under § 10 of the Act, under which the Corps claims jurisdiction * * * is limited to "navigable * * * waters of the United States." Since this is the precise phrase which was defined by the Supreme Court in *The Daniel Ball*, and which was used in that case and others to describe the reach of the federal commerce power over navigable waters prior to the enactment of the first Rivers and Harbors Act in 1890, we must assume that Congress intended the phrase to have the meaning which it had acquired in contemporary judicial interpretation. Indeed, virtually all courts which have interpreted the various provisions of the Rivers and Harbors Act of 1899 have begun with the basic definition of "navigable waters of the United States" set forth in *The Daniel Ball*.

Minnehaha Creek Watershed Dist. v. Hoffman, 597 F.2d 617, 622 (8th Cir. 1979). The relevant language of The Daniel Ball v. United States, 77 U.S. (10 Wall.) 557 (1871), is in the note following Phillips Petroleum Co. v. Mississippi in Chapter One.

4. If a body of water is subject to regulation under the Rivers and Harbors Act, must the public be allowed access to that body of water? The Hawaii Kai Marina was developed by dredging and filling Kuapa Pond, a shallow lagoon separated from the Pacific Ocean by a barrier beach. In early Hawaiian history, this body of water was used as a fish pond. Openings were made in the barrier beach, sluice gates added, and when water entered the pond during high-tide, mullet and other fish would enter the pond; the gates were then closed, and the fish were trapped in the pond. Under Hawaiian law, such fishponds are private property.

In 1961, Kaiser Aetna acquired rights to the fishpond and surrounding land. As part of its development of the area, it dredged and filled parts of the pond, removed the sluice gates, and increased the depth of the access channels to the ocean waters. At that time, it was told by the Corps that a Rivers and Harbors Act permit was not needed for its development activities in the pond. In 1972, Kaiser Aetna planned additional development activities in the pond and, at that time, was told by the Corps that a permit would be required. The Corps also claimed that, as a result of the earlier improvements, the waters had become "navigable waters of the United States" and that Kaiser Aetna could not deny the public access to the pond.

The United States Supreme Court held that, without compensation required by the Fifth Amendment "takings" clause, the federal government could not compel Kaiser Aetna to open the pond to the public. Although development activities in the waters of the pond might be subject to Rivers and Harbors Act permit requirements, it did not follow that the private waters of the pond became public waters merely because the developer connected them to navigable waters of the United States. Kaiser-Aetna v. United States, 444 U.S. 164 (1979).

Would the result of the case have been different if the Corps had required, as a condition for permission to connect the pond to the bay, that the owners of Kaupa Pond grant public access to the pond? See Nollan v. California Coastal Commission, infra, Chapter Three.

U.S. ARMY CORPS OF ENGINEERS REGULATIONS

Part 329 -- Definition of Navigable Waters of the United States

33 C.F.R. § 329.4. General definition.

Navigable waters of the United States are those waters that are subject to the ebb and flow of the tide and/or are presently used, or have been used in the past, or may be susceptible for use to transport interstate or foreign commerce. A determination of navigability, once made, applies laterally over the entire surface of the waterbody, and is not extinguished by later actions or events which impede or destroy navigable capacity. * * *

33 C.F.R. § 329.8. Improved or natural conditions of the waterbody.

Determinations are not limited to the natural or original condition of the waterbody. Navigability may also be found where artificial aids have been or may be used to make the waterbody suitable for use in navigation.

(a)   Existing improvements: artificial water bodies.

(1) An artificial channel may often constitute a navigable water of the United States, even though it has been privately developed and maintained, or passes through private property. The test is generally as developed above, that is, whether the waterbody is capable of use to transport interstate commerce. * * * A canal or other artificial waterbody that is subject to ebb and flow of the tide is also a navigable water of the United States. * * *

(3) Private ownership of the lands underlying the waterbody, or

of the lands through which it runs, does not preclude a finding of navigability.* * *

33 C.F.R. § 329.12. Geographic and jurisdictional limits of oceanic and tidal waters.

(a) Ocean and coastal waters. The navigable waters of the United States over which Corps of Engineers regulatory jurisdiction extends include all ocean and coastal waters * * *

(1) Baseline defined. * * *

> (2) Shoreward limit of jurisdiction. Regulatory jurisdiction in coastal areas extends to the line on the shore reached by the plane of the mean (average) high water. Where precise determination of the actual location of the line becomes necessary, it must be established by survey with reference to the available tidal datum, preferably averaged over a period of 18.6 years. Less precise methods, such as observation of the "apparent shoreline" which is determined by reference to physical markings, lines of vegetation, or changes in type of vegetation, may be used only where an estimate is needed of the line reached by the mean high water.

(b) Bays and estuaries. Regulatory jurisdiction extends to the entire surface and bed of all water bodies subject to tidal action. Jurisdiction thus extends to the edge (as determined by paragraph (a)(2) of this section) of all such waterbodies, even though portions of the waterbody may be extremely shallow, or obstructed by shoals, vegetation, or other barriers. Marshlands and similar areas are thus considered "navigable in law," but only so far as the area is subject to inundation by the mean high waters. The relevant test is therefore the presence of the mean high tidal waters, and not the general test described above, which generally applies to inland rivers and lakes.

33 C.F.R. § 329.13. Geographic limits: Shifting boundaries.

Permanent changes of the shoreline configuration result in similar alterations of the boundaries of the navigable waters of the United States. Thus, gradual changes which are due to natural causes and are perceptible only over some period of time constitute changes in the bed of a waterbody which also change the shoreline boundaries of the navigable waters of the United States. However, an area will remain "navigable in law," even though no longer covered with water, whenever the change has occurred suddenly, or was caused by artificial forces intended to produce that change. For example, shifting sand bars within a river or estuary remain part of the navigable water of the United States, regardless that they may be dry at a particular point in time.

(3.) Regulated Activities

UNITED STATES v. MEMBERS OF THE ESTATE OF BOOTHBY
United States Court of Appeals, First Circuit 1994
16 F.3d 19

[The United States sued to enforce the denial of permits and an eviction order issued to four houseboat owners under section 10 of the Rivers and Harbors Act. The houseboats were located in La Parguera, a beautiful and ecologically important bay in Puerto Rico. Earlier, in 1978, the Corps and Puerto Rico entered into an agreement that brought to a halt the construction of stilt houses along the shore; but, after the moratorium on stilt houses took effect, numerous houseboats appeared on the bay. Although the houseboats were certified as "navigable" by the Coast Guard and used for occasional trips about the bay, the Army Corps of Engineers determined that the houseboats were "permanently moored structures" within the meaning of 33 C.F.R. § 322.2(b) (1993) and thus subject to the permitting requirements of the Act. After the houseboat owners requested the issuance of permits, the Corps refused to issue them. The district court upheld the Corps' action and the houseboats owners appealed] * * *

Appellants berate the district court for considering motive, intent, and environmental factors, rather than limiting the inquiry strictly to capacity to navigate. But navigability is only one element in the statutory assessment. Since neither the statute nor the regulations place restrictions on the Corps' discretion to issue permits * * *, the agency was fully entitled to take into account other pertinent factors.

We are confident that, under this standard, motive and consequence qualify.* * * [The district] court spotted a pattern of deceit: the houseboats were put in place to circumvent the ban on stilt houses; they were primarily intended to serve as vacation homes, pure and simple; the gadgets attached to them over time were meant to camouflage the scheme rather than for seafaring per se; and the occasional jaunts about the bay represented perfunctory attempts to satisfy the terms of the statute.* * *

Nor can the agency attention to the impact of the houseboats on the ecosystem of La Parguera be faulted. Agency officials understood what appellants evidently do not: that the Rivers and Harbors act has been transformed into an instrument of environmental policy.* * *

In any event, the finding that the houseboats constitute "structures" is not necessary to the ultimate determination that the houseboats constitute "obstructions." Section 10's permitting requirements may be triggered by something other than those items enumerated in the second clause of the section, if that "something" plausibly can be deemed an obstruction to navigation. * * *

Affirmed. Costs to appellee

Notes and Questions

1. Ecological factors were first recognized as legitimate considerations in the Corps' enforcement of the Rivers and Harbors Act in 1970. In the landmark case, Zabel v. Tabb, 430 F.2d 199, 211-14 (5th Cir. 1970), cert. denied, 401 U.S. 910 (1971), the court held that the Corps' authority under Section 10 was supplemented by NEPA's mandate that ecological considerations be taken into account in agency permitting actions.

2. There is no implied private right of action for those allegedly injured by a violation of Section 10 of the Rivers and Harbors Act of 1899. California v. Sierra, 451 U.S. 287 (1981). Furthermore, in United States v. Sexton Cove Estates, Inc., 526 F.2d 1293 (5th Cir. 1976) and United States v. Joseph G. Moretti, Inc., 526 F.2d 1306, 1310-11 (5th Cir. 1976), the Fifth Circuit held that a corporate officer could not be held personally liable for the costs of any restoration necessitated by a corporate violation of the Rivers and Harbors Act of 1899. Under what circumstances should an officer of a corporation be held personally liable for activities of the corporation? Does a rule of non-liability provide developers with a means of avoiding the costs of destructive environmental activity?

C. SECTION 404 OF THE CLEAN WATER ACT

Although the Corps has considerable jurisdiction under the Rivers and Harbors Act of 1899, that jurisdiction essentially is limited to activities occurring below the mean high water line on navigable bodies of water. This geographic limitation leaves significant water areas outside the scope of the Act. As concern for the preservation of other water bodies and land/water interfaces or wetlands increased, new legislation was proposed to expand the Corps' authority. In 1972, amendments to the Federal Water Pollution Control Act (FWPCA)[2] were passed. One provision in those amendments, Section 404 (33 U.S.C. § 1344), gives the Corps the power to regulate the discharge of dredge and fill material into navigable waters. Section 404 **does not** supersede the Corps authority under the Rivers and Harbors Act of 1899, and the permit process of the two acts is virtually identical. In Section

---

[2] The Act was originally called The Federal Water Pollution Control Act. See S. Rep. No. 1236, 92nd Cong., 2nd Sess. 99 (1972). In 1977 Congress approved the shortened title of "Clean Water Act." H.Rep. No. 830, 95th Cong., 1st Sess. 1 (1977). Thus, the references "FWPCA" and "CWA" refer to the same basic legislation. Generally, "CWA" will be used as the shorthand reference in these materials.

404, the phrase "navigable waters" is used; but, in the definitional section of the FWPCA, "navigable waters" are defined as "waters of the United States." 33 U.S.C. § 1362(7).

A major and continuing issue in the implementation of Section 404 is what is the meaning of "waters of the United States," and how does it differ from the meaning of "navigable waters of the United States" as used in the Rivers and Harbors Act of 1899 and elsewhere.[3]

Section 404 has one other feature that should be noted at this point to help you in the reading of the statutory provisions that follow. Section 404 creates an interesting, but perhaps inherently unstable, relationship between two governmental entities -- the EPA and the Corps. Except in areas to which Section 404 is applicable, the EPA is the governmental agency designated to administer the Act. With reference to activities covered by Section 404, the EPA and the Corps share the administrative responsibilities. Thus, the reference in Section 404 (33 U.S.C. § 1344) to the "Administrator" is a reference to the Administrator of the EPA.

This interagency relationship is the subject of later material in this chapter; at this point, however, it will suffice to point out that the EPA, not the Corps, has the ultimate administrative authority to construe the phrase "waters of the United States" and thus determine the ultimate reach of Section 404. 43 Op. Att'y. Gen. 15 (Sept. 5, 1979). See also Memorandum Of Agreement Between The Department Of Army And The Environmental Protection Agency Concerning Federal Enforcement For The Section 404 Program Of The Clean Water Act (1989).

(1.) Selected Provisions of the Clean Water Act

[Section 301]

33 U.S.C. § 1311. Effluent limitations.
(a) Illegality of pollutant discharges except in compliance with law

---

[3] An examination of the legislative history would appear helpful. It seems to suggest that the departure from the traditional definition was intentional. The Conference Report of the Senate-House stated that:

> The conferees fully intend that the term "navigable waters" be given the broadest possible constitutional interpretation unencumbered by agency determinations that have been made or may be made for administrative purposes.

1 Legislative History of the FWPCA of 1972, at 327 (1973). However, the United States Supreme Court in the SWANCC case, which appears later in this chapter, stated that there was noting in the legislative history, including this statement, to signify that Congress intended to exert any more than its commerce power over navigation. Solid Waste Agency of Northern Cook County v. Army Corps of Engineers___U.S.___(2001).

Except as in compliance with this section and [section] * * * 1344 of this title, the discharge of any pollutant by any person shall be unlawful.* * *

* * *

[Section 404]

33 U.S.C. § 1344. Permits for dredged or fill material

(a) Discharge into navigable waters at specified disposal sites

The Secretary may issue permits, after notice and opportunity for public hearings for the discharge of dredged or fill material into the navigable waters at specified disposal sites. * * *

(b) Specification for disposal sites

Subject to subsection (c) of this section, each such disposal site shall be specified for each such permit by the Secretary (1) through the application of guidelines developed by the Administrator, in conjunction with the Secretary, which guidelines shall be based upon criteria comparable to the criteria applicable to the territorial seas* * * and the ocean under section 1343(c) of this title, and (2) in any case where such guidelines under clause (1) alone would prohibit the specification of a site, through the application additionally of the economic impact of the site on navigation and anchorage.

(c) Denial or restriction of use of defined areas as disposal sites

The Administrator is authorized to prohibit the specification (including the withdrawal of specification) of any defined area as a disposal site, and he is authorized to deny or restrict the use of any defined area for specification (including the withdrawal of specification) as a disposal site, whenever he determines, after notice and opportunity for public hearings, that the discharge of such materials into such area will have an unacceptable adverse effect on municipal water supplies, shellfish beds and fishery areas (including spawning and breeding areas), wildlife, or recreational areas. Before making such determination, the Administrator shall consult with the Secretary. The Administrator shall set forth in writing and make public his findings and his reasons for making any determination under this subsection.

(d) "Secretary" defined

The term "Secretary" as used in this section means the Secretary of the Army, acting through the Chief of Engineers.

(e) General permits on State, regional, or nationwide basis

(1) In carrying out his functions relating to the discharge of dredged or fill material under this section, the Secretary may, after notice and opportunity for public hearings, issue general permits on a State, regional, or nationwide basis for any category of activities involving discharges of dredged or fill material if the Secretary determines that the activities in such category are similar in nature, will cause only minimal adverse environmental effects when performed separately, and will have only minimal cumulative adverse effect on the environment. Any general permit issued under this subsection shall (A) be based on the guidelines described in subsection (b)(1) of this section, and (B) set forth the requirements and standards which shall apply to any activity authorized by such general permit.

(2) No general permit issued under this subsection shall be for a period of more than five years after the date of its issuance and such general permit may be revoked or modified by the Secretary if, after opportunity for public hearing, the Secretary determines that the activities authorized by such general permit have an adverse impact on the environment or such activities are more appropriately authorized by individual permits.

(f) Non-prohibited discharge of dredged or fill material.

(1) Except as provided in paragraph (2) of this subsection, the discharge of dredged or fill material --

(A) from normal farming, silviculture, and ranching activities such as plowing, seeding, cultivating, minor drainage, harvesting for the production of food, fiber, and forest products, or upland soil and water conservation practices;

(B) for the purpose of maintenance, including emergency reconstruction of recently damaged parts, of currently serviceable structures such as dikes, dams, levees, groins, riprap, breakwaters, causeways, and bridge abutments or approaches, and transportation structures;

* * *

is not prohibited by or otherwise subject to regulation under this section or section 1311(a) or 1342 of this title (except for effluent standards or prohibitions under section 1317 of this title).

(2) Any discharge of dredged or fill material into the navigable waters incidental to any activity having as its purpose bringing an area

of the navigable waters into a use to which it was not previously subject, where the flow or circulation of navigable waters may be impaired or the reach of such waters be reduced, shall be required to have a permit under this section.

[Section 502]

33 U.S.C. § 1362. Definitions

Except as otherwise specifically provided, when used in this chapter: * * *

(5) The term "person" means an individual, corporation, partnership, association, State, municipality, commission, or political subdivision of a State, or any interstate body.

(6) The term "pollutant" means dredged spoil, solid waste, * * * biological materials, * * *rock, sand * * * discharged into water. * * *

(7) The term "navigable waters" means the waters of the United States, including the territorial seas.

(8) The term "territorial seas" means the belt of seas measured from the line of ordinary low water along that portion of the coast which is in direct contact with the open sea and the line marking the seaward limit of inland waters, and extending seaward a distance of three miles.

(9) The term "contiguous zone" means the entire zone established or to be established by the United States under article 24 of the Convention of the Territorial Sea and the Contiguous Zone.

(10) The term "ocean" means any portion of the high seas beyond the contiguous zone. * * *

(12) The term "discharge of a pollutant" and the term "discharge of pollutants" each means (A) any addition of any pollutant to navigable waters from any point source, (B) any addition of any pollutant to the waters of the contiguous zone or the ocean from any point source other than a vessel or other floating craft. * * *

(14) The term "point source" means any discernible, confined and discrete conveyance, including but not limited to any pipe, ditch, channel, tunnel, conduit, well, discrete fissure, container, * * * or vessel or other floating craft, from which pollutants are or may be discharged. * * *

(16) The term "discharge" when used without qualification includes a discharge of a pollutant, and a discharge of pollutants.

* * *

(19) The term "pollution" means the man-made or man-induced alteration of the chemical, physical, biological, and radiological integrity of water.

(2.) The Geographic Scope of Section 404

(a.) Tidelands

LESLIE SALT CO. v. FROEHLKE
United States Court of Appeals, Ninth Circuit, 1978
578 F.2d 742

SNEED, CIRCUIT JUDGE:

[The facts of this case appear above in the Rivers and Harbors Act section of this chapter] * * *

C. Scope of Corps' Jurisdiction Under FWPCA

The scope of regulatory authority under the FWPCA presents a substantially different issue. The district court's holding that the Corps' regulatory jurisdiction under the FWPCA is "coterminous" with that under the Rivers and Harbors Act, extending to "the former line of MHHW of the bay in its unobstructed, natural state," is faulty. Sierra Club v. Leslie Salt, supra, 412 F. Supp. at 1102-03. In its opening brief in this appeal, Leslie properly concedes that:

> * * * the Corps' jurisdiction under Section 404 of the FWPCA is broader than its jurisdiction under the Rivers and Harbors Act in that it encompasses existing marshlands located above as well as below the lines of mean high water and mean higher high water which are currently subject to tidal inundation.

Brief for Appellant Leslie Salt Co. at 60.[4] * * *

---

[4] Leslie's concession is well taken, since the case law clearly supports an expansive reading of the term "navigable waters" as used in the FWPCA, 33 U.S.C. § 1251, et seq. In United States v. Holland, 373 F. Supp. 665 (M.D. Fla. 1974), the district court, in an excellent analysis, held that the discharge of "sand, dirt and dredged soil on land which, although above the mean high water line, was periodically inundated with the waters of Papy's Bayou" was within the reach of the FWPCA, since Congress intended to control the discharge of pollutants into waters at the source of the discharge, regardless of its location vis-a-vis the MHW or MHHW lines. The court stated that:

Where the parties differ is on the question of whether the Corps' jurisdiction covers waters which are no longer subject to tidal inundation because of man-made obstructions such as Leslie's dikes. These are the waters which the district court apparently wanted to include under the aegis of the FWPCA through the use of the historic MHHW line "in its unobstructed, natural state."

* * * [T]he court below actually placed undue limits on the FWPCA when it stated that "the geographical extent of the Corps' jurisdiction under the Rivers and Harbors Act is coterminous with that under FWPCA." Sierra Club v. Leslie Salt Co., supra, 412 F. Supp. at 1102. It is clear from the legislative history of the FWPCA that for the purposes of that Act, Congress intended to expand the narrow definition of the term "navigable waters," as used in the Rivers and Harbors Act. This court has indicated that the term "navigable waters" within the meaning of the FWPCA is to be given the broadest possible constitutional interpretation under the Commerce Clause. * * *

The water in Leslie's salt ponds, even though not subject to tidal action, comes from the San Francisco Bay to the extent of eight to nine billion gallons a year. We see no reason to suggest that the United States may protect these waters from pollution while they are outside of Leslie's tide gates, but may no longer do so once they have passed through these gates into Leslie's ponds. Moreover, there can be no question that activities within Leslie's salt ponds affect interstate commerce, since Leslie is a major supplier of salt for industrial, agricultural, and domestic use in the western United States. Much of the salt which Leslie harvests from the Bay's waters at the rate of about one million tons annually enters interstate and foreign commerce.

Our suggestion that the full extent of the Corps' FWPCA jurisdiction over the "waters of the United States" is in some instances not limited to

* * *

the mean high water line is no limit to federal authority under the FWPCA. While the line remains a valid demarcation for other purposes, it has no rational connection to the aquatic ecosystems which the FWPCA is intended to protect. Congress has wisely determined that federal authority over water pollution properly rests on the Commerce Clause and not on past interpretations of an act designed to protect navigation. And the Commerce Clause gives Congress ample authority to reach activities above the mean high water line that pollute the waters of the United States.

The defendants' filling activities on land periodically inundated by tidal waters constituted discharges entering "waters of the United States" and, since done without a permit, were thus in violation of 33 U.S.C. § 1311(a).

Holland, supra, 373 F. Supp. at 676.

The legislative history of the FWPCA reviewed by the Holland court amply supports its conclusion.

the MHW or the MHHW line is reinforced by regulations published by the Corps on July 19, 1977 and found at 33 C.F.R. § 323.2, as published at 42 Fed. Reg. 37144-37145.

Without determining the exact limits of the scope of federal regulatory jurisdiction under the FWPCA, we find that the regulations at 33 C.F.R. § 323.2 are reasonable, consistent with the intent of Congress, and not contrary to the Constitution. We therefore hold that the Corps' jurisdiction under the FWPCA extends at least to waters which are no longer subject to tidal inundation because of Leslie's dikes without regard to the location of historic tidal water lines in their unobstructed, natural state. We express no opinion on the outer limits to which the Corps' jurisdiction under the FWPCA might extend.

Our holdings with respect to the Rivers and Harbors Act of 1899 and the FWPCA dispose of the declaratory judgment sought by Leslie in its case.* * *

The decision of the district court with respect to the Rivers and Harbors Act of 1899 is reversed. The decision of the district court with respect to the FWPCA is reversed in part and modified in part. The action of the Sierra Club against Leslie Salt is remanded for further proceedings not inconsistent with this opinion.

Reversed in part, Modified in part, and Remanded in part.

Notes and Questions

1. How would you summarize the relationship between FWPCA Section 404 and Section 10 of the Rivers and Harbors Act? Consider the following:

> Acknowledging the "established role" of the U.S. Army Corps of Engineers in the dredging and maintenance of navigable channels and ports, Section 404 of the 1972 Amendments ordains a separate permit program for the discharge of dredged or fill material.* * * [T]here is no difficulty reconciling the key features of the Rivers and Harbors Act with Section 404: * * * The Section 10 permit program, addressing obstructions to navigation and channel alterations, differs from Section 404 in coverage but is administered under exactly the same procedures, even to the extent of using the same forms. The principal difference is that Section 404 reaches wetlands not traditionally considered navigable waters while Section 10 is thought to require some impairment of navigable capacity without regard to whether there has been a discharge.

W. Rodgers, Environmental Law 318-19 (2d Ed. 1994). After reading the *SWANCC* decision, which appears later in this chapter, ask yourself is this formulation of the difference between the Rivers and Harbors Act, Section 10, and the CWA, Section 404 still accurate?

2.   Is *Leslie Salt* consistent with *Phillips Petroleum Company*, supra?

(b.) Coastal Wetlands

Approximately 30% of all wetlands in the lower 48 states are coastal wetlands. These coastal wetlands cover an estimated 27 million acres and include a wide variety of freshwater and salt water types. Most coastal wetlands located in the continental United States are found in the southeast, roughly 81% . Of these, 51% are in the Gulf of Mexico states and remaining 30% in the South Atlantic states. The entire Pacific coast (excluding Alaska) contains   less than 2% of these coastal wetlands. The ten states with the most coastal wetlands, in descending order, are : Florida, Louisiana, South Carolina, Texas, North Carolina, Georgia, Alabama, New Jersey, California, and Maine.

Coastal wetlands constitute an important, integral component of the ecology of coastal regions. The most immediate, and most apparent, are the estuarine salt marshes readily visible along much of the Eastern and Gulf coastlines. In addition to their water filtration and purification functions, these wetlands serve as critical habitat for important fisheries, waterfowl populations, and coastal animals.   For example, these wetlands are important producers of shellfish and 2/3 of the major U.S. commercial fisheries depend upon estuaries and their associated wetlands as spawning grounds or nurseries. Many Eastern and Gulf marshes are characterized by saltwater cordgrass (*Spartina alterniflora*), while a related species (*Spartina foliosa*) is found in the less common tidal marshes on the West Coast. Along the southern coast of Florida, saltwater cordgrass is replaced by mangrove swamps.

Adjacent to the marshes flooded by the daily ebb and flow of the tide are the high marsh areas, flooded only by high-tides or spring tides. These areas are characterized by a dark green grasslike rush, called black grass (*Juncus gerardi*) on the Northeast coast, salt meadow cordgrass (*Spartina patens*) on the Mid-Atlantic and Southeastern coasts, black needle rush (*Juncus roemerianus*) on the lower Southern coast, and cactus-like pickerelweed, saltwort and other high marsh species on the West Coast.

Further inland lie a variety of freshwater marshes, ranging from the vast Florida Everglades and extensive Louisiana marsh systems to smaller pocosins. Because many of these wetlands are transitional belts that link the dry uplands with coastal rivers, estuaries, and other waters, during many parts of the year the surface of many of these wetlands will be dry. Their identity as transitional wetlands may be determinable only by the presence of water tolerant vegetation and soils that have the ability to absorb significant quantities of water.

Considerable scientific evidence establishes that these inland coastal marshes are an extremely important link in the maintenance of the level of coastal water quality necessary to provide the habitat critical to healthy fish, waterfowl, and coastal animal populations. Even the small pocosins, which are freshwater swamps found within the southeast coastal plain, play an important role in stabilizing water quality in the coastal estuaries and in balancing the salinity of estuarine waters. At the same time, these marshes are usually privately owned, desirable for either agricultural use or other types of development, and thus in the greatest jeopardy. And it is these wetland areas that present important policy and legal issues: What are the limits of the EPA's and the Corps' Section 404 authority? In order for an area to be wetlands, what at a minimum must be present at the site? What types of activities within wetland areas are subject to regulation by the Corps? Under what circumstances should the Corps issue a permit authorizing the modification or destruction of a privately owned wetland? What are the consequences of a failure to acquire or abide by a necessary Section 404 permit?

A COASTAL WETLANDS PROBLEM

Striped Bass Aquaculture Corporation has purchased 300 acres of river bottom land adjacent to the Broad River. The Broad River is a coastal navigable river subject to some tidal fluctuation.

For over sixty years the land purchased by Striped Bass has been used for rice growing. Striped Bass plans to use the area for a hybrid striped bass farm and is seeking your advice on questions relating to the application of Section 404 of the CWA to their land and plans.

Prior to 1930, portions of the tract were heavily wooded, with the remainder farmed for various crops. During times of high and flood waters, the river would spill over its banks and cover a large portion of the tract, often with devastating results to the crops. In the 1930s, the then owner of the land decided that the land was most suitable for growing rice. A series of levees and dikes were constructed to divide the tract into different rice fields. The various fields captured runoff water from the uplands and were also flooded with water pumped from the ground and the river. Occasionally, river flood waters would spill over the levees into the rice fields.

In 2001, Striped Bass purchased the tract with plans to develop a fish farm. In order to make the tract suitable for a fish farm, Striped Bass must build additional levees to reduce the size of the individual rice fields and deepen somewhat the water level of the various fields. The total area covered by the new levees will be nine acres. Once the area is suitable for fish farming, Striped Bass will stock the fish ponds (the former rice fields) with hybrid striped bass, feed the fish and, when the fish reach sufficient size, harvest the fish using long nets. Occasionally, the ponds will have to be drained and the bottom cleaned.

According to Striped Bass, the Corps claims that Striped Bass needs a Section 404 permit to make the changes it wishes. Striped Bass would like to know:

1. Is this area subject to regulation by the Army Corps of Engineers under the Section 404 program?

2. Are any of Striped Bass' planned activities exempt or allowed to take place without a permit?

1986 ARMY CORPS OF ENGINEERS REGULATIONS

PART 328 -- Definition of Waters of the United States

33 C.F.R. § 328.1. Purpose.

This section defines the term "waters of the United States" as it applies to the jurisdictional limits of the authority of the Corps of Engineers under the Clean Water Act.

33 C.F.R. § 328.2. General scope.

Waters of the United States include those waters listed in § 328.3(a). The lateral limits of jurisdiction in those waters may be divided into three categories. The categories include the territorial seas, tidal waters, and non-tidal waters (see 33 C.F.R. § 328.4 (a), (b), and (c), respectively).

33 C.F.R. § 328.3. Definitions.

For the purpose of this regulation these terms are defined as follows:

(a) The term "waters of the United States" means

(1) All waters which are currently used, or were used in the past, or may be susceptible to use in interstate or foreign commerce, including all waters which are subject to the ebb and flow of the tide;
(2) All interstate waters including interstate wetlands;
(3) All other waters such as intrastate lakes, rivers, streams (including intermittent streams), mudflats, sandflats, wetlands, sloughs, prairie potholes, wet meadows, playa lakes, or natural

ponds, the use, degradation or destruction of which could affect interstate or foreign commerce including any such waters:

(i) Which are or could be used by interstate or foreign travelers for recreational or other purposes; or

(ii) From which fish or shellfish are or could be taken and sold in interstate or foreign commerce; or

(iii) Which are used or could be used for industrial purpose by industries in interstate commerce;

(4) All impoundments of waters otherwise defined as waters of the United States under the definition;

(5) Tributaries of waters identified in paragraphs (a) (1)-(4) of this section;

(6) The territorial seas;

(7) Wetlands adjacent to waters (other than waters that are themselves wetlands) identified in paragraphs (a) (1)-(6) of this section;

(8) Waters of the United States do not include prior converted cropland[5] * * *

(b)   The term "wetlands" means those areas that are inundated or saturated by surface or ground water at a frequency and duration sufficient to support, and that under normal circumstances do support, a prevalence of vegetation typically adapted for life in saturated soil conditions. Wetlands generally include swamps, marshes, bogs, and similar areas.

(c)   The term "adjacent" means bordering, contiguous, or neighboring. Wetlands separated from other waters of the United States by man-made dikes or barriers, natural river berms, beach dunes and the like are "adjacent wetlands."

(d)   The term "high-tide line" means the line of intersection of the land with the water's surface at the maximum height reached by a rising tide. The high-tide line may be determined, in the absence of actual data, by a line of oil or scum along shore objects, a more or less continuous deposit of fine shell or debris on the foreshore or berm, other physical markings or characteristics, vegetation lines, tidal gages, or other suitable means that delineate the general height reached by a

---

[5] Prior converted croplands are defined by the Soil Conservation Service as areas that, prior to December 23, 1985, were drained or otherwise manipulated for the purpose, and having the effect, of making production of a commodity crop possible. Such areas are inundated for no more than 14 consecutive days during the growing season and do not include prairie potholes or playa wetlands. Such areas are distinguished from "farmed wetlands," which continue to be considered "waters of the United States."

rising tide. The line encompasses spring high-tides and other high-tides that occur with periodic frequency but does not include storm surges in which there is a departure from the normal or predicted reach of the tide due to the piling up of water against a coast by strong winds such as those accompanying a hurricane or other intense storm.

(e) The term "ordinary high water mark" means that line on the shore established by the fluctuations of water and indicated by physical characteristics such as clear, natural line impressed on the bank, shelving, changes in the character of soil, destruction of terrestrial vegetation, the presence of litter and debris, or other appropriate means that consider the characteristics of the surrounding areas.

(f) The term "tidal waters" means those waters that rise and fall in a predictable and measurable rhythm or cycle due to the gravitational pulls of the moon and sun. Tidal waters end where the rise and fall of the water surface can no longer be practically measured in a predictable rhythm due to masking by hydrologic, wind, or other effects.

33 C.F.R. § 328.4. Limits of jurisdiction.

(a)   Territorial Seas. The limit of jurisdiction in the territorial seas is measured from the baseline in a seaward direction a distance of three nautical miles. (See 33 C.F.R. 329.12).

(b)   Tidal Waters of the United States. The landward limits of jurisdiction in tidal waters:

(1) Extends to the high-tide line, or
(2) When adjacent non-tidal waters of the United States are present, the jurisdiction extends to the limits identified in paragraph (c) of this section.

(c)   Non-Tidal Waters of the United States. The limits of jurisdiction in non-tidal waters:

(1)   In the absence of adjacent wetlands, the jurisdiction extends to the ordinary high water mark, or
(2)   When adjacent wetlands are present, the jurisdiction extends beyond the ordinary high water mark to the limit of the adjacent wetlands.
(3)   When the water of the United States consists only of wetlands the jurisdiction extends to the limit of the wetland.

33 C.F.R. § 328.5. Changes in limits of waters of the United States.

Permanent changes of the shoreline configuration result in similar alterations of the boundaries of waters of the United States. Gradual changes which are due to natural causes and are perceptible only over some period of time constitute changes in the bed of a waterway which also change the boundaries of the waters of the United States. For example, changing sea levels or subsidence of land may cause some areas to become waters of the United States while siltation or a change in drainage may remove an area from waters of the United States. Man-made changes may affect the limits of waters of the United States; however, permanent changes should not be presumed until the particular circumstances have been examined and verified by the district engineer. Verification of changes to the lateral limits of jurisdiction may be obtained from the district engineer.

UNITED STATES v. RIVERSIDE BAYVIEW HOMES, INC.
Supreme Court of the United States, 1985
474 U.S. 121

MR. JUSTICE WHITE delivered the opinion of the Court.

This case presents the question whether the Clean Water Act, 33 U.S.C. § 1251, et seq., together with certain regulations promulgated under its authority by the Army Corps of Engineers, authorizes the Corps to require landowners to obtain permits from the Corps before discharging fill material into wetlands adjacent to navigable bodies of water and their tributaries.

I

* * *

Respondent Riverside Bayview Homes, Inc. (hereafter respondent), owns 80 acres of low-lying, marshy land near the shores of Lake St. Clair in Macomb County, Michigan. In 1976, respondent began to place fill materials on its property as part of its preparations for construction of a housing development. The Corps of Engineers, believing that the property was an "adjacent wetland" under the 1975 regulation defining "waters of the United States," filed suit in the United States District Court for the Eastern District of Michigan, seeking to enjoin respondent from filling the property without the permission of the Corps.

The District Court held that the portion of respondent's property lying below 575.5 feet above sea level was a covered wetland and enjoined respondent from filling it without a permit. * * *

Respondent * * * appealed, and the Sixth Circuit reversed. 729 F.2d 391 (1984). * * *

We granted certiorari to consider the proper interpretation of the Corps' regulations defining "waters of the United States" and the scope of the Corps' jurisdiction under the Clean Water Act, both of which were called into question by the Sixth Circuit's ruling. * * * We now reverse.

II

The question whether the Corps of Engineers may demand that respondent obtain a permit before placing fill material on its property is primarily one of regulatory and statutory interpretation: we must determine whether respondent's property is an "adjacent wetland" within the meaning of the applicable regulation, and, if so, whether the Corps' jurisdiction over "navigable waters" gives it statutory authority to regulate discharges of fill material into such a wetland. * * *

III

Purged of its spurious constitutional overtones, the question whether the regulation at issue requires respondent to obtain a permit before filling its property is an easy one. * * * The plain language of the regulation [33 C.F.R. § 323.2(c)] refutes the Court of Appeals' conclusion that inundation or "frequent flooding" by the adjacent body of water is a sine qua non of a wetland under the regulation. Indeed, the regulation could hardly state more clearly that saturation by either surface or ground water is sufficient to bring an area within the category of wetlands, provided that the saturation is sufficient to and does support wetland vegetation.

* * *

[R]espondent's property is a wetland adjacent to a navigable waterway. Hence, it is part of the "waters of the United States" as defined by 33 C.F.R. § 323.2 (1985), and if the regulation itself is valid as a construction of the term "waters of the United States" as used in the Clean Water Act, a question which we now address, the property falls within the scope of the Corps' jurisdiction over "navigable waters" under Section 404 of the Act.

IV

A

An agency's construction of a statute it is charged with enforcing is entitled to deference if it is reasonable and not in conflict with the expressed intent of Congress. Accordingly, our review is limited to the question whether it is reasonable, in light of the language, policies, and legislative history of the Act for the Corps to exercise jurisdiction over wetlands adjacent to but not regularly flooded by rivers, streams, and other hydrographic features more conventionally identifiable as "waters."[6]

On a purely linguistic level, it may appear unreasonable to classify "lands," wet or otherwise, as "waters." Such a simplistic response, however, does justice neither to the problem faced by the Corps in defining the scope of its authority under Section 404(a) nor to the realities of the problem of water pollution that the Clean Water Act was intended to combat. In determining the limits of its power to regulate discharges under the Act, the Corps must necessarily choose some point at which water ends and land begins. Our common experience tells us that this is often no easy task: the transition from water to solid ground is not necessarily or even typically an abrupt one. Rather, between open waters and dry land may lie shallows, marshes, mudflats, swamps, bogs -- in short, a huge array of areas that are not wholly aquatic but nevertheless fall far short of being dry land. Where on this continuum to find the limit of "waters" is far from obvious.

Faced with such a problem of defining the bounds of its regulatory authority, an agency may appropriately look to the legislative history and underlying policies of its statutory grants of authority. Neither of these sources provides unambiguous guidance for the Corps in this case, but together they do support the reasonableness of the Corps' approach of defining adjacent wetlands as "waters" within the meaning of Section 404(a). Section 404 originated as part of the Federal Water Pollution Control Act Amendments of 1972, which constituted a comprehensive legislative attempt "to restore and maintain the chemical, physical, and biological integrity of the Nation's waters." CWA § 101, 33 U.S.C. § 1251. This objective incorporated a broad, systemic view of the goal of maintaining and improving water quality: as the House Report on the legislation put it, "the word 'integrity' * * * refers to a condition in which the natural structure and function of ecosystems are maintained." H.R. Rep. No. 92-911, p. 76 (1972). Protection of aquatic ecosystems, Congress recognized, demanded broad federal authority to control pollution, for "[w]ater moves in hydrologic cycles and it is essential that discharge of pollutants be controlled at the source." S. Rep. No. 92-414, p. 77 (1972).

In keeping with these views, Congress chose to define the waters covered by the Act broadly. Although the Act prohibits discharges into "navigable waters," see CWA §§ 301(a), 404(a), 502(12), 33 U.S.C. §§ 1311(a), 1344(a), 1362(12), the Act's definition of "navigable waters" as "the waters of the United States" makes it clear that the term "navigable" as used in the Act is of limited import. In adopting this definition of

---

[6] We are not called upon to address the question of the authority of the Corps to regulate discharges of fill material into wetlands that are not adjacent to bodies of open water, see 33 C.F.R. §§ 323.2(a)(2) and (3) (1985), and we do not express any opinion on that question.

"navigable waters," Congress evidently intended to repudiate limits that had been placed on federal regulation by earlier water pollution control statutes and to exercise its powers under the Commerce Clause to regulate at least some waters that would not be deemed "navigable" under the classical understanding of that term. See S. Conf. Rep. No. 92-1236, p. 144 (1972); 118 Cong. Rec. 33756-33757 (1972) (statement of Rep. Dingell).

Of course, it is one thing to recognize that Congress intended to allow regulation of waters that might not satisfy traditional tests of navigability; it is another to assert that Congress intended to abandon traditional notions of "waters" and include in that term "wetlands" as well. Nonetheless, the evident breadth of congressional concern for protection of water quality and aquatic ecosystems suggests that it is reasonable for the Corps to interpret the term "waters" to encompass wetlands adjacent to waters as more conventionally defined. Following the lead of the Environmental Protection Agency, see 38 Fed. Reg. 10834 (1973), the Corps has determined that wetlands adjacent to navigable waters do as a general matter play a key role in protecting and enhancing water quality:

> The regulation of activities that cause water pollution cannot rely on * * * artificial lines * * * but must focus on all waters that together form the entire aquatic system. Water moves in hydrologic cycles, and the pollution of this part of the aquatic system, regardless of whether it is above or below an ordinary high water mark, or mean high-tide line, will affect the water quality of the other waters within that aquatic system.

> For this reason, the landward limit of Federal jurisdiction under Section 404 must include any adjacent wetlands that form the border of or are in reasonable proximity to other waters of the United States, as these wetlands are part of this aquatic system. 42 Fed. Reg. 37128 (1977).

We cannot say that the Corps' conclusion that adjacent wetlands are inseparably bound up with the "waters" of the United States -- based as it is on the Corps' and EPA's technical expertise -- is unreasonable. In view of the breadth of federal regulatory authority contemplated by the Act itself and the inherent difficulties of defining precise bounds to regulable waters, the Corps' ecological judgment about the relationship between waters and their adjacent wetlands provides an adequate basis fo r a legal judgment that adjacent wetlands may be defined as waters under the Act.

This holds true even for wetlands that are not the result of flooding or permeation by water having its source in adjacent bodies of open water. The Corps has concluded that wetlands may affect the water quality of adjacent lakes, rivers, and streams even when the waters of those bodies do not actually inundate the wetlands. For example, wetlands that are not flooded by adjacent waters may still tend to drain into those waters. In such circumstances, the Corps has concluded that wetlands may serve to filter and purify water draining into adjacent bodies of water, see 33 C.F.R. § 320.4(b)(2)(vii) (1985), and to slow the flow of surface runoff into lakes, rivers, and streams and thus prevent flooding and erosion, see §§ 320.4(b)(2)(iv) and (v). In addition, adjacent wetlands may "serve significant natural biological functions, including food chain production, general habitat, and nesting, spawning, rearing and resting sites for aquatic * * * species." 33 C.F.R. § 320.4(b)(2)(i) (1985). In short, the Corps has concluded that wetlands adjacent to lakes, rivers, streams and other bodies of water may function as integral parts of the aquatic environment even when the moisture creating the wetlands does not find its source in the adjacent bodies of water. Again, we cannot say that the Corps' judgment on these matters is unreasonable, and we therefore conclude that a definition of "waters of the United States" encompassing all wetlands adjacent to other bodies of water over which the Corps has jurisdiction is a permissible interpretation of the Act. Because respondent's property is part of a wetland that actually abuts on a navigable waterway, respondent was required to have a permit in this case.[7]

* * *

[The Court found that the history of the Clean Water Act of 1977 also supported the conclusion that the Corps' assertion of authority over waters not actually navigable was a reasonable interpretation of Section 404. When the Clean Water Act was before Congress, the Corps' assertion of jurisdiction over wetlands was specifically brought to Congress' attention and Congress rejected measures aimed at curbing the Corps' jurisdiction in large part because of its concern for the protection of wetlands.]

C

We are thus persuaded that the language, policies, and history of

---

[7] Of course, it may well be that not every adjacent wetland is of great importance to the environment of adjoining bodies of water. But the existence of such cases does not seriously undermine the Corps' decision to define all adjacent wetlands as "waters." If it is reasonable for the Corps to conclude that in the majority of cases, adjacent wetlands have significant effects on water quality and the aquatic ecosystem, its definition can stand. That the definition may include some wetlands that are not significantly intertwined with the ecosystem of adjacent waterways is of little moment, for where it appears that a wetland covered by the Corps' definition is in fact lacking in importance to the aquatic environment -- or where its importance is outweighed by other values -- the Corps may always allow development of the wetland for other uses simply by issuing a permit. See 33 C.F.R. § 320.4(b)(4) (1985).

the Clean Water Act compel a finding that the Corps has acted reasonably in interpreting the Act to require permits for the discharge of fill material into wetlands adjacent to the "waters of the United States." The regulation in which the Corps has embodied this interpretation by its terms includes the wetlands on respondent's property within the class of waters that may not be filled without a permit; and, as we have seen, there is no reason to interpret the regulation more narrowly than its terms would indicate. Accordingly, the judgment of the Court of Appeals is

Reversed.

Note

The *Riverside Bayview Homes* opinion did not answer the question of the meaning of "waters of the United States" and the jurisdictional reach of Section 404 and lower courts continued to struggle with these issues. In some coastal areas of the country, isolated, wholly intrastate, nonnavigable ponds and wetlands are an important ecological feature. The Corps determined that such areas were "waters of the United States" and activities within such areas subject to Section 404 permit requirements. One means used by the Corps to establish the necessary nexus between such waters and interstate commerce was the presence of migratory birds and migratory bird habitat –the so-called "migratory bird rule." This was challenged in a number of lawsuits filed in the 1990s. In 2000, the United States Supreme Court granted certiorari in one of the cases, *Solid Waste Agency of Northern Cook County v. United States Army Corps of Engineers*, which appears below.

SOLID WASTE AGENCY OF NORTHERN COOK COUNTY
v.
UNITED STATES ARMY CORPS OF ENGINEERS
Supreme Court of the United States, 2001
___U.S.___

CHIEF JUSTICE REHNQUIST *delivered the opinion of the Court.*

Section 404(a) of the Clean Water Act (CWA or Act) * * * regulates the discharge of dredged or fill material into "navigable waters." The United States Army Corps of Engineers (Corps) has interpreted § 404(a) to confer federal authority over an abandoned sand and gravel pit in northern Illinois which provides habitat for migratory birds. We are asked to decide whether the provisions of § 404(a) may be fairly extended to these waters, and, if so, whether Congress could exercise such authority consistent with the Commerce Clause, U.S. Const., Art. I, § 8, cl. 3. We answer the first question in the negative and therefore do not reach the second.

Petitioner, the Solid Waste Agency of Northern Cook County (SWANCC), is a consortium of 23 suburban Chicago cities and villages that united in an effort to locate and develop a disposal site for baled nonhazardous solid waste. The Chicago Gravel Company informed the municipalities of the availability of a 533-acre parcel, bestriding the Illinois counties Cook and Kane, which had been the site of a sand and gravel pit mining operation for three decades up until about 1960. Long since abandoned, the old mining site eventually gave way to a successional stage forest, with its remnant excavation trenches evolving into a scattering of permanent and seasonal ponds of varying size (from under one-tenth of an acre to several acres) and depth (from several inches to several feet).

The municipalities decided to purchase the site for disposal of their baled nonhazardous solid waste. * * * [B]ecause the operation called for the filling of some of the permanent and seasonal ponds, SWANCC contacted federal respondents (hereinafter respondents), including the Corps, to determine if a federal landfill permit was required under § 404(a) of the CWA, 33 U.S.C. § 1344(a).

Section 404(a) grants the Corps authority to issue permits "for the discharge of dredged or fill material into the navigable waters at specified disposal sites." *Ibid.* The term "navigable waters" is defined under the Act as "the waters of the United States, including the territorial seas." The Corps has issued regulations defining the term "waters of the United States" to include:

> waters such as instrastate lakes * * * wetlands, sloughs, prairie potholes, wet meadows, playa lakes, or natural ponds, the use, degradation or destruction of which could affect interstate commerce * * *

In 1986, in an attempt to "clarify" the reach of its jurisdiction, the Corps stated that § 404(a) extends to intrastate waters:

> a. Which are or would be used as habitat by birds protected by Migratory Bird Treaties; or
> b. Which are or would be used as habitat by other migratory birds which cross state lines; or
> c. Which are or would be used as habitat for endangered species;
> * * *

This last promulgation has been dubbed the "Migratory Bird Rule."

The Corps initially concluded that it had no jurisdiction over the site because it contained no "wetlands," or areas which support "vegetation typically adapted for life in saturated soil conditions," 33 CFR § 328.3(b) (1999). However, after the Illinois Nature Preserves Commission informed the Corps that a number of migratory bird species had been observed at the site, the Corps reconsidered and ultimately asserted jurisdiction over the balefill site pursuant to subpart (b) of the "Migratory Bird Rule." The Corps found that approximately 121 bird species had been observed at the site, including several known to depend upon aquatic environments for a significant portion of their life requirements. * * *

Despite SWANCC's securing the required water quality certification from the Illinois Environmental Protection Agency, the Corps refused to issue a § 404(a) permit. The Corps found that SWANCC had not established that its proposal was the "least environmentally damaging, most practicable alternative" for disposal of nonhazardous solid waste; that SWANCC's failure to set aside sufficient funds to remediate leaks posed an "unacceptable risk to the public's drinking water supply"; and that the impact of the project upon area-sensitive species was "unmitigatable since a landfill surface cannot be redeveloped into a forested habitat."

Petitioner filed suit under the Administrative Procedure Act, 5 U.S.C. § 701 *et seq.,* in the Northern District of Illinois challenging both the Corps' jurisdiction over the site and the merits of its denial of the § 404(a) permit. The District Court granted summary judgment to respondents on the jurisdictional issue, and petitioner abandoned its challenge to the Corps' permit decision. On appeal to the Court of Appeals for the Seventh Circuit, petitioner renewed its attack on respondents' use of the "Migratory Bird Rule" to assert jurisdiction over the site. Petitioner argued that respondents had exceeded their statutory authority in interpreting the CWA to cover nonnavigable, isolated, intrastate waters based upon the presence of migratory birds and, in the alternative, that Congress lacked the power under the Commerce Clause to grant such regulatory jurisdiction.

The Court of Appeals began its analysis with the constitutional question, holding that Congress has the authority to regulate such waters based upon "the cumulative impact doctrine, under which a single activity that itself has no discernible effect on interstate commerce may still be regulated if the aggregate effect of that class of activity has a substantial impact on interstate commerce." 191 F.3d 845, 850 (C.A.7 1999). The aggregate effect of the "destruction of the natural habitat of migratory birds" on interstate commerce, the court held, was substantial because each year millions of Americans cross state lines and spend over a billion dollars to hunt and observe migratory birds. Ibid. The Court of Appeals then turned to the regulatory question. The court held that the CWA reaches as many waters as the Commerce Clause allows and, given its earlier Commerce Clause ruling, it therefore followed that respondents' "Migratory Bird Rule" was a reasonable interpretation of the Act. See id., at 851-852.

We granted certiorari, 529 U.S. 1129 (2000), and now reverse.

Congress passed the CWA for the stated purpose of "restor[ing] and maintain[ing] the chemical, physical, and biological integrity of the Nation's waters." 33 U.S.C. § 1251(a). In so doing, Congress chose to "recognize, preserve, and protect the primary responsibilities and rights of States to prevent, reduce, and eliminate pollution, to plan the development and use (including restoration, preservation, and enhancement) of land and water resources, and to consult with the Administrator in the exercise of his authority under this chapter." § 1251(b). Relevant here, § 404(a) authorizes respondents to regulate the discharge of fill material into "navigable waters," 33 U.S.C. § 1344(a), which the statute defines as "the waters of the United States, including the territorial seas," § 1362(7). Respondents have interpreted these words to cover the abandoned gravel pit at issue here because it is used as habitat for migratory birds. We conclude that the "Migratory Bird Rule" is not fairly supported by the CWA.

This is not the first time we have been called upon to evaluate the meaning of § 404(a). In United States v. Riverside Bayview Homes, Inc., 474 U.S. 121 (1985), we held that the Corps had § 404(a) jurisdiction over wetlands that actually abutted on a navigable waterway. In so doing, we noted that the term "navigable" is of "limited import" and that Congress evidenced its intent to "regulate at least some waters that would not be deemed 'navigable' under the classical understanding of that term." Id., at 133. But our holding was based in large measure upon Congress' unequivocal acquiescence to, and approval of, the Corps' regulations interpreting the CWA to cover wetlands adjacent to navigable waters. See id., at 135-139. We found that Congress' concern for the protection of water quality and aquatic ecosystems indicated its intent to regulate wetlands "inseparably bound up with the 'waters' of the United States." Id., at 134.

It was the significant nexus between the wetlands and "navigable waters" that informed our reading of the CWA in Riverside Bayview Homes. Indeed, we did not "express any opinion" on the "question of the authority of the Corps to regulate discharges of fill material into wetlands that are not adjacent to bodies of open water. * * * Id., at 131-132, n. 8, 106 S.Ct. 455. In order to rule for respondents here, we would have to hold that the jurisdiction of the Corps extends to ponds that are *not* adjacent to open water. But we conclude that the text of the statute will not allow this.

Indeed, the Corps' *original* interpretation of the CWA, promulgated two years after its enactment, is inconsistent with that which it espouses here. Its 1974 regulations defined § 404(a)'s "navigable waters" to mean "those waters of the United States which are subject to the ebb and flow of the tide, and/or are presently, or have been in the past, or may be in the future susceptible for use for purposes of interstate or foreign commerce.* * *" 33 CFR § 209.120(d)(1). The Corps emphasized that "[i]t is the water body's capability of use by the public for purposes of transportation or commerce which is the determinative factor." § 209.260(e)(1). Respondents put forward no persuasive evidence that the Corps mistook Congress' intent in 1974.[8]

Respondents next contend that whatever its original aim in 1972, Congress charted a new course five years later when it approved the more expansive definition of "navigable waters" found in the Corps' 1977 regulations. In July 1977, the Corps formally adopted 33 CFR § 323.2(a)(5) (1978), which defined "waters of the United States" to include "isolated wetlands and lakes, intermittent streams, prairie potholes, and other waters that are not part of a tributary system to interstate waters or to navigable waters of the United States, the degradation or destruction of which could affect interstate commerce." Respondents argue that Congress was aware of this more expansive interpretation during its 1977 amendments to the CWA. Specifically, respondents point to a failed House bill, H.R. 3199, that would have defined "navigable waters" as "all waters which are presently used, or are susceptible to use in their natural condition or by reasonable improvement as a means to transport interstate or foreign commerce." 123 Cong. Rec. 10420, 10434 (1977). They also point to the passage in § 404(g)(1) that authorizes a State to apply to the Environmental Protection Agency for permission "to administer its own individual and general permit program for the discharge of dredged or fill material into the navigable waters (other than those waters which are presently used, or are susceptible to use in their natural condition or by reasonable improvement as a means to transport interstate or foreign commerce ***, including wetlands adjacent thereto) within its jurisdiction ***" 33 U.S.C. § 1344(g)(1). The failure to pass legislation that would have overturned the Corps' 1977 regulations and the extension of jurisdiction in § 404(g) to waters "other than" traditional "navigable waters," respondents submit, indicate that Congress recognized and accepted a broad definition of "navigable waters" that includes nonnavigable, isolated, intrastate waters.

Although we have recognized congressional acquiescence to

---

[8] Respondents refer us to portions of the legislative history that they believe indicate Congress' intent to expand the definition of "navigable waters." Although the Conference Report includes the statement that the conferees "intend that the term 'navigable waters' be given the broadest possible constitutional interpretation," S. Conf. Rep. No. 92- 1236, p. 144 (1972), U.S.Code Cong. & Admin.News 1972 pp. 3668, 3822, neither this, nor anything else in the legislative history to which respondents point, signifies that Congress intended to exert anything more than its commerce power over navigation. Indeed, respondents admit that the legislative history is somewhat ambiguous. See Brief for Federal Respondents 24.

administrative interpretations of a statute in some situations, we have done so with extreme care. "[F]ailed legislative proposals are 'a particularly dangerous ground on which to rest an interpretation of a prior statute.'" * * * A bill can be proposed for any number of reasons, and it can be rejected for just as many others. The relationship between the actions and inactions of the 95th Congress and the intent of the 92d Congress in passing § 404(a) is also considerably attenuated. * * *

We conclude that respondents have failed to make the necessary showing that the failure of the 1977 House bill demonstrates Congress' acquiescence to the Corps' regulations or the "Migratory Bird Rule," which, of course, did not first appear until 1986. * * *

Section 404(g) is equally unenlightening. In Riverside Bayview Homes we recognized that Congress intended the phrase "navigable waters" to include "at least some waters that would not be deemed 'navigable' under the classical understanding of that term." Id., at 133. But § 404(g) gives no intimation of what those waters might be; it simply refers to them as "other ... waters." Respondents conjecture that "other * * * waters" must incorporate the Corps' 1977 regulations, but it is also plausible, as petitioner contends, that Congress simply wanted to include all waters adjacent to "navigable waters," such as nonnavigable tributaries and streams. The exact meaning of § 404(g) is not before us and we express no opinion on it, but for present purposes it is sufficient to say, as we did in Riverside Bayview Homes, that " § 404(g)(1) does not conclusively determine the construction to be placed on the use of the term 'waters' elsewhere in the Act (particularly in § 502(7), which contains the relevant definition of 'navigable waters') * * *" Id., at 138, n. 11.

We thus decline respondents' invitation to take what they see as the next ineluctable step after Riverside Bayview Homes: holding that isolated ponds, some only seasonal, wholly located within two Illinois counties, fall under § 404(a)'s definition of "navigable waters" because they serve as habitat for migratory birds. As counsel for respondents conceded at oral argument, such a ruling would assume that "the use of the word navigable in the statute * * * does not have any independent significance." Tr. of Oral Arg. 28. We cannot agree that Congress' separate definitional use of the phrase "waters of the United States" constitutes a basis for reading the term "navigable waters" out of the statute. We said in Riverside Bayview Homes that the word "navigable" in the statute was of "limited import" and went on to hold that § 404(a) extended to nonnavigable wetlands adjacent to open waters. But it is one thing to give a word limited effect and quite another to give it no effect whatever. The term "navigable" has at least the import of showing us what Congress had in mind as its authority for enacting the CWA: its traditional jurisdiction over waters that were or had been navigable in fact or which could reasonably be so made.   See, *e.g.,* United States v. Appalachian Elec. Power Co., 311 U.S. 377, 407-408 (1940).

Respondents--relying upon all of the arguments addressed above-- contend that, at the very least, it must be said that Congress did not address the precise question of § 404(a)'s scope with regard to nonnavigable, isolated, intrastate waters, and that, therefore, we should give deference to the "Migratory Bird Rule." See, *e.g.,* Chevron U.S.A. Inc. v. Natural Resources Defense Council, Inc., 467 U.S. 837(1984). We find § 404(a) to be clear, but even were we to agree with respondents, we would not extend Chevron deference here.

Where an administrative interpretation of a statute invokes the outer limits of Congress' power, we expect a clear indication that Congress intended that result.   See Edward J. DeBartolo Corp. v. Florida Gulf Coast Building & Constr. Trades Council, 485 U.S. 568, 575 (1988). * * *

Twice in the past six years we have reaffirmed the proposition that the grant of authority to Congress under the Commerce Clause, though broad, is not unlimited.   See United States v. Morrison, 529 U.S. 598 (2000); United States v. Lopez, 514 U.S. 549 (1995).   Respondents argue that the "Migratory Bird Rule" falls within Congress' power to regulate intrastate activities that "substantially affect" interstate commerce.   They note that the protection of migratory birds is a "national interest of very nearly the first magnitude," Missouri v. Holland, 252 U.S. 416, 435 (1920), and that, as the Court of Appeals found, millions of people spend over a billion dollars annually on recreational pursuits relating to migratory birds.   These arguments raise significant constitutional questions.   For example, we would have to evaluate the precise object or activity that, in the aggregate, substantially affects interstate commerce.   This is not clear, for although the Corps has claimed jurisdiction over petitioner's land because it contains water areas used as habitat by migratory birds, respondents now, *post litem motam,* focus upon the fact that the regulated activity is petitioner's municipal landfill, which is "plainly of a commercial nature."   Brief for Federal Respondents 43.   But this is a far cry, indeed, from the "navigable waters" and "waters of the United States" to which the statute by its terms extends.

These are significant constitutional questions raised by respondents' application of their regulations, and yet we find nothing approaching a clear statement from Congress that it intended § 404(a) to reach an abandoned sand and gravel pit such as we have here.   Permitting respondents to claim federal jurisdiction over ponds and mudflats falling within the "Migratory Bird Rule" would result in a significant impingement of the States' traditional and primary power over land and water use. * * * Rather than expressing a desire to readjust the federal-state balance in this manner, Congress chose to "recognize, preserve, and protect the primary responsibilities and rights of States * * * to plan the development and use * * * of land and water resources* * *." 33 U.S.C. § 1251(b).   We thus read the statute as written to avoid the significant constitutional and federalism questions raised by respondents' interpretation, and therefore reject the request for administrative deference.

We hold that 33 CFR § 328.3(a)(3) (1999), as clarified and applied to petitioner's balefill site pursuant to the "Migratory Bird Rule," 51 Fed.Reg. 41217 (1986), exceeds the authority granted to respondents under § 404(a) of the CWA.   The judgment of the Court of Appeals for the Seventh Circuit is therefore

Reversed.

JUSTICE STEVENS, *with whom* **JUSTICE SOUTER**, **JUSTICE GINSBURG**, *and* **JUSTICE BREYER** *join, dissenting.*

* * *

In its decision today, the Court draws a new jurisdictional line, one that invalidates the 1986 migratory bird regulation as well as the Corps' assertion of jurisdiction over all waters except for actually navigable waters, their tributaries, and wetlands adjacent to each. * * *

Because of the statute's ambitious and comprehensive goals, it was, of course, necessary to expand its jurisdictional scope.   Thus, although Congress opted to carry over the traditional jurisdictional term "navigable waters" from the RHA and prior versions of the FWPCA, it broadened the *definition* of that term to encompass all "waters of the United States." § 1362(7).   Indeed, the 1972 conferees arrived at the final formulation by specifically deleting the word "navigable" from the definition [of waters of the United States] that had originally appeared in the House version of the Act.   The majority today undoes that deletion.

The Conference Report explained that the definition in § 502(7) was intended to "be given the broadest possible constitutional interpretation." S. Conf. Rep. No. 92-1236, p. 144 (1972), reprinted in 1 Leg. Hist. 327.   The Court dismisses this clear assertion of legislative intent with the back of its hand. *Ante,* at 680, n. 3.   The statement, it claims, "signifies that Congress intended to exert [nothing] more than its commerce power over navigation." *Ibid.*

The majority's reading drains all meaning from the conference amendment.   By 1972, Congress' Commerce Clause power over "navigation" had long since been established.   The Daniel Ball, 10 Wall. 557(1871)* * * Why should Congress intend that its assertion of federal jurisdiction be given the "broadest possible constitutional interpretation" if it did not intend to reach beyond the very heartland of its commerce power? The activities regulated by the CWA have nothing to do with Congress' "commerce power over navigation." Indeed, the goals of the 1972 statute have nothing to do with *navigation* at all. * * *

Viewed in light of the history of federal water regulation, the broad § 502(7) definition, and Congress' unambiguous instructions in the Conference Report, it is clear that the term "navigable waters" operates in the statute as a shorthand for "waters over which federal authority may properly be asserted." * * *

IV

Because I am convinced that the Court's miserly construction of the statute is incorrect, I shall comment briefly on petitioner's argument that Congress is without power to prohibit it from filling any part of the 31 acres of ponds on its property in Cook County, Illinois. The Corps' exercise of its § 404 permitting power over "isolated" waters that serve as habitat for migratory birds falls well within the boundaries set by this Court's Commerce Clause jurisprudence.

In United States v. Lopez, 514 U.S. 549, 558-559 (1995), this Court identified "three broad categories of activity that Congress may regulate under its commerce power": * * * (3) activities that "substantially affect" interstate commerce. Ibid. The migratory bird rule at issue here is properly analyzed under the third category. In order to constitute a proper exercise of Congress' power over intrastate activities that "substantially affect" interstate commerce, it is not necessary that each individual instance of the activity substantially affect commerce; it is enough that, taken in the aggregate, the *class of activities* in question has such an effect. Perez v. United States, 402 U.S. 146 (1971) (noting that it is the "class" of regulated activities, not the individual instance, that is to be considered in the "affects" commerce analysis); see also Hodel, 452 U.S., at 277, 101 S.Ct. 2352; Wickard v. Filburn, 317 U.S. 111, 127-128 (1942).

The activity being regulated in this case (and by the Corps' § 404 regulations in general) is the discharge of fill material into water. The Corps did not assert jurisdiction over petitioner's land simply because the waters were "used as habitat by migratory birds." It asserted jurisdiction because petitioner planned to *discharge fill* into waters "used as habitat by migratory birds." Had petitioner intended to engage in some other activity besides discharging fill (*i.e.,* had there been no activity to regulate), or, conversely, had the waters not been habitat for migratory birds (*i.e.,* had there been no basis for federal jurisdiction), the Corps would never have become involved in petitioner's use of its land. There can be no doubt that * * * the discharge of fill material into the Nation's waters is almost always undertaken for economic reasons.

See V. Albrecht & B. Goode, Wetland Regulation in the Real World, Exh. 3 (Feb.1994) (demonstrating that the overwhelming majority of acreage for which § 404 permits are sought is intended for commercial, industrial, or other economic use).

Moreover, no one disputes that the discharge of fill into "isolated" waters that serve as migratory bird habitat will, in the aggregate, adversely affect migratory bird populations. * * * Nor does petitioner dispute that the particular waters it seeks to fill are home to many important species of migratory birds, including the second-largest breeding colony of Great Blue Herons in northeastern Illinois, App. to Pet. for Cert. 3a, and several species of waterfowl protected by international treaty and Illinois endangered species laws, Brief for Federal Respondents 7.

In addition to the intrinsic value of migratory birds * * * it is undisputed that literally millions of people regularly participate in birdwatching and hunting and that those activities generate a host of commercial activities of great value. The causal connection between the filling of wetlands and the decline of commercial activities associated with migratory birds is not "attenuated," * * * it is direct and concrete. * * *

Because I would affirm the judgment of the Court of Appeals, I respectfully dissent.

Notes and Questions

1. What exactly is the holding of SWANCC? May the Corps continue to assert Section 404 jurisdiction over isolated freshwaters and wetlands so long as the interstate commerce nexus can be established without using the migratory bird rule? Or, is the Court saying that the Corps lacks the authority under the CWA to regulate such waterbodies and wetlands?

2. If the SWANCC opinion is given a broad reading, then many believe that it will have a devastating effect on federal regulation of activities adversely affecting wetlands. Although the annual rate of wetlands loss has declined in the past decade, during the period from 1986 to 1997, the annual loss was still 58,500 acres. More importantly, 90% of all losses during that period consisted of freshwater wetlands. Freshwater wetlands just inland from the coastline experienced the greatest development pressures. See generally T. Dahl, Status and Trends of Wetlands In the Conterminous United States 1986-1997, 10-11, 33, 45-60 (U.S. Fish and Wildlife Service 2000). If SWANCC is read broadly, one prediction is that only 20% of the nation's wetlands would remain subject to Section 404 permit requirements. Freshwater wetlands would be most impacted.

3. The Corps' response to *SWANCC* was a memorandum sent to all Corps offices stating that

> *2.* * * * [E]ffective immediately, [lower Corps offices]* * * *are prohibited from developing local practices for determining the extent of * * * [CWA] regulatory jurisdiction and from utilizing local practices that were not in effect prior to the *SWANCC* decision.

> *3.* The Court's decision in *SWANCC* effectively precludes assertion of Section 404 jurisdiction over certain isolated waters. This has necessarily focussed increased attention on the geographic extent of Section 404 jurisdiction, and on the potential "tributary" status of waters, and the potential "adjacent" status of wetlands. * * *

Memorandum For All Commanders, Major Subordinate Commands And District Commands, "Prohibition on the Development of Local Operating Procedures Addressing Jurisdictional Determinations in Light of the SWANCC Decision," (CECW-OR, May 11, 2001). In light of this memorandum, under what circumstances may a local district assert Section 404 jurisdiction over isolated waters? New Section 404 regulations are under consideration and may be issued in 2002.

4. As might be expected, the lower court reaction to SWANCC has been mixed.

> Courts interpreting SWANCC have reached varying results, the primary rift being whether the Migratory Bird Rule was the decision's only casualty, or whether the holding limited the Corps' jurisdiction even further. The Fifth Circuit took the latter position in Rice v. Harken Exploration Co., 250 F.3d 264 (5th Cir. 2001) * * * [It, however,] appears that the remainder of the courts considering the issue have reached the opposite conclusion: that SWANCC struck the Migratory Bird Rule, pushing "isolated waters" that may *affect* interstate commerce out of the Corps' jurisdiction, without altering the Corps' reach where its jurisdiction is based upon a water's use or potential use as a channel of interstate commerce. * * *

> At least six lower courts * * * have * * * declin[ed] to read SWANCC as a broad reduction of the Corps' authority to regulate waters under the Act. * * *

United States v. Lamplight Equestrian Center, Inc., 2002 WL 360652 (N.D. III. March 8, 2002). (emphasis in original). But see, United States v. Rapanos, 2002 WL 373332 (E.D. Mich. February 21, 2002) (Corps may not regulate wetlands not directly adjacent to navigable waters).

5. In SWANCC, the Court avoids deciding the constitutional question of whether Congress has the power under the Commerce Clause to regulate activities affecting wholly instrastate, isolated waters and wetlands. If Congress chooses to enact new legislation expressly giving the Corps and the EPA that authority, is it likely that the Supreme Court would find such legislation unconstitutional? If a connection to interstate commerce is essential, what type and how minimal of a connection will suffice?

6. Is the purpose of Section 404 to protect against unnecessary wetland loss? If Section 404 is not a wetlands protection mechanism, what is it? Assuming Congress does have the constitutional authority to protect wetlands, why hasn't Congress passed specific wetlands protection legislation?

(c.) Wetland Identification and Delineation

Pursuant to its Section 404 authority, the EPA has issued the following guidelines for identifying "wetlands areas and values * * * POTENTIAL IMPACTS ON SPECIAL AQUATIC SITES

40 C.F.R. § 230.41. Wetlands.

(a) (1) Wetlands consist of areas that are inundated or saturated by surface or ground water at a frequency and duration sufficient to support, and that under normal circumstances do support, a prevalence of vegetation typically adapted for life in saturated soil conditions.

(2) Where wetlands are adjacent to open water, they generally constitute the transition to upland. The margin between wetland and open water can best be established by specialists familiar with the local environment, particularly where emergent vegetation merges with submerged vegetation over a broad area in such places as the lateral margins of open water, headwaters, rainwater catch basins, and groundwater seeps. The landward margin of wetlands also can best be identified by specialists familiar with the local environment when vegetation from the two regions merges over a broad area.

(3) Wetland vegetation consists of plants that require saturated soils to survive (obligate wetland plantsas well as plants, including certain trees, that gain a competitive advantage over others because they can tolerate prolonged wet soil conditions and their competitors cannot. In addition to plant populations and communities, wetlands are delimited by hydrological and physical characteristics of the environment. These characteristics should be considered when information about them is needed to supplement information available

about vegetation, or where wetland vegetation has been removed or is dormant.

(b) Possible loss of values: The discharge of dredged or fill material in wetlands is likely to damage or destroy habitat and adversely affect the biological productivity of wetlands ecosystems by smothering, by dewatering, by permanently flooding, or by altering substrate elevation or periodicity of water movement. The addition of dredged or fill material may destroy wetland vegetation or result in advancement of succession to dry land species. It may reduce or eliminate nutrient exchange by a reduction of the system's productivity, or by altering current patterns and velocities. Disruption or elimination of the wetland system can degrade water quality by obstructing circulation patterns that flush large expanses of wetland systems, by interfering with the filtration function of wetlands, or by changing the aquifer recharge capability of a wetland. Discharges can also change the wetland habitat value for fish and wildlife as discussed in subpart D. When disruptions in flow and circulation patterns occur, apparently minor loss of wetland acreage may result in major losses through secondary impacts. Discharging fill material in wetlands as part of municipal, industrial or recreational development may modify the capacity of wetlands to retain and store floodwaters and to serve as a buffer zone shielding upland areas from wave actions, storm damage and erosion.

* * *

Note and Questions

A wetlands determination really involves two separate decisions. One is the basic determination of what constitutes wetlands. The Corps regulation, 33 CFR § 328.3 (b), embodies a three parameter test for a wetland--hydrology, vegetation, and soil conditions. But the regulation leaves unanswered the questions of specifically what hydrological conditions, types of vegetation, and soils must be present before an area is to be classified as "wetlands." For how long a period of time must the area be "inundated or saturated?" As the EPA regulation illustrates, different plant types are more or less tolerant of different degrees of saturated soil conditions. How water tolerant must a plant be to be classified as "vegetation typically adapted for life in saturated soil conditions"? If the hydrology or vegetation is absent, due to the season during which the determination is being made or the existence of drought or unusually dry conditions, what types of soils are indicative of "wetlands?"

The second decision is where to draw the line between the "wetlands" and the uplands. Depending on the terrain and hydrology of the area, the transition between wetlands and uplands may be more or less pronounced. The more gradual the transition, the more discretion the wetlands delineator may have in drawing the line between the regulated area and unregulated uplands.

The generalities of the Corps and EPA regulations must be translated into specific plant and soil types and hydrological features to guide wetlands delineators, inform affected landowners and provide some uniformity in the making of wetland determinations and delineations. To accomplish these ends the Corps developed a field manual in 1987.

The content of the field manual has been a source of continuing debate and controversy since the Corps issued its 1987 Wetlands Delineation Manual. When the Corps started using this field manual, the other two agencies with wetlands regulatory responsibilities --the EPA and the Natural Resources Conservation Service (NRCS) (formally known as the Soil Conservation Service)--each took their own approach to wetlands delineation in executing their regulatory responsibilities.[9] Uniformity existed within an agency, not necessarily among them. However, through a joint effort, an interagency manual was published in January 1989. But application of this manual's wetlands criteria would have significantly increased the amount of land classifiable as wetlands, and many affected property owners, particularly farmers, vehemently protested. Responding to the protests, Congress passed legislation that precluded the Corps' use of the 1989 manual. See Energy And Water Development Appropriations Act of 1992, Pub. L. 102-104, 105 Stat. 510, 518 (1991) (The Johnston Amendment). This legislation did not address the use of the 1989 manual by the other agencies. The Corps reverted to using the 1987 manual, but the EPA decided to use the 1989 manual and NRCS continued using its own National Food Security Act Manual and regulations.

In 1991, responding to pressure from the administration and property owners, the EPA proposed another wetlands delineation manual; but, the proposed manual was withdrawn after scientists, environmental organizations, and others severely criticized the proposed manual as unscientific. It was estimated that use of this manual would open over one-half of the country's remaining wetlands to unrestricted development.

To eliminate the potential confusion in having agencies using different wetlands delineation manuals, in 1993 both the EPA and the Corps agreed to adhere to the 1987 manual until a new, acceptable one was developed, Amended Memorandum of Agreement Concerning the Determination of Geographic Jurisdiction of the Section 404 Program, 56 Fed. Reg. 4995 (Tuesday, January 19, 1993) and, later in 1994, the

---

[9] NRCS has primary responsibility for Food Security Act programs, two of which are conservation programs for the protection of wetlands. To protect wetlands, the programs provide incentives and penalties for farmers. See 16 U.S.C. §§ 3801-3862.

NRCS and the Fish and Wildlife Service also agreed to use the 1987 manual when implementing FSA wetland conservation provisions. See Memorandum of Agreement Among the Departments of Agriculture, Interior, Army and EPA Concerning Delineation of Wetlands under Section 404 of the Clean Water Act and Subtitle B of the Food Security Act. Thus, at the present time, a single manual is used by all agencies to implement section 404. For a detailed discussion of wetlands delineation, see, e.g., National Research Council, Wetlands: characteristics and boundaries 65-89 (1995).

The crux of the ongoing debate about what is a wetland and how it is to be delineated is captured in the following excerpt from a 1991 letter by then North Carolina Governor Martin to the EPA:

> There seems to be an assumption running through these * * * [manuals] that there exists a scientifically measurable entity called "wetlands" and that the various editions of the manual identify differing subsets of these wetlands as "jurisdictional wetlands." Nothing could be further from the truth. Scientific methods can be used to measure soil moisture, water movement, flora and fauna and water quality parameters and, in principle, the interaction between these elements. However, wetlands exists as an interface between land and water. Since all sites contain features of both elements, the "delineation" of a "wetland" is a process of social agreement and is not a scientifically measurable entity.

(3.) Covered Activities

For an activity to be subject to Section 404 jurisdiction, two requirements must be satisfied. First, the place in which the activity is occurring must be within the geographic reach of Section 404. It must be an activity within "waters of the United States." Second, it must be the type of activity that is subject to regulation. It must be a "discharge of dredged or fill material."

Along the Southeastern and Gulf coasts, much of the coastal land is part of a low coastal plain containing many freshwater wetlands which play a significant role in maintaining the overall quality of coastal estuaries and rivers. Frequently, coastal development projects will include plans to alter these wetlands during construction of golf courses and related amenities. In order to avoid the Section 404 permit process, developers, using modern technology, may attempt to drain the wetland and install ditches around the perimeter of the wetland to keep it dry. Once the hydrology is changed and the wetland dries up, the vegetation dies. Is the area still a wetland? Does a developer need a Section 404 permit to drain a wetland when the intent is to ultimately convert the wetland to a nonwetland use?

A similar situation arises in connection with agricultural conversions of wetlands to croplands. Using large bulldozers and other land-clearing equipment, the wetland vegetation may be cut off at ground level and carried away for disposal on an upland site. Once the area is cleared, soil will be plowed and cultivated with a crop such as soybeans. As a result of this change in use, there will be an increase in runoff into adjacent streams and estuary waters. The increased runoff may change the salinity of the streams and estuary waters and will carry many nutrients into the waters, causing algae blooms and other undesirable effects. Do these land-clearing activities involve "discharges of dredge material" subject to Section 404 permit requirements?

U.S. ARMY CORPS OF ENGINEERS REGULATIONS

33 C.F.R. § 323.2 Definitions.

For the purpose of this part, the following terms are defined:

* * *

(c) The term "dredged material" means material that is excavated or dredged from waters of the United States.

(d) (1) Except as provided below in paragraph (d)(3), the term discharge of dredge material means any addition of dredged material into, including redeposit of dredged material other than incidental fallback within, the waters of the United States. The term includes, but is not limited to the following:

> (i) The addition of dredged material to a specified discharge site located in waters of the United States;

> (ii) The runoff or overflow from a contained land or water disposal area;

> (iii) Any addition, including redeposit other than incidental fallback of dredged material, including excavated material, into waters of the United States which is incidental to any activity, including mechanized landclearing, ditching, channelization, or other excavation.

(2)(i) The Corps and EPA regard the use of mechanized earth-moving equipment to conduct landclearing, ditching, channelization, in-stream mining or other earth-moving activity in waters of the United States as resulting in a discharge of dredged material unless project-specific evidence shows that the activity results in only incidental fallback. * * *

> (ii) Incidental fallback is the redeposit of small volumes of dredged material that is incidental to excavation activity in waters

of the United States when such material falls back to substantially the same place as the initial removal. Examples of incidental fallback include soil that is disturbed when dirt is shoveled and the back-spill that comes off a bucket when such small volume of soil or dirt falls into substantially the same place from which it was initially removed.

(3) The term discharge of dredge material does not include the following:

* * *

(ii) Activities that involve only the cutting or removing of vegetation above the ground (e.g. mowing, rotary cutting, and chainsawing) where the activity neither substantially disturbs the root system nor involves mechanized pushing, dragging, or similar activities that redeposit excavated soil material.

(iii) Incidental fallback.

(3) Section 404 authorization is not required for the following:

(i) Any incidental addition, including redeposit, of dredged material associated with any activity that does not have the effect of destroying or degrading an area of the waters of the United States as defined in paragraph (d)(5) of this section: however, this exception does not apply to any person preparing to undertake mechanized landclearing, ditching, channelization or other excavation activity in a water of the United States, which would result in a redeposit of dredged material, unless the person demonstrates to the satisfaction of the Corps, or EPA, as appropriate, prior to commencing the activity involving the discharge, that the activity would not have the effect of destroying or degrading any area of the waters of the United States * * *

(ii) incidental movement of dredged material occurring during normal dredging operations, defined as dredging for navigation in navigable waters of the United States * * *; however, this exception is not applicable to dredging activities in wetlands.   * * *

(5) * * * an activity associated with a discharge of dredge material destroys an area of the waters of the United States if it alters the area in such a way that it would no longer be a water of the United States.

(6) * * * an activity associated with a discharge of dredge material degrades an area of the waters of the United States if it has more than a *de minimis* (i.e., inconsequential) effect on the area by causing an identifiable individual or cumulative adverse effect on an aquatic function.

(e) The term "fill material" means any material used for the primary purpose of replacing an aquatic area with dry land or of changing the bottom elevation of an waterbody. * * *

(f) The term "discharge of fill material" means the addition of fill material into waters of the United States. The term generally includes, without limitation, the following activities: Placement of fill that is necessary for the construction of any structure in a water of the United States; the building of any structure or impoundment requiring rock, sand, dirt, or other material for its construction; site-development fills for recreational, industrial, commercial, residential, and other uses; causeways or road fills; dams and dikes; artificial islands; property protection and/or reclamation devices such as riprap, groins, seawalls, breakwaters, and revetments; beach nourishment; levees; fill for structures such as sewage treatment facilities, intake and outfall pipes associated with power plants and subaqueous utility lines; and artificial reefs. The term does not include plowing, cultivating, seeding and harvesting for the production of food, fiber, and forest products (See § 323.4 for the definition of these terms).

* * *

(As amended February 15, 2001) See also EPA regulations, 40 C.F.R. § 232.2.

Notes and Questions

1. The current version of the regulation above was the end product of a series of challenges to the Corps assertion of jurisdiction over activities involving minimal discharges during the process of ditching, channeling, or clearing of wetlands. The regulation, in original, broader version, was referred to as the *Tulloch* rule because it was promulgated as part of the settlement of National Wildlife Federation v. Tulloch, Civ. No. C90-713-CIV-S-BO (E.D.N.C. 1992). In 1998, the United States Court of Appeals for the District of Columbia Circuit affirmed a lower court ruling that the *Tulloch* rule exceeded the statutory authority of the Corps because it impermissibly regulated "incidental fallback." See National Mining Association v. U.S. Army Corps of Engineers, 145 F. 3d 1399 (D.C. Cir. 1998). In May 1999, the Corps promulgated its first amended *Tulloch* rule, which closely resembled the present rule. That version of the rule was challenged by the National Association of Home Builders on the ground that it violated the lower court's injunction by asserting unqualified authority to regulate mechanized landclearing. The challenge was dismissed and the district court stated that the rulemaking was consistent with its and the Court of Appeals' decisions. While that suit was pending, in response to comments the Corps made some modifications to the regulation giving it its present form.

2.   The obvious purpose of the revised *Tulloch* rule is to severely limit the types of activities that can take place in freshwater wetlands without first having obtained a Section 404 permit. But, if the message of *SWANCC* is that many freshwater wetlands are not waters of the United States, how important is the revised *Tulloch* rule? Was the larger battle fought in *SWANCC* and won by those engaged in large-scale mechanized landclearing activities?

3.   Save Our Community v. EPA, 741 F.Supp. 605 (N.D. Tex. 1990), presented the issue of whether the draining or dewatering of wetlands is a regulated activity if the draining or dewatering does not itself involve any discharge. The case involved six or seven artificially created ponds which the Corps determined to be subject to Section 404 jurisdiction. The defendant planned to drain the ponds using a mechanized pump and, following drainage, to remove the levees and dikes that allowed the retention of runoff water.   Once that was accomplished, the defendant planned to seek redetermination of the site's status as a jurisdictional wetland.

The Corps' and the EPA's position was that they had no authority under Section 404 to regulate the drainage of the ponds under these circumstances. The district court, however, disagreed. According to the district court:

> [S]ignificant case law indicates that activities that will significantly alter or destroy a wetland require a permit from the Corps.* * *

> It would seem to stand logic on its head * * * to permit a landowner to avoid the Section 404 process by completely draining a wetland and then claiming "Permit for what wetland?"

> * * * to allow the draining of ponds and the redetermination of the site as a non-wetland would "permit the very evil that * * * regulation is intended to prevent: the destruction of wetlands to eliminate the permit requirement.

Id. at 613, 615. The Fifth Circuit, however, did not think so. It reversed the district court and held that a *discharge* of dredged or fill material is a necessary statutory requirement. Save Our Community v. EPA, 971 F.2d 1155 (5th Cir. 1992).

4.   If the Court of Appeals is correct, is a drained and dewatered area still a "wetland"? In a 1986 Regulatory Guidance Letter, the Corps stated that:

> *3.*   * * * We do not intend to assert jurisdiction over those areas that once were wetlands and part of an aquatic system, but which, in the past, have been transformed into dry land for various

purposes. * * *

4. The use of the phrase "normal circumstances" is meant to respond to those situations in which an individual would attempt to eliminate the permit review requirements of Section 404 by destroying the aquatic vegetation. * * *

Regulatory Guidance Letter No.86: Clarification of "Normal Circumstances" in Wetlands Definition (27 August 1986). Later in an April 10, 1990, memorandum the Corps took the position

3. * * *If the Corps has reason to believe that someone intends to use, or is using, one or more pumps to remove water from a wetland, or is removing wetland vegetation, or both, for the apparent purpose of eliminating 404 jurisdiction over the area, the "under normal circumstances" concept preserves 404 jurisdiction over the areas notwithstanding the drainage or vegetation removal. Consequently, even if the pumping or vegetation removal might conceivably be accomplished without any regulated 404 discharge, the area still cannot be filled or developed in any manner which does involve a 404 discharge unless a 404 permit is obtained. * * *

Memorandum to all Division and District Counsels, "Evading 404 Jurisdiction by Pumping Water from Wetlands," (Lance Wood, Assistant Chief Counsel, April 10, 1990). Can these Corps documents and the Fifth Circuit's decision be fully reconciled? Does this mean that, once an area is Section 404 jurisdictional wetlands, it remains jurisdictional wetlands forever? If the hydrology of such an area is permanently altered by otherwise legal ditching, pumping, or otherwise draining, shouldn't the "existing circumstances" become "normal circumstances" at some point in time?

5. Although the draining of Section 404 jurisdictional wetlands does not require a Section 404 permit, if, in the process of ditching such wetlands, there is more than an incidental discharge, then a Section 404 permit is necessary. In United States v. Deaton, 209 F.3d 331 (4th Cir. 2000), the defendant argued that the digging of drainage ditches and the piling of the excavated dirt on either side of the ditch, a practice known as sidecasting, did not result in a regulated discharge. The defendant argued that there was no "addition of any pollutant" when excavated wetlands material was sidecast because there was no introduction of new material into the area, or an increase in the amount of material present in the wetlands. The court, however, said

the statute does not prohibit the addition of material; it prohibits the "addition of any pollutant." The idea that there could be an addition of a pollutant without the addition of material seems to us to be entirely unremarkable, at least when an activity transforms some material form a nonpollutant to a pollutant, as occurred here. In the course of digging a ditch across the Deaton property, the contractor removed earth and vegetable matter from the wetland. Once it was removed, that material became "dredged spoil," a statutory pollutant and a type of material that was not previously present on the Deaton property. * * *

In deciding to classify dredge spoil as a pollutant, Congress determined that plain dirt, once excavated from the waters of the United States, could not be redeposited into those waters without causing harm to the environment. * * *

Id. at 335-36.

(4.) Exempted Activities

Remember the vast majority of coastal wetlands are lost through agricultural conversions and not through other development activities. If a farmer changes from one wetland crop, for example rice, to another wetland crop, such as soybeans, must the farmer get a Section 404 permit before making that crop conversion?

Read Section 404(f) carefully. What are the justifications underlying the exemptions created by Section 404(f)? Is it that these activities do not represent any significant threat to water quality? Read Section 404(f)(2). Under what circumstances is an otherwise exempted activity "recaptured" by Section 404(f)(2) and subject to the permit requirements of Section 404? Would Section 404(f)(2) recapture any of the exempted activities in the Striped Bass Problem? Should Section 404(f)(2) be amended to specifically exempt fish farm activities?

(5.) Corps Permit Process

Corps regulations basically authorize two types of permits: general permits and individual permits. General permits (nationwide and regional) are automatic authorizations of certain categories of activities. See 33 C.F.R. § 330 (Nationwide Permit Program). For such activities, except those affecting wetlands and a few others, the person may proceed without notifying the Corps. Obviously, since no individual review of a general permit activity is conducted, there is considerable disagreement about what types of activities should be the subjects of general permits.

If an activity is not within the purview of a general permit, the person must apply to the Corps for an individual permit. The application for an individual permit may necessitate the preparation of an EIS, which requires extensive, expensive, time   consuming studies.

Although NEPA places the obligation of preparing an EIS on the Corps, unless the applicant finances the necessary studies, the Corps will not process the permit application. Regulatory Guidance Letter No. 87-5: Environmental Impact Statement (EIS) Costs that can be Paid by the Applicant (May 28, 1987).

Most Section 404 permit applications do not require the preparation of an EIS, but only the preparation of a less formal EA. Whether an EIS or only an EA is required may depend upon whether all aspects of the entire project or only some components of the project must be considered and evaluated.

When an individual permit is requested and the application complete, the application is subjected to an intensive "public interest" review. This public interest review is explored further in this section.

Most applications for an individual permit are granted, although frequently the application is significantly modified during the review process as the Corps' views become better known to the applicant. Some applications, especially those seeking to modify wetlands, are highly controversial. Even if the applicant is successful, the applicant in such cases finds the process both lengthy and expensive.

Public Interest Review

The first step in the process of evaluating an application for a permit is the public interest review. The factors that are to be considered are set forth in the Corps' regulations. The number and type of factors deemed relevant has grown dramatically since the initiation of the Section 404 program.

U.S. ARMY CORPS OF ENGINEERS REGULATIONS

33 C.F.R. § 320.4. General policies for evaluating permit applications.

The following policies shall be applicable to the review of all applications for DA permits. Additional policies specifically applicable to certain types of activities are identified in 33 C.F.R. Parts 321-324.

(a) Public Interest Review. (1) The decision whether to issue a permit will be based on an evaluation of the probable impacts, including cumulative impacts, of the proposed activity and its intended use on the public interest. Evaluation of the probable impact which the proposed activity may have on the public interest requires a careful weighing of all those factors which become relevant in each particular case. The benefits which reasonably may be expected to accrue from the proposal must be balanced against its reasonably foreseeable detriments. The decision whether to authorize a proposal, and if so, the conditions under which it will be allowed to occur, are therefore determined by the outcome of this general balancing process. That decision should reflect the national concern for both protection and utilization of important resources. All factors which may be relevant to the proposal must be considered including the cumulative effects thereof: among those are conservation, economics, aesthetics, general environmental concerns, wetlands, historic properties, fish and wildlife values, flood hazards, floodplain values, land use, navigation, shore erosion and accretion, recreation, water supply and conservation, water quality, energy needs, safety, food and fiber production, mineral needs, considerations of property ownership and, in general, the needs and welfare of the people. For activities involving 404 discharges, a permit will be denied if the discharge that would be authorized by such permit would not comply with the Environmental Protection Agency's 404(b)(1) guidelines. Subject to the preceding sentence and any other applicable guidelines and criteria (see §§ 320.2 and 320.3), a permit will be granted unless the district engineer determines that it would be contrary to the public interest.

(2) The following general criteria will be considered in the evaluation of every application:

(i) The relative extent of the public and private need for the proposed structure or work;
(ii) Where there are unresolved conflicts as to resource use, the practicability of using reasonable alternative locations and methods to accomplish the objective of the proposed structure or work; and
(iii) The extent and permanence of the beneficial and/or detrimental effects which the proposed structure or work is likely to have on the public and private uses to which the area is suited.

(3) The specific weight of each factor is determined by its importance and relevance to the particular proposal. Accordingly, how important a factor is and how much consideration it deserves will vary with each proposal. A specific factor may be given great weight on one proposal, while it may not be present or as important on another. However, full consideration and appropriate weight will be given to all comments, including those of federal, state, and local agencies, and other experts on matters within their expertise.

(b) Effect on wetlands. (1) Most wetlands constitute a productive and valuable public resource, the unnecessary alteration or destruction of which should be discouraged as contrary to the public interest. * * *

(2) Wetlands considered to perform functions important to the public interest include:

(i) Wetlands which serve significant natural biological functions, including food chain production, general habitat and nesting, spawning, rearing and resting sites for aquatic or land species;

(ii) Wetlands set aside for study of the aquatic environment or as sanctuaries or refuges;

(iii) Wetlands the destruction or alteration of which would affect detrimentally natural drainage characteristics, sedimentation patterns, salinity distribution, flushing characteristics, current patterns, or other environmental characteristics;

(iv) Wetlands which are significant in shielding other areas from wave action, erosion, or storm damage. Such wetlands are often associated with barrier beaches, islands, reefs and bars;

(v) Wetlands which serve as valuable storage areas for storm and flood waters;

(vi) Wetlands which are ground water discharge areas that maintain minimum baseflows important to aquatic resources and those which are prime natural recharge areas;

(vii) Wetlands which serve significant water purification functions; and

(viii) Wetlands which are unique in nature or scarce in quantity to the region or local area.

(3) Although a particular alteration of a wetland may constitute a minor change, the cumulative effect of numerous piecemeal changes can result in a major impairment of wetland resources. Thus, the particular wetland site for which an application is made will be evaluated with the recognition that it may be part of a complete and interrelated wetland area. * * *

(4) No permit will be granted which involves the alteration of wetlands identified as important by paragraph (b)(2) of this section or because of provisions of paragraph (b)(3), of this section unless the district engineer concludes, on the basis of the analysis required in paragraph (a) of this section, that the benefits of the proposed alteration outweigh the damage to the wetlands resource. In evaluating whether a particular discharge activity should be permitted, the district engineer shall apply the Section 404(b)(1) guidelines (40 C.F.R. Part 230. 10(a) (1), (2), (3)).

* * *

(g) Consideration of property ownership. Authorization of work or structures by DA does not convey a property right, nor authorize any injury to property or invasion of other rights.

(1) An inherent aspect of property ownership is a right to reasonable private use. However, this right is subject to the rights and interests of the public in the navigable and other waters of the United States,

including the federal navigation servitude and federal regulation for environmental protection.

(2) Because a landowner has the general right to protect property from erosion, applications to erect protective structures will usually receive favorable consideration. However, if the protective structure may cause damage to the property of others, adversely affect public health and safety, adversely impact floodplain or wetland values, or otherwise appears contrary to the public interest, the district engineer will so advise the applicant and inform him of possible alternative methods of protecting his property. Such advice will be given in terms of general guidance only so as not to compete with private engineering firms nor require undue use of government resources.

(3) A riparian landowner's general right of access to navigable waters of the United States is subject to the similar rights of access held by nearby riparian landowners and to the general public's right of navigation on the water surface. In the case of proposals which create undue interference with access to, or use of, navigable waters, the authorization will generally be denied.

* * *

(h) Activities affecting coastal zones. Applications for DA permits for activities affecting the coastal zones of those states having a coastal zone management program approved by the Secretary of Commerce will be evaluated with respect to compliance with that program. No permit will be issued to a non-federal applicant until certification has been provided that the proposed activity complies with the coastal zone management program. * * *

Questions

1. Just how does the Corps go about weighing these factors? Is everything just thrown into the pot, stirred up, and then tasted to see if the public benefits outweigh foreseeable detriments? If so, how could a court ever effectively review a Corps decision on the balance between benefits and detriments?

2. When the Corps engages in its public interest review and determines the benefits to be derived, does the Corps consider the benefits to be derived from the project as a whole or only that portion of the project that involves the filling of wetlands? If a developer plans to build a housing project for low income families, and the plan calls for a road to be built by filling wetlands, does the Corps look at the benefit to be derived from the road or from the project as a whole?

3. May the Corps consider the socioeconomic effects of a project

that are not related to its physical impacts? See, e.g., Mall Properties, Inc. v. Marsh, 672 F.Supp. 561 (D. Mass. 1987), appeal dismissed, 841 F.2d 440 (1st Cir. 1988) (district court held it was improper for Corps to deny a permit to build a shopping mall on ground it adversely affects the neighboring local economy).

After-The-Fact Permits

When someone without a permit is discovered engaging in activities for which a Section 404 permit is required, the Corps will issue a cease and desist order. Among the options the person faces is to seek an *after-the-fact* permit, which is subject to the full public interest review process. In addition, the Corps regulations provide:

* * *

(e) After-the-fact permit applications. (1) Following the completion of any required initial corrective measures, the district engineer will accept an after-the-fact permit application unless he determines that one of the exceptions listed in subparagraphs i-iv below is applicable. Applications for after-the-fact permits will be processed in accordance with the applicable procedures in 33 C.F.R. Parts 320-325. * * *

33 C.F.R. § 326.3(e).

Should the Corps evaluate the permit application first, decide whether it would grant the permit and upon what conditions, and then order those corrective measures that would be consistent with the proposed permit? Isn't there a danger of economic waste by doing it the other way?

Note on the Relationship Between the EPA and the Corps

When Congress enacted the FWPCA (CWA) in 1972, it did something rather unique. In Section 404, Congress divided the authority over Section 404 matters between the EPA and the Corps. Reread Section 404 carefully and make an outline of the division of authority between the EPA and the Corps.

Although neither the Corps nor the EPA is satisfied with their Section 404 relationship, the Corps is perhaps the most troubled by it. One Corps official, speaking at a 1988 ELI-ABA conference on Section 404, said that Section 404 is broken and it would not be fixed until one of three things happened: (1) Congress amends Section 404 to give the Corps exclusive Section 404 authority, (2) Congress amends Section 404 to give the EPA exclusive authority, or (3) the Corps accepts, without objection, all EPA's interpretations of Section 404, something the Corps is unwilling to do absent a direct statutory mandate by Congress. Despite agency objections to the administrative structure of Section 404 and the occasional interagency warfare, Congress has not seen fit to amend the section to give exclusive authority to either the EPA or the Corps or to adjust the existing statutory relationship between the two. See GOA, Wetlands: Corps of Engineers Administration of the Section 404 Program (July 1988).

The EPA sees itself as having an obligation to protect the environment from degradation; the Corps sees its role as determining whether, after consideration of all the relevant factors, the proposed project, for which a permit is requested, is in the "public interest." The EPA-Corps philosophical disagreement is most pronounced on the questions of "no practicable alternative" and "mitigation" measures. Neither entity will readily give ground on these issues, issues that will be explored in the following set of materials starting with the EPA Guidelines.

"No Practicable Alternatives," "Water Dependency," and "Mitigation"

EPA GUIDELINES

Subpart B -- Compliance with the Guidelines

40 C.F.R. § 230.10. Restrictions on discharge.

Note. -- Because other laws may apply to particular discharges and because the Corps of Engineers or State 404 agency may have additional procedural and substantive requirements, a discharge complying with the requirement of these Guidelines will not automatically receive a permit.

Although all requirements in § 230.10 must be met, the compliance evaluation procedures will vary to reflect the seriousness of the potential for adverse impacts on the aquatic ecosystems posed by specific dredged or fill material discharge activities.

(a) Except as provided under Section 404(b)(2), no discharge of dredged or fill material shall be permitted if there is a practicable alternative to the proposed discharge which would have less adverse impact on the aquatic ecosystem, so long as the alternative does not have other significant adverse environmental consequences.

(1) For the purpose of this requirement, practicable alternatives include, but are not limited to:

(i) Activities which do not involve a discharge of dredged or fill

material into the waters of the United States or ocean waters;
(ii) Discharges of dredged or fill material at other locations in waters of the United States or ocean waters;

(2) An alternative is practicable if it is available and capable of being done after taking into consideration cost, existing technology, and logistics in light of overall project purposes.   If it is otherwise a practicable alternative, an area not presently owned by the applicant which could reasonably be obtained, utilized, expanded or managed in order to fulfill the basic purpose of the proposed activity may be considered.

(3) Where the activity associated with a discharge which is proposed for a special aquatic site (as defined in Subpart E)[10] does not require access or proximity to or siting within the special aquatic site in question to fulfill its basic purpose (i.e., is not "water dependent"), practicable alternatives that do not involve special aquatic sites are presumed to be available, unless clearly demonstrated otherwise. In addition, where a discharge is proposed for a special aquatic site, all practicable alternatives to the proposed discharge which do not involve a discharge into a special aquatic site are presumed to have less adverse impact on the aquatic ecosystem, unless clearly demonstrated otherwise.

* * *

(c) Except as provided under Section 404(b)(2), no discharge of dredged or fill material shall be permitted which will cause or contribute to significant degradation of the waters of the United States. * * * Under these Guidelines, effects contributing to significant degradation considered individually or collectively, include:

(1) Significantly adverse effects of the discharge of pollutants on human health or welfare, including but not limited to effects on municipal water supplies, plankton, fish, shellfish, wildlife, and special aquatic sites;

(2) Significantly adverse effects of the discharge of pollutants on life stages of aquatic life and other wildlife dependent on aquatic ecosystems, including the transfer, concentration, and spread of pollutants or their by-products outside of the disposal site through biological, physical, and chemical processes;

(3) Significantly adverse effects of the discharge of pollutants on

---

[10] Special aquatic sites includes wetlands, coral reefs, mud flats, vegetated shallows, and sanctuaries and refuges. 40 C.F.R. § 230.40, et seq. (1992).

aquatic ecosystem diversity, productivity, and stability.   Such effects may include, but are not limited to, loss of fish and wildlife habitat or loss of the capacity of a wetland to assimilate nutrients, purify water, or reduce wave energy; or

(4) Significantly adverse effects of discharge of pollutants on recreational, aesthetic, and economic values.

(d)   Except as provided under Section 404(b)(2), no discharge of dredged or fill material shall be permitted unless appropriate and practicable steps have been taken which will minimize potential adverse impacts of the discharge on the aquatic ecosystem. Subpart H identifies such possible steps.

U.S. ARMY CORPS OF ENGINEERS REGULATIONS

33 C.F.R. § 320.4.

* * *

(r) Mitigation.[11] (1) Mitigation is an important aspect of the review and balancing process on many Department of the Army permit applications.   Consideration of mitigation will occur throughout the permit application review process and includes avoiding, minimizing, rectifying, reducing, or compensating for resource losses. Losses will be avoided to the extent practicable. Compensation may occur on-site or at an off-site location. * * *

(2) All compensatory mitigation will be for significant resource losses which are specifically identifiable, reasonably likely to occur, and of importance to the human or aquatic environment. Also, all mitigation will be directly related to the impacts of the proposal, appropriate to the scope and degree of those impacts, and reasonably enforceable.* * *

PERMIT ELEVATION: PLANTATION LANDING RESORT, INC.

Plantation Landing Resort, Inc. filed a permit application seeking a Corps permit.   In its application, it described its project as a fully integrated, contiguous, waterfront recreational resort complex consisting of 339 condominium dwellings, 398 townhouse units, a

---

[11] The 1990 Memorandum Of Agreement Between the Environmental Protection Agency and the Department of Army Concerning the Determination of Mitigation Under the Clean Water Act Section 404(b)(1) Guidelines defines mitigation to include minimization and compensatory mitigation. According to the memorandum, the Corps must first determine "that potential impacts have been avoided to the maximum extent appropriate and practicable; remaining unavoidable impacts will then be mitigated to the extent appropriate and practicable by requiring steps to minimize impacts and, finally, compensate for aquatic resource values."

motel, a restaurant, a cafe, a bar, a diving and fishing shop, a convenience store, and a marina. The application sought permission to fill or otherwise alter 22 acres of tidal marsh and 37 acres of shallow bay bottom.   The EPA and the National Marine Fisheries Service (NMFS), Department of Commerce, opposed the granting of the permit on the grounds that there were "practicable alternatives" to the proposed alteration of wetlands and bay bottom.   Despite these objections, after the public interest review the New Orleans District (NOD) Engineer decided to grant the requested permit.   The EPA and the Department of Commerce then sought to have the case elevated to the Corps' headquarters (HQUSACE) for a national policy level review of the issue of practicable alternatives.   The request for elevation was granted.   The Director of Civil Works, Army Corps of Engineers, reviewed the NOD permit decision and sent the following letter to NOD.

DEPARTMENT OF THE ARMY
U.S. Army Corps of Engineers
WASHINGTON, DC 20134-1000

    21 APR 1989

FOR: Commander, U.S. Army Engineer District, New Orleans

SUBJECT: Permit Elevation, Plantation Landing Resort, Inc.

* * *

    Please re-evaluate the subject permit case in light of the guidance provided in the attachment, and take action accordingly.

FOR THE COMMANDER

Attachment   Patrick J. Kelly
                                                    Brigadier General
                                                    Director of Civil Works

* * *

6.   The 404(b)(1) analysis for the Plantation Landing Resort, Inc., application, even when read in conjunction with the Statement of Findings (SOF) and the Environmental Assessment (EA), does not deal with the issues of practicable alternatives and water dependency in a satisfactory manner.* * *

7.   One significant problem in the NOD's approach to the 404(b)(1) review is found in the following, which is the only statement in NOD's 404(b)(1) evaluation document presenting a project-specific reference to the Plantation Landing case with respect to the practicable alternative

requirement of the Guidelines:

> Several less environmentally damaging alternatives were identified in the Environmental Assessment. The applicant stated and supplied information indicating that these alternatives would not be practicable in light of his overall project purposes. Recent guidance from LMVD[12] states that the applicant is the authoritative source of information regarding practicability determinations, therefore no less environmentally damaging practicable alternatives are available. (NOD's "Evaluation of Section 404(b)(1) Guidelines," Attachment 1, Paragraph 1.a.)

This statement appears to allow the applicant to determine whether practicable alternatives exist to his project. Emphatically, that is not an acceptable approach for conducting the alternatives review under the 404(b)(1) Guidelines. *The Corps is responsible for controlling every aspect of the 404(b)(1) analysis.* While the Corps should consider the views of the applicant regarding his project's purpose and the existence (or lack of) practicable alternatives, the Corps must determine and evaluate these matters itself, with no control or direction from the applicant, and without undue deference to the applicant's wishes.

* * *

9. A reading of the entire record indicates that NOD accepted the applicant's assertion that the project *as proposed* must be accepted by the Corps as the basis for the 404(b)(1) Guidelines practicability analysis. The applicant proposed a *fully-integrated, waterfront, contiguous* water-oriented recreational complex, in the form the applicant proposed. Consequently, NOD apparently presumed that no alternative site could be considered if it could not support in one, contiguous waterfront location the same sort of fully integrated recreational complex that the applicant proposed to build. The EA addresses this point specifically, as follows:

> There appear to be alternative sites for the placement of each component of the project. However, alternate sites are not preferable by the applicant because he owns the project site and wishes to realize commercial values from it. Real estate investigations revealed that Grand Isle at present does not offer a less damaging alternative site which satisfies the applicant's purpose and need as proposed on his own property. (EA at pages 89-90)

---

[12] Lower Mississippi Valley Division.

* * *

11. The effect of NOD's deferring to and accepting the applicant's definition of the basic purpose of his project as a *contiguous, fully integrated*, and entirely *waterfront* resort complex *in the form the applicant had proposed* was to ensure that no practicable alternative could exist. Nevertheless, the administrative record nowhere provides any rationale for why the applicant's proposed complex had to be "contiguous" or "fully integrated" or why all features of it had to be "waterfront." * * *

12. When an applicant proposes to build a development consisting of various component parts, and proposes that all those component parts be located on one contiguous tract of land (including waters of the United States), a question of fact arises: i.e., *whether all component parts, or some combination of them, or none, really must be built, or must be built in one contiguous block, for the project to be viable.* The applicant's view on that question of fact should be considered by the Corps, but the Corps must determine (and appropriately document its determination) whether in fact some component parts of the project (e.g., those proposed to be built in waters of the United States) could be dropped from the development altogether, or reconfigured or reduced in scope, to minimize or avoid adverse impacts on waters of the United States. * * *   [T]he Corps must not presume that the Plantation Landing Resort necessarily needs to be built in one contiguous tract of land, or that it must be "fully integrated," or that all components of it must be "waterfront," or otherwise that the project must be built in the form or configuration proposed by the applicant. Once again, the applicant bears the burden of proof for all the tests of 40 CFR 320.10 to demonstrate to the Corps that his project, or any part of it, should be built in the waters of the United States. * * *

15. In addition, the LMVD transmittal letter of 11 March 1987 contains the following statement:

> * * * minimization of cost is a legitimate factor in determining applicant's purpose and the purpose of the project.

While the applicant's wish to minimize his costs is obviously a factor which the Corps can consider, that factor alone must not be allowed to control or unduly influence the Corps' definition of project purpose or "practicable alternative," or any other part of the 404(b)(1) evaluation. * * *   This is an important point, because often wetland property may be less expensive to a developer than comparably situated upland property. The Guidelines obviously are not designed to facilitate a shift of development activities from uplands to wetlands, so the fact that an applicant can sometimes reduce his costs by developing wetland property is not a factor which can be used to justify permit issuance under the Guidelines. On the other hand, the 404(b)(1) Guidelines do address the factor of cost to an applicant in the concept of the "practicability" of alternatives, defined at 40 CFR 230.10(a)(2). As the Guidelines' preamble states on this point, "If an alleged alternative is unreasonably expensive to the applicant, the alternative is not "'practicable'." (45 Fed. Reg. at page 85343, Dec. 24, 1980)

16. The 404(b)(1) Guidelines define the concept of practicable alternative. * * *   This provision indicates that a site not presently owned by the applicant but which could be obtained, utilized, etc., to fulfill the basic purpose of the proposed activity qualifies as a practicable alternative. Consequently, the definition of "basic purpose" and "overall project purposes" is central to proper interpretation and implementation of the Guidelines' "practicable alternative" test. Moreover, part of the "practicable alternative" test of 40 CFR 230.10(a) is the "water dependency" provision, quoted in paragraph 4, supra, which also is based upon the concept of a project's "basic purpose." That is, the water dependency test states that a practicable alternative is presumed to exist for any proposed activity which does not have to be cited within or require access or proximity to water to fulfill its basic purpose (thus a 404 permit could not be issued unless the presumption is rebutted). (40 CFR 230.10(a)(3)).

17. Acceptance of the applicant's proposal to build a *fully-integrated, contiguous, waterfront* recreational resort complex led NOD to conclude that:

> "* * * the Corps considers the project to be water dependent in light of the applicant's purpose" (SOF, page 7).

This determination had the effect of finding that 339 condominium dwellings, 398 townhouse units, a motel, a restaurant, a cafe, a bar, a diving and fishing shop, and a convenience store, were all "water dependent," merely because they were said to be "integrated" with and "contiguous" to marina facilities. This approach is unacceptable, and contrary to Corps policy since 1976. If the approach used by NOD in the instant case were to gain general acceptance, then proponents of virtually any and all forms of development in wetlands could declare their proposals "water dependent" by proposing to "integrate" them with and to build them "contiguous" to a marina, or simply by adding the expression "waterfront" as a prefix to words such as "home," "motel," "restaurant," "bar," etc. The approach used by NOD in the instant case would render completely meaningless the water dependency provision of the Guidelines.

18. NOD's basis for declaring all aspects of the Plantation Landing Resort proposal to be water dependent was the following:

Individually most components comprising the proposed recreational complex are not dependent upon water to function. However, waterfront availability of proposed facilities is demanded by the public as clearly demonstrated by the success of similar waterfront facilities in adjoining gulf coastal states. Also local demand for waterfront housing is evident by the proposed expansion of Pirates Cove on Grand Isle and the presently ongoing installation of Point Fourchon at Fourchon. (EA at page 85).

One of the primary reasons why regulation of the filling of wetlands is an important Corps environmental mission is precisely because a strong economic incentive (i.e., "demand") exists to fill in many coastal wetlands for housing developments, condominium resorts, restaurants, etc. The fact that "demand" exists for the filling in of wetlands for waterfront development, is irrelevant to the question of whether any proposed development in a special aquatic site is water dependent under the 404(b)(1) Guidelines. Waterfront development can take place without the filling in of special aquatic sites.* * *

20. It follows that the "basic purpose" of each component element of the proposed Plantation Landing Resort must be analyzed in terms of its actual, non-water-dependent function. The basic purpose of the condominium housing is housing (i.e., shelter); the basic purpose of the restaurant is to feed people; etc. The Corps will *not* conclude that housing, restaurants, cafes, bars, retail facilities, or convenience stores are water dependent; they are essentially non-water-dependent activities. Moreover, they do not gain the status of water-dependent activities merely because the applicant proposes to "integrate" them with a marina, or proposes that any of these non-water-dependent facilities should be "waterfront" or built on waterfront land. The concepts of "integration," "contiguity," and "waterfront" must not be used to defeat the purpose of the "water dependency" and "practicable alternatives" provisions of the Guidelines, nor to preclude the existence of practicable alternatives.

* * *

24. Of course, notwithstanding all of the above, in a particular, given case (which might or might not be the Plantation Landing Resort application) the Corps public interest review and the 404(b)(1) Guidelines may allow the District Engineer to grant a permit for the filling of wetlands, even for a non-water-dependent activity. This would occur only if the applicant has clearly rebutted the presumptions against filling wetlands found at 40 CFR 230.10, and has clearly rebutted the presumptions of 230.10(a) with convincing evidence that no practicable alternative exists which would preclude his proposed fill. In such a circumstance the mitigation requirements of 40 CFR 230.10(b), (c), and (d) come into play. * * *

Notes and Questions

1.   If EPA or FWS disagree with a Corps' district engineer's decision on a permit application, those agencies can seek review of the decision by higher authorities within the Army. The procedure and criteria for seeking such review are set forth in memoranda of agreement (MOAs) between the Corps, EPA, and FWS.   See, e.g.,Memorandum of Agreement Between the Army and EPA Concerning Section 404(q) of the Clean Water Act (August 11, 1992). (The procedure for elevation of either policy issues or individual permit decisions is addressed in the memorandum). For a more detailed discussion of the process, see generally W. Want, Law of Wetlands Regulation § 6.11 (1998).

2.   Whether a project is "water dependent" and whether "practicable alternatives" exist is intrinsically linked to the way in which the "basic purpose" of a project or its components is characterized and the definition of the "overall project purposes." *Plantation Landing Resort, Inc.* discusses in detail the concept of *basic purpose*. The concept of *overall project purpose* and its role in the permit decision process was addressed in the 1991 *Permit Elevation: Twisted Oaks Joint Venture*.

In *Twisted Oaks*, the district engineer characterized the overall project purpose as "to provide an upscale, water orientated, residential development having water related recreational amenities to allow the applicant to realize a profit on its investment." On elevation, with one change, the Corps accepted the district engineer's characterization of the project. The language relating to the applicant's realization of a profit on its investment was deemed inappropriate because it "suggests that judgments of practicality will incorporate profitability circumstances too specific to the particular applicant." The acceptable characterization was "to provide a *viable*, upscale, water orientated, residential development having water related amenities." Although the definition included a water dependent element, that did not make the overall project purpose "water dependent." A practical alternatives analysis was required, but the search for alternatives was for those which would satisfy the acceptable overall project purpose.

Recently, in *Permit Elevation: Naples Reserve Golf Club, Collier County Florida*, 16 January 2001, Corps stated that

> the overall project purpose must not be so specific that it precludes any reasonable possibility of other sites being potentially practicable to the applicant * * * The ideal overall project purpose statement would have been something like: "To construct a viable mid-priced housing development, with two associated regulation golf courses in the Collier County, Florida area." * * *

* * * it would be inappropriate for the Corps to attempt to decide whether the market in the area supported one or two golf courses. That is for the applicant to decide. It would have been inappropriate for the applicant to demand a certain layout for its golf course and for every dwelling on the project. * * *

Id. at 5-6. Although the Corps will not defer to the applicant's statement of the overall project purpose, by proposing an integrated project that includes water related elements, the applicant can significantly influence the shape of the alternatives analysis that will be undertaken.

Interestingly, the EPA has a different reading of its 404(b)(1) guidelines. According to the EPA.

The Section 404(b)(1) Guidelines use the terms "basic purpose" and "overall project purposes" interchangeably * * * the two terms are *not intended to have distinct meanings* * * * [W]e * * * read both phrases to have the same meaning, which is a generic, basic purpose test.

Two Forks Dam: Final Determination of the U.S. EPA's Asst. Adm'r for Water Pursuant to § 404(c) of the Clean Water Act Concerning the Two Forks Water Supply Impoundments, Jefferson & Douglas Counties Colo., Nov. 23, 1990. The divergent views of the EPA and the Corps remain unreconciled.

3. At the heart of the permit review procedure is the "no practicable alternatives" test. If a project is not "water dependent," the EPA regulation creates a presumption that there exists a practicable alternative that avoids destruction or modification of wetlands.

The first question then is when is a project "water dependent?" Significant deposits of phosphate are located in the coastal regions of North Carolina and Florida. Many of these mineral deposits are found twenty or more feet under tidal and non-tidal navigable waters and wetlands. Portions of these waters and wetlands are important fish habitat. In order to recover the phosphate the overburden must be removed, which in the case of wetlands would be all of the wetland vegetation. Is phosphate mining in this setting a water dependent activity?

4. If a project is not water dependent, then the applicant must demonstrate there is "no practicable alternative" to what is being proposed. In order to be a "practicable alternative" does the alternative have to satisfy all the specifics of the applicant's proposal? In determining the existence of "practicable alternatives," are only sites that are available at the time of filing of the permit application to be considered?

In Bersani v. United States Environmental Protection Agency, 674 F. Supp. 405 (N.D.N.Y. 1987), aff'd sub. nom., Bersani v. Robichaud, 850 F.2d 36 (2d Cir. 1988), the plaintiff argued that "available" means "presently available."

Under this interpretation, the permitting authority would be required to limit its consideration of the alternative sites to those sites which are available to the applicant *at the time the agency makes its decision on the permit application*. Thus, Pyramid claims that the EPA engaged in impermissible "backdating" when it decided that the availability determination should be made at the time the applicant "entered the market," "began its investigation," or "comprehensively evaluated the area." Pyramid argues that this interpretation gives the EPA unlimited power to block proposals merely because some alternative was available in the past.

The EPA counters this argument by noting that Pyramid's interpretation of the regulations undercuts the purpose underlying the practicable alternatives test and that it is reasonable and consistent to expect applicants planning non-water dependent projects to demonstrate that construction on uplands was considered before the use of wetlands was contemplated. Plaintiffs, however, argue that the regulations do not impose any pre-application obligation on the applicant to investigate the use of uplands, rather, they maintain that the burden is on the Corps to determine whether an alternative "is available."

Pyramid also bases its conclusion on the language of the regulation itself which states that "an alternative is practicable if it is available." The EPA contends that the term "is available" can refer to any time period in which the guidelines are applied. The Final Determination focused on the point in time when the applicant actually examined the alternatives. This interpretation guards against manipulation by developers.

* * *

[T]he court finds that the EPA's interpretation of the regulations was reasonable.

* * *

Id at. 418.

5. In 1993, the EPA and the Corps issued a memorandum providing guidance as to the role of cost considerations in evaluating whether an alternative is practicable. The memorandum states:

a. Analysis Associated with Minor Impacts

The Guidelines do not contemplate that the same intensity of analysis will be required for all types of projects but instead envision a correlation between the scope of the evaluation and the potential extent of adverse impacts upon the aquatic environment * * * the level of analysis required may vary with the nature and complexity of each individual case:

* * *

b. Relationship between the Scope of Analysis and the Scope/Cost of the Proposed Project

the determination of what constitutes an unreasonable expense should generally consider whether the projected cost is substantially greater than the costs normally associated with the particular type of project. * * * [Also] to the extent that individual homeowners and small businesses may typically be associated with small projects with minor impacts, the nature of the applicant may * * * be a relevant consideration in determining what constitutes a practicable alternative. * * *

EPA/U.S. Department of Army, Memorandum To The Field: Appropriate Level Of Analysis Required For Evaluating Compliance With The Section 404(b)(1) Guidelines Alternatives Requirements (August 1993).

6.   If a project is indeed water dependent, should there still be an investigation of practicable alternatives to the proposed project? If so, who has the burden of establishing the existence of such alternatives? In a 1992 regulatory guidance letter the Corps stated that non-water dependent activities are not subject to the rebuttable presumptions contained in 40 C.F.R. § 230.10(a)(3), but must be consistent with the EPA guidelines. To be consistent "proposed discharge must be the least environmentally damaging practicable alternative." Army Corps of Engineers, Regulatory Guidance Letter No. 92-2, Water Dependency and Cranberry Production (26 June 1992).

7.   In addition to the intra-agency oversight provided by the Corps' elevation procedure, interagency oversight also exists. The EPA has the power to veto the issuance of a Section 404 permit by the Corps. See CWA Section 404(c), 33 U.S.C. § 1344(c). However, considerations of the need for interagency co-operation, the practical necessity of relying on the Corps' district and field personnel to make initial determinations and permit decisions, and the EPA's own limited resources, as a practical matter, means that it rarely exercises the power. See, e.g., GAO, Wetlands: The Corps of Engineers' Administration of the Section 404 Program 4, 48, 51 (July 28, 1988). Nonetheless, veto authority does

provide the EPA with the ability to significantly shape the implementation of the Section 404 program.

MITIGATION POLICY

Prior to 1989, the Corps' policy was that mitigation could be used to satisfy the public interest test and other requirements for a Section 404 permit. The EPA, on the other hand, contended that mitigation could only be considered as the last step in evaluation of a permit application. According to the EPA, a sequencing approach must be used. This approach requires the Corps to first determine that potential adverse impacts have been avoided to the maximum extent practicable. Second, they must determine that any unavoidable impacts are minimized. And, third, compensatory mitigation must be required for any unavoidable losses of special aquatic sites. In a 1989 Memorandum of Agreement, the Corps agreed to follow the EPA sequencing approach. The agreement also attempted to clarify and give general guidance regarding the level of mitigation necessary to demonstrate compliance with the Section 404(b)(1) guidelines. The agreement stressed that the level of mitigation deemed "appropriate" is based solely on the values and functions of the wetlands impacted. Compensatory mitigation should provide, at a minimum, one-for-one replacement. In the absence of more definitive information on the functions and values of specific wetlands sites, a minimum of one-to-one acreage replacement may be used as a reasonable surrogate for no net loss of functions and values. However, this ratio may be greater where the value of the area impacted is demonstrably high and the replacement wetlands are of lower functional value or where the likelihood of success of the mitigation project is low. Conversely, the ratio may be less than one-to-one for areas where the functional value of the area impacted is demonstrably low and the likelihood of success associated with the mitigation proposal is high. For projects involving mitigation plans with high levels of scientific uncertainty, long-term monitoring, reporting, and potential remedial action should be required. See Memorandum of Agreement Between the Environmental Protection Agency and the Department of the Army Concerning Mitigation Under the Clean Water Act Section 404(b)(1) Guidelines (1990).

1. Does a "mitigation policy" reflect a basic value judgment that development must be allowed to go forward? If so, is the only real issue how best to compensate for the loss or adverse impact upon public resources?

2. If compensatory mitigation is permitted, should it be "in kind" or "out of kind"? What factors would be relevant in that decision? Should it be "off-site" or "on-site"? What factors would be relevant?

3. To what extent should, or can, the government rely upon self-

monitoring of mitigation projects by permittees? Would the filing of mitigation progress reports be beneficial? Should citizen groups be allowed to sue to enforce mitigation agreements that were not being observed by permittees? Once the project is finished and the development sold to a third party, who is responsible for performance of the mitigation agreement? Would a requirement of satisfactorily completing the mitigation project run with the land (development project)? If the original developer runs into financial difficulties, would the mitigation agreement be enforceable against a purchaser of the project? Is it realistic to expect developers to manage mitigation wetlands for long periods of time? Should enforceable contracts and performance bonds be conditions for the issuance of the permit? Should a "wetland maintenance fund" be established?

4. If it takes decades before mitigation wetlands can achieve the complexity of structure and function of natural wetlands, is replacement on a one-to-one basis a sound policy? If mitigation is permitted, should mitigation policy require two acres of mitigation wetlands for each acre of destroyed wetlands? This is the general policy expressed in the New Jersey Administrative Code, N.J. Admin. Code tit. 7, § 7E-1.6 (1987).

5. In January 1989, the EPA announced a "no net loss" wetlands policy.[13] What should be the criteria for "no net loss"? How do you evaluate a wetland's values and determine its functions? Can any evaluation be anything more than a very crude estimate of the wetland's actual value? For a discussion of these issues, see, e.g., National Research Council, Wetlands: characteristics and boundaries 215-26 (1995); see also, National Research Council, Compensating for Wetlands Losses Under the Clean Water Act, 108-14 (pre-publication copy 2001).

6. The term "mitigation" can be used to refer to (1) methods of reducing potential harm to or destruction of wetlands and (2) ways of repairing, restoring, or compensating for damage to wetlands. Included with mitigation are "restoration" -- repairing or re-establishing an existing wetlands area, "enhancement" -- improving the quality of an existing wetlands area to make it more suitable for additional species, and "creation" -- establishing wetlands where none existed before.

The central issue is whether the government should allow the continued destruction of existing wetlands conditioned upon promises or guarantees that other wetlands will be restored or new wetlands created. Both restoration and creation rest upon imperfect science and raise institutional problems. See, e.g. J. Kusler and H. Groman, Mitigation: An Introduction, National Wetlands Newsletter 2-3 (Sept-Oct

---

[13] As of January 2002, "no net loss" policy is that the Corps will seek to achieve a 1:1 ratio for the whole 404 program, and not necessarily on an individual project basis. See, 67 Fed. Reg., 2020, 2064, 2092-93 (January 15, 2002).

1986).

7. When a Section 404 permittee alters or destroys wetlands and compensation is required, mitigation banks offer one means of providing compensation. Mitigation banks are sites at which a public or private entity has created, enhanced, restored or preserved wetlands. These sites would constitute wetland credits that could be used to satisfy the permittee's compensation requirement. Such sites could be owned and operated by the permittee itself or some other public or private entity. In the later situation, a permittee would purchase the necessary credits from the mitigation bank. Such banks are referred to as entrepreneurial banks.

Since 1992, the number of mitigation banks has increased dramatically. As of July 31, 1992, there were only 46 mitigation banks in the United States. Seventy-five percent of the banks were government owned and operated and provided wetland compensation for state highway construction, port facilities, or other public works projects. Only one was an entrepreneurial bank selling credits for general sale, with the remainder of the privately owned banks controlled by developers to provide compensation associated with their own projects. By 2002, there were approximately 230 federally approved mitigation banks, some of which were still under construction, and several hundred additional proposed banks. Sixty of the existing banks were entrepreneurial. Mitigation credit costs vary greatly, ranging from $7,500 to $60,000 per acre depending on the type of project, local conditions and other factors. Although the costs per acre are high, generally it is less than the cost of similar mitigation undertaken by individual landowners. See EPA's fact sheet distributed at November 17, 1997 wetlands workshop. For an extensive discussion of the mitigation banking, see L. Marsh et. al. (Eds), Mitigation Banking: theory and practice (1996); ELI, Wetland Mitigation Banking (1993).

8.   Should the federal government encourage the use of mitigation banks?   What public policy and regulatory issues does the encouragement of such projects raise? See ELI, Wetland Mitigation Banking (1993); see also James McElfish, Jr. and Sara Nicholas, "Structure and Experience of Wetland Mitigation Banks," 20-27 in Mitigation Banking: theory and practice (1996). In 1995, the Section 404 regulatory agencies issued federal guidance for mitigation banks, see Federal Guidance for the Establishment, Use, and Operation of Mitigation Banks, 60 Fed. Reg. 58605 (Nov. 28, 1995).

9. Another, more recent mitigation option being promoted by wetlands-protection agencies is the "in-lieu-fee." Under this option, the developer simply writes a check, with the money being deposited in the account of a non-profit natural resources organization or a government agency. The fund established is then to be used for environmental

purposes. This is a very desirable option for a developer since once the check is written, the developer no longer has any mitigation responsibilities. "In-lieu-fee" programs raise serious policy questions: Are the "fees" sufficient to cover actual costs of replacing the wetlands that will be lost? Are "in-lieu-fees" used to purchase and preserve existing wetlands and not for restoration or replacement efforts? For a comprehensive discussion of "in-lieu-fees" issues, see R. Gardner, "Money For Nothing: The Rise Of Wetlands Fee Mitigation, 19 Va. Envir. L. J. 1 (2000). In 2000 the EPA, Corps, and FWS issued a guidance for in-lieu fee arrangements. Federal Guidance on the Use of In-Lieu Fee Arrangements for Compensatory Mitigation Under Section 404 of the Clean Water Act and Section 10 of the Rivers and Harbors Act, 65 Fed. Reg. 66914 (November 7, 2000). The guidance authorizes the use of in-lieu-fee agreements under certain conditions. It states that the funds collected should be used for replacing wetlands functions and values and not to finance non-mitigation programs and priorities. Also, the funds should ensure a minimum of one-for-one acreage replacement. Simple purchase and preservation of existing wetlands will not satisfy compensatory mitigation requirements except in extraordinary circumstances. Under this guidance, in-lieu-fee arrangements closely resemble mitigation banking compensation.

10. Finally, what is really important is how well the current wetlands compensatory mitigation policy is working. A recent study conducted at the request of EPA by a committee formed by the National Research Council reached the following conclusions:

4. It appears that the performance standards sought in compensatory mitigation have not often be well defined.

5. * * *

4. The literature and testimony provided to the committee indicate that the national goal of "no net loss" for permitted wetlands conversions is not being met.

* * *

Permit followup is sparse, or too infrequent * * * Compliance monitoring is commonly known to be non-existent after 5 years * * *

National Research Council, Compensating for Wetlands Losses Under the Clean Water Act, 102 (pre-publication copy 2001).

(6.) Judicial Review of Corps Permit Decisions

When a Corps permit decision is challenged, the scope of review is not as circumscribed as when a court is reviewing an administrative decision made under NEPA. In Sierra Club v. United States Army Corps of Engineers, 772 F.2d 1043, 1051 (2nd Cir. 1985), the Second Circuit explained this important distinction as follows:

III. SCOPE OF REVIEW

Since judicial review is not specifically provided for under either NEPA or the Clean Water Act, review is under the Administrative Procedure Act, 5 U.S.C. § 706. Under that law challenged agency action must be set aside if found to be "arbitrary, capricious, an abuse of discretion, or otherwise not in accordance with law." 5 U.S.C. § 706(2)(A).

A. Review Under NEPA

When reviewing an administrative decision made under NEPA, the purpose is to ensure that the agency has considered the environmental consequences of its proposed action. Strycker's Bay Neighborhood Council v. Karlen, 444 U.S. 223, 227 (1980). To conform with NEPA, a reviewing court need only find that the agency considered the environmental consequences of its proposed actions. An agency making a decision under this statute does not have to accord environmental concerns any more weight in the decision making process than other appropriate concerns. If an agency decides that the economic or social benefits of a project outweigh its environmental costs, its choice must be affirmed so long as the procedural requirements of NEPA were followed, that is, environmental consequences were considered. Id. at 227.

In weighing whether an agency has met NEPA's expressed objectives the test is not whether the district court, this Court or even the Supreme Court would have reached the decision under review had we been decision makers within the agency. Rather, the judicial role is relegated to affirming the agency's decision so long as a rational basis is presented for the decision reached. Bowman Transp. Inc. v. Arkansas-Best Freight Sys., Inc., 419 U.S. 281, 290 (1974). Consistent with our concept of federalism, a reviewing court's scope is so limited because it may not "interject itself within the area of the discretion of the executive as to the choice of the action to be taken." Kleppe v. Sierra Club, 427 U.S. 390, 410 n.21 (1976).

B. Review Under the Clean Water Act

The purpose of judicial review under the Clean Water Act differs slightly because of its enabling statute. Like NEPA, the Clean Water Act requires that an environmental concern -- here the impact on the aquatic environment -- be considered at an early enough stage in the policymaking process to affect the agency decision. But the Clean

Water Act provides for a more intrusive power of review, one whose purpose is to prohibit agency action whenever certain environmental impact thresholds are met. Instead of simply insisting procedurally that the agency weigh environmental concerns, the Clean Water Act specifically prohibits an agency from sanctioning a project that it finds will have a significant adverse impact on the marine environment. Therefore, when an agency approves a project that the record before a reviewing court reveals will have a significant adverse impact on marine wildlife, the agency determination must be reversed.

C. Review In General

* * *

Normally, an agency's action is held to be arbitrary and capricious when it relies on factors Congress did not want considered, or utterly fails to analyze an important aspect of the problem, or offers an explanation contrary to the evidence before it, or its explanation -- as is apt here -- is so implausible that it cannot be ascribed to differing views or agency expertise. See Motor Vehicles Mfrs. Ass'n. v. State Farm Mut., 463 U.S. 29, 43 (1983). While a reviewing court may not supply the basis for the agency's decision -- lest it interfere with matters entrusted to the executive branch -- it will uphold a decision of less than ideal clarity if the "path which [the agency] followed can be discerned." Colorado Interstate Gas Co. v. FPC, 324 U.S. 581, 595 (1945). See also SEC v. Chenery Corp., 332 U.S. 194, 196 (1947). * * *

In deciding whether economic or social benefits outweigh the environmental costs, what weight does the agency assign to each? Isn't the arbitrary and capricious standard the only one a court could possibly use since it is almost impossible to weigh intangibles such as social costs and environmental costs?

A number of statutes other than CWA Section 404 and NEPA may be relevant to the decision to grant or deny a Section 404 permit. See 33 C.F.R. § 320.3.

D. PROCEDURES AND REMEDIES FOR VIOLATIONS OF THE RIVERS AND HARBORS ACT OF 1899 AND SECTION 404

By an agreement allocating enforcement responsibilities, the EPA is the lead agency for violations involving unpermitted discharges, while the Corps acts as the lead enforcement agency for all violations of Corps issued permits. A lead agency's decision with regard to any issue in a particular case is final for that case. See Memorandum of Agreement Between Department of the Army and the Environmental Protection Agency Concerning Federal Enforcement of the Section 404 Program of the Clean Water Act (January 17, 1989). Does this arrangement diminish or modify the EPA's statutory authority?

(1.) Cease and Desist Letters

Depending on the nature of the alleged violation,the first step in a Section 404 enforcement proceeding will be either an EPA administrative compliance order,[14] 33 U.S.C. § 1319(a)(3), or a cease and desist letter sent by the Corps to the alleged violator, 33 U.S.C. § 1344(s). In neither case is either considered to be final agency action subject to judicial review. See, e.g. Fiscella and Fiscella v. United States, 717 F. Supp. 1143 (E.D. Va. 1989; Southern Pines Assoc. v. United States, 20 Envtl. L. Rep. 20,003 (E.D. Va. 1989), aff'd, 912 F.2d 713 (4th Cir. 1990). Although, judicial review must await the initiation of government enforcement proceedings, violators of such directives are subject to greater administrative fines and vulnerable to civil and criminal sanctions.

(2.) Administrative Penalties

Under the CWA , the agencies may impose administrative penalties for violations. Most enforcement authority is vested in the EPA, which may impose penalties for unpermitted violations of the CWA. 33 U.S.C. § 1319(g). The Corps authority is limited to penalizing violations of Corps orders or of permit conditions. 33 U.S.C. § 1344 (s). The amount of the EPA administrative penalty that may be imposed depends on whether the violation is a Class I or Class II violation. Penalties for Class I violations may not exceed $10,000 per violation, and the maximum penalty may not exceed $25,000. 33 U.S.C. § 1319 (g)(2)(A). Class II violations, which are available for more serious violations, "may not exceed $10,000 per day for each day during which the violation continues," with the maximum penalty not to exceed $125,000. 33 U.S.C. § 1319(g)(2)(B). For violations of Corps orders or permit conditions, the Corps may impose a maximum penalty of $25,000 per day for each violation. 33 U.S.C. § 1344(s)(4). Such administrative penalties, of course, are subject to judicial review. 33 U.S.C. § 1319(g)(8)(A), (B).

(3.) Criminal and Civil Penalties

Both the Rivers and Harbors Act of 1899, 33 U.S.C. § 406, and the Clean Water Act, § 309, permit the imposition of criminal penalties upon violators in some circumstances. See, e.g. United States v. Pozsgai, 897 F.2d 524 (3rd Cir.), cert. denied, 498 U.S. 812 (1990)($200,000 fine and three-year prison sentence); United States v. Jones, 21 ER 297 (E.D. Md. 1990) ($1,000,000 fine); United States v. Marathon Dev. Corp., 867 F.2d

---

[14] Under Section 309(a)(3) of the CWA, the EPA is authorized to issue administrative compliance orders.

96 (1st Cir. 1989) ($100,000 criminal fine, six months in prison and one year's probation).

The Clean Water Act also provides for the imposition of civil penalties. But the requirement of a civil jury trial in such cases, Tull v. United States, 481 U.S. 412 (1987), has made the use of this sanction less practical. The government is much more likely to seek the imposition of administrative penalties, under 33 U.S.C. § 1319(g), and equitable orders, neither of which requires a jury trial. See generally Atlas Roofing Co. v. Occupational Safety and Health Review Comm'n, 430 U.S. 442 (1977).

(4.) Equitable Relief

(a.) Injunctions

If a developer is illegally filling wetlands or violating permit conditions, what equitable remedies are available? If a preliminary injunction is one possible remedy, what must be established before the court will grant such equitable relief? Who has the burden of proof and upon what issues? Must the government show irreparable harm to the wetlands before the court will issue an injunction? If irreparable harm is necessary, how does the government establish that irreparable harm will result if the preliminary injunction is not granted? How does the restoration remedy fit into the court's decision about whether to grant a preliminary injunction? If a statute has specific provision for the issuance of injunctive relief as a remedy for a violation, should the burden on the government to show irreparable harm be less than when the statute fails to make such a specific provision for injunctive relief? If the burden is less, how would you articulate the difference in the nature of the government's burden? Does the Clean Water Act require strict enforcement of its provisions? Is there a difference between the remedies available, and what the government must show, if the defendant violates the Rivers and Harbors Act and not the Clean Water Act?

The courts are divided on the issue of what the government must establish before the government is entitled to have a preliminary injunction issued prohibiting alleged violations of Section 404 of the CWA. The court in United States v. Lambert, 695 F.2d 536 (11th Cir. 1983), adheres to the traditional view of the prerequisites for a preliminary injunction. According to the court:

> The grant or denial of a preliminary injunction is a decision within the sound discretion of the district court. On appeal from the grant or denial of a preliminary injunction we do not review the intrinsic merits of the case. "It is the function of the trial court to exercise its discretion in deciding upon and delicately balancing the equities of

the parties involved." * * * We consider the court's decision under the abuse of discretion standard of review.

The court must exercise its discretion in light of the following four prerequisites for a preliminary injunction: "(1) a substantial likelihood that plaintiff will prevail on the merits, (2) a substantial threat that plaintiff will suffer irreparable injury if the injunction is not granted, (3) that the threatened injury to plaintiff outweighs the threatened harm the injunction may do to defendant, and (4) that granting the preliminary injunction will not disserve the public interest." Canal Authority v. Callaway, 489 F.2d 567, 572 (5th Cir. 1974). Because a preliminary injunction is "an extraordinary and drastic remedy," its grant is the exception rather than the rule and plaintiff must clearly carry the burden of persuasion. Texas v. Seatrain International, S.A., 518 F.2d 175, 179 (5th Cir. 1975).

It must be emphasized that the subject of this appeal is the denial of an injunction pending a final hearing and decision by the court. The purpose of such a preliminary injunction is "merely to preserve the relative positions of the parties until a trial on the merits can be held." University of Texas v. Camenisch, 451 U.S. 390, 395 (1981). * * * Preservation of the status quo enables the court to render a meaningful decision on the merits. Canal Authority, 489 F.2d at 573. Thus the harm considered by the district court is necessarily confined to that which might occur in the interval between ruling on the preliminary injunction and trial on the merits. * * *

Id. at 539-40.

The district court in United States v. D'Annolfo, 474 F.Supp. 220 (D. Mass. 1979), however, had a different view of the government's burden at a hearing on a request for a preliminary injunction. According to Judge McNaught:

The standard of requiring a demonstration of immediate irreparable harm, employed in civil litigation as a condition precedent to the granting of injunctive relief, is not a prerequisite to the allowance of an injunction to the plaintiff in this case. "When the government acts to enforce a statute or make effective a declared policy of Congress, the standard of public interest and not the requirements of private litigation measure the propriety and need for injunctive relief." United States v. Shafer, 132 F.Supp. 659 (D. Md. 1955), aff'd, 229 F.2d 124 (4th Cir. 1956), cert. denied, 351 U.S. 931 (1956).

Id. at 222. Does *D'Annolfo* mean that there is a presumption of irreparable harm when the government is seeking to enforce the Rivers and Harbors Act, Sections 9 and 10, or the CWA, Section 404? If the government must prove irreparable harm, what type of evidence must the government introduce to establish that requirement? Consider the materials on mitigation and the following materials on restoration.

In United States v. Schmott, 734 F. Supp. 1035 (E.D.N.Y. 1990), the government requested and was granted a preliminary injunction against a marina adjoining Jamaica Bay (an urban wildlife refuge within New York City) from storing boats or building docks in Schmitt Cove because the government established a likelihood of injury and success on the merits resulting from defendants' violations of the Rivers and Harbors Act and the Clean Water Act (i.e., failure to secure dock construction permits).

The court reviewed conflicting precedents and held:

> that irreparable harm is presumed when the Government seeks a preliminary injunction pursuant to a statute which expressly authorizes entry of an injunction upon a showing of a violation of law by the Government. Since 33 U.S.C. § 406 expressly authorizes the entry of an injunction for a violation of the Rivers and Harbors Appropriation Act proven by the Attorney General, the Government is not required to demonstrate irreparable harm in order for a preliminary injunction to issue. However, 33 U.S.C. § 1344(s)(3) does not expressly authorize the entry of an injunction for a violation of the Clean Water Act as alleged in the complaint and the Government must demonstrate irreparable harm in order for an injunction to issue with respect to its Clean Water Act claim.

Id. at 1049. The court found that the government proved irreparable harm, and as such, a preliminary injunction was granted for the CWA violations, too.

The district court in United States v. Ciampitti, 583 F. Supp. 483 (D.N.J. 1984), declined the invitation to decide whether irreparable harm must be shown by the government on the ground that, whether it was required or not, the government had established such harm in this case. The court, however, specifically stated that:

> It is axiomatic that the public interest under the Clean Water Act requires strict enforcement of the statute so as to clean up the nation's waters and preserve the surrounding ecological environment. * * *

Id. at 499.

(b.) Restoration Orders

In United States v. Weisman, 489 F. Supp. 1331 (M.D. Fla. 1980),to provide easier access to his house, the defendant constructed a dirt fill roadway on tidal wetlands after the Corps denied the necessary Section

404 permit. The roadway was almost completed by the time the Corps discovered the violation. The district court ordered restoration. First, the court found that the removal of the road would confer *maximum environmental benefits* in that it would restore the flow of water over the property to its original rate, thus preventing drying out of the land and impairment of the ecologically important detritus production. Second, removal of the construction was found methodologically *feasible and cost-effective* at the cost of $19,635. Finally, restoration would have the requisite *equitable relation to the wrong committed* since Weisman had flagrantly violated federal law, had refused to consider a less damaging alternative (a pre-existing road in another location), and was financially able to pay for the restoration.

Notes and Questions

1. Although some wetland vegetation can be restored, that does not necessarily mean the damaged wetland area can be restored so that it fully performs its original wetland functions. What type and degree of proof of ability to restore or inability to restore, depending on who has the burden of proof, should a court require when faced with the question of whether to order restoration as part of the sanctions imposed on a developer who fills wetlands without the necessary Section 404 permit?

2. If Weisman was not able to pay for the restoration, would he be able to keep his road? For a discussion of the restoration remedy, see, e.g., M. Rouvalis, Restoration of Wetlands Under Section 404 of the Clean Water Act: An Analytical Synthesis of Statutory and Case Law Principles, 15 B.C. Envtl. Aff. L. Rev. 295 (1988). In United States v. Sunset Cove, Inc., 514 F.2d 1089 (9th Cir.), cert. denied, 423 U.S. 865 (1975), defendant, believing a river to be non-navigable, placed fill material at the mouth of the river without obtaining a Rivers and Harbors Act permit. The district court ordered total removal of the illegal fill. The Ninth Circuit, however, said:

> Such an operation is, as a practical matter, far beyond the resources of Sunset or its principals. Here, we believe the court might have tempered the law with a touch of equity.

> The judgment should be modified to require the removal of as much of the riprap as will permit nature, in a reasonable period of time, to take its course and approximately re-establish former topographic conditions. * * *

Id. at 1090. If Sunset had flagrantly violated the Rivers and Harbors Act by knowingly filling a navigable river, would the court's decision have been any different?

(5.) Citizens Suits

In some circumstances, Section 305 of the CWA, 33 U.S.C. § 1365(a), allows private citizens to bring an action to enforce the CWA. The In Gwaltney of Smithfield, Ltd. v. Chesapeake Bay Foundation, 484 U.S. 49 (1987), the Supreme Court held that the statutory phrase "to be in violation" requires citizen-plaintiffs to "allege a state of either continuous or intermittent violation -- that is, a reasonable likelihood that a past polluter will continue to pollute in the future." Id. at 57.

SECTION 4. STATE REGULATION OF WETLANDS ACTIVITIES

A. STATE WETLANDS REGULATORY PROGRAMS

The United States Supreme Court decision in *SWANCC* drastically changed the landscape of wetlands regulation. Prior to the *SWANCC*, virtually all wetlands in the nation were subject to the regulatory requirements of Section 404. After *SWANCC* that was no longer true, leaving a gap to be filled either by additional federal legislation or state regulatory programs. The problem, however, was that such federal legislation, even assuming it would be within the federal commerce power, was unlikely to be forthcoming in the near future and, in many states, state law and programs existing at the time of *SWANCC* did not fill the gap.

Although a substantial number of states had some type of wetland protection statute, many of the existing state regulatory programs did not include isolated freshwater wetlands in their coverage. Almost all twenty-nine coastal states[15] had in place programs regulating the alteration or destruction of coastal and estuarine wetlands, approximately sixteen of which also included within their coverage freshwater wetlands adjacent to navigable waters and tributaries of navigable waters;[16] but, only about fourteen of the programs were sufficiently comprehensive to include isolated wetlands as well.[17] Even

---

[15] This includes the Great Lakes States, Illinois, Indiana, Ohio, Michigan, Minnesota, and Wisconsin.

[16] As of October 1, 2001, Georgia and Wisconsin were examples of such state wetlands regulatory programs that did not include isolated wetlands, but did include freshwater wetlands adjacent to navigable waters and tributaries of navigable waters. Limited staffing and funding may limit the effectiveness of the programs.

[17] As of October 1, 2001, comprehensive state wetlands programs existed in Connecticut, Florida, Maine, Maryland, Massachusetts, Michigan, Minnesota, New Hampshire, New Jersey, New York, Oregon, Pennsylvania, Rhode Island, Virginia, Vermont, and Washington.

when the program included such wetlands, in some instances coverage was limited by wetlands' acreage thresholds. For example, in New York, the area of freshwater wetlands impact had to be greater than 12.4 acres. For an excellent discussion of the nature of state programs at the time of *SWANCC*, see generally, J. Kusler, The *SWANCC* Decision and the States–Fill in the Gaps or Declare Open Season, 23 National Wetlands Newsletter 9 (March-April 2001). For a more detailed description of individual state wetlands and coastal laws, see generally W. Want, Law of Wetlands Regulation Chapter 13 (2001).[18] However, the lack of a comprehensive program did not mean that a state lacked any imput into Corps 'decisions that would authorize isolated wetlands activities. Before *SWANCC*, Section 401 of the CWA afforded states the opportunity to veto the issuance of any permit if the activity would be inconsistent with state water quality standards.

B. SECTION 401 OF THE CLEAN WATER ACT AND WETLANDS

Section 401of the CWA requires that

[a]ny applicant for a federal license or permit to conduct any activity * * * which may result in any discharge into the navigable waters, shall provide the licensing or permitting agency a certification from the State in which the discharge originates or will originate * * * that any such discharge will comply with * * * [state effluent limitations and water quality standards promulgated in accordance with other sections of the Clean Water Act].

33 U.S.C. § 1341(a)(1). If the state denies the certification, the denial acts as an absolute veto of the federal license or permit application. The state denial is not reviewable by the permitting or licensing agency nor by the federal courts. The state decision is thus reviewable only through the state courts. See, e.g., Sun Enterprises, Ltd. v. Train, 532 F.2d 280 (2d Cir. 1976). Thus, through the 401 certification process a state may wield tremendous power over the issuance of federal permits or licenses.

In 1990, the EPA stated that:

Section 401 applies to wetlands because wetlands are "navigable waters" within the meaning of the Clean Water Act. Historically, however, states have rarely used the Section 401 certification process as a means of protecting wetlands. In an effort to force states to take a more active role in protecting their wetlands, EPA

---

[18] Much relevant, informative material relating to state wetlands regulatory programs and related matter can be found at the excellent website maintained by The Association of State Wetlands Managers <www.aswm.org>.

mandated that states take steps to include wetlands within the scope of their required CWA water quality standards. By the end of the fiscal year 1993, the minimum requirements for States are

> * * * to include wetlands in their definition of "State waters," establish beneficial uses for wetlands, adopt existing narrative and numeric criteria for wetlands, adopt narrative biological criteria for wetlands, and apply antidegradation policies to wetlands. * * *

EPA Memorandum, Final Document: National Guidance on Water Quality Standards for Wetlands (July 30, 1990).

Although states may adopt water quality standards that are more restrictive than the EPA's Section 404 guidelines, not only are they not required to do so, but legislation in a number of states precludes the adoption of standards that are stricter than the prevailing federal standards. See generally, J. McElfish, Jr., "Minimal Stringency: Abdication of State Innovation," 12 Envir. L. Rep. 10003 (1995)(approximately 24 states have enacted such laws in some form).

By 2001, a number of states had completed this process and were actively using their Section 401 certification authority. One prominent example is the response of some state's to the Corps' former Nationwide Permit 26.[19] With some restrictions and limitations, this permit authorized dredge and fill activities in small, isolated wetlands. Using their Section 401 authority, states, such as North Carolina, denied certification to this nationwide permit, thereby forcing anyone proposing to engage in such activities to apply to the Corps for an individual Section 404 permit and undergo the complete permit review process.

In states relying on Section 401 water quality certifications to exercise some regulatory control over wetlands activities, the *SWANCC* decision presented significant problems. On one hand, if isolated waters and wetlands were no longer "waters of the United States" and no longer subject to Section 404 permit requirements, then a state Section 401 water quality certification was no longer necessary. If the state agency lacked any independent enforcement authority, the state had no control over such activities. On the other hand, if, as a matter of state law, state water quality standards applied to isolated waters and wetlands and violation of those standards constituted an independent violation of state law, anyone engaging in activities that violated those

---

[19] Nationwide Permit 26 had a long contentious history dating back to the late 1970s. In response to environmental concerns it was amended in both 1984 and 1996 to limit its scope of application, in each case reducing the wetlands acreage allowed to be impacted. In 1996 the Corps announced its decision to phase out this nationwide permit and replace it with a one–Nationwide Permit 39(residential, commercial, and institutional developments), which went into effect in 2000.

standards would still be subject to state imposed penalties. But, if there was no independent state permitting authority, then there was no process through which to obtain pre-activity approval of activities in isolated waters and wetlands. Anyone engaging in such activities took the risk that the state would make an *ex post facto* finding that the activity violated state water quality standards and impose financial and criminal penalties. These problems and others led some coastal states, without an existing comprehensive wetlands regulatory program, to take steps to fill the *SWANCC* created gap.

C. STATE REGULATION IN THE POST-SWANCC WORLD

In states in which the relevant state agency lacked the basic authority to either establish a permit program or to regulate activities in isolated waters and wetlands, corrective legislation was needed. Late in 2001 some states were in the process of considering such legislation. See, e.g. South Carolina Senate Bill 550 (2001).[20] In states in which, the necessary statutory authority existed, but the state had not established a permit program, relying instead on the Section 401 certification process, the regulatory bodies needed to institute a permit program or some other mechanism through which activities, subject to appropriate conditions and mitigation requirements, could receive pre-activity approval. See, e.g.15 North Carolina Administrative Code 2H.1300 (2001). The final outcome of some of these efforts, which in the case of newly promulgate administrative rules or regulations are sure to be challenged in the state courts, remains to be seen. What is clear is that the basic uniformity of wetlands protection that was at the core of Section 404 has been lost and, at best, will be replaced by varying, individual state and local regulatory programs, subject to the vagaries of state and local funding and staffing.

Note on State Takeover of the 404
Program for Nonnavigable Waters

Section 404 provides for the transfer to the states of federal Section 404 permit-issuing authority over discharges in 404 jurisdictional areas shoreward of the mean high-tide line and the ordinary high water mark. To qualify, states must be willing to administer a program meeting certain statutory requirements. 33 U.S.C. § 1344(g)(l). Only two states, Michigan and New Jersey, have assumed Section 404 permitting responsibility under this provision of the CWA

---

[20] To close the gap created by SWANCC, The Association of State Wetlands Managers offer a Model State Wetland Statute, which can be found at their website <www.aswm.org>

SECTION 5. A RETROSPECTIVE LOOK

Now that you have finished the Section 404 materials, you should take a brief retrospective look at Section 404.

Although the rate of loss has declined, the nation continues to lose important and irreplaceable wetlands resources. When North America was first settled by Europeans, the continental United States contained approximately 215 million acres of wetlands. By 1997, only 105.5 million acres were left. Of the remaining wetland acreage, less than 10% were coastal freshwater and saltwater wetlands. The vast majority of these coastal wetlands are concentrated in the southeastern and Gulf states, extending from North Carolina to Texas. See, e.g., A. Southworth, Conserving Southeastern Coastal Wetlands, in Audubon Wildlife Report, 223, 223-29 (1989). In 1987, it was estimated that wetlands were disappearing at the rate of 400,000 acres each year; but, by 1997 the rate of loss declined by eighty percent to an average of 58,500 acres. See U.S. Fish and Wildlife Service, Status and Trends of Wetlands in the Conterminous United States 1986-1997, 9 (2001).

The implementation and enforcement of wetlands protection measures through the Section 404 program was an important factor in this decline. But the program, as you now realize, is a very controversial one. Most fundamentally, it conflicts with deeply ingrained notions about private property and the right of an individual to use private property with minimal interference by governmental bodies. The conflict between this traditional American value and wetlands protection is heightened by the fact that many perceive nonhumans -- animals, birds, fish, plants and other nonhuman entities -- as the primary beneficiaries of the Section 404 program. Also, many wetland areas are still viewed by many people as wastelands that contain only mosquitoes and other noxious insects, snakes, and animals. Thus, long term public support for the program may not be as solid as support for other aspects of the CWA, the Clean Air Act, or similar legislation. And, of course, private property rights advocates continue to assert that compensation must be paid to private property owners whose use of their lands are restricted by wetlands protection legislation and regulations.

Until the decision in *SWANCC*, the assertion of federal jurisdiction over activities in small, isolated waters and wetlands was an especially irritating thorn in the side of those subject to the program. Under EPA and Corps practices, areas that are dry at the surface 365 days a year may still be deemed a wetland. Opponents of the program claim that as many as two-thirds of the applicants for Section 404 permits did not know that their property contained wetlands when it was purchased. In addition, the program reached every water or wetland no matter how small it might be. To some, activities in such areas seemed to be matters of local and state concern not national, federal concern. See, e.g. V. Albrecht and B. Goode, All is not well with Section 404, 18 National Wetlands Newsletter 14 (1996).

SWANCC tests the national commitment to wetlands preservation. If ecologically important wetlands or water areas are now beyond the reach of the current Section 404 program, will either Congress or the individual states respond with programs that gather in these waters and wetlands under a protective umbrella? In the first twenty years of the Section 404 program, its supporters generally found a sympathetic ear in the courts and later in the agencies. In response, opponents pressed for legislation limiting the Section 404 program, but were unsuccessful. Bills were introduced, but no acceptable compromise could be reached. In the late 1990s the opponents found a more receptive judicial audience to their arguments and the courts dramatically narrowed the scope of the program. Now the program advocates seek congressional assistance. But, there is no assurance that any reopening of the wetlands issues will in fact result in a more expansive program. And, even if such legislation were to pass Congress and be signed into law, there is the distinct possibility a conservative United States Supreme Court might hold such legislation beyond the scope of Congress' Commerce Clause powers and therefore unconstitutional.

So, *SWANCC* has opened a new, uncertain chapter in the battle over wetlands protection. The only certainty is that uniform, national, comprehensive wetlands protection represented by the pre-SWANCC Section 404 program has unraveled. In the absence of congressional legislation, protection of many ecologically important wetlands areas may now be in the hands of the individual states and programs varying in scope and degree of enforcement.

Chapter Three

COMPREHENSIVE MANAGEMENT OF
COASTAL DEVELOPMENT

SECTION 1. INTRODUCTION

Starting in the 1960s, public and Congressional awareness of the tremendous stress being placed upon coastal lands and water mounted. Population pressures, increased industrialization, pollution, and growing commercial and recreational uses threatened to overwhelm the capabilities of state and local governments to manage development effectively and to resolve conflicting uses of coastal resources. The unclear division of federal, state and local authority over some coastal lands, waters, and other resources and the lack of co-ordination between federal, state, and local agencies made planning and implementation of efficient, balanced, orderly coastal resources development difficult. Congressional concern led to the passage of the Marine Resources and Engineering Development Act of 1966. One significant feature of this Act was the establishment of the Commission on Marine Science, Engineering and Resources or, as it was called for its chairman, the Stratton Commission. The Stratton Commission's report laid the foundation for the Coastal Zone Management Act of 1972.

The Stratton Commission concluded that effective management—ultimately a state responsibility—was the primary problem in the coastal zone. However, the federal government's role should not be to compel a state to develop a special organization to deal with its coastal management problems. Instead, the report concluded that the federal government should encourage state action by establishing guidelines, facilitating federal cooperation with state authorities, and providing appropriate financial assistance. The Commission recommended the enactment of a coastal management act to provide policy objectives for the coastal zone and authorize federal grants-in-aid to facilitate the establishment of state authorities empowered to manage the coastal water and adjacent land.

SECTION 2. THE COASTAL ZONE MANAGEMENT ACT OF 1972 (CZMA)

A. HISTORY OF THE CZMA

Participation voluntary

The federal Coastal Zone Management Act of 1972 was enacted during the same period as other major federal environmental legislation, but differed substantially from legislation like the Clean Air Act or the Clean Water Act. First, state participation in coastal zone management planning was completely voluntary, and federal standards or management would not be imposed if the state did not develop a plan. Second, although there was a recognized national interest in effective coastal management, Congress also recognized that the type of land use planning and management required was primarily within the traditional domain of state and local governments.

land use mgt in coastal areas is state/local responsibility

The CZMA provides federal funding for states to develop and administer coastal programs according to guidelines set out in the Act. The states are given great flexibility in their approaches to coastal management. Acceptable federal models range from direct state control of land and water use regulation to state review of locally or regionally implemented programs. In addition, the CZMA gives the states substantial discretion in designating the geographic scope of its coastal zone in its management program.

Federal funding for program development is a traditional incentive for state cooperation in reaching coastal management goals. The CZMA provides, however, an additional incentive for state participation–the so-called federal consistency requirement—a kind of reverse preemption provision that assures a state that, with certain exceptions, federal agency activities or federally-sponsored activities affecting the coastal zone will be consistent with the state-created and federally-approved coastal management plan.

The Washington coastal program was the first to receive federal approval in 1976. All thirty-five eligible states and territories (including the Northern Marianas, Puerto Rico, the Virgin Islands, Guam, and American Samoa) participated in the federal program during the initial program development period of the 1970s. The 1990 amendments to the CZMA created incentives for the final states to develop programs. Currently, 33 programs have been approved bringing 95,331 miles of coast, representing 99.9% of the nation's shoreline, under the management of the Act. The development of Indiana's program will incorporate 45 of the remaining 108 miles of national coastline into the program. Only Illinois is not participating.

The CZMA is administered by the National Oceanic and Atmospheric Administration (NOAA) in the Department of Commerce. The policies of the CZMA reflect the national interests in the coastal zone and the purposes served by coastal management planning. Initially, the CZMA simply declared the national policy "to preserve, protect, develop, and where possible, to restore or enhance, the resources of the Nation's coastal zone for this and succeeding generations" and to assist the states in this effort. 16 U.S.C. § 1452. Subsequent amendments have provided a detailed enumeration of the policies fostered by the CZMA.

With the Arab oil embargo and consequential energy crisis, the 1973-74 political atmosphere made energy independence an objective of national importance. The Federal Energy Administration, the Federal Power Commission, and the Energy Research and Development Administration objected to and criticized the states' failure to identify coastal areas that were particularly suitable for energy development. NOAA acknowledged the problem but, it adopted the view that the CZMA did not obligate states to designate specific energy development sites. The 1976 amendments were a response to this situation.

The major new initiative contained in these amendments was the Coastal Energy Impact Program (CEIP), a 10-year program to provide financial assistance to coastal states likely to be impacted by outer continental shelf energy development. Only coastal states participating in the CZMA program were eligible to receive CEIP funds. The three part program provided planning grants, loans and bond guarantees to assist coastal states in financing public services and facilities necessitated by coastal energy activity, and grant money to ameliorate the negative effects of outer continental shelf development. The 1976 amendments also specifically extended the states' consistency review authority to federal offshore oil and gas exploration and development.

The 1980 amendments again highlighted Congress' concern that coastal states incorporate the national interest in the development and implementation of their CZMPs. States were now required to use an increasing proportion of their federal funds, up to a ceiling of 30%, to address the following new coastal policies: (1) protecting coastal resources; (2) managing improper coastal development; (3) siting facilities related to national defense, energy, fisheries, recreation, ports, and transportation; (4) increasing access to coastal recreation; (5) redeveloping damaged urban forests; (6) simplifying procedures to allow for quicker governmental decisions; (7) continuing to foster cooperation with affected federal agencies, local governments, and public citizens; and (8) assisting the management of living marine resources.

Other important changes contained in the 1980 amendments were a reduction in CZMA funds from $101 million to $86 million annually, the encouragement of special area management planning, and the establishment of a new grant program inducing coastal states to inventory and designate resources of national significance and to establish specific, enforceable standards for this effort. Finally, the amendments continued authorization of the CZMA through fiscal year 1985.

The Coastal Management Reauthorization Act of 1985 (passed in 1986) contained amendments establishing new procedures for review and acceptance of changes in a state's coastal program. In addition, the Act established the National Estuarine Reserve Research System, set specific requirements for the designation of an area as a national estuarine reserve, and authorized the Secretary of Commerce to make grants to coastal states to allow them to acquire land and water rights in such areas as are needed to ensure long-term management.

The Coastal Zone Act Reauthorization Amendments of 1990 (passed in 1991) made major changes in the consistency provisions which went far to clarify the provision and which effectively overruled the Supreme Court's narrow interpretation of consistency in Secretary of Interior v. California, 464 U.S. 312 (1984). In addition, the Coastal Energy Impact Program was repealed and replaced by a more limited Coastal Zone Management Fund. Finally, a new Coastal Zone Enhancement Grant Program was created. This program was designed to encourage states to improve their plans in one or more of eight areas of coastal concern. These areas are: (1) coastal wetlands protection; (2) natural hazards management; (3) public access improvements; (4) coastal growth and development impact; (5) special area management planning; (6) ocean resources planning; (7) siting of coastal energy and government facilities; and (8) reduction of marine debris. The Amendments also establish a Coastal Non-Point Pollution Program. This program requires shoreline states to develop plans for protecting coastal water from non-point source pollution from land uses. The EPA has developed uniform national guidelines which the states must follow in developing these plans. Finally, the 1990 amendments to the CZMA authorized grants to encourage participation of states without approved coastal programs.

The 1996 amendments to the CZMA made few major changes, but inserted several provisions concerning the promotion of aquaculture. Although several bills have been introduced, the latest reauthorization of the Act is still pending.

For further discussion of the history of CZMA, see, e.g., S. Rep. No. 753, 92nd Cong., 2d Sess. (1972); H.R. Conf. Rep. No. 1544, 92 Cong., 2d Sess. (1972); U.S. Commission on Marine Science, Engineering and Resources, Our Nation and the Sea (Jan. 1969); D. Brower and D. Carol, Coastal Zone Management as Land Planning (1984); W. Allayand, Integrated Planning for Water Quality Management 36 (1979); B. Millemann, And Two if By Sea: Fighting the Attack on America's Coasts (Coastal Alliance 1986).

B. DEVELOPMENT AND IMPLEMENTATION OF STATE COASTAL MANAGEMENT PROGRAMS

The Department of Commerce, primarily through the National Oceanic and Atmospheric Administration's (NOAA) Office of Ocean and Coastal Resource Management (OCRM), administers the federal CZMA grant program and approves or disapproves individual state programs. The CZMA provisions on administrative grants   set out the basic requirements for approval of a state coastal management program.

CZMA § 306. Administrative Grants
16 U.S.C. § 1455(d).

(d) Mandatory adoption of State management program for coastal zone

Before approving a management program submitted by a coastal state, the Secretary shall find the following:

* * *

(2) The management program includes each of the following required program elements:

required state Program elements

    (A) An identification of the boundaries of the coastal zone subject to the management program.

    (B) A definition of what shall constitute permissible land uses and water uses within the coastal zone which have a direct and significant impact on the coastal waters.

    (C) An inventory and designation of areas of particular concern within the coastal zone.

    (D) An identification of the means by which the State proposes to exert control over the land uses and water uses referred to in subparagraph (B), including a list of relevant State constitutional provisions, laws, regulations, and judicial decisions.

    (E) Broad guidelines on priorities of uses in particular areas, including specifically those uses of lowest priority.

    (F) A description of the organizational structure proposed to implement such management program, including the responsibilities and interrelationships of local, area wide, State, regional, and interstate agencies in the management process.

    (G) A definition of the term "beach" and a planning process for the protection of, and access to, public beaches and other public coastal areas of environmental, recreational, historical, esthetic, ecological, or cultural value.

    (H) A planning process for energy facilities likely to be located in, or which may significantly affect, the coastal zone, including a process for anticipating the management of the impacts resulting from such facilities.

(I)   A planning process for assessing the effects of, and studying and evaluating ways to control, or lessen the impact of, shoreline erosion, and to restore areas adversely affected by such erosion.

(3) The State has--

(A)   coordinated its program with local, area wide, and interstate plans applicable to areas within the coastal zone * * * .

(B)   established an effective mechanism for continuing consultation and coordination between the [state] management agency * * * and with local governments, interstate agencies, regional agencies, and area wide agencies within the coastal zone to assure the full participation of those local governments and agencies in carrying out the purposes of this chapter; * * *

(8) The management program provides for adequate consideration of the national interest involved in planning for, and managing the coastal zone, including the siting of facilities such as energy facilities which are of greater than local significance. In the case of energy facilities, the Secretary shall find that the State has given consideration to any applicable national or interstate energy plan or program.

(9) The management program includes procedures whereby specific areas may be designated for the purpose of preserving or restoring them for their conservation, recreational, ecological, historical, or esthetic values.

(10) The State, acting through its chosen agency or agencies (including local governments, area wide agencies, regional agencies, or interstate agencies) has authority for the management of the coastal zone in accordance with the management program. Such authority shall include power--

(A)   to administer land use and water use regulations to control development to ensure compliance with the management program, and to resolve conflicts among competing uses; and

(B)   to acquire fee simple and less than fee simple interests in land, waters, and other property through condemnation or other means when necessary to achieve conformance with the management program. * * *

(12) The management program contains a method of assuring that local land use and water use regulations within the coastal zone do not unreasonably restrict or exclude land uses and water uses of regional benefit.

(13)   The management program provides for--
   (A)   the inventory and designation of areas that contain one or more coastal resources of national significance; and
   (B)   specific and enforceable standards to protect such resources.

(14)   The management program provides for public participation in permitting processes, consistency determinations, and other similar decisions.

(15)   The management program provides a mechanism to ensure that all State agencies will adhere to the program.

(16)   The management program contains enforceable policies and mechanisms to implement the applicable requirements of the Coastal Nonpoint Pollution Control Program of the State required by section 1455b of this title.

CZMA § 307.   Coordination and cooperation
16 U.S.C. § 1456(b)

(b) Adequate consideration of views of Federal agencies.   The Secretary shall not approve the management program submitted by a state pursuant to section 306 [16 U.S.C. § 1455] unless the views of Federal agencies principally affected by such program have been adequately considered.

* * *

American Petroleum Institute v. Knecht, which follows, is an early *American Petroleum* important judicial consideration of the nature of coastal management programs.   The 1977 approval of the California coastal management program was challenged for failure to give adequate consideration to energy facility siting.   Reread relevant sections of the CZMA at 16 U.S.C. §§1455(d)(2), (3), (8), and (12) which require the Secretary of Commerce to find that a coastal program includes specific provisions relating to such issues as energy facility siting, consideration of the views of federal agencies, and consideration of the national interest.

Increased interest in potential oil and gas deposits off the California coast, especially on the federal outer continental shelf, led to inclusion of a substantial oil and gas element in the California program. But rather than designating certain areas of the coastal zone as suitable for energy facilities, the program provided siting policies and a planning process. Do such general provisions provide "adequate consideration of the national interest" in energy facility siting? Does the CZMA require state programs to accommodate energy facilities? Who determines what is a state's fair share of needed energy facilities?

AMERICAN PETROLEUM INSTITUTE v. KNECHT
United States District Court, C.D. Cal., 1979.
456 F. Supp. 889, aff'd, 609 F.2d 1306 (9th Cir. 1979).

KELLEHER, *District Judge.*

Plaintiffs American Petroleum Institute, Western Oil and Gas Association, and certain oil company members * * * brought this action * * * seeking declaratory and injunctive relief against defendants' imminent grant of "final approval" of the California Coastal Zone Management Program ("CZMP") pursuant to §306 of the Coastal Zone Management Act of 1972, as amended ("CZMA") * * * .

In brief, plaintiffs contend that the California Program cannot lawfully be approved by the federal defendants under §306 of the CZMA, principally for two reasons. First, the CZMP is not a "management program" within the meaning of § 304(11) of the Act in that * * * it fails to satisfy the requirements of §§ 305(b) and 306(c),(d), and (e), and regulations promulgated thereunder, as regards content specificity.

[handwritten left margin: Plaintiff / Co's program not suitable for approval. ① not a mgmt program ② fails to satisfy oil/energy production requirements]

* * *

FACTS

* * *

The Court has before it for determination both preliminarily and for ultimate disposition questions of the highest importance, greatest complexity, and highest urgency. They arise as the result of high legislative purpose, low bureaucratic bungling, and present inherent difficulty in judicial determination. In other words, for the high purpose of improving and maintaining felicitous conditions in the coastal areas of the United States, the Congress has undertaken a legislative solution, the application of which is so complex as to make it almost wholly unmanageable. In the course of the legislative process, there obviously came into conflict many competing interests which, in typical fashion, the Congress sought to accommodate, only to create thereby a morass of problems between the private sector, the public sector, the federal bureaucracy, the state legislature, the state bureaucracy, and all of the administrative agencies appurtenant thereto. Because the action taken gives rise to claims public and private which must be adjudicated, this matter is now involved in the judicial process.

* * *

LEGISLATIVE HISTORY OF THE CZMA

A seemingly unbridgeable gulf between the parties concerning the proper construction of the CZMA establishes the cutting edge of this action. First, noted at the outset of this memorandum of decision, plaintiffs complain that the California Program fails to qualify for final approval under § 306 because it lacks the requisite specificity Congress intended management programs to embody, especially with respect to the substantive requirements of §§ 305(b) and 306(c), (d), and (e), so as to enable private users in the coastal zone subject to an approved program to be able to predict with reasonable certainty whether or not their proposed activities will be found to be "consistent" with the program under § 307(c). Second, plaintiffs contend that a proper understanding of § 306(c)(8), particularly in light of the 1976 Amendments, compels the conclusion that in requiring "adequate consideration" Congress intended that an approvable program affirmatively accommodate the national interest in planning for and siting energy facilities and that the CZMP fails so to do. The Court here addresses each of these contentions.

A. The Definition of "Management Program"

Any attempt to resolve this underlying dispute, out of which most of the issues in this lawsuit arise, must begin with Congress' definition of a "management program" in § 304(11) of the Act:

The term "management program" includes, but is not limited to, a comprehensive statement in words, maps, illustrations, and other media of communication, prepared and adopted by the state in accordance with the provisions of this title, setting forth *objectives, policies and standards to guide* public and private uses of lands and waters in the coastal zone.

[Emphasis supplied.] This definition is exactly as originally contained in the Senate version of the CZMA (S. 3507). In its report on S. 3507, the Committee on Commerce stated:

"Management program" is the term to refer to the Process by which a coastal State * * * proposes * * * to manage land and water uses in the coastal zone so as to reduce or minimize a direct, significant, and adverse effect upon those waters, including the development of criteria and of the governmental structure capable of implementing such a program. In adopting the term "Management program" the Committee seeks to convey the importance of a *dynamic* quality to the planning undertaken in this Act that permits adjustments as more knowledge is gained, as new technology develops, and as social aspirations are more clearly defined. The Committee does *not* intend to provide for management programs that are *static* but rather to create a *mechanism for continuing review* of coastal zone programs on a regular basis and to provide a framework for the allocation of resources that are available to carry out these programs.

S. Rep. No. 753, 92d Cong., 2d Sess. (1972), U.S. Code Cong. & Admin. News 1972, pp. 4776, 4784 [emphasis supplied]. * * *

[Margin note: Court agrees, no "zoning map" needed nor did it need specific criteria ... needs" standards to guide"]

The Court agrees with defendants that Congress never intended that to be approvable under § 306 a management program must provide a "zoning map" which would inflexibly commit the state in advance of receiving specific proposals to permitting particular activities in specific areas. Nor did Congress intend by using the language of "objectives, policies, and standards" to require that such programs establish such detailed criteria that private users be able to rely on them as predictive devices for determining the fate of projects without interaction between the relevant state agencies and the user. To satisfy the definition in the Act, a program need only contain standards of sufficient specificity "to guide public and private uses."

The CZMA was enacted primarily with a view to encouraging the coastal states to plan for the management, development, preservation, and restoration of their coastal zones by establishing rational processes by which to regulate uses therein. Although sensitive to balancing competing interests, it was first and foremost a statute directed to and solicitous of environmental concerns. "The key to more effective use of the coastal zone in the future is introduction of management systems permitting conscious and informed choices among the various alternatives. The aim of this legislation is to assist in this very critical goal." S. Rep. No. 753, U.S. Code Cong. & Admin. News 1972, p. 4781 (Legislative History at 198). See H. Rep. No. 1049, 92d Cong., 2d Sess. (1972) (Legislative History at 313 and 315).

[Margin note: Energy amend. did not require States to become more specific]

The Amendments of 1976 made clear the national interest in the planning for, and siting of, energy facilities. Apparently neither the Act nor the Amendments thereto altered the primary focus of the legislation: the need for a rational planning process to enable the state, not private users of the coastal zone, to be able to make "hard choices." "If those choices are to be rational and devised in such a way as to preserve future options, the program must be established to provide guidelines which will enable the selection of those choices." H. Rep. No. 1049 (Legislative History at 315). The 1976 Amendments do not require increased specificity with regard to the standards and objectives contained in a management program. * * *

[Margin note: Findings ↓ Court rejects opinion that Ca plan is not specific enough]

In conclusion, to the extent plaintiffs' more specific challenges to the Acting Administrator's § 306 approval are premised on an interpretation of congressional intent to require that such programs include detailed criteria establishing a sufficiently high degree of predictability to enable a private user of the coastal zone to say with certainty that a given project must be deemed "consistent" therewith, the Court rejects plaintiffs' contention. * * *

B. Adequate Consideration of the National Interest

Plaintiffs' fundamental grievance with the California Program stems from its assertion that the Program fails to satisfy the mandate of § 306(c)(8) that before the Secretary grant approval to a management program under § 306 she find that it

> provides for adequate consideration of the national interest involved in planning for, and in the siting of, facilities (including energy facilities in, or which significantly affect, such state's coastal zone) which are necessary to meet requirements which are other than local in nature.

Plaintiffs urge that the CZMA, particularly in light of the 1976 Amendments, requires an "affirmative commitment" on the part of the state before § 306 approval is proper. The California Program allegedly fails adequately to make that commitment in that its general lack of specificity, coupled with what plaintiffs characterize as California's overall antipathy to energy development (as embodied in the policies and practices of its Coastal Commission), combine to give the Coastal Commission a "blank check" effectively to veto any or all exploration and development activities subject to § 307(c)(3) simply by finding such activity not to be "consistent" with the CZMP. * * *

The Coastal Zone Management Act Amendments of 1976, Pub.L. 94-370 ("1976 Amendments"), while largely prompted by the 1973 Arab oil embargo and while expressly recognizing the national interest in the planning for and siting of energy facilities, nevertheless did not alter the requirement of "adequate consideration" in § 306(c)(8) or make any changes in the degree of specificity required under the Act. Rather, recognizing that coastal states like California were currently burdened by the onshore impacts of Federal offshore (OCS) activities and likely to be burdened further by the plans for increased leases on the OCS, Congress sought to encourage or induce the affected states to step up their plans vis-a-vis such facilities.

The primary means chosen to accomplish this result was the Coastal Energy Impact Program ("CEIP") contained in new § 308. * * * The Congress was particularly careful to circumscribe the role of the federal government in particular siting decisions. Thus, § 308(l) provides:

> The Secretary shall not intercede in any land use or water use decision of any coastal state with respect to the siting of any energy facility or public facility by making siting in a particular location a prerequisite to, or a condition of, financial assistance under this

section.

This provision is consistent with the approach of the CZMA as a whole to leave the development of, and decisions under, a management program to the state, subject to the Act's more specific concern that the development and decision-making process occur in a context of cooperative interaction, coordination, and sharing of information among affected agencies, both local, state, regional, and federal. This last, especially as regards energy facility planning, is the policy behind the Energy Facility Planning Process ("EFPP") of § 305(b)(8) and the Interstate Grants provision of new § 309 (which encourages the coastal states to give high priority to coordinating coastal zone planning utilizing "interstate agreements or compacts"). It should be noted that the only amendment to the national interest requirement of § 306(c) (8) effectuated by the 1976 Amendments is the additional requirement that in fulfilling its obligation to provide "adequate consideration of the national interest" in the case of energy facilities, the state also give such consideration "to any applicable interstate energy plan or program" established under § 309.

The Court rejects plaintiffs' argument that affirmative accommodation of energy facilities was made a quid pro quo for approval under § 306 by the 1976 Amendments. In addition to the above, the Court notes that Congress itself did not assume that such siting was automatically to be deemed necessary in all instances. For instance, in its report on H.R. 3981, the Committee on Merchant Marine and Fisheries stated that the addition of the EFPP in § 305(b)(8)

> reflects the Committee's finding that increasing involvement of coastal areas in providing energy for the nation is likely, as can be seen in the need to expand the Outer Continental Shelf petroleum development. State coastal zone programs should, therefore, specifically address how major energy facilities are to be located in the coastal zone *if* such siting is necessary. Second, the program shall include methods of handling the anticipated impacts of such facilities. The Committee in no way wishes to accelerate the location of energy facilities in the coasts; on the contrary, it feels a disproportionate share are there now. * * * There is no intent here whatever to involve the Secretary of Commerce in specific siting decisions.

H. Rep. No. 94-878 at 45-46 (Legislative History at 931-32) [emphasis supplied]. * * *

The Senate Committee on Commerce, in reporting S. 586 to the full Senate, stated:

The Secretary of Commerce (through NOAA) should provide

guidance and assistance to States under this section 305(b)(8), and under section 306, to enable them to know what constitutes "adequate consideration of the national interest" in the siting of facilities necessary to meet requirements other than local in nature. The Committee wishes to emphasize, consistent with the overall intent of the Act, that this new paragraph (8) <u>requires a State to develop, and maintain a planning process, but does not imply intercession in specific siting decisions</u>. *The Secretary of Commerce (through NOAA), in determining whether a coastal State has met the requirements, is restricted to evaluating the adequacy of that process.*

[handwritten margin note: State only needs a planning process for energy siting]

S. Rep. No. 94-277 at 34, U.S. Code Cong. & Admin. News 1976, p. 1801 (Legislative History at 760) [emphasis supplied].

Consistent with this mandate, NOAA has promulgated revised program approval regulations * * *.

In its response to several reviewers' suggestion that § 306(c)(8) be interpreted to require that facilities be accommodated in a State's coastal zone, the agency reiterated the position it has maintained since the inception of the CZMA that

the purpose of "adequate consideration" is to achieve the act's "spirit of equitable balance between State and national interests." As such, consideration of facilities in which there may be a national interest must be undertaken within the context of the act's broader finding of a "national interest in the * * * beneficial use, protection, and development of the coastal zone" (Section 302(a)). Subsection 302(g) of the Act gives "high priority" to the protection of natural systems. Accordingly, while the primary focus of subsection 306(c)(8) is on the planning for and siting of facilities, adequate <u>consideration of the national interest in these facilities must be based on a balancing of these interests relative to the wise use, protection and other development of the coastal zone</u>. As the Department of Energy noted in its comments on the proposed regulations:

The Act presumes a balancing of the national interest in energy self-sufficiency with State and local concerns involving adverse economic, social, or environmental impacts.

43 Fed. Reg. 8379.

* * *

The Court notes further in this regard that the standards established by the Coastal Act * * * for making energy facilities siting decisions, in the words of the Coastal Commission staff, "establish the general findings that must be made to authorize coastal dependent industrial facilities, liquefied natural gas terminals, oil and gas developments, refineries, petrochemical facilities and electric power plants." FEIS, Part II (Chapter 9) at 66. The key to the California approach, and one which the Acting Administrator and this Court find acceptable under the CZMA, is that the standards require that "findings" be made upon which specific siting decisions ensue. For instance, in dealing with the siting of oil tanker facilities, § 30261(a) requires that

Ca looks at each siting separately

> [t]anker facilities shall be designed to (1) minimize the total volume of oil spilled, (2) minimize the risk of collision from movement of other vessels, (3) have ready access to the most effective feasible containment and recovery equipment for oil spills, and (4) have onshore deballasting facilities to receive any fouled ballast water from tankers where operationally or legally required.

As can readily be seen from these provisions, whether a particular tanker facility siting proposal will be deemed "consistent" with these requirements of the California Program will turn on specific findings of a factual nature. The California Program sensibly does not attempt to map out in advance precisely what type or size tanker facilities will be found to meet these requirements in particular areas of its almost 1,000-mile coastline. Rather, by its very nature, the Coastal Act encourages plaintiffs with a particular facility in mind to address themselves to the standards set forth in the Coastal Act and to plan such a facility in cooperation and communication with the Coastal Commission from the inception. This approach seems consonant with the overall approach of the CZMA itself. * * * To the extent plaintiffs seek not guidance with respect to the way in which coastal resources will be managed but instead a "zoning map" which would implicitly avoid the need to consult with the state regarding planned activities in or affecting its coastal zone, the Court rejects their position. While wholly sympathetic to the legitimate concerns of corporate officers and planners who must conform their activities to the standards of the CZMP, the Court nevertheless concludes that the Acting Administrator's finding that the Program satisfies § 306(c)(8) is supportable and hence not arbitrary or capricious. It proceeds from a correct interpretation of the CZMA.

energy co's should develop proposal in conjunction w/ Ca

NO ZONING MAP NEEDED

* * *

[U]nder our so-called federal system, the Congress is constitutionally empowered to launch programs the scope, impact, consequences and workability of which are largely unknown, at least to the Congress, at the time of enactment; the federal bureaucracy is legally permitted to execute the congressional mandate with a high degree of befuddlement as long as it acts no more befuddled than the Congress must reasonably have anticipated; if ultimate execution of the congressional mandate requires interaction between federal and state bureaucracy, the resultant maze is one of the prices required under the system. * * *

Findings

The administrative action is affirmed; the petition is denied, each side to bear its costs.

Notes and Questions

1. In a section of the opinion not included above the court considered the standard of review appropriate to the administrative decision in dispute:

> That deference is due an agency's interpretation of its own regulations and the statute is charged with administering is indisputable. * * * The principle of deference itself is premised on the twin notions of agency expertise and congressional acquiescence in that interpretation.

456 F. Supp. at 906. The court ultimately found both factors important in its decision to give "considerable deference" to the interpretations made by the federal defendants of their regulations:

> * * * Congress placed responsibility for administering the CZMA in the Department of Commerce with the clear expectation that such responsibility ultimately would be delegated to NOAA, an agency favored by Congress expressly because of its technical expertise in matters relating to the Nation's coasts. Moreover, during enactment of the 1976 Amendments Congress applauded NOAA's administration of the Act and directed it to promulgate regulations further clarifying the requirements of the Act.

Id. at 908. What other factors in the case led the reviewing court to defer to NOAA's construction of the statute and implementing regulations?

2. State programs are generally presented in the format of the Environmental Impact Statement (EIS) which is required by the National Environmental Policy Act for all major federal actions that significantly affect the environment. In API v. Knecht, API attacked the adequacy of the EIS for not considering relevant information and available alternatives and not discussing potential and unavoidable adverse impacts of approving and implementing the California plan. Upholding the adequacy of the EIS, Judge Kelleher stated:

> [T]he "essence" of the CZMP, in accordance with * * * the CZMA, is sensitivity to environmental concerns in establishing standards for utilization of the coastal zone; consequently, fewer and less

detailed environmental studies would be expected because the Program emphasizes environmental preservation. API v. Knecht, 456 F. Supp. 889 (C.D. Cal. 1978).

Was the court correct in its assessment of the "essence" of coastal planning and its conclusion that the CZMA is "first and foremost a statute directed to and solicitous of environmental concerns"? Did the court foreclose the necessity of considering alternatives that might have better accommodated both the environment and development?

3.   Implementing these coastal management policies requires states to prioritize coastal uses and make choices among uses where they conflict.   To what extent did Congress, in the CZMA, grant or delegate to the states the authority to carry out these policies?   Can states effectively make these choices between competing land and water uses in the coastal zone within constitutional limitations?

Due to the inactivity of its port for commercial shipping in the late 1970s, the City of Rochester, New York, developed plans to turn the port into a recreational and marine area. To further this plan, the port was zoned to "create a harbor district, in which the permitted uses will be those water dependent and commercial uses which will enhance the character as an attractive and recreational harbor."   The zoning ordinance prohibited all manufacturing, warehouse and distribution centers, and commercial cargo and shipping terminals.   Pittston Warehouse Corporation sought to initiate a new "roll-on/roll-off trailer ship" service between Rochester and Canada, but Rochester passed a resolution specifically prohibiting this type service. Pittston challenged the constitutionality of the ordinances. Among the city's arguments was the claim that the CZMA provides support for cities to exercise their police power for purposes of improving the harbor environment, promoting public access, and enhancing the recreational character of the area. In Pittston Warehouse Corp. v. City of Rochester, 528 F. Supp. 653 (D.C. W.D.N.Y. 1981), the court held that the ordinances violated the Commerce Clause and are "invalid insofar as they impede or obstruct the free flow of interstate and international commerce." Can this case be reconciled with Norfolk Southern Corporation v. Oberly, 822 F.2d 388 (3rd Cir. 1987) which held that the Delaware coastal program did not violate the Commerce Clause by prohibiting any new "offshore gas, liquid, or solid bulk transfer facilities" in the coastal zone, even in areas designated by the Coast Guard for such purposes?

4.   As amended in 1990, the definition of "coastal zone" provides:

The term "coastal zone" means the coastal waters (including the lands therein and thereunder) and the adjacent shorelands (including the waters therein and thereunder), strongly influenced by each other and in proximity to the shorelines of the several coastal states, and includes islands, transitional and intertidal areas, salt marshes, wetlands, and beaches. The zone extends, in Great Lakes waters, to the international boundary between the United States and Canada and, in other areas, seaward to the outer limit * * * of State title and ownership under the Submerged Lands Act. * * * The zone extends inland from the shorelines only to the extent necessary to control shorelands, the uses of which have a direct and significant impact on the coastal waters, and to control those geographical areas which are likely to be affected by or vulnerable to sea level rise. * * *

16 U.S.C. § 1453(1). How far inland should state coastal zone boundaries extend? See Woodruff, Longley & Reed, Inland Boundary Determinations for Coastal Management Purposes, 4 Coastal Zone Mgmt. J. 189 (1978). The definition leaves considerable room for variation of landward boundaries from one coastal state to another. For example, North Carolina's Coastal Area Management Act defines the inland portion of the coastal zone as the area encompassed by all the counties bounded by coastal waters; Hawaii's coastal zone includes the entire state; California, on the other hand, defines the land portion of its coastal zone as a 1000-yard strip extending inland from its coastal waters; Massachusetts' coastal zone extends landward 100 feet beyond the first major land transportation route encountered (e.g., a road, highway, or rail line), and also includes all of Cape Cod, Martha's Vineyard, Nantucket, and Gosnold.

5.   The CZMA "[e]xclude[s] from the coastal zone * * * lands the use of which is by law subject solely to the discretion of or which is held in trust by the Federal Government, its officers, or agents." See 16 U.S.C. § 1453(1). In California Coastal Commission v. Granite Rock Company, 480 U.S. 572 (1987), a mining company argued that the California Coastal Commission lacked the authority to impose environmental permit conditions upon its mining activities. The mining activities would be conducted in accordance with federal regulations on unpatented mining claims located in a national forest. According to the company, the Commission's permit requirements were per se preempted by Forest Service regulations, the Mining Act of 1872, and by the exclusion of federal lands from the definition of "coastal zone." The United States Supreme Court rejected this broad challenge to the Coastal Commission's authority. The Court concluded "that even if all federal lands are excluded from the CZMA definition of coastal zone the CZMA does not automatically preempt all state regulation of activities on federal lands." Id. at 593. The federal laws applicable to the activity were viewed by the Court as "land use" regulations which would not preempt the state's "environmental" regulation imposing conditions aimed at carrying out the activity in the least environmentally damaging manner.

6.   CZMA § 307(f), 16 U.S.C. § 1456(f), provides that federal, state, and local requirements established under the federal Clean Air and Clean Water Acts shall be the air and water pollution control requirements applicable to state coastal management programs. Are state and local governments prevented by § 307(f) from adopting more stringent coastal air pollution regulations as part of an approved state coastal program?   As long as the CZMA's inter-governmental coordination requirements are met, both the federal Clean Air and Clean Water Acts allow state and local governments to impose air and water pollution standards stricter than those promulgated by the federal Environmental Protection Agency. See 33 U.S.C. § 1370; 42 U.S.C. § 7416; Hildreth, The Operation of the Federal Coastal Zone Management Act as Amended, 10 Nat. Res. Law. 211, 215 n.25 (1977).

7.   Some states, such as North Carolina and California, have passed comprehensive coastal management legislation to create their coastal management program; other states, such as Florida, have "networked" existing legislation and regulations under the umbrella of an executive order or policy statement. The CZMA gives states a great deal of flexibility in programmatic approaches. CZMA § 306(d)(11), 16 U.S.C. § 1455(d)(11), recognizes three general approaches a state may adopt:

(A) State establishment of criteria and standards for local implementation, subject to administrative review and enforcement of compliance;
(B) Direct state land and water use planning and regulation; or
(C) State administrative review for consistency with the management program of all development plans, projects, or land and water use regulations, including exceptions and variances thereto, proposed by any state or local authority or private developer, with power to approve or disapprove after public notice and an opportunity for hearings.

Two of these approaches leave most coastal land and water use decisions at the local level. What problems are likely to result from leaving the management of the coastal zones under local control?

8.   Once the state's management plan has been approved, what must the state do to amend it? The federal district court decision in Save Our Dunes v. Pegues, 642 F. Supp. 393 (M.D. Ala. 1985), rev'd on other grounds, 834 F.2d 984 (4th Cir. 1987), posed a threat to continued federal CZMA funding of previously-approved state coastal programs that had been amended or modified without specific federal approval of the amendments or modification. The court strictly interpreted CZMA § 306(g), 16 U.S.C. § 1455(g) [now (e)], as it then read as prohibiting further CZMA program administration grants until such state program changes have been federally approved. According to the court, a supplemental environmental impact statement must be prepared if the

changes can significantly affect the environment "in qualitative or quantitative terms," which would have made the amendment approval process potentially a quite elaborate one. With federal funds delayed or cut off, state programs could deteriorate to the point of withdrawal of federal approval, thereby losing the benefits of federal consistency as well. Consider whether the following 1990 amendments on program amendment or modification solve the problems caused by the court's analysis.

16 U.S.C. § 1455(e). A coastal state may amend or modify a management program which it has submitted and which has been approved by the Secretary under this section, subject to the following conditions:

(1) The State shall promptly notify the Secretary of any proposed amendment, modification, or other program change and submit it for the Secretary's approval. The Secretary may suspend all or part of any grant made under this section pending State submission of the proposed amendments, modification, or other program change.

(2) Within 30 days after the date the Secretary receives any proposed amendment, the Secretary shall notify the State whether the Secretary approves or disapproves the amendment, or whether the Secretary finds it is necessary to extend the review of the proposed amendment for a period not to exceed 120 days after the date the Secretary received the proposed amendment. The Secretary may extend this period only as necessary to meet the requirements of the National Environmental Policy Act of 1969. If the Secretary does not notify the coastal state that the Secretary approves or disapproves the amendment within that period, then the amendment shall be conclusively presumed as approved.

(3)(A) Except as provided in subparagraph (B), a coastal state may not implement any amendment, modification, or other change as part of its approved management program unless the amendment, modification, or other change is approved by the Secretary under this subsection.
(B) The Secretary, after determining on a preliminary basis, that an amendment, modification, or other change which has been submitted for approval under this subsection is likely to meet the program approval standards in this section, may permit the State to expend funds awarded under this section to begin implementing the proposed amendment, modification, or change. This preliminary approval shall not extend for more than 6 months and may not be renewed. A proposed amendment, modification, or change which has been given preliminary approval and is not finally approved under this paragraph shall not be considered an

enforceable policy for purposes of section 307 [16 U.S.C. § 1456].

9. All changes in state coastal programs are not formal amendments or modifications requiring federal approval. A "change" may be either an "amendment" or a "routine program implementation." See 15 C.F.R. §§ 923.80-84. Plan "amendment" involves "substantial changes in, or substantial changes to[,] enforceable policies related to" certain aspects of a coastal management plan, and requires approval * * * by NOAA. Id. § 923.80(c). A "routine program implementation" is a "[f]urther detailing of a State's program that is the result of implementing" the approved program and is not subject to the approval process of an amendment. Id. § 923.84(a).

10. The CZMA established the Estuarine Sanctuaries Program, which has evolved through the 1985 CZMA amendments into the National Estuarine Research Reserve (NERR) System. 16 U.S.C. § 1461. Estuarine Reserves are designated "to enhance public awareness and understanding of estuarine areas, and provide suitable opportunities for public education and interpretation * * *." The NERR system is intended to comprise estuaries that represent all eleven of the country's biological and geographic regions and that will serve as "living laboratories" for long-term research and education. The CZMA provides funds to the states for acquisition, management, education and interpretive programs, and research within the reserves. CZMA §§ 315, 16 U.S.C. § 1461, authorizes the Secretary of Commerce to grant coastal states up to fifty percent of the costs of acquiring and operating estuarine reserves. What are some alternative mechanisms for comprehensively managing sensitive estuarine areas? See, e.g., 16 U.S.C. § 1425(3) (special area management plans encouraged by the 1980 CZMA amendments). Compare the purposes and management approach of estuarine research reserves to the National Estuary Program, 33 U.S.C. § 1330. Under this program, the EPA chooses estuaries of "national significance" and convenes a management conference to develop a comprehensive conservation and management plan for the estuary that recommends corrective action and a compliance schedule. The management conference includes state, regional and federal agencies, local governments, affected industries, public and private educational institutions, and the public. Estuary plans are to be incorporated into states' coastal management programs.

C. INTERGOVERNMENTAL COOPERATION - THE FEDERAL CONSISTENCY REQUIREMENT

(1.) History And Development Of The Consistency Doctrine

Federal grants to assist states in developing and administering coastal management programs provided an initial impetus for states to participate in coastal zone planning. These funds have continually decreased. The so-called federal consistency requirement provides the major incentive for states to continue and maintain their federally-approved programs. Section 307(c), prior to the 1990 amendments, provided that federal actions and activities "directly affecting" a state's coastal zone be conducted in a manner consistent with the state coastal program to the maximum extent practicable. The section also required that federal permitting, OCS exploration and development, and federal assistance to state and local governments for activities affecting a state's coastal zone must be consistent with the coastal program.

In Secretary of the Interior v. California, 464 U.S. 312 (1984), the state of California and others sued the Secretary of Interior on the grounds that a proposed sale of oil and gas leases on outer continental shelf (OCS) tracts off the California coast could not be conducted without the Department of Interior making a consistency determination as required by CZMA § 307(c)(1). California's position was that the lease sale required a showing by the Secretary of Interior that the sale would be "consistent" to the "maximum extent practicable" with the California coastal zone management plan. The Secretary argued that the proposed lease sale was not an "activity directly affecting" the California coastal zone and therefore, no consistency determination was required by the CZMA.

Development of oil and gas OCS resources is divided by statute into four distinct stages by the provisions of the Outer Continental Shelf Lands Act (OCSLA). The first is the five-year leasing plan prepared by the Department of Interior. 43 U.S.C. § 1344. The second stage is the lease sale itself. 43 U.S.C. § 1337. A successful lease purchaser acquires only the right to conduct limited preliminary activities on the OCS, such as geophysical and other surveys. The issue in this suit was whether the sale and these consequent preliminary activities "directly affected" the coastal zone. The third stage consists of actual exploration. However, exploration cannot take place until exploration plans have been submitted for review and approved by the Secretary of Interior. At this stage the Outer Continental Shelf Lands Act, 43 U.S.C. § 1340(c)(2), itself, as well as § 307(c)(3)(B) of the CZMA, refer to the CZMA consistency requirement, and a consistency determination is specifically required. The final stage is the actual development and production of an OCS oil and gas well. Again, before such activities can be undertaken, the lessee must submit another plan for approval by the Secretary. These activities are also specifically subject to the consistency requirement of the CZMA. At all four stages, it is important to note, the OCSLA requires that affected states are given the opportunity to comment upon the plans. In fact, at both the lease stage and the development and production stage, the Governor of any affected state may submit recommendations regarding the size, timing, or location of any proposed lease sale or development and production activity, and the recommendations must be accepted by the Secretary of Interior unless the Secretary finds the recommendations do not strike a reasonable balance between national interests and state and local interests.

In a 5-4 decision of the Court, Justice O'Connor delivered a majority opinion that left the consistency doctrine in a state of confusion. The Court rejected the state's argument that "leasing sets in motion a chain of events that culminates in oil and gas development, and that leasing therefore directly affects' the coastal zone within the meaning of § 307(c)(1)." 464 U.S. at 319. The Court noted that the lease sale authorized only preliminary exploration "that has no significant effect on the coastal zone" and is only one "in a series of decisions that may culminate in activities directly affecting that zone." The Court went on to suggest that only federal activities conducted *in* the coastal zone could have direct effects. "Section 307(c)(1)'s directly affecting' language was aimed at activities conducted or supported by federal agencies on federal lands physically situated in the coastal zone but excluded from the zone as formally defined by the Act." 464 U.S. at 330. Ultimately, however, the Court was persuaded by the fact that although consistency of OCS activities during the exploration and development stages is addressed in both the OCSLA and CZMA, neither act requires consistency review at the lease sale stage. The Court stated:

> As we have noted, the logical paragraph to examine in connection with a lease sale is not § 307(c)(1), but § 307(c)(3). Nevertheless, even if OCS lease sales are viewed as involving an OCS activity "conduct[ed]" or "support[ed]" by a federal agency, lease sales can no longer aptly be characterized as "directly affecting" the coastal zone. Since 1978 the sale of a lease grants the lessee the right to conduct only very limited, "preliminary activities" on the OCS. It does not authorize full-scale exploration, development, or production. Those activities may not begin until separate federal approval has been obtained, and approval may be denied on several grounds. If approval is denied, the lease may then be canceled, with or without the payment of compensation to the lessee. In these circumstances, the possible effects on the coastal zone that may eventually result from the sale of a lease cannot be termed "direct."

It is argued, nonetheless, that a lease sale is a crucial step. Large sums of money change hands, and the sale may therefore generate momentum that makes eventual exploration, development, and production inevitable. On the other side, it is argued that consistency review at the lease sale stage is at best inefficient, and at worst impossible: Leases are sold before it is certain if, where, or how exploration will actually occur.

The choice between these two policy arguments is not ours to make; it has already been made by Congress. In the 1978 OCSLA amendments Congress decided that the better course is to postpone consistency review until the two later stages of OCS planning, and to rely on less formal input from State Governors and local governments in the two earlier ones. It is not for us to negate the lengthy, detailed, and coordinated provisions of CZMA § 307(c)(3) (B), and OCSLA §§ 1344-1346 and 1351, by a superficially plausible but ultimately unsupportable construction of two words in CZMA § 307(c)(1).

Id. at 342-43.

Since prospective lease purchasers acquire no rights to explore, produce, or develop any portion of the OCS, no CZMA consistency review is required. The Court held that § 307(c)(1) did not mandate consistency review for OCS lease sales, but some agencies read the case more broadly. The U.S. Army Corps of Engineers, for example, adopted the interpretation that federal activities must be conducted *in* the coastal zone to have direct effects. See, e.g., Corps Ocean Dumping Regulations, 53 Fed. Reg. 14902 (Apr. 26, 1988).

After several years and a number of proposed amendments to CZMA § 307 to reverse Secretary of the Interior v. California, the 1990 Coastal Management Act Reauthorization Amendments readdressed the federal consistency requirement and provided for a presidential exemption.

CZMA § 307(c)-(d). Coordination and Cooperation
16 U.S.C. § 1456(c)-(d)

(c) Consistency of Federal activities with State management programs; Presidential exemption; certification.

(1) (A) Each Federal agency activity within or outside the coastal zone that affects any land or water use or natural resource of the coastal zone shall be carried out in a manner which is consistent to the maximum extent practicable with the enforceable policies of approved State management programs. A Federal agency activity shall be subject to this paragraph unless it is subject to paragraph (2) or (3).

(B) After any final judgment, decree, or order of any Federal court that is appealable under section 1291 or 1292 of Title 28, or under any other applicable provision of Federal law, that a specific Federal agency activity is not in compliance with subparagraph (A), and certification by the Secretary that mediation under subsection (h) of this section is not likely to result in such compliance, the President may, upon written request from the Secretary, exempt from compliance those elements of the Federal agency activity that are found by the Federal court to be inconsistent with an approved State program, if the President determines that the activity is in the paramount interest of the United States. No such exemption shall be granted on the basis of a lack of appropriations unless the President has specifically requested such appropriations as part of the budgetary process, and the Congress has failed to make available the requested appropriations.

(C) Each Federal agency carrying out an activity subject to paragraph (1) shall provide a consistency determination to the relevant State agency designated under section 1455(d)(6) of this title at the earliest practicable time, but in no case later than 90 days before final approval of the Federal activity unless both the Federal agency and the State agency agree to a different schedule.

(2) Any Federal agency which shall undertake any development project in the coastal zone of a state shall insure that the project is, to the maximum extent practicable, consistent with the enforceable policies of approved state management programs.

(3) (A) After final approval by the Secretary of a state's management program, any applicant for a required Federal license or permit to conduct an activity, in or outside of the coastal zone, affecting any land or water use or natural resource of the coastal zone of that state shall provide in the application to the licensing or permitting agency a certification that the proposed activity complies with the enforceable policies of the state's approved program and that such activity will be conducted in a manner consistent with the program. At the same time, the applicant shall furnish to the state or its designated agency a copy of the certification, with all necessary information and data. Each coastal state shall establish procedures for public notice in the case of all such certifications and, to the extent it deems appropriate, procedures for public hearings in connection therewith. At the earliest practicable time, the state or its designated agency shall notify the Federal agency concerned that the state concurs with or objects to the applicant's certification. If the state or its designated agency fails to furnish the required notification within six months after receipt of its copy of the applicant's certification, the state's concurrence with the certification shall be conclusively presumed. No license or permit shall be granted by the Federal agency until the state or its designated agency has concurred with the applicant's certification or until, by the state's failure to act, the concurrence is conclusively presumed, unless the

Secretary, on his own initiative or upon appeal by the applicant, finds, after providing a reasonable opportunity for detailed comments from the Federal agency involved and from the state, that the activity is consistent with the objectives of this chapter or is otherwise necessary in the interest of national security.

(B) After the management program of any coastal state has been approved by the Secretary under section 1455 of this title, any person who submits to the Secretary of the Interior any plan for the exploration or development of, or production from, any area which has been leased under the Outer Continental Shelf Lands Act (43 U.S.C. § 1331 et seq.) and regulations under such Act shall, with respect to any exploration, development, or production described in such plan and affecting any land or water use or natural resource of the coastal zone of such state, attach to such plan a certification that each activity which is described in detail in such plan complies with the enforceable policies of such state's approved management program and will be carried out in a manner consistent with such program. No Federal official or agency shall grant such person any license or permit for any activity described in detail in such plan until such state or its designated agency receives a copy of such certification and plan, together with any other necessary data and information, and until--

(i) such state or its designated agency, in accordance with the procedures required to be established by such state pursuant to subparagraph (A), concurs with such person's certification and notifies the Secretary and the Secretary of the Interior of such concurrence;

(ii) concurrence by such state with such certification is conclusively presumed as provided for in subparagraph (A), except if such state fails to concur with or object to such certification within three months after receipt of its copy of such certification and supporting information, such state shall provide the Secretary, the appropriate federal agency, and such person with a written statement describing the status of review and the basis for further delay in issuing a final decision, and if such statement is not so provided, concurrence by such state with such certification shall be conclusively presumed; or

(iii) the Secretary finds, pursuant to subparagraph (A), that each activity which is described in detail in such plan is consistent with the objectives of this chapter or is otherwise necessary in the interest of national security.

If a state concurs or is conclusively presumed to concur, or if the Secretary makes such a finding, the provisions of subparagraph (A) are not applicable with respect to such person, such state, and any Federal license or permit which is required to conduct any activity affecting land uses or water uses in the coastal zone of such state which is described in detail in the plan to which such concurrence or finding applies. If such state objects to such certification and if the Secretary fails to make a finding under clause (iii) with respect to such certification, or if such person fails substantially to comply with such plan as submitted, such person shall submit an amendment to such plan, or a new plan, to the Secretary of the Interior. With respect to any amendment or new plan submitted to the Secretary of the Interior pursuant to the preceding sentence, the applicable time period for purposes of concurrence by conclusive presumption under subparagraph (A) is 3 months.

(d) Applications of local governments for Federal assistance; relationship of activities with approved management programs

State and local governments submitting applications for Federal assistance under other Federal programs, in or outside of the coastal zone, affecting any land or water use of natural resource of the coastal zone shall indicate the views of the appropriate state or local agency as to the relationship of such activities to the approved management program for the coastal zone. Such applications shall be submitted and coordinated in accordance with the provisions of section 6506 of title 31. Federal agencies shall not approve proposed projects that are inconsistent with the enforceable policies of a coastal state's management program, except upon a finding by the Secretary that such project is consistent with the purposes of this chapter or necessary in the interest of national security.

Problem

The Minerals Management Service (MMS) of the Department of Interior had routinely granted the suspension of more than thirty five-year oil and gas leases granted between 1968 and 1984 off the California coast, resulting in the extension of the primary terms of the leases. From 1992 to 1999, the MMS directed suspension of the leases on its own initiative. As the directed suspensions were about to end in 1999, the leaseholders again filed a request for lease suspension. The California Coastal Commission (CCC) has challenged the issuance of the suspension of the leases (which have never been subject to consistency review). The CCC's position is that MMS may not approve the suspensions unless the state concurs with the lessee's certification of consistency. The Secretary of Interior takes the position that the suspensions have no affect on the coastal zone. How should this question be resolved under the provisions of the amended CZMA? See California v. Norton, 150 F. Supp. 2d 1046 (N.D. Cal. 2001).

Notes and Questions

1. Section 307(c) originally required federal consistency with "approved state management programs." The 1990 Amendments

require consistency only with "the enforceable policies of approved State management programs." Is there a difference? The amended CZMA defines "enforceable policy" as "State policies which are legally binding through constitutional provisions, laws, regulations, land use plans, ordinances, or judicial or administrative decisions, by which a State exerts control over private and public land and water uses and natural resources in the coastal zone." 16 U.S.C. § 1453(6a).

2. The consistency requirement was originally placed in the CZMA to provide an inducement to the states to develop coastal management plans. If a state developed a plan that met CZMA guidelines and adequately considered the national interest, the state received some assurance that its coastal policy choices would not be readily overturned by federal officials with a differing philosophy of coastal development. Of course, intergovernmental interactions are never as smooth in reality as they are in theory. The use of the consistency requirement by states to oppose development of oil and gas on the continental shelf has been one of the more controversial issues between state and federal governments.

Some critics depict the consistency requirement as a state veto power over federal activities and suggest that it is an unconstitutional violation of the Supremacy Clause. Do you agree? Does your analysis differ if you consider use of the consistency provision by the states as the implementation of a federal statute rather than the imposition of state requirements? For a complete discussion of this debate concerning the consistency requirement, see Whitney, Johnson & Perles, State Implementation of the Coastal Zone Management Consistency Provisions - Ultra Vires or Unconstitutional?, 12 Harv. Envtl. L. Rev. 67 (1988); Archer and Bondareff, Implementation of the Federal Consistency Doctrine - Lawful and Constitutional: A Response To Whitney, Johnson & Perles, 12 Harv. Envtl. L. Rev. 115 (1988); Kuhse, The Federal Consistency Requirement of the Coastal Zone Management Act of 1972: It's Time to Repeal This Fundamentally Flawed Doctrine, 6 Ocean and Coastal Law Journal 77 (2001).

In practice, there has been little evidence that the states have abused any preemptive authority the consistency provisions may have given them. States concur with nearly all consistency certifications, and the few that incur objections are generally resolved through negotiations to develop conditions or mitigating measures. Regulations adopted in December 2000 encourage further cooperation by allowing a state to issue a "conditional concurrence." The state must included in its concurrence letter the conditions that must be satisfied and explain why the conditions are necessary to ensure consistency with enforceable state policies. If the conditions are not met, then the letter will be treated as an objection. See 15 C.F.R. § 930.4.

3. The CZMA contains no provision analogous to the federal consistency provision requiring that states act consistently with their own coastal management programs. Some states have, however, enacted consistency requirements as part of the state program. For example, the Alaska Coastal Management Program (ACMP) requires that "uses and activities" of state agencies in the coastal zone must be consistent with the standards of the ACMP. Alaska Stat. 46.40.200 (1991). In Trustees for Alaska v. Alaska, 851 P.2d 1340 (Alaska 1993), the Alaska Supreme Court required the state to determine the consistency of an oil and gas lease sale in Camden Bay with the ACMP prior to proceeding. The court refused to allow the state's Department of Natural Resources (DNR) to defer until later stages of the process findings on the consistency of oil and gas development with ACMP standards concerning geophysical hazards, historic and archeological resources, and transportation. The court noted that later assessments on a site-by-site basis "may tend to mask appreciation of any cumulative environmental threat that would otherwise be apparent if DNR began with a comprehensive identification of those hazards. Second, * * * the more segmented an assessment of environmental hazards, the greater the risk that prior permits will compel DNR to approve later, environmentally unsound permits."

4. What kind of effects on the coastal zone trigger the consistency requirement? Are environmental effects in the coastal zone necessary? Are economic effects on the coastal zone enough? For example, does an OCS lease sale that affects an offshore fishery and has only economic effects in the coastal zone require consistency? In cases prior to the 1990 amendments to the CZMA, two federal courts came to opposite conclusions. See Kean v. Watt, 13 Env'tl. Law. Rep. 20618 (D.N.J. 1982) (holding that the Act is not concerned with the economic health of a coastal industry, i.e., offshore fishing) and Conservation Law Foundation v. Watt, 560 F.Supp. 561 (D.C. D.Mass. 1983) aff'd sub nom., Massachusetts v. Watt, 716 F.2d 946 (1st Cir. 1983) (finding that social and economic effects are within the scope of the Act). Does the 1990 amendment deleting the requirement of "direct" effects change the analysis? Current regulations provide:

> The term "effects on any coastal use or resource" means any reasonably foreseeable effect any coastal use or resource resulting from a federal action. Effects are not just environmental effects. But include effects on coastal uses. Effects include both direct effects which result from the activity and occur at the same time and place as the activity, and indirect (cumulative and secondary) effects which result from the activity and are later in time or farther removed in distance, but are still reasonably foreseeable. Indirect effects are effects resulting from the incremental impact of the federal action when added to other past, present, and reasonably foreseeable

actions, regardless of what person(s) undertake(s) such actions. 15 C.F.R. § 930.11(g).

5. If an activity is consistent with a state's coastal management program, may the federal government deny, limit, or condition assistance to the activity? See Cape May Greene, Inc. v. Warren, 698 F.2d 179 (3rd Cir. 1983) (EPA was arbitrary and capricious in conditioning funding for an indispensable sewage treatment plant on the denial of new hookups for development in the contiguous floodplain that had already been approved and found by the state to be in compliance with the coastal management program) and Shanty Town Associates Ltd. v. EPA, 843 F.2d 782 (4th Circ. 1988) (holding, in a similar factual situation, that the EPA had not acted arbitrarily because of the EPA's factual finding that the prohibition on new hookups was necessary to protect water quality). Does 16 U.S.C. § 1456(d) help to clarify this issue? See also Blumm, Wetlands Protection and Coastal Planning: Avoiding the perils of Positive Consistency, 5 Colum. J. Envtl. L. 69 (1978).

6. What authority does NOAA have to sanction states for acting inconsistently with its approved state program? NOAA is required to conduct a "continuing review" of state performance (generally, every three years) assessing the "extent to which the state has implemented and enforced the program approved by the Secretary, addressed coastal management needs * * *, and adhered to the terms of any grant, loan, or cooperative agreement." 16 U.S.C. § 1458(a). The 1990 CZMA amendments clarified the conditions for NOAA's suspension of financial assistance to state coastal programs and the circumstances for withdrawal of approval of state programs:

16 U.S.C. § 1458(c) Interim sanctions.

(1) The Secretary may suspend payment of any portion of financial assistance extended to any coastal state under this title, and may withdraw any unexpended portion of such assistance, if the Secretary determines that the coastal state is failing to adhere to (A) the management program or a State plan developed to manage a national estuarine reserve * * * or a portion of the program or plan approved by the Secretary, or (B) the terms of any grant or cooperative agreement funded under this title.

(2) Financial assistance may not be suspended under paragraph (1) unless the Secretary provides the Governor of the coastal state with-- (A) written specifications and a schedule for the actions that should be taken by the State in order that such suspension of financial assistance may be withdrawn; and (B) written specifications stating how those funds from the suspended financial assistance shall be expended by the coastal state to take the actions

referred to in subparagraph (A).

(3) The suspension of financial assistance may not last for less than 6 months or more than 36 months after the date of suspension.

(d) Final sanctions. The Secretary shall withdraw approval of the management program of any coastal state and shall withdraw financial assistance available to that State under this title as well as any unexpended portion of such assistance, if the Secretary determines that the coastal state has failed to take the actions referred to in subsection (c)(2)(A).

(e) Notice and hearing. Management program approval and financial assistance may not be withdrawn under subsection (d), unless the Secretary gives the coastal state notice of the proposed withdrawal and an opportunity for a public hearing on the proposed action. Upon the withdrawal of management program approval under this subsection (d), the Secretary shall provide the coastal state with written specifications of the actions that should be taken, or not engaged in, by the state in order that such withdrawal may be canceled by the Secretary.

9. In 1987, NOAA conducted a periodic review of the California Coastal Management Program (CCMP) as required by the CZMA, 16 U.S.C. § 1458(a). NOAA conditioned continued administrative grants on the Coastal Commission's preparing and submitting "for approval guidelines that would provide greater predictability for parties seeking consistency determinations for proposed activities affecting the Outer Continental Shelf. The Commission refused, contending that it would lose necessary flexibility and that the current case-by-case, negotiated process was preferable." In California v. Mack, 693 F. Supp. 821 (N.D. Cal. 1988), California sought to enjoin NOAA's enforcement of the grant conditions. The court held that:

> * * *NOAA does not have authority to revisit the approvability of a plan. In other words, once NOAA determines that a program satisfies the requirements of the CZMA and grants final approval, it may no longer examine the content of the approved program, only the adequacy of its execution. Only if NOAA determines that the state is not, in fact, satisfactorily implementing its plan, and the state refuses to remedy this deficiency, may NOAA withdraw approval . * * * In short, a careful reading of the enforcement provisions of the CZMA leaves the clear impression that NOAA may not use its power over funding to accomplish indirectly what it may not accomplish directly: enforce alteration of the approved program itself. * * *

Thus, the question here is one of degree. Clearly Congress

realized that NOAA, through its control of federal financial assistance, would wield considerable influence over state coastal programs. But it is also clear that Congress did not intend to confer on NOAA the ability to manipulate the coastal policy of the states. "There is no attempt to diminish state authority through federal preemption. The intent of this legislation is to enhance state authority by encouraging and assisting the states to assume planning and regulatory powers over their coastal zones." S. Rep. No. 753, 92d Cong., 2d Sess. 1* * *. Accordingly, this Court concludes that, whatever authority NOAA may have to impose implementation requirements as conditions to grants, it may not revisit the question of the management program's adequacy by forcing a state to choose between modifying the program and losing federal financial assistance under the CZMA.

Was NOAA attempting to reverse the position it took in API v. Knecht?

(2.) The Consistency Requirement

Problem One

Perfect Prawns, Inc., (PPI) a non-profit corporation chartered by the Commonwealth of Puerto Rico, wishes to operate a mariculture shrimp farm in a bay on the island of Vieques. To accomplish this, PPI plans to place floating cages anchored on the bottom on no more than five acres, two percent, of the bay's area. The perimeter of this area would be outlined by mooring buoys, and a wooden dock for boat launching would also be constructed. The shrimp farm operation would involve the maintenance of approximately 37,500 pounds of a species of shrimp, exotic to the waters of the bay, in the cages for each growing period of approximately 186 days.

PPI applied to the Corps of Engineers for a permit for the proposed project, and submitted a certification that its project is consistent with Puerto Rico's Coastal Management Plan (CMP). The Puerto Rico Planning Board (PRPB), its coastal management agency, objected to PPI's project on the ground that it is not consistent with the enforceable policies contained in Puerto Rico's CMP. Of specific concern to PRPB is that Appellant's proposed project would jeopardize the ecological communities existing in the proposed area as well as other systems close to the area by virtue of introducing exotic species with their associated diseases, and would also affect the water quality of the bay by the increase of nutrients from food and animal waste resulting from the concentrated culture of shrimp. The PRPB also noted its concern that permitting this mariculture project, which would be the first in Puerto Rico, would set a precedent. The PRPB then presented the alternative of considering an upland site for the project and/or the conducting of a complete monitoring study.

PPI asserted that its plan provided adequate protection against escape or introduction of exotic species and that water quality standards would not be violated. PPI further argued that the project was in the national interest by providing a sustainable use of the coastal zone to produce high quality seafood and help "eliminate the stress of harvesting in the wild." The project would also directly further the national policy to promote aquaculture facilities in the coastal zone. Finally, PPI alleges that, because of the Navy's commitment to assist in economic development on Vieques, this project is necessary in the interest of national security.

When PPI's permit was denied, PPI appealed the negative consistency determination. Experts for both PPI and the PRPB provided evidence supporting their positions. The Department of Defense was solicited for comment and replied: "The proposed project is not necessary in the interest of national security as no national defense or other national security interest would be significantly impaired if the activity were not permitted to go forward as proposed." Can the negative consistency determination be overridden?

See In the Consistency Appeal of Vieques Marine Laboratories from an Objection by the Puerto Rico Planning Board, U.S. Department of Commerce, Office of the Secretary 1996.

Problem Two

The Department of the Interior has announced it will hold a lease sale of several large offshore tracts containing deposits of phosphate. The tracts are 4 to 15 miles offshore of State A. In the same area, there is a commercial shrimping and seasonal recreational mackerel fishery in which both State A's and State B's fishermen participate. Although State A has not objected to the lease sale, adjacent State B's coastal zone management agency objects to the proposed leasing as being inconsistent with the state's federally approved coastal zone management program. The state program restricts any activities that may interfere with established fisheries. The program also contains a policy statement giving priority to exploitation of renewable, over nonrenewable, resources. It further provides that "facilities serving the commercial fishing and recreation boating industry shall be protected and, where feasible, upgraded." The state contends that the proposed mining activities will interfere with commercial shrimping and recreational fishing and will have an adverse impact upon the onshore facilities serving the commercial fishing industry. In addition, the turbidity caused by the mining may impact sea grass beds in state waters which serve as nursery and feeding areas for the shrimp and for numerous species of fish.

Before the Department of the Interior holds the lease sale, must it supply the state coastal commission with a certification that the sale is consistent to the maximum extent practicable with the state coastal zone management plan? If not, how would the state raise its objection to the proposed sale? Does the state have a legitimate objection to the proposed sale? If it does, does that mean that the sale must be canceled? Must the Department of Interior seek a Presidential exemption? On what grounds may the President exempt the leasing activity? Do those grounds exist here?

Assume the sale is held, and Phosphate, Inc. purchases the tract and applies for a federal permit to begin mining operations. Must Phosphate, Inc. supply a consistency certification with its federal permit application? Assuming the Minerals Management Service refuses to issue the permit without the consistency certification and Phosphate, Inc. continues to believe that such a certification is not required, what legal action should Phosphate take to force the issuance of a permit? Assuming, on the other hand, that Phosphate's mining operations are in fact inconsistent with the state coastal zone management plan, may Phosphate nonetheless appeal the denial of the permit? To whom does Phosphate, Inc. appeal and upon what grounds may the permit be issued notwithstanding the inconsistency of the company's proposed operations with the state coastal zone management plan?

How would your analysis be affected if State A was issuing the phosphate mining lease in state territorial waters, but Phosphate, Inc. was required to acquire a permit from the U.S. Army Corps of Engineers under the Clean Water Act and the Rivers and Harbors Act before it could proceed?

* * *

The CZMA provides for both mediation and appeals processes.

CZMA § 307(h). Mediation of Disagreements
16 U.S.C. § 1456(h)

In case of serious disagreement between any Federal agency and a coastal state * * * in the administration of [an approved] management program * * * the Secretary * * * shall seek to mediate the differences in such disagreement. The process of such mediation shall * * * include public hearings which shall be conducted in the local area concerned.* * *

Findings by a state that a federally permitted activity, an OCS exploration or development plan, or a federal assistance program is inconsistent with a state coastal program may also be appealed to the Secretary of Commerce. See 16 U.S.C. §§ 1456(c)(3)(A)-(B), (d), supra. NOAA regulations provide the basis of review for determining when the

Secretary can override a state's consistency objection by finding the activity consistent with the objectives of the CZMA or necessary in the interest of national security.

15 C.F.R. § 930.121. Consistent with the objectives or purposes of the Act.

A federal license or permit activity, or a federal assistance activity, is "consistent with the objectives or purposes of the Act" if it satisfies the following three requirements:

(a) The activity furthers the national interest as articulated in § 302 or § 303 of the Act, in a significant or substantial manner;

(b) The national interest furthered by the activity outweighs the adverse coastal effects, when those effects are considered separately or cumulatively;

(c) There is no reasonable alternative available which would permit the activity to be conducted in a manner consistent with the enforceable policies of the management program. When determining whether a reasonable alternative is available, the Secretary may consider but is not limited to considering, previous appeal decisions, alternatives described in objection letters and alternatives and other new information described during the appeal.

15 C.F.R. § 930.122. Necessary in the interest of national security.

A federal license or permit activity, or a federal assistance activity which, although inconsistent with a State's management program, is "necessary in the interest of national security" if a national defense or a national security interest would be significantly impaired if the activity were not permitted to go forward as proposed. Secretarial review of national security issues shall be aided by information submitted by the Department of Defense or other interested Federal agencies. The views of such agencies, while not binding, shall be given considerable weight by the Secretary. The Secretary will seek information to determine whether the objected-to activity directly supports national defense or other essential national security objectives.

* * *

The appeals process often results in rulings important to interpretation of the CZMA and the consistency requirement. The regulations above reflect December 2000 revisions. Section 15 C.F.R. § 930.121 added the requirement that the activity "further the national interest . . . *in a significant or substantial manner*." Would this change the analysis in the following cases?

IN THE CONSISTENCY APPEAL OF JESSIE W. TAYLOR FROM AN OBJECTION BY THE STATE OF SOUTH CAROLINA
(Taylor Decision)
U.S. Department of Commerce, Office of the Secretary
December 30, 1997

Jessie W. Taylor (Appellant) requested that the Secretary of Commerce (Secretary) override the State of South Carolina's (State) objection to his proposal to fill wetlands on his property for commercial development, and to mitigate the adverse wetland impacts through his purchase of mitigation credits in a wetland mitigation bank. This appeal arises under the consistency provisions of the Coastal Zone Management Act (CZMA). The CZMA is administered by the National Oceanic and Atmospheric Administration (NOAA), an agency within the Department of Commerce. Section 307 of the CZMA, 16 U.S.C. § 1456, provides that any applicant for a required Federal license to conduct an activity affecting any land or water use or natural resource of the approved state's coastal zone shall provide to the permitting agency a certification that the proposed activity complies with the enforceable policies of a state's coastal management program. This requirement furthers state coastal management efforts by fostering coordination and cooperation among coastal states, Federal agencies, and Federal license or permit applicants.

* * *

I. Background

In 1982, the Appellant purchased 0.62 acres of commercial property, part of a larger block of commercial property, for the purpose of building a commercial storage facility on the site. The site is situated in a developed commercial area.* * * Subsequently, the owners of adjacent property (lots 21, 24 and 25) elevated their lots above the natural grade through the placement of fill material, and one owner built a commercial structure to house a business known as Lube City next to the Appellant's property.

Notwithstanding the placement of fill on lots 21, 24 and 25, the collection of lots 21-25, together, contain 2.2 acres of wetlands. Thus, the Appellant owns 0.60 acres of a larger 2.2 acre wetland area. In 1987, the Appellant was permitted to cut, clear and clean underbrush from his property. The natural water drainage has continued to change since the placement of fill material on the adjacent property, and has interfered with water drainage from the Appellant's property. The Appellant states: "Because of activities of adjacent property owners in the past, the [Appellant's] property, through no fault of his own, has developed wetland characteristics." Robert Mikell, OCRM Director of Planning and Federal Certification, states: "These wetlands are valuable habitat, provide stormwater functions, serve as hydrologic buffers, and possibly aquifer recharge."

In 1995, the Appellant applied to the Corps for a permit for the placement of fill material on his property under section 404 of the Clean Water Act. The Corps concluded that the activity was a candidate for authorization if an acceptable mitigation proposal was submitted by the Appellant and certified by the South Carolina Bureau of Ocean and Coastal Resource Management (OCRM). The South Carolina Department of Health and Environmental Control Environmental Quality Control, waived water quality certification and review of the activity. No objections to the activity were received from the commenting public. The Appellant proposed to compensate for wetland impacts by purchasing mitigation credits in a wetland mitigation bank known as Vandross Bay Mitigation Bank. * * *[T]he Appellant completed [a] mitigation worksheet * * * provided by the Corps. In conjunction with that Federal permit application, and pursuant to CZMA § 307(c) (3) (A), the Appellant certified that the activity is consistent with South Carolina's coastal management program.

OCRM reviewed the Appellant's proposed activity and informed the Corps of its intent to find the activity inconsistent with South Carolina's coastal management program. OCRM also identified the coastal management program policies at issue. The State indicated that it did not consider the Appellant's offer of mitigation. Specifically, Robert Mikell, Director of Planning and Federal Certification, OCRM, stated:

> Because the project was not eligible for wetland master planning we are forced to use the policies of the Management Program. These policies do not allow for an alteration of this type of wetland. Consequently, the offsite mitigation proposal made by the applicant is irrelevant in this case and cannot be considered until the project can be made consistent.

The Appellant filed an unsuccessful administrative appeal at the state level. After reviewing the Appellant's appeal, OCRM formally objected to the Appellant's activity on the grounds that it is inconsistent with the South Carolina coastal management program.* * *

Under section 307(c) (3) (A) of the CZMA and 15 C.F.R. § 930.131, OCRM's consistency objection precludes the Corps from issuing a permit for the activity unless the Secretary of Commerce finds that the activity is either consistent with the objectives or purposes of the CZMA (Ground I), or necessary in the interest of national security (Ground II).

II. Request for a Secretarial Override

In accordance with CZMA § 307(c) (3) (A) and 15 C.F.R. Part 930, Subpart H, the Appellant filed with the Department of Commerce an appeal from OCRM's objection to his proposed activity. The Appellant requested that the Secretary override the State's objection, asserting that the activity is consistent with the objectives or purposes of the CZMA. Both the Appellant and the State provided an initial set of comments on the merits of the appeal.

The sole effect of overriding a state's objection is to authorize the Federal agency from whom the license or permit in question is sought to issue the license or permit notwithstanding the State's consistency objection.* * *

NOAA requested comments on the merits of the appeal from interested Federal agencies and the public. The Corps and EPA responded, whereas the FWS and NMFS did not respond. No comments were received from the general public.

After the public and Federal agency comment periods closed, NOAA provided the Appellant and OCRM with an opportunity to file final responses to any submission filed in the appeal. Both the Appellant and OCRM submitted final briefs. * * *

III. Compliance with the CZMA and its Implementing Regulations

The scope of my review of the State's objection is limited to determining whether the objection was properly lodged, i.e., whether the State complied with the requirements of the CZMA and implementing regulations in filing its objection. I have not considered whether the State was correct in its determination that the proposed activity was inconsistent with its coastal management program. Similarly, resolution of whether OCRM's denial of certification of the Corps permit is unconstitutional is also beyond the scope of this appeal.

* * *

The project is inconsistent because it would result in the permanent alteration of 0.60 acres of productive freshwater wetlands through the placement of fill material for the purpose of commercial development. The Office of OCRM has not been able to identify any alternatives to the proposed project.

* * * I find that the State Objection Letter adequately describes how the activity is inconsistent with the [state coastal management plan]. The policy is clear. With one exception, commercial proposals that require fill or other permanent alteration of salt, brackish or freshwater wetlands are inconsistent with the state's coastal management program. The exception has two prongs: there must be no feasible alternatives and the facility must be water-dependent. The administrative record reflects that the activity is clearly not water-

dependent; moreover, the Appellant argued prior to the date of the State Objection Letter that water-dependency should be an irrelevant consideration.

* * *

IV. Grounds for Overriding a State Objection

I now examine the grounds provided in the CZMA for overriding OCRM's objection. I will override OCRM's objection only if I find that the Appellant's proposed activity is consistent with the objectives of the CZMA (Ground I), or otherwise necessary in the interest of national security (Ground II). The Appellant asserts that the activity satisfies the requirements of Ground I. The four elements of Ground I [prior to the revised regulations of December 2000 were]:

1.   The proposed activity furthers one or more of the competing national objectives or purposes contained in CZMA
2.   The proposed activity's individual and cumulative adverse coastal effects are not substantial enough to outweigh its contribution to the national interest.
3.   The proposed activity will not violate the Federal Water Pollution Control Act (Clean Water Act) or the Clean Air Act.
4.   There is no reasonable alternative available that would permit the proposed activity to be conducted in a manner consistent with the State's coastal management program.

To find that the proposed activity satisfies Ground I, I must determine that the activity satisfies all four of the elements specified above. If the activity fails to satisfy any one of the four elements, I must find that the activity is not consistent with the objectives or purposes of the CZMA.

1. Element 1: Activity Furthers One or More Objectives of the CZMA

To satisfy Element 1, I must find that the proposed activity furthers one or more of the competing national objectives or purposes contained in CZMA §§ 302 or 303. Congress has broadly defined the national interest in coastal zone management to include both the protection and the development of the coastal zone. In past consistency appeal decisions, the Secretary has found a wide range of activities that satisfy these competing goals.[1]

The Appellant argues that Element 1 is satisfied because the

---

[1] Previous consistency appeal decisions have found that activities satisfying Element 1 include, in part, oil and gas exploration, the siting of railway transportation facilities, the construction of a commercial marina, and the construction of a food market.

proposed activity meets the CZMA goals of effective management and development of the coastal zone. Among other things, the Appellant cites the CZMA policy that new commercial development should be located in or adjacent to areas where such development already exists.

The State, on the other hand, argues that the project does not further one or more of the competing national objectives or purposes of the CZMA. The State points out that the activity is not water dependent, and indicates that it could not identify any overriding public benefits that would be gained from the activity. The State also highlights the need to conserve urban wetlands.

I agree with the State that the proposed activity is not coastal-dependent. Previous consistency appeal decisions have held that certain non-coastal-dependent activities at issue in those cases do not promote the national interest and objectives of the CZMA. However, those previous decisions involved limited residential projects, which are distinguishable from the activity under consideration in this case. This appeal involves a proposal for commercial development.

I also agree with the State that the activity will not further the national interest in preserving and protecting natural resources of the coastal zone. My consideration of the activity's adverse coastal effects under Element 2 of Ground I elaborates on this point. However, the CZMA reflects a competing national interest in encouraging development of coastal resources.

I am persuaded by the evidence in the record that the Appellant's activity will foster development of the coastal zone, albeit non-coastal-dependent development. The CZMA recognizes development as one of the competing uses of the coastal zone and its resources. In addition, the proposed commercial activity would be located in areas where development already exists. Any negative impacts or reasonably foreseeable future harm from that development are more properly considered under Element 2 of Ground I, rather than under this element. Accordingly, I find that the proposed activity satisfies Element 1 of Ground I because it furthers one or more of the CZMA's objectives or purposes.

2. Element 2: The Activity Will Not Cause Individual and Cumulative Adverse Coastal Effects Substantial Enough to Outweigh Its Contribution to the National Interest.

* * *

A. Adverse Coastal Effects

The adverse effects of the proposed activity must be analyzed both in terms of the activity itself, and in terms of its cumulative effects. That is, I must look at the activity in combination with other past, present and reasonably foreseeable future activities affecting the coastal zone.

In this case, the coastal resource at issue is the wetland area on the Appellant's property. In evaluating the adverse effects of the activity, relevant factors include the quantity of wetland loss, the nature of the wetland loss, and the effects of the wetland loss on the remaining ecosystem. Similarly, the mitigation worksheet provided by the Corps identified the following factors for consideration: the dominant effect of the activity, the lost wetland values, the duration of effects, the location of the activity and the area of impact.

The Appellant's proposal to fill wetlands follows similar actions taken by his neighbors and others in the surrounding area. As Robert Mikell, OCRM Director of Planning and Federal Certification, stated: "At one time the wetland was probably much larger in size, but urban development has resulted in the area being reduced to this area of approximately 2.2 acres in size." In other words, the State's management of the coastal zone has transformed this area into a commercial area.* * *

Nevertheless, the Appellant's activity would remove the wetlands on his property. Among other things, these wetlands collect and assimilate stormwater from adjacent property. The State asserts that "these wetlands are valuable habitat, provide stormwater functions, serve as hydrologic buffers, and possible aquifer recharge."

The Federal agency comments on this appeal were minimal. The FWS and NMFS did not respond to the agency's request for comments. EPA responded that it had no comments regarding the appeal. However, the Corps stated: "We are not aware of any basis for recommending that the Commerce Department override the determination made by the South Carolina Department of Health and Environmental Control's Office of Ocean and Coastal Resource Management." The Corps provided no further explanation.

To analyze the cumulative adverse effects, I must look at the activity in combination with other past, present and reasonably foreseeable future activities affecting the coastal zone. The Appellant asserts that the cumulative impacts of his activity are non-existent. He asserts that allowing economic use of wetlands in a developed area is sound policy.

I agree with the State that the project, without the Appellant's proposed mitigation measure, will cause adverse cumulative impacts. As indicated above, the commercial development of the area has reduced the larger wetlands to an isolated 2.2 acre area. It is reasonable to conclude that the State's management of the coastal zone at Surfside Beach has resulted in wetland loss that increases the need to preserve remaining wetlands. The value of preserving these wetlands, however, is limited by their size, nature, and commercial location.

The Appellant has proposed to compensate for the loss of the 0.6 acres of wetlands that would be filled by purchasing mitigation credits in a wetland mitigation bank known as Vandross Bay Mitigation Bank. While the State has determined that its coastal management policies prevent it from considering the Appellant's offer of mitigation, I am able to consider this aspect of the Appellant's proposal. The Vandross Bay Mitigation Bank provides an established mechanism for mitigating wetland losses. The amount of mitigation was determined using a worksheet provided by the Corps that considered the dominant effect of the activity (fill), the lost wetland values, the duration of effects, the location of the activity and the area of impact. The Appellant asserts that his proposed mitigation measure will preserve approximately 2.85 acres of the highest quality wetlands, 2.85 acres which will have a higher value for wildlife habitat and environmental protection than the 0.6 acres proposed to be filled. The Appellant argues that his mitigation proposal will minimize any adverse environmental impacts of his activity. The State offered no argument or facts contrary to the Appellant's assertion. In fact, the State noted that for activities where its coastal management program allowed the consideration of wetlands offsets, credits from the Vandross Bay Mitigation Bank have been allowed for approved projects.

Based on all of the materials in the record, those submitted by the Appellant, OCRM and the Federal agencies, I find that the Appellant's proposed activity, including the Appellant's proposed mitigation measure, will not cause individual and cumulative adverse effects on the natural resources of South Carolina's coastal zone as a result of the filling of wetlands. In fact, I find that the Appellant's proposed activity with mitigation would appear to have a net beneficial effect on the resources of the coastal zone since the fill of 0.6 acres of low quality wetlands would be more than offset by the creation and preservation of approximately 2.85 acres of high quality wetlands. Further, the activity including the proposed mitigation measure would lessen rather than increase cumulative impacts on the natural resources of the coastal zone.

B. Contribution to the National Interest

The national interests to be balanced in Element 2 are limited to those recognized in or defined by the objectives or purposes of the CZMA. The CZMA identifies two broad categories of national interest to be served by proposed activities. The first is the national interest in preserving and protecting natural resources of the coastal zone. The second is encouraging development of coastal resources.

* * *

In Element 1, I found that the Appellant's activity furthers one or more objectives of the CZMA. Specifically, I found that the activity will promote economic development and will be located in an area of other economic development. After considering the scope and nature of the Appellant's activity, I conclude that the Appellant's activity will make a minimal contribution to the national interests identified in the CZMA.

C. Balancing

In Element 2, an activity's adverse coastal effects are weighed against its contribution to the national interest. In this case, I found that the Appellant's proposed activity, including his mitigation offset, will not cause any adverse effects on the natural resources of the coastal zone, and, in fact, will have a net positive impact. I also found the proposed activity will have a minimal contribution to the national interest. * * *

Since I have found that the proposed activity, including the proposed mitigation measure, will have no adverse coastal effects, there is nothing to outweigh the activity's minimal contribution to the national interest. This finding is based on the administrative record, which includes the factual circumstances presented in this case and the proposed mitigation measure. Accordingly, the Appellant has satisfied Element 2.

3. Element 3: Activity Will Not Violate the Clean Water Act or the Clean Air Act

* * * I am persuaded that the Appellant will not violate the Clean Water Act or the Clean Air Act because he cannot proceed with his activity except in compliance with the CWA and CAA. * * * The proposed activity therefore satisfies Element 3 of Ground I.

4. Element 4: No Reasonable, Consistent Alternatives Available

* * * When a state is objecting to an activity as being inconsistent with the State's coastal management program, the state is required to propose alternative measures (if they exist) which would permit the activity to be conducted in a manner consistent with its coastal management program.   In this case, the State Objection Letter states simply that OCRM has not been able to identify any alternatives to the proposed activity.* * * Accordingly, I find that there are no reasonable, available alternatives which would permit the Appellant's proposed activity to be conducted in a manner consistent with the State's coastal management program, and that the Appellant has satisfied Element 4 of Ground I.

V. Conclusion

* * *

I hereby find, for the reasons stated above, that the proposed activity is consistent with the objectives and purposes of the CZMA. Accordingly, the Corps may issue the permit for the activity, which includes the Appellant's mitigation as a necessary permit condition. This decision does not enable the Corps to license or permit any other activity. Of course, the Corps may impose more restrictive or protective conditions on the activity.

IN THE CONSISTENCY APPEAL OF THE VIRGINIA ELECTRIC AND POWER COMPANY FROM AN OBJECTION BY THE NORTH CAROLINA DEPARTMENT OF ENVIRONMENT, HEALTH AND NATURAL RESOURCES

U.S. Department of Commerce, Office of the Secretary, 1994.

EXECUTIVE SUMMARY

Introduction

The Virginia Electric and Power Company (VEPCO), on behalf of the City of Virginia Beach, Virginia (City), has appealed to the Secretary of Commerce to override the State of North Carolina's objection to the City's proposal to withdraw water from Lake Gaston for the City's water supply needs. This issue has had a long and contentious history, and the decision was reached only after a thorough consideration of all the evidence in the record. As explained in more detail below, the Secretary overrides North Carolina's objection, thereby allowing the City to obtain federal permits to build a pipeline for the withdrawal of up to 60 million gallons a day (mgd) of water from Lake Gaston.

VEPCO's appeal arises under the Coastal Zone Management Act (CZMA), an act administered by the National Oceanic and Atmospheric Administration (NOAA), an agency within the Department of Commerce. Section 307 of the CZMA provides that any applicant for a required federal license to conduct an activity affecting any land or water use or natural resource of the coastal zone, shall provide to the permitting agency a certification that the proposed activity complies with the enforceable policies of a state's coastal zone management program.

VEPCO has requested approval from the Federal Energy Regulatory Commission (FERC) for the City's project. Because North Carolina has objected to the project, FERC may not grant a license or permit, unless the Secretary of Commerce finds that the activity is consistent with the objectives of the CZMA or is otherwise necessary in the interest of national security.

Background

The City, located on the coast of southeastern Virginia, is the largest city in Virginia, with more than 400,000 residents. The City has no water supply of its own and, historically, has purchased all of its water from the adjacent city of Norfolk. A series of droughts plaguing southeastern Virginia over the past 15 years has caused water shortages throughout the area. In response, the City has adopted mandatory year round water restrictions and imposed a moratorium on extensions of its water system. Numerous water studies have shown that southeastern Virginia will need at least an additional 60 mgd of water by the year 2030.

More than a decade ago, after several years of study, the City embarked upon a project to withdraw potable water from Lake Gaston for the consumption of its residents and those of neighboring cities. Lake Gaston, which lies approximately 80 miles west-southwest of the City, is a man-made lake formed by damming a portion of the Roanoke River. Lake Gaston is part of a hydroelectric project constructed in the 1950s by VEPCO, under a license granted by FERC. Lake Gaston lies partly in Virginia and partly in North Carolina. The proposed project involves the permanent, consumptive withdrawal of up to 60 mgd of water from Lake Gaston, which is the equivalent of 22 billion gallons per year.

To gain access to Lake Gaston, the City proposes to construct a pipeline. The proposed pipeline would originate in a branch of Lake Gaston in Brunswick County, Virginia, at a location approximately 400 yards north of the Virginia-North Carolina border, run 76 miles across southeastern Virginia, and end at Lake Prince in Isle of Wight County, Virginia. The proposed pipeline would be located entirely within Virginia. In 1983, in order to construct the pipeline, the City applied to the U.S. Army Corps of Engineers (Corps) for a permit under two federal statutes, the Clean Water Act and the Rivers and Harbors Act. The Norfolk District Corps of Engineers issued the permit after conducting an environmental assessment pursuant to the National Environmental Policy Act (NEPA), and concluded that the project would have no significant environmental effects.

The State of North Carolina (State) challenged the adequacy of the Corps' NEPA review in the federal courts. A decision issued in July 1991, ultimately upheld the issuance of the Corps permit.

To install and operate its water intake facility for Lake Gaston, the City must also obtain permission from VEPCO, and VEPCO, in turn, must obtain approval from FERC. VEPCO applied to FERC on February 20, 1991, to obtain the necessary permit approval for the pipeline project. The State of North Carolina requested that the City and VEPCO submit a certification that the proposed project was consistent with North Carolina's coastal management program, a program which had been approved under the CZMA. The City and VEPCO jointly submitted such a certification.

On September 9, 1991, the State objected to the City's and VEPCO's consistency certification on the ground that the proposed project is inconsistent with several enforceable policies contained in the State's coastal management program. Specifically, the State alleged that the project is not consistent with its guidelines for estuarine waters and public trust areas because the proposed withdrawal of water would significantly increase the number of low flow days experienced by the lower Roanoke River system in coastal North Carolina. This increase, the State asserted, would cause significant adverse effects on its coastal zone, including the Roanoke River striped bass fishery.

Under the CZMA, the State's consistency objection precludes any federal agency from issuing any license or permit necessary for the City's proposed project, unless the Secretary of Commerce (Secretary) finds that the activity is either consistent with the objectives or purposes of the CZMA (Ground I) or is necessary in the interest of national security (Ground II).

On October 3, 1991, VEPCO, on behalf of the City, filed with the Secretary a notice of appeal from the State's objection to the City's proposed project. The City argued that the project satisfies both Ground I and Ground II and raised several threshold issues. On December 3, 1992, then-Secretary of Commerce Barbara Franklin, relying on a Department of Justice opinion, terminated the appeal on the basis that North Carolina lacked the authority under the CZMA to review a proposed project that would occur wholly within Virginia. In February, 1993, the Department of Justice was asked again whether its previous opinion still represented its view, and Justice responded affirmatively. Subsequently, the Department of Justice withdrew its opinion, and on January 7, 1994, the Department of Commerce reopened the appeal.

Upon consideration of the entire record, which included submittals by the City and North Carolina, written information from federal agencies and the public, and views given during a public hearing, the

Secretary made the following findings.

DECISION

* * *

IV. THRESHOLD ISSUES

In accordance with prior consistency appeals, I have not considered whether the State was correct in its determination that the proposed activity was inconsistent with its coastal management program. Rather, the scope of my review[2] of the State's objection is limited to determining whether the objection was properly lodged, i.e., whether the State complied with the requirements of the CZMA and implementing regulations in filing its objection.

A. Compliance with the CZMA and its Implementing Regulations

The City has raised certain threshold issues related to whether the State's objection complies with the requirements of the CZMA. The City argues that because certain key provisions of the CZMA do not apply to the proposed pipeline project, the project is not subject to consistency review

1. The City argues that because VEPCO has not applied for a federal license or permit the right to review is not triggered.

According to the CZMA, the City must first have applied for a federal license or permit in order to trigger the State's right to review an activity for consistency purposes. The City contends that VEPCO has not applied for any such required federal license or permit. The City admits, however, that VEPCO, on the City's behalf, must obtain FERC's approval to transfer easements to the City. NOAA regulations define the term "license or permit" to include approvals.[3] Nonetheless, the City argues that these regulations should not be given effect because they exceed

---

[2] The term "appeal" is a misnomer. More precisely, I examine the State's objection for compliance with the CZMA and its regulations in order to determine whether the objection was properly lodged. I then determine whether an appellant has filed a perfected appeal. Then, based on all relevant information in the administrative record, I conduct a de novo inquiry of whether the activity is consistent with the objectives of the CZMA or necessary in the interest of national security.

[3] The term "license or permit" is defined by NOAA regulations as:

[A]ny authorization, certification, approval, or other form of permission which any federal agency is empowered to issue to an applicant * * * [It includes] [r]enewals and major amendments of federal license and permit activities not previously reviewed by the State agency * * * 15 C.F.R. § 930.51.

the authority of the CZMA.

I reject the City's argument. NOAA's consistency regulations constitute a reasonable interpretation of the term "license or permit" and thus are entitled to substantial deference. In addition, Congress has endorsed the regulations at issue. NOAA's interpretation is also consistent with other federal statutes, including the Administrative Procedure Act, which define the term "license" to include agency approvals. Therefore, I find NOAA's regulations interpreting the term "license or permit" to include approvals are valid and should be given effect. Because the City admits that FERC approval is required for the project at issue, I find that VEPCO has applied for a required federal license or permit.

B. Interstate Consistency

The second threshold issue raised by the City is that of interstate consistency. * * * "Federal consistency" is the term used to describe the mechanism by which a state can review federal activities, including federally licensed or permitted activities, to determine whether they are consistent with the state's coastal management program. The issue raised by the City is whether, under the CZMA, a state (North Carolina) has a right to review, i.e., comment on and possibly object to, a federally licensed or permitted activity occurring totally within another state (the Lake Gaston pipeline in Virginia) in order to determine if the activity has negative effects on the coastal environment of the reviewing state (North Carolina). This issue is referred to as "interstate consistency."

The two parties have raised three issues regarding interstate consistency. First, Virginia Beach argues that interstate consistency is not authorized by the CZMA. Thus, North Carolina cannot review the Lake Gaston project even if that activity affects its coastal zone, because the project is located in Virginia.

Contrarily, North Carolina believes that interstate consistency is authorized by the CZMA and that it can therefore review the Lake Gaston project if that project affects its coastal zone. Second, in addition to asserting that North Carolina has no right to review activities occurring outside its borders, the City also asserts that I am precluded from considering the interstate consistency issue because that issue was already decided when the Corps considered Virginia Beach's application for a permit related to this project. Finally, the State argues that whether interstate consistency is authorized does not have to be reached in this case because the project occurs within its own borders and thus is not an interstate application of federal consistency. Several non-party commentators submitted comments to me in this appeal supporting the positions of both North Carolina and Virginia Beach on the issue of interstate consistency. * * *

2. Does this project occur in Virginia only, or in both Virginia and North Carolina?

The State argues that the project does not involve interstate consistency because the project will occur in both North Carolina and Virginia. That is to say, the State argues that I need not decide whether it has a right to review an activity occurring in another state, because the activity is also occurring within its own borders. The State asserts that the largest part of the reservoir is in North Carolina, and that the removal of water from Lake Gaston is itself part of the project. In contrast, the City argues that the project will occur totally within the state of Virginia, but concedes that there may be only minimal effects in North Carolina.

This is a question of first impression for a consistency appeal decision. In practice, however, NOAA has considered projects to be occurring at the site where the physical activity required for the project takes place, i.e., the site of construction, the site of a discharge pipe, or the site of dredging and disposal of dredged material. This is true even for projects affecting water bodies shared by two or more states, as evidenced by NOAA's handling of several past consistency appeals (which were withdrawn for other reasons before decisions were reached). The State has, however, confused the effects of the project with the location of the project. If the FERC permit is issued, the City will be granted easements to allow it to build a pipeline and intake pipe in Virginia, from which it will extract water from the Virginia portion of Lake Gaston.

The State's request would, in effect, have me determine as a threshold matter that because the pipeline may cause detrimental effects in North Carolina, the project therefore occurs in North Carolina, and thus it can be reviewed without implicating interstate consistency. Like former Secretary Franklin, I decline to accept this argument. A project does not "occur" in a state merely because its effects might be felt there. I concur with Secretary Franklin's decision that "the proposed activity will occur wholly within the boundaries of the Commonwealth of Virginia."

Having made this threshold determination, I will, however, subsequently consider the effects of the pipeline when I balance the effects against the national interest in the project. The project's effects are thoroughly considered in Element 2 of Ground I of this decision.

3. Does the CZMA authorize one state to review for consistency with its coastal management program an activity occurring totally within another state?

a. Plain Meaning of the Statute

Interpretation of any statute begins with the plain language of that statute. The CZMA, as amended by the 1990 Coastal Zone Act Reauthorization Amendments (hereinafter CZARA), makes it clear that Congress meant to place no geographical boundaries upon the states' use of federal consistency. Two terms are particularly significant for purposes of my examination of the plain meaning of the CZMA: "affect" and "that state." At issue regarding the word "affect" is whether an activity occurring totally within one state, which will affect the coastal zone of another state, can be reviewed for consistency by the state that will be affected. * * *

The fact that Congress [in 16 U.S.C. § 1456(c)] used the term "in or outside of the coastal zone" to describe activities "affecting" the coastal zone indicates that the only test for determining whether a state can review a federal activity for consistency is whether that activity affects the reviewing state's coastal zone. In other words, the focus is not on the activity's location, but rather on its effects. The activity's location is irrelevant to the analysis of the activity's effects on the coastal zone. "Affecting" is the limiting factor in this section of the CZMA, not political and/or geographical lines.

The second significant term for purposes of my analysis is "that state." The section cited above provides that an applicant for a federal permit for an activity affecting the coastal zone of "that state" shall provide a consistency certification. The City argues that the term "that state" refers only to the state in which the activity is being conducted (in this case, Virginia), and therefore, the statute does not authorize interstate consistency review.[4]

---

[4] The City makes an often-heard argument that this view of section 307(c)(3)(A) would lead to Louisiana reviewing for consistency with its coastal management program activities occurring considerably north of Louisiana along the Mississippi-Missouri river system. While theoretically possible, this argument is a red herring. There must be a nexus between the activity wherever located and the reviewing state's coastal zone. The activity must cause an effect in the coastal zone of the reviewing state. This limiting factor may be reviewed at two critical junctures in the consistency process. First, OCRM has advised that, if a state has not indicated in its coastal management program the geographic location of activities outside of its coastal zone that it will review for consistency, the preferred method for state review is for a state to request from the Director of OCRM permission to review the activity as an unlisted activity. The standard for allowing such review is that the requesting state must show that the activity can be "reasonably expected to affect" the land and water uses or natural resources of its coastal zone. Clearly, the farther away an activity is from the coastal zone in question, the harder that showing will be. Second, if review is allowed and a state finds the activity inconsistent with its coastal management program, upon appeal, the Secretary will examine the activity within the statutory and regulatory parameters of his review and could find the activity (1) consistent with the objectives of the CZMA or (2) otherwise necessary in the interest of national security.

I decline to adopt the City's narrow reading of "that state." Rather, I find that the more reasoned approach to interpreting the term is to refer to the beginning of the sentence, where the term "state" is first used. The sentence begins with the phrase, "After final approval of a state's coastal management program, any applicant * * * ." Reading this phrase in conjunction with the use of the term "that state" later in the sentence convinces me that "that state" refers to any state with an approved coastal zone management program. This is consistent with the legislative history and the policies and purposes of the CZMA discussed below.

Therefore, based on the plain language of the statute, I find that the CZMA authorizes interstate consistency review.

b. Additional Statutory Arguments

The City also argues that allowing interstate consistency review would diminish states' "jurisdiction, responsibility, [and] rights" regarding water resources.[5] It asserts that North Carolina, by its objection to the City's consistency determination, uses a federally delegated authority in an area that should be left to the state of Virginia. This argument erroneously suggests that the CZMA gives a state with a federally approved coastal management program direct authority over activities occurring within another state.

While the CZMA does not give one state direct authority to control activities in another state, the CZMA does grant to states with federally approved coastal management programs the right to seek conditions on or prohibit the issuance of federal permits and licenses that would "affect" their state. Thus, Congress has, in effect, granted to states with a federally approved coastal management program, in exchange for their protecting the nation's coasts, the right to ensure that federal permitees and licensees will not further degrade those coasts. The ability to prevent the granting of federal permits and licenses is a federal authority which has been granted to coastal states, not a state authority which has been usurped from the states. However, as a safeguard to a state's unrestrained use of this authority, an applicant can, as the City has, appeal for an override by the Secretary of Commerce.

The City has also advanced the argument that Congress has by adding the term "enforceable policies" to section 307 of the CZMA limited a state's review to the geographical area where, under state law,

---

[5] The City cites another portion of the CZMA, section 307(e)(1), as supporting its reading of section 307(c)(3)(A). This section reads, in pertinent part:

Nothing in this title shall be construed * * * to diminish either Federal or state jurisdiction, responsibility, or rights in the field of planning, development, or control of water resources . * * *

the reviewing state's enforceable policies are in effect. Thus, the City argues that the definition of enforceable policies limits a state's objection to activities occurring within the reviewing state because that is the only place the reviewing state's enforceable policies would have effect under state law. The City's interpretation of "enforceable policies" is incongruous with the language of section 307. Where possible, one must read various parts of a law consistently; and one must read the term "enforceable policies" in the context of the section in which it appears. As discussed above, in its 1990 amendments to section 307, Congress explicitly clarified that federal consistency under section 307 applies to activities both "in and outside" a state's coastal zone. It is thus illogical that Congress meant to limit this explicit recognition of the broad scope of federal consistency review merely by using the term "enforceable policies."

Furthermore, the City's argument is contrary to the spirit of the CZMA provisions enacted by Congress. By granting states the authority to review federal licenses and permits, Congress has deliberately given states broader authority than they would otherwise have. Similarly, Congress also made clear that enforceable policies included in a state's federally approved coastal management plan should apply, through federal consistency, to activities occurring both "in and outside" of the coastal zone. Congress thereby ensured the broadest possible protection for federally sanctioned activities that might harm a state's coastal zone.

Finally, at the same time that Congress added the term "enforceable policies" to section 307, it made it clear that the amendments to sections 307(c)(3)(A) and (B) were made "solely for the purpose of conforming these existing provisions with the changes to section 307(c)(1) made to overturn the [Secretary of Interior v. California] Supreme Court decision" and "to codif[y] the existing regulatory practice [15 C.F.R. §§ 930.39(c) and 930.58(a) (4).]". Thus, the term "enforceable policies" should not be construed to change NOAA's long-standing position that the CZMA authorizes interstate consistency.

I find, therefore, that contrary to the City's contention, the addition of the term "enforceable policies" in the 1990 CZARA amendments does not preclude interstate consistency review.

c. Legislative History

While I have found that the plain language of the CZMA supports interstate consistency, the parties have extensively quoted the legislative history of the CZMA to support their positions. Before addressing their arguments, a review of some of this history may be instructive.

As mentioned above, on May 2, 1989, * * * General Counsel of NOAA issued a legal opinion concluding that interstate consistency is authorized by the CZMA. That opinion gives a long and thorough legislative and regulatory history of the CZMA on this issue. In 1992, after the CZMA was amended, NOAA General Counsel * * * again reviewed this issue in light of the amendments and concluded, after a thorough review of the legislative history of the amendments, that the amendments "confirm that the 'affects' test of the CZMA consistency provision is not subject to geographic limitation." I thoroughly agree with that conclusion and hereby incorporate that opinion by reference.

d. Comparison to Clean Water Act and Clean Air Act

The City argues that the CZMA does not apply to interstate situations because, unlike the Clean Air Act (CAA) and the Clean Water Act (CWA), the CZMA does not have an explicit mechanism for resolution of interstate disputes. Contrary to the City's claim, the CZMA, although not containing a provision labeled specifically as an interstate dispute mechanism, does have a general method for addressing disputes, including interstate disputes.

The CWA and CAA require that an activity in one state be consistent with the policies of a neighboring state if there will be effects in the neighboring state. If the activity is inconsistent, those statutes prohibit the activity without a finding by the Administrator of EPA that the activity is permissible. Likewise, under the CZMA, a federal agency is prohibited from issuing a license in the face of a state's consistency objection unless the Secretary of Commerce decides that, despite the state's objection, the activity is consistent with the objectives of the CZMA (Ground I) or otherwise necessary in the interest of national security (Ground II). Input from neighboring states is allowed under all three statutes.

Further, the CWA and CAA regulatory schemes are distinguishable from that of the CZMA. Pursuant to the CAA and CWA, the federal government establishes minimum national standards and the states are granted authority to achieve those standards through their laws and policies. Because one state's actions under those laws could prevent a neighboring state from achieving the minimum federal standards, states are given the ability to review the laws and policies of other states.

The CZMA envisions a different type of federal/state partnership. There are no national standards under the CZMA. Instead, because of the unique coastal resources of each state, the CZMA encourages each state to develop its own standards, with enforceable policies, to implement the policies and goals of the [CZMA]. Under the CZMA States do not have the ability to review other State's (laws and policies or the object to approvals granted under those state laws.) There is no delegation of federal authority for the development of those programs. However, as discussed above, a type of federal authority is granted to the states in that states are able to review federal actions, such as the granting of federal permits and licenses, for consistency with their state programs.

Thus, I find that while there are important differences between the regulatory schemes of the CZMA and the CWA and CAA, Congress provided resolution mechanisms for interstate conflicts under all three acts. For CZMA section 307(c)(3)(A) conflicts, Congress provided Secretarial override of a state's objection as a mechanism for resolution of a state's objection.

Conclusion for Interstate Consistency

For the reasons stated above, including the plain language of the statute and legislative history, I find that the CZMA authorizes North Carolina to review for consistency with its federally approved coastal management program Virginia Beach's proposed Lake Gaston project, although that activity occurs totally within Virginia, if that project affects any land or water use or natural resource in North Carolina's coastal zone.

Further, a proper reading of the policies and goals of the CZMA supports my conclusion. Congress enacted the CZMA in order to more effectively protect the nation's coasts by encouraging states to exercise their full authority over the lands and waters of the coastal zone, both for the state and for the national interest. This congressional objective is expressed in a number of policies in the CZMA.[6] To implement these policies, states were encouraged to develop management plans for their coasts which were to give "full consideration to ecological, cultural, historic, and esthetic values as well as the needs for compatible economic development * * *."

The City's view that interstate consistency is not authorized under the CZMA is a narrow interpretation of the CZMA that would thwart or make incomplete the implementation of CZMA policies. Just as the beauty of the coast knows no boundaries, neither does the ecology of the coast, nor the threats to the coast. An interpretation that restricts consistency review to the state where the activity is taking place undermines the policies of the CZMA by eliminating states' abilities to

---

[6] Those policies included:

to encourage the participation and cooperation of the public, state and local governments, and interstate and other regional agencies, as well as of the Federal agencies having programs affecting the coastal zone, in carrying out the purposes of this title. Section 303(4) of the CZMA.

consider transboundary effects on their coastal zones.

It is difficult to believe that if Virginia thought its coastal zone was being threatened by an activity requiring a federal license or permit occurring in a neighboring state, it would not at that point appreciate the ability, pursuant to the CZMA, to review that activity for consistency with Virginia's coastal management program. One's view of using the CZMA in an interstate situation will often depend on where one stands in the particular matter under consideration. * * *

[The following section is excerpted from the Executive Summary]

C. Conclusions Regarding Threshold Issues

The Secretary determined that threshold issues raised by Virginia Beach and the State of North Carolina did not preclude him from considering the merits of this case.

Ground I: Consistent with the Objectives or Purposes of the CZMA

To find that the proposed activity satisfies Ground I, the Secretary must determine that the project satisfies all four of the elements specified in the regulations implementing the CZMA. If the project fails to satisfy any one of the four elements, it is not consistent with the objectives or purposes of the CZMA and federal licenses or permits may not be granted. * * *

The Secretary made the following findings with regard to Ground I:

1. The proposed project will foster development of the coastal zone and coastal zone resources, and thus furthers more than one of the objectives or purposes of the CZMA.

2. The proposed project's individual and cumulative adverse effects on the coastal zone are outweighed by its contribution to the national interest. While the record shows that the project's effects on water flow in the Roanoke River will have individual and cumulative adverse effects on striped bass, those effects will likely be small. The record shows that the project's effects on water quality will be minimal, and will minimally affect striped bass. The record shows that the project's effects on coastal wetlands and on other coastal resources and uses will be minimal.

The proposed project will contribute significantly to the national interest because it will allow the beneficial use of water resources of the coastal zone. Providing potable water for human consumption to a major metropolitan area constitutes a very high priority use among all beneficial uses of water. The record shows that the project will contribute significantly to the national interest because of the extent to which it will further and support economic development in the coastal zone, and the extent to which it will alleviate southeastern Virginia's projected water deficit.

In sum, although the project will affect the Roanoke River striped bass fishery, as well as other coastal resources and uses, the evidence shows that the individual and cumulative adverse effects of the project are outweighed by the national interest contribution of alleviating the City's water supply shortage and encouraging economic development.

3. The proposed project will not violate the Clean Water Act or the Clean Air Act.

4. There are no reasonable alternatives available which would permit the project to be conducted in a manner consistent with the State of North Carolina's coastal management program. The proposed alternatives failed for one or more reasons. The State failed to describe some alternatives with sufficient specificity. Some alternatives were unreasonable, i.e., environmental advantages of the alternative did not outweigh the increased cost of the alternative over the proposed project. Finally, some alternatives were found to be unavailable either because of technical or legal barriers or because an alternative did not meet the primary purpose of the project, which is to provide up to 60 mgd of additional water to southeastern Virginia.

Ground II: Necessary in the Interest of National Security

Although southeastern Virginia is home to the largest naval complex in the world, the record demonstrates that there would be no significant impairment to a national defense or other national security interest if the City's project is not allowed to go forward as proposed. Therefore, the Secretary found that the requirements of Ground II have not been met.* * *

VI. CONCLUSION AND SECRETARIAL DECISION

I hereby find, for the reasons stated, that the proposed project is consistent with the objectives and purposes of the CZMA, thereby meeting the requirements of Ground I. Accordingly, the proposed project may be permitted by federal agencies.

* * *

EXXON CORP. v. FISCHER
United States Court of Appeal, Ninth Circuit, 1987
807 F.2d 842, amended on denial of rehearing, 817 F.2d 1429 (1987)

KOZINSKI, Circuit Judge.

We review a declaratory judgment in favor of Exxon entered against the individual members and executive director of the California Coastal Commission (Coastal Commission). That judgment declared invalid the Coastal Commission's objection to Exxon's proposed exploratory drilling program.

Facts

* * *

On January 24, 1983, Exxon successfully bid for the right to explore for oil in the OCS opposite Santa Barbara, California. Following the procedure described above, it submitted to the Department of the Interior a plan proposing three exploratory wells (labeled A, B and C). Recognizing that a small part of its plan (e.g., transport to and from the wells) would affect the coastal zone, Exxon also submitted a "consistency certificate." This certificate asserted that these comparatively minor effects of the Plan would not violate California's Coastal Zone Management Program (CZMP). The Interior Department reviewed the plan and then, pursuant to the CZMA, sent it to the Coastal Commission, together with Exxon's consistency certificate.

[margin note: Ca objected to Exxon exploratory drilling during thresher shark fishing season (drilling allowed offseason)]

The Coastal Commission began to review Exxon's plan for consistency with the state's CZMP. After public hearings, the Commission voted on July 27, 1983, to object to the plan as inconsistent with the CZMP. Exxon appealed this decision to the Secretary, but voluntarily dismissed the appeal in November 1983 when the Commission agreed to let Exxon drill well A and to reconsider its objections to wells B and C.

[margin note: Exxon said cost + schedule not feasible + refused plan]

After drilling well A, Exxon recertified that its plan was consistent with the CZMP. The Coastal Commission again objected, relying on the disruptive effect this drilling would have on the thresher shark fishery during the fishing season, which runs from May through early November. The Commission allowed Exxon to drill during the off-season (Thanksgiving through April) but Exxon, citing cost and scheduling problems, refused.

Exxon did announce at a public hearing before the Coastal Commission that it no longer intended to drill well C, but the Commission decided that even well B alone would violate the CZMP. Exxon again appealed to the Secretary on March 9, 1984. It also brought this action against the Coastal Commission in district court. In the *Exxon sought* district court action, Exxon sought a declaration that the Commission's *declaration* objection to the drilling of well B violated the CZMA because the drilling *well B would* would not affect any land or water use within California's coastal zone. *not violate CZMA*

On November 14, 1984, the Secretary dismissed Exxon's appeal. The Secretary found, pursuant to the four-part test established in the applicable regulation, 15 C.F.R. § 930.121 (1986), that well B was not consistent with the CZMA's purposes. Although it would further the national goal of energy self-sufficiency, although its contribution to the national interest would outweigh its effects on the coastal zone and although it would not violate the Clean Air or Clean Water Acts, the Secretary sustained the Coastal Commission's objections because he found that drilling during the off-season was a reasonably available alternative. Exxon did not seek review of the Secretary's decision.

About a year later, on October 10, 1985, the district court entered summary judgment for Exxon, holding that the Commission had violated the CZMA by objecting to aspects of the plan that did not affect the coastal zone.

Contentions of the Parties

Appellants level several attacks on the judgment below. They argue that the eleventh amendment bars a federal court from considering Exxon's case; that Exxon is precluded from raising its objection because it already did so before the Secretary; and that the Coastal Commission was perfectly within its rights under the CZMA in objecting to Exxon's plan because of the harmful effects the drilling might have on an important coastal industry.

Exxon vigorously contests each point. It argues that the district court had jurisdiction because the case raises a question of federal law; that the Secretary never resolved the contested interpretation of the CZMA in his review of the Commission's objection; and that the CZMA simply does not allow what it characterizes as "economic protectionism" by California in favoring fishermen over oilmen. * * *

Appellants argue that the Secretary's decision estops Exxon from arguing that well B would not "affect land uses" in California's coastal zone under section 1456. Exxon argues that the Secretary's decision is irrelevant to this suit. It contends that the Secretary was ruling on a wholly different issue, namely Exxon's claim that its plan for drilling well B was "consistent with the objectives of" the CZMA. Exxon argues that the suit before us is not another effort at proving that its plan is consistent with the CZMA's objectives, but an attempt to show that the Commission's objection was invalid from the start.

Whether the Secretary's decision should be given preclusive effect hinges on three factors: (1) whether the Secretary was acting in a judicial capacity; (2) whether the issue presented to the district court was actually litigated before the Secretary; and (3) whether its resolution was necessary to the Secretary's decision.

The district court concluded that the Secretary was not acting in a judicial capacity when he reached his decision, primarily because the CZMA required "the Secretary to assess and then balance costs and benefits as would a policy maker." Exxon Corp. v. Fischer, No. CV 84-2362 PAR, slip op. at 28 (C.D.Cal. Oct. 15, 1985). It is true that the law the Secretary was applying required a weighing of cost and benefits. And it is also true that he solicited comments from non-parties. But Exxon was given a hearing, with a full opportunity to present its case and attempt to rebut opposing evidence. K. Davis, 4 Administrative Law 53-54, 79 (2d ed. 1983) (key criterion is opportunity to present and rebut evidence and argument). Exxon took full advantage of these procedures by, for example, introducing its own thresher shark catch statistics for the area where it wanted to drill. See Secretary of Commerce, Decision and Finding in the Consistency Appeal of Exxon Company U.S.A. to an Objection From the California Coastal Commission 13 (Nov. 14, 1984) (hereinafter Sec'y Dec.). Equally important, the Secretary made his findings and conclusions after receiving and carefully considering Exxon's "Supporting Statement" which, like an appellate brief, contained Exxon's arguments and responses with appropriate references to the record compiled before the Coastal Commission. Id. at 7-8. Moreover, the point here in dispute is one of law; it did not call for the exercise of policy judgment. We conclude that the Secretary was acting in a judicial capacity insofar as he addressed the issue presented to the district court.

We also conclude that the issue was actually litigated before the Secretary. Exxon squarely presented the question of whether California's objection was proper under the CZMA. See Sec'y Dec. at 12 ("appellant maintains * * * that such drilling does not affect 'land or water uses' of the coastal zone"). Moreover, the Secretary resolved the issue adversely to Exxon. For one thing, the Secretary himself raised the issue through his very broad construction of the phrase "natural resources of the coastal zone." Id. at 11. His decision reflects both parties' positions on this point, id. at 12-13, and concludes that the effects will not be substantial. Id. at 14. Later in his decision, the Secretary notes that he found the effects of the drilling on coastal zone uses would be limited. Id. at 18.

Finally, a finding on this issue was necessary to the Secretary's decision. The Secretary noted that "in order to accord full effect to the statutory provisions quoted above [16 U.S.C. §§ 1456(c)(3)(B), 1453(10) and (18)], I will consider the adverse effects of the activity on coastal resources and land and water uses, as defined by the CZMA* * *." Sec'y Dec. at 12. The Secretary then proceeded to weigh the benefits of Exxon's proposed plan against the impact it would have. He found the effects of Exxon's drilling on "land and water uses in the coastal zone * * * not substantial." Id. at 14. Nevertheless, he determined that they could be avoided altogether if Exxon were to drill only from Thanksgiving through April. On that basis, he sustained the Coastal Commission's challenge. The Secretary's weighing process necessarily rested on a determination that the state's objection was valid under the CZMA and that the interests it sought to protect were encompassed by the statute. Otherwise, there was nothing to which the Secretary could have legitimately subordinated Exxon's interest.

We do not decide whether Exxon was required to submit this question to the Secretary first, or whether it could have bypassed secretarial review of the issue by going directly to the district court. We hold only that Exxon, having litigated the issue before the Secretary, cannot relitigate the issue in a collateral proceeding. Exxon's proper course to seek judicial review pursuant to the Administrative Procedure Act. See 15 C.F.R. §930.130(d) (1986).

Since this is Exxon's only basis for arguing that the Commission violated the CZMA in objecting to well B, we must reverse the district court's judgment.

Conclusion

The district court's judgment is reversed and the case is remanded for entry of judgment in favor of defendants.

Notes and Questions

1. Is the secretarial appeal process mandatory? Does the appeal represent an administrative remedy that must be exhausted before objection to an applicant's consistency determination can be appealed to the courts?

In Acme Fill Corporation v. San Francisco Bay Conservation and Development Commission (BCDC), 187 Cal.App.3d 1056, 232 Cal.Rptr. 348(1986), the court of appeals found that the petitioner was required to exhaust the administrative remedy provided under the CZMA before a state court challenge to the authority of the BCDC's exercise of consistency review authority. The court based its decision on the fact that although a Secretarial appeal involved different issues, it could have provided petitioner with the relief he sought.

What legal questions does the Secretarial appeal process leave unresolved? In the Consistency Appeal Of Chevron U.S.A., Inc., From

An Objection By The State Of Florida, U.S. Department Of Commerce, Office Of The Secretary (1993), the Secretary addressed this issue:

> * * * As in previous decisions, I do not consider in this appeal whether Florida was correct in its determination that the proposed activity is inconsistent with the state's coastal management program, nor do I consider whether the state's objection is correct as a matter of other state law. Rather, once I have found that the state's objection complies with the CZMA and its implementing regulations, I consider only whether Chevron's proposed project, notwithstanding Florida's objection, is either consistent with the objectives or purposes of the CZMA or otherwise necessary in the interest of national security. The consistency appeals process, therefore, is not the proper forum for an argument on the validity or appropriateness of Florida's consistency determination.

2. What is the standard of review and who bears the burden of proof in Secretarial appeals? See In the Drilling Discharge Consistency Appeal Of Mobil Oil Exploration & Producing Southeast, Inc. From An Objection By The State of North Carolina, U.S. Department of Commerce, Office Of The Secretary (1994) (petitioner bears the burden of proof and is responsible for the adequacy of information to establish by a preponderance of the evidence that the grounds for override have been met).

3. So-called "interstate consistency" is one of the more controversial applications of the CZMA. Was the consistency requirement intended to allow states to exert control over another state's activities? Regulations adopted in December 2000 recognize the requirement of consistency for "interstate coastal effects." 15 C.F.R. § 930.150(a) provides:

> A federal activity may affect coastal uses or resources of a State other than the State in which the activity will occur. Effective coastal management is fostered by ensuring that activities having such reasonably foreseeable interstate coastal effect are conducted consistent with the enforceable policies of the management program of each affected State.

4. The Secretarial appeal of the Lake Gaston project was found proper even though no "permit," only approval, was required to be issued by a federal agency. However, in New Jersey v. Long Island Power Authority, 30 F.d. 403 (3rd Cir. 1994), the court held that approval by the Coast Guard of an Operations Plan to ship nuclear power plant fuel through New Jersey waters did not trigger the consistency requirement. The submission of the Operational Plan was voluntary, and the failure of the agency to exercise discretionary enforcement power did not constitute an agency action under the CZMA. Id. at 420-

421. New regulations defines licenses or permits in terms of "any *required* authorization, certification, approval, lease, or other form of permission which any Federal agency is empowered to issue * * * " (emphasis added). See 15 C.F.R. § 930.51(a).

A consistency determination may also be required for renewals and major amendments which affect a coastal use or resource, particularly if the original activity was not reviewed by the state's agency, if the state program has changed since the original review, or if the effects of the activity will be substantially different than those originally reviewed by the state. See 15 C.F.R. § 930.51(b)-(e).

5. Can the state enjoin a federal permittee's activities that are inconsistent with the state coastal plan? In February 1986, John DeLyser applied to the Corps of Engineers for a permit to build a dock and boathouse on pilings. The permit was issued, but DeLyser instead began construction of a two-story residence with sanitary facilities. The Corps issued a cease and desist order and required DeLyser to submit an after-the-fact permit application. Because the state of New York found the project inconsistent with its coastal management plan, the Corps denied the permit. DeLyser's appeal to the Secretary of Commerce was also unsuccessful. Despite the adverse rulings, DeLyser completed the building and took up residence. The Corps declined to enforce its order citing consideration of funding allocations and the failure of any party other than the state to object to the structure. Does the state have an implied right of action under the CZMA to require DeLyser to remove the unauthorized structure? See State of New York v. DeLyser, 759 F. Supp 982 (W.D.N.Y. 1991)(holding that the state had no authority under the CZMA to require removal of the structure).

6. Does the CZMA allow private citizens or local governments to sue to enjoin construction of developments that are inconsistent with a federally approved state coastal management plan? See Town of North Hempstead v. Village of North Hills, 482 F. Supp. 900, 905 (E.D. N.Y. 1979) (finding the CZMA "is neither a jurisdictional grant, nor a basis for stating a claim upon which relief can be granted, the court dismissed CZMA claim against the village by neighboring town); see also Save Our Dunes v. Alabama Department of Environmental Management, 834 F.2d 984 (11th Cir. 1987), rev'g, Save Our Dunes v. Pegues, 661 F. Supp. 18 (M.D. Ala. 1987) (plaintiffs held not to have standing to appeal coastal permit decision).

7. How much discretion do agencies have in determining a federal activity is consistent "to the maximum extent practicable"? NOAA's regulations provide that federal activities must be "fully consistent with the enforceable policies of [state] programs unless full consistency is prohibited by existing law applicable to the Federal agency. * * * The Act was intended to cause substantive changes in Federal agency

decision making within the context of the discretionary powers residing in such agencies. Accordingly, whenever legally permissible, Federal agencies shall consider the enforceable policies of management programs as requirements to be adhered to in addition to existing Federal agency statutory mandates." 15 C.F.R. § 930.32(a).

Assume the U.S. Army Corps of Engineers decides to engage in a project in the coastal zone to which the state objects as being inconsistent with its federally approved coastal zone management program. After the state objects, the Army Corps of Engineers sends the appropriate state agency a letter in which the Corps asserts that the project "is consistent to the maximum extent practicable" with the state program. Does that end the matter? May the Corps proceed with its project? What right does the state have to participate in the determination of whether the activity indeed is consistent to the maximum extent possible? See 15 C.F.R. § 930.39 (content of a consistency determination); § 930.41(providing guidelines for state response and grounds for disagreement), § 930.39(d) (authorizing the federal agency to apply its more restrictive standards), § 930.36 and § 930.44-.45 (providing for mediation). See also, Commonwealth of Puerto Rico v. Muskie, 507 F. Supp. 1035, 1058-59 (D.P.R. 1981) (holding that the federal government violated the CZMA by inadequately evaluating the consistency of the effects of refugee transfers on the coastal zone).

8. For federal agency action to be consistent with a state coastal management program, are federal agencies required to get state permits required by legislation included in the state plan? Compare Minnesota v. Hoffman, 543 F.2d 1198 (8th Cir. 1976), cert. denied 430 U.S. 977 (1977) (Clean Water Act section 404 exempts the U.S. Army Corps of Engineers from state requirements relating to the discharge of dredged spoil) with the more recent cases, Friends of the Earth v. United States Navy, 841 F.2d 927 (9th Cir. 1988) (Navy must have a state permit under Washington's Shoreline Management Act before continuing with dredging and filling related to a homeport project) and Sierra Club v. Marsh, 692 F. Supp. 1210 (S.D. Cal. 1988) (The California Coastal Act will not be applied when it is hostile to the federal purpose of discharging its obligation to protect endangered species). See also California Coastal Comm'n v. Granite Rock Co., 480 U.S. 572 (1987).

The EPA proposed to designate eight sites in the New York Bight as dredged material disposal sites in June 1988. The agency stated that the ocean dumping designation process did not have to comply with the consistency provisions of the CZMA. The notice of proposed rulemaking claimed that the CZMA is preempted by the Marine Protection, Research, and Sanctuaries Act of 1972 (MPRSA or Ocean Dumping Act). The EPA cited the opinion in Chemical Waste Management v. U.S. Dept. of Commerce, Civ. No. 86-624 (D.C.D.C. 1986) which found that the CZMA did not authorize a state to impose unilateral conditions on the EPA dumping site process. This case was in fact dismissed in a consent decree and the permit sought was denied by the EPA. The opposite legal conclusion to the Chemical Waste Management case was reached in County of San Mateo v. Port of Oakland, No. 329870, slip op. (Sup. Ct. Cal. June 9, 1988), which found the CZMA not to have been preempted by the MPRSA.

SECTION 3. PERVASIVE ISSUES IN COASTAL MANAGEMENT PLANNING AND REGULATION

A. EFFECTS OF GOVERNMENT INFRASTRUCTURE FUNDING

Barrier islands and spits are arguably the most sensitive and unstable lands in the coastal zone. Until the 1950s only ten percent of the barrier islands were developed, but that situation has changed radically. Today, a third of the developable acreage and shoreline is developed, with an additional 5,000 to 6,000 acres being developed each year. Much of this development could not take place without federal and state assistance and subsidies. Federal and state programs, including flood insurance, transportation programs, sewage treatment facility funding, and disaster relief, have tended to subsidize and encourage growth on barriers. Development on barriers also involves tremendous costs with average annual storm damage to coastal property amounting to billions of dollars and disaster relief creating additional public costs.

The Coastal Barrier Resources Act (CBRA), 16 U.S.C. §§ 3501-3510, enacted in 1982, is the first federal environmental law that coordinates environmental protection with federal fiscal policy. CBRA's goal is to preserve the natural resources of coastal barrier islands, minimize danger to human life from poorly located coastal barrier development, and to end federal support for such development. The heart of the Act is the restriction of new federal assistance or expenditures within designated coastal barrier areas. These areas, known as the Coastal Barrier Resources System (CBRS), have been designated through Congressionally-adopted maps of the areas in § 3503 of CBRA. Restricted or prohibited programs include new federal flood insurance coverage, government loans, and other forms of federal assistance and subsidies. Without such federal assistance, the costs of development and the risks of development must be borne by the developer and the purchaser of newly developed coastal barrier island property. See Jones, The Coastal Barrier Resources Act: A Common Cents Approach to Coastal Protection, 21 Envtl. L. 1015 (1991); Creel, Barrier Islands: The Conflict Between Federal Programs that Promote Conservation and Those that Promote Development, 33 S. Car. L. Rev. 373 (1981).

Topsail

In Bostic v. United States, 753 F.2d 1292 (4th Cir. 1985) developers and landowners of property on Topsail Island, North Carolina, complained that CBRA wrongly designated their land as part of an undeveloped coastal barrier. Their objection centered on the fact that the alleged wrongful designation disqualified them from receiving federal flood insurance. The *Bostic* court held, however, that since a § 3503 map designated the island as an undeveloped coastal barrier, Congress unquestionably intended to include it in the CBRS. Such a designation, said the court, reduces federal expenditure and discourages development which would otherwise occur. This is accomplished because developers tend not to build in a coastal barrier area if their only recourse, when federal flood insurance is not available, is to purchase insurance in the private market which can be prohibitively expensive.

Some states have followed the lead of the federal government. For example, the coastal infrastructure policy of Florida's Coastal Zone Protection Act of 1985 reinforced the expenditure limitation approach previously ordered by the governor in 1981. Section 380.27, West's Fla. Stat. Ann., mandates that no state funds be used for constructing bridges or causeways to coastal barrier islands that are not currently accessible by bridge or causeway. The coastal infrastructure policy also emphasizes state-local cooperation by prohibiting state allocation of funds to expand infrastructure unless the construction is consistent with the approved coastal management element of local government comprehensive plans. Section 163.3178, West's Fla. Stat. Ann., states the intent of the legislature that local governments also cooperate in developing funding policies. Local governments are instructed to design their comprehensive plans to "limit public expenditures in areas that are subject to destruction in natural disaster."

B. THE "TAKINGS" ISSUE: PUBLIC AND PRIVATE INTERESTS IN CONFLICT

Coastal land comprises some of the most valuable property in the country to private owners. However, poorly conceived or implemented development of private coastal property subjects owners to natural hazards, may damage adjacent properties, endangers or impedes access to important public resources, and may result in enormous public expense for disaster relief. There seems to be little doubt that there is strong justification for conscientious regulation of coastal development.

However, the economic impact of coastal regulation seems great when compared to potential value of coastal development. Coastal wetlands may be virtually valueless to a private owner if they cannot be filled. Beachfront land may be wedged between the high water line and a highway, leaving little flexibility for locating a structure.

Restrictive building zones may incorporate the entire lot. In addition, new regulations may disproportionately affect unimproved lots in developed coastal areas. Government attempts to promote or preserve public resource values of the coasts often may conflict with private property interests. All these factors make regulation of the coast particularly susceptible to claims that regulation "goes too far" in impairing the use and value of coastal land. Two recent U.S. Supreme Court cases highlight these issues.

(1.) Basic Principles Of Takings Analysis

Fifth Amendment To The United States Constitution

"nor shall private property be taken for public use, without just compensation."

LUCAS v. SOUTH CAROLINA COASTAL COUNCIL
Supreme Court of the United States, 1992
505 U.S. 1003

JUSTICE SCALIA delivered the opinion of the Court.

In 1986, petitioner David H. Lucas paid $975,000 for two residential lots on the Isle of Palms in Charleston County, South Carolina, on which he intended to build single family homes. In 1988, however, the South Carolina Legislature enacted the Beachfront Management Act, S.C. Code §§ 48-39-250 et seq. (Supp. 1990) (Act), which had the direct effect of barring petitioner from erecting any permanent habitable structures on his two parcels. See § 48-39-290(A). A state trial court found that this prohibition rendered Lucas's parcels "valueless." This case requires us to decide whether the Act's dramatic effect on the economic value of Lucas's lots accomplished a taking of private property under the Fifth and Fourteenth Amendments requiring the payment of "just compensation."

I

A

South Carolina's expressed interest in intensively managing development activities in the so-called "coastal zone" dates from 1977 when, in the aftermath of Congress's passage of the federal Coastal Zone Management Act of 1972, 86 Stat. 1280, as amended, 16 U. S.C. §§ 1451 et seq., the legislature enacted a Coastal Zone Management Act of its own. See S.C. Code §§ 48-39-10 et seq. (1987). In its original form, the South Carolina Act required owners of coastal zone land that qualified as a "critical area" (defined in the legislation to include beaches and immediately adjacent sand dunes, § 48-39-10(J)) to obtain a permit from the newly created South Carolina Coastal Council prior to committing the land to a "use other than the use the critical area was devoted to on [September 28, 1977]." S.C. Code § 48-39-130(A).

In the late 1970's, Lucas and others began extensive residential development of the Isle of Palms, a barrier island situated eastward of the City of Charleston. Toward the close of the development cycle for one residential subdivision known as "Beachwood East," Lucas in 1986 purchased the two lots at issue in this litigation for his own account. No portion of the lots, which were located approximately 300 feet from the beach, qualified as a "critical area" under the 1977 Act; accordingly, at the time Lucas acquired these parcels, he was not legally obliged to obtain a permit from the Council in advance of any development activity. His intention with respect to the lots was to do what the owners of the immediately adjacent parcels had already done: erect single-family residences. He commissioned architectural drawings for this purpose.

The Beachfront Management Act brought Lucas's plans to an abrupt end. Under that 1988 legislation, the Council was directed to establish a "baseline" connecting the landward-most "point[s] of erosion * * * during the past forty years" in the region of the Isle of Palms that includes Lucas's lots. S.C. Code § 48-39-280(A)(2) (Supp. 1988).[7] In action not challenged here, the Council fixed this baseline landward of Lucas's parcels. That was significant, for under the Act construction of occupiable improvements[8] was flatly prohibited seaward of a line drawn 20 feet landward of, and parallel to, the baseline, S.C. Code § 48-39-290(A) (Supp. 1988). The Act provided no exceptions.

B

Lucas promptly filed suit in the South Carolina Court of Common Pleas, contending that the Beachfront Management Act's construction bar effected a taking of his property without just compensation. Lucas did not take issue with the validity of the Act as a lawful exercise of

---

[7] This specialized historical method of determining the baseline applied because the Beachwood East subdivision is located adjacent to a so-called "inlet erosion zone" (defined in the Act to mean "a segment of shoreline along or adjacent to tidal inlets which is influenced directly by the inlet and its associated shoals," S.C. Code § 48-39-270(7) (Supp. 1988)) that is "not stabilized by jetties, terminal groins, or other structures," S.C. Code § 48-39-280(A)(2). For areas other than these unstabilized inlet erosion zones, the statute directs that the baseline be established "along the crest of the primary oceanfront sand dune." § 48-39-280(A)(1).

[8] The Act did allow the construction of certain nonhabitable improvements, e.g., "wooden walkways no larger in width than six feet," and "small wooden decks no larger than one hundred forty-four square feet." S.C. Code § 48-39-290(A)(1) and (2) (Supp. 1988).

South Carolina's police power, but contended that the Act's complete extinguishment of his property's value entitled him to compensation regardless of whether the legislature had acted in furtherance of legitimate police power objectives. Following a bench trial, the court agreed. Among its factual determinations was the finding that "at the time Lucas purchased the two lots, both were zoned for single-family residential construction and * * * there were no restrictions imposed upon such use of the property by either the State of South Carolina, the County of Charleston, or the Town of the Isle of Palms." The trial court further found that the Beachfront Management Act decreed a permanent ban on construction insofar as Lucas's lots were concerned, and that this prohibition "deprive[d] Lucas of any reasonable economic use of the lots, * * * eliminated the unrestricted right of use, and render[ed] them valueless." The court thus concluded that Lucas's properties had been "taken" by operation of the Act, and it ordered respondent to pay "just compensation" in the amount of $1,232,387.50.

The Supreme Court of South Carolina reversed. It found dispositive what it described as Lucas's concession "that the Beachfront Management Act [was] properly and validly designed to preserve * * * South Carolina's beaches." 404 S.E.2d 895, 896 (1991). Failing an attack on the validity of the statute as such, the court believed itself bound to accept the "uncontested * * * findings" of the South Carolina legislature that new construction in the coastal zone -- such as petitioner intended -- threatened this public resource. Id., at 898. The Court ruled that when a regulation respecting the use of property is designed "to prevent serious public harm," id., at 899 (citing, inter alia, Mugler v. Kansas, 123 U.S. 623 (1887)), no compensation is owing under the Takings Clause regardless of the regulation's effect on the property's value.

Two justices dissented. They acknowledged that our *Mugler* line of cases recognizes governmental power to prohibit "noxious" uses of property * * * [b]ut they would not have characterized the Beachfront Management Act's "primary purpose [as] the prevention of a nuisance." 304 S.C., at 395, 404 S.E.2d, at 906 (Harwell, J., dissenting). To the dissenters, the chief purposes of the legislation, among them the promotion of tourism and the creation of a "habitat for indigenous flora and fauna," could not fairly be compared to nuisance abatement. Id., at 906. As a consequence, they would have affirmed the trial court's conclusion that the Act's obliteration of the value of petitioner's lots accomplished a taking.

We granted certiorari.

II

[The Court's discussion of the ripeness of Lucas's claim is omitted.]

III

A

Prior to Justice Holmes' exposition in Pennsylvania Coal Co. v. Mahon, 260 U.S. 393 (1922), it was generally thought that the Takings Clause reached only a "direct appropriation" of property, Legal Tender Cases, 12 Wall. 457, 551 (1871), or the functional equivalent of a "practical ouster of [the owner's] possession." Transportation Co. v. Chicago, 99 U.S. 635, 642 (1879). See also Gibson v. United States, 166 U.S. 269, 275-276 (1897). Justice Holmes recognized in *Mahon*, however, that if the protection against physical appropriations of private property was to be meaningfully enforced, the government's power to redefine the range of interests included in the ownership of property was necessarily constrained by constitutional limits. 260 U.S., at 414-415. If, instead, the uses of private property were subject to unbridled, uncompensated qualification under the police power, "the natural tendency of human nature [would be] to extend the qualification more and more until at last private property disappear[ed]." Id., at 415. These considerations gave birth in that case to the oft-cited maxim that, "while property may be regulated to a certain extent, if regulation goes too far it will be recognized as a taking." Id.

Nevertheless, our decision in *Mahon* offered little insight into when, and under what circumstances, a given regulation would be seen as going "too far" for purposes of the Fifth Amendment. In 70-odd years of succeeding "regulatory takings" jurisprudence, we have generally eschewed any "'set formula'" for determining how far is too far, preferring to "engag[e] in * * * essentially ad hoc, factual inquiries." Penn Central Transportation Co. v. New York City, 438 U.S. 104, 124 (1978) (quoting Goldblatt v. Hempstead, 369 U.S. 590, 594 (1962)). We have, however, described at least two discrete categories of regulatory action as compensable without case-specific inquiry into the public interest advanced in support of the restraint. The first encompasses regulations that compel the property owner to suffer a physical "invasion" of his property. In general (at least with regard to permanent invasions), no matter how minute the intrusion, and no matter how weighty the public purpose behind it, we have required compensation. * * *

The second situation in which we have found categorical treatment appropriate is where regulation denies all economically beneficial or productive use of land. * * * As we have said on numerous occasions, the Fifth Amendment is violated when land-use regulation "does not substantially advance legitimate state interests *or denies an owner economically viable use of his land*." Agins, supra, at 260 (citations omitted) (emphasis added).[9]

We have never set forth the justification for this rule. Perhaps it is simply, as Justice Brennan suggested, that total deprivation of beneficial use is, from the landowner's point of view, the equivalent of a physical appropriation. See San Diego Gas & Electric Co. v. San Diego, 450 U.S., at 652 (Brennan, J., dissenting). "[F]or what is the land but the profits thereof [?]" 1 E. Coke, Institutes ch. 1, § 1 (1st Am. ed. 1812). Surely, at least, in the extraordinary circumstance when no productive or economically beneficial use of land is permitted, it is less realistic to indulge our usual assumption that the legislature is simply "adjusting the benefits and burdens of economic life," Penn Central Transportation Co., 438 U.S., at 124, in a manner that secures an "average reciprocity of advantage" to everyone concerned. Pennsylvania Coal Co. v. Mahon, 260 U.S., at 415. And the functional basis for permitting the government, by regulation, to affect property values without compensation---that "Government hardly could go on if to some extent values incident to property could not be diminished without paying for every such change in the general law," id., at 413---does not apply to the relatively rare situations where the government has deprived a landowner of all economically beneficial uses.

On the other side of the balance, affirmatively supporting a compensation requirement, is the fact that regulations that leave the owner of land without economically beneficial or productive options for its use -- typically, as here, by requiring land to be left substantially in its natural state -- carry with them a heightened risk that private property is being pressed into some form of public service under the guise of mitigating serious public harm. See, e.g., Annicelli v. South Kingstown, 463 A.2d 133, 140-141 (R.I. 1983) (prohibition on construction adjacent to beach justified on twin grounds of safety and "conservation of open space"); Morris County Land Improvement Co. v. Parsippany-Troy Hills Township, 40 N.J. 539, 552-553, 193 A.2d 232, 240 (1963) (prohibition on filling marshlands imposed in order to preserve region as water detention basin and create wildlife refuge). As Justice Brennan explained: "From the government's point of view, the benefits flowing

---

[9] Regrettably, the rhetorical force of our "deprivation of all economically feasible use" rule is greater than its precision, since the rule does not make clear the "property interest" against which the loss of value is to be measured. When, for example, a regulation requires a developer to leave 90% of a rural tract in its natural state, it is unclear whether we would analyze the situation as one in which the owner has been deprived of all economically beneficial use of the burdened portion of the tract, or as one in which the owner has suffered a mere diminution in value of the tract as a whole * * * . The answer to this difficult question may lie in how the owner's reasonable expectations have been shaped by the State's law of property -- i.e., whether and to what degree the State's law has accorded legal recognition and protection to the particular interest in land with respect to which the takings claimant alleges a diminution in (or elimination of) value. * * *

to the public from preservation of open space through regulation may be equally great as from creating a wildlife refuge through formal condemnation or increasing electricity production through a dam project that floods private property." San Diego Gas & Elec. Co., supra, at 652 (Brennan, J., dissenting). The many statutes on the books, both state and federal, that provide for the use of eminent domain to impose servitudes on private scenic lands preventing developmental uses, or to acquire such lands altogether, suggest the practical equivalence in this setting of negative regulation and appropriation. [citations omitted]

We think, in short, that there are good reasons for our frequently expressed belief that when the owner of real property has been called upon to sacrifice all economically beneficial uses in the name of the common good, that is, to leave his property economically idle, he has suffered a taking.

B

The trial court found Lucas's two beachfront lots to have been rendered valueless by respondent's enforcement of the coastal-zone construction ban. Under Lucas's theory of the case, which rested upon our "no economically viable use" statements, that finding entitled him to compensation. Lucas believed it unnecessary to take issue with either the purposes behind the Beachfront Management Act, or the means chosen by the South Carolina Legislature to effectuate those purposes. The South Carolina Supreme Court, however, thought otherwise. In its view, the Beachfront Management Act was no ordinary enactment, but involved an exercise of South Carolina's "police powers" to mitigate the harm to the public interest that petitioner's use of his land might occasion. 404 S.E.2d, at 899. By neglecting to dispute the findings enumerated in the Act or otherwise to challenge the legislature's purposes, petitioner "concede[d] that the beach/dune area of South Carolina's shores is an extremely valuable public resource; that the erection of new construction, inter alia, contributes to the erosion and destruction of this public resource; and that discouraging new construction in close proximity to the beach/dune area is necessary to prevent a great public harm." Id., at 898. In the court's view, these concessions brought petitioner's challenge within a long line of this Court's cases sustaining against Due Process and Takings Clause challenges the State's use of its "police powers" to enjoin a property owner from activities akin to public nuisances. See Mugler v. Kansas, 123 U.S. 623 (1887) (law prohibiting manufacture of alcoholic beverages); Hadacheck v. Sebastian, 239 U.S. 394 (1915) (law barring operation of brick mill in residential area); Miller v. Schoene, 276 U.S. 272 (1928) (order to destroy diseased cedar trees to prevent infection of nearby orchards); Goldblatt v. Hempstead, 369 U.S. 590 (1962) (law effectively preventing continued operation of quarry in residential area).

It is correct that many of our prior opinions have suggested that "harmful or noxious uses" of property may be proscribed by government regulation without the requirement of compensation. For a number of reasons, however, we think the South Carolina Supreme Court was too quick to conclude that principle decides the present case. The "harmful or noxious uses" principle was the Court's early attempt to describe in theoretical terms why government may, consistent with the Takings Clause, affect property values by regulation without incurring an obligation to compensate--a reality we nowadays acknowledge explicitly with respect to the full scope of the State's police power. See, e.g., Penn Central Transportation Co., 438 U.S., at 125 (where State "reasonably conclude(s) that 'the health, safety, morals, or general welfare' would be promoted by prohibiting particular contemplated uses of land," compensation need not accompany prohibition); see also Nollan v. California Coastal Commission, 483 U.S., at 834-835 ("Our cases have not elaborated on the standards for determining what constitutes a 'legitimate state interest[,]' [but] [t]hey have made clear * * * that a broad range of governmental purposes and regulations satisfy these requirements"). We made this very point in Penn Central Transportation Co., where, in the course of sustaining New York City's landmarks preservation program against a takings challenge, we rejected the petitioner's suggestion that *Mugler* and the cases following it were premised on, and thus limited by, some objective conception of "noxiousness":

> "[T]he uses in issue in *Hadacheck*, *Miller*, and *Goldblatt* were perfectly lawful in themselves. They involved no 'blameworthiness, * * * moral wrongdoing or conscious act of dangerous risk-taking which induce[d society] to shift the cost to a pa[rt]icular individual.' Sax, Takings and the Police Power, 74 Yale L.J. 36, 50 (1964). These cases are better understood as resting not on any supposed 'noxious' quality of the prohibited uses but rather on the ground that the restrictions were reasonably related to the implementation of a policy -- not unlike historic preservation -- expected to produce a widespread public benefit and applicable to all similarly situated property."

[438 U.S., at 133-134, n. 30.] "Harmful or noxious use" analysis was, in other words, simply the progenitor of our more contemporary statements that "land-use regulation does not effect a taking if it 'substantially advance[s] legitimate state interests' * * *." Nollan, supra, at 834 (quoting Agins v. Tiburon, 447 U.S., at 260); see also Penn Central Transportation Co., supra, at 127; Euclid v. Ambler Realty Co., 272 U.S. 365, 387-388 (1926).

The transition from our early focus on control of "noxious" uses to our contemporary understanding of the broad realm within which government may regulate without compensation was an easy one, since the distinction between "harm-preventing" and "benefit-conferring" regulation is often in the eye of the beholder. It is quite possible, for example, to describe in either fashion the ecological, economic, and aesthetic concerns that inspired the South Carolina legislature in the present case. One could say that imposing a servitude on Lucas's land is necessary in order to prevent his use of it from "harming" South Carolina's ecological resources; or, instead, in order to achieve the "benefits" of an ecological preserve. Compare, e.g., Claridge v. New Hampshire Wetlands Board, 485 A.2d 287, 292 (1984) (owner may, without compensation, be barred from filling wetlands because landfilling would deprive adjacent coastal habitats and marine fisheries of ecological support), with, e.g., Bartlett v. Zoning Comm'n of Old Lyme, 282 A.2d 907, 910 (1971) (owner barred from filling tidal marshland must be compensated, despite municipality's "laudable" goal of "preserv[ing] marshlands from encroachment or destruction"). Whether one or the other of the competing characterizations will come to one's lips in a particular case depends primarily upon one's evaluation of the worth of competing uses of real estate. See Restatement (Second) of Torts § 822, Comment g, p. 112 (1979) ("[p]ractically all human activities unless carried on in a wilderness interfere to some extent with others or involve some risk of interference"). A given restraint will be seen as mitigating "harm" to the adjacent parcels or securing a "benefit" for them, depending upon the observer's evaluation of the relative importance of the use that the restraint favors. See Sax, Takings and the Police Power, 74 Yale L.J. 36, 49 (1964) ("[T]he problem [in this area] is not one of noxiousness or harm-creating activity at all; rather it is a problem of inconsistency between perfectly innocent and independently desirable uses"). Whether Lucas's construction of single-family residences on his parcels should be described as bringing "harm" to South Carolina's adjacent ecological resources thus depends principally upon whether the describer believes that the State's use interest in nurturing those resources is so important that *any* competing adjacent use must yield.

When it is understood that "prevention of harmful use" was merely our early formulation of the police power justification necessary to sustain (without compensation) *any* regulatory diminution in value; and that the distinction between regulation that "prevents harmful use" and that which "confers benefits" is difficult, if not impossible, to discern on an objective, value-free basis; it becomes self-evident that noxious-use logic cannot serve as a touchstone to distinguish regulatory "takings" -- which require compensation -- from regulatory deprivations that do not require compensation. A fortiori the legislature's recitation of a noxious-use justification cannot be the basis for departing from our categorical rule that total regulatory takings must be compensated. If it were, departure would virtually always be allowed. The South Carolina Supreme Court's approach would essentially nullify *Mahon*'s affirmation of limits to the noncompensable exercise of the police power. Our cases provide no support for this: None of them that employed the logic of "harmful use" prevention to sustain a regulation involved an allegation that the regulation wholly eliminated the value of the claimant's land. See Keystone Bituminous Coal Ass'n, 480 U.S., at 513-514 (Rehnquist, C.J., dissenting).

Where the State seeks to sustain regulation that deprives land of all economically beneficial use, we think it may resist compensation only if the logically antecedent inquiry into the nature of the owner's estate shows that the proscribed use interests were not part of his title to begin with. This accords, we think, with our "takings" jurisprudence, which has traditionally been guided by the understandings of our citizens regarding the content of, and the State's power over, the "bundle of rights" that they acquire when they obtain title to property. It seems to us that the property owner necessarily expects the uses of his property to be restricted, from time to time, by various measures newly enacted by the State in legitimate exercise of its police powers; "[a]s long recognized, some values are enjoyed under an implied limitation and must yield to the police power." Pennsylvania Coal Co. v. Mahon, 260 U.S., at 413. And in the case of personal property, by reason of the State's traditionally high degree of control over commercial dealings, he ought to be aware of the possibility that new regulation might even render his property economically worthless (at least if the property's only economically productive use is sale or manufacture for sale). See Andrus v. Allard, 444 U.S. 51, 66-67 (1979) (prohibition on sale of eagle feathers). In the case of land, however, we think the notion pressed by the Council that title is somehow held subject to the "implied limitation" that the State may subsequently eliminate all economically valuable use is inconsistent with the historical compact recorded in the Takings Clause that has become part of our constitutional culture.

* * * Any limitation [prohibiting all economically beneficial use of land] cannot be newly legislated or decreed (without compensation), but must inhere in the title itself, in the restrictions that background principles of the State's law of property and nuisance already place upon land ownership. A law or decree with such an effect must, in other words, do no more than duplicate the result that could have been achieved in the courts—by adjacent landowners (or other uniquely affected persons) under the State's law of private nuisance, or by the State under its complementary power to abate nuisances that affect the public generally, or otherwise.

On this analysis, the owner of a lake bed, for example, would not be entitled to compensation when he is denied the requisite permit to engage in a landfilling operation that would have the effect of flooding others' land. Nor the corporate owner of a nuclear generating plant, when it is directed to remove all improvements from its land upon discovery that the plant sits astride an earthquake fault. Such regulatory action may well have the effect of eliminating the land's only economically productive use, but it does not proscribe a productive use that was previously permissible under relevant property and nuisance principles. The use of these properties for what are now expressly prohibited purposes was always unlawful, and (subject to other constitutional limitations) it was open to the State at any point to make the implication of those background principles of nuisance and property law explicit. See Michelman, Property, Utility, and Fairness, Comments on the Ethical Foundations of "Just Compensation" Law, 80 Harv. L. Rev. 1165, 1239-1241 (1967). In light of our traditional resort to "existing rules or understandings that stem from an independent source such as state law" to define the range of interests that qualify for protection as "property" under the Fifth (and Fourteenth) amendments, Board of Regents of State Colleges v. Roth, 408 U.S. 564, 577 (1972); see, e.g., Ruckelshaus v. Monsanto Co., 467 U.S. 986, 1011-1012 (1984); Hughes v. Washington, 389 U.S. 290, 295 (1967) (Stewart, J., concurring), this recognition that the Takings Clause does not require compensation when an owner is barred from putting land to a use that is proscribed by those "existing rules or understandings" is surely unexceptional. When, however, a regulation that declares "off-limits" all economically productive or beneficial uses of land goes beyond what the relevant background principles would dictate, compensation must be paid to sustain it.

The "total taking" inquiry we require today will ordinarily entail (as the application of state nuisance law ordinarily entails) analysis of, among other things, the degree of harm to public lands and resources, or adjacent private property, posed by the claimant's proposed activities, see, e.g., Restatement (Second) of Torts § 826, 827, the social value of the claimant's activities and their suitability to the locality in question, see, e.g., id., § 828(a) and (b), 831, and the relative ease with which the alleged harm can be avoided through measures taken by the claimant and the government (or adjacent private landowners) alike, see, e.g., id., § 827(e), 828(c), 830. The fact that a particular use has long been engaged in by similarly situated owners ordinarily imports a lack of any common-law prohibition (though changed circumstances or new knowledge may make what was previously permissible no longer so, see Restatement (Second) of Torts, supra, § 827, comment g. So also does the fact that other landowners, similarly situated, are permitted to continue the use denied to the claimant.

It seems unlikely that common-law principles would have prevented the erection of any habitable or productive improvements on petitioner's land; they rarely support prohibition of the "essential use" of land, Curtin v. Benson, 222 U.S. 78, 86 (1911). The question, however, is one of state law to be dealt with on remand. We emphasize that to win its case South Carolina must do more than proffer the legislature's declaration that the uses Lucas desires are inconsistent with the public interest, or the conclusory assertion that they violate a common-law maxim such as sic utere tuo ut alienum non laedas. As we have said, a "State, by ipse dixit, may not transform private property into public property without compensation * * *." Webb's Fabulous Pharmacies, Inc. v. Beckwith, 449 U.S. 155, 164 (1980). Instead, as it would be required to do if it sought to restrain Lucas in a common-law action for public nuisance, South Carolina must identify background principles of nuisance and property law that prohibit the uses he now intends in the circumstances in which the property is presently found. Only on this showing can the State fairly claim that, in proscribing all such beneficial uses, the Beachfront Management Act is taking nothing. * * *

The judgment is reversed and the cause remanded for proceedings not inconsistent with this opinion.

So ordered.

[Justice Kennedy's concurring opinion, Justice Blackmun's and Justice Steven's dissenting opinions, and Justice Souter's statement are omitted.]

Notes and Questions

1. In the late 1800s and early 1900s, the taking requirement was viewed quite literally. Unless the government appropriated private property for its own use, no compensable taking occurred. Regulation of property uses did not constitute a "taking." This approach is derived from the law of nuisance and starts with the basic proposition that no one can obtain a vested right to injure or endanger the public. Thus, the abatement or prevention of a noxious use is not a taking of property since a use that adversely affects the public interest cannot be a vested private property right. Using this approach the economic consequences of government action are irrelevant. The chief proponent of this view was the elder Justice Harlan.

Justice Holmes, however, viewed the "taking" issue as one of a battle between economic interests and the forces of social change. In his view, the distinction between an unconstitutional taking and a valid regulation was simply one of degree. Thus, his focus was upon the degree of economic harm inflicted as a result of the state regulation. If the economic harm was substantial, a "taking" occurred.

With two such dramatic differences in "takings" theory appearing in earlier United States Supreme Court decisions, the natural question is upon which, if any, has the Court settled? Which theory dominates *Lucas*?

2. The Court in *Lucas* cites and discusses Penn Central

Transportation Company v. New York City, 438 U.S. 104 (1978). *Penn Central* was an unsuccessful "taking" challenge to New York City's Landmark Preservation Law. In that opinion, the United States Supreme Court discussed some of the factors that are relevant in the determination of whether a particular limitation on the use of private property is a valid, noncompensable exercise of the state's police power or is a violation of the Fifth Amendment to the United States Constitution.

> In engaging in these essentially ad hoc, factual inquiries, the Court's decisions have identified several factors that have particular significance. The economic impact of the regulation on the claimant and, particularly, the extent to which the regulation has interfered with distinct investment-backed expectations are, of course, relevant considerations. See Goldblatt v. Hempstead, 369 U.S. at 594. So, too, is the character of the governmental action. A "taking" may more readily be found when the interference with property can be characterized as a physical invasion by government, see, e.g., United States v. Causby, 328 U.S. 256 (1946), than when interference arises from some public program adjusting the benefits and burdens of economic life to promote the common good.

Id. at 124. What is the underlying theory of takings in *Penn Central?* When would *Penn Central's* multi-factor approach be applied to a takings claim?

3. Other than common law nuisance, what are the "background principles" of property law to which Justice Scalia refers? The Court specifically recognizes easements: "[W]e assuredly would permit the government to assert a permanent easement that was a pre-existing limitation on the landowner's title." Lucas, 505 U. S. 1003, at 1028-29. However, Justice Scalia wrote a strong dissent to the Court's denial of certiorari in Stevens v. City of Cannon Beach, 510 U.S. 1207 (1994). Stevens sought review of an Oregon Supreme Court decision finding that Stevens did not suffer a compensable taking when he was denied permits to build a seawall on the dry sand beach that was necessary to further develop his land. The Oregon court found that the doctrine of custom was a background principle of state property law and that Stevens never had the right to obstruct the dry sand beach that was subject to public use based on custom. Justice Scalia found the reliance on Thornton v. Hay, 254 Or. 584, 462 P.2d 671 (1969), problematic both substantively and procedurally:

> I believe that petitioners have sufficiently preserved their due process claim, and believe further that the claim is a serious one. Petitioners, who owned this property at the time *Thornton* was decided, were not parties to that litigation. Particularly in light of

the utter absence of record support for the crucial factual determinations in that case, whether the Oregon Supreme Court chooses to treat it as having established a "custom" applicable to Cannon Beach alone, or one applicable to all "dry-sand" beach in the State, petitioners must be afforded an opportunity to make out their constitutional claim by demonstrating that the asserted custom is pretextual. If we were to find for petitioners on this point, we would not only set right a procedural injustice, but would hasten the clarification of Oregon substantive law that casts a shifting shadow upon federal constitutional rights the length of the State.

4. Is legislation enacted prior to a party's acquisition of land a "background principle"? The majority opinion in Palazzolo v. Rhode Island, 121 S.Ct. 2448 (2001), addressed this question directly, but since the Court found that there was no "total taking," the Court's pronouncement may be no more than dicta. Justice Kennedy wrote:

> * * * In *Lucas* the Court observed that a landowner's ability to recover for a government deprivation of all economically beneficial use of property is not absolute but instead is confined by limitations on the use of land which "inhere in the title itself." This is so, the Court reasoned, because the landowner is constrained by those "restrictions that background principles of the State's law of property and nuisance already place upon land ownership." It is asserted here that *Lucas* stands for the proposition that any new regulation, once enacted, becomes a background principle of property law which cannot be challenged by those who acquire title after the enactment.
>
> We have no occasion to consider the precise circumstances when a legislative enactment can be deemed a background principle of state law or whether those circumstances are present here. It suffices to say that a regulation that otherwise would be unconstitutional absent compensation is not transformed into a background principle of the State's law by mere virtue of the passage of title.* * * A regulation or common-law rule cannot be a background principle for some owners but not for others. The determination whether an existing, general law can limit all economic use of property must turn on objective factors, such as the nature of the land use proscribed. * * * A law does not become a background principle for subsequent owners by enactment itself.* * *

5. On remand of *Lucas*, the South Carolina Supreme Court found no common law basis for prohibiting Lucas' proposed use of the land and remanded the case to the trial court for a determination of the actual damages Lucas sustained for the temporary taking of his property. What was the period of the temporary taking? What types of

evidence should be presented before the trial court in this kind of a case? See Lucas v. South Carolina Coastal Council, 309 S.C. 424, 424 S.E.2d 484 (1992) (instructing the trial court that the relevant period for determining damages was from the time of the enactment of the statute through the date of the state supreme court's order in 1992).

6. If a state objects to an applicant's consistency determination, the Corps of Engineers cannot issue a CWA § 404 permit for filling a wetland. If the applicant then brings an action because the property is valueless unless it can be filled, who is responsible for the alleged "taking"? See Anton v. South Carolina Coastal Council, 321 S.C. 481, 469 S.E.2d 604 (1995) (dismissing the case and holding that any loss suffered was the result of the Corps' permit denial, not the action of the Coastal Council).

* * *

NOLLAN v. CALIFORNIA COASTAL COMMISSION
The Supreme Court of the United States, 1987
483 U.S. 825

[The Nollans owned a beachfront lot near a public beach. A concrete seawall parallel to the shoreline separated the beach portion of their property from the rest of the lot. They decided to demolish an existing, run-down structure and replace it with a three-bedroom house. The Coastal Commission granted them permission to do so only on the condition that they record an easement on behalf of the public to pass along the beach. The Commission reasoned that the new construction would create a "psychological barrier" when combined with other buildings, causing the public to believe that the beach was not open to the public. The Nollans sought judicial review, arguing that the permit condition was an unconstitutional taking. The California court held that the collective burden on public beach access caused by projects like Nollan's justified requiring a dedication in this case. The court also rejected Nollan's "taking" claim.]

JUSTICE SCALIA delivered the opinion of the Court.

* * *

Had California simply required the Nollans to make an easement across their beachfront available to the public on a permanent basis in order to increase public access to the beach, rather than conditioning their permit to rebuild their house on their agreeing to do so, we have no doubt there would have been a taking. To say that the appropriation of a public easement across a landowner's premises does not constitute the taking of a property interest but rather, (as Justice Brennan contends) "a mere restriction on its use," is to use words in a manner that deprives them of all their ordinary meaning. Indeed, one of the principal uses of the eminent domain power is to assure that the government be able to require conveyance of just such interests, so long as it pays for them. * * *

Given, then, that requiring uncompensated conveyance of the easement outright would violate the Fourteenth Amendment, the question becomes whether requiring it to be conveyed as a condition for issuing a land-use permit alters the outcome. We have long recognized that land-use regulation does not effect a taking if it "substantially advance[s] legitimate state interests" and does not "den[y] an owner economically viable use of his land." [citations omitted] Our cases have not elaborated on the standards for determining what constitutes a "legitimate state interest" or what type of connection between the regulation and the state interest satisfies the requirement that the former "substantially advance" the latter. They have made clear, however, that a broad range of governmental purposes and regulations satisfies these requirements. [citation omitted] The Commission argues that among these permissible purposes are protecting the public's ability to see the beach, assisting the public in overcoming the "psychological barrier" to using the beach created by a developed shorefront, and preventing congestion on the public beaches. We assume, without deciding, that this is so—in which case the Commission unquestionably would be able to deny the Nollans their permit outright if their new house (alone, or by reason of the cumulative impact produced in conjunction with other construction) would substantially impede these purposes, unless the denial would interfere so drastically with the Nollan's use of their property as to constitute a taking.

The Commission argues that a permit condition that serves the same legitimate police-power purpose as a refusal to issue the permit should not be found to be a taking if the refusal to issue the permit would not constitute a taking. We agree. Thus, if the Commission attached to the permit some condition that would have protected the public's ability to see the beach notwithstanding construction of the new house -- for example, a height limitation, a width restriction, or a ban on fences -- so long as the Commission could have exercised its police power (as we have assumed it could) to forbid construction of the house altogether, imposition of the condition would also be constitutional. Moreover (and here we come closer to the facts of the present case), the condition would be constitutional even if it consisted of the requirement that the Nollans provide a viewing spot on their property for passersby with whose sighting of the ocean their new house would interfere. Although such a requirement, constituting a permanent grant of continuous access to the property, would have to be considered a taking if it were not attached to a development permit, the Commission's assumed power to forbid construction of the house in order to protect the public's view of the beach must surely include the power to condition construction upon some concession by the owner, even a concession of property right, that serves the same end. If a prohibition designed to accomplish that purpose would be a legitimate exercise of the police power rather than a taking, it would be strange to conclude that providing the owner an alternative to that prohibition which accomplishes the same purpose is not.

The evident constitutional propriety disappears, however, if the condition substituted for the prohibition utterly fails to further the end advanced as the justification for the prohibition. When that essential nexus is eliminated, the situation becomes the same as if California law forbade shouting fire in a crowded theater, but granted dispensations to those willing to contribute $100 to the state treasury. While a ban on shouting fire can be a core exercise of the State's police power to protect the public safety, and can thus meet even our stringent standards for regulation of speech, adding the unrelated condition alters the purpose to one which, while it may be legitimate, is inadequate to sustain the ban. Therefore, even though, in a sense, requiring a $100 tax contribution in order to shout fire is a lesser restriction on speech than an outright ban, it would not pass constitutional muster. Similarly here, the lack of nexus between the condition and the original purpose of the building restriction converts that purpose to something other than what it was. The purpose then becomes, quite simply, the obtaining of an easement to serve some valid governmental purpose, but without payment of compensation. Whatever may be the outer limits of "legitimate state interests" in the takings and land-use context, this is not one of them. In short, unless the permit condition serves the same governmental purpose as the development ban, the building restriction is not a valid regulation of land use but "an out-and-out plan of extortion."

The Commission claims that it concedes as much, and that we may sustain the condition at issue here by finding that it is reasonably related to the public need or burden that the Nollans' new house creates or to which it contributes. We can accept, for purposes of discussion, the Commission's proposed test as to how close a "fit" between the condition and the burden is required, because we find that this case does not meet even the most untailored standards. The Commission's principal contention to the contrary essentially turns on a play on the word "access." The Nollans' new house, the Commission found, will interfere with "visual access" to the beach. That in turn (along with other shorefront development) will interfere with the desire of people who drive past the Nollans' house to use the beach, thus creating a "psychological barrier" to "access." The Nollans' new house will also, by a process not altogether clear from the Commission's opinion but presumably potent enough to more than offset the effects of the psychological barrier, increase the use of the public beaches, thus creating the need for more "access." These burdens on "access" would be alleviated by a requirement that the Nollans provide "lateral access" to the beach.

Rewriting the argument to eliminate the play on words makes clear that there is nothing to it. It is quite impossible to understand how a requirement that people already on the public beaches be able to walk across the Nollans' property reduces any obstacles to viewing the beach created by the new house. It is also impossible to understand how it lowers any "psychological barrier" to using the public beaches, or how it helps to remedy any additional congestion on them caused by construction of the Nollans' new house. We therefore find that the Commission's imposition of the permit condition cannot be treated as an exercise of its land-use power for any of these purposes. Our conclusion on this point is consistent with the approach taken by every other court that has considered the question, with the exception of the California state courts.

Justice Brennan argues that imposition of the access requirement is not irrational. In his version of the Commission's argument, the reason for the requirement is that in its absence, a person looking toward the beach from the road will see a street of residential structures including the Nollans' new home and conclude that there is no public beach nearby. If, however, that person sees people passing and repassing along the dry sand behind the Nollans' home, he will realize that there is a public beach somewhere in the vicinity. The Commission's action, however, was based on the opposite factual finding that the wall of houses completely blocked the view of the beach and that a person looking from the road would not be able to see it at all. * * *

We are left, then, with the Commission's justification for the access requirement unrelated to land-use regulation:

> Finally, the Commission notes that there are several existing provisions of pass and repass lateral access benefits already given by past Faria Beach Tract applicants as a result of prior coastal permit decisions. The access required as a condition of this permit is part of a comprehensive program to provide continuous public access along Faria Beach as the lots undergo development or redevelopment.

That is simply an expression of the Commission's belief that the public interest will be served by a continuous strip of publicly accessible beach along the coast. The Commission may well be right that it is a good idea, but that does not establish that the Nollans (and other coastal residents) alone can be compelled to contribute to its realization. Rather, California is free to advance its "comprehensive program," if it wishes, by using its power of eminent domain for this "public purpose," see U.S. Const., Amdt. V; but if it wants an easement across the Nollans' property, it must pay for it.

Reversed.

JUSTICE BRENNAN, *with whom* *JUSTICE MARSHALL* *joins, dissenting*.

Appellants in this case sought to construct a new dwelling on their beach lot that would both diminish visual access to the beach and move private development closer to the public tidelands. The Commission reasonably concluded that such "buildout," both individually and cumulatively, threatens public access to the shore. It sought to offset this encroachment by obtaining assurance that the public may walk along the shoreline in order to gain access to the ocean. The Court finds this an illegitimate exercise of the police power, because it maintains that there is no reasonable relationship between the effect of the development and the condition imposed.

The first problem with this conclusion is that the Court imposes a standard of precision for the exercise of a State's police power that has been discredited for the better part of this century. Furthermore, even under the Court's cramped standard, the permit condition imposed in this case directly responds to the specific type of burden on access created by appellants' development. Finally, a review of those factors deemed most significant in takings analysis makes clear that the Commission's action implicates none of the concerns underlying the Takings Clause. The Court has thus struck down the Commission's reasonable effort to respond to intensified development along the California coast, on behalf of landowners who can make no claim that their reasonable expectations have been disrupted. The Court has, in short, given appellants a windfall at the expense of the public. * * *

Even if we accept the Court's unusual demand for a precise match between the condition imposed and the specific type of burden on access created by the appellants, the State's action easily satisfies this requirement. First, the lateral access condition serves to dissipate the impression that the beach that lies behind the wall of homes along the shore is for private use only. It requires no exceptional imaginative powers to find plausible the Commission's point that the average person passing along the road in front of a phalanx of imposing permanent residences, including the appellants' new home, is likely to conclude that this particular portion of the shore is not open to the public. If, however, that person can see that numerous people are passing and repassing along the dry sand, this conveys the message that the beach is in fact open for use by the public. * * * The burden produced by the diminution in visual access—the impression that the beach is not open to the public—is thus directly alleviated by the provision for public access over the dry sand. The Court therefore has an unrealistically limited conception of what measures could reasonably be chosen to mitigate the burden produced by a diminution of visual access. * * *

With respect to the permit condition program in general, the Commission should have little difficulty in the future in utilizing its expertise to demonstrate a specific connection between provisions for access and burdens on access produced by new development. * * * In the future, alerted to the Court's apparently more demanding requirement, it need only make clear that a provision for public access directly responds to a particular type of burden on access created by a new development. Even if I did not believe that the record in this case satisfies this requirement, I would have to acknowledge that the record's documentation of the impact of coastal development indicates that the Commission should have little problem presenting its findings in a way that avoids a takings problem.

Nonetheless it is important to point out that the Court's insistence on a precise accounting system in this case is insensitive to the fact that increasing intensity of development in many areas calls for farsighted, comprehensive planning that takes into account both the interdependence of land uses and the cumulative impact of development. As one scholar has noted:

> Property does not exist in isolation. Particular parcels are tied to one another in complex ways, and property is more accurately described as being inextricably part of a network of relationships that is neither limited to, nor usefully defined by, the property boundaries with which the legal system is accustomed to dealing. Frequently, use of any given parcel of property is at the same time effectively a use of, or a demand upon, property beyond the border of the user. Sax, Takings, Private Property, and Public Rights, 81 Yale L.J. 149, 152 (1971) (footnote omitted).

As Congress has declared, "The key to more effective protection and use of the land and water resources of the coastal zone [is for the states to] develo[p] land and water use programs for the coastal zone, including unified policies, criteria, standards, methods, and processes for dealing with land and water use decisions of more than local significance." 16 U.S.C. § 1451(I). This is clearly a call for a focus on the overall impact of development on coastal areas. State agencies therefore require considerable flexibility in responding to private desires for development in a way that guarantees the preservation of public access to the coast. They should be encouraged to regulate development in the context of the overall balance of competing uses of the shoreline. The Court today does precisely the opposite, overruling an eminently reasonable exercise of an expert state agency's judgment, substituting its own narrow view of how this balance should be struck. Its reasoning is hardly suited to the complex reality of natural resource protection in the twentieth century. I can only hope that today's decision is an aberration, and that a broader vision ultimately prevails.

I dissent.

JUSTICE BLACKMUN, *dissenting*.

* * *

I disagree with the Court's rigid interpretation of the necessary correlation between a burden created by development and a condition imposed pursuant to the State's police power to mitigate that burden. The land-use problems this country faces require creative solutions. These are not advanced by an "eye for an eye" mentality. The close nexus between benefits and burdens that the Court now imposes on permit conditions creates an anomaly in the ordinary requirement that a State's exercise of its police power need be no more than rationally based. In my view, the easement exacted from appellants and the problems their development created are adequately related to the governmental interest in providing public access to the beach. Coastal development by its very nature makes public access to the shore generally more difficult. Appellants' structure is part of that general development and, in particular, it diminishes the public's visual access to the ocean and decreases the public's sense that it may have physical access to the beach. These losses in access can be counteracted, at least in part, by the condition on appellants' construction permitting public passage that ensures access along the beach.

* * *

For these reasons, I respectfully dissent.

Notes and Questions

1. The debate between the Court's majority and Justices Brennan and Blackmun illustrates an extremely important point concerning government regulation of the use of privately-owned land. Intelligent, well-informed public officials may in good faith disagree about the validity of specific types of land use regulation. Even the wisest lawyers acknowledge great uncertainty about the scope of this Court's takings jurisprudence. Yet, in First English Evangelical Lutheran Church of Glendale v. County of Los Angeles, 482 U.S. 304 (1987), the United States Supreme Court held that a private property owner is entitled to compensation for the time during which the property owner was unable to use her property due to a governmental regulation that is ultimately held to be invalid or withdrawn. Local governments and

officials must pay the price for the necessarily vague standards in this area of the law.

2. To what extent may the government condition private access to public resources on the private party's grant of some reciprocal right to the public? Assuming that the public has the right to use the wet sand area seaward of the mean high tide line and that a beachfront owner wants to construct seawalls or similar structures that will prevent the natural movement of the mean high tide line landward, ultimately eliminating the wet sand area, could the government condition the grant of a permit to construct a seawall or similar structure on the beachfront owner granting the public an easement landward of the seawall or similar structure? If such a seawall was constructed before any permits for construction were required, could the government require, in the absence of a grant of a public easement landward of the seawall, that the seawall be torn down?

3. Why should the relationship required by the Nollan majority be necessary? Are Justice Brennan's and Justice Blackmun's points about tradeoffs well taken? Must regulation do no more than require that specific externalities of an activity be internalized? In Dolan v. City of Tigard, 512 U.S. 374 (1994), the Supreme Court reinforced this requirement and further defined the essential nexus as a "rough proportionality" between the dedication of property and the "nature and extent" of the impact of the proposed development.

C. COASTAL CONSTRUCTION REGULATION TO PROTECT BEACHES AND DUNE SYSTEMS

"Coastal property may present such unique concerns for a fragile land system that the State can go further in regulating its development and use than the common law of nuisance might otherwise permit." Lucas v. South Carolina Coastal Council, 505 U.S. 1003, at 1035 (1992) (Kennedy, J., concurring).

The U.S. Army Corps of Engineers estimates that about one-fourth of the United States coast is severely eroding or subsiding. Some estimates of the effects of global warming suggest that sea level rise in the next half century may inundate low-lying coastal areas. In spite of this, population continues to grow at record rates along beaches and shores, generally exacerbating erosion problems while subjecting lives and property to dangers of shoreline retreat. These costs are balanced against the high value of beachfront property and the contribution that recreational use of the shores makes to the economy.

States are attempting to deal with the problems of protecting lives and property, protecting the economic values of the beaches, and preserving the beach and dunes systems through a number of approaches. These approaches can be grouped in three general categories: 1) restoration; 2) armoring; and 3) retreat.

(1.) Restoration

From Coney Island to Miami Beach, there are recreational beaches that are such an integral part of a local or state economy that restoration is an economic necessity. The high cost of this management technique is justified by the revenues generated by the beaches. The process is not only expensive, but also perpetual. Restored beaches require renourishment approximately every three years. In a recent comprehensive study by the National Research Council (NRC), Beach Renourishment and Protection (1995), the NRC supports beach renourishment as a viable method for protecting the shoreline from erosion and for restoring lost beach. The report also contains important warnings:

> Although proven engineered shore protection measures exist, there are no quick, simple, or inexpensive ways to protect the shore from natural forces, to mitigate the effects of beach erosion, or to restore beaches, regardless of the technology or approach selected. Available shore protection measures do not treat some of the underlying causes of erosion, such as relative rise in sea level and interruption of sand transport in the littoral systems, because they necessarily address locale-specific erosion problems rather than their underlying systemic causes.

Problem

State A has historically restored its eroded sandy shorelines by dumping or pumping offshore sand on the beach. Before such a project, state law requires establishment of the current mean high water on the eroded beach. Both the common law theory of avulsion and the state's laws support the principle that title to beach created seaward of the mean high line is in the state and open to the public.

More sophisticated technologies are being developed for beach renourishment that more closely approximate natural functions. Feeder beaches, for example, may provide a source of sand for the littoral system that benefits beaches miles away. Offshore artificial reefs are also being developed to dissipate wave energy, lessening erosion and allowing more suspended sand to deposit on the shoreline. As these beaches benefit from the remote feeder beach or offshore reef, the beaches appear to accrete by natural processes and have more stability. Who owns the newly accreted beach? Does the public reap the benefit of such technology? How should the costs and benefits of such projects be allocated? Is public beach access enhanced? Do beachfront property owners receive a windfall? Do common law principles deal adequately with such new approaches?

(2.) Armoring

Armoring is a term that encompasses seawalls, rip-rap, and other fixed structures intended to stabilize the shoreline. Although armoring can provide short-term protection to endangered structures, evidence indicates that armoring may increase the rate of erosion of adjacent beaches. In general, armoring is not a preferred management tool, but is often the only solution when a storm leaves a structure teetering on the brink of destruction. One might argue that all permits for armoring should be denied because shoreline property owners have assumed this risk of erosion and armoring is a potentially dangerous approach for long-term management. Such a policy is difficult to apply in individual cases, however, because of the moral, economic, and political dilemmas that arise.

Problem

Joe Snowbird bought a coastal lot for his future retirement home in 1961, prior to any state regulation of armoring shores or filling wetlands. Over the subsequent 30 years, storms, government inlet dredging, and other development contributed to the erosion of Joe's property, causing the mean high water mark to move inland more than 60 feet. In 1998, Joe applied to the State Coastal Commission for a permit to bulkhead and backfill his lot to recover enough of the lot to construct a house. The bulkhead was necessary not only to protect the future structure from continuing erosion, but also to meet the state's requirements for coastal setback and the local government's requirements for setback from the highway. However, tidelands are designated as critical areas by the state coastal protection law and the particular beach area is a nesting area for endangered sea turtles.

(a) Should Joe be able to recover his eroded lot? Did he assume the risk of erosion when he acquired the property? Did the risk include erosion only from natural forces? If he is able to recover the lot, is he appropriating state property?

(b) Does your analysis change if most of the other lots in the area are bulkheaded? Does it matter whether the lots were bulkheaded before or after any regulation was in place?

(c) Would your analysis change if Joe had bought a developed lot and the bulkhead is necessary to protect the structure from the retreating shoreline? Is it relevant whether the threatened structure is a 100-unit condominium, rather than a single-family dwelling?

(d) If the permit is denied and Joe is unable to build his retirement home, he is likely to bring suit alleging a regulatory taking. Is he entitled to compensation?

SOUTH CAROLINA COASTAL CONSERVATION LEAGUE AND SIERRA CLUB V. SOUTH CAROLINA DEPARTMENT OF HEALTH AND ENVIRONMENTAL CONTROL
South Carolina Court of Appeals, 2001
548 S.E.2d 887

SHULER, J. The circuit court affirmed a summary judgment order of the Administrative Law Judge Division (ALJD), upholding a permit issued by the Department of Health and Environmental Control (DHEC) allowing Port Royal Plantation to refurbish a groin field and construct new groins along the beach on Hilton Head Island. South Carolina Coastal Conservation League (SCCCL) and Sierra Club appeal, arguing the South Carolina Beachfront Management Act prohibits such construction. We reverse.

Facts/Procedural History

In April 1996 Port Royal Plantation applied to the Office of Ocean and Coastal Resource Management (OCRM), a division of DHEC, for a permit to construct four new groins and refurbish a series of seventeen existing groins (a "groin field") along approximately 8,000 feet of shoreline at Hilton Head.[10] OCRM issued the permit on October 2, 1996.

SCCCL and Sierra Club filed a petition for administrative review of the permit decision and requested a contested case hearing before the ALJD. The petition named Port Royal Plantation and OCRM as respondents, and the administrative law judge (ALJ) granted the Town of Hilton Head's motion to intervene. Thereafter, the parties filed cross-motions for summary judgment. Prior to the hearing, the parties stipulated to the relevant facts and agreed that the only issue remaining was a question of law for the court: Whether the Beachfront Management Act prohibited the proposed construction.

By order dated June 16, 1998, the ALJ found the permit to refurbish the groin field and construct new groins valid. SCCCL and Sierra Club appealed this decision to the OCRM's Coastal Zone Management Appellate Panel, which adopted the order of the ALJ and affirmed on December 17. SCCCL and Sierra Club subsequently sought judicial review in the circuit court, which likewise affirmed DHEC's grant of the

---

[10] A groin is a structure built on the beach, often of large rocks or timber, running perpendicular to the shore and extending into the ocean. It is designed to retard erosion by trapping littoral drift, i.e., the shifting sand along the shore that results from wave action. A "groin field" is a series of two or more groins in close proximity which exert overlapping areas of influence.

permit in an order filed February 7, 2000. This appeal followed.

Law/Analysis

The sole issue in this appeal is whether the groin construction and refurbishment permit issued by DHEC to Port Royal Plantation violates the statutory provisions of the Beachfront Management Act. We believe it does.

In 1977 our Legislature passed the Coastal Zone Management Act (CZMA) to "protect, preserve, restore and enhance the coastal resources of South Carolina." 23A S.C. Code Ann. Regs. 30-1(C)(1) (Supp. 2000); see Beard v. S.C. Coastal Council, 304 S.C. 205, 207, 403 S.E.2d 620, 621 (1991) ("Like the 1988 Beachfront Management Act, the purpose of the 1977 Act was to protect, restore and enhance the coastal environment."). To accomplish this goal, the CZMA created a state agency, the South Carolina Coastal Council, to administer and enforce its provisions. The Council's regulatory authority, however, was inadequate to forestall extensive private beachfront development along the coast and, as a result, erosion became a serious threat.

Realizing the gravity of the problem, the Legislature enacted the Beachfront Management Act in 1988. Promulgated to further the coastal protection afforded under the CZMA, the Act was a direct response to a report by the Blue Ribbon Committee on Beachfront Management that determined South Carolina's beach/dune system was in crisis.[11] Specifically, the report noted that "over fifty-seven miles of our beaches [were] critically eroding," thereby threatening "life, property, the tourist industry, vital State and local revenue, marine habitat, and a national treasure[.]"

To combat the erosional threat, the Beachfront Management Act devised a statutory scheme to restore the beach/dune system by promoting gradual retreat from the beachfront over a forty-year period. To this end, the legislation directed DHEC to "develop and institute a comprehensive beach erosion control policy," and prohibited the use of any "critical area," including the beach, without first obtaining a permit from DHEC. [12]

In general, three methods are used to manage the problem of shoreline erosion: armoring the beach with "hard" erosion control devices; renourishing the beach with sand; and retreating from the

---

[11] The beach/dune system is defined as "all land from the mean highwater mark of the Atlantic Ocean landward to the 40 year setback line described in § 48-39-280."

[12] "Critical areas" are defined as any of the following: (1) coastal waters, (2) tidelands, (3) beach/dune systems, and (4) beaches.

beach altogether. Enactment of the Beachfront Management Act evidences a clear legislative choice favoring the latter two policies. See, e.g., § 48-39-290(B)(2) (governing all construction, reconstruction and alterations between the baseline[13] and the setback line, [14] thereby prohibiting the construction of new erosion control devices seaward of the setback line except for the protection of a pre-existing public highway and strictly regulating the repair or replacement of such devices if destroyed); § 48-39-250(5) ("The use of armoring in the form of hard erosion control devices such as seawalls, bulkheads, and rip-rap to protect erosion-threatened structures adjacent to the beach has not proved effective. . . . In reality, these hard structures, in many instances, have increased the vulnerability of beachfront property to damage from wind and waves while contributing to the deterioration and loss of the dry sand beach which is so important to the tourism industry."); § 48-39-260(3) (stating that the policy of South Carolina is to "severely restrict the use of hard erosion control devices to armor the beach/dune system and to encourage the replacement of hard erosion control devices with soft technologies as approved by [DHEC] which will provide for the protection of the shoreline without long-term adverse effects").[15]

Reflecting this preference, the Beachfront Management Act expressly states that "no new construction or reconstruction is allowed seaward of the baseline," as determined by DHEC, except the following:
    (1) wooden walkways no larger in width than six feet

---

[13] The baseline of a standard [non-inlet] erosion zone generally is fixed at the crest of the primary oceanfront sand dune. Where alterations have occurred, either natural or man-made, DHEC must establish the baseline using the best scientific and historical data available indicating where the crest would have been located had the shoreline not been altered.

[14] The setback line is established by DHEC landward of the baseline at a distance forty times the average annual erosion rate or not less than twenty feet.

[15] DHEC regulations explicitly embrace this patent expression of legislative intent. See 23A S.C. Code Ann. Regs. at 30-1(C)(2) ("Hard erosion control devices can result in increased erosion, a lowering of the beach profile ... and a decrease in the ability of the beach/dune system to protect upland property from storms and high tides. Often the result of attempting to protect upland property with hard erosion control structures is that dry sand beaches disappear, thereby placing many millions of tourist dollars in jeopardy and destroying this natural legacy for future generations."); 23A S.C. Code Ann. Regs. at 30-1(C)(4) ("It has been clearly demonstrated that the erosion problems of this State are caused by a persistent rise in sea level, a lack of comprehensive beach management planning, and poorly planned oceanfront development, including construction of hard erosion control structures, which encroach upon the beach/dune system."); 23A S.C. Code Ann. Regs. at 30-1(C)(6) (The CZMA, as amended, "rejects construction of new erosion control devices and adopts retreat and renourishment as the basic state policy towards preserving and restoring the beaches of our state."); 23A S.C. Code Ann. Regs. at 30-11(D)(2) ("[DHEC] shall promote soft-solutions to erosion within the context of a policy of retreat of development from the shore and prevent the strengthening and enlargement of existing erosion control structures.").

(2) small wooden decks no larger than one hundred forty-four square feet
(3) fishing piers which are open to the public * * *
(4) golf courses
(5) normal landscaping
(6) structures specifically permitted by special permit as provided in subsection (D)
(7) pools may be reconstructed if they are landward of an existing, functional erosion control structure or device * * * [16]

We agree with SCCCL and Sierra Club that this section precludes OCRM from issuing any permits for the construction or refurbishment of groins, which clearly are constructed seaward of the baseline and do not fit within a statutory exception.

Although Respondents acknowledge, as did the circuit court and ALJD, that this conclusion stems from a "literal reading" of [the statute], they argue the section should not be interpreted in isolation from other provisions of the Beachfront Management Act. We agree. However, even construing the Act as a whole, Respondents' arguments are unavailing.

Initially, we believe Respondents are correct in asserting that groins, as defined herein, are not "erosion control structures or devices" as defined in the Act. On its face, the statutory definition of "erosion control structures or devices" does not reference groins and enumerates only three types: seawalls, bulkheads, and revetments. See § 48-39-270(1). However, because the word "include" may be seen as one of limitation or enlargement, we must turn to rules of construction to ascertain the Legislature's true intent * * *

In our view, the statutory collocation suggests an intent to circumscribe the definitional meaning of "include" by stating:

(1) Erosion control structures or devices include:
(a) seawall: a special type of retaining wall that is designed specifically to withstand normal wave forces;
(b) bulkhead: a retaining wall designed to retain fill material but not to withstand wave forces on an exposed shoreline;
(c) revetment: a sloping structure built along an escarpment or in front of a bulkhead to protect the shoreline or bulkhead from

---

[16] Subsection (D) authorizes DHEC to issue "special permits" to build or rebuild structures other than erosion control structures or devices only if such structures are not located on the "active beach." The active beach is defined as "that area seaward of the escarpment or the first line of stable natural vegetation, whichever first occurs, measured from the ocean." Groins, therefore, by definition constructed on the active beach, are excluded from this statutory exception.

erosion.

In other words, the legislative decision to set forth each erosion control structure mentioned in a separate, individually-defined format reinforces the inference that lawmakers intended "include" to limit the definition. . . . [T]he Legislature meant to exclude other structures also designed to deter erosion when they only listed seawalls, bulkheads, and revetments in the statute.

This conclusion is supported by the fact that the three structures designated in the statute, namely seawalls, bulkheads, and revetments, parallel the shoreline and function as a barrier to "armor" it against the elements and retain sand in an effort to inhibit erosion, while groins are constructed perpendicular to the shore and operate to impede erosion by controlling the natural movement of sand that results from waves hitting the beach at an angle. See generally § 48-39-250(5) ("Armoring in the form of hard erosion control devices such as seawalls, bulkheads, and rip-rap to protect erosion-threatened structures adjacent to the beach has not proved effective. These armoring devices have given a false sense of security to beachfront property owners."); § 48-39-260(3) (policy of the state is to "severely restrict the use of hard erosion control devices to armor the beach/dune system"); 23A S.C. Code Ann. Regs. at 30-1(D)(23) ("Groins are usually perpendicular to the shore and extend from the shoreline into the water far enough to accomplish their purpose."). * * *

Having determined groins are not "erosion control structures or devices" as contemplated by the Beachfront Management Act, it is readily apparent that some statutory sections are not relevant to our analysis. For example, section 48-39-290(B)(2), governing construction, reconstruction and alteration of erosion control devices, does not apply. Section 48-39-120(B), authorizing DHEC to issue permits for erosion control structures, similarly is inapplicable. On the other hand, subsection 48-39-290(A)(6)(D) does apply, because it concerns permits "to build or rebuild a structure other than an erosion control structure or device." However, because it bans all construction on the "active beach," the subsection still operates to preclude the development or refurbishment of groins. See § 48-39-290(A)(6)(D).

Although Respondents do not rely on section 48-39-120(F) in their brief, both the circuit court and ALJD construed this section as authorizing DHEC to issue permits for the construction and reconstruction of new or existing groins. The section provides:

[DHEC], for and on behalf of the State, may issue permits not otherwise provided by state law, for erosion and water drainage structure in or upon the tidelands, submerged lands and waters of the State below the mean high-water mark as it may deem most advantageous to the State for the purpose of promoting the public health, safety and welfare, the protection of public and private property from beach and shore destruction and the continued use of tidelands, submerged lands and waters for public purposes.

The statute does not define "erosion and water drainage structure." Even assuming, arguendo, that the term "erosion and water drainage structure" could be interpreted to encompass groins, subsection (F) may not be employed to validate construction expressly prohibited by the clear language of section 48-39-290(A).* * *

The circuit court's analysis of subsection (F) is similarly misplaced. In finding the groin permit valid, the circuit court relied in part on DHEC's interpretation of the provision, which would "allow the construction or reconstruction of groins in conjunction with beach nourishment." While we agree with the circuit court that the construction given a statute by the agency charged with its administration is entitled to the utmost consideration on appeal such that it will not be overruled absent compelling reasons, an agency's construction "affords no basis for the perpetuation of a patently erroneous application of [a] statute." Thus, because DHEC's interpretation of section 48-39-120(F) conflicts directly with the express language of section 48-39-290(A), it cannot serve as a basis for upholding Port Royal's permit.* * *

Respondents urge this Court to uphold Port Royal's permit because groins purportedly extend the life of beach renourishment projects, a declared goal of the Beachfront Management Act (stating policy of South Carolina is to "promote carefully planned nourishment as a means of beach preservation and restoration where economically feasible"). In particular, Respondents claim an absolute ban on all groin construction and reconstruction would lead to "a result so absurd that it could not have been intended" by the Legislature, because groins are essential to the preservation of newly deposited beach sand. We need not decide whether groins in fact enhance such projects, a determination inappropriate for summary judgment, because, in the absence of ambiguity or contrary statutory provisions, the plain language . . . must control.

Finally, Respondents argue the Court is required to read the 1999 South Carolina Beach Restoration and Improvement Trust Act in conjunction with the Beachfront Management Act to glean the Legislature's true intent regarding the construction or reconstruction of groins. We disagree.

In making this argument, Respondents rely on * * * a definition of renourishment which reads in part:

"Beach renourishment" means the artificial establishment and periodic renourishment of a beach with sand * * * to include where considered appropriate and necessary by [OCRM], groin construction and maintenance to extend the life of such projects.

Although we agree this provision is indicative of some purposeful consideration of groins, this Court may not disregard the otherwise clear intent of the Legislature.

The General Assembly enacted the Beach Restoration and Improvement Trust Act for the express purpose of establishing a "trust" to provide matching funds to qualifying local governments for beach restoration projects. In so doing, the Legislature chose not to amend the Beachfront Management Act, but rather to create the fund in a separate chapter of Title 48. Indeed, the definition of beach renourishment therein is prefaced by the unambiguous phrase "as used in this chapter." In our view, these decisions evince a legislative intent to leave the mandatory provisions of the Beachfront Management Act intact. * * *

In the final analysis, we believe our construction of section 48-39-290 fully comports with the purpose and policy of the Beachfront Management Act. ([T]he "final management plan for the State's coastal zone," states that the "trapping of sand by a groin can have severe impacts on the adjacent shoreline down the beach"); ("Erosion is a natural process which becomes a significant problem for man only when structures are erected in close proximity to the beach/dune system. It is in both the public and private interests to afford the beach/dune system space to accrete and erode in its natural cycle. This space can be provided only by discouraging new construction in close proximity to the beach/dune system and encouraging those who have erected structures too close to the system to retreat from it."); (the policy of South Carolina is to "severely restrict the use of hard erosion control devices to armor the beach/dune system and to encourage the replacement of hard erosion control devices with soft technologies[17] as approved by [DHEC] which will provide for the protection of the shoreline without long-term adverse effects"); (the policy of our state is to "encourage the use of erosion-inhibiting techniques which do not adversely impact the long-term well-being of the beach/dune system"); ("[DHEC] shall be guided by the prohibitions against construction contained in Section 48-39-290 and Section 48-39-300 * * * These structures interfere with the natural system and impact the highest and best uses of the system * * * ").

---

[17] "Soft" solutions or technologies, as defined by DHEC, consist of beach nourishment and sand scraping.

Conclusion

Because we hold as a matter of law that the Beachfront Management Act prohibits DHEC from issuing permits for the construction or reconstruction of new or existing groins, the grant of summary judgment to Respondents is reversed and the case remanded to the circuit court for entry of an order granting summary judgment to SCCCL and Sierra Club.

REVERSED AND REMANDED.

(3.) Retreat

The third beach management option is one that is necessary where beach and dune systems are so dynamic that neither restoration nor armoring is feasible, when the economic costs of restoration cannot be justified, or when environmental concerns outweigh justifications for armoring or restoration.   Retreat may involve strict construction regulations within the sensitive beach/dune system or complete construction prohibitions within particularly sensitive or hazardous areas. Approximately half the coastal states have enacted statutes creating coastal construction zones that regulate or prohibit construction. Some zones are established as lines drawn at a fixed distance from a baseline, usually the mean high water line, the vegetation line, or a line associated with the primary dune. Fluctuating high hazard zones are usually based on local erosion rates. See Houlahan, Comparison of State Construction Setbacks to Manage Development in Coastal Hazard Areas, 17 Coastal Management 219 (1989).

Notes and Questions

1. Early setback lines generally prohibited or limited construction in areas within a prescribed distance from a baseline, usually the mean high water line, the vegetation line, or a line associated with the primary dune. The distances were relatively arbitrary and generally ranged from 40 to 100 feet. As understanding of beach and dune processes increased and as coastal engineering became more sophisticated, delineation of setback lines has also become more sophisticated and highly technical. Many states now have a second type of regulatory setback line based on complicated calculations of seasonal shoreline fluctuations, vulnerability to storms and storm surges, and the rate of shoreline erosion. See, e.g., Island Harbor Beach Club, Ltd. v. Department of Natural Resources, 495 So.2d 209 (Fla.Dist.Ct.App.1986) (finding that because of the complexity of the technical and scientific issues and the high degree of scientific uncertainty involved, agency determinations of coastal construction control lines should be given great deference), review denied, 503 So. 2d 327 (Fla. 1987). How does

this complexity affect landowners' expectations of how they can use their land? Is it relevant whether control lines are established and recorded on public records or whether they are delimited on a case-by-case basis?

2. Retreat strategies generally apply only to undeveloped beachfront property. Existing development is usually "grandfathered-in" to lessen the impact of the regulation. Two major problems have arisen in relation to grandfathering of existing structures. First, in areas that were almost fully developed prior to the new regulation, new prohibitions on development that apply only to the remaining undeveloped lots may be unreasonable. See, e.g., Lucas v. South Carolina Coastal Council, supra; but see, West's Fla. Stat. Ann. § 161.053(5)(b) (creating a variance from some Coastal Construction Control Line (CCCL) permitting requirements where existing adjacent structures form a "reasonably continuous and uniform construction line" seaward of the CCCL and the existing structures have not been "unduly affected by erosion"). Would the conclusion in *Lucas* have been the same if it concerned the first house to be constructed?

The second problem concerning existing structures relates to the determination of when they may become subject to the new regulatory scheme. South Carolina's Beachfront Management Act places new limitations on rebuilding structures that are "destroyed beyond repair" and originally banned their reconstruction within the dead zone or seaward of the baseline. Destroyed beyond repair means "more than sixty-six and two-thirds percent of the replacement value of the habitable structure * * * has been destroyed." See S.C. Code 1992 § 48-39-270(11). Reacting to the widespread impact of the Act on beachfront homeowners in the wake of Hurricane Hugo, the South Carolina legislature amended the BMA in 1990 to give the Coastal Council the authority to issue special permits to allow reconstruction of habitable structures under certain conditions, even if they were located seaward of the baseline. The Florida Coastal Zone Protection Act provides that CCCL and thirty-year erosion zone requirements will apply to all new construction except "modification, maintenance, or repair to any existing structure within the limits of the existing foundation which does not require * * * any additions to, or repair or modification of, the existing foundation." See West's Fla. Stat. Ann. § 161.053(12) (1991).

How does the Supreme Court's reasoning in *Lucas* affect states' treatment of existing nonconforming development? Can states continue to justify differential treatment of developed and undeveloped land? Does *Lucas* suggest that states should be less restrictive on new activity in developed areas or more restrictive on existing development where regulation is justified? Is it realistic to think that nonconforming structures should continue to be allowed because they are really only temporary (until the next big storm) and will be required to conform in the future?

3. Coastal building codes have come under considerable scrutiny recently because of the damages hurricanes have caused to substandard housing. The National Flood Insurance Program (NFIP), established by the National Flood Insurance Act of 1968, 42 U.S.C. §§ 4001-4128, has led to widespread adoption of minimum federal building standards for flood prone areas, including beaches. The NFIP is intended to reduce federal flood disaster relief by supplying guaranteed flood insurance coverage to communities that adopt building standards and land use controls that minimize flood damages and property losses. State and local regulation may be stricter than federally-imposed safety and building standards, and governments are encouraged to adopt land use regulations that guide development away from flood hazard areas.

In addition to guaranteeing flood insurance for communities participating in the NFIP, the program also imposes penalties for nonparticipation. If a community with areas susceptible to flooding does not join the program, federal agencies, such as the Small Business Administration and the Veterans Administration, are prohibited from providing federal assistance for development in flood-prone areas. See 42 U.S.C. § 4106(a). The NFIP has been held neither to be an unconstitutional coercion or imposition of strict federal building standards on the states nor to be a taking of private property as a result of diminished property values in nonparticipating communities. See Adolph v. Federal Emergency Management Agency, 854 F.2d 732 (5th Cir. 1988); Texas Landowners Rights Ass'n v. Harris, 453 F. Supp. 1025 (D.D.C. 1978), aff'd mem., 598 F.2d 311 (D.C. Cir.), cert. denied, 444 U.S. 927 (1979).

D. CRITERIA FOR COASTAL DEVELOPMENT

(1.) Water Dependency

The CZMA, at 16 U.S.C. § 1455(d)(2), requires states to identify in their coastal management programs:

(B) A definition of what shall constitute permissible land uses and water uses within the coastal zone which have a direct and significant impact on the coastal waters. * * *

(E) Broad guidelines on priorities of uses in particular areas, including specifically those uses of lowest priority.

Both in defining permissible coastal zone uses and establishing priorities of uses, water dependency has often been identified as a factor. How narrowly should this term be construed? How should water dependency be evaluated in the case of multiple use developments?　Should multi-use projects be allowed only if the primary purpose is water dependent?　Who makes this determination and what criteria are applied?　Consider these questions in light of the following case and notes.

EASTLAKE COMMUNITY COUNCIL v.
CITY OF SEATTLE

Court of Appeals of Washington, 1992
64 Wash. App. 273, 823 P.2d 1132

PETRICH, C.J.

The Shorelines Hearing Board by summary judgment approved the issuance of a master use permit by the City of Seattle to the Dally Development Corporation.　The permit authorized the construction of an office building on the shores of Lake Union.　The Eastlake Community Council and the Floating Homes Association, together with individual members of these groups (Eastlake Association) appeal from the superior court's affirmance of the Board's decision.　They contend that the proposed development runs afoul of the Seattle Shoreline Master Program and the Shoreline Management Act because it lacks a qualified water dependent use * * *.

On December 11, 1989 the City of Seattle's Department of Construction and Land Use approved Dally's request for a land use permit to construct a building containing an office complex and a rowing club along the Lake Union Shoreline.　Dally intends to utilize the top three floors of the complex for office space and the bottom floor is to be used by the Pocock Rowing Foundation as a rowing facility.　In order to ensure permit approval, Dally also secured an off-site parking lease through the Fuhrman Avenue Parking Associates.

On review at the request of Eastlake Association, the Shorelines Hearing Board heard motions for partial summary judgment by Dally and the City of Seattle and approved the issuance of the permit. The Eastlake Association voluntarily dismissed the remaining issues and sought review in the Thurston County Superior Court.

On January 17, 1991 the superior court affirmed the decision of the Board * * *. Eastlake Association filed this appeal, seeking direct review by the Supreme Court, and the case was subsequently transferred to this division. * * *

SHORELINE MANAGEMENT ACT

Eastlake Association argues that the approval and affirmation of Dally's substantial development permit conflicts both with the policies of the Shoreline Management Act, as set out in RCW 90.58.020 as well as the Board's prior interpretation of these policies. The relevant portion of RCW 90.58.020 delineates public policy relating to shoreline development and sets out a number of uses which are given priority, including "industrial and commercial developments which are particularly dependent on their location on or use of the shorelines of the state and other development that will provide an opportunity for substantial numbers of the people to enjoy the shorelines of the state." RCW 90.58.020.[18] Under Eastlake Association's reading of the act, the proposed offices must be an integral part of the water dependent use, or the entire project must provide for substantial public access to the shoreline.

This particular section of the Shoreline Management Act has been construed in the past by the Supreme Court as permitting commercial shoreline development that is not water dependent and did not provide for public access to the shoreline. In Department of Ecology v. Ballard Elks, 527 P.2d 1121 (1974), the Supreme Court considered a case where the Shoreline Hearings Board ordered the City of Seattle to issue a permit allowing construction of a clubhouse over the water of Shilshole Bay. The clubhouse was to contain a restaurant, a cocktail lounge, a billiard room, a gymnasium, and swimming pool facilities, none of which would be open to the public. In support of its decision to order the issuance of the building permit, the Board found that the development would not have a detrimental effect upon the shoreline and it would provide an opportunity for substantial numbers of people to enjoy the shoreline. The Supreme Court affirmed the Board's decision, noting that the Board acted "with a practical eye upon the densely developed portion of shoreline in the immediate vicinity of the subject property," and followed the relevant guidelines and policies of the Shoreline Management Act as set out in RCW 90.58.020.

In support of their argument, Eastlake Association cites the

---

[18] The relevant portion of RCW 90.58.020 provides:

In the implementation of this policy the public's opportunity to enjoy the physical and aesthetic qualities of natural shorelines of the state shall be preserved to the greatest extent feasible consistent with the overall best interest of the state and the people generally. To this end uses shall be preferred which are consistent with control of pollution and prevention of damage to the natural environment, or are unique to or dependent upon use of the state's shoreline. Alterations of the natural condition of the shorelines of the state, in those limited instances when authorized, shall be given priority for single family residences [and their appurtenant structures], ports, shoreline recreational uses including but not limited to parks, marinas, piers, [and other improvements facilitating public access to shorelines of the state, industrial and commercial developments which are particularly dependent on their location on or use of the shorelines of the state] and other development that will provide an opportunity for substantial numbers of the people to enjoy the shorelines of the state. (Bracketed material did not appear in the court's footnote.)

Shorelines Hearing Board's decision in SHB No. 156 (1975), which articulated a different interpretation of RCW 90.58.020. In Adams v. City of Seattle, SHB No. 156 (1975), the Board affirmed the denial of a permit application to build offices above a yacht moorage on Lake Union, stating that "any office building which is not an integral part of, or related to, a water-dependent use would be inconsistent with the policy of the Act unless the entire development would provide an opportunity for substantial numbers of the people to enjoy the shoreline of the state.'" *Adams*, at 3. According to the Board in *Adams*, the proposed development was inconsistent with the policies behind the Shoreline Management Act as set out in RCW 90.28.020 because it was a non-water-dependent use that did not provide for public enjoyment of the shorelines, and was not related to the water dependent use to which it was attached.

In the order being appealed from, the Board explicitly overruled the *Adams* decision to the extent that it required an integral relation with a water dependent use. In reaching its decision to overturn the Board recognized that it had recently held in another case that general office use is not inconsistent with RCW 90.58.020. * * * The plain language of the statute clearly does not compel the conclusion that a shoreline office building must be an integral part of, or be related to the water dependent use built in conjunction with the offices. Therefore, Eastlake Association's contention that the Board order was in violation of the Shoreline Management Act is without merit. * * *

POCOCK AGREEMENT

Although Eastlake Association does not dispute that a rowing club is a water-dependent use, it contends that the agreement with the rowing club is insufficiently certain to constitute a water-dependent use under § 23.60.600(C)(2) of the Seattle Municipal Code. It argued that since the permit does not contain an explicit "condition" requiring that the ground floor be reserved for the rowing club and that the facility be occupied, it does not meet the requirements under the Seattle Municipal Code.[19]

The Board in its Order Granting Summary Judgment In Part correctly pointed out that inclusion of rowing facilities in the development is an element of the permit rather than a condition. The

---

[19] The relevant portion of the Master Use Permit issued to Dally provides as follows:

Construct: four story structure containing 26,300 sf of floor area. The 8,000 sf ground floor level and 4,000 sf of outdoor area along with the entire submerged tidelands will be used by a water-dependent user, the 'George Pocock Rowing Foundation.' The remaining 16,300 sf of upper story floor area will be used as administrative office. Accessory parking will be provided in the Fuhrman avenue Parking Association lot located south of Fuhrman Avenue East.

Board stated that since it is an element of the permit, the inclusion of the rowing facility is required if development under the permit is to proceed * * *. In its order the Board stated that any change in the development plan through either a revision or the issuance of a new permit would be reviewable by the Board and that any change inconsistent with the Shoreline Management Act or the Seattle Shoreline Master Program would not be upheld.

Eastlake Association cites no authority supporting the proposition that the lack of a long term commitment is fatal to a permit of this type. In its order, the Board noted that it has previously held that no property interest is required in order for a permit to issue. While not directly on point, these cases tend to indicate that absolute certainty of future use is not required for a permit to issue under the act, since a party need not even own the property in order to obtain approval to develop it.

Under WAC 173-17-050 "[A] person who fails to conform to the terms of a permit issued under RCW 90.58.140, * * * may be subject to a civil penalty" imposed by either the Department of Ecology or the local government. A party failing to adhere to the Shoreline Management Act or the local master plan is also subject to more severe penalties under WAC 173-17-050, which provides:

> Order to cease and desist. Local government and/or the department shall have the authority to serve upon a person a cease and desist order if an activity being undertaken on shorelines of the state is in violation of chapter 90.58 RCW or the local master program.

In the event that the Pocock Rowing Foundation no longer occupied the bottom floor of the proposed building, Dally Development would be in violation of the terms of the existing permit and would thus be subject to fines under WAC 173-17-050.

The agreement with the Pocock Rowing Foundation is clearly sufficient to satisfy the water dependent use requirement of the Shoreline Management Act as implemented by the Seattle Shoreline Master Plan. * * *

The Shoreline Hearings Board granting partial summary judgement is affirmed.

Notes and Questions

1. The court in the *Eastlake* case states that fines and other penalties would apply if the water dependent use were discontinued. Are the penalties likely to be so large as to constitute a true economic incentive for compliance with the permit?

2. In 1000 Friends of Oregon v. Land Conservation and Development Commission, 302 Or. 526, 731 P.2d 1015 (1987), a public interest group challenged the permit issued to a project that was characterized an "integrated marina project," including a marina, dry boat storage, motel, RV park, restaurant, and shops, as not meeting Oregon's water-dependency requirement. The Oregon Supreme Court found:

> The Botts Marsh project was designed as an integrated marina complex. In adopting its exceptions to Goal 16 [of the State Plan], the county was required to demonstrate a public need for such a complex. 1000 Friends does not challenge in this court [the] finding that such a need exists. Neither does it contend that alternative sites exist for the complex as a whole. Rather, it suggests that the complex be broken up and its component uses placed at various upland locations.
>
> We agree with respondents that the third criterion under Goal 16 does not require this course of action, which would destroy the integrity of the project and largely defeat the purpose for which it was designed. The county was entitled to reject such an alternative. The manner in which it went about making its finding that Botts Marsh was the only suitable site for the marina complex was sufficient to demonstrate that "no alternative upland locations exist," thereby satisfying the third criterion of the dredge and fill conditions under Goal 16.

Is the permit applicant's definition of the project controlling? How many other uses can be "tacked" to the water-dependent use? See also Chapter Two on permitting criteria under CWA § 404.

3. What are the policies underlying the water-dependency requirement? How should water dependency be defined? Is a seafood restaurant water-dependent? Is a site for mooring a barge water-dependent? Is a floating seafood restaurant located on a barge water-dependent? What about the parking lot for the floating restaurant? Water dependency may be a basis for establishing the priority of certain uses as well as a standard for excluding other uses from coastal locations. Should water-dependency serve as a criterion for inclusion or exclusion of a use? Is water dependency an unworkable criterion that should be irrelevant, simply allowing economic factors to control the best use of coastal property?

(2.) Cumulative And Secondary Impacts

CONSERVANCY, INC. v. A. VERNON ALLEN BUILDER

First District Court of Appeals for Florida, 1991
580 So. 2d 772

WIGGENTON, *Judge.*

The Conservancy, Inc., and Florida Audubon Society bring this appeal from the final order of the Department of Environmental Regulation granting a dredge and fill permit. Although we affirm a number of the issues raised on appeal, we must on one point reverse and remand for further proceedings.

In April 1988, appellee A. Vernon Allen Builder, Inc. (Builder) submitted its application to the Department of Environmental Regulation (DER or Department) for a dredge and fill permit. The permit application was for the excavation and re-disposition of approximately 1,155 cubic yards of material within Gordon Pass in order to embed a sewage pipeline system along the bottom of Gordon Pass extending from the City of Naples mainland south to Keewaydin (Key) Island. The pipeline will be part of a sewage force-main system which will provide sewer service to present and future development on Key Island.

Gordon Pass is located between the City of Naples and Key Island, a coastal barrier island designated by the United States Congress as a unit to be protected within the coastal barrier resource system pursuant to the provisions of the Coastal Barrier Resources Act (CBRA). The purposes of such congressional designation include prohibiting federal funding of any projects that would enable development on designated coastal barrier islands due to their importance to the estuarine system and public health and safety. Key Island forms the southern shore of Gordon Pass. As a coastal barrier island, Key Island enables the existence and functioning of the estuarine system to the west and serves as a buffer to wave action from the Gulf of Mexico. As numerous witnesses and experts confirmed before the hearing officer, Key Island is a dynamic, evolving and inseparable part of the estuarine system. In turn, the estuarine system is dependent upon and cannot be separated from Key Island for its existence.

The northern tip of Key Island is within the city limits of Naples and contains the Keewaydin Club, a vacation resort long ago developed for an existing small private club. Its existence is so limited that its impact was determined to be minimal by Congress so as to require that Key Island be designated as an undeveloped coastal barrier island entitled to protection pursuant to the CBRA. The proposed subaqueous sewage pipeline is intended to serve the club's existing facilities which presently utilize septic tanks, as well as a proposed new development of 75 exclusive estate homes intended to be built by Builder. * * *

Appellants have raised four issues on appeal challenging DER's decision to grant the dredge and fill permit. We affirm Points I, III and IV. * * * [T]he more troublesome issue involves the hearing officer's exclusion of the proffered evidence regarding the cumulative impacts of the permitted project. It is on this point that we must reverse and remand for further proceedings.

The issue of "cumulative impacts" was initially indirectly addressed in the Department's Notice of Intent, wherein the Builder was advised to make other permit applications before constructing the sewer pipelines if it felt that denial of the other permits would result in unnecessary expenditure of resources. * * *

Thereafter, the hearing officer ruled on the matter in regard to appellees' motion to strike appellants' amended petition. In a pre-hearing order, the hearing officer stated that when the Intent to Issue was filed, the Department was very much aware that the proposed subaqueous sewer main was intended to service a planned 75-unit single-family development. She also ruled that any effect this future planning might have on the design of the system as proposed by the Builder was an appropriate matter for consideration. However, any matters relating to the development beyond the design plans would have to be shown to be probative before they would be considered at the hearing. To that end, the order provided:

> If it can be demonstrated that the sewer main line is currently designed for even more development beyond the proposed 75 units, this aspect of the design and how the design increase affects the review criteria will also be considered at the hearing. However, any extrapolation which predicts future harms from proposed development is irrelevant, and will not be considered as probative evidence during the formal hearing. * * *

> * * * In Chapter 403, Florida Statutes, the Legislature specifically set forth the criteria to be considered by DER in its review of an application for a dredge and fill permit. The statutes, the small size of the proposed project, and the representation by the applicant that the pipeline permit is not necessarily related to future development, required that the evidentiary and review limitations be imposed. * * *

Furthermore, in her conclusions of law, the hearing officer made the following additional observations on this point:

> Of particular concern to the Petitioners at hearing was the indirect

or secondary impacts from the proposed projects. In the context of this dredge and fill application, the secondary impacts would be any impact to DER jurisdictional waters not caused by the actual dredging and filling necessary to embed the sewer pipeline. In this case, DER considered the project's secondary impacts by requiring the applicant to have emergency shut-off valves on each side of the pass to limit potential environmental harm from the use of the pipeline within a sewage transfer system. A total review of the proposed development in this proceeding is not allowed by the statutory grant of authority nor is it relevant. The petitioners' concerns regarding construction activities beyond this permit is not before the agency by way of any permit application and is therefore not ripe for DER review. DER has no power to require the applicant to submit all permits for review at one time.

* * *

In refusing to disturb the hearing officer's ruling on this issue, the Secretary of DER rejected appellants' exceptions to the hearing officer's ruling on cumulative impacts. * * *

He went on to conclude that the rule of del Campo [v. Department of Environmental Regulation, 452 So. 2d 1004 (Fla. 1st DCA 1984)]:

Only requires the impact of future development to be considered where the likelihood of future development is highly probable given the economic waste of the permitted activity in the absence of such future development. Thus, in Caloosa Property Owners' Asso. v. Department of Environmental Regulation [citation omitted], the court held that the Department was not required to consider the impacts of future development where there was no evidence establishing a reasonable likelihood of prospective development in the same area. * * *

At the hearing in this case, expert testimony was introduced showing that the capacity of the pipeline was appropriate for the loading from the planned 75-unit development, but too small to handle the large additional development which Petitioners claimed would occur. * * * Therefore, there was competent, substantial evidence to support the Hearing Officer's conclusion that evidence of impacts of development beyond the planned 75-unit single-family development should be excluded because there was no reasonable likelihood that the pipeline would be economic waste in the absence of such future development.

* * *

On the other hand, appellee DER urges that appellants' argument is an attempt to expand the scope of both section 403.919[20] and previous cases dealing with the Department's examination of impacts that are generally classified as secondary or cumulative. DER explains that "secondary" impacts are those that may result from the permitted activity itself, and "cumulative" impacts are impacts that may result from the additive effects of many similar projects. It, in turn, contends that section 403.919 should be considered to refer to cumulative rather than secondary impacts. However, it does recognize that the distinction is blurred somewhat in cases such as the present one where at least some of the claimed impacts could be considered under either category, in that they include both additional dredge and fill projects (cumulative impacts) and projects or developments that may be facilitated by the installation of the pipe (secondary impacts). * * *

DER's arguments on this point illuminate the difficulties encountered by it and the hearing officer "in attempting to maintain absolute conceptual separations of the permits while simultaneously recognizing that the outcome of each one inextricably influences the outcome of the others." J.T. McCormick v. City of Jacksonville, 12 FALR 960, 981 (Jan. 22, 1990). Thus, it becomes clear that the resolution of the issue involved herein is not limited strictly to analyzing the alleged cumulative impacts, but, rather, depends as well on a consideration of secondary impacts and the subtle tension that exists between the two analyses.

The cumulative impact doctrine was elucidated by the Department in Peebles v. State of Florida, Department of Environmental Regulation, 12 FALR 1961 (1990). Therein, * * * the Secretary of DER ruled that

> in order to [show] entitlement to a dredge and fill permit, an applicant must show that he has provided reasonable assurance that water quality standards will not be violated and that the project is not contrary to the public interest, and both of those tests must take into consideration the cumulative impacts of similar projects which are existing, under construction, or reasonably expected in the future. * * * The applicant's burden of proof includes the burden of giving reasonable assurance that cumulative impacts do not cause a project to be contrary to the public interest or to violate

---

[20] Section 403.919 is as follows:

Equitable distribution. -- The department, in deciding whether to grant or deny a permit for an activity which will affect waters, shall consider:
(1) The impact of the project for which the permit is sought. (2) The impact of projects which are existing or under construction or for which permits or jurisdictional determinations have been sought. (3) The impact of projects which are under review, approved, or vested pursuant to s. 380.06, or other projects which may reasonably be expected to be located within the jurisdictional extent of waters, based upon land use restrictions and regulations.

water quality standards.

Id. at 1965-1966. The Secretary went on to explain in *Peebles* that the role of the cumulative impact analysis is such that the Department is required to take into consideration "the cumulative impacts of similar projects which are existing, under construction, or reasonably expected in the future," citing again to the language in section 403.919. The Secretary emphasized that the cumulative impact doctrine "is not a third test, but rather a factor to be considered in determining whether reasonable assurance has been provided that the project will not result in violations of water quality standards and will not be contrary to the public interest." He went on to recount that the cumulative impact doctrine was originally developed as department policy and subsequently codified by the legislature in 1984 as section 403.919.
* * * In explaining section 403.919, entitled "Equitable Distribution," the Secretary observed that, as the title suggests,

> * * * the purpose of cumulative impact analysis is to distribute equitably that amount of dredging and filling activity which may be done without resulting in violations of water quality standards and without being contrary to the public interest. In order to determine whether the allocation to a particular applicant is equitable, the determination of the cumulative impact is based in part on the assumption that reasonably expected similar future applications will also be granted.

However, in addition to employing a cumulative impact analysis, it has been the Department's policy, for purposes of applying and balancing the statutory public interest criteria in section 403.918, to look "at the actual jurisdictional area to be dredged and filled, and any other relevant activities that are `very closely linked or causally related to the proposed dredging and filling.'" Thus, in *McCormick*, the DER Secretary declined to adopt the hearing officer's recommendation not to consider any impacts of the overall landfill project in his review of the dredge and fill permit application to construct an access road to the project. Indeed, the Secretary observed:

> Specifically in the context of permitting access roads and bridges, it has been the policy of the Department to consider what will be at the end of the bridge or road. * * * Of course, if the activities or impacts proposed at the end of the bridge or road are remote in distance or conceptual relationship from the dredge and fill activity, those activities or impacts should be weighed accordingly in applying the statutory balancing test.

This particular policy, which clearly employs the secondary impact analysis, was specifically countenanced by this court in *del Campo*.

Based on the foregoing, we do not consider unreasonable DER's position that the cumulative impact doctrine is codified in section 403.919, which requires the Department to take into consideration only those impacts created by the cumulative effects of similar future projects, and not the "secondary" impacts caused or enabled by the project, such as the development in the instant case. However, it is also clear from the Department's decision in *McCormick* that the Department in certain cases is willing to apply a secondary impact analysis and to consider the impact of the total development as enabled by the proposed dredge and fill permit, which consideration is essential to the Department's evaluating whether the applicant has provided the requisite "reasonable assurances" required by section 403.918. In fact, the statement of Department policy set forth in *McCormick* is clearly consistent with that set forth in *del Campo* wherein the Department conceded that it "`has maintained as a matter of law that in reviewing a permit application for a portion of a project it may consider the impacts of associated development, even where no application has been received for that development."' 452 So. 2d at 1006 (Smith, J., specially concurring and dissenting in part).

In the instant case, we disagree with appellees that the contemplated development of 75 estate homes is speculative and is not closely linked or causally related to the proposed dredging and filling. We perceive there to be little difference between the Department's aforestated need to "consider what will be at the end of the bridge or road," and the necessity here to consider what will be at the end of the pipeline, especially when the evidence, proffered or admitted, suggests that the development enabled by the dredge and fill permit could have devastating environmental impacts. Such evidence would be highly relevant to the Department's consideration of whether the applicant has carried its burden of giving reasonable assurances under section 403.918 that water quality standards will not be violated and the project is not contrary to the public interest. Thus, the Department's consideration of the proposed development solely in relation to the design of the pipeline system itself neglected the necessity in this case to consider potential secondary impacts.

Consequently, it was error for the hearing officer to exclude the evidence proffered by appellants for the reasons set forth in her recommended order. Accordingly, this case must be reversed and remanded for further proceedings and reevaluation of the proffered evidence in a manner consistent with this opinion.

Notes and Questions

1. How are secondary and cumulative impacts distinguished? Which are more speculative? Can they legitimately be distinguished? If so, why? In the broader context of coastal development, what

impacts, in addition to environmental impacts, should be considered?

2.   To what extent should remote impacts be considered? How should uncertainty or lack of information be factored into the process? The experience under the National Environmental Policy Act (NEPA) may be helpful. In general, an environmental impact statement need not consider purely speculative impacts or remote "worst case" possibilities. See, e.g., Robertson v. Methow Valley Citizens Council, 490 U.S. 332 (1989). Keep in mind, however, that NEPA merely requires consideration of environmental impacts in the decision making process and is not imposing a substantive permitting requirement. How should this affect the analysis?

3.   How would you factor consideration of cumulative impacts into the permitting process? Does it only become a factor when development has proceeded to the point that the environmental systems are severely stressed? Should it be a consideration in the first development in an area? In the footnote in *Conservancy*, the Florida Statute incorporating cumulative impact analysis entitled "Equitable Distribution" is quoted. Does this name adequately reflect the analysis required by the statute? Does it equitably apportion environmental impacts among present and future users? Compare the Florida approach to the regulations of the Council on Environmental Quality which define cumulative impacts as "the impact on the environment which results from the incremental impact of the action when added to other past, present, and reasonably foreseeable future actions."

Chapter Four

U.S. RIGHTS AND JURISDICTION OVER OCEAN WATERS AND RESOURCES

SECTION 1. INTRODUCTION: THE REAL MAP OF THE UNITED STATES

Map-makers today have a difficult time keeping up with the rapidly changing world scene. Nation-states are dividing or disappearing, and national boundaries seem to be constantly shifting. The careful purchaser of a world map or a globe will first check to make sure that it displays the unified Germany and the new states created from the rubble of the former Soviet Union, and the break-up of the former Yugoslavia and other changes in Africa and Asia.

Yet the typical newly updated world maps still overlook some of the most significant recent changes in the planet's political geography. These maps still display the familiar basic pattern: boundary lines and pale colors covering the continents and large islands, yet nothing but a wash of light blues for the majority of the earth's surface, that part covered by the world's oceans. The clear implication in this pattern is that nations are confined to dry land, and that the ocean is undivided space beyond national boundaries. For centuries this picture of the world has indeed reflected reality: the untamed ocean seaward of a very narrow belt of coastal waters was not considered national space but was free and open for use by any nation. As true as this implication used to be, it is, today, a serious misrepresentation.

A much more accurate picture of the world's geography would show 200-mile offshore national zones blanketing forty percent of the global ocean. The differences between such a map and the normal depiction are startling and crucial to a true understanding of the political world and certainly essential to a full appreciation of the topics covered in this book. The general-circulation maps of popular atlases are correct in the implicit assumption that national sovereignty, or total governmental power, is basically limited to the land and inland waters (although even this assumption is incorrect if it does not include at least a narrow strip of offshore territory for coastal nations). But, in the last quarter century, an oceanic revolution has occurred resulting in the acquisition by coastal nations of a broad competence to govern nearly all types of human activities and events that occur within 200 nautical miles from shore. Some important governance rights and jurisdictions for these nations extend even beyond 200 miles.

Few nations have been affected as much by the new allocation of oceanic governmental competence as has the United States. The total U.S. coastline, including that of its islands, is not the longest in the world. However, the 200-mile spaces off its coasts are the largest, and probably the richest, ocean spaces of any nation's. Within these vast ocean areas, the United States now has the primary governmental authority to make laws and regulations concerning virtually all activities and events other than ship traffic, aircraft overflight, and the laying of some types of cables and pipelines on the sea's floor. For example, like other coastal nations, the United States has exclusive rights in its 200-mile ocean areas to regulate all fishing, exploration for and exploitation of oil and gas and other minerals, and the production of energy. It also has important jurisdictions and responsibilities regarding the quality of the marine environment in these areas. A truly accurate map of the United States ought to include the sea areas that fall within its primary governmental authority. See Figure 4-1.

Figure 4-1: The United States Exclusive Economic Zones
U.S. Department of State

In this chapter, we summarize the recent revolution in international ocean law that has given us this new picture of the political world and especially what it means for the expanded governance roles of the United States in its offshore seas. First, however, a review of some general notions of public international law is in order.

SECTION 2. INTRODUCTION TO INTERNATIONAL LAW

Public international law is the law that regulates the behavior of nation-states (and, to some extent, international organizations, such as the United Nations) in their relations with one another. It is a primitive legal system, one that has no legislature or executive and no compulsory-jurisdiction court, yet it is quite effective, especially in providing the structure for the international community of nation states, the so-called Global Village. Even though there is no institutionalized police force or other formal enforcement machinery to ensure compliance with international law, Professor Louis Henkin is certainly correct when he states: "It is probably the case that *almost all nations observe almost all principles of international law and almost all their obligations almost all of the time*." L. Henkin, How Nations Behave 47 (2d ed. 1979) (emphasis in original). We are not here concerned with why this is true, but instead leave that question to International Law courses. Much more important for our purposes are the sources of public international law. In a legal system without statutes or binding court decisions, where do the rules of law come from and how are they created?

A. SOURCES OF INTERNATIONAL LAW

The most-often-cited list of international law sources is found in Article 38 of the Statute of the International Court of Justice, sometimes referred to as the "World Court" or the ICJ. Only nation-states can be parties to contentious cases before the ICJ and then only if they have expressly consented to the Court's jurisdiction. The ICJ Statute, a treaty to which almost all the world's nations are parties, requires the Court to apply international law in deciding the disputes before it. According to Article 38, the three primary sources of international law are (1) international agreements, or treaties, (2) custom, and (3) general principles of law.

International agreements (treaties). Agreements between nation-states have frequently been analogized to contracts between individuals in a domestic legal system. Many international agreements or treaties are indeed similar to contracts. For example, two neighboring states might agree to buy and sell territory; one state can sell goods to another; states often agree to cultural exchanges; and so forth. But the international agreements we will be most concerned with in this chapter are those sometimes called "law making" treaties.

Law-making treaties are those that attempt to provide something like legislation in the community of nation-states, a society that has no legislature. Typically, such a treaty is negotiated at a conference called for that purpose by the interested states. The goal of the conferees is to devise a set of legal rules to regulate an activity or group of related activities of concern to them.

But "law making" treaties, while often reading like statutes, are not legislation. The major, and crucial, difference is that a treaty, like all international agreements, is binding only on those states that have explicitly assented to it, while a statute is law for everyone within the legislature's jurisdiction, including those who object to it and even for those individuals who, as legislators, might actually have voted against it. For a treaty to be an effective law-making instrument, therefore, it is essential that all directly concerned states, and not just a majority, become parties to it. As you might expect, this often requires some fancy negotiating and artfully drafted rules.

The 1982 United Nations Convention on the Law of the Sea, which is the subject of much of the discussion later in this Chapter, is one of the most prominent examples of a law-making treaty.

Custom. Customary rules of international law are said to arise from patterns of actions and words of nation-states in the conduct of their relations with each other over time. This so-called "state practice" creates expectations within the international community that all members of that community will conform their behavior to these rules out of a sense of obligation. These rules, or norms, can therefore be characterized as legally binding.

To those of us raised and trained in a highly structured national society with sophisticated institutions to create, interpret, and enforce law, custom as a source of law might seem rather illusory. It is not. Humans have lived in loosely structured groups, organized in ways that seem primitive to us, far longer than they have lived in today's civilized societies. These simpler communities, nevertheless, had laws, and all, or nearly all, of these laws were based on customary practices. A member of the group would understand which promises were binding, the extent to which private property and community property were recognized, what forms of physical force used against another member were unacceptable, and so forth, without the requirement of legislative votes or written codes.

The global community of nations is a relatively unstructured society with a primitive legal system, one that has long depended on its members recognizing and adhering to customary norms of law. Among these customary rules is one that has been around for so long that it retains its Latin designation: *pacta sunt servanda*, or the obligation of a nation to obey its international agreements in good faith. Others include a more recently evolved rule forbidding aggressive use of force against another nation-state and standards for treatment by a nation of foreigners present within its territory.

How is a customary norm created? How does one discover or identify a rule of customary international law? A couple of recent examples in the law of the sea illustrate the process and also how rapidly custom can create a new rule. In 1945, President Truman claimed for the United States jurisdiction and control over the natural resources of the continental shelves off U.S. coasts. The United States was thus claiming ownership rights to resources under the high seas beyond, often far beyond, the outer edge of its three-mile territorial sea. At the time, this claim was most certainly not legal under international law; nothing in customary or treaty practices would have then validated this unilateral assertion of rights. The response of the members of the international community, however, was one of general approval, largely through imitation and tolerance, and by no later than the mid-1950s the pattern of actions and words of approval had clearly created a rule of international law granting to coastal nations sovereign rights to the natural resources of their adjacent continental shelves. This claim-and-response process is a standard way for customary international law to come about and, in the twentieth century, one that can be considerably accelerated by modern communications technology.

A similar (and, as we shall see, related) customary law of the sea is the more recent recognition of the package of offshore rights and jurisdictions of coastal nations within 200 nautical miles of their coasts. Lying beyond the territorial sea, this area is called the exclusive economic zone (EEZ). The claim-and-response process that called the EEZ into existence occurred over a period of the three decades between the mid-1940s and the mid-1970s. This process was quite a bit more complicated than the one that created the continental shelf doctrine and will be discussed in further detail below.

Unlike laws contained in treaties, which bind only the parties to them, customary norms bind all members of the international community (except, it is often asserted, those who have persistently objected to the formation of a rule of customary law while it is in the process of formation).

General principles of law. This is a somewhat controversial and little-used source of law. It is generally understood to refer to those common principles recognized within the various domestic systems of law throughout the world. Examples often cited are res judicata, estoppel, and restitution based on unjust enrichment. When applied by the ICJ and other international tribunals, general principles are considered useful in helping to fill in the frequent gaps in the coverage of international treaty and customary law. General principle of law may also refer to general principles of international law.

Article 38 of the ICJ Statute also lists two more secondary sources of international law that can be used to assist in the identification of the three primary sources. The first of these secondary sources is *judicial decisions*. The Statute specifically states that an ICJ decision is not binding on any nation other than the parties to the case before it. Neither is the Court bound to follow its own prior judgments. In other words, there is no stare decisis or system of precedent for international judicial decisions. Nevertheless, not surprisingly, the ICJ and the lawyers that practice before it tend to treat its previous judgments as very persuasive, and certainly these judgments are among the judicial decisions that Article 38 lists as helpful secondary sources of international law. Other international and regional courts and tribunals have proliferated, and the relevant decisions of these courts are within the scope of the sources of international law. It is also clear that Article 38's reference to judicial decisions includes those decisions of national courts in those cases where these courts analyze, interpret, or apply rules of international law. For example, the United States Supreme Court has frequently examined and applied international law, at least indirectly, and its opinions are thus appropriately viewed as secondary-source judicial decisions under Article 38.

The other secondary source of international law consists of the writings of highly regarded *publicists* or scholars in the field of international law. In American legal practice, we often look to and cite such scholarly authorities as Corbin, Prosser, and the American Law Institute's Restatements of the Law to help us determine what our domestic law is or should be, so this secondary source of international law should not be surprising to us.

These two secondary sources have been quite important in the development and evolution of the law of the sea.

It should be pointed out that resolutions or declarations of the United Nations General Assembly are not law, although they sometimes purport to state rules of law. Yet an examination of the U.N. delegations' voting patterns favoring or opposing a particular law-stating resolution might show that the resolution itself is an important piece of state practice evidencing a customary law or an interpretation of a law-making treaty, so U.N. resolutions can be helpful in the search for law.

In general, you should note that the sources of international law, unlike much of domestic law, require the explicit assent (treaties) or implicit consent (custom, general principles) of the entities bound by the rules, and this requirement goes a long way toward explaining why international law is so widely obeyed. Some system of order and law is perceived to be in the interest, at least the long-term interest, of all members of the international community. Even when a nation-state wishes to avoid some accepted rule of treaty or custom, it almost never simply refuses to recognize the rule. Instead, it nearly always employs lawyers to make legal arguments favoring its position. Is international law really law? If not, it is hard to explain why virtually every nation today acts as if it is, and what more can an abstract institution such as law ask for to validate its existence?

B. SOVEREIGNTY AND JURISDICTION

Perhaps the most basic principle of international law is sovereignty. Many of the norms of international customary and treaty law are connected, in one way or another, with this vital concept. Nations and governments (and would-be nations and governments) argue, negotiate, and, too frequently, fight about sovereignty. This should not be particularly surprising because the international rules on sovereignty determine, among other things, the existence of nation-states and, very importantly for our study, the particular parts of the planet's surface that are under the sovereign governmental power of each nation-state. Until fairly recently, international law allowed acquisition of territorial sovereignty by conquest, or the use of military force. Theoretically, at least, conquest is not a legal means for a nation-state to acquire territory under present rules of international law. However, it is still permissible, as it has been for centuries, to acquire territory by voluntary cession from another nation, by prescription, and by occupation of (now nearly non-existent) unclaimed land.

Closely related to sovereignty are the international law principles of jurisdiction, or power to make or enforce laws. A nation-state has jurisdiction to prescribe and enforce its laws throughout the territory subject to its sovereignty. It also has jurisdiction beyond its boundaries over its nationals and over ships and aircraft flying its flag. While there are other debatable bases for a state to assert its jurisdiction, these are the principles that are universally recognized.

This section of the chapter has briefly introduced a few relevant concepts of public international law. With these in mind, we can now proceed to a deeper examination of the law of the sea.

SECTION 3. LAW OF THE SEA: THE LATE TWENTIETH-CENTURY REVOLUTION

The law of the sea is that part of public international law made up of norms concerning human activities and human-sponsored events on and under the world's oceans and seas. It is an ancient sub-field of international law, one that had evolved slowly for centuries, until the middle of the twentieth century, when it began to move suddenly in stunning new directions. The story of this remarkable revolution is a fascinating one.

A. A BRIEF HISTORY OF THE LAW OF THE SEA TO 1945

Imagine an animated map of the history of world ocean geography beginning in the early seventeenth century, with each year whizzing by, say, every four seconds. For about 20 minutes, the map would not change much, would hardly seem animated at all. With only a few flashing blips here and there, nearly the entire ocean would remain the familiar undivided light blue of free seas subject to no nation's sovereignty or jurisdiction; only a fluttering narrow line of color along the coasts would indicate national control in the seas. Suddenly, beginning in the mid-twentieth century, the map would explode in a fireworks display of color, starting at the coasts and blooming seaward until, two-and-a-half minutes later, nearly forty percent of the formerly light blue expanse would be covered with the many hues of coastal nation zones and the lines delineating them. We would then have arrived at today's ocean world.

Scholars frequently mark the beginning of the free seas era -- 20 minutes in our map's running time, about 300 years in actual time -- with the publication in 1609 of a tract entitled Mare Liberum, Latin for "Free Seas," authored by a young Dutch jurist, Hugo Grotius. (Mare Liberum later became a chapter in Grotius's famous text, De Jure Belle Ac Pacis, a work that would earn him the title, "the father of international law.") Grotius was almost certainly hired to write his tract by the Dutch East India Company, which at the time was having its vessels' passage to the East Indies impeded by Portugal. Spain and Portugal, supported by a papal bull, had for a century or so claimed to have divided the world ocean between their two nations, with Portugal's half covering the ocean areas east of a mid-Atlantic line. Grotius argued in Mare Liberum that the ocean was too wild to be occupied by nations and that the limitless extent of its resources made their ownership absurd. Bolstering his arguments with natural law concepts, he forcefully concluded that the seas were free and open for navigation and fishing by any nation.

It is, frankly, doubtful that Hugo Grotius' brief actually created the free seas age that is today under such serious attack, but it is not a bad starting point for a discussion of the history of the law of the sea. In reality, by the early seventeenth century, the Age of Exploration and Discovery was almost over, and those few nations with the will and capability to navigate the global ocean for colonization and profit probably saw a free seas principle as advantageous to their adventurous plans. In any case, by sometime in the 1600s, the view that the open ocean was not subject to the sovereignty or control of nation states, that it could be used freely without restriction from other nations, had become the sort of article of faith that we might call law.

The only widely recognized exception to this free seas rule over the next three centuries was the *territorial sea*, a narrow offshore belt of national authority for coastal states. The territorial sea gradually solidified as a concept in the eighteenth century. Its maximum breadth has long been a subject of some dispute, sometimes said to be the range of a land-based cannon in that century. More likely, the "cannon-shot rule" formed the basis in logic for coastal nation authority but did not provide any specific distance measurement for the width of the territorial sea. Eventually, following a claim-and-response process conducted by belligerent and neutral nations through decades of naval warfare, one English league, or three nautical miles, became a much-cited customary standard, but certainly not a universal one. For example, Scandinavian countries claimed four-mile territorial seas, based on the length of the Scandinavian league. By the opening years of the twentieth century, however, it could be confidently asserted that three nautical miles was the maximum allowable breadth for the territorial sea under customary international law.

If we freeze-frame a year in the early twentieth century -- let us say 1914, on the eve of the First World War -- we should see that the geographical picture of the world ocean remains the same basic scene we have been observing on our animated map for twenty minutes, or three hundred years: only a skinny line of territorial sea along the coasts of the continents making the slightest incursion in the vast unbounded expanse of blue that is by now known as the *high seas*. On the high seas, freedom of vessel navigation, surface and submerged, is perhaps the most important tenet of the freedom rule. Freedom to fish is next, and even the newfangled flying machines will be accorded the freedom to fly over the high seas.

Within the three-mile territorial sea, however, each coastal country has sovereignty over the waters, the seabed, the living and mineral resources located there, and the airspace over it. Only one important exception to the coastal nation's sovereignty has evolved: foreign vessels on the sea's surface must be granted the right of innocent passage through the territorial sea. That is, in general, passage for foreign ships that does not threaten the peace and security of the coastal nation cannot be impeded by the coastal nation. The right of innocent passage is, however, reserved for traditional surface traffic only and was not granted to the newer sub-surface or overflight transits.

In *internal waters*, which sometimes included arms of the ocean such as bays and gulfs, the coastal nation could exercise as complete a sovereignty as it could over its land, lakes, and rivers. Coastal states frequently granted relatively unrestricted access by foreign ships to their internal-water ports, but it is doubtful that the law of the sea recognized a right of such access.

The end of the First World War led to the creation of the League of Nations and its commitment to decolonization. Subsequent years saw the attempt to codify the customary principles of the law of the sea as summarized above. The League collapsed and the world was soon headed for another global conflict.

The United States emerged from World War II in 1945 as the only naval superpower. No nation at the time would seem to have had a greater stake in the continuance of the broadest definition and application of the freedom of the seas, which for the naval powers of any generation has always meant the freedom to send its warships just about anywhere on the ocean. Ironically, however, it was the United States that, only weeks after the end of the war, triggered the international law revolution that has seriously eroded and continues to threaten the traditional freedoms of the high seas.

In September 1945, President Truman issued two proclamations concerning the ocean areas off the U.S. coasts. One of these proclamations set forth the established right of the United States to set conservation rules for its own citizens and vessels fishing in the high seas outside U.S. territorial seas and urged international agreements with other nations whose vessels were also fishing these areas. In the other presidential proclamation, often referred to since then as "*the Truman Proclamation*," the president claimed for the United States exclusive jurisdiction and control over the natural resources of the continental shelves adjacent to U.S. coasts. As noted earlier, this claim was almost certainly illegal at the time because it asserted national authority over resources of the seabed extending often far beyond the three-mile border of the U.S. territorial sea and thus under the waters of the "free" high seas. In the wake of a devastating war that had depended more than any other prior conflict on access to petroleum, President Truman's desire to bring under U.S. control the rich oil deposits of the continental shelf was perhaps understandable. Recognizing the United States' new naval power role, the Truman Proclamation was careful not to claim any right to infringe on the freedom of the high seas in the waters above the continental shelf.

What perhaps was not foreseen, however, was the effect the continental shelf claim would have on the claim-and-response process of customary international law. Eventually, it would help turn the old order of the seas into a shambles.

B. UNCLOS I AND II: THE 1958 GENEVA CONVENTIONS

Background: The Path to Codification

Despite the frequent claim by us humans that we are the most advanced form of life on earth, we are pathetically maladapted to the planet's major environment, the ocean. Only by using our tool-making skill have we been able to exist for any length of time in the marine environment. Technology, from hollowed-out logs to sophisticated submersibles, is what enables air-breathing, land-crawling humans to survive, precariously, on and under the sea. And, until recently, we have not been particularly successful at that. Over the centuries, of course, relatively few people have ventured to sea in ships and other vessels to transport cargo and passengers and messages and to hunt for wild fish. And we still have not set up any permanent habitation in floating towns or seabed cities. We will probably colonize the moon first. Nevertheless, it is the late-twentieth-century advances in technology (the technological boom following World War II) that, among other things, really got human beings more involved in the oceans. Some of these advances have allowed drilling for oil and gas farther out to sea and deeper than ever before and have led to the serious contemplation of commercially mining the deep seabed. Other technological improvements have led to the transportation of oil in huge tanker vessels that barely resemble traditional ships. Perhaps most importantly for our study, as we shall see, technology created world-ranging, very efficient fishing fleets. In sum, humankind's highly developed tool-making skills were, by the 1950s, encouraging human society to expand outward from its land base into the offshore seas. And with society comes law.

Of course, technological advances were only part of the relevant setting in mid-century. Other events and trends on the world scene would add crucial ingredients to the recipe for revolution in the international law of the sea. Chief among these was the entry into the international community of several new nations. The United Nations, created in 1945, successfully continued the League of Nations' efforts to encourage and oversee the birth into independence of the former colonies. These new states, almost all poor countries, joined a growing group of less developed nations that came to be called the Third World. None had global navies or world-ranging fishing fleets and therefore had no perceived special interest in the traditional high seas freedoms. But most were coastal nations, and they looked with suspicion or envy at the activities of the technologically richer nations whose vessels and aircraft were exercising the "freedoms of the high seas" just offshore.

Most upsetting to many coastal countries, including some developed nations, such as the United States, were the distant water fishing fleets of a few countries, such as the Soviet Union and Japan, which, with increasing frequency, could be observed fishing on the high seas just outside other nations' territorial seas for fish stocks that were viewed, by history and geography, as "belonging to" coastal states and their fishermen. Coastal countries also often resented the presence of foreign naval fleets off their coasts and some were suspicious of foreign oceanographic vessels conducting operations there.

One result of this tension between the many coastal countries and the few maritime states was a new claim-and-response process that, to the latter states at least, threatened to infringe on their traditional high seas freedoms. Many newly independent nations claimed 12-mile territorial seas, and some established states increased their territorial sea claims to 12 miles. Others, with the 1945 Truman Proclamation as an analogous precedent, asserted exclusive fishing zones beyond their territorial seas.

The most ambitious post-war claims to extended coastal nation jurisdiction were asserted by Chile, Ecuador, and Peru (known in this context for some time thereafter as the "CEP countries"). In 1947, Chile lodged the first 200-mile claim in the face of a post-war Japanese return to the whaling grounds off the South American country's long coast. Although the Chilean claim was only to the natural resources of its new offshore zone, reflecting to some extent the limited nature of the

Truman Proclamation, the same year saw Peru, Chile's neighbor to the north, assert what some observers characterized as a 200-mile territorial sea. In 1952, based on the CEP countries' Santiago Declaration, which proclaimed the legality and rightness of 200-mile zones, Ecuador extended its territorial sea to 200 miles.

The international response to these initial 200-mile claims, unlike the nearly immediate favorable response to the 1945 Truman Proclamation on the Continental Shelf, was opposition, especially from the maritime nations with large navies or fishing fleets. In the beginning, then, the acceptance of the these very expansive jurisdictional claims was slow in coming. The "200-mile Club" of nations did, however, gradually start to gather Third World members, first in Latin America and then in Africa.

In the midst of this unsettling trend toward greater national jurisdiction in the ocean, the International Law Commission determined that the law of the sea was ripe for codification. The ILC is a group of international law experts operating within the United Nations system and charged with codifying and progressively developing international law. In the mid-1950s, the ILC studied the traditions and trends in the law of the sea and drafted four proposed law-making treaties. Under the call and sponsorship of the U.N. General Assembly, the First United Nations Conference on the Law of the Sea (UNCLOS I) gathered in Geneva in 1958 to consider the ILC drafts. More than 80 nation-state delegations participated in these deliberations and, following a few weeks of negotiations, adopted the four 1958 Geneva Conventions on the Law of the Sea.

As a package, these four law-making treaties painted a somewhat surprisingly traditional picture of the law of the sea, with little indication of the extended-national-jurisdiction trend other than the important recognition of the continental shelf doctrine inspired by the Truman Proclamation. The other major indication of the new trend was the inability of the delegations in Geneva to agree on the maximum breadth of the territorial sea. Of course, the United States, as a major naval power, and other maritime countries wanted to retain the three-mile limit, while the CEP countries and their imitators would like to have seen recognition of 200-mile limits. A growing number of coastal nations preferred a 12-mile breadth. In 1960, the Second United Nations Conference on the Law of the Sea (UNCLOS II) met again in Geneva in an attempt to resolve this issue, but failed.

The Geneva Conventions on the Law of the Sea:
The Old Picture

Collectively, the 1958 Geneva Conventions provide us with a law of the sea snapshot -- by now, as old-fashioned as a tintype, the last portrait of the old order of the oceans. Nevertheless, they were for many years cited as generally accurate codifications or articulations of the customary law of the sea, and the United States today technically remains a party to the four treaties adopted at UNCLOS I. They are important landmarks in our animated map of the historical sweep of ocean geography, and we ought to examine them, at least in summary form. See Figure 4-2.

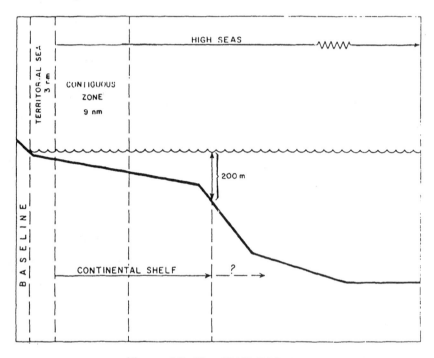

Figure 4-2. The UNCLOS I picture
Jacobson, Law of the Sea--What Now? 37 Naval War College Review 82, 88 (1984)

The Convention on the Territorial Sea and the Contiguous Zone codified most of the traditional notions of national jurisdiction in the offshore oceans. That is, the sovereignty of coastal nations is limited to its internal waters, including bays of the ocean, and its territorial sea, subject only to the right of innocent passage for foreign-flag vessels transiting on the surface through the territorial sea. Because of the inability of the UNCLOS delegations to come to agreement on the maximum breadth of the territorial sea, the treaty makes no mention of its allowable width. It does, however, authorize a "contiguous zone," which can extend beyond the territorial sea to a maximum limit of 12 nautical miles.

The *contiguous zone* is a concept drawn from our animated map's offshore "flutterings," those occasional assertions of various sorts of special authority by coastal countries in the waters outside their territorial seas. The 1958 treaty allows coastal nations to exercise enforcement jurisdiction to prevent and punish violations of its customs, fiscal, immigration, and sanitary laws applicable to its territory or territorial sea. It does not authorize adoption of substantive laws on these topics in the zone, only enforcement actions.

Because the contiguous zone is far more limited in its grant of authority to coastal nations than the sovereignty of the territorial sea and cannot extend beyond 12 miles, it is often persuasively argued that, despite the failure of the UNCLOS I and II delegations to establish a specific territorial sea width, it certainly can be no more than 12 miles under the Convention on the Territorial Sea and Contiguous Zone.

That convention also sets down several important rules on drawing baselines from which the breadth of the territorial sea (meaning whatever distance a coastal nation was claiming) was to be measured. The so-called normal baseline was established as the mean low-water line of the coast. The treaty allows coastal countries to draw exceptional, "non-normal" baselines along the outer points of especially convoluted coastlines and across the mouths of rivers and bay openings. "Bay" is a legal term applicable to coastal indentations, be they designated as gulfs or inlets or estuaries or even bays, deep enough and narrow enough at their mouths to justify, according to simple geometric limits, the drawing of baselines joining their outer headlands. "Historic" bays, not defined in the treaty, are allowed to ignore the limits. Baselines are significant for many reasons, not the least of which are that the waters landward of them are, of course, internal waters and that the outer boundaries of the territorial sea and the contiguous zone can be extended seaward by the use of "non-normal" baselines.

The Convention on the Continental Shelf codified the continental shelf doctrine, the custom created by the 1945 Truman Proclamation's claim, and the favorable response of the international community. The doctrine recognizes coastal nations' sovereign rights in the natural resources of the seabed and subsoil of the continental shelves adjacent to their coasts. "Sovereign rights" lie somewhere in between sovereignty and jurisdiction.

The convention gives to the coastal nation the exclusive right to explore the continental shelf and the exclusive right to exploit its resources. This concept is crucial to the new directions the law of the sea was even then embarking upon because, like the contiguous zone but with more significance, it demonstrated that the ancient barrier between the national sovereignty of the territorial sea and the community freedoms of the high seas beyond the territorial sea could be breached by the extension of less-than-sovereign national authority into the high seas.

Again, however, a major issue arose on the geographical limits of this national extension of authority. Geologically, the continental shelf is the submerged top of the continental platform and ends where the continental slope begins its steeper plunge toward the deep seabed. This outer natural boundary is, however, not precise enough for legal definition, so the treaty chose to establish the 200-meter isobath, a depth line that approximates the average natural limit and is also close to the 100-fathom line marked on nautical charts, as the initial outer boundary for the legal continental shelf. But, to provide for future growth of ocean technology, the Continental Shelf Convention also allows the further extension of the legal continental shelf beyond the 200-meter isobath to the depths of exploitability of the natural resources of the seabed and subsoil. Although some critics have argued that the combined legal continental shelves of the coastal nations could thereby some day cover the entire seabed, most authorities agreed that they could extend no farther than the inner edge of the deep seabed ("where the ball stops rolling," as one perceptive wag put it). In any event, as we shall see, the several questions raised by the exploitability test have no doubt been rendered moot by more recent developments.

The Convention on the High Seas was, as its Preamble states, almost entirely a codification or "restatement" of the customary law of the sea as it existed in 1958. In the convention, the high seas are defined as the area seaward of the outer boundary of the territorial sea. Four specific "freedoms of the high seas" are listed: (1) freedom of navigation (meaning both surface and submerged); (2) freedom to fish; (3) freedom of overflight; and (4) freedom to lay cables and pipelines on the sea floor. The treaty makes clear, however, that customary international law might recognize other freedoms, and the International Law Commission's deliberations leading to its draft of the High Seas Convention indicate that freedom of scientific research could be a "fifth freedom." In the exercise of their freedoms of the high seas, nation-states must give reasonable regard to other states in their exercise of the same freedoms.

For many years, these provisions not only guided the conduct of its parties, including the United States, but were also frequently said by the ICJ and publicists to reflect customary law binding on all states. Thus, no nation-state could unreasonably interfere with most high seas activities of other states and their flag vessels and aircraft. The convention includes a short list of exceptions to this broad rule of noninterference, such as control of piracy and drug trafficking, but perhaps its principal significance lay in its strong reaffirmation of the traditional Grotian notion that the rule of freedom of the seas reigned throughout the vast expanse of the ocean beyond relatively narrow territorial seas. This was a victory for the maritime states, who undoubtedly hoped to nip in the bud the trend toward expansion of national jurisdiction into the high seas. Of course, the continental shelf doctrine, the contiguous zone, and the failure of UNCLOS I to agree on a territorial sea breadth were at the same time important reflections of that very trend.

The Convention on Fishing and Conservation of the Living Resources of the High Seas and its eventual fate, when viewed from our historical perspective, reveal a lot about the extension-of-national-jurisdiction trend and the failure of the 1958 Geneva conventions to stop it or even slow it down. Of the four treaties, the Fishing Convention is the clearest attempt to resolve the growing tension between the maritime countries (especially the United States), who wanted to preserve the greatest extent of the freedoms of navigation and overflight, and non-maritime coastal states, who particularly resented the prospect of foreign fishing fleets continuing to exercise the freedom to fish the high seas off their shores.

The Fishing Convention would allow coastal nations to unilaterally set nondiscriminatory conservation rules for all fishing for threatened stocks in the high seas beyond their territorial seas, provided that negotiations for international agreement on such rules had failed and provided further that fishing regulations would eventually be set by compulsory and binding international arbitration.

Although the Fishing Convention received the requisite two-thirds favorable vote for adoption at UNCLOS I and gathered enough ratifications to come into force, it was effectively a failure. None of the leading distant water fishing nations became parties and, since the treaty could not be legitimately characterized as a codification or articulation of customary international law, these states had no obligation to observe high seas fishing regulations set unilaterally by the countries off whose coasts they fished. Thus, if high seas fishing were to regulated at all, it would have to be by bilateral or multilateral international agreement.

After UNCLOS I and II: The Revolution Continues

If the International Law Commission and the maritime powers hoped that the four 1958 Geneva conventions would calm the gathering law of the sea storm, they were soon disappointed. Only ten years after UNCLOS II, the United Nations General Assembly would call for a third conference on the law of the sea. Why? What happened to the carefully crafted set of treaties that made them so unsatisfactory so soon? In a nutshell: the trend toward expanded national jurisdiction in the ocean proceeded unabated in the wake of the first two conferences. Newly independent and established coastal states alike, mostly Third World countries, continued to ignore the traditional three-mile limit for territorial seas and opted for the increasingly popular 12-mile breadth, and a growing number claimed more, sometimes far more. Exclusive fishing zones layered outward from territorial seas became more common, and, most disturbing, the 200-Mile Club continued to recruit new members. Although the primary concern of the coastal nations was to gain control of offshore marine resources, especially living resources, the claims to extended jurisdiction often included assertions of authority to regulate other activities. Any extension of the territorial sea, of course, automatically asserted sovereignty (minus the right of innocent passage) over the broadened area. This chipping away at the freedoms of the high seas naturally concerned the maritime countries. Even where the extended jurisdiction claims were by their terms limited to resources, the naval and maritime powers worried about "creeping jurisdiction," a process by which the initially limited claims might gradually evolve into assertions of rights to regulate navigation and overflight.

By the mid-1960s, the expansionist trend had become so alarming to the United States, as the world's pre-eminent naval power, and the Soviet Union, by then having achieved a global navy of its own, that these two Cold War adversaries took the extraordinary step of jointly addressing the problem. The two superpowers decided that a new international effort was needed to try to compromise the interests of the naval and maritime powers in maintaining broad freedoms of navigation and overflight, on the one side, and, on the other, the interests of coastal states in having substantial control over fisheries in the high seas off their coasts. The United States and the U.S.S.R. began to lobby for a new international conference in which fishing would be traded for the preservation of navigation freedoms.

Fortuitously, at the same time events in another field of ocean activity would add to the pressure for a new law of the sea conference and in fact would provide the trigger mechanism for the U.N. General Assembly's 1970 call for a third conference.

It had been known for a century, ever since the famous H.M.S. Challenger oceanographic expedition, that large areas of the deep ocean floor were covered with fist-sized nodules composed mainly of manganese. In the 1950s and '60s, investigators pointed out that the nodules also contained smaller traces of more valuable minerals, particularly, nickel, copper, and cobalt. With the technology boom again playing a significant role, interest in the commercial possibilities for mining manganese nodules arose. But this new interest in the deep seabed, almost all of which lay beyond the limits of national jurisdiction, raised fears that a land-grab rush to "colonize" the bottom of the sea would ensue.

In one of the modern law of the sea's defining moments, the Maltese ambassador to the United Nations, Arvid Pardo, rose to address the General Assembly at its annual meeting in November 1967. Ambassador Pardo informed the delegations there of the potentially vast wealth that lay deep beneath the seas and of his nation's concern that the technologically rich nations of the world would rush to exploit the manganese nodules for their own benefit. He proposed that the seabed beyond national jurisdiction be set aside for peaceful purposes, that it and its resources be declared the "common heritage of mankind," and that its potential wealth be realized for the benefit of all mankind, especially the poorest countries.

Ambassador Pardo's speech was received in the U.N., the great majority of whose members were now less developed Third World countries, with overwhelming approval. Within three years, the General Assembly took several significant actions concerning the deep seabed and its resources. Among these were (1) the Principles Declaration, which declared the deep seabed beyond national jurisdiction "the common heritage of mankind"; (2) the Moratorium Resolution, which purported to make illegal any mining of the deep seabed until an international mining scheme, with the common heritage idea as its guiding principle, could be established; and (3) the Conference Resolution, which called for the convening of a new law of the sea conference to establish the mining regime. The target date for this new conference was 1973. The General Assembly had also created a Seabed Committee and assigned to it the task of preparing the way for what would be the Third United Nations Conference on the Law of the Sea (UNCLOS III), the most ambitious undertaking in the history of international negotiations.

C. UNCLOS III

The Third United Nations Conference on the Law of the Sea began its deliberations in late 1973 and would not conclude its work with the adoption of a treaty until nearly ten years later. It was the largest and most complex international law-making conference ever attempted. Three numbers define the immensity of the challenge that faced the delegations at UNCLOS III: 85, 150, and 70.

85: After meeting in several sessions, the General Assembly's Seabed Committee set an agenda for the upcoming conference that listed about 85 items and subitems. It had become clear in the committee's meetings that the conference would need to address far more than the issues, themselves daunting enough, that surrounded the task of establishing a seabed mining regime. Indeed, the agenda disclosed that the new conference would review the entire range of rules that make up the law of the sea. Virtually every use of the oceans and seas including ship navigation, fishing, overflight, marine scientific research, protection of the marine environment, and exploitation of the nonliving resources of the continental shelf and of the deep seabed showed up on the agenda.

150: More than 150 national delegations, collectively representing almost every place and person on the planet, would participate in the negotiations at UNCLOS III. No one wanted to be left out of this venture. As the joint efforts of the United States and the Soviet Union had indicated, maritime states were increasingly desperate to find ways to use the conference to check the erosion of high seas freedoms. Coastal countries, with the 200-mile claimants in the lead, wanted to establish recognition of expanded national jurisdiction in the seas. Landlocked states, together with those that would come to style themselves "geographically disadvantaged states," sought rules guaranteeing access to their neighbors' offshore zones. Third World countries saw UNCLOS III as yet another arena in which to pursue the goal of a New International Economic Order, especially concerning the mining and distribution of the supposed riches of the deep seabed, while those many fewer nations who saw themselves as mining states were anxious to preserve access to the seabed and reward for providing the technology and management skills that would allow mining to occur. In short, every member of the international community saw an important, even vital, stake in the UNCLOS III negotiations.

70: This number is the approximate percentage of our planet's surface that is covered by the global ocean.

We could perhaps add two more numbers: 0 and 100. These represent the most daunting aspect of the challenge, the so-called "package deal." No issue (0) would be resolved unless all (100 percent) were resolved. That meant that UNCLOS III would adopt no treaty on any aspect of the law of the sea unless and until the conference had satisfactorily come to an agreement on all agenda items. This extraordinary procedure is explained by the varying degrees of importance placed on different issues by each negotiating state or group of states. Each could see certain ocean interests of others that it might be willing to trade for a rule or regime protecting its own special interests. A nation with rich fishing grounds off its coasts, for example, might be willing to agree to allow maritime states greater navigation rights in exchange for treaty provisions authorizing extended coastal state jurisdiction over offshore living resources.

The United States was in a unique position in the UNCLOS III negotiations. Not only was it the world's greatest naval power; it was also one of the most significant coastal countries. It had coastal fishermen and distant water fishermen. Its companies were, they said, preparing to mine the deep seabed. Its world-ranging oceanographic institutions were among the most prominent. Its citizens were as interested as those of other coastal states in the condition of the offshore marine environment. In fact, you could probably find a group of concerned U.S. citizens for each item on the conference agenda.

First and foremost for the U.S. delegation, however, was the interest in preserving the traditional freedoms of navigation and overflight for its naval and air forces. In the early 1970s, the Cold War and the Soviet adversary still dominated U.S. foreign policy. The United States considered it essential that the trend toward extended national authority not be allowed to interfere with the freedom of the United States to send its forces anywhere throughout the world ocean to counter Soviet aggression and influence and to ward off threats from any other quarter. By the time the first substantive session of the conference convened in 1974 in Caracas, it had become clear that any eventual treaty would endorse some sort of 200-mile zone, and the Americans of course wanted to ensure that the treaty would also maintain traditional navigational freedoms in these extensive ocean areas. But the U.S. delegation's primary worry was the status of transit rights through international straits.

The straits issue hinged on the growing popularity of 12-mile territorial seas. Although the United States continued to argue that three miles was the maximum breadth for the territorial sea, this argument was becoming increasingly anachronistic. But recognition of 12-mile, rather than three-mile, territorial seas would mean that over 100 international straits could become blanketed by the territorial seas of the bordering nations, erasing high seas channels that would exist if the three-mile limit were law. And, it should be recalled, there was no right of innocent passage for submerged submarines beneath the territorial sea or for aircraft above it. The Strait of Gibraltar sets the Cold War problem for the United States. The Strait is about eight nautical miles across at it narrowest. With a maximum of three-mile territorial seas for Spain and Morocco, U.S. nuclear missile submarines, considered to be the primary deterrent to Soviet nuclear attack, could legally pass through the Strait of Gibraltar submerged, retaining the secrecy of their locations; with 12-mile territorial seas, the traditional rule would require the submarines to pass through on the surface, disclosing their locations, at least for a time.

In addition, many coastal states took the position that no foreign warships, whether or not on the surface, were entitled to innocent passage, or they defined innocent passage in such a way as to require prior notification of passage from foreign warships.

The main tasks of the U.S. delegation to UNCLOS III, therefore, were to negotiate a special set of rules for straits passage, maintain the freedoms of navigation and overflight in any zones of extended national authority, and retain the right of innocent passage for warships. The delegation was also under pressure to promote the ambitions of potential seabed-mining companies, to weigh the concerns of the U.S.'s coastal fishermen (who favored a 200-mile fishing zone) and its distant water tuna fleets (which did not), to somehow safeguard the marine environment without unduly interfering with vessel navigation, to make sure the treaty protected marine mammals, and to balance and prioritize all these interests and concerns, along with a multitude of others, so that the eventual law of the sea treaty would, as nearly as possible, represent the optimum set of U.S. ocean interests.

The UNCLOS III negotiations were long and arduous for all delegations. By 1976, however, most of the navigational and fisheries issues had been tentatively negotiated favorably for the United States. In that year, despite strong reservations from the Executive Branch and its UNCLOS III delegation, the U.S. Congress passed the Magnuson-Stevens Fishery Conservation and Management Act, which established a 200-mile exclusive fishing zone for the United States (see Chapter Six) and effectively ensured that 200-mile zones would not only be part of any future law of the sea treaty but would also become accepted in customary international law within a few years.

But 1976 also saw the conference deadlock on what had become the other main branch of the "package deal," the mass of knotty issues surrounding the deep seabed mining regime. The seabed problem was incredibly complicated and the negotiations had become as much an ideological debate between the developed world and the developing world as an attempt to establish a workable mining code. With great oversimplification, it can be said that the seabed negotiators were in three camps. The developed countries, those few that could see themselves or their companies soon having the technology to mine the seabed, in general preferred a mining scheme that would grant them relatively easy access to seabed minerals and adequately compensate them for their investment of money, time, and talent. The developing countries would have preferred an international agency that would be the sole mining entity and that would distribute the proceeds of mining in accordance with the broadest concept of the common heritage principle. The third camp, which overlapped considerably with the second, was made up of those nations whose domestic land-based mining industries would have to compete for markets with the recovered seabed minerals, and these states insisted that the treaty's mining regime must include production limits.

The United States was, of course, in the first camp. As a nation with a free-enterprise economy, it resisted the idea of a monopolistic international mining entity and was opposed to production limits. It was, however, willing to work a seabed compromise in 1976, mainly because it was anxious to ensure that there would be a law of the sea treaty containing the already-negotiated navigational provisions. But there would be no treaty until the package was complete.

The United States and its seabed allies did compromise their positions on seabed mining and by 1980, the conference was nearly ready to adopt its treaty. In 1981, however, the new U.S. presidential administration ordered a complete review of the draft treaty in light of its perceptions of U.S. ocean interests. The year-long review effectively put the conference on hold, and when the reconstituted U.S. delegation presented its recommendations (or, some said, demands) for a number of substantial changes in the draft treaty, it met heavy resistance. Certain last-minute changes were made in an attempt to meet some of the U.S. objections, but the conference then adopted its treaty in April 1982. At U.S. insistence, the adoption of the treaty was put to a vote of the delegations, even though, in a widely admired and precedent-setting negotiations procedure, the delegations had to that date, through all the long years of the conference, settled on the various parts of the complex document by non-voting consensus.

The vote was 130 in favor and 4 opposed, with 17 abstentions. The United States voted against adoption of the treaty, citing the "flawed" deep seabed mining regime. To the Reagan Administration, the earlier seabed compromise, still largely intact in the treaty, was unacceptable.

The 1982 United Nations Convention on the Law of the Sea is a highly significant milestone in the history of international agreements. The official U.N. publication of the treaty is 200 pages long and its nearly 450 articles, do indeed, cover almost every aspect of ocean use worldwide.

When the 1982 Convention was opened for signature in December 1982, it received 119 signatures the first day, a world record. By its terms it would not come into force until one year after the 60th ratification. On November 16, 1993, Guyana became the 60th ratifier, so the treaty became binding on the ratifying states on November 16, 1994. By September 2001, the 1982 U.N. Convention on the Law of the Sea had gathered 137 parties.

The United States did not sign, nor has it yet ratified or acceded to the Convention. As will be discussed in more detail below, however, in late 1994 the Clinton Administration transmitted the Convention to the Senate and, as the U.S. Constitution requires, requested that body's consent to ratification (technically, accession). By fall 2001, the Senate Foreign Relations Committee had not acted on the presidential request. The United States thus still remains outside the Convention and has no direct rights or duties under its provisions. Yet the 1982 Convention, together with the conference that brought it into being, has had a major impact on the customary international law of the sea, which does bind the United States. In the next section of this chapter, we will try to explain why this is so and then present the new portrait of the law of the sea painted by the treaty.

D. THE 1982 U.N. CONVENTION ON THE LAW OF THE SEA

Treaty and Custom

Although treaty and custom are truly separate sources of international law, the two are interrelated in often intricate ways. Start with a basic proposition: treaties, as agreements between and among nation states, are state practice. And state practice, you will recall, is the genesis for and evidence of customary international law. It is frequently argued, for example, that the existence of many bilateral treaties with consistent provisions–on, say, the immunity from seizure of coastal fishing vessels in wartime–is state practice evidencing a customary rule of law and that this customary rule binds even those nation states not parties to any of the treaties. Also, treaties can, in general, override a customary norm for the treaty parties; for instance, nations have frequently bound themselves by treaty to restrict their fishing efforts on the high seas even though the customary rule of freedom to fish would allow no restriction. It is said that the emergence of a new customary norm can overrule prior treaty law. For example, 200-mile exclusive fishing zones override the freedom to fish beyond the territorial sea guaranteed in the 1958 High Seas Convention. (How this occurs, though, is somewhat of a mystery; the best analysis suggests some sort of implied amendment of the pre-existing treaty.)

For our purposes, we need to focus on the customary law implications of the 1982 U.N. Convention on the Law of the Sea and the conference that brought it into existence, UNCLOS III. The present and recent state of customary law of the sea was heavily influenced by state practice that occurred (1) prior to UNCLOS III, (2) during UNCLOS III, and (3) after UNCLOS III. Let's look at a few important examples.

We have already examined briefly the state practice leading up to the conference. It was, you will recall, characterized by a growing number of coastal nation claims to expanded offshore sovereignty or jurisdiction and resistance to these claims by the maritime states. Although this extended jurisdiction trend was clearly in evidence by the time UNCLOS III opened, it had not yet achieved the sort of widespread uniformity of claim-and-response necessary to create a new set of customary law rules. In addition to the extended jurisdiction trend, many argued, state practice, at least the practice represented by the votes and speeches of national delegations in the U.N. General Assembly, had declared the seabed beyond national jurisdiction as the "common heritage of mankind," but with no clear agreement on exactly what that enticing phrase meant.

State practice during UNCLOS III, both within and outside the conference, played an especially crucial role in creating the new customary law of the sea. Remember that over 150 nations, collectively representing nearly the entire international community, participated in UNCLOS III. It was, in effect, a town meeting of the Global Village. There, almost all members of the community got a chance to tell each other what they thought the law of the sea was and what it should be. And this they did, for almost ten long years. Thus, the conference discussions and negotiations were themselves highly important state practice that expressed and formed notions of rights and duties and greatly informed the search for customary law in a time of confusion and change for the law of the sea. The expectations of permissible and nonpermissible national behavior created by this process were significantly bolstered by the more traditional types of law-making state practice that were occurring outside the conference meeting halls. Encouraged by the validation of the extended jurisdiction trend taking place within the UNCLOS III negotiations, more coastal nations joined the trend as the conference proceeded. Among these nations was the United States, which, as noted above, adopted its own 200-mile limit, an exclusive fishing zone, in 1976. This congressional action by the country whose naval interests had previously made it the most formidable opponent of 200-mile zones, quickly prompted numerous other coastal nations to join the club. Within a couple of years, it could by said with some confidence that national 200-mile zones, with a common core of exclusive competence to manage living resources, were a part of the customary law of the sea.

Meanwhile, the negotiations within UNCLOS III settled by consensus upon a definition of an allowable zone of coastal nation rights, jurisdictions, and duties that could extend out to 200 miles offshore, called the exclusive economic zone (EEZ). As we shall see, this concept of the 200-mile zone allows the coastal state to manage, or govern, not just fisheries but most types of activities that occur there.

During UNCLOS III, coastal states also continued, within and outside the conference, to provide additional support for the 12-mile territorial sea, although the United States kept to its contention that three miles was the maximum allowable breadth.

Following adoption of the 1982 Convention at the close of UNCLOS III, nations continued to generally adapt their actions and behavior to conform to the rules laid down in the Convention, even though it was not a binding treaty. (There have been some disturbing variances, discussed below.) Even the United States proclaimed its own 200-mile EEZ in 1983 and extended its territorial sea to 12 miles in 1988. This general compliance further entrenched the negotiated rules into the body of customary law.

Beyond state practice was further evidence of the new customary rules found in the post-UNCLOS III maritime boundary cases of the

International Court of Justice and in the writings of international law scholars. For instance, the most recent Restatement of Foreign Relations Law of the United States relies heavily on the not-yet-in-force 1982 Convention to define the basic principles of the international law of the sea.

Certainly, some detailed, heavily negotiated provisions of the Convention are not part of customary law. Nor are most of the treaty's articles and annexes on the deep seabed mining regime, since custom cannot create the institutions necessary for the regime to operate, and the same can be said for the treaty's innovative and complex dispute settlement scheme. And there is continuing controversy over whether some parts of the Convention -- for example, the straits transit rules -- are part of customary law.

Yet it can now be said that the provisions of the 1982 Convention provide the best evidence of what the international law of the sea is today, either by treaty for the Convention's now-numerous parties or (with some important exceptions) by customary law for the few that have not become parties, including the United States. The new portrait it paints is, in very significant respects, quite different from the 1958 snapshot we looked at earlier.

SECTION 4. THE POLITICAL GEOGRAPHY
OF THE OCEANS TODAY

Because the main focus of this section is on United States law as it relates to governing the sea and seabed off U.S. shores, the following discussion will emphasize the rights and obligations of coastal nations, such as the United States, currently recognized by the international law of the sea, as principally reflected and articulated in the 1982 U.N. Convention on the Law of the Sea. The ocean zones within which coastal nations now have substantial governance rights—those newly colored sea areas on our animated map's picture of the present geography of the ocean—are (1) internal waters, (2) the territorial sea, (3) the contiguous zone, (4) the exclusive economic zone, and (5) the continental shelf. See Figure 4-3. Discussion of the two zones lying essentially beyond national jurisdiction, the high seas and the deep seabed, will be limited.

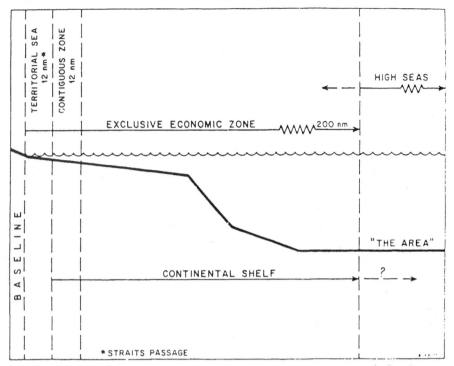

Figure 4-3. The UNCLOS picture
Jacobson, Law of the Sea--What Now? 37 Naval War College Review 82, 88 (1984)

A. INTERNAL WATERS

Of all the ocean zones discussed here, only internal waters have not changed at all from the 1958 picture. Coastal ocean areas that lie landward of the inner boundary of the territorial sea are internal waters and thus subject to the complete sovereignty of the coastal nation. They are part of the nation's territory and all persons and things located there are within the widest scope of the national government's territorial jurisdiction.

As you will recall, the inner boundary of the territorial sea is called the baseline from which the breadth of the territorial sea is measured. The rules for drawing this baseline also remain virtually unchanged from those found in the 1958 Geneva Convention on the Territorial Sea and Contiguous Zone. The normal baseline is the mean low-water line of the coast, but non-normal baselines can be drawn across river mouths, the openings of bays, and along the outer points of complex coastlines. The 1982 Convention has added a couple of new allowances for delta areas and offshore reefs, but otherwise the new baseline provisions are the same. The 1982 Convention also authorizes the use of special archipelagic baselines around the island groups of those nations composed entirely of islands, but since the United States is mainly a continental nation, this set of rather complicated rules and formulas does not apply to U.S. island groups, such as Hawaii, and therefore they will not be discussed here.

B. THE TERRITORIAL SEA

With the territorial sea, the present picture begins to change noticeably from the 1958 version. First, a definite maximum territorial sea breadth, measured from the baseline, is now set at 12 nautical miles in the 1982 treaty and by custom.

Second, and crucially for the United States, the treaty contains several articles establishing a special regime for transit through most straits blanketed by territorial seas. This special regime essentially replaces the traditional right of innocent passage that still applies to non-strait areas of the territorial sea. Although the straits articles are not without some ambiguity on their face, a proper reading of them in context and with reference to the drafting history shows that the treaty will allow near-high seas freedoms of navigation and overflight to foreign vessels and aircraft passing through straits, such as the Strait of Gibraltar, that are commonly used for international navigation, even if these straits are completely covered by the territorial seas of the bordering nations. Thus, submarines may transit in their normal, or submerged, mode. This is a negotiated exception to the general innocent passage requirement that submarines surface and show their flags. The Convention's straits transit provisions also allow aircraft to pass over such straits and even surface vessels will have a freedom of passage greater than the right of innocent passage.

A subject of a still ongoing debate is whether the 1982 Convention's straits transit rules are now also a part of the customary law of the sea. The United States, which has not yet acceded to the treaty, insists that they are. Other nations disagree, arguing that the straits transit regime is not a reflection or articulation of custom, but was instead an UNCLOS III exchange for the naval and maritime states' assent to the inclusion in the treaty of other provisions, notably those that would establish a deep seabed mining regime. These nations have insisted that the United States cannot take advantage of the Convention's straits transit rules unless it buys the whole "package deal" by becoming a party to the Convention in its entirety. In the oft-quoted colorful imagery of one Third World advocate, "You cannot pick and choose from the basket of fruit."

Except for the straits transit regime, which applies only to territorial seas in straits used for international navigation, the present content of coastal state authority remains essentially the same as it was codified in 1958: absolute sovereignty, subject only to the right of innocent passage by foreign vessels, including warships, on the surface. Because the maritime states had become concerned about what they considered to be unwarrantedly narrow unilateral interpretations of the innocent passage rights by some coastal nations, the 1982 Convention defines the term in some detail.

As noted above, the United States extended its territorial sea to 12 miles by presidential proclamation in 1988. President Reagan was careful in his proclamation to state that this extension was consistent with customary international law as reflected in the 1982 U.N. Convention on the Law of the Sea. At the same time, he made it clear that the United States would recognize 12-mile territorial seas of other coastal nations only if they were consistent with the U.S. view of customary international law, including the straits transit regime.

In extending the U.S. territorial sea from three to 12 miles, the 1988 presidential proclamation by its terms limited its effect to U.S. relations with other countries and specifically refrained from any attempt to change the domestic law of the United States as it applied to its territorial sea. The proclamation thus created an interesting set of domestic law issues, especially concerning federal/state relations, and these issues are addressed in the last sections of this chapter.

C. CONTIGUOUS ZONE

The 1982 Convention on the Law of the Sea, like the 1958 Geneva Convention on the Territorial Sea and the Contiguous Zone, allows coastal nations to exercise certain limited enforcement jurisdiction, such as drug interdiction, in a contiguous zone beyond the territorial sea. The 1958 treaty, however, limited the outer boundary of the contiguous zone to 12 nautical miles from the territorial sea baseline. The 1982 Convention allows extension of the contiguous zone out to 24 miles from the baseline. Present-day customary law almost certainly has adjusted to the new outer limit.

When President Ronald Reagan extended the U.S. territorial sea from three to 12 miles in 1988, he did not extend the U.S. contiguous zone's outer boundary from 12 to 24 miles. This was, to some observers, a curious omission, but it was not an oversight. The reasoning of the Reagan administration was that the United States, as a party to the still-binding 1958 Geneva Convention on the Territorial Sea and the Contiguous Zone, could not validly claim a contiguous zone beyond the 12-mile line. This rationale for failure to claim a contiguous zone out to 24 miles was not particularly convincing. After all, in 1983, President Reagan proclaimed a U.S. EEZ, which, because it denied freedom to fish far beyond the U.S. territorial sea, seemingly violated the 1958 Geneva Convention on the High Seas, to which the United States is still a party. The justification for both a 200-mile EEZ and a 24-mile contiguous zone should be the same: Customary law has changed to recognize both and also to instigate an implied amendment to the 1958 Geneva Conventions. In recognition of this, President Clinton in September 1999 declared a contiguous zone to a distance of 24 miles from the baselines of the U.S. by Presidential Proclamation.

D. THE EXCLUSIVE ECONOMIC ZONE

Coastal nation claims to 200-mile exclusive economic zones (EEZs) or similar 200-mile zones, particularly during the 1970s and '80s, are what caused the spectacular two-minute fireworks display on our animated map of the history of the ocean's political geography. This explosive series was, of course, due to UNCLOS III's unmistakable embrace of the 200-mile zone concept and the 1976 enactment by the U.S. Congress of a 200-mile exclusive fisheries zone. If all coastal nations were to claim 200-mile zones, these would collectively cover nearly forty percent of the world ocean. As shown in Table A, approximately 127 coastal countries make an extended offshore boundary claim generally based on the right to a 200-mile EEZ. The national rights and jurisdictions asserted by them usually, but not always, track those authorized by the 1982 U.N. Convention on the Law of the Sea's EEZ provisions.

TABLE A

Summary of National Claims to Maritime Zones*

Distance (nautical miles)	Territorial Sea	Contiguous Zone	EEZ	Fisheries Zones**
3	3			
6	3			
12	114			
18		3		
24		55		
200	6		94	5
Other	1 (4)***	1 (10) 1 (14)	1 (unspecified) 6 (indicated by coordinates) 5 (by agreement)	1 (50 meter isobath) 1 (25) 1 (32 or 52) 1 (41)

*Statistics derived from Report of the Secretary General to the General Assembly, Oceans and the Law of the Sea (9 March 2001), Annex II.
**Only indicated if no additional claim to an EEZ of the same distance.
***Distance of claim indicated in parentheses.

So-called "200-mile zones" claimed by the great majority of coastal states are zones that lie seaward of the territorial sea and extend out to 200 miles from the territorial sea's inner boundary, the "baseline from which the breadth of the territorial sea is measured." Thus, the typical EEZ is 188 miles wide, measured from the outer limit of the 12-mile territorial sea out to the 200-mile line. In addition, some coastal states' EEZs and exclusive fishing zones are further restricted, in whole or in part, by the similar zones of other countries on bodies of water less than 400 miles wide. Because present customary international law, as reflected in the 1982 Convention, limits the breadth of the territorial sea to 12 nautical miles, the few remaining claims to 200-mile territorial seas are illegal.

According to a fairly uniform consensus of authority, the rights and jurisdictions authorized by current custom for coastal nations out to 200 miles are those articulated in the EEZ articles of the 1982 Convention. While some argue persuasively that certain details of the treaty's EEZ provisions are not part of customary law, the general assignment or recognition of national governmental authority described in the treaty is certainly present customary international law.

The core description of coastal nation authority in the EEZ is set out in Article 56(1) of the 1982 Convention:

In the exclusive economic zone, the coastal State has:

(a)   sovereign rights for the purpose of exploring and exploiting, conserving and managing the natural resources, whether living or non-living, of the waters superjacent to the sea-bed and of the sea-bed and its subsoil, and with regard to other activities for the economic exploitation and exploration of the zone, such as the production of energy from the water, currents and winds;

(b)   jurisdiction and provided for in the relevant provisions of this Convention with regard to:

(i)   the establishment and use of artificial islands, installations and structures;
(ii)   marine scientific research;
(iii) the protection and preservation of the marine environment;

(c)   other rights and duties provided for in this Convention.

This summary list of EEZ rights and jurisdictions is fleshed out in other articles of the Convention. Although the Convention and the customary law it reflects do not grant to coastal nations full sovereignty in their EEZs, international law now permits an EEZ nation the primary governance role for nearly all types of activities that occur in the zone. Let's look at the most important of these activities.

Fishing

Within its EEZ, a coastal nation has "sovereign rights" to the living resources located there. Whatever else the term "sovereign rights" means in this context, it certainly means the exclusive right to manage fisheries and a preferential right for the EEZ nation's fishermen to harvest the fish. The coastal nation can thus adopt laws regulating fishing within its EEZ and enforce these laws there. While it has extremely broad discretion in exercising these rights, they are not unlimited. International law, as reflected in the 1982 Convention, also imposes some duties on EEZ fisheries managers. These include the duties both to conserve the living resources of the EEZ and to promote their "optimum utilization." The latter duty requires the EEZ country to allow foreign fishing for any "surplus" fish, within conservation limits, beyond the capacity of the coastal country's vessels to harvest.

The coastal nation must also coordinate with other affected nations in managing stocks of fish whose habitats or migratory ranges overlap the boundary between the EEZs of neighbor nations ("transboundary stocks") and stocks that migrate into the high seas beyond the EEZ ("straddling stocks"), where the vessels of other countries still have the freedom to fish. In addition, all affected nations are obligated to cooperate in the management of "highly migratory species," such as tuna, which frequently migrate throughout broad areas of the high seas and several EEZs. Again, the management objectives are conservation and optimum utilization. In several sessions spanning the years 1993-95, a United Nations conference produced a new important international agreement devoted to implementing the 1982 Convention's charge that states coordinate and cooperate in the management of straddling stocks and highly migratory species on the high seas. The 1995 Agreement on Straddling Fish Stocks and Highly Migratory Fish Stocks attempts to require coordination of conservation and management measures for these stocks on both sides of the outer boundaries of national 200-mile EEZs and fishing zones. The Agreement urges the creation of effective regional organizations, includes innovative enforcement provisions, and adopts what is perhaps the most detailed "hard law" version of the precautionary approach, an emerging principle of international environmental law that requires resource managers to exercise caution in the face of scientific uncertainty. As of September 2011, this significant international agreement had received 29 ratification—only one ratification short of the 30 necessary to come into force. The United States has already ratified it, however, and has begun implementation of some of its provisions. The 1995 Agreement on Straddling Fish Stocks and Highly Migratory Fish Stocks is discussed further in Chapter Six.

The 1982 Convention on the Law of the Sea contains one article, Article 66, on the management of anadromous stocks, such as salmon, which spawn in inland waters but migrate widely in the open sea. The country in whose waters these stocks spawn has the "primary interest and responsibility" for them. Although salmon often migrate beyond 200 miles from shore, especially in the North Pacific Ocean, fishing for them is not allowed beyond the EEZ, except where this would cause economic dislocation for another country whose vessels have been engaged in fishing them on the high seas. In this case, Article 66 purports to impose on the country of origin obligations to consult and to cooperate in minimizing the economic dislocation. This highly negotiated article is probably now a part of customary international law, but that remains a somewhat arguable proposition.

The 1982 Convention specially authorizes EEZ countries and international organizations to protect marine mammals to a greater degree than the general rules on optimum utilization of living resources would otherwise require. (See Chapter Eight.)

The EEZ provisions of the 1982 Convention do not apply to so-called sedentary species of the sea bottom. These species are, however, treated in that part of the Convention on the coastal nation's continental shelf rights and are discussed below.

In its initial 1976 congressional assertion of a 200-mile exclusive fishing zone, the United States claimed exclusive "jurisdiction" over living resources within its new zone and over anadromous stocks originating in U.S. waters throughout their entire migratory ranges. In deference to the important U.S. distant water tuna fleet, however, Congress refused at that time to assert jurisdiction over tuna passing through the U.S. zone. Following the 1983 presidential proclamation of an EEZ, Congress changed "jurisdiction" to "sovereign rights" for living resources in the zone, and has now included tuna and other highly migratory species within these sovereign rights even when such species are in the high seas. The legislation also claims exclusive U.S. management authority, even beyond the EEZ, over anadromous stocks of U.S. origin, but this claim is probably illegal under the rules reflected in Article 66.

We discuss the United States' fisheries management laws and practices in Chapter Six.

Non-living Resources

The 1982 U.N. Convention on the Law of the Sea recognizes the same "sovereign rights" of the EEZ nation in the zone's non-living natural resources as it does in the zone's living resources; this includes resources of the seabed and subsoil, as well as the water column. The treaty, however, sets forth the international law concerning exploration for and exploitation of offshore non-living resources much more completely in its articles on the continental shelf; further, customary law's continental shelf doctrine, which that part of the treaty in general reflects, is the traditional framework for addressing coastal nation rights and jurisdictions over the continental shelf. Consequently, we will address these rights and related jurisdictions in our later discussion of the legal continental shelf.

You should nevertheless note at this point that there is a large, and sometimes confusing, overlap of EEZ and continental shelf law.

Marine Scientific Research

According to the 1982 Convention, no marine scientific research can occur within the EEZ without the coastal nation's consent and researchers must apply for consent at least six months before the start of their proposed projects. This "consent regime," however, has some important exceptions and qualifications. These include an implication of consent if the coastal nation does not respond to a research request within four months, together with a general admonition to coastal states to give their consent "in normal circumstances," and to research projects that have as their purpose the expansion of scientific knowledge of the marine environment "for the benefit of all mankind." On the other hand, any research of direct significance to the exploration for or exploitation of the EEZ's or continental shelf's natural resources can be denied consent at the coastal nation's discretion.

A researcher granted consent must still comply with a long list of obligations listed in the Convention. These obligations are generally designed to keep the coastal state fully informed of the project as it progresses and provide the opportunity for coastal state participation.

As noted earlier, the United States proclaimed its EEZ in 1983. President Reagan, while recognizing that the Convention's consent regime for marine scientific research was part of customary law, refused to assert the regime on behalf of the United States. This refusal was designed to underscore U.S. commitment to the unrestricted conduct of marine scientific research beyond the territorial sea and, it was undoubtedly hoped, to provide an example to other coastal nations. So far, many coastal countries have not taken the hint and continue to exercise control over research in their EEZs.

Vessel Navigation and Overflight

The 1982 Convention and current customary law continue to allow freedom of surface and submerged vessel navigation as well as overflight in the EEZ. The treaty's incorporation of these high seas freedoms into the EEZ was an important UNCLOS III victory for U.S. negotiators and those of other naval and maritime countries. However, some coastal nations, such as Brazil, contend that neither the Convention nor customary law permits military maneuvers in the EEZ without the consent of the coastal nation, especially if these maneuvers involve the use of weapons or explosives. The United States maintains that the freedoms of navigation and overflight, on the high seas and in the EEZ, encompass the freedom to conduct military exercises if done with reasonable regard for the rights and freedoms of other nations. On this issue, the United States probably still has the winning argument.

Protection of the Marine Environment

With the exception of the 1982 Convention's Part XI on the deep seabed mining regime, the treaty devotes a greater number of its articles to Part XII on protection and preservation of the marine environment than to any other part. (In fairness, though, it should be conceded that, if the Convention's annexes are included, the complex dispute settlement scheme garners more articles.) Collectively, the marine environment articles purport to impose an impressive array of duties on all nation states to prevent, reduce, and control ocean pollution from all sources subject to their jurisdiction, including land-based sources, vessels, and offshore installations. The treaty also requires nations to cooperate globally and regionally to establish rules and standards for protecting the marine environment.

The rights of coastal nations to control vessel source pollution in their EEZs is limited by the treaty's (and custom's) recognition of freedom of navigation within EEZs. The Convention requires its parties to act through "the competent international organization" or general diplomatic conference to establish uniform rules and standards for protecting the marine environment from vessel-source pollution. The "competent international organization" is understood to mean the International Maritime Organization (IMO). And only in carefully restricted situations, in which a foreign flag vessel in the EEZ has clearly committed a violation that has caused or is threatening to cause serious damage, is the coastal nation authorized to interfere with the vessel's passage. The treaty gives primary jurisdiction for enforcing the vessel-source rules and standards to flag states and, in certain circumstances even where the offense is committed outside the internal waters, territorial sea, or EEZ of the port nation, to countries whose ports are visited by offending vessels.

The 1982 Convention on the Law of the Sea recognizes and encourages other international agreements designed to protect and preserve the marine environment. These certainly include the 1970 London (Dumping) Convention and the growing number of regional treaties applicable to the world ocean's various seas and special areas.

Further, the 1992 U.N. Conference on Environment and Development (UNCED, or the so-called "Earth Summit"), referred to the marine environment articles of the Law of the Sea Convention as a basis or framework for further development of international rules for protecting and preserving the marine environment.

We address the U.S. laws and practices on protecting and preserving its offshore marine environment in Chapter Eight.

Artificial Structures

In its EEZ, a coastal nation has the exclusive right to construct and authorize and control the construction and use of artificial islands and of other installations and structures built to allow it to exercise its other EEZ rights and jurisdictions. This right includes such structures as oil drilling platforms and, presumably, marine scientific stations, energy production platforms, and fishing devices. The EEZ nation must, however, give due regard to the rights and freedoms of other countries in the EEZ. The rights and freedoms of others include the freedoms of navigation and overflight. They also include the high seas freedom to lay submarine cables and pipelines if these are compatible with the coastal country's rights and jurisdictions in its EEZ and on its continental shelf.

E. THE CONTINENTAL SHELF

In most respects, the qualitative extent of coastal nation rights in the natural resources of the continental shelf remains today the same as that asserted in the 1945 Truman Proclamation and later codified in the 1958 Continental Shelf Convention. Quantitatively, however, there are some rather startling differences between the physical extent of today's legal continental shelf and that recognized in 1958.

Recall that the 1958 Continental Shelf Convention set the outer limit of the coastal nation's legal (as contrasted to the physical) continental shelf at the 200-meter depth line, or beyond that isobath to the limit of "exploitability" of the natural resources. Although the 200-meter isobath in some locations lies hundreds of miles from the coast, the average is between 40 and 50 miles offshore. Influenced by the development of the EEZ concept, the 1982 Law of the Sea Convention establishes the minimum outer limit of the legal continental shelf, measured from the territorial sea baseline, at 200 miles! In many offshore areas, this means that the legal continental shelf extends far beyond the geologic continental shelf and, indeed, often encompasses parts of the deep seabed. Furthermore, under an almost incomprehensively complex and heavily negotiated article, the 1982 Convention allows extension of the coastal state's continental shelf beyond 200 miles where the geologic continental margin (shelf, slope, and rise) extends farther than the 200-mile distance line. As we shall see, however, the coastal nation's rights are somewhat qualified on the far "outer continental shelf."

In general, it can no doubt be confidently asserted that the 200-mile minimum continental shelf boundary is now part of customary international law. The 1982 Convention's complicated formulas for delimiting the boundary of the outer shelf beyond 200 miles might not, in their intricate detail, yet be part of custom; nevertheless, customary law probably does recognize the basic notion that the legal continental shelf can extend seaward of 200 miles to the edge of the geologic continental margin.

The substance of the coastal country's rights in its continental shelf are expressed in both the 1958 and 1982 treaties as "sovereign rights for the purpose of exploring it and exploiting its natural resources." These rights exist without any declaration by the coastal state, and no one may undertake these activities without the consent of the coastal nation.

The natural resources of the continental shelf are the non-living resources of the seabed and subsoil, such as oil and gas, together with "sedentary species" of living resources. Sedentary species are those "organisms which, at the harvestable stage, either are immobile on or under the sea-bed or are unable to move except in constant physical contact with the sea-bed or the subsoil." This is a rather strange definition, with no basis in categories recognized by the science of marine biology. Nevertheless, it has caused few problems, and again the definition in the 1982 Convention is identical to that of the 1958 Convention. The United States has gotten away for some time with its claim that "sedentary species" include such questionable (but economically significant) animals as lobsters and crabs.

An interesting point about the continental shelf's sedentary species that is often overlooked or not mentioned in the literature on international fisheries law is that the coastal nation's management of these species is not qualified by the duties to conserve and optimally utilize them. These duties are found in the 1982 Convention's EEZ articles which, by the treaty's terms, do not apply to sedentary species. The treaty's continental shelf articles, however, do not mention the duties to conserve or utilize. Of course, the 1958 Continental Shelf Convention did not impose any such obligations, and it is therefore not surprising that the negotiators of the 1982 treaty chose not to cut back on rights of coastal countries already recognized by international law.

The main economic value of the planet's continental shelves lies in their oil and gas deposits, which are still the most valuable commercially exploited resources of the seabed and subsoil. Hard mineral mining on or beneath the continental shelf or deep seabed will not be economically viable on any large scale until well into the next century.

With respect to any exploitation of non-living resources undertaken in a coastal nation's "outer continental shelf" beyond 200 miles, the 1982 Convention will require the coastal nation to contribute a small percentage, eventually a maximum of seven percent, of the value of the production to a fund to benefit developing countries. It is debatable whether this duty is currently a part of customary international law, or whether it will ever become part of customary international law.

Note that the coastal nation's continental shelf rights are limited to natural resources of the seabed and subsoil. Therefore, they do not include rights to sunken ships or their cargoes, and this distinction has been upheld in fascinating U.S. case law involving fabulous treasures and old Spanish galleons. Instead, the rights in these objects are in general governed by the law of salvage and other rules of admiralty law. However, the removal of objects of an archaeological and historical nature from the seabed of the contiguous zone without the coastal nation's consent might, according to the 1982 Convention, be an infringement of that country's laws.

The United States, having invented the legal continental shelf doctrine, has an elaborate system of laws and regulations for the exploration and exploitation of the non-living resources of its continental shelf. We treat these in Chapter Five.

SECTION 5. THE DEEP SEABED BEYOND THE CONTINENTAL SHELF

Much time and energy was expended during the years of UNCLOS III in a largely successful attempt to compromise the often widely separated positions of the delegation blocs on the major topic that instigated the conference: the international mining regime for the deep seabed beyond national jurisdiction. Yet it is the part of the 1982 Convention, Part XI, devoted to that regime that caused the United States to vote against adoption of the treaty by the conference and to refuse to sign or ratify it after its adoption by an overwhelming majority over U.S. objection. We do not have the space in a book addressing essentially domestic ocean and coastal law of the United States to examine in detail the 1982 Convention's complex provisions that make up Part XI and its Annexes. Moreover, as we shall see, many of the Convention's seabed mining provisions have been modified in response to U.S. objections. Nevertheless, it is important to have a general understanding of the original provisions of Part XI in order to comprehend why the United States objected to them so strongly, rejecting a treaty that otherwise was quite favorable to other U.S. ocean interests.

After all, the 1982 U.N. Convention on the Law of the Sea is, except for its deep seabed mining regime, very good to the United States in its dual role as both a major naval power and one of the most important coastal countries. The treaty recognizes freedom of navigation and overflight throughout the high seas and EEZs and generous transit passage rights through and over all important international straits; at the same time, it would confirm a broad array of rights and jurisdictions in the U.S. EEZ, which is the largest and probably the richest EEZ on the planet. The treaty would also tend to stabilize a rapidly evolving and unpredictable law of the sea, which would certainly be in the interests of the United States, the most important ocean user of our era. What, then, is so bad about Convention's deep seabed provisions to have caused the United States to refuse to endorse the treaty?

In announcing his administration's decision in mid-1982 to refuse to sign or ratify the treaty, President Reagan did, indeed, recognize that the Convention's non-seabed parts were acceptable to the United States, but he went on to list serious U.S. objections to Part XI. The most important of these were the following:

(1) The treaty would restrict access by private mining companies to deep seabed minerals under a so-called "parallel system." The parallel system would require a miner to submit two roughly equal proposed mining sites to an International Seabed Authority (ISA), an international agency to be established by the Convention. If approved by the ISA, the applicant would be allowed to mine one of the sites, while the ISA would "bank" the other and it would be mined by the ISA's operating arm, "the Enterprise," or by a developing country.

(2) The Convention would mandate the transfer of mining technology, albeit on fair commercial terms, from private mining companies to the Enterprise or developing-country miners.

(3) Richer nations would be obligated to finance the immense costs of mining by the Enterprise and developed countries.

(4) The treaty's production limits for seabed minerals -- a concession to those countries with land-based sources of the same minerals -- are anti-competitive and unfair.

(5) The United States does not have as large a role in ISA decision-making as, according to the Reagan administration, it deserved.

(6) Some of the "common heritage" proceeds realized by the ISA could, by the Convention's terms, be paid to national liberation organizations, such as the PLO.

(7) The mining regime could, in the future, be amended over U.S.

objections.

Basically, the objections of the United States to the 1982 Convention can be characterized as ideological. The presidential administration of Ronald Reagan strongly favored the free-enterprise system as a general tenet and (correctly) viewed the Convention's deep seabed mining regime, which does not sufficiently reward technological innovation and investment and requires private miners to compete with the semi-monopolistic Enterprise, as not reflective of free enterprise principles.

In addition, the Reagan administration took the position, with some justification, that the favorable non-seabed parts of the Convention had, by 1982, become customary international law, while the mining regime could be created only by the Convention and bind only the parties to it. According to this thinking, therefore, the United States could take advantage of the new customary law of the sea it liked and, by refusing to become a party to the Convention, reject the deep-seabed mining provisions and the ISA, which it did not like at all. As for the legal status of the deep seabed, the United States has argued that customary law deems this to be subject to the freedom of the high seas and thus that the minerals of the seabed, like the fish of the high seas, are free for the taking. Other nations asserted that international law now applies the common heritage principle to the deep seabed beyond national jurisdiction and that this means there can be no mining of the seabed except under the auspices of the ISA.

In the waning days of the UNCLOS III negotiations, the U.S. Congress, with approval of the Executive Branch, enacted the Deep Seabed Hard Mineral Resources Act. Under this Act, the United States could issue licenses to its own nationals and companies to mine the deep seabed. The Act made no territorial claims to the seabed beyond the U.S. continental shelf and seemed to recognize the common heritage notion. It also encouraged other countries to enact similar legislation with the potential for reciprocal recognition of national licenses. The United States and other like-minded industrialized countries also pursued the potential for an international agreement among themselves to establish a seabed mining system.

Ironically, in the years since the United States took its position in opposition to the 1982 Convention's Part XI, changed circumstances reduced the significance of the Convention's deep seabed regime. First, world market prices for the important minerals of the seabed have plummeted since UNCLOS III and nearly every recent economic study of the potential for a true deep seabed mining industry has concluded that commercial mining of the deep seabed is not likely to occur until some time in the future. Second, the end of the Cold War and the current disrepute of centrally managed economies caused many nations to look more favorably at the principles of market driven systems and thus with increased sympathy for the U.S. position opposing the 1982 Convention's seabed regime. There was also a growing realization that the Convention cannot succeed in achieving its hoped-for status as a constitution for the world ocean unless the most important ocean nation, the United States, is a party to it.

The result of these developments was a series of efforts to make the Convention more palatable to the United States and other industrialized countries. These efforts originally took place in meetings of the Preparatory Commission, a body established by UNCLOS III to prepare the procedural way for the International Seabed Authority, and more significantly, in informal consultations among interested U.N. members sponsored by the United Nations Secretary General. The latter process has eventually concocted a way to remove from the Convention or change many of the deep seabed mining provisions to which the United States objected.

With the active participation of representatives of the Bill Clinton presidential administration, the consultations sponsored by the Secretary General produced a new Agreement that, if successfully implemented (a rather tricky and complex process), will effectively and significantly modify all provisions of the 1982 Convention's deep seabed regime to which President Reagan objected. This Agreement was adopted by the General Assembly and signed by the United States. In early October 1994, President Clinton submitted the new Agreement, together with the 1982 Convention itself, to the U.S. Senate and requested its advice and consent to ratification of both. Despite considerable effort by the Clinton Administration to persuade the Senate to consider and approve the ratification of the 1982 Convention and the Part XI modification Agreement, the Senate has still not acted. The delay has allowed the provisional U.S. membership in the International Seabed Authority to terminate.

SECTION 6. U.S. JURISDICTION IN THE HIGH SEAS

Internal waters and the territorial sea are part of the sovereignty of the United States. With the exception of the right of innocent passage in the territorial sea, the United States thus has the greatest recognized extent of governmental authority over these areas. The United States and other coastal countries also exercise a form of territorial jurisdiction over their continental shelves and their EEZs, too, since these zones are geographically described areas of the planet's surface. How did the coastal countries acquire its governmental authority over these zones? The International Court of Justice has stated that a coastal nation has sovereign rights to explore and exploit the natural resources of the continental shelf because the shelf is the "natural prolongation" of the land territory. This justification cannot explain the EEZ's 200-mile boundary; nor, for that matter, can it any longer explain the legal continental shelf, which also is now delimited primarily by an arbitrary distance line. The basic answer to this rather philosophical question is that the world's coastal countries (the great majority of the members of the international community) acquired their authority in their expanded offshore zones at the expense of international community space, by operation of international law, and by the consensus implicit in the development of customary law.

But sixty percent of the world ocean still lies beyond these coastal nation zones. The waters there remain high seas where the traditional freedoms of the seas are generally intact. (The legal status of the seabed beneath these waters, however, is subject to some debate, as noted above.) These freedoms include the freedom of surface and submerged navigation, the freedom of overflight, the freedom to fish, and the freedom to lay submarine cables and pipelines. In addition, the 1982 Convention on the Law of the Sea newly lists the freedom of scientific research and the "freedom to construct artificial islands and other installations permitted under international law." Except for the freedoms of navigation and overflight, the freedoms of the high seas are, according to the Convention, subject to certain qualifications.

For example, the freedom to fish is restricted in the Convention by the duty to conserve the living resources of the high seas and to cooperate with other nations to this end. The treaty also requires nations whose nationals fish the high seas to recognize the rights and duties of coastal nations with respect to straddling stocks, highly migratory species, anadromous stocks, and marine mammals. If the 1995 Agreement on Straddling Fish Stocks and Highly Migratory Fish Stocks succeeds in achieving widespread ratification by coastal states and those states whose nationals fish the high seas, some of these 1982 Convention obligations should be largely fleshed out.

The high seas freedoms to lay submarine cables and pipelines and to construct artificial installations are subject to the treaty's provisions on the continental shelf. The freedom to conduct scientific research is subject to the "consent regime" applicable to the EEZ and to the exclusive right of the coastal nation to explore its continental shelf.

Even in the waters of the high seas beyond the geographical limits of their EEZs, the United States and other coastal nations have some limited jurisdiction to exercise their governmental authority to make or enforce law. United States nationals are subject to U.S. law there. Moreover, persons and events on U.S. flag vessels and aircraft are governed by U.S. law while on or over the high seas. Although this flag-state jurisdiction is something like nationality jurisdiction, it has also been analogized to territorial jurisdiction, with the ship or aircraft "assimilated to the territory" of the flag nation.

Warships of any nation are empowered by international law to seize pirate ships or aircraft on or over the high seas. Piracy is a long-recognized international crime committed by individuals for private ends, a crime that is witnessing a resurgence in some areas, such as the Gulf of Thailand and the Caribbean Sea. Similarly, any country's warships can board any ship if there is a reasonable basis for suspecting that the ship is engaged in the slave trade or that it is a ship without nationality.

A coastal nation also has the right of hot pursuit into the high seas. "Hot pursuit" is continuous pursuit by the coastal country's warships or military aircraft of a foreign ship reasonably suspected of violating the laws or regulations of the coastal country. The traditional rule requires that the pursuit be commenced within the internal waters, territorial sea, or contiguous zone of the pursuing country, but it has been extended to pursuit starting in the EEZ or over the continental shelf for violations of the coastal nation's laws and regulations applicable to those zones. Following hot pursuit into the high seas, the pursuing ships or aircraft may validly stop and arrest the suspect ship.

In general, however, no nation may interfere with any other nation's exercise of the freedoms of the high seas. The law of the sea requires that each nation exercising its high seas freedoms give "due regard" to the interests of other nations in their exercise of these freedoms.

SECTION 7. THE FUTURE OF THE LAW OF THE SEA

As indicated above, one of the major goals of the United States in embarking on the UNCLOS III negotiations was to stem the tide of coastal nation expansionism in the oceans. The world's mightiest naval power and its rival, the U.S.S.R., together with other maritime nations, feared that the expansionist trend, if unchecked, could lead to a world ocean divided into "national lakes," vast areas of coastal nation authority that could, among other dire things, seriously interfere with the freedoms of navigation and overflight.

Was the U.S. goal achieved? Certainly a glance at our two portraits of the law of the sea, the 1958 snapshot and the current customary law picture at least roughly reflected in the 1982 U.N. Convention on the Law of the Sea, starkly illustrate the force of the historic move by national governments into the sea. Yet the 1982 treaty purports to preserve the freedoms of navigation and overflight within EEZs and, crucially for the naval and maritime states, to establish favorable regimes for passage through and over straits and archipelagic waters.

But the 1982 Convention will not grant its treaty-law rights and freedoms to the United States unless and until that nation becomes a party. While the Clinton Administration signaled its willingness to accede to the treaty, little progress has been made in achieving the Senate's consent to ratification. It continues to be difficult to say whether the United States will soon, or ever, become a party to the 1982 Convention.

Customary international law or other treaties will set the rights and duties of those countries that remain outside the Convention. We earlier stated the widely accepted position that the 1982 Convention generally mirrors present-day customary law. If so, and if it remains so for the foreseeable future, the United States and the other naval and maritime nations can rest easy even if they do not become parties to the Convention. Extensive areas of coastal nation authority in the offshore seas will not seriously interfere with navigation and overflight. The fact that the great majority of the world's nations have now become parties to the Convention clearly enhances the prospect that it will set the standard for the general law of the sea for some decades to come.

But, as we have seen, the customary law of the sea has been changing rapidly over the past generation. Indeed, the pace of change wrought by state practice can be accurately portrayed as revolutionary, and revolutions are not easily stopped. There are, in fact, several indications that the trend of coastal nation expansionism, although considerably slowed by the adoption of the 1982 Convention and its widespread ratification, is not frozen in place but still retains some of its momentum. Many coastal nations have adopted domestic laws that assert their expanded rights and jurisdictions in their offshore seas. Only rarely, however, do these domestic laws expressly recognize the duties, such as the duties to conserve and optimally utilize living resources, that current international law supposedly imposes on them there. Other coastal countries have claimed more extensive continental shelves than international law now allows. Still others have effectively claimed more ocean space than the law permits by manipulating or abusing the rules for drawing baselines from which the territorial sea, the contiguous zone, the EEZ, and the continental shelf are measured.

But probably the greatest potential for reassertion of the national expansionist trend lies in the possibility that coastal countries will begin claiming authority over resources and events in areas even farther seaward of these now-established zones. There are pressures urging some coastal nations to extend management authority over straddling stocks of fish, those whose migratory patterns are astride the boundary between the EEZ and the high seas, into high seas areas beyond the EEZ. For instance, some members of U.S. fishing communities had urged the United States to assert its fisheries control beyond 200 miles into the so-called "donut hole" of high seas in the middle of the Bering Sea. Instead, a special agreement of the United States, Russia, and other concerned nations, has established an international fishing regime in the donut hole. And the 1995 Agreement on Straddling Fish Stocks and Highly Migratory Fish Stocks, if widely ratified, should stem some of the expansionist tide in other areas of the global ocean.

To some, the most threatening of the recent expansionist developments is Chile's claim to a *mar presencial*, or "presential sea." The presidential sea remains a rather amorphous concept, but it is certainly some sort of assertion by Chile to a special national presence zone that, on a map delineating the area, extends to the middle of the southern Pacific Ocean! Thus far, Chile's claim, unlike its 1947 claim to the first 200-mile zone, has not been emulated by other coastal countries.

It should, however, be remembered that the great majority of coastal nations do not have global navies or world-ranging fishing or oceanographic fleets. Therefore, they have no clearly perceived interest in preserving broad freedoms of the high seas. Precedential claims by one or more of these countries could conceivably trigger another round of claims to even more national authority in even wider geographic areas of the world ocean. At the moment, this potential is no doubt considerably restrained by the 1982 U.N. Convention on the Law of the Sea and its implementation of the "common heritage" notion for the seabed beyond national jurisdiction. Still, there is a constant risk that state practice could re-energize the expansionist trend in the future and that a larger proportion of the ocean could thereby be brought under national dominance.

However, as the future law of the sea picture develops, the currently recognized bundle of coastal nation governance authority in the ocean will not be undone or rolled back. The United States, whose coastal length and configuration give it the world's largest geographic area of offshore authority, will almost certainly remain the chief beneficiary of this reality. With too little fanfare, the United States has already entered its new Ocean Age, an era that, like the free seas age that Hugo Grotius introduced in 1609, could well last for centuries.

In the following chapters of this book, we will examine in some detail just what the various levels and branches of this nation's government have done and are doing to exercise the rights and jurisdictions granted to it by today's international law of the sea. The remainder of this chapter traces the history of federal-state relations in the United States' offshore areas, beginning with the landmark decision of the Supreme Court in United States v. California, 332 U.S. 19 (1947).

SECTION 8. DIVISION OF AUTHORITY OVER U.S. OCEAN RESOURCES PRIOR TO 1953

The ownership of the resources in the territorial (marginal) sea, the area formerly extending three miles seaward from the low tide line of the United States coastline, was the subject of a substantial disagreement between the federal and state governments. The original thirteen states viewed themselves as having jurisdiction over and ownership of the resources in this area, subject only to the overriding constitutional power of the federal government to regulate matters of navigation, commerce, and foreign affairs. This view was initially accepted by the federal government, but in 1945 this policy was reversed. The federal position became that the federal government, not the individual states, had jurisdiction over all resources located in the territorial sea. The states' ownership and authority, according to the federal government, ended at the low tide line. Thus, although state boundaries might extend through the territorial sea, none of the submerged lands or resources seaward of the low tide line were owned by the state.

Prior to 1945, a few states, acting upon their belief that territorial sea resources and profits to be derived from their exploitation belonged to them, had granted leases for offshore oil and gas exploration. In 1945, the federal government moved to challenge the validity of the states' claims and filed suit against the state of California asserting that the federal government owned the offshore areas that were the subject of California oil and gas exploration leases. The result of the litigation is the following historic United States Supreme Court decision.

UNITED STATES v. CALIFORNIA
Supreme Court of the United States, 1947
332 U.S. 19

MR. JUSTICE BLACK *Delivered the Opinion of the Court.*

The United States by its Attorney General and Solicitor General brought this suit against the State of California. * * * The complaint alleges that the United States "is the owner in fee simple of, or possessed of paramount rights in and powers over, the lands, minerals, and other things of value underlying the Pacific Ocean, lying seaward of the ordinary low water mark on the coast of California and outside of the inland waters of the State, extending seaward three nautical miles and bounded on the north and south, respectively, by the northern and southern boundaries of the State of California." It is further alleged that California, acting pursuant to state statutes, but without authority from the United States, has negotiated and executed numerous leases with persons and corporations purporting to authorize them to enter upon the described ocean area to take petroleum, gas, and other mineral deposits, and that the lessees have done so, paying to California large sums of money in rents and royalties for the petroleum products taken. The prayer is for a decree declaring the rights of the United States in the area as against California and enjoining California and all persons claiming under it from continuing to trespass upon the area in violation of the rights of the United States.

California has filed an answer to the complaint. It admits that persons holding leases from California or those claiming under it, have been extracting petroleum products from the land under the three mile ocean belt immediately adjacent to California. The basis of California's asserted ownership is that a belt extending three English miles from low water mark lies within the original boundaries of the state, Cal. Const. 1849, Art. XII; that the original thirteen states acquired from the Crown of England title to all lands within their boundaries under navigable waters, including a three-mile belt in adjacent seas; and that since California was admitted as a state on an "equal footing" with the original states, California at that time became vested with title to all such lands.

* * *

After California's answer was filed, the United States moved for judgment as prayed for in the complaint on the ground that the purported defenses were not sufficient in law. The legal issues thus raised have been exhaustively presented by counsel for the parties, both by brief and oral argument. Neither has suggested any necessity for the introduction of evidence, and we perceive no such necessity at this stage of the case. It is now ripe for determination of the basic legal issues presented by the motion.

* * * The crucial question on the merits is not merely who owns the bare legal title to the lands under the marginal sea. The United States here asserts rights in two capacities transcending those of a mere property owner. In one capacity it asserts the right and responsibility to exercise whatever power and dominion are necessary to protect this country against dangers to the security and tranquility of its people incident to the fact that the United States is located immediately adjacent to the ocean. The Government also appears in its capacity as a member of the family of nations. In that capacity it is responsible for conducting United States relations with other nations. It asserts that proper exercise of these constitutional responsibilities requires that it have power, unencumbered by state commitments, always to determine what agreements will be made concerning the control and use of the marginal sea and the land under it. In the light of the foregoing, our question is whether the state or the Federal Government has the paramount right and power to determine in the first instance when, how, and by what agencies, foreign or domestic, the oil and other resources of the soil of the marginal sea, known or hereafter discovered may be exploited.

California claims that it owns the resources of the soil under the three-mile marginal belt as an incident to those elements of sovereignty which it exercises in that water area. The state points out that its original Constitution, adopted in 1849 before that state was admitted to the Union, included within the state's boundary the water area extending three English miles from the shore. Cal. Const. 1849, Art. XII, 1; that the Enabling Act which admitted California to the Union ratified the territorial boundary thus defined; and that California was admitted "on an equal footing with the original States in all respects whatever," 9 Stat. 452. With these premises admitted California contends that its ownership follows from the rule originally announced in Pollard's Lessee v. Hagan, 3 How. 212, 44 U.S. 212; see also Martin v. Waddell, 16 Pet. 367, 410, 41 U.S. 367, 410. In the Pollard case it was held, in effect, that the original states owned in trust for their people the navigable tidewaters between high and low water mark within each state's boundaries, and the soil under them, as an inseparable attribute of state sovereignty. Consequently, it was decided that Alabama, because admitted into the Union on "an equal footing" with the other states, had thereby become the owner of the tidelands within its boundaries. Thus the title of Alabama's tidelands grantee was sustained as valid against that of a claimant holding under a United States grant made subsequent to Alabama's admission as a state.

The Government does not deny that under the Pollard rule, as explained in later cases, California has a qualified ownership of lands under inland navigable waters such as rivers, harbors, and even tidelands down to the low water mark.* * * It stresses that the thirteen original colonies did not own the marginal belt; that the Federal Government did not seriously assert its increasingly greater rights in this area until after the formation of the Union; that it has not bestowed any of these rights upon the states, but has retained them as appurtenances of national sovereignty. And the Government insists that no previous case in this Court has involved or decided conflicting claims of a state and the Federal Government to the three-mile belt in a way which requires our extension of the Pollard inland water rule to the ocean area.

* * * From all the wealth of material supplied, however, we cannot say that the thirteen original colonies separately acquired ownership to the three-mile belt or the soil under it, even if they did acquire elements of the sovereignty of the English Crown by their revolution against it.

At the time this country won its independence from England there was no settled international custom or understanding among nations that each nation owned a three-mile water belt along its borders. Some countries, notably England, Spain, and Portugal, had, from time to time, made sweeping claims to a right of dominion over wide expanses of ocean. And controversies had arisen among nations about rights to fish in prescribed areas. But when this nation was formed, the idea of a three-mile belt over which a littoral nation could exercise rights of ownership was but a nebulous suggestion. Neither the English charters granted to this nation's settlers, nor the treaty of peace with England, nor any other document to which we have been referred, showed a purpose to set apart a three-mile ocean belt for colonial or state ownership. Those who settled this country were interested in lands upon which to live, and waters upon which to fish and sail. There is no substantial support in history for the idea that they wanted or claimed a right to block off the ocean's bottom for private ownership and use in the extraction of its wealth.

It did happen that shortly after we became a nation our statesmen became interested in establishing national dominion over a definite marginal zone to protect our neutrality.[1] Largely as a result of their efforts, the idea of a definite three-mile belt in which an adjacent nation can, if it chooses, exercise broad, if not complete dominion, has apparently at last been generally accepted throughout the world, although as late as 1876 there was still considerable doubt in England about its scope and even its existence. That the political agencies of this nation both claim and exercise broad dominion and control over our three-mile marginal belt is now a settled fact. And this assertion of national dominion over the three-mile belt is binding upon this Court.

Not only has acquisition, as it were, of the three-mile belt, been accomplished by the national Government, but protection and control of it has been and is a function of national external sovereignty. The belief that local interests are so predominant as constitutionally to require state dominion over lands under its land-locked navigable waters finds some argument for its support. But such can hardly be said in favor of state control over any part of the ocean or the ocean's bottom. This country, throughout its existence has stood for freedom of the seas, a principle whose breach has precipitated wars among nations. The country's adoption of the three-mile belt is by no means incompatible with its traditional insistence upon freedom of the sea, at least so long as the national Government's power to exercise control consistently with whatever international undertakings or commitments it may see fit to assume in the national interest is unencumbered. The three-mile rule is but a recognition of the necessity that a government next to the sea must be able to protect itself from dangers incident to its location. It must have powers of dominion and regulation in the interest of its revenues, its health, and the security of its people from wars waged on or too near its coasts. And insofar as the nation asserts its

---

[1] Secretary of State Jefferson in a note to the British minister in 1793 pointed to the nebulous character of a nation's assertions of territorial rights in the marginal belt, and put forward the first official American claim for a three-mile zone which has since won general international acceptance. Reprinted in H. Ex. Doc. No. 324, 42nd Cong., 2nd Sess. (1872) 553-554. See also Secretary Jefferson's note to the French Minister, Genet, reprinted American State Papers, 1 Foreign Relations (1883), 183, 384, Act of June 5, 1794, 1 Stat. 381; 1 Kent, Commentaries, 14th ed., 33-40.

rights under international law, whatever of value may be discovered in the seas next to its shores and within its protective belt, will most naturally be appropriated for its use. But whatever any nation does in the open sea, which detracts from its common usefulness to nations, or which another nation may charge detracts from it, as a question for consideration among nations as such, and not their separate governmental units. What this Government does, or even what the states do, anywhere in the ocean, is a subject upon which the nation may enter into and assume treaty or similar international obligations. The very oil about which the state and nation here contend might well become the subject of international dispute and settlement.

The ocean, even its three-mile belt, is thus of vital consequence to the nation in its desire to engage in commerce and to live in peace with the world; it also becomes of crucial importance should it ever again become impossible to preserve that peace. And as peace and world commerce are the paramount responsibilities of the nation, rather than an individual state, so if wars come, they must be fought by the nation. The state is not equipped in our constitutional system with the powers or the facilities for exercising the responsibilities which would be concomitant with the dominion which it seeks. Conceding that the state has been authorized to exercise local police power functions in the part of the marginal belt within its declared boundaries, these do not detract from the Federal Government's paramount rights in and power over this area. Consequently, we are not persuaded to transplant the Pollard rule of ownership as an incident of state sovereignty in relation to inland waters out into the soil beneath the ocean, so much more a matter of national concern. If this rationale of the Pollard case is a valid basis for a conclusion that paramount rights run to the states in inland waters to the shoreward of the low water mark, the same rationale leads to the conclusion that national interests responsibilities, and therefore national rights are paramount in waters lying to the seaward in the three-mile belt.

* * *

The question of who owned the bed of the sea only became of great potential importance at the beginning of this century when oil was discovered there. As a consequence of this discovery, California passed an Act in 1921 authorizing the granting of permits to California residents to prospect for oil and gas on blocks of land off its coast under the ocean. This state statute, and others which followed it, together with the leasing practices under them, have precipitated this extremely important controversy, and pointedly raised this state-federal conflict for the first time. Now that the question is here, we decide for the reasons we have stated that California is not the owner of the three-mile marginal belt along its coast, and that the Federal Government rather than the state has paramount rights in and power over that belt, an incident to which is full dominion over the resources of the soil under that water area, including oil.

* * * Even assuming that Government agencies have been negligent in failing to recognize or assert the claims of the Government at an earlier date, the great interests of the Government in this ocean area are not to be forfeited as a result. The Government, which holds its interests here as elsewhere in trust for all people, is not to be deprived of those interests by the ordinary court rules designed particularly for private disputes over individually owned pieces of property; and officers who have no authority at all to dispose of Government property cannot by their conduct cause the Government to lose its valuable rights by their acquiescence, laches, or failure to act.

* * *

We hold that the United States is entitled to the relief prayed for. The parties, or either of them, may, before September 15, 1947, submit the form of decree to carry this opinion into effect, failing which the Court will prepare and enter an appropriate decree at the next term of Court.

It is so ordered.

Mr. Justice JACKSON took no part in the consideration or decision of this case.

[Dissenting opinions of Justices Frankfurter and Reed have been omitted.]

Notes and Questions

1. United States v. California was decided on national security grounds. Justice Black, author of the majority opinion, wrote that "[t]he three-mile rule is but a recognition of the necessity that a government next to the sea must be able to protect itself from dangers incident to its location." 332 U.S. at 35. The United States has rarely been attacked by sea. Even conceding the possibility of attack, is it not feasible for the states to recognize the superior power of the federal government to deal with external threats and yet control the marginal seas for domestic purposes?

Did United States v. California overrule the old Alabama case, Pollard v. Hagan, 44 U.S. (3 How.) 212 (1844), which seemed to give the states control of the tidelands? If not, how was *Pollard* distinguished from *California*?

What justification did the Court give for holding that the actions of federal officers could not cause the government to lose its rights?

2. United States v. California was a complex case, both in terms of the events leading up to it and its outcome. E. Bartley explained the unexpected legal twist in the Supreme Court's holding:

> The California pleadings were stated almost entirely in terms of property concepts. Since the case of the United States was premised on that line of reasoning, there was no reason for California to do otherwise.
>
> These were lawyers arguing, on the legal bases with which they were familiar, a concept of title and all that title implies. It appears that they saw no reason to argue the larger but ephemeral concept of "paramount rights," a doctrine of far greater importance to the general theory of federalism than the more prosaic and legalistic concept of title. Whether the outcome could or would have been different if the State of California had chosen to devote the bulk of its pleadings to this more inclusive theory is a matter for pure conjecture. * * * The fact remains that the case was argued entirely on one basis and decided on another.

E. Bartley, The Tidelands Oil Controversy 166 (1953).

The final outcome of United States v. California was ambiguous. At the following term, the government proposed a decree which would have given the United States proprietorship, as well as paramount rights, in the marginal sea. California objected, however, and the word "proprietorship" was deleted. Therefore though neither California nor the United States had title to the area, the United States was entitled to an injunction to prevent further removal of oil under California leases. See R. Hardwicke, C. Illig & C. Patterson, The Constitution and the Continental Shelf, 26 Tex. L. Rev. 304, 405 (1947).

3. The dispute which generated the litigation in United States v. California also resulted in a number of other Supreme Court decisions. In United States v. Louisiana, 339 U.S. 699 (1950), the Court rejected claims by Louisiana which were similar to those made by California. In addition to the 3-mile belt, Louisiana also claimed the seabed to a distance of 24 additional nautical miles on the basis of a 1938 state statute extending the states' seabed boundaries that distance. Following the reasoning of *California*, the Court held that statute had no effect on the national government's paramount rights.

In United States v. Texas, 339 U.S. 707 (1950), the issues were somewhat different, as Texas was never a territory but, prior to statehood, had been an independent nation with a constitution claiming a 3 marine league territorial sea. In spite of this difference in Texas history, the Court held that Texas, once it became a state, could have no greater rights of sovereignty than the other states—an unusual application of the Equal Footing Doctrine.

For discussions of United States v. Louisiana and United States v. Texas, see R. Morris, The Forging of the Union Reconsidered: A Historical Refutation of State Sovereignty Over Seabeds, 74 Col. L. Rev. 1056, 1058-59 (1974); and C. Dinkins, Texas Seashore Boundary Law: The Effect of Natural and Artificial Modifications, 10 Hous. L. Rev. 43 (1972).

4. United States v. California was a landmark case and prompted an extensive response among academic observers. See, e.g., J. Hanna, The Submerged Lands Cases, 3 Stan. L. Rev. 193 (1950); C. Illig, Offshore Lands and Paramount Rights, 14 U. Pitt. L. Rev. 10 (1952); W. Metcalfe, The Tidelands Controversy: A Study in Development of a Political-Legal Problem, 4 Syracuse L. Rev. 39 (1952); J. Thomason, United States v. California, Paramount Rights of the Federal Government in Submerged Coastal Lands, 26 Tex. L. Rev. 304 (1947). For an historical perspective on ownership and control of the marginal sea before United States v. California, see G. Ireland, Marginal Seas Around the States, 2 La. L. Rev. 252 (1940); H. Fraser, The Extent and Delimitation of Territorial Waters, 11 Cornell L.Q. 455 (1926).

SECTION 9. THE HISTORY OF THE SUBMERGED LANDS ACT OF 1953

* * * In 1952, Congress sent Senate Joint Resolution Twenty to President Truman quitclaiming all federal interests in the submerged lands to the coastal states, and restoring to the coastal states the ownership of the submerged lands in the three-mile limit. President Truman, a firm proponent of federal ownership of offshore resources, vetoed the Senate Joint Resolution because "it would turn over to certain States, as a free gift, very valuable lands and mineral resources (owned by) the United States as a whole." No attempt was made to override the veto, and numerous similar bills introduced in Congress which would have quitclaimed the lands and resources underlying the three-mile marginal belt were also consistently opposed as "giveaway" legislation.

With General Eisenhower's election to the presidency, Truman's efforts to preserve federal ownership of submerged lands were quickly reversed. On May 22, 1953, President Eisenhower signed the SLA into law. This Act granted the states ownership to and proprietary use of all lands under their navigable waters for a distance of three geographical miles from their coastlines, or to the historic seaward boundaries as they existed at the time the states became members of the Union. * * *

G. Jones, The Development of Outer Continental Shelf Energy Resources, 11 Pepperdine L. Rev. 9, 38-39 (1983).

SECTION 10. SELECTED PROVISIONS OF THE SUBMERGED LANDS ACT OF 1953

43 U.S.C. § 1301. Definitions

When used in this subchapter and subchapter II of this chapter--

(a) The term "lands beneath navigable waters" means --

(1) all lands within the boundaries of each of the respective States which are covered by nontidal waters that were navigable under the laws of the United States at the time such State became a member of the Union, or acquired sovereignty over such lands and waters thereafter, up to the ordinary high water mark as heretofore or hereafter modified by accretion, erosion, and reliction;

(2) all lands permanently or periodically covered by tidal waters up to but not above the line of mean high tide and seaward to a line three geographical miles distant from the coast line of each such State and to the boundary line of each such State where in any case such boundary as it existed at the time such State became a member of the Union, or as heretofore approved by Congress, extends seaward (or into the Gulf of Mexico) beyond three geographical miles, and

(3) all filled in, made, or reclaimed lands which formerly were lands beneath navigable waters, as hereinabove defined; * * *

(c) The term "coast line" means the line of ordinary low water along that portion of the coast which is in direct contact with the open sea and the line marking the seaward limit of inland waters;

* * *

(e) The term "natural resources" includes, without limiting the generality thereof, oil, gas, and all other minerals, and fish, shrimp, oysters, clams, crabs, lobsters, sponges, kelp, and other marine animal and plant life but does not include water power, or the use of water for the production of power;

(f) The term "lands beneath navigable waters" does not include the beds of streams in lands now or heretofore constituting a part of the public lands of the United States if such streams were not meandered in connection with the public survey of such lands under the laws of the United States and if the title to the beds of such streams was lawfully patented or conveyed by the United States or any State to any person;

43 U.S.C. § 1311.   Rights of the States

(a) Confirmation and establishment of title and ownership of lands and resources; management, administration, leasing, development, and use

It is determined and declared to be in the public interest that (1) title to and ownership of the lands beneath navigable waters within the boundaries of the respective States, and the natural resources within such lands and waters, and (2) the right and power to manage, administer, lease, develop, and use the said lands and natural resources all in accordance with applicable State law be, and they are, subject to the provisions hereof, recognized, confirmed, established, and vested in and assigned to the respective States or the persons who were on June 5, 1950, entitled thereto under the law of the respective States in which the land is located, and the respective grantees, lessees, or successors in interest thereof;

(b)   Release and relinquishment of title and claims of the United States; payment to States of moneys paid under leases

(1) The United States Releases and relinquishes unto said States and persons aforesaid, except as otherwise reserved herein, all right, title, and interest of the United States, if any it has, in and to all said lands, improvements, and natural resources; (2) the United States releases and relinquishes all claims of the United States, if any it has, for money or damages arising out of any operations of said States or persons pursuant to State authority upon or within said lands and navigable waters; and (3) the Secretary of the Interior or the Secretary of the Navy or the Treasurer of the United States shall pay to the respective States or their grantees issuing leases covering such lands or natural resources all moneys paid thereunder to the Secretary of the Interior or to the Secretary of the Navy or to the Treasurer of the United States and subject to the control of any of them or to the control of the United States on May 22, 1953, except that portion of such moneys which (1) is required to be returned to a lessee; or (2) is deductible as provided by stipulation or agreement between the United States and any of said States; * * * .

43 U.S.C. § 1312.   Seaward boundaries of States

The seaward boundary of each original coastal State is approved and confirmed as a line three geographical miles distant from its coast line or, in the case of the Great Lakes, to the international boundary. Any State admitted subsequent to the formation of the Union which has not already done so may extend its seaward boundaries to a line three geographical miles distant from its coast line, or to the international boundaries of the United States in the Great Lakes or any other body of water traversed by such boundaries. Any claim heretofore or hereafter asserted either by constitutional provision, statute, or otherwise, indicating the intent of a State so to extend its boundaries is hereby approved and confirmed, without prejudice to its claim, if any it has, that its boundaries extend beyond that line. Nothing in this section is to be construed as questioning or in any manner prejudicing the existence of any State's seaward boundary beyond three geographical miles if it was so provided by its constitution or laws prior to or at the time such State became a member of the Union, or if it has been heretofore approved by Congress.

43 U.S.C. § 1314. Rights and powers retained by the United States; purchase of natural resources; condemnation of lands

(a) The United States retains all its navigational servitude and rights in and power of regulation and control of said lands and navigable waters for the constitutional purposes of commerce, navigation, national defense, and international affairs, all of which shall be paramount to, but shall not be deemed to include, proprietary rights of ownership, or the rights of management, administration, leasing, use, and development of the lands and natural resources which are specifically recognized, confirmed, established and vested in and assigned to the respective States and others by Section 1311 of this title. * * *

Notes and Questions

1. After the passage of the SLA, a number of coastal states, relying on 43 U.S.C. §1312, asserted claims to submerged lands and resources extending beyond three miles from the coastline. Texas successfully claimed an "historic boundary" extending three marine leagues into the Gulf of Mexico; but Louisiana's, Mississippi's, and Alabama's similar claims were rejected. United States v. Louisiana, 363 U.S. 1 (1960). See also United States v. Louisiana, 389 U.S. 155 (1967); United States v. Louisiana, 394 U.S. 1 (1969). It was also determined that Florida's Gulf of Mexico boundary was three marine leagues, but its Atlantic Ocean boundary was settled by consent decree at three geographical miles from shore. United States v. Florida, 363 U.S. 121 (1960); United States v. Florida, 420 U.S. 531 (1975). The other Atlantic and Pacific coast states' boundaries also extend only three miles seaward from the coast.

2. The Submerged Lands Act created a number of boundary problems, the most serious of which was the definition of "inland waters." Coastlines, unfortunately, are rarely straight. Bays, estuaries, and shallow indentations make straight boundary lines impossible. The act, in Section 1301(c), mentioned "inland waters" but failed to provide a definition. At issue was whether the 3-mile marginal sea was to be measured from a line following the sinuosities of the coast, or a straight line drawn from headland to headland. Why did states with deeply

indented coastlines favor the straight baseline method?

In 1963 the United States filed an amended complaint against the State of California and sought a supplemental decree defining "inland waters." The U.S. Supreme Court granted the supplemental decree in United States v. California, 381 U.S. 139 (1965). California, using the straight baseline method, claimed a huge area as inland water. The Supreme Court ruled that by eliminating the definition of inland waters from the bill, Congress intended to leave the meaning of the term to the courts. The Court then held that the definition should conform to the one adopted by the 1958 Geneva Convention on the Territorial Sea and the Contiguous Zone. The Convention adopted a 24-mile closing line rule for bays and a semicircle test for the sufficiency of water enclosed as the definition of inland waters. Professor A. Shalowitz, in Boundary Problems Raised by the Submerged Lands Act, 54 Colum. L. Rev. 1021, 1031-32 (1954), explained the test:

> Since bays in nature are seldom exactly circular, recourse is had to the theory of equivalence and the rule adopted that if the area of a bay in nature is greater than the area of the semicircle formed with the distance between the headlands as a diameter, the bay is a closed bay, or intra-territorial, and the seaward boundary of inland waters is a headland-to-headland line. But if the area of the bay is less than the area of the semicircle, the bay is an open bay, or extra-territorial, and the boundary line of inland waters would be the ordinary low-water mark following the sinuosities of the coast.

When the Court applied the Convention's test to the California coast it found that only Monterey Bay qualified as inland water. The remainder of the huge expanse of ocean claimed by California, the Court held, was open sea and therefore measured by the baseline method more favorable to the federal government.

For purposes of reporting oil and hazardous substance spills discussed in Chapter 8, Section 311 of the federal Clean Water Act defines "inland waters of the United States" as "waters of the United States lying inside the baseline from which the territorial sea is measured" and the "contiguous zone" as the zone "established by the United States under Article 24 of the Convention on the Territorial Sea and the Contiguous Zone." 33 U.S.C. §§ 1321(a)(9), (16). The contiguous zone is defined the same way for other purposes of the Clean Water Act. See 33 U.S.C. § 1362(9). Despite President Reagan's 1988 proclamation of a twelve nautical mile territorial sea, virtually all federal statutes define the territorial sea as extending seaward "three miles." 33 U.S.C. §§ 1362(8), 2701(35).

3. In United States v. Louisiana, 394 U.S. 11 (1969), the Supreme Court defined the prerequisites for a claim of historic bay status. These

were:

(a) the exercise of authority over the area by the state claiming the historical right
(b) the continuity of this exercise of authority
(c) the attitude of foreign states

United States v. Alaska, 422 U.S. 184 (1975) (lower Cook Inlet held not to be an "historic bay"); United States v. Louisiana, 470 U.S. 93 (1985) (Mississippi Sound is an historic bay). See generally Comment, The Doctrine of Historic Bays: Apply an Anachronism in the Alabama and Mississippi Boundary Case, 23 San Diego L. Rev. 763 (1986).

In United States v. Maine, 469 U.S. 504 (1985) (Rhode Island and New York boundary case), the Court determined that Long Island, although in reality an island, would be considered a peninsula attached to the New York mainland. The decision classified Long Island Sound as a closed bay and therefore part of the inland waters of New York and Connecticut. The baseline drawn from Long Island to Watch Hill on the mainland, however, defeated the Rhode Island claim to Block Island Sound as part of its territorial sea.

The Supreme Court in United States v. Maine, 475 U.S. 89 (1986), rejected Massachusetts' claim that Nantucket Sound is within the state's internal waters rather than partly territorial sea and partly high seas as the United States argued. The state claim rested entirely on the doctrine of "ancient title." Under that doctrine, occupation as an original mode of territorial acquisition and an assertion of exclusive authority vests the occupant with clear title if the "occupation" began before freedom of the high seas became part of international law. The doctrine is recognized by Juridical Regime of Historic Waters, Including Historic Bays, 2 Y.B. Int'l L. Comm'n 1 (1962), a United Nations study upon which the Supreme Court has relied in prior federal-state boundary determinations. See, e.g., United States v. Louisiana, 470 U.S. 93, 101 (1985). Assuming, arguendo, the legitimacy of claims based on "ancient title," Justice Marshall dismissed Massachusetts 'claim on the grounds that the state failed to demonstrate the "existence of acts, attributable to the sovereign, manifesting an assertion of exclusive authority over the waters claimed." 475 U.S. at 98.

In United States v. Alaska, 521 U.S. 1 (1997), the Court rejected most of Alaska's claims to submerged lands in the Beaufort Sea off Alaska's Arctic coast. Alaska could not treat the alluvial formation known as Dinkum Sands as an island nor use straight baselines between barrier islands in Prudhoe Bay to extend its coastline seaward for Submerged Lands Act purposes.

4. Important maritime boundaries between the United States and

neighboring countries have been resolved as well. On October 12, 1984, the International Court of Justice (ICJ) handed down its landmark decision delimiting the U.S.-Canada maritime boundary in the Gulf of Maine. Delimitation of the Maritime Boundary in the Gulf of Maine Area (Canada v. United States), 1984 ICJ 246. Pursuant to this decision, Canada is entitled to the lion's share of Georges Bank's multimillion dollar scallop fishery located on its rich Northeast Peak; both countries share several stocks of groundfish divided in two by the new boundary. As a practical result, this decision profoundly affects optimum management of these resources and consequently mandates international cooperation in conservation and management. Moreover, as the delimitation marked the first single boundary ever drawn for both the continental shelf and the water column, this decision provided a significant milestone in the law of international maritime boundaries. See, e.g., J. Bubier and A. Rieser, U.S. and Canadian Groundfish Management in the Gulf of Maine-Georges Bank Region, 10 Ocean Mgmt. 83 (1986); B. Shibles, Implications of an International Legal Standard for Transnational Management of Gulf of Maine-Georges Bank Fishery Resources, 1 Ocean and Coastal L. J. 1 (1994).

Reflecting a century-old conflict, the dispute over Gulf of Maine resources began in earnest in 1977 when the U.S. and Canada simultaneously expanded their fishery jurisdictions to 200 nautical miles. In the Gulf of Maine, the new jurisdictions incorporated some of the world's richest fishing grounds, including that of the prized Georges Bank, over which the claims clashed irreconcilably. Bilateral negotiations failed to resolve the dispute, forcing the two countries to seek outside binding settlement. In a Special Agreement submitted November 1981, the two countries asked a five-member Chamber of the ICJ to delimit by a single boundary both the continental shelf and the water column of the Gulf of Maine, pursuant to Article 26 of the Statute of the ICJ.

The ICJ based its delimitation almost exclusively on geography. In so doing, it clarified the rule of customary international law which requires that maritime boundary delimitations, in the absence of agreement, be based on equitable principles adjusted to account for relevant circumstances in order to achieve an equitable result. See, e.g., Case Concerning the Continental Shelf (Tunisia v. Libya), 1982 ICJ 18. The court drew an initial boundary based on the equitable principle of coastline geography. The line bisecting the angle formed by the Nova Scotia and North American continent coastal parallels provided the initial delimitation. In making this initial delimitation, the ICJ rejected application of the equidistance principle as defined in Article 6 of the 1958 Convention on the Continental Shelf even though both countries are parties to the treaty. The 1958 Convention governed only the continental shelf and was thus found inapplicable to the dual-purpose boundary. Furthermore, the court found that equidistance had not become a general rule of maritime boundary delimitation in customary international law and the court was thus under no obligation to follow it.

Relevant circumstances considered by the ICJ in making its initial delimitation equitable were again geographical: the boundary was adjusted by the proportional lengths of coastlines. In flatly refusing to consider certain nongeographical circumstances proposed by both parties, the court further emphasized the relationship of geography to equitable delimitations. Thus historical fishing patterns, socio-economic dependence on fishery resources, and naturally existing ecological boundaries delimiting fishery resources, were all deemed irrelevant to achieving an equitable result.

In 1978 the United States and Mexico were able to resolve their overlapping 200-mile claims in the Gulf of Mexico by a treaty utilizing the equidistant method of boundary line calculation finally ratified by the United States Senate in October 1997. The EEZ boundaries completely surround a triangular "western gap" of high seas and continental shelf in the middle of the Gulf of Mexico, approximately 135 miles long. In 2000, the two countries adopted a treaty dividing the area with an equidistance line and reserving a buffer zone on each side of the boundary to deal with possible transboundary oil and gas deposits.

5.   Another boundary problem under the Submerged Lands Act was the problem of ambulatory boundaries. Not only are ocean coastlines irregular, they are subject to change. In United States v. Louisiana, 394 U.S. 11 (1969), the U.S. Supreme Court held that if erosion takes place so that the historic boundary is more than three marine leagues from the present coastline, the present three-league line becomes the new boundary; in other words, the state loses territory. In places where accretion has extended the coastline, the historic seaward boundary of the state did not extend beyond three leagues. However, for most of the states, their SLA boundaries were ambulatory.

What effect would these shifting territories have on state leases near the boundary line? Would the lessee have to renegotiate his lease with the federal government? See G. Swan, Remembering Maine: Offshore Federalism in the United States and Canada, 6 Cal. W. Int'l L.J. 296, 315 (1976).

Some (but not all) artificial coastline extensions, such as harbors and breakwaters, may help the states. Compare United States v. California, 447 U.S. 1 (1980) with United States v. Alaska, 503 U.S. 569 (1992). For qualifying artificial extensions, the marginal sea is measured from their farthest seaward extent.

R. Krueger, in The Background of the Continental Shelf and the

Outer Continental Shelf Lands Act, 10 Nat. Resources J. 442, 463 (1970), criticized the concept of ambulatory boundaries:

> The concept of an ambulatory boundary is a sound one from an international standpoint. If the United States or any other country increases its land mass artificially, there are good reasons, such as national defense, for extending its territorial sea appropriately. It is not, however, a good rule of law with respect to federal-state relationships. It could lead to further federal-state litigation over boundaries and title and may have an inhibiting influence on beneficial coastal developments. It has been recommended that the federal government and the various states adopt appropriate legislation to fix their offshore boundaries.

As part of the Budget Reconciliation Act of 1985, P.L. 99-272, § 8005, Congress amended Section 2(b) of the Submerged Lands Act, 43 U.S.C. § 1301(b), to provide that once they are fixed by a decree of the Supreme Court, the coordinates delineating a federal-state offshore boundary "shall remain immobilized * * * and shall not be ambulatory." This provision does not appear to apply to lateral seaward boundaries between states, but a Supreme Court decree fixing such boundaries could itself provide that the decreed boundary shall be fixed rather than ambulatory with physical changes in the coastline. See generally New Jersey v. New York, 1998 WL 259994 (U.S. Sup. Ct. May 26, 1998); Texas v. Louisiana, 426 U.S. 465 (1976).

6. Section 1313 of the Submerged Lands Act led to the third supplemental decree granted in United States v. California, 436 U.S. 32 (1978). The last sentence of § 1313(a) exempted from the grant to the states "any rights the United States has in lands presently occupied by the United States under claim of right." The United States claimed dominion over the submerged lands and waters within the Channel Islands National Monument, situated inside the three-mile marginal sea off the southern California mainland. The United States had maintained and controlled the monument for decades and claimed that this was "actual occupation" under § 1313(a).

The Supreme Court held that the United States did not have dominion, and that title to the disputed area was in California. The Court noted that the entire purpose of the Submerged Lands Act would have been nullified if the "claim of right" exemption saved claims based solely on paramount rights obtained in the 1947 United States v. California decision. Thus, the exception in § 1313(a) applies only if the United States' claim rests on some basis other than paramount rights. The United States failed to show any other basis of ownership.

What other bases might the United States have for claiming ownership within the three-mile marginal sea?

7. In Douglas v. Seacoast Products, Inc., 431 U.S. 265 (1977), the U.S. Supreme Court defined coastal state "ownership" under the Submerged Lands Act. Ownership consists of the right to exploit offshore resources subject to encumbrances previously created by the exercise of the commerce, navigation, national defense, and international affairs powers of the federal government. Justice Rehnquist, dissenting, preferred an alternative reading of the act -- that the reservation of powers clause only gives fair warning of the possibility that the government may, at some time in the future and in furtherance of the specifically enumerated powers, find it necessary to intrude upon state ownership and control of coastal submerged lands. See T. Schoenbaum & F. Parker, Federalism in the Coastal Zone: Three Models of State Jurisdiction and Control, 57 N.C. L. Rev. 231 (1979).

In Zabel v. Tabb, 430 F.2d 199 (5th Cir. 1970), cert. denied, 401 U.S. 910 (1971), the court held that Congress has the power under the Commerce Clause to regulate state submerged lands for conservation purposes and that it had not given up this power in the Submerged Lands Act. See Annotation, 25 A.L.R. Fed. 684 (1975). Thus the multiple uses of state submerged lands and the waters overhead are controlled by federal and state law. See, e.g., Barber v. Hawaii, 42 F.3d 1185 (9th Cir. 1994) (Hawaii statutes and regulations governing anchorage and mooring in the state's ocean waters upheld); Coastal Petroleum v. Chiles, 701 So.2d 619 (Fla .App.1997) (state legislative drilling prohibition imposed on previously issued state offshore oil and gas leases upheld); Coastal Petroleum Co. v. Department of Environmental Protection, 672 So.2d 574 (Fla. App.1996) (bond requirement to protect state submerged lands during exploratory drilling imposed after the state issued offshore oil and gas leases held invalid); Fanning v. Oregon Division of State Lands, 151 Or. App.609, 950 P.2d 353 (1997) (forfeiture of a state lease issued for commercial kelp harvesting in state ocean waters); James v. Alaska, 950 P.2d 1130 (Alaska 1997) (state regulation of subsistence fishing upheld); Kaneohe Bay Cruises, Inc. v. Hirata, 75 Haw. 250, 861 P.2d 1 (1993) (Hawaii statutory ban on commercial "thrill craft" operations in two ocean bays on weekends and holidays upheld); Murphy v. Dept. of Natural Resources, 837 F. Supp. 1217 (S.D. Fla. 1994) (state control of houseboats through leasing of submerged lands and water column upheld); Stop the Outfall Pipe v. Massachusetts Water Resources Authority, 419 Mass. 1, 642 N.E.2d 568 (1994) (state agency approved sewage outfall pipe does not violate the Massachusetts Ocean Sanctuaries Act).

8. The Submerged Lands Act, unfortunately, raised nearly as many questions as it answered. One of the most important unanswered questions was ownership of lands beyond the marginal sea. In the same year as the SLA, Congress passed the Outer Continental Shelf Lands Act of 1953 which basically ratified and codified the Truman Proclamation. Jurisdiction over and ownership of the resources of the

continental shelf was asserted in the federal government. See R. Breeden, Federalism and the Development of Outer Continental Shelf Mineral Resources, 28 Stan. L. Rev. 1107, 1112-14 (1976).

9. In United States v. California and subsequent cases, the Supreme Court held in favor of federal paramount rights within three geographical miles (or leagues) of the coastline. The basis of these paramount rights was, in large part, national security. Congress subsequently enacted the Submerged Lands Act and the Outer Continental Shelf Lands Act discussed above, the latter asserting federal jurisdiction over the outer continental shelf beyond the three miles of seabed returned to the states under the Submerged Lands Act. Why, then, did the 13 Atlantic states in United States v. Maine, 420 U.S. 515 (1975), unsuccessfully attempt to claim state ownership of the outer continental shelf? Is not the national security argument even stronger when applied to the outer continental shelf?

The explanation of the Atlantic states' position is threefold. First, the 13 defendants in Maine were the original colonies who felt they had stronger historical claims to offshore lands. See D. Flaherty, Virginia and the Marginal Sea: An Example of History in the Law, 58 Va. L. Rev. 694 (1972). Second, the paramount rights doctrine of United States v. California was and is suspect. Justice Frankfurter, in his *California* dissent, accused the majority of confusing the concepts of dominium and imperium. Dominium concerns ownership; imperium is the superior right of the federal government to act as sovereign in international affairs. See Note, States' Rights in the Outer Continental Shelf Denied by the United States Supreme Court, 30 U. Miami L. Rev. 203, 210 (1975); D. Christie, State Historic Interests in the Marginal Seas, 2 Territorial Sea Journal 151 (1992). Third, the Submerged Lands Act did not foreclose more expansive state ownership based on historic claims under Section 1312 quoted above.

The Submerged Lands Act was ambiguous not only in specific sections, but as a whole. The situation after passage of the act was reviewed in Note, Right, Title and Interest in the Territorial Sea: Federal and State Claims in the United States, 4 Ga. J. Int'l & Comp. Law 463, 469 (1974):

Both federal and state interests found support for their positions in the Act. States asserted that this Act was a congressional recognition that broad rights to these lands and waters had always existed in the states and that upon each states' entry into the Union the federal government had relinquished these broad rights to the states rather than retaining them in the federal government. The federal theory maintained that this Act merely granted limited authority over these lands back to the states, leaving most aspects of authority still vested in the hands of the federal government.

The history of federal-state and federal-provincial relations offshore in Australia and Canada is remarkably similar to that of the United States. See R. Hildreth, Managing Ocean Resources: Canada, 6 Int'l J. of Estuarine & Coastal Law 199 (1991); R. Hildreth, Managing Ocean Resources: New Zealand and Australia, 6 Int'l J. of Estuarine & Coastal Law 89 (1991); R. Hildreth, Managing Ocean Resources: United States, 6 Int'l J. of Estuarine & Coastal Law 313 (1991). Regional approaches to ocean governance are receiving increasing attention in those countries as well. See B. Cicin-Sain, M. Hershman, R. Hildreth & J. Isaacs, Improving Ocean Management Capacity in the Pacific Coast Region: State and Regional Perspectives (National Coastal Resources Institute 1991); R. Hildreth, Regional Ocean Resources Management, 3 Proceedings of Coastal Zone '91 at 2583.

Problem

On December 27, 1988 President Ronald Reagan issued the Presidential Proclamation extending the territorial sea of the United States from three miles to twelve miles. The legislators in your state are interested in how this extension could affect state authority over offshore waters and resources. They have asked you to describe the division of state-federal authority over living and nonliving ocean resources as it existed before the issuance of the proclamation and after. If the proclamation has not changed the division, they wish to know what difficulties you perceive in persuading Congress to pass legislation extending state authority to the limits of the new territorial sea.

SECTION 11. SUBMERGED CULTURAL RESOURCES IN MARGINAL SEAS

New technologies and improved research techniques have led to the discovery of an increasing number of vessels in recent years, and conflicts concerning ownership and jurisdiction over these vessels have led to complex court cases. Both the federal government and the coastal states view ancient shipwrecks off the coasts of the United States as having significance beyond the monetary value of the recoverable cargo. The historic importance of such shipwrecks is illustrated by the designation of the site of the wreck of the *USS Monitor* as a national marine sanctuary. Marine archaeologists portray private salvage of historic wrecks as the equivalent of "looting" an archaeological or historic site. Private salvors do not perceive themselves as looters and point out that without their investment of resources and capital, historic wrecks would never be located.

During the last two decades, numerous shipwreck cases have addressed the appropriateness of the application of the maritime law of salvage or finds as well as issues of jurisdiction, preemption, ownership, and Eleventh amendment immunity of states from suit. Didn't passage of the Submerged Lands Act give states clear ownership of historic shipwrecks? Prior to the passage of the Abandoned Shipwreck Act (ASA) of 1987, 43 U.S.C. § 2101 et seq., a split of opinion existed over whether the state received title or even the right to regulate ownership and recovery of abandoned shipwrecks situated on offshore submerged lands. Historically, such rights were governed by federal admiralty principles. According to the district court in Cobb Coin v. Unidentified Wrecked and Abandoned Sailing Vessel, 525 F. Supp. 186, 214-16 (S.D. Fla. 1981), the "paramount rights" ceded by the United States to the individual coastal states through the Submerged Lands Act included the right to determine the disposition of the natural resources in the area, not historic wreck sites that may be found there. However, in Subaqueous Exploration v. Unidentified Wrecked Vessel, 577 F. Supp. 597, 612-13 (D. Md. 1983), the district court held that the rights and powers granted to the states by the Submerged Lands Act included the right to regulate the ownership and recovery of *abandoned* shipwrecks situated on submerged lands within a state.

In the ASA, Congress resolved the issue in an interesting two-step process. First, Congress asserted title of the United States to all abandoned shipwrecks. 43 U.S.C. § 2105(a). Congress then transferred title to the state of ". . . any abandoned shipwreck that is— (1) embedded in submerged lands of a State; (2) embedded in coralline formations protected by a State on submerged lands of a State; or (3) on submerged lands of a State and is included in or determined eligible for inclusion in the National Register." Id. §2105(c). Shipwrecks located on public lands of the United States remained the property of the United States and shipwrecks located on lands owned by Indian tribes became the property of the tribe. Id. §2105(d).

The ASA did not define "abandoned" or totally clarify all the jurisdictional issues surrounding the shipwreck controversy. The U.S. Supreme Court first addressed the application of the ASA in California v. Deep Sea Research, 523 U.S. 491 (1998), known as the Brother Jonathan case.

CALIFORNIA AND STATE LANDS COMMISSION v. DEEP SEA RESEARCH
U.S., Supreme Court, 1998
523 U.S. 491

JUSTICE O'CONNOR delivered the opinion of the Court.

* * *

The dispute before us arises out of respondent DSR's assertion of rights to both the vessel and cargo of the *Brother Jonathan*, a 220-foot, wooden-hulled, double side-wheeled steamship that struck a submerged rock in July 1865 during a voyage between San Francisco and Vancouver. It took less than an hour for the *Brother Jonathan* to sink, and most of the ship's passengers and crew perished. The ship's cargo, also lost in the accident, included a shipment of up to $2 million in gold and a United States Army payroll that some estimates place at $250,000. * * *

Shortly after the disaster, five insurance companies paid claims totaling $ 48,490 for the loss of certain cargo. It is unclear whether the remaining cargo and the ship itself were insured. Prior to DSR's location of the vessel, the only recovery of cargo from the shipwreck may have occurred in the 1930's, when a fisherman found 22 pounds of gold bars minted in 1865 and believed to have come from the *Brother Jonathan*. The fisherman died, however, without revealing the source of his treasure. There appears to be no evidence that either the State of California or the insurance companies that paid claims have attempted to locate or recover the wreckage.

In 1991, DSR filed an action in the United States District Court for the Northern District of California seeking rights to the wreck of the *Brother Jonathan* and its cargo under that court's *in rem* admiralty jurisdiction. California intervened, asserting an interest in the *Brother Jonathan* based on the Abandoned Shipwreck Act of 1987 (ASA) * * *. According to California, the ASA applies because the *Brother Jonathan* is abandoned and is both embedded on state land and eligible for inclusion in the National Register of Historic Places (National Register). California also laid claim to the *Brother Jonathan* under Cal. Pub. Res. Code Ann. § 6313 (hereinafter § 6313), which vests title in the State "to all abandoned shipwrecks * * * on or in the tide and submerged lands of California."

* * *

The District Court held two hearings on the motions. The first focused on whether the wreck is located within California's territorial waters, and the second concerned the possible abandonment, embeddedness, and historical significance of the shipwreck, issues relevant to California's claims to the res. For purposes of the pending motions, DSR stipulated that the *Brother Jonathan* is located upon submerged lands belonging to California.

After the hearings, the District Court concluded that the State failed to demonstrate a "colorable claim" to the *Brother Jonathan* under federal law, reasoning that the State had not established by a preponderance of the evidence that the ship is abandoned, embedded in the sea floor, or eligible for listing in the National Register as is required to establish title under the ASA. As for California's state law claim, the court determined that the ASA pre-empts § 6313. Accordingly, the court issued a warrant for the arrest of the *Brother Jonathan*, appointed DSR custodian of the shipwreck subject to further order of the court, and ordered DSR to take possession of the shipwreck as its exclusive salvor pending the court's determination of "the manner in which the wreck and its cargo, or the proceeds therefrom, should be distributed."

* * *

The Court of Appeals for the Ninth Circuit affirmed the District Court's orders. The court first concluded that § 6313 is pre-empted by the ASA because the state statute "takes title to shipwrecks that do not meet the requirements of the ASA and which are therefore within the exclusive admiralty jurisdiction of the federal courts." With respect to the State's claim under the ASA, the court presumed that "a federal court has both the power and duty to determine whether a case falls within its subject matter jurisdiction" * * *

By concluding that the State must prove its claim to the *Brother Jonathan* by a preponderance of the evidence in order to invoke the immunity afforded by the Eleventh Amendment, the Ninth Circuit diverged from other Courts of Appeals that have held that a State need only make a bare assertion to ownership of a res. We granted certiorari to address whether a State's Eleventh Amendment immunity in an *in rem* admiralty action depends upon evidence of the State's ownership of the res, and to consider the related questions whether the *Brother Jonathan* is subject to the ASA and whether the ASA pre-empts § 6313.

II

The judicial power of federal courts extends "to all Cases of admiralty and maritime Jurisdiction." Art. III, § 2, cl. 1. The federal courts have had a unique role in admiralty cases since the birth of this Nation, because "maritime commerce was * * * the jugular vein of the Thirteen States." F. Frankfurter & J. Landis, The Business of the Supreme Court 7 (1927). Accordingly, "the need for a body of law applicable throughout the nation was recognized by every shade of opinion in the Constitutional Convention." *Ibid.* * * * That jurisdiction encompasses "maritime causes of action begun and carried on as proceedings *in rem*, that is, where a vessel or thing is itself treated as the offender and made the defendant by name or description in order to enforce a lien."

The jurisdiction of the federal courts is constrained, however, by the Eleventh Amendment, under which "the Judicial power of the United States shall not be construed to extend to any suit in law or equity, commenced or prosecuted against one of the United States by Citizens of another State, or by Citizens or Subjects of any Foreign State." * * * According to this Court's precedents, a State may not be sued in federal court by one of its own citizens and a state official is immune from suit in federal court for actions taken in an official capacity.

The Court has not always charted a clear path in explaining the interaction between the Eleventh Amendment and the federal courts' *in rem* admiralty jurisdiction. Early cases involving the disposition of "prize" vessels captured during wartime appear to have assumed that federal courts could adjudicate the *in rem* disposition of the bounty even when state officials raised an objection. As Justice Story explained, in admiralty actions *in rem*,

> "the jurisdiction of the [federal] court is founded upon the possession of the thing; and if the State should interpose a claim for the property, it does not act merely in the character of a defendant, but as an actor. Besides, the language of the [Eleventh] Amendment is, that 'the judicial power of the United States shall not be construed to extend to any suit *in law or equity*.' But a suit in the admiralty is not, correctly speaking, a suit in law or in equity; but is often spoken of in contradistinction to both." 2 J. Story, Commentaries on the Constitution of the United States § 1689, pp. 491-492 (5th ed. 1891).

Justice Washington, riding Circuit, expressed the same view in *United States v. Bright, 24 F. Cas. 1232, 1236* (No. 14,647) (CC Pa. 1809), where he reasoned:

> "In cases of admiralty and maritime jurisdiction the property in dispute is generally in the possession of the court, or of persons bound to produce it, or its equivalent, and the proceedings are in rem. The court decides in whom the right is, and distributes the proceeds accordingly. In such a case the court need not depend upon the good will of a state claiming an interest in the thing to enable it to execute its decree. All the world are parties to such a suit, and of course are bound by the sentence. The state may interpose her claim and have it decided. But she cannot lie by, and, after the decree is passed say that she was a party, and therefore not bound, for want of jurisdiction in the court."

Although those statements might suggest that the Eleventh Amendment has little application in *in rem* admiralty proceedings, subsequent decisions have altered that understanding of the federal courts' role. In *Ex parte New York*, 256 U.S. 490 (1921) (New York I), the Court explained that admiralty and maritime jurisdiction is not wholly exempt from the operation of the Eleventh Amendment, thereby rejecting the views of Justices Story and Washington.* * *

The Court's most recent case involving an *in rem* admiralty action, *Florida Dept. of State v. Treasure Salvors, Inc.,* 458 U.S. 670 (1982), addressed whether the Eleventh Amendment "bars an in rem admiralty action seeking to recover property owned by a state." A plurality of the Court suggested that * * * the State's possession of maritime artifacts was unauthorized, and the State therefore could not invoke the Eleventh Amendment to block their arrest. As the plurality explained, "since the state officials do not have a colorable claim to possession of the artifacts, they may not invoke the Eleventh Amendment to block execution of the warrant of arrest."

That reference to a "colorable claim" is at the crux of this case. Both the District Court and the Ninth Circuit interpreted the "colorable claim" requirement as imposing a burden on the State to demonstrate by a preponderance of the evidence that the *Brother Jonathan* meets the criteria set forth in the ASA. Other Courts of Appeals have concluded that a State need only make a bare assertion to ownership of a res in order to establish its sovereign immunity in an *in rem* admiralty action.

By our reasoning, however, either approach glosses over an important distinction present here. In this case, unlike in *Treasure Salvors*, DSR asserts rights to a res that is not in the possession of the State. The Eleventh Amendment's role in that type of dispute was not decided by the plurality opinion in *Treasure Salvors*, which decided "whether a federal court exercising admiralty *in rem* jurisdiction may seize property held by state officials under a claim that the property belongs to the State." * * *

Nor did the opinions in *New York I* or *New York II* address a situation comparable to this case. The holding in *New York I* explained that, although the suit at issue was styled as an *in rem* libel action seeking recovery of damages against tugboats chartered by the State, the proceedings were actually "in the nature of an action *in personam* against [the Superintendent of Public Works of the State of New York], not individually, but in his [official] capacity." The action in *New York II* was an *in rem* suit against a vessel described as being "at all times mentioned in the libel and at present * * * the absolute property of the State of New York, in its possession and control, and employed in the public service of the State for governmental uses and purposes * * *"

* * *

It is true that statements in the fractured opinions in *Treasure Salvors* might be read to suggest that a federal court may not undertake *in rem* adjudication of the State's interest in property without the State's consent, regardless of the status of the res. Those assertions, however, should not be divorced from the context of *Treasure Salvors* * * *.

* * * Although the Eleventh Amendment bars federal jurisdiction over general title disputes relating to State property interests, it does not necessarily follow that it applies to *in rem* admiralty actions, or that in such actions, federal courts may not exercise jurisdiction over property that the State does not actually possess.

* * *[A] requirement that a State possess the disputed res in such cases is "consistent with the principle which exempts the [State] from suit and its possession from disturbance by virtue of judicial process." Based on longstanding precedent respecting the federal courts' assumption of *in rem* admiralty jurisdiction over vessels that are not in the possession of a sovereign, we conclude that the Eleventh Amendment does not bar federal jurisdiction over the *Brother Jonathan* and, therefore, that the District Court may adjudicate DSR's and the State's claims to the shipwreck. We have no occasion in this case to consider any other circumstances under which an *in rem* admiralty action might proceed in federal court despite the Eleventh Amendment.

III

There remains the issue whether the courts below properly concluded that the *Brother Jonathan* was not abandoned for purposes of the ASA.* * * In light of our ruling that the Eleventh Amendment does not bar complete adjudication of the competing claims to the *Brother Jonathan* in federal court, the application of the ASA must be reevaluated. Because the record before this Court is limited to the preliminary issues before the District Court, we decline to resolve whether the *Brother Jonathan* is abandoned within the meaning of the ASA. We leave that issue for reconsideration on remand, with the clarification that the meaning of "abandoned" under the ASA conforms with its meaning under admiralty law.

Our grant of certiorari also encompassed the question whether the courts below properly concluded that the ASA pre-empts § 6313, which apparently operates to transfer title to abandoned shipwrecks not covered by the ASA to the State. Because the District Court's full consideration of the application of the ASA on remand might negate the need to address the pre-emption issue, we decline to undertake that analysis.

Accordingly, the judgment of the Court of Appeals assuming jurisdiction over this case is affirmed, its judgment in all other respects is vacated, and the case is remanded for further proceedings consistent with this opinion.

It is so ordered.

JUSTICE STEVENS, concurring.

In *Florida Dept. of State v. Treasure Salvors, Inc.* both the four Members of the plurality and the four dissenters agreed that the District Court "did not have power . . . to adjudicate the State's interest in the property without the State's consent." Our reasons for reaching that common conclusion were different, but I am now persuaded that all of us might well have reached a different conclusion if the position of Justices Story and Washington (that the Eleventh Amendment is no bar to any *in rem* admiralty action) had been brought to our attention. I believe that both opinions made the mistake of assuming that the Eleventh Amendment has the same application to an *in rem* admiralty action as to any other action seeking possession of property in the control of state officers.

* * *

Having given further consideration to the special characteristics of *in rem* admiralty actions, and more particularly to the statements by Justice Story and Justice Washington quoted at pages 9 and 10 of the Court's opinion, I am now convinced that we should have affirmed the *Treasure Salvors* judgment in its entirety. Accordingly, I agree with the Court's holding that the State of California may be bound by a federal court's *in rem* adjudication of rights to the *Brother Jonathan* and its cargo.

JUSTICE KENNEDY, with whom *JUSTICE GINSBURG* and *JUSTICE BREYER* join, concurring.

I join the opinion of the Court. In my view, the opinion's discussion of *Florida Dept. of State v. Treasure Salvors, Inc.*, does not embed in our law the distinction between a State's possession or nonpossession for purposes of Eleventh Amendment analysis in admiralty cases. In light of the subsisting doubts surrounding that case and Justice Stevens' concurring opinion today, it ought to be evident that the issue is open to reconsideration.

Notes and Questions

1. Congress found both the law of salvage and the law of finds unsuitable for preservation of historic shipwrecks; the ASA specifically provides that neither shall apply to abandoned shipwrecks that have been transferred into state ownership. ASA §2106(a). In *The Brother Jonathan*, the Supreme Court found that "abandoned" under the ASA has the same meaning as under admiralty law, i.e., a shipwreck is abandoned if the title has been affirmatively renounced or when an inference of abandonment can be made from the circumstances.

Therefore, in spite of the statutory language rejecting the application of admiralty law to ships transferred to the states by the ASA, a large body of admiralty law concerning abandonment still remains relevant to determining, as a threshold issue, whether a vessel falls within the ASA. Fairport Int'l Exploration v. The Shipwrecked Vessel known as The Captain Lawrence, 177 F.3d 491 (2000) provides an excellent legal analysis of the term abandonment. The case specifically addressed the issue of the burden of proof in establishing abandonment under the ASA and found: "The uniform rule in admiralty is that a finding of abandonment requires proof by clear and convincing evidence." Id. at 501.

2. In *The Brother Jonathan*, the state of California relied on Florida Department of State v. Treasure Salvors, Inc., 458 U.S. 670 (1982), where four members of the plurality and four dissenters had agreed that Treasure Salvors could not sue Florida in federal admiralty court to recover property owned by the state without the state's consent. In that case, however, the state official was found to have acted beyond his authority and the state did "not have even a colorable claim to the artifacts." Subsequent cases have found federal courts to have no in rem admiralty jurisdiction where the state presents a "colorable claim." How did the Supreme Court distinguish *The Brother Jonathan*? Why does *The Brother Jonathan* call the result of *Treasure Salvors* into question?

3. In a number of earlier cases, the state's "colorable claim" was based on a state law, like Cal. Pub. Res. Code § 1603, rather than the ASA or the SLA. Are such laws likely to survive a pre-emption challenge when used to assert jurisdiction over shipwrecks that do not fall within the ASA? Note that even before *The Brother Jonathan*, it was estimated that only about five percent of the shipwrecks in state waters were affected by the ASA.

4. When is a ship "embedded"? In Zych v. Unidentified, Wrecked and Abandoned Vessel, Believed to be the Seabird, 941 F.2d 525 (7th Cir.1991), the Seventh Circuit Court of Appeals remanded the case for a determination of whether the ship was "embedded" within the definition of the ASA. The court directed that "embedded" is defined as "firmly affixed in the submerged lands or in coralline formations such that the use of tools of excavation is required in order to move the bottom sediments to gain access to the shipwreck, its cargo, and any part thereof[.]" ASA § 2102(a). The term is to be interpreted consistently with the common law exception from the law of finds.

Chapter Five

OCEAN ENERGY AND
MINERAL RESOURCES

SECTION 1. OUTER CONTINENTAL SHELF
OIL AND GAS DEVELOPMENT

A. INTRODUCTION

Oil and gas are the principal non-living continental shelf resources. Exploration for and development of oil and gas reserves may conflict with the preservation and management of other coastal and ocean resources or other potential uses of ocean and coastal areas. Often, there is significant opposition to offshore oil and gas leasing, exploration, and development. Some state legislatures have banned oil and gas development in state ocean waters. See Coastal Petroleum v. Chiles, 701 So.2d 619 (Fla.App.1997), cert. denied, 118 S. Ct. 2369 (1998). The November 1989 Report of National Research Council of the National Academy of Sciences, National Academy of Engineering, and the Institute of Medicine concluded that the available scientific and technical information bearing on potential environmental impacts is currently inadequate for decisions about development and production in the three federal Outer Continental Shelf (OCS) areas it studied. National Research Council, The Adequacy of Environmental Information For Outer Continental Shelf Oil And Gas Decisions: Florida and California (1989).

This information and concerns generated by the 1989 Exxon Valdez tanker spill led to congressionally imposed moratoria on OCS drilling and related activities in several offshoreareas, and the administrative cancellation of a number of proposed lease sales. In response to the moratoria, oil companies holding existing leases subjected to the moratoria sought damages for the breach of their lease rights. In addition, bills were introduced to require the federal government to buyback OCS leases if the holders were not permitted to exercise their OCS lease rights. The expense of such buybacks could be substantial as the decision of the U.S. Supreme Court in Mobil Oil Exploration & Producing Southeast, Inc. v. United States, 530 U.S. 604 (2000), excerpted below illustrates.

The future course of OCS oil and gas operations is unclear. Many different factors will shape our energy policy and OCS operations' role in that policy. One key factor will be the status of Middle Eastern oil supplies. As long as these supplies remain secure, environmentalists and coastal state interests may continue to be able to marshall support for limiting OCS oil and gas activities. However, even among these groups there are differing views about the desirability of OCS oil and gas activities. On one hand, OCS oil and gas activities do pose some risk of oil spills and other damage to sensitive environments; but, on the other hand, some data suggests that the environmental risks of OCS activities are significantly less than the risks associated with oil tanker traffic. Dependency on Middle Eastern oil supplies means that large numbers of vulnerable oil tankers will be moving through American waters on a daily basis. Historically all but one major oil spill in U.S. waters, the Santa Barbara Channel oil spill, has resulted from a tanker mishap. A second factor is our desire to utilize more environmentally friendly fuels such as natural gas. Such a policy led the Clinton Administration in 1994 to support the drilling of an exploratory natural gas well off the Gulf coast of Florida. A third factor is the fiscal one. Lease sales, royalties, bonus, and rents constitute the third largest non-tax source of revenue for the federal government. Periodic concerns about federal budget deficit could make it difficult to forgo such a large source of revenue and to implement any federal buyback program.

B. OUTER CONTINENTAL SHELF LANDS ACT

Continental shelf oil and gas resources seaward of the outer limit of state waters are under the control of the federal government and managed pursuant to the Outer Continental Shelf Act of 1953:

The Outer Continental Shelf Lands Act was passed in 1953, after a series of events, from the middle 1940's to early 1950's, raised the issue of Tidelands Oil and Federal/State conflict over offshore resource jurisdiction to the public consciousness.

On September 28, 1945, President Harry S. Truman issued a Proclamation on the Continental Shelf stating that the Government of the United States "regards the natural resources of the subsoil and seabed of the continental shelf beneath the high seas contiguous to the coasts of the United States and appertaining to the United States, subject to its jurisdiction and control." Although not so stated in the Proclamation, the continental shelf was considered to be that area contiguous to the Continent covered by no more than 100 fathoms (600 feet; 200 meters) of water. The Truman Proclamation and the claim of the United States was subsequently recognized by the Geneva Convention on the Continental Shelf.

However, a number of jurisdictional problems arose between the U.S. Federal Government and certain State Governments. In 1947 the Supreme Court, rejecting prior rulings in this area, held that the Federal Government had "paramount rights" over the area 3 miles seaward from the normal low water mark on the California coast. Similar decisions were made in Louisiana and Texas cases in 1950. In effect, then, the Court had decided that these States had no title to, or property interest in, the submerged lands off of their respective coasts outside their inland waters.

However, there was a real question whether the Mineral Leasing Act of 1920 applied to the Outer Continental Shelf and whether it was necessary for the Congress to explicitly confer this authority on the Interior Department.

Congressional Action, 1953

To resolve these jurisdictional issues statutorily, Congress passed two acts in 1953 which helped to clarify the distinction in Federal-State control. The Submerged Lands Act of 1953 gives the coastal States exclusive rights to the resources up to 3 geographical miles from the coast. Subsequent court cases provided that, for historic reasons, the boundaries of Texas and Florida extended for three marine leagues (approximately 10 1/2 [land] miles) from their coast lines into the Gulf of Mexico. The Act also reaffirmed the jurisdiction, power and control of the United States beyond that point.

Although the Submerged Lands Act established coastal and seaward boundaries for Federal and State governmental jurisdiction, it was silent on the matter of Federal leasing for Outer Continental Shelf mineral resources. To remedy this situation, Congress passed the Outer Continental Shelf Lands Act of 1953 (OCSLA).

This legislation defines the OCS as all lands lying seaward and outside of State waters (3 miles) "and of which the subsoil and seabed (belong) to the United States and are subject to its jurisdiction and control." It also establishes very general guidelines and directives for the Secretary of the Interior in managing the resources of the OCS and in leasing tracts for oil and gas, and other mineral exploration and development.

H.R. No. 95-590, 95th Cong. 2nd Sess. (1977).

Although a number of federal agencies play active roles in the management of OCS living and nonliving resources, the primary responsibility for the management of OCS oil and gas resources is within the Department of the Interior. The Minerals Management Service of the Department of Interior administers the leasing provisions of the OCSLA and oversees the development of a tract once it has been leased.

(1.) Environmental Issues in Lease Sales,
Exploration, and Development

Possible adverse impacts of OCS oil and gas operations upon state beaches, waters, and coastal resources, and the lack of any significant offsetting economic benefits to most coastal states, have resulted in substantial opposition to such operations. At each stage of the process, state objections to OCS oil and gas plans are interposed and, not infrequently, litigation erupts with state, tribal, local, fishing and environmental interests on one side and federal agencies and oil and gas interests on the other. See E. Fitzgerald, The Seaweed Rebellion: Federal-State Conflicts Over Offshore Energy (2001).

Since OCS operations must comply with a large number of statutory requirements, there are numerous legal avenues available to attempt to thwart OCS development. In most situations, opponents have not been able to prevent OCS oil and gas leasing or drilling. Delay, modification of the most objectionable features of OCS plans, and sometimes Congressional action withdrawing highly sensitive areas from a leasing plan are usually the realistic goals of OCS litigation. The monetary and energy stakes are too high to expect that OCS drilling can be totally precluded.

NEPA, the Endangered Species Act (ESA), and CZMA are at the core of much of the environmental OCS litigation. The role of CZMA is discussed further in Chapter Three and in Mobil Oil Exploration & Producing Southeast, Inc. v. United States, 530 U.S. 604 (2000), excerpted below. The following case and notes discuss the relationship of the requirements of OCSLA, NEPA, and ESA.

TRIBAL VILLAGE OF AKUTAN v. HODEL
United States Court of Appeals, Ninth Circuit, 1988
869 F.2d 1185, cert. denied,
Cowper v. Secretary of Interior, 493 U.S. 873 (1989)

The Tribal Village of Akutan and two other tribal villages, the Trustees for Alaska and twelve other environmental organizations, and the State of Alaska and seven organizations concerned with the preservation of Alaska's fisheries (Alaska), appeal the district court's grant of summary judgment in favor of the Secretary of the Interior, the Department of the Interior, the National Marine Fisheries Service and nineteen intervenors (Secretary). Appellants have sued to enjoin the Secretary from conducting Lease Sale 92 in the North Aleutian Basin (also referred to as Bristol Bay) on the grounds that the Secretary has failed to comply with the National Environmental Policy Act (NEPA), the Endangered Species Act (ESA), and the Outer Continental Shelf Lands Act (OCSLA).

I. FACTS

The development and operation of offshore oil wells is controlled by OCSLA, which establishes a national policy of making the outer continental shelf "available for expeditious and orderly development, subject to environmental safeguards, in a manner which is consistent with the maintenance of competition and other national needs." The Act establishes four distinct stages in the administrative process: (1) formulation of a five-year leasing plan by the Secretary; (2) lease sales; (3) exploration by the lessees; and (4) development and production. Secretary of the Interior v. California, 464 U.S. 312, 337 (1984). "Each stage involves separate regulatory review that may, but need not, conclude in the transfer to lease purchasers of rights to conduct additional activities on the OCS [outer continental shelf]." Id. at 337.

During the first stage of OCSLA, the Secretary prepares a Five-Year OCS Oil and Gas Lease-Sale Schedule. The Secretary must request comments from federal agencies and governors of affected states before submitting the proposed program of lease sales to the President and Congress. In the second stage, the Secretary conducts lease sales of tracts on the outer continental shelf. Before soliciting bids and awarding leases, the Secretary must comply with a detailed combination of investigating, consulting and reporting requirements. Most significantly, the Secretary's review of environmental consequences must meet both NEPA standards and ESA requirements (while not mentioned in OCSLA, ESA "applies of its own force and effect"). Under OCSLA, the Secretary must also consult with the governor of any affected state, and accept the governor's recommendations if the Secretary believes they strike a reasonable balance between the national interest and the well-being of the citizens of the affected state.

After the lease sale has been completed, the highest qualified bidder is granted a lease which entitles him to conduct limited preliminary activities such as geophysical surveys. However, "by purchasing a lease, lessees acquire no right to do anything more. Under the plain language of the OCSLA, the purchase of a lease entails no right to proceed with full exploration, development, or production * * * ; the lessee acquires only a priority in submitting plans to conduct these activities." Secretary of the Interior v. California, 464 U.S. at 339.

Prior to embarking on the third stage of the OCSLA process -- exploration of the lease sale area -- a lessee must submit an exploration plan and an environmental report, which are subject to further review. There is yet another round of review before the lessor may enter into the final stage -- development and production of oil. "If [the lessee's] plans, when ultimately submitted, are disapproved, no further exploration or development is permitted." Id. This four-level review process gives the Secretary a "continuing opportunity for making informed adjustments" to the process of developing offshore oil wells in order to ensure all activities are conducted in an environmentally sound manner. Village of False Pass, 733 F.2d at 616 (quoting Sierra Club v. Morton, 510 F.2d 813, 828 (5th Cir. 1975)).

In November 1974, the Secretary began studying the possibility of leasing tracts for oil and gas production in the North Aleutian Basin off the southwest coast of Alaska. This region is important economically and ecologically. The fisheries of the North Aleutian Basin are "among the most productive in the world," Alaska Outer Continental Shelf Region, Minerals Management Service, U.S. Dep't of the Interior, 1 Final Environmental Impact Statement, North Aleutian Basin Sale 92 III-C-1 (1985) [hereinafter cited as FEIS], important both for commercial and sport fishing. The area is also the home of endangered species of marine mammals and birds. Eighty percent of the current eastern population of Pacific gray whales migrates through the Bristol Bay's Unimak Pass during the spring and fall.

After twice canceling plans for lease sales in the bay at Alaska's request, the Secretary submitted a five-year oil and gas leasing schedule in 1982 which proposed the lease sale of all 32.5 million acres of the North Aleutian Bay. This lease sale, denominated Lease Sale 92, was scheduled for April 1985. In March 1984, in response to concerns expressed by the Governor of Alaska, the Secretary restricted leasing to the southwest corner of the region by deleting nearly 83 percent of the acreage from the sale.

The Secretary then proceeded to follow the statutory pre-lease process: He solicited resource reports from federal and state agencies; solicited comments from the oil industry, governmental agencies, environmental groups and the general public; prepared both a draft and final environmental impact statement as required by NEPA; obtained biological opinions from the Fish and Wildlife Service and the National Marine Fisheries Service, as required by ESA; conducted public hearings; and consulted at length with the Governor of Alaska and other state officials.

In his formal recommendations to the Secretary, the Governor objected to the timing, size, location and terms of the proposed lease sale of the remaining 5.6 million acres. He requested a number of changes, including an additional eight-year delay in the sale and the deletion of all tracts within twenty-five miles of the Alaska Peninsula. Letter from Governor, State of Alaska, to Donald Hodel, Secretary, Department of the Interior (November 5, 1985) at 2, Excerpts of Record (ER) at 33. The Secretary rejected both recommendations, see U.S. Dep't of the Interior, Statement of the Reasons for the Decision on Sale 92 (Dec. 1985), ER at 35 [hereinafter cited as Statement of Reasons], although he accepted the Governor's other mitigating measures. On December 16, 1985, the Secretary published a final notice of sale in the Federal Register.

Litigation began later that month, as appellants filed three suits, later consolidated by the district court, to enjoin the Secretary from proceeding with Lease Sale 92. Appellants claimed the proposed sale violated OCSLA, NEPA, ESA and the Alaska National Interest Lands Conservation Act (ANILCA), 16 U.S.C. §§ 3101-3233. * * * [T]he district court concluded that the Secretary had violated section 810 of ANILCA, 16 U.S.C. § 3120, and that such a violation automatically entitled plaintiffs to injunctive relief.

Appellees immediately obtained a partial stay of the district court's preliminary injunction to prevent cancellation of the sale pending appeal. In Tribal Village of Akutan v. Hodel, 792 F.2d 1376 (9th Cir. 1986), vacated, 480 U.S. 943 (1987), we upheld the preliminary injunction. * * * While a petition for certiorari in Akutan was pending in the Supreme Court, the Court reversed *Gambell II* [the case relied upon for the injunction], holding that section 810 of ANILCA, establishing procedures to protect Alaskan natives' use of public lands, does not apply to land in the outer continental shelf; and that violations of the Act do not require an automatic injunction. Amoco Production Co. v. Village of Gambell, 480 U.S. 531. The Court then granted certiorari in *Akutan*, and remanded to this court. 480 U.S. 943 (1987). The Secretary did not seek to vacate the preliminary injunction but, instead, agreed to an expedited resolution of the remaining issues. We remanded to the district court, which granted summary judgment for the Secretary on all counts, but enjoined the lease sale pending appeal. We denied the Secretary's motion to vacate the injunction.

Appellants make three claims. First, they contend that the Secretary's rejection of the Governor's key recommendations to delay and limit the area of the sale was arbitrary and capricious, thus violating section 19 of OCSLA, 43 U.S.C. § 1345. Second, they claim that the environmental impact statement prepared for Lease Sale 92 was so flawed by methodological and procedural errors that it did not satisfy the requirements of NEPA. Finally, they claim that the Secretary violated ESA by rejecting some of the reasonable and prudent alternatives recommended by the National Marine Fisheries Service (NMFS), and by relying on a biological opinion which was itself fundamentally flawed. We consider each claim in turn.

As the district court granted summary judgment on all these claims, we stand in the district judge's shoes in reviewing his decision: "[W]e may affirm a summary judgment only if, viewing the evidence in the light most favorable to the party against whom it is granted, we find no genuine issue of material fact, and we find that the prevailing party is clearly entitled to judgment as a matter of law."

II. The OCSLA Claim

Section 19 of OCSLA, 43 U.S.C. § 1345, entitles the governor of an affected state to submit recommendations "regarding the size, timing, or location of a proposed lease sale" to the Secretary. The Secretary must accept these recommendations "if he determines, after having provided the opportunity for consultation, that they provide for a reasonable balance between the national interest and the well-being of the citizens of the affected State." Section 1345(d) provides that the Secretary's acceptance or rejection of the recommendations shall be final "unless found to be arbitrary or capricious."

As we noted in California v. Watt, the scope of our review is limited: "In determining whether the Secretary's rejection of the Governor's recommendations was arbitrary or capricious, we must consider whether the decision was based on a consideration of the relevant factors and whether there was a clear error of judgment." 683 F.2d at 1268. The court must decide whether the Secretary "articulate[d] a rational connection between the facts found and the choice made," and "whether the Secretary made the decision in accordance with his duty under law."

Alaska contends that the district court made two errors in determining that the Secretary's rejection of the Governor's recommendations was not arbitrary or capricious. First, Alaska claims that the district court misinterpreted section 19 of OCSLA. Under Alaska's reading of the statute, if the governor has balanced the national interest and the well-being of the citizens of the state in an objectively reasonable way, the Secretary must defer to the governor's recommendations. A reviewing court should therefore determine whether the governor's recommendations fall within the range of reason, not whether the Secretary was arbitrary or capricious in rejecting them.

This analysis is in accord with neither the statutory language nor our precedents. The plain language of section 19 limits the court to reviewing the rationality of the Secretary's determination; the court cannot "substitute its judgment for that of the [Secretary]." California v. Watt, 683 F.2d at 1269 (dismissing a similar argument that the Secretary must accept the governor's recommendations if they "provided for a reasonable balance between national and state interests."). Even if we agreed that the Governor's recommendations were reasonable, we could not conclude the Secretary was arbitrary or capricious simply because he chose to reject them.

Alaska offers a second reason for reversing the Secretary's decision: It was made without due consideration of the Governor's recommendations and in reliance on flawed data. Alaska alleges the Secretary made a number of specific errors: He disregarded OCSLA's requirement to base the determination of national interest "on the desirability of obtaining oil and gas supplies in a balanced manner and on the findings, purposes, and policies of this subchapter" as required by section 19(c) of OCSLA; he failed to make sufficient findings concerning the protection of fisheries; he relied on erroneous economic calculations in refusing to delay the sale at least eight more years; and he based his refusal to defer the sale of 137 near-shore tracts on a flawed oil spill risk analysis.

None of these contentions has merit. As the district court held, the Secretary adequately balanced the nation's interest in developing oil and gas supplies against its policy of protecting the environment, see

Statement of Reasons at 2-35, and specifically discussed the importance of preserving the bay's fisheries. Contrary to appellants' suggestion, the Secretary carefully compared the costs and benefits of the proposed lease sale with those of the governor's plan. In making his cost-benefit analysis, the Secretary relied on experts' assessments of the net economic value of the lease sales and the probability and impact of oil spills. In attacking the accuracy of the experts' calculations, Alaska uncovers no fundamental flaws or irrationality; rather, Alaska only succeeds in showing it prefers the results reached by a different methodology.

Finally, Alaska argues that the Secretary did not give the Governor a meaningful opportunity to comment on the net economic value calculations used in planning Lease Sale 92. Although the Secretary formally solicited the Governor's comments on the original lease sale proposal, the Secretary did not resubmit the proposal to the Governor after making minor revisions in net economic value calculations. However, as the Governor had a fair opportunity to comment on the original lease sale proposal, which was not altered in any significant way, OCSLA does not require a second round of consultation.

Because the Secretary complied with the duties imposed by statute, and "articulate[d] a rational connection between the facts found and the choice made," we agree with the district court that the Secretary's decision to reject the Governor's suggestions was not arbitrary or capricious.

III. The NEPA Claim

NEPA is a procedural statute designed to "ensure that federal agencies are fully aware of the impact of their decisions on the environment." Section 102 of NEPA, 42 U.S.C. § 4332, requires all agencies of the federal government to "include in every recommendation or report on proposals for legislation and other major Federal actions significantly affecting the quality of the human environment, a detailed statement by the responsible official on * * * the environmental impact of the proposed action * * * [and] alternatives to the proposed action." 42 U.S.C. §§ 4332 (2)(C)(i) and (iii). Before preparing an environmental impact statement, the responsible federal official "shall consult with and obtain the comments of any Federal agency which has jurisdiction by law or special expertise with respect to any environmental impact involved." 42 U.S.C. § 4332(2)(C).

Our review of an environmental impact statement is governed by the Administrative Procedure Act, which empowers a court to strike down agency actions taken "without observance of procedure required by law." In applying this standard, the district court must determine whether the environmental impact statement contains a "reasonably thorough discussion of the significant aspects of the probable environmental consequences," and provides information which is reasonably sufficient to encourage informed public participation and to "enable the decisionmaker to consider the environmental factors and make a reasoned decision." A court may not strike down an environmental impact statement because of minor technical deficiencies. Findings of fact underlying the district court's decision may not be overturned unless they are clearly erroneous, while the legal adequacy of an environmental impact statement is a question of law, which we review de novo.

Appellants contend that the environmental impact statement prepared for Lease Sale 92 suffered from three fundamental errors, two methodological and one procedural. The alleged methodological errors infected the preparation of the oil spill risk analysis. First, appellants claim the Secretary's analysis was based on a significant underestimation of the amount of oil that might be spilled in the environmentally sensitive near-shore tracts. Because of this error, they argue, the Secretary was unable to make an accurate assessment of the benefits that would accrue from deleting these tracts from the lease sale area. Second, appellants allege that the analysis did not consider such variables as seasonal changes in the weather and the movement of seasonal fish and wildlife. Finally, appellants point to a procedural error: In failing to disclose all of the underlying assumptions on which the oil spill risk analysis was based, the Secretary violated his duty to "make available to the public, information of the proposed project's environmental impact and encourage public participation in the development of that information." Trout Unlimited v. Morton, 509 F.2d 1276, 1282-83 (9th Cir. 1974).

The Secretary vigorously contests these claims. He argues that the oil spill risk analysis was adequate given the inherently speculative character of such analyses at an early stage in the planning process; that there are serious methodological flaws in appellant's own methodology; and that, in any event, the difference between the Secretary's results and those of the appellants is statistically insignificant.

The question of whether the Secretary's analysis was adequate to meet the requirements of NEPA is largely disposed of by our reasoning in Village of False Pass v. Clark, 733 F.2d 605 (9th Cir. 1984). In that case, appellants argued that the environmental impact statement prepared for a proposed lease sale of offshore drilling locations violated NEPA because it failed to consider a worst case scenario of a 100,000-barrel oil spill. Holding that such an analysis was unnecessary at the lease sale stage, we announced the general principle that the amount and specificity of information necessary to meet NEPA requirements varies at each of OCSLA's stages. This principle has been adopted by other circuits and approved by the Supreme Court.

Prior to exploration, it is difficult to make so much as an educated guess as to the volume of oil likely to be produced or the probable location of oil wells. Without this information, an oil spill risk analysis can never be more than speculative, regardless of what methodology is used. More accurate information will be available at later stages of the exploration process, and the Secretary can make appropriate alterations in the oil development plan at that time. Furthermore, any technical deficiencies at the lease sale stage are unlikely to result in environmental damage, as a lease sale "does not directly mandate further activity that would raise an oil spill problem," Village of False Pass, 733 F.2d at 616. We reached a similar conclusion in California v. Watt, where we approved an environmental impact statement even though its oil spill risk analysis was based on a fifty percent underestimation of oil reserves. We noted that "additional Environmental Impact Statements will be required at the later exploration, production, and development stages, and these will, of course, be based on the latest reserve estimates available at the time they are prepared." Id. at 1268.

Under the standard applicable to the lease sale stage, we conclude that the Secretary's environmental impact statement for Lease Sale 92 was adequate to meet the requirements of NEPA. As the district court observed, the Secretary provided "a reasoned analysis of the evidence before [him]," Friends of Endangered Species v. Jantzen, 760 F.2d 976, 986 (9th Cir. 1985), in compliance with the statutory procedure. We need not consider whether the oil spill risk analysis was in fact flawed by a deficiency in methodology; we need only consider whether use of the particular methodology employed in preparing the oil risk spill analysis is reasonable. As we previously stated, "NEPA does not require that we decide whether an [environmental impact statement] is based on the best scientific methodology available, nor does NEPA require us to resolve disagreements * * * as to methodology." The Secretary may refine his analysis based on information learned during later stages of exploration.

Appellants also make a procedural challenge, claiming that the Secretary violated NEPA by failing to provide the public with adequate information on oil spill risks. The Secretary contends that the twelve-page discussion of methodology in the environmental impact statement * * * adequately fulfilled his responsibilities. We agree. NEPA does not require the environmental impact statement to disclose all assumptions underlying a particular methodology. In light of the speculative nature of the oil spill risk analysis at the lease sale stage, the omission of information regarding the Secretary's selection of the number and location of oil spill points, and the amount of oil assumed to have spilled from each point, is immaterial.[1]

IV. THE ESA CLAIMS

Section 7(a)(2) of the Endangered Species Act, 16 U.S.C. § 1536(a)(2), requires federal agencies, with the assistance of the Secretary, to "insure that any action authorized, funded, or carried out by such agency * * * is not likely to jeopardize the continued existence of any endangered species or threatened species. * * *" The federal agency undertaking such an activity must consult the service having jurisdiction over the relevant endangered species;[2] the service then issues a biological opinion that details how the proposed action "affects the species or its critical habitat," including the impact of "incidental takings" of the species.[3] If a species might be endangered by the agency action, the service suggests "reasonable and prudent alternatives" to the agency's proposal. The agency is not required to adopt the alternatives suggested in the biological opinion; however, "[i]f [the Secretary] deviates from them, he does so subject to the risk that he has not satisfied the standard of section 7(a)(2)." Village of False Pass v. Watt, 565 F. Supp. 1123, 1160-61 (D. Alaska 1983), aff'd, 733 F.2d 605 (9th Cir. 1984).

Because ESA contains no internal standard of review, our review is governed by the Administrative Procedure Act. We may set aside the actions of the Secretary or the NMFS only if they were "arbitrary, capricious, an abuse of discretion, or otherwise not in accordance with

---

[1] The omission of speculative information from an environmental impact statement prepared at the lease sale stage is permissible; however, an environmental impact statement which is incomplete due to the omission of ascertainable facts, or the inclusion of erroneous information, violates the disclosure requirement of 42 U.S.C. § 4332(2)(C).

[2] The U.S. Fish and Wildlife Service (FWS) and the National Marine Fisheries Service (NMFS) are jointly responsible for administering the ESA. * * *

[3] An incidental taking "refers to takings that result from, but are not the purpose of, carrying out an otherwise lawful activity conducted by the Federal agency or applicant." 50 C.F.R. § 402.02 (1987).

the law." The Secretary need not justify his decisions by clear and convincing evidence, as the appellants erroneously claim. We review the district court's application of this standard de novo.

Appellants contend that the Secretary failed to fulfill his responsibilities under section 7(a)(2) by rejecting one of the NMFS's "reasonable and prudent alternatives" for the protection of gray whales. In its biological opinion, the NMFS determined that a "major oil spill in the waters of the southeastern Bering Sea during peak migration periods of gray whales is likely to jeopardize the continued existence of the species." Nat'l Marine Fisheries Service, Nat'l Oceanic and Atmospheric Admin., U. S. Dep't of Commerce, Endangered Species Act Section 7 Consultation -- Biological Opinion 13 (March 21, 1984) [hereinafter Biological Opinion], reprinted in 2 FEIS at H-4. To "reduce the risk of oil spills to gray whales," the NMFS recommended adoption of the Minerals Management Service's recommendation "of leasing deferrals within a 50-mile radius of Unimak Pass and the Pribilof Islands, and within 25 miles of shore along the Alaska Peninsula." Biological Opinion at 20. The Secretary did not fully adopt this proposal. While he deleted "virtually all tracts within 50 miles of Unimak Pass," he did not provide the full 25 mile offshore buffer zone advised by NMFS. Instead, he deleted all tracts within 11 miles of shore and adopted alternative measures he considered sufficient to prevent preliminary activities from endangering the whales.

The Secretary's departure from the suggestions in the biological opinion does not by itself constitute a violation of ESA; he satisfied section 7(a)(2) if he took alternative, reasonably adequate steps to insure the continued existence of any endangered or threatened species. We once again make this determination in light of OCSLA's multi-stage structure. As the D.C. Circuit noted in North Slope Borough v. Andrus, 642 F.2d 589, 609 (D.C. Cir. 1980), mandatory stage-by-stage review prevents the telescoping of any and every projected hazard to endangered life and to the environment into one overwhelming statutory obstacle. * * * By ensuring graduated compliance with environmental and endangered life standards, OCSLA makes ESA requirements more likely to be satisfied both in an ultimate and a proximate sense."

The Secretary's responsibilities are not identical at every step of the OCSLA process. We must first determine, therefore, what actions ESA requires at the lease sale stage. We discussed this in depth in Village of False Pass v. Clark, where appellants raised an ESA challenge to the Secretary's proposed sale of oil leases in the St. George Basin of the Bering Sea, a refuge for rare gray and right whales. Because the NMFS had phrased its "reasonable and prudent alternatives" in general, rather than specific terms, the Secretary did not explicitly reject the service's recommendations. Appellants nevertheless contended that the Secretary had violated ESA by failing "to adopt 'concrete measures' at the lease sale stage, such as tract deletion or seasonal drilling restrictions, to protect gray and right whales under ESA from oil spills and seismic testing." We disagreed. As "[t]he lease sale decision itself could not directly place gray or right whales in jeopardy," we concluded that concrete steps were not necessary, and "the Secretary could properly limit his action at the lease sale stage to a plan for later implementation." In *Village of False Pass*, the Secretary's plan included an agreement with NMFS for further monitoring after the lease sale and the inclusion of special disclaimers in the Final Notice of Sale specifying the Secretary's "continuing control of any post-sale drilling." Id. We ruled that such a plan was legally adequate, so long as the Secretary recognized his continuing obligation to implement the plan and to take other steps necessary to fulfill his ESA responsibilities at each stage of the OCSLA process.

Applying the standards established by *Village of False Pass* to appellants' ESA claims, we conclude that the steps taken by the Secretary to comply with ESA requirements were adequate, and his decision to reject some of NMFS's "reasonable and prudent alternatives" was neither arbitrary nor capricious. We agree with the district court that the Secretary's explanation for declining to delete 250 miles of offshore tracts was well reasoned and supported by the record: The Secretary "pointed out that exploration-stage spills are most unlikely, that deletion of nearshore tracts would only marginally reduce the threat to endangered whales from such spills, and that seasonal or ad hoc drilling restrictions can provide adequate protection."

Instead of deleting all the offshore tracts recommended by NMFS, the Secretary adopted other mitigating measures.* * * For example, he agreed to consult informally with NMFS following the lease sale and to initiate formal consultations once the development and production stages began. He modified the Final Notice of Sale to inform lessees that the Secretary might limit or suspend drilling activities whenever migrating whales were near enough to be subject to the risk of oil spills. Finally, he minimized disturbances to the whales by requiring operators and lessees to post whale lookouts when conducting seismic tests. The district court observed that "[t]hese steps and the [Secretary's] explanation appear to have satisfied NMFS's parent agency, NOAA* * * for in its final ESA comments on the sale NOAA did not reiterate those recommendations."

We once again note that the risks to endangered species during the lease sale stage are virtually nonexistent. Only limited preliminary activities are permitted during this stage, such as geological, geophysical and other surveys "which do not result in any physical penetration of the seabed of greater than 500 feet and which do not result in any significant adverse impact on the natural resources of the Outer Continental Shelf [OCS]." Geophysical contractors conducting these surveys are subject to regulation under the Marine Mammal Protection Act (MMPA), 16 U.S.C. §§ 1361-1407, which flatly prohibits the taking of any marine mammal on the high seas except under circumstances not applicable here.

Nor does the Secretary's rejection of some NMFS recommendations at the lease sale stage create a risk of oil spills at later stages. As with NEPA, the Secretary must comply with ESA at every step of the oil development process.   Before the lessees can proceed to the exploration stage, the Secretary must "implicitly conclude that any approval does not affect an endangered species [and] take appropriate steps to insure, on the basis of his previous consultation with the [NMFS], the absence of jeopardy to an endangered species; or reinitiate formal consultation." Lessees must pass through the same approval and review process prior to the production and development stage. While there may be "minor changes in the Secretary's discretion" at later stages in the OCSLA process, such changes are relatively insignificant.

In light of the protective steps implemented at the lease sale stage, the improbability of an oil spill risk arising at this stage and the opportunity for the Secretary to take further action at later stages in the process, we conclude that the Secretary has fulfilled his responsibility to "insure that agency action * * * is not likely to jeopardize the continued existence of any endangered species." 16 U.S.C. § 1536(a)(2).

Appellants make the additional claim that NMFS's biological opinion violated section 7(b)(4) of the ESA, 16 U.S.C. § 1536(b)(4), by failing to specify the impact of any incidental takings of endangered whales. The NMFS concluded that any incidental taking would be prohibited under pertinent provisions of the ESA and section 101(a)(3)(B) of the MMPA and therefore did not include a statement specifying the impact of incidental takings. The NMFS's interpretation of its obligation under section 7(b)(4) was correct. Furthermore, despite the omission of any formal statement about incidental taking, the biological opinion does consider the effect of such adverse impact on the whales. For example, in its discussion of right whales, the opinion states that "[b]ecause this species is nearly extinct, we believe that adverse impacts to small numbers * * * probably would have severe adverse effects on the entire population." Therefore, we conclude that the NMFS's omission of a formal statement concerning incidental takings of endangered species was not arbitrary or capricious, and did not violate the ESA.

V. CONCLUSION

The development of gas and oil reserves in an environmentally sound manner is a complex process: the Secretary must consider vast amounts of often speculative data and balance the demands of numerous interested parties in making plans that extend many years into the future. Under OCSLA's segmented approach, we must uphold the Secretary's actions so long as they meet the standards applicable to each stage. As the Supreme Court has noted, this approach was intended "to forestall premature litigation regarding adverse environmental effects that all agree will flow, if at all, only from the latter stages of OCS exploration and production." Secretary of the Interior v. California, 464 U.S. 312, 341 (1984). Applying this analytical framework, we approve the Secretary's decision to go forward with Outer Continental Shelf Lease Sale 92, and affirm the district court's judgment.

Note on OCSLA and NEPA

For purposes of discussion, OCS development frequently is divided into four stages: five-year program, leasing, exploration, and development and production, with a fifth, shut down of fully exploited fields receiving increasing attention. One question is whether an EIS must be prepared at each stage. Only one provision in OCSLA mandates the preparation of an EIS, and that provision is directed at development and production plans in frontier areas. 43 U.S.C. §. 1351(e)(1) provides:

At least once the Secretary shall declare the approval of a development and production plan in any area or region * * * of the outer Continental Shelf, other than the Gulf of Mexico, to be a major federal action.

Although nowhere else in OCSLA is there a direct mandate for application of NEPA, the lease sale provisions imply that NEPA requirements must be met and an EIS prepared prior to any lease sale. See, e.g., 43 U.S.C. § 1346. Finally, OCSLA does state:

(a) Except as otherwise expressly provided in this Act, nothing in this Act shall be construed to amend, modify, or repeal any provision of * * * the National Environmental Policy Act * * *

43 U.S.C. § 1866(a). In light of this statutory structure, the courts have little difficulty finding that NEPA applies, and an EIS is required as part of the leasing process, see, e.g., Conservation Law Foundation v. Andrus, 623 F.2d 712, 716 (1st Cir. 1979); Natural Resources Defense Council v. Morton, 458 F.2d 827, 836 (D.C. Cir. 1972); New York v. Kleppe, 9 E.R.C. 1769, 1778 (E.D.N.Y. 1976), and to any frontier oil and gas production and development plan approval, see, e.g., Village of False Pass v. Clark, 733 F.2d 605, 609, 614, 615-16 (9th Cir. 1984).

NEPA also applies to the intermediate stage of the approval of an exploration plan 30 C.F.R. § 250.203(g). Potential adverse environmental impacts of exploration activities is an express concern of the OCSLA. 43 U.S.C. § 1340(c)(1) states:

> * * * The Secretary shall approve * * * [an exploration] plan * * * within thirty days of its submission, except that the Secretary shall disapprove such plan if he determines that (A) any proposed activity under such plan would result in a condition described in section 1334(a)(2)(A)(i) of this title, and (B) such proposed activity cannot be modified to avoid such condition. * * *

The condition described in 43 U.S.C. § 1334(a)(2)(A)(i) is

> * * * [the proposed] activity * * * would probably cause serious harm or damage to life (including fish and other aquatic life), to property * * * or to the marine, coastal, or human environment.

An important question is to what extent the irreversible commitment of resources at the leasing stage may affect the balancing of environmental cost against economic interest at later stages in oil and gas development when the environmental cost could have been predicted or determined before the commitment of resources? Will the opportunity to defer the gathering of information about environmental impacts, by itself, create a shift in NEPA balancing because of investments after leases are issued? If so, should a higher standard of NEPA review be imposed at the initial stage of a multi-stage project like OCS oil and gas development?

Note on OCSLA and ESA

The presence of endangered fish, sea turtle, and bird populations and marine mammals in areas in which operations may take place means that the ESA and Marine Mammal Protection Act (MMPA) can have an effect on the location, timing, and extent of OCS oil and gas activities.

The ESA mandates that:

Each federal agency shall, in consultation with * * * the Secretary [of Interior or Commerce] insure that any action authorized, funded or carried out by such agency * * * is not likely to jeopardize the continued existence of any endangered specie or threatened species or result in the destruction or adverse modification of any habitat of such species which is determined by the Secretary * * * to be critical, unless such agency has been granted an exemption.
* * *

Section 7(a)(2) [16 U.S.C. § 1536(a)(2)]. The MMPA's mandate, which is discussed later in Chapter 7, is similar to that of the ESA.

The ESA phrase "insure that any action" suggests a continuing obligation for all federal agencies to avoid adversely affecting threatened or endangered species. See, e.g., Sierra Club v. Lyng, 694 F. Supp. 1260, 1270 (E.D. Tex. 2000). According to the implementing regulations, "action" includes the granting of licenses, * * * leases * * * [or] permits. * * *" 50 C.F.R. § 402.2 (2000). Thus the ESA is applicable to all stages of the OCS oil and gas process. See Village of False Pass v. Clark, 733 F.2d 605, 611-12 (9th Cir. 1984).

The act further provides that:

the Federal agency and the permit or license applicant shall not make any irreversible or irretrievable commitment of resources with respect to the agency action which has the effect of foreclosing the formulation or implementation of any reasonable and prudent alternative measures which would not violate subsection (a)(2) of this section.

16 U.S.C. § 1536(d) (emphasis added). See 50 C.F.R. § 402.09 (prohibition is in force during the consultation process and continues until the requirements of Section 7(a)(2) are satisfied). In the OCSLA context, a lease sale is not considered an "irreversible or irretrievable commitment of resources" because the Secretary has the authority to halt any future potentially harmful activities. See, e.g., Conservation Foundation v. Andrus, 623 F.2d. 712, 715 (1st Cir. 1979); North Slope Borough v. Andrus, 642 F.2d 589, 612 (D.C. Cir. 1980). In addition, leasing activities themselves do not pose any threat to any endangered species. It is the later stages of the OCS oil and gas process that present the dangers. Exploration and development/production plans thus would result both in potentially jeopardizing activities and constitute "irreversible or irretrievable commitment of resources."

The ESA mandates that federal agencies consult with the FWS or the National Marine Fisheries Service whenever their actions may affect a species identified as endangered. 16 U.S.C. § 1536. However, this procedural duty seems only to require a level of compliance similar to that which exists in the NEPA context, with any judicial review applying the "arbitrary and capricious" standard. See, e.g., Cabinet Mountains Wilderness v. Peterson, 685 F.2d 678, 687 (D.C. Cir. 1982), in addition to the principal case.

In the context of some OCS activities, the ESA may lack any real teeth. Although the ESA will halt activities that clearly jeopardize an endangered species, e.g. TVA v. Hill, 437 U.S. 153 (1977), the risks associated with offshore oil and gas activities are usually perceived as minimal due to the low probability of occurrence. Whenever OCS activities do potentially affect endangered species, the ESA provides various mechanisms that allow projects to proceed nonetheless. E.g., 16 U.S.C. §§ 1536(b)(4) and (o) (Secretary may issue biological opinions or incidental take permits setting out certain conditions that will minimize impacts to endangered species).[4]

Note on Alaskan Natives' OCS Rights

In People of Village of Gambell v. Clark, 746 F.2d 572 (9th Cir. 1984), Alaskan natives challenged OCS oil and gas development in Norton Sound because it would adversely affect their aboriginal right to subsistence hunting and fishing. The court found this claim to be without merit, stating (incorrectly as it turned out) that even if the natives did have an aboriginal right to hunt and fish, it had been extinguished by the Alaskan Native Claims Settlement Act, 43 U.S.C. §§ 1601-1628, 1603(b). See also Inupiat Community of the Arctic Slope v. U.S., 746 F.2d 570 (9th Cir. 1984), cert. denied, 474 U.S. 820 (1985). The court (wrongly) accepted the second contention of the natives that the Alaska National Interest Land Conservation Act (ANILCA), 16 U.S.C. § 3120, applied to OCS lands and waters. In doing this, the court recognized that the Secretary of Interior had a duty to see that the utilization of the OCS for oil and gas development caused the least possible adverse impact upon rural Alaskan residents who depend upon subsistence resource uses for their survival. See Tribal Village of Akutan v. Hodel, 16 ELR 20245 (D. Ak. 1986), aff'd, 869 F.2d 1185 (9th Cir. 1988),

---

[4] Also, whenever an agency's activities would be halted by the ESA, the head of that agency can petition a special Endangered Species Committee for an exemption. The exemption available is narrowly drawn and therefore difficult to obtain. See 16 U.S.C. §§ 1536(e), (f), (g) and (h); see also 16 U.S.C. § 1536(j) (creates narrow exemption for national security purposes).

in which the district court had enjoined the Bristol Bay OCS lease sale because the Interior Secretary had applied an incorrect standard under ANILCA in approving a lease sale "unlikely" to affect subsistence life styles.

In a unanimous 9-0 decision, the Supreme Court, in Amoco Production Co. v. Village of Gambell, 480 U.S. 531 (1987), lifted an injunction that had halted exploration in Norton Sound and the Navarin Basin of the Bering Sea in connection with a dispute over native Alaskan subsistence fishing and hunting rights. Several Alaskan native villages, including Gambell and Stebbins, brought suit to enjoin the Secretary of the Interior's sale of oil and gas leases for federal outer continental shelf land off Alaska. The villages claimed that the Secretary had failed to consider the possible adverse impacts of exploration on subsistence hunting and fishing as required by section 810(a) of ANILCA, 16 U.S.C. § 3120. The U.S. District Court for the District of Alaska granted the Secretary's motion for summary judgment and the villages appealed. The Ninth Circuit affirmed in part, reversed in part, and remanded, 746 F.2d 572 (1984), upon which the District Court denied the villages' consolidated motion for a preliminary injunction. The villages again appealed and the Ninth Circuit once more reversed and remanded, granting the injunction. 774 F.2d 1414 (1985).

In the majority opinion, Justice White held that the villages were not entitled to a preliminary injunction and that ANILCA, which sets forth procedures to be followed before allowing lease, occupancy, or disposition of public lands that would significantly restrict Alaskan natives' use of lands for subsistence, does not apply to the outer continental shelf. By ANILCA's plain language, section 810(a) applies only to federal lands within the State of Alaska's boundaries, and includes coastal waters only out to the three mile limit. The Court remanded to the Ninth Circuit native claims to aboriginal rights on the OCS.

The Ninth Circuit Court of Appeals then held that the federal government's paramount interest in oil and gas leasing on the Outer Continental Shelf subordinates, but does not extinguish, aboriginal subsistence hunting and fishing rights. People of the Village of Gambell v. Hodel, 869 F.2d 1273 (9th Cir. 1989). On remand, the Ninth Circuit said the district court must decide: first, whether the native villages possess aboriginal subsistence rights in the Outer Continental Shelf; second, if so, whether oil and gas drilling will significantly interfere with those rights; and, third, whether the Outer Continental Shelf Lands Act -- which extended federal jurisdiction to the Outer Continental Shelf -- extinguishes subsistence rights in the Outer Continental Shelf as a matter of law. The court did not rule out the possibility that Alaskan natives may have aboriginal rights to offshore resources. The court found that the United States had exerted sufficient control over the Outer Continental Shelf constituting sovereignty and requiring recognition of aboriginal rights. The court said the Alaska Native Claims Settlement Act, which extinguishes certain aboriginal titles, applies to the geographical boundaries of the state but, like ANILCA, also does not apply to the Outer Continental Shelf, contrary to its earlier ruling. See also Native Village of Eyak v. Trawler Diane Marie, Inc., 154 F.3d 1090 (9th Cir. 1998), cert. denied, —U.S.— (6/14/99), finding no exclusive aboriginal rights to groundfish off Alaska.

Note on Fisheries and Offshore Oil and Gas Development

A significant threat to coastal and ocean fisheries is water pollution, particularly oil pollution. Consequently, proposals to conduct offshore oil and gas drilling in or near rich fishing grounds raise substantial public concern. An oil well blowout, such as the 1969 Santa Barbara Channel blowout, is risk inherent in offshore drilling operations. Such events however are rare. Ships and tankers, river and urban runoff, coastal refinery operations, and other sources account for over 98% of all worldwide spillage of oil into ocean waters. Staff of House Comm. on Outer Continental Shelf, 94th Cong., 2nd Sess., A Study on the Effects of Offshore Oil and Gas Development on the Coastal Zone, 132-34 (Comm. Print 1976). Nevertheless, blowouts, disposal of drilling muds, underwater noise, increased vessel traffic, and other aspects of offshore drilling are threats to the nation's fisheries and the rest of the marine environment. Thus, the nation's need for continued, assured supplies of oil and gas must be balanced against the potential short and long term damage to ocean fisheries.

As part of the Secretary of Interior's responsibilities in overseeing OCS development, the Secretary has "a duty to see that gas and oil exploration and drilling is conducted without unreasonable risk to the fisheries. His duty includes the obligation not to go forward with a lease sale in a particular area if it would create unreasonable risks in spite of all feasible safeguards." Massachusetts v. Andrus, 594 F.2d 872, 889 (1st Cir. 1979). See also 43 U.S.C. § 1334(a)(1); M. Bean, The Evolution of National Wildlife Law 177 2d ed. (1983). After issuing a lease, the Secretary may cancel it, with compensation, if

> continued activity pursuant to such lease * * * would probably cause serious harm to life (including fish and other aquatic life) * * * or the marine coastal, or human environment.

43 U.S.C. § 1334(a)(2)(A)(i). See North Slope Borough v. Andrus, 642 F.2d 589 (D.C. Cir. 1980); Conservation Law Foundation v. Andrus, 623 F.2d 712 (1st Cir. 1979).

When conflicts do arise, it is left to the Secretary to balance the competing interests. See Massachusetts v. Andrus, 594 F.2d 872, 889 (1st Cir. 1979). However, if oil and gas operations would jeopardize the continued existence of a threatened marine species or its habitat, the Endangered Species Act mandates that the project be altered or an exemption from the requirements of the act secured. 16 U.S.C. § 1536. In addition, 1986 and 1996 amendments to the Fishery Conservation and Management Act require the Interior Secretary to respond specifically and in detail to the Commerce Secretary and regional fisheries management council fishery habitat protection recommendations. 16 U.S.C. § 1855(b)(1)(c) and (4); see H. Kennedy, The 1986 Habitat Amendments to the Magnuson Act: A New Procedural Regime for Activities Affecting Fisheries Habitat, 18 Envtl. L. Rev. 339, 343-44 (1988).

Although the fate of marine life is to be considered when permitting OCS development, the need for oil and gas, the potential revenue to the federal treasury, other short-term economic and political pressures, and the lack of adequate scientific information about the impacts of OCS upon marine life may tip the balance in close cases in favor of going forward with OCS oil and gas operations. For an extensive discussion of potential conflicts between offshore oil and gas operations and fisheries, see G. Jones, Harvesting the Ocean's Resources: Oil or Fish?, 60 S. Cal. L. Rev. 587 (1987).

Notes and Questions

1. Massachusetts v. Andrus, 594 F.2d 872 (1st Cir. 1979), also illustrates a comprehensive approach to OCS litigation as in the *Akutan* case excerpted above, in addition to attacking the Department of the Interior's regulatory programs and the department's compliance with NEPA procedures, the plaintiffs utilized the mandates of specific resource protection statutes and comprehensive management programs. The conflict in federal agency mandates and priorities was argued to be a substantial barrier to OCS development. What benefits did the plaintiffs in *Andrus* gain from this new approach? Consider the following excerpt from D. Finn, Interagency Relationships in Marine Resource Conflicts: Some Lessons from OCS Oil and Gas Leasing, 4 Harv. Envtl. L. Rev. 359, 369-72 (1980):

Following the decision of the First Circuit, Interior prepared a supplemental environmental impact statement (EIS) specifically considering marine sanctuary alternatives and fisheries issues. But before the draft of this document (DSES) was circulated for public review and comment, one of the plaintiffs in the still pending litigation formally petitioned the Secretary of Commerce to designate Georges Bank as a marine sanctuary. The petition requested that the entire Georges Bank area be designated as a sanctuary and called for undefined but strict regulation of all potentially conflicting activities to make fisheries production and conservation the primary objectives of federal management of the area. After receiving the sanctuary nomination, NOAA which had previously submitted critical comments on the proposed sale and accompanying environmental analyses selected Georges Bank as an "active candidate" for designation as a marine sanctuary. It then provided its comments on the DSES to Interior, specifically directing Interior's attention to the sanctuary nomination and finding Interior's discussion of the marine sanctuary alternative inadequate.

NOAA then published an "issue paper" discussing the merits of designating Georges Bank as a marine sanctuary. This paper became the basis for a series of public workshops held to consider the nomination. The chief management alternative presented in the issue paper was to designate all of Georges Bank as a sanctuary. NOAA would allow oil and gas operations in areas included in Lease Sale No. 42, but would subject such operations to additional regulations, which would presumably be similar to the additional actions that NOAA had proposed Interior should take if a sanctuary were not designated.

In response to NOAA's actions on the marine sanctuary petition, Interior claimed that it had "exclusive authority" under the amended OCSLA to ensure that oil and gas activities would not unduly affect the marine resources of the area. Interior argued that any attempt by NOAA to designate Georges Bank as a sanctuary, before experience under lease indicated that such resources were actually being injured, would be an attempt to "preempt" Interior's primary regulatory authority. Interior pointed out that it already had a mandate under the amended OCSLA to ensure that "oil and gas exploration and development are conducted without unreasonable risk to the fisheries and the other resources * * *" and "to assure environmental protection." * * *

For several weeks, Interior and NOAA proceeded with their separate plans for management of Georges Bank while conducting negotiations toward a unified position. On September 21, 1979, the Departments of the Interior and Commerce announced an agreement under which Interior would adopt certain additional safeguards: NOAA would withdraw Georges Bank as an active candidate for marine sanctuary designation; and Interior, NOAA, and the Environmental Protection Agency (EPA) would draw up a memorandum of understanding for continued interagency coordination.

In most respects, the agreement between NOAA and Interior was a victory for Interior. In its comments on the DSES, NOAA had presented a strong case that there would be an unreasonable risk to commercial fishery resources and endangered whales if its recommendations were not followed. Under the agreement, however, few of NOAA's recommendations were adopted.

* * *

The plaintiffs in the still pending litigation challenged both the substantive adequacy of the agreed measures and the procedural validity of the actions of Interior and NOAA. They claimed that both Interior and NOAA had failed to give proper consideration to the possible nomination of Georges Bank as a sanctuary. Indeed, the plaintiffs claimed that NOAA's failure to proceed further on the nomination petition itself was a "major federal action" requiring preparation of an EIS. Finally, the plaintiffs sought to prevent Interior from "interfering" further with NOAA's sanctuary designation process. They argued that these deficiencies rendered the lease sale proposal defective and should prevent the sale until Interior and NOAA had adequately discharged their responsibilities.

The plaintiffs were unsuccessful in asserting these claims in their motion for a new preliminary injunction delaying the sale then scheduled for November 6, 1979. The District Court concluded that Interior had adequately considered the marine sanctuary alternative and that NOAA had acted within its discretion in concluding its agreement with Interior.

On appeal the Circuit Court agreed that Interior had adequately discharged its responsibility to analyze the environmental aspects of the proposed sale, including the marine sanctuary alternative. The court also indicated that NOAA's actions regarding the sanctuary supported the proposition that the Secretary of Interior had adequate opportunity to consider the marine sanctuary alternative.

On December 22, 1980 the district court accepted an agreement between the parties in Massachusetts v. Andrus:

Terms of Agreement

The settlement agreement gives the state and the conservation group access to federal studies already done, underway, or planned in the future on Georges Bank. "This allows us more convenient access to scientific work before it is formally released," according to Douglas Foy, executive director of the Conservation Law Foundation.

The agreement also commits the National Oceanic and Atmospheric Administration of the Commerce Department to re-evaluate the nomination of a proposed marine sanctuary for the area, with recommendations due by Dec 1, 1981. The marine sanctuary proposal was dropped when Interior and Commerce agreed on the Georges Bank plan last year.

Under the settlement, the use of best available and safest technology will be required for all drilling operations on the Georges Bank. The agreement requires Interior to develop new standards defining best available and safest technology for drilling operations before such activities are approved.

Finally, the settlement requires Interior to make a "good faith consideration" for approval and funding of all future study recommendations by the Biological Task Force, which was set up to protect the rich fishery resources in the area. Interior must give the plaintiffs specific reasoning for its final determinations on Biological Task Force recommendations and must apprise the plaintiffs each time it decides whether to do an environmental impact statement on development and production plans.

Stephen Leonard, chief of the environmental protection division in the Massachusetts Attorney General's office, stated that 22 oil companies challenged the settlement in court because they wanted the lawsuit dismissed and did not want approval of the agreement.

"The challenge to legality of Lease Sale 42 is over," Leonard said, but the state and the conservation group will watch carefully and challenge, if necessary, the ocean discharge permits to be issued by the Environmental Protection Agency for drilling wastes, exploration plans to be approved by Interior, and endangered species findings to be submitted by NOAA.

Reactions to Settlement

"We feel we have accomplished what we set out to do when we filed this three years ago. We've made sure that at this pre-drilling stage a number of mechanisms are set up to protect Georges Bank from environmental damage," Foy said. However "this is not the end of the battle over the quality of protection for fisheries on Georges Bank. This was the first round in an extended series of efforts to force adequate protection," he concluded.

Massachusetts Attorney General Francis X. Bellotti * * * said the agreement is the latest in a "long legal process by which we have assured that everything possible is being done to protect this extraordinary natural resource."

Interior Secretary Cecil Andrus said, "I believe the agreement we have reached with the Commonwealth of Massachusetts and the other plaintiffs provides for a resolution of this litigation in the best interests of all concerned."

A petroleum industry spokesman * * * told BNA, "It sounds like the Justice Department has given away the store in agreeing to this out-of-court settlement. The specifics of the settlement will certainly provide the Conservation Law Foundation with more opportunities for litigating the approval of exploration, development, and production plans."

Oil and gas exploration is to begin along the bank in 1981, but it will be years before oil actually flows from the area, according to Leonard.

15 Envtl. Rptr. 1347 (1981). See D. Finn, Georges Bank: The Legal Issues, 23 Oceanus 30 (1980). In the end, what did the plaintiffs gain from their efforts to protect fishing on Georges Bank?

2. Should federal agencies be allowed to resolve disputes over OCS development without interference from the courts?

Another issue raised by interagency relationships is the possibility of informal resolution of such conflicts within the executive branch, with no opportunity for public scrutiny or participation. In the Georges Bank case, for example, NOAA's comments on Interior's FSES and statements made by its own Administrator indicated that the agency opposed the lease sale, believing that it would present an unreasonable risk to fisheries and a potential hazard to endangered whales. A marine sanctuary designation could have diminished these dangers; thus NOAA should have continued with the designation process. At the very least, preparation of a draft EIS on marine sanctuary alternatives would have put the agency in a better position to determine whether designation of a marine sanctuary was justified.   There is some reason, therefore, to question whether NOAA performed its responsibility to implement the Marine Sanctuaries Act in good faith.

D. Finn, Interagency Relationships in Marine Resource Conflicts: Some Lessons from OCS Oil and Gas Leasing, 4 Harv. Envtl. L. Rev. 359, 377 (1980).

3. Should U.S. ocean areas be managed on a regional area-wide, multiple-use basis to reduce conflicts like Massachusetts v. Andrus? See B. Cicin-Sain, M. Hershman, R. Hildreth and I. Isaacs, Improving Ocean Management Capacity in the Pacific Coast Region: State and Regional Perspectives (1990); R. Hildreth, Regional Ocean Resources Management, Coastal Zone '91 Proceedings 2583 (1991).

4. What are the onshore impacts of offshore oil drilling? Are the effects positive or negative? What mechanisms are available to state and local governments for planning and controlling onshore impacts? NEPA? The public trust doctrine? See Atlantic Richfield Co. v. State Lands Comm'n, 21 ELR 21320 (Cal. Super. Los Angeles County, Jan. 24, 1990); Boone v. Kingsbury, 206 Cal. 148, 273 p. 797 (1928), cert. denied; Workman v. Boone, 280 U.S. 517 (1929); Coastal Petroleum v. Chiles, 701 So.2d 619 (Fla. App. 1997), cert. denied, 118 S. Ct. 2369 (1998); R. Hildreth, The Public Trust Doctrine and Ocean and Coastal Resources Management, 8 J. of Envtl. L. & Litigation 221 (1993); R. Hildreth, Marine Use Conflicts Arising from Development of Seabed Hydrocarbon and Minerals: Some Approaches from the United States West Coast, 12 Ocean & Shoreline Management 271 (1989); R. Hildreth, The Public Trust Doctrine and Conflict Resolution in Coastal Waters: West Coast Developments, Coastal Zone '89 Proceedings 2604 (1989). The state navigation servitude? State coastal zone management programs? See Western Oil and Gas Association v. Sonoma County, 905 F.2d 1287 (9th Cir. 1990) (land use ordinances in California that regulate onshore facilities used to support offshore oil and gas development were not subject to challenge by the oil industry association because the plaintiffs had not demonstrated that the ordinances will interfere with their bidding rights for OCS leases); Louisiana v. Lujan, 777 F. Supp. 486 (E.D. La. 1991) (rejecting the state's challenge to a Gulf of Mexico lease sale based on negative impacts on coastal wetlands and inadequately estimated socioeconomic impacts onshore).

5. Outer Continental Shelf Lands Act Section 8(g). In a 1984 case with important political and fiscal implications, a federal district court in Texas was called upon to decide what was meant by a "fair and equitable" division of revenues from OCS oil and gas produced from so called "8(g)" lands. Texas v. Secretary of the Interior, 580 F. Supp. 1197 (E.D. Tex. 1984); see 43 U.S.C. 1337(g)(4). At stake in the litigation was $1 billion. 8(g) lands are the innermost three mile strip of federal offshore lands which lies immediately adjacent to state owned offshore lands. Texas argued that the just and equitable division of monies from these lands should be made after a broad analysis, taking into account things such as the onshore economic impacts of offshore development and the enhancement in value of federal tracts that has occurred because of prior state offshore leasing. The Secretary of Interior claimed that only a single factor should be used in determining a "fair and equitable" allocation of 8(g) monies, that being the drainage of oil and gas from beneath state lands. The court sided with Texas as to which approach should be used, and based upon the facts and circumstances presented in the immediate case, called for a 50/50 division of the 8(g) monies between Texas and the federal government.

Section 8(g) was amended in 1986. Future bonuses, rentals and royalties subject to 8(g) would also be split 73%-federal, 27%-states, except that future royalties from existing 8(g) leases would be distributed on the basis of surface acreage actually within three miles of state waters but at a 50% rate. Could amended section 8(g) reduce tensions between the federal and state governments over OCS oil and gas development? See Alabama v. U.S. Dept. of Interior, 84 F.3d 410 (11th Cir. 1996). See generally R. Hildreth, Federal-State Offshore Revenue Sharing Deserves Attention and Expansion, 21 Ocean Devel. and Int'l L. 241 (1990); R. Hildreth, Federal-State Revenue Sharing and Resource Management Under Outer Continental Shelf Lands Act Section 8(g), 17 Coastal Management 171 (1989).

(2.) Suspension and Termination of OCS Lease Rights

(a.) Exploration Stage

MOBIL OIL EXPLORATION & PRODUCING SOUTHEAST, INC. v. UNITED STATES
The Supreme Court of the United States, 2000
530 U.S. 604

JUSTICE BREYER delivered the opinion of the Court.

Two oil companies, petitioners here, seek restitution of $156 million they paid the Government in return for lease contracts giving them rights to explore for and develop oil off the North Carolina coast. The rights were not absolute, but were conditioned on the companies' obtaining a set of further governmental permissions. The companies claim that the Government repudiated the contracts when it denied them certain elements of the permission-seeking opportunities that the contracts had promised. We agree that the Government broke its promise; it repudiated the contracts; and it must give the companies their money back.

I

A

A description at the outset of the few basic contract law principles applicable to this case will help the reader understand the significance of the complex factual circumstances that follow. "When the United States enters into contract relations, its rights and duties therein are governed generally by the law applicable to contracts between private individuals." *United States v. Winstar Corp.*, 518 U.S. 839, 895, 116 S.Ct. 2432, 135 L.Ed.2d 964 (1996) (plurality opinion) (internal quotation marks omitted). The Restatement of Contracts reflects many of the principles of contract law that are applicable to this case. As set forth in the Restatement of Contracts, the relevant principles specify that, when one party to a contract repudiates that contract, the other party "is entitled to restitution for any benefit that he has conferred on" the repudiating party "by way of part performance or reliance." Restatement (Second) of Contracts § 373 (1979) (hereinafter Restatement). The Restatement explains that "repudiation" is a "statement by the obligor to the obligee indicating that the obligor will commit a breach that would of itself give the obligee a claim for damages for total breach." *Id.,* § 250. And "total breach" is a breach that "so substantially impairs the value of the contract to the injured party at the time of the breach that it is just in the circumstances to allow him to recover damages based on all his remaining rights to performance." *Id.,* § 243.

As applied to this case, these principles amount to the following: If the Government said it would break, or did break, an important contractual promise, thereby "substantially impair[ing] the value of the contract[s]" to the companies, *ibid.,* then (unless the companies waived their rights to restitution) the Government must give the companies their money back. And it must do so whether the contracts would, or would not, ultimately have proved financially beneficial to the companies. The Restatement illustrates this point as follows:

"A contracts to sell a tract of land to B for $100,000. After B has made a part payment of $20,000, A wrongfully refuses to transfer title. B can recover the $20,000 in restitution. The result is the same even if the market price of the land is only $70,000, so that performance would have been disadvantageous to B." *Id.,* § 373, Comment *a,* Illustration 1.

B

In 1981, in return for up-front "bonus" payments to the United States of about $158 million (plus annual rental payments), the companies received 10-year renewable lease contracts with the United States. In these contracts, the United States promised the companies, among other things, that they could explore for oil off the North Carolina coast and develop any oil that they found (subject to further royalty payments) provided that the companies received exploration and development permissions in accordance with various statutes and regulations to which the lease contracts were made "subject." * * * The statutes and regulations, the terms of which in effect were incorporated into the contracts, made clear that obtaining the necessary permissions might not be an easy matter. In particular, the Outer Continental Shelf Lands Act (OCSLA), 67 Stat. 462, as amended, 43 U.S.C. § 1331 *et seq.* (1994 ed. and Supp. III), and the Coastal Zone Management Act of 1972 (CZMA), 16 U.S.C. § 1451 *et seq.,* specify that leaseholding companies wishing to explore and drill must successfully complete the following four procedures.

First, a company must prepare and obtain Department of the Interior approval for a Plan of Exploration. 43 U.S.C. § 1340(c). Interior must approve a submitted Exploration Plan unless it finds, after "consider[ing] available relevant environmental information," § 1346(d), that the proposed exploration

"would probably cause serious harm or damage to life (including fish and other aquatic life), to property, to any mineral * * *, to the national security or defense, or to the marine, coastal, or human environment." § 1334(a)(2)(A)(i).

Where approval is warranted, Interior must act quickly--within " thirty days" of the company's submission of a proposed Plan. § 1340(c)(1).

Second, the company must obtain an exploratory well drilling permit. To do so, it must certify (under CZMA) that its Exploration Plan is consistent with the coastal zone management program of each affected State.   16 U.S.C. §   1456(c)(3).   If a State objects, the certification fails, unless the Secretary of Commerce overrides the State's objection.   If Commerce rules against the State, then Interior may grant the permit. § 1456(c)(3)(A).

Third, where waste discharge into ocean waters is at issue, the company must obtain a National Pollutant Discharge Elimination System permit from the Environmental Protection Agency. 33 U.S.C. § § 1311(a), 1342(a).   It can obtain this permit only if affected States agree that its Exploration Plan is consistent with the state coastal zone management programs or (as just explained) the Secretary of Commerce overrides the state objections. 16 U.S.C. § 1456.

Fourth, if exploration is successful, the company must prepare, and obtain Interior approval for, a Development and Production Plan--a Plan that describes the proposed drilling and related environmental safeguards. 43 U.S.C. § 1351. Again, Interior's approval is conditioned upon certification that the Plan is consistent with state coastal zone management plans--a certification to which States can object, subject to Commerce Department override. § 1351(a)(3).

C

The events at issue here concern the first two steps of the process just described--Interior's consideration of a submitted Exploration Plan and the companies' submission of the CZMA "consistency certification" necessary to obtain an exploratory well drilling permit.   The relevant circumstances are the following:

1. In 1981, the companies and the Government entered into the lease contracts.   The companies paid the Government $158 million in up-front cash "bonus" payments.

2. In 1989, the companies, Interior, and North Carolina entered into a memorandum of understanding. In that memorandum, the companies promised that they would submit an initial draft Exploration Plan to North Carolina before they submitted their final Exploration Plan to Interior.   Interior promised that it would prepare an environmental report on the initial draft.   It also agreed to suspend the companies' annual lease payments (about $250,000 per year) while the companies prepared the initial draft and while any state objections to the companies' CZMA consistency certifications were being worked out, with the life of each lease being extended accordingly.

3. In September 1989, the companies submitted their initial draft

Exploration Plan to North Carolina.   Ten months later, Interior issued the promised ("informal" pre-submission) environmental report, after a review which all parties concede was "extensive and intensive." App. 179 (deposition of David Courtland O'Neal, former Assistant Secretary of the Interior) (agreeing that the review was "the most extensive and intensive" ever "afforded an exploration well in the outer continental shelf (OCS) program").   Interior concluded that the proposed exploration would not "significantly affec[t]" the marine environment or "the quality of the human environment." *Id.,* at 138-140 (U.S. Dept. of Interior Minerals Management Service, Environmental Assessment of Exploration Plan for Manteo Area Block 467 (Sept.1990)).

4. On August 20, 1990, the companies submitted both their final Exploration Plan and their CZMA "consistency certification" to Interior.

5. Just two days earlier, on August 18, 1990, a new law, the Outer Banks Protection Act (OBPA), § 6003, 104 Stat. 555, had come into effect. That law prohibited the Secretary of the Interior from approving any Exploration Plan or Development and Production Plan or to award any drilling permit until (a) a new OBPA-created Environmental Sciences Review Panel had reported to the Secretary, (b) the Secretary had certified to Congress that he had sufficient information to make these OCSLA-required approval decisions, and (c) Congress had been in session an additional 45 days, but (d) in no event could he issue an approval or permit for the next 13 months (until October 1991). § 6003(c)(3).   OBPA also required the Secretary, in his certification, to explain and justify in detail any differences between his own certified conclusions and the new Panel's recommendations.   § 6003(c)(3)(A)(ii)(II).

6. About five weeks later, and in light of the new statute, Interior wrote a letter to the Governor of North Carolina with a copy to petitioner Mobil.   It said that the final submitted Exploration Plan "is deemed to be approvable in all respects."   It added:

> "[W]e are required to approve an Exploration Plan unless it is inconsistent with applicable law or because it would result in serious harm to the environment.   Because we have found that Mobil's Plan fully complies with the law and will have only negligible effect on the environment, we are not authorized to disapprove the Plan or require its modification." App. to Pet. for Cert. in No. 99-253, at 194a (letter from Regional Director Bruce Weetman to the Honorable James G. Martin, Governor of North Carolina, dated Sept. 28, 1996).

But, it noted, the new law, the "Outer Banks Protection Act (OBPA) of 1990 ... prohibits the approval of any Exploration Plan at this time." It concluded, "because we are currently prohibited from approving it, the Plan will remain on file until the requirements of the OBPA are met." In the meantime a "suspension has been granted to all leases offshore the State of North Carolina." *Ibid.* See also App. 129-131 (letter from Lawrence H. Ake, Minerals Management Service, to William C. Whittemore, Mobil Exploration & Producing U.S. Inc., dated Sept. 21, 1990 (notice of suspension of leases, citing 30 CFR § 250.10(b)(7) (1990) as the basis for the suspensions)).

About 18 months later, the Secretary of the Interior, after receiving the new Panel's report, certified to Congress that he had enough information to consider the companies' Exploration Plan. He added, however, that he would not consider the Plan until he received certain further studies that the new Panel had recommended.

7. In November 1990, North Carolina objected to the companies' CZMA consistency certification on the ground that Mobil had not provided sufficient information about possible environmental impact. A month later, the companies asked the Secretary of Commerce to override North Carolina's objection.

8. In 1994, the Secretary of Commerce rejected the companies' override request, relying in large part on the fact that the new Panel had found a lack of adequate information in respect to certain environmental issues.

9. In 1996, Congress repealed OBPA. § 109, 110 Stat. 1321-177.

D

In October 1992, after all but the two last-mentioned events had taken place, petitioners joined a breach-of-contract lawsuit brought in the Court of Federal Claims. On motions for summary judgment, the court found that the United States had broken its contractual promise to follow OCSLA's provisions, in particular the provision requiring Interior to approve an Exploration Plan that satisfied OCSLA's requirements within 30 days of its submission to Interior. The United States thereby repudiated the contracts. And that repudiation entitled the companies to restitution of the up-front cash "bonus" payments it had made. *Conoco Inc. v. United States,* 35 Fed.Cl. 309 (1996).

A panel of the Court of Appeals for the Federal Circuit reversed, one judge dissenting. The panel held that the Government's refusal to consider the companies' final Exploration Plan was not the "operative cause" of any failure to carry out the contracts' terms because the State's objection to the companies' CZMA "consistency statement" would have prevented the companies from exploring regardless. 177 F.3d 1331 (C.A.Fed.1999).

We granted certiorari to review the Federal Circuit's decision.

II

The record makes clear (1) that OCSLA required Interior to approve "within thirty days" a submitted Exploration Plan that satisfies OCSLA's requirements, (2) that Interior told Mobil the companies' submitted Plan met those requirements, (3) that Interior told Mobil it would not approve the companies' submitted Plan for at least 13 months, and likely longer, and (4) that Interior did not approve (or disapprove) the Plan, ever. The Government does not deny that the contracts, made "pursuant to" and "subject to" OCSLA, incorporated OCSLA provisions as promises. The Government further concedes, as it must, that relevant contract law entitles a contracting party to restitution if the other party "substantially" breached a contract or communicated its intent to do so. See Restatement § 373(1); 11 W. Jaeger, Williston on Contracts § 1312, p. 109 (3d ed.1968) (hereinafter Williston); 5 A. Corbin, Contracts § 1104, p. 560 (1964); see also *Ankeny v. Clark,* 148 U.S. 345, 353, 13 S.Ct. 617, 37 L.Ed. 475 (1893). Yet the Government denies that it must refund the companies' money.

This is because, in the Government's view, it did not breach the contracts or communicate its intent to do so; any breach was not "substantial"; and the companies waived their rights to restitution regardless. We shall consider each of these arguments in turn.

A

The Government's "no breach" arguments depend upon the contract provisions that "subject" the contracts to various statutes and regulations. Those provisions state that the contracts are "subject to" (1) OCSLA, (2) "Sections 302 and 303 of the Department of Energy Organization Act," (3) "all regulations issued pursuant to such statutes and in existence upon the effective date of" the contracts, (4) "all regulations issued pursuant to such statutes in the future which provide for the prevention of waste and the conservation" of Outer Continental Shelf resources, and (5) "all other applicable statutes and regulations." * * * The Government says that these provisions incorporate into the contracts, not only the OCSLA provisions we have mentioned, but also certain other statutory provisions and regulations that, in the Government's view, granted Interior the legal authority to refuse to approve the submitted Exploration Plan, while suspending the leases instead.

First, the Government refers to 43 U.S.C. § 1334(a)(1)(A), an OCSLA provision that authorizes the Secretary to promulgate regulations providing for "the suspension * * * of any operation or activity * * * *at the request of a lessee,* in the national interest, to facilitate proper development of a lease." (Emphasis added.) This provision, as the emphasized terms show, requires "the request of a lessee," *i.e.,* the companies. The Government does not explain how this requirement was satisfied here. Hence, the Government cannot rely upon the provision.

Second, the Government refers to 30 CFR § 250.110(b)(4) (1999), formerly codified at 30 CFR § 250.10(b)(4) (1997), a regulation stating that "[t]he Regional Supervisor may * * * direct * * * a suspension of any operation or activity * * * [when the] suspension is necessary for the implementation of the requirements of the National Environmental Policy Act or to conduct an environmental analysis." The Government says that this regulation permitted the Secretary of the Interior to suspend the companies' leases because that suspension was "necessary * * * to conduct an environmental analysis," namely, the analysis demanded by the new statute, OBPA.

The "environmental analysis" referred to, however, is an analysis the need for which was created by OBPA, a later enacted statute. The lease contracts say that they are subject to then-existing regulations and to certain future regulations, those issued pursuant to OCSLA and § § 302 and 303 of the Department of Energy Organization Act. This explicit reference to future regulations makes it clear that the catchall provision that references "all other applicable * * * regulations," *supra,* at 2433, must include only statutes and regulations already existing at the time of the contract, see 35 Fed.Cl., at 322–323, a conclusion not questioned here by the Government. Hence, these provisions mean that the contracts are not subject to future regulations promulgated under other statutes, such as new statutes like OBPA. Without some such contractual provision limiting the Government's power to impose new and different requirements, the companies would have spent $158 million to buy next to nothing. In any event, the Court of Claims so interpreted the lease; the Federal Circuit did not disagree with that interpretation; nor does the Government here dispute it.

Instead, the Government points out that the regulation in

question--the regulation authorizing a governmental suspension in order to conduct "an environmental analysis"--was not itself a *future* regulation. Rather, a similar regulation existed at the time the parties signed the contracts, 30 CFR § 250.12(a)(iv) (1981), and, in any event, it was promulgated under OCSLA, a statute exempted from the contracts' temporal restriction. But that fact, while true, is not sufficient to produce the incorporation of future statutory requirements, which is what the Government needs to prevail. If the pre- existing regulation's words, "an environmental analysis," were to apply to analyses mandated by *future* statutes, then they would make the companies subject to the same unknown future requirements that the contracts' specific temporal restrictions were intended to avoid. Consequently, whatever the regulation's words might mean in other contexts, we believe the contracts before us must be interpreted as excluding the words "environmental analysis" *insofar as* those words would incorporate the requirements of future statutes and future regulations excluded by the contracts' provisions. Hence, they would not incorporate into the contracts requirements imposed by a new statute such as OBPA.

Third, the Government refers to OCSLA, 43 U.S.C. § 1334(a)(1), which, after granting Interior rulemaking authority, says that Interior's "regulations * * * shall include * * * provisions * * * for the suspension * * * of any operation * * * pursuant to any lease * * * *if there is a threat of serious,* irreparable, or immediate *harm* or damage to life * * * , to property, to any mineral deposits * * * , or to the marine, coastal, or *human environment.*" (Emphasis added.)

The Government points to the OBPA Conference Report, which says that any OBPA-caused delay is "related to * * * environmental protection" and to the need "for the collection and analysis of crucial oceanographic, ecological, and socioeconomic data," to "prevent a public harm." H.R. Conf. Rep. No. 101-653, p. 163 (1990), U.S.Code Cong. & Admin.News 1990, pp. 722, 842; see also Brief for United States 32. At oral argument, the Government noted that the OBPA mentions "tourism" in North Carolina as a "major industry * * * which is subject to potentially significant disruption by offshore oil or gas development." § 6003(b)(3). From this, the Government infers that the pre-existing OCSLA provision authorized the suspension in light of a "threat of * * * serious harm" to a "human environment."

The fatal flaw in this argument, however, arises out of the Interior Department's own statement--a statement made when citing OBPA to explain its approval delay. Interior then said that the Exploration Plan "fully complies" with current legal requirements. And the OCSLA statutory provision quoted above was the most pertinent of those current requirements. * * * The Government did not deny the accuracy of Interior's statement, either in its brief filed here or its brief filed in the Court of Appeals. Insofar as the Government means to suggest that the new statute, OBPA, *changed* the relevant OCSLA standard (or that OBPA language and history somehow constitute findings Interior must incorporate by reference), it must mean that OBPA in effect created a *new* requirement. For the reasons set out * * * however, any such new requirement would not be incorporated into the contracts.

Finally, we note that Interior itself, when imposing the lengthy approval delay, did not rely upon any of the regulations to which the Government now refers. Rather, it relied upon, and cited, a different regulation, 30 CFR § 250.110(b)(7) (1999), which gives Interior the power to suspend leases when "necessary to comply with judicial decrees prohibiting production or any other operation or activity." The Government concedes that no judicial decree was involved in this case and does not rely upon this regulation here.

We conclude, for these reasons, that the Government violated the contracts. Indeed, as Interior pointed out in its letter to North Carolina, the new statute, OBPA, *required* Interior to impose the contract-violating delay. See App. 129 ("The [OBPA] contains provisions that specifically prohibit the Minerals Management Service from approving any Exploration Plan, approving any Application for Permit to Drill, or permitting any drilling offshore the State of North Carolina until at least October 1, 1991"). It therefore made clear to Interior and to the companies that the United States had to violate the contracts' terms and would continue to do so.

Moreover, OBPA changed pre-existing contract-incorporated requirements in several ways. It delayed approval, not only of an Exploration Plan but also of Development and Production Plans; and it delayed the issuance of drilling permits as well. It created a new type of Interior Department environmental review that had not previously existed, conducted by the newly created Environmental Sciences Review Panel; and, by insisting that the Secretary explain in detail any differences between the Secretary's findings and those of the Panel, it created a kind of presumption in favor of the new Panel's findings.

The dissent argues that only the statements contained in the letter from Interior to the companies may constitute a repudiation because "the enactment of legislation is not typically conceived of as a 'statement' of anything to any one party in particular," and a repudiation requires a "statement by the obligor to the obligee indicating that the obligor will commit a breach." *Post,* * * * n. 4 (quoting Restatement §

250). But if legislation passed by Congress and signed by the President is not a "statement by the obligor," it is difficult to imagine what would constitute such a statement. In this case, it was the United States who was the "obligor" to the contract.   See App. to Pet. for Cert. in No. 99-253, at 174a (lease, identifying "the United States of America" as the "Lessor"). Although the dissent points out that legislation is "addressed to the public at large," *post,* * * * n. 4, that "public" includes those to whom the United States had contractual obligations.   If the dissent means to invoke a special exception such as the "sovereign acts" doctrine, which treats certain laws as if they simply created conditions of impossibility, see *Winstar,* 518 U.S., at 891- 899, 116 S.Ct. 2432 (principal opinion of SOUTER, J.), 923-924, 116 S.Ct. 2432 (SCALIA, J., concurring in judgment), it cannot do so here. The Court of Federal Claims rejected the application of that doctrine to this case, see and the Government has not contested that determination here.   Hence, under these circumstances, the fact that Interior's repudiation rested upon the enactment of a new statute makes no significant difference.

We do not say that the changes made by the statute were unjustified.   We say only that they were changes of a kind that the contracts did not foresee.   They were changes in those approval procedures and standards that the contracts had incorporated through cross-reference. The Government has not convinced us that Interior's actions were authorized by any other contractually cross- referenced provision.   Hence, in communicating to the companies its intent to follow OBPA, the United States was communicating its intent to violate the contracts.

B

The Government next argues that any violation of the contracts' terms was not significant;   hence there was no "substantial" or "material" breach that could have amounted to a "repudiation."   In particular, it says that OCSLA's 30-day approval period "does not function as the 'essence' of these agreements." Brief for United States 37.   The Court of Claims concluded, however, that timely and fair consideration of a submitted Exploration Plan was a "necessary reciprocal obligation," indeed, that any "contrary interpretation would render the bargain illusory." 35 Fed.Cl., at 327. We agree.

We recognize that the lease contracts gave the companies more than rights to obtain approvals. They also gave the companies rights to explore for, and to develop, oil.   But the need to obtain Government approvals so qualified the likely future enjoyment of the exploration and development rights that the contract, in practice, amounted primarily to an *opportunity* to try to obtain exploration and development rights in accordance with the procedures and under the standards specified in the cross-referenced statutes and regulations. Under these circumstances, if the companies did not at least buy a promise that the Government would not deviate significantly from those procedures and standards, then what did they buy? Cf. *id.*, at 324 (the companies bought exclusive rights to explore and develop oil "*if they met* " OCSLA requirements (emphasis added)).

The Government's modification of the contract-incorporated processes was not technical or insubstantial. It did not announce an (OBPA-required) approval delay of a few days or weeks, but of 13 months minimum, and likely much longer. The delay turned out to be at least four years. And lengthy delays matter, particularly where several successive agency approvals are at stake. Whether an applicant approaches Commerce with an Interior Department approval already in hand can make a difference (as can failure to have obtained that earlier approval). Moreover, as we have pointed out, OBPA changed the contract-referenced procedures in several other ways as well. * * *

The upshot is that, under the contracts, the incorporated procedures and standards amounted to a gateway to the companies' enjoyment of all other rights. To significantly narrow that gateway violated material conditions in the contracts. The breach was "substantia[l]," depriving the companies of the benefit of their bargain. Restatement § 243. And the Government's communication of its intent to commit that breach amounted to a repudiation of the contracts.

C

The Government argues that the companies waived their rights to restitution. It does not deny that the United States repudiated the contracts *if* (as we have found) OBPA's changes amounted to a substantial breach. The Government does not claim that the United States retracted its repudiation. Cf. *id.*, § 256 (retraction will nullify the effects of repudiation if done before the other party either changes position in reliance on the retraction or communicates that it considers the repudiation to be final). It cannot claim that the companies waived their rights simply by urging performance. *Id.*, § 257 (the injured party "does not change the effect of a repudiation by urging the repudiator to perform in spite of his repudiation"); see also 11 Williston § 1334, at 177-178. Nor has the Government convinced us that the companies' continued actions under the contracts amount to anything more than this urging of performance. See 2 E. Farnsworth, Contracts § 8.22, p.

544 (2d ed.1998) (citing *United Cal. Bank v. Prudential Ins. Co.,* 140 Ariz. 238, 282-283, 681 P.2d 390, 433-434 (App.1983) (urging performance and making "efforts of its own to fulfill the conditions" of the contract come to the same thing)); cf. 11 Williston § 1337, at 186-187. Consequently the Government's waiver claim must come down to a claim that the companies *received* at least partial performance. Indeed, acceptance of performance under a once-repudiated contract can constitute a waiver of the right to restitution that repudiation would otherwise create. Restatement § 373, Comment *a;* cf. Restatement of Restitution § 68, Comment *b* (1936).

The United States points to three events that, in its view, amount to continued performance of the contracts. But it does not persuade us. First, the oil companies submitted their Exploration Plan to Interior two days *after* OBPA became law. * * * The performance question, however, is not just about what the oil companies did or requested, but also about what they actually received from the Government. And, in respect to the Exploration Plan, the companies received nothing.

Second, the companies subsequently asked the Secretary of Commerce to overturn North Carolina's objection to the companies' CZMA consistency certification. And, although the Secretary's eventual response was negative, the companies did at least receive that reply. * * * The Secretary did not base his reply, however, upon application of the contracts' standards, but instead relied in large part on the findings of the new, OBPA-created, Environmental Sciences Review Panel. See App. 224, 227, n. 35, 232-233, 239, 244 (citing the Panel's report). Consequently, we cannot say that the companies received from Commerce the kind of consideration for which their contracts called.

Third, the oil companies received suspensions of their leases (suspending annual rents and extending lease terms) pending the OBPA-mandated approval delays. * * * However, a separate contract--the 1989 memorandum of understanding--entitled the companies to receive these suspensions. See App. to Brief for United States 2a (letter from Toni D. Hennike, Counsel, Mobil Exploration & Producing U.S. Inc., to Ralph Melancon, Regional Supervisor, U.S. Dept. of Interior Minerals Management Service, dated Feb. 21, 1995 (quoting the memorandum as a basis for the requested suspensions)). And the Government has provided no convincing reason why we should consider the suspensions to amount to significant performance of the lease contracts in question.

We conclude that the companies did not receive significant postrepudiation performance. We consequently find that they did not waive their right to restitution.

D

Finally, the Government argues that repudiation could not have hurt the companies. Since the companies could not have met the CZMA consistency requirements, they could not have explored (or ultimately drilled) for oil in any event. Hence, OBPA caused them no damage. As the Government puts it, the companies have already received "such damages as were actually caused by the [Exploration Plan approval] delay," namely, none. Brief for United States 43-44; see also 177 F.3d, at 1340. This argument, however, misses the basic legal point. The oil companies do not seek damages for breach of contract. They seek restitution of their initial payments. Because the Government repudiated the lease contracts, the law entitles the companies to that restitution whether the contracts would, or would not, ultimately have produced a financial gain or led them to obtain a definite right to explore. See * * * If a lottery operator fails to deliver a purchased ticket, the purchaser can get his money back--whether or not he eventually would have won the lottery. And if one party to a contract, whether oil company or ordinary citizen, advances the other party money, principles of restitution normally require the latter, upon repudiation, to refund that money. Restatement § 373.

III

Contract law expresses no view about the wisdom of OBPA. We have examined only that statute's consistency with the promises that the earlier contracts contained. We find that the oil companies gave the United States $158 million in return for a contractual promise to follow the terms of pre-existing statutes and regulations. The new statute prevented the Government from keeping that promise. The breach "substantially impair[ed] the value of the contract[s]." *Id.,* § 243. And therefore the Government must give the companies their money back.

For these reasons, the judgment of the Federal Circuit is reversed. We remand the cases for further proceedings consistent with this opinion.

It is so ordered.

JUSTICE STEVENS, *dissenting.*

Since the 1953 passage of the Outer Continental Shelf Lands Act

(OCSLA), 43 U.S.C. § 1331 *et seq.,* the United States Government has conducted more than a hundred lease sales of the type at stake today, and bidders have paid the United States more than $55 billion for the opportunity to develop the mineral resources made available under those leases. The United States, as lessor, and petitioners, as lessees, clearly had a mutual interest in the successful exploration, development, and production of oil in the Manteo Unit pursuant to the leases executed in 1981. If production were achieved, the United States would benefit both from the substantial royalties it would receive and from the significant addition to the Nation's energy supply. Self-interest, as well as its duties under the leases, thus led the Government to expend substantial resources over the course of 19 years in the hope of seeing this project realized. *Conoco, Inc. v. United States,* 35 Fed.Cl. 309, 315, n. 2 (1996); see also U.S. Dept. of Interior, Minerals Management Service, Mineral Revenues 1999, Report on Receipts From Federal and American Indian Leases 35 (reporting more than $64 billion in royalties from federal offshore mineral leases from 1953-1999).

From the outset, however, it was apparent that the Outer Banks project might not succeed for a variety of reasons. Among those was the risk that the State of North Carolina would exercise its right to object to the completion of the project. [2] That was a risk that the parties knowingly assumed. They did not, however, assume the risk that Congress would enact additional legislation that would delay the completion of what would obviously be a lengthy project in any event. I therefore agree with the Court that the Government did breach its contract with petitioners in failing to approve, within 30 days of its receipt, the plan of exploration petitioners submitted. As the Court describes, * * * the leases incorporate the provisions of the OCSLA into their terms, and the OCSLA, correspondingly, sets down this 30-day requirement in plain language. 43 U.S.C. § 1340(c).

I do not, however, believe that the appropriate remedy for the Government's breach is for petitioners to recover their full initial investment. When the entire relationship between the parties is considered, with particular reference to the impact of North Carolina's foreseeable exercise of its right to object to the project, it is clear that the remedy ordered by the Court is excessive. I would hold that petitioners are entitled at best to damages resulting from the delay caused by the Government's failure to approve the plan within the requisite time.

* * *

The Federal Water Pollution Control Act, 86 Stat. 816, 33 U.S.C. § 1251 *et seq.,* requires lessees to obtain a National Pollutant Discharge Elimination System (NPDES) permit from the Environmental Protection Agency (EPA) before lessees may move forward with any exploration plan that includes discharging pollutants into the ocean, § § 1311(a), 1342(a). The EPA cannot issue an NPDES permit, however, before the lessee has certified to the State's satisfaction that the discharge would comply with the State's CZMA requirements. Unless the Secretary of Commerce overrides any state objection arising during this process, 16 U.S.C. § 1456(c)(3), lessees will not receive the necessary permit.

After the State of North Carolina filed its formal CZMA objections on November 19, 1990 (indicating that the State believed a contract still existed), petitioners promptly sought in December 1990--again under statutory terms incorporated into the contracts--to have the Secretary of Commerce override the objections, 43 U.S.C. § 1340(c)(1), to make it possible for the exploration permits to issue. In a response explainable solely on the basis that the Government still believed itself to be performing contractually obligatory terms, the Secretary of Commerce undertook to evaluate petitioners' request that the Secretary override the State's CZMA objections. This administrative review process has, I do not doubt, required a substantial expenditure of the time and resources of the Departments of Commerce and Interior, along with the 12 other administrative agencies whose comments the Secretary of Commerce solicited in evaluating the request to override and in issuing, on September 2, 1994, a lengthy "Decision and Findings" in which he declined to do so.

* * *

Indeed, petitioners have pending in the United States District Court for the District of Columbia at this very moment their appeal from the Secretary of Commerce's denial of petitioners' override request of North Carolina's CZMA objections. *Mobil Oil Exploration & Producing Southeast, Inc. v. Daley,* No. 95-93 SSH (filed Mar. 8, 2000).

Absent, then, any repudiation, we are left with the possibility that the nature of the Government's breach was so "essential" or "total" in the scope of the parties' contractual relationship as to justify the remedy of restitution. As above, I would reject the suggestion that the OBPA somehow acted *ex proprio vigore* to render a total breach of the parties' contracts. * * * The OBPA was not passed as an amendment to statutes that the leases by their terms incorporated, nor did the OBPA state that its terms were to be considered incorporated into then existing leases; it was, rather, an action external to the contract, capable of affecting the parties' actions but not of itself changing the contract terms. The OBPA did, of course, impose a legal duty upon the Secretary of the Interior to take actions (and to refrain from taking actions) inconsistent with the Government's existing legal obligations to the lessees. Had the Secretary chosen, despite the OBPA, to issue the required approval, he presumably could have been haled into court and compelled to rescind the approval in compliance with the OBPA requirement. But that this possibility remained after the passage of the OBPA reinforces the conclusion that it was not until the Secretary actually took action inconsistent with his contractual obligations that the Government came into breach.

The result of such a proceeding may well have been the issuance of a judicial decree enjoining the Secretary's actions. Ironically, the Secretary would then have been authorized under the regulatory provisions expressly incorporated into the parties' contracts to suspend the leases. 30 CFR § 250.10(b)(7) (1990) ("The Regional Supervisor may also direct * * * suspension of any operation or activity, including production, because * * * (7)[t]he suspension is necessary to comply with judicial decrees prohibiting production or any other operation or activity, or the permitting of those activities * * * "). Indeed, this was the very provision the DOI relied on in explaining why it was suspending petitioners' leases. App. 129-130.

* * *

Whether the breach was sufficiently "substantial" or material to justify restitution depends on what impact, if any, the breach had at the time the breach occurred on the successful completion of the project. See E. Farnsworth, Contracts § 8.16 (3d ed. 1999) ("The time for determining materiality is the time of the breach and not the time that the contract was made * * * Most significant is the extent to which the breach will deprive the injured party of the benefit that it justifiably expected"). In this action the answer must be close to none. Sixty days after the Government entered into breach--from September 19, 1990, to November 19, 1990--the State of North Carolina filed its formal objection to CZMA certification with the United States. App. 141-148. As the OCSLA makes clear, "The Secretary *shall not grant any license or permit for any activity described* in detail in an exploration plan and affecting any land use or water use in the coastal zone of a State with a coastal zone management program * * * unless the State concurs or is conclusively presumed to concur with the consistency certification accompanying such plan * * * , or the Secretary of Commerce makes the finding [overriding the State's objection]." 43 U.S.C. § 1340(c)(2) (emphasis added); see also § 1351(d). While this objection remained in effect, the project could not go forward unless the objection was set aside by the Secretary of Commerce. Thus, the Government's breach effectively delayed matters during the period between September 19, 1990, and November 19, 1990. Thereafter, implementation was contractually precluded by North Carolina.

This fact does not, of course, relieve the Government of liability for breach. It does, however, make it inappropriate to conclude that the Government's pre-November 19 actions in breach were sufficiently "material" to the successful completion of the parties' project to justify giving petitioners all of their money back. * * *

IV

The risk that North Carolina would frustrate performance of the leases executed in 1981 was foreseeable from the date the leases were signed. It seems clear to me that the State's objections, rather than the enactment of OBPA, is the primary explanation for petitioners' decision to take steps to avoid suffering the consequences of the bargain they made. As a result of the Court's action today, petitioners will enjoy a windfall reprieve that Congress foolishly provided them in its decision to pass legislation that, while validly responding to a political constituency that opposed the development of the Outer Banks, caused the Government to breach its own contract. Viewed in the context of the entire transaction, petitioners may well be entitled to a modest damages recovery for the *two months* of delay attributable to the Government's breach. But restitution is not a default remedy; it is available only when a court deems it, in all of the circumstances, just. A breach that itself caused at most a delay of two months in a protracted enterprise of this magnitude does not justify the $156 million draconian remedy that the Court delivers.

Accordingly, I respectfully dissent.

(b.) Production Stage

UNION OIL CO. OF CALIFORNIA v. MORTON
United States Court of Appeals, Ninth Circuit, 1975
512 F.2d 743

CHOY, *CIRCUIT JUDGE*:

Four major oil companies brought this action to set aside an order of the Secretary of the Interior denying them permission to construct a drilling platform in the Santa Barbara Channel which they allege is necessary for full exercise of their rights under a federal oil and gas lease. The companies also seek to enjoin the Secretary from further interference with enjoyment of their lease rights. The district court held that the Secretary's order was within his statutory authority and was not arbitrary, capricious, or an abuse of discretion, and dismissed the complaint. We vacate the decision of the district court and remand for further proceedings.

Factual Background

In February 1968, the four companies (hereinafter "Union") paid over $61 million for oil and gas rights on tract OCS-P 0241. The leased tract lies on the continental shelf in the Santa Barbara Channel, beyond the jurisdiction of the State of California. The Interior Department granted the lease under the authority of the Outer Continental Shelf Lands Act, 43 U.S.C. § 1331 et seq.

The lease gives Union the right to erect floating drilling platforms, subject to the provisions of the Act and to "reasonable regulations" not inconsistent with the lease issued by the Secretary. Two platforms, A and B, were installed, each supporting many productive wells. In September 1968, Union sought permission to install a third platform, C. The Secretary approved the application, and the Army Corps of Engineers issued the necessary permit. In January 1969, before platform C was installed, a blow-out occurred on one of the wells on platform A. The blowout caused the disastrous Santa Barbara oil spill which killed birds and marine organisms, damaged beaches and seafront properties, and restricted fishing and recreational activities in the area.

On February 7, 1969, the Secretary ordered all activities on this and certain other leases suspended pending further environmental studies. After these studies were completed, the Secretary announced on September 20, 1971, that Union would not be allowed to install platform C, because operation of that platform would be "incompatible with the concept of the Federal Sanctuary [which the Secretary had proposed to Congress]." He stated that all operations would remain suspended on certain other Channel leases, pending action by Congress canceling the leases. See Gulf Oil Corp. v. Morton, 493 F.2d 141 (9th Cir. 1973).

The Department formally notified the companies the following month that the Secretary "has determined that the installation of Platform 'C' would be inconsistent with protection of the environment of the Santa Barbara Channel and has directed [the Regional Supervisor] to withdraw the approval of September 16, 1968." This suit resulted. On November 3, 1972, just prior to trial, the Secretary issued a statement further clarifying the environmental concerns contributing to his decision.

* * *

We upheld the Secretary's suspension of the leases pending congressional action in Gulf Oil, supra. Because Congress had not acted within a reasonable time to cancel the leases in question, however, we declared the suspension invalid after October 18, 1972. 493 F.2d at 149. This appeal is limited to the validity of the order withdrawing permission for Union to install platform C.

The Act

The Outer Continental Shelf Act authorizes the Secretary to issue oil and gas leases on the outer continental shelf to the highest bidder. 43 U.S.C. § 1337(a). A lease issued under this Act, like a mineral lease granted under the Mineral Leasing Act of 1920, 30 U.S.C. § 181 et seq., does not convey title in the land, nor does it convey an unencumbered estate in the oil and gas. The lease does convey a property interest enforceable against the Government, of course, but it is an interest lacking many of the attributes of private property. Oil and gas deposits beneath the continental shelf are precious resources belonging to the entire nation. Congress, although encouraging the extraction of these resources by private companies, provided safeguards to insure that their exploitation should inure to the benefit of all. These safeguards are not limited to those provided by covenants in the lease; Congress also authorized the Secretary to maintain extensive, continuing regulation of the oil companies' day to day drilling operations.

Careful study of the Act confirms that Congress intended to exercise both proprietary powers of a landowner and the police powers of a legislature in regulating leases of publicly owned resources. Cf. Forbes v. United States, 125 F.2d 404, 408 (9th Cir. 1942). The Secretary, to whom Congress has delegated these powers, may prescribe at any time those rules which he finds necessary for the conservation of natural resources. 43 U.S.C. § 1334(a)(1). Exercising its legislative power, Congress has provided criminal penalties for knowing violation of these rules. 43 U.S.C. § 1334(a)(2). In addition, those rules in effect at the time a lease is executed are incorporated statutorily into the terms of the lease. 43 U.S.C. § 1334(a)(2). The Secretary, like a private property owner, may obtain cancellation of the lease if the lessee breaches such a rule. 43 U.S.C. § 1334(b)(1). Violation of rules issued after the lease has been executed does not enable the Secretary to cancel the lease, however. The property rights of the lessee are determined only by those rules in effect when the lease is executed. See generally W. Christopher, The Outer Continental Shelf Lands Act: Key to a New Frontier, 6 Stan. L. Rev. 23, 43-47 (1953).

* * *

Suspension: Regulation or Taking?

Pursuant to 43 U.S.C. § 1334(a)(1), the Secretary issued a regulation on August 22, 1969, authorizing emergency suspension of any operation which threatens immediate, serious, or irreparable harm or damage to life, including aquatic life, to property, to the leased deposits, to other valuable mineral deposits or to the environment. Such emergency suspension shall continue until in his judgment the threat or danger has terminated." 30 C.F.R. § 250.12. Refusal to allow installation of a previously approved platform could be justified only as a suspension of operations under this regulation.

The regulation properly provides for "conservation of the natural resources of the outer Continental Shelf," as we have construed that phrase. Nevertheless, Union points to the distinction between a suspension and a revocation, asserting that the Secretary did not in fact merely suspend operations, because a suspension by definition possesses a "temporary nature." The structure of the Act demonstrates that Congress intended vested rights under the lease to be invulnerable to defeasance by subsequently issued regulations. Although 30 C.F.R. § 250.12 provides expressly that a "suspension" shall be limited in time only by the Secretary's judgment that the environmental threat has ended, and although 43 U.S.C. § 1334(a)(1) authorizes regulations providing not only for suspensions but for any other action affecting operations which the Secretary determines "necessary and proper" for "conservation of natural resources," Congress clearly did not intend to grant leases so tenuous in nature that the Secretary could terminate them, in whole or in part, at will.

Congress itself can order the leases forfeited even now, subject to payment of compensation. But without congressional authorization, the Secretary or the executive branch in general has no intrinsic powers of condemnation. Congress' clear concern to distinguish police power regulation from invasion of property rights in these leases convinces us that Congress did not confer powers of condemnation upon the Secretary by implication.

The degree to which the Government may interfere with the

enjoyment of private property by exercise of its police power without having to pay compensation is not a simple question. The courts, under a variety of tests, have recognized that regulation of private property can become so onerous that it amounts to a taking of that property. If, as Union contends, platform C is a necessary means for the extraction of oil from a portion of the leased area, refusal to permit installation of that platform now or at any time in the future deprives Union of all benefit from the lease in that particular area. We therefore conclude that an open-ended suspension of the right granted Union to install a drilling platform would be a pro tanto cancellation of its lease.

Such a taking by interference with private property rights is within the constitutional power of Congress, subject to payment of compensation. See Dugan v. Rank, 372 U.S. 609 (1963). But Congress no more impliedly authorized the Secretary to take the leasehold by prohibiting its beneficial use than by condemnation proceeding. A suspension for which the fifth amendment would require compensation is therefore unauthorized and beyond the Secretary's power.

Whether the Secretary has taken Union's property depends on the conditions of the suspension. If operations are suspended indefinitely, property rights have been taken. To determine whether the suspension is indefinite, or, on the other hand, is a temporary suspension whose termination is conditioned by the occurrence of certain future events, we must examine the justifications which the Secretary has offered for the suspension. The Secretary explained the suspension most recently in his statement of November 3, 1972:

The following were the primary factors that led to my decision denying the platform applications:

(1) construction of the proposed platform and drilling wells would increase the risk of oil pollution in the Santa Barbara Channel by reason of:

(a) the risks inherent in offshore oil drilling;

(b) location of the Channel in an active seismic belt, and

(c) with regard to Platform "C," the fact that the platform would be located on the damaged Dos Quadros [sic] structure;

(2) oil pollution in the Santa Barbara Channel would have adverse consequences both short and longer term, because of the

characteristics of the Channel environment; the following attributes of the Channel that would be affected by oil pollution were given particular consideration:

(a) animal and plant marine life;

(b) commercial and sport fisheries;

(c) recreational use;

(d) beaches and shore line of the Channel;

(e) birds;

(3) the lack of systems and equipment which are completely effective in controlling and removing oil pollution under all weather and sea conditions;

(4) the suitability of the Dos Quadros [sic] structure (leases OCS-P 0241 and 0240) for unitization and the suitability of leases OCS-P 0240 and 0166 for unitization;

(5) additional platforms would increase interference with other uses of the Channel for recreational and commercial fishing;

(6) additional platforms would be aesthetically undesirable.

Factors 2, 4, 5, and 6 amount simply to a weighing of conflicting interests which the Secretary should have undertaken before the lease was granted. For the Secretary to offer these factors now to justify suspending Union's drilling activities asserts in effect that he can cancel the lease because he has changed his mind. These enumerated interests are not temporary concerns which the passage of time may eliminate.

Factors 1 and 3, however, suggest conditions which the development of new technology or further study may lessen as threats to the environment. Further study of seismic risks in the Channel, or of the geology of the Dos Quadros structure, for example, may produce evidence of environmental risks unanticipated at the time the lease was executed. Knowledge of these newly discovered risks might induce Congress to cancel the lease. A suspension also might provide time for an improved pollution control technology to be developed. A suspension whose termination was conditioned on the occurrence of events or the discovery of new knowledge which can be anticipated within a reasonable period of time would be a valid exercise of the Secretary's regulatory power, and not a fifth amendment taking.

The vague assertion of potential risks advanced in the Secretary's 1972 statement is totally inadequate to enable this court to decide whether such justifications for a suspension do exist, however, and whether they sufficiently restrict the duration of the suspension to avoid the need for compensation. The trial court decided without explanation that the suspension deprived Union of no property rights. We are uncertain as to the basis for this conclusion.

In view of the insufficient nature both of the Secretary's explanation for the suspension and the district court's justification of its judgment, we vacate the decision of the district court and remand the case to the district court for a determination whether the Secretary is taking property rights from Union. The court should allow the Secretary to prepare and present an amended statement of the grounds on which he bases the suspension. The court may, at its discretion, receive additional evidence and testimony in support of and in opposition to the Secretary's amended justification. The court should then determine whether each justification advanced by the Secretary is appropriate under 30 C.F.R. § 250.12, whether the Secretary has offered sufficient evidence to demonstrate that his decision was not arbitrary and capricious or an abuse of discretion, and whether the duration of a suspension based on the grounds offered is sufficiently conditioned on the occurrence of future events to avoid fifth amendment requirements of compensation.

If the trial court finds that the suspension, as limited by the Secretary's amended statement, complies with these requirements, Union's complaint should be dismissed. Otherwise, the order of suspension should be set aside as beyond the Secretary's statutory powers. 5 U.S.C. § 706(2)(C).

Because of the Secretary's continuing supervisory obligations, injunctive relief against further interference with Union's operations would be inappropriate.

Vacated and remanded.

Notes and Questions

1. In *Union Oil*, what exactly was the district court directed to determine? If a valid suspension order is one that is "sufficiently conditioned on the occurrence of future events," must it be certain that

those events will in fact occur, or are only probable?

2. Congress attempted to clarify the rights of lessor and lessee in the OCS Lands Act Amendments of 1978. The section dealing with suspension and termination of leases provides in part (43 U.S.C. § 1334(a)):

* * *

The regulations prescribed by the Secretary under this subsection shall include, but not be limited to, provisions --

(1) for the suspension or temporary prohibition of any operation or activity, including production, pursuant to any lease or permit (A) at the request of a lessee, in the national interest, to facilitate proper development of a lease or to allow for the construction or negotiation for use of transportation facilities, or (B) if there is a threat of serious, irreparable, or immediate harm or damage to life (including fish and other aquatic life), to property, to any mineral deposits (in areas leased or not leased), or to the marine, coastal, or human environment, and for the extension of any permit or lease affected by suspension or prohibition under clause (A) or (B) by a period equivalent to the period of such suspension or prohibition, except that no permit or lease shall be so extended when such suspension or prohibition is the result of gross negligence or willful violation of such lease or permit, or of regulations issued with respect to such lease or permit;

(2) with respect to cancellation of any lease or permit

(A) that such cancellation may occur at any time, if the Secretary determines, after a hearing, that --

i) continued activity pursuant to such lease or permit would probably cause serious harm or damage to life (including fish and other aquatic life), to property, to any mineral (in areas leased or not leased), to the national security or defense, or to the marine, coastal, or human environment;

(ii) the threat of harm or damage will not disappear or decrease to an acceptable extent within a reasonable period of time; and

(iii) the advantages of cancellation outweigh the advantages of continuing such lease or permit in force;

(B) that such cancellation shall not occur unless and until operations under such lease or permit shall have been under suspension, or temporary prohibition, by the Secretary, with due extension of any lease or permit term continuously for a period of five years, or for a lesser period upon request of the lessee;

(C) that such cancellation shall entitle the lessee to receive such compensation as he shows to the Secretary as being equal to the lesser of (i) the fair value of the canceled rights as of the date of cancellation, taking account of both anticipated revenues from the lease and anticipated costs, including costs of compliance with all applicable regulations and operating orders, liability for cleanup costs or damages, or both, in the case of an oil spill, and all other costs reasonably anticipated on the lease, or (ii) the excess, if any, over the lessee's revenues, from the lease (plus interest thereon from the date of receipt to date of reimbursement) of all consideration paid for the lease and all direct expenditures made by the lessee after the date of issuance of such lease and in connection with exploration or development, or both, pursuant to the lease (plus interest on such consideration and such expenditures from date of payment to date of reimbursement).

3. Why weren't the above provisions applied by the Court in *Mobil Oil*? See R. Craig, *Mobil Oil Exploration*, Environmental Protection, and Contract Repudiation: It's Time to Recognize the Public Trust in the Outer Continental Shelf, 30 ELR 11104 (2000). Under 43 U.S.C. §§ 1334(c) and (d), a lease is subject to cancellation for violation of any regulation no matter when the regulation was issued, not, as under the original act, only for violations of regulations "in force and in effect on the date of the issuance of the lease." Is it constitutional for Congress to avoid paying compensation for a canceled lease by putting a lessee on notice that his lease may be canceled for violation of subsequently issued regulations? In practice, would a court cancel a producing lease for a negligent violation or a trivial violation? Is cancellation in such circumstances required by the terms of the Act if requested by the Secretary and the violation is proven?

4. What proprietary rights, if any, does a lessee retain under the above statutory provisions? Has the leasehold become so tenuous as to discourage new ventures by industry? Alternative bidding systems could lessen the impact of cancellation. For example, the Secretary of Interior could be required to lease some of the area offered for lease each year by a bidding system other than the bonus bid/fixed royalty method, which has been the usual system. Lessees under an

alternative bidding system such as variable royalty bidding would not be required to make such a high initial capital outlay as under the bonus bid system, and so would not have as much at stake in a suspension or termination.

SECTION 2. OCEAN MINERALS MINING

A. OCS AND EEZ MINERALS MINING

Historically, scientific and mining industry attention has focused more on manganese nodules than on polymetallic sulfides. Nonetheless, polymetallic sulfides have recently dominated discussions of deep seabed mining issues, because they contain high concentrations of strategically important minerals, such as cobalt, zinc, copper, and silver. First discovered at seafloor spreading centers in the Eastern Pacific, polymetallic sulfides precipitate out of hot aqueous solutions emitted at "smokers" (hydrothermal vents in the ocean floor), accumulating in vast deposits. Active vent sites are inhabited by unique, previously unknown life forms not dependent on photosynthesis for their existence. See generally J. Edmond and K. Von Damm, Hot Springs on the Ocean Floor, Sci. Am., Apr. 1983, at 78. There is some question as to the actual need for the U.S. to mine the oceans for strategic minerals given the "magnitude of domestic onshore deposits, the international availability of certain minerals, and the decline in international demand." Implications of a United States Claim to a 200 Mile Exclusive Economic Zone (summary of a workshop), Center for Ocean Management Studies at the University of Rhode Island at 9-10 (Apr. 11-12, 1983).

Shortly after President Reagan issued his 1983 EEZ proclamation, officials at the Minerals Management Service of the Interior Department announced plans to lease a Pacific Ocean seabed site potentially rich in polymetallic sulfides for exploration and eventual mineral extraction. This proposed lease sale would have been one of the first offerings of hardrock minerals from the seabed under U.S. jurisdiction, and it would have opened up some 12,000 square miles (7.68 million acres) of the Gorda Ridge off Northern California and Southern Oregon for competitive bidding. The 250-mile-long Gorda Ridge stretches from 35 to 250 miles off the coastlines of those states and is unique among potential deposit sites thus far discovered in that it lies mostly within the U.S. EEZ. In contrast, a preliminary Interior Department assertion of jurisdiction over the Juan de Fuca Ridge off the Washington State coast was withdrawn after the Canadian government protested that the site lay beyond U.S. jurisdiction.

Although no lease sale of Gorda Ridge minerals so far has been held, the Interior Department did proceed to develop an OCS minerals regulatory regime predicated on the Department's authority under OCSLA section 8(k)(1) (43 U.S.C. § 1337(k)(1)). Section 8(k)(1) states:

> The Secretary is authorized to grant to qualified persons offering the highest cash bonuses on a basis of competitive bidding any leases of any mineral other than oil, gas and sulphur in any area of the Outer Continental Shelf not then under lease for such mineral upon such royalty, rental, and other terms and conditions as the Secretary may prescribe at the time of offering the area for lease.

In response to the question of whether the Presidential Proclamation on the EEZ was intended to affect the Department of Interior's jurisdiction under the OCSLA, the Department responded that

> the OCSLA definition of "Outer Continental Shelf" includes all lands seaward of those granted to the States in the Submerged Lands Act * * * to which the United States claims jurisdiction and control under international law. The Presidential Proclamation on the EEZ formally claimed U.S. jurisdiction to a minimum of 200 nautical miles from its coasts.

53 Fed. Reg. 25246 (July 5, 1988). Such an assertion of authority, the Department further asserted, is consistent with existing international law, "which now accepts that the continental shelf extends to a minimum of 200 nautical miles for all nations, essentially concurrent with the 200-mile EEZ."* * * Id.

One set of regulations addresses geological and geophysical prospecting and scientific research activities relating to minerals other than oil, gas and sulphur. 53 Fed. Reg. 25246 (July 5, 1988); 30 CFR part 280. The regulations require a permit for all prospecting-related research and some types of scientific research activities.

The second set of regulations addresses leasing and post-lease operations. 53 Fed. Reg. 31,442 (Aug. 18, 1988); 30 C.F.R. parts 281, 282. The regulations authorize the issuance of leases with a 20 year initial term. Notices of proposed leasing will be sent to the governors of affected states in addition to being published in the Federal Register. If a lease will be near the federal-state boundary offshore, joint management agreements are suggested.

It is anticipated that an EIS will be prepared when the initial lease sale in a given area is offered. In addition, the 1990 amendments to

CZMA arguably require that all OCS mineral activities that affect any land or water use or natural resource of the coastal zone be conducted in a manner that is consistent with the state's federally approved coastal zone management plan, unless either a Presidential exemption is obtained or the Secretary of Commerce overrides any state consistency objection.

Through a judicial proceeding, MMS may cancel a lease or suspend operations for noncompliance with the lease regulations or the OCSLA. Leases may also be cancelled in some circumstances to protect from harm aquatic life, property, minerals, national security, or the environment. If a lease is cancelled for violation of lease regulations or the OCSLA, no compensation is paid to the lessee, but if it is cancelled for environmental or other reasons, then compensation is paid in accordance with a formula contained in the regulations.

OCSLA section 8(k) was amended in 1994 by P.L. 103-426 to authorize negotiated contracts rather than competitive lease sales when OCS sand and gravel resources are needed for public works projects such as beach and coastal wetlands restoration.

For commentary discussing the evolution of the OCSLA minerals mining regime, see D. Fischer, Federal-State Conflict Over Ocean Hard Minerals Governance, 16 Ocean and Shoreline Management 61 (1991); D. Fischer, Hard Mineral Resource Development Policy in the U.S. Exclusive Economic Zone: A Review of the Role of the Coastal States, 19 Ocean Development and International Law 101 (1988); D. Fischer, Structuring a U.S. Offshore Hard Mineral Development Policy: Reflections on a Seabed Tenure System, 19 Ocean Development and International Law 59 (1988); D. Fischer, Two Alternatives in National Governance of Marine Hard Minerals in the U.S. Exclusive Economic Zone, 19 Ocean Development and International Law 287 (1988); R. Hildreth, Legal Regimes for Seabed Hard Mineral Mining: Evolution at the Federal and State Levels, 20 Ocean Development and International Law 141 (1989); R. Hildreth, Marine Use Conflicts Arising from Development of Seabed Hydrocarbons and Minerals, 12 Ocean and Shoreline Management 271 (1989); R. Hildreth, Ocean Resources and Intergovernmental Relations in the 1980s: Outer Continental Shelf Hydrocarbons and Minerals, in Silva, ed., Ocean Resources and U.S. Intergovernmental Relations in the 1980s at 155, 160, 172-73, 193-94 (1986); J. Jacobson and T. Hanlon, Regulation of Hard-Mineral Mining on the Continental Shelf, 50 Oregon Law Review 425 (1971).

B. DEEP SEABED MINERALS MINING

In June 1980 Congress passed the Deep Seabed Hard Mineral Resources Act (DSHMRA) (30 U.S.C. § 1401 et seq.). The act was intended to improve the investment climate for private ocean mining interests during the interim period prior to the effective date of any law of the sea treaty adopted by the United Nations Conference on the Law of the Sea (UNCLOS). At the time of passage, it appeared likely that such a treaty would someday regulate sea bed mining on an international level.

The act deals with the mining of manganese nodules, fist-sized lumps of minerals found primarily on the deep seabed in international waters at depths of 12,000 to 20,000 feet. The nodules contain manganese, iron, nickel, copper, and cobalt. Some estimates place the potential supply of nodules as high as 1.5 trillion tons. Manganese, cobalt, and nickel are considered to be "strategic" to U.S. industrial and national security interests, because they are used to impart strength and temperature and corrosion resistance to steel alloys. The U.S. currently imports virtually all of its supply of these metals from a handful of foreign sources, many of them in the Third World. The act is premised on the belief that the U.S. must develop its own source of these "strategic" minerals to ensure a supply in the event of worldwide shortages, price dislocations or political disruptions.

It was Congress' view that substantial investment and a relatively long lead time are needed to develop fully the technology and capability necessary for commercial exploitation of the nodule resource. Congress feared that this private investment would not take place because of the uncertainty as to the nature of an UNCLOS treaty regime and the degree of seabed access the treaty rules would provide to investing U.S. companies. Therefore, Congress enacted this legislation with the stated purposes of both encouraging the completion of a law of the sea treaty and creating a domestic legal regime to encourage private investment and technology development. The act also creates an interim regulatory program to ensure that ocean mining is conducted in a manner which conserves the resources, protects the environment, and promotes safety at sea.

The act requires a U.S. miner to obtain a license from the Administrator of the National Oceanic and Atmospheric Administration (NOAA) to explore for nodules and a permit before the miner may engage in commercial recovery. Each license or permit gives the holder the exclusive right to explore or mine a specific area, but only as against other U.S. citizens. As interpreted by the U.S., present international law does not prohibit a foreign miner, in exercise of freedom of the seas, from exploiting the same area.

Exploration licenses are issued to qualified applicants on a first come, first served basis. The holder of a ten year license to explore a specific area then has a preference to secure a permit to commercially recover nodules from the explored area. To date four licenses have been issued for deep seabed exploration in the Clarion-Clipperton zone of the south Pacific Ocean, two of which have been relinquished for economic considerations.

The Administrator of NOAA is directed to consult with regional fishery management councils prior to issuance of any license or permit if it appears that a fishery resource could be adversely affected. In contrast to certain other federal legislation, the act makes no provision for the approval by or consultation with coastal states prior to license issuance. However, since the act requires any shore based processing of minerals to take place in the U.S., deep seabed mining may have some effects on U.S. coastal areas. In such circumstances, applicable CZMA consistency requirements will have to be satisfied.

A "reciprocating states" provision allows the Administrator of NOAA to designate other nations as reciprocating states, if they meet certain criteria. The U.S. and the designated nations would coordinate their respective license and permit programs to avoid conflicts over mining areas. To become a reciprocating state, another nation must create a domestic regulatory system for its miners that is compatible with the U.S. act and that respects licenses and permits issued by the U.S. Germany enacted seabed mining legislation similar to the U.S. approach.

The "reciprocating states" provision makes it possible for the U.S., together with other technologically advanced nations such as Japan, France, Germany, and the United Kingdom, to create a reciprocating states regime to regulate ocean mining as an alternative to an international regime under the Law of the Sea treaty. A multinational reciprocating states system may be viewed by some as more favorable to U.S. and private mining company interests, because it would eliminate conflicts between the handful of nations with ocean mining capability and, at the same time, avoid obligations and restrictions likely to be present under the Law of the Sea treaty.

The multinational reciprocating system, or a "mini-treaty" among the mining nations, would also have drawbacks, however. The other nations of the world could still claim rights to the deep seabed nodules as part of the "common heritage of mankind." The U.S. could also lose the strategic benefits of other provisions of the Law of the Sea treaty, such as right of passage through the world's international straits. And, of course, there would be a loss of goodwill between the U.S. and much of the Third World. Extensive seabed claims by coastal Third World nations would be another possible consequence of the mini-treaty or reciprocal approach.

Commercial recovery of nodules will impact the ocean environment in several ways. Some mining methods likely to be used may stir up and distribute sediments and other debris in the lower part of the water column. A surface plume of bottom debris will result when nodules are collected at the ship and the finer debris is dumped back in the ocean. Heavy metals found in the sediments could be taken up into the food chain at this point and eventually become accumulated in the larger predator species such as tuna. The clouding of the water and the increase in surface nutrients may affect fish larvae and fish migrations. It is even possible that heavy metals from the bottom sediments could undergo thermal or chemical alteration at the surface, with toxic results to some marine life. There will also be additional surface discharges of solid and chemical wastes if the nodules are processed by factory ships at sea.

Because of these and other potential environmental impacts, several provisions of the act address environmental concerns. NOAA was directed to expand its Deep Ocean Mining Environmental Study to collect basic scientific information on the ocean environment. Programmatic environmental impact statements must be prepared by NOAA in certain circumstances. Finally, a site-specific EIS must be prepared for each license or permit NOAA issues. The act also contains other provisions for the protection of the environment and for the application of other federal laws such as the Clean Water Act to deep seabed mining operations.

The act has been reauthorized several times without significant change. NOAA regulations governing permits for commercial recovery of deep seabed mineral resources define the "deep seabed" as the area beyond any nation's continental shelf. As written, the commercial recovery regulations lack specific regulatory standards. NOAA addressed the information deficit by requiring licensees and permittees to conduct monitoring programs to ensure early and accurate detection of significant adverse impacts on the environment. The regulations do not define significant adverse impact, leaving it to case-by-case determination. Moveover, NOAA concluded that the occurrence of such impacts due to commercial scale mining is unlikely. The commercial recovery regulations also contain extensive state consultation provisions even though the act itself does not require them. However, commercial recovery remains a distant prospect at best.

Notes and Questions

1. NEPA requires an environmental impact statement for all "major Federal actions significantly affecting the quality of the human environment." 42 U.S.C. § 4332(2)(c). Does the coverage of NEPA include only those areas clearly under U.S. jurisdiction? Can the deep seabed be considered a "human environment"?

2. Deep sea hydrothermal vents provide an oasis-like environment for highly specialized and bizarre life forms, unique in that they are dependent on geothermal rather than solar energy for sustenance. Scientists believe that some of these creatures may be remnants of the earth's earliest life forms, and thus an irreplaceable scientific treasure. Could the Endangered Species Act be extended to cover primitive deep sea creatures whose only habitat lies far from U.S. shores? If so, is it likely that mining will proceed without first learning much more about these animals? See J. Flipse, Deep Ocean Mining Pollution Mitigation (Texas A&M Sea Grant Program 1981).

3. Who owns manganese nodules resting on the ocean floor beyond the continental shelf of any coastal nation?

> The legal premises of the Act are that, pursuant to customary international law, exploration for and recovery of seabed mineral resources beyond the limits of national jurisdiction is protected by the principle of freedom of the seas, that ownership of the resources involved would vest upon capture, and that no sovereign claim to the seabed itself is necessary to support a claim to harvest the resources thereon, any more than a sovereign claim to the seabed would be necessary to sustain a claim to mid-oceanic fishing rights.

D. Arrow, The Proposed Regime for the Unilateral Exploitation of Deep Seabed Mineral Resources, 21 Harv. Int'l L.J. 337-38 (1980). As described by Arrow, are the Act's legal premises correct? As a matter of property law, especially if the common heritage principle discussed in Chapter 4 has become customary international law? As a matter of international law? See D. Arrow, The Customary Norm Process and the Deep Seabed, 9 Ocean Dev. and Int'l L.J. 1 (1981).

4. For additional reading, on deep seabed mining, see National

Oceanic and Atmospheric Administration, Deep Seabed Mining: Report to Congress (1987); M. Ball, Law of the Sea: Federal-State Relations 71-73 (1978); Senate Commerce Committee, Congress and the Nation's Oceans: Marine Affairs in the 94th Congress 131-32 (1977); R. Frank, Deepsea Mining and the Environment (1976); R. Frank, Environmental Aspects of Deepsea Mining, 15 Va. J. Int'l L. 815 (1975).

Chapter Six

FISHERIES AND MARINE ECOSYSTEMS

SECTION 1. INTRODUCTION

In 1976, Congress adopted the Fishery Conservation and Management Act, declaring a 200-mile zone of exclusive U.S. fishing authority. Fishing pressure on certain coastal fish stocks from foreign distant-water fishing fleets had grown enormously in the previous decade. Congress believed it could not afford to wait for the conclusion of the Third United Nations Conference on the Law of the Sea (UNCLOS III), at which the nations of the world were in the process of accepting the 200-mile Exclusive Economic Zone (EEZ) regime on behalf of coastal nations. The 1976 Act declared an exclusive Fishery Conservation Zone, extending 197 miles from the seaward limit of the territorial sea. The original Fishery Act asserted exclusive management authority over all marine life, other than birds, marine mammals, and highly migratory species of tuna, and made foreign fishing a matter of U.S. consent, rather than right. As numerous other countries followed suit and declared similar exclusive fishery zones, the era of freedom of fishing on the high seas came rapidly to a close.

In addition to the foreign fishing controls, the Fishery Conservation and Management Act enacted a regulatory system for the domestic marine fishing industry, both commercial and recreational sectors. The new program was the first federal effort to manage the fishery resources in waters above the U.S. continental shelf. Until this time, fishery management was almost exclusively the concern of the individual states, which adopted regulations to conserve fish stocks and to prevent conflicts among different sectors of the fishing industry. The new national program adopted a regional structure for regulating fisheries in waters beyond the marine limits of the states.

Although initial controversy over the Act focused on its impact on foreign fishing, implementation of the domestic regulatory program proved to be the most problematic aspect of the new law. In grappling with the difficulties of managing diverse fishery resources and a growing

435

domestic industry, the Congress has amended the Act many times since 1976. In 1983, President Reagan by proclamation established a 200-mile Exclusive Economic Zone, Proclamation No. 5030, 48 Fed. Reg. 10601 (1983), and the Act was amended to reflect this change. In 1990, further amendments brought tunas and other highly migratory fish species under U.S. management authority. By the late 1990s, the policy emphasis had shifted from 'Americanization' of all U.S. fisheries to the conservation and rebuilding of overfished fish stocks. The 1996 Sustainable Fisheries Act made major substantive changes to the Act, to refocus implementation toward the goals of conservation and ecosystem protection. The Act was renamed in 1980 in honor of the late Senator Warren G. Magnuson, its original sponsor in the Senate, and again in 1996, to include Senator Ted Stevens. It is now the Magnuson-Stevens Fishery Conservation and Management Act (hereafter the "Magnuson-Stevens Act" or "MSA").

While the Secretary of Commerce is legally responsible for implementing the MSA, the National Marine Fisheries Service (NMFS), an agency within the Commerce Department's National Oceanic and Atmospheric Administration, works with eight regional fishery management councils to develop plans and regulations for fisheries within their respective regions of the EEZ. The regional councils are very controversial bodies. Composed largely of members of the fishing industry and state fishery officials, the councils have significant authority to determine policies and regulations for commercial and recreational fisheries within their areas. NMFS has had difficulty at times asserting national interests over regional and industry interests in the fishery resources of the U.S. because of the council system.

A flood of litigation engulfed the Fisheries Service after the 1996 Sustainable Fisheries Act amendments and a 1996 amendment to the Regulatory Flexibility Act of 1980, making compliance with its economic impact analytical requirements subject to judicial review. The Endangered Species Act and the National Environmental Policy Act have also emerged as major legal levers for requiring an ecosystem-based approach to managing the fisheries of the U.S. EEZ.

This chapter introduces some basic concepts and tools in fisheries management, highlights the major elements of the federal management program for domestic fisheries under the Magnuson-Stevens Act, and explores the challenges presented by the ecosystem-related goals of the Act.

SECTION 2. REGULATION OF U.S. FISHERIES

A. BACKGROUND ON FISHERIES MANAGEMENT

(1.) Overfishing and the Economics of Fishing

The Magnuson-Stevens Act directs the Secretary of Commerce and the regional councils to identify those fish stocks under their jurisdiction that are approaching an "overfished" condition or are already overfished and to institute programs either to prevent the overfishing or to end it and to rebuild the fishery. 16 U.S.C. §§ 1853(a)(10), 1854(e). The Act defines "overfishing" and "overfished" as "a rate or level of fishing mortality that jeopardizes the capacity of a fishery to produce the maximum sustainable yield in such fishery. Id. at § 1802(29).

How does a fishery become overfished? What are the methods available to counteract these causes and keep fishing within sustainable limits?

In addition to the heavy impact of increased demand and improved technology upon fisheries, the basic economic structure of an unregulated fishery contributes to the tendency to overfish. This economic structure also leads to substantial economic waste in the fishing industry.

Under microeconomic theory, a fishery with free access to all fishermen will inevitably become exploited to the point of depletion. In his famous article, The Tragedy of the Commons, 162 Science 1243 (1968), Garrett Hardin drew upon an earlier article in economics analyzing the problem of the open access resource in the context of a fishery. See H. Gordon, The Economic Theory of a Common-Property Resource: The Fishery, 62 J. Pol. Econ. 124 (1954). Diagram A depicts a typical population growth pattern for a fish stock.

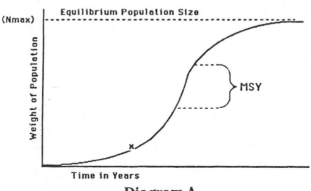

Diagram A

[Adapted from F. Bell, Food From The Sea: The Economics and Politics of Ocean Fisheries, 92 (1978).]

In an ideal environment containing a single species of fish, the population will start out at a low level (the bottom left of the diagram). As the population gets established, mature fish increasingly become available for reproduction. Then there is a period of rapid growth of the stock. Eventually, the stock will reach the maximum level that the particular environment can support, the environment's carrying capacity. At that point, the population is at its equilibrium population (Nmax). Shortage of food and habitat, predation pressure, and other factors come into play and the population size reaches a plateau. This biological limit is different for different species of fish with different life strategies. It is also difficult to predict for a given stock because natural mortality and environmental conditions which affect population size are difficult variables to measure and to factor into a stock assessment. For further explanations of fish population dynamics see, e.g., T. Pitcher and P. Hart, Fisheries Ecology 77-109 (1982).

If we assume that our fishery is an unregulated, open fishery with an equilibrium population, the question is: what will prevent the fishermen in that fishery from exploiting the fish population until, over time, it falls to the level of point x, at which the spawning stock is so depleted that it is unable to replenish itself? The answer is that in an unregulated fishery, only economic constraints may prevent exactly that from occurring.

In an unregulated fishery, no one is forcing fishermen to operate in a manner that conserves the fish stock. So, lacking any assurance that all of his competitors will also act to conserve the fishery resource, there is simply no incentive for an individual fisherman (or government in a multinational fishery) to act to conserve the resource. In fact, the opposite is true. The unregulated, open access environment acts as a disincentive for any fisherman to conserve.

In an open fishery, each fisherman has the incentive to engage in maximum fishing efforts and to take as large a share of the resource as she can before someone else does. A conservation-conscious fisherman who limits his catch to allow the fish stock to replenish would not find this restraint matched by a similar restraint by all other fishermen. More likely some, perhaps most, would continue to exploit the stock in the same manner as before, ignoring conservation efforts. All the conservationist fisherman's efforts would produce would be a lessening of competition for the other fishermen and a reduction of their costs as the conserving fisherman's efforts slowed the rate of depletion making it less expensive for them to harvest the stock.

Of course, as the stock becomes depleted, more and more capital and labor are required to harvest the same, or even a lesser, amount of fish. Thus, the unregulated, open fishery is characterized by economic waste. Within such a fishery, the fishing will continue until the break-even point is reached. At that point the marginal cost of catching the fish equals the marginal price consumers are willing to pay. Unfortunately, by the time the break-even point is reached, the fishing efforts will already be depleting the stock.

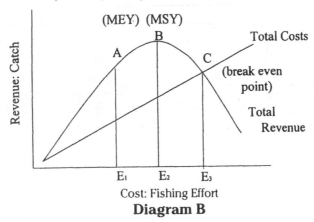

Diagram B

Diagram B illustrates the relationship of catch to fishing effort (number of boats, days at sea, etc.). The vertical axis represents the catch or value ("yield") of fish. It assumes that the revenue derived from selling the fish is directly proportional to the yield; that is, the unit price of the fish does not vary with harvest size. The horizontal axis represents fishing effort and its associated costs, again assuming that costs are directly proportional to fishing effort. In this diagram, point A is the point of maximum profit because a high amount of yield is achieved at a relatively low level of effort (E1) and the profit is greater than the costs. This point is sometimes referred to as the maximum economic yield (MEY). At Point B, effort has increased (E2) and so has the catch. But the costs have increased more than the catch because as the fish stock is reduced by fishing, fish get harder to catch and the costs go up. The value of the catch is still higher than the costs incurred, but the difference is not as much as at Point A. Point B is often called the maximum sustainable yield (MSY) because, in theory, if effort stays at E2 the stock can maintain its size through reproduction and recruitment and the catch will remain at this level from season to season. (In Diagram A, the MSY is in the range represented by the dotted lines.) However, if effort increases to E3, the catch and revenues will decrease and will meet the growing costs at Point C, the so-called break-even point, where the value of the catch is the same as the cost of the fishing effort. At this level of fishing effort, there is no profit and a declining fish stock. This is the point at which overfishing occurs. If fishing effort again increases, the catches will decline further. The fishery is now losing money as well as seriously depleting the stock, perhaps approaching collapse.

Diagram B shows that MSY is not synonymous with MEY. The MEY represents the point on the curve at which the increase in fishing cost per unit matches the increase in revenues. Fishing beyond this point results in a decline in revenues at such a rate as to constitute economic waste. Thus, an MEY-based management scheme might prove to be the most economically efficient course of action. However, there are reasons why a nation might choose an MSY approach over an MEY approach. What do you see as the disadvantages of an MEY-based management scheme? What is the management standard under the Magnuson-Stevens Act--MSY, MEY or some other value? For additional discussion of the economics of fishing, see, e.g., L. Anderson, The Economics Of Fisheries Management (1986); and S. Iudicello, M. Weber, and R. Wieland, Fish, Markets, and Fishermen: The Economics of Overfishing (1999).

(2.) Basic Regulatory Tools for Fishing

The most common tools of fishery regulation are total quotas, closed seasons and areas, and gear restrictions. Each has problems * * *. Consider first *total quotas*. Assume that a management agency decides to limit catch to the economically efficient level. On the surface, this appears to be a plausible way to regulate. However, if that effort is reduced, the new equilibrium average revenue will be higher than the average cost. That is, to the degree that catch restrictions are successful, the stock size will increase and hence catch and revenue per vessel will go up. Seeing the potential profits, other boats will be motivated to enter the fishery and those already fishing will try to catch more. With the total quota in effect, however, the boats will have to be prepared to take their catch as quickly as possible because all fishing ceases when the limit is reached. They will use bigger boats, more nets, and additional equipment, which can only mean an increase in the annual cost of maintaining and operating a representative vessel. A successful quota, therefore, sows the seeds of its own destruction as far as economic efficiency is concerned. The resulting profits encourage activities that will increase costs until they equal average revenue and hence all profits are once again removed. The desired catch will be achieved, but at a higher cost than is necessary.

Closed seasons and *closed areas* have the same problem. In addition, they cannot even guarantee that the proper amount of fish will be harvested. If a management agency wanted to achieve the optimal yield by these methods, it would have to reduce the length of the season or the areas in which fishing can take place so that the amount of fishing that could be done in the allowed time or area would result in the desired catch. In the very short run this may be effective because fishermen will have no way to adjust their rate of fishing. However, as the stock increases as a result of the reduced effort, the resulting extra profits will encourage fishermen to increase the amount of effort. Because of limits on time and area, this can only be done by increasing the annual cost of this effort. The end result is a fleet with the capacity to harvest more than the optimal catch and which tends to harvest fish at a higher average cost than is necessary. Therefore, not only does economic inefficiency result, but the biological effectiveness of the regulation is eroded as well.

This type of regulation often results in a race between the fishermen, who are motivated to increase their catching power, and the regulator, who must then impose further restrictions. The Pacific halibut fishery provides a good example. Before regulation, the normal season was several months. But as fishermen adapted to successively shorter seasons by improving their vessels and equipment, the season was finally restricted to several weeks.

Under *gear restrictions*, regulators try to limit catch by restricting the type of amount of equipment that the fishermen can use. To the extent that these restrictions affect the fishermen's ability to operate, they will increase the annual cost of maintaining and operating a vessel. With the increased costs, some vessels will be forced to leave the fishery. A new equilibrium will be achieved when the fleet has decreased sufficiently to increase catch per vessel to cover the higher costs. Under these regulations, therefore, the fleet will operate at a lower level of effort. However, the fish that are caught will not be harvested as cheaply as possible. In addition, these measures usually only have a short-term effect. As fishermen adjust to input restrictions, they learn how to increase their fishing power within the constraints of the controls. Here again, there will often be a race between regulators and fishermen, with the former trying to reduce the effectiveness of the latter, while the latter try to increase their fishing power subject to the constraints, and in doing so increase cost per boat.

economic waste

Taxes, *individual quotas*, and *licenses* (sometimes considered together as "limited entry" approaches) can also be used to encourage the desirable amount of fishing. If a tax were levied on each ton of fish harvested, annual revenue per boat after taxes would be decreased; in turn this would reduce the number of boats since revenues will no longer cover costs. The reduction in the fleet would continue until average revenue per boat again equaled average cost. Under the tax approach, the fishermen will have an incentive to keep costs as low as possible; thus the actual cost of catching the fish will be minimized. It is important to note, however, that the tax approach is very unpopular with fishermen. Moreover, it can also be difficult to implement because changes in prices and/or costs will necessitate a change in the tax rate in order to keep the fleet at the desired level.

Individual (as opposed to total) quotas could also be used as a regulatory device. After the desired total catch is determined, it could be divided into shares which would be assigned to individual fishermen. These shares would give each of them the right to harvest a certain amount of fish each year. Since each can catch only a specified amount, it would be to the individual fisherman's advantage to take the allowable catch as cheaply as possible. Under an ideal individual quota system, the allotted shares would be freely transferable between fishermen, so that those who are more efficient could purchase the right to harvest from others. This would further decrease the real cost of harvesting the allotted catch while at the same time benefiting both the buyer and the seller of the quotas.

L. Anderson, "Marine Fisheries" in Current Issues In Natural Resources Policy 149, 161-63 (P. Portney, ed. 1982).

Under the Magnuson-Stevens Act, limited entry programs are "optional," in that a regional council has the discretion to consider them as alternatives to other management approaches. However, if a council does consider limited entry it must take into account social, cultural and economic factors in the fishery. These include present participation in the fishery; historical fishing practices in, and dependence on, the fishery; the economics of the fishery; the capability of vessels used to participate in other fisheries; the cultural and social framework relevant to the fishery; and any other relevant considerations. 16 U.S.C. § 1853(b)(6).

License programs forbid fishing to those not specifically licensed to do so. The object is to set the number of licenses so that those allowed to fish will harvest the optimal catch. The problems with this approach are not difficult to discern. For example, if boats are licensed, and if the restriction on the number of boats is successful in increasing the profitability of the fishery, then the participants will have an incentive to increase their fishing power by manipulating unlicensed inputs, such as size of boat, fish-finding equipment, and so on. Where such substitutions are possible, therefore, limited license programs are very similar in design and effect to limitations on gear. Measures to prevent fishermen from increasing their catch by attaching the licenses to specifically defined units of fishing effort (i.e., a boat of specific length with a certain amount of gear) might work, but would require an accurate definition of a unit of effort, especially in a fleet composed of different types and ages of vessels. In addition, they may also inhibit technological advance * * *.

In summary, limited entry approaches differ from total quotas, closed seasons and areas, and gear restrictions. They have a potential to minimize the costs of harvesting the desired catch. This is especially true of taxes and individual quotas. There are other differences among them, however, including ease of implementation, political acceptability, and the distribution of costs and benefits among fishermen and general consumers. In actual fisheries management in the United States, it is usually the latter that determine which type of regulation is selected.

It is hard to explain exactly why the pattern of regulation has developed as it has. However, the explanation may be that the individuals responsible for the original programs were primarily biologists or industry representatives with no training in fisheries economics. They viewed the problem as one of reducing catch, with no consideration for economic efficiency. In addition, in the realm of international management, the only types of control that could be agreed upon were those which were viewed as helping the stocks without favoring any one nation. Total quotas, closed seasons and areas, and gear restrictions were fairly easy to implement and yet appeared to accomplish these objectives.

Once the pattern was set, it was hard to break, even after jurisdiction was extended. Fisheries administrators were not easily convinced that economic efficiency was important and therefore there was no real incentive to look at other types of regulation. Employment, nondiscriminatory access to the stocks, the way of life in fishing communities, as well as concern with biological aspects of conservation, were deemed more important.

Furthermore, many fishermen and fisheries administrators feel that fisheries are the last frontier and that fishing should be an inalienable right. They therefore opposed individual quotas and limited licenses. Hard to believe as it may seem, private property rights in fisheries were viewed as socialistic even though they are an integral part of the market system! In addition, individual quotas and licenses were opposed because no one relished the possibility that they personally would be precluded from free entry to the fishery. Similarly, taxes were not popular for obvious reasons.

Because of industry opposition and a lack of support for efficiency as a primary objective of management, limited entry programs have not been widely implemented. Licenses have been tried in several instances, but the programs usually amount to prevention of further entry into an already overcapitalized fleet, with little effective effort to reduce fleet size. The fact that license programs are closer to normal practice than taxes or individual quotas may explain why they have been adopted. Unfortunately, however, because license programs are similar to gear restriction programs when inputs can be easily substituted for one another, the former are generally less effective in obtaining efficiency than taxes or individual quotas.

L. Anderson, "Marine Fisheries" in Current Issues in Natural Resources Policy 149, 163-65 (P. Portney, ed. 1982). For additional discussion of these issues, see also National Research Council, Sharing the Fish: Toward an National Policy on Individual Fishing Quotas (1999).

B. THE FISHERY MANAGEMENT PLANNING PROCESS

(1.) Fishery Management Plans and the National Standards

(a.) The Basic Elements of the FMP Process

The Magnuson-Stevens Act charges eight regional fishery management councils with preparing fishery management plans (FMPs) for fish stocks under their jurisdiction. The FMPs are required to have a number of basic elements: an assessment of the condition of the fish stock to be managed and the fishery for it and the regulations that are needed to conserve the stock and manage the fishery. The councils choose the particular conservation and management regulations and other requirements. The Secretary of Commerce, acting through the NMFS, then implements the FMP if it meets the requirements of the Act. If the Secretary finds, however, that there is an emergency, he is authorized to promulgate regulations in response, regardless of whether a FMP exists. 16 U.S.C. § 1855(c)(1). This power extends to "interim measures" to address overfishing. Id.

Section 303 describes these required and discretionary provisions, 16 U.S.C. § 1853. The FMP must include, inter alia, (1) conservation and management measures which are necessary and appropriate for the conservation and management of the fishery, to prevent overfishing and rebuild overfished stocks, and to protect, restore and promote the long-term health and stability of the fishery; (2) a description of the fishery; (3) a specification of the maximum sustainable yield and optimum yield from the fishery; (4) objective and measurable criteria for identifying when the fishery is overfished and measures to prevent or end overfishing and rebuild the fishery; (5) a description and identification of the essential fish habitat for the fishery, measures to minimize to the extent practicable adverse effects on such habitat caused by fishing, and other actions to encourage conservation and enhancement of such habitat; (6) a fishery impact statement which assesses the likely effect of the management measures on affected fishing communities and participants; and (7) an allocation of any reduced catches or recovery benefits in a rebuilding plan that is fair and equitable among all the sectors of the fishery.

When the regional councils develop plan provisions and accompanying proposed regulations to meet the above requirements, the Secretary of Commerce, acting through the Fisheries Service, is required immediately to request public comment on the submission for 60 days and review it to determine whether it is consistent with the Act's national standards, the other provisions of the Act, and any other applicable law. 16 U.S.C. § 1854 (a)(1), (b). The Secretary is then required to approve, disapprove or partially disapprove the council's submission within 30 days of the end of the public comment period.

If the Secretary disapproves or partially disapproves a submission, he or she must specify the applicable law with which it is inconsistent, how it is inconsistent, and recommendations the council could take to conform the plan provisions to these requirements. If, however, the council is not given notice within 30 days of the end of the public comment period, the plan provisions take effect as if approved. Id. at § 1854(a)(3). If the plan provision is disapproved in whole or in part, the council may submit a revised plan or amendment for review. The Act does not specify how long the Secretary must wait for a revised submission, nor how many submissions he or she must review for approval or disapproval before acting to implement plan provisions. The Act gives the Secretary the power to prepare a needed FMP or amendment if the council fails to develop and submit one "after a reasonable period of time," or if the council submits a plan or a revision and the Secretary disapproves it and the council fails to submit a revised or further revised plan or amendment. 16 U.S.C. § 1854(c).

The national standards for all FMPs and implementing regulations are contained in section 301(a), 16 U.S.C. § 1851:

16 U.S.C. § 1851. National standards for fishery conservation and management

(a) In general

Any fishery management plan prepared, and any regulation promulgated to implement any such plan, pursuant to this subchapter shall be consistent with the following national standards for fishery conservation and management:

(1) Conservation and management measures shall prevent overfishing while achieving, on a continuing basis, the optimum yield from each fishery for the United States fishing industry.

(2) Conservation and management measures shall be based upon the best scientific information available.

(3) To the extent practicable, an individual stock of fish shall be managed as a unit throughout its range, and interrelated stocks of fish shall be managed as a unit or in close coordination.

(4) Conservation and management measures shall not discriminate between residents of different States. If it becomes necessary to allocate or assign fishing privileges among various United States fishermen, such allocation shall be (A) fair and equitable to all such fishermen; (B) reasonably calculated to promote conservation; and (C) carried out in such manner that no particular individual, corporation, or other entity acquires an excessive share of such privileges.

(5) Conservation and management measures shall, where practicable, consider efficiency in the utilization of fishery resources; except that no such measure shall have economic allocation as its sole purpose.

(6) Conservation and management measures shall take into account and allow for variations among, and contingencies in, fisheries, fishery resources, and catches.

(7) Conservation and management measures shall, where practicable, minimize costs and avoid unnecessary duplication.

(8) Conservation and management measures shall, consistent with the conservation requirements of this Chapter (including the prevention of overfishing and rebuilding of overfished stocks), take into account the importance of fishery resources to fishing communities in order to (A) provide for the sustained participation of such communities, and (B) to the extent practicable, minimize adverse economic impacts on such communities.

[handwritten margin notes:] • places economic interests above enum'tl? • what is practicable? • Conservatn & mgmt emphasis? "consistent w/ conservatn requirements"

(9) Conservation and management measures shall, to the extent practicable, (A) minimize bycatch and (B) to the extent bycatch cannot be avoided, minimize the mortality of such bycatch.

(10) Conservation and management measures shall, to the extent practicable, promote the safety of human life at sea.

(b) Guidelines--The Secretary shall establish advisory guidelines (which shall not have the force and effect of law), based on the national standards, to assist in the development of fishery management plans.

———

The guidelines required by section 301(b), 16 U.S.C. § 1851(b), on how the Secretary interprets the national standards are published in 50 C.F.R. Part 600. For a discussion of the changes made to the national standards guidelines after 1996, see the preamble in NMFS, NOAA, Final Rule, National Standard Guidelines, 63 Fed. Reg. 24212 (May 1, 1998).

A Closer Look at the Regional Fishery Management Councils

The 1976 Fishery Conservation and Management Act was heralded as a promising new approach to managing a public resource because of the structure of the regional councils. See, e.g., W. Rogalski, The Unique Federalism of the Regional Councils Under the Fishery Conservation and Management Act of 1976, 9 B.C. Envt'l Aff. L. Rev. 163 (1980).

The Congress intended the regional councils to take the lead in designing the management approaches for the fisheries under their jurisdiction, except for fisheries for highly migratory fish species in the Atlantic or Caribbean. 16 U.S.C. § 1852(h). The Magnuson-Stevens Act requires the voting members of each council to include each constituent state's chief marine fisheries official, the NMFS regional administrator, and individuals nominated by the governors and appointed by the Secretary who "by reason of their occupational or other experience, scientific expertise or training, are knowledgeable regarding the conservation and management, or the commercial or recreational harvest, of the fishery resources of the geographical area concerned." Id. § 1852(b).

In making appointments, the Secretary must, "to the extent practicable, ensure a fair and balanced apportionment, on a rotating or other basis, of the active participants (or their representatives) in the commercial and recreational fisheries under the jurisdiction of the Council," reporting annually to Congress on how the required balance among active industry members has been achieved. Id. § 1852(b)(2)(B). Appointed members may serve a maximum of three consecutive 3-year terms. Voting members are compensated at the daily rate for GS-15, step 7 of the General Schedule. Non-voting members of the council include representatives of the Coast Guard, the State Department, and the interstate fishery commission.

Each council determines its organization, practices and procedures and is required to establish a scientific and statistical committee, a fishing industry advisory committee, and other advisory panels as needed to carry out its functions. Id. § 1852(g). The councils hire their own scientific and administrative staffs who receive and analyze information from the NMFS science centers, the fishing industry, and academic and consulting institutions. Councils must hold public hearings in their geographical areas to allow interested persons an opportunity to participate in the development of FMPs and amendments and in meeting other requirements of the Act. Id. § 1852(h)(3). The councils and their committees and panels are exempt from the Federal Advisory Committee Act, 5 U.S.C. App. 2, but must follow procedures outlined in the Act regarding notice and conduct of their meetings. Id. § 1852(i).

As you read the following cases and materials, ask yourself how well this decentralized and industry-centered model has worked and, in light of the difficulties experienced, why it has it survived largely unchanged since 1976. While the experience has varied across the eight regional councils, in at least one of the most important fishing regions of the country, New England, the decisionmaking process created under the Act was insufficient to prevent the overfishing and depletion of the most popular fish stocks: the Gulf of Maine and Georges Bank stocks of cod, haddock, and flounders that make up the traditional groundfish catch.

A detailed account of the management of New England groundfish under the New England Regional Fishery Management Council is given in P. Shelley, J. Atkinson, E. Dorsey, and P. Brooks, The New England Fisheries Crisis: What Have We Learned? 9 Tulane Envt'l L.J. 221 (1996). The authors note that during the decade from 1983 to 1993, despite a large increase in the number of licensed fishing vessels, total groundfish landings fell by 60%, with haddock landings dropping 94%. Early in this period, scientists warned NMFS and the regional council that overfishing was causing very serious declines in fish populations. In 1986, NMFS disapproved the regional council's new FMP which proposed to continue the same strategy of managing catches, not by setting and enforcing a total quota on landings, but through indirect controls of minimum mesh and fish sizes and closed spawning areas. But shortly thereafter,

> [I]n a key moment of weakness, NMFS backed down from its conservation-oriented position in the midst of overwhelming political pressure from the New England congressional delegation and approved margii l and ineffectual changes to the Council's 1986 plan. NMFS did not attempt to directly reassert its management prerogatives to protect the region's groundfish under the FCMA again until the agency was sued by [the Conservation Law Foundation] in 1991.* * *

Shelley et al., at 227. The result of the lawsuit was a consent decree requiring a plan to reduce fishing effort and rebuild the stocks. Conservation Law Foundation v. Mosbacher, __ F.Supp.__, 1991 WL 501640 (D. Mass. 1991). Several intervenors representing the commercial fishing industry challenged the Secretary's authority to enter into the consent decree on a number of grounds, all of which were rejected. Conservation Law Foundation v. Franklin, 989 F.2d 54 (1st Cir. 1993). This rebuilding plan was implemented in 1994 as Amendment 5 to the groundfish FMP and reduced effort by limiting the number of days at sea each licensed vessel could fish. However, by the time the planned reductions in fishing effort went into effect under Amendment 5, the cuts were insufficient to allow the stocks to rebuild. Amendment 7 reduced the target fishing mortality rate to almost zero, cut further the groundfish fleet's allowable days at sea, and closed large areas of the Georges Bank to fishing. See Amendment 7 Notice of Final Rule, 61 Fed. Reg. 27710 (May 31, 1996). When Associated Fisheries of Maine, Inc. challenged Amendment 7 as having a disastrous effect on the small trawler fleet of Maine based on a shaky scientific and economic analysis, the district court found:

Amendment 7 regrettably will have a harsh effect on the fishing industry, a significant means of support for many coastal families and communities, and part of our social, cultural and economic heritage. But it is a rational, though controversial, choice within the Secretary's statutory mandate, and it has been promulgated according to the procedures required by the applicable statutes. Based on a careful review of the administrative record in this case, I find that the Secretary acted within the scope of his broad discretion to promulgate regulations implementing fishery management plans.

Associated Fisheries of Maine, Inc. v. Daley, 954 F. Supp. 383 (D.Me. 1997), aff'd, 127 F.3d 104 (1998).

What caused the fisheries disaster in New England? Could it have been prevented by stronger management actions taken earlier? Was the Act's mandate too ambiguous? After the amendments described in the following sections were enacted, New England groundfish management became no less controversial, nor any more precautionary, leading to further litigation. A federal court decision found that the Secretary and the NMFS had failed to prevent overfishing and minimize bycatch along the New England coast, in violation of the Sustainable Fisheries Act. Conservation Law Foundation v. Evans, __ F.Supp.3d__, No. 00-1134, slip op. at 1 (D.D.C. Dec. 28, 2001).

(b.) Overfishing and Optimum Yield Definitions

The most important requirement for each FMP is that it prevent overfishing while achieving optimum yield "for the United States fishing industry." For the first twenty years of the Act's implementation, the goal of achieving optimum yield, as it was variously defined in the many FMPs, took center stage. The Act contained a definition of OY but not of overfishing. This focus led in many key fisheries to the institutionalization of a condition of overfishing. The Act's ability to constrain the growth of the commercial fishing industry turned out to be limited, necessitating a series of emergency actions followed by a substantial overhaul in the 1996 Sustainable Fisheries Act. The Act now contains an express definition of "overfished" and "overfishing." Also, the definition of optimum yield has been changed to preclude setting OY at a level that exceeds the maximum sustainable catch level.

16 U.S.C. § 1802. Definitions

* * *

(28)   The term "optimum", with respect to the yield from a fishery, means the amount of fish which--

(A)   will provide the greatest overall benefit to the Nation, particularly with respect to food production and recreational opportunities, and taking into account the protection of marine ecosystems;

(B)   is prescribed on the basis of the maximum sustainable yield from the fishery, as reduced by any relevant economic, social, or ecological factors; and

(C)   in the case of an overfished fishery, provides for rebuilding to a level consistent with producing the maximum sustainable yield in such fishery.

(29) The terms "overfishing" and "overfished" mean a rate or level of fishing mortality that jeopardizes the capacity of a fishery to produce the maximum sustainable yield on a continuing basis.

Congress did more in the 1996 amendments than just provide a definition of "overfishing" and require expressly that the councils stop it. Congress also increased the role of the Fisheries Service in meeting the overfishing provisions. Under section 304(e), 16 U.S.C. § 1854(e), the Secretary of Commerce is now required to report annually to Congress and councils on the status of fisheries and identify those within each council's geographical area of authority that are either overfished or are approaching a condition of being overfished, using the criteria specified in the applicable FMP or international agreement. "A fishery shall be classified as approaching a condition of being overfished if, based on trends in fishing effort, fishery resource size, and other appropriate factors, the Secretary estimates that the fishery will become overfished within two years." Id. § 1854(e)(1). Within one year of receiving notice that a fishery is overfished, the responsible council must submit a plan amendment or proposed regulations to end or prevent overfishing and to rebuild the affected stocks. Id. § 1854(e)(4). The council's submission must specify a rebuilding period that is as short as possible taking into account the nature of the stocks and their ecosystem and the needs of fishing communities, not to exceed 10 years, unless the biology of the stock, environmental conditions, or international management measures dictate otherwise. If the council does not submit a plan or regulations to stop overfishing or to rebuild the affected stocks within one year, the Secretary is required to prepare such amendment and regulations to stop overfishing and rebuild the stocks within 9 months. Id. § 1854(e)(5). At the council's request the Secretary can implement interim measures to reduce overfishing until a full rebuilding or overfishing plan can be put into place. The Secretary must also regularly review the rebuilding and overfishing plans to ensure their effectiveness, and notify the council if insufficient progress toward these goals is being made, recommending further measures the council should consider to achieve adequate progress, triggering again the one-year time period for action. Id. § 1854(e)(7).

(2.) The Quota-Setting Process

In the early years of the Magnuson-Stevens Act, litigation challenging decisions under the Act focused on the allocation of fishing quotas among competing sectors of the fishery, for example, the recreational and commercial sectors, or different components of the commercial fishery. See, e.g., C & W Fish Co., Inc. v. Fox, 931 F.2d 1556 (D.C. Cir. 1991); American Factory Trawlers Assoc. v. Baldrige, 831 F.2d 1456 (9th Cir. 1987). One commentator reviewing these and other cases in 1993 concluded that courts appeared unwilling "to delve into the intricacies of fishery management," including whether the best available science is being properly used, and that "even relatively scant evidence may be enough to support management measures on judicial review." In his view, this was unlikely to change, absent the adoption of a standard requiring management measures to be supported by a "preponderance of the scientific evidence." E.V.C. Greenberg, Ocean Fisheries, in C. Campbell-Mohn, B. Breen, and J.W. Futrell, eds., Sustainable Environmental Law (1993), 7.5 text at n. 376.

After that prediction was made, the courts began to consider more closely industry challenges to the scientific basis for commercial quotas they believed were too low. In Fishermen's Dock Cooperative, Inc. v. Brown, 867 F.Supp. 385 (E.D. Va. 1994), District Court Judge Robert Doumar invalidated the 1994 commercial fishing quota for summer flounder of 16 million pounds and ordered that it be reset at 19 million pounds. He found that the quota set by the council and approved by the Secretary deviated downward from the figure reached using the "best scientific information available". Id. at 386. The following appeal resulted.

FISHERMEN'S DOCK COOPERATIVE, INC. v. BROWN
United States Court of Appeals for the Fourth Circuit
75 F.3d 164, 1996

SENIOR CIRCUIT JUDGE **PHILLIPS:**

The Secretary of Commerce (the Secretary) appeals a district court order that invalidated the Department of Commerce's commercial catch quota for summer flounder for 1994 and that imposed another quota in its place. Because the district court misapplied the statutory requirement that the Department set the quota in accord with the "best scientific information available," and consequently erred in invalidating the agency-set quota, we reverse.

I

This case involves a challenge by a coalition of commercial fishers (the Coalition) to the 1994 commercial catch quota for summer flounder promulgated by the Department of Commerce (the Department). The Department sets the quota every year through a complex process mandated by the Magnuson Fishery Conservation and Management Act and by federal regulations. Within the Department of Commerce are eight regional fishery management councils, established by the Act, whose job it is to develop plans for the conservation and management of the fish in each council's respective section of the American coastal waters. Among these bodies is the Mid-Atlantic Fishery Management Council ("the Council"), which has among its responsibilities the management of the summer flounder fishery, including the annual setting of the commercial catch quota.

Before it could set annual quotas, the Council was required to develop a Fishery Management Plan for Summer Flounder, which it did in 1992. Amendments to the plan were promulgated in 1993 and 1994 as well. As part of this Plan, the Council had to set for each of several years a "target fishing mortality rate." The fishing mortality rate is a statistic called F that expresses the depletion of the stock of fish attributable to fishers, whether by capture or by discard of fatally wounded fish or otherwise, in a given year. For 1994, the Fishery Management Plan set a target F of 0.53 and thus required that the commercial catch quota for 1994 be set at a level that would ensure that the actual F would not exceed 0.53.

The process of setting the quota began, for present purposes, with the holding of a Stock Assessment Workshop, a gathering of marine scientists whose mission it was to estimate the size, age structure, and any other relevant characteristics of current populations of various species of fish off the Atlantic coast. The numbers produced by the Workshop for summer flounder were then presented to the Summer Flounder Monitoring Committee (the Monitoring Committee), a subunit of the Council, on September 1, 1993 with recommendations from Council staff. The Monitoring Committee is a group of scientists constituted by the Department who are required to recommend, among other things, a commercial catch quota. The quota for 1994 was to be based on the scientific information from the Workshop and was to be designed to ensure that the "fishing mortality rate," F, did not exceed the 0.53 level previously announced as the 1994 target by the Fishery Management Plan. The Monitoring Committee recommended a quota of 16,005,560 pounds. That recommendation then went to the Demersal Species Committee of the Council and to the Atlantic States Marine Fisheries Commission, an interstate organization with which the Council cooperates. Those two bodies, meeting jointly on September 23, approved the Monitoring Committee's recommendation and passed it on to the Council which, in turn, recommended it to the Regional Director for approval. After the requisite notice and comment, during which no objections pertinent to this appeal seem to have been filed, the quota became final in early 1994.

At the heart of the case is the way the Monitoring Committee used the Workshop's data regarding the "recruitment" of summer flounder -- that is, the number of new flounder expected to appear in the population in 1994. At the Committee's annual quota-setting meeting, staff member Wendy Gabriel had presented the Committee with the geometric mean of the previous five years' estimated recruitments and the values one standard deviation above and below that mean. Then, on recommendation of Council staff, and specifically following the lead of Gabriel's presentation of the recruitment statistics to the Committee, the Committee chose to recommend that the quota be set on the basis of a conservative estimate of recruitment. In particular, the staff had recommended, and the Committee then chose to use, an estimate of recruitment equal to the figure one standard deviation below the geometric mean rather than a recruitment estimate equal to that geometric mean. As a direct consequence, the Committee recommended that the previous year's quota be increased for 1994 only to about 16 million pounds (a 28% increase) whereas incorporation of the geometric-mean estimate would have boosted the quota to about 19 million pounds.

The lower quota was ratified at every step of review and published in the Federal Register accompanied by four justifications that closely reflected those articulated in the original staff recommendation. As articulated in the Federal Register, the four reasons for using the lower estimate were the following:

First, the summer flounder population was composed mainly of fish aged 2 and under; so an overestimate in recruitment would have great power to cause an overestimate in overall stock size and thus "would result in quotas that would exceed the target fishery mortality rate (F level)." Second, "the probability of achieving the target F level is higher at the lower harvest level" with staff estimating an 80% probability that the proposed quota would keep actual F under target F. Third, three risky assumptions--that the previous year's quota would prove to have been adhered to, that all landings get reported, and that discard rates would not increase-- underlay the estimate of the stock size and suggested that the stock-size curve might be overly optimistic. Fourth, since the target F was scheduled to decrease dramatically for 1996, it was better to err on the safe side now so as to minimize the chances of having to reduce the 1996 quota even more than was already anticipated. In short, the Council believed that the uncertainty in the recruitment estimates was so great and the long-term flounder population so fragile a resource for the fishers, especially in light of a coming reduction in the target fishing mortality rate for 1996, that a low estimate of recruitment was the prudent estimate.

In challenging the quota, the Coalition argued that use of the lower estimate rather than the geometric mean in calculating the quota constituted a failure to use the best scientific information available as required by 16 U.S.C. § 1851(a)(2). After holding a three-day hearing to have the administrative record explained, the district court agreed and held that the quota, therefore, represented an arbitrary and capricious decision on the part of the Department. The court concluded that only the geometric-mean estimate could constitute the best scientific information available in this case. On this basis, the court held that "the 1994 commercial catch quota is invalidated to the extent that it deviates downward from the figure reached using the best scientific information available, which was 19.05 million pounds for 1994," Fishermen's Dock Cooperative v. Brown, 867 F. Supp. 385, 386 (E.D. Va. 1994), and ordered that the quota be reset at that figure. The key parts of the district court's opinion read as follows:

> The Court finds that the use of figures one standard deviation below the mean was arbitrary and capricious. The use of a figure one standard deviation below the mean was chosen not because it was the best scientific information available, but solely because it increased the percentages of reaching not a balanced result but a result which protected the summer flounder stock to the detriment of the fishermen.

> * * * The Council chose to implement a quota one standard deviation below the geometric mean, resulting in a quota of 16.005 million pounds rather than a quota of 19.05 million pounds, a sixteen percent difference. Defendant's designees explained that using the lower figure increased the probability of reaching 0.53, the target fishing mortality for 1994, from 59% at the geometric mean to 81% with the lower figure.

> This Court finds that the Council's decision to implement a quota one standard deviation below the geometric mean failed to utilize the best scientific information available, and therefore was arbitrary and capricious. * * *. The commercial catch quota * * * should be reset using the figure derived from the best scientific information available--19.05 million pounds, the geometric mean, replacing the quota set at one standard deviation below the mean, or 16.005 million pounds* * * Accordingly, this Court * * * ORDERS that the 1994 summer flounder commercial catch quota be invalidated to the extent that it is less than 19.05 million pounds.

Fishermen's Dock, 867 F. Supp. at 396-97.

This appeal by the Secretary followed. A number of environmental organizations and recreational fishers' organizations have filed an amicus brief in support of the Secretary's position.

* * *

III

The district court held that, at least in the circumstances of this case, the statutory requirement that the agency use the "best scientific information available" translated to a rule of law that the agency use the geometric mean as its estimate of recruitment in setting the commercial catch quota for 1994. The Secretary argues on appeal that the agency's action in this case was in no way arbitrary, capricious, or otherwise illegal and that, even if it was, the district court overreached its authority in imposing a new quota rather than remanding to the agency.

We agree with the essentials of the Secretary's primary argument. In explaining why, it is important at the outset to point out the limited scope of the Coalition's challenge to the agency action. It does not challenge the Fishery Management Plan or its target fishing mortality rate for 1994. It does not challenge the procedures used in producing the quota or the scientific validity of the data underlying the quota. It challenges only the Department's choice to rely on one estimate of recruitment rather than another, and contends that the district court was correct to hold that there was only one estimate consistent with use of the best scientific information available as required by 16 U.S.C. § 1851(a)(2). We disagree on that basic point. The district court's holding that the available scientific information on recruitment dictated one and only one possible quota reveals a critical misunderstanding of the nature of the information available.

The Act mandates that the agency conform to several "national standards," [including standards 1,2 and 6] * * * No one contends that the Council's Fishery Management Plan is inconsistent with the above statutory standards. [the court goes on to describe the FMP's requirement for setting the catch quotas and other restrictions necessary to ensure that the fishing mortality rate set in the plan is not exceeded. 50 C.F.R. 625.20 (regulations implementing the FMP).]

* * *

* * * [t]he [FMP] regulations call for the Demersal Species Committee, the Council, and the Regional Director (both before and after public comment), each in turn, to consider what quota is *"necessary to assure that the applicable fishing mortality rate specified in paragraph (a) of this section is not exceeded."* (Emphasis added.) This quoted language appears four separate times in that subsection.

The sum of these provisions is that the Monitoring Committee is required to seek a fairly high level of confidence that the quota it recommends will not result in an F greater than 0.53, even as it must be equally concerned to provide the fishing industry with an "optimum yield" both in the current year and over the long term. Although the regulatory language repeatedly calls for the Council to "assure" that the target F is "not exceeded," it cannot be taken to require 100% assurance. If taken literally, that language could mean that the Monitoring Committee would have to recommend something close to closing of the fishery to "assure" an acceptable F. But, of course, the statute does not contemplate regulatory overkill. It anticipates an "optimum yield" for the fishing industry that is consistent with reasonable assurance that the actual F will be less than or equal to the target F.

Also, while the language assumes that such a quota can be established on the basis of the "best scientific information available"-- and so requires that the quota be set on that basis--it appears to say nothing about how that term is to be defined. It only mandates the constitution of committees of scientists to provide and evaluate such information. In this case, the Monitoring Committee had before it, among other things, three estimates or predictions of recruitment for 1994 that were derived from research that, at least for purposes of this appeal, everyone agrees constituted the best scientific information available. One of the estimates was the geometric mean of the estimated recruitments for the years 1988 through 1992; that is, the midpoint of the probability curve of all possible recruitment estimates for 1994 as derived from the estimated actual recruitments of the previous five years. The other two estimates for 1994 were produced by traveling one standard deviation above and below the geometric mean along the curve of 1994 recruitment estimates. As is always true of the single standard-deviation points along a normal curve, these high and low estimates represented the upper and lower limits of a range of estimates within which there was a 68% probability that the true recruitment would eventually lie. The geometric mean was just the middle value in that range, and the single-standard-deviation values were simply standard statistical markers for indicating the degree of uncertainty in the data.

Thus, to illustrate, if the geometric mean were about 30 million fish with a standard deviation of about 10 million, all the Monitoring Committee would know from the three estimates presented to it was that the best science available predicted a 68% chance that the actual recruitment for 1994 would be somewhere between 20 million and 40 million fish. No single point estimate on the curve had any assigned probability of being the ultimately correct one. But any range of estimates on the curve had a particular and easily derived probability of containing the ultimately correct number.

One of the properties of the curve, then, was that it could provide the scientists and the administrators with the available research's best conclusions as to the ranges within which the actual 1994 recruitment was likely to lie. But another even more important property was that that curve apparently implied another curve; and this second curve provided, for any chosen point estimate of recruitment, the probability that the quota derived from that point estimate would ultimately produce an actual F for 1994 of 0.53 or less. Crucially for this case, that latter curve in fact indicated that the 19-million-pound quota, derived from the estimate at the geometric mean, carried a 59% chance of eventually producing a 1994 F of 0.53 or less, whereas the 16-million-pound quota, derived from the estimate one standard deviation below the mean, carried an 81% chance of eventually producing a 1994 F of 0.53 or less. And no one disputes the validity of these probabilities; no one suggests that they rested on anything but the best scientific information available.

On the basis of this best available scientific information, then, the Monitoring Committee had to estimate what the true recruitment would be. If it estimated too high and set the quota accordingly high, then the smaller actual recruitment would be decimated by fishers operating under the high quota, with the result that F would exceed 0.53. Alternatively, the Monitoring Committee could estimate that actual recruitment would be low and thereby increase its chances of not exceeding target F. Since the Fishery Management Plan called for assurance that target F would not be exceeded but not such absolute assurance as would result in previously undershooting target F and denying the fishing industry its "optimum yield," the Agency's decisionmakers necessarily had some discretion to decide what precise degree of assurance it would seek within the uncertainty of the data.

In exercising that discretion, these decision-makers consistently offered the four reasons recited above for recommending use of the lower of the two recruitment estimates and thus the lower of the two quotas that they had considered in light of the data presented: first, the truncated age structure of the summer flounder population, which magnified the risk to target F involved in any overestimate of the size of the recruitment class; second, the general proposition that a lower recruitment estimate provided a higher probability of assuring that actual F would turn out to be less than or equal to target F; third, the recognition that certain assumptions underlying the estimate of the flounder stock size might be overly optimistic; and, fourth, the belief that, since target F was to decrease significantly in 1996, it was better to deal with the current uncertainty in recruitment estimates by erring on the conservative side rather than risking an exacerbation of the painful quota decrease that had to come soon in any case.[1]

---

[1] The Coalition argues in passing that this last justification is an unauthorized acceleration of the Fishery Management Plan's call for a reduction in target F in 1996 (not 1994). That argument is correct as far as it goes. But the Department's mandate in setting quotas is to manage great uncertainties in data as best as it can while taking the

These reasons do not justify the precise choice of an 81% probability of success or the choice to plug into the formula the specific recruitment estimate located at the one-standard-deviation-below-the-geometric-mean mark. Nor do they consistently explain why the choice of a conservative recruitment estimate was the best way to modify the quota rather than using a higher recruitment estimate but then simply lowering the quota itself to take account of all the uncertainties in the data. But they do reflect the Monitoring Committee's understanding that the recruitment estimate was the main source of uncertainty along the way to making a stock-size estimate and then setting a quota; and they do justify setting a quota that, taking that uncertainty into account, offered a high probability--if not 100% assurance-of achieving the regulatory goal of not exceeding target F. Moreover, at the Monitoring Committee's meeting and later in the process, the point was made that, "happenstantial" as the lower figure might be, it had the benefit of both providing a high probability of staying under target F and still allowing a substantial (28%) increase in the quota from the year before. It thus showed commercial fishers that the Department's measures were not simply relentless attacks on the industry but beneficial over the long term for all concerned as the Act contemplated. The option of setting the quota so as to provide a 90% or 95% probability of success was also considered but rejected as too heavy a short-term burden on the fishing industry.

In this situation, to assert, as the district court did, that the "best scientific information" required use of the geometric-mean estimate to dictate a quota that had only a 59% chance of not causing F to be exceeded, rather than use of an estimate that would provide an 81% chance of not causing F to be exceeded, is to misconstrue what the best scientific information really shows in the context of the statute and regulations. A quota "based on" that information and designed to "assure" that the target F was not exceeded while still providing the fishing industry with an "optimum yield" could not properly be determined by a court in judicial review to be, as a matter of law, only one that happened to provide a 59% chance of not exceeding F. The district court was correct that the specific choice of an 81% probability largely because it happened to correspond to one of the three recruitment estimates presented to the committee--when those three estimates were presented merely as indicators of the degree of uncertainty in the data--was, in a sense, arbitrary. But, within the terms of the statute and regulations, so would have been the choice of a 59% probability.

---

long view of the state of fishery and its users, whether fishers or conservationists or anyone else. In that context, it seems fair to allow the Department to bolster its decision to err on the safe side with its observation that, if in fact its estimate proved to be low, it would at least have the benefit of easing the transition to the new target F in 1996.

When the regulations say that the Committee's recommendation should "assure" that target F is not exceeded, they do not say what probability of success (as derived from the best scientific information available) constitutes "assurance" of success. As long as everyone agrees, as everyone does, that the regulations do not require 100% assurance, the choice of how much assurance to indulge in must be a policy choice left to the reasonable exercise of the discretion of the statutorily authorized decision-makers. And that choice inevitably contains a degree of arbitrariness.

In the event, those decisionmakers seem to have allowed themselves to gravitate to a specific number--within the general range suggested by their reasoning--largely because that number happened to have been on the table as a standard deviation. If allowing themselves to gravitate in that way constituted arbitrariness in the selection of the final number within the acceptable range of assurance, then the Monitoring Committee indulged only in the kind of arbitrariness that is inherent in the exercise of discretion amid uncertainty and not in the kind of arbitrariness that the statute condemns when it exists in tandem with capriciousness.

To dispute this conclusion, the Coalition cites a handful of cases for the proposition that the APA requires a tighter connection than the agency has articulated here between the specific regulation adopted and the regulation's justifications. But evaluation of agency reasoning is inevitably an ad hoc enterprise, and the Coalition's cited cases simply do not present factual situations similar enough to our case to suggest that the agency failed to justify itself adequately. In fact, these cases do little but reaffirm the requirement that the agency have engaged in reasoned decision-making within the specific regulatory context.

* * *

IV

Our independent review of the record satisfies us that the agency's process of setting the 1994 quota was conducted in good faith, pursued with a proper understanding of the law, based on the best scientific information available, and adequately justified by the agency. If there was an inevitable element of arbitrariness in the decision, there was not the least caprice. The district court could not properly hold that the quota was not based on the best scientific information available where, as we hold, the record demonstrates that the agency fully understood the meaning of the data before it and chose to adopt a quota that, on the basis of that information, offered a high probability of meeting its regulatory mandate while also allowing the fishing industry to increase its harvest for 1994 over that of 1993. Accordingly, we will reverse the district court's judgment, uphold the Department's 1994 commercial catch quota, and dismiss the Coalition's action.

REVERSED.

Notes and Questions on Judicial Review of Fisheries Regulations

1. Although he was ultimately reversed, District Court Judge Doumar certainly proved wrong the prediction that courts would not "delve into the intricacies of fisheries management." See Greenberg, *supra*. After denying both parties' motions for summary judgment, he ordered the parties to conduct a trial on whether NMFS used the best scientific information available in setting the 1994 summer flounder quota. After the trial he made several findings of fact. While noting that other courts have been reluctant to find that the best scientific information available was not utilized, he found that the 'best scientific information available' requirement should be interpreted in light of the "dual objectives" of the Act: to conserve fishery resources and to promote fishing. In his view, this required him to reject as arbitrary the choice of a recruitment estimate one standard deviation below the mean, because it caused the quota to be lower than what it would have been had the geometric means of the estimates been used. The Fourth Circuit reversed, but Doumar's opinion is interesting in the degree to which he examines the data and assumptions used in the stock assessments and the way he uses the Act's policy goals to help define what constitutes the best scientific information. After the 1996 amendments, is he correct that the dual objectives of the Act have equal weight in defining the best available information? See NRDC v. Daley, 209 F.3d 747 (D.C.Cir. 2000), *infra* at C.(1.)(p. 471).

In the summer founder cases, Judge Doumar set a precedent for in-depth, skeptical review of fisheries management decisions by the courts, under the Magnuson-Stevens Act, and under the judicial review provisions of the Regulatory Flexibility Act (RFA), as amended by the Small Business Regulatory Enforcement Fairness Act of 1996, 5 U.S.C. §§ 601 et seq. In North Carolina Fisheries Assoc. v. Daley, 16 F.Supp.2d 647 (E.D.Va. 1997), Judge Doumar reviewed the quota-setting and deductions-for-overages process for summer flounder for 1996 and 1997. He found them deficient because NMFS had conducted an insufficient analysis of the economic impact of the summer flounder quotas on small businesses under the RFA and National Standard 8, remanded the quota, and ordered the Secretary to carry out the required economic review. 16 F.Supp.2d at 658.

After NMFS submitted the required analysis, Judge Doumar appointed an independent expert to review the adequacy of the analysis. In the meantime, NMFS issued the 1998 quota and adjustments, which were in turn challenged by the plaintiffs. Judge

Doumar applied the standard of review announced in Associated Fisheries of Maine v. Daley, 127 F.3d 104, 116 (1st Cir. 1997), that under the RFA, the Secretary's judgments are not arbitrary and capricious if he "made a reasonable, good faith effort to canvas major options and weigh their probable effects." See M.J. McDevitt, Comment, Impact of the Regulatory Flexibility Act on the Implementation and Judicial Review Provisions of the Magnuson-Stevens Fishery Conservation and Management Act, 6 Ocean & Coastal L.J. 371 (2001). Doumar found that the Secretary had prepared an analysis that was "utterly lacking in compliance with the requirements of the RFA" for failing to consider a community any smaller than the entire state of North Carolina and to consider available data indicating a large difference between the number of licensed fishermen and those who actually fish for flounder. North Carolina Fisheries Assoc. v. Daley, 27 F.Supp.2d 650 (E.D.Va. 1998). He set aside the penalty adjustment to the 1998 quota for overfishing in 1997, increasing the quota, and ordered the Secretary to issue the annual quotas at the beginning of the year. Id.

In a third installment of the case, Judge Doumar reviewed the actions of NMFS in revising the summer flounder quotas in light of the D.C. Circuit's decision in an environmental group's challenge to the summer flounder quotas. In NRDC v. Daley, 209 F.3d 747 (D.C. Cir. 2000), see infra at C.(1.), environmental groups this time challenged the 1999 summer flounder quota as too high to prevent overfishing. The court agreed and remanded the 1999 quota, ordering the Secretary to set it and all future quotas at a level that provides at least a 50% probability of not exceeding the target fishing mortality rate (i.e., the overfishing threshold) established in the FMP. After the Secretary issued the new quota specifications for the coming year (2001), well after the start of the fishing year due to difficulties in obtaining the most recent information on landings, the fishing industry challenged the specification process as a violation of the Judge's previous orders. North Carolina Fisheries Assoc. v. Daley, 152 F.Supp.2d 870 (E.D.Va. 2001).

This time, however, Judge Doumar, noting the D.C. Circuit's order to lower the quota, did not sanction the agency by effectively increasing it. Instead, he ordered the Secretary not to make any additional adjustments to North Carolina's future summer flounder quotas on the basis of overages in 2000, despite the FMP's requirement of this payback process, and to pay the reasonable attorneys' fees incurred in the latest case. 152 F.Supp.2d at 881. Four months later, after the plaintiffs challenged the Secretary's reduction of the quotas to below the overfishing threshold (in order to make up for higher past quotas), Federal District Court Judge Friedman of the Eastern District of Virginia held that the Secretary had violate neither National Standard 1 nor 2. North Carolina Fisheries Assoc. v. Evans, 172 F.Supp.2d 792 (E.D.Va. 2001). After considering the reasons NMFS gave for setting the interim biomass levels as it did and in applying its standard approach to assessing the flounder stock, the court held that "[b]ased on the evidence presented by the parties, this Court cannot say that the Secretary's decisions with respect to the fish mortality rate and biomass targets were unreasonable or devoid of justification." Id. at 802. Did Judge Friedman return to a more typical standard of judicial review? See also question 4 below.

2. The Magnuson-Stevens Act gives federal district courts exclusive jurisdiction over "any case or controversy arising under the provisions of [the] Act." 16 U.S.C. § 1861(d). The judicial review provisions allow challenges to FMP regulations and implementing actions, including closures, only if petitions for such review are filed within 30 days after promulgation of the regulations or publication of the action in the Federal Register. 16 U.S.C. § 1855(f). Why should challenges be limited to such a short time period? For a discussion of the legislative history of this provision, see Note, Judicial Review of Fishery Management Regulations Under the Fishery Conservation and Management Act of 1976, 52 Wash. L. Rev. 599 (1977).

The Act requires the Secretary to file the administrative record within 45 days of the filing of the petition for review and the court, upon motion, to "expedite the matter in every possible way." Id. § 1855(f)(4). Challengers, however, may not obtain a preliminary injunction when challenging FMP regulations or actions. 16 U.S.C. § 1855(f)(1)(A). Why do you think Congress excluded preliminary injunctions as a interim remedy for aggrieved parties? See Kramer v. Mosbacher, 878 F.2d 134 (4th Cir. 1989).

Even if a petition for review is timely, the court may only set aside the regulation or action on a ground specified in section 706(2)(A)-(D) of the Administrative Procedure Act, that is, if the court finds that the agency action, findings, and conclusions were arbitrary, capricious, an abuse of discretion, or otherwise not in accordance with law; contrary to constitutional right or power; in excess of statutory jurisdiction or authority; or without observance of procedure required by law. 5 U.S.C. § 706(2)(A-(D).

In the years following enactment of the Sustainable Fisheries Act and the Small Business Regulatory Enforcement Fairness Act, both of 1996, the number of legal challenges to federal fisheries actions increased enormously. Plaintiffs have used these laws, and the requirements of the National Environmental Policy Act of 1969 (NEPA) and the Endangered Species Act of 1973 (ESA), to open the federal fishery management process to increased judicial scrutiny under a broader set of environmental and social policy goals than was probably anticipated by Congress in 1976. For the impact of NEPA on the Magnuson-Stevens Act, see section C.(3.)(b.) below and ch. 7 (ESA).

3. Challengers must exhaust their administrative remedies before they can challenge the FMP regulations in federal court, including filing

a formal request with the Secretary for an amendment where the regional council made no such recommendations. See Midwater Trawlers Co-op v. Mosbacher, 727 F. Supp. 12 (D.D.C. 1989). Once review is granted, the Secretary's decision is reviewed for reasonableness, not de novo. Washington Crab Producers v. Mosbacher, 924 F.2d 1438 (9th Cir. 1991). The court will not overturn the Secretary's decision to approve or disapprove an FMP or amendment unless the record shows that the Secretary's findings with respect to the National Standards or other applicable law were arbitrary and capricious or an abuse of discretion.

4. The councils and NMFS have come to rely on a process called a "framework adjustment" under most FMPs, whereby the FMP or a major FMP amendment serves as a framework plan to guide specific management actions to be taken every year, usually requiring the annual specification of quotas and other management measures, as was the case in the summer flounder FMP. The annual specifications are then implemented as "framework adjustments" rather than amendments to the FMP, in order to streamline the notice-and-comment process prior to implementation. See 50 C.F.R. § 600.340. When a framework adjustment process is used, it may be several years after the adoption of the FMP or amendment that authorized it. See, e.g., 50 C.F.R. § 648.90 (framework adjustments to the New England groundfish FMP). In that case, the 30-day petition for review requirement begins to run when the framework adjustment is published. When a framework adjustment is challenged, is the challenger limited to issues concerning the specifics of the adjustment regulation, or may he or she raise issues about the underlying FMP or amendment?

In a challenge to the Framework 33 regulation issued under the New England groundfish FMP, the plaintiffs challenged the framework's failure to implement the rebuilding fishing mortality targets of the recently-approved Amendment 9, and Amendment 9's failure to contain bycatch minimization provisions as required by the 1996 Sustainable Fisheries Act. Conservation Law Foundation v. Evans, No. 00-1134, slip op. (D.D.C. Dec. 28, 2001). The court held these latter claims were not time-barred by § 1855(f) because "a party against whom a rule is applied may bring a substantive challenge to a rule at the time of its application[,]" citing, e.g., Independent Community Bankers v. Board of Governors of the Federal Reserve, 195 F.3d 28, 34 (D.C.Cir. 1999). Id. at 18-19.

5. In his 2001 summer flounder decision, District Court Judge Friedman concluded that the fishing industry plaintiffs were really challenging the quota-setting policies adopted under Amendment 2 to the summer flounder FMP, approved in 1992 and continued in a 1999 amendment, which was designed to meet the Sustainable Fisheries Act (SFA). These claims therefore were time-barred under § 1855(f). (Judge Doumar had considered their challenges to each year's quotas

as part of his supervision of NMFS's compliance with his order that the quotas be issued on a timely basis.) While denying review, Judge Friedman noted that plaintiffs whose SFA-based challenges to past NMFS actions are time-barred by §1855(f) could have recourse by petitioning for rulemaking under section 553(e) of the Administrative Procedure Act, and then suing to review if the agency denies the petition. 172 F.Supp.2d at 799. Are parties likely to find satisfaction through this route? Note Connecticut's challenge to the denial of its petition for rulemaking to alter the summer flounder FMP described below in B.(4). NMFS set the 2002 summer flounder total quota at 24.3 million pounds, a quota the Monitoring Committee found to have a 50% change of achieving the target fishing mortality rate of 0.26. NMFS also amended the regulations to allow it to deduct overages based on the landings as of Oct. 31 in a given year. NMFS, 2002 Specifications for Summer Flounder, 66 Fed. Reg. 66348 (Dec. 26, 2001).

6. Congress gave North Carolina a seat on the Mid-Atlantic Fishery Management Council in the 1996 amendments to the MSA. 16 U.S.C. § 1852(a)(1)(B). The Mid-Atlantic council develops the summer flounder FMP in cooperation with an interstate fisheries commission.

Notes on Enforcing Fishery Management Regulations

1. Enforcing the FMP regulations has proven to be as daunting a challenge as developing and approving them for implementation. A 1987 NOAA study raised the enforcement issue.

> In certain fisheries there is said to be widespread cheating on regulations. This is, to put it plainly, stealing valuable U.S. property from law abiding fishermen, the public owners, and from the taxpayer by increasing enforcement cost and diminishing revenues from unreported income. These unlawful practices seriously undermine the fundamental objectives of conservation and fair allocation. There are a number of contributing factors, including economic pressure, perception that risk of getting caught and punished is less than the rewards of violation, the respect of peers for large catches, inadequate funding, and a lack of understanding of the value of the management regime. Whatever factors contribute to these practices, it is plain that more aggressive and effective steps must be taken to discourage them.

Department of Commerce, NOAA Fishery Management Study 18 (June 30, 1987).

In the 1990 amendments, Congress made several changes to enhance the enforcement authority of the NMFS and the Coast Guard. The Act now allows a maximum civil penalty of $100,000 per violation, up from $25,000. 16 U.S.C. § 1858(a). Most significantly, the Act now provides specific authority for the revocation or suspension of, or the imposition of conditions on, a fishing vessel permit, or the denial of a new permit. 16 U.S.C. § 1858(g). Why is it important for the Secretary to have the authority to revoke a fishing vessel's permit? Before imposing such sanctions, the Secretary must afford the violator an opportunity for a hearing on the facts concerning the underlying violation. If a hearing was offered or held prior to the levying of a civil penalty, an additional hearing is not required before the permit sanctions are imposed. With the opportunity for a hearing, is it likely that a permit sanction will be levied in a manner timely enough to impose a real cost on the violator? See J. Sutinen, A. Rieser and J. Gauvin, Measuring and Explaining Noncompliance in U.S. Fisheries, 21 Ocean Devt & Intl. L. 335 (1990).

NOAA's civil enforcement procedures governing actions for monetary penalties and for revocation or suspension of fishing permits under section 308, 16 U.S.C. § 1858, are set out in 15 C.F.R. Part 904. Criminal sanctions are not authorized for violations of the fishery regulations, but they may be imposed for persons who interfere with inspections or enforcement activities. Id. § 1859. Penalties are imposed after an adjudicatory hearing in front of a Department of Commerce administrative law judge. Over time, these officers have become very familiar with the nature of fisheries violations and their appropriate penalties.

Civil forfeitures of the fishing vessel, gear, or illegal catch are allowed under the Act. 16 U.S.C. § 1860. In Gulf of Maine Trawlers v. United States, 674 F. Supp. 927 (D.Me. 1987), the court held that prior court approval was not required under the Act for the sale of seized fish; the Act permits sale of fish, subject to approval and direction of appropriate court, for at least fair market value. These regulations did not exceed the Secretary's authority, where prompt sale was necessary to preserve value. Jensen v. United States, 743 F. Supp. 1091 (D.N.J. 1990).

2.   In Lovgren v. Byrne, 787 F.2d 857 (3rd Cir. 1986), the Third Circuit Court of Appeals rejected appellant's arguments that NMFS' regulations authorizing warrantless search of dockside facilities exceeded the authority conferred on the agency by the MFCMA and violated the Fourth Amendment. In rejecting appellant's Fourth Amendment claim, the court found that Lovgren "had little if any reasonable expectation of privacy on his dock," that government interests for the searches were "compelling," and that the act and regulations were carefully tailored to avoid "unnecessary intrusion on privacy." Id. at 865.

(3.) Reforming the Regional Councils

In the 1990s, some plaintiffs challenging particular FMP regulations also questioned the constitutionality of the Magnuson-Stevens Act's council process and its use of both state and federal officers in potential violation of the Appointments Clause and the separation of powers doctrine. See, e.g., Northwest Environmental Defense Center v.

Brennan, 958 F.2d 930, 937-38 (9th Cir. 1992)(plaintiffs lacked standing to raise the constitutional issues). In State of Connecticut v. U.S. Dept of Commerce, 204 F.3d 413, 416-17 (2d Cir. 2000), Connecticut challenged the Secretary's failure to grant its petition for rulemaking to set quotas for summer flounder on a coastwise, rather than a state-by-state basis. (Under the existing state-by-state quota system, Connecticut's share is 2.25%.) Judge Calabresi affirmed the district court's decision for the Secretary, but made the following comments on the constitutional claim:

> In part, but not only, because of this superfluous interpretation of the statute, Connecticut now asserts, for the first time, important constitutional challenges to the validity of the Magnuson-Stevens Act. * * * We appreciate Connecticut's reasons for wanting the constitutionality of the statute to be evaluated at this time. But we believe that any such immediate consideration would make difficult an adequate treatment of the complex questions at stake and hence would not be in the best interest of the parties or of the administration of justice. To the extent that Connecticut's arguments depend on a reading of the statute that we find unnecessary to the district court's result, the State's claims are premature. And to the extent that the standing issues at stake involve factual determinations, we are necessarily handicapped by not having full findings as to these facts from the district court. * * * Accordingly, we decline to express a view on the constitutional challenges that Connecticut has made to the validity of the statute.

> In doing this, we take note that Connecticut is in no way precluded from raising, in an appropriately made facial challenge to the statute, brought in the district court, any of the constitutional claims we opt not to consider today. This is so for two independent reasons. First, the statute applies to a number of regulatory actions other than those involved in this case, a fact that makes the application of *res judicata* to any such challenge extremely dubious. Second, the Secretary, by asking us to postpone consideration of the constitutional issues to a later time, has, we conclude, waived whatever arguments in favor of preclusion might exist.

> Should such a facial challenge be made, the district court would be able to evaluate the standing questions involved and make the factual findings necessary to a determination of some of them. It would also, with the benefit of full briefing, including that of relevant friends of the court, be able to treat in a coherent and complete way the fundamental and important issues raised by Connecticut.

> Accordingly, and confident that, despite the arguments for doing otherwise, this is one of those occasions when not deciding is deciding best, we decline to consider Connecticut's constitutional claims and express no view on any of them * * *

Was Judge Calabresi inviting the State to try again? On July 24, 2000, Connecticut filed suit for declaratory and injunctive relief against enforcement of the MSA (and of the Atlantic Coastal Fisheries Cooperative Management Act), claiming that both on their face and as applied violate the Fifth and Tenth Amendments of the U.S. Constitution "because the regulatory system established by the MSA permits fishermen and states in direct competition with Connecticut's fishermen to regulate their activities in violation of the Fifth Amendment and requires Connecticut to participate in the unconstitutional scheme naming members to and participating in the Council in violation of the Tenth Amendment; and because the Atlantic Coastal Fisheries Cooperative Management Act requires the State to enforce FMPs in State waters in violation of the Tenth Amendment." Complaint at 2, State of Connecticut v. U.S. Dept of Commerce, No. 1386 (D.Conn. July 24, 2000).

The complaint notes that the summer flounder quotas are set by the Mid-Atlantic Council, comprised of representatives from New York, New Jersey, Delaware, Maryland, Virginia, North Carolina, and Pennsylvania, but not from Connecticut or other New England states. It claims that by requiring the Governor to nominate individuals from commercial and recreational fisheries for appointments to the regional council and requiring the principal state fisheries official to serve on the council, "Connecticut is required to participate in an unconstitutional delegation of regulatory authority to members of the regulated community in violation of the Due Process Clause * * * [and] of the Tenth Amendment of the Fifth Amendment to the U.S. Constitution." By granting authority to the Mid-Atlantic Council for summer flounder, scup, black sea bass, and bluefish fisheries, the Secretary "allows a consortium of states and business interests other than Connecticut to regulation Connecticut's interests in violation of the Tenth Amendment."

Some critics of the decision-making structure of the Magnuson-Stevens Act argue that it gives too much authority to those with a financial interest in any resulting fishery regulation. Prior to the 1996 amendments, some commentators concluded that the financial interests of some council members made them less willing to accept conservation restrictions on fisheries in which they had a stake. See R.J. McManus, America's Saltwater Fisheries: So Few Fish, So Many Fishermen, 9 Nat. Resources & Envt. 13 (Spring 1995); World Wildlife Fund, Managing U.S. Marine Fisheries: Public Interest or Conflict of Interest? (Aug. 1995). For a discussion of the conflict of interest issue, see T. Cloutier, Comment, Conflicts of Interest on Regional Fishery Management Councils: Corruption or Cooperative Management?, 2 Ocean & Coastal L.J. 101 (1996).

The Act requires council voting members to disclose their financial interests in fisheries after their nomination for an appointment and to keep up-to-date their financial disclosure forms, which are kept on file at the council offices. 16 U.S.C. § 1852(j). This requirement covers financial interests "in any harvesting, processing, or marketing activity that is being, or will be, undertaken within a fishery over which the council concerned has jurisdiction." Id. § 1852(j)(2). Failure to make disclosures in accordance with the Secretary's regulations will not serve as grounds for invalidation of the council's action. Id. § 1852 (j)(6).

The Sustainable Fisheries Act amended the council process to require recusal prior to voting of a member with a financial interest in a council decision if that decision would have "a significant and predictable effect on such financial interest." Id. § 1852(j)(7)(A). A council decision is to be considered to have such an effect "if there is a close causal link between the council decision and an expected and substantially disproportionate benefit to the financial interest of the affected individual relative to the financial interests of other participants in the same gear type or sector of the fishery." Id. The recusing member can still participate in the council's deliberations, however, and may indicate for the record how he or she would have voted. Id. Voting members in compliance with NOAA regulations on disclosure are exempt from federal conflict of interest laws of 18 U.S.C. § 208. Id. § 1852(j)(8). Intentional failures to disclose, false disclosures, or failures to recuse are punishable by civil penalties. 16 U.S.C. § 1857(1)(O). The Secretary may remove for cause, after notice and opportunity for a hearing, any member who violates this prohibition. 16 U.S.C. § 1852(b)(6).

When President Bill Clinton signed the 1996 amendments to the Magnuson-Stevens Act into law, he offered the following statement:

Section 107 does not provide adequate protections against conflicts of interest on the part of members of the fishery management councils. A council member will be able to vote in many situations where the member could derive a significant financial gain from the matter. Further, the conflict provisions will not be consistent with other Government-wide conflict laws.

President's Statement on Signing the Sustainable Fisheries Act, Public Papers of the President, Oct. 11, 1996, 32 Weekly Comp. Pres. Doc. 2040.

What is lacking in these new safeguards? NOAA regulations on the financial disclosure requirements are found in 50 C.F.R. § 600.235.

Is any kind of financial disclosure requirement likely to reduce the tendency of the regional councils to make risk-prone decisions even in the face of clear scientific information about the effect of fishing rates on fish stock recovery? Are risk-prone decisions merely due to the inability of sectors of the fishing industry to put long-term interests above short-term economic considerations? Is the problem merely that the 'foxes are guarding the chicken coop,' or are there more subtle factors involved? For a fascinating discussion of the cognitive psychology of resource users who are trapped in a commons dilemma, see B.H. Thompson, Jr., Tragically Difficult: The Obstacles to Governing the Commons, 30 Envtl L. 241 (2000).

Should Congress amend the Act to require council members to reflect a balanced representation among those representing not only commercial and recreational fisheries, but the broader public interest?

C. THE SUSTAINABLE FISHERIES ACT OF 1996

As noted above, the 1996 Sustainable Fisheries Act added provisions to the Magnuson-Stevens Act that require the regional councils and the Secretary of Commerce to stop overfishing, to rebuild overfished stocks, and to address the ecological impacts of fisheries. These amendments reflect a recognition by the United States that fisheries management can no longer afford to be concerned only with achieving the maximum sustainable harvests from exploited fish stocks and allocating that harvest among competing user groups. The major elements of the Act that add ecological concerns to the management process are the bycatch reduction provisions and the essential fish habitat requirements. In addition, the new provisions on fishing gear registration provides at least some check on the introduction of new fishing technology that may have unacceptably high levels of impact on the surrounding habitat and associated species. Finally, Congress required the Fisheries Service to convene an expert panel to prepare a report on the degree to which ecosystem goals, principles, and policies are applied and can be applied under the Magnuson-Stevens Act. See Ecosystem Principles Advisory Panel, Ecosystem-Based Fishery Management, A Report to Congress (Nov. 15, 1998); M. Macpherson, Integrating Ecosystem Management Approaches into Federal Fishery Management Through the Magnuson-Stevens Fishery Conservation and Management Act, 6 Ocean & Coastal L.J. 1 (2001)(see pp. 490-93, infra).

(1.) Preventing Overfishing and Rebuilding Overfished Stocks

After the 1996 amendments, the pace and intensity of judicial review of fishery management decisions increased dramatically, reflecting in part the resistance of the fishing industry to the tough new controls on overfishing, but also the entry of environmental non-governmental organizations (NGOs) into debates over the management and protection of marine fisheries. These groups have used litigation to push NMFS and the councils to adopt a more ecosystem-based approach. The 1996 amendments' reinvigoration of the conservation goal of the Act provided a basis for this intervention. In A.M.L. International, Inc. v. Daley, 107 F.Supp.2d 90 (D.Mass. 2000), the court described the genesis and impact of the amendments:

In 1996, Congress ushered in a new era in fisheries management by making significant revisions to the Magnuson-Stevens Act through the Sustainable Fisheries Act. See Pub.L. No. 104-297, 110 Stat. 3559 (1996). The Magnuson-Stevens act was revised because, "it was very clear that major changes were needed. Despite numerous efforts to improve the law over the past two decades, the sad reality [was] that the act did not prevent the current crisis in* * * groundfish stocks, a crisis for the conservation of both fish stocks and fishing families." See 142 Cong.Rec. H11418, 11439 (September 27, 1996) (statement of Rep. Studds). Indeed, Congress recognized that revisions to the Magnuson-Stevens act were critical in order to "put our fisheries back onto a sustainable path and literally avert an environmental catastrophe on a national level * * *. We are precariously close to fisheries failures in many of our most commercially important fish stocks, and it is imperative that we take immediate action if we are to avert disasters." See 142 Cong.Rec. S10794, 10811-12 (September 18, 1996) (statement of Sen. Kerry).

Perhaps the most significant revision to the Magnuson-Stevens Act was the removal of some discretion regarding "overfished" fisheries.[2] If the Secretary determines at any time that a fishery is overfished, the Secretary must immediately notify the appropriate fishery council, and request that action be taken to end overfishing in the fishery and to implement conservation and management measures to rebuild affected stocks of fish. Once a council has been notified that a particular stock is overfished, it has only one year to prepare a fishery management plan to end overfishing and rebuild the stocks.[3] The primary purpose of a plan is to establish conservation and management measures which are "necessary and appropriate for the conservation and management of the fishery, to prevent overfishing and rebuild overfished stocks, and to protect, restore, and promote the long-term health and stability of the fishery." The ultimate goal, therefore, of any fishery management plan is to establish measures which achieve a rate or level of fishing mortality that allows the fishery to produce the maximum sustainable yield on a continuing basis.[4]

---

[2]   The Magnuson-Stevens Act defines overfishing as "a rate or level of fishing mortality that jeopardizes the capacity of a fishery to produce the maximum sustainable yield on a continuing basis." See 16 U.S.C. § 1802(29); 50 C.F.R. § 600.310(d)(1)(i). Maximum Sustainable Yield ("MSY") is the "largest long-term average catch or yield that can be taken from a stock under prevailing ecological and environmental conditions."

[3]   Significantly, Congress imposed the one-year time limit on fishery councils because of the perceived inability of fishery councils to quickly enact needed conservation measures. Indeed, Congress recognized that "it actually took a lawsuit by two Massachusetts environmental groups to force the notoriously slow New England Fishery Management council to draft and implement a fishery management plan that contained the teeth needed to stem continued overfishing and stock decimation." See 142 Cong.Rec. S10906, 10901 (September 19, 1996) (statement of Sen. Chafee).

[4]   The Magnuson-Stevens Act requires that fishery management plans must ultimately "prevent overfishing." As discussed above, "overfishing" means a rate of mortality that jeopardizes the capacity of a fishery to produce MSY on a continuing basis. The Magnuson-Stevens Act also calls for fishery management plans to specify the "optimum yield.." The statute defines "optimum yield" as the amount of fish which will

A.M.L. Int'l v. Daley, 1007 F.Supp.2d at 94.

Congress clearly intended to change the way in which fisheries were managed, to require the councils and NMFS to set limits on fishing that would allow stocks to rebuild to levels that could produce a long-term sustainable catch level. But several questions remained, including: how much discretion did the councils and NMFS have to set the pace of the rebuilding, in order to reduce economic hardship on the industry? The following case, again involving the summer flounder FMP, is one of the most significant Magnuson-Stevens Act precedents established by environmental NGOs through litigation after the 1996 amendments. What principle does it establish?

NATURAL RESOURCES DEFENSE COUNCIL v. DALEY
United States Court of Appeals, D.C. Circuit, 2000
209 F.3d 747

CHIEF ~~JUSTICE~~ *Judge* *EDWARDS*:

* * *

B. The Summer Flounder Fishing Quota

From a commercial standpoint, the summer flounder is one of the most important species of flounder in the United States.   All parties agree that the summer flounder fishery is "overfished" and has been for some time.   The Mid-Atlantic Fishery Management Council (MAFMC), covering New York, New Jersey, Delaware, Pennsylvania, Maryland, Virginia, and North Carolina, developed the original summer flounder management plan with the assistance of two other regional Management Councils and the Atlantic States Marine Fisheries Commission ("the Commission"), a consortium of 15 coastal states and the District of Columbia.   The Service approved the original management plan in 1988; however, the Service has amended the plan several times.   At the time relevant to the instant case, the plan was designed to achieve a fishing mortality rate equal to F submax by 1998.

Pursuant to the management plan, the Service must set a quota each year fixing the total weight of summer flounder that may be harvested by commercial and recreational fishers.   This quota is referred to as the "total allowable landings" for the year, or "TAL."   The Service allocates 60% of the TAL to commercial fisheries and 40% of the

---

provide the greatest overall benefit to the nation, with respect to food production and recreational opportunities, and taking into account the protection of marine ecosystems. Optimum yield is prescribed on the basis of the MSY from the fishery, as reduced by any relevant social, economic, or ecological factor. More importantly, the optimum yield for an overfished fishery must rebuild to a level consistent with producing the maximum sustainable yield.

quota to recreational fisheries, and states receive allocations based upon their share of the summer flounder fishery. States may subdivide their allocated commercial quota between "incidental" and "directed" catch. Directed fisheries intentionally harvest summer flounder. Fishers who catch juvenile flounder, or who are part of the directed fishery for another species and catch summer flounder unintentionally, have harvested incidental catch.

* * *

There is a relatively direct relationship between the TAL and the likelihood of achieving the target F. In general, the higher the TAL, the less likely a plan is to achieve the target F. In other words, the lower the target F, the lower the TAL must be to attain the target F. The basic dispute between the parties concerns whether the 1999 TAL provides a sufficient guarantee that the target F for summer flounder will be achieved.

For 1999, the summer flounder fishery management plan mandated a target F equivalent to F submax, which was 0.24. The Summer Flounder Monitoring Committee, a MAFMC committee, had recommended a TAL of 14.645 million pounds, while MAFMC had recommended a TAL of 20.20 million pounds. The Service rejected MAFMC's recommendation as "unacceptably risk-prone" for several reasons: (1) it had an "unacceptably low probability" of 3% of achieving the target F; (2) it had a 50% probability of achieving an F of 0.36, which was "significantly higher" than the target F; (3) the proposal relied on unpredictable data; and (4) MAFMC had "yet to specify a harvest level that has achieved the annual target F." The Service also rejected the Summer Flounder Monitoring Committee's recommendation of a 14.645 million pound TAL. Although the Committee's recommendation had a 50% chance of achieving the target F, the Service rejected the proposal without any meaningful explanation.

On October 21, 1998, the Service proposed a TAL of 18.52 million pounds. All parties agree that, at most, the Service's proposal afforded only an 18% likelihood of achieving the target F. * * *

Between the time of proposal of the 1999 TAL and its adoption, the Service concluded that it did not have the authority to impose any incidental catch restrictions on the states. Therefore, the Service merely *recommended* that the states adopt the incidental catch proposal [of allocating 32.7% of the TAL to incidental catch], making the proposal entirely voluntary. The Commission, the body representing 15 coastal states and the District of Columbia, also declined to command the states to adopt the proposal. According to an advisor to the Service's Assistant Administrator for Fisheries, this development "result[ed] in an unknown but probably substantial reduction in the likelihood that [MAFMC's] rebuilding schedule will be achieved," and he therefore recommended that the Service adopt the Summer Flounder Monitoring Committee's recommended 14.645 million pound TAL.

The Service rejected this recommendation and, on December 31, 1998, issued the final TAL, adopting its initial proposal. The Service acknowledged that the Summer Flounder Monitoring Committee's recommended quota had a 50% chance of achieving the target F, while the Service's TAL had only an 18% chance of achieving the target F.

* * *

Appellants filed suit in District Court on January 29, 1999, seeking, *inter alia,* (1) a declaratory judgment that defendants violated the Fishery Act, the Administrative Procedure Act ("APA"), and NEPA, and (2) remand to the agency to impose a new summer flounder TAL. The District Court upheld the Service's adoption of the 18.52 million pound TAL, deferring to the agency under Chevron U.S.A. Inc. v. Natural Resources Defense Council, Inc., 467 U.S. 837, 104 S.Ct. 2778, 81 L.Ed.2d 694 (1984). The District Court first determined that [National Standards #1 and #8] in the Fishery Act evinced competing interests between advancing conservation and minimizing adverse economic effects and that Congress offered no insight as to how to balance these concerns. See Natural Resources Defense Council, Inc. v. Daley, 62 F.Supp.2d 102 (D.D.C.1999), at 106-07. In addition, the trial court found that the Fishery Act expressed no clear intent as to the particular level of certainty a TAL must guarantee to be consistent with [National Standard #1]. Given these perceived ambiguities, the District Court deferred to the Service pursuant to *Chevron* Step Two. This appeal followed.

* * *

As for the Service's disputed interpretations of the Fishery Act, we are guided by the Supreme Court's seminal decision in *Chevron U.S.A., Inc.,* [which] governs review of agency interpretation of a statute which the agency administers. Under the first step of *Chevron* the reviewing court "must first exhaust the 'traditional tools of statutory construction' to determine whether Congress has spoken to the precise question at issue." The traditional tools include examination of the statute's text, legislative history, and structure; as well as its purpose. This inquiry using the traditional tools of construction may be characterized as a search for the plain meaning of the statute. If this search yields a clear result, then Congress has expressed its intention as to the question, and deference is not appropriate. If, however, "the statute is silent or ambiguous with respect to the specific issue," Congress has not spoken clearly, and a permissible agency interpretation of the statute merits judicial deference.

Although agencies are entitled to deferential review under *Chevron*

Step Two, our judicial function is neither rote nor meaningless:

> [W]e will defer to [an agency's] interpretation[ ] if [it is] reasonable and consistent with the statutory purpose and legislative history. However, a court will not uphold [an agency's] interpretation "that diverges from any realistic meaning of the statute."

This case presents a situation in which the Service's quota for the 1999 summer flounder harvest so completely diverges from any realistic meaning of the Fishery Act that it cannot survive scrutiny under *Chevron* Step Two.

As an initial matter, we reject the District Court's suggestion that there is a conflict between the Fishery Act's expressed commitments to conservation and to mitigating adverse economic impacts. Compare [National Standard #1] (directing agency to "prevent overfishing" and ensure "the optimum yield from each fishery"); with [National Standard #8] (directing agency to "minimize adverse economic impacts" on fishing communities). The Government concedes, and we agree, that, under the Fishery Act, the Service must give priority to conservation measures. It is only when two different plans achieve similar conservation measures that the Service takes into consideration adverse economic consequences. This is confirmed both by the statute's plain language and the regulations issued pursuant to the statute. See id.§ 1851(a)(8) (requiring fishery management plans, "consistent with the conservation requirements of this chapter," to take into account the effect of management plans on fishing communities) (emphasis added); 50 C.F.R. § 600.345(b)(1) (1999) ("*[W]here two alternatives achieve similar conservation goals,* the alternative that * * * minimizes the adverse impacts on [fishing] communities would be the preferred alternative.") (emphasis added).

The real issue in this case is whether the 1999 TAL satisfied the conservation goals of the Fishery Act, the management plan, and the Service's regulations. In considering this question, it is important to recall that the Service operates under constraints from three different sources. First, the statute requires the Service to act both to "prevent overfishing" and to attain "optimum yield." 16 U.S.C. § 1851(a)(1). Overfishing is commonly understood as fishing that results in an F in excess of F submax. Since F submax for 1999 was equivalent to 0.24, this constraint required the Service to issue regulations to prevent F from exceeding 0.24. Second, any quota must be "consistent with" the fishery management plan adopted by the Service. In this case the fishery management plan called for an F of 0.24. Therefore, the quota had be to "consistent with" achieving that F. Third, the Service is required to adopt a quota "necessary to assure that the applicable specified F will not be exceeded." The "applicable specified F" for 1999 was F submax , or 0.24.

All of these constraints, then, collapse into an inquiry as to whether the Service's quota was "consistent with" and at the level "necessary to assure" the achievement of an F of 0.24, and whether it reasonably could be expected to "prevent" an F greater than 0.24. In other words, the question is whether the quota, as approved, sufficiently ensured that it would achieve an F of 0.24. Appellants argue that the quota violates applicable standards under both *Chevron* Step One and *Chevron* Step Two * * *

Appellants' *Chevron* Step One "plain meaning" argument is virtually indistinguishable from their *Chevron* Step Two reasonableness argument. Appellants acknowledge that the statutory terms "assure," "prevent," and "consistent with" do not mandate a precise quota figure. However, appellants contend that a TAL with only an 18% likelihood of achieving the target F is so inherently unreasonable that it defies the plain meaning of the statute. This is an appealing argument on the facts of this case, because, as we explain below, the Service's action is largely incomprehensible when one considers the principal purposes of the Fishery Act. Nonetheless, we still view this case as governed by *Chevron* Step Two. The statute does not prescribe a precise quota figure, so there is no plain meaning on this point. Rather, we must look to see whether the agency's disputed action reflects a reasonable and permissible construction of the statute. In light of what the statute *does* require, short of a specific quota figure, it is clear here that the Service's position fails the test of *Chevron* Step Two.

The 1999 quota is unreasonable, plain and simple. Government counsel conceded at oral argument that, to meet its statutory and regulatory mandate, the Service must have a "fairly high level of confidence that the quota it recommends will not result in an F greater than [the target F]." We agree. We also hold that, at the very least, this means that "to assure" the achievement of the target F, to "prevent overfishing," and to "be consistent with" the fishery management plan, the TAL must have had at least a 50% chance of attaining an F of 0.24. This is not a surprising result, because in related contexts, the Service has articulated precisely this standard.

The disputed 1999 TAL had at most an 18% likelihood of achieving the target F. Viewed differently, it had at least an 82% chance of resulting in an F greater than the target F. Only in Superman Comics' Bizarro world, where reality is turned upside down, could the Service reasonably conclude that a measure that is at least four times as likely to fail as to succeed offers a "fairly high level of confidence."

Rather than argue that the quota alone provided enough assurance, the Service contends instead that two additional measures were adopted to increase the likelihood of achieving the target F. These measures were: (1) the provision relating to minimum mesh size; and

(2) the recommendation that states voluntarily allocate a certain portion of the directed commercial fishery toward incidental catch. There is nothing in this record, however, to indicate that the proposals on mesh size and voluntary state action would improve the level of confidence so as to assure a reasonable likelihood of achieving the target F.

* * *

As we noted at the outset of this opinion, the Service's quota for the 1999 summer flounder harvest so completely "diverges from any realistic meaning" of the Fishery Act that it cannot survive scrutiny under *Chevron* Step Two. The Service resists this result by suggesting that we owe deference to the agency's "scientific" judgments. While this may be so, we do not hear cases merely to rubber stamp agency actions. To play that role would be "tantamount to abdicating the judiciary's responsibility under the Administrative Procedure Act." The Service cannot rely on "reminders that its scientific determinations are entitled to deference" in the absence of reasoned analysis "to 'cogently explain' " why its additional recommended measures satisfied the Fishery Act's requirements. Indeed, we can divine no scientific judgment upon which the Service concluded that its measures would satisfy its statutory mandate.

Here, the adopted quota guaranteed only an 18% probability of achieving the principal conservation goal of the summer flounder fishery management plan. The Service offered neither analysis nor data to support its claim that the two additional measures aside from the quota would increase that assurance beyond the at-least-50% likelihood required by statute and regulation.

Notes and Questions

1. Why did the NMFS set a summer flounder quota that had only an 18% chance of meeting the 'prevent overfishing' target? Chief Justice Edwards said the court could "divine no scientific judgment upon which the Service concluded that its measures would satisfy" the Magnuson-Stevens Act. What judgment was the agency relying upon if not a scientific one?

2. The court also rejected the agency's reliance on the assumption that the states, who manage the summer flounder fisheries in state waters according to the federal plan, would voluntarily comply with the recommendation they allocate 32.7% of the quota to incidental catch, that is, the unintended catch and discard of undersized flounders, and thus increase the probability of meeting the target fishing mortality rate. This would mean the states would "count" that amount of the quota taken and therefore not available for landing by the fishery. The court

concluded this was an unsupported assumption, given the evidence in the record that several states had commented that the incidental catch allowance was too high, unenforceable, and beyond the agency's power to compel. Federal and interstate management of the summer flounder fishery is very controversial. As mentioned previously, the State of Connecticut has challenged the constitutionality of the Magnuson-Stevens Act because of its objections to the way quotas are set for the summer flounder fishery. See State of Connecticut v. Daley, 53 F.Supp.2d 147 (D.Conn. 1999), aff'd, 204 F.3d 413 (2d Cir. 2000).

3. What happens when the definition of "overfishing" and the associated rebuilding requirements of an FMP point to a fishing mortality rate or target spawning stock biomass size that require setting a quota that is too low to allow an existing commercial fishery to operate, effectively shutting it down?

In addition to the overfishing provisions, the 1996 amendments added a national standard requiring conservation and management measures to "consistent with the conservation requirements of this Act (including the prevention of overfishing and rebuilding of overfished stocks), take into account the importance of fishery resources to fishing communities in order to (A) provide for the sustained participation of such communities, and (B) to the extent practicable, minimize adverse economic impacts on such communities." 16 U.S.C. § 1853(a)(8). Also, as noted previously, the Regulatory Flexibility Act, 5 U.S.C. § 601 et seq. was amended to include a judicial review provision for parties to challenge agency compliance with the act's requirements for analysis of proposed rulemaking for impact on small businesses.

The fishermen of New England developed a fishery for the spiny dogfish, once considered a "trash" species, after the traditional groundfish species (cod, haddock, and flounder) were overfished and made subject to severe regulatory restrictions. After the Secretary of Commerce declared the spiny dogfish as "overfished" in 1998, he then partially approved a joint FMP submitted by the New England and Mid-Atlantic Fishery Management Councils that contained a definition of overfishing, set a 5-year rebuilding schedule, identified essential fish habitat, and proposed measures to control fishing mortality. The disapproved measure was a target spawning stock biomass of 180,000 metric tons, one of the objective and measurable criteria contained in the overfishing definition (the others were a minimum spawning stock biomass threshold and a maximum and target fishing mortality thresholds). Spawning stock biomass (SSB) is the amount of fish mature enough to reproduce in a given fishery. For spiny dogfish, estimates of large, mature, female dogfish are used to estimate SSB. In the years since 1989 when the fishery was still growing, estimates of the biomass of mature female spiny dogfish declined by more than 50%. The Secretary disapproved the councils' proposed target biomass level as too low to be a rebuilding target because the best scientific information at the time indicated that 200,000 metric tons was the level most likely to produce MSY.

In the following case, the court considered a challenge to the quota restrictions adopted to implement the rebuilding plan, which included trip limits of around 300 pounds, equivalent only to a incidental catch, effectively eliminating a fishery targeting spiny dogfish. The court had to decide what effect the provisions requiring consideration of adverse economic impacts have on the rebuilding mandates of the Magnuson-Stevens Act.

A.M.L. INTERNATIONAL, INC. v. DALEY
United States District Court, D. Massachusetts, 2000
107 F.Supp.2d 90

DISTRICT JUDGE **HARRINGTON:**

The fishing industry is, and has always been, an extremely important part of this nation's heritage. The United States is the world's fifth largest fishing nation, harvesting approximately ten billion pounds of fish, and producing approximately $3.5 billion in dockside revenues each year. The United States is the third largest seafood exporter, with exports valued at over $3 billion annually.

[T]he spiny dogfish] [is] a small shark whose habitat extends from Nova Scotia to Florida. The vast majority of the spiny dogfish fishing industry, however, exists in the New England and mid-Atlantic waters. The directed fishery of the spiny dogfish has emerged only within the last fifteen years. During this time, commercial landings have increased approximately ten-fold. Since 1990, the United States fishing industry has landed and processed an average of forty (40) million pounds of spiny dogfish each year. Indeed, in 1999, more than forty (40) percent of all fish caught by weight in the Northwest Atlantic were spiny dogfish.

The plaintiffs in this case are New England and mid-Atlantic companies which harvest, process and export spiny dogfish. The plaintiffs constitute the vast majority of the spiny dogfish fishing and processing industry. Last year, the plaintiffs processed over forty (40) million pounds, and generated revenues in excess of $20 million from sales of spiny dogfish. Additionally, the plaintiffs represent many individuals whose livelihood depends on the harvest, processing and sale of spiny dogfish.

This dispute arose when the Secretary of the United States Department of Commerce ("the Secretary"), through the National Marine Fisheries Service ("NMFS"), imposed regulatory restrictions through the implementation of the spiny dogfish Fishery Management Plan

("SDFMP") on the spiny dogfish fishing industry. The Secretary acknowledges that the quota restrictions contained in the plan will likely have the effect of shutting down the spiny dogfish industry for at least the next five years.

The plaintiffs bring this case, therefore, seeking to invalidate the SDFMP. The plaintiffs argue that the actions of the Secretary were arbitrary, capricious, an abuse of discretion or otherwise not in accordance with the law. This Court is now faced with the weighty task of either declaring the plan invalid as a matter of law, or upholding the actions of the Secretary. This Court is well aware that the latter decision may well cause the collapse of the spiny dogfish fishing and processing industry.

* * *

National Standard Eight ("NS-8") states that "conservation and management measures shall, *consistent with the conservation requirements of this Act* (including the prevention of overfishing and rebuilding of overfished stocks), take into account the importance of fishery resources to fishing communities in order to (A) provide for the sustained participation of such communities, and (B) *to the extent practicable,* minimize adverse economic impacts on such communities." See 16 U.S.C. § 1851(8); 50 C.F.R. § 600.345(a) (emphasis added).

NS-8 explicitly acknowledges that deliberations regarding the importance of fishery resources to affected fishing communities "*must not compromise the achievement of conservation requirements.*" See *50 C.F.R. § 600.345(b)* (emphasis added). All other things being equal, however, where two alternatives achieve similar conservation goals, the alternative which provides the greater potential for sustained participation of communities and minimizes the adverse economic impacts is preferred. See 50 C.F.R. § 600.345(b).

The plaintiffs argue that the SDFMP does not comply with NS-8 because (1) there was no attempt to minimize economic consequences, (2) the descriptions of economic impacts, fishery demographics and the fishing communities are inadequate, (3) the consideration of alternative measures was inadequate, and most importantly, (4) the plan shuts down an entire industry. For example, the plaintiffs assert that they will suffer revenue losses of thirty (30) to one hundred (100) percent, and the elimination of at least two hundred (200) jobs in the processing sector.

The record, however, establishes that the Secretary and the councils considered the importance of the fishery to numerous communities. Indeed, the Secretary concluded that without the measures contained in the SDFMP, data indicates that the fishery will collapse completely within two or three years. A collapsed fishery will not be economically viable for decades, creating drastically worse economic consequences than the temporary measures contained in the SDFMP.

Furthermore, the record establishes that the councils and the Secretary considered twelve (12) alternative schemes. The Secretary, councils, and technical committees concluded that the rebuilding schedule ultimately contained in the SDFMP is most likely to rebuild the fishery to a level consistent with producing MSY on a long-term basis. Furthermore, NS-8 specifically states that a fishery management plan does not have to contain an exhaustive listing of all communities that might be affected. See 50 C.F.R. § 600.345(c)(3).

The Magnuson-Stevens Act requires the SDFMP to contain management measures which will rebuild this overfished fishery to levels consistent with achieving MSY (in this case SSBmax) within a time period as short as possible but not exceeding ten (10) years. See 16 U.S.C. § § 1853(a)(10),1854(e)(4)(A),1802(28)(C), 1802(29). Given this ultimate objective, the SDFMP, *to the extent practicable,* minimizes adverse economic impacts on fishing communities. See 16 U.S.C. § 1851(8); 50 C.F.R. § 600.345(a). Finally, the fact that implementation of the SDFMP will result in a closure of the spiny dogfish directed fishery is, in itself, not a violation of NS-8.

* * *

D. Regulatory Flexibility Act

The Plaintiffs argue that that Secretary's approval of the SDFMP and interim final rule was arbitrary, capricious or otherwise contrary to the law because it violated the Regulatory Flexibility Act ("RFA"),5 U.S.C. § 601 et seq. Congress enacted the RFA to encourage administrative agencies to consider the potential impact of nascent federal regulations on small businesses. See Associated Fisheries, 127 F.3d at 111. The RFA requires an agency to prepare a Regulatory Flexibility Analysis ("RF-Analysis") which, among other things, must identify the potential economic impact of agency regulation on small entities, and discuss alternatives which might minimize adverse economic consequences.[Small entities are defined as small businesses, nonprofit enterprises, and small governmental jurisdictions, 5 U.S.C. 601(6).]See 5 U.S.C. § § 603, 604;Associated Fisheries, 127 F.3d at 111-12.

An RF-Analysis is required only, (1) when "an agency is required by [law] to publish general notice of proposed rulemaking for any proposed rule," or (2) when "an agency promulgates a final rule ... after being required by [law] to publish a general notice of proposed rulemaking." See 5 U.S.C. § § 603(a), 604(a). The Secretary may incorporate into an RF-Analysis "any data or analysis contained in any other impact statement or analysis required by law." See Associated Fisheries, 127 F.3d at 115.

The RFA does not command an agency to take specific substantive measures, but rather, only to give explicit consideration to less onerous options. See Associated Fisheries, 127 F.3d at 114. Among other things, a final RF-Analysis must contain "a description of the steps the agency has taken to minimize the significant economic impact on small entities *consistent with the stated objectives of applicable statutes,* including a statement of the factual, policy and legal reasons for selecting the alternative adopted in the final rule and why each one of the other significant alternatives to the rule considered by the agency which affect the impact on small entities was rejected." See 5 U.S.C. § 604(a)(5) (emphasis added).

In this case, the Secretary was required to, and did, prepare an RF-Analysis prior to the final rule which implemented the SDFMP. The record indicates that the Secretary and the councils were and are aware that implementation of the SDFMP, which greatly reduces landings, may result in the "elimination of [spiny dogfish] processing operations for the remaining dogfish processors and the potential loss of approximately two hundred (200) jobs." See Final Rule, 65 Fed.Reg. 1557, 1566 (January 11, 2000). The plaintiffs do not argue, therefore, that the Secretary is unaware of the potential devastating consequences to small businesses. Rather, the plaintiffs claim that the Secretary has violated the RFA by failing to adequately consider and describe other significant alternatives and measures to the final rule implementing the SDFMP. See 5 U.S.C. § 604(a)(5).

First, the RFA does not require that an RF-Analysis address every alternative, but only that it address significant ones. See 5 U.S.C. § § 603(c), 604(a)(5). Even so, as discussed above, the record indicates that at least twelve (12) alternative rebuilding schedules were considered and rejected by the Secretary and the councils. In short, the alternatives were rejected because they did not meet target fishing mortality levels, did not meet other requirements of the Magnuson-Stevens Act, or did not provide long-term economic benefits greater than those of the proposed action. See Final Rule, 65 Fed.Reg. 1557, 1567 (January 11, 2000).

The mandate of the RFA is to minimize significant economic impacts on small entities *consistent with the applicable statute. See* 5 U.S.C. § § 603, 604. Congress has emphasized that the RFA should *not* be construed to undermine other legislatively mandated goals. *See Associated Fisheries,* 127 F.3d at 113. The intent of the RFA is not to limit regulations having adverse economic impacts on small entities. Rather, "the intent is to have the agency focus special attention on the impacts its proposed actions would have on small entities, to disclose to the public which alternatives it considered, to consider public comments on impacts and alternatives, and to require the agency to state its reasons for not adopting an alternative having less of an adverse impact on small entities." See Associated Fisheries, 127 F.3d at 116; see also Final Rule, 61 Fed.Reg. 27,710, 27,721 (May 31, 1996).

In this case, the objective of the Magnuson-Stevens Act is clear. The SDFMP must provide for measures which will rebuild the fishery to a level consistent with achieving MSY (in this case SSBmax) within a time period as short as possible but not exceeding ten (10) years. As this Circuit has recognized, what the fishing industry desires is inconsistent with what the Magnuson-Stevens Act obliges the Secretary to do. See Associated Fisheries, 127 F.3d at 117. "Of necessity, given the distressed condition of * * * this fishery, *any* alternative consistent with the Secretary's conservation mandate under the Magnuson-Stevens Act will produce economic hardships for the industry." See id. (emphasis added).

The RF-Analysis completed by the Secretary meets all of the requirements of the RFA. See 5 U.S.C. § § 603, 604.

* * *

F. Closing the Directed Spiny Dogfish Fishery

Much of the plaintiffs' argument is based on the fact that the implementation of the SDFMP will likely result in the closure of the spiny dogfish directed fishery for at least the next five years. Indeed, the record indicates that some members of the NEFMC and state agencies are confused about the requirements and priorities of the Magnuson-Stevens Act. The National Standards and the RFA *must be consistent with the ultimate conservation requirements of the Magnuson-Stevens Act.* Any fishery management plan must, first and foremost, contain measures which prevent overfishing and rebuild overfished stocks. Where the Secretary has designated a fishery as overfished, measures *must* provide for rebuilding to a level consistent with producing the maximum sustainable yield, or suitable proxy, within a time period as short as possible but not exceeding ten (10) years.

The requirements of the RFA as well as the National Standards pertaining to adverse economic impacts, efficiency, and bycatch, are to be applied *to the extent practicable* given this primary conservation objective.[5] Measures contained in a fishery management plan may well

---

[5]   When Congress amended the Magnuson-Stevens Act in 1996, it specifically recognized that concepts contained in other National Standards should be consistent with the primary conservation goal of the statute. For example, Congress "demote[d]

result in the closure of a fishing industry. This terrible and unfortunate consequence, however, was readily anticipated by Congress when it amended the Magnuson- Stevens Act in 1996.[6]

This Court sympathizes greatly with those individuals involved in the spiny dogfish fishing and processing industry. Nevertheless, this Court concludes that the Secretary implemented the SDFMP and the interim final rule in a reasoned manner, pursuant to statute, and supported by substantial evidence in the record. The Secretary examined the pertinent evidence, considered the relevant factors, and articulated a satisfactory explanation for his actions. The Secretary adequately explained his actions and responded to relevant public comment. After a thorough and searching inquiry of the administrative record, this Court is satisfied that the Secretary made reasoned decisions founded on a reasoned evaluation of the relevant factors. As such, this Court finds that the actions of the Secretary were not arbitrary, capricious or otherwise contrary to law.

VII. Conclusion

As a sick person must undergo painful surgery and then convalesce for a short time in order to regain his health, a sick fishery must suffer this drastic procedure and then conserve itself for a short time in order to recover its full vitality. For the reasons stated above, the plaintiffs' Motion for Summary Judgment is denied, and the defendant's Cross-Motion for Summary Judgment is granted.

-----

the role of efficiency in fishery management * * * by changing National Standard Five from one of promoting efficiency * * * to merely considering efficiency." See 142 Cong.Rec. S10794, 10814 (September 18, 1996) (statement of Sen. Gorton). Significantly, Congress recognized that "there is no requirement in the Magnuson-Stevens Act to require fishery management councils to try to minimize the adverse economic impacts of fisheries regulations on fishing communities * * * [It is] clear that these economic considerations are not designed to trump conservation considerations in the process of developing fishery management plans." See 142 Cong.Rec. S10794, 10825 (September 18, 1996) (statement of Sen. Snowe) (emphasis added). Even if there were an internal conflict between the overarching conservation mandates of the Magnuson-Stevens Act and another provision, this Circuit has recognized that "the job of the courts and the administrator is to implement the central aim of the statute." See Commonwealth of Massachusetts v. Daley, 170 F.3d 23, 30 (1st Cir.1999). In fact, the balancing of any conflicting objectives is primarily for the Secretary; his decision on this issue, and even more so on the exigencies of enforcement, are matters on which he enjoys great latitude. See id. At 31.

[6] Congress recognized that "rebuilt stocks in New England and elsewhere will eventually provide benefits to producers and consumers, but, at the present, efforts to halt overfishing, restore the depleted resource, and conserve habitats will decrease revenues to fishermen and drive some out of business. The industry will have to sustain some losses in the short term if it is to remain viable in the long term." See 140 Cong.Rec. E964 (May 18, 1994) (extension of remarks by Rep. Hamilton) (emphasis added).

Questions

1. Does this decision settle the issue? Are fishing industry groups likely to stop challenging FMP regulations on economic grounds?

2. The New England council had reportedly adopted a SSB target of 180,000 metric tons in order to reduce the overall number of spiny dogfish because of that species' predation on juvenile cod. Adult cod, also the subject of a rebuilding plan, are even greater predators of juvenile cod. How should management efforts take account of these inter-species and intra-species interactions? Is fisheries management on an ecosystem basis achievable? See discussion below at (3.) (p. 490).

(2.) Bycatch Reduction and Essential Fish Habitat

Two other provisions of the 1996 amendments enlarge the goal of federal fisheries management beyond that of a single-species MSY: the bycatch and essential fish habitat requirements.

Bycatch

The Magnuson-Stevens Act defines "bycatch" as "fish which are harvested in a fishery, but which are not sold or kept for personal use, and include economic discards and regulatory discards. Such term does not include fish released alive under a recreational catch and release fishery management program." 16 U.S.C. § 1802(2). "Economic discards" are those fish that are "the target of a fishery, but which are not retained because they are of an undesirable size, sex, or quality, or for other economic reasons." Id. at § 1802(9). "Regulatory discards" are defined as "fish harvested in a fishery which fishermen are required by regulation to discard whenever caught, or are required by regulation to retain but not sell." Id. at § 1802(32).

The Act defines "fish" as "finfish, mollusks, crustaceans, and all other forms of marine animal and plant life *other than* marine mammals and birds. Id. at § 1802(12)(emphasis added). Therefore, the bycatch requirements of the Act do not apply to marine mammals and other wildlife. The incidental mortality of these species in commercial fisheries can be the subject of FMP regulations, as the Secretary of Commerce has frequently used the regional councils or their FMPs to implement the Marine Mammal Protection Act and Endangered Species Act provisions affecting marine wildlife. These laws are covered in the next chapter.

National Standard 9 provides the basic requirements regarding bycatch. "Conservation and management measures shall, *to the extent practicable*, (A) minimize bycatch and (B) to the extent bycatch cannot be avoided, minimize the mortality of such bycatch." 16 U.S.C. § 1851(a)(9)(emphasis added). Also, all FMPs are required to include "a standardized reporting methodology to assess the amount and type of bycatch occurring in the fishery, and include conservation and management measures that, *to the extent practicable* and in the following priority-- (A) minimize bycatch; and (B) minimize the mortality of bycatch which cannot be avoided[.]"   16 U.S.C. § 1853(a)(11)(emphasis added).

What does it mean to minimize bycatch "to the extent practicable"? Is "practicable" a technological feasibility standard or one that takes costs into account? In a statement on the House floor during debates on the reauthorization, Congressman Don Young of Alaska said Councils should make "reasonable efforts," but that:

> it is not the intent of Congress that the councils ban a type of fishing gear or a type of fishing in order to comply with this standard. 'Practicable' requires an analysis of the costs of imposing a management action; the Congress does not intend that this provision will be used to allocate among fishing gear groups, nor to impose costs on fishermen and processors that cannot be reasonably met.

14 Cong. Rec. H11437 (daily ed. September 27, 1996).

The guidelines on the bycatch National Standard is found at 50 CFR § 600.350--National Standard Guideline on Bycatch. It provides further insight into the nature of the fish bycatch problem.

> * * * Bycatch can, in two ways, impede efforts to protect marine ecosystems and achieve sustainable fisheries and the full benefits they can provide to the Nation.   First, bycatch can increase substantially the uncertainty concerning total fishing-related mortality, which makes it more difficult to assess the status of stocks, to set the appropriate OY and define overfishing levels, and to ensure that OYs are attained and overfishing levels are not exceeded.   Second, bycatch may also preclude other more productive uses of fishery resources.

50 C.F.R. § 600.350(b).

To help the regional councils determine how far it is practicable to minimize bycatch, NOAA offers the following guidance:

> (i) A determination of whether a conservation and management measure minimizes bycatch or bycatch mortality to the extent practicable, consistent with other national standards and maximization of net benefits to the Nation, should consider the following factors:

> (A) Population effects for the bycatch species.

(B) Ecological effects due to changes in the bycatch of that species (effects on other species in the ecosystem).

(C) Changes in the bycatch of other species of fish and the resulting population and ecosystem effects.

(D) Effects on marine mammals and birds.

(E) Changes in fishing, processing, disposal, and marketing costs.

(F) Changes in fishing practices and behavior of fishermen.

(G) Changes in research, administration, and enforcement costs and management effectiveness.

(H) Changes in the economic, social, or cultural value of fishing activities and nonconsumptive uses of fishery resources.

(I) Changes in the distribution of benefits and costs.

(J) Social effects.

(ii) The Councils should adhere to the precautionary approach * * * when faced with uncertainty concerning any of the factors listed in this paragraph.

Id. at § 600.350(d)(3).

In addition to the above general requirements for all FMPs, Congress enacted separate provisions addressing bycatch and regulatory discards in fisheries of the North Pacific and in the shrimp trawl fishery in the Gulf of Mexico and South Atlantic. 16 U.S.C. §§ 1862(f),(g); 1881d(d). In the North Pacific, the council is authorized to develop a program of individual vessel discard quotas and other incentive-based programs to reduce bycatch and discards in all North Pacific fisheries. For the shrimp fishery, Congress required the Secretary to undertake a bycatch reduction program.

One of the most controversial bycatch problems subject to the Magnuson-Stevens Act is the catch of juvenile red snapper in the Gulf of Mexico shrimp fishery, the most valuable commercial fishery in the Gulf of Mexico. In 1995, for example, approximately 5,000 large shrimp trawlers and over 20,000 smaller vessels harvested 219.8 million pounds of shrimp. The ex vessel value of their catch was $437.4 million. 62 Fed. Reg. 35774 (July 2, 1997). Estimates of finfish bycatch, however, range between 4 and 10 pounds of fish for every pound of shrimp. The Gulf of Mexico Fishery Management Council adopted Amendment 2 to the Gulf of Mexico shrimp FMP requiring the use of "bycatch reduction devices" in shrimp trawl nets. See 62 Fed. Reg. 18536 (April 16, 1997). In April, 2001, the Texas Shrimp Association filed a formal petition with

NMFS for emergency rules to reduce the annual red snapper quota from 9.12 million pounds to 3 million pounds and to shorten the red snapper recreational fishing season. The Association argued that the bycatch reduction devices are not reducing mortality on red snapper sufficiently to rebuild the stocks, and the shrimp industry fears further reductions in their catches unless the directed snapper fishery is reduced. NMFS denied the petition. 66 Fed. Reg. 53579 (Oct. 23, 2001).

Essential Fish Habitat

To address the need for conservation of the habitat on which fish and other marine species depend, the 1996 amendments to the Magnuson-Stevens Act added the following findings on the significance of habitat to fisheries:

Certain stocks of fish have declined to the point where there survival is threatened, and other stocks of fish have been so substantially reduced in number that they could become similarly threatened as a consequence of (A) increased fishing pressure, (B) the inadequacy of * * * conservation and management practices and controls, or (C) direct and indirect habitat losses which have resulted in a diminished capacity to support existing fishing levels.

16 U.S.C. § 1801(a)(2).

One of the greatest long-term threats to the viability of commercial and recreational fisheries is the continued loss of marine, estuarine, and other aquatic habitats. Habitat considerations should receive increased attention for the conservation and management of fishery resources of the United States.

16 U.S.C. § 1801(a)(9).

The Act establishes the concept of "essential fish habitat," defined as "those waters and substrate necessary to fish for spawning, breeding, feeding or growth to maturity." 16 U.S.C. § 1802 (10). The councils are now required in their FMPs to:

describe and identify essential fish habitat for the fishery based on the guidelines established by the Secretary * * *, minimize to the extent practicable adverse effects on such habitat caused by fishing, and identify other actions to encourage the conservation and enhancement of such habitat[.] * * *

16 U.S.C. § 1853(a)(7).

The Secretary of Commerce has significant responsibilities under the Magnuson-Stevens Act to safeguard the essential fish habitats the councils identify in their FMPs. The Secretary is required to furnish other federal agencies with information that will further the conservation and enhancement of essential fish habitat. 16 U.S.C. §

1855(b)(1)(D). The Act also creates an interagency consultation process under which all other federal agencies must consult with the Secretary regarding actions they propose to authorize, fund or undertake "that may adversely affect any essential fish habitat identified under this Act." Id. at § 1855(b)(2).

The councils are authorized to make recommendations to the Secretary and to federal or state agencies on activities that they believe may affect the habitat, including essential fish habitat, of a fishery resource under their authority. 16 U.S.C. § 1855(b)(3)(A). The councils are required to comment on and make recommendations if the affected habitat is that of an anadromous fishery resource under its authority and the council believes the adverse effect will be substantial. Id. at § 1855(b)(3)(B). If the Secretary receives information from a council or other agency, or determines from other sources that a proposed action threatens identified EFH, the Secretary is required to recommend measures to the responsible agency that can be taken to conserve that habitat. Id. § 1855(b)(4)(A). The receiving agency is not required to follow exactly those recommendations. It must, however, provide a detailed response in writing to the commenting council and the Secretary which explains the reasons for not following the recommendations and describes the measures it will take to avoid, mitigate, or offset the impact of the proposed activity on the habitat. Id. § 1855(b)(4)(B).

NOAA's rules establishing guidelines for the regional councils in preparing FMP amendments to describe and identify essential fish habitat and the procedure the Secretary, the regional councils, and other federal and state agencies will use to review and consult on federal and state activities that may adversely affect identified habitat are found at 50 C.F.R. 600 Subparts J and K--Essential Fish Habitat (EFH). See NMFS, NOAA Essential Fish Habitat Final Rule, 67 Fed. Reg. 2343 (Jan 17, 2002).

While the councils can only comment on and make recommendations regarding activities of other agencies that could affect essential fish habitat, the Act requires the councils to adopt conservation and management measures that "minimize to the extent practicable adverse effects on such habitat *caused by fishing*, and identify other actions to encourage the conservation and enhancement of such habitat[.]" 16 U.S.C. § 1853(a)(7)(emphasis added).

To make these determinations, the NOAA rules offer the following:

(iii) * * * Councils must act to prevent, mitigate, or minimize any adverse effects from fishing, to the extent practicable, if there is evidence that a fishing activity adversely affects EFH in a manner that is more than minimal and not temporary in nature, * * *.

(iv) In determining whether it is practicable to minimize an adverse effect from fishing, Councils should consider the nature and extent of the adverse effect on EFH and the long and short-term costs and benefits of potential management measures to EFH, associated fisheries, and the nation, consistent with national standard 7 [minimizing costs and avoiding unnecessary duplication].

50 C.F.R. § 600.815(a)(2)(ii),(iii).

Options that the councils may consider as management measures to control the adverse effects of fishing on EFH include, but are not limited to, seasonal and area restrictions on fishing equipment, gear modifications or prohibitions; time/area closures and designation of zones as marine protected areas; and limits on harvest of prey species and species that provide habitat for other species assemblages or communities. Id. at § 600.815(a)(2)(iv).

Activities that an FMP could identify as non-fishing activities that may adversely affect EFH include dredging, filling, excavation, mining, impoundment, discharge, water diversions, thermal discharges, actions that contribute to non-point source pollution and sedimentation, introduction of potentially hazardous materials or exotic species, and conversion of aquatic habitat that may eliminate, diminish, or disrupt the functions of EFH. Id. at § 600.815(a)(3).

In accordance with the Secretary's guidelines, the councils had to submit amendments to their 36 existing FMPs by October 11, 1998, to identify EFH, the adverse impacts to EFH from both fishing and non-fishing sources, and measures to conserve and enhance EFH. The three Secretarial FMPs prepared directly by the NMFS for Atlantic highly migratory species were to be amended in a similar fashion.

Notes and Questions

1. After the Secretary approved the councils' EFH amendments, environmental NGOs challenged the adequacy of five of them. The district court found that all councils had identified EFHs within each of their jurisdictions, yet none adopted further measures that would restrict fishing gear in order to minimize adverse effects of fishing related activities on EFH. The amendments were sufficient for meeting the requirements of section 303(a)(7) of the MSA but the environmental impact and alternatives analysis required by NEPA was inadequate. American Oceans Campaign v. Daley, No. 99-982, slip op. at 6 (D.D.C. Sept. 14, 2000). See also Testimony of S. Chasis, Senior Attorney, Natural Resources Defense Council, Before the Subcommittee on Fisheries Conservation, Wildlife and Oceans of the House Committee on Resources on Implementation of the EFH Provisions of the Sustainable Fisheries Act, March 9, 2000, 2000 WL 27989.

2. Bycatch rates and the extent of impacts on habitat vary among fishing gear types and methods. In the era of open access fisheries, fishermen were encouraged to innovate and develop new methods and

gears with little consideration of the potential ecological impacts. The Magnuson-Stevens Act now requires 90-days advanced notice before a new fishing gear may be employed or a new fishery engaged in if that gear or fishery is not on the list of existing fisheries and gears prepared by the Secretary. 16 U.S.C. §1855(a). If the council has concerns about the proposed new gear or fishery, it can request the Secretary to promulgate emergency regulations prohibiting it. The Secretary can do likewise for the Atlantic highly migratory species for which the Secretary has direct management responsibility under section 302(a)(3). The criterion for such emergency prohibition is that the council or Secretary determines that the unlisted gear or fishery "would compromise the effectiveness of conservation and management efforts" under the Act. 16 U.S.C. § 1855(a). The regulations may remain in effect for only six months, unless extended for an additional six months while the council prepares an FMP or FMP amendment to address the gear or fishery concerns. 16 U.S.C. § 1855(c)(3).

Does the new provision effectively shift the burden of proof that a new fishing gear or fishery is ecologically sustainable? When NMFS banned the use of drift gillnets in the Atlantic tunas and swordfish fishery in 1999 to reduce bycatch of marine mammals and to rebuild swordfish stocks, a fishermen with a federal, limited access swordfish permit sued, claiming the drift gillnet ban was a Fifth Amendment regulatory taking of his property interests. The U.S. Court of Federal Claims held that the plaintiff had no Fifth Amendment-protected property interest in the continued use of drift gillnets to take swordfish, as this interest was not a right inherent in his fishing permit or in the ownership of his fishing gear or vessel, but a collateral interest. Conti v. United States, 48 Fed.Cl. 532, 539 (Ct. Claims 2001). The plaintiff appealed.

3. Do the EFH provisions provide a basis for managing fisheries with a view to the marine ecosystems of which they are a part? What does ecosystem-based management entail and how can it be achieved under the Magnuson-Stevens Act?

(3.) Ecosystem-Based Fishery Management

(a.) The Ecosystem Principles Advisory Panel Report to Congress

Responding to calls for further changes to the Act to apply ecosystem principles in fishery conservation and management activities, Congress required the Secretary in 1996 to establish an advisory panel of ecosystem experts and fisheries interests. The panel's task was to report to Congress on the extent to which ecosystem principles are being applied in management and research activities under the Act and to propose actions by the Secretary and Congress to expand the application of such principles. The Panel submitted its report in late 1998. As commentator Marian Macpherson explains,

"Ecosystem management" can have different meanings to

different people.   While there is a general consensus that ecological issues should be the foundation of ecosystem management, some commentators believe that social and economic issues also play a role. The "ecological" approach to fishery management would look at the interactions between organisms and their environment and the effects of those interactions on the distribution and abundance of organisms. Yet ecosystem management might also encompass institutional, informational, and administrative concepts, such as stakeholder involvement in decision-making.

In 1998, the Ecosystem Principles * * * Advisory Panel's report identified the goal of ecosystem-based management as "to maintain ecosystem health and stability," describing ecosystem health as, 'the capability of an ecosystem to support and maintain a balanced, integrated, adaptive community of organisms having a species composition, diversity and functional composition comparable to that of the natural habitat of the region.' The panel's report conceptualized ecosystem-based management as an approach that would require recognition and consideration of the complex interactions and interdependencies in a fishery, and that would allow for the maintenance of such natural complexities.

The panel concluded that in order to manage for ecosystems, managers must both understand the basic characteristics of ecosystems, and develop an ability to manage activities that affect ecosystems in a manner consistently with goals. Pursuant to an ecosystem-based approach, managers would "consider all interactions that a target fish stock has with predators, competitors, and prey species; the effects of weather and climate on fisheries biology and ecology; the complex interactions between fishes and their habitat; and the effects of fishing on fish stocks and their habitat." The report identified eight principles for understanding ecosystems and six key policies for promoting ecosystem-based management.   The eight principles [are]: (1.) The ability to predict ecosystem behavior is limited; (2.) Ecosystems have real thresholds and limits which, when exceeded, can effect major system restructuring; (3.) Once thresholds and limits have been exceeded, changes can be irreversible; (4.) Diversity is important to ecosystem functioning; (5.) Multiple scales interact within and among ecosystems; (6.) Components of ecosystems are linked; (7.) Ecosystem boundaries are open; [and] (8.) Ecosystems change with time.

The key concepts embodied in these principles include recognition of our limited understanding of and ability to predict ecosystem functioning, the importance of diversity, the complexity of interactions and downstream impacts, and the recognition that ecosystems are in flux.

The policies, which are based on the overriding concepts of ecosystem exhaustibility, uncertainty, and human interaction, include: (1.) Change the burden of proof; (2.) Apply the precautionary approach; (3.) Purchase 'insurance' against unforeseen, adverse ecosystem impacts; (4.) Learn from management experiences; (5.) Make local incentives compatible with global goals; and, (6.) Promote participation, fairness, and equity in policy and management.

* * *

The panel recommended the use of two key management approaches: a new overarching planning mechanism they called a Fishery Ecosystem Plan (FEP), and reserved areas called Marine Protected Areas (MPAs). According to the Panel's suggestions, an FEP would (1) describe the physical, biological, and human components of the ecosystem to be managed, (2) direct how to use such information, and (3) set policies with management options. An FEP might, for example, include "zoning" an ecosystem for various types of uses. Presumably, FMPs would then fall under the umbrella of a broader, more programmatic FEP. The MPA concept was less well-defined. The panel believed that MPAs could be developed in a variety of ways along a continuum of possible management regimes that would vary from more to less protective. It is reasonable to assume that MPAs could range in scope from areas permanently closed to all fishing, to areas where gear types are prohibited or other less, sweeping protections are in place.

C. Information

The Panel identified several areas where additional information is needed to support a more ecosystem-oriented management regime. Recognizing an "urgent need for better understanding of ecosystem processes in general, and about the state and dynamics of specific ecosystems," the panel recommended a "substantial expansion of existing programs that collect data on trends and dynamics of marine ecosystems and which characterize the biological and physical relationships pertinent to ecosystem-based management." Areas of focus could include monitoring of non-fish components of ecosystems; developing better understandings of food webs; and assessing the impacts of fishing in terms of effects on the genetic composition of the target stock, disturbances to food webs, and gear's alteration of habitat.

The Panel also recommended research tailored to developing incentives for humans to become "prudent predators," including research into (1) social and economic importance of fisheries and other ecosystem uses, to improve understanding of motivations for behavior and facilitate development of incentives, (2) studies to identify factors that determine success or failure of governance systems, and (3) management experiments to test approaches for involving stakeholders in governance, making decisions when faced with multiple objectives, and considering differing societal perspectives across sectors.

In addition to these new research agendas, the panel recommended a change in the current system of calculating total removals. The panel concluded that current management practices probably calculate total removals too low, and recommended that the measure of total removals should include fish, bycatch, predation, and fish caught and released in recreational fisheries with some determination of mortality rates for such fish.

M. Macpherson, Integrating Ecosystem Management Approaches into Federal Fishery Management Through the Magnuson-Stevens Fishery Conservation and Management Act, 6 Ocean & Coastal L.J. 1, 2-3, 27-28 (2001) (footnotes omitted). See also, National Research Council, Sustaining Marine Fisheries (1999).

(b.) NEPA as a Lever for Ecosystem-Based Fishery Management

While advisory panels were preparing reports and recommendations on ecosystem-based approaches, environmental NGOs sought to force fishery managers to adopt such an approach through litigation. One of the legal levers they choose to use was the National Environmental Policy Act of 1969 (NEPA). In their challenges to NMFS and council decisions after the 1996 Sustainable Fisheries Act, failure to comply with NEPA duties has been a central claim. The councils and NMFS had developed the practice of preparing environmental assessments and a finding of "no significant impact" (FONSI) to accompany framework adjustments and amendments to FMPs, even for those implementing the new requirements of the Sustainable Fisheries Act. See 50 C.F.R. § 600.335 (National Standard 6 guidelines). Environmental plaintiffs argued this was inadequate. NEPA requires all federal agencies to prepare an environmental impact statement (EIS) whenever they propose "major federal actions significantly affecting the quality of the human environment." 42 U.S.C. § 4332(2)(C). The Council on Environmental Quality has promulgated authoritative regulations providing additional guidance to agencies on complying with NEPA. 40 C.F.R. 1500-1508. NMFS' parent agency, NOAA, has issued agency guidance for NMFS' compliance with NEPA in NOAA Administrative Order 216-6, and gives criteria for when an EA may be prepared instead of an EIS. Adm. Order 216-6 at §§ 6.11, 6.05.a.2.

The challenge to EFH amendments described above is an example of this strategy. NMFS' environmental assessments on the EFH amendments had compared a very limited set of alternatives, either the status quo (no EFH identification and protective measures) or the councils' proposed amendments (broad identification of EFH but no further protective measures). In American Oceans Campaign (AOC) v. Daley, No. 99-982, slip op. (D.D.C. Sept. 14, 2000), the court held that while the five councils' EFH amendments, which included little or no assessment of fishing gear impacts on EFH, were adequate under the Magnuson-Stevens Act EFH provisions, their NEPA assessments were insufficient and violated the mandates and principles underlying NEPA. The court enjoined the enforcement of the amendments until NMFS fulfilled it order "to perform a new and thorough EA or EIS as to each EFH amendment." Id. at 42-43.

In exchange for the plaintiffs' dropping their appeal of the MSA ruling, NMFS entered into a court-approved joint stipulation and order, agreeing to prepare full EISs for all of the fisheries that were challenged in the lawsuits, including an analysis of the impacts of fishing on EFH, including direct and indirect effects, an analysis of the impacts of a full range of reasonable alternatives for meeting the requirement of section 303(a)(7), 16 U.S.C. § 1853(a)(7), to "minimize, to the extent practicable, adverse effects on [EFH] caused by fishing" and a decision whether action is needed to meet that requirement. AOC v. Daley, No. 99-982, Joint Stipulation and Order (Dec. 2001). In guidance to his regional administrators, the D.D.C. Assistant Administrator for Fisheries directed them to prepare the EISs "in the context of the best scientific information that is available today" even though the EFH FMP amendments were completed in 1998. Memorandum from W.T. Hogarth, Ph.D., Director, NMFS, to Regional Administrators, Guidance for Developing Environmental Impact Statements for Essential Fish Habitat per the AOC v. Daley Court Order, Jan. 22, 2001.

In a major victory for environmental plaintiffs, a federal district court agreed that NEPA effectively enlarges the scope of fisheries management to require consideration of the entire marine ecosystem, in this case, that of the North Pacific, home of the United States' largest single-species fishery, the Alaska pollock fishery.

GREENPEACE v. NATIONAL MARINE FISHERIES SERVICE
United States District Court, W.D. Washington, 1999
55 F.Supp.2d 1248

DISTRICT JUDGE ZILLY:

* * *

The North Pacific is home to the largest commercial fishing industry in the United States. The most abundant fish in the region, and the major component of the North Pacific fishing industry, is the walleye pollock (pollock). Pollock is a bottom-dwelling fish and a member of the cod family. Mature female pollock are approximately 40 cm in length, and males are longer. Pollock have a fairly short life-span and a high mortality rate, in part because they are sometimes highly cannibalistic.

The estimated biomass of pollock in the North Pacific ecosystem has fluctuated significantly since the 1960s. In the east Bering Sea, for example, the estimated biomass was less than 2 million metric tons (mmt) in the mid-1960s, rose to nearly 8 mmt in 1971, declined to 4 mmt in 1978, peaked at 14 mmt in 1984, declined to 8 mmt in 1990, increased again to over 12 mmt in 1993, and dropped to 7 mmt in 1997. The fishing effort directed toward pollock has also fluctuated. From 1964 to 1970, the pollock catch in the BSAI rose from approximately 200,000 to 1 million mt. In the late 1980s, the total catch peaked at approximately 2.7 mmt. A significant portion of this catch came from what later was designated as Steller sea lion critical habitat. By the mid-1990s, the total pollock catch in the BSAI had declined to approximately 1.25 mmt, but much of the catch came from within Steller sea lion critical habitat. Scientists believe that the pollock population changes stem in large part from climate changes which have effected [sic] the rest of the North Pacific ecosystem as well. In part because of these changes, Steller sea lions have become increasingly dependent on pollock as their major source of prey.

* * *

[The court describes claims based on the Endangered Species Act.]

This case also involves claims by plaintiffs based on the National Environmental Policy Act (NEPA). NEPA requires that an environmental impact statement (EIS)[7] be prepared on proposals for legislation and

---

[7] An EIS is "an action-forcing device to insure that [NEPA's] policies and goals * * * are infused into the ongoing programs and actions of the Federal Government. It shall provide full and fair discussion of significant environmental impacts and shall inform decisionmakers and the public of the reasonable alternatives which would avoid or

other major federal actions significantly affecting the quality of the human environment. The Fishery Management Plans (FMPs), such as those for the fisheries in this case, undisputedly constitute major federal actions requiring an EIS. Accordingly, NMFS published an EIS for the GOA fishery in 1978, in connection with the FMP for that year. The Bering Sea EIS was published in 1981. These FMPs and their accompanying EISs address numerous issues, including when, where, and how the fish are caught, TAC levels, bycatch, habitat destruction, socioeconomic issues, and other marine mammals affected.

NEPA requires continuing environmental analysis for changes to ongoing federal actions, such as the dozens of amendments to the FMPs for the North Pacific fisheries. If an agency finds that a change is not substantial, however, it can prepare an Environmental Assessment (EA) and Finding of No Significant Impact (FONSI) rather than a supplemental environmental impact statement (SEIS).[8] The key difference, for present purposes, between an EA/FONSI and an SEIS is that the latter must consider a broad range of alternatives to the proposed federal action, while an EA can simply approve the action as proposed. NMFS had prepared EAs/FONSIs for all prior amendments to the FMPs, and had never prepared an SEIS until December 1998.

During the approximately twenty years since the original EISs were prepared, however, there have been dramatic changes to the North Pacific ecosystem. Steller sea lions were listed as a threatened species nine years after preparation of the original EISs, and the western population was classified as endangered sixteen years after their preparation. In fact, the original EISs considered the Steller sea lion population as being at an optimal sustainable level. This period also saw significant population declines of fur seals, harbor seals, and several species of whales, birds and fish in the North Pacific ecosystem. This area went through a major climate change during this period, which significantly affected the prevalence of various fish species, which in turn affected the focus of the fishing industry. When the original EISs were prepared, the fishing fleet was dominated by foreign vessels; it is now almost entirely composed of American vessels. This change has significantly altered the fishing industry's economic effects on Alaskan communities. The size and capacity of the trawlers used has also

---

minimize adverse impacts or enhance the quality of the human environment." 40 C.F.R. § 1502.1.

[8] An Environmental Assessment is a concise public document that helps an agency determine whether an EIS is necessary, facilitates preparation of an EIS when one is necessary, and aids in the agency's NEPA compliance. 40 C.F.R. § 1508.9. A Finding of No Significant Impact briefly presents "the reasons why an action * * * will not have a significant effect on the human environment and for which an [EIS] therefore will not be prepared." 40 C.F.R. § 1508.13.

increased considerably, which allows more fish to be caught in a shorter amount of time. This highlights only a small fraction of the changes which occurred in the North Pacific in the 1980s and 1990s.

These extensive changes in the North Pacific led to sharp criticism within NMFS over the adequacy of the existing documents for NEPA compliance. Some NMFS employees have urged the preparation of a supplemental EIS since the early 1990s. NMFS did not take its first formal step towards doing so, however, until March 1997, when NMFS issued a notice of intent to prepare an SEIS regarding the BSAI and GOA groundfisheries. NMFS announced that the SEIS would "incorporate[ ] the following: The amendments to the groundfish FMPs; the annual process for determining the TAC specifications; and the public process in place for implementing new regulations, revising existing ones, and incorporating new information." After 18 months of preparation, the agency issued a draft EIS for public review and comment in September 1998. The final SEIS (FSEIS) was issued on December 18, 1998. It discussed in great detail the new developments regarding the North Pacific fisheries, from the changes in the way the fisheries occur to the listings of the Steller sea lion and several other species under the ESA, to the new scientific information obtained since the prior EISs had been prepared. The critical "alternatives" section of the FSEIS, however, analyzed this information only under a range of alternative TAC levels. Plaintiffs contend that this narrow scope violates NEPA; the defendants argue that this approach fulfills their NEPA obligations.

* * *

C. History of NEPA Compliance/Decision to Prepare SEIS

In support of their argument that NEPA required preparation of a broad SEIS, plaintiffs rely on the history of NEPA compliance in this case. They point out that the Final Supplemental EIS, which NMFS issued in December 1998, was the first EIS prepared regarding the North Pacific groundfisheries in almost twenty years. Since the original EISs were prepared, significant changes occurred within the fishing industry and the FMPs for the GOA and BSAI were each amended more than forty times. The North Pacific ecosystem also underwent major changes, including the steep decline of the Steller sea lion population.

Since the early 1990s, there has been criticism within NMFS regarding the overall adequacy of the existing documents for NEPA compliance. For example, the record contains a draft letter, written in 1990, stating that the environmental analysis in the original documents "would be considered grossly inadequate by today's standards." Another memorandum, written in 1992, around the time of the emergency listing of the Steller sea lions as a threatened species, called for the preparation of a supplemental EIS, since the existing one treated

Steller sea lions as being at "optimum sustainable population levels." Despite these criticisms, however, NMFS did not begin preparation of an SEIS on the groundfisheries until March 1997, when it published a notice of intent to prepare an SEIS.[9] In this scoping notice, NMFS relied on the "[n]ew information about the ecosystem, impacts of the fisheries, and management tools" to explain its decision to prepare an SEIS. NMFS also noted the major changes made to the FMPs as relevant to its decision to prepare an SEIS. NMFS therefore seems to have acknowledged that an SEIS was necessary under both the "substantial changes to the action" and the "significant new information" prongs of 40 C.F.R. § 1502.9(c).

D. Scope of the SEIS

In support of its motion for summary judgment, NMFS relies on the fact that the SEIS undisputedly included a great deal of new "information relevant to environmental concerns and bearing on the proposed action or its impacts." 40 C.F.R. § 1502.9(c)(1)(ii). They correctly note that the "Affected Environment" section of the SEIS discussed the various components of the North Pacific ecosystem, updating the information known about each component. For example, the SEIS contains twelve pages on the ESA Section 7 Consultations regarding the Steller sea lion, providing a detailed history of the data available and the actions taken based on that data. The SEIS also discussed the changes made to the structure and composition of the fisheries, providing a high level of detail about such things as the various Alaskan communities affected by the fishing industry and the types of vessels used in the industry.

The plaintiffs, however, point out that the SEIS *analyzed* this detailed new information, not by looking at a range of alternatives reflecting the broad scope of the FMPs, but instead only under a range of alternatives dealing with one particular aspect of the FMPs: TAC levels. The SEIS considered the environmental effects on the North Pacific ecosystem of using four alternative TAC levels: (A) the status quo method of setting TAC levels annually, for each species complex, within the optimum yield (OY) range based on the biological status of the species and "other ecological and socio-economic aspects of the fisheries"; (B) setting TAC levels at the lower end of the OY range; (C) setting TAC levels at the upper end of the OY range; and (D) no directed groundfishing. As a result of this approach, the EIS did not consider how the vast array of new information about the affected environment relates to the other aspects of the fisheries that the FMPs regulate, such as "time and area closures, gear restrictions, bycatch limits of prohibited species, and

---

[9] The regulations require an agency to publish in the Federal Register a notice of intent to prepare an EIS. 40 C.F.R. § 1508.7. This scoping notice should, among other things, invite public participation, determine the breadth and depth of the significant issues to be analyzed in the EIS, and provide a tentative schedule for EIS preparation. Id.

allocations of TACs among vessels delivering to different types of processors groups, gear types, and qualifying communities."

1. Federal Action Under Review

The plaintiffs argue that this approach violates NEPA for a number of reasons. NEPA requires preparation of an SEIS when "[t]he agency makes substantial changes in the proposed action that are relevant to environmental concerns;" or when "[t]here are significant new circumstances or information relevant to environmental concerns and bearing on the proposed action or its impacts." 40 C.F.R. § 1502.9(c). Applying these standards to the present case, plaintiffs argue that the FMPs as a whole, not the method used to set TAC-levels, is "the proposed action" about which there are significant new circumstances and to which substantial changes have been made. In support of this argument, plaintiffs point to the scoping notice, which indicated that the SEIS would analyze:

> * * * decisions about location and timing of each fishery, harvestable amounts, exploitation rates, exploited species, groupings of exploited species, gear types and groupings, allocations, product quality, organic waste and secondary utilization, at-sea and on-land organic discard, species at higher and lower trophic levels, habitat alterations, and relative impacts to coastal communities, society, the economy, and the domestic and foreign groundfish markets.

As prepared, however, the SEIS discussed these issues generally, but did not consider a range of alternatives dealing with them. Plaintiffs argue that by narrowing the range of alternatives to those specifically dealing with TAC levels rather than the FMPs as a whole, NMFS failed to "take a hard look" at the environmental consequences of the agency action, the FMPs.

NMFS responds that the federal action under review in the SEIS was not the FMPs generally, but rather was merely the more limited issue of "setting of TACs in the GOA and BSAI groundfish fisheries." They argue that the scoping notice reflected this narrow focus as well: "NMFS announces its intention to prepare a supplemental environmental impact statement (SEIS) on the Federal action by which the total allowable catch (TAC) specifications and prohibited species catch limits * * * are annually established and apportioned." .[They argue a] "proposed alternative is reasonable only if it will bring about the ends of the federal action" being considered. Citizens Against Burlington, Inc. v. Busey, 938 F.2d 190 (D.C.Cir.1991). "When the purpose is to accomplish one thing, it makes no sense to consider the alternative ways by which another thing might be achieved." City of Angoon v. Hodel, 803 F.2d 1016, 1021-22 (9th Cir.1986). Thus, NMFS argues that the range of alternatives was properly tailored to meet this definition of the federal action at issue.

NMFS's argument is legally flawed. Although NMFS contends that the scoping notice and the SEIS clearly establish that the federal action under review was only the setting of TAC levels, both documents are in fact ambiguous on this point. The language quoted above, on which NMFS relies, indicates a narrow scope. On the other hand, the scoping notice also stated that "[t]he SEIS will analyze the *process by which* annual TAC specifications and prohibited species catch limits are determined, together with the procedures for implementing changes to these processes." The notice then defines "the process" as including the numerous elements relied on by plaintiffs, quoted above.

The SEIS itself reflects similar ambivalency. The section describing the "purpose" of the SEIS detailed the changes that have occurred since the original EISs were prepared for the original FMPs (1978 and 1981). These include changes in the following: 1) the BSAI and GOA ecosystems and our understandings of them; 2) the marine species and population frequencies of marine mammal, seabird, and fish in the biological assemblages of the BSAI and GOA; 3) the marine species listed under the Endangered Species Act, some of which may be affected by the BSAI and GOA groundfish fisheries; 4) the information about the biological characteristics of the groundfish stocks; 5) the information about the ecosystem impacts of the fisheries; 6) the fishery management tools that are being used or are available; 7) the characteristics of the groundfish fleets; and 8) the distributions of catch by fleet, area and season.

Plaintiffs are correct that this discussion demonstrated a need for a broad SEIS, which analyzed the effect of this myriad of changes on the North Pacific ecosystem. The SEIS then continued: "A programmatic SEIS was developed to analyze and display the effects of the fisheries on the affected human (biological, physical, and economic) environment * * * The scope of actions in this analysis includes a range of levels for setting of TACs in the GOA and BSAI groundfish fisheries." This language implies both a broad scope (programmatic SEIS) and a narrow one (scope of action concerns TAC levels). While the SEIS contained language indicating that the federal action under review was merely the setting of TAC levels, the weight of the language pointed to a broader scope.[10]   Furthermore, as discussed below, a narrow SEIS dealing

---

[10] Additionally, the SEIS refers repeatedly to the fact that it is a "programmatic analysis" of the fisheries as they affect the environment. The government's counsel conceded at oral argument that the document should be treated as a programmatic analysis. Programmatic analyses look to the environmental consequences of a project as a whole, and do not necessarily contain the same level of detail or specificity as a site or project-specific EIS. Instead, they often form the basis for tiering future NEPA documents focusing on specific facets under review. NMFS's description of the SEIS as

only with TAC levels would not satisfy NEPA. The FMPs involve "a myriad of interrelated regulations to manage the fisheries." In light of the significant changes to these FMPs and the new information about the broad range of issues covered by these regulations, the Court concludes as a matter of law that NEPA required a broad programmatic SEIS in order to fairly evaluate the dramatic and significant changes which have occurred in the GOA and BSAI groundfisheries.

2. Cumulative Effects Analysis

The plaintiffs correctly argue that NEPA required creation of a document that thoroughly analyzed the cumulative effects of the FMPs:

> Cumulative impact is the impact on the environment which results from the incremental impact of the action when added to other past, present, and reasonably foreseeable future actions.... Cumulative impacts can result from individually minor but collectively significant actions taking place over a period of time.

40 C.F.R. § 1508.7. If several actions have a cumulative environmental effect, this consequence must be considered in an EIS." *Blue Mountain,* 161 F.3d at 1214 (internal quotation omitted). Plaintiffs therefore argue that the SEIS needed to analyze the changes to the FMPs.

Each amendment to the FMPs may have been individually minor and therefore properly dealt with in an EA/FONSI rather than in an SEIS. See Greenpeace Action v. Franklin, 14 F.3d 1324, 1332 (9th Cir.1992) (1991 amendments too minor to warrant an EIS). Nevertheless, NEPA does not permit NMFS to continue making individually minor but collectively significant changes to the FMPs without preparing an SEIS analyzing these changes. "Significance exists [and thus an EIS must be prepared] if it is reasonable to--anticipate a cumulatively significant impact on the environment. Significance cannot be avoiding by * * * breaking [an action] down into small component parts." 40 C.F.R. § 1508.27(b)(7). By preparing only EA/FONSIs for each FMP amendment, NMFS tried to avoid "significance" for many years. The Court has no doubt that the vast changes to the FMPs have reached the threshold of "cumulatively significant impact on the environment," thereby requiring preparation of an SEIS addressing these vast changes. For the same reasons, NMFS cannot then break the FMPs down "into small component parts" by analyzing only the setting of TAC levels rather than these FMPs in their entirety. The Court therefore concludes that NEPA's cumulative effects provision requires a programmatic analysis of the FMPs in their current form.

"a programmatic analysis" provides further support for the conclusion that the SEIS must be a broad document considering the FMPs as a whole.

E. Range of Alternatives Considered

1. Fully Informed Decisions

The Court's determination that the SEIS must be treated as a broad, programmatic analysis of the FMPs as a whole leads directly to its conclusion that the range of alternatives considered was inadequate. One of the goals of the NEPA process is "to identify and assess the reasonable alternatives to proposed actions that will avoid or minimize adverse effects of these actions upon the quality of the human environment." 40 C.F.R. § 1500.2(e). The regulation regarding alternatives, 40 C.F.R. § 1502.14, provides:

> Based on the information and analysis presented in the sections on the Affected Environment (§ 1502.15) and the Environmental Consequences (§ 1502.16), [the alternatives section] should present the environmental impacts of the proposal and the alternatives in comparative form, thus sharply defining the issues and providing a clear basis for choice among options by the decisionmaker and the public.

40 C.F.R. § 1502.14.[11] The SEIS in this case, however, does not "sharply [define] the issues and [provide] a clear basis for choice among options" related to the FMPs. It does not help future decision-makers assess whether the fisheries should continue to be conducted under the current structure of the FMPs, or whether other alternatives would be more beneficial. The Environmental Protection Agency's final comments on the SEIS correctly note that NEPA's requirement that NMFS "rigorously explore and objectively evaluate all reasonable alternatives," dictates inclusion of more comprehensive alternatives which look at and programmatically address all elements of the FMP (i.e. location and timing of each fishery, harvestable amounts, exploitation rates, exploited species, groupings of exploited species, gear types and groupings,

---

[11] The section further provides that agencies shall:

(a) Rigorously explore and objectively evaluate all reasonable alternatives, and for alternatives which were eliminated from detailed study, briefly discuss the reasons for their having been eliminated.

(b) Devote substantial treatment to each alternative considered in detail including the proposed action so that reviewers may evaluate their comparative merits.

(c) Include reasonable alternatives not within the jurisdiction of the lead agency.

(d) Include the alternative of no action.

(e) Identify the agency's preferred alternative or alternatives, if one or more exists, in the draft statement and identify such alternative in the final statement unless another law prohibits the expression of such a preference.

(f) Include appropriate mitigation measures not already included in the proposed action or alternatives.

40 C.F.R. § 1502.14.

allocations, product quality, organic waste and secondary utilization, at-sea and on-land organic discard, species at higher and lower trophic levels, habitat alterations, and relative impacts to coastal communities, society, the economy, and the domestic and foreign groundfish markets) and varies TAC levels outside of the present status quo range.

As written, however, the SEIS does not provide decision-makers with any way of assessing the trade-offs between gear-restrictions and bycatch, for example, or the way that the timing of the various fisheries interact.   The difficulty of the issues presented in the [ESA-required] Biological Opinion and its Reasonable and Prudent Alternatives highlight the need for consideration of the range of environmental effects of the various regulations contained in the FMPs. One important goal of NEPA is to help "public officials make decisions that are based on understanding of environmental consequences." 40 C.F.R. § 1500.1(c). The SEIS does not provide the information necessary for decision-makers to make fully informed choices.   The SEIS is therefore inadequate under NEPA.

2. "Practical Analysis" of Fisheries

NMFS contends that by analyzing the fisheries under various TAC levels, the SEIS nevertheless considered the full range of environmental impacts from the fisheries as conducted under the array of regulations contained in the FMPs. Specifically, NMFS argues that this Court should defer to NMFS's determination "that an examination of the fishery under alternative TAC levels would *result in a practical analysis* of the environmental impacts of the fisheries."   NMFS contends that this determination is entitled to substantial deference, and therefore that analysis of alternative TAC levels fulfills NEPA's purpose of ensuring informed decision-making regarding the FMPs in their entirety.

The case law providing for substantial deference to an agency's determination of the scope of an EIS, however, does not support NMFS's argument.   NMFS relies on cases involving deference to an agency's decision about the scope of the federal action under review. See, e.g., Kleppe v. Sierra Club, 427 U.S. 390, 96 S.Ct. 2718, 49 L.Ed.2d 576 (1976) (deference to agency's determination that no regional proposal for federal action existed and therefore no regional EIS was necessary); Marsh, 490 U.S. at 376-77, 109 S.Ct. 1851 (deference to agency's determination that new information did not require preparation of a supplemental EIS).   These cases do not require the Court to defer to NMFS's assertion that an analysis of TAC levels will provide a practical analysis of the fisheries.   The SEIS completely lacks any explanation of *why* and *how* analysis of TAC levels "results in a practical analysis" of the impact of the fisheries, as governed by a myriad of regulations.   NMFS merely stated: "Analysis of the 'process' or actual procedure employed by the NMFS in developing annual TAC specifications would not be as illustrative of the impacts that could occur to the environment as a result of a change from the current TAC levels under the current baseline." Id. Judicial deference to such an unexplained assertion on a critical point would render judicial review meaningless.   Even under "arbitrary and capricious" review, the appropriate inquiry is "whether the agency 'considered the relevant factors and *articulated a rational connection* between the facts found and the choice made.'" *Pyramid Lake*, 898 F.2d at 1414 (emphasis added).   Here, the government's failure to explain the connection between setting various TAC levels and the impact of other fishery regulations is not entitled to deference, and even if the Court were to defer, the result would be the same.   The Court cannot excuse NMFS's total failure to analyze or explain this critical point.   The Court concludes that an analysis of the fisheries under various TAC levels was not sufficient to fulfill NEPA's requirements.[12]

3. Programmatic Analysis

Clearly, a programmatic analysis would not require consideration of detailed alternatives with respect to each aspect of the plan--otherwise a programmatic analysis would be impossible to prepare and would merely be a vast series of site specific analyses. See *Robertson,* 35 F.3d at 1306 ("specific analysis is better done when a specific development action is to be taken, not at the programmatic level.").   The level of detail necessary in an EIS is directly related to the scope of the federal action under review. California v. Block, 690 F.2d 753, 761 (9th Cir.1982). Thus, if a multi- step project is proposed that nevertheless has a very broad scope at the initial stage, a high level of detail may be required even in a programmatic EIS. Id. at 765.   In the present case, however, the programmatic EIS was necessary because of the significant cumulative effects of the amendments to the FMPs over the years, rather than because there were particular new amendments pending.   The programmatic EIS should therefore present a more general picture of the environmental effects of the plans, rather than focusing narrowly on one aspect of them.

F. NEPA Conclusion

The administrative record in this case demonstrates that NMFS's employees faced a very difficult task in preparing this SEIS. The "Affected Environment" section synthesized a great deal of new

---

[12] This conclusion is even stronger when one realizes that the three of the four "alternatives" were closely related to the status quo.   As the DPA final comments correctly point out, "Not only were the alternatives limited to variations of TAC, but three of the four existed within the current status quo range: Alternative A maintained the entire range, Alternative B low-balled the existing range, and Alternative C high-balled the existing range.   Alternative D, which called for ceasing all fishing activities * * * seems unreasonable and therefore unlikely to be considered."

information regarding the North Pacific ecosystem, and took an important step toward full compliance with NEPA. The Act, however, requires NMFS to analyze the ways in which the groundfisheries effect [sic] the North Pacific ecosystem, and to provide decisionmakers and the public with a document that will help further informed decision-making as to the consequences of these plans. The present SEIS, by focusing its analysis only on TAC levels, does not fulfill this mandate.

* * *

NEPA required preparation of a programmatic supplemental environmental impact statement analyzing the environmental impacts of the FMPs as a whole on the North Pacific ecosystem.

Pursuant to NEPA, the Court will also enter an order remanding the Environmental Impact Statement to NMFS for action consistent with this Order.

Notes and Questions

1. This decision is a precedent on a par with NRDC v. Daley, 209 F.3d 747 (D.C. Cir. 2000), excerpted above in section (C.)(1.)(p.471). Does the ruling apply only to fisheries that take place in marine ecosystems in which a species listed under the Endangered Species Act that is potentially affected by the fishery also occurs? See chapter 7 for more on the impact of the Endangered Species Act on marine fisheries management.

2. To meet the court's order, NMFS and the North Pacific Fishery Management Council released for public comment a 3,400-page Draft Programmatic Supplemental EIS (PSEIS) for the Bering Sea/Aleutian Islands and Gulf of Alaska Groundfish in Jan., 2001. Testimony of D. Fluharty before the U.S. House Committee on Resources, Subcommittee on Fisheries Conservation, Wildlife and Oceans, Hearing on Ecosystem-Based Fishery Management and Reauthorization of the Magnuson-Stevens Fishery Conservation and Management Act, June 14, 2001. On Nov. 27, 2001, NMFS announced its intent to revise the draft PSEIS, after reviewing more than 21,000 comment letters, to restructure the alternatives from single-focus to more comprehensive, multi-component alternatives and include additional analysis of cumulative and other impacts. How difficult is it to meet the court's expectations for an EIS that considers impacts of the FMPs as a whole on the entire North Pacific marine ecosystem?

 (c.) Marine Protected Areas and Fishery Management Plans

NMFS's Final Rules on EFH, 50 C.F.R. § 600, Subpart J, identify marine reserves or marine protected areas (MPAs) as one tool that might be used to protect fish habitat. MPAs are a controversial approach to protecting marine ecosystems and managing resources. They are viewed as 'anti-fishing', even though they can benefit fisheries by protecting spawning grounds and other habitat required for healthy fish populations. A study by the National Academy of Sciences released in 2001 concluded that marine reserves show "promise as components of an ecosystem-based approach for conserving the ocean's living assets" and that a growing body of research documents their effectiveness in "conserving habitats, fostering the recovery of overexploited species, and maintaining marine communities." National Research Council, Marine Protected Areas: Tools for Sustaining Ocean Ecosystems 1, 175 (2001). The report noted that implementation of the EFH provisions by the councils and NMFS has included some consideration of fishery reserves as a component of management, including consideration by the Pacific council to protect rockfish, the South Atlantic and Gulf of Mexico councils to protect coral reef fish species, and the Gulf council to evaluate their effectiveness in protecting grouper populations. The councils have also adopted some restrictions on trawling to protect the sea bottom and places where crabs congregate in the North Pacific and to protect juvenile groundfish habitat on the Georges Bank off New England. The report notes, however, that this work has been driven by single-species concerns and gear conflicts, not by an overarching ecosystem-based agenda, nor by a desire to obtain baseline information on unfished areas for comparison with fished areas to improve our understanding of the impacts of fishing. Id. at 165.

In May, 2000, President Clinton issued Executive Order 13158 on Marine Protected Areas. 65 Fed. Reg. 34909 (May 31, 2000). The Order finds that "[a]n expanded and strengthened comprehensive system of marine protected areas throughout the marine environment would enhance the conservation of our Nation's natural and cultural marine heritage and the ecologically and economically sustainable use of the marine environment for future generations." Id. at Section 1. The Order directs federal agencies, consistent with domestic and international law, to strengthen the management, protection, and conservation of existing MPAs and establish new or expanded MPAs; develop a scientifically based, comprehensive national system of MPAs representing diverse U.S. marine ecosystems, and the Nation's natural and cultural resources; and avoid causing harm to MPAs through federally approved activities. Id. at Sections 3 - 5.

Several national marine sanctuaries have already been designated under the National Marine Sanctuaries Act, 16 U.S.C. 1431 et seq. Few, if any, restrictions on fishing have been adopted to protect sanctuary resources, and the regional councils have argued they have primary authority to determine whether any restrictions are warranted (under the EFH provisions and otherwise). Does the Executive Order's requirement that federal agencies whose actions affect resources protected by an MPA avoid harm to those resources, to the maximum extent practicable and to the extent permitted by law, require NMFS to assess the effect of fishing gear on areas like the Stellwagen National Marine Sanctuary in the Gulf of Maine, regardless of what the New England council concludes in its EFH amendment? For further discussion of the marine sanctuaries program, see chapter 8.

Note on the Northwest Hawaiian Islands Coral Reef Ecosystem Reserve

In amendments to the National Marine Sanctuaries Act in 2000, Pub. L. 106-513, Congress authorized the President to designate any Northwest Hawaiian Islands coral reef or coral reef ecosystem as a reserve to be managed by the Secretary of Commerce, Pub. L. 106-513, 6(g)(1), 16 U.S.C. § 6401note(g)(1). Upon the President's designation, the Secretary is then required to initiate designation of the reserve as a national marine sanctuary. Id. at § 6401note(g)(2). After a public review process involving several hearings in Hawaii and extensive public comment, President Clinton created the Northwest Hawaiian Islands Coral Reef Ecosystem Reserve by Executive Order 13178, 65 Fed. Reg. 76903 (Dec. 4, 2000). The Reserve encompasses an area approximately 1200 nautical miles long and 100 nautical miles wide of the marine waters and submerged lands of the Northwest Hawaiian Islands. The Order created the largest nature preserve in the U.S. and one of the only true marine reserves under federal authority. The Reserve protects more than 70% of all coral reefs under U.S. jurisdiction and thus greatly advances international efforts to protect coral reefs worldwide. After the National Oceanic and Atmospheric Administration, on behalf of the Secretary, held seven public hearings and a 30-day public comment period on the Reserve, President Clinton followed with a second order to put in final form the Reserve, Exec. Order 13196, 66 Fed. Reg. 7395 (Jan. 23, 2001).

Certain conservation measures included in the Northwest Hawaiian Islands Coral Reef Ecosystem Reserve are controversial as they restrict activities throughout the Reserve and create Reserve Preservation Areas around various atolls, islands, and banks within the Reserve where extractive uses are prohibited. Changes to the Reserve made in the second order, however, clarify that certain fisheries are allowed to continue although capped at levels achieved in the 5 years preceding the date of the Reserve's original designation. Native Hawaiian fishers are allowed a one-time reasonable increase in fishing under their existing bottomfish permits. The taking of coral, permitted under the regional council's Precious Corals FMP, is now prohibited by the Reserve.

The Bush Administration began a review of the Reserve in 2001, creating uncertainty whether the new Secretary of Commerce would follow the Executive Order and initiate a sanctuary designation process to effectuate its objectives. While this review was underway, the Western Pacific Fishery Management Council submitted to the Secretary a new plan, the Coral Reef Ecosystem Protection FMP, which the council argues makes the Reserve unnecessary. Critics of the draft plan, however, note that it would allowed a significant expansion of extractive activities in the Reserve rather than offer comparable or superior levels of protection.

In Greenpeace Foundation v. Mineta, 122 F.Supp.2d 1123 (D.Hawai'i 2000), Judge Samuel P. King concluded that management of the crustacean and bottomfish fisheries at the Northwest Hawaiian Islands, under FMPs prepared by the Western Pacific Fishery Management Council, violated the Endangered Species Act and NEPA. Judge King found the FMP had failed to keep lobster fishery within sustainable limits that took account of the potential dietary needs of the Hawaiian monk seal, a critically endangered species endemic to the NWHI. The lobster fishery, which crashed in recent years, was enjoined from reopening while NMFS prepared a new EIS and conducted a new biological consultation under section 7 of the Endangered Species Act. Does the Secretary have a duty to consider this decision in reviewing whether to approve the proposed Coral Reef Ecosystem FMP?

D. MANAGING HIGHLY MIGRATORY SPECIES

The Magnuson-Stevens Act defines "highly migratory species" (HMS) as tunas, oceanic sharks, and billfishes (swordfish, marlins, and sailfishes). 16 U.S.C. § 1802(20). The Act provides a different management regime for highly migratory species because their extensive, trans-oceanic migrations makes their effective management a subject of international cooperation. The Magnuson-Stevens Act assigns responsibility for managing Atlantic sharks and other "highly migratory species" exclusively to the Secretary of Commerce. 16 U.S.C. § § 1852(a)(3), 1854(g). The Act's basic jurisdictional provision states that "except as provided for in section 102, the United States claims, and will exercise in the manner provided for in this Act, sovereign rights and exclusive fishery management authority over all fish, and all Continental Shelf fishery resources, within the exclusive economic zone." Id. at § 1811. In section 102, the United States commits itself to "cooperate directly or through appropriate international organizations with those nations involved in fisheries for highly migratory species with a view to ensuring conservation and shall promote the achievement of optimum yield of such species throughout their range, both within and beyond the exclusive economic zone." Id. at § 1812.

Prior to 1990, the Act excluded from the claim of sovereign rights and exclusive management authority highly migratory species of fish, which the Act defined as tuna. See D. Hoover, A Case Against International Management of Highly Migratory Marine Fishery

Resources: The Atlantic Bluefin Tuna, 11 B.C. Env. Aff. L. Rev. 11 (1983).

Because highly migratory species are apex predators (i.e., animals that have evolved without predators), are far-ranging, and are managed under international agreements, effective management has been difficult to achieve. Compounding these difficulties is the intense competition among the different gears and user groups in the U.S. fishery for Atlantic bluefin tuna, a species for which the international regime has been particularly ineffective, and the rapid growth of the shark fishery in response to demand of the Asian markets.

Sharks

Responsibility for managing all non-Atlantic highly migratory species under U.S. jurisdiction rests with the regional fishery management councils. For example, tuna and swordfish fisheries carried out by Hawaii-based longline vessels in waters of the western Pacific region are covered by the FMP for the Pelagic Fisheries of the Western Pacific Fishery Management Council. 50 C.F.R. Part 660. One of the bycatch species in that fishery is the blue shark, which crew members would discard after cutting off the fins and later sell for shipment to the Asian market. Management regulations for fisheries in the Atlantic, Gulf of Mexico, and Caribbean waters banned the practice, but the Western Pacific council resisted pressure to do so, arguing that the blue shark was not in danger of overfishing. While NMFS was considering a petition for rulemaking to prohibit the practice of shark finning in the Pacific region, Congress enacted H.R. 5461, on Dec. 21, 2000. The amendments add a prohibition to section 307(1) of the Magnuson-Stevens Act, 16 U.S.C. § 1857(1)(P), on removing any fin of a shark and discarding the carcass at sea, to have custody, control or possession of such fin aboard a fishing vessel without the carcass, or to land any such fin without the carcass. The section contains a rebuttable presumption that any shark fins found on board a fishing vessel were taken, held or landed in violation of this section if the total weight of shark fins found on board exceeds 5% of the total weight of shark carcasses found on board.

Directed Shark Fisheries under the Atlantic Highly Migratory Species FMP

In addition to the ten national standards, the highly migratory species provisions require the Secretary to consider a number of factors, to "minimize, to the extent practicable, any disadvantage to United States fishermen in relation to foreign competitors", and to "diligently pursue, through international entities (such as the International Commission for the Conservation of Atlantic Tunas [ICCAT]) comparable international fishery management measures with respect to fishing for highly migratory species." Id. at § 1854(g)(1)(C),(F).

When a coalition of shark fishermen and shark fishing organizations challenged the 1997 commercial harvest quotas for Atlantic sharks, the plaintiffs alleged, inter alia, that NMFS failed to comply with these requirements in its efforts at ICCAT. The Secretary of Commerce countered that these claims raised non-justiciable political questions because they asked the court to intrude into the foreign policy prerogatives of the executive branch contrary to the Supreme Court's political question doctrine applied in Baker v. Carr, 369 U.S. 186 (1962). The court agreed that the plaintiffs' challenge to the ICCAT efforts was non-justiciable. It noted that even if the claim was justiciable, the Secretary was entitled to summary judgment on the claim because NMFS was pursuing international cooperation at ICCAT and with Mexican scientists. "Although the secretary's efforts in this regard may come too late and comprise too little, I believe that they satisfy the minimum required by § 1854(g)(1)(F) * * *." Southern Offshore Fishing Ass'n v. Daley, 995 F.Supp. 1411, 1428, n. 25 (M.D.Fla. 1998). The court went on to find that the decision to reduce commercial quotas by 50% did not violate the national standards nor constitute an arbitrary action despite the inconclusiveness of the stock assessments. In the court's view, the record included ample evidence suggesting that these shark species may have already lost their ability to replenish and are headed for extinction. The court did, however, remand the 1997 regulations for further economic impact analysis on small businesses and potential alternatives under the Regulatory Flexibility Act, 5 U.S.C. §§ 603, 604.

After NMFS submitted the required analysis, Judge Merryday questioned its adequacy and appointed a special master to review it. When NMFS then issued regulations for 1999 that further reduced the shark quotas in light of the overfished condition of the shark stocks, the plaintiffs challenged them. The court enjoined the regulations and harshly criticized the agency for its "willing[ness] to pursue its institutional objectives without acknowledging applicable Congressional and judicial limitations * * * Although the preservation of Atlantic shark species is a benevolent, laudatory goal, conservation does not justify government lawlessness." The court reinstated the 1997 commercial quota pending further judicial review. Southern Offshore Fishing Ass'n v. Daley II, 55 F.Supp.2d 1336 (M.D.Fla. 1999). The parties eventually entered a settlement agreement, under which NMFS agreed to submit its shark stock assessment to an independent peer review panel.

Atlantic bluefin tuna

Atlantic tunas are managed by NMFS under the authority of the Magnuson-Stevens Act and the Atlantic Tunas Convention Act, 16 U.S.C. § 971 et seq., which gives the Secretary of State authority to participate in the International Commission for the Conservation of Atlantic Tunas (ICCAT) and requires the Secretary of Commerce power to issue regulations that implement ICCAT's binding recommendations. Id. §§ 971c, 971d(a). The ATCA gives the State and Commerce departments broad discretion to develop tuna conservation programs, "except that no regulation * * * may have the effect of increasing or decreasing any allocation or quota of fish or fishing mortality level to the United States agreed to pursuant to a recommendation of the Commission." 16

U.S.C. §§ 971d(c)(1)(A), 971d(c)(3)(K).

In November, 1998, ICCAT adopted a 20-year rebuilding program for the Atlantic bluefin tuna, setting an annual total allowable catch of 2,500 metric tons (m.t.), inclusive of dead discards. The annual landing quota allocated to the U.S. is 1,387 m.t. Regulations subdivide the U.S. bluefin quota among the several categories of the domestic fishery as percentage shares based on historical allocations. 50 C.F.R. Part 635.

Even before ICCAT adopted the rebuilding program, management of the Atlantic bluefin tuna had become the most highly politicized fishery management process involving U.S. fishing interests. For an account of domestic and international tuna politics, see Carl Safina, Song for the Blue Ocean 78-116 (1997). For a description of the bluefin harpoon fishery of Cape Cod, see Douglas Whynott, Giant Bluefin (1995).

On Sept. 30, 1997, the Secretary issued a report to Congress as required by 16 U.S.C. § 1854(e)(1), identifying the Atlantic bluefin tuna and several other highly migratory species as "overfished." Before the ICCAT meeting in November, 1998, NMFS prepared a draft FMP for Atlantic highly migratory species, describing several alternative approaches to rebuilding the fishery. The plan was based on the assumption that the 1996 Sustainable Fisheries Act required an overfished stock to be rebuilt in a time period that is "as short as possible, taking into account * * * recommendations of international organizations in which the United States participates," but not exceeding 10 years "except in cases where * * * management measures under an international agreement in which the United States participates dictate otherwise." 16 U.S.C. § 1854(e)(4)(A). Does this provision allow the Secretary to adopt a 20-year rebuilding program, or does the Act require the Secretary to push ICCAT for a faster rebuilding program?

The final Highly Migratory Species FMP was adopted in 1999. Final rules implementing the FMP for Atlantic Tunas, Swordfish, and Sharks (the HMS FMP) were published on May 28, 1999, 64 Fed. Reg. 29090, and are codified at 50 C.F.R. Part 635. The regulations included, inter alia, limits on the number of bluefin tuna that could be caught and kept per fishing trip that limited longliners to incidental catch only, an area ban on fishing during the month of June where high concentrations of bluefin tuna are known to occur, annual quotas for blue sharks and subquotas for porbeagle sharks, and an requirement that all pelagic longline vessels install a vessel monitoring system (VMS) on their vessels to ensure compliance with the time/area and fishery closures. Pelagic longliners fishing south of a certain latitude could retain only one large or medium bluefin per trip.

The association representing offshore tuna and swordfish fishing vessels challenged the regulations, arguing they violated National Standards 1(optimum yield/overfishing), 8 (effect on fishing communities), and 9 (reduce bycatch) and disadvantaged domestic fishermen in relation to their foreign competitors. The court upheld all the measures except the vessel monitoring system. It found that NMFS had failed to explain why it was necessary to require VMS on all pelagic longline vessels "regardless of whether the vessels would encounter closure-restricted areas, and because NMFS failed to demonstrate that it gave adequate consideration to significant, practicable alternatives." Blue Water Fisherman's Association v. Mineta, 122 F.Supp.2d 150, 169 (D.D.C. 2000). The court rejected the claim of a violation of the international parity requirement of the MSA, 16 U.S.C. § 1854(g)(1)(C), finding:

> * * * The Magnuson-Stevens Act requires the Secretary to "evaluate the likely effects, if any, of conservation and management measures on participants in the affected fisheries and minimize, to the extent practicable, any disadvantage to United States fishermen in relation to foreign competitors." 16 U.S.C. § 1854(g)(1)(C). Because I have found that the VMS requirements are not valid under National Standards Seven and Eight, I will evaluate only the June Closure and pelagic shark quotas against the international parity provision.

> * * *

> Defendant contends that the conservation benefits from enforced quotas justify any potential disadvantages imposed upon domestic fishers. The record demonstrates that NMFS implemented the blue shark quota and the porbeagle shark subquota to provide conservation benefits and prevent overfishing. I cannot second-guess NMFS's justifications; I may strike a regulation only if rational justifications are lacking. "Merely because [certain species] are also harvested beyond [United States waters] is no reason why the Secretary should not regulate them within the bounds of his authority under the [Magnuson-Stevens] Act. When Congress passed the Magnuson Act it was well aware of the existence of international fishery management agreements, especially * * * the International Convention for the Conservation of Atlantic Tunas [ICCAT]." National Fisheries Inst. v. Mosbacher, 732 F.Supp. at 221, cited in Southern Offshore Fishing Ass'n v. Daley, 995 F.Supp. 1411, 1428 (M.D.Fla.1998) (Congress did not intend the Secretary "to suspend his conservation and management obligations whenever fish stocks become lethally subject to both foreign and domestic harvest").

> * * *

NMFS issued emergency regulations under the HMS FMP closing portions of the Atlantic Ocean known as the Northeast Distant Statistical

Area, a 2.6 million square nautical mile area near the Grand Banks off Newfoundland to pelagic longline fishing for highly migratory species in 2001. See 66 Fed. Reg. 36711 (July 13, 2001); 16 U.S.C. § 1855(c)(Secretary's emergency powers). The rules were designed to reduce bycatch of loggerhead and leatherback sea turtles in response to a biological opinion prepared under section 7 of the Endangered Species Act, 16 U.S.C. § 1536(a)(2), and National Standard 9's requirement to minimize bycatch, 16 U.S.C. § 1851(a)(9).

Holders of federal highly migratory species limited fishing permits challenged NMFS' authority to extend the Magnuson-Stevens Act beyond the EEZ, the scientific data and methods relied on in issuing the regulations, and the closure's unfair burden on their sector of the fishery. In Blue Water Fishermen's Ass'n v. NMFS, 158 F.Supp.2d 118 (D.Mass. 2001), the court found that the agency had jurisdiction beyond the EEZ to implement measures in cooperation with international efforts to conserve highly migratory species under the Magnuson-Stevens Act, §§1811(a) and 1812, and the Atlantic Tunas Convention Act of 1975, 16 U.S.C. § 971d(a). The court noted, however, that the Magnuson-Stevens Act precludes courts from enjoining the implementation of FMP regulations pending judicial review, but affords plaintiffs expedited review. 16 U.S.C. § 1855(f)(1)(A), (4).

In Atlantic Fish Spotters Ass'n v. Daley, 8 F.Supp.2d 113 (D.Mass. 1998), the owners of spotter aircraft and fishing vessels challenged NMFS regulations banning the use of spotter aircraft by those holding general category Atlantic bluefin tuna fishing permits but not by those holding harpoon or purse seine permits. The district court held that the regulations were arbitrary and capricious because the record lacked evidence supporting the agency's claim that the aircraft skewed the data on bluefin tuna abundance, induced the catching of juvenile tuna, and posed safety risks.

E. RESTRICTING ACCESS AND REDUCING CAPACITY

(1.) Limited Entry Under the Magnuson-Stevens Act

The Magnuson-Stevens Act, in section 303 (b)(6), 16 U.S.C. § 1853 (b)(6), specifically allows the regional councils and the Secretary of Commerce to adopt and implement systems for limiting the number of fishing vessels or other units of fishing effort that may be used in a fishery. In developing such systems, the council and the Secretary must take into account the present participation in the fishery; historical fishing practices in, and dependence on, the fishery; the economics of the fishery; the capability of fishing vessels used in the fishery to engage in other fisheries; the cultural and social framework of the fishery and any affected fishing communities; and any other relevant considerations.

Most fisheries managed under the Act are now under a limited access permit program. Fishing vessels are permitted to catch and land managed species only if they obtain a limited access permit for that fishery. Limited access permits are generally available only to vessels with a record of landings before the "control date." That is the date established by NMFS regulations after which landings will not qualify a vessel for a permit unless circumstances beyond the control of the permit applicant prevented the vessel from making or documenting the necessary landings. What happens when state fishery law prevents a vessel from harvesting certain species and thus establishing a catch record? See F/V Robert Michael, Inc. v. Kantor, 961 F.Supp. 11 (D.Me. 1997).

States have adopted various programs to limit access to state fisheries through license limitations and other schemes. For a discussion of legal methods for limiting entry into fisheries and the federal constitutional law claims raised against them in state courts, see M. Lansford and L.S. Howarth, Legal Impediments to Limited Entry Fishing Regulation in the Gulf States, 34 Nat. Resources J. 411, 415-24 (1994). Alaska's extensive limited entry licensing system was upheld against claims of violations of federal and state equal protection clauses. See Commercial Fisheries Entry Comm'n v. Apokedak, 606 P.2d 1255 (Alaska 1980). For more on the design and early challenges to Alaska's limited entry system, see R. Groseclose and G. Boone, An Examination of Limited Entry as a Method of Allocating Commercial Fishing Rights, 6 U.C.L.A.-Alaska L. Rev. 201 (1977); Owers, Court Tests of Alaska's Limited Entry Law, 11 UCLA-Alaska L. Rev. 87 (1981).

(2.) Individual Fishing Quotas

Individual fishing quotas (IFQs) are perhaps the most controversial form of limited access or capacity reduction regulation. When the quotas are made transferable and fisherman can sell them on the open market, they are called individual transferable quotas (ITQs). The Mid-Atlantic Fishery Management Council was the first regional council to recommend adoption of ITQ program for a federally managed fishery. The Secretary of Commerce approved for implementation the council's surf clam and ocean quahog ITQ program in 1990. The Magnuson Act at the time had no specific criteria or guidelines for ITQ program design. In Sea Watch International v. Mosbacher, 762 F. Supp. 370 (D.D.C. 1991), the court addressed a number of issues of first impression and for which the Magnuson Act gave little guidance at the time. Congress revisited these issues in the 1996 reauthorization of the Magnuson Act and they became the focus of the new language added regarding IFQs. The plaintiffs in Sea Watch claimed, inter alia, that the ITQ system amounted to a privatization of the surf clam and quahog resource, thereby transferring private ownership interests in a fishery, a result prohibited by Magnuson Act. The court found:

* * * The present ITQ system differs only in degree from the system of aggregate quotas and transferable permits previously in use and

unchallenged by plaintiffs, and the interests created by it fall short of actual full-scale ownership. * * * The new quotas do not become permanent possessions of those who hold them, any more than landing rights at slot-constrained airports become the property of airlines, or radio frequencies become the property of broadcasters. These interests remain subject to the control of the federal government which, in the exercise of its regulatory authority, can alter and revise such schemes, just as the Council and the Secretary have done in this instance. An arrangement of this kind is not such a drastic departure from ordinary regulation, nor is it so akin to the sale of government property, that the Court must require a more precise expression of congressional intent to uphold it.

762 F. Supp. at 376.

The plaintiffs had cited a number of instances in which NMFS had referred to the ITQs as property rights. To this argument the court noted that those references had used the term "property" only as an analogy and were always qualified with references to the possibility that management could change and not rely on ITQs. Id. at n. 10.

The plaintiffs also claimed that the ITQ program violated National Standard 4 by discriminating against owners of smaller fishing fleets. The court concluded:

Plaintiffs next contend that the ITQ system violates National Standard 4 because it is intended to drive a particular group of individuals, the single vessel and small fleet owners, out of the fisheries. Since Amendment 8 permits owners to catch their entire ITQ with a few vessels, the argument runs, it will result in lower average costs to the owners of large fleets, and provide them with an unfair competitive advantage. Moreover, it is alleged, small fishermen lack the capital to purchase sufficient ITQs to operate their vessels at full capacity, and ultimately will be driven out of business. It is quite possible that scale economies and transferability of ITQs will produce some consolidation. It is also possible that small fishermen enjoy advantages of their own, and nothing prevents coalitions of small owners from pooling their allocations to obtain efficiencies. Moreover, single vessel or small fleet owners may happen to have substantial allocations depending upon their history. Even where a fisherman with a small allocation decides to exit, transferability of the ITQ provides at least some compensation. There is nothing intentionally invidious or inherently unfair in the plan adopted by the Council and the Secretary. "Inherent in an allocation is the advantaging of one group to the detriment of another." 50 C.F.R. § 602.14(c)(3)(i).

Id. at 377.

To the plaintiffs contention that the IFQ program would lead to consolidation of quota in the hands of a few fishermen in violation of the

National Standard 4 prohibition against "excessive shares," the court responded:

> Plaintiffs * * * allege that two fishermen now hold ITQs totalling forty percent of the annual catch quota for ocean quahogs, and that fragmentation of the remaining shares will necessarily result in further consolidation, as holders of smaller shares sell their interest. This figure does give pause, although the raw number may not be economically significant. The defendants have acknowledged that increased efficiency due to consolidation was one of the explicit objectives of Amendment 8. However, the Act contains no definition of "excessive shares," and the Secretary's judgment of what is excessive in this context deserves weight, especially where the regulations can be changed without permission of the ITQ holders. The record reflects that the Council and the Secretary considered the problem, and addressed it by providing for an annual review of industry concentration, with the possibility of referral to the Department of Justice.

Notes and Questions

1. Do you agree that the ITQ is more akin to "ordinary regulation" than a property right? What does the economic theory underlying the ITQ approach say regarding the nature of the allocated interest? For a discussion of the ITQ system in the surf clam and ocean quahog fisheries, see generally Note, Protecting Common Property Resources Through the Marketplace: Individual Transferable Quotas for Surf Clams and Ocean Quahogs, 16 Vt. L. Rev. 1127 (1991). For a discussion of the nature of the right created, see Note, Harnessing Market Forces in Natural Resources Management: Lessons From the Surf Clam Fishery, 21 B.C. Envl. L.Rev. 335, 354-58 (1994). For an earlier discussion of the nature of the right created by limited access programs, see Note, Legal Dimensions of Entry Fishery Management, 17 William & Mary L. Rev. 757, 767 (1976).

2. The 1996 Sustainable Fisheries Act defines an IFQ as "a federal permit under a limited access system to harvest a quantity of fish, expressed by a unit or units representing a percentage of the total allowable catch of a fishery that may be received or held for exclusive use by a person.* * *" 16 U.S.C. § 1802(21). The Act provides that an IFQ shall not confer any right of compensation to the holder of the IFQ if it is revoked or limited at any time. Id. at § 1853(d)(3).

3. In October, 1994, the Internal Revenue Service prevented the issuance of halibut and sablefish IFQs to approximately 300 Alaska fishermen who owed back taxes or who had failed to file returns. The IRS issued a Notice of Levy to NMFS asserting a lien for nearly nine million dollars in unpaid taxes, interest, and penalties. The Justice Department concluded that the halibut IFQs, although not yet delivered to the qualifying fishermen, "constitute a right to intangible property--i.e., a valuable and transferable legal right to catch and land certain

quantities" and as such were property or rights to property which are subject to the tax lien or levy. Office of Legal Counsel, Dep't of Justice, Internal Revenue Service Notices of Levy on Undelivered Commerce Dep't Fishing Quota Permits, 1995 WL 944019 (Jan. 26, 1995). See J. Weiss, Comment, A Taxing Issue: Are Limited Entry Fishing Permits Property? 9 Alaska L. Rev. 93 (1992).

4. How are IFQs treated in divorce proceedings? New Zealand's highest court ruled that an IFQ constitutes matrimonial property to which both partners have a right to equal shares in the event of divorce. Although the IFQ was granted to the husband after the couple separated, the court noted that the IFQ was granted based on fishing history which occurred before the separation and in which the wife participated and assisted. Batterham v. Batterham, High Court, Auckland, [1993] 1 N.Z.L.R. 742. The Supreme Court of Alaska ruled that a federal IFQ is property subject to division as marital property, but that the husband's interest is separate property to the extent the size of his quota share was calculated on the basis of landings he made prior to the marriage. Ferguson v. Ferguson, 928 P.2d 597 (Alaska 1996). In Johns v. Johns, 945 P.2d 1222 (Alaska 1997), the court retained jurisdiction over the husband's state permits for herring roe for which he qualified during marriage that were currently valueless but could become marketable and transferable.

5. National Standard 4 requires any fishery allocation to be fair, conservation-oriented, and calculated to prevent any one individual or company from obtaining an excessive share. 16 U.S.C. § 1851(a)(4). Recall that in Sea Watch International, two fishermen held 40% of the ocean quahog quota. Is it sufficient for the Secretary and the Mid-Atlantic Council to rely on an annual review of concentrations and possible referral to the Department of Justice's Antitrust Division to meet the no "excessive share" standard? What standards would apply under the Sherman Antitrust Act? See W. Milliken, Comment, Individual Transferable Fishing Quotas and Antitrust Law, 1 Ocean & Coastal L. J. 35 (1994).

6. The Secretary of Commerce may not implement a limited access system unless the program receives approval by a majority of the appropriate regional council members present and voting. 16 U.S.C. § 1854 (c)(3). Also, the Secretary may by regulation set the level of fees that may be charged for fishing permits required in a FMP. However, the level of fees charged for the permits may not exceed the administrative costs incurred in issuing the permits. 16 U.S.C. § 1854 (d)(1). For IFQ programs, the Secretary is allowed to collect a fee to cover the actual costs "directly related to the management and enforcement" of the program, but the fee may not exceed 3 percent of the ex vessel value of the fish harvested under it. Id. at § 1854(d)(2).

7. The North Pacific Fishery Management Council developed an ITQ plan for the Gulf of Alaska halibut and sablefish fixed gear fisheries which received the Secretary's approval in January, 1993, for

implementation in 1994 and 1995. 58 Fed. Reg. 59375 (Nov. 9, 1993). When it went into effect, this program was the world's largest individual quota program in number of participants. D. Fluharty, Magnuson Fishery Management and Conservation [sic] Act Reauthorization and Fishery Management Needs in the North Pacific Region, 9 Tulane Env'l L. J. 301, 310 (1996). By setting restrictions on transfers of ITQ ownership to owners of vessels in the same vessel category and fishing area, the plan addressed one of the chief concerns of ITQ opponents -- that the individual allocations will become concentrated in the hands of a small number of large-scale operators, to the detriment of the family-scale operators. 50 C.F.R. § 676.21. The North Pacific council also created a Western Alaska Community Development Quota (CDQ) Program, allocating a fixed portion of the annual total allowable catch (TAC) to the native Alaskan villages of western Alaska. 50 C.F.R. § 676.24. One objective of the CDQ was to allocate at least a portion of the fish resources of the Bering Sea to the communities closest to them, but which were unlikely on their own to develop the fishing fleet to take advantage of that proximity, or to have the money to purchase quota shares. Fluharty supra at 310-11. The communities use their quotas to generate economic development, primarily in partnership with the trawlers owned by companies based in the Seattle, Washington area. Does the idea of reserving a portion of the TAC for allocation as an IFQ to a coastal community rather than an individual vessel owner have other potential applications? Could such a mechanism help reduce the economic and social impacts of IFQs on those fishermen who do not benefit from the initial allocation of quota shares? See A. Rieser, Property Rights and Ecosystem Management in U.S. Fisheries: Contracting for the Commons?, 24 Ecology L.Q. 813 (1997).

ALLIANCE AGAINST IFQs v. BROWN
United States Court of Appeals, Ninth Circuit, 1996
84 F. 3d 343, *cert. denied*, 520 U.S. 1185, 1997

KLEINFELD, CIRCUIT JUDGE.

* * *

Commercial ocean fishing combines difficult and risky labor with large capital investments to make money from a resource owned by no one, the fish. Unlimited access tends to cause declining fisheries. The reason is that to get title to a fish, a fisherman has to catch it before someone else does. Pierson v. Post, 3 Caines 175, 2 Am. Dec. 264 (N.Y.1805). This gives each fishermen an incentive to invest in a fast, large boat and to fish as fast as possible. As boats and crews get more efficient, fewer fish escape the fishermen and live to reproduce. "The result is lower profits for the too many fishermen investing in too much capital to catch too few fish." Terry L. Anderson and Donald R. Leal, Free Market Environmentalism, 123 (1991).

* * * The Secretary of Commerce, pursuant to the Magnuson Act and the Northern Pacific Halibut Act of 1982 ("Halibut Act"), 16 U.S.C. § 773 et seq., promulgated regulations to limit access to sablefish and halibut fisheries in the Gulf of Alaska and the Bering Sea and Aleutian Islands area.

The Secretary of Commerce implemented by regulation a management plan for sablefish and pacific halibut fishing. The basic scheme is that any boat that fishes commercially for the regulated fish in the regulated area must have an individual quota share (IFQ) permit on board, specifying the individual fishing quota allowed for the vessel, and anyone who receives the regulated fish must possess a "registered buyer permit."

The regional director of the National Marine Fisheries Service (NMFS) in the Department of Commerce assigns to each owner or lessee of a vessel which made legal landings of halibut or sablefish during 1988, 1989, or 1990, a quota share (QS) based on the person's highest total legal landings of halibut and sablefish during 1984 to 1990. Each year, the regional director allocates individual fishing quotas (IFQs) by multiplying the person's quota share by the annual allowable catch. Subject to some restrictions, the quota shares and individual fishing quotas can be sold, leased and otherwise transferred. If someone who did not fish in the regulated waters during 1988 to 1990 wants a quota share, he has to buy it from someone who did.

Like any governmental regulatory scheme, this one substitutes a governmental decision for myriad individual decisions to determine who shall be permitted to make money in the regulated industry. The plaintiffs are people who suffer from the economic impact of the regulation. Some have invested in fishing vessels and fished in the regulated waters for halibut or sablefish, but not during the critical three years which would give them a quota share. Some have consistently fished for the regulated fish in the regulated waters, but did not own or lease the boats. Of those who acquired quota shares under the scheme, some probably never fished, and just invested in fishing boats to get investment tax credits and depreciation. The regulatory scheme has the practical effect of transferring economic power over the fishery from those who fished to those who owned or leased fishing boats. For these reasons, among others, the case is troubling and difficult.

* * *

Where we review regulations promulgated by the Secretary of Commerce under the Magnuson Act, our only function is to determine whether the Secretary "has considered the relevant factors and articulated a rational connection between the facts found and the choice made." We determine only if the Secretary acted in an arbitrary and capricious manner in promulgating such regulations. We cannot substitute our judgment of what might be a better regulatory scheme, or overturn a regulation because we disagree with it, if the Secretary's reasons for adopting it were not arbitrary and capricious.

Plaintiffs urge us to adopt a more onerous standard of review and cite Atwood v. Newmont Gold Co., Inc., 45 F.3d 1317 (9th Cir.1995), as support. *Atwood* is distinguishable, because we were reviewing an ERISA plan fiduciary's duty, not those of the Secretary of Commerce, and were doing so in light of facts indicating a conflict of interest.

* * *

Plaintiffs argue that the allocation of quota shares to vessel owners and lessees violates the statutory requirement that allocation be "fair and equitable to all such fishermen." 16 U.S.C. § 1851(a)(4). The statute requires that a fishery management plan comply with a number of national standards. * * *

Plaintiffs make the sensible argument that a crew member is just as much of a fisherman as a vessel owner. If all the quota shares go to vessel owners and lessees during that period, and none to the crew, as the Secretary's approved plan provides, then this violates the statutory command of fairness and equity to "all" the fishermen.

As the quoted section of this statute shows, the Secretary's duty was not solely limited to allocating quota shares fairly and equitably among the fishermen. The plan also had to "prevent overfishing while achieving, on a continuing basis, the optimum yield," be "reasonably calculated to promote conservation," "promote efficiency," "minimize costs and avoid unnecessary duplication," and achieve several other criteria. There is a necessary tension, perhaps inconsistency, among these objectives. The tension, for example, between fairness among all fishermen, preventing overfishing, promoting efficiency, and avoiding unnecessary duplication, necessarily requires that each goal be sacrificed to some extent to meeting the others.

The Council and Secretary directed their attention to the fairness problem plaintiffs raise, but decided that the other standards imposed by the statute required allocation of quota shares to boat owners and lessees as opposed to all the fishermen. The Council thought that equity to people who had invested in boats, and the greater ease of ascertaining how much fish boats, as opposed to individual fishermen, had taken, favored allocating quota shares according to owner and lessees of boats:

> There is no question that the IFQ program will restructure the current fixed gear fishery for halibut and sablefish. Some fishermen will be better off and some will be worse off under the IFQ program. * * * In brief, those persons benefited by receiving an initial allocation are vessel owners or lease holders. * * * The Council's rationale for this particular allocation is that vessel owners and lease holders are the participants who supply the means to harvest fish, suffer the financial and liability risks to do so, and direct the fishing operations.

* * *

The advantaging of one group to the detriment of another is inherent in allocation. * * * The Council considered allocating [quota share] to crew members but decided against it because of the practical difficulties of documenting crew shares. Instead, the Council decided to give eligibility for initial allocations only to vessel owners and lease holders because they have a capital investment in the vessel and gear that continues as a cost after crew and vessel shares are paid from a fishing trip.

[NOAA, Preamble to the Final Rules]

The Secretary thought that the problem of overfishing resulted more from investment in boats than occupational choices of fishermen, so the administrative remedy should be measured by ownership and leasing of boats:

The Council's consideration of "present participation" also included the form of involvement in the fishery (e.g., as a vessel owner, crew member, or processor). As explained under national standard 4, above, the Council perceived vessel owners and lease holders as the most directly involved persons in terms of capital investment. The conservation and management problems resolved by this program stem largely from excess capital in the fisheries. Therefore, it is reasonable to define the group of persons who make the capital investment decision to either enter or exit a fishery as "present participants" for initial allocation purposes.

Id.

The Secretary promulgated a regulation [the National Standards Guidelines] requiring that allocations be "rationally connected with the achievement of [optimum yield] or with the furtherance of a legitimate [fishery management plan] objective." In consideration of the fact that "[i]nherent in an allocation is the advantaging of one group to the detriment of another," the regulation provided:

The motive for making a particular allocation should be justified in terms of the [fishery management plan]; otherwise, the disadvantaged user groups or individuals would suffer without cause. * * *
(B) An allocation of fishing privileges may impose a hardship on one group if it is outweighed by the total benefits received by another group or groups. An allocation need not preserve the status quo in the fishery to qualify as fair and equitable, if a restructuring of fishing privileges would maximize overall benefits.

Id.

Congress required the Secretary to exercise discretion and

judgment in balancing among the conflicting national standards in section 1851. "[U]nless the Secretary acts in an arbitrary and capricious manner promulgating such regulations, they may not be declared invalid." Alaska Factory Trawler Ass'n v. Baldrige, 831 F.2d 1456, 1460 (9th Cir. 1987). Although the Secretary's approval of the plan sacrificed the interest of non-owning crew members to boat owners and lessees, the Secretary had a reason for doing that which was consistent with the statutory standards. Controlling precedent requires that a plan not be deemed arbitrary and capricious, "[e]ven though there may be some discriminatory impact," if the regulations "are tailored to solve a gear conflict problem and to promote the conservation of sablefish." Id. The Secretary is allowed, under this authority, to sacrifice the interests of some groups of fishermen, for the benefit as the Secretary sees it of the fishery as a whole. Id.

The plan adopted will undoubtedly have an adverse impact on the lives of many fishermen who have done nothing wrong. Their entirely legitimate interest in making a living from the fishery has been sacrificed to an administrative judgment about conservation of fish and efficiency of the industry. That is, however, an unavoidable consequence of the statutory scheme. Despite the harshness to the fishermen who were left out, there is no way we can conclude on this record that the Secretary lacked a rational basis for leaving them out. The Secretary considered their interests, "considered the relevant factors and articulated a rational connection between the facts found and the choice made." Washington Crab, 924 F.2d at 1441. Because this standard was met, we do not have the authority to substitute our judgment for the Secretary's with regard to allocation of all the quota shares to boat owners and lessees.

* * *

This is a troubling case. Perfectly innocent people going about their legitimate business in a productive industry have suffered great economic harm because the federal regulatory scheme changed. Alternative schemes can easily be imagined. The old way could have been left in place, where whoever caught the fish first, kept them, and seasons were shortened to allow enough fish to escape and reproduce. Allocation of quota shares could have been on a more current basis, so that fishermen in 1996 would not have their income based upon the fish they had caught before 1991. Quota shares could have been allocated to all fishermen, instead of to vessel owners and lessees, so that the non-owning fishermen would have something valuable to sell to vessel owners. But we are not the regulators of the north pacific halibut and sablefish industry. The Secretary of Commerce is. We cannot overturn the Secretary's decision on the ground that some parties' interests are injured. Government regulation of an industry necessarily transfers economic rewards from some who are more efficient and hardworking to others who are favored by the regulatory scheme. We have authority to overturn the Secretary's decisions only if they are arbitrary and capricious, or contrary to law. In this case, they are not.

Notes and Questions

1. Note the degree of deference afforded the Secretary of Commerce in fashioning the ITQ allocation scheme. The court refused the plaintiffs' request for the more searching standard of review it had recently applied in reviewing the ERISA plan fiduciary's duty when the facts indicated a conflict of interest. Does the Secretary have a fiduciary's duty under the Magnuson-Stevens Act as trustee of the public's marine resources? Had the Secretary made sure that crew members were represented on the North Pacific council during the years it was creating the halibut-sablefish limited access plan? Is a high degree of deference appropriate when the regulations are creating quasi-private property rights in the harvesting of public fish resources?

2. Applicants for individual quota share permits under the Alaska program had to prove they were either owners or lessees of vessels that had made legal landings of halibut or sablefish during 1988-1990. Applicants whose applications NMFS denied had the right to an administrative appeal. 60 C.F.R. § 676.20. What kind of procedure is NMFS required to give a disappointed applicant, given the importance of the IFQ permit to his or her livelihood? Does the Due Process Clause of the U.S. Constitution require NMFS to provide compulsory process (i.e., the appeals officer has subpoena power) as part of the administrative adjudication of the application?

In Dell v. Dept of Commerce, 191 F.3d 460 (Table), 1999 WL 604217 (9th Cir. 1999)(unpublished opinion), Dell was granted a quota share initially as the lessee of a fishing vessel. The owner of the vessel (and Dell's former father-in-law), however, appealed the decision to NMFS, claiming that Dell was his employee, not lessee. The appeals officer concluded that the relationship between the two claimants was that of owner and captain, not lessor and lessee. She held that the vessel owner was entitled to the IFQ, and NMFS denied Dell's application. When Dell challenged the agency's decision, the district court granted summary judgment for NMFS, and the Ninth Circuit affirmed, finding that while Dell had a "protectable [private] property interest in obtaining IFQ permits," citing Foss v. NMFS, 161 F.3d 584, 589 (9th Cir. 1998), the regulations' appeals procedures without compulsory process were more than adequate to protect them, the risk of erroneous deprivation of the permit was very low, and the government had an interest in a timely and efficient resolution of IFQ applications, thus meeting the test of Matthews v. Eldridge, 424 U.S. 319, 334-35 (1976). In dissent, Judge Reinhardt argued that without the ability to compel production of documents in the possession of his former wife, Dell was denied a fair resolution of his appeal, and that society's interest in speedy resolution of fishing license claims did not outweigh Dell's interest in a fair hearing. Do you agree? Once the moratorium on new IFQ programs expires (see note 5), should Congress amend the Magnuson-Stevens Act to require a compulsory process for IFQ appeals?

3. The *Alliance Against IFQs* decision leaves no doubt that IFQ

programs have significant redistributive effects on power and wealth among different sectors of the fishing industry.

> Under an ITQ program, the redistribution of economic resources in a fishery occurs because overfishing and overcapitalization is controlled using free market forces to create a smaller, more efficient fishery. The market in ITQs encourages less efficient fishers to sell off their quota shares and leave the fishery. Generally, the sector of the fishing industry made up of smaller, community-based operations is less efficient. The redistributive effects of ITQs can be mitigated by Congress and NMFS, but such measures come at a cost to efficiency. Therefore, the question for any government interested in implementing an ITQ program is how many local fishers can be sacrificed in order to remove overfishing and overcapitalization* * * Whether ITQs become the management tool of choice and the manner in which the tool is utilized ultimately depend on the degree to which we value the environmental and economic benefits afforded by ITQs over certain [smaller, community-based] fishers' livelihood.

N. Black, Note, Balancing the Advantages of Individual Transferable Quotas Against Their Redistributive Effects: The Case of Alliance Against IFQs v. Brown, 9 Geo. Int'l Envt'l L. Rev. 727, 745-46 (1998).

4. The halibut-sablefish IFQ program attempts to maintain the existing structure of the fishery by restricting the sale of quota shares to vessels within the same size and gear category and by setting a cap on the total percentage of the TAC any one quota share holder could hold. 50 C.F.R. §§ 679.41(e),(g). Also, amendments to the program set aside some quotas for purchase by crew members.

5. In the 1996 Sustainable Fisheries Act, Congress placed a moratorium on the submission, approval or implementation of any new federal ITQ programs until October 1, 2000. 16 U.S.C. § 1853(d)(1). Even before the moratorium was enacted, Congress had attached a rider to the appropriations bill for fiscal year 1997, prohibiting the use of funds to develop new IFQ programs. Section 208 of the Omnibus Consolidated Appropriations Act of 1997, Pub.L. No. 104-208, 110 Stat. 3009 (1996).

During the moratorium, Congress called upon the National Academy of Sciences (NAS) to conduct a comprehensive review of the experience to date with IFQs, and to evaluate a number of issues, including the desirability of limiting or prohibiting the transferability of IFQs, mechanisms to minimize their adverse effects on fishing communities, and methods for ensuring fair and equitable treatment of vessel owners, crew, and processors in the initial allocation of fishing quotas. P.L. 104-297, § 108(f), 16 U.S.C. § 1853 note.

The moratorium and NAS study was a compromise between the proponents of IFQs and those who favored either their complete prohibition under the Act or their non-transferability and 'sunset' after no more than seven years. The debate became a forum for the intense intra-regional competition over the fishery resources of the North Pacific Ocean off Alaska. Senators from Washington State, who favored the ability of the North Pacific council to develop IFQ programs, clashed with members of the Senate from Alaska, who feared Alaska-based fishing interests would not fare as well as the large (and largely overcapitalized and foreign-owned) Seattle-based catcher-processor fleet in any initial allocation of IFQs for the lucrative North Pacific pollock fishery. The catcher-processor sector was promoting IFQs as a way to reduce the number of vessels in their fishery and to lengthen their season. See S. Hsu and J. Wilen, Ecosystem Management and the 1996 Sustainable Fisheries Act, 24 Ecology L. Q. 799 (1997). See also D. Dana, Overcoming the Political Tragedy of the Commons: Lessons Learned from the Reauthorization of the Magnuson Act, 24 Ecology L.Q. 833 (1997).

6. The National Academy of Sciences study was released in 1999. National Research Council, Sharing the Fish: Toward a National Policy on Individual Fishing Quotas (1999). The Committee recommended that the moratorium be lifted and that IFQs be made an option in fisheries management, if regional councils find them to be warranted by a particular fishery's condition, and if appropriate measures are imposed to avoid potential adverse effects. The report urged that the councils and the Secretary of Commerce gives careful consideration to issues of initial allocation, transferability, and accumulation of shares when IFQ programs are developed. The report gave detailed recommendations on how these issues could be addressed in the design and implementation of a program.

7. During the moratorium, some of the companies that owned catcher-processors in the North Pacific pollock fishery, but who also had vessels engaged in the smaller Pacific whiting fishery off the coasts of Washington, Oregon, and California under the jurisdiction of the Pacific Fishery Management Council, looked for a solution to a similar problem of overcapitalization of that fishery. The council had set a total allowable level of fishing (TAC) for whiting, adopted a limited entry licensing program, and an allocation of part of the TAC to each sector, but there were still more vessels and fishing power than was needed to catch the TAC. In 1997, the companies in the catcher-processor sector developed a private agreement among themselves to end their wasteful practice of racing against each other for the fish. They created a non-profit cooperative and a contractual agreement not to harvest any more than a specific percentage of their sector allocation, which was 34% of the TAC. Their agreement was reviewed and approved by the Anti-trust Division of the U.S. Justice Department. By all accounts, this arrangement eliminated the race to fish. It allowed the companies to reduce the number of vessels in the fishery and to fish at a rate that allowed greater efficiency and product quality in their processing and reduced levels of bycatch because they could move vessels away from areas where bycatches were high. See J. LeBlanc, U.S. Fishery

Cooperatives: Rationalizing Fisheries Through Privately Negotiated Contracts, a presentation to the National Fishery Law Symposium, University of Washington Foundation, Seattle, Wash., Nov. 2001.

In 2000, Congress extended the moratorium on IFQs until October 1, 2002, but authorized the Gulf of Mexico and North Pacific regional fishery management councils to study the possibility of quota management programs for fisheries under their jurisdiction. Pub. L. 106-554, § 1(a)(4) [Div.B, Title I, § 144(a)(1),(2)], Dec. 21, 2000; 114 Stat. 2763, 2763A-238, amending 16 U.S.C. § 1853(d). This extension was adopted in lieu of bills introduced by Senators Kerry (D-Mass.) and Snowe (R-Maine) that would have lifted the moratorium and enacted specific criteria for individual quota programs. See, e.g., S. 2973, S. 2832, and S. 637 introduced in the 107th Congress. The Snowe bill, S. 637, for example, would had authorized the adoption and approval of individual quota programs only if they expired after 5 years, created non-transferable quotas, could be held only by citizens and active participants in the fishery, and were twice approved by a two-thirds majority of votes cast by eligible permit holders.

8. How are IFQ systems likely to affect the ability of managers to take account of the ecosystems of which the target fish stocks are components? With increasing awareness of the importance of predator-prey relationships among species, the dangers of bycatch, the potential competition between a commercial fishery and marine wildlife, and the significance of habitat for fisheries and for marine biodiversity, many commentators call for greater application of a precautionary approach to fisheries. See, e.g., National Research Council, Sustaining Marine Fisheries 7 (1999). Does the creation of IFQs make it more or less likely that managers can exercise caution and protect marine ecosystems especially where large areas of uncertainty surround our understanding of the dynamics of such systems? Consider the following:

> The trend toward ecosystem-based management reflects recognition of two ideas crucial to the debate over ITQs. The first is that good fishing returns require management that ensures the health of the larger ecosystem of which the fish stock is a part. Even if humans only value the fish actually taken from the environment, humans still need to attend to the ecosystem effects of fishing to guarantee sustainable yields. Effective management of a marine ecosystem requires scientific data beyond the population dynamics of the commercially harvested fish stock and how much "surplus" fish those populations can produce. The second idea is that ecosystems have valuable components beyond the fish caught, marketed, and consumed. The other valuable CPRs [common-pool resources] of the ocean include the diversity of species and habitats. Fishing can harm other species and habitats and alter marine ecosystems in ways not fully understood. To protect the health and productivity of a marine ecosystem, restraints are needed to supplement total

catch limits, including fish size limits, measures to prevent or minimize bycatch, restrictions on damaging fishing gears, and finally, closed areas to protect vital habitats.

Catching a species of fish for sale realizes one value of a rich and diverse marine ecosystem. If the right to engage in this activity is held exclusively by a group of individuals in the form of an ITQ, and these are traded actively in a market, there is a serious risk that all other valuable components of the ecosystem, which have no direct market value and whose contribution to the ecosystem's productivity is not understood, will be ignored. The value of the ecosystem itself is likely to be discounted by managers when setting regulations such as the total catch limit from which the annual, individual harvesting rights will be calculated.

Protecting the broader ecosystem does not necessarily require the adoption of one particular institutional arrangement. * * * Carol M. Rose has observed that environmentalists use the image of a particular resource as part of a larger ecosystem to argue against rights-based regulatory tools like ITQs.[13] The effect of such measures, environmentalists fear, will be to elevate the significance of the propertized component and, in effect, over-value them. This overvaluation may lead people to ignore that their entitlements overlap the entitlements of others interested in the same resource or ecosystem. It may even cause the disintegration of the "larger and intricately interrelated ecosystem," as holders of one entitlement overstate what they "own" and block other management actions aimed at protecting other components of the same ecosystem.[14]

However, the need for management sensitive to the broader ecosystem may suggest, that, if property rights approaches are to be used to prevent resource depletion and spillover effects, these rights should take a particular form. These approaches should emphasize less the individual nature of the property right and more the community nature of the right. In fisheries management, for example, property rights could be allocated to a community, rather than an individual. Communities are more likely to embody a broader range of values and will therefore balance harvesting decisions against broader spatial and temporal views of the ecosystem. Communities can also enforce

---

[13] See Carol M. Rose, The Several Futures of Property: Of Cyberspace and Folk Tales, Emission Trades and Ecosystems, 83 Minn. L. Rev. 129, 174-77 (1998).

[14] Id. at 173. This result may be aided by the introduction of a rhetoric and mentality of entitlement when property-like policy instruments are used.

limits on individual appropriators through informal norms and sanctions.

* * *

The end of the ocean resource frontier is signaled by the increasing number of spillover effects between users, including fisheries bycatch levels, habitat destruction, and changes in biological relations among trophic levels (such as predator-prey relations) that now threaten the integrity of whole marine ecosystem.[15] Having reached the end of the frontier, environmental law scholars and policymakers must recognize that property rights accorded any one individual cannot adequately take account of the entire ecosystem. Nor can one individual acting alone, even when given incentives through a permanent property right, take sufficient actions to ensure that all of the interconnecting components of a functioning ecosystem remain intact. Even a large number of individuals with the same new incentives, acting independently, cannot collectively address and account for all of these interacting components. Therefore, the individual property right seems more consistent with the previous era of resource use, a time when the policy goal was to design incentives to capture the flow of benefits from fish populations without an excess investment in physical capital.[16]

The collapse of fish stocks and the subsequent cascading effects that have been felt throughout the marine environment have made it apparent that fisheries must also be managed on the basis of the entire ecosystem. The institutions of management must abandon the frontier mentality and emphasize common resource approaches. The original Fishery Conservation and Management Act of 1976 in one sense perpetuated the frontier mindset by encouraging the Americanization of all fisheries, including those used previously only by foreign fishing fleets. The Sustainable Fisheries Act of 1996 may have begun the process of adapting existing regimes toward what land-based managers have already recognized as the ecosystem approach.

If new management approaches use property rights, those property rights must be created in a manner informed by a wider sense of social justice. The new property rights must

---

[15] See Susan Hanna. The New Frontier of American Fisheries Governance, 20 Ecological Econ. 221-222 (1997).

[16] Hanna describes physical capital as the fishing vessels and equipment which are applied to the ecosystem's natural capacity to extract benefits in the form of landed catch. See id. At 222.

acknowledge the importance of the distribution of benefits as well as endangered species, endangered cultures, and all groups dependent upon and affected by the condition of the natural environment. In the modern fisheries commons, property rights should not be designed to alienate fishermen and free them from the interference of the community. Instead, a link should be established between rights and responsibilities.

The ITQ is firmly rooted in the principles of what Joseph Sax calls the "transformative economy," where nature is seen as a discrete entity waiting for the investment of time and human energy to transform it into something of value.[17] The vision of property embodied in the ITQ is the traditional notion of an individual property right, that views nature as something that can be "separated into components and dedicated to [the] production of particular commodities through monocultural practices or parcelization."[18] With the end of the fisheries frontier and the recognition of the legitimate claims of other components of marine ecosystems, new fisheries management should include property rights that reflect an ecological view of property, what Sax calls the "economy of nature." Advances in science and the observation of the adverse effects of parcelization highlight that the marine environment is of far greater value when all its ecological components operate "as a whole, complexly-functioning entity."

The marine environment, with its fish stocks, physical environment, and other biological components, is not waiting for human interaction to make it productive. As Sax has described land when viewed ecologically, the marine environment is also "already at work, performing important services in its unaltered state .... Transformation diminishes the functioning of this economy and, in fact, is at odds with it." The marine environment is, like land, part of a community which extends beyond the dominion of the owner, where use rights must be determined by physical nature, not humankind, and where public and exclusive owners have a custodial and affirmative protective role for ecological functions.

Recognizing the economy of nature in the oceans requires active involvement of the community in determining how the marine

---

[17] Joseph L. Sax, Property Rights and the Economy of Nature: Understanding Lucas v. South Carolina Council, 45 STAN. L. REV. 1433, 1442 (1993).

[18] See Lee P. Breckenridge. Reweaving the Landscape: The Institutional Challenges of Ecosystem Management for Lands in Private Ownership, 19 VT. L. REV. 363, 385 (1995).

system should be used. It cannot be left to the discretion of the individual owner of an ITQ, because a system of ITQs does not provide the capital needed to sustain systems of resource use. The institutions of a sustainable marine governance system must at the least force resource users to recognize that the fishery is an integrated system and that other stakeholders must share in the decision-making.

A. Rieser, Prescriptions for the Commons: Environmental Scholarship and the Fishing Quotas Debate, 23 Harv. Envtl. L. Rev. 393, 405-06, 418-21 (1999).

(3.) Reducing Fishing Capacity by Congressional Action

(a.) The American Fisheries Act of 1998

While the IFQ moratorium was in place, Congress enacted the American Fisheries Act of 1998, Pub.L. No. 105-277, section 208(e), 112 Stat. 2681, 2681-625 (1998)(provisions at 16 U.S.C. § 1851 notes). The American Fisheries Act bill, S.1221, was introduced in the 105th Congress by Senator Stevens as part of the Omnibus Consolidated and Emergency Supplemental Appropriations for Fiscal Year 1999.

A complex piece of legislation, the American Fisheries Act (AFA) achieved a major restructuring of the largest North Pacific fishery, the Alaska pollock fishery. Due to its timing, however, it was subject to very little debate. The AFA requires owners of all U.S.-flag fishing vessels to meet a 75% U.S.-controlling interest standard. It also eliminated certain exceptions to restrictions on the flagging of foreign-rebuilt vessels. These exceptions had purportedly allowed a huge build-up in the at-sea processing sector of the fishery. The AFA identified a specific list of fishing vessels by name and federal number that are eligible to participate in the Bering Sea and Aleutian Islands pollock fishery. For some of those vessels not eligible to participate, the Act includes a vessel buy-back program for nine catcher/processor vessels, financed by a combination of up to $90 million dollars in taxpayer funds and private industry funds borrowed from the government but repaid through a landings fee.

The AFA redefined the pollock allocations for the major (competing) sectors of the fishery: for the offshore component --40% for catcher/processors and 10% for catcher vessels delivering to motherships; for the inshore processing component --50% for catcher vessels delivering to onshore processing plants (located in Alaska). Ten percent of the total pollock quota is to be allocated as a directed fishery allowance to the western Alaska community development quota program created under section 305(i), 16 U.S.C. § 1855(i). The Act also authorized and defined terms for cooperatives for both fishing vessel owners and fish processors participating in the Alaska pollock fishery. (See discussion at note #7 above following Alliance Against IFQs decision.) The AFA prohibited entry into any fishery managed under the

Magnuson-Stevens Act of new vessels over 165 feet in length or 750 tons, or with engines of greater than 3,000 horsepower, unless the vessel's entry is specifically approved by the Secretary of Commerce and the regional fishery management council. Vessels fishing in the U.S. EEZ under the jurisdiction of the Western Pacific Fishery Management Council or tuna purse seine vessels fishing outside the U.S. EEZ are excluded from these size limits.

The AFA creates huge winners and losers. Some fishers tried to capitalize even further from the Act. In Myers v. F/V American Triumph, 260 F.2d 1067 (9th Cir. 2001), plaintiffs brought an in rem class action in admiralty against the fishing vessel F/V American Triumph for conversion of the ferae naturae fish the vessel had caught from 1989 through 1998. During that period, the vessel held a Certificate of Documentation and Fishery Endorsement, issued by the U.S. Coast Guard pursuant to 46 U.S.C. § § 12101-12122. Despite the fact that the vessel had been constructed in a foreign shipyard, the Coast Guard believed the vessel was covered by an exception allowing some vessels rebuil in foreign shipyards to qualify for a certificate under the Commercial Fishing Industry Vessel Anti-Reflagging Act of 1987, 46 U.S.C. § 12108 notes. Once the Coast Guard learned that the vessel had not actually qualified for the exception because it was not under written contract for purchase before July 28, 1997, it issued a notice of intent to invalidate the certificate. During the ten years that the vessel had the certificate, it landed fish worth as much as $150 million. Before the Coast Guard could act, however, Congress enacted the American Fisheries Act, which, inter alia, exempted the American Triumph from the contract condition. The plaintiff claimed that the fish should have belonged to him and to other members of the class. He also claimed the vessel had engaged in intentional and negligent interference with business opportunity, misrepresentation, and unjust enrichment. The court found that the fact that the vessel had a certificate during the period in question was dispositive. The certificate was "conclusive evidence of qualification to be employed in the [fishery]" which the plaintiff could not controvert. In upholding the lower court's dismissal of the action, the Ninth Circuit held: "Once the Coast Guard gave notice that it might cancel the Vessel's Certificate, Myers saw an opportunity to capture the Vessel's income from the past years. He cannot succeed because the Vessel had an incontrovertible right to take fish during the years in question." Id. at 1069.

The FY 2002 Commerce appropriations bill included language amending section 213 of the AFA to delete a sunset provision on the allocation and entitlement provisions of the Act. The change make permanent the prohibition on direct pollock fishing by non-AFA catcher/processors, even though these vessels may have some history of pollock catches prior to 1998. H.R. Conf. Rep. 107-278, 2001 WL 1402218.

(b.) *The Congressional Ban on Large Freezer Trawlers in the North Atlantic*

The American Fisheries Act is an example of Congress using the budget appropriations process, rather than the reauthorization and amendment process, or the Secretary and regional councils process, to determine which vessels should be permitted to participate in U.S. fisheries in the EEZ and at what level. Another such effort did not meet with as much success as the American Fisheries Act apparently has. In American Pelagic Fishing Co., L.P. v. United States, 49 Fed. Cl. 36 (Ct. Cl. 2001), the U.S. Court of Federal Claims held that a series of legislative riders introduced by Senator Snowe of Maine, which effectively precluded the owner of a fishing trawler from fishing for Atlantic mackerel and herring in the U.S. EEZ, effected a taking of the owner's property interest in the use of its vessel. Applying the *Penn. Central* analysis for a regulatory taking, the court found the owner had a reasonable investment-backed expectation that he would be able to use the vessel for such purpose (he had obtained a permit from NMFS), an economic impact of $40 million, and the legislation was retroactive and aimed specifically at the plaintiff's vessel, the Atlantic Star. (The riders had prohibited NMFS from using appropriations to issue or renew fishing permits or other authorizations for any vessel greater than 165 feet in length or of more than 750 tons, with an engine capacity of 3000 horsepower or more. Id. at 42.) The court distinguished its recent decision in Conti v. US, 48 Fed.Cl. 532 (2001), holding that NMFS' ban on swordfish drift gillnet fishing was not a taking, because Conti's permits were not revoked nor was he denied all use of his vessel. Id. at 47-48.

(4.) Vessel and Permit Buyback Programs

In Sustaining Marine Fisheries, the National Research Council's Committee on Ecosystem Management for Sustainable Marine Fisheries found:

> Excess fishing capacity and overcapitalization reduce the economic efficiency of the fisheries and usually are associated with overfishing. Substantial global reductions in fleet capacity are the highest priority for dealing with uncertainty and unexpected events in fisheries and to help reduce overfishing. However, overcapacity is a symptom of socioeconomic incentive systems and management regimes, not a fundamental property of fisheries.   Overcapacity has been created unintentionally by many national and international institutions through lack of property rights, subsidies, and other activities that circumvent market forces.
>
> Fishers adapt ingeniously to regulations designed to reduce fishing capacity, by improving technology, fishing "smarter" or harder, and modifying their techniques. So fishing capacity is difficult to manage directly without also changing other

socioeconomic and management incentives. ...[M]anagers' primary focus [should] not be on direct management of fishing capacity alone. Instead, managers and policy makers should focus on developing or encouraging socioeconomic and other management incentives that reward conservative use of marine resources and their ecosystem and should learn to understand and address the problems of subsidies. Direct management of fishing capacity is more appropriate in extreme or urgent circumstances or as a first step in establishing a more sustainable system of using marine resources. Then the degree of overcapacity can be used as one indicator of the sustainability of a fishery.

* * * Simple buy-back programs have often been ineffective and even counterproductive in the past when large amounts of money have been spent to buy out the least efficient vessels. If there are no incentives to reduce fishing power further, the remaining individuals may invest additional capital and increase overall fleet capacity.

Id. at 121-122.

The 1996 Sustainable Fisheries Act added section 312, entitled "Transition to Sustainable Fisheries" authorizing the Secretary, at the request of a council or the governor of a state, to conduct a voluntary fishing capacity reduction program if the Secretary determines the program (1) is necessary to prevent or end overfishing, rebuild stocks, or achieve measurable and significant improvements in the conservation and management of the fishery, (2) is consistent with the FMP in effect for the fishery, and (3) that the FMP will prevent the replacement of fishing capacity removed through the program through a moratorium on new entrants, restrictions on vessel upgrades, and other effort control measures. The FMP must also establish a specified or target TAC to trigger closure of the fishery. 16 U.S.C. § 1861a(b). The objective of the program is to obtain the "maximum sustained reduction in fishing capacity at the least cost and in a minimum period of time." Id. at § 1861a(b)(2). Vessel buy-back programs are one way to reduce capacity in fisheries. See Congressional Research Service, Commercial Fishing: Economic Aid and Capacity Reduction, ENR Report 97-441 (1997). Section 312 authorizes the Secretary to "buy out" either or both fishing vessels and fishing permits, and may fund such programs with appropriations or funds provided under an industry fee system, provided a two-thirds majority of those participating in a referendum among all permit holders or vessel owners vote in favor of the industry fee system. Id. at § 1861a(e). Under an industry fee program, the fishers who remain in the fishery pay for the buyouts, as they are the chief beneficiaries of the capacity reduction plan.

As of 2001, no buy-back programs have been implemented under section 312. NMFS is developing guidelines for fishing capacity reduction programs. Proposed rules were published on Feb. 11, 1999, 64 Fed. Reg. 6854. Most vessel and permit buy-back programs are instituted after a fishery becomes overfished. Some critics argue that a greater effort should be made to reduce effort through capacity reduction before this point, in order to prevent declines in stocks to an overfished status. How would you design such a program?

SECTION 3. TRIBAL FISHING RIGHTS

In 1979, The U.S. Supreme Court held that Northwest Indian tribes that had signed treaties with the U.S. in 1854 were entitled to have an opportunity to catch up to 50% of the harvestable salmon at their traditional off-reservation fishing sites. Washington v. Washington State Commercial Passenger Fishing Vessel Association, 443 U.S. 658 (1979). Since 1979, federal salmon management under the Magnuson-Stevens Act has incorporated this ruling in its allocation of salmon catches. See, e.g., Washington State Charterboat Assoc. v. Baldrige, 702 F.2d 820, 823 (9th Cir. 1983), cert. denied 464 U.S. 1053 (1984).

The courts have interpreted Indian treaty fishing rights to include the right to harvest shellfish as well as anadromous species. This ruling has required the State of Washington to manage its Dungeness crab and other shellfish fisheries to take account of this obligation. United States v. Washington, 873 F. Supp. 1422 (W.D. Wash. 1994), modified, 135 F.3d 618 (9th Cir. 1998).

In Washington v. Daley, 173 F.3d 1158 (9th Cir. 1999), the court heard an appeal of the dismissal of a case challenging regulations allocating certain groundfish species to four Northwest tribes. The court provided this background on the case (some citations not included):

> The Pacific Coast Groundfish Management Plan ("the Plan"), first adopted in 1982, manages whiting fisheries. Pacific whiting, also known as Pacific hake and found off the west coast of North America, is used to make seafood products such as imitation crab. Whiting, sablefish and rockfish are among more than 80 species of groundfish whose allocation is governed by the Plan. Since 1989, the Pacific Council has allocated portions of the sablefish and rockfish harvests to the four Tribes that each have a reservation on the Pacific coast of Washington state--the Makah, Hoh and Quileute tribes and the Quinault Indian Nation.

> In 1995 the Makah tribe petitioned the Pacific Council to set aside a harvest of 25,000 metric tons of whiting. The Makah claimed that their treaty with the United States secures to them the right to harvest whiting within their "usual and accustomed" fishing grounds, which extend roughly westward from the northwest coast of Washington to 125 degrees 44' West

longitude. See United States v. Washington, 730 F.2d 1314 (9th Cir.1984). In October 1995, the Fisheries Service and the General Counsel to the National Oceanic and Atmospheric Administration advised the Pacific Council that the Tribes have treaty rights to harvest groundfish in their "usual and accustomed" grounds. In November 1995, after hearing testimony from members of the fishing industry and the Attorney General's office of the State of Oregon, the Pacific Council voted against recognition of the Tribes' treaty rights in the whiting fishery on the ground "that a treaty tribe's right to harvest fish from its [usual and accustomed] area only exists for those species to which the tribe can show historical catch or access at the time the treaty was signed."

The Secretary rejected the Pacific Council's recommendations as contrary to "other applicable law"--specifically, the treaties with the Tribes. The Secretary therefore published a proposed amendment to the Plan's implementing regulations to establish a "framework process" to "accommodate treaty rights" in the groundfish fishery. The Secretary also proposed other modifications to the groundfish regulations and sought public comment on the 1996 allocation of whiting to the Makah.

On June 6, 1996, the Secretary published the final rule, which established the framework for implementing the Tribes' treaty rights in the groundfish fishery and allocated 15,000 metric tons of whiting to the Makah. The final rule provides that, for purposes of the Plan, the "usual and accustomed fishing areas" of the Tribes extend west from Washington's Pacific coast to 125 degrees 44' West longitude and from the international boundary with Canada on the north (the most northerly portion of the Makah's treaty area) to 46 degrees 53' North latitude (the most southerly portion of the Quinaults' treaty area). The Secretary noted that federal salmon and halibut regulations had recognized the same areas as "usual and accustomed" tribal fishing grounds. The Secretary also noted that the western boundary was determined by extending south the line of the Makah's adjudicated western boundary.

Washington v. Daley, 173 F.3d at 1162-63.

The States of Washington and Oregon and three fishing industry groups challenged the Secretary's rules allocating groundfish catches to the tribes, and the following decision resulted.

MIDWATER TRAWLERS COOP. v. DEP'T OF COMMERCE
United States District Court, W.D. Washington, 2000
139 F.Supp.2d 1136, aff'd in part and rev'd in part, __F.3d(9th Cir. 2002)

DISTRICT JUDGE **ROTHSTEIN:**

B. Treaty Right to Harvest Pacific Whiting

Midwater argues that in 1996, when the Final Rule was adopted, no court had "affirmatively and precisely held that Indian fishing rights applied to Pacific whiting." Midwater's Memorandum in Support of Motion for Summary Judgment at 13. On this basis, Midwater argues that there was no "applicable law" on this question and, therefore, the federal defendants acted unreasonably by promulgating regulations recognizing such a right. Id. This argument lacks merit.

First, Midwater advances a flawed definition of "applicable law." Although Fishery Management Plans and regulations promulgated under the Magnuson Act must be consistent with the provisions of the Magnuson Act and "other applicable law," 16 U.S.C. § 1853(a)(1)(C), 1854(a)(1)(B), "other applicable law" includes the Stevens Treaties negotiated between the United States and the Tribes in the 1850s.[19] See, e.g., Parravano v. Babbitt, 70 F.3d 539, 544 (9th Cir.1995); Washington Crab Producers, Inc. v. Mosbacher, 924 F.2d 1438, 1440-41 (9th Cir.1990). The Secretary need not await a specific adjudication prior to carrying out his obligation to promulgate regulations consistent with treaty rights.

Second, Judge Rafeedie determined in 1994 that tribal rights are not limited by species of fish or by whether the Tribes harvested that species at the time of the Stevens Treaties. See Shellfish I, 873 F.Supp. at 1430. In the Final Rule, the Secretary cited Judge Rafeedie's decision as support for recognizing the Tribes' treaty right to whiting. 61 Fed.Reg. 28788. Judge Rafeedie's decision on this point has since been affirmed by the Ninth Circuit. See Shellfish II, 157 F.3d at 643-44.

* * *

The federal defendants did not act arbitrarily and capriciously in recognizing the Tribes' right to harvest Pacific whiting.

---

[19] The Stevens Treaties at issue here are the Treaty of Neah Bay (Makah), and the Treaty of Olympia (Quinault, Quileute, and Hoh). Article 4 of the Treaty of Neah Bay provides: The right to taking fish ... at usual and accustomed grounds and stations is further secured to said Indians in common with all citizens of the United States ... 12 Stat. 939 (Jan. 31, 1855). The Treaty of Olympia contains similar language. 12 Stat. 971.

C. "Usual and Accustomed" Fishing Areas

The Final Rule provides that, for purposes of the FMP, the U & A fishing areas of the Tribes extend west from Washington's coast to 125 44' West longitude, i.e., approximately 40 miles into the ocean. Midwater contests this determination on two grounds. First, Midwater argues that no tribe has the right to usual and accustomed fishing areas beyond Washington's territorial waters, i.e., beyond three miles of the coast.

* * *

Midwater argues that the treaty parties could not have meant to ensure fishing rights to the entire U & A grounds and stations because, when the Stevens Treaties were signed, no nation had control of the high seas beyond three miles of the shore. Midwater further argues that, regardless of original intent, the Magnuson Act must have extinguished the treaty rights by establishing the United States' sovereign rights and exclusive marine fishery management jurisdiction out to 200 nautical miles. See 16 U.S.C. § 1811. Midwater's interpretation is contrary to the Magnuson Act's language, basic tenets of treaty interpretation, and the understanding of the Tribes and the United States.

The Magnuson Act requires that FMPs and regulations promulgated under the Act be consistent with other applicable law, which law expressly includes Indian treaty rights. See, e.g., Washington Crab Producers, 924 F.2d at 1444. The Act itself requires that FMPs describe the "nature and extent" of any "Indian treaty fishing rights." 16 U.S.C. § 1853(a)(2). The fishing rights in the Stevens Treaties are " 'not a grant of rights to the Indians, but a grant of rights from them--a reservation of those not granted.' " Shellfish I, 873 F.Supp. at 1430. One of the Tribes' reserved rights is the right to fish in their U & A areas irrespective of management authority. Cf. Washington v. Washington Passenger Fishing Vessel Ass'n, 443 U.S. 658, 696, 99 S.Ct. 3055, 61 L.Ed.2d 823 (1979) (noting that Magnuson Act "place[s] a responsibility on the United States, rather than the State, to police the take of fish ... to assure compliance with the treaties").

Furthermore, neither the United States nor the Tribes disputes the tribal right to fish within the federal fisheries management jurisdiction. Absent extraordinarily strong evidence to the contrary, the court will defer to the treaty parties' interpretation. See Sumitomo Shoji America, Inc. v. Avagliano, 457 U.S. 176, 184, 102 S.Ct. 2374, 72 L.Ed.2d 765 (1982).

* * *

D. Challenge to Language Added to Final Rule

The State of Washington challenges the following language, which was added to the Final Rule at the request of the Quileute:

> The Secretary recognizes the sovereign status and co-manager role of Indian tribes over shared federal and tribal fishery resources. Accordingly, the Secretary will develop tribal allocations and regulations under this paragraph, in consultation with the affected tribe(s) and, insofar as possible, with tribal consensus.

50 C.F.R. § 660.324(d); 61 Fed.Reg. at 28791.

Washington contends that the additional language violates the Magnuson Act's grant of exclusive management authority over a certain area to the United States, is inconsistent with the open public process required by the Act, and was adopted without the required notice and opportunity for comment.

1. Sovereign and Co-Manager Status over "Shared" Resources

The Magnuson Act grants to the United States exclusive management authority over all fish within the exclusive economic zone ("EEZ"). 16 U.S.C. § 1811(a). Washington acknowledges the sovereign status of the Tribes and their treaty right to fish for groundfish within the EEZ. Washington also recognizes the Tribes' authority to manage their own tribal fisheries. Washington argues, however, that the challenged language confers upon the Tribes an additional legal interest in the fishery resources.

The court does not read the challenged language in the same way. The challenged clause does not create title to the fish or in any way alter the Tribes current "legal status vis-a-vis the resource." The parties all agree that the Tribes have no claim of a property ownership interest in the fish. See Foss v. NMFS, 161 F.3d 584, 587 (9th Cir.1998) (citing Douglas v. Seacoast Products, Inc., 431 U.S. 265, 284, 97 S.Ct. 1740, 52 L.Ed.2d 304 (1977)) (noting that any claim of owning fish themselves is "pure fantasy"). Furthermore, the unchallenged portion of the Final Rule contains language that has a similar effect to that of the challenged portion: that the Tribes "will * * * manage[ ]" their fishery allocation, thereby making them, in effect, co-managers of the shared resources. Compare 61 Fed.Reg. 10308 (March 13, 1996) with 61 Fed.Reg. at 28791. The federal defendants note that tribal management of such fishery allocations has occurred since at least 1990 ([when it] provid[ed] for tribal management of its own sablefish fishery).

Washington argues that if the challenged clause is interpreted in this innocuous fashion, then the language constitutes surplusage that should be stricken. The court does not, however, monitor economy of language. The Secretary did not act arbitrarily and capriciously by adding language that provides no more than a statement acknowledging the practical realities of fisheries management.

* * *

Notes

1. In USA v. State of Washington, 143 F.Supp.2d 1218 (W.D. Wash. 2001), Judge Rothstein upheld NMFS's use of a methodology for allocating the U.S.'s share of whiting between tribal and non-tribal fishers the Makah had proposed in 1999. The method uses a sliding scale to define the tribal portion as a percentage of the overall U.S. whiting allocation, with a 17.5% tribal harvest ceiling. Id. at 1224. Judge Rothstein held the method to be within the tribe's treaty right to a fair share of whiting, rejecting Oregon's claim that the allocation should be based on the whiting's estimated biomass distribution within the tribal fishing grounds. On appeal, the Ninth Circuit ruled that the allocation methodology was a political compromise that did not meet the Act's requirement that it be based on the best scientific information available, remanding the allocation for further scientific justification. Midwater Trawlers Coop v. Dept. of Commerce, No. 00-35717, slip op. at 7 (9th Cir. Mar. 5, 2002), WL 338406.

2.   In Village of Eyak v. Trawler Diane Marie, Inc., 154 F.3d 1090 (9th Cir. 1998), several Native Alaskan villages located in the Prince William Sound and lower Cook Inlet regions of Alaska challenged the Secretary's sablefish and halibut IFQ regulations. They claimed the regulations and federal management program violated their rights to exclusive use and occupancy of portions of the Outer Continental Shelf (OCS) under unextinguished aboriginal title and use extending back over 7,000 years. The court held that the villages' claims to the OCS were barred by the federal paramountcy doctrine. The doctrine reasons that because the Constitution gives the federal government jurisdiction over foreign commerce, foreign affairs, and national defense, it must have paramount rights in offshore areas as an attribute of these external sovereign powers. See, e.g., United States v. California, 332 U.S. 19 (1947), discussed above in Chapter 4.

SECTION 4. MANAGEMENT OF FISHERIES IN STATE WATERS

A. THE BASIS OF STATE FISHERIES AUTHORITY

Traditionally, the management of coastal and internal waters fisheries was the province of the individual coastal states. While state regulation was certainly common, the legal nature of the states' interests in fishery resources was always somewhat unclear. That they had an important interest was uncontested, at least from the time of the Supreme Court's decision in Manchester v. Massachusetts, 139 U.S. 240 (1891), where the Court upheld Massachusetts restrictions on the menhaden seine net fishery in Buzzards Bay. The Court held that if Congress "does not by affirmative legislation assert its right or will to assume control of menhaden fisheries in such bays, the right to control such fisheries must remain with the State which contains such bays." Id. at 266.

Confusion stemmed, at least in part, from the Court's earlier opinions in cases like McCready v. Virginia, 94 U.S. 391 (1876), upholding a Virginia law which prohibited citizens of other states from planting oysters in a Virginia tidewater river. There the Court held that the citizens of a state collectively own "the tide-waters * * * and the fish in them, so far as they are capable of ownership while running." Id. at 394. This ownership rationale has been used over the years in defense of state regulations that discriminate against out-of-state or nonresident interests. See Haavik v. Alaska Packers Assn., 263 U.S. 510 (1924) (upholding fishing licenses discriminating between residents and nonresidents); Foster Packing Co. v. Haydel, 278 U.S. 1 (1942) (Louisiana shrimp local processing requirement before out-of-state shipment violates Commerce Clause); Toomer v. Witsell, 334 U.S. 385 (1948) (shrimp landing and packing requirement violated Commerce Clause as did a nonresident licensing fee one hundred times greater than resident fee.) As Justice Reed stated in his dissent in the equal protection case Takahashi v. Fish and Game Commission, 334 U.S. 410 (1948), "Whether the philosophical basis of * * * the power over fish and game, is a theory of ownership or trusteeship for its citizens or residents or conservation of natural resources or protection of its * * * coasts is not material. The right to control [fishing] rests in sovereign governments and, in the United States, it rests with the individual states in the absence of federal action by treaty or otherwise." Id. at 428, n. 3.

In Douglas v. Seacoast Products, Inc., 431 U.S. 265 (1977), the Court considered the validity of two Virginia statutes that limited the right of nonresidents and aliens to catch menhaden in state coastal and inland waters. The statutes were challenged by a New Jersey-based company, owned almost exclusively by foreign stockholders, whose vessels were enrolled and licensed by the federal government. Under the applicable statutes the vessels were enrolled and licensed to be employed in the mackerel fishery, a license that entitled the holder to catch fish of any description, 46 U.S.C. § 325 (1976). The company asserted that the Virginia statutes purporting to limit its fishing operations in Virginia coastal and inland waters were preempted by the federal enrollment and licensing statutes. The state argued that the federal statutes only granted the company the right to navigate in state waters and no more. The Court held, however, that the federal statute granted the company the right to fish in Virginia waters on the same terms as Virginia residents and thus the conflicting Virginia statute was preempted.

Although the case turned on the Supremacy Clause analysis of the state laws under the federal enrollment and licensing statutes, one very interesting aspect of the decision is the Court's treatment of the state's argument that the Submerged Lands Act of 1953, as well as a number of prior U. S. Supreme Court decisions, recognize that "the States have title or ownership interest in the fish swimming in their territorial waters." Id. at 283. And, "that because the States 'own' the fish, they may exclude federal licensees." Id. The Court made two responses to this argument. First, the Submerged Lands Act expressly retained for the federal government all constitutional powers of regulation and control for purposes of commerce, navigation, national defense, and international affairs. Since the grant of the federal fisheries license was pursuant to the federal government's commerce power, the Submerged Lands Act did not affect the validity of the license. Second, the Court said:

> * * * it is pure fantasy to talk of "owning" wild fish, birds, or animals. Neither the States nor the Federal Government, any more than a hopeful fisherman or hunter, has title to these creatures until they are reduced to possession by skillful capture. The "ownership" language of [earlier United States Supreme Court] cases such as those cited by appellant must be understood as no more than 19th-century legal fiction expressing "the importance to its people that a State have the power to preserve and regulate the exploitation of an important resource." [Citations omitted.] Under modern analysis, the question is simply whether the State has exercised its police power in conformity with the federal laws and Constitution. * * * Virginia has failed to do so here.

While the Court may have laid to rest the ownership theory for constitutional analysis of state non-residency discriminations, the legal basis for state fishery jurisdiction has continued to challenge the courts and fishery managers.

B. STATE JURISDICTION UNDER THE MAGNUSON-STEVENS ACT

The authority of a state to regulate fishing vessels and activities within state waters is confirmed by section 306(a) of the Magnuson-Stevens Act, 16 U.S.C. § 1856(a). See below. The one exception to this state law savings clause is the Secretary's power to preempt state authority in state waters and impose federal FMP regulations there if the Secretary finds the state is undermining the effectiveness of an approved FMP and the fishery is largely a federal waters fishery. 16 U.S.C. § 1856(b). State authority to enforce regulations on fishing in the EEZ is provided for in section 306(a)(3), 16 U.S.C. § 1856(a)(3).

Prior to the 1976 enactment of the Act, many states regulated fisheries through laws that applied to fishing vessels licensed by state law, often without regard to whether they fished only in state waters, or through landing laws, which applied to all fish landed in the state regardless of where they were caught. In 1996, Congress made several changes to section 306(a) with respect to state authority in the EEZ. Before the amendments, this section contained only a one sentence statement that a state *may not* regulate a fishing vessel outside the state's boundaries either directly or indirectly unless the vessel is registered under the laws of the state. Although short, the language was subject to different interpretations.

Congress' intent in the original Magnuson Act in 1976 apparently was to allow states to continue to regulate fishing beyond state waters through direct regulation and enforcement at sea and by dockside enforcement of possession and landing laws. The wording of the 1976 Act needed revision to more accurately reflect Congress' intent. Federal courts in Florida, a state with extensive fisheries regulation that often applies beyond state waters, concluded that section 306(a) reflected a Congressional intent to occupy the field of fisheries regulation in the EEZ, leaving no room for concurrent state jurisdiction, even for vessels registered under state laws. See Southeastern Fisheries Assoc. v. Chiles, 979 F.2d 1504 (11th Cir. 1992).

In an effort to clarify its intent, the Congress replaced this sentence with an affirmative statement: "A State *may* regulate a fishing vessel outside the boundaries of the State in the following circumstances * * * ." This statement is then followed by three paragraphs that define three alternative scenarios under which a state could regulate fishing outside it waters.

The intent of this change was to make it clear to federal and state courts that Congress did not intend to displace all state regulation of fisheries in the EEZ either by the enactment of the Magnuson-Stevens Act or by the Secretary of Commerce's approval of an FMP and implementing regulations. Such displacement would occur only if the state and federal regulations conflicted with one another.

16 U.S.C. § 1856. State jurisdiction

(a) In general.

(1) Except as provided in subsection (b), nothing in this Act shall be construed as extending or diminishing the jurisdiction or authority of any State within its boundaries.

* * *

(3) A State may regulate a fishing vessel outside the boundaries of the State in the following circumstances:

(A) The fishing vessel is registered under the laws of that State, and

(i) there is no fishery management plan or other applicable Federal fishing regulations for the fishery in which the vessel is operating; or (ii) the State's laws and regulations are consistent with the fishery management plan and applicable Federal fishing regulations for the fishery in which the vessel is operating.

(B) The fishery management plan for the fishery in which the fishing vessel is operating delegates management of the fishery to a State and the State's laws and regulations are consistent with such fishery management plan. If at any time the Secretary determines that a State law or regulation applicable to a fishing vessel under this circumstance is not consistent with the fishery management plan, the Secretary shall promptly notify the State and the appropriate Council of such determination and provide an opportunity for the State to correct any inconsistencies identified in the notification. If, after notice and opportunity for corrective action, the State does not correct the inconsistencies identified by the Secretary, the authority granted to the State under this subparagraph shall not apply until the Secretary and the appopriate Council find that the State has corrected the inconsistencies. For a fishery for which there was a fishery management plan in place on August 1, 1996 that did not delegate management of the fishery to a State as of that date, the authority provided by this subparagraph applies only if the Council approves the delegation of management of the fishery to the State by a three-quarters majority vote of the voting members of the Council.

(C) The fishing vessel is not registered under the laws of the State of Alaska and is operating in a fishery in the exclusive economic zone off Alaska for which there was no fishery management plan in place on August 1, 1996, and the Secretary and the North Pacific Council find that there is a legitimate interest of the State of Alaska in the conservation and management of such fishery. The authority provided under this subparagraph shall terminate when a fishery management plan under this Act is approved and implemented for such fishery.

(b) Exception.

(1) If the Secretary finds, after notice and an opportunity for a hearing in accordance with section 554 of title 5, United States Code, that--

(A) the fishing in a fishery, which is covered by a fishery management plan implemented under this Act, is engaged in predominately within the exclusive economic zone and beyond such zone; and

(B) any State has taken any action, or omitted to take any action, the results of which will substantially and adversely affect the carrying out of such fishery management plan; the Secretary shall promptly notify such State and the appropriate Council of such finding and of his intention to regulate the applicable fishery within the boundaries of such State (other than its internal waters), pursuant to such fishery management plan and the regulations promulgated to implement such plan.

(2) If the Secretary, pursuant to this subsection, assumes responsibility for the regulation of any fishery, the State involved may at any time thereafter apply to the Secretary for reinstatement of its authority over such fishery. If the Secretary finds that the reasons for which he assumed such regulation no longer prevail, he shall promptly terminate such regulation.

* * *

Notes and Questions

1. A court will resolve any legal challenge to a state's fisheries enforcement actions beyond state waters by determining how much authority Congress intended the states to have in the EEZ. As the principal statement of this intent, is section 306 clear? Does it dispel all uncertainty over the scope of state regulation in the EEZ?

2. Would defendants in state fisheries law enforcement actions still be able to argue that "registered under the laws of the state" refers to federal enrollment and licensing laws and not state fishing licensing laws? Such challenge is unlikely to succeed, as several courts have now concluded that the term covers a wide variety of state laws that require licenses, permits, and other acknowledgments from the state before a fishing vessel can operate in its waters. In People v. Weeren, 26 Cal.3d 654, 163 Cal. Rptr. 255, 607 P.2d 1279 (1990), cert. denied, 449 U.S. 839 (1980), the California Supreme Court reasoned that the Congress meant to incorporate the variety of state fishing registration schemes such as California's, "premis[ing] continued state jurisdiction on the undefined and generic concept of local 'registration'." Id. at 1286. This broad reading of the term was appropriate because to do otherwise, at least when no FMP was in place, would leave important food resources without effective controls.

3. As "registered under the laws of the state" is not defined in the Act, how broadly may states define vessel registration under their own laws? May they cover fishing vessels registered and home-ported in other states and owned by citizens of another state? For contrasting views on the Congressional intent behind the state registration requirement, compare Comment, The Fishery Conservation and Management Act of 1976: State Regulation of Fishing Beyond the Territorial Sea, 31 Me. L. Rev. 303 (1980) and Comment, Alaska's

Regulation of King Crab on the Outer Continental Shelf, 6 U.C.L.A. Alaska L. Rev. 375, 405 (1977).

4. During the reauthorization of the Magnuson Act in 1996, the Senate Commerce Committee reported out a bill in May, 1996 that included the following language:

For the purposes of this paragraph, the term 'registered under the law of that State' means that-

i) the owner, captain, or vessel holds a fishing license, or other document that is a prerequisite to participating in the fishery, issued by the State;

ii) the vessel is numbered by the State in accordance with chapter 123 of title 46, United States Code; or

iii) the documentation of the vessel under chapter 121 of title 46, United States Code, identifies the vessel's homeport as located in the State.

The Senate, however, adopted a substitute bill that deleted the above definition. If this definition had been enacted, would it preclude the more expansive definitions of "registered" that would automatically make a fishing vessel "registered" if it transits state waters with fish or shellfish in its hold, regardless of its intended port of landing? If someone were to challenge such a state law definition of "registered," is the court likely to use the Senate Commerce Committee's language as guidance in reviewing state regulation for consistency with an FMP or considering proposed FMP delegations to states under section 306(a)(3)(B)?

5. Litigation under section 306(a) is more likely to focus on whether the state regulation applied to state-registered fishing vessels is "consistent" with the FMP and applicable federal fishing regulations for the fishery in which the vessel is operating than on the permissible scope of state registration laws. 16 U.S.C. § 1856(a)(3)(A). What does the term "consistent" with the FMP mean? The Senate Commerce Committee bill had language requiring the state regulations to be consistent *with the purposes of* the FMP. Does the deletion of this language signify a stricter standard? How far can state regulations differ from the measures adopted to achieve the Council's objectives for a fishery?

In a discussion on the Senate floor prior to voting on the 1996 amendments, the bill's floor manager, Senator Ted Stevens of Alaska, said the new language of section 306(a)(3) protected the existing authority of the states to impose more stringent regulations as long as they are "not irreconcilable" with the FMP. Are the terms "consistent" and "not irreconcilable" the same?

For a discussion of the policy implications of allowing state fishery regulation in the EEZ, see E. Greenberg and M. Shapiro, Federalism in the Fishery Conservation Zone: A New Role for the States in an Era of Federal Regulatory Reform, 55 S. Cal. L. Rev. 641 (1982).

6. The 1996 amendments to section 306(a) allow a state to regulate fishing vessels in the EEZ that are not licensed or registered under state law. This may happen if the applicable council adopts an FMP delegating management of the fishery to the state. The council must approve the delegation by a three-quarters majority and the state's regulations must be consistent with the FMP. Section 306(a)(3)(B), 16 U.S.C. § 1856(a)(3)(B). This provision was modeled on a federal-state cooperative arrangement contained in the North Pacific Council's FMP for Alaska king and tanner crabs. It extends the option of delegating EEZ management to all the councils and their constituent states, not just the North Pacific council and Alaska.

The Act also allows the State of Alaska to regulate fishing vessels that are not registered under Alaskan law but operate in a fishery in the EEZ off Alaska, even in the absence of an FMP delegating such authority to it, if there was no FMP in place by August 1, 1996. Before it may do so, the North Pacific council and Secretary of Commerce must find that Alaska has a "legitimate interest in the conservation and management of such fishery." In the event an FMP is adopted by the North Pacific Council, the authority of the State is terminated. Section 306(a)(3)(C), 16 U.S.C. § 1856(a)(3)(C).

This provision originated in the House bill in order to address an incident occurring in 1995. At that time there was no FMP for scallops in the EEZ off Alaska. A North Carolina-based fishing vessel, the M/V MR. BIG, renounced its Alaskan vessel registration and continued to catch scallops in the EEZ after the State of Alaska's quotas had been reached and the fishery closed. Alaska could not enforce the closure against the vessel because it was not registered under Alaska law, as then required by the Magnuson Act. At the request of the North Pacific council, NMFS adopted regulations prohibiting retention of scallops in EEZ off Alaska until the council could develop other management measures to replace the prohibition. The owner of the MR. BIG challenged the authority of NMFS to plug this loophole with emergency regulations and lost. Trawler Diane Marie, Inc. v. Kantor, 918 F. Supp. 921 (E.D.N.C.1995), aff'd, 91 F.3d 134 (4th Cir. 1996). To prevent similar situations from occurring, Congress chose to give Alaska blanket authority to regulate non-state registered fishing vessels until such time as an FMP is adopted. The authority is not extended, however, to other states. Why not?

7. Although the Secretary's state waters preemption power under section 306(b), 16 U.S.C. § 1856, has been used infrequently, it remains an important lever to ensure that state law loopholes don't undermine enforcement of an FMP. Should the Secretary's power to preempt state fisheries laws be limited to fisheries "predominately" within the EEZ or

beyond?   For NOAA's procedures for the Secretary's preemption authority, see 50 C.F.R. § § 600.605 to 600.630.

C. INTERSTATE COORDINATION AND COOPERATION

Although section 306(b), 16 U.S.C. § 1856, limits the power of the Secretary to insist on cooperative management of fisheries that occur solely in state waters, a 1993 enactment requires Atlantic coastal states to adopt fishery regulations to implement cooperative interstate plans.

> The Atlantic Coastal Fisheries Cooperative Management Act (the "Cooperative Act"), 16 U.S.C. § 5101 et seq., permits Eastern Coastal states to participate in the management of Atlantic Ocean fisheries under a dual federal-state management regime. The Magnuson-Stevens Act expressly delegates exclusive regulatory authority within three miles of a state's coastline, traditionally recognized as state territorial waters ("State Waters"), to the individual states. *See* 16 U.S.C. § § 1856(a)(1), (a)(2)(A). The Atlantic States Marine Fisheries Commission (the "States Commission"), which is comprised of representatives from the Eastern Coast states, prepares Coastal Fishery Management Plans ("CFMPs"). CFMPs do not require separate federal approval, but the states themselves are required under the Cooperative Act to implement and enforce CFMPs through state legislation.   If a state fails to implement or otherwise comply with a CFMP, the Secretary, upon certain conditions, may intervene to impose a moratorium on fishing in the noncompliant state's State Waters.

New York v. Evans, 162 F.Supp.2d 161(E.D. NY 2001).

The ACFCMA was modeled on the 1983 Atlantic Striped Bass Conservation Act, Pub. L. 98-613, Oct. 31, 1984, 98 Stat. 3187, which is largely credited with allowing the recovery of the severely depleted striped bass. The Striped Bass Act required the Atlantic states to enact protective regulations for striped bass recommended by the interstate commission or risk a federal shut-down of the fishery in state waters. The ACFCMA allows the Commission to use the moratorium threat to ensure each state complies with interstate plans adopted by the states for weakfish, bluefish, summer flounder, and a number of other important state-waters fisheries.

Some interests have questioned the power that the Act gives to the Atlantic States Marine Fisheries Commission and the Secretary. They argue that the 1942 Atlantic States Marine Fisheries Compact that created the Commission was a voluntary arrangement for coordinating state fisheries regulations for coastal migratory fish stocks.   The interstate compact was approved by Congress, P.L. No. 77-539, 56 Stat. 267 (1942) and Pub. L. No. 81-721, 64 Stat. 467 (1950) (amendment to original compact).

The critics argue that the ACFCMA transforms the interstate compact into a vehicle for federal enforcement of the interstate plans and that cooperation is no longer voluntary. In North Carolina Fisheries Assoc. v. Brown, 917 F. Supp. 1108 (E.D. Va. 1996), the plaintiff commercial fisheries trade association, sought to enjoin the federal moratorium on weakfish fishing in the EEZ, which had been promulgated under the ASFCMA to support the interstate weakfish plan. The plaintiffs questioned the constitutionality of the Act as well as whether the statutory requirements had been met before the EEZ moratorium went into effect. The court ruled that the Commission's plan did not make the requisite finding that the moratorium was necessary thus the moratorium action was beyond the Secretary's authority. Id. at 1118. By finding that the statutory prerequisites had not been met, the court found it unnecessary to reach the constitutional issues.

The constitutional arguments included a claim that the ACFCMA violates the 10th Amendment's protection of state sovereignty. The Act purportedly infringes upon a state's sovereignty because it attempts "to commandeer state governments into the service of federal regulatory processes" through federal sanctions directed at the state. See New York v. United States, 505 U.S. 144 (1992) (Low-Level Radioactive Waste Policy Amendments Act of 1985 requiring states to develop plans for nuclear waste disposal violated the 10th Amendment). (Note the similarity of these claims to those raised regarding the Magnuson-Stevens Act's council process by Connecticut in a case filed in 2000. See section 2.(B.)(4.) above.) Do you see a 10th Amendment problem with the ACFCMA? What is the result if a state fails to comply with the interstate plan?

Another constitutional claim argues that the ACFCMA effectively amended the 1942 Compact to give the Commission more power than the states had agreed to. What powers does the Commission have under the Act that it did not under the Compact? Does the Commission make the final determination whether a particular state regulation is necessary for the conservation and management of the interstate coastal fishery?

In Ace Lobster Co. v. Evans, 165 F.Supp.2d 148 (D.R.I. 2001), the court rejected claims that the Secretary of Commerce exceeded his authority under the Atlantic Coastal Fisheries Cooperative Management Act (ACFCMA), or violated the National Standards of the MSFCMA when he issued lobster trap regulations setting a uniform cap of 1800 on the number of traps each licensed vessel can fish in the designated offshore area (30 to 200 miles) instead of limits that reflected a percentage of their historical trap numbers. The court found that the overall trap limit is a reasonable interim conservation measure until such time as the Secretary can secure enough information to develop a fair, individualized, historical trap limit for those lobstermen.

For background on the transition from management of the

American lobster fishery by the regional councils under the MSA to interstate cooperative management under the ACFCMA, see Erik T. Barstow, Comment, American Lobster Fishery Management Under the Atlantic Coastal Fisheries Cooperative Management Act: An Attempt at Cooperative Fishery Jurisdiction, 4 Ocean & Coastal L.J. 113 (1999).

How well is the "dual federal-state management regime" under the Magnuson-Stevens Act and the Atlantic Coastal Fisheries Cooperative Management Act working?

NEW YORK v. EVANS
United States District Court, E.D. New York, 2001
162 F. Supp.2d 161

DISTRICT JUDGE GARAUFIS:

Plaintiffs have brought suit seeking invalidation of U.S. Department of Commerce (the "Secretary") final regulations implementing federal quotas for the summer 2000 and 2001 scup fisheries.[20] Plaintiffs intend by this lawsuit to compel the Secretary to allocate a specific percentage of the overall summer scup quota to each state participating in the fishery. Plaintiffs now move for partial summary judgment on the grounds that the summer 2000 regulations are arbitrary and capricious. Because this court concludes that the Secretary's action is not arbitrary and capricious, the motion is denied and this claim is dismissed.

* * *

II. Factual Background

1. The Dual Regime

During the summer months, scup school primarily in State Waters and in Federal Waters during the winter months. In early 1995, the Fisheries Service concluded "that the scup stock is overexploited and at a low abundance level." In response, the Fisheries Service adopted a scup FMP (the "Federal Plan") proposed jointly by the Mid-Atlantic Fishery Management Council (the "Federal Council") and the States Commission, with input from the New England and South Atlantic Fishery Management Councils. The Federal Plan divided the fishing year

---

[20] Scup (also known as porgy) is a schooling fish species found in the Northwest Atlantic Ocean primarily between Cape Cod, Massachusetts and Cape Hatteras, North Carolina. "Fishery" is defined under the Magnuson-Stevens Act as "(A) one or more stocks of fish which can be treated as a unit for the purposes of conservation and management and which are identified on the basis of geographical, scientific, technical, recreational and economic characteristics; and (B) any fishing for such stocks." 16 U.S.C. § 1802.

into two winter periods and one summer period and set targets for fishing quotas to protect the fish stock. The States Commission then adopted an identical plan as a scup CFMP (the "State Plan").

On May 22, 1997 the Secretary published final regulations implementing a regulatory amendment (the "Regulatory Amendment") allocating state-by-state on a percentage basis the summer period's overall federal scup quota. Under the Regulatory Amendment the Secretary would announce in the Federal Register each state's attainment of its scup quota; the state would then close its scup fishery, thereby prohibiting vessels licensed to fish under state permits from selling scup to fish dealers. Upon attainment of every state's quota, the Secretary would close the scup fishery in Federal Waters and forbid vessels licensed to fish under federal permits from selling scup to fish dealers. The States Commission adopted an addendum to the State Plan subdividing the overall summer quota into state-by-state allocations identical to the Regulatory Amendment. Under this dual regime, any scup caught in either Federal or State Waters were counted against both the Federal Plan quota and the State Plan quota of the state where the fish were sold to fish dealers. Any fish sold in excess of a state's quota was recorded as an "overage." While the Regulatory Amendment did not expand the Secretary's power to regulate in State Waters, a state's overages during one year's summer period would be subtracted by the Secretary from that state's Federal Plan quota for the next summer as a penalty.

2. Massachusetts Litigation

In June 1997, Massachusetts filed an action in federal district court to set aside the Secretary's Federal Plan to the extent that it established a state- by-state allocation of the summer quota. See Com. of Mass. by Div. of Marine Fisheries v. Daley, 10 F.Supp.2d 74 (D.Mass.1998). Massachusetts claimed that the state-by-state allocations were discriminatory. The state argued that the data used to determine the allocations underestimated its appropriate share because scup caught and sold by small scale fishermen and dealers, who were not required to (and in fact did not) report amounts of scup caught and sold to the state or to the Fisheries Service, constituted 90% of the state's scup fishery. The district court set aside the federal state-by-state allocations of the summer quota as discriminatory to Massachusetts local fisherman.

In February 1999, the First Circuit affirmed the district court's decision on other grounds. Mass. v. Daley, 170 F.3d 23, 31-32 (1st Cir.1999). The court acknowledged that "if the state-by-state quotas were shown to be necessary to achieve the [Magnuson-Stevens Act's] main conservation goal, we would decide the case in favor of the Secretary." Id. at 30. Nonetheless, the court held against the Secretary because the administrative record did not "explain why the state-by-state quota was necessary at all." Id. at 30. The court held that state-by-state allocation of the summer quota was not invalid per se, but required adequate justification in the administrative record.: "nothing in this opinion precludes the adoption--subject always to swift judicial review--of state-by-state quotas on an emergency basis, or through further proceedings in the ordinary course, or both." Id. at 32. Instead of remanding the case back to the Secretary, the court set aside the regulations to the extent they implemented Federal Plan state-by-state allocations but left intact the regulations implementing the Federal Plan's overall coastwide quota. Id.

Even before the district court decision, Massachusetts had ignored the Federal and State Plan dual regime. In January 1998, the Fisheries Service determined that Massachusetts' 1997 summer scup landings exceeded its 1997 Federal Plan allocation by over one million pounds. Subtracting Massachusetts' overages from the following year's allocation, the Fisheries Service determined that no commercial quota was available to Massachusetts for the 1998 summer period. Under the procedures envisioned by the Federal Plan, the Secretary would have closed the Massachusetts scup fishery for the 1998 summer period.

Daley, however, invalidated the Federal Plan state-by-state allocations of the summer quota effectively prohibiting calculation and enforcement of Massachusetts' overages. See Daley, 10 F.Supp.2d at 79. Thus constrained, the Secretary regulated the summer scup fishery in 1998 exclusively through enforcement of the overall coastwide summer quota. When this quota had been met, the Secretary closed Federal Waters to further scup fishing. During the 1998 summer period, Massachusetts continued to ignore the Federal and State Plan conservation measures and landed almost 900,000 pounds of scup.

On November 5, 1998 the States Commission informed the Secretary that Massachusetts had not complied with the State Plan 1997 and 1998 state-by-state summer quotas. Recognizing that Daley foreclosed enforcement of the Federal Plan state-by-state allocations, but believing that the corresponding State Plan quotas had been left undisturbed, the States Commission asked the Secretary, pursuant to the Cooperative Act, to enforce the summer quotas in the State Plan. By letter dated May 4, 1999, the States Commission advised that Massachusetts' summer scup fishery should be closed to compensate for its 1997 and 1998 overages totaling 1,725,719 pounds.

In June 1999 the States Commission forwarded to the Secretary a proposed emergency rule re-instituting state-by-state allocations to the Federal Plan for the 1999 summer scup fishery. Based on new data provided by Massachusetts, the States Commission's proposed rule increased Massachusetts' Federal Plan allocation of scup from 15% to

21.5883% of the 1999 summer quota to approximately 210,000 pounds.

On June 1, 1999 Massachusetts opposed the States Commission's request that the Secretary implement a moratorium on fishing in Massachusetts waters and denied that it had failed to comply with the State Plan. Massachusetts further opposed the States Commission's proposed rule and rejected its increased allocation as discriminatory under *Daley.* By letters dated June 10, 1999 the Secretary informed the States Commission and the Federal Council that *Daley* prevented the Secretary from imposing a moratorium on fishing in Massachusetts waters and from enacting the proposed emergency rule re-establishing state-by-state allocations.

Instead of adopting the emergency rule, the Secretary set a Federal Plan coastwide quota for the summer of 1999 at 987,055 pounds. Massachusetts announced it would take up to 500,000 pounds of scup in the summer of 1999 notwithstanding the Federal and the State Plans. New York and Rhode Island, citing the lack of Federal Plan state- by-state allocations and Massachusetts' unwillingness to abide by the State Plan, also disregarded the Federal Plan quota and allowed fishing in their respective State Waters up to the limits set forth in the States Commission's emergency rule. As a result, the 1999 Federal Plan summer quota was exceeded by over 300,000 pounds.

On January 28, 2000 the Fisheries Service published proposed specifications, setting the Federal Plan 2000 summer coastwide quota just under one million pounds, to be reduced to approximately 685,000 pounds by reason of the 1999 overages. On April 5, 2000 the States Commission issued another emergency rule which set a State Plan 2000 quota of approximately 1.3 million pounds for the summer, with a decreased "discard rate,"[21] and no assessment for previous overages. The States Commission informed the Secretary that this emergency regulation was the result of an agreement by all states "achieved after a lot of hard bargaining." The States Commission urged the Secretary not to implement the proposed Federal Plan 2000 coastwide quota, but rather to let the states "implement the emergency action as the only way to provide against a runaway summer fishery in 2000."

The Secretary did not consent to the States Commission's request. On May 24, 2000 the Secretary published final regulations establishing the Federal Plan 2000 coastwide summer quota at 685,628 pounds. Two months later, the Secretary closed the scup fishery to all federal permit

---

[21] "Discards" are fish that are caught which, for regulatory or other reasons, are not landed and sold, but instead are discarded, usually dead. A "discard rate" is a percentage reduction to a quota in order to take into account the diminution of the stock due to discards. A lower discard rate translates into a smaller reduction of the quota allowing for more fish to be caught, landed and sold.

holders because the Federal Plan 2000 summer quota had been exceeded. Nevertheless, the states permitted scup fishing in State Waters up to the limits of the quotas set forth in the States Plan 2000 emergency rule. As a result, the Federal Plan 2000 summer quota was exceeded by over 500,000 pounds.

On June 23, 2000, New York filed this action, later joined by Rhode Island, seeking invalidation of the Federal Plan 2000 coastwide summer quota as arbitrary and capricious.

III. Discussion

* * *

It is well documented that scup are overfished, and the parties do not dispute that fact. Under the Magnuson-Stevens Act the Secretary must act to counteract the inimical effects of such overfishing. The imposition of a coastwide quota is justified as a conservation measure which would allow for some fishing while rebuilding the fishery: "[t]he coastwide quota is a conservation measure, because it represents the maximum amount of fish that may be harvested while preventing overfishing and enabling this overfished resource to rebuild to its target level." This rationale alone is sufficient to defeat Plaintiffs' motion. Plaintiffs cannot show that the Federal Plan 2000 coastwide summer quota is without justification in the administrative record. Accordingly, this court must conclude that the regulation challenged here is not arbitrary and capricious.[22]

3. The Challenges to the Secretary's Decision Lack Merit

Even though the Federal Plan 2000 coastwide summer quota finds ample justification in the administrative record, Plaintiffs argue on several grounds that the Secretary's decision to promulgate a coastwide quota in lieu of state-by-state allocations is nonetheless arbitrary and capricious. These arguments-- that the state-by-state allocations were necessary to prevent overfishing, that there was adequate support in the administrative record for the state-by-state allocations, and that the Secretary had the power to enact the state-by-state allocations but failed to do so--bring to stark relief the lack of cooperative restraint and the absence of effective central leadership which together may well doom this troubled fishery to a tragedy of the commons.[23] Nonetheless, this

---

[22]   In addition, it is noted that neither Daley decision found coastwide quotas to be arbitrary and capricious.   See Daley 10 F.Supp.2d at 79; Daley 170 F.3d at 28.

[23]   See Garrett Hardin, The Tragedy of the Commons, 162 Science 1243 (1968). The tragedy ensues when "the rational but independent pursuit by each decisionmaker of its own self-interest leads to results that leave all decisionmakers worse off than they would have been had they been able to agree collectively on a different set of policies."

court is constrained to do no more here than determine whether or not the Secretary entirely ignored important aspects of the problem, explained its decision in terms contrary to the evidence before it, or relied on factors that Congress did not intend for it to consider. See Motor Vehicle Mfrs. Assn., 463 U.S. at 43, 103 S.Ct. 2856; see also Sierra Club, 772 F.2d at 1051. Plaintiffs have failed to show that the Secretary's promulgation of the Federal Plan 2000 coastwide summer quota was deficient under any of these tests.

a. The Secretary's Decision Entirely Ignores Important Aspects of the Problem

According to Plaintiffs, the Secretary entirely ignored the fact that a coastwide quota encourages a "derby-style"[24] summer fishing season and overfishing contrary to the conservation rationale of the Magnuson-Stevens Act. As early as July 21, 1999 the Fisheries Service asserted the need for new state-by-state allocations. The Secretary, through the Fisheries Service, explained the value of state-by-state allocations to the enforcement of the overall quota in the administrative record. Plaintiffs argue that the Fisheries Service's acknowledgment that state-by-state allocations are preferable to a coastwide quota renders the Secretary's failure to implement the former measures arbitrary and capricious. If the state-by-state allocations better conserve the fishery, Plaintiffs argue, any alternative is arbitrary and capricious as contrary to the Magnuson-Stevens Act's overarching conservation rationale.

This argument rests on the unfounded premise that state-by-state allocations are more effective than a coastwide quota. The first state-by-state allocations of the summer scup quota were ignored in 1997 and subsequently invalidated in 1998. In fact, there is no evidence in the administrative record that a state-by-state allocation of the summer scup quota has ever been effective. Furthermore, it is the states that have continued to allow fishing in State Waters after the Federal Plan's quota is reached and Federal Waters are closed; these states cannot now be heard to complain of a Federal Plan quota that does not guard against such overfishing, especially when the Secretary cannot enforce a Federal Plan quota in State Waters.

Moreover, even if Plaintiffs could show that federal state-by-state allocations are more effective, this fact alone would not warrant invalidation of the Secretary's action. See Marsh v. Ore. Natural Res. Council, 490 U.S. 360, 378, 109 S.Ct. 1851, 104 L.Ed.2d 377 (1989) ("When

---

Natural Res. Def. Council, Inc. v. Costle, 568 F.2d 1369, 1378 n. 19 (D.C.Cir.1977).

[24] "Derby-style" fishing is "a race to fish" in which fishermen are encouraged due to limitations on a fishery to attempt to catch as much of a species as quickly as possible in order to maximize their harvest before a season or fishery is closed.

specialists express conflicting views, an agency must have discretion to rely on the reasonable opinions of its own qualified experts, even if, as an original matter, a court might find contrary views more persuasive."). Plaintiffs' alternative to the coastwide quota only serves to call into doubt the wisdom of the Secretary's decision. Where a challenge to an agency action "fairly conceptualized, really centers on the wisdom of the agency's policy, rather than on whether it is a reasonable choice within a gap left open by Congress, the challenge must fail." *Chevron*, 467 U.S. at 866, 104 S.Ct. 2778. The Secretary's assessment of which fishery conservation and management measures are in the nation's best interest is "a classic example of a factual dispute the resolution of which implicates substantial agency expertise," *Marsh*, 490 U.S. at 376, 109 S.Ct. 1851, not to be second guessed by Plaintiffs or this court, *Chevron*, 467 U.S. at 866, 104 S.Ct. 2778 ("[F]ederal judges--who have no constituency--have a duty to respect legitimate policy choices made by those who do."). While the Secretary's lack of initiative in failing to re-establish state-by-state allocations may be lamentable, the Secretary did not ignore an aspect of the problem, and coastwide quota retains its presumption of validity based on the ample justification found in this administrative record.

b.　The Secretary's Explanation Why State-By-State Allocations Were Not Justified Is Contrary to the Evidence

Plaintiffs next argue that the Secretary's decision to replace the state-by-state allocations, explained in terms of *Daley,* was contrary to the justification for the allocations based on the overfishing in the summer of 1999 in the administrative record. This is not the case. The First Circuit required that the justification for any federal state-by-state allocation "must demonstrate that the state-by-state quotas incorporate the best available scientific information and serve a conservation purpose. The administrative record must also show that if the new state-by-state quota system has some discriminatory effect among the states, any discrimination is necessary to conserve the scup resource." The overfishing in the summer of 1999 alone does not provide justification for federal state-by-state allocations. As discussed above, the overfishing occurred in State Waters after the Federal Plan 2000 quota was reached and Federal Waters were closed to scup fishing. It is unclear that federal state-by-state allocations can effectively address this problem. Because the administrative record in May of 2000 did not clearly satisfy this standard, the Secretary's decision not to implement state- by-state quotas until the record could be supplemented was merely cautious, not erroneous.

Further, ample justification for the Secretary's decision to opt against state-by-state allocations once again appears in the administrative record. [Adm.Rec.] at 2403 (rejecting Council and States Commission proposals due to inflated quota and decreased discard rate); 1412 ("[E]ven if it was determined that emergency action was warranted, the time frame for developing proposed measures made it impossible for [Fisheries Service] to take any sort of action by May 1[, 2000].")) Plaintiffs fail to show that the Secretary relied upon an erroneous interpretation of *Daley,* or that state-by-state allocations were justified in the administrative record. There is, therefore, no basis for concluding that the decision to implement a coastwide quota was explained in terms contrary to the evidence before the Secretary.

c. The Secretary Relied on Factors Congress Did Not Intend For It To Consider

Finally, Plaintiffs contend that the Secretary was prompted to reject state- by-state allocations and adopt a coastwide quota by an improper desire to avoid further litigation, and which is a factor Congress did not intend for the Secretary to consider. The administrative record clearly reflects that the Secretary took great pains to conform his actions to the *Daley* decisions. There is no indication that apprehension of further litigation prompted agency action. In fact, the Secretary demonstrated a willingness to work toward future state-by-state allocations, despite the First Circuit's admonitions that they would be "subject to swift judicial review." *Daley,* 170 F.3d at 32. This court will not equate adherence to court mandates with an impermissible formulation of agency regulations based on an aversion to litigation.

Furthermore, the administrative record suggests that other permissible factors, rather than fear of litigation, motivated the Secretary's decision. The Magnuson-Stevens Act itself, with its power-sharing ideal, is a particularly blunt tool with which to battle the tragedy of the commons. See William Funk, Bargaining Toward the New Millennium: Regulatory Negotiation and the Subversion of the Public Interest, 46 Duke L.J. 1351, 1374-75 (1997) (arguing that negotiated rulemaking betrays the public interest and debases agency authority). The lack of coordinated effort between the States Commission, Federal Council and the Secretary under this power-sharing regime is apparent throughout the administrative record. Examples of agendas contrary to the Magnuson-Stevens Act's conservation mandate, decision making based solely on expediency, and political wrangling permeate the minutes of Federal Council and States Commission meetings. Finally, logistical difficulties plague the amendment process and delay promulgation of regulations and emergency measures. The administrative record reflects that the existence of these factors, rather than fear of future litigation, counseled against adopting the States Commission's emergency rule and limited the Secretary's ability to formulate a solution involving state-by-state allocations. "[The Fisheries Service] will have no option except to monitor the summer period coastwide quota * * *").

* * *

Notes and Questions

1. A 1998 stock assessment indicated that scup are overexploited and at a record low biomass; the spawning stock biomass is less than one-tenth of the biomass threshold, which was established in the FMP as the maximum biomass size observed by federal fisheries scientists. See NMFS, Final Specifications for 2000 Scup Fisheries, 65 Fed. Reg. 33486, 33489 (May 24, 2000). NMFS disapproved both the rebuilding schedule and the bycatch provision for scup in the Mid-Atlantic council's FMP amendment as insufficient under the Sustainable Fisheries Act. Id. Given the intense competition among the states for what remains of this stock, what are the prospects for its rebuilding to a level that can support MSY?

2. Note that in State of Connecticut v. Daley, the court distinguished the 1st Circuit's holding in Massachusetts v. Daley, discussed above in Evans, when it rejected Connecticut's challenge to the Secretary's failure to adopt a coast-wide quota for the summer flounder fishery. The State wanted the Secretary to replace the existing state-by-state quota system that gives Connecticut only a 2.25% share of the total allowable catch with one coast-wide quota that fishers in every state could compete for. 53 F.Supp.2d 147 (D.Conn. 1999), aff'd 204 F.3d 413 (2d Cir. 2000). The summer flounder fishery is managed under the same FMP as scup and black sea bass. See 50 C.F.R. Part 648. What would make the state-by-state quota fair in one fishery (summer flounder) and discriminatory in another (scup)?

D. CONSTITUTIONAL LIMITS ON STATE REGULATION

Two cases discussing constitutional limitations on state regulation -- Toomer v. Witsell, 334 U.S. 385 (1948) and Takahashi v. Fish and Game Commission, 334 U.S. 410 (1948) -- were both decided in 1948. The principal issue in both was the validity of state legislation that discriminated against nonresidents. *Toomer* concerned a challenge to two South Carolina statutes, the first of which imposed a state license fee upon fishermen who were nonresidents of South Carolina that was one hundred times greater than the fee for South Carolina residents. The alleged justification for the difference was the need to conserve the supply of shrimp in South Carolina waters, a justification not supported by the record. The United States Supreme Court held that there was no reasonable relationship between any potential harm to the South Carolina shrimp fishery associated with the fishing efforts of nonresidents in South Carolina waters and the large difference in the fees charged residents and nonresidents. The nonresident licensing fee statute violated the Privileges and Immunities Clause, Art. IV, sec. 2, U.S. Constitution.

Takahashi concerned a challenge to a California statute barring the issuance of fishing licenses to resident aliens who were Japanese. The Court held that this statute violated the Equal Protection Clause of the Fourteenth Amendment. According to the Court, the Equal Protection Clause guaranteed resident aliens the same right to livelihoods as state citizens.

A second issue in *Toomer* involved a South Carolina statute that required all boats licensed to trawl for shrimp in state waters to dock in a state port, unload the shrimp, and pack and stamp the catch before shipping or transporting the catch to another state. The Court found that the costs of nonresident shrimpers would be materially increased by requiring them to follow this procedure in South Carolina rather than unloading their catch in their out-of-state home ports. In addition, the effect of the statute was to divert to South Carolina ports work that might otherwise be done in the out-of-state ports. Such legislation, the Court held, imposes an improper burden on interstate commerce and thus violates the commerce clause of Art. I, § 8, U.S. Constitution.

Prior to the Supreme Court's decision in *Douglas*, states used the ownership theory to shield their treatment of out-of-state fishing vessels and companies from constitutional scrutiny. Since *Douglas*, states have had to craft their restrictions more carefully in order to enable their regulations to qualify as "evenhanded regulations" necessary for the conservation of natural resources. After a relatively quiet period in terms of constitutional claims against fishing regulations, new constitutional questions have begun to surface as states deal with dwindling fish stocks by, among other means, banning the use of particular fishing gears or fishing vessel type and/or size.

Notes and Questions

1. In Atlantic Prince, Ltd. v. Jorling, 710 F. Supp. 893 (E.D.N.Y. 1989), the court found that a New York law prohibiting squid trawlers greater than 90 feet in length from fishing in state waters violated the Commerce Clause by limiting non-resident fishing without promoting environmental protection. The local fishing fleet contained no vessels over 90 feet in length and there was evidence in the record to suggest that the State had intended to shield the smaller in-state fleet from competition. In Davrod Corp. v. Coates, 971 F.2d 778 (1st Cir. 1992), the Court of Appeals upheld a similar 90-foot limit, even though it excluded a Rhode Island freezer-trawler vessel by a margin of six inches, which had been squid fishing in the waters of Massachusetts' Nantucket Sound. The court reasoned, in part, that the presence of vessels of 90 feet in the Massachusetts' fleet that could theoretically be affected by the restriction, were they to switch from offshore lobster to squid fishing, negated any discriminatory or unreasonable burden on interstate commerce. In his dissent, Judge Coffin concluded that since there were no Massachusetts freezer-trawlers of any size, by banning squid freezer-trawlers from Massachusetts waters, the law manifestly discriminated against out-of-state interests, disproportionately

benefiting shore-based squid processors in Massachusetts. In his view, a remand was in order to determine whether less discriminatory alternatives to conserving squid, such as a shorter squid season, were available.

2.   In Ampro Fisheries, Inc. v. Yaskin, 606 A.2d 1099 (NJ 1992), the court upheld regulations prohibiting purse-seine fishing for menhaden for other than bait purposes closer than 1.2 nautical miles from the Atlantic coastline. The rule also prohibited menhaden fishing for industrial production purposes in the Delaware, Raritan, and Sandy Hook Bays, fishing which had previously been permitted. The rule was enacted after the one New Jersey-based menhaden processing plant owned by Seacoast Products closed.   The plaintiff, a Virginia commercial fishing company with plants in Virginia, North Carolina, and on the Gulf of Mexico, operated more than a dozen fishing vessels, nine of which were licensed by New Jersey for taking menhaden. The court found that Ampro's fishing rights were protected by the Commerce Clause but that the regulation did not discriminate against interstate commerce and was reasonable: "New Jersey should not be prevented from correcting in-shore problems simply because New Jersey fleets have withdrawn from the state." The court noted also that other states in the region had already restricted purse-seining close to shore. "Absent evidence of economic protectionism directed at out-of-state fishing fleets or clear abuse of authority, courts do well to recognize that the complex regulation of fisheries resources is within the primary jurisdiction of the councils established under state and federal law."

Should Commerce Clause analysis turn on whether any in-state commercial vessels are affected by the fishing restriction? Does New Jersey's closure of state waters to commercial menhaden fishing once the only in-state commercial menhaden company has closed or left the state suggest a discriminatory intent or effect? Can a state law be said to "regulate evenhandedly" when no state residents are constrained by it because none are engaged in the restricted fishery? What was New Jersey's purpose in enacting the ban? Is the State restricting the access of nonresidents to an interstate natural resource for the benefit of residents interested in menhaden only as prey for their recreational fisheries for bluefish, striped bass, and weakfish?

3.   If the Mid-Atlantic Fishery Management Council were to adopt the Atlantic States Marine Fisheries Commission's recommended interstate menhaden plan, and that plan affirmatively allowed purse seining for menhaden and allocated a portion of the total annual quota to vessels of that gear type, would the New Jersey law discussed in *AMPRO* be preempted by the FMP? See *Davrod,* supra note 1, for discussion of plaintiff's claim of preemption by federal squid regulations.

Several states have adopted state-wide bans on the use of certain types of fishing nets, often of the so-called "gillnet" variety. In many instances, these acts have been adopted by citizen initiatives, after campaigns by sport fishing groups. The state courts have had little trouble upholding the constitutionality of these laws under current constitutional doctrine.

4. In Lane v. Chiles, 698 So.2d 260 (Fla. 1997), the Supreme Court of Florida upheld the constitutionality of Article X, § 16, of the Florida Constitution, the "net ban" amendment adopted through the citizen initiative process. The court found that fishing was not a fundamental right and commercial fishermen were not a suspect class, thus the rational basis test rather than the strict scrutiny standard applied. The court found that the net ban bore a reasonable relationship to a permissible governmental objective and was not discriminatory or oppressive. Lane also claimed that the ban deprived him of his right to due process by denying a right to engage in a lawful occupation and his right to possess and enjoy private property, his nets, which had been taken without just compensation. The court rejected these claims as well, finding:

> [A] state regulation violates a protected liberty interest if it completely interferes with the right to engage in a lawful occupation. However, that is not the case with respect to Article X Section 16. The amendment satisfies the rational basis test in that it serves to accomplish a legitimate governmental objective. The amendment is designed to conserve marine resources and it attempts to meet that objective by a reasonable regulation on commercial fishing. While citizens of differing views could argue the wisdom of the amendment, it would be hard to say that the amendment is without any rational basis.

> Moreover, the amendment does not completely prevent the plaintiffs from engaging in their chosen occupation. Commercial fishermen can still fish with nets beyond the territorial limits set by the amendment and they can still fish with nets of a smaller size within the territorial limits. Article X, Section 16 is widely known as the "net ban amendment" but despite this reference the amendment does not actually ban all net fishing. It is more accurate to say the amendment restricts certain methods of net fishing.

> * * * Article X, Section 16 is a valid exercise of the police power and it operates uniformly to prohibit all persons from using certain kinds of fishing equipment in certain areas of the State waters. It does not set arbitrary restrictions that apply only to some persons or classes of persons and not others.

> Furthermore, the amendment does not prohibit all possible uses for the property and equipment in question. State statutes that limit fishing seasons, restrict permitted gear, and define certain zones for particular activities have been upheld. The State clearly has an interest in preserving and protecting the resources of the State, which are commonly owned by the people, and restrictions on the

harvest of marine fish does not constitute a taking of property from particular individuals.

5.   In Louisiana Seafood Management Council v. Louisiana Wildlife and Fisheries Commission, No. 97-137 (La. 1998), 1998 WL 251240, the court upheld the constitutionality of a commercial gillnet ban in the face of challenges based on the Takings Clause, the Commerce Clause, and the Equal Protection Clause. The Louisiana and Florida gillnet restrictions reflect a trend in state fisheries law in the Gulf of Mexico. See A. Renard, Will Florida's New Net Ban Sink or Swim?: Exploring the Constitutional Challenges to State Marine Fishery Restrictions, 10 J. Land Use & Envtl. L. 273, 290 (1995).

6.   In Carlson v. Alaska Commercial Fisheries Entry Commission, 919 P. 2d 1337 (Ak. 1996) (Carlson II), a class action suit by nonresident commercial fishers challenged Alaska's practice of charging nonresident commercial licensing and limited entry permit fees that were three times greater than the fees charged resident fishermen. The class claimed the fee differential violated the Commerce Clause and Privileges and Immunities Clause of the U.S. Constitution.

In *Carlson I*, the superior court agreed with the State that the fee was not unconstitutional.   When the class appealed, the Alaska Supreme Court reversed and remanded, imposing on the State the burden of persuasion on the Commerce and Privileges and Immunities Clauses issues.   The court left open the question of whether the Commerce Clause governed the case, noting that earlier U.S. Supreme Court cases had suggested that the Commerce Clause does not apply to fish until the fish are actually harvested. Carlson *I*, 798 P.2d at 1276 n. 4 (citing McCready v. Virginia, 94 U.S. 391, 396 (1876); Toomer v. Witsell, 334 U.S. 385, 394-395, reh'g denied, 335 U.S. 837 (1948)). Carlson II, 919 P.2d __ at n. 25.

The superior court held:

Commercial fishing is a sufficiently important activity to come within the purview of the Privileges and Immunities Clause, and license fees which discriminate against nonresidents are prima facie a violation of it * * *. Thus the questions here are whether the state has a substantial reason for the discrimination, and whether the 3:1 fee ratio bears a sufficiently close relationship to the goal.

Carlson I, 798 P.2d 1269, at 1274 (citations omitted).

On remand the superior court granted summary judgment to the State. On appeal a second time, the Alaska Supreme Court held that the fee differential did not raise a Commerce Clause issue but did raise an issue under the Privileges and Immunities Clause. It remanded the Privileges and Immunities Clause challenge to the superior court, requiring it to judge the differential fees using a method comparing the fees being paid by nonresidents with the expenditures of state revenues to which the nonresidents make no contribution (the costs to residents) rather than a pro rate formula.

Justice Rabinowitz dissented in *Carlson II*, arguing that the Supreme Court's reasoning in Oregon Waste Systems v. Dep't of Envtl. Quality, 511 U.S. 93 (1994), was applicable, given the very close relationship of the Privileges and Immunities and Commerce Clauses. Under that reasoning, Justice Rabinowitz argued, the State could not attribute a share of the State's oil revenues, which are the equivalent to general state tax revenues, to resident fishermen in calculating their contribution to commercial fisheries management. He noted that:

> The justification advanced by the State [the compensatory tax theory] in this case suffers from precisely the same defect alluded to in both *Armco* and *Oregon Waste Systems*. Specifically, a fisher from Oregon who purchases a commercial license in Alaska will no doubt be under an obligation to pay Oregon income taxes, a portion of which probably will have been used for conservation costs in that state. Accordingly, the fee discrepancy places the Oregon fisher, as a nonresident, at a competitive disadvantage. In other words, both the Alaska fisher and the Oregon fisher are obliged to contribute to a general tax fund from which their respective States may draw monies to support local fisheries, but only the Oregon fisher is being called upon to pay enhanced fees.

919 P.2d at 1349.

For a discussion of the *Carlson II* decision, see Oliver F.C. Murray, Note, *Carlson v. State*: Fair Fees for Fishing Far From Home, 4 Ocean & Coastal L.J. 157 (1998).

Chapter Seven

MARINE WILDLIFE AND BIODIVERSITY

SECTION 1. INTRODUCTION

This chapter explores the major U.S. laws aimed at preserving marine wildlife: the Marine Mammal Protection Act of 1972 and the Endangered Species Act of 1973. The evolution of these laws reflects both the development of more pragmatic approaches to marine wildlife conservation and a sober recognition of the irreversibility of the losses associated with any extinctions within the marine realm. Efforts to apply these lessons to the international community have brought U.S. marine wildlife policies into conflict with the nation's commitment to global trade. These tensions and recognitions are examined in the following materials.

SECTION 2. PROTECTED MARINE WILDLIFE

A. WHALES AND WHALING

In the 20th century, the United States policy with respect to whaling underwent a dramatic change. By the middle of the 19th century, the U.S. had become one of the world's largest high seas whaling nations, with its New England-based fleet of factory whaling ships, peaking in effort from 1820 to 1860, roaming the world's oceans in search of whaling grounds to replace the decimated whale populations of the Northwest Atlantic. See N. Philbrick, In the Heart of the Sea: The Tragedy of the Whaleship Essex (2000). As whale populations around the globe began to disappear, some whaling nations including the U.S. adopted in 1931 a largely ineffective international agreement to prevent wasteful whaling practices and promote their full utilization. See Michael J. Bean and Melanie J. Rowland, The Evolution of National Wildlife Law 478-79 (3rd ed. 1997).

Attempts to strengthen the agreement failed, but World War II brought a temporary cessation to whaling. After the war, as the major whaling fleets were resuming their activities, the U.S. joined other major whaling nations in signing the International Convention for the Regulation of Whaling in 1946. The Convention sought both to promote the increase of whale populations and the "orderly development of the whaling industry." It established the International Whaling Commission (IWC) as the body through which the member states would establish regulations on seasons, catches as methods of whaling, effective in all waters in which whales are found. Id. at 479. Regulations were adopted through amendments to the Schedule, an appendix of the Convention. A three-fourths majority of the members is necessary to amend the Schedule, but member nations, however, may opt out of an amendment by filing an objection to it within 90 days of the vote. Due to this provision and the ineffectiveness of the control measures adopted, large numbers of various whale populations were killed by whaling vessels, leading to a succession of bans on the commercial take of particular species, including the blue and humpback whales in 1966, of fin and sei whales of the North Pacific in 1975, and other species in 1976. Id. at 480.

By the early 1970s, the U.S. was promoting the idea of a global moratorium on all commercial whaling. While this campaign was underway, it sought a mechanism to use its economic power to force whaling nations to comply with the IWC's quotas through the threat of import restrictions. In 1971, Congress enacted the Pelly Amendment to the Fishermen's Protection Act of 1967, 22 U.S.C. §1978(a). Once the IWC adopted a moratorium on all commercial whaling in 1982, the U.S. also used this legislation to compel nations to withdraw their objections to the moratorium. The Executive Branch and the Congress, however, held different views on the suitability of the embargo as a tool for marine conservation.

JAPAN WHALING ASSOC. v. AMERICAN CETACEAN SOCIETY
United States Supreme Court, 1986
478 U.S. 221

JUSTICE **WHITE:**

For centuries, men have hunted whales in order to obtain both food and oil, which, in turn, can be processed into a myriad of other products. Although at one time a harrowing and perilous profession, modern technological innovations have transformed whaling into a routine form of commercial fishing, and have allowed for a multifold increase in whale harvests worldwide.

Based on concern over the effects of excessive whaling, 15 nations formed the International Convention for the Regulation of Whaling (ICRW), Dec. 2, 1946, 62 Stat. 1716, T.I.A.S. No. 1849 (entered into force Nov. 10, 1948). The ICRW was designed to "provide for the proper conservation of whale stocks and thus make possible the orderly development of the whaling industry," id., at 1717, and today serves as the principal international mechanism for promoting the conservation and development of whale populations.   See generally Smith, The International Whaling Commission: An Analysis of the Past and Reflections on the Future, 16 Nat. Resources Law. 543 (1984).   The United States was a founding member of the ICRW; Japan joined in 1951.

To achieve its purposes, the ICRW included a Schedule which, *inter alia*, regulates harvesting practices and sets harvest limits for various whale species.   In addition, the ICRW established the International Whaling Commission (IWC), which implements portions of the Convention and is authorized to amend the Schedule and set new harvest quotas. The quotas are binding on IWC members if accepted by a three-fourths' majority vote.   Under the terms of the Convention, however, the IWC has no power to impose sanctions for quota violations.   Moreover, any member country may file a timely objection to an IWC amendment of the Schedule and thereby exempt itself from any obligation to comply with the limit unless and until the objection is withdrawn.   All nonobjecting countries remain bound by the amendment.

Because of the IWC's inability to enforce its own quota and in an effort to promote enforcement of quotas set by other international fishery conservation programs, Congress passed the Pelly Amendment to the Fishermen's Protective Act of 1967. 22 U.S.C. § 1978. Principally intended to preserve and protect North American Atlantic salmon from depletion by Danish fishermen in violation of the ban imposed by the International Convention for the Northwest Atlantic Fisheries, the Amendment protected whales as well.   The Amendment directs the Secretary of Commerce to certify to the President if "nationals of a foreign country, directly or indirectly, are conducting fishing operations in a manner or under circumstances which diminish the effectiveness of an international fishery conservation program * * *" 22 U.S.C. § 1978(a)(1).   Upon certification, the President, in his discretion, may then direct the Secretary of the Treasury to prohibit the importation of fish products from the certified nation. § 1978(a)(4).   The President may also decline to impose any sanctions or import prohibitions.

After enactment of the Pelly Amendment, the Secretary of Commerce five times certified different nations to the President as engaging in fishing operations which "diminish[ed] the effectiveness" of IWC quotas. None of the certifications resulted in the imposition of sanctions by the President.   After each certification, however, the President was able to use the threat of discretionary sanctions to obtain commitments of future compliance from the offending nations.

Although "the Pelly Amendment * * * served the useful function of quietly persuading nations to adhere to the decisions of international fishery conservation bodies," H.R.Rep. No. 95-1029, supra, at 9, U.S.Code Cong. & Admin.News 1978, pp. 1768, 1773, Congress grew impatient with the Executive's delay in making certification decisions and refusal to impose sanctions.   As a result, Congress passed the Packwood Amendment to the Magnuson Fishery Conservation and Management Act, 16 U.S.C. § 1801 et seq. (1982 ed. and Supp. III). This Amendment requires the Secretary of Commerce to "periodically monitor the activities of foreign nationals that may affect [international fishery conservation programs]," 22 U.S.C. § 1978(a)(3)(A); "promptly investigate any activity by foreign nationals that, in the opinion of the Secretary, may be cause for certification * * *," § 1978(a)(3)(B); and "promptly conclude; and reach a decision with respect to; [that] investigation." § 1978(a)(3)(C).

To rectify the past failure of the President to impose the sanctions authorized--but not required--under the Pelly Amendment, the Packwood Amendment removes this element of discretion and mandates the imposition of economic sanctions against offending nations. Under the Amendment, if the Secretary of Commerce certifies that "nationals of a foreign country, directly or indirectly, are conducting fishing operations or engaging in trade or taking which diminishes the effectiveness of the International Convention for the Regulation of Whaling," 16 U.S.C. § 1821(e)(2)(A)(i), the Secretary of State must reduce, by at least 50%, the offending nation's fishery allocation within the United States' fishery conservation zone. Although the Amendment requires the imposition of sanctions when the Secretary of Commerce certifies a nation, it did not alter the initial certification process, except for requiring expedition.   It was also provided that a certificate under the Packwood Amendment also serves as a certification for the purposes of the Pelly Amendment.

In 1981, the IWC established a zero quota for the Western Division stock of Northern Pacific sperm whales.   The next year, the IWC ordered a 5- year moratorium on commercial whaling to begin with the 1985-1986 whaling season and last until 1990. In 1982, the IWC acted to grant Japan's request for a 2-year respite--for the 1982-1983 and 1983-1984 seasons--from the IWC's earlier decision banning sperm whaling.

Because Japan filed timely objections to both the IWC's 1981 zero quota for Northern Pacific sperm whales and 1982 commercial whaling moratorium, under the terms of the ICRW, it was not bound to comply with either limitation. Nonetheless, as the 1984-1985 whaling season grew near, it was apparently recognized that under either the Pelly or Packwood Amendment, the United States could impose economic sanctions if Japan continued to exceed these whaling quotas.

Following extensive negotiations, on November 13, 1984, Japan and the United States concluded an executive agreement through an exchange of letters between the Charge d'Affaires of Japan and the Secretary of Commerce. Subject to implementation requirements, Japan pledged to adhere to certain harvest limits and to cease commercial whaling by 1988. In return and after consulting with the United States Commissioner to the IWC, the Secretary determined that the short-term continuance of a specified level of limited whaling by Japan, coupled with its promise to discontinue all commercial whaling by 1988, "would not diminish the effectiveness of the International Convention for the Regulation of Whaling, 1946, or its conservation program." Accordingly, the Secretary informed Japan that, so long as Japan complied with its pledges, the United States would not certify Japan under either Amendment.

Several days before consummation of the executive agreement, several wildlife conservation groups filed suit in District Court seeking a writ of mandamus compelling the Secretary of Commerce to certify Japan.[1] Because in its view any taking of whales in excess of the IWC quotas diminishes the effectiveness of the ICRW, the District Court granted summary judgment for respondents and ordered the Secretary of Commerce immediately to certify to the President that Japan was in violation of the IWC sperm whale quota. Thereafter, Japan's Minister for Foreign Affairs informed the Secretary of Commerce that Japan would perform the second condition of the agreement--withdrawal of its objection to the IWC moratorium--provided that the United States obtained reversal of the District Court's order.

A divided Court of Appeals affirmed. Recognizing that the Pelly and Packwood-Magnuson Amendments did not define the specific activities which would "diminish the effectiveness" of the ICRW, the court looked to the Amendments' legislative history and concluded, as had the District Court, that the taking by Japanese nationals of whales in excess of quota automatically called for certification by the Secretary. We granted certiorari, and now reverse.

* * *

The issue before us is whether, in the circumstances of these cases,

---

[1] In addition, plaintiffs also requested (1) a declaratory judgment that the Secretary's failure to certify violated both the Pelly and Packwood Amendments, because any whaling activities in excess of IWC quotas necessarily "diminishes the effectiveness" of the ICRW; and (2) a permanent injunction prohibiting any executive agreement which would violate the certification and sanction requirements of the Amendments. 604 F.Supp. 1398, 1401 (DC 1985). The Japan Whaling Association and Japan Fishing Association (Japanese petitioners), trade groups representing private Japanese interests, were allowed to intervene.

either the Pelly or Packwood Amendment required the Secretary to certify Japan for refusing to abide by the IWC whaling quotas. We have concluded that certification was not necessary and hence reject the Court of Appeals' holding and respondents' submission that certification is mandatory whenever a country exceeds its allowable take under the ICRW Schedule.

Under the Packwood Amendment, certification is neither permitted nor required until the Secretary makes a determination that nationals of a foreign country "are conducting fishing operations or engaging in trade or taking which diminishes the effectiveness" of the ICRW. It is clear that the Secretary must promptly make the certification decision, but the statute does not define the words "diminish the effectiveness of" or specify the factors that the Secretary should consider in making the decision entrusted to him alone. Specifically, it does not state that certification must be forthcoming whenever a country does not abide by IWC Schedules, and the Secretary did not understand or interpret the language of the Amendment to require him to do so. Had Congress intended otherwise, it would have been a simple matter to say that the Secretary must certify deliberate taking of whales in excess of IWC limits.

Here, as the Convention permitted it to do, Japan had filed its objection to the IWC harvest limits and to the moratorium to begin with the 1985-1986 season. It was accordingly not in breach of its obligations under the Convention in continuing to take whales, for it was part of the scheme of the Convention to permit nations to opt out of Schedules that were adopted over its objections. In these circumstances, the Secretary, after consultation with the United States Commissioner to the IWC and review of the IWC Scientific Committee opinions, determined that it would better serve the conservation ends of the Convention to accept Japan's pledge to limit its harvest of sperm whales for four years and to cease all commercial whaling in 1988, rather than to impose sanctions and risk continued whaling by the Japanese. In any event, the Secretary made the determination assigned to him by the Packwood Amendment and concluded that the limited taking of whales in the 1984 and 1985 coastal seasons would not diminish the effectiveness of the ICRW or its conservation program, and that he would not make the certification that he would otherwise be empowered to make.

The Secretary, of course, may not act contrary to the will of Congress when exercised within the bounds of the Constitution. If Congress has directly spoken to the precise issue in question, if the intent of Congress is clear, that is the end of the matter. Chevron U.S.A. Inc. v. Natural Resources Defense Council, Inc., 467 U.S. 837, 843 (1984). But as the courts below and respondents concede, the statutory language itself contains no direction to the Secretary automatically and regardless of the circumstances to certify a nation that fails to conform to the IWC whaling Schedule. The language of the Pelly and Packwood Amendments might reasonably be construed in this manner, but the Secretary's construction that there are circumstances in which certification may be withheld, despite departures from the Schedules and without violating his duty, is also a reasonable construction of the language used in both Amendments. We do not understand the Secretary to be urging that he has *carte blanche* discretion to ignore and do nothing about whaling in excess of IWC Schedules. He does not argue, for example, that he could refuse to certify for any reason not connected with the aims and conservation goals of the Convention, or refuse to certify deliberate flouting of schedules by members who have failed to object to a particular schedule. But insofar as the plain language of the Amendments is concerned, the Secretary is not forbidden to refuse to certify for the reasons given in these cases. Furthermore, if a statute is silent or ambiguous with respect to the question at issue, our longstanding practice is to defer to the "executive department's construction of a statutory scheme it is entrusted to administer," *Chevron,* supra, 467 U.S., at 844, unless the legislative history of the enactment shows with sufficient clarity that the agency construction is contrary to the will of Congress.

IV

Contrary to the Court of Appeals and respondents' views, we find nothing in the legislative history of either Amendment that addresses the nature of the Secretary's duty and requires him to certify every departure from the IWC's scheduled limits on whaling. The Pelly Amendment was introduced in 1971 to protect Atlantic salmon from possible extinction caused by overfishing in disregard of established salmon quotas. Under the International Convention for the Northwest Atlantic Fisheries (ICNAF), zero harvest quotas had been established in 1969 to regulate and control high seas salmon fishing. Denmark, Germany, and Norway, members of the ICNAF, exercised their right to file timely objections to the quotas, however, and thus were exempt from their limitations. Although respondents are correct that Congress enacted the Pelly Amendment primarily as a means to enforce those international fishing restrictions against these three countries, particularly Denmark, they fail to establish that the Amendment requires automatic certification of every nation whose fishing operations exceed international conservation quotas.

Both the Senate and House Committee Reports detail the "conservation nightmare" resulting from Denmark's failure to recognize the ICNAF quota; a position which "effectively nullified" the ban on high seas harvesting of Atlantic salmon. In addition, Danish operations were seen as leading to the "eventual destruction of this valuable sports fish," a matter of "critical concern" to both the Senate and House Committees. There is no question but that both Committees viewed Denmark's excessive fishing operations as "diminish [ing] the effectiveness" of the ICNAF quotas, and envisioned that the Secretary would certify that nation under the Pelly Amendment. The Committee Reports, however, do not support the view that the Secretary must certify every nation that exceeds every international conservation quota.

* * *

Subsequent amendment of the Pelly Amendment in 1978 further demonstrates that Congress used the phrase, "diminish the effectiveness," to give the Secretary a range of certification discretion. The 1978 legislation expanded coverage of the Pelly Amendment "to authorize the President to embargo wildlife products from countries where nationals have acted in a manner which, directly or indirectly, diminishes the effectiveness of any international program for the conservation of endangered or threatened species." H.R.Rep. No. 95-1029, p. 8 (1978), U.S.Code Cong. & Admin.News 1978, p. 1772. This extension was premised on the success realized by the United States in using the Amendment to convince other nations to adhere to IWC quotas, thus preserving the world's whale stocks. Id., at 9.

* * *

It may be that in the legislative history of these Amendments there are scattered statements hinting at the *per se* rule advocated by respondents, but read as a whole, we are quite unconvinced that this history clearly indicates, contrary to what we and the Secretary have concluded is a permissible reading of the statute, that all departures from IWC Schedules, regardless of the circumstances, call for immediate certification.

V

We conclude that the Secretary's construction of the statutes neither contradicted the language of either Amendment, nor frustrated congressional intent. In enacting these Amendments, Congress' primary goal was to protect and conserve whales and other endangered species. The Secretary furthered this objective by entering into the agreement with Japan, calling for that nation's acceptance of the worldwide moratorium on commercial whaling and the withdrawal of its objection to the IWC zero sperm whale quota, in exchange for a transition period of limited additional whaling. Given the lack of any express direction to the Secretary that he must certify a nation whose whale harvest exceeds an IWC quota, the Secretary reasonably could conclude, as he has, that, "a cessation of all Japanese commercial whaling activities would contribute more to the effectiveness of the IWC and its conservation program than any other single development."

We conclude, therefore, that the Secretary's decision to secure the certainty of Japan's future compliance with the IWC's program through the 1984 executive agreement, rather than rely on the possibility that certification and imposition of economic sanctions would produce the same or better result, is a reasonable construction of the Pelly and Packwood Amendments. Congress granted the Secretary the authority to determine whether a foreign nation's whaling in excess of quotas diminishes the effectiveness of the IWC, and we find no reason to impose a mandatory obligation upon the Secretary to certify that every quota violation necessarily fails that standard. Accordingly, the judgment of the Court of Appeals is

Reversed.

*JUSTICE **MARSHALL**, with whom JUSTICE **BRENNAN**, JUSTICE **BLACKMUN**, and JUSTICE **REHNQUIST** join, dissenting.*

Since 1971, Congress has sought to lead the world, through the repeated exercise of its power over foreign commerce, in preventing the extermination of whales and other threatened species of marine animals. I deeply regret that it will now have to act again before the Executive Branch will finally be compelled to obey the law. I believe that the Court has misunderstood the question posed by the case before us, and has reached an erroneous conclusion on a matter of intense worldwide concern. I therefore dissent.

Congress began its efforts with the Pelly Amendment, which directs that "[w]hen the Secretary of Commerce determines that nationals of a foreign country, directly or indirectly, are conducting fishing operations in a manner or under circumstances which diminish the effectiveness of an international fishery conservation program, the Secretary of Commerce shall certify such fact to the President." 22 U.S.C. § 1978(a)(1). That Amendment, although apparently mandatory in its certification scheme, did not provide for a mandatory response from the President once the certification was made. Rather, the President was empowered, in his discretion, to impose sanctions on the certified nations or not to act at all. § 1978(a)(4).

This executive latitude in enforcement proved unsatisfactory. Between 1971 and 1978, every time that a nation exceeded international whaling quotas--on five occasions--the Secretary of Commerce duly certified to the President that the trespassing nation had exceeded whaling quotas set by the International Whaling Commission and had thus diminished the effectiveness of the conservation program. Although the offending nations had promised immediate compliance, the Secretary apparently believed that he was obliged to certify the past violations. Yet on the basis of those assurances, the President each time exercised his option under the Pelly Amendment to impose no sanctions on the violators. Id., at 193, 195.

Unhappy with the President's failure to sanction clear violations of international whaling agreements, Congress responded in 1979 with the Packwood Amendment. That Amendment provides that if the Secretary of Commerce certifies that a country is diminishing the effectiveness of the International Convention for the Regulation of Whaling, the Secretary of State must reduce the fishing allocation of the offending nation by at least 50 percent. 16 U.S.C. § 1821(e)(2). It also provides certain time limits within which the Executive Branch must act in imposing the mandatory sanctions. The automatic imposition of sanctions, it seemed, would improve the effectiveness of the Pelly Amendment by providing a definite consequence for any nation disregarding whaling limits.

In 1984, the Secretary of Commerce for the first time declined to certify a case of intentional whaling in excess of established quotas. Rather than calling into play the Packwood Amendment's mandatory sanctions by certifying to the President Japan's persistence in conducting whaling operations, Secretary Baldrige set about to negotiate with Japan, using his power of certification under domestic law to obtain certain promises of reduced violations in future years. In the resulting compromise, the Secretary agreed not to certify Japan, provided that Japan would promise to reduce its whaling until 1988 and then withdraw its objection to the international whaling quotas. Arguing that the Secretary had no discretion to withhold certification, respondents sought review of the Secretary's action in federal court. Both the District Court, and the Court of Appeals, found that Congress had not empowered the Secretary to decline to certify a clear violation of International Whaling Commission (IWC) quotas, and ordered the Secretary to make the statutory certification. This Court now renders illusory the mandatory language of the statutory scheme, and finds permissible exactly the result that Congress sought to prevent in the Packwood Amendment: executive compromise of a national policy of whale conservation.

I

* * *

The Secretary would rewrite the law. Congress removed from the Executive Branch any power over penalties when it passed the Packwood Amendment. Indeed, the Secretary's compromise in these cases is precisely the type of action, previously taken by the President, that led Congress to enact the mandatory sanctions of the Packwood Amendment: in 1978, five nations had been found to have exceeded quotas, but the President had withheld sanctions upon the promise of future compliance with international norms. Here, the future "compliance" is even less satisfactory than that exacted in the past instances: instead of immediate compliance, the Secretary has settled for continued violations until 1988. And in 1988 all that Japan has promised is to withdraw its formal objection to the IWC moratorium; I see no indication that Japan has pledged to "cease commercial whaling by 1988," or to "dismantle its commercial whaling industry." The important question here, however, is not whether the Secretary's choice of sanctions was wise or effective, but whether it was authorized. The Court does not deny that Congress intended the consequences of actions diminishing the effectiveness of a whaling ban to be governed exclusively by the sanctions enumerated in the Packwood Amendment, with the optional addition of those provided in the Pelly Amendment. Thus, when the Secretary's action here, well intentioned or no, is seen for what it really is--a substitute of his judgment for Congress' on the issue of how best to respond to a foreign nation's intentional past violation of quotas--there can be no question but that the Secretary has flouted the express will of Congress and exceeded his own authority. On that basis alone, I would affirm the judgment of the Court of Appeals.

* * *

I would affirm the judgment below on the ground that the Secretary has exceeded his authority by using his power of certification, not as a means for identifying serious whaling violations, but as a means for evading the constraints of the Packwood Amendment. Even focusing, as the Court does, upon the distinct question whether the statute prevents the Secretary from determining that the effectiveness of a conservation program is not diminished by a substantial transgression of whaling quotas, I find the Court's conclusion utterly unsupported. I am troubled that this Court is empowering an officer of the Executive Branch, sworn to uphold and defend the laws of the United States, to ignore Congress' pointed response to a question long pondered: "whether Leviathan can long endure so wide a chase, and so remorseless a havoc; whether he must not at last be exterminated from the waters, and the last whale, like the last man, smoke his last pipe, and then himself evaporate in the final puff." H. Melville, Moby Dick 436 (Signet ed. 1961).

Notes and Questions

1. How do you explain the difference in the two opinions? Do they reflect differences in philosophy concerning statutory interpretation or in the degree of deference the court should give the Executive Branch in the area of foreign affairs?

2. Are trade sanctions the right approach to international conservation? If not, what course should the U.S. pursue to promote

the conservation and protection of marine wildlife? See Section 3., infra.

3. A variety of U.S. laws now provides the basis for protection of whales under U.S. jurisdiction and on the high seas. The principal statutes providing protection within U.S. waters are the Endangered Species Act, 16 U.S.C. §§1531 et seq., and the Marine Mammal Protection Act, 16 U.S.C. §§1361 et seq. Two national marine sanctuaries have been created to provide additional protection to whales. The Hawaiian Islands Humpback Whale Sanctuary protects Pacific humpback whales while in waters around Hawaii during their winter breeding season. The Stellwagen Bank National Marine Sanctuary Act created a protected area off the coast of Massachusetts that serves as an important summer feeding ground for humpback, North Atlantic right, and other species of whales.

4. The United States used the Pelly Amendment in the 1980s to threaten sanctions against countries that hunt for whales despite the IWC moratorium on commercial whaling. See G.S. Martin, Jr. and J.W. Brennan, Enforcing the International Convention for the Regulation of Whaling: The Pelly and Packwood-Magnuson Amendments, 17 Denv. J. Int'l L.& Pol'y 293 (1989). By 2001, Japan was killing 440 minke whales in Antarctic waters under the rubric of scientific research. Although a majority of IWC members continues to pass resolutions criticizing Japan's research program as unjustified, the IWC has no power to prohibit it under the terms of the Convention, and the U.S. perennially faces the question whether to invoke sanctions. In August, 2000, the U.S. cancelled a bilateral fisheries consultation meeting with Japan in protest of Japan's expansion of its whaling to other species. When Norway resumed commercial whaling in the late 1990s, the pressure on the IWC to lift the moratorium increased, and by 2001, Japan had recruited several countries to join or rejoin the IWC and vote with the pro-whaling members. A three-fourths majority is required to amend the Schedule and lift the moratorium. See W. Aron, W. Burke, and M. Freeman, The Whaling Issue, 24 Marine Policy 179 (2000).

5. The conflicting policies of preserving Native cultures and communities and marine mammal populations were brought sharply into focus in 1976 when the IWC voted to ban all whale hunting, including that for subsistence purposes, on bowhead whales. In Adams v. Vance, 570 F.2d 950 (D.C. Cir. 1978), the Court of Appeals held that the native Alaskan plaintiffs had not met the extraordinary burden of proof necessary to support an injunction ordering the U.S. to object to the IWC's vote, given the significant intrusion into foreign affairs such an injunction would represent. In Metcalf v. Daley, 214 F.3d 1135 (9th Cir. 2000), the Ninth Circuit held that the Commerce Secretary had violated the National Environmental Policy Act (NEPA) in preparing an environmental assessment on the resumption of whale hunting by the

Makah Tribe after substantial resources had already been committed to support the tribe's proposal for a subsistence hunting quota on gray whales at the IWC. See R. Fowles, Note, Metcalf v. Daley: Consideration of the Significant Impact on the Gray Whale Population in an Environmental Assessment, 6 Ocean & Coastal L.J. 397 (2001). See also M.L. Chiropolos, Inupiat Subsistence and the Bowhead Whale: Can Indigenous Hunting Cultures Coexist With Endangered Animal Species, 5 Colo. J. Int'l Envtl. L. & Pol'y 213 (1994). Japan has requested that the IWC consider whaling carried out by its coastal villages to be for subsistence. See Aron et al., supra.

B. THE MARINE MAMMAL PROTECTION ACT

In 1972, Congress responded to urgent calls for action from members of the scientific and conservation communities who believed the mammals inhabiting the world's oceans were in jeopardy. By enacting the Marine Mammal Protection Act, it established one of the first comprehensive federal programs to address an entire class of wildlife. The law Congress passed reflected a diverse array of viewpoints on the significance of marine mammals and their role in the environment. During the legislative debates, there were those who considered marine mammals a natural resource that through careful management can be utilized in a sustained manner for food and other commercial uses. Others believed these animals should be put off-limits to exploitation because of their intelligence, their complex social interactions, or their beauty. Congress responded to these conflicting views with a statute that was so complex and replete with ambiguities that it would take at least twenty years, extensive litigation, and several amendments to resolve them. Over this period, the goals of the Act would expand beyond controlling domestic activities affecting marine mammals to exerting an influence on practices throughout the world.

A philosophy of preservation is reflected in the Act's provision for a permanent moratorium on the taking and importation of marine mammals in the United States. 16 U.S.C. § 1371(a). The resource management philosophy is found in the Act's inclusion of certain exceptions to the moratorium and in the authority of the Secretaries of Commerce (for whales, porpoises, and seals, but not walruses) and of Interior (for all other marine mammals), to permit or otherwise authorize takings of marine mammals that will not be to the disadvantage of the species or population stock in question. 16 U.S.C. § 1371(a)(1).

While the statutory definition of "taking" covers a wide range of activities affecting marine mammals, from hunting to harassment, 16 U.S.C. § 1362(13), the statutory exceptions and exemption also cover a broad range. Id. at § 1371(a). The exceptions allows, under certain circumstances, takings for scientific research, public display, Alaskan

Native subsistence hunting, and injury and death incidental to commercial fishing and other ocean uses.   For two decades, implementation of the Act reflected the uneasy compromise between preservation and management.   When Congress, in the 1994 amendments, adopted a regulatory regime for incidental takes in all non-tuna commercial fisheries, the resource management philosophy appeared to become the dominant paradigm.

For a discussion of the legislative history of the 1972 Marine Mammal Protection Act, see S. Gaines and D. Schmidt, Wildlife Population Management Under the Marine Mammal Protection Act of 1972, 6 ELR 50096, 50103-08 (1976).   The 1994 amendments are described in N. Young and S. Iudicello, Blueprint for Whale Conservation: Implementing the Marine Mammal Protection Act, 3 Ocean & Coastal L. J. 149, 167-202 (1997).   A detailed and comprehensive examination of the MMPA is presented in Michael J. Bean and Melanie J. Rowland, The Evolution of National Wildlife Law 109-149 (3rd ed. 1997).

(1). The Moratorium on Taking and Statutory Exceptions

(a.) Basic Policies of the Act

16 U.S.C. § 1361. Congressional findings and declaration of policy

The Congress finds that--

(1) certain species and population stocks of marine mammals are, or may be, in danger of extinction or depletion as a result of man's activities;

(2) such species and population stocks should not be permitted to diminish beyond the point at which they cease to be a significant functioning element in the ecosystem of which they are a part, and, consistent with this major objective, they should not be permitted to diminish below their optimum sustainable population. Further measures should be immediately taken to replenish any species or population stock which has already diminished below that population. In particular, efforts should be made to protect essential habitats, including the rookeries, mating grounds, and areas of similar significance for each species of marine mammal from the adverse effect of man's actions;

(3) there is inadequate knowledge of the ecology and population dynamics of such marine mammals and of the factors which bear upon their ability to reproduce themselves successfully;

(4) negotiations should be undertaken immediately to encourage

the development of international arrangements for research on, and conservation of, all marine mammals;

(5)   marine mammals and marine mammal products either--

(A) move in interstate commerce, or

(B) affect the balance of marine ecosystems in a manner which is important to other animals and animal products which move in interstate commerce, and that the protection and conservation of marine mammals and their habitats is therefore necessary to insure the continuing availability of those products which move in interstate commerce; and

(6)   marine mammals have proven themselves to be resources of great international significance, esthetic and recreational as well as economic, and it is the sense of the Congress that they should be protected and encouraged to develop to the greatest extent feasible commensurate with sound policies of resource management and that the primary objective of their management should be to maintain the health and stability of the marine ecosystem. Whenever consistent with this primary objective, it should be the goal to obtain an optimum sustainable population keeping in mind the carrying capacity of the habitat.

* * *

(b.) *Definition of Taking*

UNITED STATES v. HAYASHI
United States Court of Appeals, Ninth Circuit, 1993
5 F.3d 1278

REINHARDT, CIRCUIT JUDGE:

David Hayashi appeals his conviction of taking a marine mammal in violation of 16 U.S.C. § 1372(a)(2)(A). We hold that the Marine Mammal Protection Act (MMPA) and the regulations implementing the act do not make it a crime to take reasonable steps to deter porpoises from eating fish or bait off a fisherman's line. Therefore, we conclude that insufficient evidence supported Hayashi's conviction, and we reverse.

I

On the morning of January 24, 1991, Hayashi, a part-time commercial fisherman, and his son were fishing for Ahi off the coast of Waianae, Hawaii. A group of four porpoises began to eat the tuna off

Hayashi's and his son's lines. Hoping the impact of the bullets hitting the water would scare the porpoises away from their catch, Hayashi fired two rifle shots into the water behind the porpoises. The shots did not hit the porpoises. When the Hayashis reeled in their lines, they discovered that a porpoise had in fact eaten a part of at least one of the tuna.

A state enforcement officer reported to the National Marine Fisheries Service (NMFS) that occupants of Hayashi's vessel had fired at dolphins. In February 1991, NMFS agents interviewed Hayashi and his son, taking written statements from each. An April 22, 1991 information charged Hayashi with knowingly taking a marine mammal in violation of the MMPA, 16 U.S.C. § 1372(a)(2)(A).

In July 1991, after denying Hayashi's motion to dismiss the information for unconstitutional vagueness, the magistrate judge tried and convicted Hayashi on stipulated facts. The submitted facts consisted of the Hayashis' statements, and an NMFS agent's report and notes on the interviews of the father and son. Hayashi appealed to the district court, [and] * * * without oral argument, the district court affirmed.

II

The MMPA declares it unlawful for any person to "take" a marine mammal in United States waters. See 16 U.S.C. § 1372(a)(2)(A). "The term 'take' means to harass, hunt, capture, or kill, or attempt to harass, hunt, capture, or kill any marine mammal." 16 U.S.C. § 1362(13). The MMPA prescribes both civil and criminal penalties, but the latter apply only to persons who "knowingly" violate any provision of the act. See 16 U.S.C. § 1375(b).

The government agrees that the only definition of "take" with possible application to Hayashi is "to harass" or "attempt to harass." The statute itself fails to define "harass." Various agencies of the federal government have promulgated regulations implementing the MMPA. The regulations applicable to porpoises, issued by the NMFS, do not define "harass" but further define "take" as including:

> The collection of dead animals, or parts thereof; the restraint or detention of a marine mammal, no matter how temporary; tagging a marine mammal; the negligent or intentional operation of an aircraft or vessel, or the doing of any other negligent or intentional act which results in disturbing or molesting a marine mammal; and feeding or attempting to feed a marine mammal in the wild.

50 C.F.R. § 216.3. The "disturbing or molesting" example is the only regulatory definition potentially applicable to Hayashi's act of firing a rifle into the water behind a group of porpoises to scare them away

from his fishing lines. [The "feeding" language was not part of the regulatory definition at the time of the incident.] We conclude that the regulation does not reach the conduct underlying Hayashi's conviction.

* * *

B

As noted above, the government contends that Hayashi committed a criminal "taking" by "harassing" the porpoises; "harass" is left undefined by the statute. See 16 U.S.C. § 1362(13). If we look to the administrative regulations, the only form of "taking" specified in 50 C.F.R. § 216.3 that is potentially applicable to Hayashi's act of firing into the water behind the porpoises to divert them from his fishing lines is the prohibition of any "intentional act which results in disturbing or molesting a marine mammal." However, "disturb" and "molest" are not much more definitive than "harass." All three are very general terms, requiring us to resort to their context to ascertain their meaning.

Following the "familiar principle of statutory construction that words grouped in a list should be given related meaning," we look to the other statutory and regulatory examples of "taking." Third Nat'l Bank in Nashville v. Impac Ltd., 432 U.S. 312, 322, (1977). The statute groups "harass" with "hunt," "capture," and "kill" as forms of prohibited "taking." The latter three each involve direct, sustained, and significant intrusions upon the normal, life-sustaining activities of a marine mammal; killing is a direct and permanent intrusion, while hunting and capturing cause significant disruptions of a marine mammal's natural state. Consistent with these other terms, "harassment," to constitute a "taking" under the MMPA, must entail a similar level of direct and sustained intrusion.

Interpreting "harassment" under the MMPA to involve a sustained, direct, and significant intrusion also comports with a common understanding of the term "take," of which "harass" is simply one form. To "take" a marine mammal strongly suggests a serious and sustained diversion of the mammal from its natural routine. Congressional concern in passing the MMPA about marine mammals "in danger of extinction or depletion as a result of man's activities" supports this conception of "take." Killing, capturing, and hunting fit the common understanding of the term. "Harassment" under the MMPA, to constitute a "taking," must entail a similarly significant level of intrusiveness.

* * *

This emphasis upon protecting natural animal behavior comports with the MMPA emphasis upon marine mammals as essential components of the natural marine ecosystem. See MMPA § 2(2), Pub.L. 92-522, 86 Stat. 1027 (1972) (marine mammals "should not be permitted to diminish beyond the point at which they cease to be a significant functioning element in the ecosystem of which they are a part"). The concern that underlies the prohibition against disturbing mammals was for mammals as a part of nature, not for mammals acting in ways that endanger human life or property.

Interpreting the act and regulations otherwise, as prohibiting isolated interference with abnormal marine mammal activity, would lead to absurdity. Under such a broad interpretation, anyone who acted to prevent or in any way interfered with any marine mammal activity would face potential criminal prosecution. Nothing could legally be done to save a modern-day Jonah from the devouring whale, or to deter a rampaging polar bear from mauling a child. Neither could a porpoise intent on swimming into severely contaminated waters, or into the propellers of a motorized boat, be diverted by the selfless actions of a good Samaritan. These are but examples of what the unreasonably broad interpretation advocated by the government would lead us to. Our conclusion that only sustained and serious disruptions of normal mammal behavior fall under the term "harass" comports with a more reasonable understanding of the extent and scope of the MMPA.

Applying our interpretation to the act for which Hayashi was convicted, we conclude that there was insufficient evidence to find a criminal "taking" by "harassment." The stipulated facts, consisting almost entirely of Hayashi's and his son's statements to the NMFS investigator, show that Hayashi did not fire at the porpoises, nor did he hit them. He simply fired two successive shots behind and outside the area of the porpoises to discourage them from eating bait and hooked tuna from his fishing lines--an act that is not a part of the porpoise's normal eating habits. Even if the shots succeeded in scaring away the porpoises--and the stipulated facts do not tell us whether the porpoises were aware of, or reacted to, the shots--any diversion from eating off the fisherman's lines is not of the significance or sustained effect required for a "taking" under the MMPA. Hayashi's conduct was not the kind of direct, sustained disruption of a porpoise's customary pursuits required to find a criminal "taking." Reasonable acts to deter porpoises from eating fish or bait off a fisherman's line are not criminal under the MMPA.

* * *

III

We hold that reasonable actions--those not resulting in severe, sustained disruption of the mammal's normal routine--to deter porpoises from eating fish or bait off a fishing line are not rendered criminal by the MMPA or its regulations. Because the evidence shows that Hayashi's action was reasonable, we conclude that insufficient evidence supported his conviction. We reverse.

***BROWNING**, CIRCUIT JUDGE, dissenting.*

The majority unjustifiably restricts the breadth of the Marine Mammal Protection Act to avoid subjecting Hayashi to a criminal prosecution the majority regards as unreasonable. The gloss imposed by the majority to limit the scope of "taking," a key jurisdictional term in the Act, has no source in the language, structure or legislative history of the Act and derives little support from the various circumstances collected to sustain it. It ignores the structure and purpose of the Act and substantially weakens it as an instrument for effectuating the public policy determined by Congress.

I

Much more is at stake in defining the statutory term "taking" than Hayashi's freedom to fire his rifle at dolphins to protect a tuna caught by his son. The meaning assigned to this term defines the authority of the Secretary of Interior and the Secretary of Commerce to regulate private and public activities affecting marine mammals. The authority granted the Secretary by the Act to prohibit acts harmful to marine mammals and to develop and encourage means of ensuring their survival is keyed directly or indirectly to the concept of "taking." A cramped construction of the term "taking" will therefore restrict most aspects of the scheme envisioned by Congress for the protection of marine mammals, from the monitoring of marine mammal populations to research into more humane fishing techniques.

The references in the Act to the term "taking" confirm its importance. The substantive provisions of the Act open with a moratorium on the "taking and importation of marine mammals and marine mammal products." 16 U.S.C. § 1371(a). The Secretary is authorized to allow exceptions to the moratorium by issuing permits "for taking and importation" of marine mammals, as detailed in the Act. 16 U.S.C. §§ 1371, 1374. What is prohibited and what is permitted are stated in terms of "taking" and will be fixed by the definition of that term. 16 U.S.C. §§ 1372, 1375, 1376. The Secretary's regulatory judgments are to be based upon the past and projected impact of "taking" upon the well-being of the species or stocks and the purposes and policies of the Act. 16 U.S.C. § 1373(a). * * *

II

The scheme of the Act is to define "taking" broadly, thus giving ample scope to the regulatory scheme, and at the same time, to introduce the flexibility that is essential to the effective administration of the Act by authorizing the Secretary to approve particular conduct that would otherwise be prohibited although consistent with the purposes of the Act and required by changing circumstances. The statutory language, the legislative history, the Secretary's regulations, and the type of conduct approved by the Secretary in the past all point to an interpretation of the jurisdictional term "taking" sufficiently broad to encompass Hayashi's act of deliberately firing his rifle near feeding dolphins to frighten them off.

* * *

The term "harass" performs the specific function of broadening the definition of "taking" and therefore the Act itself. * * * When the Act was amended in 1988, Congress again emphasized that "[t]aking of marine mammals, as defined in the Act, is not limited to capturing or killing them, but includes harassment of the mammals as well. H.Rep. No. 970, 100th Cong., 2nd Sess. (1988), reprinted in 1988 U.S.C.C.A.N. 6154, 6158.

* * *

III

Congress included a system of exceptions and exemptions in the Act to enable the Secretary to administer effectively the Act's broad prohibition of activity that might prove harmful to marine mammals. These provisions grant the Secretary the necessary authority to achieve the overall objective of protecting marine mammals while affording reasonable protection to other interests. The statutory structure and the manner in which the Secretary has administered it offer additional, significant support for a broad reading of the jurisdictional term "taking," and specifically for application of the Act to the conduct involved in this case.

* * *

In the exercise of these powers, the Secretary has from time to time issued regulations dealing with the general problem presented by the facts of this case. A regulation issued in 1980 authorized commercial fishermen in specified categories to "take such steps as are necessary to protect [their] catch" from marine mammals. 50 C.F.R. § 216.24(d)(5)(ii). In 1988, Congress added an exemption to the Act under which commercial fishermen in certain fisheries who registered with the Secretary would be exempt from the statutory prohibition against incidental taking of marine mammals until October 1, 1993. See 16 U.S.C. § 1383a. The Secretary adopted regulations pursuant to the 1988 exemption permitting such fishermen to "intentionally take marine mammals to protect catch, gear, or person during the course of commercial fishing operations," upon securing an exemption certificate or complying with reporting requirements. 50 C.F.R. §§ 229.4(a),

229.6(c)(5), 229.7(d) (emphasis added).

* * *

The regulations enforcing the 1988 exemption contradict the majority's conclusion that the Act prohibits only direct and sustained intrusions on a marine mammal's life-sustaining activities. The authorization to "take" marine mammals to protect a fisherman's catch is expressly limited to conduct "not expected to cause death or injury to a marine mammal." 50 C.F.R. §§ 229.6(c)(5), 229.7(d). This limitation makes it clear conduct necessary to protect a catch and not expected to threaten the life of a porpoise was nonetheless included within the statute's prohibition against "taking."

Equally important, the 1988 exemption illustrates an essential element of the structure of the Act which the majority ignores--the use of the Secretary's power to authorize controlled exceptions in appropriate circumstances and under proper conditions to the statute's broad prohibition of conduct potentially harmful to marine mammals, without irreversibly limiting the application of the Act to such conduct in other circumstances and under other conditions. With its approval of Hayashi's conduct, the majority not only limits the scope of the Act, but also the ability of the Secretary to protect marine mammals while accommodating the needs of commercial fishermen.

Notes and Questions

1. Why was the majority at pains to distinguish Mr. Hayashi's actions from an intentional "taking" of a marine mammal? Does the dissent's explanation of the statutory context of the "taking" prohibition give a more convincing account of congressional intent? For a critique of the *Hayashi* decision, see R. Kurz, Note, The Taking Of Marine Mammals Under The Marine Mammal Protection Act: Domestic and International Implications, 14 J. Energy Nat. Resources & Envtl. L. 395 (1994).

2. In its 1994 amendments, Congress apparently rejected the *Hayashi* court's reasoning in a new definition of "harassment" that defined two levels of harassment to accommodate actions like those in the *Hayashi* case. Harassment prohibited by the MMPA is "any act of pursuit, torment, or annoyance which (i) has the potential to injure a marine mammal or ... stock in the wild; or (ii) has the potential to disturb a marine mammal or ... stock in the wild by causing disruption of behavioral patterns, including, but not limited to, migration, breathing, nursing, breeding, feeding, or sheltering." 16 U.S.C. § 1362(18). Micahel J. Bean and Melanie J. Rowland, The Evolution of National Wildlife Law 119 (3rd ed. 1997).

3. Also in the 1994 amendments, Congress added an express exception to the takings prohibition for non-lethal deterrence actions to prevent damage to fishing gear, or to protect personal safety or public and private property, as long as the deterrence actions are consistent with guidelines published by the Secretary of Commerce. For endangered or threatened species listed under the Endangered Species Act, the measures must be consistent with specific control measures recommended by the Secretary. 16 U.S.C. § 1371(a)(4)(A),(B). The Secretary of Commerce may prohibit certain deterrent measures that have a significant adverse effect on marine mammals, but deterrent actions may be taken even against mammals designated as "depleted" (that is, below its "optimum sustainable population") under the Act. Id. at § 1371(a)(4)(C), (D). The Act defines the key management term "optimum sustainable population" as "the number of animals which will result in the maximum productivity of the population or the species, keeping in mind the carrying capacity of the habitat and the health of the ecosystem of which they form a constituent element." 16 U.S.C. § 1362(9).

4. Judge Browning 's dissent mentions the 5-year exemption from the incidental take provisions Congress adopted for commercial fisheries in the 1988 amendments. This exemption was replaced in the 1994 amendments by the regulatory regime for incidental takes which classifies fisheries by the degree of their interaction with marine mammals and sets limits on their takes based on estimates of "potential biological removal levels" and other standards. See discussion, infra, in 2.B(2.) of this Section.

5. The penalties for violating the Act's prohibitions are significant. Each unlawful taking or importation of a marine mammal is a separate offense, punishable by a civil fine of up to $10,000. 16 U.S.C. § 1375(a)(1). Any person who "knowingly" violates the regulations or applicable permit conditions is subject to criminal fines of up to $20,000 or imprisonment of up to one year, or both. Id. at § 1375(b). A vessel used in the commission of a violation may be seized and its cargo seized and forfeited, and a civil fine of up to $25,000 assessed against the vessel. Id. at § 1376(a),(b). The Secretary of the Treasury may pay half of any fine, up to $2,500, as a reward to any person who provides information leading to a conviction under the Act. Id. at § 1376 (b). For NOAA's civil procedures, see 15 C.F.R. § § 904.100 et seq.

(c.) Standards for Marine Mammal Management

Interpretations of the Act's key management standard "optimum sustainable population" (OSP) proved difficult in the early years of the Act's implementation. 16 U.S.C. § 1362(9). Early commentators on the Act described the OSP standard as follows:

The use of "population" rather than the conventional management term "yield" as the basis criterion reflects the protectionist focus on the maintenance of live animals in their natural state. Yet the implicit assumption that a certain population level for each species is optimal, and that the populations should be actively managed for that level, adopts the managerial view that positive control is preferable to abstention from human interference and is often necessary to protect the integrity of the ecosystem.

As a dynamic synthesis of the opposing philosophies of management and protection, OSP appears to mean a population that is at a level of maximum ecological productivity, that is at the limit of the environment to sustain healthy populations indefinitely, and that does not adversely affect the ecosystem of which it is a part. A population defined in this way will normally be the largest sustainable population of the species in a given region.

S. Gaines and D. Schmidt, Wildlife Population Management Under the Marine Mammal Protection Act of 1972, 6 Env'l. L. Rep. 50096, 50101(1976).

After much consideration, NMFS adopted regulations defining OSP in a manner that emphasizes the variable "maximum productivity" over the other variable "health of the marine ecosystem":

Optimum sustainable population is a population size which falls within a range from the population level of a given species or stock which is the largest supportable within the ecosystem to the population level that results in maximum net productivity. Maximum net productivity is the greatest net annual increment in population numbers or biomass resulting from additions to the population due to reproduction and/or growth less losses due to natural mortality.

50 C.F.R. § 216.3. Is this definition consistent with the Act's requirement that marine mammals be "protected and encouraged to develop to the greatest extent feasible commensurate with sound policies of resource management * * * ?" 16 U.S.C. § 1361. See J. Nafziger, The Management of Marine Mammals After the Fishery Conservation and Management Act, 14 Willamette L. J. 153, 171 (1978) (NMFS's definition emphasizes productivity rather than populations contrary to the legislative intent but has been accepted by leading marine mammal scientists).

In 1981 amendments, Congress revised the Act to focus upon a single management standard, that is, the maintenance of a species at its optimum sustainable population. This replaced the former three-part management standard: to prevent the further decline of a species or population stock that had declined to a significant degree over a period of years, to prevent the decline of a species or population stock which, if continued or resumed, would place the species or stock within the provisions of the Endangered Species Act of 1973, and to protect a species or population stock that was below its optimum carrying capacity within its environment.

The 1981 amendments clarified the meaning of another population term in the MMPA, "depleted." Now, if the Secretary determines that a species or population stock (defined as "a group of marine mammals of the same species or smaller taxa * * * that interbreed when mature" (16 U.S.C. § 1362(1)) is below OSP, it is considered "depleted." If the species or stock is listed as endangered or threatened under the Endangered Species Act, it is "depleted" for purposes of the MMPA. 16 U.S.C. § 1362(1). A depleted status has significant consequences. The moratorium cannot be waived or a permit granted to take or import a depleted species or stock, except for scientific research or photographic purposes or for enhancing the survival or recovery of a species or stock. 16 U.S.C. § 1371(a)(3)(B). Also, the Native taking of a depleted species or stock may be restricted. 16 U.S.C. § 1371(b). Incidental takes in commercial fishing may, however, be authorized for species considered depleted due to their listing under the Endangered Species Act. U.S.C. § 1371(a)(5)(E).

A process for making depleted status determinations, including by citizen petition, is set forth in § 1383b. Once classified as depleted, the Secretary must prepare a conservation plan to restore the species or stock to its optimum sustainable population. 16 U.S.C. § 1383b(b). These plans are similar to the recovery plans required under the Endangered Species Act. 16 U.S.C. § 1533(f).

(d.) Statutory Exemptions and Exceptions From the Takings Prohibition

As the court noted in *Hayashi*, the MMPA excludes from the moratorium certain categories of marine mammal takings or importation, allowing the Secretary to issue permits for these exempted actions. The categories include scientific research, public display, conservation efforts, incidental takings in the course of commercial fishing operations, and the taking by Native Alaskans for either subsistence purposes or for the creating and selling of authentic native articles of handicrafts and clothing. 16 U.S.C. § 1371(a)(1), (b).

(i.) Scientific Research and Public Display

The Secretary of Commerce can issue a scientific research permit under expedited procedures. In the 1994 amendments, Congress authorized the Secretary to issue "general authorization and implementing regulations" allowing scientific research that results only in disturbance, and not injury, to marine mammals.   16 U.S.C. 1374(c)(3)(C). This change eliminated the need for scientists to obtain an individual permit for much of their research on whale behavior. In Hawaii County Green Party v. Clinton, 124 F.Supp.2d 1173 (D.Haw. 2000), environmental groups sought to enjoin the Navy's testing of its SURTASS low-frequency active sonar system in the whale breeding and calving grounds around Hawaii under research permits issued by NMFS. A previous case had been dismissed, 14 F.Supp.2d 1198 (D.Haw. 1998), and the plaintiffs sought to reopen the case, challenging the testing and other commitments to deploy the system under NEPA and the MMPA. The motions were denied on jurisdictional grounds, but the court noted and expressed concern regarding reports that researchers had recommended that the Navy avoid testing in active breeding areas. Id. at 1179. See further references on this issue in subsection (3.) of this Section.

The public display exemption, allowing animals to be taken under NMFS permits by aquaria and other commercial or educational facilities, is controversial. In Animal Protection Institute of America v. Mosbacher, 799 F. Supp. 173 (D.D.C. 1992), plaintiff animal rights groups challenged permits issued for the importation of beluga and false killer whales because NMFS had not ascertained their OSPs prior to the issuance. The court, however, found no abuse of discretion in the process followed and that the Secretary had information at hand to indicate that the populations were not depleted or listed under the Endangered Species Act.

During the 1994 amendment and reauthorization process, much of the controversy over the public display of captive marine mammals came to the forefront, perhaps inspired by the 1993 movie, "Free Willy." Proponents of bills to eliminate or severely restrict public display facilities did not, however, prevail. Instead, the aquaria and public display industry successfully lobbied Congress to loosen the Act's restrictions and to significantly reduce the oversight of the Secretaries of Commerce and Interior of their facilities. The Act requires public display permittees to offer a program for education or conservation that is based on "professionally recognized standards of the public display community," to be registered or permitted under 7 U.S.C. §§ 2131 et seq., and to maintain facilities that are open to the public on a regularly scheduled basis without restrictions other than an admission fee. 16 U.S.C. § 1374(c)(2)(A). The Act no longer requires the Secretaries to make individualized determinations that a particular facility or program had sufficient educational content to warrant the continued captivity of the affected animal.   Once a display permit is obtained, no further permits are required for the permittee to sell, export or otherwise transfer possession of the marine mammal to someone meeting the general requirements of § 1374(c)(2)(A). Id. at § 1374(c)(2)(B).

Further, the Act allows the export of captive marine mammals for scientific research or public display to any foreign facility that meets requirements comparable to those applied under § 1374(c)(2)(A) to domestic facilities.

What constitutes "professionally recognized standards of the public display community"? Does this concept include only facilities on the scale of Sea World in California, or does it encompass the smaller roadside aquaria that may not have professional caretakers and state-of-the-art facilities? Some commentators anticipate litigation over the definition of this term. See G. Chmael II, K. Ainsworth, and R. Kramer, The 1994 Amendments to the Marine Mammal Protection Act, 9-Spg. Nat. Resources & Env't 18 (1995).

Are tourboat operators offering wild dolphin feeding trips subject to the Act and eligible for public display permits? In 1990, NMFS issued a policy declining to review any application for a public display permit for operations involving feeding wild dolphin populations, based on information that feeding can harm wild populations and thus constitute a "take." 56 Fed. Reg. 20341 (1990). A federal district court invalidated the regulations in Strong v. United States, 811 F. Supp. 246 (S.D. Tex. 1992), and the following appeal resulted.

STRONG v. SECRETARY OF COMMERCE
U.S. Court of Appeals, Fifth Circuit, 1993
5 F.3d 905

Erv and Sonja Strong conduct a commercial tourboat business to transport tourists into the bay by boat for the purpose of feeding dolphins. By this suit the Strongs have challenged the validity of a rule promulgated under the Marine Mammal Protection Act by the Secretary of Commerce which defines the feeding of marine mammals in the wild as prohibited activity. The district court permanently enjoined enforcement of the regulation. 811 F. Supp. 246. We uphold the regulation and vacate the injunction.

By this statute, Congress has prohibited the taking of marine mammals without a permit. The term "take" is defined to mean "to harass, hunt, capture, or kill, or to attempt to harass, hunt, capture, or kill any marine mammal." § 1362(12). Congress has directed the Secretary to promulgate regulations with respect to taking and importing of each species of marine mammal. § 1373. Pursuant to that authorization the National Marine Fisheries Service in the Department of Commerce sought the opinions of informed experts on the effect of feeding dolphins, finally concluding that harm was a real possibility and that habitual feeding cruises should be restricted as harassment of the mammal.

The appeal before us does not contest the denial of a permit to conduct feeding cruises. The position of the Strongs is that the Secretary of Commerce has no authority to consider feeding to be a form of harassment or to regulate same. We think the contention asked too much, and that the district court's order infringes upon the authority of the Secretary.

* * *

Here, the precise question addressed by the challenged regulation is whether feeding marine mammals in the wild constitutes a "take." 50 C.F.R. § 216.3. The district court rejected the decision of the agency because "to feed" is not among the dictionary definitions of "harass." But "disturb" is synonymous with "harass" and the agency has been given substantial scientific evidence that feeding wild dolphins disturbs their normal behavior and may make them less able to search for food on their own. It is therefore clearly reasonable to restrict or prohibit the feeding of dolphins as a potential hazard to them. The regulation was promulgated by the agency within its authority.

* * *

Notes and Questions

1. After the district court decision in *Strong*, the Congress enacted Pub. L. 102-567, Title III, Section 306, requiring the National Academy of Sciences, with the cooperation of the Marine Mammal Commission, to study the effects of wild dolphin feeding in the eastern Gulf of Mexico and to report to Congress in 1994. Does this action undermine NMFS' determination that the scientific evidence already supported a ban?

2. How much and what kind of human interaction with marine mammals did Congress consider appropriate in enacting the MMPA? Has that understanding changed through the 1994 amendments to the public display permit provisions?

3. What rules should govern whale-watching? Does approaching a whale to allow passengers to watch and photograph it constitute "harassment"? In 1992, NMFS proposed rules and draft guidelines imposing minimum approach distances, 57 Fed.Reg. 34101 (1992), but withdrew them in the face of voluminous public comment. 58 Fed.Reg. 16519 (1993). The approach distances were then republished as non-mandatory guidelines. In the 1994 MMPA amendments, Congress enacted a minimum approach distance of no closer than 100 yards for humpback whales in U.S. waters surrounding Hawaii. See C.B. Bridgewater, Comment, The Next Step in North Atlantic Whale Protection: A Closer Look at Whale-Watch Guidelines for the Northeast, 6 Ocean & Coastal L.J. 347 (2001).

(ii.) Native Alaskan Subsistence Hunting and Handicrafts

The MMPA provides that the Act does not apply with respect to takings of any marine mammal by any Indian, Aleut, or Eskimo who resides in Alaska and who dwells on the coast of the North Pacific Ocean or Arctic Ocean if such taking--

(1) is for subsistence purposes; or

(2) is done for purposes of creating and selling authentic native articles of handicrafts and clothing: Provided, That only authentic native articles of handicrafts and clothing may be sold in interstate commerce: And provided further, That any edible portion of marine mammals may be sold in native villages and towns in Alaska or for native consumption. For the purposes of this subsection, the term "authentic native articles of handicrafts and clothing" means items composed wholly or in some significant respect of natural materials, and which are produced, decorated, or fashioned in the exercise of traditional native handicrafts without the use of pantographs, multiple carvers, or other mass copying devices. Traditional native handicrafts include, but are not limited to weaving, carving, stitching, sewing, lacing, beading, drawing, and painting; and

(3) in each case, is not accomplished in a wasteful manner.

16 U.S.C. § 1371(b).

Why did Congress provide so much detail in describing the kinds of products that qualify for the exemption? Is the intent clear?

In Didrickson v. Department of Interior, 982 F.2d 1332 (9th Cir. 1992), plaintiffs challenged Interior Department regulations defining "authentic native articles of handicrafts and clothing" which required the items to be ones "commonly produced on or before December 21, 1972" (the effective date of the MMPA) and excluded all items made from sea otters.   50 C.F.R. § 18.3.   Federal authorities had confiscated the following items the plaintiffs had made from sea otter pelts: growling teddy bears, pillows, hats, mittens, fur flowers, and a parka and hat with metal snaps and zippers. The court invalidated the regulations on the grounds that the Act's very explicit description of authentic native articles did not place any restriction on what marine mammals may be used to fashion the handicrafts or clothing, nor that they be of a kind made or sold prior to 1972.

The validity of the federal regulations defining "taken in a 'wasteful' manner" was upheld in United States v. Clark, 912 F.2d 1087 (9th Cir. 1990), precluding the practice of taking walrus for only a few body parts, such as the ivory tusks and flippers.

The administration of the Pribilof Islands fur seal herds under the North Pacific Fur Seal Convention raises some interesting questions with respect to the relationship of the Federal Government's trust responsibilities for Native Alaskans vis-à-vis its duty to conserve and manage fur seals and fisheries. See Int'l Fund for Animal Welfare v. Baldrige, 594 F. Supp. 129 (D. D.C. 1984) (planned seal kill on Pribilof Islands did not violate MMPA or NEPA and was consistent with Fur Seal Convention, which takes precedence where planned kill does not meet OSP standards). Pribilovians are allowed to take fur seals if taken for subsistence purposes and not accomplished in a wasteful manner. 50 C.F.R. § 216.17.

(iii.) Small Takes During OCS Exploration and Other Activities

For years, U.S. citizens engaging in non-fishing ocean activities such as seismic research or oil and gas development on the Outer Continental Shelf, which interfered with or otherwise harmed marine mammals, were subject to the Act's prohibitions and were, at least in theory, potentially liable for civil and criminal penalties. After amendments in 1981, the Act now makes an exception to the moratorium and prohibitions for these incidental but unintentional takes, if the U.S. citizen makes a specific application to the Secretary. 16 U.S.C. §§ 1371(a)(5)(A)-(D). See 50 C.F.R. Part 216, Subpart I.

The Secretary must insure that the total taking will have only a "negligible impact" on the species and will not have an unmitigable impact on its availability for subsistence uses by Alaska natives. 16 U.S.C. § 1371(a)(5)(A)(i). In issuing the authorizing regulations, the Secretary need only follow a notice and comment process, but must prescribe the permissible methods of taking and other means of minimizing the impact on the species or stock and its habitat, with particular attention to rookeries, mating grounds, and other important areas. The regulations must also specify monitoring and reporting requirements. 16 U.S.C. § 1371(a)(5)(A). The authorization cannot exceed five years. A one-year authorization is available for takes by harassment of small numbers of marine mammals if the Secretary makes the same determinations as for other small-numbers takes. Id. The most controversial decision NMFS faces under this provision is with respect to the Navy's proposed worldwide deployment of its SURTASS low-frequency active sonar program to detect "stealth" submarines. See NMFS, Taking Marine Mammals Incidental to Navy Operations of Surveillance Towed Array Sensor System Low Frequency Active Sonar, Proposed Rules, 66 Fed. Reg. 15375 (Mar. 19, 2001). See also M. Jasny, Sounding the Depths: Supertankers, Sonar, and the Rise of Undersea Noise (Natural Resources Defense Council) (1999); E.M. McCarthy, International Regulation of Transboundary Pollutants: The Emerging Challenge of Ocean Noise, 6 Ocean & Coastal L.J. 257 (2001). The Navy released a final Overseas EIS in 2001. EPA Notice of Receipt of Final

EIS, 65 Fed. Reg. 8788 (Feb. 2, 2001).

In the 1986 amendments, Section 1371(a)(5) was modified to allow these small number takings for depleted as well as non-depleted species. 16 U.S.C. § 1371(a)(5)(A). This change was made to conform to a 1982 change in the Endangered Species Act (ESA) that allowed the authorization of incidental takings of species listed as endangered or threatened under that Act. 16 U.S.C. § 1539(a)(1)(B). Since ESA-listed species are automatically considered "depleted" under the MMPA, without this amendment the MMPA would have precluded the ESA incidental takes, as the more restrictive provisions of the MMPA and ESA take precedence. See 16 U.S.C. § 1543. The intent was to allow appropriate activities that are non-lethal and do not jeopardize the species' survival.

The Act now also allows government officials to make non-lethal removals of individual "nuisance" animals, as well as lethal takes in a humane manner to protect the animal's welfare or the public health and welfare. 16 U.S.C. § 1379(h). The nuisance problem was particularly acute in the case of the sea lion "Herschel" at the Ballard Locks in Seattle, Washington, who, with his cohorts, was eating large numbers of returning coho salmon and steelhead trout.

(e.) Effect Upon State Law

The MMPA provides that "[n]o State may enforce, or attempt to enforce, any State law or regulation relating to the taking of any species * * * of marine mammal within the State unless the Secretary has transferred authority for the conservation and management of that species * * * to the State * * *." 16 U.S.C. § 1379(a). How does this treatment of state authority compare with the Magnuson-Stevens Fishery Conservation and Management Act? The Federal Clean Water and Clean Air Acts?

Like the moratorium on takings and importations, which the Secretary may waive, the Act's displacement of state law is not necessarily permanent. A State may apply to have its management authority for a particular species reinstated. 16 U.S.C. § 1379(b). It must, however, prove to the Secretary's satisfaction that it has laws and regulations in place that are consistent with the MMPA and international treaty obligations. Id. If the State wishes to authorize any takings, it must ensure that they are humane, and are based upon a determination that the species is at its optimum sustainable population and will remain so even after any takings. Id. The taking may not be for scientific research, public display, or enhancing the survival of the species or stock unless such taking is undertaken either by or on behalf of the state. 16 U.S.C. § 1379(b)(1)(E). The regulations on procedures for the transfer of marine mammal management authority to states can be found in 50 C.F.R. Part 403. The MMPA exempts the transfer of management authority to states from the requirement to prepare an environmental impact statement. 16 U.S.C. § 1379(g).

The preemptive effect of § 1379(a) applies to state laws on importations as well as takings. This prevents a state from prohibiting the importation of a marine mammal product if the Secretary has waived the moratorium and granted a permit to the importing company. In Fouke Co. v. Mandel, 386 F. Supp. 1341 (D. Md. 1974), a Maryland law prohibiting importation into the state of seal skins was found to be implicitly preempted by § 1379(a), even though the provision referred only to "taking." For a criticism of this ruling, see Note, Federal Preemption: A New Method for Invalidating State Laws Designed to Protect Endangered Species, 47 U.Colo. L. Rev. 261 (1976).

What effect does the Act have upon state laws aimed at preserving marine wildlife rather than authorizing hunting or other takes? In State of Alaska v. Arnariak, 941 P.2d 154 (Ak. 1997) the defendant charged with violating a state law prohibiting discharge of firearms in a walrus sanctuary claimed that the state law was preempted by the MMPA. The court held that the Act did not preempt state laws aimed at regulating state lands such as state wildlife sanctuaries. A strong dissenting opinion argues that the Act's preemption clause is broad and covers all state laws relating to marine mammals, including state sanctuary laws.

California applied for a transfer of management authority over sea otters shortly after the MMPA was enacted. For an account of this effort, see J. Armstrong, The California Sea Otter: Emerging Conflicts in Resources Management, 16 San Diego L. Rev. 249 (1979). California eventually withdrew its application when the sea otter was listed as "threatened" under the Endangered Species Act. Alaska's efforts to return management authority to the state met with significant problems after the court in People of Togiak v. United States, 470 F. Supp. 423 (D.D.C. 1979), ruled that the Federal Government could not transfer authority to the state if Native Alaskans were not afforded the same opportunities to hunt marine mammals as under the native take exception to the MMPA.

In 1981, Congress overhauled the state authority transfer provision to make it easier to return authority to the states. The revised provision now contains a very detailed review provision and substantive standards for state transfers. The provision also now allows native subsistence takes to be regulated by a state after transfer. It contains a specific provision for Alaska should it ever again seek a return of state management authority. 16 U.S.C. § 1379(f). The Act requires Alaska to adopt a statute making "subsistence" a priority consumptive use over sport and commercial hunting, using the definition of subsistence found in the Alaska National Interest Lands Conservation Act, 16 U.S.C. § 3113.

Despite these changes, none of the states, including Alaska, has sought a return of their management authority from the Federal Government. Even after a transfer of authority to a state, the Secretary retains regulatory authority over, inter alia, commercial fishing incidental takes in the EEZ, with authority to enter into a "cooperative allocation agreement" with a state for any transboundary stock. 16 U.S.C. § 1379(d).

In Jones v. Gordon, 792 F.2d 821 (9th Cir. 1986), affirming and modifying 621 F. Supp. 7 (D. Alaska 1985), the court invalidated a NMFS public display permit to SeaWorld allowing the capture of killer whales because the agency had failed to prepare or to justify not preparing an environmental impact statement in conjunction with the permit issuance. The State of Alaska joined the plaintiffs' challenge to the SeaWorld permits. Should the states have a special role in reviewing proposed permits to capture marine mammals from state waters? A bill introduced in the House of Representatives in 1993, the "Marine Mammal Public Display Reform Act" (H.R. 585, 103rd Cong., 1st Sess.), would have given a state 30 days in which to disapprove a proposed public display permit if animals were to be taken from state waters designated as "protected," i.e., as having special value or requiring protection from certain activities under state law. Even absent this amendment, could a state use the federal consistency provision of the Coastal Zone Management Act, 16 U.S.C. § 1456(c), to object to a NMFS permit allowing a commercial resort facility to display dolphins, if a state law prohibiting such displays is one of the enforceable policies of the state's approved coastal management program? Would such a state law be preempted by the MMPA's Section 1379(a)?

(2.) Reconciling Marine Mammal and Fishing Conflicts

The most significant exception to the MMPA's moratorium on the taking of marine mammals is that provided for their incidental taking in the course of commercial fishing operations. 16 U.S.C. § 1371(a)(2). The Secretary may either issue permits under Section 1374 according to regulations promulgated under Section 1373, or may grant "authorizations" under Section 1387 and its implementing regulations. Takes allowed under either route are subject to the following overriding policy standard:

> In any event it shall be the immediate goal that the incidental kill or incidental serious injury of marine mammals permitted in the course of commercial fishing operations be reduced to insignificant levels approaching a zero mortality and serious injury rate; provided that this goal shall be satisfied in the case of the incidental taking of marine mammals in the course of purse seine fishing for yellowfin tuna by a continuation of the application of the best marine mammal safety techniques and equipment that are economically

and technologically practicable.

16 U.S.C. § 1371(a)(2). The second clause of this standard was added in 1981, in the aftermath of Committee for Humane Legislation, Inc. v. Richardson, 540 F.2d 1141 (D.C. Cir. 1976), in which the court invalidated the general permit issued by NMFS to the American Tunaboat Association. The permit had allowed the killing of an unlimited number of dolphins in the purse-seine yellowfin tuna fishery (which sets its nets around schools of dolphins) because the agency was unable to determine either the stocks' OSPs or the impact of the proposed takes upon these levels. After that decision, NMFS significantly increased the restrictions on the U.S. yellowfin tuna purse-seine fishery to meet the requirements of the Act. The U.S. yellowfin tuna purse-seine fishery is now regulated by a general permit dating from 1980, extended indefinitely by the Act subject to compliance with a number of operational conditions, including the duty to use the "best marine mammal safety techniques and equipment that are economically and technologically practicable" and to carry official observers. 16 U.S.C. § 1374(h)(2). Further legal developments with regard to the tuna-dolphin conflict are described in Section 3 of this chapter, where the Act's provisions affecting the importation of tuna products from non-U.S. purse-seine fisheries are examined.

The overall goal of the MMPA from its inception was to reduce eventually marine mammal deaths and injury in all fisheries operations to insignificant levels. The 1972 Act's mechanism for individually permitting incidental takes in commercial fisheries under Section 1374, however, proved unworkable. The federal courts ruled that the Act did not allow the Secretary to issue permits for incidental mortality for fisheries that encountered either depleted stocks or those whose population sizes were unknown. Kokechik Fishermen's Ass'n v. Secretary of Commerce, 839 F.2d 795 (D.C. Cir. 1988), cert. denied, Verity v. Center for Env'l Educ., 488 U.S. 1004 (1989). Because so little information had been collected about the extent of commercial fisheries takes and their impact on mammal populations, this ruling threatened to tie up many economically significant U.S. fisheries.

Congress quickly amended the Act in 1988 to provide a five-year interim exemption to the incidental take provision while the NMFS collected more information on the extent of mortality and injuries in commercial fisheries. 16 U.S.C. §§ 1383a, 1381. During the interim period, a regulatory regime was developed in consultation with the industry, conservation groups, and the Marine Mammal Commission, which oversees implementation of the Act under 16 U.S.C. § 1402. This regime was added to the Act by the 1994 amendments, along with many other provisions addressing a number of issues that had arisen since 1988. The amendments attempted to put in place a more practical approach to the reality of marine mammal deaths in commercial fisheries. See G. Chmael II, K.W. Ainsworth, R. Kramer, The 1994 Amendments to the Marine Mammal Protection Act, 9-SPG Nat. Resources & Env't 18 (1995) and N. Young and S. Iudicello, Blueprint for Whale Conservation: Implementing the 1994 Amendments to the Marine Mammal Protection Act, 3 Ocean & Coastal L.J. 149 (1997).

The new regime requires the Secretary to prepare and revise annually a list of commercial fishing operations that have frequent, occasional, or remote likelihood of incidentally taking marine mammals. Fisheries in either the frequent or occasional categories must then register for authorizations to incidentally take the affected marine mammals and must comply with any regulations required to reduce the incidence of such takes to insignificant levels within five years. These regulations also may require that fishing vessels subject to the authorization carry observers. The Secretary has the authority also to issue emergency regulations if she determines that the incidental taking is having an immediate and significant adverse impact upon a stock. See 50 C.F.R. Part 229, Authorization for Commercial Fisheries under the MMPA of 1972.

The 1994 amendments also require the Secretary of Commerce to prepare stock assessments on all marine mammal stocks that occur in U.S. waters. 16 U.S.C. § 1386. These assessments must describe the stock's geographic range; estimate its population size, reproduction or "productivity" rates, and rates of mortality due to human activities; and determine its "potential biological removal level" (PBR). The Secretary must also categorize the status of the stock as either "strategic" or as being at a level of human-caused mortality and serious injury that is not likely to cause the stock to be reduced below its optimum sustainable population. Id. at § 1386(a)(5). The assessments and PBR determinations are made through a public process, and the Secretary is assisted by scientific review groups convened from each of the three major marine regions of the U.S.: Alaska, the Pacific, and the Atlantic. Id. at § 1386(b),(d). Assessments for strategic stocks must be reviewed at least annually; all other stocks, unless significant new information is available, must be reviewed at least once every three years. Id. at § 1386(c).

The Act defines these key population terms as follows:

16 U.S.C. § 1362. Definitions

For the purposes of this chapter--

* * *

(19) The term "strategic stock" means a marine mammal stock--

    (A) for which the level of direct human-caused mortality exceeds the potential biological removal level;

    (B) which, based on the best available scientific information, is declining and is likely to be listed as a threatened species under the Endangered Species Act of 1973 within the foreseeable future; or

    (C) which is listed as a threatened species or endangered species under the Endangered Species Act of 1973, or is designated as depleted under this chapter.

(20) The term "potential biological removal level" means the maximum number of animals, not including natural mortalities, that may be removed from a marine mammal stock while allowing that stock to reach or maintain its optimum sustainable population. The potential biological removal level is the product of the following factors:

    (A) The minimum population estimate of the stock.

    (B) One-half the maximum theoretical or estimated net productivity rate of the stock at a small population size.

    (C) A recovery factor of between 0.1 and 1.0.

(26) The term "net productivity rate" means the annual per capita rate of increase in a stock resulting from additions due to reproduction, less losses due to mortality.

(27) The term "minimum population estimate" means an estimate of the number of animals in a stock that--

    (A) is based on the best available scientific information on abundance, incorporating the precision and variability associated with such information; and

    (B) provides reasonable assurance that the stock size is equal to or greater than the estimate.

Under the new regime governing incidental taking of marine mammals in U.S. commercial fishing operations, the immediate goal is to reduce such mortality or serious injury to insignificant levels "approaching a zero mortality and serious injury rate" within seven years after April 30, 1994. 16 U.S.C. § 1387(b)(1). To achieve that end, the Secretary of Commerce must classify commercial fisheries based on the frequency of incidental mortalities and injuries and issue authorizations to vessels in the frequent and occasional categories that submit registration forms. These vessels agree to comply with the take reduction plan and any emergency regulations the Secretary issues and to take an observer on board if required. Id. at § 1387(c)(3). The Secretary is authorized to work with the states and the appropriate regional fishery management council to integrate the authorizations into existing fishery licensing and related programs. Id. at § 1387(c)(5).

The Act requires the Secretary to develop and implement take reduction plans to assist in the recovery or prevent the depletion of each strategic stock which interacts with a commercial fishery on either a frequent or occasional basis, as determined by the Secretary's classification process.   16 U.S.C. § 1387(f)(1).   The Secretary is authorized to prepare a plan for other stocks that interact with a fishery that has a high level of mortality and serious injury across a number of marine mammal stocks. Id. See 50 C.F.R. Part 220.

The take reduction plans are the vehicle by which the Act's goal are to be achieved. If the affected stock is strategic, the plan's immediate goal shall be to reduce, within six months of implementation, the incidental mortality or serious injury rate to levels less than the PBR level established for that stock under the stock assessment process of § 1386. The long-term goal must be to reduce incidental takes within five years to incidental levels approaching a zero mortality and serious injury rate, "taking into account the economics of the fishery, the availability of existing technology, and existing state or regional fishery management plans." Id. at §1387(f)(3).   The plans must include recommended regulatory or voluntary measures for reducing death and injury and recommended dates for achieving the plan's objectives. The plans are to be prepared by take reduction teams composed of representatives of the commercial fisheries and conservation communities, scientists, and others, consisting of "to the maximum extent practicable, * * * an equitable balance among representatives of resource user interests and nonuser interests." Id. at § 1387(f)(6)(C). The teams are not subject to the Federal Advisory Committee Act, but their meetings must be publicized and open to the public.

For strategic stocks for which the incidental take rate is estimated to be equal to or greater than the PBR level, the team has six months to develop a draft plan. These plans are to be developed by consensus, but in the event a consensus cannot be reached, the team is to advise the Secretary in writing on the possibilities the team considered and the views of the majority and minority of its members. Id. at § 1387(f)(7). The Secretary is required to take the plan into consideration and publish the plan in the Federal Register for public comment with an indication of changes proposed to it. If the team fails to submit a draft plan within six months, the Secretary must publish a proposed plan and implementing regulations for public comment.   If the incidental rates are less than the estimated PBR level, the team has eleven months to prepare the plan. Id. at § 1387(f)(8).

A review of the take reduction planning process is presented in N. Young and S. Iudicello, Blueprint for Whale Conservation: Implementing the 1994 Amendments to the Marine Mammal Protection Act, 3 Ocean & Coastal L.J. 149, 203-216 (1997). Rules governing the implementation of § 1387 are codified in 50 C.F.R. Part 229. Final rules to implement the Gulf of Maine harbor porpoise take reduction plan appear in 50 C.F.R. § 229.33, published in 62 Fed. Reg. 43302 (1997). Rules governing the implementation of § 1387 are published in 50 C.F.R. Part 229. For contrasting views on the effectiveness of this process and of NMFS's implementation of the take reduction teams' recommendations, compare N.M. Young, The Conservation of Marine Mammals Using a Multi-Party Approach: An Evaluation of the Take Reduction Team Process, 6 Ocean & Coastal L.J. 293 (2001), with Statement of S.B. Young, The Humane Society of the U.S., to the House Resources Comm., Subcomm. on Fisheries Conservation, Wildlife and Oceans regarding reauthorization of the MMPA, Oct. 11, 2001, 2001 WL 26186986. The Humane Society sued NMFS in 2000 for failure to implement effective take reduction measures to protect Northern right whales from entanglement in fishing gear in the waters off New England. The court denied plaintiffs' motion for an injunction based on NMFS's assurances that it would promptly issue regulations to implement recommendations in the June 2001 biological opinions prepared under the Endangered Species Act for the fisheries of the Northeast. Humane Society of the U.S. v. Mineta, D.Mass. No. 00-CV12069DPW. The right whale take reduction regulations were published in the Federal Register on Dec. 21, 2000, 65 Fed. Reg. 80368 (to be codified at 50 C.F.R. § 229.32). Regulations implementing the 2001 biological opinions' recommendations were published in Jan. 2002. See 67 Fed. Reg. 1133, 1300.

In addition to this focus on protection of mammal stocks through regulations, the 1994 amendments give the Secretary of Commerce the discretionary authority to protect marine mammal habitats. 16 U.S.C. § 1361(2), (5)(B). See 140 Cong. Rec. H2724 (daily ed. April 26, 1994)(statement of Rep. Studds). The Act requires three ecosystem studies--for the Gulf of Maine, the Bering Sea, and for the Pacific region pinniped-fishery interactions-- to help the Secretary in meeting one of the Act's principal goals, to maintain marine mammals as a "significant functioning element of the ecosystem." 16 U.S.C. §§ 1380(c),(d); 1389. For a discussion of the potential role of habitat conservation planning under the Marine Mammal Protection Act, see S. Alker, Comment, The Marine Mammal Protection Act: Refocusing the Approach to Conservation, 44 UCLA L. Rev. 527 (1996).

C. MARINE ENDANGERED SPECIES

The Endangered Species Act of 1973 (ESA), as amended, despite its acknowledged limitations, is the legal basis for most of the protection afforded wildlife and the ecosystems upon which they depend. Although most of the Act's principles and programs have been worked out in the context of terrestrial species and ecosystems, the increasing intensity of marine uses and the decline of many marine wildlife species and ecosystems have given its mandates increasing prominence in marine conservation efforts. Because many marine wildlife species are also marine mammals, implementation of the ESA and the MMPA may in some instances appear indistinguishable, especially under their similar incidental take provisions. The ESA's mandate to all federal agencies, however, to insure their actions neither jeopardize the survival and recovery of an endangered or threatened species nor adversely modify its critical habitat, coupled with its citizen suit provision, provides a stronger lever in favor of species preservation, albeit one limited by the effectiveness of agency efforts and enforcement and its interpretation of what is the "best scientific evidence available."

(1.) Species Listing and the Designation of Critical Habitat

The process for listing a species under the ESA is described in Section 4, 16 U.S.C. § 1533. A species is "endangered" when it is in "danger of extinction throughout all or a significant part of its range," and is "threatened" when it is "likely to become an endangered species within the foreseeable future." 16 U.S.C. §§ 1532(6),(20), 1533(c). The Secretary is required to determine whether any species is either endangered or threatened because of any of the following factors, any one of which is sufficient to support a listing determination: (a) the present or threatened destruction, modification, or curtailment of its habitat or range; (b) overutilization for commercial, recreational, scientific, or educational purposes; (c) disease or predation; (d) the inadequacy of existing regulatory mechanisms; or (e) other natural or manmade factors affecting its continued existence. 16 U.S.C. § 1533(a)(1). For species for which programmatic responsibilities have been vested in the Secretary of Commerce, the Secretary of Interior is to accept the recommendations of the Commerce Secretary with respect to listings. 16 U.S.C. § 1533(a)(2). Listing decisions are to be made "solely on the basis of the best scientific and commercial data available * * * after conducting a review of the status of the species and after taking into account those efforts, if any, being made by any State or foreign nation." 16 U.S.C. § 1533(b).

The Act requires the Secretary also to designate the critical habitat of a species concurrently with its listing "to the maximum extent prudent and determinable." 16 U.S.C. § 1533(a)(3)(A). Critical habitat designations are also required to be based on the best scientific data available, but the Secretary must also consider the economic impact of the designation, unlike the listing determination, which is to be made without regard to economic or commercial considerations. 16 U.S.C. § 1533(b)(2). The Secretary is allowed to exclude any area from critical habitat upon determining that the benefits of such exclusion outweigh the benefits of specifying the area as critical, unless the area's exclusion will result in the species' extinction. Id.

Section 4 allows persons to petition the Secretary under the Administrative Procedure Act, 5 U.S.C. § 553(e), to determine whether the status of a species warrants its listing or to revise a critical habitat designation. 16 U.S.C. § 1533(b)(3)(C),(D).

The ESA divides responsibility for endangered and threatened species between the Secretaries of the Interior and of Commerce. 16 U.S.C. § 1533(a)(2). The Secretaries have delegated their authority under the Act to the Fish and Wildlife Service (FWS) and the National Marine Fisheries Service (NMFS). See 50 C.F.R. § 402.01(b). NMFS is responsible for species of the order Cetacea (whales and dolphins) and the suborder Pinnipedia (seals and sea lions) except walrus. FWS has responsibility for the polar bear, walrus, sea otter, manatee, and dugong. They share responsibility for sea turtles (which nest on land but live at sea). Because NMFS also administers the Marine Mammal Protection Act and the Magnuson-Stevens Fishery Conservation and Management Act, its decisions whether to list a species or designate critical habitat often involve reviewing the extent to which species protection can be afforded under these laws. This review can lead to actions under those statutes to address whatever threats the species faces, obviating the need for listing as endangered or threatened under the ESA, a much more controversial action. If the petitioner for listing or designation is dissatisfied with the decision, the petitioner may challenge it under the Administrative Procedure Act, but the petitioner must show that the agency's finding that adequate protection is afforded by the other statutes is "arbitrary, capricious, an abuse of discretion, or otherwise not in accordance with law." As the following case illustrates, this can be a difficult burden to sustain.

COOK INLET BELUGA WHALE v. DALEY
United States District Court, District of Columbia, 2001
156 F.Supp.2d 16

ROBERTSON, DISTRICT JUDGE:

This Administrative Procedure Act case presents a challenge to the decision of the Secretary of Commerce and the National Marine Fisheries Service (NMFS) to list the Cook Inlet Beluga Whale as "depleted" under the Marine Mammal Protection Act, but not as "endangered" or "threatened" under the Endangered Species Act (ESA). The Secretary determined that the recent Beluga Whale population decrease, which everyone agrees is attributable almost exclusively to over-hunting, can be arrested using the statutory protection afforded "depleted" marine mammal species and a legislative moratorium on Native American takings.[2] Because the plaintiffs have not sustained their burden of showing that that determination was "arbitrary, capricious, an abuse of discretion, or otherwise not in accordance with law," summary judgment will be entered in favor of the government.

Factual and Procedural Background

The Cook Inlet Beluga Whale (*Delphinapterus leucas*) is a genetically distinct, geographically isolated marine mammal with a remnant population that inhabits Cook Inlet from late April or early May until October or November. NMFS estimates that in the mid-1980's, between 1000 and 1300 whales inhabited the inlet. Today, the population is estimated at between 300 and 400 whales. It is not disputed that the single most significant factor in the population decline has been Native American hunting: NMFS estimates that between 1995 and 1997 the Native American subsistence harvest averaged 77 whales per year. That is why, in March 1999, the plaintiffs filed a petition to list the Cook Inlet Beluga Whale under the Endangered Species Act (ESA).

* * *

Within thirty days of plaintiffs' request for an ESA listing, the NMFS published formal notice that action under the ESA "may be warranted." That notice triggered a one year status review period. On October 19, 1999, the NMFS published a proposed rule, not under the ESA, but under the Marine Mammal Protection Act (MMPA), to list the whale as "depleted." (The final rule was issued May 31, 2000). Under the MMPA, 16 U.S.C. § 1362, the Secretary can designate a species as "depleted" if the species is listed as endangered or threatened under the ESA or if the Secretary determines that the stock is below its Optimum Sustainable Population. Once a marine mammal has been listed as "depleted," the Secretary is authorized to promulgate regulations limiting takings by Native Americans, but a listing under the MMPA does not have the regulatory, economic and environmental fallout of a listing as "threatened" or "endangered" under the ESA.

---

[2] A temporary legislative moratorium on Native American takings of Cook Inlet beluga whales was signed into law May 21, 1999. Pub.L. 106-31, § 3022, 113 Stat. 57, 100. The moratorium was made permanent in December, 2000. Pub.L. 106-553, § 1(a)(2), 114 Stat. 2762 (Dec. 21, 2000). Because the statute contains an exception for takings under a cooperative agreement between NMFS and the affected Alaska Native organizations, the protection it affords (or fails to afford) is co-extensive with that of the MMPA listing.

On June 22, 2000, the NMFS determined that an ESA listing was "not warranted." It is that determination which, in plaintiffs' submission, was "arbitrary, capricious, an abuse of discretion, or otherwise not in accordance with law."

Argument

"In exercising its narrowly defined duty under the APA, the Court must consider whether the agency acted within the scope of its legal authority, adequately explained its decision, based its decision on facts in the record, and considered the relevant factors." National Park and Conservation Ass'n v. Stanton, 54 F.Supp.2d 7, 11 (D.D.C.1999). Plaintiffs argue that the agency decision in this case improperly applied the law and facts to the five-factor determination; failed to apply the best scientific and commercial data available; and improperly considered political and economic factors.

I. Statutory Factors

A decision whether or not to list a species shall be made "solely on the basis of the best scientific and commercial data available * * * after conducting a review of the status of the species and after taking into account those efforts, if any, being made by any State or foreign nation." 16 U.S.C. § 1533(b). Applying this standard, the Secretary must list a species as endangered or threatened if "any of § 1533(a)(1)'s five factors are sufficiently implicated." Southwest Center for Biological Diversity v. Babbitt, 215 F.3d 58, 60 (D.C.Cir.2000). Each of the five factors is considered below.

(A) The present or threatened destruction, modification, or curtailment of the species' habitat or range.

The agency's conclusion that "no indication exists that the range has been, or is threatened with being modified or curtailed to an extent that appreciably diminishes the value of the habitat for both survival and recovery of the species," 65 Fed.Reg. 38778, 38781 (June 22, 2000), was not arbitrary or capricious. There is no dispute that the Cook Inlet, the whale's habitat, has changed over time in response to the increasing demand of municipal, industrial, and recreational activities, but there is no record basis for concluding that these changes have had a deleterious effect on the whale. Plaintiffs can point only to the fact that the whales have increasingly inhabited the upper inlet in recent decades. The agency concedes that this change in whale behavior might be in response to human activities, but no data suggest that the change threatens extinction. The agency is not required to conduct further testing to determine the effect of various environmental factors, such as oil drilling, on the whale population. "The 'best available data' requirement makes it clear that the Secretary has no obligation to conduct independent studies." Southwest Center for Biological Diversity, 215 F.3d at 60.

(B) Overutilization

All agree that Native American harvesting has been the most significant factor in the declining whale population. The agency has found "that a failure to restrict the subsistence harvest would likely cause CI beluga whales to become in danger of extinction in the foreseeable future." 65 Fed.Reg. 38778, 38783 (June 22, 2000). But the agency has also concluded that "overutilization" does not support ESA listing because it has been stopped--by designating the whale as "depleted" under the MMPA. Plaintiffs attack that conclusion as unreasonable.

Although plaintiffs are correct that the agency has used low population as evidence to support other listing decisions, NMFS is not required by law to list any species with a historically small or a declining population, and the NMFS decision in this case is not inconsistent with agency precedent. It seems clear that the agency must list under the ESA (1) if the current population qualifies as "threatened" or "endangered" without considering any further decline, see, e.g., Friends of Wild Swan, Inc. v. U.S. Fish Wildlife Service, 945 F.Supp. 1388, 1398 (D.Or.1996) (the agency "determines for listing decisions whether a species 'is an endangered species' "); 65 Fed.Reg. 26167, 26171 (May 5, 2000) (listing white abalone where the population decline resulted in "extremely low" reproduction chances); 57 Fed.Reg. 47620, 47620 (Oct. 19, 1992) (ESA listing not warranted where "given present abundance estimates and levels of take, [ ] the population will remain viable in perpetuity"), or (2) if the current population will continue to decline, even with the MMPA listing, to levels warranting listing, see, e.g., Defenders of Wildlife v. Babbitt, 958 F.Supp. 670 (D.D.C.1997) requiring listing where lynx population not only had declined from its historic numbers, but was continuing to decline). But neither of those conditions has been shown to exist.

If the moratorium fails to control Native American harvesting in he future, ESA listing will be warranted. That much is agreed. But plaintiffs have been unable to point to anything in the record indicating that the current whale population is unsustainable if the harvest is indeed restricted successfully. Nor have plaintiffs successfully rebutted a study by Breiwick and DeMaster (1999), who examined the effects of stochastic events on the population dynamics of small populations of whales subject to subsistence harvests and reported no extinctions in populations with maximum environment stochasticity and a 3 percent harvest rate. 65 Fed.Reg. 38778, 38782-38783 (June 22, 2000). Plaintiffs disagree with Breiwick and DeMaster and cite to Dr. Lande (whose declaration was stricken as extra-record material) for the proposition that NMFS did not have the necessary data to model stochastic events. Even if Dr. Lande's opinions had been before the agency, however, "[w]hen specialists express conflicting views, an agency must have discretion to rely on the reasonable opinions of its own qualified experts even if, as an original matter, a court might find contrary views more persuasive." Marsh v. Oregon Natural Resources Council, 490 U.S. 360, 378, 109 S.Ct. 1851, 104 L.Ed.2d 377 (1989). Whether the Breiwick and DeMaster study was an adequate model or not and whether its substitution of additional mortality for random events was reasonable or not are the sorts of agency decisions courts will rely on unless "there is 'simply no rational relationship' between the model chosen and the situation to which it is applied." American Iron & Steel Institute v. Environmental Protection Agency, 115 F.3d 979, 1004 (D.C.Cir.1997).

Plaintiffs argue that harvesting will still occur even after the MMPA "depleted" listing because some hunting will be permitted under co-management agreements between the agency and Native American organizations and some hunting will occur illegally. Proposed regulations governing co-management agreements, however, limit Native American hunts to two strikes annually, 65 Fed.Reg. 59164, 59165-66 (Oct. 4, 2000), and there is no reason to believe that the MMPA's enforcement mechanisms, which are identical to those of the ESA, will be less effective in controlling illegal takings. Plaintiffs' concerns are reasonable, and enforcement should be carefully monitored, but the record contains support for the agency's conclusion that future takings will be minimal and that the current population is sustainable.

(C) Disease or Predation

The agency concedes that both disease or predation "occur in the CI beluga population and may affect reproduction and survival," but it has concluded that these factors are not causing the stock to be threatened or endangered. Plaintiff has not shown that conclusion to be arbitrary or capricious. Nothing in the record indicates that disease threatens recovery of the Beluga Whale stocks. Plaintiffs have not rebutted the agency's finding that "[n]o quantitative data exist on the level of removals from this population due to killer whale predation or its impact." Id. "Even if the available scientific and commercial data were quite inconclusive, [the Secretary] may--indeed must--still rely on it at that stage." Southwest Center for Biological Diversity, 215 F.3d at 60.

(D) Inadequacy of Existing Regulatory Mechanisms

We have found nothing in the record, and plaintiff has identified nothing, showing that there are inadequacies in existing regulatory mechanisms or, if there were, what the effects of such inadequacies would be. Plaintiffs argue that the MMPA is inadequate to ensure that illegal hunting does not occur and to adequately protect Cook Inlet from damaging development activities, but that argument simply asserts plaintiffs' policy preference for a remedy under the ESA and begs the question of whether ESA listing is required.

(E) Other Natural or Manmade Factors Affecting its Continued Existence

Plaintiffs argue that there are many other factors--strandings, oil spills, takings through commercial fishing, effects of pollutants, ship strikes, noise, urban runoff, etc.--that put the species at risk and that it was arbitrary and capricious for the agency to determine that "[t]he best available information * * * indicates that these activities, alone or cumulatively, have not caused the stock to be in danger of extinction and are not likely to do so in the foreseeable future." 65 Fed.Reg. 38778, 38783 (June 22, 2000). They point to a snippet in the record indicating that "other factors could be contributing to the decline," and argue that the agency failed to adequately consider the cumulative effects of all of the potential factors combined with the small population size of the Cook Inlet Beluga Whale.

It is true that the absence of "conclusive evidence" of a real threat to a species does not justify an agency's finding that ESA listing is not warranted. Defenders of Wildlife, 958 F.Supp. at 679. But neither is listing required simply because the agency is unable to rule out factors that could contribute to a population decline. It was not arbitrary or capricious for the agency to place its principal reliance on the cessation of Native American hunts and the Breiwick and DeMaster conclusion that the Cook Inlet Beluga Whale population could sustain itself, even accounting for stochastic events.

II . Other Arguments

(A) IUCN Criteria

The agency's decision is not rendered arbitrary by the fact that criteria adopted by the International Union for the Conservation of Nature and Natural Resources (IUCN) would have supported a different conclusion. The IUCN criteria are widely used, by NMFS among others, to classify species that are at a high risk of extinction. But the agency's obligations arise under the five statutory criteria of the ESA, and not the IUCN criteria. The agency adequately explained its decision to depart from the IUCN recommendation in its final decision. 65 Fed.Reg. 38778, 38779 (June 22, 2000).

(B) Political Considerations

Plaintiffs' allegation that the listing decision was impermissibly affected by political considerations is not supported by the record. The record does contain an agency memorandum reciting that the whales "presently meet some or all of the qualifications for listing under both the ESA and MMPA," and stating that one of the advantages of an MMPA listing is that "interest among the Alaska congressional delegation is high, which opposes an ESA listing." And, one of the agency's own experts stated that the evidence "towards a listing * * * are compelling" and that "most knowledgeable scientists would support a listing decision in the absence of politics." These bits of evidence show that the agency's decision was a difficult one and that political considerations may have been lurking in the corridors. They do not establish that, but for "politics," the whale would have been listed under the ESA or that political considerations became part of the decision making process.

Notes and Questions

1. For a discussion of this case, see S. Edmonds, Comment, A Whale's Tale: Efforts to Save the Cook Inlet, Alaska Beluga Whale, 7 Ocean & Coastal L.J. __ (2001).

2. Footnote 2 of the opinion indicates that the a legislative moratorium on Native American takings of Cook Inlet beluga whales was signed into law on May 21, 1999. This law, known as the Stevens Amendment, was enacted as a section of the Emergency Supplemental Appropriations Act Act. Pub. L. 106-31, § 3022, 113 Stat. 57, 100. NMFS received two petitions to list Cook Inlet beluga whales and to designate critical habitat in March 1999, after a sharp decline in abundance was detected between 1994 and 1998 (from 653 to 347 animals), about a 50% reduction, of about 15% per year. 65 Fed. Reg. 38778, 38778 (June 22, 2000). Both petitions asked NMFS to promulgate regulations to govern the subsistence harvest. Before receiving the petitions, the NMFS Alaska Regional Office had requested the legislative action, on the advice of the Marine Mammal Commission that the MMPA rulemaking to set limits would take too long. MMPA sections 101(b) and 103(d) require regulations that prescribe limits on subsistence harvests of Alaska Natives be made on the record after opportunity for an agency hearing. See 50 C.F.R. Part 228 (procedural regulations for such hearings and regulations).

3. The MMPA allows Alaska Natives to take marine mammals for subsistence or handicraft purposes as long as the take is not done in a wasteful manner. 16 U.S.C. § 1371(b). The Marine Mammal Commission reported in 2000 that beluga whale muktuk (a Native Alaskan delicacy made from whale skin and blubber) has been sold

through commercial outlets, under the language of Act permitting edible portions of marine mammals taken by Alaska Natives to be sold in Native villages and towns. The city of Anchorage, located on the upper end of Cook Inlet and the largest city in Alaska, is included within the definition of a Native village under the current interpretation of the MMPA. Marine Mammal Commission, 1999 Annual Report to Congress 33. Because of the high demand for muktuk it has significant cash value, and the Native subsistence exemption provided no mechanism for setting limits on hunting for market, absent an effective co-management agreement between the NMFS and the Alaska Native communities. Although 1994 amendments to the MMPA, in section 119, authorize the creation of co-management agreements to control Native takes, enforcement difficulties prevented these arrangements from being effective. Designating the stock as "depleted" under the MMPA or listing it as threatened or endangered under the ESA would give NMFS the authority to set hunting limits and enforce them. 16 U.S.C. § 1371. Establishing regulations to limit Native hunting under either section 10(e) of the ESA or section 101(b) of the MMPA requires a lengthy rulemaking process. Publication of the depleted determination is only the first step. Following the determination of depleted that was at issue in the above case, 65 Fed. Reg. 34590 (May 31, 2000), NMFS held a formal adjudicatory (on-the-record) hearing regarding proposed regulations on the subsistence harvest before an administrative law judge in Anchorage, Alaska on Nov. 15, 2000. The proposed regulations would limit Native hunting to two strikes annually until the stock is no longer considered depleted, require a co-management agreement between NMFS and an Alaska Native organization pursuant to the MMPA's section 119, and prohibit the sale of Cook Inlet beluga whale products. 65 Fed. Reg. 59164 (Oct. 4, 2000).

4. How demanding is the requirement that the Secretary base the determinations whether any of the five factors is present on the "best scientific and commercial data available"? What is the Secretary's obligation if the best available data is simply not good enough? In Southwest Center for Biological Diversity v. Babbitt, 215 F.3d 58 (D.C. Cir. 2000), the court held that the "Secretary has no obligation to conduct independent studies" to improve the data base. 215 F.3d at 60. The requirement "merely prohibits the Secretary from disregarding available scientific evidence that is in some way better than the evidence he relies on. Even if the available scientific and commercial data were quite inconclusive, he may-- indeed must-- still rely on it at that stage." Id. (quoting City of Las Vegas v. Lujan, 891 F.2d 927,933 (D.C. Cir. 1989), in the context of emergency listings under 16 U.S.C. 1533(b)(7)). For a critique of the requirement to base listing decisions "solely" on the basis of the best available science, see H. Doremus, Listing Decisions Under the Endangered Species Act: Why Better Science Isn't Always Better Policy, 75 Wash. U. L.Q. 1029 (1997). NMFS and the Fish and Wildlife Service published joint regulations in 1980

governing their listing and habitat designations. 50 C.F.R. Part 424.

5.   May the agency consider listing only the Cook Inlet stock of beluga whales?   Ever since the 1978 ESA amendments, the Act's definition of "species" has been broad, including "any subspecies of fish or wildlife or plants, and any distinct population segment of any species of vertebrate fish or wildlife which interbreeds when mature. 16 U.S.C. § 1532(16).   By allowing the Secretaries to list subspecies and populations, the Act gives them the authority to vary the classification of distinct groups within a given species, reflecting differing degrees of population declines and risks of extinction.   NMFS and the Fish and Wildlife Service issued a joint policy interpreting the term "distinct population segment" for purposes of listing, delisting, and reclassifying vertebrates under the ESA. 61 Fed. Reg. 4722 (Feb. 7, 1996). The policy sets out three elements to be considered in deciding the status of a possible "distinct population segment" (DPS) as endangered or threatened under the ESA: (1) discreteness of the population segment in relation to the remainder of the species to which it belongs; (2) the significance of the population segment to the species to which it belongs; and (3) the population segment's conservation status in relation to the ESA criteria for listing. NMFS determined that the Cook Inlet beluga whale, one of five stocks of beluga whale, is a distinct population segment under these criteria and therefore would qualify as a "species" under the ESA.

6.   A status review of another Alaska marine mammal, the Steller sea lion (Eumetopias jubatus), commenced in 1993, 58 Fed. Reg. 58318, (Nov. 1, 1993), led to its reclassification in 1997 into two DPSs and the downgrading of the population west of 144 degrees W. longitude to endangered status. 62 Fed. Reg. 24345 (May 5, 1997). The species throughout its range had been listed as threatened in 1990. 55 Fed. Reg. 12645 (April 5, 1990).

7.   The Fish and Wildlife Service and NMFS use the "distinct population segment" concept to facilitate the listing process and, in some commentators' view, to diffuse political opposition that a wider species definition and listing might engender. See, e.g., K. Siegel, Comment, Challenging the 'Distinct Population Segment' Definition of Atlantic Salmon Under the Endangered Species Act, 2 Ocean & Coastal L.J. 341, 361-62 (1997) ("Having removed all but the downeast rivers from consideration through the definition of the DPS, the impacts of dams on the New England rivers where they actually pose threats to the species * * * need not be addressed."); D. Rohlf, There's Something Fishy Going on Here: A Critique of the NMFS's Definition of Species Under the ESA, 24 Envtl. L. 617, 633 (1994). What is the likelihood of a successful challenge to a NMFS decision to list only those population segments of a species that inhabit areas not affected by politically powerful user groups? For a discussion of the FWS's application of the

DPS concept, see Southwest Center for Biological Diversity v. Babbitt, 926 F.Supp. 920 (D.Ariz. 1996).

8.   The Section 4 listing provision allows persons to petition the Secretary to remove a species from the endangered species list as well as to list it. 16 U.S.C. § 1533(b)(3)(A). In 1994, the eastern North Pacific stock of the North Pacific gray whale became one of the first marine species to be removed from the endangered species list, after the Northwest Indian Fisheries Commission and others petitioned for its removal. NMFS determined the stock had recovered to between 60 and 90% of its carrying capacity. 59 Fed. Reg. 31094 (June 16, 1994). A petition to relist the gray whale was filed in March 2001 on behalf of Australians for Animals, The Fund for Animals, and several other groups, who claimed the gray whale was inadequately protected under the MMPA and the subsistence takes policies of the International Whaling Commission (which had granted a gray whale quota in 1997 on a joint request from the U.S. and Russia on behalf of the Makah Tribe and native peoples in Russia). NMFS found that the petition did not present substantial scientific or commercial information to warrant listing as either threatened or endangered.   The best available information shows that the gray whales are within their MMPA-required population levels. 66 Fed. Reg. 32305 (June 14, 2001).

9.   Some of the most controversial ESA listing decisions concern several runs of the five species of Pacific salmon whose habitats have been greatly modified by hydroelectric development of the river systems of the Pacific Northwest, timber harvesting, and agriculture. Decisions not to list a species as endangered or threatened are subject to the citizen suit provision of § 1540(g), which allows any person to commence a civil suit against the Secretary for alleged failure to perform acts or duties under Section 4 which are not discretionary, as well as to enjoin violations of the Act by other persons or agencies.

In Oregon Natural Resources Council v. Daley, 6 F.Supp.2d 1139 (D.Or. 1998), the court invalidated NMFS's final rule that the Oregon Coast unit of coho salmon did not warrant listing as a threatened species under the ESA based on proposed state conservation measures identified in the Oregon Coastal Salmon Restoration Initiative, which relied largely on voluntary measures aimed at avoiding an ESA listing. In August 1998, pursuant to the court order, NMFS announced its decision to list the Oregon Coast coho "evolutionary significant unit" (ESU) as threatened, but excluded the nine Oregon hatchery populations, which were part of the ESU, from the listing. 63 Fed. Reg. 42587 (Aug. 10, 1998). This listing was challenged. In Alsea Valley Alliance v. Evans, 161 F.Supp.2d 1154 (D.Ore. 2001), the court held that the decision to list only naturally spawning salmon as "threatened" was arbitrary and capricious. In response to the ruling, NMFS announced it would begin a rulemaking process to determine what standards should be applied to salmon populations that include hatchery-reared fish.

10. Once a species or population segment is listed under the Act three major provisions of the Act are then triggered. Section 9's prohibition against taking the listed species and the civil penalties for doing so are invoked. 16 U.S.C. §§ 1538(a), 1540(a). The Secretary assumes the responsibility to develop protective regulations and recovery plans for the conservation and survival of the listed species "us[ing] all methods and procedures which are necessary to bring any [listed] species to the point" where the species would no longer require listing. 16 U.S.C. §§ 1533(d),(f); 1532(3). And finally, it becomes incumbent upon any federal agency to insure that its actions are not likely "to jeopardize the continued existence of" the listed species or result in the adverse modification of its critical habitat, and to consult with the Secretary and seek her biological opinion to insure no jeopardy. 16 U.S.C. § 1536(a),(b). Citizens can challenge the adequacy of agency performance of these duties under the citizen suit provision. 16 U.S.C. § 1540(g). What is the standard of proof for such challenges? Will the courts enforce substantive as well as procedural requirements of the Act? See Section 2(C)(4.), infra.

Once a species is listed, what obligation are the Secretaries under to designate critical habitat? What additional protection from extinction does the designation of critical habitat provide a listed species?

SIERRA CLUB v. U.S. FISH & WILDLIFE SERVICE
United States of Appeals, Fifth Circuit, 2001
245 F.3d 434

HIGGINBOTHAM, CIRCUIT JUDGE:

The Gulf sturgeon is a large, wide-ranging fish that can reach up to fifty years of age and five-hundred pounds in size. The sturgeon is one of the few anadromous species in the Gulf of Mexico, migrating between fresh and salt water. The sturgeon spends spring and summer in the Gulf Coast rivers from Louisiana to Florida. In the winter months, the sturgeon returns to the waters of the Gulf of Mexico to feed. Although the sturgeon once supported a major commercial fishery, habitat destruction and overfishing conspired to bring about a population collapse. This alarming decrease in population led to the sturgeon's listing as a threatened species in 1991.

The listing of the sturgeon as a threatened species triggered the "critical habitat" provisions of the ESA. The ESA requires the Secretary of the Interior to "designate any habitat of such species which is then considered to be critical habitat" concurrently with the listing of the threatened species, unless a statutory exception applies. Although the Secretary invoked two one-year statutory extensions from the listing date, no critical habitat was designated for the sturgeon by the deadline.

In 1994, the Orleans Audubon Society filed suit in the United States District Court for the Eastern District of Louisiana, seeking to compel the Department of the Interior to decide whether to designate critical habitat for the sturgeon.   While the litigation was pending, the Department assured the Orleans Audubon Society and the district court that it was in the process of designating critical habitat for the sturgeon. The FWS prepared a draft proposal to this effect, which stated that critical habitat designation would provide additional benefit to the sturgeon.   The court ordered the Department on August 9, 1995, to "take all appropriate action," prompting the Department to render a decision.

On August 23, 1995, the FWS and the NMFS signaled an abrupt change of course.   The Services decided not to designate critical habitat for the sturgeon, finding that it was "not prudent" to do so. The Services concluded that designation would not provide additional benefit to the species beyond other statutory regimes and conservation programs in place. In the wake of this decision, the Gulf States Marine Fisheries Commission approved a comprehensive Recovery/Management Plan for the Gulf sturgeon.

The Orleans Audubon Society amended its complaint to challenge the Services' refusal to designate critical habitat.   The district court found that the Services had failed to articulate a rational basis for their finding that designation was "not prudent." Although the Services' decision described various programs that would ostensibly provide benefit to the sturgeon in lieu of designation, the court found no evidence in the record to support this assertion. It therefore remanded to the Services for action in accordance with the best scientific evidence available.

On February 27, 1998, the Services decided on remand that critical habitat designation remained "not prudent." The Services found that designation would not provide any additional benefit to the sturgeon. The Sierra Club challenged this decision in the U.S. District Court for the Eastern District of Louisiana. Although the district court conceded that the regulation on which the Services based much of their reasoning, 50 C.F.R. § 402.02, appeared to conflict with the language of the ESA, the district court granted summary judgment in favor of the Services. The court found that the Services's conclusions were "minimally rational" and supported by the best scientific evidence available.   Sierra Club appeals the court's ruling.

II

In 1973, Congress enacted the ESA as a "means whereby the

ecosystems upon which endangered species and threatened species depend may be conserved," and "to provide a program for the conservation of such endangered species and threatened species." The ESA defines "conservation" as "the use of all methods and procedures which are necessary to bring any endangered species or threatened species to the point at which the measures provided [by the ESA] are no longer necessary." As the district court observed, the objective of the ESA is to enable listed species not merely to survive, but to recover from their endangered or threatened status.[3]

To achieve this objective, Congress required the Secretary of the Interior to designate a "critical habitat" for all listed species. The ESA defines occupied critical habitat as "the specific areas within the geographic area occupied by the species, at the time it is listed ... on which are found those physical or biological features (I) essential to the conservation of the species and (II) which may require special management considerations or protection." In addition to "occupied habitat," the ESA contemplates the designation of "unoccupied critical habitat." Unoccupied habitat is composed of the "specific areas outside the geographical area occupied by the species at the time it is listed * * * upon a determination by the Secretary that such areas are essential for the conservation of the species."

Once a species has been listed as endangered or threatened, the ESA states that the Secretary "shall" designate a critical habitat "to the maximum extent prudent or determinable." The ESA leaves to the Secretary the task of defining "prudent" and "determinable." According to Interior Department regulations, critical habitat designation is "not prudent" where either of two conditions is met: "(i) [t]he species is threatened by taking or other human activity, and identification of critical habitat can be expected to increase the degree of such threat to the species, or (ii)[s]uch designation of critical habitat would not be beneficial to the species." Although the ESA does not define the scope of the "not prudent" exception, the statute requires the Secretary to make the designation decision "on the basis of the best scientific data available and after taking into consideration the economic impact, and any other relevant impact, of specifying any particular area as critical habitat."

Critical habitat designation primarily benefits listed species through the ESA's consultation mechanism. Section 7(a)(2) of the statute requires federal agencies to consult with the Secretary to "insure that any action authorized, funded, or carried out by such agency * * * is not

---

[3] *See* 50 C.F.R. § 402.02 (2000) (" 'Recovery' means improvement in the status of listed species to the point at which listing is no longer appropriate under the criteria set out in" the ESA) (emphasis omitted); 63 Fed.Reg. At 9968 ("[T]he Act defines 'conservation' to mean recovery of the species").

likely to jeopardize the continued existence of any endangered species or threatened species or result in the destruction or adverse modification" of that species's critical habitat. Thus, regardless of whether critical habitat is designated, an agency must consult with the Secretary where an action will "jeopardize the continued existence" of a species. If critical habitat has been designated, the statute imposes an additional consultation requirement where an action will result in the "destruction or adverse modification" of critical habitat.

Although the ESA does not elaborate on the two consultation scenarios discussed above, 50 C.F.R. § 402.02 defines each in terms of the effects of agency action on both the survival and recovery of the species. Thus, to "jeopardize the continued existence of" a species is "to engage in an action that reasonably would be expected, directly or indirectly, to reduce appreciably the likelihood of *both the survival and recovery* of a listed species in the wild." This "jeopardy standard" is similar to the regulation's description of "destruction or adverse modification" of critical habitat. The regulation defines "destruction or adverse modification" as "a direct or indirect alteration that appreciably diminishes the value of critical habitat for *both the survival and recovery* of a listed species."

III

The 1998 critical habitat decision by the Services relied on the "not prudent" exception to the ESA. The Services noted, first, that "[c]ritical habitat, by definition, applies only to Federal agency actions." They observed that agencies would have to engage in "jeopardy consultation" under the ESA where agency action could jeopardize the existence of a listed species. The Services reasoned that virtually any federal action that would adversely modify or destroy the Gulf sturgeon's critical habitat would also jeopardize the species' existence and trigger jeopardy consultation. Relying on the definitions of the destruction/adverse modification and jeopardy standards in 50 C.F.R. § 402.02, the Services concluded that designation of critical habitat would provide no additional benefit to the sturgeon beyond the protections currently available through jeopardy consultation.

The Services also considered the merits of critical habitat designation in light of federal and state statutory prohibitions against taking members of the species; the water quality standards set by Gulf Coast states; the federal Clean Water Act; and the priority tasks of the Recovery/Management Plan established for the sturgeon. The Services concluded that, where the protections afforded by these measures proved insufficient to safeguard the survival of the sturgeon, jeopardy consultation would be sufficient.

The Services further noted that it was rare for agency action to adversely modify or destroy critical habitat without also jeopardizing the existence of the species.   The Services concluded that these rare instances might involve federal action in the unoccupied critical habitat of an endangered species. Because critical habitat designation would protect the survival and recovery of the endangered species in a manner not afforded by jeopardy consultation, designation would be beneficial in those instances.   Since the sturgeon is merely a *threatened* species, however, the Services reasoned that expansion of its population into unoccupied critical habitat would not be necessary for both survival and recovery. Later in the decision, the Services stated: "Protection of unoccupied habitat is * * * essential for full recovery, but not for survival of the Gulf sturgeon." Designation of unoccupied habitat was therefore deemed not prudent.

IV

A

Sierra Club contends that the regulation which informs much of the Services' 1998 decision facially conflicts with the ESA. We review a regulation interpreting the ESA under Chevron, U.S.A., Inc. v. Natural Resources Defense Council, Inc.[467 U.S. 837 (1984).] * * *

With the appropriate standard of review in mind, we turn to the merits of Sierra Club's challenge to 50 C.F.R. § 402.02. Sierra Club observes that the regulation defines the jeopardy and destruction/adverse modification standards in terms of both survival and recovery. Arguing that the regulation consequently equates the two consultation standards, Sierra Club asserts that 50 C.F.R. § 402.02 violates a cardinal principle of statutory construction-- i.e., "to give effect, if possible, to every clause and word of a statute * * * rather than to emasculate an entire section."[4] Sierra Club argues that the ESA contemplates two separate standards and that the regulation impermissibly conflates the two consultation standards.

We are unpersuaded by this argument. The mere fact that both definitions are framed in terms of survival and recovery does not render them equivalent. Significantly, the destruction/adverse modification standard is defined in terms of actions that diminish the "*value of critical habitat* " for survival and recovery. Such actions conceivably possess a more attenuated relationship to the survival and recovery of the species. The destruction/adverse modification standard focuses on the action's effects on critical habitat. In contrast, the jeopardy standard addresses the effect of the action itself on the survival and recovery of the species.

---

[4] *Bennett v. Spear*, 520 U.S 154, 173 (1997).

The language of the ESA itself indicates two distinct standards;[5] the regulation does not efface this distinction.

Sierra Club also contends that the regulation "sets the bar too high" for the destruction/adverse modification standard. Sierra Club argues that the regulation's requirement that an action affect both survival and recovery conflicts with the ESA. According to Sierra Club, the ESA requires consultation where an action affects recovery alone; it is not necessary for an action to affect the survival of a species.

On this point, we are in agreement with Sierra Club. The ESA defines "critical habitat" as areas which are "essential to the conservation" of listed species. "Conservation" is a much broader concept than mere survival. The ESA's definition of "conservation" speaks to the recovery of a threatened or endangered species.[6] Indeed, in a different section of the ESA, the statute distinguishes between "conservation" *and* "survival."[7] Requiring consultation only where an action affects the value of critical habitat to both the recovery and survival of a species imposes a higher threshold than the statutory language permits.

The legislative history of the ESA affirms the inconsistency of 50 C.F.R. § 402.02 with the statute. A 1978 regulation defined "critical habitat" for purposes of the ESA as "any air, land or water area * * * the loss of which would appreciably decrease the likelihood of the *survival and recovery* of a listed species or a distinct segment of its population*

---

[5] *See Greenpeace v. National Marine Fisheries Serv.*, 55 F.Supp.2d 1248, 1265 (W.D.Wash.1999) ("Although there is considerable overlap between the two, the Act established two separate standards to be considered."); *Conservation Council for Hawai'i v. Babbitt*, 2 F.Supp.2d 1280, 1287 (D.Haw.1998) ("[T]he ESA clearly established two separate considerations, jeopardy and adverse modification, but recognizes * * * that these standards overlap to some degree.").

[6] *Compare* 16 U.S.C.A. § 1532(3) (defining "conservation" as "the use of all methods and procedures which are necessary to bring any endangered species or threatened species to the point at which the measures provided pursuant to this chapter are no longer necessary"), *with* 50 C.F.R. § 402.02 (" 'Recovery' means improvement in the status of listed species to the point at which listing is no longer appropriate under the criteria set out in" the ESA).

[7] *See* 16 U.S.C.A. § 1533(f)(1) (stating that recovery plans should be crafted "for the conservation and survival" of endangered and threatened species); *see also Sullivan v. Stroop*, 496 U.S. 478 (1990) ("[I]dentical words used in different parts of the same act are intended to have the same meaning."); *United States Ass'n of Texas v. Timbers of Inwood Forest Assocs., Ltd.*, 484 U.S. 365, 371 (1998) ("Statutory construction * * * is a holistic endeavor. A provision that may seem ambiguous in isolation is often clarified by the remainder of the statutory scheme - because the same terminology is used elsewhere in a context that makes its meaning clear * * *.").

* *"[8] Although Congress was aware of this regulatory interpretation of the statute, it chose not to adopt this approach when it amended the ESA in 1978 to define critical habitat. Instead, Congress employed the current statutory definition, which is grounded in the concept of "conservation." As a House Report accompanying a subsequent appropriations bill indicated, the 1978 amendments "significantly altered" the agency definition of critical habitat, which was phrased in terms of effects on both survival and recovery. The Services' definition of the destruction/adverse modification standard in terms of survival and recovery is consequently an attempt to revive an interpretation that was rejected by Congress.

We further note that 50 C.F.R. § 402.02 renders it less likely that critical habitat will be designated. Because of the higher threshold imposed by defining the destruction/adverse modification standard in terms of both survival and recovery, federal agencies would be required to consult with the Department of Interior less frequently than if the standard were defined in terms of recovery alone. Because the jeopardy standard already requires agencies to consult with the Department where their actions would affect both the survival and recovery of a species, it is less likely that the Services would discern additional benefit from designating critical habitat. Consequently, the Services are more likely to find designation "not prudent." This result is in tension with the avowed intent of Congress that a "not prudent" finding regarding critical habitat would only occur under "rare" or "limited" circumstances. In practice, the Services have inverted this intent, rendering critical habitat designation the exception and not the rule.[9] The rarity of designation is attributable, in part, to the manner in which the Services have defined the jeopardy and destruction/adverse modification standards.[10]

---

[8] 50 C.F.R. § 402.02 (1978) (emphasis added). The 1978 regulation also contained a definition of "destruction or adverse modification" that is virtually identical to the current definition. The 1978 definition read: "a direct or indirect alteration of critical habitat which appreciably diminishes the value of that habitat for survival and recovery of a listed species." *Id.* The only salient difference between the two definitions is that the current definition refers to "*both* survival and recovery." *See* 50 C.F.R. § 402.02 (2000) (emphasis added).

[9] *See* S.Rep. No. 106-126, at 2, 4 (1999) (observing the infrequency of critical habitat deisgnation in practice and noting that the "not prudent" exception was intended to be exercised "only rarely"); Thomas F. Darin, Comment, *Designating Critical Habitat Under the Endangered Species Act: Habitat Protection Versus Agency Discretion*, 24 Harv. Envt'l L.Rev. 209, 224 (2000) (noting that, by 1999, the Services had only designated critical habitat for 120 out of 1,181 listed species).

[10] *See* Pamela Baldwin, *The Role of Designation of Critical Habitat Under the Endangered Species Act*, CRS Report for Congress, at 5-6 (1999) (tracing the infrequency of critical habitat designation to the Service's definition of the destruction/adverse modification standard); Darin, *supra* n. 58, at 224 (noting that the "not prudent" rationale

Based on the manifest inconsistency between 50 C.F.R. § 402.02 and Congress's "unambiguously expressed intent" in the ESA, we find the regulation's definition of the destruction/adverse modification standard to be facially invalid.[11]

<h1 style="text-align:center">B</h1>

We now turn to the substance of the 1998 decision. The district court found the 1998 decision to be valid, despite the facial conflict between 50 C.F.R. § .402.02 and the ESA. The court found that the decision was not arbitrary and capricious because "the agencies considered all of the necessary factors, which extend beyond the scope of the regulation, and articulated minimally rational conclusions that are supported by the factual record." The court further noted that the decision was based on the best scientific data available.

Sierra Club contests the court's findings, arguing that the Services' reliance on 50 C.F.R. § 402.02 went to the heart of its decision. Sierra Club contends that the agency further misinterpreted the ESA by concluding that designation of unoccupied habitat is never beneficial for threatened species * * * We address each of these contentions in turn.

<h1 style="text-align:center">1</h1>

In addition to our power to review agency interpretations under *Chevron*, we may review the reasonableness of an agency's decision-making process under the Administrative Procedure Act (APA). We reverse agency action that is "arbitrary, capricious, an abuse of discretion, or otherwise not in accordance with law." Review is generally limited to the record in existence at the time the agency made its decision * * *

* * * The Services expressly found that designation of unoccupied critical habitat was necessary to the recovery, but not the survival, of the sturgeon. In this instance, the invalid regulation directly informed the Services' conclusion that designation was not warranted. Moreover, the Services' evaluation of the merits of critical habitat designation was premised on the view that jeopardy consultation was "functionally equivalent" to consultation under the destruction/adverse modification standard. This position was based on the fact that 50 C.F.R. § 402.02

---

was the most common reason for not designating critical habitat and stating that the FWS employed a "strained interpretation" of that exception).

[11] We emphasize that our holding applies only to the definition of "destruction or adverse modification." The remainder of 50 C.F.R. § 402.02 - including the regulation's definition of "jeopardize the continued existence of" - is unaffected by our ruling.

defined both standards in terms of survival and recovery. As we have concluded that the regulatory definition of the destruction/adverse modification standard is flawed, this "functional equivalence" argument is untenable.[12] The 1998 decision also considered the benefits of designation in light of existing protections outside the ESA consultation mechanism (e.g., state and federal clean water laws). However, this analysis was further guided by the "survival and recovery" threshold.

2

We note that the Services' reliance on 50 C.F.R. § 402.02 also led them to erroneous conclusions regarding the benefit of designation for threatened species. Submerged in the 1998 decision is the contention that designation would only be "beneficial" in relation to the unoccupied habitat of certain endangered species. The Services reasoned that "[s]ince *threatened* species such as the Gulf sturgeon are, by definition, not currently at risk of extinction, but are rather anticipated to become so in the foreseeable future, unoccupied critical habitat would not be immediately required for their survival." This conclusion was based, in part, on the regulation's definition of the destruction/adverse modification standard in terms of both survival and recovery.

Although we find the Services' reasoning to be flawed on the preceding basis alone, we note an additional source of error: the Services' argument would effectively prevent all threatened species from receiving critical habitat designation. It is difficult to reconcile this result with the ESA, which states that critical habitat "shall" be designated for threatened, as well as endangered, species. The agency's interpretation would read these provisions out of the statute. In light of the preceding errors, it is of no moment that the Services may have based their conclusions on the "best scientific data available." Given the extent of the Services' reliance on an invalid regulation, we conclude that the 1998 decision was arbitrary and capricious.

* * *

---

[12] We also question the rationale underlying the entire 1998 decision - i.e., that designation is not "beneficial" to a species where it is less beneficial than other existing protections. As the Ninth Circuit observed in a recent opinion, "[n]either the Act nor the implementing regulations sanctions nondesignation of habitat when designation would be merely *less* beneficial to the species than another type of protection." *Natural Resources Defense Council v. Department of Interior*, 113 F.3d 1121, 1127 (9th Cir.1997). However, as the ESA is ambiguous on this point, we are unprepared to conclude that the Services' interpretation is an impermissible construction of the statute. *See Chevron U.S.A., Inc. v. Natural Resources Defense Council, Inc.*, 467 U.S. 837, 843 (1984).

Notes and Questions

1. Why would the FWS or NMFS be reluctant to designate critical habitat for a listed species? In 1999, the FWS announced its intention to develop policy and revise regulations, if necessary, to clarify the role of habitat in endangered species conservation. 64 Fed. Reg. 31871 (June 14, 1999). In the notice, the Service noted that "[w]hile attention to and protection of habitat is paramount to successful conservation actions, we have long believed that, in most circumstances, the designation of "official" critical habitat is of little additional value for most listed species, yet it consumes large amounts of conservation resources." Id. at 31872.

2. How much information must the Secretary have about the biology and ecology of a species before its critical habitat is "determinable" within the meaning of section 4(a)(3) of the ESA, 16 U.S.C. § 1533(a)(3)? See 50 C.F.R. § 424.12(a).

3. In 2001, NMFS received a petition asking it to revise the critical habitat for the Pacific population of Northern right whales to include an area of approximately 200,000 square kilometers of the Southeastern Bering Sea. See 66 Fed. Reg. 29773 (June 1, 2001)(NMFS 90-finding and request for public comment). The petition was denied in Feb. 2002. See 67 Fed. Reg. 7660 (Feb. 20, 2002). What issues would the extended critical habitat have raised?

NMFS also received a petition to designate critical habitat for the Western Arctic stock of bowhead whales (*Balaena mysticetus*), which was listed as endangered in June, 1970, prior to the addition of critical habitat provisions to the ESA by the 1978 amendments. The areas that would be included are the bowheads' summering area in the Beaufort Sea off Alaska's North Slope, between Point Barrow and the Canadian border, from mean high tide to about 170 km offshore. NMFS determined that the petition presented substantial scientific information "indicating that the action may be warranted" and sought public comment. 66 Fed. Reg. 28141, 28142 (May 22, 2001).

(2.) Prohibition on Taking Listed Species

Like the Marine Mammal Protection Act (MMPA), the Endangered Species Act protects certain fish and wildlife by prohibiting a broad range of public and private activities that could constitute a "take" of a listed species. 16 U.S.C. § 1538(a)(1). The Act defines the term "take" as meaning to harass, harm, pursue, hunt, shoot, wound, kill, trap, capture or collect, or to attempt to engage in any such activity." Id. at § 1532(19). Federal regulations interpreting the term "harm" under the ESA, however, also encompass "significant habitat modification or degradation." This interpretation was upheld by the Supreme Court in

Sweet Home Chapter of Communities for a Great Oregon v. Babbitt, 515 U.S. 687 (1995). NMFS published regulations adopting a consistent interpretation of the term "harm" that includes habitat destruction for marine listed species, including Pacific salmon and steelhead stocks. 63 Fed. Reg. 60727 (Nov. 8, 1999) (codified at 50 C.F.R. § 222.102). Under these regulations, an action that changes or degrades the habitat of a listed marine species where it actually kills or injures the species by significantly impairing essential behavior patterns, including breeding, spawning, rearing, migrating, feeding, and sheltering, will be a violation of the Act. Given the range of activities that occur in coastal waters and the shared jurisdiction between state and federal governments, section 9 has the potential to alter state as well as private actions in significant ways.

STRAHAN v. COXE
United States Court of Appeals, First Circuit, 1997
127 F.3d 155, cert. denied, 119 S. Ct. 81 and 437 (1998)

TORRUELLA, CHIEF JUDGE

* * *

BACKGROUND

I. Status of the Northern Right Whale

Strahan is an officer of GreenWorld, Inc., an organization dedicated to the preservation and recovery of endangered species. Strahan, 939 F.Supp. at 966 & n. 6. Strahan brought suit on behalf of the Northern Right whale, listed as an endangered species by the federal government. See 50 C.F.R. § 222.23(a). Northern Right whales are the most endangered of the large whales, Strahan, 939 F.Supp. at 968, presently numbering around 300, 62 Fed.Reg. 39157, 39158 (1997). Entanglement with commercial fishing gear has been recognized as a major source of human-caused injury or death to the Northern Right whale. Final Recovery Plan for the Northern Right Whale (Eubalaena Glacialis), NMFS (December 1991)("Right Whale Recovery Plan") at 24; see also Strahan, 939 F.Supp. at 972. Collision with ships is also a significant cause of Northern Right whale death. See Right Whale Recovery Plan at 10; Strahan, 939 F.Supp. at 972.

The majority of Northern Right whales are present in Massachusetts waters only during spring feeding. Strahan, 939 F.Supp. at 968. The district court found, based on statements made by defendants as well as on affidavits from three scientists, that Northern Right whales have been entangled in fixed fishing gear in Massachusetts coastal waters at least nine times. See Strahan, 939 F.Supp. at 984 ("On May 15, 1983, a Right whale was observed 'thrashing around' a location three miles east of Manomet Point in Plymouth, MA because of its entanglement in ropes attached to lobster buoys. * * * Right whales were also found entangled in lobster and other fishing gear in Massachusetts waters on June 16, 1978, May 13, 1982, October 14, 1985, May 15, 1983, August 29, 1986, August 7, 1993, November 17, 1994, and August 17, 1995. At least one of these whales was not expected to survive its injuries from the gear."). Moreover, a Northern Right whale mortality was reported off Cape Cod, Massachusetts in May 1996. 61 Fed.Reg. 41116, 41117 (Aug. 7, 1996).

The NMFS issued a final interim rule proposing to close off entirely the critical habitat of the Northern Right whale and to modify fishing practices to enhance the viability of the Northern Right whale. Taking of Marine Mammals Incidental to Commercial Fishing Operations; Atlantic Large Whale Take Reduction Plan Regulations, 62 Fed.Reg. 39157, 39158-39159 (July 22, 1997). The report accompanying the proposed rule recognized that entanglement with fishing gear is one of the leading causes of the depletion of the Northern Right whale population and indicated that more than half of the Northern Right whale population bear scars indicating unobserved and unrecorded earlier entanglement. Id. The report calls for a ban on gillnet fishing and lobster pot fishing, the two manners of fishing at issue in this case, during the Northern Right whales' high season in the Cape Cod Bay Critical Habitat from January 1 to May 15 of each year, and in the Great South Channel from April 1 to June 30, until modified fishing equipment is developed that will diminish the risk of injury and death to the Northern Right whale. Id. at 39159- 39160.

II. Massachusetts' Regulatory Authority Scheme

The Massachusetts Division of Marine Fisheries ("DMF") is vested with broad authority to regulate fishing in Massachusetts's coastal waters, Mass. Gen. L. c. 130, which extend three nautical miles from the shoreline, see Strahan, 939 F.Supp. at 974. Nearly all commercial fishing vessels must receive a permit from DMF in order to take fish, including shellfish, from Massachusetts coastal waters. 322 C.M.R. §§ 7.01-7.05, 8.08. DMF is a division of the Department of Fisheries, Wildlife and Environmental Law Enforcement, which is part of the Executive Office of Environmental Affairs. The Division of Fisheries and Wildlife, a subcomponent of the Department of Fisheries, Wildlife and Environmental Law Enforcement, "has authority over all endangered species of Massachusetts including marine mammals."

The DMF has limited the use of gillnets and lobster pot fishing gear in certain areas * * *"In 1994, in response to the alarming depletion of the Harbor porpoise, DMF ordered that all sink gillnets be removed from coastal waters north of Cape Ann every November and from Massachusetts Bay and Cape Cod Bay every March." 939 F.Supp. at 975 (citing DMF Rules Update (Nov. 2, 1994)).

In addition, the DMF has established a 500-yard "buffer zone" around Northern Right whales in Massachusetts coastal waters. 322 C.M.R. § § 12.00-12.05 (1993). Defendant Coates admitted that he had "issued a limited number of scientific research permits to some whale watch vessels exempting them from the 500 yard buffer zone surrounding right whales for scientific research purposes upon application."

* * *

DISCUSSION

II. Endangered Species Act

A. Statutory and Regulatory Background

The Endangered Species Act was enacted with the purpose of conserving endangered and threatened species and the ecosystems on which they depend. See 16 U.S.C. § 1531. The ESA is "the most comprehensive legislation for the preservation of endangered species ever enacted by any nation." TVA v. Hill, 437 U.S. 153, 180 (1978) * * * The Northern Right whale has been listed as endangered pursuant to the ESA. See 50 C.F.R. § 222.23(a).

As it relates to this litigation, the ESA prohibits any person from "tak[ing] any [endangered] species within the United States or the territorial sea of the United States." § 1538(a)(1)(B). In addition, the ESA makes it unlawful for any person "to attempt to commit, solicit another to commit, or cause to be committed, any offense defined" in the ESA. See § 1538(g). The term "'take' means to harass, harm, pursue, hunt, shoot, wound, kill, trap, capture, or collect, or to attempt to engage in any such conduct." § 1532(19). " 'Take' is defined * * * in the broadest possible manner to include every conceivable way in which a person can 'take' or attempt to 'take' any fish or wildlife." S.Rep. No. 93-307, at 7 (1973); see also Babbitt v. Sweet Home Chapter of Communities for a Great Oregon, 515 U.S. 687, 703-04 (1995) (citing Senate and House Reports indicating that "take" is to be defined broadly). The Secretary of the Interior has defined "harm" as "an act which actually kills or injures wildlife. Such act may include significant habitat modification or degradation where it actually kills or injures wildlife by significantly impairing essential behavioral patterns, including breeding, feeding, or sheltering." See 50 C.F.R. § 17.3 (1994); Sweet Home, at 695-701 (upholding the regulation as a reasonable interpretation of the statutory language). The term "person" includes "any officer, employee, agent, department, or instrumentality * * * of any State, municipality, or political subdivision of a State * * * [or] any State, municipality, or political subdivision of a State* * * " 16 U.S.C. §

1532(13).

Under the ESA regulatory scheme, the National Marine Fisheries Service ("NMFS"), part of the National Oceanic and Atmospheric Administration ("NOAA") within the Department of Commerce, is responsible for species of the order Cetacea (whales and dolphins) under the ESA and the MMPA. See ESA, 16 U.S.C. §§ 1532(15), 1540; MMPA, 16 U.S.C. §§ 1362(12), 1377; Incidental Take of Endangered, Threatened and Other Depleted Marine Mammals, 54 Fed.Reg. 40,338 (1989). Under the ESA, the Secretary of Commerce, acting through the NMFS, may permit the taking of an endangered species if that taking is "incidental to, and not the purpose of, the carrying out of an otherwise lawful activity." § 1539(a)(1)(B). Pursuant to an application for an incidental take permit, an applicant must submit a conservation plan discussing the impact of the incidental takings, the steps the applicant will take to minimize the impact, and the alternatives considered with reasons why the alternatives would not be implemented. See § 1539(2)(A).

On August 31, 1995, the NMFS implemented a prohibition on any taking of a Northern Right whale incidental to commercial fishing operations. See Taking of Threatened or Endangered Marine Mammals Incidental to Commercial Fishing Operations; Interim Permit, 60 Fed.Reg. 45,399 (NMFS) (Aug. 31, 1995). In addition, the NMFS recently implemented a ban on approaches within 500 yards of a Northern Right whale. See North Atlantic Northern Right Whale Protection; Interim Final Rule, 62 Fed.Reg. 21562 (Apr. 25, 1997). This restriction brings the federal approach distance in line with the Massachusetts 500 yard approach prohibition. See 322 Code Mass. Reg. § 12.05.

Furthermore, the NMFS has proposed an interim final rule, modifying 50 C.F.R. pt. 229 and set to become effective November 15, 1997, 62 Fed.Reg. 39157 (July 22, 1997), that restricts the use of gillnet and lobster pot fishing gear during specific times of the year unless the gear conforms to marking and design requirements set forth within the provision. See 62 Fed.Reg. at 39184. * * * These proposed restrictions, however, do not impact on the district court's and this court's consideration of whether Massachusetts, through its fishing licensure scheme, has violated the provisions of the ESA.

B. Legal Challenges

The district court's reasoning, in finding that Massachusetts' commercial fishing regulatory scheme likely exacted a taking in violation of the ESA, was founded on two provisions of the ESA read in conjunction. The first relates to the definition of the prohibited activity of a "taking," see § 1538(a)(1)(B), and the second relates to the solicitation or causation by a third party of a prohibited activity, such as a taking, see § 1538(g). The district court viewed these provisions, when read together, to apply to acts by third parties that allow or authorize acts that exact a taking and that, but for the permitting process, could not take place. Indeed, the district court cited several opinions that have also so held. See, e.g., * * * Palila v. Hawaii Dep't of Land and Nat. Resources, 639 F.2d 495, 497-98 (9th Cir.1981) (holding state's practice of maintaining feral goats and sheep in palila's habitat constituted a taking and ordering state to remove goats and sheep); Loggerhead Turtle v. County Council of Volusia County, 896 F.Supp. 1170, 1180-81 (M.D.Fla.1995) (holding that county's authorization of vehicular beach access during turtle mating season exacted a taking of the turtles in violation of the ESA). The statute not only prohibits the acts of those parties that directly exact the taking, but also bans those acts of a third party that bring about the acts exacting a taking. We believe that, contrary to the defendants' argument on appeal, the district court properly found that a governmental third party pursuant to whose authority an actor directly exacts a taking of an endangered species may be deemed to have violated the provisions of the ESA.

The defendants argue that the statute was not intended to prohibit state licensure activity because such activity cannot be a "proximate cause" of the taking.   The defendants direct our attention to long-standing principles of common law tort in arguing that the district court improperly found that its regulatory scheme "indirectly causes" these takings. Specifically, the defendants contend that to construe the proper meaning of "cause" under the ESA, this court should look to common law principles of causation and further contend that proximate cause is lacking here. The defendants are correct that when interpreting a term in a statute which is, like "cause" here, well-known to the common law, the court is to presume that Congress intended the meaning to be interpreted as in the common law. We do not believe, however, that an interpretation of "cause" that includes the "indirect causation" of a taking by the Commonwealth through its licensing scheme falls without the normal boundaries.

The defendants protest this interpretation. Their first argument is that the Commonwealth's licensure of a generally permitted activity does not cause the taking any more than its licensure of automobiles and drivers solicits or causes federal crimes, even though automobiles it licenses are surely used to violate federal drug laws, rob federally insured banks, or cross state lines for the purpose of violating state and federal laws. The answer to this argument is that, whereas it is possible for a person licensed by Massachusetts to use a car in a manner that does not risk the violations of federal law suggested by the defendants, it is not possible for a licensed commercial fishing operation to use its gillnets or lobster pots in the manner permitted by the Commonwealth without risk of violating the ESA by exacting a taking. Thus, the state's licensure of gillnet and lobster pot fishing does not involve the intervening independent actor that is a necessary component of the other licensure schemes which it argues are comparable. Where the state has licensed an automobile driver to use that automobile and her license in a manner consistent with both state and federal law, the violation of federal law is caused only by the actor's conscious and independent decision to disregard or go beyond the licensed purposes of her automobile use and instead to violate federal, and possibly state, law. The situation is simply not the same here. In this instance, the state has licensed commercial fishing operations to use gillnets and lobster pots in specifically the manner that is likely to result in a violation of federal law. The causation here, while indirect, is not so removed that it extends outside the realm of causation as it is understood in the common law.

The defendants' next argument need only detain us momentarily. They contend that the statutory structure of the ESA does not envision utilizing the regulatory structures of the states in order to implement its provisions, but that it instead leaves that implementing authority to NMFS. The point that the defendants miss is that the district court's ruling does not impose positive obligations on the Commonwealth by converting its regulation of commercial fishing operations into a tool of the federal ESA regulatory scheme. The Commonwealth is not being compelled to enforce the provisions of the ESA. Instead, the district court's ruling seeks to end the Commonwealth's continuing violation of the Act.

Defendants also contend that the district court's ruling is erroneous because it fails to give deference to the position of NMFS, the federal agency charged with enforcing the ESA. The defendants' position is flawed for two reasons. First, the ESA gives NMFS, through the Secretary, discretion in authorizing takings incidental to certain commercial activity; the Act does not give a federal court, having determined that a taking has occurred, the same discretion in determining whether to grant injunctive relief. Second, the fact that NMFS has expressly declined to ban gillnet or lobster pot fishing in Cape Cod Bay does not reflect a policy determination by NMFS that such a ban is unnecessary. For these two reasons, we find the defendants' deference arguments without merit.

* * *

The defendants * * * contend that the district court ignored evidence of the significant efforts made by the Commonwealth to "minimize Northern Right Whale entanglements in fishing gear," and evidence of other causes of takings of Northern Right whales. With respect to the determination of whether a taking has occurred, the district court quite rightly disregarded such evidence. Given that there was evidence that any entanglement with fishing gear injures a

Northern Right whale and given that a single injury to one whale is a taking under the ESA, efforts to minimize such entanglements are irrelevant. For the same reasons, the existence of other means by which takings of Northern Right whales occur is irrelevant to the determination of whether the Commonwealth has engaged in a taking.

Finding neither any error of law nor any clear error with respect to the factual findings, we believe that the district court properly applied the ESA to the facts presented and was correct in enjoining the Commonwealth so as to prevent the taking of Northern Right whales in violation of the ESA.

* * *

Notes and Questions

1. Why did Massachusetts' enactment of right whale protection regulations, which preceded the adoption of the federal regulations noted in the opinion, fail to be a mitigating factor in determining whether the State's licensing of commercial fishing gear that adversely modified the right whale's critical habitat violated section 9's takings prohibition? Note that the Endangered Species Act differs from the Marine Mammal Protection Act on the issue of whether states may enact their own regulations regarding the taking of endangered marine wildlife. In section 6(f), 16 U.S.C. § 1535(f), the ESA preempts inconsistent state laws and regulations on the importation or exportation of listed species, but specifically authorizes state laws or regulations respecting the taking of a listed species that are more restrictive than the exemptions or permits provided for under the ESA.

2. The district court in Strahan v. Coxe, 939 F.Supp. 963, aff'd in part and vacated in part, 127 F.3d 155, ordered the Commonwealth of Massachusetts to apply for a general incidental take permit under section 10 of the ESA, 16 U.S.C. § 1539(a)(1)(B), and an incidental take authorization under section 118 of the MMPA, 16 U.S.C. § 1387. Section 10 allows the Secretary to authorize what would otherwise be a violation of Section 9 of the ESA, 16 U.S.C. § 1538(a)(1)(B), if the taking would be incidental to and not the purpose of the carrying out of an otherwise lawful activity and the applicant submits a conservation plan. 16 U.S.C. § 1539(a)(1)(B). The conservation plan must indicate the impact of the taking, actions to be taken to mitigate these impacts, and why alternative actions are not being utilized. 16 U.S.C. § 1539(a)(2). The Secretary is to issue the permit if she determines that the impacts will in fact be minimized and that the taking will not appreciably reduce the likelihood of the survival and recovery of the species in the wild. If the permittee fails to fulfill the permit requirements, the Secretary must revoke the permit. Id.

Pursuant to the court's order, Massachusetts applied for a general incidental take permit under either section 7 of the ESA, 16 U.S.C §1536(b)(4) (the interagency consultation provision), section 10, 16 U.S.C. § 1539(a)(1)(b) (the incidental take permit provision), or sections 101(a)(5)(E)(i) or 118 of the MMPA, 16 U.S.C. §§ 1371(a)(5)(E)(i) and 1387 (the small take exemption and commercial fisheries incidental take authorizations). NMFS denied the application because the sections were either inapplicable or it could not make the requisite findings. See NMFS, Notice of Denial of Application for a Small Take Exemption, 62 Fed. Reg. 5385 (Feb. 5, 1997).

In April, 1997, NMFS proposed a take reduction plan and implementing regulations for takes of four large whale stocks that occur incidental to certain commercial fisheries, including the Massachusetts-licensed fisheries at issue in Strahan v. Coxe, under section 118 of the MMPA, 16 U.S.C. § 1387. See 62 Fed. Reg. 16519 (April 7, 1997). These stocks include the North Atlantic right whale and the humpback, fin and minke whales stocks of the western North Atlantic. Final rules are codified in 50 C.F.R. § 229.32. Once these rules were final, and after the lobster pot and trap fisheries were reclassified from Category III to Category I under section 118, the gillnet and lobster fisheries were authorized to have incidental takes as long as they complied with the regulations. The plan was developed by NMFS in consultation with a take reduction team convened in 1996 under section 118 of the MMPA. NMFS had previously approved a right whale recovery plan in Dec., 1991 and designated critical habitat for right whales in 1994. See NMFS, Final Rule Designating Critical Habitat for the Northern Right Whale, 59 Fed. Reg. 28793 (June 3, 1994). The 1991 recovery plan had recognized entanglement in fishing gear as a significant source of human-induced mortality or injury to the right whale and recommended that NMFS develop gear modifications to reduce the risk of entanglement and implement seasonal or geographic restrictions on the use of certain fishing gears in known whale habitats. NMFS did not implement these recommendations, however, until the take reduction plan was significantly revised in 1999 and 2001 after a number of new whale entanglements that were covered extensively in the news media.

3. In 1994, Greenworld's Max Strahan sued both the U.S. Coast Guard and the NMFS for their alleged failure to address the impact of Coast Guard activities on right whales and other endangered marine mammals, including ship strikes during search and rescue missions, and to prepare adequate recovery plans. Strahan v. Linnon, 967 F.Supp. 581 (D.Mass. 1997). The federal district court ordered the Coast Guard to comply with the ESA, NEPA, and the MMPA in 1995. 967 F.Supp. at 609. The Coast Guard prepared an EIS, revised its procedures to reduce the likelihood of ship strikes, and conducted ESA consultations with NMFS to determine if these actions were likely to jeopardize the continued existence of northern right whales. The Coast Guard's

conservation program and NMFS's actions to implement the recovery plan were later deemed adequate by the district court, and the federal defendants were granted summary judgment. NMFS's consultations with the U.S. Coast Guard resulted in the requirement of the following measures: posting lookouts, reducing speed, providing training, and improving vessel operations to avoid interactions with the listed species. Endangered Species Act Implementation: Hearing Before the House Comm. on Resources, 105th Cong., 2d Sess., March 5, 1998 (statement of Rolland D. Schmitten, Ass't Administrator for Fisheries, National Oceanic and Atmospheric Administration).

(3.) Regulations to Prevent Takings

Before the lobster and gillnet fisheries of the Northeast came under ESA scrutiny, the other major U.S. fisheries most affected by the ESA were the shrimp fisheries of the Gulf of Mexico and South Atlantic. Several species of sea turtle are listed under the ESA, and NMFS has implemented regulations requiring special equipment in shrimp nets, turtle excluder devices (TEDs), to reduce the incidental mortality and injury of sea turtles in this fishery. Challenges to the scientific basis of the TEDs regulations have been unsuccessful.

STATE OF LOUISIANA v. VERITY
United States Court of Appeals, Fifth Circuit, 1988
853 F.2d 322

SMITH, CIRCUIT JUDGE:

Five species of sea turtles--the Kemp's ridley, loggerhead, leatherback, green, and hawksbill--frequent the Gulf of Mexico and the Atlantic Ocean, off the southeast coast of the United States. All of these species are listed as either "endangered" or "threatened" under the Endangered Species Act of 1973 ("ESA"). Upon inclusion of any species on the list as endangered, section 9 of the ESA prohibits any person from "taking" any such species within the United States, the territorial waters of the United States, or upon the high seas. In the case of sea turtles, it is equally forbidden to take threatened and endangered species. 50 C.F.R. §§ 222.21, 227.71. In addition to these prohibitions, the ESA permits the Secretaries of Commerce and the Interior to promulgate protective regulations.

On June 29, 1987, the Commerce Department, through its National Marine Fisheries Service ("NMFS"), promulgated final regulations requiring shrimp trawlers in the Gulf and South Atlantic to reduce the incidental catch and mortality of sea turtles in shrimp trawls. The regulations attempt to supplement ESA's prohibitions against the "taking" of protected species, and were to become effective for Louisiana on March 1, 1988. Specifically, the regulations require shrimpers operating in offshore waters *and* in vessels 25 feet or longer to install and use certified "turtle excluder devices," or "TEDs", in each of their trawls. 50 C.F.R. § 227.72(e)(2), (6)(i) (1987). If the vessel is less than 25 feet or is trawling in inshore waters, the shrimper may limit each towing period to 90 minutes or less as an alternative to using a TED. *Id*. at § 227.72(e)(3), (6)(ii) (1987).

The reason for the regulations is simple: Researchers have found that during shrimping operations sea turtles are caught in the large nets, or trawls, pulled behind commercial shrimping vessels. The nets drag the turtles behind the boats and thereby prevent them from surfacing for air. According to one study, once a turtle is within the mouth of a shrimp trawl, the animal's initial reaction is to attempt to outswim the device. Of course, this strenuous effort consumes oxygen but affords the turtle no opportunity to replenish the supply. Once trapped, if the exhausted turtle is not released quickly, it will drown. Research cited in the administrative record indicates that trawl times in excess of 90 minutes are highly likely to result in the death of a captured turtle.

The TED requirement thus applies without exception to large shrimping vessels that operate offshore, as these vessels frequently pull their nets for long hours prior to bringing their catches aboard. All of the presently certified TEDs are coated mesh, rope, or rigid frame devices inserted into the cone-shaped shrimp nets at an angle, at the point where the trawl begins to narrow. When a captured turtle reaches the TED, the device deflects the turtle to an escape portal in the top or bottom of the net. The alternative measure of restricting tow-time to 90-minute intervals applies both to smaller vessels, which tend to pull fewer nets at a time and for shorter durations, and to inshore areas, where TED use by either large or small vessels may be impaired by often heavier concentrations of underwater debris.

In October 1987, the State of Louisiana filed a complaint in federal district court, contending that both the TED and tow limit requirements are invalid. The State's complaint alleged that the regulations are arbitrary and capricious, [and] unsupported by the record.

* * *

The core of appellants' challenge on appeal concerns the sufficiency of the administrative record to support the TED and trawling-period regulations. In particular, they assert that the record insufficiently demonstrates the impact of shrimp trawling on sea turtle mortality, the efficacy of the regulations as applied to inshore Louisiana waters, and the impact of the regulations on the Louisiana economy. Appellants also challenge the regulations insofar as the administrative record supporting them fails to address serious causes of sea turtle mortality other than shrimping * * *

1. The Impact of Shrimp Trawling on Sea Turtle Mortality.

The relationship of shrimping to sea turtle mortality is strongly demonstrated by data contained in the administrative record. Since 1973, on-board observers have documented the capture and drowning of sea turtles by shrimp trawlers. Using extrapolations based upon more than 27,000 hours of shrimp trawl observation, experts have concluded that more than 47,000 endangered and threatened sea turtles are caught in shrimp trawls each year; 11,179 of these turtles drown in the shrimpers' nets. Tag returns on the Kemp's ridley also provide a fertile source of information: 84% of the Kemp's ridley turtles tagged by scientists and later recovered were captured by shrimp trawlers.

The capture and mortality statistics for Louisiana waters were derived largely from the so-called Henwood-Stuntz study, a series of extrapolations based upon 16,785 hours of observer effort in the Gulf of Mexico. Of this total, 4,333 hours were spent on shrimp boats off the Louisiana shore. During the Louisiana observation period, 12 sea turtles were taken, 5 of which had died by the time the trawl was retrieved. This mortality rate of 42% is among the highest of any state, the Gulf-wide rate being 29%. More than one-third of the turtles that were observed to have died in Gulf shrimp trawls, died off Louisiana.

Although the observers spent substantial hours on the shrimp boats, their efforts recorded the results of only a small fraction of the annual shrimping effort. Each year, commercial shrimpers are estimated to spend 2,063,074 hours trawling off Louisiana. Using a simple ratio of $5/4,333 = X/2,063,074$ and solving for X, a total of 2,381 endangered and threatened turtles would be estimated to be killed annually off Louisiana alone.

"Stranding" data further supports the conclusion that shrimping is responsible for large numbers of sea turtle deaths. Beginning in 1980, volunteers established the Sea Turtle Stranding and Salvage Network ("Network") to monitor the number and types of sea turtle carcasses stranded on beaches and in marshes and bayous. More than 8,300 dead sea turtles, including nearly 600 Kemp's ridleys, were reported to NMFS by the Network. Although determining the precise cause of a stranded sea turtle's death is difficult, a causal link to shrimping appears reasonable in light of the fact that strandings occur predominantly in areas adjacent to shrimping grounds, and that the number of sea turtle strandings increases dramatically with the advent of the shrimping season.

In addition, the administrative record established that, based upon tag returns between 1966 and 1984, 32% of the Kemp's ridley turtles incidentally captured are caught in Louisiana waters, by far the highest rate of any state or country.   Twenty-two percent of the Kemp's ridley strandings in the Gulf occur in Louisiana.   In a 1984 study, 12 out of 15 Louisiana shrimpers interviewed said they caught from 1 to 2 sea turtles each year.

In challenging the administrative fact-finding that links shrimp trawling to sea turtle mortality, appellants assert that the Secretary failed to consider the best scientific data available before issuing the regulations. The Henwood-Stuntz extrapolations heavily relied upon by the agency are flawed, appellants contend, because one of the field samples on which they are based is unscientifically small.   Specifically, appellants point out that researchers conducting the study recorded a mere two capturings of the Kemp's ridley turtles during the entire time test trawls were pulled off Louisiana's shores. The insufficiency of this sample is borne out, they believe, by the discrepancy between the Henwood- Stuntz extrapolations and observations made by the Louisiana Department of Wildlife and Fisheries.   From 1967 until 1986, the Louisiana Department conducted a total of 36,837 trawl samples, but in none of these was a single sea turtle ever reported to have been captured.   At the very least, appellants conclude, the methodology of Henwood-Stuntz is prone to grossly over-estimating the killing of sea turtles in shrimp trawls.

Although we believe appellants' challenge is not totally without merit, we are mindful that under the arbitrary-and-capricious standard, our deference to the agency is greatest when reviewing technical matters within its area of expertise, particularly its choice of scientific data and statistical methodology. In reviewing such technical choices, "[w]e must look at the decision not as the chemist, biologist or statistician that we are qualified neither by training nor experience to be, but as a reviewing court exercising our narrowly defined duty of holding agencies to certain minimal standards of rationality." Avoyelles Sportsmen's League, Inc. v. Marsh, 715 F.2d 897, 905 (5th Cir.1983) (quoting Ethyl Corp. v. EPA, 541 F.2d 1, 36 (D.C.Cir.) (en banc), cert. denied, 426 U.S. 941(1976)).   Accordingly, where, as here, the agency presents scientifically respectable conclusions which appellants are able to dispute with rival evidence of presumably equal dignity, we will not displace the administrative choice.   Nor will we remand the matter to the agency in order that the discrepant conclusions be reconciled.

From our admittedly lay perspective, the Henwood-Stuntz method of extrapolating the magnitude of sea turtle takings in shrimp trawls does not necessarily appear unreasonable.   There are more than 18,000 domestic shrimp vessels operating in the Gulf and South Atlantic.   Each of these vessels simultaneously pulls from 1 to 4 trawls, generally for 2 to 6 hours at a time. Shrimping occurs in the Gulf year-round, with most activity concentrated between June and December.   Therefore, while the 16,785 hours of observer effort invested in the Henwood-Stuntz study represents the equivalent of less than one hour of fishing by the entire shrimping fleet, we recognize that the size of the industry realistically precludes statistical findings based totally upon actual observation rather than extrapolation.

We are also unpersuaded by appellants' mischaracterization of the data base from which Henwood-Stuntz extrapolations were made. Appellants' attack is accomplished by isolating a narrow range of data concerning the most endangered of the five protected species--the Kemp's ridley--and concluding that the data concerning this single species in waters off a single state was insufficient to justify the regulations.   As already indicated, however, the regulations are intended to prevent the illegal taking of all of the five endangered and threatened sea turtle species, whose habitats are not confined by state boundaries but may encompass thousands of square miles of sea. Because each local area, indeed each shrimper, is responsible for catching only a few sea turtles each year, it is only by aggregating this information that the relevant statistics can be approximated.

* * *

4. The Secretary's Failure To Regulate Other Major Causes of Sea Turtle Mortality.

Appellants argue that the TED regulations are arbitrary and capricious because they do not address other serious causes of sea turtle mortality. As we understand this argument, however, appellants are in fact raising two separate points.   First, they appear to be urging us to adopt a novel proposition that regulations failing to address all of the causes of a problem are, for that reason, arbitrary and capricious. In doing so, they ignore the well-established rule that regulations need not remedy all evils, or none.   Nor must the government "choose between attacking every aspect of a problem or not attacking the problem at all." Dandridge v. Williams, 397 U.S. 471, 486-87 (1970). Thus, the agency's decision to attack one of the major causes of sea turtle mortality through regulation is entirely within its discretion. That dredges, commercial fishermen from other nations, and pollution also contribute to sea turtle deaths does not undermine the validity of these restrictions.

Appellants' second contention is based upon the proposition * * * that regulations issued under the ESA must halt, or even reverse, the population depletion of an endangered species. * * * appellants believe the administrative record in the instant case is * * * deficient: There is no finding that the regulations will ultimately save sea turtles from extinction; nor does the record show that sea turtles saved from drowning in shrimpers' nets will ultimately survive the other causes of sea turtle mortality for such time as to replenish or increase their numbers.

An essential part of appellants' argument assumes that the ESA authorizes the Secretary to issue protective regulations only if found actually to save an endangered species from extinction. We believe, however, that this assumption finds no support in the statutory grant of regulatory authority. To be sure, that statute mandates the Secretary to "issue such regulations as he deems necessary and advisable to provide for the conservation of [threatened] species." "Conservation" is elsewhere defined in the ESA as "all methods and procedures which are necessary to bring endangered species or threatened species to the point at which the measures provided pursuant to this chapter are no longer necessary." 16 U.S.C. § 1532(3).

In addition to this mandatory duty, however, the ESA also provides the Secretary discretionary authority to prohibit by regulation the taking of *any* threatened species of fish and wildlife. 16 U.S.C. § § 1533(d), 1538(a)(1).   This regulatory authority supplements the statutory prohibition against the taking of endangered species, see 16 U.S.C. § 1538(a)(1), the enforcement of which is not conditioned upon any showing that the prohibition will itself operate to restore the species to a level considered unendangered. Rather, Congress simply presumes that prohibited takings will deplete the species. We must honor that legislative determination.

In sum, therefore, regulations aimed at preventing the taking of a protected species cannot be invalidated on the ground that the record fails to demonstrate that the regulatory effort will enhance the species' chance of survival * * * [T]he record need only show that such regulations do in fact prevent prohibited takings of protected species. Here, the record developed by the Secretary amply satisfies this burden.

* * *

Notes and Questions

1. In 1988, Congress directed NMFS to request the National Academy of Sciences to prepare a study of its sea turtle regulations. The resulting report endorsed the agency's approach of requiring TEDs in shrimp nets used in U.S. waters, noting that the incidental take of adults and juveniles in fisheries, not habitat destruction of nesting beaches, was the leading cause of sea turtle population declines. See Michael J. Bean and Melanie J. Rowland, The Evolution of National Wildlife Law 224, n. 148 (3rd ed. 1997), citing National Research Council, Decline of the Sea Turtles: Causes and Prevention (1990).

2. Note that the TEDs regulations were issued under the authority

of sections 4(d) and 11(f) of the ESA, 16 U.S.C. §§ 1533(d) and 1540(f). The plaintiffs in *Verity* did not challenge the agency's authority to promulgate the regulations, only whether there was sufficient evidence to justify them. See Bean and Rowland, supra note 1. Should the NMFS make greater use of this regulatory authority to implement the endangered species' recovery plans prepared under section 4(f)(1), 16 U.S.C. § 1533(f)(1), which describe the scientific evidence supporting the need for recovery efforts? Does the agency have a duty to carry out the recommendations of the recovery plans? See generally, F. Cheever, The Road to Recovery: A New Way of Thinking About the Endangered Species Act, 23 Ecol. L.Q. 1 (1996); Bean and Rowland, supra note 1, at 210-212.

(4.) Federal Agency Duties

In addition to the ESA's prohibition against takings, in section 7 the Act directs the Secretaries of Interior and Commerce and all other federal agencies to carry out programs to conserve endangered and threatened species. 16 U.S.C. § 1536 (a)(1). Section 7 also requires all federal agencies to insure that their actions do not jeopardize the continued existence of listed species. This directive "has been the single most significant provision" of the ESA. Bean and Rowland, supra, at 240. It was the basis for the Supreme Court's decision prohibiting the Tennessee Valley Authority from completing the Tellico Dam because it would jeopardize the snail darter's continued existence. TVA v. Hill, 437 U.S. 153 (1978). Section 7 has also played a dramatic role in U.S. fisheries management.

16 U.S.C. § 1536. Interagency Cooperation

(a) Federal agency actions and consultations

* * *

(2) Each Federal agency shall, in consultation with and with the assistance of the Secretary, insure that any action authorized, funded, or carried out by such agency (hereinafter in this section referred to as an "agency action") is not likely to jeopardize the continued existence of any endangered species or threatened species or result in the destruction or adverse modification of habitat of such species which is determined by the Secretary, after consultation as appropriate with affected States, to be critical, unless such agency has been granted an exemption for such action by the [Endangered] Committee pursuant to subsection (h) of this section. In fulfilling the requirements of this paragraph each agency shall use the best scientific and commercial data available.

* * *

(4) Each Federal agency shall confer with the Secretary on any agency action which is likely to jeopardize the continued existence of any species proposed to be listed under section 1533 of this title or result in the destruction or adverse modification of critical habitat proposed to be designated for such species. This paragraph does not require a limitation on the commitment of resources as described in subsection (d) of this section.

(b) Opinion of Secretary

(1) (A) Consultation under subsection (a) (2) of this section with respect to any agency action shall be concluded within th 90-day period beginning on the date on which initiated or, subject to subparagraph (B), within such other period of time as is mutually agreeable to the Secretary and the Federal agency.

* * *

(4) If after consultation under subsection (a)(2) of this section, the Secretary concludes that--

(A) the agency action will not violate such subsection, or offers reasonable and prudent alternatives which the Secretary believes would not violate such subsection;

(B) the taking of an endangered species or a threatened species incidental to the agency action will not violate such subsection; and

(C) if an endangered species or threatened species of a marine mammal is involved, the taking is authorized pursuant to section 1371(a)(5) of this title;

the Secretary shall provide the Federal agency and the applicant concerned, if any, with a written statement that--

(i) specifies the impact of such incidental taking on the species,

(ii) specifies those reasonable and prudent measures that the Secretary considers necessary or appropriate to minimize such impact,

(iii) in the case of marine mammals, specifies those measures that are necessary to comply with section 1371(a)(5) of this title with regard to such taking, and

(iv) sets forth the terms and conditions (including, but not limited to, reporting requirements) that must be complied with by the Federal agency or applicant (if any), or both, to implement the measures specified under clauses (ii) and (iii).

* * *

(d) Limitation on commitment of resources

After initiation of consultation required under subsection (a) (2) of this section, the Federal agency and the permit or license applicant shall not make any irreversible or irretrievable commitment of resources with respect to the agency action which has the effect of foreclosing the formulation or implementation of any reasonable and prudent alternative measures which would not violate subsection (a) (2) of this section.

* * *

GREENPEACE FOUNDATION v. MINETA
U.S. District Court , D. Hawaii, 2000
122 F.Supp.2d 1123

KING, DISTRICT JUDGE.

The Hawaiian monk seal (*Monachus schauinslandi*) ("monk seal") is an endangered species. Statistics on the status of the monk seal paint a grim picture. Recent population estimates indicate that the current monk seal population numbers at approximately 1,300 to 1,400. A 1997 National Marine Fisheries Service ("NMFS") report noted that the seal population at French Frigate Shoals ("FFS") atoll, which is home to one of the largest monk seal colonies, has declined nearly 55% since 1989. The survival rate of monk seal pups is another portent of the bleak outlook for the monk seal. In the mid-1980's, approximately 90% of seal pups at FFS survived to age two. The survival rate declined to about 10% in the mid- 1990's. Indeed, NMFS scientists agree that "[t]he overall status of the Hawaiian monk seal is extremely grave."

The monk seal is endemic to Hawaii. It inhabits eight areas in the Northwestern Hawaiian Islands ("NWHI"): FFS, Laysan Island, Lisianski Island, Pearl and Hermes Reef, Midway Atoll, Kure Atoll, Necker Island, and Nihoa Island. Defendant NMFS has designated the NWHI as the monk seal's "critical habitat."

An active lobster fishery and bottomfish fishery operate in the NWHI. NMFS and the Western Pacific Regional Fishery Management Council ("Council") manage each fishery via separate Fishery Management Plans ("FMP") prepared pursuant to the Magnuson-Stevens Fishery

Conservation and Management Act. NMFS adopted the FMP for the Crustacean Fisheries of the Western Pacific Region ("Crustacean FMP") in 1983, and the FMP for the Bottomfish and Seamount Groundfish Fisheries of the Western Pacific Region ("Bottomfish FMP") in 1986. The lobster fishery harvests spiny lobster (*Panulirus marginatus*) and slipper lobster (*Scyllarides squammosus*). The bottomfish fishery targets snappers, groupers, and jacks. Monk seals are known to prey on the species harvested by the fisheries.

Plaintiffs Greenpeace Foundation, Center for Biological Diversity, and Turtle Island Restoration Network ("Plaintiffs") brought this suit against Defendants Norman Mineta, Secretary of Commerce; and Penelope D. Dalton, Assistant Administrator of the NMFS (collectively, "Defendants"). The target of the suit is the embattled NMFS, whom Plaintiffs allege is violating the Administrative Procedure Act ("APA"), by managing the fisheries in a manner that does not comply with Sections 7 and 9 of the Endangered Species Act ("ESA"). * * *

The crux of the ESA claims is that the fisheries are depleting the monk seal's food supply and interacting with monk seals in an injurious manner. Cast in the language of the ESA, the claims allege that (1) NMFS has been remiss in performing its Section 7 duty to consult with the Secretary of Commerce regarding the impact of the FMPs on protected species, and (2) the operation of the fisheries has resulted in "takes" of monk seals in violation of Section 9.

* * *

II. ENDANGERED SPECIES ACT

A. Section 7

Section 7 of the ESA requires every federal agency to "insure that any action authorized, funded, or carried out by such agency * * * is not likely to jeopardize the continued existence" or "result in the destruction or adverse modification of habitat" of listed species. To fulfill its obligation under Section 7, an agency must consult with the Secretary of Commerce. See id. An agency must use "the best scientific and commercial data available" in conducting the consultation. Id.

Consultation can be informal or formal. Informal consultation is an optional process designed to assist an agency in determining whether formal consultation is required. If an agency determines during informal consultation that the proposed action is not likely to adversely affect listed species or critical habitat, and the Director concurs, the consultation process is terminated, and no further action is required. See id. If, however, the agency determines that the proposed action may affect listed species or critical habitat, formal consultation is required.

After consultation is complete, the Secretary must prepare a biological opinion. The biological opinion must include a "detailed discussion of the effects of the action on listed species or critical habitat" and the Secretary's "opinion on whether the action is likely to jeopardize the continued existence of a listed species or result in the destruction or adverse modification of critical habitat," (a "jeopardy opinion"), or whether the proposed action poses no threat of jeopardy or adverse modification (a "no jeopardy opinion"). If new information reveals effects of the action that may affect listed species or critical habitat in a manner or to an extent not previously considered, the agency must reinitiate consultation. Consultation must also be reinitiated if the action is modified in a manner that causes an effect to a listed species or its habitat that was not previously considered.

Plaintiffs contend that NMFS ignored the best scientific and commercial data available in preparing the biological opinions on the Crustacean FMP. In reviewing whether NMFS's past consultation efforts satisfied Section 7 requirements, the Court applies the standard set forth in the APA, which requires that an agency action be set aside if it is "arbitrary, capricious, an abuse of discretion or otherwise not in accordance with law."

NMFS issued the first biological opinion on the Crustacean FMP in 1981. The theme pervading the opinion is that insufficient information prevented detailed assessment of the impact of the FMP on the monk seal. The opinion identified spiny lobster as a prey species for monk seals, but it could not ascertain its relationship to the monk seal diet. The opinion stated that monk seals are "opportunistic feeders supported by a diverse prey base." NMFS believed that monk seals could adapt to other prey species if lobster were to become unavailable. However, the available information did not permit NMFS to assess the amount of shift in the monk seal's diet from lobster to other prey caused by lobster fishing or the impact of that stress. NMFS opined that the lobster fishery did have the "potential of reducing the lobster populations to levels at which lobsters are no longer available to monk seals." NMFS further admitted that the maximum sustainable yield ("MSY") and optimum yield ("OY") estimates of the lobster population calculated by the Council were too high and rested on the erroneous assumption that the lobster stocks in the NWHI were unexploited. The opinion warned: "[I]f OY is overestimated the fishery could result in depletion of the lobster resources. Therefore the FMP does not insure the availability of lobster to monk seals." The opinion concluded that "[t]here is insufficient information available for the Council to be able to insure that the proposed activity will not jeopardize the continued existence of the monk seal* * *" NMFS stressed that the opinion was not to be construed as a "no jeopardy opinion" and that it "in no way alleviate[d] the Council of its obligation under Section 7(a)(2) of the ESA to insure that the activities conducted under the spiny lobster FMP are not likely to jeopardize the continued existence of the threatened and endangered species which occur in the NWHI* * *" Despite this conclusion, the opinion paradoxically recommended implementation of the FMP.[13]

The conclusions of the 1981 biological opinion are difficult to reconcile with the recommendation of NMFS that the FMP be implemented. NMFS has an affirmative obligation under Section 7(a)(2) to insure that agency action will not jeopardize the continued existence of listed species or adversely modify their habitat. Certainly, an agency's assessment of proposed action is limited by the best scientific and commercial information available. Data on the role of lobster in the monk seal's diet was admittedly sparse at the time the 1981 biological opinion was prepared. Nonetheless, when an agency concludes after consultation that it cannot insure that the proposed action will not result in jeopardy, and yet proceeds to implement such action, the agency has flouted the plain requirements of Section 7.

The next biological opinion prepared in connection with the lobster fishery, issued in 1996, assessed the impact of Amendment 9 to the Crustacean FMP. Amendment 9 established a new harvest guideline system that allowed fishermen to retain berried and undersized lobsters in a catch. The rationale was that the retention limits then in effect resulted in waste from mortality of lobsters that are captured and released without contributing to the protection of the reproductive potential of lobster stocks. The new proposed harvest management program was based on the existing model for calculating the exploitable lobster population. The models indicated that stocks of spiny lobster would remain healthy over the long term. At the same time, the opinion noted a "continuing decline in pup production, and total seal counts over the past six years, [which] is cause for significant concern." NMFS attributed the decline to several factors, one of which was the reduction of the availability of prey such as lobster due to lobster fishing. The availability of lobster had been particularly low at FFS for a number of years. NMFS maintained, as it did before and does today, that "monk seals appear to be very opportunistic and catholic feeders." However, NMFS still had not elucidated the importance of lobsters to the monk seal's diet. Regarding the effect of Amendment 9

---

[13] The biological opinion reasoned that implementing the Crustacean FMP was preferable to taking no action because the FMP would regulate the fishing industry, whereas the fishery would operate and expand without restriction in the absence of FMP. NMFS constructs a false dichotomy. If conservation of the monk seal is a high priority objective for NMFS, an unconsidered alternative would have been to regulate lobster fishing by banning it until more information regarding the impacts of lobster fishing on listed species was available.

on the monk seal, the opinion stated: "[G]iven the relatively healthy status of the stocks of lobsters and the small contribution of French Frigate Shoals to the fishery, it is expected that catch competition with monk seals at French Frigate Shoals would not likely occur." The opinion concluded that the annual harvest guidelines formulated under the proposed harvest rate strategy would protect the reproductive capacity and existing stock of lobster in the NWHI.

The 1996 opinion in many ways perpetuated the errors of the 1981 opinion. As a memorandum from one NMFS scientist to another regarding the 1996 opinion reveals, NMFS takes the position in the opinion that its knowledge of monk seal behavior had not advanced much in the past fifteen years. And so management of the lobster fishery remained relatively unchanged. The harvest management system under Amendment 9 was predicated on the existing model of calculating the exploitable population of lobster, with the addition of a guideline permitting retention of berried and undersized lobsters. NMFS ignored the flaws of that model, as evidenced by its observation in the 1996 opinion that the status of the lobster stocks was relatively healthy. In fact, the lobster stocks showed signs of stress. From 1983 to 1991, the catch per unit effort ("CPUE") declined from 2.71 to 0.56 legal spiny and slipper lobsters per trap haul. NMFS closed the lobster fishery in 1991 and 1993. It reopened the fishery briefly in 1994, but aborted the season shortly after it began when it realized that its harvest quota was too high. In the year before the 1996 biological opinion issued, the CPUE was an anemic 0.60. Such data should have alerted NMFS that the existing model of calculating the exploitable lobster population was in need of revision. NMFS ignored the data.

Moreover, the 1996 opinion overemphasized the importance of the status of the lobster stocks at FFS. A 1992 NMFS report on the status of the monk seal found that monk seals at FFS may depend on the availability of food at Gardner Pinnacles and Necker Island, where most of the lobster harvest has occurred for many years. The 1996 opinion did not examine the availability of lobster in those areas of the NWHI.

A review of the 1996 opinion convinces the Court that NMFS did not adequately discharge its duties under Section 7(a)(2). If, in the 1981 opinion NMFS was uncertain of the impact of the FMP because it knew too little about the monk seal diet, by 1996 it was emboldened by its ignorance to draw definitive conclusions about the impact. NMFS reiterated in the 1996 opinion that the available information still had not clarified the importance of lobster in the monk seal diet; yet, in a departure from its conclusion in 1981, NMFS this time concluded that no jeopardy to the monk seal would result. NMFS arrived at this conclusion despite the fact that the fishery operated up to the 10- and 20-fathom isobath areas of Maro Reef, FFS, and Necker Island--all within the critical habitat of the monk seal, which by then had been designated. The explanation for the reversal in judgment is that the 1996 opinion focused on Amendment 9 alone. But ESA regulations require NMFS to consider "the effects of [agency action] as a whole." While Amendment 9 might be an innocuous measure as far as monk seal survival is concerned, it is appended to an FMP that NMFS could not insure would be consistent with the continued existence of the monk seal. In making a "no jeopardy" determination in the 1996 opinion, NMFS essentially affirmed that the existing model of calculating lobster stocks was workable. The available data indicated it was not. By neglecting such data, and by failing to evaluate the Crustacean FMP's impact on prey availability for the monk seal in all areas of the NWHI (not just FFS), NMFS was arbitrary and capricious in reaching the conclusions contained in the 1996 biological opinion.

* * *

NMFS has failed to fulfill its "rigorous" affirmative duty under Section 7 to "insure" that implementation of the Crustacean FMP does not result in jeopardy or adverse modification. NMFS cannot speculate that no jeopardy to monk seals or adverse modification of their critical habitat will occur because it lacks enough information regarding the impact of the fishery on seals. Such a conclusion is arbitrary and capricious. Accordingly, the Court grants summary judgment to Plaintiffs and denies summary judgment to Defendants on the claim that past consultation on the Crustacean FMP violates Section 7(a)(2) and the APA.

B. Section 9

Section 9(a)(1)(B) of the ESA makes it unlawful for any person to take any endangered species of wildlife within the United States or the territorial seas of the United States. "Take" is defined as "harass, harm, pursue, hunt, shoot, wound, kill, trap, capture, or collect, or to attempt to engage in any such conduct." The term "harm" includes "significant habitat modification or degradation which actually kills or injures fish or wildlife by significantly impairing essential behavioral patterns, including breeding, spawning, rearing, migrating, feeding or sheltering." 50 C.F.R. § 222.102; see also Babbitt v. Sweet Home Chapter of Communities for a Great Oregon, 515 U.S. 687, 115 S.Ct. 2407, 132 L.Ed.2d 597 (1995) (upholding ESA regulation that included "significant habitat modification" in the definition of "harm").

1. The Lobster Fishery

Plaintiffs claim that the lobster fishery adversely modifies the habitat of the monk seal by depleting the lobster population in the NWHI. It is undisputed that the fishery removes prey from the critical habitat of the monk seal. The question is whether the removal of prey results in adverse habitat modification. Plaintiffs offer circumstantial evidence that it does. One study revealed that monk seals at FFS dive deeper and travel farther to forage than seals at Pearl and Hermes Reef because there is less food available at FFS. Another study found that monk seals at FFS consume more cephalopods than seals elsewhere because other prey is less available to them. Decreased prey availability has been hypothesized to be a cause of the decline in the reproduction, survival, and condition of surviving immature seals. Plaintiffs also rely on studies of the monk seal's diet. One study found that lobster contains amino acids and macrominerals important to bodily functions of the monk seal. Fatty acid signature analysis of monk seal blubber suggests that lobster comprises a significant part of the monk seal's diet.

The information in the record is insufficient to establish as a matter of law that lobster is absolutely critical to the diet of the monk seal. Plaintiffs may of course rely on circumstantial evidence to show a causal link between lobster fishing and the monk seal population. Circumstantial evidence was the basis for the findings of adverse habitat modification in Palila v. Hawaii Department of Land & Natural Resources, 471 F.Supp. 985 (D.Haw.1979), aff'd, 639 F.2d 495 (9th Cir.1981), and Sierra Club v. Lyng, 694 F.Supp. 1260 (E.D.Tex.1988), aff'd in relevant part, Sierra Club v. Yeutter, 926 F.2d 429 (5th Cir.1991). The difference is that the agency action in those cases destroyed or modified a feature of the species' habitat that was decidedly critical to the continued existence of the species. In *Palila*, this Court found that mamane trees were clearly essential to the endangered Palila's survival. *See Palila*, 471 F.Supp. at 989; see also Palila v. Hawaii Dep't of Land & Natural Resources, 73 F.Supp.2d 1181, 1182 (D.Haw.1999). In Lyng, the court found that the very shelter upon which the red-cockaded woodpecker depended for survival was threatened by the Forest Service's management of the Texas national forests.

Here, it is not certain that lobster plays such an essential role in the monk seal diet that a reduction of lobster prey dooms the monk seal to extinction. The studies Plaintiffs rely upon do not prove otherwise. Studies of monk seal foraging behavior may indicate a decrease in prey availability in general, but they do not show that it is a reduction in the availability of *lobster* that causes monk seals to consume other prey. Indeed, one study hypothesized that monk seals were consuming more octopi because fewer teleosts (ray-finned fish) were available. Nor do the data based on fatty acid signature analysis prove that the monk seal relies heavily on lobster as part of its diet. Dr. Sara Iverson, the researcher conducting the studies, submits a declaration to the Court in which she states that her findings "cannot be conclusive and should not be used as a basis for decisions concerning possible interactions between fisheries and monk seals." Dr. Iverson emphasizes that her research is "preliminary" and that it has not been peer reviewed. She anticipates an additional three years of research before she can make "firm and defensible conclusions" about the importance of various prey in the monk seal diet.[14]

The Court agrees that preliminary findings are not a basis for a conclusive determination that lobster comprises a significant and essential portion of the monk seal diet. On the basis of the currently available scientific information, this Court cannot find as a matter of law that the removal of lobster from the monk seal's critical habitat results in "harm" to the monk seal within the meaning of Section 9. The role of lobster in the monk seal diet is a question of fact that precludes summary judgment on the Section 9 claim.

The ruling does not assure victory for NMFS. NMFS's position is essentially that it is innocent of Section 9 violations because it is not aware of any data that confirms that it is in violation of Section 9; such is a head-in-the-sand attitude we do not condone.[15] It is also a position in conflict with the underlying philosophy of the ESA. But to this problem we assign the requirements of NEPA and Section 7 of the ESA, not section 9.[16]

Because a material question of fact exists, the Court DENIES summary judgment to Plaintiffs and DENIES summary judgment to Defendants on the Section 9 claim with respect to the lobster fishery.

* * *

Notes and Questions

1. In Greenpeace Foundation v. Mineta, Judge King noted that with respect to federal fisheries management, the National Marine Fisheries Service consults with itself. Because it has responsibility for approving

---

[14] Dr. Iverson has presented her preliminary findings to NMFS's Monk Seal Recovery Team, but chiefly for the purpose of demonstrating fatty acid signature analysis as an innovative technique of examining diets in free-ranging animals, and to report on the progress of her research.

[15] With all this talk of seals, fish and lobsters, we break the monotony by tendering a fact about a terrestrial member of the animal kingdom. The legend that ostriches bury their heads when faced with danger is just that: a legend. The real story is that ostriches lie on the ground with their necks outstretched to avoid detection. *See* Flightless Birds, in *Compton's Interactive Encyclopedia* (1996).

[16] Under NEPA, federal agencies are under a duty "to gather information and do independent research when missing information that is 'important,' 'significant,' or 'essential' to a reasoned choice among alternatives." Section 7 of the ESA requires agencies to use the "best scientific and commercial data available" in conducting consultation on agency action. Moreover, an agency has a correlative duty to conduct independent research and to make projections of impact to protected species based on existing information.

and implementing FMPs and amendments that authorize the fisheries potentially affecting the listed species, NMFS is both the action agency and the consulting agency under section 7(a)(2). Can the agency simultaneously meet its mandates under the Magnuson-Stevens Act and the ESA? Note that the Magnuson-Stevens Act requires the Secretary of Commerce, upon receipt of an FMP or amendment, to "immediately commence a review of the plan or amendment to determine whether it is consistent with the national standards, the other provisions of this Act, and any other applicable law; ..." 16 U.S.C. § 1854(a). When in the FMP process is the agency required to prepare a biological opinion? See 50 C.F.R. Part 402 (ESA interagency consultation guidelines).

2. In *Mineta*, the plaintiffs also charged NMFS with failing to comply with the National Environmental Policy Act (NEPA) in authorizing the Hawaii lobster and bottomfish fisheries in monk seal critical habitat. Judge King enjoined the fishery until NMFS prepared an adequate EIS and biological opinion. He noted that NMFS faced a similar charge in the same court with respect to its management of the Hawaii longline fishery for tuna and swordfish. In that case, Judge David A. Ezra partially enjoined the operation of the longline fishery until NMFS complied with the ESA and NEPA with respect to the incidental hooking and mortality of sea turtles. See Leatherback Sea Turtle v. NMFS, Civ. No. 99-00152DAE, slip op. (D. Haw. Oct. 18, 1999).

3. When a federal agency has sued a municipality to force its remediation of a serious environmental problem and then must fulfill the ESA's interagency consultation requirements before it can assist with that cleanup, how likely is the agency to conclude that the cleanup facilities it proposes to license will increase the jeopardy of a listed species? In The Bays' Legal Fund v. Browner, 828 F.Supp. 102 (D.Mass. 1993), plaintiff Max Strahan and others sought to stop further construction of a nine-mile outfall tunnel under Boston Harbor and Massachusetts Bay to discharge treated sewage effluent into the Massachusetts and Cape Cod Bays, waters inhabited by the seriously endangered Northern Right whale and several other endangered marine species. After the municipal sewerage agency awarded contracts for the tunnel's construction, the EPA initiated formal consultation with NMFS pursuant to section 7, 16 U.S.C. § 1536(a)(2). The plaintiffs contended that the discharge from the outfall would increase nutrient levels and perhaps cause harmful phytoplankton blooms in the bays, adversely affecting the endangered species there. Proceeding with the outfall in the face of this possibility violated the ESA. The court rejected this claim, concluding:

> These experts put everyone on notice of potential threats to the food source of endangered species in the bays. If and when there is concrete, scientific evidence that substantiates the likelihood of a threat, it will be appropriate to reconsider the wisdom, not to

mention the legality, of the outfall tunnel as a means of effluent discharge. Until then, however, the ESA does not require the cessation of activities because of "concerns" that some may have. Such a grave response is only required by statute when there is a "likelihood" of an adverse impact to endangered species. See 16 U.S.C. § 1536(a), (c). Nothing in the experts' affidavits comes near to meeting that standard. Therefore, I conclude that, at present, there is insufficient evidence to show that the discharge of nutrients from the outfall tunnel will harm endangered species in the bays.

828 F.Supp. at 109.

The court also rejected the claim that continued construction of the outfall tunnel before NMFS's completion of its formal biological opinion precluded the development of reasonable and prudent alternatives the opinion might identify if it determined that the project threatened the survival of endangered species in the bays. The court held that alternative means of removing the wastewater were not precluded, short of halting construction altogether, which the court found not to be a reasonable or prudent alternative, "given the adverse impact that such non-action has already had on coastal water quality." The defendants' decision to allow construction to proceed was not arbitrary and capricious. 828 F.Supp. at 113.

For criticism of the *Bays' Legal Fund* decision, see J. Kopf, Comment, Steamrolling Section 7(d) of The Endangered Species Act: How Sunk Costs Undermine Environmental Regulation, 23 B.C. Envtl. Aff. L. Rev. 393 (1996); S. Williams, Note, The Bays' Legal Fund v. Browner: Should the Courts Allow an Agency's Poor Timing to Imperil Endangered Species?, 1 Ocean & Coastal L.J. 123 (1994). For background on the Boston Harbor sewage treatment litigation, see A. Savage, Comment, Boston Harbor: The Anatomy of a Court-Run Cleanup, 22 B.C. Envtl. Aff. L. Rev. 365 (1995).

4. The continuing decline of the Steller sea lion in Alaska raises questions on the effectiveness of Section 7 consultation in the fishery management context. Do the objectives of the ESA or those of the Magnuson-Stevens Act take precedence? What is the appropriate role of the regional fishery management council in developing measures to mitigate the adverse effects of fisheries they manage on imperiled species and their critical marine habitat, especially where their habitat includes a prey species that is subject to an intensive fishery?

In Greenpeace Action v. Franklin, 982 F.2d 1342 (9th Cir. 1992), the court ruled NMFS had fulfilled its duties under the ESA when it found that a large increase in the annual catch of Alaska pollock, a prey species of the Steller sea lion, despite uncertainty about the effect of commercial pollock fishing on the sea lion, would not jeopardize the threatened sea lion if measures were taken to reduce the potential impact. In 1997, after a status review, NMFS's downgraded the western population of Steller sea lions to endangered, 62 Fed. Reg. 24345 (May 5, 1997), in view of the western population's precipitous decline since 1994 to fewer than 34,000. Greenpeace again sued NMFS over its implementation of the ESA for the North Pacific fisheries under the Magnuson-Stevens Act. Greenpeace was joined by the Sierra Club and the American Oceans Campaign in the suit, which the plaintiffs claimed was necessary to prevent collapse of the entire North Pacific ecosystem, not just extinction of its top predator, the Steller sea lion. H. Jung, Environmentalists File Suit to Protect Steller Sea Lions, Anchorage Daily News, April 16, 1998, A1.

While the litigation was pending, NMFS issued a new biological opinion that for the first time found that the pollock fisheries were likely to jeopardize sea lions and adversely affect their critical habitat. In 1999, Federal District Court Judge Zilly upheld the jeopardy determinations but found that NMFS had failed to explain how the reasonable and prudent alternatives (RPAs), drawn up by the North Pacific Fishery Management Council, would mitigate these effects, remanding them to the agency. Greenpeace v. NMFS, 55 F.Supp.2d 1248 (W.D.Wash. 1999). In Jan., 2000, Judge Zilly found that new biological opinions on all the fisheries of the area were insufficiently comprehensive and failed to analyze the full scope of the fishery management plans and the potential cumulative effects of the fisheries. Greenpeace v. NMFS, 80 F.Supp.2d 1137 (W.D. 2000), and in July, 2000, he enjoined fishing within the sea lion's critical habitat until NMFS prepared an adequate biological opinion. After NMFS issued a jeopardy opinion in Nov., 2000, with an extensive RPA spreading the fishery in space and time to reduce its impact on prey availability within the critical habitat, Senator Stevens of Alaska attached an amendment to an FY 2001 appropriations bill requiring phased implementation or replacement of the new measures and a National Academy of Sciences review of the scientific underpinning of the biological opinion. He also added authorization of $30 million in disaster relief for Alaska fishing communities and $30 million of additional research funds to test the validity of the competing theories about what is causing the sea lion's decline, including the nutritional stress and localized prey depletion theory relied on by NMFS, climate regime shifts, and the effect of killer whale predation on the Bering Sea ecosystem. Consolidated Appropriations - FY 2001, Pub. L. 106-554, Dec. 21, 2000, 114 Stat. 2763, § 209(c)(2). See NMFS, Emergency Interim Rule, Steller Sea Lion Protection Measures for the Groundfish Fisheries Off Alaska, 67 Fed. Reg. 956 (Jan. 8, 2002).

5. Often the scientific understanding of a listed species' relationship to its ecosystem is inadequate to pinpoint the cause of a species' continued decline. How much scientific certainty does Section

7 require? In Greenpeace v. NMFS, Judge Zilly held that this standard requires far less than conclusive proof. Greenpeace v. NMFS, 55 F.Supp.2d 1248 (W.D.Wash. 1999). See also Judge King's decision in Greenpeace Foundation v. Mineta, supra. Does the agency's duty under Section 7 to use the best scientific and commercial data available in making jeopardy and adverse habitat impact determinations include an obligation to conduct scientific research to provide information upon which to make those determinations? See, e.g., Roosevelt Campobello Int'l Park Comm'n v. EPA, 684 F.2d 1041 (1st Cir. 1982)(EPA violated duty to use best scientific data available in insuring that construction of oil refinery was unlikely to jeopardize endangered whales or eagles when it failed to conduct real time simulation studies of supertanker passage through narrow and hazardous channel). Does NMFS have special obligations to get the necessary information because it is also responsible for the protection and recovery of endangered marine species?

For a discussion of U.S. management of the Bering Sea in light of evolving principles of international environmental law regarding ecosystem management, see T. Smith, Comment, United States Practice and the Bering Sea: Is It Consistent with a Norm of Ecosystem Management?, 1 Ocean & Coastal L.J. 141 (1995).

SECTION 3. INTERNATIONAL TRADE AND MARINE WILDLIFE PROTECTION

The U. S. Congress has a long history of authorizing trade sanctions to enforce international fisheries and wildlife conservation agreements and resolutions, beginning with the Pelly Amendment to the Fishermen's Protection Act of 1967, 22 U.S.C. § 1978(a), and extending to the High Seas Driftnet Enforcement Act of 1992, 16 U.S.C. §§ 1826a-1826c. The latter enactment amended the Magnuson-Stevens Act to require sanctions against nations whose vessels or nationals engage in large-scale driftnet fishing in waters beyond the Exclusive Economic Zone of any nation. See Humane Society of the United States v. Clinton, 44 F.Supp.2d 260 (CIT 1999) (Secretary of Commerce unlawfully withheld decision to identify Italy as nation engaged in large-scale driftnet fishing beyond the EEZ); 236 F.3d 1320 (CIT 2001)(discussed in subsection C, infra). Officials in the Executive Branch, however, are often reluctant to impose the sanctions called for in these laws, and environmental groups have sought judicial orders requiring action. In Japan Whaling Association v. American Cetacean Society, 478 U.S. 221 (1978), excerpted above in subsection 2.A, the U.S. Supreme Court, in a 5-to-4 decision, held that the Pelly Amendment gave the Secretary of Commerce discretion not to impose sanctions against Japan for refusing to comply with whaling quotas set by the International Whaling Commission.

After *Japan Whaling Association*, Congress enacted provisions mandating trade embargoes and other sanctions to support marine mammal and endangered species protection efforts. By far the most controversial trade sanction provisions have been those aimed at "leveling the playing field" for U.S. fisheries subject to incidental take restrictions and other regulations under the MMPA and ESA. Often these fisheries compete in the U.S. market with foreign fisheries not subject to as stringent domestic conservation measures. See R. McLaughlin, Settling Trade-Related Disputes Over the Protection of Marine Living Resources: UNCLOS or the WTO?, 10 Geo.Int'l Envtl L.Rev. 29 (1997). Also, to avoid the increasingly stringent MMPA regulations, many U.S. tuna vessels changed to foreign flags of registry. See Marine Mammal Commission, 1990 Annual Report to Congress 99 (1991). Protection of marine mammals vulnerable to tuna fisheries in the Eastern Tropical Pacific Ocean required Congress to tighten the MMPA's application to foreign-caught tuna.

A. PACIFIC DOLPHINS AND TUNA IMPORTS

The tuna-dolphin controversy has played a major role in the development of U.S. and international marine resources law and policy, and its intersection with international trade law. Following a long series of enactments aimed at using the U.S. market as leverage for international dolphin conservation efforts, Congress shifted away from the embargo approach in favor of a promising new international regulatory regime.

DEFENDERS OF WILDLIFE v. HOGARTH
United States Court of International Trade, 2001
177 F. Supp.2d 1336

BARZILAY, DISTRICT JUDGE:

I. INTRODUCTION

In this case, the court is asked to evaluate the latest actions taken by the government of the United States in its long effort to protect dolphins endangered as a result of certain tuna-fishing practices. This government action began in 1972, with the passage of the United States Marine Mammal Protection Act ("MMPA"), driven by intense interest in and activity on behalf of dolphins by U.S. individuals and environmental groups, some of whom find themselves on opposite sides of the question at bar in the current case.[17]

---

[17] For a detailed history of the numerous U.S. statutory enactments and international efforts to protect dolphins, including the inevitable unintended and unforeseen consequences, and the backlashes and conflicts, see Richard W. Parker, *The Use and Abuse of Trade Leverage to Protect the Global Commons: What We Can Learn From the*

* * *

II . BACKGROUND

The ETP is a seven million square mile stretch of ocean running from the coast of southern California to Peru. Yellowfin tuna swim beneath dolphins in these waters. Because dolphins surface for air and are hence more visible than tuna, fishermen in the ETP use dolphin sightings as an aid to catch tuna. One common method of fishing for tuna in the ETP involves lowering a commercial fishing net, called a purse seine, into the water around a group of dolphins. Once the net encircles the dolphins, a drawstring around the bottom of the net is closed to catch the yellowfin tuna below. During this process dolphins may become entrapped in the net. While some dolphins are released alive, others suffocate by the time a release can be made. Although certain safety devices in the nets and other changes in fishing practice have significantly decreased the number of dolphin mortalities associated with the purse seine method, some dolphin deaths continue to occur.

A. Background Legislation

In the early 1970s, an estimated 350,000 dolphins were killed annually due to purse seine fishing. Congress passed the MMPA in 1972 in response to public concern over the ETP yellowfin tuna fishing industry. 16 U.S.C. § 1361 (1972). Congressional findings indicated that

(1) certain species and population stocks of marine mammals are, or may be, in danger of extinction or depletion as a result of man's activities; [and that] * * *

(6) marine mammals have proven themselves to be resources of great international significance, esthetic and recreational as well as economic, and it is the sense of the Congress that they should be protected and encouraged to develop to the greatest extent feasible commensurate with sound policies of resource management and that the primary objective of their management should be to maintain the health and stability of the marine ecosystem.

16 U.S.C. § 1361(1), (6). The MMPA centered on the principle of fisheries management to foster a sustainable population. The act

Tuna-Dolphin Conflict, 12 GEO. INT'L ENVTL. L.REV. 1, 6 (1999). ("For nearly ten years, the tuna-dolphin issue has been identified with trade and environment conflict. Nearly lost in the legal conflict has been the story of the quiet emergence of one of the most innovative and effective environmental regimes in the world - a regime which has reduced dolphin mortality by over 99% while eliciting a very high level of compliance from all fisheries and flag states in the fishery.")

primarily relied on a permit system to regulate fishing practices.

In 1988, Congress enacted the Marine Mammal Protection Act Amendments of 1988, Pub.L. No. 100-711, 102 Stat. 4755 (1988) ("1988 Amendments"), which specified criteria to be satisfied for the regulatory program of a tuna- harvesting nation to be considered comparable to that of the United States, and thus have access to the U.S. market. In 1990, Congress enacted the Dolphin Protection Consumer Information Act, ("DPCIA"). The DCPIA made it a violation of section 5 of the Federal Trade Commission Act ("FTCA") for any producer, importer, exporter, distributor, or seller of any tuna product sold in or exported from the United States to label that product as "dolphin-safe" if the product contained tuna harvested (a) on the high seas by a vessel engaging in driftnet fishing, or (b) in the ETP by a vessel using the purse seine method, unless the tuna was accompanied by various statements demonstrating that no dolphin was intentionally encircled during the trip in which the tuna was caught.

Pursuant to the 1988 Amendments, in August of 1990, [under court order, see Earth Island Institute v. Mosbacher, 746 F.Supp.964 (N.D.Ca. 1990); aff'd, 929 F.2d 1449, 1452 (9th Cir. 1991)] the United States imposed an embargo on Mexico for failure to achieve comparability with U.S. tuna harvesting standards. Mexico then requested the establishment of a dispute settlement panel in accordance with the General Agreement on Tariffs and Trade ("GATT"). The panel concluded that the U.S. tuna embargoes violated GATT. However, the panel's decision was not adopted by the GATT Council, and was not pursued further by Mexico in the World Trade Organization ("WTO"), GATT's successor. In 1993, the European Union ("EU") brought a GATT challenge relating to the tuna embargo provisions of the MMPA. A GATT panel again ruled against the United States, but again the GATT Council did not adopt the decision.

In June of 1992, the United States entered into the La Jolla Agreement, a non-binding international agreement setting forth programs to protect dolphins from harm in the ETP, and allowing the practice of purse seine fishing with dolphin mortality caps. Six months later, Congress enacted the International Dolphin Conservation Act of 1992 ("IDCA"), which amended the MMPA by (a) imposing a five-year moratorium upon the harvesting of tuna with purse seine nets; and (b) lifting tuna embargos upon those nations making a declared commitment to implement the moratorium and take further steps to reduce dolphin mortality. The La Jolla Agreement led to the signing of the Panama Declaration, under which the United States and eleven other nations made affirmative commitments to strengthen the protection of dolphins by (a) reducing dolphin mortality to levels approaching zero, with the goal of eliminating dolphin mortality in the ETP; (b) establishing annual dolphin mortality limits ("DMLs"); (c) avoiding bycatch of immature yellowfin tuna and other non-target species such as sea turtles;   (d) strengthening national scientific advisory committees;   (e) creating incentives for vessel captains; and (f) enhancing the compliance of participating nations to these commitments. The Panama Declaration also sought to negotiate a new binding agreement to establish the International Dolphin Conservation Program ("IDCP"), contingent upon the United States amending its laws to (a) lift the embargoes imposed under the MMPA; (b) permit the sale of both dolphin-safe and non- dolphin safe tuna in the United States market; and (c) change the definition of "dolphin-safe tuna" to mean "tuna harvested without dolphin mortality," rather than tuna harvested without any dolphin encirclement. *Panama Declaration* at Annex I.

In 1997, Congress enacted the International Dolphin Conservation Program Act ("IDCPA"), which is the subject of this litigation. Pub.L. No. 105-42, 111 Stat. 1122 (1997). The act stated three purposes: (a) to give effect to the Panama Declaration; (b) "to recognize that nations fishing for tuna in the [ETP] have achieved significant reductions in dolphin mortality;" and (c) "to eliminate the ban on imports of tuna from those nations that are in compliance with the [IDCP]." The IDCPA amended the MMPA yet again and revised the criteria for banning imports. A nation would be permitted to export tuna to the United States if it provided documentary evidence that (a) it participates in the IDCP and is a member of the Inter-American Tropical Tuna Commission ("IATTC"); (b) it meets its obligations under the IDCP and the IATTC; and (c) it does not exceed certain DMLs. Furthermore, the IDCPA changed the "dolphin-safe" labeling standard by amending the DPCIA. Pursuant to this amendment, the Secretary of Commerce was directed to make initial and final findings of "whether the intentional deployment on or encirclement of dolphin with purse seine nets is having a significant adverse impact on any depleted dolphin stock in the eastern tropical Pacific Ocean." 16 U.S.C. § 1385(g)(2). These findings would in turn be used to determine whether to revise the definition of "dolphin-safe" tuna. *See* 16 U.S.C. § 1385(d). The IDCPA provided that it would become effective when the Secretary of State certified that a legally-binding instrument establishing the IDCP had been adopted and was put into force. *See* PL 105-42 at § 8, 111 Stat. at 1139.[18]

---

[18] This provision, basing the effective date of the statute on the completion of a legally binding international agreement, is not the only noteworthy feature of the legislation. It amends the existing dolphin protective scheme for the specific purpose of supporting international efforts to protect dolphins and other species. It empowers the Secretaries of State and Commerce to "seek to secure a binding international agreement to establish an International Dolphin Conservation Program..." Although the language is specific with regard to some of the required features of such a program, it clearly contemplates that the parameters of the program await future negotiation and completion. For that reason, the language of the various provisions refer continually to the International Dolphin Conservation Program and its requirements in several contexts, including the documentation required for a nation's commercial fishing product to be

The IDCPA and the subsequent international agreement represented a change in policy on the part of the United States. Congress clearly endorsed the idea that a new approach was needed. It understood that the embargo had limited leverage on the international community. As Sen. Chafee pointed out, "the ETP is completely outside the jurisdiction of the United States. We cannot simply go in and tell others how to fish. Instead our best chance of promoting conservation is through a multilateral, rather than unilateral, forum." 143 Cong. Rec. S8294-02, 8304 (1997). Congress, however, was not abandoning its efforts to preserve the ecosystem. The safer procedures of seine-net fishing gaining acceptance among those fishing in the ETP, and embodied in the Panama Declaration, pointed to a more effective regime. That regime directly contributed to the reduction in dolphin mortality witnessed in the past decade. It also had the benefit of protecting the entire ecosystem, and not just one species. As the House Committee Report noted, alternative methods imperiled species other than dolphins, including sharks, billfish, sea turtles, and a great number of immature tuna. H.R. Rep. 105- 74(I), at 37.

With the IDCPA Congress endorsed, and charged the Executive Branch with executing, a simple trade-off. The U.S. would lift the existing embargo if other nations agreed to bind their vessels to the new, more protective practices. In addition, the crucial compromise struck during Senate consideration of the bill provided a fail-safe. While the embargo could be lifted immediately, the "dolphin-safe" label would remain in place pending a scientific review by the Department of Commerce. That review is now the subject of litigation in the Northern District of California. See Brower v. Daley, 93 F.Supp.2d 1071 (N.D.Cal.2000) aff'd 257 F.3d 1058 (9th Cir.2001). Following enactment of the IDCPA, in May of 1998, the eight nations that signed the Panama Declaration signed the Agreement on the International Dolphin Conservation Program ("International Agreement"). The International Agreement became effective on February 15, 1999, after four nations (United States, Panama, Equador, and Mexico) deposited their instruments of "ratification, acceptance, or adherence with the depository for the agreement." Art XXVII; *see also IDCPA* at § 8, 111

---

imported in the United States. Other references to the international program appear in sections dealing with such topics as the setting of dolphin mortality limits, what specialized fishing equipment may be required, and the requirement to consult with the international governing body if the United States needs to take steps to reduce unusual incidental mortality or serious injury to dolphins. Overall, the act attempts to balance the goals of opening the United States' market to the international fishing industry in exchange for its adopting more protective fishing practices and closely monitoring the results of this liberalization by requiring scientific research into the health of dolphin populations. However, even during the important monitoring process, the act requires consultation with the international governing body when the Secretary of Commerce undertakes the scientific research necessary to trigger the change in the meaning of the dolphin-safe tuna label.

Stat. at 1139.

B. The Initial Finding, the Proposed Rule, and the Interim-Final Rule.

In May of 1999, Commerce, acting through the NMFS and the NOAA, published its initial finding pursuant to the IDCPA. See Taking of Marine Mammals Incident to Commercial Fishing Operations; Tuna Purse Seine Vessels in the Eastern Tropical Pacific Ocean (ETP); Initial Finding, 64 Fed.Reg. 24590, 24591 (May 7, 1999) ("Initial Finding"). In the Initial Finding, Commerce allowed for the change in the meaning of the tuna label when it determined that no sufficient evidence existed to conclude that intentional encirclement of dolphins with purse seine nets was having an adverse effect on depleted dolphin stock in the ETP. The *Initial Finding* was challenged in the Northern District of California. See Brower v. Evans, 257 F.3d at 1060. The district court granted the plaintiffs' motion for summary judgment, holding that the Secretary abused his discretion when he triggered a change in the dolphin-safe label standard on the ground that he lacked sufficient evidence of significant adverse impacts.[19] See Brower v. Daley, 93 F.Supp.2d at 1089.

On June 14, 1999, Commerce published a proposed rule to implement the IDCPA. Taking of Marine Mammals Incidental to Commercial Fishing Operations; Tuna Purse Seine Vessels in the Eastern Tropical Pacific Ocean (ETP), 64 Fed.Reg. 31806 (June 1999) ("*Proposed Rule*"). Commerce accepted public comments on the *Proposed Rule* through July 14, 1999. Several plaintiff organizations submitted written comments on the Proposed Rule and testified at the public hearings. Commerce then published its interim-final rule. Taking of Marine Mammals Incidental to Commercial Fishing Operations; Tuna Purse Seine Vessels in the Eastern Tropical Pacific Ocean (ETP), 65 Fed.Reg. 30 (Jan 3, 2000) ("Interim-Final Rule").

On April 12, 2000, Commerce found that the Government of Mexico met the requirements of MMPA section 101(a)(2)(B) and (C) to import yellowfin tuna harvested in the ETP by purse seine vessels into the United States. Notice of this finding was published in the Federal Register on May 8, 2000. Taking and Importing of Marine Mammals, 65 Fed.Reg. 26585 (May 8, 2000).

* * *

---

[19] The trial court judge noted the extremely specific terms of the statute requiring research into the stress impact on dolphins of purse seine net fishing, the lack of any preliminary data from such projects, and concluded, "the Secretary acted contrary to the law and abused his discretion when he triggered a change in the dolphin safe label standard on the ground that he lacked sufficient evidence of significant adverse impacts." 93 F.Supp.2d at 1089.

IV. DISCUSSION

A. The Interim-Final Rule is in Accordance with Law.

Plaintiffs contend that the *Interim-Final Rule* violates the MMPA, as amended, and is therefore not in accordance with law. First, Defenders claim that Commerce ignored the plain language of the IDCPA by permitting sundown sets upon dolphins upon completion of the backdown procedure a half-hour *after* sundown, instead of *before* sundown, as stated in the IDCPA. Second, Plaintiffs assert that the *Interim-Final Rule's* triggers for imposition of embargoes upon exporting nations are unauthorized and contrary to the statutory language of the IDCPA. Third, according to Defenders, the tracking and verification programs detailed in the *Interim-Final Rule* are defective. Finally, Plaintiffs assert that, contrary to Congressional direction given in the IDCPA, Defendants have refused to implement positive incentives toward reducing dolphin mortality, and have even instituted incentives to maintain dolphin mortality at a certain level.

* * *

[The court found that the regulation on sundown sets was consistent with the intent of Congress, practical considerations, and the International Agreement. Also, the regulations pertaining to actions that would trigger an embargo, which allowed exporting nations to exceed dolphin mortality limits under "extraordinary cirucmstances" and implemented the dolphin mortality limits through per-stock per-year limits, did not contravene Congress' clear and broad mandate in the IDCPA. Similarly, the regulations implementing the tracking and verification programs for tuna labeled as dolphin safe, to prevent circumvention of the International Agreement, reflected a reasonable interpretation of the statute. The court also held that Commerce's interpretation of the statute as not requiring it to implement incentives toward reducing dolphin mortality was not arbitrary and capricious. The language of the statute stating that the objective of the tuna-dolphin program is to "progressively reduc[e] dolphin mortality to a level approaching zero through the setting of annual limits and the goal of eliminating dolphin mortality", 16 U.S.C. 1371(a)(2)(B)(iii), is merely hortatory in nature, not demanding that a system of reduction incentives be firmly entrenched in the rules. The court went on, as follows:]

In addition to stating that no incentives exist in the *Interim-Final Rule* itself, Defenders cite several examples in which the *Interim-Final Rule* mandates a "penalty" for lack of intentional sets on dolphins. For instance, 50 C.F.R. § 216.24(c)(9)(iv)(A) provides,

A vessel assigned a full-year DML that does not make a set on dolphins by April 1 or that leaves the fishery will lose its DML for the remainder of the year, unless the failure to set on dolphins is due to *force majeure* or other extraordinary circumstances as determined by the International Review Panel.

Subsection (B) of that same provision states that a vessel assigned a DML for the second half of the year "will be considered to have lost its DML if the vessel has not made a set on dolphins before December 31 * * *" 50 C.F.R. § 216.24(c)(9)(vi) provides that a vessel desiring to fish in the ETP on a limit basis may apply for a per-trip DML from the Administrator, and that

> [i]f a vessel assigned a per-trip DML does not set on dolphins during that trip, the vessel will be considered to have lost its DML unless this was a result of *force majeure* or other extraordinary circumstances as determined by the International Review Panel. After two consecutive losses of a DML, a vessel will not be eligible to receive a DML for the next fishing year.

Defenders further claim that the *Interim-Final Rule* provides a more severe penalty for not utilizing a DML than for exceeding a DML. Section 216.24(c)(9)(iv)(C) provides that any vessel losing its DML for 2 consecutive years will not be eligible to receive a DML for the following year. Yet, section 216.24(c)(9)(v) provides that a vessel exceeding its assigned DML will merely have its DML reduced for the subsequent year by 150% of the overage. Defenders conclude that not only are there no incentives to reduce dolphin mortality, but "the system is rigged to keep dolphin deaths at current unsustainable levels."

The court does not disagree that the *Interim-Final Rule* permits the maintenance of dolphin mortality at existing levels. Indeed, if a vessel seeks to preserve its allowed DML, it must make a set on dolphins. Yet, Defenders' claims that Commerce rigged the system to ensure the preservation of current dolphin mortality levels are no more than speculative. Defenders's argument conflates Dolphin sets and DMLs. The basic policy choice represented in the IDCPA is that improved techniques make dolphin sets safe if done properly. Even though DMLs are assigned to those vessels that set upon dolphins, it is to promote safe fishing practices. Assigning DMLs to vessels brings those vessels within the goals of the international agreement and promotes a reduction in dolphin mortality. Therefore, the regulations can be seen as entirely consistent with the IDCPA. Defenders have provided no evidence that Commerce has "illogically and illegally" contravened the IDCPA. The court defers to the agency's "greater familiarity with the ever-changing facts and circumstances surrounding the subjects regulated," and holds that the lack of specific incentives to eliminate dolphin mortality in the *Interim-Final Rule* are not arbitrary and capricious.

B. Defendants did not violate NEPA in promulgating the Interim-Final Rule and in Negotiating the Agreement on the International Dolphin Conservation Program.

* * *

C. The Affirmative Finding with regard to Mexico

Under the IDCPA, Congress directed the Department of Treasury to lift the embargo against tuna imports from a country if the Secretary of Commerce made specific positive findings with regard to that country. 16 U.S.C. § 1371(a)(2)(B). The statute requires a country meet the following criteria: 1) the nation participates in the International Dolphin Conservation Program, and is either a member of the Inter-American Tropical Tuna Commission or has initiated all steps required of applicant nations; 2) the nation is meeting the obligations of the IDCP and the obligations of membership in the IATTC, including all financial obligations; 3) the total dolphin mortality limits (DMLs), and per-stock per year dolphin mortality limits permitted for that nation's vessels under the IDCP do not exceed the limits determined for 1997, or for any year thereafter, consistent with the objective of progressively reducing dolphin mortality to a level approaching zero through the setting of annual limits; 4) the nation provides directly or asks the IATTC to release complete and accurate information to the Secretary in a timely manner to allow determination of compliance with the IDCP and relevant parts of the Dolphin Protection Consumer Information Act; 5) the nation is not consistently failing to take enforcement actions on violations which diminish the effectiveness of the IDCP.

Plaintiffs contend the Secretary of Commerce's affirmative findings for Mexico were flawed on five counts. First, Plaintiffs assert Mexico is not meeting its obligations under the IDCP and IATTC in four ways.[20] The second claimed flaw in the Secretary's Mexican affirmative finding is that Mexico is failing to meet its financial obligations under the IATTC; third, the Secretary disregarded the increased Dolphin Mortality Limits assigned to Mexico in 2001; fourth, that severe problems exist in the Mexican tracking and verification system; and fifth, that the Secretary's findings ignore repeated and serious violations of the IDCP by Mexican vessels due to lax Mexican enforcement.

This court evaluates Defenders' assertions that the Secretary's

---

[20] The four ways are: 1) Mexican regulations incorrectly define sundown sets; 2) Mexico is not conducting research for purpose of seeking ecologically sound means of capturing large yellowfin tunas not in association with dolphins; 3) Mexican regulations provide no incentives to vessel owners or their captains to reduce dolphin mortality; and 4) Mexico's intransigence has hampered important scientific research on stress impacts on affected dolphin populations.

affirmative finding was flawed under the APA's "arbitrary and capricious" standard. In addition, the court acknowledges that the findings are based on unique circumstances. The Secretary is making findings using a domestic standard embodied in the law and the international standards to which the U.S. law makes reference. When Plaintiffs' claims are examined using the appropriate standard of review it is clear many of them do not have merit, and none withstand scrutiny.

1. Mexican violations of IDCP obligations

* * *

Incentives: Plaintiffs' contention that Mexico is not in compliance with the IDCP for failure to provide incentives to vessel owners in their regulations "with the goal of eliminating dolphin mortality in this fishery," does not withstand scrutiny. Pls.' Br. at 56. Under the IDCP, the incentive program is one of several methods to "limit total incidental dolphin mortality in the purse-seine tuna fishery in the Agreement Area to no more than five thousand annually." Art V(1). While the hard cap of five thousand is an immediate restriction, the multiple methods specified in the agreement to achieve a lower future total are not all required to be immediately effective. The incentive program, like some of the other methods for mortality reduction, are multilateral efforts that were not fully described at the program's inception. Therefore, clearly, the parameters of the incentive program are not in place, and are not required to be at this point. Consequently, the Secretary of Commerce was not acting contrary to the law when he did not hold Mexico to such a stringent standard with regard to incentives for vessel captains and owners.

* * *

3. Mexican increased DML

Plaintiffs claim Mexico is not adhering to the Dolphin Mortality Limits (DMLs). In 2000, the Mexican fleet was assigned a DML of 1826. For 2001, the Mexican total DML is 2565. Defenders assert that the increase in the DML assigned under the international agreement violates the statutory requirement by exceeding its total annual limits "for any year thereafter." The Secretary relied on a determination made by the IATTC that "no Mexican tuna purse-seine vessel that was allocated a Dolphin Mortality Limit during the 1999 fishing year exceeded its DML." Though the Plaintiffs are not clear on exactly why an increase from one year to the next is contrary to the statutory requirements, it appears there are two different understandings of what it means to exceed the limits for 1997 or any year thereafter. Plaintiffs view this language as a one-way ratchet; the 1997 limits can never be exceeded, nor can any subsequent allocation exceed the 1997 limit. An alternative reading would understand the language to mean that governments are bound by annual allocations, and cannot exceed those allocations in the corresponding year. In addition, as the Defendant points out, whether Mexico exceeds its allocation for 2001 is not relevant to the determination of the Secretary in 2000. The limited question is whether the Secretary's determination that Mexico did not violate the DML's assigned to its vessels between 1997 and 1999 was arbitrary or capricious. There is significant evidence in the record to support that conclusion, and therefore the Secretary's determination was proper.

* * *

5. Mexican failure to take enforcement actions

Plaintiffs claim Mexico is failing to "consistently take enforcement actions" because the IATTC has reported "repeated and serious" violations by Mexican vessels. Plaintiffs do not specify how the discovery of violations, which will happen in nearly all enforcement situations, equates to failure to take enforcement actions. While it is possible violations could become so pervasive that they would indicate non-compliance by Mexico, the IATTC and the U.S. government have not reached that conclusion. * * *

Plaintiffs also state, "unregulated vessels under 400 tons are illegally setting nets on dolphins." The IDCP and the IDCPA, however, do not govern actions by vessels under 400 tons. IDCP Annex IV.2.c ("Each Party shall provide * * * a list of vessels under its jurisdiction of carrying capacity greater than 363 metric tons (400 short tons) that have requested a full-year DML."); 16 U.S.C. § 1385(d)(2)(A) ("[A] tuna product that contains tuna harvested in the eastern tropical Pacific Ocean by a vessel using purse seine nets is dolphin safe if * * * the vessel is of a type and size that the Secretary has determined, consistent with the International Dolphin Conservation Program, is not capable of deploying its purse seine nets on or to encircle dolphins.") Therefore, neither the United States or Mexican government is obliged to monitor or restrict the actions of these smaller vessels, and the Secretary was not acting in an arbitrary and capricious manner or contrary to law in not considering actions by Mexican vessels less than 400 tons.

V. CONCLUSION

For the foregoing reasons, Plaintiffs' motion for summary judgment on the record is denied and the action is dismissed. Judgment will be entered accordingly.

Notes and Questions

1. Before the 1997 IDCPA was enacted authorizing Commerce to lift the embargoes against foreign purse-seine caught tuna and implement the International Dolphin Conservation Program, conservation plaintiffs had to go to court to compel Commerce to impose embargoes under the 1988 amendments to the MMPA. In Earth Island Institute v. Mosbacher, 746 F.Supp. 964 (E.D.Cal. 1990), Judge Henderson ordered Commerce to impose an embargo on Mexico, finding:

> Congress clearly believed that banning the importation into the United States of tuna caught by foreign nations with incidental marine mammal taking rates in excess of U.S. rates would help to protect the dolphin population. Congress believed that the ban would encourage foreign fleets to adopt dolphin- safe practices * * * The 1988 amendments to the MMPA * * * were designed to address the "foreign fleet problem." The amendments were designed to limit agency discretion to determine "comparability" as to the incidental taking rate of foreign nations to that of the U.S. fleet by establishing precise and clear standards for these determinations.* * * From the legislative history, it is clear that the Congress was frustrated with what it considered to be agency foot-dragging in implementing the import ban * * * Congress clearly intended the statutory scheme it established to reduce unnecessary dolphin deaths. The Secretary of Commerce's failure to enforce the statute's clear requirements interferes with this scheme, and therefore assures the continued slaughter of dolphins. The statute was intended to use access to the U.S. market as an incentive for foreign nations to reduce marine mammal deaths. The Secretary, contrary to Congressional intent, has not provided that incentive.

746 F. Supp. at 968, 971.

The Ninth Circuit Court of Appeals upheld Judge Henderson's decision in Earth Island Institute v. Mosbacher, 929 F.2d 1449 (9th Cir. 1991). Why was the Secretary so resistant to using the tuna embargo provisions of the MMPA? One answer may lie in the aftermath of the Earth Island Institute decision.

After Congress amended the MMPA in 1988 to require embargoes of intermediary nations from which yellowfin tuna products are exported to the U.S. but which are unable to certify that those products were not caught by countries with high incidental mortality rates, 16 U.S.C. § 1371(a)(2)(ii), Earth Island Institute again sued for implementation. This time, Judge Henderson order the Commerce and Treasury Departments to ban the importation of all yellowfin tuna and tuna products from more than twenty intermediary nations. Earth

Island Institute v. Mosbacher, 785 F. Supp. 826 (N.D.Cal. 1992). In the meantime, Mexico challenged its embargo as a primary nation under the dispute resolution provisions of the General Agreement on Tariffs and Trade (GATT), Oct. 30, 1947, 61 Stat. A-11, T.I.A.S. 1700, 55 U.N.T.S. 194. In September, 1991, a GATT dispute panel concluded that the embargoes were not authorized under any of the exceptions to the GATT and were discriminatory, thereby violating U.S. commitments to free trade under the treaty. GATT, United States-Restrictions on Imports of Tuna (adopted Sept. 3, 1991)(Panel Report No. DS21/R), reprinted in 30 I.L.M. 1594 (1991). See S. Fleischer, The Mexico-U.S. Tuna/Dolphin Dispute in GATT: Exploring the Use of Trade Restrictions to Enforce Environmental Standards, 3 Transnat'l L. & Contemp. Probs. 515 (1993). Mexico did not seek to have the panel's opinion adopted by the GATT after the U.S. State Department negotiated with Mexico to seek a compromise. At the time of the negotiations, Mexico was also considering adoption of the North American Free Trade Agreement. J. Floum, Commentary, Defending Dolphins and Sea Turtles: On the Front Lines in an "Us-Them" Dialectic, 10 Geo. Int'l Envtl L.Rev. 943, 954 (1998).

An apparent solution to the immediate source of conflict came when Congress adopted in late 1992 the International Dolphin Conservation Act, Pub.L. 102-523, October 26, 1992, 16 U.S.C. §§ 1411-1418. The bill amended the MMPA to authorize the State Department to enter into bilateral agreements with all tuna fishing countries to implement a five-year global moratorium on dolphin-encircling purse seining, beginning in 1994. 16 U.S.C. § 1412(a). The amendment lifted all current embargoes and prohibited future ones for those countries agreeing to the global ban. Under these agreements, dolphin mortalities would be zero for the period from March, 1994 through February, 1999. The moratorium would affect all fishing on dolphins regardless of whether the harvests were intended for domestic consumption or export. Embargoes would be instituted automatically, however, if countries failed to comply with these agreements. See L.C. Perkins, Comment, International Dolphin Conservation under U.S. Law: Does Might Make Right? 1 Ocean & Coastal L.J. 213 (1995).

While these bilateral agreements were under discussion, the Inter-American Tropical Tuna Commission (IATTC), the organization of tuna-fishing countries responsible for the conservation of Pacific tunas, adopted an agreement, known as the Panama Declaration, to reduce dolphin deaths through international quotas, a large-scale research program on alternative fishing methods, and an international compliance monitoring and observer program. Ten of the thirteen members approved the new agreement, which would progressively reduced dolphin mortality quotas, from 19,500 in 1993 to less than 5,000 in 1999. Through the year 2000, however, the IATTC would permit 45,000 more dolphin kills than would be killed under the five-year moratorium. Declaration of Panama, Oct. 4, 1995, reprinted in Cong. Rec. S. 397 (daily ed. Jan. 21, 1997). See N. Young, W. Irvin, and M. McLean, The Flipper Phenomenon: Perspectives on the Panama Declaration and the "Dolphin Safe" Label, 3 Ocean & Coastal L.J. 57, 83-100 (1997).

The conflict intensified after a GATT panel ruled in May, 1994 on a European Union challenge brought on behalf of its members subject to the MMPA intermediary nation embargoes that these embargoes were inconsistent with the treaty. GATT: Dispute Settlement Panel, Report on United States Restrictions on Imports of Tuna (1994)(unadopted), reprinted in 33 I.L.M. 839 (1994). See S. Charnovitz, Dolphins and Tuna: An Analysis of the Second GATT Panel Report, 24 Envtl. L.Rep. 10567 (1994) and P. Yechout, In the Wake of *Tuna II*: New Possibilities for GATT-Compliant Environmental Standards, 5 Minn. J. Global Trade 247 (1996).

Although GATT did not make the panel reports final or subject the U.S. to any sanctions, the decisions did fuel the continuing controversy over the tuna embargoes. After several years of negotiations and debate, Congress enacted the 1997 International Dolphin Conservation Program Act, Pub. L. 105-42, to lift the embargoes and implement the IATTC's Panama Declaration, which the U.S. delegation had worked for within the IATTC. See President William J. Clinton, Statement at Signing the International Dolphin Conservation Program Act (August, 15, 1997), 33 Weekly Comp. Pres. Doc. 1251 (1997). The 1997 amendments passed each chamber by large margins, but the votes fail to reveal the serious disagreements over the embargo-lifting amendments. What accounts for the deep division among environmental groups over the approach of the Panama Declaration? See generally J. Floum, Commentary, Defending Dolphins and Sea Turtles: On the Front Lines in an "Us-Them" Dialectic, 10 Geo. Int'l Envtl L.Rev. 943 (1998).

2. Upon signing the 1997 amendments, President Clinton noted that dolphin mortality in the Eastern Tropical Pacific tuna fisheries had already been reduced by more than 98% from previous levels. President William J. Clinton, Statement at Signing the International Dolphin Conservation Program Act (August, 15, 1997), 33 Weekly Comp. Pres. Doc. 1251 (1997). Commentators attribute these declines to the comparability provisions of the MMPA and the trade sanctions to enforce them, coupled with a movement among tuna consumers to boycott canned tuna products that were not "dolphin safe." See J. Floum, Commentary, Defending Dolphins and Sea Turtles: On the Front Lines in an "Us-Them" Dialectic, 10 Geo. Int'l Envtl L.Rev. 943, 945 n.8 (1998).

The Dolphin-Safe Label

After U.S. wildlife conservation groups organized a tuna consumer boycott, the U.S. tuna canning industry moved voluntarily to limit their purchase of foreign-caught tuna to those fisheries that relied on non-purse seined tuna and used the "dolphin safe" logo on their labels. Following this, the Congress enacted the Dolphin Protection Consumer Information Act of 1990, 16 U.S.C. § 1385, which makes it a violation of the Federal Trade Commission Act to include on the label of any tuna product exported from or offered for sale in the U.S. the term "dolphin safe," or any other term or symbol that falsely claims that the product was harvested using a method that is not harmful to dolphins, if that product contains tuna that was caught with driftnets on the high seas, or does not meet the Act's definition of "dolphin safe." Under the 1990 Act, tuna was "dolphin safe" only if it was caught without encirclement and capture of dolphins. 16 U.S.C. § 1385(d)(1)(1990). The International Dolphin Conservation Program Act of 1997 amended the "dolphin safe" definition to allow the importation of tuna caught with dolphin-encircling purse seines in compliance with the IATTC's protocol, but only if the Secretary of Commerce, after conducting research on the effects of repeated chasing and encirclement by fishing vessels on dolphin populations, found that such activities did not have significant adverse effects. 16 U.S.C. § 1385(d). After the Secretary made an initial finding of no effect in 1999, the following case resulted.

BROWER v. EVANS
United States Court of Appeals, 9th Circuit, 2001
257 F.3d 1058

SILVERMAN, CIRCUIT JUDGE:

* * *

In part to implement the Panama Declaration and eliminate the ban on tuna imports from countries complying with the La Jolla Agreement, on August 15, 1997, Congress enacted the International Dolphin Conservation Program Act ("IDCPA"). While there had been success in lowering dolphin mortality rates,[21] Congress remained concerned that, even if dolphins were not killed or seriously injured in the purse seine nets, the physiological stress they suffered during the year-round chase and encirclement would impede the dolphin populations' recovery. Accordingly, Congress rejected Panama Declaration language which sought an immediate change in the dolphin-safe label. Congress included in the IDCPA a requirement of specified research projects

---

[21] In 1972, the estimated annual ETP dolphin mortality rate caused by the purse seine net fishery was 423,678. By 1992, the estimated rate had dropped to 15,550. These numbers do not reflect the proportional impact on the total population.

directed toward assessing the prevalence and magnitude of fishery-induced stress in the ETP dolphins.

Through the IDCPA, Congress amended the DPCIA and required the Secretary to make Initial and Final Findings as to "whether the intentional deployment on or encirclement of dolphins with purse seine nets is having a significant adverse impact on any depleted dolphin stock in the [ETP]." The Secretary was to make the Initial Finding on the basis of research conducted before March 1, 1999, information obtained under the International Dolphin Conservation Program, and any other relevant information. The IDCPA also amended the MMPA to provide details of the required research.

* * *

On March 25, 1999, NMFS submitted its report to Congress. NMFS found that the currently depleted populations of both northeastern offshore spotted dolphins and eastern spinner dolphins were "not increasing at the rate expected based on the low rate of reported mortalities from the fishery since 1991 and the reproductive potential for these populations." NMFS noted the difficulty in attributing the cause of the low or declining growth rates. NMFS identified only one possible non-fishery related explanation for the slow or declining growth rates-a large scale environmental variability in the ocean habitat. However, NMFS discounted that explanation: "The review of environmental conditions did not disclose any large-scale oceanographic regime shifts during recent decades [and therefore] it is unlikely that [the dolphin populations'] failure to grow can be explained by large-scale environmental variability."

Turning to fishery-related explanations for the slow or declining population growth rates, NMFS identified stress, separation of cows and calves (with subsequent death of calves), as well as under-reporting of direct kills. NMFS noted that none of these potential explanations is necessarily exclusive of the others. However, NMFS reported that it did not have data from *any* of the three mandated stress research projects. Therefore, regarding stress concerns, NMFS included only the "physiological and behavioral stress in mammals" literature review. After reviewing the literature, NMFS concluded that:

> Although this review of existing literature regarding stress in mammals cannot provide a quantitative or definitive answer to the question of whether the tuna fishery is causing stress to affected dolphin populations, the available information and evidence point to the likelihood that physiological stress is induced by fisheries activities. It is therefore plausible that stress resulting from chase and capture in the ETP tuna purse-seine fishery could have a population level effect on one or more dolphin stocks.

NMFS then reported that it did not have evidence to determine whether there was physiological evidence of stress in individual dolphins from the affected dolphin populations, and that the answer probably would be available at "the completion of the necropsy sampling program." Therefore, NMFS concluded that:

> Given the information available from research vessel abundance estimates, tuna vessel abundance indices and observed fishery mortality, the quantitative answers to the question, "In the period since 1991, has there been for any depleted stock a failure to grow at the expected rate * * *" are "yes" for both northeastern offshore spotted and eastern spinner dolphins. The probabilities associated with these answers are quite high, well above the suggested thresholds * * * When considered with the qualitative answer from oceanographic studies (that it is unlikely that such a failure to grow can be explained by large- scale environmental variability) and the qualitative answer from the literature review (that it is plausible that stress resulting from chase and encirclement could have population level effects) *the information suggests but by no means conclusively that the fishery has been the source of significant adverse impact on these two populations.*[22]

On May 7, 1999, the Secretary issued his Initial Finding concluding "that there is insufficient evidence that chase and encirclement by the tuna purse seine fishery 'is having a significant adverse impact' on depleted dolphin stocks in the ETP." Pursuant to the Initial Finding, the dolphin safe label standard changed effective February 2, 2000, to permit the use of "dolphin safe" labeling when purse seine nets are used, as long as no dolphins were killed or seriously injured during the particular set in which the tuna were caught.

Earth Island challenged the validity of the Secretary's Initial Finding under the Administrative Procedure Act, as arbitrary, capricious, an abuse of discretion, and contrary to law. Earth Island claimed that the Secretary failed to obtain and consider preliminary data from the congressionally mandated stress research projects, and failed to determine whether, on the basis of the best available scientific evidence, the use of purse seine nets is having a significant adverse impact on the depleted dolphin populations. Earth Island also asserted that the Secretary failed to apply the proper legal standard to the

---

[22] The record includes a "Scientists Statement Regarding the Setting of Nets on Dophins in the [ETP]" (9/95) and "Letter from Sixteen Marine Mammal Scientists" (3/24/99) ("[A]s scientists who have conducted research on cetaceans and have observed the impacts of human activity on them * * * we believe that research on the effects of human activities on dolphins demonstrates that it is highly likely that the activities of the [ETP] tuna fleets are causing significant negative impacts on dolphins in addition to the direct mortalities counted by observers.").

scientific information available, abused his discretion, and acted arbitrarily and capriciously by failing to find significant adverse impact given the best available evidence.

The district court found that the Secretary's Initial Finding was not in accordance with the law and an abuse of discretion because the Secretary failed to (1) obtain and consider preliminary data from the congressionally mandated stress studies and (2) apply the proper legal standard to the available scientific information.

* * *

In urging this court to reverse the district court, the Secretary and amici stress that this case involves international concerns and competing policies for protecting dolphins. That it does, but it is not our role to make policy decisions about ETP dolphin conservation. Such decisions are within Congress's bailiwick, and both the Secretary and this court must defer to congressional intent as reflected in the IDCPA.

The Required Secretarial Findings

In the section entitled "Secretarial Findings", the IDCPA mandates the Secretary's course of action: "[T]he Secretary shall * * * make an initial finding regarding *whether* the intentional deployment on or encirclement of dolphins with purse seine nets is having a significant adverse impact on any depleted dolphin stock in the [ETP]." The common meaning of "whether" is "whichever of the two," Merriam Webster's Collegiate Dictionary (10th ed.1993), and should be read to mean "whether or not". Therefore, the IDCPA's mandatory language required the Secretary to make an Initial Finding whether or not the purse seine net fishery was having a significant adverse impact on any depleted ETP dolphin stock.

However, urging us to read § 1385(h)[23] as establishing a default to

---

[23] (h) Certification by captain and observer. -

  (1) Unless otherwise required by paragraph (2), the certification by the captain under subsection (d)(2)(B)(i) of this section and the certification provided by the observer as specified in subsection (d)(2)(B)(ii) of this section shall be that no dolphins were killed or seriously injured during the sets in which the tuna were caught.

  (2) The certification by the captain under subsection (d)(2)(B)(i) of this section and the certification provided by the observer as specified under subsection (d)(2)(B)(ii) of this section shall be that no tuna were caught on the trip in which such tuna were harvested using a purse seine net intentionally deployed on or to encircle dolphins, and that no dolphins were killed or seriously injured during the sets in which the tuna were caught, if the tuna were caught on a trip commencing -

the less protective label standard, the Secretary argues that he is not required to find affirmatively that there is not a significant adverse impact. The Secretary contends that if he fails to find evidence of significant adverse impact, then the less protective dolphin labeling standard will go into effect. We reject this interpretation for several reasons.

First, the Secretary's interpretation is at odds with the statute's structure. Under § 1385(g), "Secretarial Findings," the IDCPA required the Secretary to make a finding *whether or not* the fishery-related activities were adversely impacting the dolphins. This finding requires a "yes" or "no" answer: "Yes," there was a significant adverse impact or "no," there was no significant adverse impact. Section 1385(h), "Certification by Captain and Observer," does not determine the parameters or scope of the Initial Finding. Nor does it change the Secretary's burden of proof as written in § 1385(g), "Secretarial Findings".

Second, Congress rejected Panama Declaration language which sought an immediate change in the dolphin safe label. It would be inconsistent with that history and congressional concern to interpret the statute as establishing the new less-protective labeling standard as the default. Just as we may not substitute our judgment for the agency's, the agency may not ignore Congress.

Finally, this default construction should be avoided because it would lead to absurd results. Statutory interpretations "which would produce absurd results are to be avoided if alternative interpretations consistent with the legislative purpose are available." Such a default construction would render the required stress studies irrelevant. The use of a default does not encourage active, aggressive fact-finding and research or conclusive answers. For example, the Secretary could deliberately drag his feet in commencing studies or while conducting studies and then conclude there was insufficient evidence to warrant finding a significant adverse impact on the ETP dolphin stocks. Similarly, the Secretary could limit the studies' breadth and then

---

(A) before the effective date of the initial finding by the Secretary under subsection (g)(1) of this section;

(B) after the effective date of such initial finding and before the effective date of the finding of the Secretary under subsection (g)(2) of this section, where the initial finding is that the intentional deployment on or encirclement of dolphins is having a significant adverse impact on any depleted dolphin stock; or

(C) after the effective date of the finding under subsection (g)(2) of this section, where such finding is that the intentional deployment on or encirclement of dolphins is having a significant adverse impact on any such depleted stock.

16 U.S.C. § 1385(h).

discover that there was insufficient evidence to warrant finding a significant adverse impact on the ETP dolphin stocks. Following the Secretary's interpretation, under the above scenarios, the dolphin labeling standard would default to the less protective standard for the Initial Finding, because the Secretary failed to find evidence of significant adverse impact, and the less protective standard would be in place during the interim period between the Initial and Final Findings. A practical consequence of this default would be increased pressure on the Secretary to keep the same dolphin labeling standard, that is, to have the same result for the Final Finding.

We reject the Secretary's default construction and hold, as Congress required, that the Secretary must affirmatively find whether or not there is a significant adverse impact before the dolphin safe labeling standards can be relaxed.

Commencement of the Stress Studies

The deference accorded an agency's scientific or technical expertise is not unlimited. The presumption of agency expertise can be rebutted when its decisions, while relying on scientific expertise, are not reasoned. We defer to agency expertise on methodology issues, "unless the agency has completely failed to address some factor consideration of which was essential to [making an] informed decision."

* * *

Congress mandated that the agency make an Initial Finding on the basis of the specific research prescribed in 16 U.S.C. § 1414a, including stress studies. The record fails to show any compliance or valid excuse for the failure to comply. The Secretary's emphasis on other work completed before the Initial Finding, including the mandatory abundance study, the stress literature review, and environmental variability analysis is irrelevant. Completion of other studies does not relieve the Secretary from progressing with clearly mandated studies....

The agency invoked the lack of stress-related information to trigger a change in the dolphin-safe label standard. This puts the cart before the horse. The agency was required by law to conduct stress research as a *prerequisite* to its decision making. By failing to obtain and consider preliminary data from any of the mandated stress research projects before the Initial Finding, the Secretary unreasonably delayed action. In addition, by failing to obtain and consider preliminary data from any of the mandated stress research projects in its Initial Finding, the Secretary abused his discretion, and acted arbitrarily and capriciously and not in accordance with the law.

The Best Available Scientific Evidence Standard

Scientific findings in marine mammal conservation are often necessarily made from incomplete or imperfect information. The Secretary and Earth Island agree that the Initial Finding was to be determined using the "best available evidence" standard. *Cf. Conner,* 848 F.2d at 1454 (with best available data standard Congress required agency to consider the scientific information presently available and intended to give "the benefit of the doubt to the species"); Am. Tunaboat Ass'n v. Baldrige, 738 F.2d 1013 (9th Cir.1984) (discussing best available evidence standard under MMPA); Earth Island Inst. v. Brown, 865 F.Supp. 1364, 1373 n. 10 (N.D.Cal.1994) (discussing MMPA and concluding that there is no "indication that Congress intended to render all depletion determinations irrelevant simply because the available data may not always be complete or precise"). However, the Secretary determined that there was insufficient information to determine whether the fishery was having a significant adverse impact on the ETP dolphin stock. That determination was contrary to law and an abuse of his discretion.

The Endangered Species Act requires agencies to make determinations on the basis of the best scientific data available. Thus, a review of ESA case law provides insightful and analogous provisions and analysis. In Conner v. Burford, 848 F.2d 1441, 1454 (9th Cir.1988), this court held that an agency's claim of insufficient information to prepare comprehensive biological opinions violated the ESA requirement that opinions use best data available, and ordered the agency to comply with the ESA requirement. See also Greenpeace v. Nat'l Marine Fisheries Serv., 55 F.Supp.2d 1248, 1261-62 (W.D.Wash.1999) (best scientific data available standard requires less than conclusive proof; Secretary *must* issue biological opinion); Defenders of Wildlife v. Babbitt, 958 F.Supp. 670, 679-81 (D.D.C.1997) (Secretary *must* determine *whether* any species is threatened or endangered using the best available evidence).

As shown in the Report, the available information from the mandated abundance study and the stress literature review indicated that the fishery was having a significant adverse impact on the dolphin stocks. The abundance survey revealed that the dolphins were not recovering at expected levels, while the stress literature indicated that "stress resulting from chase and capture in the ETP tuna purse-seine fishery could have a population level effect on one or more dolphin stocks." The record and the Report do not provide any contradictory conclusions, and NMFS was unable to attribute the failure to recover to any source other than the fishery. In fact, NMFS specifically ruled out the only potential non-fishery explanation for the slow population recovery-a large scale change in the ocean environment. Here, *all* of the evidence indicated that dolphins were adversely impacted by the fishery.

Given the best available evidence standard and IDCPA's statutory mandate to determine *whether or not* the chase and netting of dolphins are having a significant adverse impact on the depleted ETP dolphin stocks, the Secretary cannot use insufficient evidence as an excuse for failing to comply with the statutory requirement. See, e.g., Conner, 848 F.2d at 1454; Comm. for Humane Legislation Inc. v. Richardson, 540 F.2d 1141, 1150 (D.C.Cir.1976) (NMFS's assertion that "there is no evidence that the porpoise populations would substantially increase or decrease as a result of the * * * reissuance of general permit" to set nets on dolphins was "not responsive" to statutory mandate). By claiming insufficiency of evidence, the Secretary acted contrary to law and abused his discretion.

Notes and Questions

1. Why did the Secretary make the initial finding before the required stress studies had been completed? Note that in Defenders of Wildlife, supra, the plaintiffs argued that Mexico's failure to cooperate in conducting these studies, which require the use of purse-seine vessels operating in the ETP, suggested it had not meet the conditions for lifting the embargo against its tuna products. Assuming Mexican cooperation was essential to conducting the stress studies, why would Mexico withhold its cooperation?

2. If the studies show significant adverse effects from repeated chasing and encirclement, how will that affect the international dolphin conservation program?

3. Does the development of the international dolphin conservation progam and its dramatic reductions in direct kills of dolphins vindicate Commerce's reluctance to impose embargoes as a lever for conservation? Does it support the use of embargoes? How effective has the embargo approach been in the turtle-shrimp case?

B. SEA TURTLES AND SHRIMP IMPORTS

The Congress and the Executive Branch have also differed over the appropriate role of trade sanctions in protecting sea turtles listed under the Endangered Species Act and subject to recovery regulations affecting the U.S. shrimp industry. The Endangered Species Act, like the MMPA, requires nations wishing to export shrimp to the U.S. to be certified as having an effective conservation program preventing the killing of turtles by their shrimp fishing fleets.

The U.S. State Department's resistance to this approach and its attempt to narrowly apply the import restrictions program have also been challenged by environmental group plaintiffs. At the same time, however, the affected exporting nations challenged the measures in the GATT/WTO dispute resolution bodies, resulting in further strains on the State Department's efforts to meet the ESA mandate.

TURTLE ISLAND RESTORATION NETWORK v. EVANS
United States Court of Appeals, Federal Circuit, 2002
__F.3d __, 2002 WL 434815

CLEVENGER, CIRCUIT JUDGE:

* * *

BACKGROUND

Since 1987, United States regulations have required that shrimp trawlers generally install turtle excluder devices ("TEDs") when operating in United States waters where sea turtles are to be found. 50 C.F.R. §§ 223.206, 223.207 (2001). Shrimpers sweep many other denizens of the sea ("bycatch") into their nets when they trawl for shrimp. But unlike fish or shrimp, sea turtles are reptiles and must breathe air. While sea turtles can remain submerged for up to 90 minutes at a time, trawl nets typically are deployed for periods longer than 90 minutes before being hauled up. Sea turtles will drown if they are caught in shrimp nets and held underwater for long periods of time. When fitted into trawl nets, TEDs prevent sea turtles from being retained in the nets--typically by means of a metal grid barring entry to the closed end of the net. The grid bars are spaced so as to let shrimp pass through the grid into the closed end of the net, but the much larger sea turtles cannot pass through and are instead directed out an "escape hatch" above or below the grid.

The domestic shrimp industry strongly opposed the imposition of TED requirements in United States waters. *See, e.g.*, State of Louisiana, ex rel. Guste v. Verity, 853 F.2d 322 (5th Cir.1988). However, the case before us concerns not domestic regulations, but arises instead from nearly a decade's worth of litigation over the enforcement of a statute designed to impose TEDs on shrimping vessels of foreign nations: The Departments of Commerce, Justice, and State, the Judiciary, and Related Agencies Appropriations Act, 1990, Pub.L. 101-162, Title VI, § 609, 103 Stat. 1037 (1989) (codified at 16 U.S.C. § 1537 note (2000)) ("section 609").

The full text of section 609 is as follows:

(a) The Secretary of State, in consultation with the Secretary ofCommerce, shall, with respect to those species of sea turtles the conservation of which is the subject of regulations promulgated by the Secretary of Commerce on June 29, 1987--

(1) initiate negotiations as soon as possible for the development of bilateral or multilateral agreements with other nations for the protection and conservation of such species of sea turtles;

(2) initiate negotiations as soon as possible with all foreign governments which are engaged in, or which have persons or companies engaged in, commercial fishing operations which, as determined by the Secretary of Commerce, may affect adversely such species of sea turtles, for the purpose of entering into bilateral and multilateral treaties with such countries to protect such species of sea turtles;

(3) encourage such other agreements to promote the purposes of this section with other nations for the protection of specific ocean and land regions which are of special significance to the health and stability of such species of sea turtles;

(4) initiate the amendment of any existing international treaty for the protection and conservation of such species of sea turtles to which the United States is a party in order to make such treaty consistent with the purposes and policies of this section; and

(5) provide to the Congress by not later than one year after the date of enactment of this section (Nov. 21, 1989)--

(A) a list of each nation which conducts commercial shrimp fishing operations within the geographic range of distribution of such sea turtles;

(B) a list of each nation which conducts commercial shrimp fishing operations which may affect adversely such species of sea turtles; and

(C) a full report on--

(i) the results of his efforts under this section; and

(ii) the status of measures taken by each nation listed pursuant to paragraph (A) or (B) to protect and conserve such sea turtles.

(b)(1) In General.--The importation of shrimp or products from shrimp which have been harvested with commercial fishing technology which may affect adversely such species of sea turtles shall be prohibited not later than May 1, 1991, except as provided in paragraph (2).

(2) Certification Procedure.--The ban on importation of shrimp or products from shrimp pursuant to paragraph (1) shall not apply if the President shall determine and certify to the Congress not later than May 1, 1991, and annually thereafter that--

(A) the government of the harvesting nation has provided documentary evidence of the adoption of a regulatory program governing the incidental taking of such sea turtles in the course of such harvesting that is comparable to that of the United States; and

(B) the average rate of that incidental taking by the vessels of the harvesting nation is comparable to the average rate of incidental taking of sea turtles by United States vessels in the course of such harvesting; or

(C) the particular fishing environment of the harvesting nation does not pose a threat of the incidental taking of such sea turtles in the course of such harvesting.

Section 609 is divided into two parts, (a) and (b). Part (a) directs the Secretary of State to initiate international negotiations with the aim of protecting those species of sea turtles protected by the domestic TED requirements. Part (b)(1) restricts the importation of shrimp which have been harvested in a manner that may endanger those species of sea turtles. Part (b)(2) establishes a certification procedure,[24] by which nations are exempted from the ban either if they have adopted regulatory measures reducing the incidental catch of sea turtles (e.g., a requirement that their shrimp fleets be equipped with TEDs), or if their operations do not pose any threat to sea turtles (e.g., no endangered turtles inhabit the waters fished by that nation).

This case requires us to decide whether section 609(b)(2)'s certification procedure is the only way a foreign nation may comply with section 609(b). Under the State Department's current regulations (Revised Guidelines for the Implementation of Section 609 of Public Law 101-162 Relating to the Protection of Sea Turtles in Shrimp Trawl Fishing Operations, 64 Fed. Reg. 36,946 (July 8, 1999) ("the 1999 Guidelines")), shrimp may be imported into the United States under one of two conditions. If the exporter attests that the nation in which the shrimp originated (that is, in whose waters the shrimp were harvested) has been certified under section 609(b)(2), the shrimp may be imported without further ado. Alternatively, if the country of origin has not been certified under section 609(b)(2), shrimp harvested in its waters may still

---

[24] The President has delegated his authority to certify nations under 609(b)(2) to the Secretary of State. Delegation of Authority Regarding Certification of Countries Exporting Shrimp to the United States, 56 Fed. Reg. 357 (Jan. 4, 1991).

enter the United States if both the exporter and an official of the harvesting nation attest that the individual shipment of shrimp in question was harvested under conditions that do not adversely affect sea turtles. Shipments meeting these conditions include those of aquaculture-grown shrimp, hand-caught shrimp, and shrimp harvested by vessels equipped with TEDs. Thus, under the government's interpretation of section 609, a country may export shrimp to the United States either by requiring its entire fleet to be equipped with TEDs (and becoming certified under section 609(b)(2)), or by requiring TEDs only on those vessels catching shrimp destined for the United States market.[25]

Turtle Island interprets section 609 somewhat differently. Turtle Island believes that section 609 requires the government to prohibit the importation of all shrimp from uncertified countries. Under Turtle Island's interpretation of the statute, certification is the *only* way in which shrimp may be imported into the United States. In practice, this means that in countries where shrimp and endangered sea turtles frequent the same waters, all shrimping vessels must be equipped with TEDs if that country wishes to export shrimp to the United States. Turtle Island argues that this interpretation is mandated by the plain language, intent, and legislative history of the statute.

The contest between Turtle Island and the government over the interpretation of section 609 has a long and tortured history, chiefly marked by the government's Protean efforts to escape the statutory interpretations being imposed upon it by the Court of International Trade. * * *

* * *

The Court of International Trade agreed with Earth Island that section 609(b)(1)'s embargo should be applied on a nation-by-nation basis, rather than on a shipment-by-shipment basis. The Court of International Trade's interpretation of section 609 rested on two grounds. First, the Court of International Trade refused to read the language of section 609(b)(1) in isolation. Reasoning that section 609(a) directed the Secretary of State to pursue negotiations with foreign nations, and that section 609(b)(2) required the President to determine whether a foreign nation's regulatory programs met United States standards for protection of sea turtles, the Court of International Trade concluded that section 609(b)(2) should be read *in pari materia* with

---

[25] In practice, TED-equipped vessels and non-TED-equipped vessels do not seem to fish side by side in the waters of uncertified countries. Currently, uncertified countries that export shrimp to the United States enforce TED requirements on vessels plying certain fisheries but not in other fisheries. Turtle Island Restoration Network v. Mallett, 110 F.Supp.2d 1005, 1011-13 (Ct. Int'l Trade 2000).

the other sections of section 609. As such, the import restrictions of section 609(b)(2) should be applied nation-by-nation, and not shipment-by-shipment. Earth Island Inst. v. Christopher, 942 F.Supp. 597, 603-04 (Ct. Int'l Trade 1996).

The Court of International Trade's second rationale was based on its earlier conclusion that section 609 supplemented the Endangered Species Act ("ESA") and should also be read *in pari materia* with the ESA. Earth Island Inst. v. Christopher, 890 F.Supp. 1085, 1092 (Ct. Int'l Trade 1995). The Court of International Trade took from the ESA the principle that "the plain intent of Congress in enacting this statute was to halt and reverse the trend towards species extinction, whatever the costs." Earth Island, 942 F. Supp. at 606 (quoting Earth Island, 913 F.Supp. at 576, in turn quoting Tenn. Valley Auth. v. Hill, 437 U.S. 153, 184 (1978)). Accepting (in the absence of contrary evidence from the government) Earth Island's claim that the shipment-by- shipment approach would undermine the incentive for uncertified nations to become certified, the Court of International Trade agreed with Earth Island that the 1996 Guidelines would "eviscerat[e] the goal of Congress in enacting section 609." Earth Island, 942 F. Supp. at 604. Accordingly, the Court of International Trade prohibited the government from permitting the import of shrimp unless the harvesting nation had been certified under section 609(b)(2). Id. at 617.

* * *

Meanwhile, during the period that the Court of International Trade had enjoined the government from permitting the import of TED-caught shrimp from uncertified nations, a group of such nations--India, Pakistan, Malaysia, and Thailand--brought a proceeding against the United States before the Dispute Settlement Body of the World Trade Organization ("WTO"), arguing that the enforcement of section 609 under the 1996 Guidelines violated certain provisions of the 1994 General Agreement on Tariffs and Trade ("GATT"). Ultimately, the WTO Appellate Body ruled that section 609 was a permissible conservation measure under GATT Article XX, but that the United States' enforcement of section 609 was discriminatory. United States--Import Prohibition of Certain Shrimp and Shrimp Products, 1998 WL 720123 (Oct. 12, 1998). Specifically, the WTO pointed to the fact that shrimp caught using methods identical to those employed in the United States (*i.e.*, with TEDs) were embargoed solely because they were caught in the waters of uncertified countries. And while the statute itself might permit a flexible approach, the 1996 Guidelines demanded that a country adopt a regulatory regime identical to that of the United States as the only path to certification. Furthermore, the failure of the United States to initiate serious international negotiations to protect sea turtles (as demanded by section 609(a)) supported a finding of unjustifiable discrimination.

After this court vacated the Court of International Trade's injunction against the government, the State Department issued new Guidelines reinstating importation of shrimp from uncertified countries. Revised Notice of Guidelines for Determining Comparability of Foreign Programs for the Protection of Sea Turtles in Shrimp Trawl Fishing Operations, 63 Fed. Reg. 46,094 (Aug. 28, 1998). Like the 1996 Guidelines, the 1998 Guidelines permitted import of shrimp from uncertified countries if the shipment was accompanied by a DSP 12 form attesting that the shrimp had been harvested by vessels equipped with TEDs. Its earlier victory having been negated for lack of jurisdiction, Earth Island again filed suit challenging the new regulations in the Court of International Trade, which (not surprisingly) again found that importation of shrimp from uncertified countries violated the provisions of section 609(b). Earth Island Inst. v. Daley, 48 F.Supp.2d 1064, 1081 (Ct. Int'l Trade 1999). Soon afterwards, the State Department issued its 1999 Guidelines. Designed to meet the WTO's objections, the 1999 Guidelines took a more flexible stance on which regulatory programs would merit national certification, but the 1999 Guidelines continued to permit importation of TED-caught shrimp from uncertified countries. Accordingly, the Court of International Trade yet again held that the shipment-by-shipment approach violated section 609 and entered a final declaratory judgment in favor of Turtle Island--which by now had been spun off as an independent entity from the Earth Island Institute. Turtle Island Restoration Network v. Mallett, 110 F.Supp.2d 1005, 1018 (Ct. Int'l Trade 2000).

However, although the Court of International Trade concluded "without reservation that the plaintiffs have *prevailed* " in their argument that the importation of TED-caught shrimp from uncertified nations violated the terms of section 609, the Court of International Trade denied Turtle Island injunctive relief. Moreover, the Court of International Trade refused to hold that the government's legal position was not substantially justified, barring Turtle Island from collecting attorney fees under the Equal Access to Justice Act. The Court of International Trade appeared to base these conclusions on the fact that of all the countries exporting shrimp to the United States, only Brazil and Australia were not certified, suggesting that relatively few sea turtles were being harmed in the waters of uncertified nations that served the United States shrimp market. Moreover, no nation that had previously established a nation-wide TED program had limited its regulatory program in favor of equipping only those vessels that served the United States market with TEDs. Given the absence of proof that shrimp trawling by uncertified nations was currently contributing significantly to sea turtle mortality, and in apparent recognition of the traditional reluctance of courts to intrude into matters of foreign relations, the Court of International Trade concluded, somewhat cryptically:

given the facts and circumstances of this case, which obviously transcend purely domestic concerns, this court is unable to conclude that the government's position currently is not substantially justified * * *

The court's inability means not only that plaintiff's application for any award of fees etc. cannot be granted, the motion for injunctive relief based upon the declaratory judgment in their favor must also be denied.

Id.

After the Court of International Trade issued its final judgment in Turtle Island Restoration Network v. Mallett, Malaysia renewed its challenge to the United States over enforcement of section 609 before a panel of the Dispute Settlement Body of the World Trade Organization. However, the panel ruled, and the Appellate Body affirmed, that the enforcement of section 609 under the State Department's 1999 Guidelines was justified under Article XX of GATT. These conclusions were based in part on the Court of International Trade's refusal to grant Turtle Island an injunction against the government, since under that ruling the United States continued to permit the import of TED- caught shrimp from uncertified countries. United States--Import Prohibition of Certain Shrimp and Shrimp Products, 2001 WL 671012, at 101 (Jun. 15, 2001). Moreover, the United States had initiated serious international negotiations for sea turtle protection, and now required nations to establish for certification a sea turtle program comparable in effectiveness to that of the United States--not necessarily one identical to that of the United States. United States--Import Prohibition of Certain Shrimp and Shrimp Products, 2001 WL 126572, at 38-49; 51-54 (Oct. 22, 2001). Consequently, the enforcement of section 609 was ruled a permissible conservation measure and not discriminatory under Article XX of GATT.

Turtle Island now appeals the Court of International Trade's denial of an injunction and attorney fees. The government appeals the judgment of the Court of International Trade that the importation of TED-caught shrimp from uncertified countries as permitted by the 1999 Guidelines violates section 609. We exercise appellate jurisdiction over the final decision of the Court of International Trade under 28 U.S.C. § 1295(a)(5).

I

We first consider whether the Court of International Trade reached the proper construction of section 609, as the propriety of the Court of International Trade's denial of injunctive relief and attorney fees will hinge on whether Turtle Island or the government has advocated the appropriate interpretation of the statute. We must therefore decide whether section 609(b)(1) of Pub. L. 101-162 prohibits importation of all shrimp or shrimp products from a country not certified under section 609(b)(2), or whether the government may permit the import of individual shipments from uncertified countries if exporters represent that those particular shipments were caught without the use of commercial fishing technology that may adversely affect those species of sea turtles protected by domestic law. Statutory interpretation is a matter of law that we review without deference to the interpretation reached by the Court of International Trade. SKF USA Inc. v. United States, 263 F.3d 1369, 1378 (Fed.Cir.2001).

A

We begin, as in all questions of statutory interpretation, with the plain words of the law, and in this case those words weigh heavily in the government's favor. The operative language of the embargo is found in section (b)(1), which prohibits importation of shrimp, "which have been harvested with commercial fishing technology" that may harm sea turtles, except as provided in (b)(2). The clause "which have been harvested" modifies "shrimp." "Shrimp" are discrete objects, each of which has either been harvested with technology harmful to sea turtles or not. The statute distinguishes between the former shrimp, which are embargoed, and the latter shrimp, which are not. The plain language of the statute provides no basis for embargoing shipments of shrimp which have *not* been harvested with commercial fishing technology that may harm sea turtles. Because TED-caught shrimp have not been harvested with commercial fishing technology that may harm sea turtles, the statutory language does not support embargoing TED-caught shrimp from uncertified countries. Moreover, if certification under (b)(2) was the *only* way shrimp could be imported into the United States, then "which have been harvested with commercial fishing technology which may affect adversely such species of sea turtles" in (b)(1) is largely superfluous language. We cannot see how the "harvested with commercial fishing technology" language could consistently be interpreted to permit import of some shrimp that have been harvested without adverse effect on sea turtles-- such as aquacultured or hand-caught shrimp from uncertified countries--but to ban the import of other shrimp that have been harvested without adverse effect on sea turtles--such as TED-caught shrimp from uncertified countries.

Recognizing the primacy of the plain language in the hierarchy of statutory interpretation, Turtle Island tries to advance several arguments under that rubric. It argues that its interpretation is consistent with congressional intent, with other portions of the statute, and with the law's ultimate purpose--all of which might be true but none of which states an argument based on the plain language of the statute. Turtle Island cannot escape the fact that it seeks to interpolate words into the plain language of the statute, reading 609(b)(1) as an embargo on "shrimp which have been harvested *from a nation that employs* commercial fishing technology which may affect adversely said species of sea turtles." While the text might not absolutely bar such an interpolation, this interpretation does not comport with the most direct reading of the law's words.

In any event, we do not find persuasive the argument based on conformity with the remaining sections of section 609. Turtle Island points to section 609(a), which directs the Secretary of State to negotiate with foreign *nations* to protect sea turtles, and to section 609(b)(2), which establishes a procedure for *nations* to be certified as exempt from the embargo of section 609(b)(1). The Court of International Trade drew from this structure the conclusion that, reading those sections of the law *in pari materia* with the embargo provisions, the embargo provisions must refer to other nations, and not to individual shipments of shrimp. *Earth Island,* 942 F. Supp. at 603-604. We cannot agree with this reasoning. The fact that other portions of the statute direct the Secretary of State to negotiate with and certify nations does not demand that the Secretary apply the embargo to entire nations as well. One negotiates with nations and imports shrimp, not vice versa. Congress drafted sections 609(a) and 609(b)(2) to refer to nations because the negotiation and certification provisions could not have been drafted in any other way--not because Congress made a conscious choice to focus them on nations rather than shipments. An embargo provision, on the other hand, might be drafted either to apply to shipments or to nations, and we do not think Congress was foreclosed from embargoing individual shipments of shrimp simply because it included the embargo provisions in a law that also speaks of nations. We find nothing inherently insensible about applying the negotiation and certification provisions to nations on the one hand, and the embargo provisions to particular shipments of shrimp on the other.

B

Both sides also lay claim to the legislative history of section 609. The State Department finds some congressional intent to delegate the definition of which shrimp should be embargoed, while Turtle Island finds both the nation-by- nation principle and the conclusion that section 609's principal goal is the protection of endangered sea turtle species worldwide. We cannot find support for the State Department's position. While Congress may have intended the administering agency to define which methods of harvesting shrimp may adversely affect sea turtles, we find no intent to delegate the power to define the scope of the embargo itself. But our disagreement with Turtle Island's view of the legislative history is more profound and more damaging to its case. For we find nothing in the legislative history to mandate a nation-by-nation approach, and we find little, if any, indication that minimizing sea turtle drownings was Congress's main concern when it enacted section 609.

* * *

Thus, to the extent legislative history is available, we find that Congress with remarkable unanimity was focused on protecting the domestic shrimp industry, not the sea turtle, when it enacted section 609. Many of the comments made on the Senate floor reflected deep skepticism about the effectiveness of TED requirements, and about the wisdom of placing sea turtle conservation above the economic well-being of domestic shrimpers. We therefore cannot agree with Turtle Island that the fidelity of the government's implementation of section 609 should be measured solely by how effectively the measures protect endangered sea turtles.

* * *

Whether or not Congress was correct that the domestic TED requirements handicapped domestic shrimpers, Congress was concerned with the effects of TEDs on the United States market alone. Congress enacted a measure applicable to only those sea turtles encountered by American shrimpers, and Congress enacted the embargo to protect what it saw as unfair competition in the American market. As such, Congress was concerned with those foreign vessels harvesting shrimp for the United States market, not foreign vessels harvesting shrimp for foreign markets. We find Congress's intent met by the State Department's current system of enforcing section 609(b), which regulates all imports of shrimp into the United States market. The contemporary legislative history provides no basis for extending section 609(b)'s reach in an attempt to control how shrimp bound for foreign markets are harvested.

C

We find further indication that section 609(b)(1) refers to shipments, not nations, when we compare it to similar statutes. Congress has drafted other statutes with explicit nation-by-nation embargoes, but did not do so in the case of section 609(b). Congress has enacted nation-by-nation embargoes triggered by foreign restrictions on fishing rights of U.S. vessels:

> the Secretary of the Treasury shall immediately take such action as may be necessary and appropriate to prohibit the importation into the United States ... fish or fish products, *from any fishery of the foreign nation concerned,* which the Secretary of State finds to be appropriate * * *

16 U.S.C. § 1825(b)(2) (2000) (emphasis added); by nations conducting

large-scale driftnet fishing outside their exclusive economic zones.

> The President * * * shall direct the Secretary of the Treasury to prohibit the importation into the United States of *fish and fish products* * * * *from that nation.*

16 U.S.C. § 1826a(b)(3)(A) (2000) (emphasis added); and by fishing operations or other trade threatening endangered species:

> the President may direct the Secretary of the Treasury to prohibit the bringing or the importation into the United States of *any products from the offending country* for any duration as the President determines appropriate and to the extent that such prohibition is sanctioned by the World Trade Organization....

22 U.S.C. § 1978(a)(4) (Supp. V 1999) (emphasis added).

When Congress omits from a statute a provision found in similar statutes, the omission is typically thought deliberate. See, e.g., I.N.S. v. Phinpathya, 464 U.S. 183, 190 (1984). In very similar instances, Congress has explicitly embargoed *all* imports from the offending nation, regardless of whether any particular shipment was taken in a manner that would threaten endangered species. The fact that Congress declined to include such language in section 609(b) suggests that Congress did not intend to impose a similar embargo there.

* * *

Likewise, because the meaning of section 609 is clear, we need not reach the question of how much deference we ought to accord the State Department's interpretation of section 609, or whether the State Department's interpretation would minimize potential conflicts with international trade agreements. "If the intent of Congress is clear, that is the end of the matter; for the court, as well as the agency, must give effect to the unambiguously expressed intent of Congress." Chevron U.S.A., Inc. v. Natural Res. Def. Council, Inc., 467 U.S. 837, 842-843 (1984). The intent of Congress is clear and the government's current implementation of section 609(b) carries out that intent.

CONCLUSION

However much we may respect Turtle Island's long struggle on behalf of the Earth's endangered sea turtles, we cannot find that Congress shared Turtle Island's current position when it enacted section 609 of Pub. L. 101-162. Having concluded that the State Department's interpretation of section 609 is the correct one, we must also hold both that Turtle Island is not entitled to an injunction, and that the government's legal position was substantially justified within the meaning of the Equal Access to Justice Act. We therefore reverse the Court of International Trade's judgment that the government's decision to permit the importation of TED-caught shrimp from uncertified nations is not in accordance with section 609(b) of Pub. L. 101-162, and affirm the Court of International Trade's denial of injunctive relief and attorney fees.

NEWMAN, CIRCUIT JUDGE, dissenting:

I respectfully dissent, for the majority's decision negates the statutory method of protecting endangered sea turtles. The Court of International Trade applied the statute in accordance with its terms. Whatever the political or diplomatic considerations, neither the executive agency charged with administering the statute, nor this court, has authority to depart from the statute as enacted.

* * *

The Legislative Purpose

It is not disputed that sea turtles are endangered by commercial trawl shrimping. The decline in sea turtle populations throughout the world has been dramatic; for example, as of 1990 the Kemp's ridley turtle population had declined to less than one percent of its abundance in 1947. See Decline of the Sea Turtles: Causes and Prevention, 26 National Academy of Sciences 144 (1990). The acknowledged principal cause of sea turtle deaths is capture and drowning in shrimp trawl nets. In 1987 the National Marine Fisheries Service estimated that 11,179 sea turtles were killed in southeastern United States waters each year. United States trawlers harvest eight percent of the world's supply of shrimp. Sea turtles, however, roam in warm waters worldwide, and are endangered worldwide. Globally, it was estimated that 124,000 turtles were killed each year by commercial shrimp trawlers. See *Earth Island,* 913 F.Supp. at 568.

On this background, section 609 was enacted. The statute requires nations that wish to serve the United States market to adopt turtle-protective measures no less rigorous than those imposed on our own fleet; all trawl shrimpers in United States waters are required to use turtle exclusion devices. It is generally accepted that when some trawlers use turtle exclusion devices and others do not, the turtles escaped or excluded from the nets of one trawler are often caught by trawlers without TEDs. However, if all vessels in harvest areas use turtle exclusion devices, it is estimated that the devices release "97 percent of the turtles caught in shrimp trawls." *Sea Turtle Conservation; Shrimp Trawling Requirements,* 52 Fed. Reg. 24244, 24244 (June 29, 1987). These data led to the legislation as enacted, requiring that other countries, if their shrimpers wish to sell into the United States market, protect the turtles to the same extent as required for United States vessels. At the time of enactment it was well recognized that the purpose of the legislation was to protect sea turtles in their global habitat, while assuring that United States fishermen were not competitively disadvantaged. Both goals are served by the statute's requirement that nations whose shrimp fishers wish to sell to the United States must adopt fleet-wide turtle-protection devices, and not simply place such devices on selected ships. The Report of the Senate Committee on Appropriations explained the legislation as follows:

> It calls for a ban on imports of shrimp from any nation that: (1) fails to adopt a regulatory program for turtle protection which is comparable to that of the United States; and (2) has higher incidental catches of sea turtles than U.S. shrimpers.

S. Rep. No. 101-144, at 104 (1989). Similarly, after the Conference addition of section 609(b)(2)(C) providing that certification may be based on turtle- free shrimp fishing environments, the Conference Report of the House of Representatives explained the legislation as requiring

> a ban on importation of shrimp which have been harvested with commercial fishing technology which may adversely affect species of sea turtles subject to the regulations, not later than May 1, 1991, unless the President certifies to Congress that *the harvesting nation has adopted regulations governing the incidental taking of sea turtles in the course of shrimp harvesting comparable to regulations adopted by the U.S.,* that the average rate of the incidental taking by the vessels of the harvesting nation is comparable to the average rate of incidental taking of sea turtles by U.S. vessels in the course of such harvesting or the particular fishing environment of the harvesting nation does not pose a threat of the incidental taking of sea turtles in the course of such harvesting.

H.R. Conf. Rep. No. 101-299, at 84 (1989) (emphasis added). Neither of the legislative Reports indicates that Congress intended to adopt or accept merely a shipment-by-shipment approach to importation of shrimp.

The legislative record illustrates the congressional purpose of protecting these endangered animals worldwide, while avoiding any disadvantage to domestic shrimp fishing interests due to their obligatory use of TEDs.

There were no statements, during the extensive floor discussion, contrary to the uniform goal of protecting endangered sea turtles and avoiding disadvantage to United States shrimpers. A shipment-by-shipment approach not only weakens the incentive for countries to impose TED requirements, but it removes the anticipated "level playing field" for domestic interests, for all United States shrimpers are required to use TEDs. That the legislation was designed for country-by-country certification, not shipment-by-shipment, was reiterated by Senator Breaux:

> It is patently unfair on its face to say to the U.S. industry that you must abide by these sets of rules and regulations, but other countries do not have to do anything, and, yet, we will then give them our market. That is exactly what is happening. I think the amendment ... is a good amendment. It will require other countries to do exactly what we are being required to do, and if in fact they do not, they will lose the U.S. market.

135 Cong. Rec. S12191, 12266.* * *

Since United States shrimpers produce only eight percent of the world's shrimp catch, sea turtle protection was recognized as requiring a global effort. Although the panel majority's theory that "section 609 was not enacted with the primary goal of minimizing sea turtle deaths" is not supported by the legislative record, the alternative legislative goal of protecting the domestic industry is also disserved by permitting importation from nations whose other vessels do not carry turtle-exclusion devices. In addition, I do not agree with the majority that if there is a commercial aspect to legislation, the humanitarian purpose becomes irrelevant.

The Guidelines

For the first six years after enactment, the State Department interpreted section 609 as requiring an embargo of all shrimp from a nation that harvests shrimp in turtle habitat with at least some trawlers that do not use turtle exclusion devices. This interpretation was changed in the 1996 Guidelines. "An agency interpretation of a relevant provision which conflicts with the agency's earlier interpretation is 'entitled to considerably less deference' than a consistently held agency view." I.N.S. v. Cardoza Fonseca, 480 U.S. 421, 446 n.30 (1987) (quoting Watt v. Alaska, 451 U.S. 259, 273 (1981)).

It cannot be disputed that when only some of the ships trawling for shrimp use TEDs, sea turtles that are saved by the TEDs may later be captured by the vessels without TEDs. The Commerce Department itself raised this concern. Rolland Schmitten, Fisheries Administrator for the National Marine Fisheries Service, wrote as follows:

> By requiring that TEDs be used only on those vessels that harvest shrimp for export to the U.S. market, sea turtles will be put at greater risk of incidental capture aboard non-TED equipped boats in a

nation's fleet.

This approach will also reduce the incentive for nations to adopt comprehensive national programs to reduce the incidental take of sea turtles ... [and] may also result in some certified nations abandoning the comprehensive programs they now have in place or curtailing enforcement of such programs.

Letter from R. Schmitten to Mary Beth West, Deputy Assistant Secretary of State for Oceans (July 28, 1998).

Although the government argues that the State Department has discretion to interpret the statute, citing Japan Whaling Association v. American Cetacean Society, 478 U.S. 221 (1986), in that case the Court held that the discretion exercised by the Secretary of Commerce for phased-in compliance with the national whale quota was "a reasonable construction of the language used in [the legislation]." Id. at 232. Here, the State Department's interpretation is not a reasonable construction of the statute, which clearly requires country-by-country, not shipment-by-shipment, certification. An agency's statutory interpretation cannot stand if it contravenes the clearly expressed legislative intent. See Chevron U.S.A., Inc. v. Natural Resources Defense Council, Inc., 467 U.S. 837, 842-43 (1984) ("If the intent of Congress is clear, that is the end of the matter; for the court, as well as the agency, must give effect to the unambiguously expressed intent of Congress."); Board of Governors of Fed. Reserve Sys. v. Dimension Financial Corp., 474 U.S. 361, 368 (1986).

In its brief, the Secretary of State suggests that matters of international relations and trade pressures in the World Trade Organization (WTO) have warranted more circumspect handling than section 609 may have originally contemplated. The government also states that global turtle protection is proceeding, albeit slowly. However, this court is not authorized to evaluate a pragmatic political accommodation. We, like the Executive branch, are bound by the law as Congress enacted it.

The World Trade Organization Litigation

The government makes much of the recent resolution of the challenge to section 609 in the WTO. In 1996 Malaysia, Thailand, India, and Pakistan challenged the United States' implementation of section 609 as contrary to the GATT. The WTO Appellate Body held that this statute was within an exception to GATT rules in that it related to conservation, but held that various aspects of the certification guidelines were discriminatory. Eventually, in 2001, on a second suit brought by Malaysia, the State Department's 1999 Guidelines (which authorize shipment-by-shipment certification) were accepted as in harmony with the GATT.

The government states that the WTO rulings "support" the State Department's interpretation. The government describes these WTO rulings as "the law of nations" and states that "an act of Congress ought never to be construed to violate the law of nations, if any other possible construction remains," quoting Murray v. The Charming Betsy, 6 U.S. (2 Cranch) 64, 118 (1804). However, no party asserts that WTO decisions have controlling status as United States law. The Statement of Administrative Action (SAA) accompanying the Uruguay Round Agreement Acts states that decisions of WTO panels and the WTO Appellate Body "have no binding effect under the law of the United States and do not represent an expression of U.S. foreign or trade policy." H.R. Doc. No. 103-316, at 1032 (1994). The SAA also states:

> If a[WTO] report recommends that the United States change federal law to bring it into conformity with a Uruguay Round Agreement [including the GATT], it is for the Congress to decide whether any such change will be made.

Id. The SAA is "an authoritative expression by the United States concerning the interpretation and application of the Uruguay Round Agreements and this Act in any judicial proceeding in which a question arises concerning such interpretation or application." 19 U.S.C. § 3512(d); *see also* 19 U.S.C. § 3512(a)(1) ("No provision of any of the Uruguay Round Agreements, nor the application of any such provision to any person or circumstance, that is inconsistent with any law of the United States shall have effect.").

Thus although the government appears to rely on the WTO ruling as requiring United States (and judicial) support of the current Guidelines, neither we nor the State Department has authority to rewrite the statute. *See* Suramerica de Aleaciones Laminadas C.A. v. United States, 966 F.2d 660, 668 (Fed.Cir.1992) ("if the statutory provisions at issue here are inconsistent with the GATT, it is a matter for Congress and not this court to decide and remedy"); Mississippi Poultry Ass'n, Inc. v. Madigan, 992 F.2d 1359, 1366 (5th Cir.1993) (the court must "give effect to Congress' intent, even if implementation of that intent is virtually certain to create a violation of the GATT").

I repeat, it is not before us to decide whether the State Department has pursued a path that is diplomatically preferable to that selected by the Congress. The government brief states that an increasing number of nations are requiring the use of TEDs for all their trawled shrimp. These salutary developments do not relieve the judicial obligation to implement the statutory text as Congress intended and enacted it. Thus I must, respectfully, dissent from the court's incorrect statutory interpretation.

Notes and Questions

1. As the case above notes, in May, 1998, in a challenge brought by Malaysia, India, Thailand, and Pakistan, the WTO Dispute Settlement Body issued a report concluding that the imports restrictions under Section 609 violated Article XI of the GATT and could not be considered natural resource conservation measures within the exception of GATT's Article XX because they were applied in a discriminatory manner in violation of the introductory clause ("chapeau") of XX. WTO, Report of the Panel on U.S. - Import Prohibition of Certain Shrimp and Shrimp Products, (WT/DS58/R) (May 15, 1998) published at 37 I.L.M. 832 (1998). The U.S. appealed, and on Oct. 12, 1998, the WTO Appellate Body upheld the decision of the Dispute Settlement Body but provided a somewhat different interpretation of Article XX. WTO, Report of the Appellate Body on U.S. - Import Prohibition of Certain Shrimp and Shrimp Products, (AB - 1998 - 4) (Oct. 12, 1998) published at 38 I.L.M. 118 (1999). The Appellate Body concluded that the U.S. Section 609 import bans were among the types of measures that fell within the Article XX exception. The particular manner in which the U.S. had applied them, however, violated the requirement in the chapeau that such measures not be applied in an arbitrary or unjustifiably discriminatory manner. See N.L. Perkins, Introductory Note, 38 I.L.M. 118, 118-120 (1999). The Appellate Body also held that dispute settlement panels are free to consider unsolicited information received from non-WTO members, opening the door for NGOs to submit amicus briefs as did the Center for International Environmental Law on behalf of five environmental organizations.

The Appellate Body's decision was the first indication that the WTO does not categorically disallow the use of trade restrictions that are based on the processes or production methods from which the products are derived. It also suggests that the WTO does not prohibit the use of trade measures to protect the environment or natural resources that are outside the WTO member state's territory as long as there is some jurisdictional relationship between the resource the member seeks to protect and the WTO member. Id. The Report indicates, however, that it is generally not valid for one WTO member to restrict trade based on the failure of other members to adopt identical conservation regulations. Section 609 set a standard that was too "rigid and unbendable" for achieving sea turtle protection. Members are required to examine other nations' efforts and circumstances individually. Finally, the Body criticized the U.S. for failing to pursue bilateral or multilateral negotiations on turtle conservation measures.

After the U.S. revised the Section 609 Guidelines, Malaysia brought another challenge before a WTO dispute panel. The panel this time found that the U.S. had complied with the WTO's previous reports and the measure was being applied in a manner that no longer constitutes a means of "arbitrary or unjustifiable discrimination among countries where the same conditions prevail" and is therefore within the scope of Article XX of the GATT. WTO, Report of the Panel on U.S. Import Prohibition of Certain Shrimp and Shrimp Products (WT/DS58/RW) (June 15, 2001), 2001 WL 671012 (WTO). Malaysia appealed, and on Oct. 22, 2001, the Appellate Body decided that the U.S. law fully complies with the recommendations of the dispute settlement body and meet the U.S.'s duties under Articles XI and XX of the GATT. WTO, Report of the Appellate Body, U.S. - Import Prohibition of Certain Shrimp and Shrimp Products, Recourse to article 21.5 by Malaysia (WT/DS58/RW)(Oct. 22, 2001), 2001 WL 1261572. See J.R. Schmertz and M. Meier, WTO Appellate Body Agrees With Its Panel That U.S. Sea Turtle Protection Regime Now Complies with Articles XI and XX of GATT 1994, 7 Int'l L. Update 172 (Nov. 2001).

2. In 1992, Congress enacted the High Seas Driftnet Fisheries Enforcement Act, 16 U.S.C. §§ 1826-1826g, in an effort to give force to the United Nations General Assembly resolutions of 1991 calling for a worldwide moratorium on large-scale high seas driftnets. The Act establishes a process under which the U.S. may take actions against a foreign nation whose nationals or vessels engage in such fishing practices beyond the EEZ of any nation. The process begins with the Secretary of Commerce identifying a nation and notifying the President of that identification. The President is then supposed to enter into discussions with the foreign nation "for the purpose of obtaining an agreement that will effect the immediate termination of large-scale driftnet fishing by the nationals or vessels of that nation * * *" 16 U.S.C. § 1826a(b)(2). If the negotiations fail, the President is to order the Secretary of the Treasury to prohibit the importation into the United States of fish and fish products and sport fishing equipment from that nation. 16 U.S.C. § 1826a(b)(3)(A)(ii). If the import restrictions prove ineffective, the import restrictions can be extended to any products from the offending country. 16 U.S.C. § 1826a(b)(4).

In 1995, the Humane Society of the U.S. and other groups sued in the Court of International Trade, alleging that the Secretary of Commerce had failed to identify Italy as a nation whose nationals or vessels were conducting large-scale driftnet fishing on the high seas (the Mediterranean Sea) in violation of the Act. Humane Society of the U.S. v. Brown, 901 F.Supp. 338 (CIT 1995). The court eventually agreed and held that the Secretary's decision not to identify was an abuse of discretion. Humane Society of the U.S. v. Brown, 920 F.Supp. 178 (CIT 1996). Italy was identified in March 1996 and in July, 1996, the State Department negotiated an agreement with Italy under which steps would be taken to end the fishery. The Secretary then certified to the President that Italy had ended the driftnet fishing. After Italy resumed such fishing in the 1997 and 1998 fishing seasons, the plaintiffs obtained an order of the Court of International Trade that Italy be identified for a second time, based on evidence available to the Secretary that violations of the Driftnet Fishing Act were continuing. In Humane Society of the United States v. Clinton, 44 F.Supp.2d 260 (CIT 1999), the court found that the Secretary of Commerce had "reason to believe" that illegal driftnet fishing was taking place in Italy in violation of the Act, and that the Secretary's failure to identify Italy to the President was arbitrary and capricious. The Secretary was ordered to identify Italy within 10 days. The plaintiffs appealed the court's ruling that mandamus did not lie to compel the President to order import restrictions after Italy was identified and its denial of their request for an order that the Secretary rescind the certification that Italy had ceased driftnet fishing. Humane Society of the United States v. Clinton, 236 F.3d 1320 (Fed. Cir. 2001). The plaintiffs were later awarded attorneys' fees and expenses of $42,367.79,when the court found that the U.S. was not substantially justified in refusing to identify Italy as a country it had reason to believe was engaged in driftnet fishing. Humane Society of the U.S. v. Bush, 159 F.Supp.2d 707 (CIT 2001).

Chapter Eight

POLLUTION OF COASTAL AND OCEAN WATERS

SECTION I. INTRODUCTION

This chapter examines a wide range of international treaties and United States legislation that attempts to limit the pollution of coastal and ocean waters. Some are directed at the consequences of oil and hazardous substance spills. They establish responsibility for clean-up costs, for damages to natural resources, and, in some instances, for physical, property, and economic injuries. They also create funds and mechanisms for recovery of clean-up costs and damages. Other legislation is more preventative in nature. It addresses design and safety requirements for vessels transporting oil and hazardous substances, regulates the discharge of waste into ocean waters, and creates protected ocean areas in which potential environmentally harmful activities may be prohibited. The ultimate issue is the effectiveness of this vast legal regime in protecting coastal and ocean waters from the adverse consequences that often arise from our growing population and industrial economy.

The 1982 United Nations Convention on the Law of the Sea, 21 I.L.M. 1261, obligates nations party to the convention "to protect and preserve the marine environment" (Article 192) by minimizing all sources of marine pollution "to the fullest possible extent" (Article 194(3)). These diverse sources include vessels, offshore installations, and land-based sources such as sewage treatment plants and agricultural runoff. National jurisdiction to protect the marine environment extends throughout the nation's 200-mile Exclusive Economic Zone (EEZ) (Article 56(1)(b)(iii)) and includes the obligation to avoid damaging other nations' EEZs, the high seas, and the deep seabed (Article 194(2)).

691

SECTION 2. OIL AND HAZARDOUS SUBSTANCE SPILLS IN COASTAL WATERS: LIABILITY FOR CLEAN-UP COSTS, PROPERTY DAMAGES, NATURAL RESOURCE DAMAGES, AND ECONOMIC LOSSES

A. PROBLEMS

Oil Spill Problem

Last month during a hurricane an oil tanker sank fifteen miles off the Florida coast in the Gulf of Mexico. Hundreds of thousands of barrels of oil spilled into the Gulf and were carried into state waters by Gulf Stream eddies. Large quantities of the oil settled in valuable offshore fishing grounds and penetrated coastal waters thereby destroying valuable coastal fishing grounds and breeding areas. Fortunately, massive clean-up efforts by Offshore Oil, the vessel's owner, the federal government and the state, along with favorable winds and currents, prevented the oil from reaching a number of recreational beaches.

As a result of this incident, a number of claims are being asserted against Offshore Oil. Both the federal government and the state are asserting claims for their clean-up expenses. The federal government claims clean-up costs of $20,000,000; the state claims $15,000,000. This is in addition to the $100,000,000 expended by Offshore Oil in the clean-up operation. The state is also seeking to recover an additional $80,000,000 for damages to the coastal waters and fisheries and other living resources damaged or destroyed by the oil. A group of Florida commercial fishermen have filed a class action seeking to recover over $13,000,000 for lost profits and an additional $1,200,000 for damages to fishing gear. Finally, a group of fish processors, located in Florida and Southern Alabama dependent upon catches of the commercial fishermen, are asserting a claim of $9,000,000 for lost profits because of their inability to get fish to process and to fulfill delivery contracts.

You are an attorney working for the law firm representing the fishermen, fish processors, and the State of Florida. You have been requested to write a memorandum explaining Offshore Oil's liability under both state and federal law for all of the statutory and common law claims of the fishermen, fish processors, and the State of Florida. The only applicable Florida statutes are:

§ 143-215.83. Discharges.

(a) Unlawful Discharges. -- It shall be unlawful, except as otherwise provided in this Part, for any person to discharge, or cause to be discharged oil or other hazardous substances into or upon any waters, tidal flats, beaches, or lands within this State, or into any sewer, surface water drain or other waters that drain into the waters of this State, regardless of the fault of the person having control over the oil or other hazardous substances, or regardless of whether the discharge was the result of intentional or negligent conduct, accident or other cause.

§ 143-215.90. Liability for damage to public resources.

(a) Any person who discharges oil or other hazardous substances in violation of this Article * * * and in the course thereof causes the death of, or injury to fish, animals, vegetation or other resources of the State * * * shall be liable to pay the State damages. Such damages shall be an amount equal to the cost of all reasonable and necessary investigations made or caused to be made by the Environmental Management Commission in connection with such violation and the sum of money necessary to restock with waters, replenish such resources, or otherwise restore the rivers, streams, bays, tidal flats, beaches, estuaries or coastal waters and public lands adjoining the seacoast to their condition prior to the injury as such condition is determined by the Environmental Management Commission.* * *

§ 143-215.93. Liability for damage caused.

Any person having control over oil or other hazardous substances which enters the waters of the State in violation of this Part shall be strictly liable without regard to fault, for economic losses and damages to persons or property, public or private caused by such entry.

* * *

You may consider any compensation due any of these groups from statutorily established federal funds as a liability of Offshore Oil for purposes of this question. You may also assume that applicable Florida statutes do not contain any limitation of liability provisions. Please write the memorandum, clearly explaining the basis of liability on each claim and any limitations on liability that may exist.

Hazardous Substance Spill Problem

The M/V Mermaid, a large tanker carrying a highly toxic chemical,

Tamulid, collided with a U.S. Navy carrier in the Chesapeake Bay. Both vessels were equally at fault for this collision.

The chemical spilled from the holds of the Mermaid into the Bay. Large quantities settled in areas in which there were clam beds or large populations of blue crabs. The clam beds were destroyed and the blue crabs either died or were rendered inedible. The owners of the clam beds, a number of crabbers who make a living harvesting the blue crabs, and several clam distributors and crabmeat packing houses want to know what damages they may recover under either state or federal law. (You may assume that the state statutes quoted in the above Oil Spill Problem apply and that typical common law remedies exist.)

B. STATUTORY LAW, COMMON LAW, AND MARITIME REMEDIES

The accidental or deliberate discharge of oil or chemicals into coastal or ocean waters may have complex environmental, economic, and legal implications. Fisheries, marine mammals, seabirds, and other forms of sea life may be destroyed or seriously damaged. Beaches may be fouled. The local fishing industry may collapse. Coastal businesses and their employees may be financially devastated by the economic losses associated with a loss of tourist trade and a collapsed fishing industry. As the various allegedly injured or responsible parties sort through the maze of jurisdictional and substantive legal principles that govern their rights or liabilities, the legal ramifications of such discharges frequently will be as complicated as the non-legal effects.

Federal efforts to curb water pollution are traceable back to the Rivers and Harbors Act of 1899. Section 10 regulates obstruction of navigable waters (Chapter Two), and Section 13, known as the Refuse Act, prohibits dumping of refuse. Although the Refuse Act had long been interpreted as applying only to discharges that obstructed or impeded navigation, in the 1966 case of United States v. Standard Oil Company, 384 U.S. 224 (1966), the Court declared that "refuse" encompassed all foreign substances and pollutants except those expressly excluded. The Court went on to say that the Act reached not only navigational menaces, but also pollution. However, it was not until after the disastrous 1967 *Torrey Canyon* oil spill off the coast of England that Congress finally began to consider measures for the prevention of oil spills, clean-up of spills, liability for spillers, and compensation for oil pollution damages. Its initial foray was Section 311 of the Clean Water Act (CWA), 33 U.S.C § 1321, initially passed as part of the Water Quality Improvement Act of 1970. In 1989, when the tanker *Exxon Valdez* hit a reef in the pristine waters of Prince William Sound and spilled millions of gallons of oil,[1] the legal inadequacies of Section 311 and the Trans-Alaska Pipeline Authorization Act, 43 U.S.C. § 1651, et seq, were driven home to Congress and the American people by that tragic oil spill.

In response to the *Exxon Valdez* spill, Congress passed the Oil Pollution Act of 1990 (OPA), 33 U.S.C. §§ 2701-61. OPA did not repeal Section 311 of the CWA. Section 311's National Oil And Hazardous Substances Contingency Plan, its reporting requirements, and its penalty provisions remain in place, but its clean-up and damage provisions are abrogated. OPA, which is limited to oil spills, creates a comprehensive federal scheme for recovery of clean-up costs and imposes liability for damages to natural resources. It also makes the party responsible for the discharge of oil into navigable waters strictly liable for physical injuries, property damages, and direct and some indirect economic losses that are the consequence of the oil spill.

The discharge of hazardous or toxic substances, other than petroleum products, into navigable waters is addressed by the Comprehensive Environmental Responses, Compensation and Liability Act (also known as "Superfund" or CERCLA), 42 U.S.C. §§ 9601-75, passed in 1980. CERCLA also grew out of Section 311. In its original form, Section 311's application was limited to petroleum products. In 1978 its coverage was broadened to include toxic and hazardous substances. But as part of a more comprehensive program addressing the release of hazardous substances on land and in the water, CERCLA was passed by Congress. When CERCLA went into effect, Section 311's application to discharges of non-petroleum products ceased. CERCLA establishes its own reporting requirements for releases of hazardous substances (other than petroleum products) and imposes strict liability for clean-up costs and damages to natural resources. However, unlike OPA, CERCLA contains no provisions for the recovery of private damages. Recovery of such damages is left to other applicable state or federal law. In 1996, under CERCLA, the Environmental Protection Agency (EPA) designated the first open ocean contaminated clean up site. Located off southern California's Palos Verdes Peninsula, the site was contaminated when Montrose Chemical Corporation flushed several million pounds of DDT into a sewer which emptied into the Pacific Ocean. The EPA found that the contamination posed substantial risks to marine life and to people who ate fish caught in the region. See

---

[1] For an excellent discussion of the spill and subsequent events, see A. Davidson, In The Wake Of The Exxon Valdez (1990). See also J. Wheelwright, Degrees of Disaster (1994) (analyzing the long-term effects of the spill).

A Review of Developments in U.S. Ocean and Coastal Law 1994-96, 2 Ocean & Coastal L. J. 457, 489 (1997). This became the largest U.S. environmental damages case since the *Exxon Valdez* spill, and the largest non-oilspilll environmental case in U.S. history. With a final settlement in December 2000, the polluting companies had paid a total of $137.5 million for environmental restoration.

The following materials emphasize the statutory liability scheme created by OPA and CERCLA (as it applies to spills of non-petroleum hazardous and toxic substances into coastal navigable waters), the remaining relevant aspects of CWA Section 311, and issues of the application of maritime law, common law, and state statutes to releases of either oil or other toxic and hazardous substances into coastal navigable waters.

(1.) What Is Prohibited

Although OPA and CERCLA have displaced most of CWA Section 311, subsection 311(b) continues to be a statement of the basic policy of the United States and a flat prohibition against discharges of harmful quantities of oil or hazardous substances:

> (1) The Congress hereby declares that it is the policy of the United States that there should be no discharges of oil or hazardous substances into or upon the navigable waters of the United States, adjoining shorelines, * * * or in connection with activities under the Outer Continental Shelf Lands Act or the Deepwater Port Act of 1974, or which may affect natural resources belonging to, appertaining to, or under the exclusive management authority of the United States (including resources under the Magnuson-Stevens Fishery Conservation and Management Act).* * *

> (3) The discharge of oil or hazardous substances (i) into or upon the navigable waters of the United States, adjoining shorelines * * * or (ii) in connection with activities under the Outer Continental Shelf Lands Act [43 U.S.C. § 1331 et seq.] or the Deepwater Port Act of 1974 [33 U.S.C. § 1501 et seq.], or which may affect natural resources belonging to, appertaining to, or under the exclusive management authority of the United States (including resources under the Magnuson-Stevens Fishery Conservation and Management Act [16 U.S.C. § 1801 et seq.]), in such quantities as may be harmful as determined by the President under paragraph (4) of this subsection, is prohibited, except * * * (B) where permitted in quantities and at times and locations or under such circumstances or conditions as the President may, by regulation,

determine not to be harmful. Any regulations issued under this subsection shall be consistent with maritime safety and with marine and navigation laws and regulations and applicable water quality standards.

(4)   The President shall by regulation determine for the purposes of this section those quantities of oil and any hazardous substances the discharge of which may be harmful to the public health or welfare or the environment of the United States, including but not limited to fish, shellfish, wildlife, and public and private property, shorelines, and beaches.

33 U.S.C. § 1321(b)(1),(3), and (4). The sanctions for violations include administrative, civil, and criminal penalties. 33 U.S.C. §§ 1319, 1321 (b) (5), (6).

(2.) The Obligation to Report Discharges of Oil and Hazardous Substances

CWA Section 311 remains the major federal statute governing the reporting of oil spills. It requires immediate reporting to the appropriate authorities of any prohibited discharge to assure that prompt and effective clean-up efforts are undertaken. According to subsection 311(b)(5)

(5)   Any person in charge of a vessel or of an onshore facility or an offshore facility shall, as soon as he has knowledge of any discharge of oil or a hazardous substance from such vessel or facility in violation of paragraph (3) of this subsection, immediately notify the appropriate agency of the United States Government of such discharge. * * *

33 U.S.C. § 1321(b)(5).

Before it was amended in 1978, the predecessor of current subsection 311(b)(3) of the Clean Water Act prohibited the discharge of oil in "harmful quantities." The Clean Water Act further provided that it was a crime for the captain of any vessel to fail to notify the appropriate federal agency of any such discharge. The applicable EPA regulations stated that harmful discharges included those which "* * * (b) cause a film or sheen upon or discoloration of the surface of the water. * * *" 40 C.F.R. § 110.3(b). A major reason for the adoption of this "sheen test" was its workability. Instead of having a numerical criterion, the judgment was that the sheen test was readily applicable by any person discharging oil.

The validity of this so called "sheen test" was unsuccessfully challenged in United States v. Boyd, 491 F.2d 1163 (9th Cir. 1973), a case involving the accidental discharge of approximately thirty gallons of oil. The defendant claimed that the regulation "improperly defined as 'harmful' a broader class of oil discharges than Congress intended," and thus made it unlawful to fail to report discharges that were not in fact harmful. The court, however, stated that "workability" was a permissible factor in promulgating such a regulation. In addition, the government produced evidence that spills smaller than ten barrels do have an adverse effect upon the environment. Based on this information the court held that, on the facts of the particular case, the sheen test was a valid basis for distinguishing harmful and nonharmful discharges.

The challenges to the sheen test did not end with *Boyd*. In November 1972, a vent malfunctioned on a Chevron structure located in navigable waters. Approximately 21-42 gallons of oil spilled into the water creating a sheen. An employee corrected the malfunction, recovered approximately one-half the discharge, and reported the spill. Chevron immediately notified the Coast Guard. When the Coast Guard sought to impose a $1000 penalty for the oil spill, Chevron challenged the assessment at a hearing in which a Chevron expert testified that, despite the presence of a sheen, the spill had no harmful effect upon the environment. The government did not produce any evidence that this particular spill was in fact harmful, relying only on an affidavit from a government expert that asserted " an oil spill sufficient to produce a film or sheen on the surface of the water is large enough to cause harm to the environment." The district court granted summary judgment for the government, but the Ninth Circuit Court of Appeals reversed and remanded.

Although the Court of Appeals found that the sheen test regulation was a valid workable regulation for reporting purposes, it held that subsection 311(b) substantively only prohibited discharges of "harmful quantities." Thus, absent evidence that the Chevron spill was of a harmful quantity under the circumstances, no penalty could be imposed. United States v. Chevron Oil Co., 583 F.2d 1357 (5th Cir. 1978).

The difficulty that the government had in determining what constituted harmful quantities of hazardous substances resulted in amending Section 311. Subsections 311 (b)(3) and (b)(4) then were changed to read "quantities * * * which [or as] may be harmful." See J. Battle, Environmental Law 509-11 (2d ed. 1993). The effect of these amendments was addressed in Chevron v. Yost, 919 F.2d 27 (5th Cir. 1990), which involved twelve separate oil spills from Chevron vessels in 1986. Chevron reported the spills and admitted that they created a sheen. However, Chevron denied liability for penalties under Section 311 of the Clean Water Act because the spills did not cause actual injury. The court found that the 1978 amendments to Section 311 empowered the EPA to prohibit environmentally hazardous substances upon a determination that they "may be harmful to the public health or welfare of the United States." 33 U.S.C. § 1321(b)(3) and (4). The EPA then re-promulgated the sheen test as the proper way to make that determination. The holding of United States v. Chevron Oil, 583 F.2d 1357 (5th Cir. 1978), therefore, did not control this case because that case pre-dated the 1978 amendments to Section 311. The court in *Yost* upheld the validity of the sheen test. The *Yost* court followed the reasoning of Orgulf Transport Co. v. United States, 711 F. Supp. 344 (W.D. Ky. 1989), that "[w]hether a spill resulted in actual harm to the environment is irrelevant to the determination of whether Section 311 * * * has been violated. The only pertinent inquiry is whether the spill was in a quantity which may be harmful as determined by the EPA. Because the EPA has determined that a spill of oil which creates a sheen is a quantity which `may be harmful,' such a spill is subject to the penalty provisions." Id. at 347.

Since people responsible for a spill must report it or face additional penalties, the issue has arisen whether the report can be used as evidence in any governmental action to impose penalties pursuant to subsection 311(b)(6) or in criminal prosecutions for negligent or knowing violations. The United States Supreme Court held that the penalty imposed by subsection 311(b)(6) was civil and not criminal and therefore the Fifth Amendment did not apply to use of a report in such a proceeding. United States v. Ward, 448 U.S. 242 (1980). However, subsection 311(b)(5) creates immunity in criminal prosecutions for such required reported information. See, e.g., Hazelwood v. Alaska, 836 P.2d 943 (Alaska App. 1992).

(3.) Liability for Discharges of Oil and Hazardous Substances

(a.) Liability, Defenses, and Limitations on Liability

OPA creates a comprehensive liability system which makes the responsible party strictly liable for clean-up costs and damages flowing from an oil spill. Some limited defenses are available; but, to avail itself of these defenses, the responsible party must report the oil spill if it is aware of the incident, provide all reasonable requested cooperation with officials responsible for removal of the oil, comply with any Section 311 clean-up order, and establish that it exercised due care with respect to the handling of the oil. See, e.g., National Shipping Co. of Saudi Arabia v. Moran Trade Corp. of Delaware, 122 F.3d 1062, 1997 WL 560047

(4th Cir. 1997) (unpublished opinion).

SELECTED PROVISIONS OF OIL POLLUTION ACT OF 1990

33 U.S.C. § 2701 Definitions

[Section 1001]

For the purposes of this chapter, the term --

* * *

(21) "navigable waters" means the waters of the United States, including the territorial sea; * * *

(29) "public vessel" means a vessel owned or bareboat chartered and operated by the United States, or by a State or political subdivision thereof, or by a foreign nation, except when the vessel is engaged in commerce;

(30) "remove" or "removal" means containment and removal of oil or a hazardous substance from water and shorelines or the taking of other actions as may be necessary to minimize or mitigate damage to the public health or welfare, including, but not limited to, fish, shellfish, wildlife, and public and private property, shorelines, and beaches;

(31) "removal costs" means the costs of removal that are incurred after a discharge of oil has occurred or, in any case in which there is a substantial threat of a discharge of oil, the costs to prevent, minimize, or mitigate oil pollution from such an incident;

(32) "responsible party" means the following:

(A) Vessels.

In the case of a vessel, any person owning, operating, or demise chartering the vessel. * * *

(35) "territorial seas" means the belt of the seas measured from the line of ordinary low water along that portion of the coast which is in direct contact with the open sea and the line marking the seaward limit of inland waters, and extending seaward a distance of 3 miles; * * *.

33 U.S.C. § 2702 Elements of Liability

[Section 1002]

(a) IN GENERAL. -- Notwithstanding any other provision or rule of law, and subject to the provisions of this Act, each responsible party for a vessel or a facility from which oil is discharged, or which poses the substantial threat of a discharge of oil, into or upon the navigable waters or adjoining shorelines or the exclusive economic zone is liable for the removal costs and damages specified in subsection (b) that directly result from such incident. * * *

(c) EXCLUDED DISCHARGES. -- This subchapter does not apply to any discharge --

(1) permitted by a permit issued under Federal, State, or local law;

(2) from a public vessel. * * *

33 U.S.C. § 2703 Defenses to Liability.

[Section 1003]

(a) COMPLETE DEFENSES. -- A responsible party is not liable for removal costs or damages under 33 U.S.C. § 2702 if the responsible party establishes, by a preponderance of the evidence, that the discharge or substantial threat of a discharge of oil and the resulting damages or removal costs were caused solely by --

(1) an act of God;

(2) an act of war;

(3) an act or omission of a third party, other than an employee or agent of the responsible party or a third party whose act or omission occurs in connection with any contractual relationship * * * if the responsible party establishes, by the preponderance of the evidence, that the responsible party --

(A) exercised due care with respect to the oil concerned, taking into consideration the characteristics of the oil and in light of all relevant facts and circumstances; and

(B) took precautions against foreseeable acts or omissions

of any such third party and the foreseeable consequences of those acts or omissions; or

(4) any combination of paragraphs (1), (2), and (3).

(b) DEFENSES AS TO PARTICULAR CLAIMANTS. A responsible party is not liable under 33 U.S.C. § 2702 to a claimant, to the extent that the incident is caused by the gross negligence or willful misconduct of the claimant.

(c) LIMITATION ON COMPLETE DEFENSE. Subsection (a) does not apply with respect to a responsible party who fails or refuses --

(1) to report the incident as required by law if the responsible party knows or has reason to know of the incident;

(2) to provide all reasonable cooperation and assistance requested by a responsible official in connection with removal activities; * * *

33 U.S.C. § 2704 Limits on Liability.

[Section 1004]

(a) General Rule. -- Except as otherwise provided in this section, the total of the liability of a responsible party under 33 U.S.C. § 2702 and any removal costs incurred by, or on behalf of, the responsible party, with respect to each incident shall not exceed [minimums ranging between $500,000 to $10,000,000 for most vessels, depending on tonnage, and maximums for onshore facilities of $350,000,000 and for offshore facilities of $75,000,000 plus all removal costs]. * * *

(c) Exceptions. --

(1) ACTS OF RESPONSIBLE PARTY. -- Subsection (a) does not apply if the incident was proximately caused by –

(A) gross negligence or willful misconduct of, or

(B) the violation of an applicable Federal safety, construction, or operating regulation by, the responsible party, an agent or employee of the responsible party, or a person acting pursuant to a contractual relationship with the responsible party (except where the sole contractual arrangement arises in connection with carriage by a common carrier by rail).

(2) Failure or Refusal of Responsible Party. -- Subsection (a) does not apply if the responsible party fails or refuses –

(A) to report the incident as required by law and the responsible party knows or has reason to know of the incident;

(B) to provide all reasonable cooperation and assistance requested by a responsible official in connection with removal activities; or

(C) without sufficient cause, to comply with an order issued under subsection (c) or (e) of Section 311 of the Federal Water Pollution Control Act [33 U.S.C. § 1321] * * * or the Intervention on the High Seas Act. * * *

CERCLA also imposes strict liability for clean-up costs and natural resource damages, but does not address other damage claims. CERCLA's limitation provisions are very similar to OPA's but contain different limitation amounts. 42 U.S.C. § 9607(c)(1). CERCLA limitations of liability may be lost if the discharge was the "result of willful misconduct or willful negligence within the privity or knowledge of * * *" the discharger of the hazardous substance. 42 U.S.C. § 9607(c)(2)(A)(i). The phrase -- "within the privity or knowledge" -- was derived from the Limitation of Liability Act of 1851, 46 U.S.C. § 183. What constitutes willful misconduct or willful negligence "within the privity or knowledge" of the discharger? Compare e.g., Tug Ocean Prince, Inc. v. United States, 584 F.2d 1151 (2d Cir. 1978), cert. denied, 440 U.S. 959 (1978) (finding that the combination of "various inactions and gross disregard of the potential harm" by the tug owner constituted willful misconduct), with Steuart Transp. Co. v. Allied Towing Corp., 596 F.2d 609 (4th Cir. 1979) (no willful negligence even though company made inadequate inspections, since barge had been "routinely and regularly certified by the Coast Guard"). See also G. Gilmore and C. Black, The Law of Admiralty 877-98 (1975). Does the absence of that phrase in OPA make it more or less likely that the right to limit liability under OPA will be lost? Although the limitation amounts are substantial, removal, cleanup costs, and other claims associated with major spills may greatly exceed these amounts.

Coast Guard vessel owner and operator financial responsibility regulations under OPA and CERCLA are found at 33 C.F.R. pts. 4, 130-32,

137-38.

(b.) Recovery of Damages to Natural Resources

Measuring Damages

When living natural resources that have no market value are destroyed or damaged as the result of the release of oil or hazardous substances, the difficult issues are how to determine what resources have been destroyed or damaged, the extent to which they have been destroyed or damaged, the feasibility of restoration, and the amount of the damages for resources which can not be restored within a reasonable time frame. Both CERCLA and OPA contain provisions for federal and state recovery of natural resource damages. However, the precise means of measurement of such damages remain uncertain. Department of Interior (DOI) procedures for assessing damages to natural resources resulting from a release of hazardous substances are described in the Natural Resource Damage Assessment Regulations, 43 C.F.R. § 11.10 et seq. The background of these regulations can be found in 51 Fed. Reg. 27674 (August 1, 1986).

Prior to the promulgation of these regulations, in the only previous reported case directly addressing the issue of the appropriate measure of damages for loss or damage to natural resources lacking any traditional market value, Commonwealth of Puerto Rico v. S.S. Zoe Colocotroni, 628 F.2d 652 (1st Cir. 1980), the court rejected the defendant's argument that the appropriate measure is diminution of value determined by the difference in the commercial market of the property before and after the event causing injury. The court also rejected the further argument of the defendant that restoration, as a remedy, was only appropriate when restoration costs are less than the diminution of value. Relying on the applicable Puerto Rican statute, the court determined that the appropriate measure is

> the cost reasonably to be incurred by the sovereign * * * to restore or rehabilitate the environment in the affected area to its pre-existing condition, or as closely thereto as is feasible without greatly disproportionate expenditures. The focus in determining such a remedy should be on the steps a reasonable and prudent sovereign * * * would take to mitigate the harm done by the pollution, with attention to such factors as technical feasibility, harmful side effects, compatibility with or duplication of such regeneration as is naturally to be expected, and the extent to which efforts beyond a certain point would become either redundant or disproportionately expensive. * * *

Id. at 675.

The promulgated DOI regulations, however, limited the natural resource damages recoverable to the lesser of restoration or replacement costs or diminution of use values, 43 C.F.R. § 11.35(b)(2) (1987). These regulations were held to be contrary to the intent of Congress and invalid. State of Ohio v. U.S. Dept. of the Interior, 880 F.2d. 432 (D.C. Cir. 1989). According to the court, Congress expressed a "distinct preference for restoration costs as the measure of recovery in natural resource damages cases." Id. at 459.

For oil spills, OPA provides for the recovery by the United States or a state of "[d]amages for injury to, destruction of, loss of, or loss of use of, natural resources, including the reasonable costs of assessing damage * * *." 33 U.S.C. § 2702(b)(2)(A).[2] 33 U.S.C. § 2706(d), provides:

(1) IN GENERAL. -- The measure of natural resource damages under 33 U.S.C. 2702(b)(2)(A) is --

(A) the cost of restoring, rehabilitating, replacing, or acquiring the equivalent of, the damaged natural resources;

(B) the diminution in value of those natural resources pending restoration; plus

(C) the reasonable cost of assessing those damages.

(2) DETERMINE COSTS WITH RESPECT TO PLANS. -- Costs shall be determined under paragraph (1) with respect to plans adopted under subsection (c).

(3) NO DOUBLE RECOVERY. -- There shall be no double recovery under this chapter for natural resource damages, including with respect to the costs of damage assessment or restoration, rehabilitation, replacement, or acquisition for the same incident and

---

[2] OPA defines natural resources to include:

> * * * land, fish, wildlife, biota, air, water, ground water, drinking water supplies, and other such resources belonging to managed by, held in trust by, appertaining to, or otherwise controlled by the United States (including the resources of the exclusive economic zone), any State or local government or Indian tribe, or any foreign government;

33 U.S.C. § 2701 (20)[OPA Section 1001(20)].

natural resource.

It is clear that in OPA, Congress has opted for an expansion of the common law principles for measurement of damages and for a distinct preference for restoration as a remedy. But restoration damages are only part of the damages recoverable under OPA. Lost use and nonuse values and assessment costs are also recoverable. Of these three components of recoverable OPA damages, the measurement of lost use and nonuse values are perhaps the most controversial.

Discussions of natural resource valuation are frequently confusing because of differences in terminology used by courts and commentators. In particular, there is considerable variation in the classification of components of economic value as use values or nonuse values. From a practical standpoint, the most useful distinction is between those components of use value that can be identified and measured by traditional economic analysis of behavior (or "revealed preference methods"), and existence and other nonuse values, which can be measured only by the controversial contingent valuation method.

Use values are simply the value of resources to people who use or potentially use them. Consumptive uses are those uses which consume resources, such as fishing, and nonconsumptive uses are those uses which do not reduce the availability of the resource for others, such as bird watching. Nonconsumptive uses of natural resources are generally thought to dwarf consumptive uses.

Obviously, oil spills or releases of hazardous substances can deny natural resources to many users, at least temporarily. Recreational areas may be closed due to oiled beaches, and fisheries may be closed due to the danger of oiling gear. * * *

In contrast, nonuse values are values placed on natural resources by persons who do not use them. The most significant nonuse values are existence value, option value and bequest value. Existence value is the amount that someone is willing to pay to preserve a resource, regardless of whether he has any intention to ever use it. Option value is the value of preserving the option of using the resource in the future. Bequest value is the value of preserving the resource for future generations.

There seems little doubt that existence values are real. Like constitutional rights, certain resources have value to people whether or not they will ever use them. That existence value has considerable economic importance is demonstrated by the large amounts of money that people contribute to environmental groups to preserve wilderness areas that the contributors have little hope of ever visiting. Nonuse values are likely to be most significant for long-term damages to well known natural resources with few substitutes. Nevertheless, while few economists question the reality of existence value, there is a lively debate over whether the concept is sufficiently well defined and consistent with economic theory to allow empirical measurement.

Whatever the merits of the debate among economists regarding existence value, Congress has decided that existence value should be taken into account in assessing natural resource damages. Congress rejected the option of simply using natural resources' commercial value. Similarly, Congress rejected a "narrow market value and use value based approach. * * *" OPA "makes it clear that forests are more than board feet of lumber, and that seals and sea otters are more than just commodities traded on the market." Accordingly, Congress intended OPA's measure of natural resource damages to follow the lead of the D.C. Circuit in Ohio v. United States Department of the Interior, which held that under CERCLA, natural resource damages include lost existence values. * * *

Economists have developed a number of techniques to measure the loss in value of natural resources due to oil spills or releases of hazardous substances. The least controversial techniques are those used to measure use values. These methods include use of market values and appraisals, indirect methods such as travel cost and hedonic pricing models. The most controversial method is the contingent valuation method, which is the only way to measure nonuse values.

Measurement of use values is more in accord with traditional techniques of economic measurement. Measurement of use values is more precise and reliable because economists can derive values from human behavior, and these indirect methods are thought to be more reliable than measuring attitudes through direct surveys, such as contingent valuation.

Where a competitive market reflects the full value of a resource, the most reliable measure of value is, of course, the market value. Use of market values is consistent with both traditional economic and common law approaches. It provides a relatively easy, objective standard for assigning a value to natural resources. If commercially harvested fish have been destroyed, the market for those fish provides a readily ascertainable standard for their value. If timber has been destroyed, the market price of lumber may provide an adequate measure of the damage. Furthermore, to the extent that the market reflects the value of natural resources, forcing those that damage natural resources to internalize market values of those resources will promote overall economic efficiency.

The problem with market values is that in the case of natural resources, they frequently do not reflect the true value of the resources to society. Frequently, there is no market for important natural resources, such as nongame birds, or wilderness areas. Even where there is some market for certain resources, it is likely to be imperfect. The loss of Yellowstone National Park could not be adequately measured by the value of its timber and minerals. Furthermore, markets almost completely fail to reflect existence values. Thus, market values are "necessarily * * * incomplete."

Another market-based approach to calculating the value of natural resources is the appraisal method. Appraisals can be used where there is no market for the injured resources themselves, but similar resources are traded in a market. They are commonly used to determine the value of resources for federal land acquisition. Appraisals are subject to some of the same limitations as market prices, however. There are no commercially traded commodities similar to a bald eagle, for example. Furthermore, to the extent that markets do not reflect the true value of natural resources, the price paid by the government in acquiring property will not be an accurate reflection of its value to society. Presumably, the value of a wilderness area to society is in excess of the cost of acquisition.

Indirect methods of measuring use values include the travel cost and hedonic pricing methods. Travel cost models are based on the assumption that the recreational value of a site is reflected in the expenses and opportunity costs incurred by visitors to it. When a site is damaged, visitors substitute other sites. By measuring the increase in travel costs associated with this substitution, an estimate can be derived of at least one component of the use value lost when the site is injured. The travel cost method is subject to significant limitations, however. Adequate data may be unavailable. It is difficult to isolate changes in the site due to pollution from other changes. Losses may be underestimated where visitors travel to unaffected parts of the site. There are theoretical and practical difficulties in valuing travel time. Travel cost models cannot evaluate true wilderness areas, where travel is infrequent and often discouraged. Most importantly, the travel cost method cannot measure existence value.

Hedonic pricing attempts to measure the extent to which the value of natural resources are reflected in the value of marketed commodities, such as land. For example, vacation property next to a pristine wilderness is presumably more valuable than property next to a hazardous waste site. Similarly, property values may decline due to an oil spill. Hedonic pricing attempts to use these effects to derive the changes in the value of public resources caused by pollution.

Hedonic pricing has significant limitations, however. There may not be an active private market for land next on the area affected by an oil spill. Even where there is, it is difficult to separate environmental amenities from the other attributes that contribute to the value of property. Akin to travel cost methods, hedonic pricing fails to capture existence values.

Nonuse values can be measured only by means of the contingent valuation method (CV). CV is essentially a survey, much like a public opinion survey, which asks people potentially affected by injury to natural resources how they value that injury. CV surveys use sophisticated survey techniques similar to the techniques used in opinion polling by political candidates. The survey instrument should provide a fair and accurate description of the injury. It should also provide a series of questions carefully designed to elicit respondents' valuation of the injury. One common method asks respondents how much they would pay to reverse the injury, as a surrogate for the respondents' valuation of the injury. Statistical methods are used to extrapolate from individual respondent's answers to the total value of the injury to the affected population. For a well known resource that has a few substitutes, the numbers produced by CV can be enormous.

The validity of CV is probably the most controversial issue in the field of natural resource damages. As DOI has noted, "[i]t is difficult to get a consensus on the reliability" of CV.

CV has been criticized on a number of grounds. Most fundamentally, economists prefer to measure value based on people's behavior, such as in the marketplace. They are skeptical of methods which attempt to predict behavior from expressed attitudes. Accordingly, some economists doubt whether responses to a CV survey accurately predict the true values that people assign to natural resources. Furthermore, most people have little familiarity with assessing the value of natural resources. Accordingly, some economists have questioned whether respondents to a CV survey have the information necessary to make a rational evaluation of the value of natural resources. Some studies have suggested that respondents tend to respond with a fixed amount for environmental protection, regardless of the particular problem they are questioned about, and this figure cannot be rationally separated into distinct components for different environmental problems. Nevertheless, a number of other studies have shown that the results of CV in measuring use values are consistent with such methods as travel costs or hedonic pricing, suggesting that CV should be a reliable measure of nonuse values as well.

Apart from the theoretical objections to CV, there are a number of problems that can introduce bias into a CV survey. It is generally thought important for the interviewer not to disclose the purpose of the survey or the party on whose behalf the survey is done. This might lead to "strategic behavior" on the part of respondents, who might inflate estimates of value to punish a polluter. An improperly designed survey may provide suggestions to the respondents regarding the desired answer.

In developing its natural resource damage assessment regulations, DOI carefully considered the benefits and limitations of CV and concluded that it was sufficiently reliable to be used in measuring nonuse values when "properly structured and professionally applied." * * *

Congress intended the scope of natural resource damages under OPA to follow the principles of the Ohio decision. * * * Nevertheless * * * there are a host of issues that arise in * * * [the] application [of CV]. The use of CV in particular cases is certain to be the subject of intense litigation in the future. * * *

J. Nicoll, Jr., Marine Pollution And Natural Resources Damages: The Multi-Million Dollar Damage Award and Beyond, 5 U.S.F. Maritime L. J. 323, 338-45 (1993).

What should be the criteria for determining whether a CV survey reliably calculates nonuse values? See 59 Fed. Reg. 1062, 1143-47 (Jan. 9, 1994). For additional detailed discussions of assessment of natural resources damages, see, e.g., R. Kopp and V. Smith (eds.), Valuing Natural Assets (1993); F. Cross, Natural Resource Damage Valuation, 42 Vand. L. Rev. 269 (1989); F. Halter and J. Thomas, Recovery of Damages by States for Fish and Wildlife Losses Caused by Pollution, 10 Ecology L.Q. 5, 18-30 (1982).

The recovery of natural resources damages pursuant to OPA and CERCLA is not inconsistent with traditional common law principles. The Restatement (Second) of Torts, § 929(1)(a)(1979), states:

(1) If one is entitled to a judgment for harm to land resulting from a past invasion and not amounting to a total destruction of value, the damages include compensation for

(a) the difference between the value of the land before the harm and the value after the harm, or at his election in an appropriate case, the cost of restoration that has been or may be reasonably incurred.

In comment b this rule is further explained.

b. Restoration. Even in the absence of value arising from personal use, the reasonable cost of replacing the land in its original position is ordinarily allowable as the measure of recovery. Thus if a ditch is wrongfully dug upon the land of another, the other normally is entitled to damages measured by the expense of filling the ditch, if he wishes it filled. If, however, the cost of replacing the land in its original condition is disproportionate to the diminution in the value of the land caused by the trespass, unless there is a reason personal to the owner for restoring the original condition, damages are measured only by the difference between the value of the land before and after the harm.

* * *

* * * So, when a garden has been maintained in a city in connection with a dwelling house, the owner is entitled to recover the expense of putting the garden in its original condition even though the market value of the premises has not been decreased by the defendant's invasion.

Isn't the destruction or degradation of a natural bay and its associated fish, plants, and wildlife analogous to the destruction of a city garden?

Pursuant to 33 U.S.C. § 2706(e)(1)'s mandate, the National Oceanic and Atmospheric Administration (NOAA) has issued detailed rules for the assessment of natural resource damages resulting from oil spills including calculation of non-use values by contingent valuation and other methods. See 15 C.F.R. pt. 990. With a few exceptions, the regulations were upheld in General Electric Co. v. U.S. Dept. of Commerce, 128 F.3d 767 (D.C. Cir. 1997).

Who Is Entitled To Sue For Natural Resource Damages And Proper Use Of Recoveries

. If damages are recoverable for the effects on natural resources of oil and hazardous substance spills, who is entitled to recover these damages and what, if any, limitations exist on how the recovered funds may be used? Prior to the passage of OPA and CERCLA, the federal government and the state of Virginia both sued to recover for damage to migratory waterfowl when approximately 30,000 migratory birds were killed as the result of an oil spill in Chesapeake Bay in February 1976. The district court allowed both to seek recovery under both the public trust doctrine and parens patriae.[3] See In re Steuart Transportation Co., 495 F. Supp. 38 (E.D. Va. 1980). Should private plaintiffs be allowed to sue as "surrogate plaintiffs" to recover for injury to natural resources or must the suit be brought by the proper state or federal authority? Regarding oil spills, see Alaska Sport Fishing Ass'n v. Exxon Corp., 34 F.3d 769 (9th Cir. 1994), (only the federal and state governments may recover lost use damages caused by oil spills); In re Exxon Valdez, 104 F.3d 1196 (9th Cir. 1997) (Alaskan Natives could not recover alleged noneconomic cultural damages caused by oil spill). Regarding hazardous substance spills, see Pruitt v. Allied Chemical Corporation, 523 F. Supp. 975 (E.D. Va. 1981), which appears later in this chapter.

Both OPA and CERCLA contain provisions of recovery of natural resource damages by federal "trustees" (states, Indian tribes, and foreign governments) for injury to resources belonging to those governments. See 33 U.S.C § 2706(a); 42 U.S.C. § 9607(f) (no provision for recovery by foreign governments in CERCLA). Since neither CERCLA nor OPA preempt state law,

> [t]here may be instances where two or more trustees share jurisdiction or control over natural resources. In such cases, trustees should exercise joint management or control of the shared resources. Thus, one class of trustee cannot preempt the right of other classes of trustees to exercise their trusteeship responsibilities.

---

[3] The parens patriae theory is that the state is a public trustee and the representative of the public's interest in the protection of natural resources. See, e.g., State of Maine v. M/V Tamano, 357 F.Supp. 1097 (D. Me. 1973).

H.R. Conf. Rep. No. 101-653, 101st Cong., 2d Sess. 109 (1990). Thus, it is quite likely more than one trustee may bring claims for damage to the same natural resource. Although OPA prevents double recovery, it does not provide any mechanism for resolving conflicting claims between two or more trustees or allocation of damages among such trustees. However, OPA does limit the use of recovered sums once collected.

(f) USE OF RECOVERED SUMS. -- Sums recovered * * * by a Federal, State, Indian, or foreign trustee for natural resource damages under 33 U.S.C. § 2702(b)(2)(A) shall be retained by the trustee in a revolving trust account, without further appropriation, for use only to reimburse or pay costs incurred by the trustee under subsection (c) of this section with respect to the damaged natural resources. Any amounts in excess of those required for these reimbursements and costs shall be deposited in the Fund.

Subsection (c) requires trustees to assess natural resource damages and to develop and implement plans for the restoration, rehabilitation, replacement, or acquisition of the equivalent of the damaged natural resources.

(4.) Exclusivity of the Federal Statutory Remedy

(a.) *Federal Clean-up Costs and Natural Resource Damages*

An issue related to the right of the discharger to limit liability is whether CERCLA or OPA is the exclusive remedy available to recover clean-up costs and natural resource damages for incidents covered by these statutes.[4] The extent to which CERCLA is the federal government's exclusive remedy for recovery of clean-up costs and natural resource damages is still an open question. But cf. United States v. Price, 523 F. Supp 1055 (D.N.J. 1981) (no federal common law nuisance remedy available to the federal government). Arguably it is, but CERCLA contains a savings clause, Section 302(d), 42 U.S.C. § 9652(d), which states:

Nothing in this chapter shall affect or modify in any way the obligations or liabilities of any person under other Federal or State

---

[4] When Section 311 was the governing statute, it was the exclusive remedy for recovery by the federal government of such costs and damages. See, e.g., United States v. Oswego Barge Corp., 664 F.2d 327 (2d Cir. 1981); United States v. Dixie Carriers, Inc., 627 F.2d 736 (5th Cir. 1980); Frederick E. Bouchard, Inc., v. United States, 583 F. Supp. 477 (D. Mass. 1984). Thus, the federal government could not rely on other theories such as maritime tort or public nuisance to collect damages in excess of Section 311's limits.

law, including common law, with respect to releases of hazardous substances. * * *

There is other language in CERCLA also suggesting it is not the federal government's exclusive remedy. In the very section that imposes strict liability and sets the statutory limits to liability, subsection (h) appears to preserve the federal government's maritime tort remedies. This subsection provides that:

The owner or operator of a vessel shall be liable in accordance with this section [which contains the limitation of liability provision], [and] under maritime tort law. * * *

42 U.S.C. § 9607(h). Professor Schoenbaum, however, asserts that CERCLA should not be read to allow the federal government to recover amounts in excess of the CERCLA limits. To do so, he argues, would make the limits meaningless. T. Schoenbaum, Admiralty and Maritime Law, 849 n.114 (2d ed. 1994). But cf. Cropwell Leasing Co. v. NMS, Inc., 5 F.3d 899 (5th Cir. 1993) (holding that Section 302(d) preserves the government's right to assert, in an admiralty limitation of liability proceeding, a general maritime claim for natural resource damages against a nondischarging vessel that was responsible for a collision resulting in a spill of a hazardous substance).

OPA does not expressly state that it is the federal government's exclusive remedy and it too contains a savings clause that might be read to allow recovery beyond OPA's limits under other theories. See 33 U.S.C. § 2751(e); S. Rep. No. 94, to accompany S. Rep. 686, 101st. Cong., 1st. Sess. 14 (1989). However, it is also arguable that it is inconsistent with OPA's limits to allow the federal government to do so. But see W. Duncan, The Oil Pollution Act of 1990's Effect on the Shipowner's Limitation of Liability Act, 5 U.S.F. Maritime L. J. 303, 306, n.13 (1993) (OPA is not an exclusive remedy).

(b.) *State Clean-up Costs and Natural Resource Damages*

If liability to the federal government for federal clean up costs and damages to federal natural resources is limited to the amounts specified in CERCLA or OPA, are state governments also so limited?[5] The answer

---

[5] In Steuart Transp. Co. v. Allied Towing Corp., 596 F.2d 609 (4th Cir. 1979), the court held that Section 311 of the Clean Water Act allowed Virginia, under a state statute imposing unlimited liability, to recover for oil spill cleanup costs and natural resource damages that exceeded the Section 311 limits. The court, however, left open the issue of whether Virginia's claim against the owner of the vessel was limited by the Limitation

to that question is "No."

Section 114(a) of CERCLA, 42 U.S.C. § 9614(a), states:

Nothing in this Act shall be construed or interpreted as preempting any State from imposing any additional liability or requirements with respect to the release of hazardous substances within such State.

And CERCLA Section 302(d) states:

Nothing in this Act shall affect or modify in any way the obligations or liabilities of any person under other Federal or State law, including common law, with respect to releases of hazardous substances. * * *

42 U.S.C. § 9652(d). These provisions read together give the states the authority to impose and recover damages in excess of the limits contained in CERCLA.

Both 33 U.S.C. §§ 2718 and 2752 and the legislative history of OPA make it clear that OPA is not the exclusive remedy for recovery of state clean-up costs or other damages associated with an incident covered by OPA. 33 U.S.C. § 2718 allows states to impose greater liability upon vessels or other facilities responsible for discharges of oil. It provides

(a) Preservation of State Authorities; Solid Waste Disposal Act. -- Nothing in this Act or the Act of March 3, 1851 [Limitation of Liability Act of 1851] shall --

(1) affect, or be construed or interpreted as preempting, the authority of any State or political subdivision thereof from imposing any additional liability or requirements with respect to --

(A) the discharge of oil or other pollution by oil within such State; or

(B) any removal activities in connection with such a discharge;

or

---

of Liability Act of 1851. See also Askew v. American Waterways Operators, Inc., 411 U.S. 325, 332 (1973).

(2) affect, or be construed or interpreted to affect or modify in any way the obligations or liabilities of any person under * * * State law, including common law.

Furthermore, according to the Senate Report, OPA is

designed to provide basic protection for the environment and victims damaged by spills of oil. Any State wishing to impose a greater degree of protection for its own resources and citizens is entitled to do so. * * *

S. Rep. No. 94, to accompany S. Rep. 686, 101st Cong., 1st. Sess. 6, 14 (1989). But see 33 U.S.C. § 2704(a).[6]

(5.) Preservation of Maritime Tort Remedies and the Impact of the Limitation of Liability Act of 1851

(a.) Maritime Torts

When a tort occurs in or upon navigable waters and is in some way related to a "traditional maritime activity," it generally is labeled a "maritime tort." Maritime torts have two unique characteristics. The first is jurisdictional; the second is substantive.

A maritime tort gives rise to federal admiralty jurisdiction. This is significant because 28 U.S.C. § 1333, the statute conferring admiralty jurisdiction on the federal district courts, does not have an "amount in controversy" requirement, and there is also no right to a jury trial in admiralty. However, the possible existence of admiralty jurisdiction does not preclude the prosecution of a maritime tort in an appropriate state court or in the federal court in diversity, assuming the $75,000 amount in controversy requirement is satisfied, because 28 U.S.C. § 1333 preserves these options for the plaintiff. If the action is for damages and filed in either a state court or a federal district sitting in diversity jurisdiction, a jury trial normally would be available.

Second, in the absence of a controlling federal statute, a unique branch of judge-made law -- general federal maritime law-- establishes the nature of the rights and liabilities of maritime tort plaintiffs and defendants. This is true irrespective of whether the suit is filed in state

---

[6] "Except as otherwise provided in this section, the total of the liability of a responsible party under 33 U.S.C. § 2702 and any removal costs incurred by, or on behalf of, the responsible party, with respect to each incident shall not exceed [the amounts specified in 33 U.S.C. § 2704] * * *."

or federal court, or whether admiralty or diversity jurisdiction is invoked. General federal maritime law is intended to provide a uniform body of law for determination of maritime tort claims. Unfortunately, the simplicity associated with such a theoretically uniform system does not in fact exist for two reasons. First, there are the inevitable splits between federal courts of appeals, left unresolved by the United States Supreme Court. Second, there are some situations in which state law, and not general federal maritime law, might be applied to a maritime tort. See, e.g., Askew v. American Waterways Operators, Inc., 411 U.S. 325 (1973); See generally N. Healy and D. Sharpe, Admiralty 98-99 (2d Ed. 1986).

(b.) *Preservation of Maritime Tort Remedies*

OPA does not preempt any preexisting maritime tort remedies. 33 U.S.C. § 2751 provides:

Except as otherwise provided in this chapter, this chapter does not affect --

(1) admiralty or maritime law

33 U.S.C. § 2751(e). Furthermore, the drafters of OPA explicitly stated that:

The owner or operator of a vessel shall be liable in accordance with this * * * [act], and Section 311 of the Clean Water Act, [and] under maritime tort law. * * *

S. Rep. No. 94, to accompany S. Rep. 686, 101st Cong., 1st. Sess. 6, 14 (1989). Pollution of navigable waters is a long-recognized maritime tort claim. See, e.g., Oppen v. Aetna Insurance Co., 485 F.2d 252, 257 (9th Cir. 1973), cert. denied sub. nom., Luck v. Union Oil Co., 414 U.S. 1162 (1974); United States v. M/V Big Sam, 681 F.2d 432 (5th Cir. 1982), cert. denied, 462 U.S. 1132 (1983). Since OPA's limits of liability apply only to claims under that statute, when the OPA remedy is insufficient to provide a complete recovery, claimants may seek to recover additional damages asserting a claim under maritime law.

(c.) *Maritime Law and Limitations of Liability*

Limitation of Liability Act of 1851

When a vessel is the source of spills of oil or other hazardous substances, any claims for damages under state or maritime law may be subject to the limitations contained in the Limitation of Liability Act of 1851, 46 U.S.C §§ 181-186 (1982). This act, a relic of the nineteenth century, continues to figure prominently whenever the source of any maritime tort is a vessel. Essentially, this act permits a vessel owner to limit any liability for any maritime tort committed by the vessel or its captain or crew, for which the owner would otherwise be responsible, to the value of the vessel if the tort was committed without the owner's "privity or knowledge." The value of the vessel for this purpose is the value as the vessel sits, above or below water, after the tort. Thus, if the vessel sinks, its value may be nothing! See, e.g., In re Barracuda, 281 F. Supp. 228 (S.D.N.Y. 1968) (total liability of $50.00 based on one surviving lifeboard); see generally, T. Schoenbaum, Admiralty and Maritime Law, Chapter 14 (1987); G. Gilmore and C. Black, The Law of Admiralty 877-98 (1975).

Oil Pollution Claims and the Act of 1851

The language of 33 U.S.C. § 2751, supra, that, except where otherwise provided, OPA "does not affect" admiralty and maritime law leaves open the possibility that the Limitation of Liability Act of 1851 is available to limit any recovery of any maritime claim. However, the language of 33 U.S.C. § 2718 may close that door.[7]

---

[7] 33 U.S.C. § 2718 of OPA states

> (c) Additional Requirements and Liabilities; Penalties. - Nothing in this chapter, the Act of March 3, 1851 * * * shall in any way affect, or be contrued to affect, the authority of the United States or any State of political subdivision thereof -
> > (1) to impose additional liability of additional requirements; or
> > (2) to impose, or to determine the amount of, and fine or penalty * * * for any violation of law; relating to the discharge, or substantial threat of a discharge, of oil.

33 U.S.C. § 2718(c).   Similar nulatory language appears in 33 U.S.C. § 2718, which permits the imposition of greater obligations and liabilities as a matter of state statutory or common law.   An earlier version of 33 U.S.C. § 2718(c) was more broadly worded. It stated

> (c) Limitation of Liability Act. - The Act of March 3, 1851 * * * shall not apply to removal costs and damages that directly result from an incident involving the discharge of or substantial threat of a discharge of oil. * * *

This version would clearly have precluded the application of the Limitation of Liability Act of 1851 to the recovery of clean-up costs and damages based on theories of maritime law.   The enacted version does not.

CERCLA and Maritime Torts

CERCLA contains a provision which on its face seems to permit a state to use maritime law as the basis for recovery of clean-up costs and other damages resulting from a hazardous substance spill in navigable waters. Section 107, the section imposing strict liability within the specified limits of liability, contains a subsection (h) which states: "The owner or operator of a vessel shall be liable in accordance with this section, under maritime tort law. * * *" 42 U.S.C. § 9607(h). But see, e.g., Conner v. Aerovox, Inc., 730 F.2d 835 (1st Cir. 1984) (a case involving the discharges of PCBs in which the court held that the CWA preempted any maritime tort claim predicated on general nuisance principles). Section 107(h), 42 U.S.C. § 9607(h), also states that "The owner or operator of a vessel shall be liable * * * under maritime tort law notwithstanding any provision of the Act of March 3, 1851. * * *" This section precludes raising the Act of 1851 as a limitation on liability to hazardous and toxic substance spill maritime tort claims.

(6.) Liability for Private Economic Losses and Other Damages

(a.) Oil Spill Claims

OPA is intended as a comprehensive compensation scheme for both public and private damages sustained as a consequence of an oil spill. The damages compensable under OPA include:

* * *

(B) Real or personal property. -- Damages for injury to, or economic losses resulting from destruction of, real or personal property, which shall be recoverable by a claimant who owns or leases that property.

(C) Subsistence use. -- Damages for loss of subsistence use of natural resources, which shall be recoverable by any claimant who so uses natural resources which have been injured, destroyed, or lost, without regard to the ownership or management of the resources.

(D) Revenues. -- Damages equal to the net loss of taxes, royalties, rents, fees, or net profit shares due to the injury, destruction, or loss of real property, personal property, or natural resources, which shall be recoverable by the Government of the United States, a State, or a political subdivision thereof.

(E) Profits and earnings capacity. -- Damages equal to the loss of profits or impairment of earning capacity due to the injury, destruction, or loss of real property, personal property, or natural resources, which shall be recoverable by any claimant.

(F) Public services. -- Damages for net costs of providing increased or additional public services during or after removal activities, including protection from fire, safety, or health hazards, caused by a discharge of oil, which shall be recoverable by a State, or a political subdivision of a State.* * *

33 U.S.C. § 2702(b)(2).

To provide assured compensation to claimants sustaining such damages, OPA establishes an Oil Spill Compensation Fund. This Fund absorbs and replaces similar pre-existing funds created to compensate victims of certain types of activity associated with the oil industry. See, e.g., Section 311(k)'s revolving fund, 33 U.S.C. § 1321(k), and the funds created by the Deepwater Port Act of 1974, 33 U.S.C. § 1517(f), Title III of the Outer Continental Shelf Lands Act Amendments of 1978, 43 U.S.C. § 1811-42. 33 U.S.C. §§ 2712-14.

OPA, with limited exceptions, requires that all compensation claims be first presented to the person responsible for the spill. See Boca Ciega Hotel v. Bouchard Transportation Co., 51 F.3d 235 (11th Cir. 1995). If the alleged spiller denies liability or does not settle the claim within a three month time period, the claimant may present the claim to the Fund or commence an action against the alleged spiller. The purpose of the Fund is to provide:

a source of compensation for claims which are not settled by the spiller by virtue of a limit or a defense. This assures compensation of victims regardless of the liability of the spiller. * * * The Fund assures that [all] the costs associated with a spill are compensated, not just those within the spiller's limits of liability, through a mechanism which spreads these excess costs to all users of oil.

[It also will provide] compensation in the event that the spiller cannot be identified or located, or is judgment proof. * * *

S. Rep. No. 94, 101st Cong., 1st Sess. 5 (1989). Thus, a person suffering economic injury would need to rely on state law or maritime law only if for some reason she chooses either not to file a claim with the Fund or suffers damages not compensable under OPA but compensable under state law or maritime law.

Claims of commercial fishermen for economic losses sustained as a result of damage to fishing gear and fish populations are compensable under OPA. How do they prove these losses? If the defendant shows that after the incident the weather was so bad that fishing would have been severely limited, would it affect the amount of damages? Would the amount of damages be affected by evidence that the fishermen refitted their vessels, moved to different waters and other species of fish, and had a profitable year? Can you think of any other factors that might influence the damages recoverable?

Coastal businesses that suffer indirect economic injuries as the result of an oil spill, however, may not be compensated under OPA if it is determined that their loss of profits is not "due to the injury, destruction, or loss of real property, personal property or natural resources. * * *" 33 U.S.C. § 2702(b)(2)(E). See, e.g., South Port Marine, LLC v. Gulf Oil Ltd., 234 F.3d 58 (1st Cir. 2000) (marina owner may recover lost ship revenues and other business disruption damages under OPA due to gasoline spill; however, punitive damages are not recoverable under OPA); Sekco Energy, Inc. v. M/V Margaret Chouest, 820 F. Supp. 1008, 1014-15 (E.D. La. 1993) (33 U.S.C. § 2702(b)(2)(E) permits recovery of lost future earnings from OCS drilling because such earnings are "property"); Petition of Cleveland Tankers, Inc., 791 F. Supp. 669, 678 (E.D. Mich. 1992); In re the Exxon Valdez, 767 F. Supp. 1509 (D. Alaska 1991); Louisiana ex. rel. Guste v. M/V Testbank, 752 F.2d 1019 (5th Cir. 1985) (en banc), cert. denied, 477 U.S. 903 (1986); Pruitt v. Allied Chemical Corp., 523 F. Supp. 975, 977-80 (E.D. Va. 1981); Burgess v. M/V Tamano, 370 F. Supp. 247, 249-50 (D. Me. 1973), aff'd mem., 559 F.2d 1200 (1st Cir. 1977). Would such plaintiffs find a maritime tort or state law remedy? The next note and case address these questions.

(b.) Recovery of Economic Losses by Fishermen and Shoreside Businesses

Whether shoreside businesses may rely on state law when making claims for recovery of economic losses suffered as a result of an oil or chemical spill is a very difficult question. The reasons for the difficulty are many. First, an oil or chemical spill in navigable waters is a maritime tort which means that generally the substantive law to be applied to claims arising from such an incident would be uniform federal maritime law and not state law. Second, although Congress has the power to legislate and statutorily modify existing general federal maritime law--the common law of admiralty-- that Congressional power is non-delegable. Thus, there is a line of cases which hold that, under the Constitution, Congress lacks the authority to authorize the states to apply their own individual common law or statutory law to maritime torts occurring within the states. E.g. Knickerbocker Ice Co. v. Stewart, 253 U.S. 149, 164 (1920). Under those cases, the provision in OPA permitting states to enact oil spill statutes that impose different, potentially greater, liabilities than those imposed by OPA would be unconstitutional. To hold otherwise would destroy the uniformity of maritime law which was the reason for the Constitution placing control over admiralty matters in the federal government. See In re Exxon Valdez, 767 F. Supp. 1509 (D. Alaska 1991). See also M. Harrington, Necessary and Proper, But Still Unconstitutional: The Oil Pollution Act's Delegation of Admiralty Power to the States, 48 Case W. Res. L. Rev. 1 (1997).

On the other hand, recent cases suggest that whether state law may be applied to maritime torts requires a balancing of the particular state and federal interests involved in any given case. E.g. Askew v. American Waterways Operators, Inc. 411 U.S. 325 (1973) (upholding the constitutionality of a Florida oil pollution liability statute). If, on balance, uniformity is deemed necessary, state law is preempted and state regulation precluded; but, if such is not the case, state law may be applied. See, e.g., American Dredging Co. v. Miller, 510 U.S. 443 (1994). In the latter situation, application of state law might allow recovery for injuries for which recovery would not exist under general federal maritime law or for amounts in excess of that recoverable under federal maritime law.

To further complicate the matter, historically, when a vessel was a source of injuries that occurred on land, the claims for such damages were not cognizable in admiralty. Such claims were not deemed maritime claims since the injury itself did not occur on navigable waters. Thus, historically, claims by shoreside fish processors and other business for recovery of economic losses associated with damage to fisheries in navigable waters would not have been governed by maritime law, but by state law, and would not have been within the admiralty jurisdiction of the federal courts. However, in 1948, Congress passed the Admiralty Extension Act of 1948, 44 U.S.C. 740, which provides:

> The admiralty and maritime jurisdiction of the United States shall extend to and include all cases of damages or injury, to person or property, caused by a vessel on navigable water, not withstanding that the damage or injury be done or consummated on land.

After 1948, assuming that indirect economic injury claims fall within the words "damages or injury, to * * * property," claims by shoreside processors and other businesses to recover lost profits associated with an oil or chemical spill would qualify as maritime tort claims and are within the admiralty jurisdiction of the federal courts. So, after 1948, claims which formally would have been governed by non-uniform state law were transformed into federal maritime claims presumably governed by a uniform general federal maritime law. But, under federal maritime case law--Robins Dry Dock & Repair Co. v. Flint, 275 U.S. 303 (1927) which is discussed in the next case--claimants are barred from recovering for purely economic losses.

This leaves the interesting question of why claims not demanding a uniform law before 1948 would suddenly rise to the level of claims demanding a uniform governing law after 1948? The apparent response of the court in the next case--Ballard Shipping Co. v. Beach Shellfish--is that uniformity is not required and state law may apply; but other courts have reached the opposite conclusion. See, e.g., In re Exxon Valdez, 767 F. Supp. 1509 (D. Alaska 1991).

BALLARD SHIPPING CO. V. BEACH SHELLFISH
United States Court of Appeals, First Circuit, 1994
32 F.3d 623

BOUDIN, *Circuit Judge*

This appeal presents the question whether federal maritime law preempts Rhode Island legislation affording expanded state-law remedies for oil pollution damage. In an able opinion, the district court held that the remedies were preempted. Discerning the law in this area is far from easy; one might tack a sailboat into a fog bank with more confidence. Yet guided in part by an important Supreme Court decision rendered after the district court's decision, we are constrained to reverse in part and to remand for further proceedings.

The basic facts of the case are not in dispute. On June 23, 1989, the M/V World Prodigy, an oil tanker owned by Ballard Shipping Co., ran aground in Narragansett Bay, Rhode Island, spilling over 300,000 gallons of heating oil into the bay. The wreck occurred when the ship strayed from the designated shipping channel and collided with a rock near Brenton Reef, about a mile south of Newport at the mouth of the bay. The oil slick prompted the State of Rhode Island to close Narragansett Bay to all shellfishing activities for a period of two weeks during and after cleanup operations.

State authorities charged the captain of the ship with entering the bay without a local pilot on board in violation of state law. Both the captain and Ballard also pleaded guilty to criminal violations of the

Federal Water Pollution Control Act, see 33 U.S.C. § 1319(c). The captain and owner were fined a total of $30,500 and $500,000, respectively. In addition, Ballard agreed to pay $3.9 million in compensation for federal cleanup costs, $4.7 million for state cleanup costs and damage to natural resources, $500,000 of which was to be available to compensate individuals, and $550,000 to settle claims for lost wages by local shellfishermen.

A number of claimants filed suit against Ballard in Rhode Island. Ballard responded on December 22, 1989, by bringing a petition in admiralty for limitation or exoneration from liability. 46 App.U.S.C. § 185. "[T]he court of admiralty in [a limitation of liability] proceeding acquires the right to marshal all claims, whether of strictly admiralty origin or not, and to give effect to them by the apportionment of the *res* and by judgment *in personam* against the owner, so far as the court may decree." Just v. Chambers, 312 U.S. 383, 386 (1941). In the present case, several claimants reasserted their claims in the admiralty action.

The claimants in the present appeal are a group of shellfish dealers who allege severe economic losses arising from the two-week hiatus in shellfishing activities, which suspended their operations during the busiest time of the shellfishing season. They alleged negligence under the general maritime law and the common law of Rhode Island, as well as a claim for economic losses pursuant to the Rhode Island Environmental Injury Compensation Act, R.I.Gen.Laws ch. 46-12.3 et seq. ("the Compensation Act").

On June 17, 1992, Ballard moved to dismiss the shellfish dealers' claims on the basis of the Supreme Court's decision in Robins Dry Dock & Repair Co. v. Flint, 275 U.S. 303 (1927), which held that compensation for economic losses standing alone is unavailable in admiralty cases. The district court granted the motion, holding that Robins preempted the contrary provisions of the state's Compensation Act, which expressly provides for recovery of purely economic losses arising from an oil spill. In re Complaint of Ballard Shipping Co., 810 F. Supp. 359 (D.R.I. 1993). The dealers now appeal from that dismissal.

We first address the federal claims brought under the general maritime law. The Constitution grants the federal courts authority to hear "all Cases of admiralty and maritime Jurisdiction." U.S. Const. Art. III, § 2. The parties agree that the dealers' federal claims fall within this group because the spill occurred on navigable waters and arose out of traditional maritime activity. See Executive Jet Aviation, Inc. v. City of Cleveland, 409 U.S. 249 (1972). Admiralty jurisdiction brings with it a body of federal jurisprudence, largely uncodified, known as maritime law. See East River S.S. Corp. v. Transamerica Delaval, 476 U.S. 858, 864 (1986).

The dealers assert that their businesses were injured when the World Prodigy spill prevented local fishermen from harvesting shellfish in Narragansett Bay and thereby precluded the dealers from purchasing the shellfish and reselling them to restaurants and other buyers. The dealers' maritime-law claims are thus purely for economic losses, unaccompanied by any physical injury to their property or person. Those federal claims, as the district court held, are squarely foreclosed by Robins Dry Dock & Repair Co. v. Flint, 275 U.S. 303 (1927).

* * *

Several courts have recognized exceptions to *Robins*, but none of the familiar examples apply in this case.[8] The district court so held, and the dealers do not challenge that conclusion on appeal. Accordingly, we agree that plaintiffs' federal claims for purely economic losses under the general maritime law are barred. The appeal thus turns upon the extent to which *Robins* bars the states from permitting a different result under state law pursuant to the exercise of the state's police powers.

* * *

On appeal, the dealers mainly stress their claims under Rhode Island's Compensation Act. The Compensation Act provides generally that owners or operators of seagoing vessels may be held liable for harms arising from negligence of the owner, operator or agents or from the violation of Rhode Island pilotage and water pollution laws. See R.I.Gen.Laws §§ 46-12.3-2, 46-12.3-3. The statute also contains the following specific provisions regarding economic loss:

(a) A person shall be entitled to recover for economic loss * * * if the person can demonstrate the loss of income or diminution of profit to a person or business as a result of damage to the natural resources of the state of Rhode Island caused by the violation of any provision [of the piloting or water pollution laws] by the owner or operator * * * of the seagoing vessel and/or caused by the negligence of the owner or operator * * * of the seagoing vessel.

---

[8] The classic exceptions include claims brought by fishermen as "favorites of admiralty," see Union Oil Co. v. Oppen, 501 F.2d 558 (9th Cir. 1974), and claims for economic losses that are intentionally caused, see Dick Meyers Towing Service, Inc., v. United States, 577 F2d 1023, 1025 (5th Cir. 1978), cert. denied, 440 U.S. 908 (1979).

(b) In any suit brought to recover economic loss it shall not be necessary to prove that the loss was sustained as a result of physical injury to the person or damage to his or her property, nor shall it be a defense to any claim that the defendant owed no special duty to the plaintiff or that the loss was the result of governmental action taken in response to the violation and/or negligence of the defendant.

(c) Without limiting the generality of the foregoing, persons engaged in commercial fishing or shellfishing and/or the processors of fish or shellfish, who can demonstrate that they have sustained a loss of income or profit as a result of damage to the environment resulting from [violations of law or negligence] * * * shall have a cause of action for economic loss. Persons employed by, or who operate businesses, who have sustained a loss of income or profit as a result of a decrease in the volume of business caused by the damage to the environment shall also be entitled to maintain an action for economic loss.

R.I.Gen.Laws § 46-12.3-4.

For the purposes of this appeal only, Ballard concedes that the dealers would have a valid cause of action under this statute, and that the Compensation Act, which became effective on September 30, 1990, may be applied retroactively to cover the 1989 M/V World Prodigy spill.[9] We think that the statutory claims effectively subsume state common law claims since the Compensation Act appears to go as far and further than common law in departing from *Robins*. Thus, we focus upon the statute.

The shipowner and captain insist, and the district court agreed, that the state claims are preempted under the doctrine of Southern Pacific Co. v. Jensen, 244 U.S. 205 (1917). *Jensen*, in a now famous passage, held that state legislation affecting maritime commerce is invalid "if it contravenes the essential purpose expressed by an act of Congress, or works material prejudice to the characteristic features of the general maritime law, or interferes with the proper harmony and uniformity of that law in its international and interstate relations." Id. at 216.

* * *

---

[9] See 1990 R.I.Pub.Laws ch. 198, § 2 (providing that the Compensation Act shall apply to all causes of action pending on or after September 30, 1990, regardless of when the violation and/or act of negligence occurred, as long as suit was commenced within the applicable statute of limitations).

In balancing the state interest in regulation against a potential overriding federal need for harmony or uniformity, we start with Rhode Island's interest in implementing its Compensation Act. No one can doubt that the state's interest in avoiding pollution in its navigable waters and on its shores, and in redressing injury to its citizens from such pollution, is a weighty one. In *Huron Portland Cement*, the Supreme Court described state air pollution laws as a classic example of police power, and continued: "In the exercise of that power, the states * * * may act, in many areas of interstate commerce and *maritime activities*, concurrently with the federal government." 362 U.S. at 442 (emphasis added).

In Askew v. American Waterways Operators, Inc., 411 U.S. 325 (1973), the Court sustained, against a maritime-law preemption challenge, a Florida statute that imposed no-fault liability on vessel owners and operators for damages to private parties caused by oil spills in territorial waters. Justice Douglas described oil spillage as "an insidious form of pollution of vast concern to every coastal city or port and to all the estuaries on which the life of the ocean and lives of the coastal people are greatly dependent." Id. at 328-29. See also Id. at 332-43.

Claimants in this case argue flatly that *Askew,* without more, sustains the Rhode Island statute; and perhaps it does. The difficulty is that Justice Douglas rejected the maritime law preemption claim on the ground that *Jensen* had nothing to do with "shoreside injury by ships on navigable waters." 411 U.S. at 344. "Historically," said Justice Douglas, "damages to the shore or to shore facilities were not cognizable in admiralty." Id. at 340. Although Congress had by statute extended admiralty jurisdiction shoreward in 1948, the Court said that this extension did not carry *Jensen* with it. Id. at 341.

If Justice Douglas meant to avoid preemption for physical damage to the shore or shore facilities, as his words seem to suggest, this might easily not embrace damage to bay waters or the beds beneath them. If instead *Askew* meant to allow a state remedy for any intangible impact or loss ultimately felt on shore, it is hard to see what would be left of preemptive federal authority since the most traditional of admiralty events--for example, a ship collision or a seaman's death--has such intangible effects ashore. However the riddle of *Askew* is solved, we think it safest to take it here merely to show, as it assuredly does, the importance of the state's interest in providing remedies for vessel-caused oil pollution damage.

The federal interest in limiting remedies is more subtle but also not without importance. The Compensation Act does not regulate the out-of-court behavior of ships or sailors--what is sometimes called "primary conduct"; rather the act is concerned with the liability imposed for conduct that is already unlawful. State regulation of primary conduct in the maritime realm is not automatically forbidden, e.g. Ray v. Atlantic Richfield Co., 435 U.S. 151, 179-80 (1978), but such regulation presents the most direct risk of conflict between federal and state commands, or of inconsistency between various state regimes to which the same vessel may be subject.

* * *

Having said all this, we think one final consideration tips the scales in favor of the Compensation Act's validity. Congress has recently enacted the Oil Pollution Act, 33 U.S.C. § 2701 et seq., which almost certainly provides for recovery of purely economic damages in oil spill cases.[10] Section 2702(b)(2)(E) of the act provides that "[d]amages equal to the loss of profits or impairment of earning capacity due to the injury, destruction, or loss of real property, personal property, or natural resources, * * * shall be recoverable by any claimant." The House Conference Report makes clear that, under Section 2702(b)(2)(E), "[t]he claimant need not be the owner of the damaged property or resources to recover for lost profits or income". H.R.Conf.Rep. No. 101-653, 101st Cong., 2d Sess. 103 (1990), U.S.Code Cong. & Admin. News 1990, p. 722. The act also expressly provides that it does not preempt state imposition of additional liability requirements. 33 U.S.C. § 2718(a).

The statute contains another substantial piece of evidence that Congress means to allow recovery of economic losses from injury to natural resources even though the claimant's own property was not damaged. In another subsection of the damage provision, there is an explicit provision for recovery of "economic losses resulting from destruction of real or personal property" by a claimant "who owns or leases that property." 33 U.S.C. § 2702(b)(2)(B). If the "natural resources" injury provision in subsection (E) were limited to those owned by the claimant, the recovery thus provided would be already covered by subsection (B) and subsection (E) would be redundant.

---

[10] We say "almost" only because one court has held to the contrary. See In re Petition of Cleveland Tankers, Inc. 791 F Supp. 669, 678-79 (E.D.Mich. 1992). Most commentators, by contrast, have read the new statute - as its language and legislative history suggest - to override the *Robins Dry Dock* rule, see McCurdy, "An Overview of OPA 1990 and Its Relationship to Other Laws," 5 U.S.F.Mar.L.J 423 (1993); Gonynor, "The Robins Dry Dock Rule: Is the 'Bright Line' Fading?" 4 U.S.F.Mar.L.J. 85 (1992).

United States v. Ven-Fuel, Inc., 758 F.2d 741, 751-52 (1st Cir. 1985) (readings that create redundancies are not favored).

The new federal statute does not apply retroactively to govern the present case. See Pub.L. No. 101-380, § 1020 (providing that the statute "shall apply to an incident occurring after the date the enactment of this Act [August 18, 1990]."). But we think that the statute is compelling evidence that Congress does not view either expansion of liability to cover purely economic losses or enactment of comparable state oil pollution regimes as an excessive burden on maritime commerce. Given the Congress' superior ability to weigh the very practical considerations relating to such a judgment, we give Congress' conclusion substantial weight. For this purpose, the non-retroactivity of the statute is irrelevant.

We hold, then, that the Rhode Island's Compensation Act as reasonably construed and applied is not preempted by the admiralty clause of the Constitution. We express no judgment on whether claimants' particular injuries were reasonably foreseeable or proximately caused by the grounding of the M/V World Prodigy, or whether claimants' claims are otherwise viable under the Rhode Island statute. That determination is for the district court in the first instance or for the state courts. *Robins Dry Dock* remains the rule in this circuit for federal claims; we simply hold that Rhode Island is free to chart a different course.

Because of the Oil Pollution Act, it may well be that the immediate problem with which we have wrestled at length in this case is a transient one; the legal regime for oil pollution accidents after August 18, 1990, will largely be a creature of the new statute. But the case before us, like all cases, is important to the litigants, and the governing legal standards have application elsewhere. Applying an imprecise federal preemption standard to a little construed state statute is no easy task. For the present, assuming that the Rhode Island statute is providently construed and applied, we think that it is not unconstitutional.

The decision of the district court dismissing plaintiffs' federal claims is affirmed; the dismissal of plaintiffs' state claims is reversed and the case is remanded for further proceedings consistent with this opinion.

Notes and Questions

1.   Does the passage of OPA remove the *Robins Dry Dock* rule as a limitation on maritime tort as well as on state law claims, of fish

processors and shoreside business? 33 U.S.C. § 2702, begins with

(a) In general

Notwithstanding any other provision or rule of law, and subject to the provisions of this chapter, each responsible party for a vessel or a facility from which oil is discharged * * * for the * * * damages specified in subsection (b). * * *

33 U.S.C. § 2702(a). Compare OPA with the language of CERCLA, Section 107(h), 42 U.S.C. § 9614(h), which is quoted in footnote 11 below. Is the absence of similar language in OPA legally significant?

2. For natural resource damages caused by events outside the scope of OPA and CERCLA, the preemptive effect of federal maritime law remains strong. See, e.g., State of Md. Dept. of Natural Resources v. Kellum, 51 F.3d 1220 (4th Cir. 1995) (state strict liability statute for damages to oyster bed caused by barge grounding preempted).

(c.) Hazardous Substance Release Claims

CERCLA is not a private damage recovery mechanism. When commercial fishermen and coastal businesses seek recovery for economic losses occasioned by a hazardous substance release such claims would have to be predicated on either maritime law or applicable state law.[11] Traditionally, federal maritime law recognized at least two theories upon which plaintiffs could recover for direct economic injuries: negligence and nuisance. See generally J. Kalo, Water Pollution And Commercial Fishermen: Applying General Maritime Law To Claims For Damages To Fisheries In Ocean And Coastal Waters, 61 N.C.L. Rev. 313, 318-31 (1983).

Prior to the passage in 1972 of CWA, the United States Supreme Court in Illinois v. Milwaukee, 406 U.S. 91, 92 (1972) [Milwaukee I], held that there also existed a federal common law public nuisance claim for water pollution. However, after the passage of CWA, the Court held that

---

[11] Section 107(h), 42 U.S.C. § 9607(h), of CERCLA appears to abolish the *Robins Dry Dock* rule when the claim arises out of a discharge of hazardous substances from a vessel. That section states:

> The owner or operator of a vessel shall be liable in accordance with this section, *under maritime tort law,* and as provided in Section 114, 42 U.S.C. § 9614, notwithstanding any provision of the Act of March 3, 1851 *or in the absence of any physical damage to the claimant* (emphasis added).

federal common law remedies had been preempted by the CWA, even though there was no provision for any federal damage remedy in the statute. Milwaukee v. Illinois, 451 U.S. 304 (1981) [Milwaukee II]; Middlesex County Sewerage Authority v. National Sea Clammers Association, 453 U.S. 1 (1981). In addition, the Court held that no implied cause of action for water pollution exists. Id. at 13-18.

National Sea Clammers Association involved a suit brought by fishermen and shellfishermen seeking damages for alleged discharges of sewage, sludge, and other waste materials into the Hudson River, New York harbor, and into an offshore area known as the New York Bight. The plaintiffs contended that the resulting pollution was causing the collapse of the fishing, clamming, and lobster industries which operate in Atlantic waters. Among other things, the district court dismissed the plaintiffs' federal common law nuisance and maritime tort claims. The Court of Appeals reversed. The Supreme Court granted the petition for certiorari, but limited certiorari to three questions:

> (i) whether FWPCA and MPRSA [Marine Protection, Resources and Sanctuaries Act] imply a private right of action independent of their citizen-suit provisions, (ii) whether all federal common-law nuisance actions concerning ocean pollution now are preempted by the legislative scheme contained in the FWPCA and the MPRSA, and (iii) if not, whether a private citizen has standing to sue for damages under the federal common law of nuisance. * * *

Id. at 10-11. The Court held no private right of action existed under either CWA [FWPCA], which applies to coastal and inland waters, or MPRSA, which applies to waters beyond the outer limits of the territorial sea. Furthermore, the Court held that "the federal common law of nuisance in the area of water pollution is entirely preempted by the more comprehensive scope of the FWPCA." Id. at 22. The existence of maritime remedies was not discussed. The Court did foreclose federal common law remedies but the expression "federal common law" can have more than one meaning. It can mean all judge-made law, which would include both maritime and nonmaritime judge-made law. However, frequently the courts have distinguished federal common law from general maritime law. See J. Kalo, Water Pollution And Commercial Fishermen: Applying General Maritime Law To Claims For Damages To Fisheries In Ocean And Coastal Waters, 61 N.C.L. Rev. 313, 346, 349 (1983).

The question of whether maritime tort law provides a private damage remedy and thus federal court jurisdiction, 28 U.S.C. § 1333, is important for three reasons. First, the existence of a maritime tort claim gives rise to federal admiralty jurisdiction and thus immediate access to the federal courts without regard to diversity of citizenship. Second, substantive federal maritime law may be more favorable than state law. Third, injury to fisheries located in waters more than three miles from a state's coast line may be beyond the reach of state law. If federal maritime law does not afford a private remedy and no federal statute creates such a remedy, fishermen whose livelihood is impaired when fishing grounds are polluted by hazardous substances may be left without any means of recovery.

When commercial lobstermen, shellfishermen, and fishermen sued to recovery damages allegedly flowing from the defendants' discharges of PCBs into Massachusetts' rivers and coastal waters, the district court dismissed maritime damages claims based on public nuisance principles. The district court found no perceptible reason to distinguish between common law claims and maritime torts in construing the preemptive effect of FWPCA and MPRSA. On appeal, the district court dismissal was upheld. Conner v. Aerovox, Inc., 730 F.2d 835 (1st Cir. 1984).

Subsequently, in 1986, the Marine Protection, Research, and Sanctuaries Act was amended. Section 106(g), 33 U.S.C. § 1416(g), was added. It states:

> Nothing in this chapter shall restrict, affect or modify the rights of any person (1) to seek damages * * * under State law, including State common law, or (2) to seek damages under other Federal law, including maritime tort law, resulting from noncompliance with any requirement of this subchapter or any permit under this subchapter.

When this provision is read together with CERCLA Section 107(h), 43 U.S.C. § 9607(h) (providing that "owners and operators of vessels shall be liable * * * under maritime tort law"), is the issue of whether commercial fishermen may predicate a damage claim on maritime tort law resolved? What if the source of the pollution is not a vessel and is not regulated by MPRSA? Do commercial fishermen have a state common law nuisance claim for damages?

In Leo v. General Electric Co., 538 N.Y.S.2d 844 (A.D. 1989), the defendant discharged PCBs into the Hudson River during a 30 year period, thus contaminating the striped bass population and other marine life and prompting a suit by commercial fishermen. The Court rejected the defendant's assertion that CERCLA and the FWCWA preempted the state's common law of nuisance. Commercial fishermen thus were entitled to sue for both injunctive relief and damages on a state common law nuisance theory. Ultimately, an out-of-court settlement was reached in 1993 with General Electric agreeing to pay New York commercial striped bass fishermen $7 million for lost income.

To what extent may state law provide a damage remedy for fish processors, onshore businesses, or recreational fishermen? Some interesting possibilities are explored in the next case.

PRUITT V. ALLIED CHEMICAL CORPORATION

United States District Court,
Eastern District of Virginia, 1981
523 F. Supp. 975

MEMORANDUM

MERHIGE, DISTRICT JUDGE

Plaintiffs bring the instant action against Allied Chemical Corporation ("Allied") for Allied's alleged pollution of the James River and Chesapeake Bay with the chemical agent commonly known as Kepone.[12]

Plaintiffs allege that jurisdiction vests with the Court pursuant to 28 U.S.C. § 1331 (federal question), § 1332 (diversity of citizenship), and § 1333 (arising in admiralty).

Plaintiffs allegedly engage in a variety of different businesses and professions related to the harvesting and sale of marine life from the Chesapeake Bay ("Bay").[13] All claim to have suffered economic harm from defendant's alleged discharges of Kepone into the James River and thence into the Bay. Plaintiffs assert their right to compensation under each of the dozen counts to their complaint. Defendant has moved to dismiss nine of those counts for failure to state a claim upon which relief can be granted. The parties have fully briefed the issues involved, and the matter is ripe for disposition.

Defendant moves to dismiss counts I, II, III, V, VII, VIII, IX, X and XII of the complaint as they apply to all plaintiffs other than those directly engaged in the harvesting of the Bay's marine life. That is, defendant

---

[12] Kepone, a pesticide, is an extremely persistent, toxic substance.

[13] Plaintiffs include commercial fishermen; seafood wholesalers, retailers, distributors and processors; restauranteurs; marina, boat tackle and baitshop owners; and employees of all the above groups.

would dismiss these nine counts as to all plaintiffs except those classified in paragraph 6A of the complaint (generally, fishermen, shell fishermen, and lessors of oysterbeds). All plaintiffs, subject to defendant's motion, claim as damages lost profits resulting from their inability to sell seafood allegedly contaminated by defendant's discharges, and from a drop in price resulting from a decline in demand for seafood coming from areas affected by Kepone. These plaintiffs can generally be described as parties suffering only indirect harm to their property or businesses as the result of Kepone pollution.[14] They or their possessions have not been caused direct, physical damage by defendant. Instead, plaintiffs allege that the stream of profits they previously received from their businesses or employment has been interrupted, and they seek compensation for the loss of the prospective profits they have been denied. As plaintiffs' claims rely on various, radically different theories of liability, the Court considers each count, or group of similar counts, separately.

Negligence and Products Liability

Counts I, II and V allege that negligence, of some degree, by defendant entitles plaintiffs to recover. Count III alleges that the effluence released by defendant were "defective and unreasonably dangerous," and that defendant should be strictly liable for any harm caused by its discharges. All of these counts arise from the Court's diversity jurisdiction and rely on theories of state tort law.

The Virginia Supreme Court has, to the Court's knowledge, never directly considered the question of recovery for loss of prospective economic benefits. It is commonly stated that the general rule both in admiralty and at common law has been that a plaintiff cannot recover for indirect economic harm. The logical basis for this rule is obscure. Although Courts have frequently stated that economic losses are "not foreseeable" or "too remote," these explanations alone are rarely apposite. As one well-respected commentator has noted, "the loss to plaintiff in each case * * * would be readily recoverable if the test of duty or remoteness usually associated with the law of negligence were applied."

The Court frankly acknowledges the fact that there exist[s] a substantial number of cases that may be construed to establish a general rule favorable to plaintiffs. As noted by the Ninth Circuit in

---

[14] In fact, none of the plaintiffs has suffered direct harm to his or its property. As discussed below, the plaintiffs not subject to defendants' motion to dismiss obviously do not own the marine life that they harvest or the water in which that life flourishes.

Union Oil Co. v. Oppen, 501 F.2d 558 (9th Cir. 1974), the general rule has found application in a wide variety of contexts:

> [T]he negligent destruction of a bridge connecting the mainland with an island, which caused a loss of business to the plaintiff who was a merchant on the island, has been held not to be actionable. * * * A plaintiff engaged in commercial printing has been held unable to recover against a negligent contractor who, while engaged in excavation pursuant to a contract with a third party, cut the power line upon which the plaintiff's presses depended. * * * A defendant who negligently injures a third person entitled to life-care medical services by the plaintiff is liable to the third person but not to the plaintiff. * * * The operators of a dry dock are not liable in admiralty to charterers of a ship, placed by its owners in the dry dock, for negligent injury to the ship's propeller where the injury deprived the charterer of the use of the ship.

501 F.2d at 563-64 (citations omitted).

Nevertheless, there also exist cases that conflict with this broadly recognized general rule. At least two of the minority cases deal with precisely the case present here: the loss of business opportunities due to pollution of streams adjoining a plaintiff's property. Moreover, even defendant concedes that a third case, *Union Oil*, supra, that provided compensation for fishermen for losses caused by pollution from oil spills, is correctly decided. Although defendant would distinguish *Union Oil* as limited solely to those who labor on the water (but not at its edge) the rationale for creation of this particular distinction is unclear.

Given the conflicting case law from other jurisdictions, together with the fact that there exists no Virginia law on indirect, economic damages, the Court has considered more theoretical sources in order to find a principled basis for its decision. There now exists a considerable amount of literature on the economic rationale for tort law. In general, scholars in the field rely on Judge Learned Hand's classic statement of negligence to argue that a principal purpose of tort law is to maximize social utility: where the costs of accidents exceeds the costs of preventing them, the law will impose liability.

The difficulty in the present case is how to measure the cost of Kepone pollution. In the instant action, those costs were borne most directly by the wildlife of the Chesapeake Bay. The fact that no one individual claims property rights to the Bay's wildlife could arguably preclude liability. The Court doubts, however, whether such a result would be just. Nor would a denial of liability serve social utility: many citizens, both directly and indirectly, derive benefit from the Bay and its marine life. Destruction of the Bay's wildlife should not be a costless activity.

In fact, even defendant in the present action admits that commercial fishermen are entitled to compensation for any loss of profits they may prove to have been caused by defendant's negligence. The entitlement given these fishermen presumably arises from what might be called a constructive property interest in the Bay's harvestable species. These professional watermen are entitled to recover despite any direct physical damage to their own property. Presumably, sportsfishermen share the same entitlement to legal redress for damage to the Bay's ecology.[15] The Court perceives no valid distinction between recognition of commercial damages suffered by those who fish for profit and personal harm suffered by those who fish for sport.[16]

The claims now considered by the Court, however, are not those of direct users of the Bay, commercial or personal. Instead, defendant has challenged the right of those who buy and sell to direct users of the Bay, to maintain a suit.

Defendant would have the Court draw a sharp and impregnable distinction between parties who exploited the Bay directly, and those who relied on it indirectly. In *Union Oil*, the Ninth Circuit suggested that it might make such a distinction if it were ever required to decide the issue. The panel in *Union Oil*, however, did not have to decide the question now facing this Court--and the Court does not perceive that there exists so simple a distinction as defendant would urge it to construct.

None of the plaintiffs here--including commercial fishermen--has suffered any direct damage to his private property. All have allegedly

---

[15] A sportsman who sued would, of course, still be required to prove his damages to a legally acceptable degree of certainty. Moreover, in a federal court he would have to satisfy any applicable jurisdictional amount. Nevertheless, the Supreme Court has stated that purely personal, aesthetic damage may be sufficiently determinate to satisfy the case or controversy clause of Article III. Association of Data Processing Service Organizations, Inc. v. Camp, 397 U.S. 150, 154 (1970).

[16] E.g. if chemicals discharged into the water had harmed fishermen's boats, rather than the Bay's fishlife, there would be no need to distinguish between a sportsman's basic right to sue for damages, and a professional waterman's right. Of course, in the instant case, a sportsman's actual damages would be considerably more speculative. Nevertheless, under the theory of liability now considered by the Court, a sportsman would still have at least a chance to prove his damages.

suffered economic loss as a result of harm to the Bay's ecology. Apart from these similarities, the different categories of plaintiffs depend on the Bay in varying degrees of immediacy. The commercial fishermen here fit within a category established in Union Oil: they "lawfully and directly make use of a resource of the sea." The use that marina and charterboat owners make of the water, though hardly less legal, is slightly less direct. (And indeed, businesses in similar situations have been held entitled to recover in other courts.) Still less direct, but far from nonexistent, is the link between the Bay and the seafood dealers, restauranteurs, and tackle shops that seek relief (as do the employees of these establishments).

One meaningful distinction to be made among the various categories of plaintiffs here arises from a desire to avoid double-counting in calculating damages. Any seafood harvested by the commercial fishermen here would have been bought and sold several times before finally being purchased for consumption.[17] Considerations both of equity and social utility suggest that just as defendant should not be able to escape liability for destruction of publicly owned marine life entirely, it should not be caused to pay repeatedly for the same damage.

The Court notes, however, that allowance for recovery of plaintiffs' lost profits here would not in all cases result in double-counting of damages. Plaintiffs in categories B, C, D, E, and F allegedly lost profits when deprived of supplies of seafood. Those profits represented a return on the investment of each of the plaintiffs in material and labor in their businesses, and thus the independent loss to each would not amount to double-counting. Conversely, defendants could not be expected to pay, as a maximum, more than the replacement value of a plaintiff's actual investment, even if the stream of profits lost when extrapolated into the future, would yield greater damages.

Tracing the stream of profits flowing from the Bay's seafood, however, involves the Court in other complexities. The employees of the enterprises named in categories B through F, for example, had no physical investment in their employers' businesses. Yet if plaintiffs' allegations are proven, these employees undoubtedly lost wages and faced a less favorable job market than they would have, but for defendant's acts, and they have thus been harmed by defendant. What is more, the number of parties with a potential cause of action against defendant is hardly exhausted in plaintiffs' complaint. In theory, parties who bought and sold to and from the plaintiffs named here also suffered

---

[17] Indeed, plaintiffs here apparently contain a representative of every level of seafood distribution between fisherman and consumer.

losses in business, as did their employees. In short, the set of potential plaintiffs seems almost infinite.

Perhaps because of the large set of potential plaintiffs, even the commentators most critical of the general rule on indirect damages have acknowledged that some limitation to liability, even when damages are foreseeable, is advisable. Rather than allowing plaintiffs to risk a failure of proof as damages become increasingly remote and diffuse, courts have, in many cases, raised an absolute bar to recovery.

The Court thus finds itself with a perceived need to limit liability, without any articulable reason for excluding any particular set of plaintiffs. * * * The Court concludes that plaintiffs who purchased and marketed seafood from commercial fishermen suffered damages that are not legally cognizable, because insufficiently direct. This does not mean that the Court finds that defendant's alleged acts were not the cause of plaintiffs' losses, or that plaintiffs' losses were in any sense unforeseeable. In fact, in part because the damages alleged by plaintiffs here were so foreseeable, the Court holds that those plaintiffs in categories G, H and I have suffered legally cognizable damages. The Court does so for several reasons. The United States Court of Appeals for the Fourth Circuit has held, in admiralty, that a defendant should "pay * * * once, but no more" for damages inflicted. While commercial fishing interests are protected by allowing the fishermen themselves to recover, it is unlikely that sportsfishing interests would be equally protected. Because the damages each sportsman suffered are likely to be both small[18] and difficult to establish, it is unlikely that a significant proportion of such fishermen will seek legal redress. Only if some set of surrogate plaintiffs is entitled to press its own claims which flow from the damage to the Bay's sport fishing industry will the proper balance of social forces be preserved. Accordingly, the Court holds that to the extent plaintiffs in categories G, H and I suffered losses in sales of goods and services to sportsfishermen as a result of defendant's tortious behavior, they have stated a legally cognizable claim.

Defendant hardly has reason to complain of the equity of the Court's holding. First, it benefitted above from the Court's exclusion of the claims of innocent businessmen in categories B through F who are probable victims of their alleged acts. Here, the Court applies different restrictions on liability for reasons of equity and efficiency previously addressed. Second, the "directness" of the harm, at least to plaintiffs in

---

[18] The net loss to any sportsman would have to take into account any enjoyment received from natural areas visited as a substitute to the Chesapeake Bay.

categories G and I,[19] is high here. Both operate on the water or at its edge. Finally, the Court is influenced by similar decisions as to liability in cases such as Maddox v. International Paper Co., 105 F. Supp. 89 (W.D. La. 1951) and Masonite Corp. v. Steede, 198 Miss. 530, 547, 23 So.2d 756 (1945). The Court's conclusion results from consideration of all these factors, and an attempt to tailor justice to the facts of the instant case.

[The district court dismissed all the admiralty claims of the plaintiffs, except those of the fishermen, shellfishermen and lessors of oysterbeds, on the basis of Robins Dry Dock & Repair Co. v. Flint, 275 U.S. 303 (1927). It also dismissed the claims of plaintiffs in categories B, C, D, E and F for recovery of indirect economic damages predicated on state nuisance law. In passing the court stated that, although Virginia recognizes nuisance as a basis of liability, it has never been decided that it could serve as a basis for recovery of indirect economic injuries.]

* * *

An appropriate order shall issue.

Notes and Questions

1. In both the *Ballard* and *Pruitt* cases, the courts dismissed some claims for indirect economic damages on the ground that federal maritime law does not permit plaintiffs to recover for indirect economic losses associated with a maritime tort but then found nonpreempted state law bases for recovery. If the Virginia James River Sportsfishing Association brings suit on behalf of all its members for the injury to recreational fishing interests, would it be allowed to recover damages? What distinction would you draw between such a suit and a suit by commercial fishing interests who are allowed to recover under both federal and state law? If the Association would not be allowed to recover damages, why should the marinas and bait and tackle shops supplying sportsfishermen be allowed to recover as "surrogate plaintiffs?" Isn't this just a ruse to allow recovery of indirect economic losses? For a further discussion of the Kepone case and related issues, see J. Kalo, Water Pollution and Commercial Fishermen: Applying General Maritime Law to Claims for Damages to Fisheries in Ocean and Coastal Waters, 61 N.C.L. Rev. 313 (1983).

2. CERCLA may abolish the *Robins Dry Dock* rule's prohibition on

---

[19] Generally boat and marina owners.

recovery of indirect economic damages when the hazardous substance responsible for the claim is discharged from a vessel. Section 107(h), 42 U.S.C. § 9614(h), makes the owner or operator of such a vessel liable under "maritime tort law [and state law] notwithstanding the absence of physical damage to the proprietary interest of the claimant." Section 107 addresses recovery of natural resource damages by federal, state, and tribal governments. Doesn't that limit the scope of the language in Section 107(h)? If not, then what limits exist to recovery of indirect economic damages?

SECTION 3. PREVENTION OF ACCIDENTAL OCEAN POLLUTION

A. TANKER DESIGN AND OPERATIONS

The Ports And Waterways Safety Act (PWSA)
33 U.S.C. § 1221 Et Seq.

The imposition of liability is an indirect method of grappling with the problems of oil in the marine environment. The PWSA as amended by the Port and Tanker Safety Act of 1978, confronted the issue of how to prevent oil pollution. It was a call for strengthened standards in ship design, construction, and operation, and a grant of authority to the Coast Guard to control ship movements. Relevant Coast Guard regulations are found in 33 C.F.R. Pts. 155-57, 160-64; 46 C.F.R. Pts. 30-32, 35, 70, 90, 172.

Vessel Construction

Title II of the Act addresses bulk cargo vessels that carry oil, hazardous substances, or inflammable or combustible liquids. The Secretary of Transportation (in whose department the Coast Guard operates) is directed to establish additional rules and regulations for vessel design, construction, alteration, repair, maintenance, and operation. These categories reach such areas as hulls, places for stowing and carrying cargo, equipment and appliances for the prevention of mitigation of damage to the marine environment, vessel inspections, and crew qualifications.

The Secretary was also given a special and immediate mandate ("as soon as practicable") to begin promulgating regulations for ship design, construction, alteration, and repair with the express purpose of protecting the marine environment. These regulations are to cover vessel maneuvering and stopping abilities, lowering the possibilities of collisions and groundings, reducing cargo losses after accidents, and such normal vessel operations as ballasting and cargo handling. These special, environmental regulations are to apply to both foreign vessels and U.S. Flag vessels operating in the foreign trade.

Traffic Control

Under Title I (33 U.S.C. § 1221 et seq.) the Coast Guard is given broad powers to control the movements of vessels in ports and areas where hazardous conditions exist. The Coast Guard may establish vessel traffic control systems, require compliance with those systems, and control vessel movements in hazardous areas or at times of adverse weather, reduced visibility, or congested traffic. Traffic controls include establishing vessel routing plans; setting vessel size, speed limits, and operating conditions; and restricting vessel operation in hazardous areas to vessels that have particular characteristics and capabilities necessary for safe operation. The Coast Guard is also authorized to deny entry into U.S. ports to vessels with histories of accidents or pollution incidents, vessels that fail to comply with vessel traffic systems or design specifications, and vessels with inadequately trained crews.

Oil Tanker Design

In the debate surrounding the 1990 Oil Pollution Act, one major point of controversy was whether double hulls should be required on oil tankers. Proponents argued that double hulls would prevent major spill disasters in the future. Strong support for their assertion was a Coast Guard study of 30 tanker groundings that occurred between 1969 and 1973. The study concluded that 96 percent of the spills caused by those groundings would have been prevented if the tankers were equipped with double hulls. The opponents of double hulls argued that water can rush in between a ruptured hull and the inner hull thereby causing the vessel to settle lower and exaggerate the leak. They also argued that explosive vapors could possibly collect between the hulls and create a bigger catastrophe than with a single hull.

The proponents won out in the end, as the PWSA [46 U.S.C. § 3703(a)] requires double hulls by the year 2010 for all tankers entering United States ports. The Act does allow an amortization period for complying with this mandate that began in 1995.[20] On the economic side, estimates for retrofitting the 153 United States tankers run as high

---

[20] In Maritrans, Inc. v. United States, 40 Ct.Cl. 790 (1998), the court held that owners of single-hulled tank barges had a protected property interest in their vessels and could bring a "takings" claim predicated upon the implementation of OPA's double-hull requirement.

as $30 million each for a total cost of about $4 billion. This estimate, however, does not take into account savings from clean-ups and liabilities associated with leakages or spills that might occur in the absence of double hulls.

More specifically, the Act states that all new tankers and barges of more than 5,000 tons that operate in United States waters must have double hulls. Any single hull tankers must be refitted with a second hull or be phased out between 1995 to 2010. All barges greater than 5,000 tons must have double hulls by the year 2015.

Other safety measures include a requirement that tanker operators participate in the United States Coast Guard's vessel monitoring and tracking system (VTS). This was added because evidence showed that the Exxon Valdez disaster might have been avoided if Exxon's tanker operators participated in the VTS. At the time of that spill, VTS participation was on a purely voluntary basis. The responsibility to determine which ports and channels will have the VTS system is bestowed on the Secretary of Transportation.

In addition, the Act authorizes the Secretary of Transportation to deny licensing to applicants refusing to disclose information contained in the National Driver Register; review criminal records of applicants for licensing; require testing and revoke licenses, certificates of registry, and merchant mariners' documents for drug and alcohol abuse; remove the individual in charge of a vessel if the two next most senior officers believe the individual to be under the influence of drugs or alcohol and incapable of commanding the vessel; periodically evaluate the staffing standards of foreign tank vessels; require appropriate vessels to participate in vessel traffic service systems and authorizes the expansion and improvement of those systems in U.S. ports; increase penalties for pilotage violations; complete a study regarding navigational safety and tanker operations, including crew size and qualifications, navigation equipment and procedures, effectiveness of tanker-free zones, and evaluation of tank vessel design and construction criteria; and set the length of crew watches and limit the use of an auto-pilot.

The Act also establishes a nationwide planning and response system for spills including spill contingency plans for facilities handling oil and hazardous substances. Relevant Coast Guard and Interior Department regulations are found at 30 C.F.R. Pt. 254; 33 C.F.R. Pts. 150, 154.

B. INTERNATIONAL CONVENTIONS

Recognizing that pollution of the seas by oil is a truly international issue, nations have negotiated a number of treaties to control intentional discharges and to minimize accidental discharges. While the emphasis internationally and in the U.S. has been on oil spills from tankers carrying oil as cargo, approximately half of the oil spills in the U.S. Pacific EEZ have been from vessels other than tankers. Globally, spills are more common than cargo spills from vessel bunker fuel oil tankers and represent one-half of the total number of pollution claims. Bunker fuel oil is always heavy and dirty and thus significantly more expensive to clean up than some lighter oils carried as cargo, which evaporate and dissipate more readily. Bunker fuel cleanup costs can easily exceed the vessel owner liability limits of some existing spill liability funds. N. Healy & D. Sharpe, Cases and Materials on Admiralty 910-11 (3rd ed. 1999). The proposed 2001 Convention on Compensation for Pollution from Ship's Bunkers would create a regime of compulsory insurance and direct action for bunker fuel spills that is compatible with the international regime for oil tankers summarized next.

The major treaties which have gone into force (some without United States ratification) include the following:

1) The 1954 Oil Pollution Prevention Convention, 327 U.N.T.S. 3, prohibited the discharge of oil and oily mixtures into the sea in certain areas. Prohibited zones were defined to include all sea areas within fifty miles of a coast, but a number of special areas extended to 100 miles offshore. An Oil Record Book was required to document discharges of oil and the surrounding circumstances. Amendments in 1969, 9 I.L.M. 1, added a rule that discharges must be en route and proscribed a rate of discharge in addition to the distance-from-land rule. Amendments in 1971, 11 I.L.M. 267, related to tank size and arrangement and created a fifty-mile prohibition zone around Australia's Great Barrier Reef.

2) The 1969 Convention On Intervention On The High Seas 9 I.L.M. 25, gives contracting nations the authority to "take such measures on the high seas as may be necessary to prevent, mitigate or eliminate grave and imminent danger to their coastline or related interests from pollution or threat of pollution of the sea by oil, following upon a maritime casualty * * * which may reasonably be expected to result in major harmful consequences."

3) The 1969 Convention on Civil Liability for Oil Pollution Damage, 9 I.L.M. 45, provides a legal basis for claims for damages to the territorial sea or coast of a state. The convention also provides a limitation of liability and defenses for shipowners and requires that all ships carrying over 2,000 tons of oil have financial security or insurance to the limit of liability.

4) The 1971 Convention Concerning an International Fund for Compensation for Oil Pollution Damage, 1110 U.N.T.S. 57, is a supplement to the 1969 Liability Convention. It supplements the 1969 liability convention's compensation limits and provides compensation to individuals who suffer pollution damage but cannot obtain compensation under the liability convention. The Fund is maintained by oil companies in each treaty nation, rather than by the oil tanker owners and operators. Under this international liability and fund regime some oil spill damage awards for economic losses and natural resources restoration are being made. The 1992 protocols specifically authorize awards for "reinstatement" of the damaged environment. However, the United States has not ratified the Liability and Fund Conventions or their 1984 and 1992 protocols.

5) The 1973 Convention for the Prevention of Pollution from Ships (MARPOL), 12 I.L.M. 1319 and its 1978 protocol, 17 I.L.M. 546, supersede the 1954 convention and extend the scope of the international pollution prevention effort to intentional discharges of harmful substances and to virtually all vessels and oil platforms. Tankers over 150 gross tons and other ships over 400 gross tons must be inspected and certified that they meet convention requirements. Fixed platforms and structures must be equipped with the same pollution control devices as ships over 400 tons. MARPOL emphasizes improved technology. Port reception facilities are required to eliminate the necessity of flushing tanks at sea. MARPOL Annex II entered into force on April 6, 1987. Annex II sets forth measures to control the discharge of noxious liquid substances carried on board vessels. Included are rules governing the discharge of cargo into receiving tanks on shore and the discharge of residues at sea (see United States v. Apex Oil Co., 132 F.3d 1287 (9th Cir. 1997)) as well as two codes mandatory under MARPOL relating to the carriage of noxious liquid substances. Under Annex II regulations, ships certified to carry certain substances will be required to be fitted with efficient pumping systems to remove cargo residues. The regulations also mandate tankwashing for the most hazardous substances before the ship leaves port. Port reception facilities are required for a few substances and the port nation is required to ensure that foreign ships comply with Annex II.

Although international efforts have had a significant effect in the area of liability and clean-up costs for pollution from oil and hazardous substances, many commentators believe that the conventions have actually provided very little relief from chronic discharges from vessels. The major weakness of the conventions is inadequate coastal-state enforcement authority, even within "prohibited" zones. Enforcement is the primary responsibility of the flag state and, unfortunately, there is very little economic incentive for a country to engage in vigorous enforcement of treaty obligations against its ships in distant waters. The 1982 Law of the Sea Convention offers increased opportunities for coastal-state and port-state enforcement, but the United States still is not a party to the convention and those provisions probably are not customary international law yet.

Regionally, the United States and twelve other countries are also parties to the 1983 Cartagena De Indias Convention for the Protection and Development of the Marine Environment of the Wider Caribbean Region 22 I.L.M. 227, and the Protocol concerning Cooperation in Combating Oil Spills in the Wider Caribbean Region, 22 I.L.M. 240, commonly called the Cartagena Convention. An additional sixteen countries are participating in a Caribbean Action Plan to implement the treaty. The convention was intended to address a number of sources of marine pollution, including vessels, dumping, seabed activities, airborne pollution, and land-based sources and to provide a dispute resolution procedure. In addition to adopting the protocol on oil spills, the parties have adopted a resolution urging nations in the region to refrain from ocean incineration, dumping, and disposal of nuclear wastes, except in accordance with the London Convention discussed below. The United States has proposed that the oil spill protocol be extended to include other hazardous substances.

For additional readings on the international regime for marine pollution control, see R. Mitchell, Intentional Oil Pollution At Sea (1994); R. Soni, Control of Marine Pollution in International Law 179-88 (1985); P. Dempsey, Compliance and Enforcement in International Law -- Oil Pollution of the Marine Environment by Ocean Vessels, 6 NW. J. Int'l L. & Bus. 459, 557-61 (1984), H. Bryant, Legal Regimes for Oil Pollution, 2 Eur. Envtl. L. Rev. 70 (1993).

C. STATE AUTHORITY AND THE CONSTITUTION'S FEDERAL SUPREMACY, COMMERCE, AND FOREIGN AFFAIRS CLAUSES

UNITED STATES v. LOCKE
The Supreme Court Of The United States, 2000
529 U.S. 89

JUSTICE KENNEDY delivered the opinion of the Court.

The maritime oil transport industry presents ever-present, all too real dangers of oil spills from tanker ships, spills which could be catastrophes for the marine environment. After the supertanker Torrey

Canyon spilled its cargo of 120,000 tons of crude oil off the coast of Cornwall, England, in 1967, both Congress and the State of Washington enacted more stringent regulations for these tankers and provided for more comprehensive remedies in the event of an oil spill. The ensuing question of federal pre-emption of the state's laws was addressed by the court in Ray v. Atlantic Richfield Co., 435 U.S. 151, 98 S.Ct. 988, 55 L.Ed.2d 179 (1978).

In 1989, the supertanker Exxon Valdez ran aground in Prince William Sound, Alaska, and its cargo of more than 53 million gallons of crude oil caused the largest oil spill in United States history. Again, both Congress and the State of Washington responded. Congress enacted new statutory provisions, and Washington adopted regulations governing tanker operations and design. Today we must determine whether these more recent state laws can stand despite the comprehensive federal regulatory scheme governing oil tankers. Relying on the same federal statute that controlled the analysis in Ray, we hold that some of the State's regulations are pre-empted; as to the balance of the regulations, we remand the case so their validity may be assessed in light of the considerable federal interest at stake and in conformity with the principles we now discuss.

I

The State of Washington embraces some of the Nation's most significant waters and coastal regions.   Its Pacific Ocean seacoast consists, in large part, of wave-exposed rocky headlands separated by stretches of beach. Washington borders as well on the Columbia River estuary, dividing Washington from Oregon. Two other large estuaries, Grays Harbor and Willapa Bay, are also within Washington's waters. Of special significance in this case is the inland sea of Puget Sound, a 2,500 square mile body of water consisting of inlets, bays, and channels. More than 200 islands are located within the sound, and it sustains fisheries and plant and animal life of immense value to the Nation and to the world.

Passage from the Pacific Ocean to the quieter Puget Sound is through the Strait Of Juan De Fuca, a channel 12 miles wide and 65 miles long which divides Washington from the Canadian Province of British Columbia. The international boundary is located midchannel. Access to Vancouver, Canada's largest port, is through the strait. Traffic inbound from the Pacific ocean, whether destined to ports in the United States or Canada, is routed through Washington's waters; outbound traffic, whether from a port in Washington or Vancouver, is directed through Canadian waters. The pattern had its formal adoption in a 1979 agreement entered by the United States and Canada. Agreement for a Cooperative Vessel Traffic Management System for the Juan De Fuca Region, 32 U.S.T. 377, T.I.A.S. No. 9706.

In addition to holding some of our vital waters, Washington is the site of major installations for the Nation's oil industry and the destination or shipping point for huge volumes of oil and its end products. Refineries and product terminals are located adjacent to Puget Sound in ports including Cherry Point, Ferndale, Tacoma, and Anacortes. Canadian refineries are found near Vancouver on Burrard Inlet and the lower Fraser River. Crude oil is transported by sea to Puget Sound. Most is extracted from Alaska's North Slope reserve and is shipped to Washington on United States flag vessels. Foreign-flag vessels arriving from nations such as Venezuela and Indonesia also call at Washington's oil installations.

The bulk of oil transported on water is found in tankers, vessels which consist of a group of tanks contained in a shipshaped hull, propelled by an isolated machinery plant at the stern. The Court described the increase in size and numbers of these ships close to three decades ago in Askew v. American Waterways Operators, Inc., 411 U.S. 325, 335, 93 S.Ct. 1590, 36 L.Ed.2d 280 (1973), noting that the average vessel size increased from 16,000 tons during World War II to 76,000 tons in 1966. (The term "tons" refers to "deadweight tons," a way of measuring the cargo-carrying capacity of the vessels.) Between 1955 and 1968, the world tanker fleet grew from 2,500 vessels to 4,300. Ibid. By December 1973, 366 tankers in the world tanker fleet were in excess of 175,000 tons, see 1 M. Tusiani, The Petroleum Shipping Industry 79 (1996), and by 1998 the number of vessels considered "tankers" in the merchant fleets of the world numbered 6,739, see U.S. Dept. Of Transp., Maritime Administration, Merchant Fleets of the World 1 (oct. 1998).

The size of these vessels, the frequency of tanker operations, and the vast amount of oil transported by vessels with but one or two layers of metal between the cargo and the water present serious risks. Washington's waters have been subjected to oil spills and further threatened by near misses. In December 1984, for example, the tanker ARCO Anchorage grounded in Port Angeles Harbor and spilled 239,000 gallons of Alaskan crude oil. The most notorious oil spill in recent times was in Prince William Sound, Alaska, where the grounding of the Exxon Valdez released more than 11 million gallons of crude oil and, like the Torrey Canyon spill before it, caused public officials intense concern over the threat of a spill.

Washington responded by enacting the state regulations now in issue.   The legislature created the Office Of Marine Safety, which it directed to establish standards for spill prevention plans to provide "the best achievable protection [BAP] from damages caused by the discharge of oil." Wash. Rev.Code § 88.46.040(3) (1994). The Office of Marine Safety then promulgated the tanker design, equipment, reporting, and operating requirements now subject to attack by petitioners. Wash. Admin. Code (WAC) § 317-21-130 et seq. (1999). A summary of the relevant regulations, as described by the Court of Appeals, is set out in the Appendix, infra.

If a vessel fails to comply with the Washington rules, possible sanctions include statutory penalties, restrictions of the vessel's operations in state waters, and a denial of entry into state waters. Wash. Rev.Code. §§ 88.46.070, 88.46.080, 88.46.090 (1994).

Petitioner International Association of Independent Tanker Owners ("Intertanko") is a trade association whose 305 members own or operate more than 2,000 tankers of both United States and foreign registry. The organization represents approximately 80% of the world's independently owned tanker fleet; and an estimated 60% of the oil imported into the United States is carried on Intertanko vessels. The association brought this suit seeking declaratory and injunctive relief against state and local officials responsible for enforcing the BAP regulations.   Groups interested in environmental preservation intervened in defense of the laws.   Intertanko argued that Washington's BAP standards invaded areas long occupied by the Federal Government and imposed unique requirements in an area where national uniformity was mandated. Intertanko further contended that if local political subdivisions of every maritime nation were to impose differing regulatory regimes on tanker operations, the goal of national governments to develop effective international environmental and safety standards would be defeated.

Although the United States declined to intervene when the case was in the District Court, the governments of 13 ocean-going nations expressed concerns through a diplomatic note directed to the United States.   Intertanko lodged a copy of the note with the District Court. The concerned governments represented that "legislation by the State of Washington on tanker personnel, equipment and operations would cause inconsistency between the regulatory regime of the U.S. Government and that of an individual state of the US. differing regimes in different parts of the U.S. would create uncertainty and confusion. This would also set an unwelcome precedent for other Federally administered countries." Note Verbale from the Royal Danish Embassy to the U.S. Dep't of State 1 (June 14, 1996).

The district court rejected all of Intertanko's arguments and upheld the state regulations. International Assn. of Independent Tanker Owners (Intertanko) v. Lowry, 947 F.Supp. 1484 (W.D.Wash.1996). The appeal followed, and at that stage the United States intervened on Intertanko's behalf, contending that the District Court's ruling failed to give sufficient weight to the substantial foreign affairs interests of the Federal Government. The United States Court Of Appeals for the Ninth Circuit held that the State could enforce its laws, save the one requiring the vessels to install certain navigation and towing equipment. 148 F.3d 1053 (1998) (the Court Of Appeals reasoned that this requirement, found in WAC § 317-21-265, was "virtually identical to" requirements declared pre-empted in Ray v. Atlantic Richfield Co., 435 U.S. 151, 98 S.Ct. 988, 55 L.Ed.2d 179 (1978)). 148 F.3d, at 1066. Over Judge Graber's dissent, the Court Of Appeals denied petitions for rehearing en banc. 159 F.3d 1220 (1998). Judge Graber, although unwilling, without further analysis, to conclude that the panel reached the wrong result, argued that the opinion was "incorrect in two exceptionally important respects: (1) The opinion places too much weight on two clauses in Title I of OPA 90 [The Oil Pollution Act of 1990] that limit OPA 90's preemptive effect. (2) Portions of the opinion that discuss the Coast Guard regulations are inconsistent with Ninth Circuit and Supreme Court precedent." Id., at 1221. We granted certiorari and now reverse. 527 U.S. 1063, 120 S.Ct. 33, 144 L.Ed.2d 835 (1999).

II

The State of Washington has enacted legislation in an area where the federal interest has been manifest since the beginning of our Republic and is now well established. The authority of Congress to regulate interstate navigation, without embarrassment from intervention of the separate States and resulting difficulties with foreign nations, was cited in the Federalist Papers as one of the reasons for adopting the Constitution. E.g., The Federalist Nos. 44, 12, 64. In 1789, the First Congress enacted a law by which vessels with a federal certificate were entitled to "the benefits granted by any law of the United States." Act of Sept. 1, 1789, ch. 11, § 1, 1 Stat. 55. The importance of maritime trade and the emergence of maritime transport by steamship resulted in further federal licensing requirements enacted to promote trade and to enhance the safety of crew members and passengers. See Act of July 7, 1838, ch. 191, 5 Stat. 304; Act of Mar. 3, 1843, ch. 94, 5 Stat. 626. In 1871, Congress enacted a comprehensive scheme of regulation for steam powered vessels, including provisions for licensing captains, chief mates, engineers, and pilots. Act of Feb. 28, 1871, ch. 100, 16 Stat. 440.

The court in Cooley v. Board of Wardens of Port of Philadelphia ex rel. Soc. For Relief of Distressed Pilots, 12 How. 299, 13 L.Ed. 996 (1852), stated that there would be instances in which state regulation of maritime commerce is inappropriate even absent the exercise of federal authority, although in the case before it the court found the challenged state regulations were permitted in light of local needs and conditions.

Where Congress had acted, however, the Court had little difficulty in finding state vessel requirements were pre- empted by federal laws which governed the certification of vessels and standards of operation. Gibbons v. Ogden, 9 Wheat. 1, 6 L.Ed. 23 (1824), invalidated a New York law that attempted to grant a monopoly to operate steamboats on the ground it was inconsistent with the coasting license held by the vessel owner challenging the exclusive franchise. And in Sinnot v. Davenport, 22 How. 227, 16 L.Ed. 243 (1859), the Court decided that the federal license held by the vessel contained "the only guards and restraints, which Congress has seen fit to annex to the privileges of ships and vessels engaged in the coasting trade." Id., at 241. The Court went on to explain that in such a circumstance, state laws on the subject must yield: "In every such case, the act of Congress or treaty is supreme; and the law of the State, though enacted in the exercise of powers not controverted, must yield to it." Id., At 243.

Against this background, Congress has enacted a series of statutes pertaining to maritime tanker transports and has ratified international agreements on the subject. We begin by referring to the principal statutes and international instruments discussed by the parties.

1. The Tank Vessel Act.

The Tank Vessel Act of 1936, 49 Stat. 1889, enacted specific requirements for operation of covered vessels. The Act provided that "[i]n order to secure effective provisions against the hazards of life and property," additional federal rules could be adopted with respect to the "design and construction, alteration, or repair of such vessels," "the operation of such vessels," and "the requirements of the manning of such vessels and the duties and qualifications of the officers and crews thereof." The purpose of the Act was to establish "a reasonable and uniform set of rules and regulations concerning * * * vessels carrying the type of cargo deemed dangerous." H.R.Rep. No. 2962, 74th Cong., 2d Sess., 2 (1936). The Tank Vessel Act was the primary source for regulating tank vessels for the next 30 years, until the Torrey Canyon grounding led Congress to take new action.

2. The Ports and Waterways Safety Act of 1972.

Responding to the Torrey Canyon spill, Congress enacted the Ports and Waterways Safety Act of 1972 (PWSA). The Act, as amended by the Port and Tanker Safety Act of 1978, 92 Stat. 1471, contains two somewhat overlapping titles, both of which may, as the Ray Court explained, preclude enforcement of state laws, though not by the same pre-emption analysis. Title I concerns vessel traffic "in any port or place under the jurisdiction of the United States." 110 Stat. 3934, 33 U.S.C. § 1223(a)(1) (1997 ed. Supp. III). Under Title I, the Coast Guard may enact measures for controlling vessel traffic or for protecting navigation and the marine environment, but it is not required to do so. Ibid.

Title II does require the Coast Guard to issue regulations, regulations addressing the "design, construction, alteration, repair, maintenance, operation, equipping, personnel qualification, and manning of vessels * * * that may be necessary for increased protection against hazards to life and property, for navigation and vessel safety, and for enhanced protection of the marine environment." 46 U.S.C. § 3703(a).

The critical provisions of the PWSA described above remain operative, but the Act has been amended, most significantly by the Oil Pollution Act of 1990(OPA), 104 Stat. 484. OPA, enacted in response to the Exxon Valdez spill, requires separate discussion.

3. The Oil Pollution Act of 1990.

The OPA contains nine titles, two having the most significance for these cases. Title I is captioned "Oil Pollution Liability, and Compensation" and adds extensive new provisions to the United States Code. See 104 Stat. 2375, 33 U.S.C. § 2701 et seq. (1994 ed. and Supp. III). Title I imposes liability (for both removal costs and damages) on parties responsible for an oil spill. § 2702. Other provisions provide defenses to, and limitations on, this liability. 33 U.S.C. §§ 2703, 2704. Of considerable importance to these cases are OPA's saving clauses, found in Title I of the Act, § 2718, and to be discussed below.

Title IV of OPA is entitled "Prevention And Removal." For the most part, it amends existing statutory provisions or instructs the Secretary of Transportation (whose departments include the Coast Guard) to take action under previous grants of rulemaking authority. For example, Title IV instructs the Coast Guard to require reporting of marine casualties resulting in a "significant harm to the environment." 46 U.S.C. § 6101(a)(5) (1994 ed. and Supp. V). Title IV further requires the Secretary to issue regulations to define those areas, including Puget Sound, on which single hulled tankers shall be escorted by other vessels. 104 Stat. 523. By incremental dates specified in the Act, all covered tanker vessels must have a double hull. 46 U.S.C. § 3703a.

4. Treaties and International Agreements.

The scheme of regulation includes a significant and intricate complex of international treaties and maritime agreements bearing upon the licensing and operation of vessels. We are advised by the United States that the international regime depends upon the principle of reciprocity. That is to say, the certification of a vessel by the government of its own flag nation warrants that the ship has complied with international standards, and vessels with those certificates may enter ports of the signatory nations. Brief for United States 3.

Illustrative of treaties and agreements to which the United States is a party are the International Convention for the Safety of Life at Sea, 1974, 32 U.S.T. 47, T.I.A.S. No. 9700, the International Convention for Prevention of Pollution from Ships, 1973, 17 I.L.M. 546, and the International Convention of Standards of Training, Certification and Watchkeeping for Seafarers, With Annex, 1978 (STCW), S. Treaty Doc. No. 96-1, C.T.I.A. No. 7624.

The United States argues that these treaties, as the supreme law of the land, have pre-emptive force over the state regulations in question here. We need not reach that issue at this stage of the case because the state regulations we address in detail below are pre-empted by federal statute and regulations. The existence of the treaties and agreements on standards of shipping is of relevance, of course, for these agreements give force to the longstanding rule that the enactment of a uniform federal scheme displaces state law, and the treaties indicate Congress will have demanded national uniformity regarding maritime commerce. See Ray, 435 U.S., at 166, 98 S.Ct. 988 (recognizing Congress anticipated "arriving at international standards for building tank vessels" and understanding "the Nation was to speak with one voice" on these matters). In later proceedings, if it is deemed necessary for full disposition of the case, it should be open to the parties to argue whether the specific international agreements and treaties are of binding, pre-emptive force. We do not reach those questions, for it may be that pre-emption principles applicable to the basic federal statutory structure will suffice, upon remand, for a complete determination.

III

In Ray v. Atlantic Richfield, supra, the Court was asked to review, in light of an established federal and international regulatory scheme, comprehensive tanker regulations imposed by the State of Washington. The Court held that the PWSA and Coast Guard regulations promulgated under that Act pre-empted a state pilotage requirement, Washington's limitation on tanker size, and tanker design and construction rules.

In these cases, petitioners relied on *Ray* to argue that Washington's more recent state regulations were preempted as well.   The Court Of Appeals, however, concluded that *Ray* retained little validity in light of subsequent action by Congress.   We disagree.   The *Ray* Court's interpretation of the PWSA is correct and controlling. Its basic analytic structure explains why federal pre-emption analysis applies to the challenged regulations and allows scope and due recognition for the traditional authority of the States and localities to regulate some matters of local concern.

At the outset, it is necessary to explain that the essential framework of *Ray*, and of the PWSA which it interpreted, are of continuing force, neither having been superseded by subsequent authority relevant to these cases.   In narrowing the pre-emptive effect given the PWSA in *Ray*, the Court Of Appeals relied upon OPA's saving clauses, finding in their language a return of authority to the States. Title I of OPA contains two saving clauses, stating:

(a) Preservation of State authorities * * *
Nothing in this Act or the Act of March 3, 1851 shall--

> (1) affect, or be construed or interpreted as pre-empting, the authority of any State or political subdivision thereof from imposing any additional liability or requirements with respect to--

>> (A) the discharge of oil or other pollution by oil within such State * * *

(c) additional requirements and liabilities; penalties
Nothing in this Act, the Act of March 3, 1851 (46 U.S.C. 183 et seq.), Or section 9509 of [the Internal Revenue Code of 1986 (26 U.S.C. § 9509]), shall in any way affect, or be construed to affect, the authority of the United States or any State or political subdivision thereof--

> (1) to impose additional liability or additional requirements * * * "relating to the discharge, or substantial threat of a discharge, of oil." 33 U.S.C. § 2718.

The Court Of Appeals placed more weight on the saving clauses than those provisions can bear, either from a textual standpoint or from a consideration of the whole federal regulatory scheme of which OPA is but a part.

The saving clauses are found in Title I of OPA, captioned Oil Pollution Liability and Compensation and creating a liability scheme for oil pollution. In contrast to the Washington rules at issue here, Title I does not regulate vessel operation, design, or manning. Placement of the saving clauses in Title I of OPA suggests that Congress intended to preserve state laws of a scope similar to the matters contained in Title I of OPA, not all state laws similar to the matters covered by the whole of OPA or to the whole subject of maritime oil transport.   The evident purpose of the saving clauses is to preserve state laws which, rather than imposing substantive regulation of a vessel's primary conduct, establish liability rules and financial requirements relating to oil spills. See Gutierrez v. Ada, 528 U.S. 250, ----, 120 S.Ct. 740, 744, 145 L.Ed.2d 747 (2000) (words of a statute should be interpreted consistent with their neighbors to avoid giving unintended breadth to an Act of Congress).

Our conclusion is fortified by Congress' decision to limit the saving clauses by the same key words it used in declaring the scope of Title I of OPA. Title I of OPA permits recovery of damages involving vessels "from which oil is discharged, or which pos[e] the substantial threat of a discharge of oil." 33 U.S.C. § 2702(a). The saving clauses, in parallel manner, permit States to impose liability or requirements "relating to the discharge, or substantial threat of a discharge, of oil." § 2718(c). In its titles following Title I, OPA addresses matters including licensing and certificates of registry, 104 Stat. 509; duties of senior licensed officers to relieve the master, id., at 511; manning standards for foreign vessels, id., at 513; reporting of marine casualties, ibid.; Minimum standards for plating thickness, id., at 515; tank vessel manning requirements, id., at 517; and tank vessel construction standards, id., at 517-518, among other extensive regulations. If Congress had intended to disrupt national uniformity in all of these matters, it would not have done so by placement of the saving clauses in Title I.

The saving clauses are further limited in effect to "this Act, the Act of March 3, 1851 * * * Or section 9509 of the Internal Revenue Code." § 2718(a) and (c).   These explicit qualifiers are inconsistent with interpreting the saving clauses to alter the pre-emptive effect of the PWSA or regulations promulgated thereunder. The text of the statute indicates no intent to allow states to impose wide-ranging regulation of the at-sea operation of tankers. The clauses may preserve a State's ability to enact laws of a scope similar to Title I, but do not extend to subjects addressed in the other Titles of the Act or other acts.

Limiting the saving clauses as we have determined respects the established federal-state balance in matters of maritime commerce between the subjects as to which the States retain concurrent powers and those over which the federal authority displaces state control. We have upheld state laws imposing liability for pollution caused by oil spills. See Askew v. American Waterways Operators, Inc., 411 U.S., at 325, 93 S.Ct. 1590. Our view of OPA's savings clauses preserves this important role for the States, which is unchallenged here. We think it quite unlikely that Congress would use a means so indirect as the savings clauses in Title I of OPA to upset the settled division of authority by allowing states to impose additional unique substantive regulation on the at-sea conduct of vessels. We decline to give broad effect to saving clauses where doing so would upset the careful regulatory scheme established by federal law. See, e.g., Morales v. Trans World Airlines, Inc., 504 U.S. 374, 385, 112 S.Ct. 2031, 119 L.Ed.2d 157 (1992); American Telephone & Telegraph Co. v. Central Office Telephone, Inc., 524 U.S. 214, 227-228, 118 S.Ct. 1956, 141 L.Ed.2d 222 (1998).

From the text of OPA and the long-established understanding of the appropriate balance between federal and state regulation of maritime commerce, we hold that the pre-emptive effect of the PWSA and regulations promulgated under it are not affected by OPA. We doubt Congress will be surprised by our conclusion, for the Conference Report on OPA shared our view that the statute " does not disturb the Supreme Court's decision in Ray v. Atlantic Richfield Co., 435 U.S. 151, 98 S.Ct. 988, 55 L.Ed.2d 179 (1978)." H.R. Conf. Rep. No. 101-653, 101, p. 122 (1990). The holding in *Ray* also survives the enactment of OPA undiminished, and we turn to a detailed discussion of that case.

As we mentioned above, the *Ray* Court confronted a claim by the operator of a Puget Sound refinery that federal law precluded Washington from enforcing laws imposing certain substantive requirements on tankers. The *Ray* Court prefaced its analysis of the state regulations with the following observation:

"The Court's prior cases indicate that when a State's exercise of its police power is challenged under the Supremacy Clause, 'We start with the assumption that the historic police powers of the States were not to be superseded by the Federal Act unless that was the clear and manifest purpose of Congress.' Rice v. Santa Fe Elevator Corp., 331 U.S. 218, 230, 67 S.Ct. 1146, 91 L.Ed. 1447 (1947)." 435 U.S., at 157, 98 S.Ct. 988.

The fragmentary quote from *Rice* does not support the scope given to it by the Court of Appeals or by respondents.

Ray quoted but a fragment of a much longer paragraph found in *Rice*. The quoted fragment is followed by extensive and careful qualifications to show the different approaches taken by the Court in various contexts. We need not discuss that careful explanation in detail, however. To explain the full intent of the *Rice* quotation, it suffices to quote in full the sentence in question and two sentences preceding it. The *Rice* opinion stated: "the question in each case is what the purpose of Congress was. Congress legislated here in a field which the States have traditionally occupied. So we start with the assumption that the historic police powers of the States were not to be superseded by the Federal Act unless that was the clear and manifest purpose of Congress." 331 U.S., at 230, 67 S.Ct. 1146 (citations omitted).

The qualification given by the word "so" and by the preceding sentences in *Rice* are of considerable consequence. As *Rice* indicates, an "assumption" of nonpre-emption is not triggered when the State regulates in an area where there has been a history of significant federal presence. See also Jones v. Rath Packing Co., 430 U.S. 519, 525, 97 S.Ct. 1305, 51 L.Ed.2d 604 (1977) ("assumption" is triggered where "the field which Congress is said to have pre-empted has been traditionally occupied by the States"); Medtronic, Inc. v. Lohr, 518 U.S. 470, 485, 116 S.Ct. 2240, 135 L.Ed.2d 700 (1996) (citing *Rice* in case involving medical negligence, a subject historically regulated by the States). In *Ray*, and in the case before us, Congress has legislated in the field from the earliest days of the Republic, creating an extensive federal statutory and regulatory scheme.

The state laws now in question bear upon national and international maritime commerce, and in this area there is no beginning assumption that concurrent regulation by the State is a valid exercise of its police powers. Rather, we must ask whether the local laws in question are consistent with the federal statutory structure, which has as one of its objectives a uniformity of regulation for maritime commerce. No artificial presumption aids us in determining the scope of appropriate local regulation under the PWSA, which, as we discuss below, does preserve, in Title I of that Act, the historic role of the States to regulate local ports and waters under appropriate circumstances. At the same time, as we also discuss below, uniform, national rules regarding general tanker design, operation, and seaworthiness have been mandated by Title II of the PWSA.

The *Ray* Court confirmed the important proposition that the subject and scope of Title I of the PWSA allows a State to regulate its ports and waterways, so long as the regulation is based on "the peculiarities of local waters that call for special precautionary measures." 435 U.S., at

171, 98 S.Ct. 988.   Title I allows state rules directed to local circumstances and problems, such as water depth and narrowness, idiosyncratic to a particular port or waterway.   Ibid. There is no pre-emption by operation of Title I itself if the state regulation is so directed and if the Coast Guard has not adopted regulations on the subject or determined that regulation is unnecessary or inappropriate. This principle is consistent with recognition of an important role for States and localities in the regulation of the nation's waterways and ports. E.g., Cooley, 12 How., at 319 (recognizing state authority to adopt plans "applicable to the local peculiarities of the ports within their limits").   It is fundamental in our federal structure that states have vast residual powers. Those powers, unless constrained or displaced by the existence of federal authority or by proper federal enactments, are often exercised in concurrence with those of the national government. Mcculloch v. Maryland, 4 Wheat. 316, 4 L.Ed. 579 (1819).

As *Ray* itself made apparent, the states may enforce rules governed by Title I of the PWSA unless they run counter to an exercise of federal authority. The analysis under Title I of the PWSA, then, is one of conflict pre-emption, which occurs "when compliance with both state and federal law is impossible, or when the state law 'Stands as an obstacle to the accomplishment and execution of the full purposes and objective of Congress.' " California v. Arc America Corp., 490 U.S. 93, 100-101, 109 S.Ct. 1661, 104 L.Ed.2d 86 (1989) (citations omitted).   In this context, Coast Guard regulations are to be given pre-emptive effect over conflicting state laws. City of New York v. FCC, 486 U.S. 57, 63-64, 108 S.Ct. 1637, 100 L.Ed.2d 48 (1988) (" '[A] federal agency acting within the scope of its Congressionally delegated authority may pre-empt state regulation' and hence render unenforceable state or local laws that are otherwise not inconsistent with federal law"). *Ray* defined the relevant inquiry for Title I pre-emption as whether the Coast Guard has promulgated its own requirement on the subject or has decided that no such requirement should be imposed at all. 435 U.S., at 171-172, 98 S.Ct. 988; see also, id., at 178, 98 S.Ct. 988 (" 'Where failure of * * * federal officials affirmatively to exercise their full authority takes on the character of a ruling that no such regulation is appropriate or approved pursuant to the policy of the statute,' States are not permitted to use their police power to enact such a regulation. Bethlehem Steel Co. v. New york State Labor Relations Board, 330 U.S. 767, 774, 67 S.Ct. 1026, 91 L.Ed. 1234 (1947)"). *Ray* also recognized that, even in the context of a regulation related to local waters, a federal official with an overview of all possible ramifications of a particular requirement might be in the best position to balance all the competing interests. Id., at 177, 98 S.Ct. 988.

While *Ray* explained that Congress, in Title I of the PWSA, preserved state authority to regulate the peculiarities of local waters if there was no conflict with federal regulatory determinations, the Court further held that Congress, in Title II of the PWSA, mandated federal rules on the subjects or matters there specified, demanding uniformity. Id., at 168, 98 S.Ct. 988 ("Title II leaves no room for the States to impose different or stricter design requirements than those which Congress has enacted with the hope of having them internationally adopted or has accepted as the result of international accord. A state law in this area * * * would frustrate the Congressional desire of achieving uniform, international standards"). Title II requires the Coast Guard to impose national regulations governing the general seaworthiness of tankers and their crews. Id., at 160, 98 S.Ct. 988. Under *Ray's* interpretation of the Title II PWSA provision now found at 46 U.S.C. § 3703(a), only the Federal Government may regulate the "design, construction, alteration, repair, maintenance, operation, equipping, personnel qualification, and manning" of tanker vessels.

In *Ray*, this principle was applied to hold that Washington's tanker design and construction rules were pre-empted. Those requirements failed because they were within a field reserved for federal regulation under 46 U.S.C. § 391a (1982 ed.), the predecessor to § 3703(a). We reaffirm *Ray's* holding on this point. Contrary to the suggestion of the Court of Appeals, the field of pre-emption established by § 3703(a) cannot be limited to tanker "design" and "construction," terms which cannot be read in isolation from the other subjects found in that section. Title II of the PWSA covers "design, construction, alteration, repair, maintenance, operation, equipping, personnel qualification, and manning" of tanker vessels. Ibid. Congress has left no room for state regulation of these matters. See Fidelity Fed. Sav. & Loan Assn. v. de la Cuesta, 458 U.S. 141, 102 S.Ct. 3014, 73 L.Ed.2d 664 (1982) (explaining field pre-emption). As the *Ray* Court stated: "[T]he Supremacy Clause dictates that the federal judgment that a vessel is safe to navigate United States waters prevail over the contrary state judgment. Enforcement of the state requirements would at least frustrate what seems to us to be the evident Congressional intention to establish a uniform federal regime controlling the design of oil tankers." 435 U.S., at 165, 98 S.Ct. 988.

The existence of some overlapping coverage between the two Titles of the PWSA may make it difficult to determine whether a pre-emption question is controlled by conflict pre-emption principles, applicable generally to Title I, or by field pre-emption rules, applicable generally to Title II. The *Ray* Court acknowledged the difficulty, but declined to resolve every question by the greater pre-emptive force of Title II. We follow the same approach, and conflict pre-emption under Title I will be applicable in some, although not all, cases. We recognize that the terms used in § 3703(a) are quite broad. In defining their scope, and the scope of the resulting field pre- emption, it will be useful to consider the type of regulations the Secretary has actually promulgated under the section, as well as the section's list of specific types of regulation that must be included. Useful inquiries include whether the rule is justified by conditions unique to a particular port or waterway. See id., at 175, 98 S.Ct. 988 (a Title I regulation is one "based on water depth in Puget Sound or on other local peculiarities"). Furthermore, a regulation within the State's residual powers will often be of limited extraterritorial effect, not requiring the tanker to modify its primary conduct outside the specific body of water purported to justify the local rule. Limited extraterritorial effect explains why *Ray* upheld a state rule requiring a tug escort for certain vessels, id., at 171, 98 S.Ct. 988, and why state rules requiring a registered vessel (i.e., one involved in foreign trade) to take on a local pilot have historically been allowed, id., at 159- 160, 98 S.Ct. 988. Local rules not pre-empted under Title II of the PWSA pose a minimal risk of innocent noncompliance, do not affect vessel operations outside the jurisdiction, do not require adjustment of systemic aspects of the vessel, and do not impose a substantial burden on the vessel's operation within the local jurisdiction itself.

IV

The field pre-emption rule surrounding Title II and § 3703(a) and the superseding effect of additional federal statutes are illustrated by the pre-emption of four of Washington's tanker regulations. We address these because the attempted reach of the state rules is well demonstrated by the briefs and record before us; other parts of the state regulatory scheme can be addressed on remand.

First, Washington imposes a series of training requirements on a tanker's crew. Wac § 317-21-230; see also Appendix, infra, at 1153. A covered vessel is required to certify that its crew has "complete[d] a comprehensive training program approved by the [State]." The State requires the vessel's master to "be trained in shipboard management" and licensed deck officers to be trained in bridge resource management, automated radar plotting aids, shiphandling, crude oil washing, inert gas systems, cargo handling, oil spill prevention and response, and shipboard fire fighting. The state law mandates a series of "weekly," "monthly," and "quarterly" drills.

This state requirement under WAC § 317-21-230 does not address matters unique to the waters of Puget Sound. On the contrary, it imposes requirements that control the staffing, operation, and manning of a tanker outside of Washington's waters.   The training and drill requirements pertain to "operation" and "personnel qualifications" and so are pre-empted by 46 U.S.C. § 3703(a).   Our conclusion that training is a field reserved to the Federal Government receives further confirmation from the circumstance that the STCW Convention addresses "training" and "qualification" requirements of the crew, Art. VI, and that the United States has enacted crew training requirements. E.g., 46 CFR pts. 10, 12, 13, 15 (1999).

The second Washington rule we find pre-empted is WAC § 317-21-250; see also, Appendix, infra, at 1153. Washington imposes English language proficiency requirements on a tanker's crew.   This requirement will dictate how a tanker operator staffs the vessel even from the outset of the voyage, when the vessel may be thousands of miles from Puget Sound.   It is not limited to governing local traffic or local peculiarities. The State's attempted rule is a "personnel qualification" pre-empted by § 3703(a) of Title II. In addition, there is another federal statute, 33 U.S.C. § 1228(a)(7), on the subject.   It provides: "[N]o vessel * * * shall operate in the navigable waters of the United States * * *, if such vessel * * * while underway, does not have at least one licensed deck officer on the navigation bridge who is capable of clearly understanding English."   The statute may not be supplemented by laws enacted by the States without compromising the uniformity the federal rule itself achieves.

The third Washington rule we find invalid under field pre-emption is a navigation watch requirement in WAC § 317-21-200. Washington has different rules for navigation watch, depending on whether the tanker is operating in restricted visibility or not.   We mention the restricted visibility rule below, but now evaluate the requirement which applies in general terms and reads: "[T]he navigation watch shall consist of at least two licensed deck officers, a helmsman, and a lookout." The general watch requirement is not tied to the peculiarities of Puget Sound;   it applies throughout Washington's waters and at all times.   It is a general operating requirement and is pre-empted as an attempt to regulate a tanker's "operation" and "manning" under 46 U.S.C. § 3703(a).

We have illustrated field pre-emption under § 3703(a) by discussing three of Washington's rules which, under the current state of the record, we can determine cannot be enforced due to the assertion of federal authority found in that section.   The parties discuss other federal statutory provisions and international agreements which also govern specific aspects of international maritime commerce. In appropriate circumstances, these also may have pre- emptive effect.

For example, the record before us reveals that a fourth state rule cannot stand in light of other sources of federal regulation of the same subject. Washington requires vessels that ultimately reach its waters to report certain marine casualties. WAC § 317-21-130; see also Appendix, infra, at 1153. The requirement applies to incidents (defined as a "collision," "allision," "near-miss incident," "marine casualty" of listed kinds, "accidental or intentional grounding," "failure of the propulsion or primary steering systems," "failure of a component or control system," "fire, flood, or other incident that affects the vessel's seaworthiness," and "spills of oil"), regardless of where in the world they might have occurred. A vessel operator is required by the state regulation to make a detailed report to the state on each incident, listing the date, location, and weather conditions. The report must also list the government agencies to whom the event was reported and must contain a "brief analysis of any known causes" and a "description of measures taken to prevent a reoccurrence." Ibid.

The State contends that its requirement is not pre-empted because it is similar to federal requirements. This is an incorrect statement of the law. It is not always a sufficient answer to a claim of pre-emption to say that state rules supplement, or even mirror, federal requirements. The Court observed this principle when Commerce Clause doctrine was beginning to take shape, holding in Sinnot v. Davenport, 22 How. 227, 16 L.Ed. 243 (1859), that Alabama could not require vessel owners to provide certain information as a condition of operating in state waters even though federal law also required the owner of the vessel "to furnish, under oath * * * all the information required by this State law." Id., at 242. The appropriate inquiry still remains whether the purposes and objectives of the federal statutes, including the intent to establish a workable, uniform system, are consistent with concurrent state regulation. On this point, Justice Holmes' later observation is relevant: "[W]hen Congress has taken the particular subject matter in hand coincidence is as ineffective as opposition, and a state law is not to be declared a help because it attempts to go farther than Congress has seen fit to go." Charleston & Western Carolina R. Co. v. Varnville Furniture Co., 237 U.S. 597, 604, 35 S.Ct. 715, 59 L.Ed. 1137 (1915).

We hold that Congress intended that the Coast Guard regulations be the sole source of a vessel's reporting obligations with respect to the matters covered by the challenged state statute. Under 46 U.S.C. § 6101, the Coast Guard "shall prescribe regulations on the marine casualties to be reported and the manner of reporting," and the statute lists the kinds of casualties that the regulations must cover. See also §

3717(a)(4) (requiring the Secretary of Transportation to "establish a marine safety information system").   Congress did not intend its reporting obligations to be cumulative to those enacted by each political subdivision whose jurisdiction a vessel enters.   The State's reporting requirement is a significant burden in terms of cost and the risk of innocent noncompliance. The Roanoke, 189 U.S. 185, 195, 23 S.Ct. 491, 47 L.Ed. 770 (1903) (the master of a vessel is in a position "such that it is almost impossible for him to acquaint himself with the laws of each individual State he may visit").   Furthermore, it affects a vessel operator's out-of-state obligations and conduct, where a State's jurisdiction and authority are most in doubt.   The state reporting requirement under WAC § 317-21-130 is pre-empted.

V

As to conflict pre-emption under Title I, Washington argues that certain of its regulations, such as its watch requirement in times of restricted visibility, are of limited extraterritorial effect and necessary to address the peculiarities of Puget Sound.   On remand, the Court of Appeals or District Court should consider whether the remaining regulations are preempted under Title I conflict pre-emption or Title II field pre-emption, or are otherwise pre-empted by these Titles or under any other federal law or international agreement raised as possible sources of pre-emption.

We have determined that Washington's regulations regarding general navigation watch procedures, English language skills, training, and casualty reporting are pre-empted.   Petitioners make substantial arguments that the remaining regulations are preempted as well.   It is preferable that the remaining claims be considered by the Court of Appeals or by the District Court within the framework we have discussed.   The United States did not participate in these cases until appeal.   Resolution of these cases would benefit from the development of a full record by all interested parties.

We infer from the record that Washington is not now enforcing its regulations.   If, pending adjudication of the case on remand, a threat of enforcement emerges, the Court of Appeals or the District Court would weigh any application for stay under the appropriate legal standards in light of the principles we have discussed and with recognition of the national interests at stake.

When one contemplates the weight and immense mass of oil ever in transit by tankers, the oil's proximity to coastal life, and its destructive power even if a spill occurs far upon the open sea, international, federal, and state regulation may be insufficient protection.   Sufficiency, however, is not the question before us.   The issue is not adequate regulation but political responsibility; and it is, in large measure, for Congress and the Coast Guard to confront whether their regulatory scheme, which demands a high degree of uniformity, is adequate. States, as well as environmental groups and local port authorities, will participate in the process. See 46 U.S.C. § 3703(a) (requiring the Coast Guard to consider the views of "officials of state and local governments," "representative of port and harbor authorities," and "representatives of environmental groups" in arriving at national standards).

The judgment of the Court of Appeals is reversed, and remand for further proceedings consistent with this opinion.

It is so ordered.

APPENDIX TO OPINION OF THE COURT

1.   Event Reporting--WAC 317-21-130. Requires operators to report all events such as collisions, allisions and near-miss incidents for the five years preceding filing of a prevention plan, and all events that occur thereafter for tankers that operate in Puget Sound.

2.   Operating Procedures--[Watch Practices WAC-317-21-200.] Requires tankers to employ specific watch and lookout practices while navigating and when at anchor, and requires a bridge resource management system that is the 'standard practice throughout the owner's or operator's fleet,' And which organizes responsibilities and coordinates communication between members of the bridge.

3.   Operating Procedures--Navigation WAC--317-21-205. Requires tankers in navigation in state waters to record positions every fifteen minutes, to write a comprehensive voyage plan before entering state waters, and to make frequent compass checks while under way.

4.   Operating Procedures--Engineering WAC--317-21-210. Requires tankers in state waters to follow specified engineering and monitoring practices.

5.   Operating Procedures--Prearrival Tests and Inspections WAC--317-21-215. Requires tankers to undergo a number of tests and inspections of engineering, navigation and propulsion systems twelve hours or less before entering or getting underway in state

waters.

6.   Operating Procedures--Emergency Procedures WAC--317-21-220. Requires tanker masters to post written crew assignments and procedures for a number of shipboard emergencies.

7.   Operating Procedures--Events WAC--317-21-225. Requires that when an event transpires in state waters, such as a collision, allision or near miss incident, the operator is prohibited from erasing, discarding or altering the position plotting records and comprehensive written voyage plan.

8.   Personnel Policies, Training--WAC--317-21-230.   Requires operators to provide a comprehensive training program for personnel that goes beyond that necessary to obtain a license or merchant marine document, and which includes instructions on a number of specific procedures.

9.   Personnel Policies--Illicit Drugs and Alcohol Use--WAC 317-21-235. Requires drug and alcohol testing and reporting.

10.   Personnel Policies--Personnel Evaluation--WAC 317-21-240. Requires operators to monitor the fitness for duty of crew members, and requires operators to at least annually provide a job performance and safety evaluation for all crew members on vessels covered by a prevention plan who serve for more than six months in a year.

11.   Personnel Policies--Work Hours WAC--317-21-245.   Sets limitations on the number of hours crew members may work.

12.   Personnel Policies--Language WAC--317-21-250. Requires all licensed deck officers and the vessel master to be proficient in English and to speak a language understood by subordinate officers and unlicensed crew.   Also requires all written instruction to be printed in a language understood by the licensed officers and unlicensed crew.

13.   Personnel Policies--Record Keeping WAC--317-21-255: requires operators to maintain training records for crew members assigned to vessels covered by a prevention plan.

14.   Management WAC--317-21-260. Requires operators to implement management practices that demonstrate active monitoring of vessel operations and maintenance, personnel

training, development, and fitness, and technological improvements in navigation.

15. Technology WAC--317-21-265. Requires tankers to be equipped with global positioning system receivers, two separate radar systems, and an emergency towing system.

16. Advance Notice of Entry and Safety Reports WAC--317-21-540. Requires at least twenty-four hours notice prior to entry of a tanker into state waters, and requires that the notice report any conditions that pose a hazard to the vessel or the marine environment." 148 F.3d, at 1053 (footnote omitted).

Notes and Questions

1. Does the Court construe Congressional intent too narrowly? Consider the following:

As distinguished from vessel design, construction, and operation, the Court recognized that Congress did intend the states to have a significant role additional to the federal government in "imposing liability for pollution caused by oil spills." [529 U.S. 89 at 106] * * * the Court * * * underemphasized Congress' role in controlling preemption questions through express statutory language. If Congress feels that the Court has misinterpreted Congressional intent with respect to the state regulatory role, Congress may redefine the state role with appropriate statutory amendments, recognizing that some amendments could also require the negotiation of changes in treaty language. * * * A broader state role is justified because marine pollution prevention, response, and liability laws lie at the intersection of environmental and maritime law. Federal environmental statutes such as OPA typically delegate significant responsibility to the states and authorize them to enforce pollution control requirements that are more stringent than federal rules. Maritime law * * * and the Court's decision in Ray v. Arco use traditional concerns for national and international uniformity, often reflected in Coast Guard regulations issued under OPA and the PWSA, in order to undercut state marine pollution control roles accepted by Congress.

R. Hildreth, C. Terenzi, & l. Thomas, Evaluation of the New Carissa Incident for Improvements to State, Federal, and International Law, 16 J. Of Envtl. L. & Litigation 101, 135-36 (2001).

2. In response to United States v. Locke, in August 2000 the

Washington State Department of Ecology repealed both the remanded and the previously invalidated rules and terminated its inspections of tankers and oil-carrying barges in the Columbia River. Furthermore, the Washington State Legislature terminated the DOES Office Of Marine Safety, which had administered the repealed rules. 2000 Wash. S.S.B. No. 6210. On the other hand, immediately following the Court's 1978 decision in Ray, Secretary of Transportation Adams issued a federal regulation closing Puget Sound to tankers greater than 125,000 dwt. 43 Fed. Reg. 12,257 (1978), extended, 44 Fed. Reg. 36,174 (June 21, 1979). Congress had restricted tanker traffic in Puget Sound even before the Court's 1978 decision. See 33 U.S.C. § 476 (Supp. I 1977).

3. As the Supreme Court held in *Ray*, a state tug assistance requirement for tankers could stand only until the Coast Guard decided whether to impose such a rule. The State of Alaska's attempt to require tug assistance was held to be preempted by the Coast Guard's then voluntary Prince William Sound vessel traffic system. See Chevron v. Hammond, no. A77-195 Civil (D. Alaska, 1978). See generally note, oil tanker regulation: a state or federal area?, 19 Nat. Resources J. 701 (1979).

4. Of what practical significance is the state authority to require pilots on registered (foreign flag and U.S. Flag vessels engaged in foreign commerce) vessels in light of the Jones Act, section 27 of the Merchant Marine Act of 1920, 46 U.S.C. § 883, requiring that goods shipped between American ports be carried on American vessels? All such coastwise or enrolled tankers will carry federally licensed pilots pursuant to Coast Guard rules adopted under 46 U.S.C. § 8502(a).

5. Some state regulation of oil tanker operations can be accomplished indirectly through the regulation of shore facilities or the use of liability programs. What other indirect methods are available for a state seeking to protect its environment from tanker source pollution? does the federal coastal zone management act discussed in chapter 3 provide yet another opportunity for indirect state regulation of oil tankers? see R. Dubey, Control of oil transport in the coastal zone: A look at Puget Sound, 56 or. L. Rev. 593, 630 (1977).

D. OFFSHORE STRUCTURES

Advances in technology permit the siting of large offshore marine structures miles from the nearest land. Such structures have been erected or placed in ocean waters as part of the effort to explore for and exploit OCS oil and natural gas deposits. Not infrequently, they are connected to the land by means of pipelines that transport oil and gas to land-based storage and processing facilities. These structures, their associated pipelines, supply vessels, and related operations are potentially significant sources of water pollution, and thus the subject of environmental regulations discussed in chapter 5 and this chapter.

The technology for offshore structures first developed to exploit offshore oil and gas deposits but it can be adapted to other uses, such as deepwater port facilities. Large tankers can discharge their cargo miles at sea through the means of a deepwater port facility. Such a facility is essentially an artificial island that is connected to land-based facilities by means of a pipeline. In 1975, the Deepwater Ports Act of 1974 became law. The legislation established licensing requirements for deepwater ports located beyond the traditional three mile limit of state waters. In addition, strong environmental safeguards were placed in the Act to address specific environmental threats posed by supertankers and superports. Although a number of Gulf States considered superport development, as of 1998, only one deepwater port, the Louisiana Loop, has been licensed and constructed. See generally R. Meltz, the Deepwater Ports Act of 1974: Half Speed Ahead, 5 Envtl. L. Rep. 50043 (1975).

Another type of offshore structure is ocean thermal energy conversion facilities which use technology that is still in the developmental stages. The process involves using warm ocean surface waters to heat ammonia. As the temperature of the ammonia rises, it vaporizes and expands. The ammonia gas is then used to drive a turbine to generate power. After passing through the turbine, the gas is cooled by deeper, colder ocean waters and converts back to a liquid form. The process then repeats itself. The Ocean Thermal Energy Act of 1980, 42 U.S.C § 9101 et. seq., establishes licensing requirements for commercial facilities, one of which is the preparation of an Environmental Impact Statement.

SECTION 4. INTENTIONAL WASTE DISPOSAL IN OCEAN AND COASTAL WATERS

A. OCEAN DUMPING FROM VESSELS

National obligations under the 1982 United Nations Convention on the Law of the Sea, 21 I.L.M.1261, to protect the marine environment include enforcement under Article 210 of global, regional, and national rules to control vessels transporting waste materials from land for disposal in the ocean. According to J. Kindt, Ocean Dumping, 13 Denver J. Int'l & Pol'y 335, 336-337 (1984):

Of the pollutants entering the world's oceans, approximately 10 percent are due to direct ocean dumping. * * * Of the 10 percent of ocean dumped materials, dredged spoils constitute 80 percent of this total. Approximately 1 to 10 percent of the dredged sediment taken from waterways and harbors has been contaminated to potentially unacceptable levels because of industrial, urban, and agricultural activities. Even non-toxic dredged spoils can physically damage marine organisms in ways ranging from inhibiting the penetration of light (due to suspended sediments) to smothering organisms on the ocean floor when large quantities are dumped.

Sludge from onshore sewage treatment plants dumped in the ocean also may contain heavy metals and organic chemicals. Under Article 216, coastal nations can control, even prohibit, dumping within their territorial seas and exclusive economic zones seaward 200 nautical miles and on their continental shelves where they extend further. However, the United States so far has chosen to only control dumping by foreign flag vessels seaward 12 nautical miles pursuant to the 1972 Ocean Dumping Act and 1972 London Dumping Convention, 11 I.L.M. 1294, discussed next.

In 1972, a group of nations already was sufficiently concerned about ocean pollution problems that they negotiated the London Convention on the Prevention of Marine Pollution by Dumping of Wastes and Other Matter (London Dumping Convention). The treaty came into force in 1975 and has been ratified by the United States. The Convention only applies to materials that are transported for the purpose of ocean disposal and does not cover the disposal of wastes derived from normal vessel operations. However, restrictions on vessel disposal of plastics, garbage, and noxious liquids are provided by the MARPOL convention mentioned above and discussed further below.

The nations party to the convention originally agreed to prohibit the dumping of materials listed in Annex I of the Convention, unless they are "rapidly rendered harmless by physical, chemical, or biological processes in the sea. * * * " (Annex I, No. 8, 26 U.S.T. At 2465). Dumping of material specifically listed in Annex II and other material was allowed only on the issuance of a prior permit. The Convention set forth a number of factors in Annex III to be considered in granting permits, including the characteristics of the waste and site, method of disposal, effect on marine organisms, other uses of the sea, and the availability of alternative methods of dumping.   However, the Convention's 1996 Protocol 36 L.L.M. 1, greatly restricts permissible dumping by prohibiting the ocean dumping of all wastes except those listed in revised Annex I. Revised Annex I only allows the dumping of dredged material, sewage sludge, fish wastes, inert geological materials, natural organic materials, abandoned vessels and platforms, and other bulky items made of iron, steel, concrete, and similar unharmful materials. Revised Annexes 2 and 3 to the 1996 Protocol deal with waste assessment and arbitral procedures. The 1996 Protocol will enter into force upon its ratification by 26 nations, including at least 15 of the 76 nations who are parties to the Convention. A number of multilateral treaties control dumping in specific ocean regions. See L. Guruschwamy & B. Hendricks, International Environmental Law in a Nutshell 270-71 (1997).

Although the oceans off the United States coast have been used as a disposal site for many years, generally only relatively small amounts of material were dumped, including the first known ocean disposal of radioactive waste done by the United States 50 miles off california in 1946. The annual amount of material (industrial wastes, sewage sludge, solid wastes, and construction and demolition debris) dumped in the early 1950s was approximately 1.7 million tons. By the mid-1960s, this figure rose to 7.4 million tons per year, a 335 percent increase. These figures do not include the amount of dredge spoil disposed; this is generally estimated to be four times, by weight, that of all other materials. Congressional Research Service, Library of Congress, Ocean Dumping Regulations: An Appraisal Of Implementation I (1976). Sources of waste material were identified as dredged material (680 million metric tons per year nationally, with 25 percent of it dumped into the ocean); sewage sludge (5.9 million wet metric tons were ocean dumped in 1979, and 2.8 million wet metric tons were discharged through the Los Angeles and Boston outfalls); industrial waste (2.6 million tons were ocean dumped in 1979); solid waste (570 million tons); nonpoint sources (vast amounts of wastes from urban runoff, mining wastes, and agriculture and silviculture runoff); and potential new sources. 12 Coastal Zone Management Newsletter No. 6, Feb. 11, 1981, at 2-3. Several probable causes of this drastic increase were identifiable:

1. There was a widely held perception, which to some degree continues today, that the ocean can serve as a vast ultimate sink for wastes. This view gave rise to the assumption that the ocean was a "safe" disposal site able to dilute and absorb otherwise harmful material.

2. Between 1930 and 1970 the population in coastal areas approximately doubled. This growth of population and associated land development led to the generation of tremendous amounts of solid waste. At the same time, this growth reduced the amount of land available for landfill disposal methods.

3. Since the late 1960s there have been growing numbers and types of controls upon air and water discharge. This has led to:

> (a) A transfer of waste disposal processes to coastal and ocean dumping, transferring pollution from one medium to another rather than eliminating it; and

> (b) Pollution controls have themselves expanded the amount of waste needing disposal. Sewage treatment has generated more sewage sludge and stack scrubbers collect large amounts of fly ash. Both of these are bulky wastes that require some type of disposal.

4. Until 1972 there was no federal regulation of ocean dumping. In many instances this encouraged use of ocean dumping over other methods of waste disposal.

In response to this dramatic increase in ocean dumping, the President's Council on Environmental Quality took a deep look at the problem presented by unregulated ocean dumping. It recommended a "comprehensive national policy on ocean dumping of wastes to ban *unregulated* dumping of all materials and strictly limit ocean disposal of any materials harmful to the marine environment." Council on Environmental Quality, Ocean Dumping: A National Policy at v (1970) (emphasis added).

In response to the report's recommendations and to implement the London Convention, Congress passed the Marine Protection, Research and Sanctuaries Act (MPRSA) of 1972, 33 U.S.C. § 1401 et seq. Titles I and II pertain to ocean dumping and are commonly referred to as the Ocean Dumping Act; Title III concerns marine sanctuaries and is discussed later.

The Ocean Dumping Act adopts a national policy of regulating the dumping of all materials into ocean waters. "Material" is broadly defined in the Ocean Dumping Act to encompass just about any variety of waste, except for vessel sewage wastes regulated under the CWA. 33 U.S.C. § 1402(c). Unless within one of the limited exceptions, material is "dumped" if it is disposed of from a vessel or aircraft. 33 U.S.C. § 1402(f).

Title I of the MPRSA, the heart of the dumping regulatory scheme, prohibits, unless authorized by permit, (1) transportation from the United States of materials for the purpose of dumping them into ocean waters, and (2) dumping of materials transported from outside the United States within twelve nautical miles of the territorial sea baseline.

33 U.S.C. § 1411. The Corps of Engineers is authorized to issue permits with respect to dredged wastes only, see, e.g., Clean Ocean Action v. York, 57 F.3d 328 (3rd Cir. 1995), and the Environmental Protection Agency (EPA) has permit authority for all other wastes. 33 U.S.C. §§ 1412, 1412a, 1413. In addition, the EPA is authorized to designate recommended dumping sites and to limit or prohibit dumping of some items or dumping at specific sites if necessary to protect "critical areas." 33 U.S.C. § 1412(c); see National Wildlife Federation v. Costle, 629 F.2d 118 (d.C. Cir. 1980) (the EPA's designation of "interim" sites based on historical usage upheld). The act specifically bans the dumping of radiological, chemical, or biological warfare agents and high-level radioactive wastes. 33 U.S.C. § 1412(a).

The Ocean Dumping Act directs the EPA to promulgate criteria to be used both by the EPA and by the Corps in evaluating whether particular dumping proposals "will unreasonably degrade or endanger human health, welfare, or amenities, or the marine environment, ecological systems, or economic potentialities." 33 U.S.C. § 1412(a); see Clean Ocean Action v. York, 57 F.3d 328 (3rd Cir. 1995). See also 33 U.S.C. § 1412(a) (emergency permits). In developing these criteria, the Administrator must consider nine statutory factors, including the need for dumping, its effects, alternatives to the dumping, and alternative uses of the ocean areas, and must apply standards created by the London Convention "to the extent that he may do so without relaxing the [Act's] requirements." 33 U.S.C. § 1412. Pursuant to this directive, the EPA has promulgated regulations for site selection and permit application evaluation. 40 C.F.R. §§ 227-28; see City Of New York v. EPA, 543 F. Supp. 1084 (S.D.N.Y. 1981) (lengthy discussion of the criteria structure).

The Corps, in evaluating permit applications for dumping "dredged material," must consider only those EPA-promulgated criteria that relate to the effects of the dumping. 33 U.S.C. § 1413(b). Adherence by the Corps to the EPA's criteria is assured by the EPA's veto power over the issuance of such permits. 33 U.S.C. § 1413(c). In the event that the EPA determines the granting of a permit by the Corps would not conform to the EPA's criteria, the Corps may request a waiver if the Corps finds "there is no economically feasible method or site available." 33 U.S.C. § 1413(d). A waiver must be granted unless the EPA concludes that the dumping will "result in an unacceptably adverse impact on municipal water supplies, shellfish beds, wildlife, fisheries (including spawning and breeding areas), or recreational activities." Id.; See Environmental Law Institute, Law of Environmental Protection 12-180 - 12-195. For a comprehensive analysis of ocean dumping and its effects on the ecosystem, see D. Squires, The Ocean Dumping Quandary (1983).

The Ocean Dumping Ban Act of 1988, Pub. L. No. 100-688, 102 Stat. 4139 (1988), provided a partial ban on ocean dumping. See M. Taylor, Ocean Dumping: A Light at the End of the Tunnel, 3 Hofstra Prop. L.J. 235 (1990). The Act prohibited the dumping of sewage sludge and industrial waste effective January 1, 1992. Regarding continued dredged material dumping, on October 31, 1992, President Bush signed H.R. 6167, the Water Resources Development Act of 1992, Pub. L. 102-580. Title V of that Act, entitled the "National Contamination Sediment Assessment and Management Act," amended the Ocean Dumping Act in a number of ways. First, Section 502 established a National Contaminated Sediment Task Force, composed of a variety of federal, state, and private interests, to review, inter alia, the extent and seriousness of aquatic sediment contamination and to report findings and recommendations to Congress. Next, the Act required the EPA, in consultation with NOAA and the Corps of Engineers, to conduct a comprehensive survey and monitoring program to assess and address aquatic sediment quality in the United States. Id. § 503. The Act also required the Corps to provide the EPA forty-five days to concur or object to Corps issuance of dredged material dumping permits. Id. § 504 (amending 33 U.S.C. § 1413(c)).

Significantly, section 505 preserved states' Rights "to adopt or enforce any requirements respecting dumping of materials" into state ocean waters, except with regard to federal projects where the EPA makes specified findings (amending 33 U.S.C. § 1416(d)). The Act also required the EPA to designate sites and times for sediment disposal so as to mitigate environmental impacts while also giving the EPA authority to prohibit dumping when necessary (amending 33 U.S.C. § 1412(c)). Further, the EPA must develop site management plans to ensure environmental safety for existing and proposed disposal sites and after January 1, 1995, it may not officially designate any disposal site without completing such plans. Id. Additionally, section 507 of the act limits dumping permits to a period of seven years (amending 33 U.S.C. § 1414(a)). Finally, the act amended the criminal penalty provisions of 33 U.S.C. § 1415(b) to allow for the seizure and forfeiture of property or proceeds involved in or resulting from any knowing violation of the Act.

With regard to offshore disposal of dredged materials, the Corps of Engineers Ocean Dumping Act (ODA) permit authority geographically overlaps its Clean Water Act (CWA) section 404 permit authority (discussed in Chapter 2) in the zone extending three nautical miles seaward from the territorial sea baseline. As D. Christie, and R. Hildreth, Coastal and Ocean Management Law in a Nutshell 293-294 (2d ed. 1999) explains:

The ODA authorizes the Corps, with the concurrence of the EPA, to issue permits for the *dumping of dredged material.* 33 U.S.C. § 1413. Under Section 404 of the CWA, the Corps also has authority to permit the *discharge of dredged materials* into navigable waters. Id. § 1344(a). Because ODA jurisdiction includes waters seaward of the territorial sea baseline and because "navigable waters" under the CWA includes waters three nautical miles seaward of that baseline, the Corps' programs for disposal of dredged material overlap in the area three miles offshore. The Corps has published regulations addressing the issue of the overlapping jurisdiction of the CWA and the ODA in the territorial sea. All disposal in the ocean or territorial sea of material that has been excavated or dredged from navigable waters will be evaluated under the ODA. Only materials determined to be deposited primarily for the purpose of fill will be evaluated under section 404 of the CWA. See 33 C.F.R. § 336.0; see also 53 Fed. Reg. 14,902, 14,905 (1988).

Whether a permit for dredged spoil disposal is evaluated under the CWA or the ODA can be significant. First, although the criteria for evaluation are virtually the same, the ODA requires that the Corps "make an independent determination as to the need for the dumping[,] * * * other possible methods of disposal[,] and * * * appropriate locations for the dumping." 33 U.S.C. § 1413(b). The CWA does not have a comparable requirement.

For comprehensive coverage of ocean dumping regulations, including the relationship between the Ocean Dumping Act and the London Dumping Convention, see A. Bakalian, Regulation and Control of United States Ocean Dumping: A Decade of Progress, An Appraisal for the Future, 8 Harv. Envtl. L. Rev. 193 (1984); S. Moore, Troubles in the High Seas: A New Era in the Regulation of U.S. Ocean Dumping, 22 Envtl. L. 913 (1992). See also D. Finn, Nuclear Waste Management Activities in the Pacific Basin and Regional Cooperation on the Nuclear Fuel Cycle, 13 Ocean Devel. & Int'l L. 213 (1983); D. Finn, Ocean Disposal of Radioactive Wastes: The Obligation of International Cooperation to Protect the Marine Environment, 21 Va. J. Int'l L. 621 (1981).

Notes and Questions

1. An important question is whether the long-range goal of the Ocean Dumping Act is to phase out all ocean dumping of wastes or to continue ocean dumping as a feasible disposal alternative under adequate regulation and control at least for dredged materials.

2.   Can ocean dumping of dredged materials affect the water quality or coastal zone of a state? If so, must the Corps' issuance of an ocean dumping permit or Corps' dumping of its own dredged materials be certified as complying with the state's water quality standards under Clean Water Act Section 401 discussed in Chapter 2 or consistent with the state's federally approved coastal zone management program as discussed in Chapter 3? see 33 U.S.C. § 1416(d); D. Christie, Coastal & Ocean Management Law in a Nutshell 288-89 (1994).

3.   Ocean incineration is regulated under the Ocean Dumping Act. The EPA denied Chemical Waste Management, Inc. (CWM) a permit to conduct a research burn at sea. 51 Fed. Reg. 20,344 (June 4, 1986). CWM proposed to burn 708,958 gallons of fuel oil containing 10-30% PCBs over a 19 day period at a site 104 miles east of the delaware river. The EPA decided to deny the permit pending promulgation of final ocean incineration regulations which address issues such as the application of other federal statutes, including the Coastal Zone Management Act (CZMA), performance and operational standards, and liability and financial responsibilities. In March 1986, CWM filed suit in the U.S. District Court for the District of Columbia challenging various conditions imposed by New Jersey in its CZMA consistency determination regarding the proposed burn. CWM also charged that the Commerce Department violated the CZMA by permitting Maryland, in whose waters none of the proposed activities would take place, to review CWM's permit application for consistency with the Maryland state coastal zone management program. The EPA's permit denial was upheld in Waste Management, Inc. v. United States Environmental Protection Agency, 669 F. Supp. 536 (D.D.C. 1987).   The EPA's interpretation of ocean incineration as dumping subject to regulation under the Ocean Dumping Act was upheld in Seaburn Inc. v. United States E.P.A, 712 F. Supp. 218 (D.D.C. 1989).

1993 amendments to the London Convention banned the ocean incineration dumping of industrial wastes and the dumping of low-level radioactive wastes. These bans are continued in the Convention's 1996 Protocol described above.

Note on MARPOL Annex V

The United States Senate, in December 1987, unanimously approved MARPOL Annex V (regulations for the Prevention of Pollution by Garbage from Ships), which entered into force 12 months later. Annex V governs the disposal of garbage generated on board vessels into the sea. It prohibits the disposal of all plastics, including but not limited to synthetic ropes, synthetic fishing nets, and plastic garbage bags (regulation 3 (1)(a)). It further regulates the disposal of garbage into the sea by limiting garbage disposal to 25 nautical miles for floatable dunnage, lining, and packing materials, 12 nautical miles for unground food wastes and other garbage (reg. 3 (1)(b)), and 3 nautical miles for ground non-plastic or food waste.

There are three exceptions to the discharge provisions: (1) disposal necessary for the purpose of securing the safety of the ship or saving life at sea; (2) escape resulting from damage to a ship or its equipment; and (3) accidental loss of synthetic fishing nets or synthetic material incidental to the repair of such nets (reg. 6).

The prohibitions apply to all ships and to fixed or floating platforms engaged in mineral exploration, exploitation, and associated offshore processing. Annex V also specifies that governments party to the convention "undertake to ensure the provision" for facilities at ports and terminals for the reception of garbage, without causing undue delay to ships and according to the needs of the ships using them" (reg. 7 (1)). Special areas can be identified under Annex V which have more stringent regulations.

To implement MARPOL Annex V, the Marine Plastic Pollution Research and Control Act of 1987 (33 U.S.C. §§ 1901-1912) took effect on December 31, 1988. The Coast Guard has issued extensive regulations implementing Annex V and the act. The regulations apply to marine craft of any size and offshore platforms. Disposal of plastic wastes at sea is prohibited and other waste discharges are restricted. The National Oceanic and Atmospheric Administration has published a guidebook for ports in meeting their responsibilities under Annex V. See generally T. Brillat & M. Liffmann, The Implications of MARPOL Annex V on the Management of Ports and Coastal Communities, 19 Coastal Management 371 (1991).

B. POINT SOURCE DISCHARGES FROM LAND AND OFFSHORE FACILITIES

At the same time the Ocean Dumping Act was pending, Congress was in the middle of a struggle to pass sweeping FWPCA (CWA) amendments. This water pollution legislation, passed into law over President Nixon's veto in October 1972, had as its original goal the elimination of polluting discharges into navigable waters by 1985. While much of this legislation was designed to deal with the nation's fresh and estuarine waters, see, e.g., California Public Interest Research Group v. Shell Oil Co., 840 F. Supp. 712 (N.D. Cal. 1993), involving oil refinery selenium discharges into San Francisco Bay, two sections deal specifically with ocean discharges: Section 403 (33 U.S.C. § 1343) regulates the offshore discharge of nondredged materials from onshore outfall pipes and other point sources except vessels. See, e.g., United States v. Weitzenhoff, 35 F.3d 1275 (9th Cir. 1993), cert. denied 513 U.S. 1128 (1995) (criminal prosecution for toxic sludge discharges into ocean off Honolulu). Section 404 (33 U.S.C. § 1344) regulates discharges of dredged materials seaward three nautical miles and authorizes the Corps of Engineers to issue permits for the discharge of dredged or fill materials at Environmental Protection Agency specified disposal sites in navigable waters. Section 404 was discussed extensively in Chapter Two.

Section 403 calls for prevention of unreasonable degradation of the marine environment and authorizes the use of effluent limitations established by the federal Environmental Protection Agency (EPA), including a prohibition of discharge, if necessary, to ensure this goal. Although Section 403 of the CWA and Section 102 of the Ocean Dumping Act are similar, they are not identical. In essence, however, the Ocean Dumping Act applies to dumping from vessels into ocean waters and does not apply to discharges from pipes and outfalls, which are subject to control under the CWA. All such discharges seaward of the inner boundary of the United States territorial sea are subject to Section 403 requirements.

Section 301 of the CWA makes unlawful the unpermitted "discharge of any pollutant by any person" except in compliance with the terms of that and other specifically enumerated sections. Thus, among other things, Section 301 prohibits the discharge of untreated sewage. Permit criteria developed pursuant to Section 403 supplement Section 301 requirements and are applicable to permit proceedings authorized by Section 402 as well as to municipal marine dischargers seeking a modification of the normally applicable secondary sewage treatment requirements provided by Section 301(h). See City of San Diego v. Whitman, 242 F.3d 1097 (9th Cir. 2001).

The administrative framework of the CWA differs fundamentally from that provided in the Ocean Dumping Act. The Ocean Dumping Act is premised on a federally run program and explicitly preempts state regulatory activity. With certain exceptions, the CWA focuses on state pollution control programs which are reviewed and approved by the EPA, thus giving states permit authority over point sources of pollution seaward to three nautical miles. See Puget Soundkeeper Alliance v. Washington DOE, 9 P.3d 892 (Wash. App. 2000); Pacific Legal Foundation v. Costle, 586 F.2d 650, 655 (9th Cir. 1978) judgment reversed on other grounds, 445 U.S. 198 (1980), rehearing denied 446 U.S.

947(1980). Beyond three nautical miles, the EPA administers the discharge permit processes for outer continental shelf (OCS) oil and gas facilities, see, e.g., BP Exploration & Oil, Inc. v. Environmental Protection Agency, 66 F.3d 784 (6th Cir. 1995), deepwater ports, see 33 U.S.C. § 1502(10), ocean thermal energy conversion facilities, see 42 U.S.C. § 9117(f), and other offshore facilities, see 33 U.S.C. § 1316. See also Sierra Club, Lone Star Chapter v. Cedar Point Oil Co., 73 F.3d 546 (5th Cir. 1996); cert. denied, 519 U.S. 811 (1996), and Texas Oil & Gas Ass'n v. EPA, 161 F.3d 923 (5th Cir. 1998.) (discharges from offshore oil and gas operations in state waters).

C. POLLUTION FROM OTHER LAND-BASED ACTIVITIES

Worldwide, about 70 to 80 percent of marine pollution comes from land-based activities (LBA) rather than vessels. These activities include industrial and sewage point source discharges like those in the previous section and more dispersed runoff pollution into rivers, estuaries, and the ocean from agriculture, forestry, mining, and urban development. The international and United States legal responses to LBA pollution, especially the runoff type, are much less developed than for vessels. Articles 207(1) and 213 of the 1982 LOS Convention very generally obligate nations party to the convention to adopt laws "to prevent, reduce, and control pollution of the marine environment" from land-based point sources and runoff. Paragraphs 17.24 through 17.29 of Agenda 21 produced by the 1992 United Nations Conference on Environment and Development (U.N. Doc. A/CONF. 151/26 (1992) contain recommendations for national action as do the 1985 Montreal Guidelines for the Protection of the Marine Environment Against Pollution from Land-Based Sources (UNEP/GC.13/9/Add.3, UNEP/GC/DEC/13/1811, UNEP ELPG No. 7 (1985) issued by the United Nations Environment Program (UNEP). More detailed is UNEP's 1995 Global Programme of Action for the Protection of the Marine Environment from Land-Based Activities (UNEP (OCA)/LBA/IG.2/7). See J. Karau, D. Vanderzwaag, & P. Wells, The Global Programme of Action for the Protection of the Marine Environment from Land-Based Activities: A Cacophony of Sounds, Will the World Listen?, in E. Borgese, A. Chircop, M. Mcconnell, & J. Morgan, eds., Ocean Yearbook 13 (1997).

Nine multilateral regional conventions for specific ocean areas address pollution from land-based activities (LBA) including the Cartagena Convention for the Caribbean Region discussed above to which the United States is a party. See L. Guruswamy & B. Hendricks, International Environmental Law in a Nutshell 237-40 (1997).

In the United States, regulation of both the point source (discussed in Section B above) and the runoff components of LBA pollution occurs primarily under the CWA. CWA runoff regulatory programs include those for concentrated animal feeding operations (see Concerned Area Residents for the Environment v. Southview Farm, 34 F.3d 114 (2d Cir. 1994) cert. denied 514 U.S. 1082 (1995), combined sewer overflows (see Northwest Environmental Advocates v. City of Portland, 56 F.3d 979 (9th Cir. 1995), cert. denied 518 U.S. 1018 (1996)), and Stormwater (See Molokai Chamber of Commerce v. Kukui (Molokai), Inc., 891 F. Supp. 1389 (D. Hawaii 1995)). Other runoff pollution sources are addressed as "nonpoint sources" (NPS) through the state-implemented land use planning and pollution prevention process of CWA Section 319 (33 U.S.C. § 1329) and the coastal NPS control provisions of the federal Coastal Zone Management Act (CZMA) (16 U.S.C. § 1455(b). The latter requires state design and implementation of enforceable NPS pollution management measures against a broad range of NPS sources and includes federal consistency requirements paralleling those of CZMA Section 307 (16 U.S.C. § 1456) discussed in Chapter Three. When the cumulative impact of point and nonpoint source pollution in a particular water body results in a violation of its state-established CWA ambient water quality standards, the CWA's complex total maximum daily load (TMDL) process (see 33 U.S.C. § 1313(d) can be invoked to force reductions in both types of pollution. See Dioxin/Organochlorine Center v. Clarke, 57 F.3d 1517 (9th Cir. 1995) (EPA imposed TMDL for dioxin in Columbia River upheld).

SECTION 5. AREA-BASED MANAGEMENT OF COASTAL AND OCEAN WATERS

A. BACKGROUND ON THE CONCEPT OF AREA-BASED MANAGEMENT

Area-based management is commonly practiced on units of land such as parks, national forests, wilderness areas, and municipal zones, but only 1% of the global marine environment has been separated from surrounding waters into discrete management areas. Generally called "marine protected areas" or "marine sanctuaries," these spatial oceanic set-asides vary greatly in management and enforcement regimes, and even such basic parameters as definition, category (purpose), and scope. There is a national and international trend to expand the use of marine protected areas in ocean resources conservation. If established and implemented correctly, marine protected areas may prove to be powerful tools for achieving many important goals. Among those goals are pollution abatement, conservation of important habitats, fisheries and marine wildlife, preservation of biodiversity, protection of cultural and historic resources such as native american artifacts and shipwrecks, and education of researchers and the public.

(1.) Elements of Marine Protected Areas

(a.) Definitions

There are many definitions of marine protected areas and marine sanctuaries available, but two are particularly important. The international community mostly refers to the World Conservation Union's (IUCN) definition for "marine protected area," defined as: any area of intertidal or subtidal terrain, together with its overlying water and associated flora, fauna, historical or cultural features, which has been reserved by law, or other effective means, to protect part or all of the marine environment.

From a U.S. National perspective, President Clinton's Executive Order No.13158, quoted further below, defined "Marine Protected Area" as:

> any area of the marine environment that has been reserved by federal, state, territorial, tribal, or local laws or regulations to provide lasting protection for part or all of the natural and cultural resources therein.

(b.) Categories

The many different categories of marine protected areas may correspond with the purposes set forth at the time of establishment or may relate to the entity in charge of managing the area. Often, the "purpose" categories are actually subcategories within a larger management infrastructure. For example, national marine sanctuaries, discussed below, are one type of marine protected area in the waters of the United States already existing under federal law. Zones within the borders of a national marine sanctuary may be created and regulated in different fashions; i.e., Particular activities including fishing, biodiversity conservation, recreation, and oil and gas exploration may be assigned to sectioned-off areas of the map, and each area may then have its own rules and regulations attached. Some national parks are also considered marine protected areas; they may actually be located within the boundaries of a national marine sanctuary (e.g. Channel Islands National Park is within Channel Islands National Marine Sanctuary). State governments may establish marine protected areas in the 3-mile limit of the state territorial waters, and may work with the federal government to manage larger marine protected areas that span both federal and state waters.

A marine reserve is another, more restrictive type of marine protected area, which can be as large as the entire marine protected area or may only be a zone within the larger marine protected area. Within a marine reserve, some or all of the biological resources are protected from removal or disturbance, virtually prohibiting all human activities. Marine reserves implemented for the purpose of protecting all living marine resources through various prohibitions on human activities are often called ecological reserves; an example of an ecological reserve is the Western Sambos Ecological Reserve within the Florida Keys National Marine Sanctuary. Marine reserves implemented for the purpose of conserving fisheries, also called no take or fishery reserves, are often very controversial when proposed because stakeholders such as commercial fishermen and others who may follow more traditional notion of freedom of the seas view these no-take zones as "fencing off the ocean," infringements on their inherent rights to fish under freedom of the seas.

However, fishery reserves are viewed as necessary by some in order to provide insurance for continuance of the ocean's species. Traditional fisheries quotas based on stock assessments have historically been set too high due to difficulties in population estimation and political pressure, especially considering the fact that there are significant problems with bycatch of non-target stocks closely associated with the target species. In theory, once a fishery reserve is functioning well, a spillover effect occurs where catch levels outside the reserve increase in both quantity and quality. In short, fishery reserves create more and bigger fish because reproducing individuals within the reserve are left alone to replenish the population and young within reserves are able to grow to a larger size before being caught. This eventually translates into maintaining the range of sizes available in the genetic pool instead of causing a population to become smaller over time by constantly over-harvesting only the larger sized individuals. In the short term, there is little doubt that fishery reserves do impact the ability of some stakeholders such as commercial fishermen to maintain a living. Some programs such as buybacks and other economic incentives may exist to alleviate these socioeconomic effects. It is also worth noting that several studies have demonstrated the necessity of involving stakeholders in the designation and management process as early as possible. Observations of various processes have indicated that stakeholder cooperation is not only necessary for the eventual success of marine reserves because often agency budgets run low for enforcement, but also because people such as commercial fishermen who have been fishing a particular area for several years represent a valuable source of knowledge that should not go unused when designing and implementing a fishery reserve.

Successfully-run marine protected areas exist worldwide, including the marine protected areas of New Zealand and the Great Barrier Reef of Australia. Studying the relative successes and failures of other countries in establishing marine protected areas will be absolutely essential to designing and refining the marine protected areas in the waters of the United States.

(2.) *National Expansion Of Marine Protected Areas*

> **Executive Order No. 13158**
> **May 26, 2000, 65 F.R. 34909**
> **Marine Protected Areas**

* * *

1. Purpose. This executive order will help protect the significant natural and cultural resources within the marine environment for the benefit of present and future generations by strengthening and expanding the nation's system of marine protected areas (MPAs). An expanded and strengthened comprehensive system of marine protected areas throughout the marine environment would enhance the conservation of our nation's natural and cultural marine heritage and the ecologically and economically sustainable use of the marine environment for future generations. To this end, the purpose of this order is to, consistent with domestic and international law: (a) strengthen the management, protection, and conservation of existing marine protected areas and establish new or expanded MPAs; (b) develop a scientifically based, comprehensive national system of MPAs representing diverse U.S. marine ecosystems, and the nation's natural and cultural resources; and (c) avoid causing harm to MPAs through federally conducted, approved, or funded activities.

2. Definitions. For the purposes of this order:

(A) "marine protected area" means any area of the marine environment that has been reserved by federal, state, territorial, tribal, or local laws or regulations to provide lasting protection for part of all of the natural and cultural resources therein.

(B) "Marine environment" means those areas of coastal and ocean waters, the great lakes and their connecting waters, and submerged lands thereunder over which the United States exercises jurisdiction, consistent with international law.

(C) The term "United States" includes the several states, the District of Columbia, the Commonwealth of Puerto Rico, the Virgin Islands of the United States, American Samoa, Guam, and the Commonwealth of the Northern Mariana Islands.

3. MPA establishment, protection, and management. Each federal agency whose authorities provide for the establishment or management of MPAs shall take appropriate actions to enhance or expand protection of existing MPAs and establish or recommend, as appropriate, new MPAs. Agencies implementing this section shall consult with the agencies identified in subsection 4(a) of this order, consistent with existing requirements.

4. National system of MPAs.

(A) to the extent permitted by law and subject to the availability of appropriations, the Department of Commerce and the Department of the Interior, in consultation with the Department of Defense, the Department of State, the United States Agency for International Development, the Department of Transportation, the Environmental Protection Agency, the National Science Foundation, and other pertinent federal agencies shall develop a national system of MPAs. They shall coordinate and share information, tools and strategies, and provide guidance to enable and encourage the use of the following in the exercise of each agency's respective authority to further enhance and expand protection of existing MPAs and to establish or recommend new MPAs, as appropriate:

(1) science-based identification and prioritization of natural and cultural resources for additional protection;

(2) integrated assessments of ecological linkages among MPAs including ecological reserves in which consumptive uses of resources are prohibited, to provide synergistic benefits;

(3) a biological assessment of the minimum area where consumptive uses would be prohibited that is necessary to preserve representative habitats in different geographic areas of the marine environment;

(4) an assessment of threats and gaps in levels of protection currently afforded to natural and cultural resources, as appropriate;

(5) practical, science-based criteria and protocols for monitoring and evaluating the effectiveness of MPAs;

(6) identification of emerging threats and user conflicts affecting MPAs and appropriate, practical, and equitable management solutions, including effective enforcement strategies, to eliminate or reduce such threats and conflicts;

(7) assessment of the economic effects of the preferred management solutions; and

(8) identification of opportunities to improve linkages with, and technical assistance to, international marine protected area programs.

(B) In carrying out the requirements of Section Four of this order, the Department of Commerce and the Department of the Interior shall consult with those states that contain portions of the marine environment, the Commonwealth of Puerto Rico, the Virgin Islands of the United States, American Samoa, Guam, and the Commonwealth of Northern Mariana Islands, tribes, regional fishery management councils, and other entities, as appropriate, to promote coordination of federal, state, territorial, and tribal actions to establish and manage MPAs.

(C) In carrying out the requirements of this section, the Department of Commerce and the Department of the Interior shall seek the expert advice and recommendations of non-federal scientists, resource managers, and other interested persons and organizations through a marine protected area federal advisory committee.   The committee shall be established by the Department of Commerce.

(D) The Secretary of Commerce and the Secretary of the Interior shall establish and jointly manage a website for information on MPAs and federal agency reports required by this order. They shall also publish and maintain a list of MPAs that meet the definition of MPA for the purpose of this order. [http://www.mpa.gov]

(E) The Department of Commerce's National Oceanic and

Atmospheric Administration shall establish a Marine Protected Area Center to carry out, in cooperation with the Department of the Interior, the requirements of subsection 4(a) of this order, and partner with governmental and nongovernmental entities to conduct necessary research, analysis, and exploration. The goal of the MPA center shall be, in cooperation with the Department of the Interior, to develop a framework for a national system of MPAs, and to provide federal, state, territorial, tribal, and local governments with information, technologies, and strategies to support the system. This national system framework and the work of the MPA Center is intended to support, not interfere with, agencies' independent exercise of their own existing authorities.

(F) To better protect beaches, coasts, and the marine environment from pollution, the Environmental Protection Agency (EPA), relying upon existing Clean Water Act authorities, shall expeditiously propose new science-based regulations, as necessary, to ensure appropriate levels of protection for the marine environment. Such regulations may include the identification of areas that warrant additional pollution protections and the enhancement of marine water quality standards. The EPA shall consult with the federal agencies identified in subsection 4(a) of this order, states, territories, tribes, and the public in the development of such new regulations.

5. Agency responsibilities. Each federal agency whose actions affect the natural or cultural resources that are protected by an MPA shall identify such actions. To the extent permitted by law and to the maximum extent practicable, each federal agency, in taking such actions, shall avoid harm to the natural and cultural resources that are protected by an MPA. In implementing this section, each federal agency shall refer to the MPAs identified under subsection 4(d) of this order.

6. Accountability. Each federal agency that is required to take actions under this order shall prepare and make public annually a concise description of actions taken by it in the previous year to implement the order, including a description of written comments by any person or organization stating that the agency has not complied with this order and a response to such comments by the agency.

7. International law. Federal agencies taking actions pursuant to this executive order must act in accordance with international law and with Presidential Proclamation 5928 of December 27, 1988 [43 U.S.C.A. § 1331 note], on the territorial sea of the United States of America, Presidential Proclamation 5030 of March 10, 1983 [16 U.S.C.A. § 1453 note], on the Exclusive Economic Zone of the United States of America, and Presidential Proclamation 7219 of September 2, 1999 [43 U.S.C.A. § 1331 note], on the contiguous zone of the United States.

* * *

William J. Clinton

B. NATIONAL MARINE SANCTUARIES

The National Marine Sanctuaries Program was created in 1972 as part of the Marine Protection, Research, and Sanctuaries Act. 16 U.S.C. § 1431 et seq. The purpose of the program is to identify marine areas of special national or international significance due to their resource or human-use values and to provide authority for comprehensive conservation and management of such areas where existing regulatory authority is inadequate to assure coordinated conservation and management. National or international significance is determined by assessment of:

> the area's natural resource and ecological qualities, including its contribution to biological productivity, maintenance of ecosystem structure, maintenance of ecologically or commercially important or threatened species or species assemblages, maintenance of critical habitat of endangered species, and the biogeographic representation of the site. * * *

Id. § 1433(b)(1)(A). The act particularly identifies the importance of maintaining natural biological communities * * * and to protect * * * natural habitats, populations, and ecological processes." Id. § 1431(b)(3). Designation of a marine area as a sanctuary, in itself, does not prohibit all development, but does require special use permits from the Department of Commerce (DOC) to authorize specific activities that are compatible with the purposes of the sanctuary. Id. § 1440.

The National Marine Sanctuaries Program got off to a slow start. The first sanctuary, the U.S.S. Monitor National Marine Sanctuary (NMS), was not designated by the DOC until 1975. During this first phase of the NMS program, designation was a slow process and sanctuaries included relatively small areas of ocean space within their boundaries and were managed for narrowly defined purposes. Eight sanctuaries were designated during the period between 1975-88: the U.S.S. Monitor, Key Largo and Looe Key off Florida, Gray's Reef off Georgia, the Channel Islands, Gulf of Farallones, and Cordell Banks in California, and Fagatele Bay in the American Samoas. Criticism of the designation process and the effectiveness of the NMS program led to reassessment of the marine sanctuaries program.

In 1988 and 1992, the program was amended substantially. NOAA was given authority to review federal agency actions that may affect a sanctuary resource. Important provisions for enforcement and liability were added that give sanctuary designation and sanctuary management plans greater authority. The amendments provide that it is unlawful to:

(1) destroy, cause the loss of, or injure any sanctuary resource managed under law or regulations for that sanctuary;

(2) possess, sell, offer for sale, purchase, import, export, deliver, carry, transport, or ship by any means any sanctuary resource taken in violation of this section. * * *

Id. § 1436. A "sanctuary resource" is "any living or nonliving resource * * * that contributes to the * * * value of the sanctuary." Id. § 1432(8). The amendments create a rebuttable presumption that all sanctuary resources on board a vessel were taken in violation of the act or regulations. Id. § 1437(e)(4). Enforcement authorities are granted broad powers to board, search, and seize vessels, and impose penalties of up to $100,000 per violation per day. Id. § 1437. In addition, persons damaging or injuring any sanctuary resources are liable for response costs and damages, with retention of damage awards for restoration work. Id. § 1442. Damages from groundings, oil spills, and toxic pollution are covered. The 1984 grounding of the Cypriot M/V Wellwood in the Key Largo National Marine Sanctuary and the 1987 sinking of the oil tanker M/V Puerto Rican near the Gulf of Farallones National Marine Sanctuary had demonstrated the need for such a liability regime. See United States v. M/V Jacquelyn L., 100 F.3d 1520 (11th Cir. 1996); United States v. M/V Miss Beholden, 856 F. Supp. 668 (S.D. Fl. 1994).

The act also allows NOAA to review any federal agency action that might impact a sanctuary resource and requires NOAA to review and revise sanctuary management plans every five years. Id. §§ 1434(d),(e).

The designation process for marine sanctuaries has been streamlined, but Congress has also accelerated the process by designating or ordering the designation of certain sanctuaries. During this second phase of sanctuary designation, the Florida Keys, Monterey Bay, Stellwagen Bank, the Hawaiian Islands Humpback Whale, the Flower Garden Banks, Olympic Coast, and Thunder Bay national marine sanctuaries have been created.

All these sanctuaries differ from those designated earlier in two ways: 1) their size, and 2) their management approach. The Stellwagen Bank Sanctuary bans sand and gravel mining in the rich fisheries and whale calving grounds off the coast of Massachusetts, Pub. L. 102-587, while the Hawaiian Humpback Whale Sanctuary includes important breeding, calving, and nursing areas for the endangered humpback whale and requires development of a comprehensive management plan. Id. The Flower Garden Banks Sanctuary includes coral reefs and rich marine life 110 miles south of the Texas coast. Pub. L. 102-251. Furthermore, Congress finalized designation of the Monterey Bay Sanctuary, banning all oil and gas activities, Pub. L. 102-587; amended the Florida Keys Sanctuary Act to prioritize research needs, establish long-term ecological monitoring, and implement a water quality program, id.; prohibited oil and gas activities within the Olympic Coast Sanctuary off Washington State; Id.; and authorized the President to establish the 100,000 square nautical mile Northwestern Hawaiian Islands Coral Reef Reserve pending its designation as a national marine sanctuary, P.L. 106-513. President Clinton's executive orders creating the reserve restrict some activities throughout the reserve and establish Reserve Preservation areas around certain islands, atolls, and banks in which all resource consumptive uses are restricted. See 66 Fed. Reg. 7395 (Jan. 18, 2001); 65 Fed. Reg. 76903 (Dec. 4, 2000). In addition, President Clinton issued an executive order directing federal agencies to work closely with local, state, territorial, tribal and other stakeholders to build existing marine protected areas into a national system. 65 Fed. Reg. 34909 (May 26, 2000). The excutive order defined "marine protected area" (MPA) very broadly to mean "any area of the marine environment that has been reserved by Federal, State, territorial, tribal, or local laws or regulations to provide lasting protection for part or all of the natural and cultural resources therein." Id. For state or territorial MPAs containing coral reefs, assistance in the development of management strategies may be available under the Coral Reef Conservation Act of 2000; Title II P.L. 106-562.

TABLE 8.1 SANCTUARIES IN THE U.S. MARINE SANCTUARIES
PROGRAM.

Year Designated	Sanctuary	Site of Protected Area (In Square Miles)	Type of Habitat	Key Species
1975	Monitor (North Carolina)	1	pelagic, open ocean, artificial reef (protection of Civil War sunken vessel	amberjack, black sea bass, red barbler, scad, corals, sea anemones, dolphin, sand tiger shark, sea urchins
1975	Key Largo* (Florida)	100	coral reefs, patch and bank reefs, mangrove-fringed shorelines and islands, sand flats, seagrass meadows	coral reef and associated reef species
1980	Channel Islands (California)	1,658	kelp forests, rocky shores, sandy beaches, seagrass, meadows, pelagic, open ocean, deep rocky reefs	California sea lion, elephant and harbor seals, blue & gray whales, dolphin, blue shark, brown pelican, western gull
1981	Gulf of the Farallones (California)	1,255	coastal beaches, rocky shores, mud and tidal flats, salt marsh, esteros, deep benthos, continental shelf and slope	dungeness crab, gray whale, steller sea lion, common murre, ashy storm-petrel

Year Designated	Sanctuary	Site of Protected Area (In Square Miles)	Type of Habitat	Key Species
1981	Gray's Reef (Georgia)	23	calcareous sandstone, sand bottom communities, tropical temperate reef	northern right whale, loggerhead sea turtle, barrel sponge, angelfish, ivory bush coral, grouper, black sea bass, coral reef and associated reef species
1981	Looe Key* (Florida)	5.32	coral reefs, patch and bank reefs, mangrove-fringed shorelines and islands, sand flats, seagrass meadows	coral reef and associated reef species
1986	Fagatele Bay (American Samoa)	0.25	tropical coral reef	crown-of-thorns starfish, blacktip reef shark, surgeon fish, hawksbill turtle, parrotfish, giant clam
1989	Cordell Bank (California)	526	rocky subtidal, pelagic, open ocean, soft sediment continental shelf and slope, seamount	krill, Pacific salmon, blue whale, Dall's porpoise, shearwater, albatross, rockfish
1990	Florida Keys (Florida)	3,674	coral reefs, patch and bank reefs, mangrove-fringed shorelines and islands, sand flats, seagrass meadows	brain and star coral, sea fan, loggerhead sponge, turtle grass, angel fish, spiny lobster, stone crab, grouper, tarpon

Year Designated	Sanctuary	Site of Protected Area (In Square Miles)	Type of Habitat	Key Species
1992	Flower Garden Banks (Texas/ Louisiana)	56	coral reefs, artificial reef, algal-sponge communities, brine seep, pelagic, open ocean	brain and star coral, manta ray, loggerhead turtle, hammerhead shark
1992	Monterey Bay (California)	5,328	pelagic, open ocean, sandy beaches, rocky shores, kelp forests, wetlands, submarine canyon	sea otter, gray whale, market squid, brown pelican, rockfish, giant kelp
1992	Hawaiian Islands (Hawaii)	1,300	humpback whale breeding, calving and nursing grounds, coral reefs, sandy beaches	humpback whale, pilot whale, hawaiian monk seal, spinner dolphin, green sea turtle, trigger fish, limu, cauliflower coral
1992	Stellwagen Bank (Massachusetts)	842	sand and gravel bank, muddy baisins, boulder fields, rocky ledges	northern right whale, humpback whale, storm petrel, white-sided dolphin, bluefin tuna, sea scallop, northern lobster
1994	Olympic Coast (Washington)	3,310	pelagic, open ocean, sandy and rocky shores, kelp forests, seastacks and islands	tufted puffin, bald eagle, northern sea otter, gray whale, humpback whale, Pacific salmon, dolphin

* Looe Key and Key Largo Marine Sanctuaries were incoporated into the Florida Keys National Marine Sanctuary

Source: Adapted from NOAA NOS. 1997. National Marine Sanctuaries Accomplishments Report.

Table 8.1 summarizes the key features of the first twelve sanctuaries to be created under the federal National Marine Sanctuaries Act. The newest national marine sanctuaries and reserves encompass extensive ocean areas under both federal and state jurisdiction. Designation of large ocean areas allows management of more of the activities that affect sanctuary resources and provides the opportunity to develop an ecosystem approach to resource management. Management plans deal with direct and indirect, as well as primary and secondary, effects on sanctuary resources. For example, the management plan for the Monterey Bay sanctuary includes a Water Quality Protection Program. That program includes an Agriculture and Rural Lands Plan to help farmers in the bay's inland watershed minimize the runoff into the bay's waters of polluting sediments and nutrients from fields and rural roads. International, as well as federal, state, and local cooperative programs are encouraged and advisory councils have become part of the management plan development process. For example, in May 2000, the International Maritime Organization approved a Monterey Bay Vessel Traffic Plan designed to facilitate safe, efficient travel by large vessels through the Monterey Bay, Gulf of the Farallones, and Channel Islands national marine sanctuaries off California. Because designation of such large areas affects numerous user groups, conflict management is an important part of plan development and implementation as the following Court opinion illustrates.

PERSONAL WATERCRAFT INDUSTRY ASSOCIATION V. DEPARTMENT OF COMMERCE

United States Court of Appeals, District of Columbia Circuit, 1995
48 F.3d 540

RANDOLPH, CIRCUIT JUDGE

These are cross-appeals from the District Court's judgment setting aside one of the regulations designed to protect and preserve the Monterey Bay National Marine Sanctuary off the central California coast. The regulation governs the use of "motorized personal watercraft"--jet skis, wet bikes, miniature speed boats, air boats, hovercraft, and the like--on the Sanctuary's waters. The District Court thought it arbitrary to regulate this sort of small craft without regulating other vessels. We reverse this portion of the Court's judgment.

I

The Monterey Bay National Marine Sanctuary encompasses 4000 square nautical miles of coastal and ocean waters, and the submerged lands thereunder. It is the nation's largest ocean sanctuary, spreading seaward as far as forty-six nautical miles, and extending along the California coast from the Gulf of Farallones in the north to San Simeon and Cambria Rock in the south. It encompasses the Monterey Peninsula, the "finest meeting of land and water in existence," so Robert Louis Stevenson believed. The area is home to thirty-one species of marine mammals, including the sea otter and twenty-one other threatened or endangered species protected under the Endangered Species Act, 16 U.S.C. §§ 1531-1544. There are large concentrations of whales, pinnipeds (e.g. seals) and seabirds. Fish stocks are substantial. Varieties of crustaceans and other invertebrates abound. Among the Sanctuary's diverse flora are forests of giant kelp growing from the seabed, with fronds towering to the surface as much as 175 feet above. Residents and visitors use the Sanctuary for kayaking, fishing, scuba diving, surfing, sailing, swimming, and other recreational activities.

Title III of the Marine Protection, Research, and Sanctuaries Act (the Act), as amended, 16 U.S.C. §§ 1431-1439, authorizes the Secretary of Commerce to designate as national marine sanctuaries discrete areas of the marine environment that are "of special national significance." 16 U.S.C. § 1433(a). In 1988, Congress directed the Secretary to issue a "notice of designation" under 16 U.S.C. § 1434(b)(1) for the waters in the vicinity of Monterey Bay "no later than December 31, 1989." Pub.L. No. 100- 627, § 205(a)(3), 102 Stat. 3213, 3217 (1988). The National Oceanic and Atmospheric Administration (NOAA), to whom the Secretary had delegated authority, complied, but not until August 3, 1990, when it published in the Federal Register a notice of proposed designation, proposed implementing regulations, and a draft environmental impact statement discussing options for managing the proposed sanctuary. 55 Fed.Reg. 31,786 (Aug. 3, 1990). The agency requested comments within sixty days (by October 2, 1990).

In June 1992, after three public hearings and after receiving more than 1200 comments, NOAA issued its Final Environmental Impact Statement and, on September 18, 1992, its final regulations formalizing the designation of the Monterey Bay National Marine Sanctuary. 57 Fed.Reg. 43,310 (Sept. 18, 1992); 15 C.F.R. pt. 944.

One of the final regulations, 15 C.F.R. § 944.5(a)(8), limits the operation of "motorized personal water craft," also known as "thrill craft," in the Monterey Bay Sanctuary to four designated zones and access routes, an area of fourteen square nautical miles. The regulation defines "motorized personal watercraft" as:

any motorized vessel that is less than fifteen feet in length as manufactured, is capable of exceeding a speed of fifteen knots, and has the capacity to carry not more than the operator and one other person while in operation. The term includes, but is not limited to, jet skis, wet bikes, surf jets, miniature speed boats, air boats and hovercraft.

15 C.F.R. § 944.3. NOAA's final regulations did not restrict the use of other types of vessels in the Monterey Bay Sanctuary. The agency stated that it was then working with the Coast Guard to determine whether such measures were needed. 57 Fed.Reg. at 43,311-12.

In July 1992, the Personal Watercraft Industry Association, an organization consisting of manufacturers and distributors, submitted comments to NOAA opposing the restrictions placed on personal watercraft. Thereafter the agency denied the Association's petition for rulemaking to rescind the "thrill craft" regulation. 58 Fed.Reg. 15,271 (Mar. 22, 1993).

* * *

On cross-motions for summary judgment, the District Court held that the restriction on personal watercraft was arbitrary and capricious because NOAA had treated personal watercraft differently from all other vessels without providing a sufficient explanation. Personal Watercraft Indus. Ass'n v. DEPArtment of Commerce, No. 93-1381, at 3 (D.D.C. Aug. 24, 1993).

* * *

The Association complains about a "study" NOAA used in determining where personal watercraft would be allowed within the Sanctuary, but it is hard to tell exactly what the complaint is. Only two paragraphs of the Association's fifty-page brief are devoted to this topic; the summary of argument ignores it entirely. The two paragraphs are under the following heading, which does not talk directly about the study: the "personal watercraft restrictions were developed after the comment period closed and never made available for public scrutiny and comment." Appellees' Brief at 47. That of course is true with respect to NOAA's final regulations, and indeed would be true in any rulemaking proceeding in which an agency formulated its final rules in response to comments. If the heading is supposed to capture a colorable argument, we fail to see it. "Rulemaking proceedings would never end if the agency's response to comments must always be made the subject of additional comments." Community Nutrition Inst. v. Block, 749 F.2d 50, 58 (D.C.Cir. 1984).

* * *

NOAA retained Dr. James W. Rote, a marine biologist and former Director of the Office of Habitat Protection at NOAA. Dr. Rote was to "gather information about current restrictions and current areas of motorized personal watercraft use in the proposed Monterey Bay National Marine Sanctuary area" and "to develop recommended zones to which motorized personal watercraft use might be restricted." In June and October 1991, Dr. Rote delivered his recommendations. The four zones he suggested were designed to encompass the areas with the highest amount of personal watercraft use. The results of Dr. Rote's study were included in the final rulemaking. 57 Fed.Reg. at 43,328- 29.

[handwritten margin note: maintain use]

* * *

The District Court agreed with the Association that the regulation treated "personal watercraft (which are narrowly defined) differently from all other vessels, and that this disparate treatment is arbitrary and unsupported by the factual record." Personal Watercraft Industry Ass'n, No. 93-1381, at 2. It is worth keeping in mind that we are dealing with a marine sanctuary and measures an agency thought were needed to protect and preserve it. The regulations did indeed single out personal watercraft from other kinds of vessels. Maybe the presence of other vessels was a cause for concern; as we shall see, NOAA thought it might be. This scarcely means that NOAA had to regulate them if it was to do anything about thrill craft. An agency does not have to "make progress on every front before it can make progress on any front." United States v. Edge Broadcasting Co., 509 U.S. 418, ----, (1993). Agencies often must contend with matters of degree. Regulations, in other words, are not arbitrary just because they fail to regulate everything that could be thought to pose any sort of problem. Las Vegas v. Lujan, 891 F.2d 927, 935 (D.C.Cir. 1989); Louisiana v. Verity, 853 F.2d 322, 332 (5th Cir. 1988). This is a common principle, well known not only in administrative law cases but also in constitutional cases raising equal protection challenges to economic regulation. See Williamson v. Lee Optical of Oklahoma Inc., 348 U.S. 483, 489 (1955). To it, the District Court here added a wrinkle--when an agency decides "to address several aspects of the problem itself in a single rulemaking, it must provide a reasoned basis for differential treatment of the various causes of the perceived problem." Personal Watercraft Industry Ass'n, No. 93-1381, at 4 n.2. This suggests that if an agency did a little, that would be permissible, but if it did more than a little, it had better have a good reason for not going all the way. We fail to see why it should matter whether the agency takes two steps instead of one, so long as it is heading in a proper direction. The patient has a headache, a sore throat and a hangnail. Are we to suppose that it would be arbitrary to treat only the headache and the sore throat in a single session, yet not be arbitrary to treat only the hangnail?

Before discussing this further, we ought to examine what made jet skis and other thrill craft the headache. The record is full of evidence that machines of this sort threatened the Monterey Bay National Marine Sanctuary. NOAA received written comments and testimony from marine scientists, researchers, federal agencies, state agencies, state and local governments, business organizations, and more than a hundred citizens on the issue of regulating these machines. Everyone agreed--personal watercraft interfered with the public's recreational safety and enjoyment of the Sanctuary and posed a serious threat to the Sanctuary's flora and fauna. The concept of a "sanctuary" entails elements of serenity, peace, and tranquility. Yet the commentaries described instances of personal watercraft operators harassing sea otters and other marine mammals, disturbing harbor seals, damaging the Sanctuary's kelp forests, menacing swimmers, divers, kayakers, and other recreational users, and generally disrupting the esthetic enjoyment of the Sanctuary. All concerned recommended either prohibiting personal watercraft outright or restricting them to specific areas in the Sanctuary. No one urged NOAA to do nothing about the problem.

When NOAA acted, did it satisfactorily explain itself? The Administrative Procedure Act required it to give a "concise general statement" of the regulation's "basis and purpose." 5 U.S.C. § 553(c). Here is part of what NOAA said:

> The small size, maneuverability and high speed of these craft is [*NOAA's explanation*] what causes these craft to pose a threat to resources. Resources such as sea otters and seabirds are either unable to avoid these craft or are frequently alarmed enough to significantly modify their behavior such as cessation of feeding or abandonment of young. Also other, more benign, uses of the Sanctuary such as sailing, kayaking, surfing and diving are interfered with during the operation of [personal watercraft].

* * *

> This regulation is intended to provide enhanced resource protection by prohibiting operation of motorized personal watercraft in areas of high marine mammal and seabird concentrations, kelp forest areas, river mouths, estuaries, lagoons and other similar areas where sensitive marine resources are concentrated and most vulnerable to disturbance and other injury from personal watercraft.

57 Fed. Reg. at 43,314, 43,321. The first paragraph is the "basis," the second the "purpose." The statement is "concise" and it is "general."

Despite NOAA's evident compliance with the Administrative Procedure Act, the Association rails against "NOAA's unsupported and unexplained distinction between personal watercraft and other similar and larger vessels," Appellees' Brief at 32. The Association is very much mistaken and its citation of, for example, National Wildlife Federation v. Costle, 629 F.2d 118, 133-35 (D.C.Cir. 1980), is therefore off the mark. NOAA did explain and support the distinction. It said that personal watercraft were small, highly maneuverable, and fast, and it indicated that they operated close to shore, in areas of high concentrations of kelp forests, marine mammals and sea birds. That differentiated all larger craft, all slower craft, all less maneuverable craft, and all craft that did not tend to use the same areas in the same manner. As if this were not enough, NOAA also stated why it had decided not to regulate vessels other than personal watercraft *at this time*. NOAA said that it was working with the United States Coast Guard "to determine the need for additional measures to ensure protection of Sanctuary resources and qualities from vessel traffic," adding that:

> These consultations aim to determine which resources are most at risk, which vessel traffic practices are most threatening and which regulations or restrictions would be most appropriate to alleviate potential threats, including those, if any, from foreign vessels.

57 Fed. Reg. at 43,311.

There for all who read the Federal Register are the reasons for NOAA's regulating personal watercraft and for not then regulating other vessels--the first category posed a clear problem, the rest needed further study, which the agency had undertaken.

The Act authorized NOAA to set down rules for the Sanctuary that it determined "may be necessary and reasonable." 16 U.S.C. § 1434(a)(1)(A). The record amply supports NOAA's judgment of September 1992, that restricting thrill craft was then necessary and reasonable. It may turn out that regulating other vessels will also be necessary and reasonable. NOAA has yet to make that determination. But nothing in Title III of the Marine Protection, Research, and Sanctuaries Act, or in the Administrative Procedure Act, or in any judicial decision, forces an agency to refrain from solving one problem while it ponders what to do about others.

* * *

As NOAA pointed out in its Final Environmental Impact Statement, personal watercraft use was a relatively new phenomenon and local governments had only just begun issuing laws to minimize conflicts between this form of water sport, and other uses of marine resources. Many local officials urged NOAA to restrict jet skis; the towns of Capitola and Pacifica, and the County of Santa Cruz had their own restrictions, but these of course applied only within their jurisdictions. NOAA's regulatory jurisdiction--over 4000 square nautical miles--was considerably more comprehensive. As one would expect, the agency therefore determined that regulating personal watercraft throughout the Sanctuary was needed to fill what would otherwise have been a "major gap in the regulatory regime governing activities in the area."

* * *

NOAA's personal watercraft regulation, 15 C.F.R. § 944.5(a)(8), is not arbitrary and capricious, and the District Court's judgment is therefore

Reversed.

Notes and Questions

1. If the designation for a sanctuary is silent on floating nuclear power plants, would the siting of such plants within the sanctuary be subject to regulation by the Secretary of Commerce?

2. Does authority to regulate activities occurring within a sanctuary include the power to meet threats from outside the sanctuary? For example, an oil spill from a source outside the sanctuary could drift across the sanctuary boundary. Ultimately, must the Secretary depend on the cooperation of other agencies to protect marine sanctuaries?

3. What values is the marine sanctuary program intended to protect? The Act states that preserving esthetic values is one reason for establishing marine sanctuaries. Could a marine sanctuary be used to protect some particularly pleasing ocean vista from the impact of visible drilling platforms?

In a tentative ruling by the U.S. District Court for the Central District of California, Judge Alicemarie Stotler rejected a claim by the Western Oil & Gas Association (WOGA) challenging the designation of the Channel Islands National Marine Sanctuary. WOGA v. Byrne, CV No. 82-5034-AHS (March 22, 1985). WOGA had asserted that the designation of the Sanctuary and the issuance of regulations which prohibit new oil and gas development within the boundaries of the Sanctuary were invalid. The claim was based on a theory that the designation and regulations had caused substantial injury to several of WOGA's members. The Court's March 1985 tentative ruling rejected these claims, saying that WOGA had failed to show that the decision by the Secretary of Commerce to designate the Sanctuary and promulgate the "no oil" regulations was arbitrary, capricious, or an abuse of discretion. Basing its ruling on statutory construction and legislative history, the Court found that the Secretary did indeed have the discretion to designate sanctuaries and promulgate regulations that would reasonably promote their purposes. Furthermore, the Court found the "no oil" regulations a necessary step to protect against oil spills, aural and visual disturbances, and air and water pollution. All of these negative aspects, wrote Judge Stotler, are attendant upon normal hydrocarbon operations and can be prohibited by regulations designed to provide comprehensive management of waters designated as marine sanctuaries.

In another Channel Islands Sanctuary oil and gas dispute, the California Coastal Commission's consistency objection to Union Oil's exploration plan to drill two new wells within the boundaries of the sanctuary was overruled by the Secretary of Commerce on appeal. The Secretary found the exploration plan to be consistent with the objectives of the CZMA and allowed federal agencies to approve exploration activities as described in the Union Oil exploration plan. 50 Fed. Reg. 872 (Jan. 7, 1985).

Could designation of a sanctuary ever result in restrictions on commercial and recreational fishing and diving activities? See Craft v. National Park Service, 34 F.3d 918 (9th Cir. 1994); United States v. Fisher, 22 F.3d 262 (11th Cir. 1994); United States v. Fisher, 977 F. Supp. 1193 (S.D. Fla. 1997) (injunctions and civil penalties imposed on divers and salvors for altering sanctuary seabeds without permits).

Which resource values should have priority in the designation of marine sanctuaries? Other factors taken into account in the designation of marine sanctuaries have included the potential threat to the resources of the area, the significance of the area for research, the value of the area in complementing other areas or programs with similar objectives, the beauty of the area, the economic value of the area which might have to be forgone if designated a sanctuary, and the economic benefit to be derived from protecting the area.

4. Given that the marine sanctuaries program provides only a limited geographical foundation for comprehensive ocean management, what other approaches are possible? Should the

multiple-use, sustained-yield approach to public lands management onshore be extended offshore to the ocean waters and seabeds subject to United States jurisdiction? Should ocean waters be managed separately from seabed resources? Should the legal regime governing the territorial sea simply be extended seaward? Or should the present outer continental shelf lands management regime merely be broadened to make it more comprehensive? Where should the balance between development and preservation be struck? How should the interests of national security and private industry be accounted for? How much management responsibility should each level of government federal, state, and local exercise? These are but a few of the important questions to be answered in the evolution of United States ocean management. See B. Cicin-Sain & R. Knecht, The Future of U.S. Ocean Policy (1999); B. Cician-Sain & R. Knecht, Integrated Coastal & Ocean Management (1998); B. Cicin-Sain, M. Hershman, R. Hildreth, & J. Isaacs, Improving Ocean Management Capacity in the Pacific Coast Region: State and Regional Perspectives (1990); U.S. Department of Commerce, Ocean Management: Seeking a New Perspective 41-45, 56 (1980).

If federal legislation were to achieve a modicum of integrated management authority over ocean resources under United States jurisdiction, what would be the next legal step in managing the ocean as an ecological unit? For an example of how emerging theories of sea use planning, integrated marine policy, large marine ecosystems, and exclusive economic zone governance can be applied to specific ocean regions, see R. Hildreth, Regional Ocean Resources Management, 3 Coastal Zone '91 at 2583.

Can internationally integrated management be achieved by treaty? Did President Reagan's rejection of the United Nations Law of the Sea Convention because of its provisions on deep seabed mining necessarily bode ill for the future of United States participation in international ocean management?

The Oceans Act of 2000 (P.L. 106-256) established a commission to review U.S. ocean policy and report its recommendations in late 2002. What specific ocean policy issues should such a commission study? What specific recommendations on those issues should the commission make?

Index

References are to Pages

ISBN 0–314–25876–0

90000